Frommer's®
Hawaii 2011

by Jeanette Foster

Wiley Publishing, Inc.

Published by:
WILEY PUBLISHING, INC.
111 River St.
Hoboken, NJ 07030-5774

ISBN 978-0-470-63236-9 (paper); ISBN 978-0-470-92145-6 (ebk); ISBN 978-0-470-40613-7 (ebk); ISBN 978-1-118-00400-5 (ebk)

Editor: Christina Summers *with* Christine Ryan
Production Editor: Erin Amick
Cartographer: Andrew Dolan
Photo Editor: Alden Gerwitz, Cherie Cincilla
Cover Photo Research: Richard Fox
Design and Layout by Vertigo Design
Graphics and Prepress by Wiley Indianapolis Composition Services

Front cover photo: A surfer takes on one of Hawaii's challenging waves © Chris Dyball / Innerlight / Getty Images.
Back cover photo: *Left:* Plumeria blossom © Pacific Stock / SuperStock, Inc.; *Middle:* Kalalau Valley, Na Pali Coast, Kauai © Don White / SuperStock, Inc.; *Right:* Lava flows into the ocean on the Big Island © Bruce Omori Photography.

For information on our other products and services or to obtain technical support, please contact our Customer Care Department within the U.S. at 877/762-2974, outside the U.S. at 317/572-3993 or fax 317/572-4002.

Wiley also publishes its books in a variety of electronic formats. Some content that appears in print may not be available in electronic formats.

Manufactured in the United States of America

5   4   3   2   1

CONTENTS

4 SUGGESTED HAWAII ITINERARIES 106

5 OAHU, THE GATHERING PLACE 126

6 HAWAII, THE BIG ISLAND 298

7 MAUI, THE VALLEY ISLE 423

8 MOLOKAI, THE MOST HAWAIIAN ISLE 569

9 LANAI, A DIFFERENT KIND OF PARADISE 605

LIST OF MAPS

ABOUT THE AUTHOR

A resident of the Big Island, **Jeanette Foster** has skied the slopes of Mauna Kea—during a Fourth of July ski meet, no less—and gone scuba diving with manta rays off the Kona Coast. A prolific writer widely published in travel, sports, and adventure magazines, she's also the editor of *Zagat's Survey to Hawaii's Top Restaurants,* and the Hawaii chapter author of *1,000 Places to See in the USA and Canada Before You Die.* In addition to writing this guide, Jeanette is the author of *Frommer's Maui; Frommer's Kauai; Frommer's Hawaii with Kids; Frommer's Portable Big Island; Frommer's Hawaii Day by Day; Frommer's Honolulu, Waikiki & Oahu; Frommer's Maui Day by Day; and Frommer's Honolulu & Oahu Day by Day.*

HOW TO CONTACT US

In researching this book, we discovered many wonderful places—hotels, restaurants, shops, and more. We're sure you'll find others. Please tell us about them, so we can share the information with your fellow travelers in upcoming editions. If you were disappointed with a recommendation, we'd love to know that, too. Please write to:

Frommer's Hawaii 2011
Wiley Publishing, Inc. • 111 River St. • Hoboken, NJ 07030-5774
frommersfeedback@wiley.com

AN ADDITIONAL NOTE

Please be advised that travel information is subject to change at any time—and this is especially true of prices. We therefore suggest that you write or call ahead for confirmation when making your travel plans. The authors, editors, and publisher cannot be held responsible for the experiences of readers while traveling. Your safety is important to us, however, so we encourage you to stay alert and be aware of your surroundings. Keep a close eye on cameras, purses, and wallets, all favorite targets of thieves and pickpockets.

FROMMER'S STAR RATINGS, ICONS & ABBREVIATIONS

Every hotel, restaurant, and attraction listing in this guide has been ranked for quality, value, service, amenities, and special features using a **star-rating system.** In country, state, and regional guides, we also rate towns and regions to help you narrow down your choices and budget your time accordingly. Hotels and restaurants are rated on a scale of zero (recommended) to three stars (exceptional). Attractions, shopping, nightlife, towns, and regions are rated according to the following scale: zero stars (recommended), one star (highly recommended), two stars (very highly recommended), and three stars (must-see).

In addition to the star-rating system, we also use **seven feature icons** that point you to the great deals, in-the-know advice, and unique experiences that separate travelers from tourists. Throughout the book, look for:

special finds—those places only insiders know about

fun facts—details that make travelers more informed and their trips more fun

kids—best bets for kids and advice for the whole family

special moments—those experiences that memories are made of

overrated—places or experiences not worth your time or money

insider tips—great ways to save time and money

great values—where to get the best deals

The following abbreviations are used for credit cards:

AE	American Express	**DISC**	Discover	**V**	Visa
DC	Diners Club	**MC**	MasterCard		

TRAVEL RESOURCES AT FROMMERS.COM

Frommer's travel resources don't end with this guide. Frommer's website, **www.frommers.com**, has travel information on more than 4,000 destinations. We update features regularly, giving you access to the most current trip-planning information and the best airfare, lodging, and car-rental bargains. You can also listen to podcasts, connect with other Frommers.com members through our active-reader forums, share your travel photos, read blogs from guidebook editors and fellow travelers, and much more.

1

THE BEST OF HAWAII

There's no place on earth quite like this handful of sun-drenched mid-Pacific islands. The Hawaii of South Seas literature and Hollywood films really does exist. Here you'll find palm-fringed blue lagoons, lush rainforests, hidden gardens, cascading waterfalls, wild rivers running through rugged canyons, and soaring volcanoes. And oh, those beaches—gold, red, black, and even green sands caressed by endless surf. The possibilities for adventure—and relaxation—are endless. Each of the six main islands is separate, distinct, and infinitely complex. There's far too much to see and do on any 2-week vacation, which is why so many people return to the Aloha State year after year.

Unfortunately, even paradise has its share of stifling crowds and tourist schlock. If you're not careful, your trip to Hawaii could turn into a nightmare of tourist traps selling shells from the Philippines, hokey faux culture like cellophane-skirted hula dancers, overpriced exotic drinks, and a 4-hour timeshare lecture before you get on that "free" snorkeling trip. That's where this guide comes in. As a Hawaii resident, I can tell the extraordinary from the merely ordinary. This book will steer you away from the crowded, the overrated, and the overpriced—and toward the best Hawaii has to offer. No matter what your budget, this guide will help ensure that every dollar is well spent.

THE best BEACHES

- **Lanikai Beach** (Oahu): Too gorgeous to be real, this stretch along the Windward Coast is one of Hawaii's postcard-perfect beaches—a mile of golden sand as soft as powdered sugar bordering translucent turquoise waters. The waters are calm year-round and excellent for swimming, snorkeling, and kayaking. Two tiny offshore islands complete the picture, functioning not only as scenic backdrops, but also as bird sanctuaries. See p. 204.

- **Hapuna Beach** (Big Island): This half-mile-long crescent regularly wins kudos in the world's top travel magazines as the most beautiful beach in Hawaii—some consider it one of the most beautiful beaches in the world. One look and you'll see why: Perfect cream-colored sand slopes down to crystal-clear waters that are great for swimming, snorkeling, and bodysurfing in summer; come winter, waves thunder in like stampeding horses. The facilities for picnicking and camping are top-notch, and there's plenty of parking. See p. 356.

PREVIOUS PAGE: **Haena Beach.**

The Hawaiian Islands

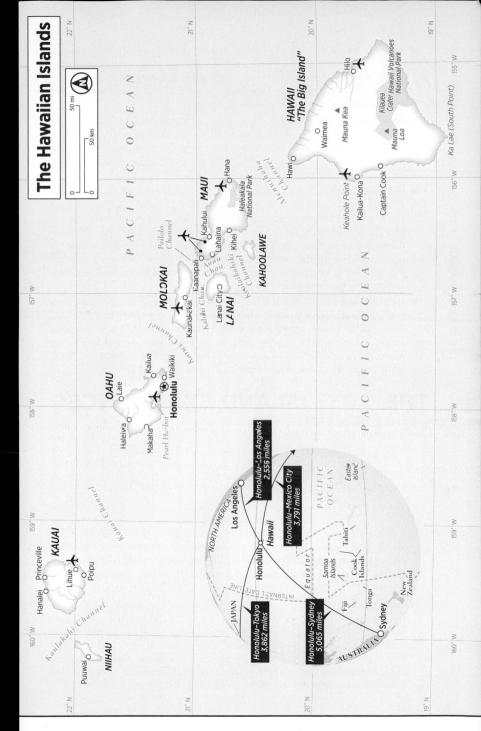

PACIFIC OCEAN

KAUAI
Hanalei
Princeville
Lihue
Poipu

Kaulakahi Channel

NIIHAU
Puuwai

Kauai Channel

OAHU
Laie
Kailua
Makaha
Haleiwa
Waikiki
Honolulu
Pearl Harbor

Kaiwi Channel

MOLOKAI
Kaunakakai

Kalohi Channel

LANAI
Lanai City

Auau Chan.

Kalohikahiki Channel

MAUI
Kahului
Lahaina
Kaanapali
Kihei
Hana
Haleakala National Park

Pailolo Channel

KAHOOLAWE

Alalakeiki Channel

Alenuihaha Channel

HAWAII "The Big Island"
Waimea
Hawi
Mauna Kea
Kiilauea Crater Hawaii Volcanoes National Park
Keahole Point
Kailua-Kona
Captain Cook
Mauna Loa
Ka Lae (South Point)

PACIFIC OCEAN

NORTH AMERICA
Los Angeles

Honolulu–Los Angeles
2,555 miles

Honolulu–Mexico City
3,791 miles

Hawaii
Honolulu

PACIFIC OCEAN

Easter Island

Equator

INTERNAT'L DATE LINE

JAPAN

Tahiti
Samoa Islands
Cook Islands

Fiji
Tonga
New Zealand

AUSTRALIA
Sydney

Honolulu–Tokyo
3,862 miles

Honolulu–Sydney
5,065 miles

o **Kapalua Beach** (Maui): On an island with many great beaches, Kapalua takes the prize. This golden crescent with swaying palms is protected from strong winds and currents by two outstretched lava-rock promontories. Its calm waters are perfect for snorkeling, swimming, and kayaking. Facilities include showers, restrooms, and lifeguards. See p. 501.

o **Papohaku Beach** (Molokai): These gold sands stretch on for some 3 miles (it's one of Hawaii's longest beaches) and are about as **wide** as a football field. Offshore the ocean churns mightily in winter, but the waves die down in summer, making the calm waters inviting for swimming. It's also great for picnicking, walking, and watching sunsets. See p. 584.

o **Hulopoe Beach** (Lanai): This golden, palm-fringed beach off the south coast of Lanai gently slopes down to the azure waters of a Marine Life Conservation District, where clouds of tropical fish flourish and spinner dolphins come to play. A tide pool in the lava rocks defines one side of the bay, while the other is lorded over by the Four Seasons Resort Lanai at Manele Bay, which sits prominently on the hill above. Offshore you'll find good swimming, snorkeling, and diving; onshore there's a full complement of beach facilities, from restrooms to camping areas. See p. 617.

o **Haena Beach** (Kauai): Backed by verdant cliffs, this curvaceous North Shore beach has starred as Paradise in many a movie. It's easy to see why Hollywood loves Haena Beach, with its grainy golden sand and translucent turquoise waters. Summer months bring calm waters for swimming and snorkeling; winter brings mighty waves for surfers. There are plenty of facilities on hand, including picnic tables, restrooms, and showers. See p. 682.

THE best ISLAND EXPERIENCES

o **Hitting the Beach:** A beach is a beach is a beach, right? Not in Hawaii. With 132 islets, shoals, and reefs, plus a general coastline of 750 miles, Hawaii has beaches in all different shapes, sizes, and colors, including black. The variety on the six major islands is astonishing; you could go to a different beach every day for years and still not see them all. For the best of a spectacular bunch, see "The Best Beaches," above.

o **Taking the Plunge:** Don mask, fins, and snorkel to explore Hawaii's magical underwater world, where exotic corals and kaleidoscopic clouds of tropical fish await you—a sea turtle may even come over to check you out. Can't swim? That's no excuse—take one of the many submarine tours offered by **Atlantis Submarines** (© **800/548-6262;** www.go-atlantis.com) on Oahu, the Big Island, and Maui. Check out the "Watersports" section in each island chapter for more information on all these underwater adventures.

o **Meeting Local Folks:** If you go to Hawaii and see only people like the ones back home, you might as well not have come. Extend yourself—leave your hotel, go out and meet the locals, and learn about Hawaii and its people. Just smile and say "Owzit?"—which means "How is it?" ("It's good," is the usual response)—and you're on your way to making a new friend. Hawaii is remarkably cosmopolitan; every ethnic group in the world seems to be represented here. There's a huge diversity of food, culture, language, and customs.

o **Feeling History Come Alive at Pearl Harbor** (Oahu): The United States could turn its back on World War II no longer after December 7, 1941, when Japanese warplanes bombed Pearl Harbor. Standing on the deck of the **USS** *Arizona* **Memorial** (© **808/422-0561;** www.nps.gov/usar)—the eternal tomb for the 1,177 sailors and Marines trapped below when the battleship sank in just 9 minutes—is a moving experience you'll never forget. Also in Pearl Harbor, you can visit the USS *Missouri* Memorial, where World War II came to an end. The Japanese signed their surrender on the deck of this 58,000-ton battleship on September 2, 1945. See p. 242.

o **Watching for Whales:** If you happen to be in Hawaii during humpback-whale season (roughly Dec–Apr), don't miss the opportunity to see these gentle giants. A host of boats—from small inflatables to high-tech, high-speed sailing catamarans—provide a range of whale-watching cruises on every island. One of my favorites is along the Big Island's Kona Coast, where **Captain Dan McSweeney's Year-Round Whale-Watching Adventures** (© **808/322-0028;** www.ilovewhales.com) takes you right to the whales year-round (pilot, sperm, false killer, melon-headed, pygmy killer, and beaked whales call Hawaii home even when humpbacks aren't in residence). A whale researcher for more than 25 years, Captain Dan frequently drops an underwater microphone or video camera into the depths so you can listen to whale songs and maybe even see what's going on. See p. 359.

o **Creeping up to the Ooze** (Big Island): Kilauea volcano has been adding land to the Big Island continuously since 1983. In 2007, the volcano goddess Pele blew smoke and plumage into the air from the main crater of Halemaumau. If conditions are right, you can walk up to the red-hot lava and see it ooze along, or you can stand at the shoreline and watch with awe as 2,000°F (1,093°C) molten fire pours into the ocean. You can also take to the air in a helicopter and see the volcano goddess's work from above. See p. 401.

Snorkeling in Hawaii.

The *USS Missouri* Memorial at Pearl Harbor.

Whale-watching.

o **Going Big-Game Fishing off the Kona Coast** (Big Island): Don't pass up the opportunity to try your luck in the sport-fishing capital of the world, where 1,000-pound marlin are taken from the sea just about every month of the year. Not looking to set a world record? Kona's charter-boat captains specialize in conservation and will be glad to tag any fish you angle, and then let it go so someone else can have the fun of fighting a big-game fish tomorrow. See p. 366.

o **Greeting the Rising Sun from atop Haleakala** (Maui): Bundle up in warm clothing, fill a thermos full of hot java, and drive up to the summit to watch the sky turn from inky black to muted charcoal as a small sliver of orange light forms on the horizon. There's something about standing at 10,000 feet, breathing in the rarefied air, and watching the first rays of sun streak across the sky. This is a mystical experience of the first magnitude. See p. 540.

o **Riding a Mule to Kalaupapa** (Molokai): If you have only a day to spend on Molokai, spend it on a mule. The trek from "topside" Molokai to Kalaupapa National Historical Park (Father Damien's world-famous leper colony) with **Molokai Mule Ride** (© **800/567-7550;** www.muleride.com) is a once-in-a-lifetime adventure. The cliffs are taller than 300-story skyscrapers, but Buzzy Sproat's sure-footed mules go up and down the narrow 3-mile trail daily, rain or shine, and he's never lost a rider or a mount on the 26 switchbacks. Even if you can't afford to mule or helicopter in, don't pass up the opportunity to see this hauntingly beautiful peninsula. If you're in good shape and brought hiking boots with you, you can get a permit (available at the trail head) and hike down the trail. The views are breathtaking: You'll see the world's highest sea cliffs and waterfalls plunging thousands of feet into the ocean. See p. 596.

o **Taking a Day Trip to Lanai** (from Maui): If you'd like to visit Lanai but have only a day to spare, consider taking a day trip. **Trilogy** (© **888/MAUI-800** [628-4800]; www.sailtrilogy.com) leads an all-day sailing, snorkeling, and whale-watching adventure. Trilogy is the only outfitter with rights to Hulopoe Beach, and the trip includes a minivan tour of the little isle (pop. 3,500). You can also take **Expeditions Lahaina/Lanai Passenger Ferry** (© **808/661-3756;** www.go-lanai.com) from Maui to Lanai, and then rent a four-wheel-drive vehicle from **Dollar Rent-A-Car** (© **800/588-7808;** www.dollar.com) for a day of backcountry exploring and beach fun. See chapter 9.

o **Soaring over the Na Pali Coast** (Kauai): This is the only way to see the spectacular, surreal beauty of Kauai. Your helicopter will dip low over razor-thin cliffs, fluttering past sparkling waterfalls and swooping down into the canyons and valleys of the fabled Na Pali Coast. The only problem is that there's too much beauty to absorb, and it all goes by in a rush. See p. 638.

THE best OF NATURAL HAWAII

o **Volcanoes:** The entire island chain is made of volcanoes; don't miss the opportunity to see one. On Oahu, the entire family can hike to the top of ancient, world-famous **Diamond Head** (p. 218). At the other end of the spectrum is fire-breathing Kilauea at **Hawaii Volcanoes National Park,** on the Big Island, where you can get an up-close-and-personal experience with the red-hot lava ooze (p. 305). On Maui, **Haleakala National Park** provides a bird's-eye view into a long-dormant volcanic crater (p. 538).

A lava flow on the Big Island.

o **Waterfalls:** Rushing waterfalls thundering downward into sparkling freshwater pools are some of Hawaii's most beautiful natural wonders. If you're on the Big Island, stop by **Rainbow Falls** (p. 400), in Hilo, or the spectacular 442-foot **Akaka Falls** (p. 392), just outside Hilo. On Maui, the Road to Hana offers numerous viewing opportunities; at the end of the drive, you'll find **Oheo Gulch** (also known as the Seven Sacred Pools), with some of the most dramatic and accessible waterfalls on the islands (p. 550). Kauai is loaded with waterfalls, especially along the North Shore and in the Wailua area, where you'll find 40-foot **Opaekaa Falls** (p. 713), probably the best-looking drive-up waterfall on Kauai. With scenic mountain peaks in the background and a restored Hawaiian village on the nearby riverbanks, the Opaekaa Falls are what the tourist-bureau folks call an eye-popping photo op.

o **Gardens:** The islands are redolent with the sweet scent of flowers. For a glimpse of the full breadth and beauty of Hawaii's spectacular range of tropical flora, I suggest spending an afternoon at a lush garden. On Oahu, amid the high-rises of downtown Honolulu, the leafy oasis of **Foster Botanical Garden** (p. 247) showcases 26 native Hawaiian trees and the last stand of several rare trees, including an East African, whose white flowers bloom only at night. On the Big Island, **Liliuokalani Gardens** (p. 398), the largest formal Japanese garden this side of Tokyo, resembles a postcard from Asia, with bonsai, carp ponds, pagodas, and even a moon-gate bridge. At Maui's **Kula Botanical Garden** (p. 543), you can take a leisurely self-guided stroll through more than 700 native and exotic plants, including orchids, proteas, and bromeliads. On lush Kauai, **Na Aina Kai Botanical Gardens** (p. 717), on some 240 acres, is sprinkled with around 70 life-size (some larger-than-life-size) whimsical bronze statues, hidden off the beaten path of the North Shore.

Kauai's Opaekaa Falls.

Foster Botanical Garden on Oahu.

○ **Marine Life Conservation Areas:** Nine underwater parks are spread across Hawaii, most notably **Waikiki Beach** (p. 200) and **Hanauma Bay** (p. 202), on Oahu; **Kealakekua Bay** (p. 365), on the Big Island; **Molokini,** just off the coast of Maui (see "Watersports" in chapter 7); and Lanai's **Manele and Hulopoe Bays** (p. 617). Be sure to bring snorkel gear to at least one of these wonderful places during your vacation.

○ **Garden of the Gods** (Lanai): Out on Lanai's north shore lies the ultimate rock garden: a rugged, barren, beautiful place full of rocks strewn by volcanic forces and molded by the elements into a variety of shapes and colors—brilliant reds, oranges, ochers, and yellows. Scientists use phrases such as "ongoing posterosional event" or "plain and simple badlands" to describe the desolate, windswept place. The ancient Hawaiians, however, considered the Gar-

Surfers on the beach at sunset.

den of the Gods to be an entirely supernatural phenomenon. Natural badlands or mystical garden? Take a four-wheel-drive trip out here and decide for yourself. See p. 623.

○ **Waimea Canyon** (Kauai): This valley, known for its reddish lava beds, reminds everyone who sees it of Arizona's Grand Canyon. Kauai's version is bursting with ever-changing color, just like its namesake, but it's smaller—only a mile wide, 3,567 feet deep, and 12 miles long. All this grandeur was caused by a massive earthquake that sent all the streams flowing into a single river, which then carved this picturesque canyon. You can stop by the road and look at it, hike down into it, or swoop through it by helicopter. See p. 635.

THE best OF UNDERWATER HAWAII

○ **Hanauma Bay** (Oahu): It can get crowded, but for clear, warm, calm waters; an abundance of fish that are so friendly they'll swim right up to your face mask; a beautiful setting; and easy access, there's no place like Hanauma Bay. Just wade in waist-deep and look down to see more than 50 species of reef and inshore fish. Snorkelers hug the safe, shallow inner bay—it's like swimming in an outdoor aquarium. Serious divers shoot "the slot," a passage through the reef, to enter Witch's Brew, a turbulent cove. See p. 202.

○ **Kahaluu Beach** (Big Island): The calm, shallow waters of Kahaluu are perfect for beginning snorkelers or those who are unsure of their swimming abilities and want the comfort of being able to stand up at any time. The sunlight through the shallow waters casts a dazzling spotlight on the colorful sea life and coral formations. If you listen closely, you can actually hear the parrotfish feeding. See p. 353.

o **Kealakekua Bay** (Big Island): Mile-wide Kealakekua Bay, at the foot of massive U-shaped sea cliffs, is rich with marine life, snorkelers, and history. A white obelisk marks the spot where, in 1778, the great British navigator Capt. James Cook, who charted most of the Pacific, was killed by Hawaiians. The bay itself is a marine sanctuary that teems with schools of polychromatic tropical fish. See p. 365.

o **Molokini** (Maui): The islet of Molokini is shaped like a crescent moon that fell from the sky. Its shallow concave side serves as a sheltering backstop against sea currents for tiny tropical fish; its opposite side is a deep-water cliff inhabited by spiny lobsters, moray eels, and white-tipped sharks. Neophyte snorkelers should report to the concave side, experienced scuba divers the other. The clear water and abundant marine life make this islet off the Makena coast one of Hawaii's most popular dive spots, so expect crowds. See "Watersports" in chapter 7.

o **Kee Beach** (Kauai): Where the road ends on the North Shore, you'll find a dandy little reddish-gold beach almost too beautiful to be real. It borders a reef-protected cove at the foot of fluted volcanic cliffs. Swimming and snorkeling are safe inside the reef, where long-nosed butterfly fish flitter about and schools of taape (bluestripe snapper) swarm over the coral. See p. 681.

THE best GOLF COURSES

o **Mauna Kea & Hapuna Golf Courses** (Big Island; ℂ **808/882-5400** for Mauna Kea Golf Course, ℂ 808/880-3000 for Hapuna Golf Course): The Mauna Kea Golf Course, located out on the Kohala Coast, is everyone's old favorite. One of the first fields of play to be carved out of the black lava, the dramatic, always-challenging, par-72, 18-hole championship course is still one of Hawaii's top three. The Arnold Palmer/Ed Seay–designed Hapuna Golf Course rests in the rolling foothills above Hapuna Beach Prince Hotel and provides a memorable links-style golf experience along with one of the best views of this unusual coast. See p. 371.

o **Mauna Lani Francis H. I'i Brown Championship Courses** (Big Island; ℂ **808/885-6655**): Mauna Lani's two resort courses, North and South, feature a combination of oceanfront and interior lava-lined holes; both

Mauna Lani golf course.

offer wonderful scenery accompanied by strategic, championship-level golf. See p. 372.

o **Kapalua Resort** (Maui; © 877/ **KAPALUA** [527-2582]): Kapalua is probably the best nationally known golf resort in Hawaii, thanks to the PGA Mercedes Championship played here each January. The Bay and Village courses are vintage Arnold Palmer designs; the Plantation Course is a strong Ben Crenshaw/Bill Coore design. See p. 524.

o **Wailea Golf Club** (Maui; © 808/ **875-7450**): On Maui's sunbaked south shore stands Wailea Resort, *the* hot spot for golf in the islands. Three resort courses complement a string of beachfront hotels: The Blue Course is an Arthur Jack

The Big Island's Merrie Monarch Hula Festival.

Snyder design, while Robert Trent Jones, Jr., is the mastermind behind the Emerald and Gold courses. All three offer outstanding views of the Pacific and the mid-Hawaiian islands. See p. 525.

o **The Lanai Courses** (Lanai): For quality and seclusion, nothing in Hawaii can touch Lanai's two resort courses. The **Experience at Koele,** designed by Ted Robinson and Greg Norman, and the **Challenge at Manele,** a wonderful Jack Nicklaus effort with ocean views from every hole, both rate among Hawaii's best courses. See p. 622.

o **Poipu Bay Golf Course** (Kauai; © 808/742-8711): On Kauai's flat, dry south shore is a 210-acre, links-style course designed by Robert Trent Jones, Jr. The course, which for years hosted the PGA Grand Slam of Golf, is not only scenically spectacular but also a lot of fun to play. A flock of native Hawaiian nene geese frequents the course's lakes, and you can often see whales, monk seals, and green sea turtles along the shore. See p. 701.

o **Princeville Golf Club** (Kauai; © 800/826-1105): Here you'll find 45 of the best tropical holes of golf in the world, all the work of Robert Trent Jones, Jr. They range along green bluffs below sharp mountain peaks and offer stunning views in every direction. The 18-hole Prince Course, one of the top three courses in Hawaii, provides a round of golf few ever forget—among 390 acres of scenic tableland bisected by tropical jungles, waterfalls, streams, and ravines. See p. 701.

THE best WAYS TO IMMERSE IN HAWAIIAN CULTURE

o **Experiencing the Hula:** For a real, authentic hula experience on Oahu, check out the **Bishop Museum** (p. 235), which stages excellent performances on weekdays, or head to the Halekulani's **House Without a Key**

THE WELCOMING lei

Nothing makes you feel more welcome than a lei. The tropical beauty of the delicate garland, the deliciously sweet fragrance of the blossoms, the sensual way the flowers curl softly around your neck—there's no doubt about it: Getting lei'd in Hawaii is a sensuous experience.

Leis are much more than just a decorative necklace of flowers—they're also one of the nicest ways to say "hello," "goodbye," "congratulations," "I salute you," "my sympathies are with you," or "I love you."

During ancient times, leis given to *alii* (royalty) were accompanied by a bow, since it was *kapu* (forbidden) for a commoner to raise his arms higher than the king's head. The presentation of a kiss with a lei didn't come about until World War II; it's generally attributed to an entertainer who kissed an officer on a dare and then quickly presented him with her lei, saying it was an old Hawaiian custom. It wasn't then, but it sure caught on fast.

Lei making is a tropical art form. All leis are fashioned by hand in a variety of traditional patterns; some are sewn with hundreds of tiny blooms or shells, or bits of ferns and leaves. Some are twisted, some braided, some strung. Every island has its own special flower lei—the lei of the land, so to speak. On Oahu, the choice is *ilima,* a small orange flower. Big Islanders prefer the *lehua,* a large, delicate red puff. On Maui, it's the *lokelani,* a small rose; on Kauai, it's the *mokihana,* a fragrant green vine and berry; on Molokai, it's the *kukui,* the white blossom of a candlenut tree; and on Lanai, it's the *kaunaoa,* a bright yellow moss. Residents of Niihau use the island's abundant seashells to make leis that were once prized by royalty and are now worth a small fortune.

Leis are available at all of the islands' airports, from florists, and even at supermarkets. You can find wonderful inexpensive leis at the half-dozen lei shops on **Maunakea Street** in Honolulu's Chinatown, and at **Greene Acres Leis** (✆ 808/329-2399), off Kaimiminani Drive in the Kona Palisades subdivision, across from the Kona Airport on the Big Island. If you plan ahead, you can also arrange to have a lei-greeter meet you as you deplane; **Greeters of Hawaii** (✆ 800/366-8559 or 808/836-3246; www.greetersofhawaii.com) serves the Honolulu (Oahu), Kona (Big Island), Kahului (Maui), and Lihue (Kauai) airports.

Leis are the perfect symbol for the islands: They're given in the moment, and their fragrance and beauty are enjoyed in the moment, but even after they fade, their spirit of aloha lives on. Welcome to Hawaii!

Canoe paddling at Ala Wai Canal.

(p. 292) at sunset to watch the enchanting Kanoelehua Miller dance beautiful hula under a century-old kiawe tree. The first week after Easter brings Hawaii's biggest and most prestigious hula extravaganza, the **Merrie Monarch Hula Festival** (p. 421), in Hilo on the Big Island; tickets sell out by January 30, so reserve early. In May, Molokai holds the **Ka Hula Piko Festival** (p. 590) at Papohaku Beach Park, a wonderful daylong affair that celebrates the hula on the island where it was born.

o **Watching the Ancient Hawaiian Sport of Canoe Paddling** (Oahu): From February to September, on weekday evenings and weekend days, hundreds of canoe paddlers gather at Ala Wai Canal and practice the Hawaiian sport of canoe paddling. Find a comfortable spot at Ala Wai Park, next to the canal, and watch this ancient sport come to life.

o **Attending a Hawaiian-Language Church Service** (Oahu): **Kawaiahao Church** (© 808/522-1333) is the Westminster Abbey of Hawaii. The vestibule is lined with portraits of the Hawaiian monarchy, many of whom were crowned in this very building. The coral church is a perfect setting in which to experience an all-Hawaiian service, held every Sunday at 9am, complete with Hawaiian song. Admission is free; let your conscience be your guide as to a donation. See p. 240.

o **Buying a Lei in Chinatown** (Oahu): There's actually a host of cultural sights and experiences to be had in Honolulu's Chinatown. Wander through this several-square-block area with its jumble of exotic shops selling herbs, Chinese groceries, and acupuncture services. Before you leave, be sure to check out the lei sellers on Maunakea Street (near N. Hotel St.), where Hawaii's finest leis go for as little as $5. If you'd like a little guidance, you can follow the walking tour described on p. 253.

o **Listening to Old-Fashioned "Talk Story" with Hawaiian Song and Dance** (Big Island): Once a month, under a full moon, **Twilight at Kalahuipua'a,** a celebration of the Hawaiian culture that includes storytelling, singing, and

13

dancing, takes place oceanside at Mauna Lani Resort (✆ 808/885-6622; www.maunalani.com/luxury-hawaii-resort-factsheet.htm). It hearkens back to another time in Hawaii, when family and neighbors would gather on back porches to sing, dance, and "talk story." See p. 422.

o **Visiting Ancient Hawaii's Most Sacred Temple** (Big Island): On the Kohala Coast, where King Kamehameha the Great was born, stands Hawaii's oldest, largest, and most sacred religious site: the 1,500-year-old **Mookini Heiau,** used by kings to pray and offer human sacrifices. This massive three-story stone temple, dedicated to Ku, the Hawaiian god of war, was erected in A.D. 480. It's said that each stone was passed from hand to hand from Pololu Valley, 14 miles away, by 18,000 men who worked from sunset to sunrise. Seeing the site is by appointment only. See p. 387.

o **Hunting for Petroglyphs** (Big Island): Archaeologists are still uncertain exactly what these ancient rock carvings mean. The majority are found in the 233-acre **Puako Petroglyph Archaeological District,** near Mauna Lani Resort on the Kohala Coast. The best time to hunt for these intricate depictions of ancient life is either early in the morning or late afternoon, when the angle of the sun lets you see the forms clearly. See p. 387.

o **Exploring Puuhonua O Honaunau National Historical Park** (Big Island): This sacred site on the southern Kona Coast was once a place of refuge and a revered place of rejuvenation. You can walk the same consecrated grounds where priests once conducted holy ceremonies and glimpse the ancient way of life in precontact Hawaii in the re-created 180-acre village. See p. 384.

o **Visiting the Most Hawaiian Isle** (Molokai): A time capsule of old Hawaii, Molokai allows you to experience real Hawaiian life in its most unsullied form. The island's people have woven the cultural values of ancient times into modern life. In addition to this rich community, you'll find the magnificent natural wonders it so cherishes: Hawaii's highest waterfall, its greatest collection of fish ponds, and the world's tallest sea cliffs, as well as sand dunes, coral reefs, rainforests, and gloriously empty beaches. The island is pretty much the same Molokai of generations ago. See chapter 8.

THE best LUXURY HOTELS & RESORTS

o **Halekulani** (Oahu; ✆ 800/367-2343; www.halekulani.com): When price is no object, this is really the only place to stay. An oasis of calm amid the buzz, this beach hotel is the finest Waikiki has to offer (heck, I think it's the finest in the state). Even if you don't stay here, pop by for a sunset mai tai to see a lovely hula dancer swaying to Hawaiian music. See p. 149.

o **Royal Hawaiian** (Oahu; ✆ 800/325-3535; www.royal-hawaiian.com): This flamingo-pink oasis, hidden away among blooming gardens within the concrete jungle of Waikiki, is a symbol of luxury. You can step back in time by staying in the rooms in the Historic Wing, which contain carved wooden doors, four-poster canopy beds, flowered wallpaper, and period furniture. One of Waikiki's best spas, **Abhasa** (✆ 808/922-8200; www.abhasa.com), is located on the property. See p. 151.

○ **Kahala Hotel & Resort** (Oahu; ℭ 800/367-2525; www.kahalaresort.com): After 11 years under the helm of the Mandarin Oriental Group, this grand old hotel changed management in 2006, after which it underwent a complete makeover, restoring the hotel's former opulence, complete with Art Deco stylings. The location alone offers a similarly wonderful compromise: Situated in one of Oahu's most prestigious residential areas, the Kahala provides the peace and serenity of a neighbor-island vacation, but with the conveniences of Waikiki just a 10-minute drive away. The lush, tropical grounds include an 800-foot crescent-shaped beach and a 26,000-square-foot lagoon (home to two bottle-nosed dolphins, sea turtles, and tropical fish). See p. 164.

○ **Four Seasons Resort Hualalai at Historic Kaupulehu** (Big Island; ℭ 888/340-5662; www.fourseasons.com/hualalai): Private pools, unimpeded ocean views, excellent food, and a new 18-hole championship golf course—what more could any mortal want? This new low-impact, high-ticket hideaway under the dormant Hualalai Volcano ups the ante with its residential resort of two-story bungalows clustered around five seaside swimming pools on a black lagoon. See p. 309.

○ **Mauna Lani Bay Hotel & Bungalows** (Big Island; ℭ 800/367-2323; www. maunalani.com): Burned out? In need of tranquillity and gorgeous surroundings? Look no further. Sandy beaches and lava tide pools are the focus of this serene seaside resort, where gracious hospitality is dispensed in a historic setting. From the lounge chairs on the pristine beach to the turndown service at night, everything here is done impeccably. The rooms are arranged to capture maximum ocean views, and they surround interior atrium gardens and pools in which endangered baby sea turtles are raised. A shoreline trail leads across the whole 3,200-acre resort, giving you an intimate glimpse into the ancient past, when people lived in lava caves and tended the large complex of fish ponds. See p. 321.

The Halekulani hotel.

Watching the sunset from Haleakala.

o **The Fairmont Orchid Hawaii** (Big Island; ✆ **800/845-9905;** www. fairmont.com/orchid): Located on 32 acres of oceanfront property, the Orchid is the place for watersports nuts, cultural explorers, families with children, or anyone who just wants to lie back and soak up the sun. This elegant beach resort takes full advantage of the spectacular ocean views and historic sites on its grounds. The sports facilities here are extensive, and there's an excellent Hawaiiana program. See p. 318.

o **The Fairmont Kea Lani Maui** (Maui; ✆ **800/659-4100;** www.fairmont. com/kealani): This is the place to get your money's worth: For the price of a hotel room, you get an entire suite—plus a few extras. Each unit in this all-suite luxury hotel has a kitchenette, a living room with entertainment center and sofa bed (great if you have the kids in tow), a marble wet bar, an oversize marble bathroom with separate shower big enough for a party, a spacious bed-room, and a large lanai that overlooks the pools, lawns, and white-sand beach. See p. 458.

o **Four Seasons Resort Maui at Wailea** (Maui; ✆ **800/334-MAUI** [6284]; www.fourseasons.com/maui): This is the ultimate beach hotel for latter-day royals, with excellent cuisine, spacious rooms, gracious service, and Wailea Beach, one of Maui's best gold-sand strips, out the front door. Every guest room has at least a partial ocean view from a private lanai. The luxury suites, as big as some Honolulu condos, are full of marble and deluxe appointments. See p. 459.

o **Hotel Hana-Maui** (Maui; ✆ **800/321-HANA** [4262]; www.hotelhanamaui. com): Picture Shangri-La, Hawaiian style: 66 acres rolling down to the sea in a remote Hawaiian village, with a wellness center, two pools, and access to one of the best beaches in Hana. Cathedral ceilings, a plush feather bed, a giant-size soaking tub, Hawaiian artwork, bamboo hardwood floors—this is luxury. The white-sand beach (just a 5-min. shuttle away), a top-notch wellness center with some of the best massage therapists in Hawaii, and numerous activities (horseback riding, mountain biking, tennis, pitch-and-putt golf) all add up to make this one of the top resorts in the state. I highly recommend this little slice of paradise. See p. 467.

o **Four Seasons Resort Lanai at Manele Bay** (Lanai; ℂ 800/321-4666; www.fourseasons.com/lanai): The well-known luxury hotel chain Four Seasons took over management of this 236-unit resort after a multimillion-dollar makeover in 2005. Perched on a sun-washed southern bluff overlooking Hulopoe Beach, one of Hawaii's best stretches of golden sand, this U-shaped hotel steps down the hillside to the pool and the beach. Designed as a traditional luxury beachfront hotel, the Manele Bay features open, airy, oversize rooms, each with a breathtaking view of the big blue Pacific. The guest rooms have been redone in the clean, crisp style of an elegant Hawaiian resort, with 40-inch flatscreen TVs, huge marble bathrooms, and semiprivate lanais. See p. 611.

o **Four Seasons Resort Lanai, The Lodge at Koele** (Lanai; ℂ 800/321-4666; www.fourseasons.com/lanai): The sister hotel to Manele Bay (see above), this luxury resort was renovated and rebranded a Four Seasons in 2006. A $50-million renovation gave all 102 guest rooms new carpeting, glass partitions in the bathroom, signature Four Seasons beds, 42-inch flatscreen TVs, new furniture, new fabrics, and high speed Internet service. This inn, which resembles a grand English country estate, was built in 1991 and needed the makeover—the new look is spectacular. See p. 612.

o **Grand Hyatt Kauai Resort & Spa** (Kauai; ℂ 800/55-HYATT [554-9288]; www.kauai.hyatt.com): This Art Deco beach hotel recalls Hawaii in the 1920s—before the crash—when gentlemen in blue blazers and ladies in summer frocks came to the islands to learn to surf and play the ukulele. The architecture and location, on the sunny side of Kauai, make this the island's best hotel. The beach is a bit too rough for swimming, but the saltwater swimming pool is the biggest on the island. An old-fashioned reading room by the sea houses club chairs, billiards, and a bar well stocked with cognac and port. Nearby diversions include golf, horseback riding, and the shops of Koloa, a former plantation town. See p. 644.

o **St. Regis Princeville Resort** (Kauai; ℂ 800/826-4400; www.stregis princeville.com): This palace of green marble and sparkling chandeliers recalls Hawaii's monarchy period of the 19th century. It's set in one of the most remarkable locations in the world, on a cliff between the crystal-blue waters of Hanalei Bay and steepled mountains; you arrive on the ninth floor and go down to get to the beach. Opulent rooms with magnificent views and all the activities of Princeville and Hanalei make this one of Hawaii's finest resorts. See p. 656.

THE best MODERATELY PRICED ACCOMMODATIONS

o **New Otani Kaimana Beach Hotel** (Oahu; ℂ 800/356-8264; www.kaimana.com): This is one of Waikiki's best-kept secrets: a boutique hotel nestled right on a lovely stretch of beach at the foot of Diamond Head, with Kapiolani Park just across the street. The Waikiki-side guest rooms are teeny-tiny, with barely room for two, but they are tastefully decorated and open onto lanais with ocean and park views. A good budget buy is the parkview studio with kitchen. You can stock up with provisions from the on-site Mini-Mart. See p. 161.

o **Ke Iki Beach Bungalows** (Oahu; ☏ 866/638-8229; www.keikibeach. com): This collection of studio and one- and two-bedroom cottages snuggled on a large lot with its own 200-foot stretch of white-sand beach between two legendary surf spots (Waimea Bay and Banzai Pipeline) has been totally renovated to the tune of $1 million. Most units are compact—the kitchens and living rooms are small and the bedrooms even smaller—but they're affordable, with rates starting at $160 a night. And with the ocean just outside, how much time are you going to spend inside anyway? The winter waves are too rough for most swimmers, but there's a large lava reef nearby with tide pools to explore and, on the other side, Shark's Cove, a relatively protected snorkeling area. Nearby are tennis courts and a jogging path. All units have full kitchens and their own barbecue areas. See p. 168.

o **Kona Tiki Hotel** (Big Island; ☏ 808/329-1425; www.konatiki.com): Right on the ocean, away from the hustle and bustle of downtown Kailua-Kona, is one of the best budget deals in Hawaii: tastefully decorated rooms with private lanais overlooking the ocean, starting at just $72 a night! Although it's called a hotel, this small, family-run operation is more like a large B&B, with plenty of friendly conversation around the pool at the morning continental breakfast buffet. See p. 314.

o **Waipio Wayside Bed & Breakfast Inn** (Big Island; ☏ 800/833-8849; www.waipiowayside.com): Jackie Horne renovated this 1938 Hamakua Sugar supervisor's home—nestled among fruit trees and surrounded by sweet-smelling ginger, fragile orchids, and blooming birds of paradise—and transformed it into a gracious B&B. Just minutes from the Waipio Valley Lookout and the village of Honokaa, this comfy five-bedroom house abounds with thoughtful touches, such as a help-yourself tea-and-cookies bar with 26 kinds of tea. Jackie's friendly hospitality and excellent continental breakfasts really round out the experience. Rooms start at $99 for two. See p. 325.

o **Old Wailuku Inn at Ulupono** (Maui; ☏ 800/305-4899; www.mauiinn. com): This 1924 former plantation manager's home, lovingly restored, provides a genuine old Hawaii experience. The theme is Hawaii of the 1920s and 1930s, with decor, design, and landscaping to match. The spacious rooms are gorgeously outfitted with exotic ohia-wood floors, high ceilings, and traditional Hawaiian quilts. A full gourmet breakfast is served on the enclosed back lanai or, if you prefer, delivered to your room. The inn is located in the old historic area of Wailuku, about 10 to 15 minutes to the beach. Once you settle in, you may not want to leave—and with rooms starting at $165 for a double, you can afford to stay awhile. See p. 435.

o **Pineapple Inn Maui** (Maui; ☏ 877/212-MAUI [6284]; www.pineapple innmaui.com): This charming inn (only four rooms, plus a cottage) is not only an exquisite find, but also a terrific value. Located in the residential Maui Meadows area, with panoramic ocean views, this two-story inn is expertly landscaped, with a lily pond in the front and a giant saltwater pool and Jacuzzi overlooking the ocean. Each of the soundproof rooms is expertly outfitted

The Waipio Wayside Bed & Breakfast Inn.

with a small kitchenette, a comfy bed, free wireless Internet access, TV/VCR, and an incredible view off your own private lanai. Prices start at $139. If you need more room, there's also a darling two-bedroom, one-bathroom cottage. See p. 456.

- **Aloha Beach House** (Molokai; © 888/828-1008 or 808/828-1100; www.molokaivacation.com): Book this place! Here is the Hawaii of your dreams. This Hawaiian-style beach house sits right on the white-sand beach of Waialua on the lush East End. Perfect for families or two couples, this two-bedroom, 1,600-square-foot beach house has a huge open living/dining/kitchen area that opens out to an old-fashioned porch for meals or just sitting in the comfy chairs and watching the clouds roll by. Plus, it's close to Mana'e Goods and Grindz, the East End's only takeout deli. See p. 579.

- **Dunbar Beachfront Cottages** (Molokai; © 800/673-0520; www.molokai-beachfront-cottages.com): Each of these green-and-white plantation-style cottages sits on its own secluded beach—you'll feel like you're on your own private island. Impeccable decor, a magical setting, and reasonable rates ($170 for two) make these cottages a must-stay. See p. 580.

- **Hotel Lanai** (Lanai; © 800/795-7211; www.hotellanai.com): Lanai's only budget lodging is a simple, down-home, plantation-era relic that has recently been Laura Ashley–ized. The Hotel Lanai is homey, funky, and fun—and, best of all, a real bargain (starting at $99 for two), compared to its ritzy neighbors. See p. 613.

- **Kauai Country Inn** (Kauai; © 808/821-0207; www.kauaicountryinn.com): This old-fashioned country inn, nestled in the rolling hills behind Kapaa, seems too good to be true. Each of the four suites (starting at just $129) is uniquely decorated in Hawaiian Art Deco, complete with hardwood floors, private bathroom, kitchen or kitchenette, your own computer with high-speed Internet connection, and lots of little extra amenities. Everything is top-drawer, from the furniture to the Sub-Zero refrigerator. The owners recently added a two-bedroom country cottage for families with young children. The grounds are immaculate, and you can pick as much organic fruit as you want. See p. 654.

o **Hanalei Surf Board House** (Kauai; (C) 808/826-9825; www.hanalei surfboardhouse.com): Book well in advance—this place is so fabulous, it will go fast! Just a block from the beach, these two incredibly decorated studio units are a steal at $195. Host Simon Potts, a former record-company executive from England, has filled his two studios (with kitchenettes) with imaginative decor choices: One of them sports a whimsical cowgirl theme, while the other is filled with Elvis memorabilia. But the best reason to stay here (besides the 2-min. walk to the beach and the 10-min. walk to downtown Hanalei) is Simon himself: His stories about the record industry will keep you howling with laughter for hours. See p. 658.

THE best PLACES TO STAY WITH THE KIDS

o **Hilton Hawaiian Village Beach Resort & Spa** (Oahu; (C) 800/HILTONS [445-8667]; www.hiltonhawaiianvillage.com): Camp Penguin, a year-round daily program of activities for children ages 5 to 12, offers a wide range of educational and fun activities (from Hawaiian storytelling to crafts) and excursions (Honolulu Zoo, Waikiki Aquarium, and so on) for $65 per half-day (no excursions) to $90 for a full day with excursions, including lunch. Everything about this hotel is kid-friendly, from the wildlife parading about the grounds to the submarine dives offered just out front. See p. 146.

o **JW Marriott Ihilani Resort & Spa at Ko Olina Resort** (Oahu; (C) 800/626-4446; www.ihilani.com): This resort on Oahu's virgin leeward coast is a haven of relaxation and tropical fun for travelers of all ages. The Keiki Beachcomber Club, for children ages 5 to 12, is available daily. Activities (9am–3pm) range from kite flying and tide-pool exploration to snorkeling and Hawaiian cultural activities. The cost ranges from $42 per child for a half-day with lunch to $60 for a full day. See p. 168.

o **Kona Village Resort** (Big Island; (C) 800/367-5290; www.kona village.com): This is a parent's dream: custom-designed programs to entertain your kids, from tots to teenagers, from dawn to well after dusk, all at no charge. There's even a dinner seating for children, so Mom and Dad can enjoy an intimate dinner for two later in the evening. See p. 310.

One of the many activities for kids at the JW Marriott Ihilani Resort & Spa.

- **The Fairmont Orchid Hawaii** (Big Island; ℂ **800/845-9905;** www. fairmont.com/orchid): The Keiki Aloha program, for kids 5 to 12 years old, features supervised activities from watersports to Hawaiian cultural games for $65 half-day and $85 for a full day. The resort has some great money-saving deals, too; for example, children 5 and under eat free at various restaurants on the property. See p. 318.

- **Hyatt Regency Maui Resort & Spa** (Maui; ℂ **800/233-1234;** www.maui. hyatt.com): The Camp Hyatt program, for kids 5 to 12 years old, operates daily from 9am to 3pm and offers young guests a range of activities, from "Olympic Games" to a scavenger hunt. The cost starts at $40 for a half-day and goes up to $70 for a full day. See p. 440.

- **Four Seasons Resort Maui at Wailea** (Maui; ℂ **800/334-MAUI** [6284]; www.fourseasons.com/maui): The most kid-friendly hotel on Maui not only offers a complimentary kids' program year-round and an everyday activities center (daily 9am–5pm), but also makes children feel welcome with extras such as complimentary milk and cookies on their first day and children's menus at all resort restaurants (and even from room service). See p. 459.

- **Grand Hyatt Kauai Resort & Spa** (Kauai; ℂ **800/55 HYATT** [554-9288]; www.kauai.hyatt.com): In addition to the Camp Hyatt program for kids 3 to 12 (costs start at $60 for a half-day with lunch or $50 without lunch, and go up to $80 for a full day), it's the collection of swimming pools (freshwater and salt, with slides, waterfalls, and secret lagoons) that makes this oceanfront Hyatt a real kids' paradise. Summertime features theater nights, when the whole family can enjoy a showing of one of the more than 400 movies filmed on Kauai. See p. 644.

THE best RESORT SPAS

- **SpaHalekulani at the Halekulani** (Oahu; ℂ **808/923-2311;** www. halekulani.com): This is Waikiki's first spa to explore the healing traditions of the Pacific islands, including Hawaii. Like everything else at the top-rated Halekulani hotel, it's truly a heavenly experience, from the time you step into the elegantly appointed, intimate spa and experience the foot massage, to the last whiff of fragrant maile, the signature scent. Spa connoisseurs should try something unique, like the Polynesian Nonu, a Samoan-inspired massage using stones. See p. 149.

- **Spa Suites at the Kahala Hotel & Resort** (Oahu; ℂ **808/739-8938;** www. kahalaresort.com): The Kahala has taken the concept of spa as a journey into relaxation to a new level, with former garden rooms converted into individual spas, each with a glass-enclosed shower, a private changing area, an infinity-edge soaking Jacuzzi tub, and a personal relaxation area. No detail is overlooked, from the warm foot bath when you arrive to the refreshing hot tea served on your personal enclosed garden lanai after your treatment. See p. 164.

- **Spa Luana at Turtle Bay Resort** (Oahu; ℂ **808/447-6868;** www.turtle bayresort.com): This Zen-like spa, positioned on the ground floor facing the ocean, has six treatment rooms, a meditation waiting area, an outdoor workout area, plus a complete fitness center and a private elevator to the rooms on the second floor, reserved for guests getting spa treatments. See p. 167.

PAMPERING IN paradise

Hawaii's spas have raised the art of relaxation and healing to a new level. The traditional Greco-Roman-style spas have evolved into airy, open facilities that embrace the tropics. Spa-goers in Hawaii want to hear the sound of the ocean, smell the salt air, and feel the caress of the warm breeze. They want to experience Hawaiian products and traditional treatments they can get only here.

Today's spas offer a wide diversity of treatments. Massage options include Hawaiian lomilomi, Swedish, aromatherapy, craniosacral (massaging the head), shiatsu (no oil, just deep thumb pressure on acupuncture points), Thai (another oilless massage involving stretching), and hot stone. There are even side-by-side massages for couples, and duo massages—two massage therapists working on you at once.

Body treatments, for the entire body or just the face, involve a variety of herbal wraps, masks, or scrubs using a range of ingredients from seaweed to salt to mud, with or without accompanying aromatherapy.

After you have been rubbed and scrubbed, most spas offer an array of water treatments—a sort of hydromassage in a tub with jets and an assortment of colored crystals, oils, and scents.

Those are just the traditional treatments. Most spas also provide a range of alternative healthcare like acupuncture and chiropractic, and more exotic treatments like ayurvedic and siddha from India or reiki from Japan. Some use cutting-edge treatments, like the Grand Wailea Resort's full-spectrum color-light therapy pod (based on NASA's work with astronauts).

Spas also have a range of fitness facilities (weights, racquetball, tennis, golf) and classes (yoga, aerobics, spinning, tai chi, kickboxing). Several even offer adventure fitness packages (from bicycling to snorkeling). For the less active, most spas also have salons dedicated to hair and nail care.

Of course, all this pampering doesn't come cheap. Massages are generally $175 to $275 for 50 minutes and $295 to $350 for 80 minutes; body treatments are in the $150 to $300 range; and alternative healthcare treatments can be as high as $250 to $350. But you may think it's worth the expense to banish your tension and stress.

o **Ihilani Spa at the JW Marriott Ihilani Resort** (Oahu; *℄* **808/679-0079;** www.ihilani.com): An oasis by the sea, this free-standing 35,000-square-foot facility is dedicated to the traditional spa definition of "health by water." The modern, multistoried spa, filled with floor-to-ceiling glass looking out on green tropical plants, combines Hawaiian products with traditional therapies to produce some of the best water treatments in the state. You'll also find a fitness center, tennis courts, and a bevy of aerobic and stretching classes. See p. 168.

o **Hualalai Sports Club & Spa at the Four Seasons Resort Hualalai at Historic Kaupulehu** (Big Island; *℄* **808/325-8000;** www.fourseasons.com/hualalai): It's easy to see why some 6,000 *Condé Nast Traveler* readers voted this 13,000-square-foot facility their favorite resort spa. Five of its sixteen treatment rooms are thatched huts (with bamboo privacy screens) nestled

Spa Kea Lani at the Fairmont Kea Lani Maui.

into a tropical garden. This is the place to come to be pampered. The fitness facilities, classes, and adventure activities are all excellent, but the attentive service and dreamy spa facilities are what you will remember long after your vacation. See p. 309.

o **Kohala Sports Club & Spa at the Hilton Waikoloa Village** (Big Island; *C* **808/886-2828;** www.hiltonwaikoloavillage.com): The Big Island's oldest (since 1989) spa has something for everyone, including 33 treatment rooms, 50 classes, and a variety of sports ranging from racquetball to indoor rock climbing. Treatments are on the cutting edge and include such unique therapies as acupuncture facials and astrological readings. Spend the day luxuriating in the lava whirlpool, steam room, and sauna before or after your treatment. See p. 322.

o **Spa Moana at the Hyatt Regency Maui Resort** (Maui; *C* **808/661-1234;** www.maui.hyatt.com): You cannot match the location: This is Hawaii's only oceanfront spa. The 20,000-square-foot spa houses 15 relaxing treatment rooms and features one of the island's best full-service fitness centers, plus a relaxation lounge, two romantic couples' suites, a salon and retail shop, and new treatments for kids and teenagers. See p. 440.

o **Spa Kea Lani at the Fairmont Kea Lani Maui** (Maui; *C* **808/875-2229;** www.fairmont.com/kealani): Come to this intimate Art Deco boutique spa (just a little over 5,000 sq. ft., with nine treatment rooms) for personal and private attention. The fitness center is just next door. See p. 458.

o **The Spa at Four Seasons Resort Maui at Wailea** (Maui; *C* **808/874-8000;** www.fourseasons.com/maui): This oasis in the luxurious Four Seasons offers a menu of pampering—from traditional Hawaiian massage to ayurvedic, plus Vichy shower treatments, body wraps, body scrubs, facials, and even ocean aquacranial massage for the ultimate in relaxation. You don't just get a massage here; you can choose from a list of therapies: hot stone, reiki, jin shin do, Swedish, aromatherapy, shiatsu, reflexology, and Thai. See p. 459.

o **Spa Grande at the Grand Wailea Resort Hotel** (Maui; *C* **808/875-1234;** www.grandwailea.com): This is Hawaii's biggest spa, at 50,000 square feet, with 40 treatment rooms. The spa incorporates the best of the Old World (romantic ceiling murals, larger-than-life Roman-style sculptures, mammoth Greek columns, huge European tubs), the finest Eastern traditions (a full Japanese-style traditional bath and various exotic treatments from India), and the lure of the Hawaiian Islands (tropical foliage, ancient Hawaiian treatments, and local products). It has everything from a top fitness center to a menu of classes and is constantly on the cutting edge of the latest trends. See p. 460.

o **ANARA Spa at the Grand Hyatt Kauai Resort** (Kauai; ℂ **808/742-1234;** www.kauai.hyatt.com): Come here to get rid of stress and to be soothed and pampered in a Hawaiian atmosphere, where the spirit of aloha reigns. An elegant 25,000-square-foot spa, ANARA (A New Age Restorative Approach) focuses on Hawaiian culture and healing, with some 16 treatment rooms, a lap pool, fitness facilities, lava-rock showers that open to the tropical air, outdoor whirlpools, a 24-head Swiss shower, Turkish steam rooms, Finnish saunas, and botanical soaking tubs. Recent renovations make this spa even more serene and relaxing. The four-handed massage (two therapists at once) is not to be missed. See p. 644.

THE best DINING, HAWAII STYLE

o **Tropical Fruit:** The **mangosteen,** the queen of fruit in Indonesia, is the sensation at the Hilo Farmers Market on the Big Island. Mangosteen's elegant purple skin and soft, white, floral-flavored flesh (like litchi, but more custardlike) make this fruit a sure winner.

The mango is always a much-anticipated feature of late spring and summer. **Hayden mangoes** are universally loved for their plump, juicy flesh and brilliant skins. **White Pirie mangoes,** with their resinous flavor and fine, fiberless flesh, are even better; this rare and ambrosial variety can be found in Honolulu's Chinatown or at roadside fruit stands in rural Oahu. Watch for the

Some of Hawaii's local produce.

Rapoza mango, a new large, sweet, fiberless fruit introduced to Hawaii several years ago.

Kahuku papayas—firm, fleshy, dark orange, and so juicy they sometimes squirt—are the ones to watch for on menus and in markets; check out the roadside stands in Kahuku on Oahu, and at supermarkets. **Sunrise papayas** from Kapoho and Kauai are also top-notch.

White, acid-free, extra-sweet, and grown on Kauai and the Big Island, **Sugarloaf pineapples** are the new rage. Hilo is the town for **litchis** (also known as lychees) in summer, but Honolulu's Chinatown markets carry them, too. **Ka'u oranges,** grown in the volcanic soil of the southern Big Island, are available in supermarkets and health food stores. Don't be fooled by their brown, ugly skin—they're juicy, thin-skinned, and sweet as honey.

o **Noodles:** Ramen, udon, saimin, pho, pasta, chow mein—Hawaii is the epicenter of ethnic noodle stands and houses, with many recommendable and inexpensive choices. **Jimbo's Restaurant** (Oahu; ✆ 808/947-2211), a neighborhood staple, is tops for freshly made udon with generous toppings and a homemade broth (p. 191). On the neighbor islands, **Nori's Saimin & Snacks** (Big Island; ✆ 808/935-9133) is the place in charming Hilo for consummate saimin of every stripe (p. 351). And noodle mania prevails at **Hamura's Saimin Stand** (Kauai; ✆ 808/245-3271), where saimin and teriyaki sticks have replaced hamburgers and pizza as the late-night comfort-food tradition (p. 662).

o **Plate Lunches: Zippy's** (21 locations throughout Oahu; call ✆ 808/973-0880 for the one nearest you) is a household word in Hawaii. Other favorite plate-lunch spots on Oahu include **Kakaako Kitchen** (✆ 808/596-7488; p. 288), which serves dinner at indoor and outdoor tables at the Ward Centre; **I ♥ Country Café** (✆ 808/596-8108; p. 182), at Ala Moana Plaza; and **Yama's Fish Market** (✆ 808/941-9994; p. 282), where the chocolate/macadamia-nut cookies and chocolate biscotti have legions of fans. On Maui, **Aloha Mixed Plate** (✆ 808/661-3322; p. 479) lets you nosh on fabulous shoyu chicken at ocean's edge—and with a mai tai, too. On Kauai, **Pono Market** (✆ 808/822-4581; p. 660), **Fish Express** (✆ 808/245-9918; p. 661), and **Koloa Fish Market** (✆ 808/742-6199; p. 660) are at the top of the plate-lunch pyramid.

Shave ice.

o **Shave Ice:** Like surfing, shave ice is synonymous with Haleiwa, the North Shore Oahu town where **Matsumoto Shave Ice** (✆ 808/637-4827; p. 291) serves mounds of the icy treat. Shave ice is even better over ice cream and adzuki beans.

○ **Other Mighty Morsels:** Poi biscotti from the **Poi Company,** available at supermarkets and gourmet outlets, are the consummate accompaniment to another island phenomenon, Kona coffee. Coffee growers of highest esteem (all based on the Big Island, of course), include **Rooster Farms** (✆ 808/328-9173), which sells and ships only organic coffees; **Bong Brothers** (✆ 808/328-9289); **Kona Blue Sky Coffee Company** (✆ 808/322-1700); **Langenstein Farms** (✆ 808/328-8356); and **Holualoa Kona Coffee Company** (✆ 800/334-0348). See "Kona Coffee Craze!" (p. 339) for details.

The buttery, chocolate-dipped shortbread cookies of **Big Island Candies** (Big Island; ✆ 808/935-8890; p. 417 are worth every calorie and every dollar. From Kauai, Hanapepe town's venerable **Taro Ko Chips Factory** (✆ 808/335-5586; p. 721) makes taro chips that neighbor islanders drive miles to find.

THE best RESTAURANTS

○ **La Mer** (Oahu; ✆ 808/923-2311; www.halekulani.com): This romantic, elegant dining room at Waikiki's Halekulani is the only AAA Five Diamond restaurant in the state. The second-floor, open-sided room, with views of Diamond Head and the sound of trade winds rustling the nearby coconut fronds, is the epitome of fine dining. Michelin award–winning chef Yves Garnier melds classical French influences with fresh Island ingredients. It's pricey but worth it. Men are required to wear jackets (they have a selection if you didn't pack one). See p. 170.

○ **Chef Mavro Restaurant** (Oahu; ✆ 808/944-4714; www.chefmavro.com): Honolulu is abuzz over the wine pairings and elegant cuisine of George Mavrothalassitis, the culinary wizard and James Beard Award–winner from Provence who turned La Mer (at the Halekulani) and Seasons (at the Four Seasons Resort Wailea) into temples of fine dining. He brought his award-winning signature dishes with him and continues to prove his ingenuity with dazzling a la carte and prix-fixe ($65–$150) menus. See p. 189.

○ **Alan Wong's Restaurant** (Oahu; ✆ 808/949-2526; www.alanwongs.com): Master strokes at this shrine of Hawaii Regional Cuisine include warm California rolls made with salmon roe, wasabi, and Kona lobster instead of rice; luau lumpia with butterfish and kalua pig; and ginger-crusted fresh onaga. Opihi shooters and day-boat scallops in season are a must, and grilled lamb chops are a perennial special. The menu changes daily, but the flavors never lose their sizzle. See p. 189.

○ **3660 on the Rise** (Oahu; ✆ 808/737-1177; www.3660.com): Ever since *Wine Spectator* gave this restaurant its Award of Excellence, this place has been packed, and with good reason. In his 200-seat restaurant, chef Russell Siu adds an Asian or local touch to the basics: rack of lamb with macadamia nuts, filet of catfish in *ponzu* sauce, and seared ahi salad with grilled shiitake mushrooms, a local favorite. See p. 192.

○ **Hoku's** (Oahu; ✆ 808/739-8780; www.kahalaresort.com/dining/hoku. cfm): Elegant without being stuffy, creative without being overwrought, the kitchen at the Kahala Hotel & Resort creates fusion cuisine that really works—European finesse with an Island touch. The ocean view, open kitchen, and astonishing bamboo floor are stellar features. Reflecting the restaurant's cross-cultural influences, the kitchen is equipped with a kiawe grill, an Indian tandoori oven, and Szechuan woks. The Sunday brunch is one of the best on Oahu. See p. 194.

o **Roy's Restaurant** (Oahu; ⓒ 808/396-7697; www.roysrestaurant.com): Good food still reigns at this busy, noisy flagship dining room in Hawaii Kai with its trademark open kitchen. Roy Yamaguchi's deft way with local ingredients, nostalgic ethnic preparations, and fresh fish makes his menu, which changes daily, a novel experience every time. See p. 195.

o **Merriman's** (Big Island, ⓒ 808/885-6822; Maui, 808/669-6400; Kauai, ⓒ 808/742-8385; www.merrimanshawaii.com): Chef Peter Merriman, one of the founders of Hawaii Regional Cuisine, displays his creativity at restaurants in Waimea (on the Big Island), Kapalua (on Maui), and his newest outpost in Poipu (on Kauai). Dishes include his signature wok-charred ahi, kung pao shrimp, or lamb from the Big Island's Kahua Ranch. Merriman was developing relationships with ranchers and farmers to supply locally sourced food to his restaurants long before it became trendy. A dinner at Merriman's is a memorable event; every course is done to perfection and the menu identifies where he got the ingredients. See p. 345, 487, and 665.

o **Son'z Maui at Swan Court** (Maui; ⓒ 808/667-4506; www.maui.hyatt. com): For 30 years, the Swan Court was *the* dining experience at the Hyatt Regency Maui. When Tri-Star Restaurant Group CEO Aaron Placourakis took over this restaurant, he and executive chef Geno Sarmiento knew they wanted to hit a home run every night with the cuisine. The restaurant already had perhaps the most romantic location in Maui, overlooking a man-made lagoon with white and black swans swimming by and the rolling surf of the Pacific in the distance. Inside, the culinary team's creative dishes, fresh local ingredients (Kula corn and strawberries, Ono Farms avocados, Hana hearts of palm, Maui Cattle Company beef, fresh Hawaiian fish, and sweet Maui onions), top-notch service, and relaxing atmosphere make this one of Maui's best restaurants. See p. 482.

o **Pineapple Grill** (Maui; ⓒ 808/669-9600; www.pineapplekapalua.com): If you had only a single night to eat on the island of Maui, this would be the place to go. In fact, if you eat here at the beginning of your Maui trip, you are definitely going to want to come back! Up-and-coming chef Ryan Luckey (a local Lahaina boy) is a genius, combining Asian/Filipino ingredients into culinary masterpieces. You'll find lots of tasty sandwiches and salads at lunch, and a continental-style breakfast in the morning—all served in a very Maui-like atmosphere overlooking the rolling hills of the Kapalua golf course out to the Pacific Ocean. See p. 488.

o **Haliimaile General Store** (Maui; ⓒ 808/572-2666; www.haliimailegeneral store.com): Bev Gannon, one of the original Hawaii Regional Cuisine chefs, is still going strong at her foodie haven in the pineapple fields. You'll dine at tables set on old wood floors under high ceilings, in a peach-colored room emblazoned with works by local artists. Gannon's Texas roots shine through in her food, a blend of eclectic American with ethnic touches that puts an innovative spin on Hawaii Regional Cuisine. See p. 495.

Dondero's restaurant.

- **Ihilani** (Lanai; © **808/565-2296**; www.fourseasons.com/manelebay/dining): A number of top Hawaii chefs (such as Philippe Padovani and Edwin Goto) have each added a bit of their own style during their tenure here, but the common denominator is the melding of Mediterranean with Island cuisine. The result is Lanai's top gourmet restaurant, in a formal atmosphere with inspiring food. The latest incarnation of this classy restaurant, overlooking the resort and the ocean beyond, is traditional Italian cuisine, priced moderately for the Four Seasons Resort Lanai at Manele Bay. See p. 613.

- **Dondero's** (Kauai; © **808/742-1234**; www.kauai.hyatt.com): If you're looking for a romantic dinner, Dondero's, at the Grand Hyatt Kauai, is hard to beat. Dine either under the stars overlooking the ocean or tucked away at an intimate table surrounded by inlaid marble floors, ornate imported tiles, and Franciscan murals. You get all this atmosphere plus the best Italian cuisine on the island, served with efficiency. It's hard to have a bad experience here. Dinners are pricey but worth every penny. See p. 664.

- **Kauai Grill** (Kauai; © **808/826-9644**): For a romantic, splurge meal, this is it! Located in the luxurious St. Regis Hotel on the North Shore, Kauai Grill has a spectacular view (dramatic Bali Hai–like peaks in the background and the rolling surf just outside), but combined with the decor (spiraling lit fabric ceiling in the shape of a nautilus shell with a ruby glass hibiscus chandelier) and the amazing cuisine of Chef Jean-George Vongerichten, this is a foodies' paradise. See p. 673.

THE best SPOTS FOR SUNSET COCKTAILS

o **Sunset Lanai Lounge,** at the New Otani Kaimana Beach Hotel (Oahu; © 808/923-1555): The hau tree here shaded Robert Louis Stevenson as he wrote poems to Princess Kaiulani; today it frames the ocean view from the Sunset Lanai Lounge. This lounge is the favorite watering hole of Diamond Head–area beachgoers, who love Sans Souci Beach, the ocean view, the mai tais, and the live music during weekend sunset hours. See p. 161.

o **Jameson's by the Sea** (Oahu; © 808/637-6272): The mai tais here are dubbed the best in surf city, and the view, though not perfect, doesn't hurt, either. Across the street from the harbor, this open-air roadside oasis is a happy stop for North Shore wave watchers and sunset-savvy sightseers. See p. 197.

o **Mai Tai Bar,** at the Royal Hawaiian (Oahu; © 808/923-7311): This bar without walls is perched a few feet from the sand, with pleasing views of the south shore and the Waianae Mountains. Surfers and paddlers ride the waves while Diamond Head acquires a golden sunset halo. Sip a mighty mai tai while Carmen and Keith Haugen serenade you. See p. 152.

o **House Without a Key,** at the Halekulani (Oahu; © 808/923-2311): Oahu's quintessential sunset oasis offers a view of Diamond Head, great hula and steel-guitar music, and the best mai tais on the island—all under a century-old kiawe tree. Even jaded locals are unable to resist the lure. See p. 292.

Huggo's on the Rocks.

o **Duke's Waikiki,** at the Outrigger Waikiki on the Beach (Oahu; ℂ **808/922-2268**): It's crowded in the evening, but who can resist Hawaiian music with Waikiki sand still on your feet? Come in from the beach or the street—it's always a party at Duke's. Entertainment here is tops, reaching a crescendo at sunset. See p. 151.

o **Beach Tree Bar & Grill,** at the Four Seasons Resort Hualalai (Big Island; ℂ **808/325-8000**): The bar on the beach seats only a handful, but the restaurant will accept the overflow. This is the finest sunset perch in North Kona, with consummate people-watching, tasty drinks, and the gorgeous ocean. The open-air restaurant, with Hawaiian music and hula dancing at sunset, also serves excellent fare. See p. 333.

o **Huggo's on the Rocks** (Big Island; ℂ **808/329-1493**): Here's a thatched-bar fantasy that's *really* on the rocks. This mound of thatch, rock, and grassy-sandy ground right next to Huggo's restaurant is a sunset lover's nirvana. Sip a tropical drink while reclining on a chaise and nosh on Island-style appetizers while the ocean laps at your feet. See p. 334.

o **Kimo's** (Maui; ℂ **808/661-4811**): An oceanfront dining room and deck, upstairs dining, and happy-hour drinks draw a fun-loving Lahaina crowd. Nibble on sashimi or nachos and take in the views of Lanai and Molokai. See p. 478.

o **Hula Grill** (Maui; ℂ **808/667-6636**): Sit outdoors at the Barefoot Bar, order drinks, nibble on macadamia nut and crab wontons, and marvel at the wonders of West Maui, where the sun sets slowly and Lanai looks like a giant whale offshore. It's simply magical. See p. 566.

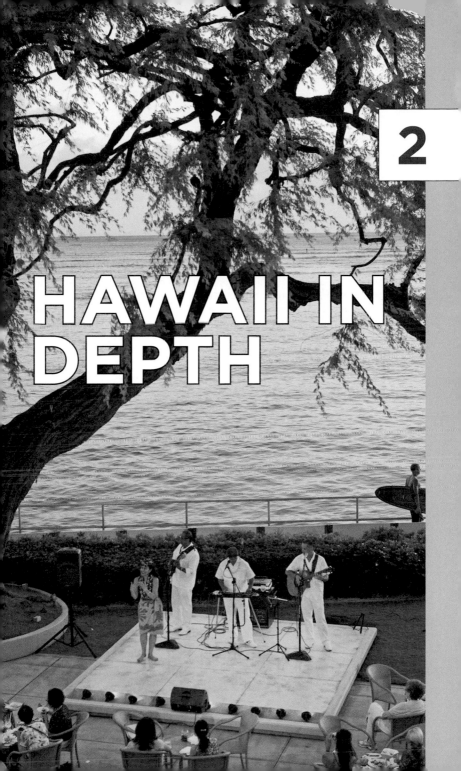

2

HAWAII IN DEPTH

S ince the Polynesians ventured across the Pacific to the Hawaiian Islands more than 1,000 years ago, these floating jewels have continued to call visitors from around the globe.

Located in one of the most remote and isolated places on the planet, the islands bask in the warm waters of the Pacific, where they are blessed by a tropical sun and cooled by gentle year-round trade winds—creating what might be the most ideal climate imaginable. Centuries of the indigenous Hawaiian culture have given the people of the islands the "spirit of aloha," a warm, welcoming attitude that invites visitors to come and share this exotic paradise. Mother Nature has carved out verdant valleys, hung brilliant rainbows in the sky, and trimmed the islands with sandy beaches in a spectrum of colors, from white to black to even green and red.

Visitors are drawn to Hawaii not only for its incredible beauty, but also for its opportunities for adventure: bicycling down a 10,000-foot dormant volcano, swimming in a sea of rainbow-colored fish, hiking into a rainforest, or watching whales leap out of the ocean as you tee off on one of the country's top golf courses. Others come to rest and relax in a land where the pace of life moves at a slower rate and the sun's rays soothe and allow both body and mind to regenerate and recharge.

Venturing to Hawaii is not your run-of-the-mill vacation, but rather an experience in the senses that will remain with you, locked into your memory, long after your tan fades. Years later, a sweet smell, the warmth of the sun on your body, or the sound of the wind through the trees will take you back to the time you spent in the Hawaiian Islands.

HAWAII TODAY
A Cultural Renaissance

A conch shell sounds, a young man in a bright feather cape chants, torchlight flickers at sunset on Waikiki Beach, and hula dancers begin telling their graceful centuries-old stories. It's a cultural scene out of the past, come to life once again—for Hawaii is enjoying a renaissance of hula, chant, and other aspects of its ancient culture.

The biggest, longest, and most elaborate celebrations of Hawaiian culture are the Aloha Festivals, which encompass more than 500 cultural events from August to October. "Our goal is to teach and share our culture," says Gloriann Akau, who manages the Big Island's Aloha Festivals. "In 1946, after the war, Hawaiians needed an identity. We were lost and needed to regroup. When we started to celebrate our culture, we began to feel proud. We have a wonderful culture that had been buried for a number of years. This brought it out again. Self-esteem is more important than making a lot of money."

PREVIOUS PAGE: **The stage at Oahu's House Without a Key.**

In 1985, native Hawaiian educator, author, and *kupuna* (respected elder) George Kanahele started integrating Hawaiian values into hotels like the Big Island's Mauna Lani and Maui's Kaanapali Beach Hotel. "You have the responsibility to preserve and enhance the Hawaiian culture, not because it's going to make money for you, but because it's the right thing to do," Kanahele told the Hawaii Hotel Association. "Ultimately, the only thing unique about Hawaii is its Hawaiianness. Hawaiianness is our competitive edge."

From general managers to maids, resort employees went through hours of Hawaiian cultural training. They held focus groups to discuss the meaning of aloha—the Hawaiian concept of unconditional love—and applied it to their work and their lives. Now many hotels have joined the movement and instituted Hawaiian cultural programs. No longer content with teaching hula as a joke, resorts now employ a real *kumu hula* (hula teacher) to instruct visitors and have a *kupuna* (elder) to take guests on treks to visit *heiau* (temples) and ancient petroglyph sites.

Lanai's Aloha Festival.

The Question of Sovereignty

The Hawaiian cultural renaissance has also made its way into politics. Many *kanaka maoli* (native people) are demanding restoration of rights taken away more than a century ago when the U.S. overthrew the Hawaiian monarchy. Their demands were not lost on President Bill Clinton, who was picketed at a Democratic political fundraiser at Waikiki Beach in July 1993. Four months later, Clinton signed a document stating that the U.S. Congress "apologizes to Native Hawaiians on behalf of the people of the United States for the overthrow of the Kingdom of Hawaii on January 17, 1893, with the participation of agents and citizens of the United States, and deprivation of the rights of Native Hawaiians to self-determination."

But even neonationalists aren't convinced that complete self-determination is possible. Each of the 30 identifiable sovereignty organizations (and more than 100 splinter groups) has a different stated goal, ranging from total independence to nation-within-a-nation status, similar to that of Native Indians. In 1993, the state legislature created a Hawaiian Sovereignty Advisory Commission to "determine the will of the native Hawaiian people." The commission plans to pose the sovereignty question in a referendum open to anyone over 18 with Hawaiian blood, no matter where they live. The question still remains unanswered.

LOOKING BACK AT HAWAII

Paddling outrigger canoes, the first ancestors of today's Hawaiians followed the stars and birds across the ocean to Hawaii, which they called "the land of raging fire." Those first settlers were part of the great Polynesian migration that settled the vast triangle of islands stretching between New Zealand, Easter Island, and Hawaii. No one is sure exactly when they came to Hawaii from Tahiti and the Marquesas Islands, some 2,500 miles to the south, but a bone fishhook found at the southernmost tip of the Big Island has been carbon-dated from A.D. 700. Chants claim that the Mookini Heiau (a temple made from stones), also on the Big Island, was built in A.D. 480.

An entire Hawaiian culture arose from these settlers, with each island becoming a separate kingdom. The inhabitants built temples, fish ponds, and aqueducts to irrigate taro plantations. Sailors became farmers and fishermen. The *alii* (high-ranking chiefs) created a caste system and established taboos—anyone who broke those taboos could be sacrificed.

The "Fatal Catastrophe"

No ancient Hawaiian ever imagined a *haole* (a white person; literally, one with "no breath") would ever appear on one of these islands. But then one day in 1778, just such a person sailed into Waimea Bay on Kauai, where he was welcomed as the god Lono.

The man was 50-year-old Capt. James Cook, already famous in Britain for "discovering" much of the South Pacific. Now on his third great voyage of exploration, Cook had set sail from Tahiti northward across uncharted waters to find

The Mookini Heiau.

James Cook.

Kealakekua Bay.

Statue of Father Damien.

the mythical Northwest Passage that was said to link the Pacific and Atlantic oceans. On his way, Cook stumbled upon the Hawaiian Islands quite by chance. He named them the Sandwich Islands, for the Earl of Sandwich, first lord of the admiralty, who had bankrolled the expedition

Overnight, stone-age Hawaii entered the age of iron. Nails were traded for fresh water, pigs, and the affections of Hawaiian women. The sailors brought syphilis, measles, and other diseases to which the Hawaiians had no natural immunity, thereby unwittingly wreaking havoc on the native population.

After his unsuccessful attempt to find the Northwest Passage, Cook returned to Kealakekua Bay on the Big Island, where a fight broke out over an alleged theft, and the great navigator was killed by a blow to the head. After this "fatal catastrophe," the British survivors sailed home. But Hawaii was now on the sea charts, and traders on the fur route between Canada and China anchored in Hawaii to get fresh water. More trade—and more disastrous liaisons—ensued.

Two more sea captains left indelible marks on the islands. The first was American John Kendrick, who in 1791 filled his ship with sandalwood and sailed to China. By 1825, Hawaii's sandalwood forests were gone, enabling invasive plants to take charge. The second captain was Englishman George Vancouver, who in 1793 left cows and sheep, which spread out to the high-tide lines. King Kamehameha I sent for cowboys from Mexico and Spain to round up the wild livestock, thus beginning the islands' *paniolo* (cowboy) tradition.

The tightly woven Hawaiian society began to unravel after the death in 1819 of King Kamehameha I, who had used guns seized from a British ship to unite the islands under his rule. One of his successors, Queen Kaahumanu, abolished the old taboos and opened the door for religion of another form.

Hawaii History & Legend

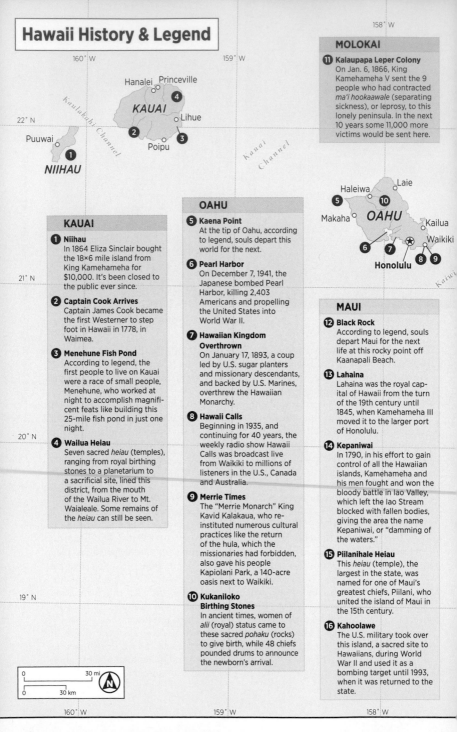

MOLOKAI

⑪ Kalaupapa Leper Colony
On Jan. 6, 1866, King Kamehameha V sent the 9 people who had contracted *ma'i hookaawale* (separating sickness), or leprosy, to this lonely peninsula. In the next 10 years some 11,000 more victims would be sent here.

KAUAI

① Niihau
In 1864 Eliza Sinclair bought the 18×6 mile island from King Kamehameha for $10,000. It's been closed to the public ever since.

② Captain Cook Arrives
Captain James Cook became the first Westerner to step foot in Hawaii in 1778, in Waimea.

③ Menehune Fish Pond
According to legend, the first people to live on Kauai were a race of small people, Menehune, who worked at night to accomplish magnificent feats like building this 25-mile fish pond in just one night.

④ Wailua Heiau
Seven sacred *heiau* (temples), ranging from royal birthing stones to a planetarium to a sacrificial site, lined this district, from the mouth of the Wailua River to Mt. Waialeale. Some remains of the *heiau* can still be seen.

OAHU

⑤ Kaena Point
At the tip of Oahu, according to legend, souls depart this world for the next.

⑥ Pearl Harbor
On December 7, 1941, the Japanese bombed Pearl Harbor, killing 2,403 Americans and propelling the United States into World War II.

⑦ Hawaiian Kingdom Overthrown
On January 17, 1893, a coup led by U.S. sugar planters and missionary descendants, and backed by U.S. Marines, overthrew the Hawaiian Monarchy.

⑧ Hawaii Calls
Beginning in 1935, and continuing for 40 years, the weekly radio show Hawaii Calls was broadcast live from Waikiki to millions of listeners in the U.S., Canada and Australia.

⑨ Merrie Times
The "Merrie Monarch" King Kavid Kalakaua, who re-instituted numerous cultural practices like the return of the hula, which the missionaries had forbidden, also gave his people Kapiolani Park, a 140-acre oasis next to Waikiki.

⑩ Kukaniloko Birthing Stones
In ancient times, women of *alii* (royal) status came to these sacred *pohaku* (rocks) to give birth, while 48 chiefs pounded drums to announce the newborn's arrival.

MAUI

⑫ Black Rock
According to legend, souls depart Maui for the next life at this rocky point off Kaanapali Beach.

⑬ Lahaina
Lahaina was the royal capital of Hawaii from the turn of the 19th century until 1845, when Kamehameha III moved it to the larger port of Honolulu.

⑭ Kepaniwai
In 1790, in his effort to gain control of all the Hawaiian islands, Kamehameha and his men fought and won the bloody battle in Iao Valley, which left the Iao Stream blocked with fallen bodies, giving the area the name Kepaniwai, or "damming of the waters."

⑮ Piilanihale Heiau
This *heiau* (temple), the largest in the state, was named for one of Maui's greatest chiefs, Piilani, who united the island of Maui in the 15th century.

⑯ Kahoolawe
The U.S. military took over this island, a sacred site to Hawaiians, during World War II and used it as a bombing target until 1993, when it was returned to the state.

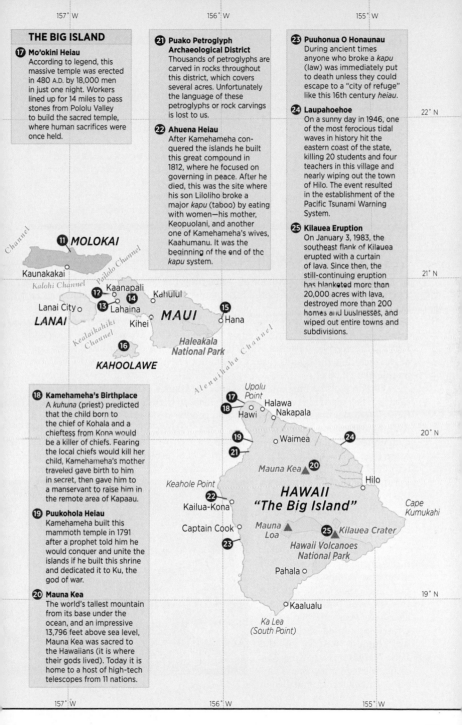

THE BIG ISLAND

17 Mo'okini Heiau
According to legend, this massive temple was erected in 480 A.D. by 18,000 men in just one night. Workers lined up for 14 miles to pass stones from Pololu Valley to build the sacred temple, where human sacrifices were once held.

21 Puako Petroglyph Archaeological District
Thousands of petroglyphs are carved in rocks throughout this district, which covers several acres. Unfortunately the language of these petroglyphs or rock carvings is lost to us.

22 Ahuena Heiau
After Kamehameha conquered the islands he built this great compound in 1812, where he focused on governing in peace. After he died, this was the site where his son Liloliho broke a major *kapu* (taboo) by eating with women—his mother, Keopuolani, and another one of Kamehameha's wives, Kaahumanu. It was the beginning of the end of the *kapu* system.

23 Puuhonua O Honaunau
During ancient times anyone who broke a *kapu* (law) was immediately put to death unless they could escape to a "city of refuge" like this 16th century *heiau*.

24 Laupahoehoe
On a sunny day in 1946, one of the most ferocious tidal waves in history hit the eastern coast of the state, killing 20 students and four teachers in this village and nearly wiping out the town of Hilo. The event resulted in the establishment of the Pacific Tsunami Warning System.

25 Kilauea Eruption
On January 3, 1983, the southeast flank of Kilauea erupted with a curtain of lava. Since then, the still-continuing eruption has blanketed more than 20,000 acres with lava, destroyed more than 200 homes and businesses, and wiped out entire towns and subdivisions.

18 Kamehameha's Birthplace
A *kuhuna* (priest) predicted that the child born to the chief of Kohala and a chieftess from Kona would be a killer of chiefs. Fearing the local chiefs would kill her child, Kamehameha's mother traveled gave birth to him in secret, then gave him to a manservant to raise him in the remote area of Kapaau.

19 Puukohola Heiau
Kamehameha built this mammoth temple in 1791 after a prophet told him he would conquer and unite the islands if he built this shrine and dedicated it to Ku, the god of war.

20 Mauna Kea
The world's tallest mountain from its base under the ocean, and an impressive 13,796 feet above sea level, Mauna Kea was sacred to the Hawaiians (it is where their gods lived). Today it is home to a host of high-tech telescopes from 11 nations.

IS EVERYONE hawaiian IN HAWAII?

The plantations brought so many different people to Hawaii that the state is now a rainbow of ethnic groups: Living here are Caucasians, African Americans, American Indians, Eskimos, Japanese, Chinese, Filipinos, Koreans, Tahitians, Vietnamese, Hawaiians, Samoans, Tongans, and other Asian and Pacific Islanders. Add to that a few Canadians, Dutch, English, French, Germans, Irish, Italians, Portuguese, Scottish, Puerto Ricans, and Spaniards.

In combination, it's a remarkable potpourri. Many people retain an element of the traditions of their homeland. Some Japanese Americans in Hawaii, generations removed from the homeland, are more traditional than the Japanese of Tokyo. And the same is true of many Chinese, Koreans, Filipinos, and others, making Hawaii a kind of living museum of various Asian and Pacific cultures.

Staying to Do Well

In April 1820, missionaries bent on converting the "pagans" arrived from New England. The missionaries clothed the natives, banned them from dancing the hula, and nearly dismantled their ancient culture. They tried to keep the whalers and sailors out of the bawdy houses, where a flood of whiskey quenched fleet-size thirsts and the virtue of native women was never safe. They taught reading and writing, created the 12-letter Hawaiian alphabet, started a printing press, and began recording the islands' history, which until then was only an oral account in memorized chants.

Children of the missionaries became the islands' business leaders and politicians. They married Hawaiians and stayed on in the islands, causing one wag to remark that the missionaries "came to do good and stayed to do well." In 1848, King Kamehameha III proclaimed the Great Mahele (division), which enabled commoners and eventually foreigners to own crown land. In two generations, more than 80% of all private land was in *haole* (foreign) hands. Sugar planters imported waves of immigrants (Chinese starting in 1852, Japanese in 1885, and Portuguese in 1878) to work the fields as contract laborers.

King David Kalakaua was elected to the throne in 1874. This popular "Merrie Monarch" built Iolani Palace in 1882, threw extravagant parties, and lifted the prohibitions on the hula and other native arts. For this, he was much loved. He also gave Pearl Harbor to the United States; it became the westernmost bastion of the U.S. Navy. In 1891, King Kalakaua visited chilly San Francisco, caught a cold, and died in

Iolani Palace.

the royal suite of the Sheraton Palace. His sister, Queen Liliuokalani, assumed the throne.

A Sad Farewell

On January 17, 1893, a group of American sugar planters and missionary descendants, with the support of U.S. Marines, imprisoned Queen Liliuokalani in her own palace, where she later penned the sorrowful lyric "Aloha Oe," Hawaii's song of farewell. The monarchy was dead.

A new republic was then established, controlled by Sanford Dole, a powerful sugar-cane planter. In 1898, through annexation, Hawaii became an American territory ruled by Dole. His fellow sugar cane planters, known as the

The statue of Queen Liliuokalani on the grounds of the state capital.

Big Five, controlled banking, shipping, hardware, and every other facet of economic life on the islands.

Oahu's central Ewa Plain soon filled with row crops. The Dole family planted pineapple on its vast acreage. Planters imported more contract laborers from Puerto Rico (1900), Korea (1903), and the Philippines (1907–31). Most of the new immigrants stayed on to establish families and become a part of the islands. Meanwhile, the native Hawaiians became a landless minority.

For nearly a century on Hawaii, sugar was king, generously subsidized by the U.S. government. The sugar planters dominated the territory's economy, shaped its social fabric, and kept the islands in a colonial plantation era with bosses and field hands. But the workers eventually went on strike for higher wages and improved working conditions, and the planters found themselves unable to compete with cheap third-world labor costs.

pidgin: 'EH FO'REAL, BRAH

If you venture beyond the tourist areas, you might hear another local tongue: pidgin English, a conglomeration of slang and words from the Hawaiian language. "Broke da mouth" (tastes really good) is the favorite pidgin phrase and one you might hear; "'Eh fo'real, brah" means "It's true, brother." You could be invited to hear an elder "talk story" (relating myths and memories). But because pidgin is really the province of the locals, your visit to Hawaii is likely to pass without your hearing much pidgin at all.

DO YOU HAVE TO SPEAK
hawaiian IN HAWAII?

Almost everyone here speaks English. But many folks in Hawaii now speak Hawaiian as well. All visitors will hear the words *aloha* and *mahalo* (thank you). If you've just arrived, you're a *malihini*. Someone who's been here a long time is a *kamaaina*. When you finish a job or your meal, you are *pau* (finished). On Friday, it's *pau hana*, work finished. You eat *pupu* (Hawaii's version of hors d'oeuvres) when you go *pau hana*.

The Hawaiian alphabet, created by the New England missionaries, has only 12 letters: the five regular vowels (*a, e, i, o,* and *u*) and seven consonants (*h, k, l, m, n, p,* and *w*). The vowels are pronounced in the Roman fashion: that is, *ah, ay, ee, oh,* and *oo* (as in "too")—not *ay, ee, eye, oh,* and *you,* as in English. For example, *huhu* is pronounced *who-who.* Most vowels are sounded separately, though some are pronounced together, as in Kalakaua: Kah-lah-*cow*-ah.

Below are some basic Hawaiian words that you'll often hear in Hawaii and see throughout this book. For a more complete list of Hawaiian words, go to www.hisurf.com/hawaiian/dictionary.html.

alii   Hawaiian royalty
aloha   greeting or farewell
halau   school
hale   house or building
heiau   Hawaiian temple or place of worship
kahuna   priest or expert
kamaaina   old-timer
kapa   tapa, bark cloth
kapu   taboo, forbidden
keiki   child
kupuna   respected elder
lanai   porch or veranda
lomilomi   massage
mahalo   thank you
makai   a direction, toward the sea
mana   spirit power
mauka   a direction, toward the mountains
muumuu   loose-fitting gown or dress
ono   delicious
pali   cliff
paniolo   Hawaiian cowboy(s)
wiki   quick

The Tourists Arrive

Tourism proper began in the 1860s. Kilauea volcano was one of the world's prime attractions for adventure travelers. In 1865, a grass Volcano House was built on the rim of Halemaumau Crater to shelter visitors; it was Hawaii's first tourist hotel. But tourism really got off the ground with the demise of the plantation era.

In 1901, W. C. Peacock built the elegant Beaux Arts Moana Hotel on Waikiki Beach, and W. C. Weedon convinced Honolulu businessmen to bankroll his plan to advertise Hawaii in San Francisco. Armed with a stereopticon and tinted photos of Waikiki, Weedon sailed off in 1902 for 6 months of lecture tours to introduce "those remarkable people and the beautiful lands of Hawaii." He drew packed houses. A tourism promotion bureau was formed in 1903, and about 2,000 visitors came to Hawaii that year.

The steamship was Hawaii's tourism lifeline. It took 4½ days to sail from San Francisco to Honolulu. Streamers, leis, and pomp welcomed each Matson liner at downtown's Aloha Tower. Well-heeled visitors brought trunks, servants, and Rolls-Royces, and stayed for months. Hawaiians amused visitors with personal tours, floral parades, and shows spotlighting that naughty dance, the hula.

Beginning in 1935 and running for the next 40 years, Webley Edwards's weekly live radio show, "Hawaii Calls," planted the sounds of Waikiki—surf, sliding steel guitar, sweet Hawaiian harmonies, drumbeats—in the hearts of millions of listeners in the United States, Australia, and Canada.

By 1936, visitors could fly to Honolulu from San Francisco on the *Hawaii Clipper*, a seven-passenger Pan American Martin M-130 flying boat, for $360 one-way. The flight took 21 hours, 33 minutes. Modern tourism was born, with five flying boats providing daily service. The 1941 visitor count was a brisk 31,846 through December 6.

World War II & Its Aftermath

On December 7, 1941, Japanese Zeros came out of the rising sun to bomb American warships based at Pearl Harbor. This was the "day of infamy" that plunged the United States into World War II.

The attack brought immediate changes to the islands. Martial law was declared, stripping the Big Five cartel of its absolute power in a single day. Japanese Americans and German Americans were interned. Hawaii was "blacked out" at night, Waikiki Beach was strung with barbed wire, and Aloha Tower was painted in camouflage. Only young men bound for the Pacific came to Hawaii during the war years. Many came back to graves in a cemetery called Punchbowl.

The attack on Pearl Harbor.

The postwar years saw the beginnings of Hawaii's faux culture. Harry Yee invented the Blue Hawaii cocktail and dropped in a tiny Japanese parasol. Vic Bergeron created the mai tai, a drink made of rum and fresh lime juice, and opened Trader Vic's, America's first themed restaurant that featured the art, decor, and food of Polynesia. Arthur Godfrey picked up a ukulele and began singing *hapa-haole* tunes on early TV shows. In 1955, Henry J. Kaiser built the Hilton Hawaiian Village, and the 11-story high-rise Princess Kaiulani Hotel opened on a site where the real princess once played. Hawaii greeted 109,000 visitors that year.

The National Memorial Cemetery of the Pacific.

Statehood

In 1959, Hawaii became the 50th state of the United States. That year also saw the arrival of the first jet airliners, which brought 250,000 tourists to the state. The personal touch that had defined aloha gave way to the sheer force of numbers. Waikiki's room count nearly doubled in 2 years, from 16,000 units in 1969 to 31,000 in 1971, and kept increasing until city fathers finally clamped down on growth. By 1980, annual arrivals had reached four million.

In the early 1980s, the Japanese began traveling overseas in record numbers, and they brought lots of yen to spend. Their effect on sales in Hawaii was phenomenal: European boutiques opened branches in Honolulu, and duty-free shopping became the main supporter of Honolulu International Airport. Japanese investors competed for the chance to own or build part of Hawaii. Hotels sold so fast and at such unbelievable prices that heads began to spin with dollar signs.

In 1986, Hawaii's visitor count passed five million. Two years later, it went over six million. Expensive fantasy megaresorts bloomed on the neighbor islands like giant artificial flowers, swelling the luxury market with ever-swankier accommodations.

The visitor count was at a record 6.7 million in 1990 when the bubble burst in early 1991 with the Gulf War and worldwide recessions. In 1992, Hurricane Iniki devastated Kauai. Airfare wars sent Americans to Mexico and the Caribbean. Overbuilt with luxury hotels, Hawaii slashed its room rates, giving middle-class consumers access to high-end digs at affordable prices—a trend that continues as Hawaii struggles to stay atop the tourism heap.

Hawaii was finally back to record-breaking visitor counts (6.9 million) in 2000. Then September 11, 2001, sent a blow to Hawaii—tourism dropped abruptly, sending Hawaii's economy into a tailspin. But people eventually started traveling again, and in 2003, visitor arrivals were up to 6.3 million. By 2005, Hawaii's economy was recovering, the number of visitors to the state shot up to 6.75 million, business was booming in construction, and real-estate sales were higher than ever.

Just 3 years later, the economic pendulum swung the opposite way. Real estate in Hawaii, as on the mainland, dropped in value and sales plummeted. Although a record number of visitors, some nine million, had come to Hawaii in 2007, the economic downturn in 2008 saw the closure of Aloha Airlines (which had served Hawaii for 61 years) and ATA Airlines, as well as the shutting down of all operations of Molokai Ranch, the island's largest employer and landowner.

THE LAY OF THE LAND

The first Hawaiian islands were born of violent volcanic eruptions that took place deep beneath the ocean's surface about 70 million years ago. As soon as the islands emerged, Mother Nature's fury began to carve beauty from barren rock. Untiring volcanoes spewed forth rivers of fire that cooled into stone. Severe tropical storms battered and blasted the cooling lava rock into a series of shapes. Ferocious earthquakes formed the islands into precipitous valleys, jagged cliffs, and recumbent flatlands. Monstrous surf and gigantic tidal waves rearranged and polished the lands above and below the reaches of the tide.

It took millions of years for nature to shape the familiar form of Diamond Head on Oahu, Maui's majestic peak of Haleakala, the waterfalls of Molokai's northern side, the reefs of Hulopoe Bay on Lanai, and the lush rainforests of the Big Island. The result is a tropical dreamscape of a landscape rich in flora and fauna, surrounded by a vibrant underwater world.

The Flora of the Islands

Hawaii is filled with sweet-smelling flowers, lush vegetation, and exotic plant life.

AFRICAN TULIP TREES   Even from afar, you can see the flaming red flowers on these large trees, which can grow to be more than 50 feet tall.

ANGEL'S TRUMPETS   These small trees can grow up to 20 feet tall, with an abundance of large pendants—white or pink flowers that resemble, well, trumpets. The flowers, which bloom continually from early spring to late fall, have a musky scent. *Warning:* All parts of the plant are poisonous and contain a strong narcotic.

ANTHURIUMS   More than 550 species exist, but the most popular are the heart-shaped red, orange, pink, white, and purple flowers with tail-like spathes. Look for the heart-shaped green leaves in shaded areas. These exotic plants have no scent but will last several weeks as cut flowers. Anthuriums are particularly prevalent on the Big Island.

BANYAN TREES   Among the world's largest trees, banyans have branches that grow out and away from the trunk, forming descending roots that grow down to the ground to feed and form additional trunks, making the tree very stable during tropical storms.

BIRDS OF PARADISE   These natives of Africa have become something of a trademark of Hawaii. They're easily recognizable by the orange and blue flowers nestled in gray-green bracts, looking somewhat like birds in flight.

BOUGAINVILLEA   Originally from Brazil, these vines feature colorful, tissue-thin bracts, ranging in color from majestic purple to fiery orange, that hide tiny white flowers. A good place to spot them is on the Big Island, along the Queen Kaahumanu Highway stretching from Kona Airport to Kailua-Kona.

BREADFRUIT TREES A large tree—more than 60 feet tall—with broad, sculpted, dark-green leaves, the famous breadfruit produces a round, head-size green fruit that's a staple in the diets of all Polynesians. When roasted or baked, the whitish-yellow meat tastes somewhat like a sweet potato.

BROMELIADS There are more than 1,400 species of bromeliads, of which the pineapple plant is the best known. "Bromes," as they're affectionately called, are generally spiky plants ranging in size from a few inches to several feet in diameter. They're popular not only for their unusual foliage, but also for their strange and wonderful flowers. Used widely in landscaping and interior decoration, bromeliads are found on every island.

COFFEE Hawaii is the only state that produces coffee commercially. Coffee is an evergreen shrub with shiny, waxy, dark-green pointed leaves. The flower is a small, fragrant white blossom that develops into half-inch berries that turn bright red when ripe. Look for coffee at elevations above 1,500 feet on the Kona side of the Big Island and on large coffee plantations on Kauai, Molokai, Oahu, and Maui.

GINGER White and yellow ginger flowers are perhaps the most fragrant in Hawaii. Usually found in clumps growing 4 to 7 feet tall in areas blessed by rain, these sweet-smelling, 3-inch-wide flowers are composed of three dainty petal-like stamens and three long, thin petals. Look for white and yellow ginger from late spring to fall. If you see ginger on the side of the road, stop and pick a few blossoms—your car will be filled with a divine fragrance the rest of the day.

Other members of the ginger family frequently seen in Hawaii include red, shell, and torch ginger. Red ginger consists of tall green stalks with foot-

long red "flower heads." The red "petals" are actually bracts, which protect the 1-inch-long white flowers. Red ginger, which does not share the heavenly smell of white ginger, lasts a week or longer when cut. Look for red ginger from spring through late fall. Shell ginger, which originated in India and Burma, thrives in cool, wet mountain forests. These plants, with their pearly white, clamshell-like blossoms, bloom from spring to fall.

Perhaps the most exotic ginger is the red or pink torch ginger. Cultivated in Malaysia as seasoning, torch ginger rises directly out of the ground. The flower stalks, which are about 5 to 8 inches in length, resemble the fire of a lighted torch. This type of ginger can bloom year-round.

HELICONIA Some 80 species of the colorful heliconia family came to

Heliconia.

Hawaii from the Caribbean and Central and South America. The bright yellow, red, green, and orange bracts overlap and appear to unfold like origami birds. The most obvious heliconia to spot is the lobster claw, which resembles a string of boiled crustacean pincers. Another prolific heliconia is the parrot's beak: Growing to about hip height, it's composed of bright-orange flower bracts with black tips. Look for parrot's beaks in spring and summer.

HIBISCUS   The 4- to 6-inch hibiscus flowers bloom year-round and come in a range of colors, from lily white to lipstick red. The flowers resemble crepe paper, with stamens and pistils protruding spirelike from the center. The yellow hibiscus is Hawaii's official state flower.

JACARANDA   Beginning around March and sometimes lasting until early May, these huge lacy-leaved trees metamorphose into large clusters of spectacular lavender-blue sprays. The bell-shaped flowers drop quickly, leaving a majestic purple carpet beneath the tree.

MACADAMIA   A transplant from Australia, macadamia nuts have become a commercial crop in recent decades in Hawaii, especially on the Big Island and Maui. The large trees—up to 60 feet tall—bear a hard-shelled nut encased in a leathery husk, which splits open and dries when the nut is ripe.

MONKEYPOD TREES   The monkeypod is one of Hawaii's most majestic trees; it grows more than 80 feet tall and 100 feet across. Seen near older homes and in parks, the leaves of the monkeypod drop in February and March.

NIGHT-BLOOMING CEREUS   Look along rock walls for this spectacular night-blooming flower. Originally from Central America, this vinelike member of the cactus family has green scalloped edges and produces foot-long white flowers that open as darkness falls and wither as the sun rises. The plant also bears an edible red fruit.

ORCHIDS   To many minds, nothing says Hawaii more than orchids. The most widely grown variety—and the major source of flowers for leis and garnish for tropical libations—is the vanda orchid. The vandas used in Hawaii's commercial flower industry are generally lavender or white, but they grow in a rainbow of colors, shapes, and sizes. The orchids used for corsages are the large, delicate cattleya; the ones used in floral arrangements are usually dendrobiums. On the Big Island, don't pass up a chance to wander through the numerous orchid farms around Hilo.

PANDANUS (HALA)   Called *hala* by Hawaiians, pandanus is native to Polynesia. Thanks to its thick trunk, stiltlike supporting roots, and crown of long, swordlike leaves, the hala tree is easy to recognize. In what is quickly becoming a dying art, Hawaiians weave the *lau* (leaves) of the hala into hats, baskets, mats, bags, and the like.

PLUMERIA   This sweet-smelling, five-petal flower, found in clusters on trees, is the most popular choice of lei makers. The Singapore plumeria has five creamy-white petals, with a touch of yellow in the center. Another popular variety, *ruba*—with flowers from soft pink to flaming red—is also used in leis. Be careful of the sap from the flower—it's poisonous and can stain clothes.

PROTEA This unusual oversize shrub comes in more than 40 varieties. The flowers of one species resemble pincushions; those of another look like a bouquet of feathers. Once dried, proteas will last for years.

SILVERSWORD This very uncommon and unusual plant is seen only on the Big Island and in the Haleakala Crater on Maui. It blooms between July and September. The silversword in bloom is a fountain of red-petaled, daisy-like flowers that turn silver soon after blooming.

Protea.

TARO Around pools, near streams, and in neatly planted fields, you'll see these green heart-shaped leaves, whose dense roots are a Polynesian staple. The ancient Hawaiians pounded the roots into poi. Originally from Sri Lanka, taro not only is a food crop, but also is grown for ornamental reasons.

The Fauna of the Islands

When the first Polynesians arrived in Hawaii between A.D. 500 and 800, scientists say they found some 67 varieties of endemic Hawaiian birds. They did not find any reptiles, amphibians, mosquitoes, lice, fleas, or even a cockroach.

There were only two endemic mammals: the hoary bat and the monk seal. The **hoary bat** must have accidentally blown to Hawaii at some point, from either North or South America. It can still be seen during its early evening forays, especially around the Kilauea Crater on the Big Island.

The **Hawaiian monk seal** was nearly slaughtered into extinction for its skin and oil during the 19th century. These seals have recently experienced a minor population explosion; sometimes they even turn up at various beaches throughout the state. They're protected under federal law. If you're fortunate enough to see a monk seal, just look; don't disturb one of Hawaii's living treasures.

The first Polynesians brought a few animals from home: dogs, pigs, and chickens (all were for eating), as well as rats (stowaways). All four species are still found in the Hawaiian wild today.

BIRDS

More species of native birds have become extinct in Hawaii in the past 200 years than anywhere else on the planet. Of 67 native species, 23 are extinct and 30 are endangered. Even the Hawaiian crow, the **alala,** is threatened.

The **ae'o,** or Hawaiian stilt—a 16-inch-long bird with a black head, black coat, white underside, and long pink legs—can be found in protected wetlands like the Kanaha Wildlife Sanctuary on Maui (where it shares its natural habitat with the Hawaiian coot), the Kealia Pond on Maui, and the Hanalei National

Wildlife Refuge on Kauai, which is also home to the Hawaiian duck. Other areas in which you can see protected birds are the Kipuka Puaulu (Bird Park) and the Olaa Rain Forest—both in Hawaii Volcanoes National Park on the Big Island—and at Goat Island bird refuge off Oahu, where you can see wedge-tailed shearwaters nesting.

Another great birding venue is Kokee State Park on Kauai. Various native birds that have been spotted include some of the 22 species of the native honey creepers. Frequently seen are the **apapane** (a red bird with black wings and a curved black bill), **iiwi** (also red with black wings but with orange legs and a salmon-colored bill), **amakihi** (a plain olive-green bird with a long, straight bill), and **anianiau** (a tiny yellow bird with a thin, curved bill). Also in the forest is the **'elepaio,** a small gray flycatcher with an orange breast and an erect tail. The most common native bird at Kokee—and the most easily seen—is the **moa,** or red jungle fowl, a chicken brought to Hawaii by the Polynesians.

To get a good glimpse of the seabirds that frequent Hawaii, drive to Kilauea Point on Kauai's North Shore. Here you can easily spot **red-** and **white-footed boobies, wedge-tailed shearwaters, frigate birds, red-tailed tropic birds,** and the **Laysan albatross.**

Hawaii's state bird is the **nene.** It's being brought back from the brink of extinction through strenuous protection laws and captive breeding. A relative of the Canada goose, the nene stands about 2 feet high and has a black head and yellow cheeks. The approximately 500 nene in existence can be seen in only three places: on Maui at Haleakala National Park, and on the Big Island at Mauna Kea State Recreation Area bird sanctuary and on the slopes of Mauna Kea.

The Hawaiian short-eared owl, the **pueo,** which grows to between 12 and 17 inches, can be seen at dawn and dusk on Kauai, Maui, and the Big Island. According to legend, spotting a pueo is a good omen.

SEA LIFE

Approximately 450 of the 680 species of fish known to inhabit the waters around the Hawaiian Islands stay close to the reef and inshore areas.

CORAL The reefs surrounding Hawaii are made up of various coral and algae. The living coral grows through sunlight that feeds a specialized algae, which, in turn, allows the development of the coral's calcareous skeleton. The reef,

---

Leapin' Lizards!

Geckos are harmless, soft-skinned, insect-eating lizards that come equipped with suction pads on their feet, enabling them to climb walls and windows to reach tasty insects such as mosquitoes and cockroaches. You'll see them on windows outside a lighted room at night or hear their cheerful chirp.

which takes thousands of years to develop, attracts and supports fish and crustaceans, which use it for food and habitat. Mother Nature can batter the reef with a strong storm, but humans have proven far more destructive.

The corals most frequently seen in Hawaii are hard, rocklike formations named for their familiar shapes: antler, cauliflower, finger, plate, and razor coral. Some coral appears soft, such as tube coral; it can be found in the ceilings of caves. Black coral, which resembles winter-bare trees or shrubs, is found at depths of more than 100 feet.

REEF FISH Of the approximately 450 types of reef fish here, about 27% are native to Hawaii and are found nowhere else in the world. During the millions of years it took for the islands to sprout up from the sea, ocean currents—mainly from Southeast Asia—carried thousands of marine animals and plants to Hawaii's reef; of those, approximately 100 species adapted and thrived.

Angelfish can be distinguished by the spine, located low on the gill plate. These fish are very shy; several species live in colonies close to coral.

Blennies are small, elongated fish, ranging from 2 to 10 inches long, with the majority in the 3- to 4-inch range. Blennies are so small that they can live in tide pools; you might have a hard time spotting one.

Butterfly fish, among the most colorful of the reef fish, are usually seen in pairs (scientists believe they mate for life) and appear to spend most of their day feeding. There are 22 species of butterfly fish, of which three (bluestripe, lemon or milletseed, and multiband or pebbled butterfly fish) are endemic. Most butterfly fish have a dark band through the eye and a spot near the tail resembling an eye, meant to confuse their predators (moray eels love to lunch on them).

Moray and **conger eels** are the most common eels seen in Hawaii. Morays are usually docile except when provoked or when there's food around. Unfortunately, some morays have been fed by divers and now associate divers with food; thus, they can become aggressive. But most morays like to keep to themselves. While morays may look menacing, conger eels look downright happy, with big lips and pectoral fins (situated so that they look like big ears) that give them the appearance of a perpetually smiling face. Conger eels have crushing teeth so they can feed on crustaceans; because they're sloppy eaters, they usually live with shrimp and crabs that feed off the crumbs they leave.

Parrotfish, one of the largest and most colorful of the reef fish, can grow up to 40 inches long. They're easy to spot—their front teeth are fused together, protruding like buck teeth that allow them to feed by scraping algae from rocks and coral. The rocks and coral pass through the parrotfish's system, resulting in fine sand. In fact, most of the white sand found in Hawaii is parrotfish waste; one large parrotfish can produce a ton of sand a year. Native parrotfish species include yellowbar, regal, and spectacled.

Scorpion fish are what scientists call "ambush predators": They hide under camouflaged exteriors and ambush their prey. Several kinds sport a venomous dorsal spine. These fish don't have a gas bladder, so when they stop swimming, they sink—that's why you usually find them "resting" on ledges and on the ocean bottom. They're not aggressive, but be very careful where you put your hands and feet in the water so as to avoid those venomous spines.

Surgeonfish, sometimes called *tang,* get their name from the scalpel-like spines located on each side of the body near the base of the tail. Several surgeonfish, such as the brightly colored yellow tang, are boldly colored; others are adorned in more conservative shades of gray, brown, or black. The only endemic surgeonfish—and the most abundant in Hawaiian waters—is the convict tang, a pale white fish with vertical black stripes.

Wrasses are a very diverse family of fish, ranging in length from 2 to 15 inches. Wrasses can change gender from female to male. Some have brilliant coloration that changes as they age. Several types of wrasse are endemic to Hawaii: Hawaiian cleaner, shortnose, belted, and gray (or old woman).

GAME FISH Hawaii is known around the globe as *the* place for big-game fish—marlin, swordfish, and tuna. Six kinds of **billfish** are found in the offshore waters around the islands: Pacific blue marlin, black marlin, sailfish, broadbill swordfish, striped marlin, and shortbill spearfish. Hawaii billfish range in size from the 20-pound shortbill spearfish and striped marlin to the 1,805-pound Pacific blue marlin, the largest marlin ever caught with rod and reel in the world.

Tuna ranges in size from small (1 lb. or less) mackerel tuna used as bait (Hawaiians call them *oioi*) to 250-pound yellowfin ahi tuna. Other local species of tuna are big-eye, albacore, kawakawa, and skipjack.

Other types of fish, also excellent for eating, include **mahimahi** (also known as dolphin fish or dorado), in the 20- to 70-pound range; **rainbow runner,** from 15 to 30 pounds; and **wahoo,** from 15 to 80 pounds. Shoreline fishermen are always on the lookout for **trevally** (the state record for a giant trevally is 191 lb.), **bonefish, ladyfish, threadfin, leatherfish,** and **goatfish.** Bottom fishermen pursue a range of **snapper**—red, pink, gray, and others—as well as **sea bass** (the state record is a whopping 563 lb.) and **amberjack** (which weigh up to 100 lb.).

WHALES Humpback whales are popular visitors who come to Hawaii to mate and calve every year, beginning in November and staying until spring—April or so—when they return to Alaska. On every island, you can take winter whale-watching cruises that will let you observe these magnificent leviathans up close. You can also spot them from shore—humpbacks

Mahimahi.

grow to up to 45 feet long, so when one breaches (jumps out of the water), you can see it for miles.

Humpbacks are among the biggest whales found in Hawaiian waters, but other whales—such as pilot, sperm, false killer, melon-headed, pygmy killer, and beaked—can be seen year-round, especially in the calm waters off the Big Island's Kona Coast.

SHARKS   Yes, there *are* sharks in Hawaii, but you more than likely won't see one unless you're specifically looking. About 40 species of sharks inhabit the waters surrounding Hawaii, ranging from the totally harmless whale shark (at 60 ft., the world's largest fish), which has no teeth and is so docile that it frequently lets divers ride on its back, to the not-so-docile, extremely uncommon great white shark. The most common sharks seen in Hawaii are white-tip or gray reef sharks (about 5 ft. long) and black-tip reef sharks (about 6 ft. long).

Hawaii's Ecosystem Problems

Officials at Hawaii Volcanoes National Park on the Big Island saw a potential problem a few decades ago with people taking a few rocks home with them as "souvenirs." To prevent this problem from escalating, the park rangers created a legend that the fiery volcano goddess, Pele, would punish these souvenir seekers with bad luck. There used to be a display case in the park's visitor center filled with letters from people who had taken rocks from the volcano, relating stories of all the bad luck that followed. Most begged Pele's forgiveness and instructed the rangers to please return the rock to the exact location that was its original home.

Unfortunately, Hawaii's other ecosystem problems can't be handled as easily.

MARINE LIFE   Hawaii's beautiful and abundant marine life has attracted so many visitors that they threaten to overwhelm it. A great example of this is Oahu's **Hanauma Bay.** Crowds flock to this marine preserve, which features calm, protected swimming and snorkeling areas loaded with tropical reef fish. Its popularity has forced government officials to limit admissions and charge an entrance fee. Commercial tour operators have also been restricted.

Another marine-life conservation area that suffers from overuse is **Molokini,** a small crater off the coast of Maui. Twenty-five years ago, one or two small six-passenger boats made the trip once a day to Molokini; today it's not uncommon to sight 20 or more boats, each carrying 20 to 49 passengers, moored inside the tiny crater. One tour operator has claimed that, on some days, it's so crowded that you can actually see a slick of suntan oil floating on the surface of the water.

Hawaii's **reefs** have faced increasing impact over the years as well. Runoff of soil and chemicals from construction, agriculture, and erosion can blanket and choke a reef, which needs sunlight to survive. Human contact with the reef can also upset the ecosystem. Coral, the basis of the reef system, is very fragile; snorkelers and divers grabbing onto it can break off pieces that took decades to form. Feeding the fish can also upset the balance of the ecosystem (not to mention upsetting the digestive systems of the fish). In areas where they're fed, the normally shy reef fish become more aggressive, surrounding divers and demanding food.

FLORA   The rainforests are among Hawaii's most fragile environments. Any intrusion—from hikers carrying seeds on their shoes to the rooting of wild boars—can upset the delicate balance of these complete ecosystems. In recent years, development has moved closer and closer to the rainforests. On the Big Island, people have protested the invasion of bulldozers and the drilling of geothermal wells in the Wao Kele O Puna rainforest for years.

FAUNA   The biggest impact on the fauna in Hawaii is the decimation of native birds by feral animals that have destroyed the birds' habitats, and by mongooses that have eaten the birds' eggs and young. Government officials are vigilant about snakes because of the potential damage they can do to the remaining bird life.

A recent pest introduced to Hawaii is the coqui frog. That loud noise you hear after dark, especially on the eastern side of the Big Island and various parts of Maui, is the cry of the male coqui frog looking for a mate. A native of Puerto Rico, where the frogs are kept in check by snakes, the coqui frog came to Hawaii in some plant material, found no natural enemies, and has spread across the Big Island and Maui. A chorus of several hundred coqui frogs is deafening (it's been measured at 163 decibels, or the noise level of a jet engine from 100 ft.). In some places, there are so many frogs that they are now chirping during daylight hours.

HAWAII IN POPULAR CULTURE

In addition to the books discussed below, those planning an extended trip to Hawaii should check out *Frommer's Honolulu, Waikiki & Oahu; Frommer's Honolulu & Oahu Day by Day; Frommer's Kauai; Frommer's Maui; Frommer's Maui Day by Day;* and *Frommer's Hawaii with Kids* (all published by Wiley Publishing, Inc.).

Books

FICTION

The first book people think about is James A. Michener's *Hawaii* (1974). This epic novel manages to put the island's history into chronological order, but remember, it is still fiction, and very sanitized fiction, too. For a more contemporary look at life in Hawaii today, one of the best novels is *Shark Dialogues,* by Kiana Davenport (1995). The novel tells the story of Pono, the larger-than-life matriarch, and her four daughters of mixed races. Davenport skillfully weaves legends and myths of Hawaii into the "real life" reality that Pono and her family face in the complex Hawaii of today. Lois-Ann Yamanaka uses a very "local" voice

Mark Twain in Hawaii: Roughing It in the Sandwich Islands.

and stark depictions of life in the islands in her fabulous novels *Wild Meat and the Bully Burgers* (1996), *Blu's Hanging* (1997), and *Heads by Harry* (1999). A great read is *Honolulu Stories: Two Centuries of Writing*, edited by Gavan Daws and Bennett Hymer (2008), which has hundreds of writers (from Mark Twain to Robert Louis Stevenson to Jack London to James Jones to second-grade school kids) all telling their stories about Hawaii's most famous city.

NONFICTION

Mark Twain's writing on Hawaii in the 1860s offers a wonderful introduction to Hawaii's history. One of his best books is *Mark Twain in Hawaii: Roughing It in the Sandwich Islands* (Mutual Publishing, 1990). A great depiction of the Hawaii of 1889 is *Travels in Hawaii*, by Robert Louis Stevenson (1973).

For contemporary voices on Hawaii's unique culture, one of the best books to get is *Voices of Wisdom: Hawaiian Elders Speak*, by M. J. Harden (1999). Some 24 different *kahuna* (experts) in their fields were interviewed about their talent, skill, or artistic practice. These living treasures talk about how Hawaiians of yesteryear viewed nature, spirituality and healing, preservation and history, dance and music, arts and crafts, canoes, and the next generation.

Native Planters in Old Hawaii: Their Life, Lore, and Environment (2004) was originally published in 1972 but is still one of the most important ethnographic works on traditional Hawaiian culture, portraying the lives of the common folk and their relationship with the land before the arrival of Westerners. This revised edition, with a great index that allows you to find anything, is an excellent resource for anyone interested in Hawaii.

Honolulu Stories: Two Centuries of Writing, edited by Gavan Daws and Bennett Hymer (2008), is a fascinating 1,000-plus-page book filled with the writings of various authors over the past 200 years. More than 350 selections—ranging from short stories, excerpts from novels, and scenes from plays, musicals, and operas to poems, songs, Hawaiian chants, cartoons, slams, and even stand-up comedy routines—are contained in this must-read for anyone interested in Hawaii. The authors range from Hawaiian kings and queens to Hawaiian chefs and commoners, including some well-known writers (translated from seven languages)—all telling their own stories about Honolulu.

FLORA & FAUNA

Because Hawaii is so lush with nature and blessed with plants, animals, and reef fish seen nowhere else on the planet, a few reference books can help you identify what you're looking at and make your trip more interesting. In the botanical world, Angela Kay Kepler's *Hawaiian Heritage Plants* (1998) is the standard for plant reference. In a series of essays, Kepler weaves culture, history, geography, botany, and even spirituality into her vivid descriptions of plants. You'll never look at plants the same way. There are great color photos and drawings to help you sort through the myriad species. Another great resource is *Tropicals*, by Gordon Courtright (1988), which is filled with color photos identifying everything from hibiscus and heliconia to trees and palms.

The other necessary reference to have in Hawaii is one that identifies the colorful reef fish you will see snorkeling. The best of the bunch is John E. Randall's *Shore Fishes of Hawaii* (1998). Two other books on reef-fish identification, with easy-to-use spiral bindings, are *Hawaiian Reef Fish: The Identification Book*, by Casey Mahaney (1993), and *Hawaiian Reef Fish,* by Astrid Witte and Casey Mahaney (1998).

To learn everything you need in order to identify Hawaii's unique birds, try H. Douglas Pratt's *A Pocket Guide to Hawaii's Birds* (1996).

HISTORY

There are many great books on Hawaii's history, but one of the best places to start is with the formation of the Hawaiian Islands, vividly described in David E. Eyre's *By Wind, By Wave: An Introduction to Hawaii's Natural History* (2000). In addition to chronicling the natural history of Hawaii, Eyre describes the complex interrelationships among the plants, animals, ocean, and people. He points out that Hawaii has become the "extinction capital of the world," but rather than dwelling on that fact, he urges readers to do something about it and carefully spells out how.

For a history of "precontact" Hawaii (before Westerners arrived), David Malo's *Hawaiian Antiquities* (1976) is the preeminent source. Malo was born around 1793 and wrote about the Hawaiian lifestyle at that time, as well as the beliefs and religion of his people. It's an excellent reference book, but not a fast read. For more readable books on old Hawaii, try *Stories of Old Hawaii,* by Roy Kakulu Alameida (1997), on myths and legends; *Hawaiian Folk Tales,* by Thomas G. Thrum (1998); and *The Legends and Myths of Hawaii,* by His Hawaiian Majesty King David Kalakaua (1992).

The best story of the 1893 overthrow of the Hawaiian monarchy is told by Queen Liliuokalani, in her book *Hawaii's Story by Hawaii's Queen Liliuokalani* (1990). When it was written, it was an international plea for justice for her people, but it is a poignant read even today. It's also a must-read for people interested in current events and the recent rally for sovereignty in the 50th state. Two contemporary books on the question of Hawaii's sovereignty are Tom Coffman's *Nation Within: The Story of America's Annexation of the Nation of Hawaii* (1998) and Thurston Twigg-Smith's *Hawaiian Sovereignty: Do the Facts Matter?* (2000), which explores the opposite view. Twigg-Smith, former publisher of the statewide newspaper *The Honolulu Advertiser,* is the grandson of Lorrin A. Thurston, one of the architects of the 1893 overthrow of the monarchy. His so-called "politically incorrect" views present a different look on this hotly debated topic.

An insightful look at history and its effect on the Hawaiian culture is *Waikiki, A History of Forgetting and Remembering,* by Andrea Feeser (2006). A beautiful art book (designed by Gaye Chan), this is not your typical coffee-table book, but a different look at the cultural and environmental history of Waikiki. Using historical texts, photos, government documents, and interviews, this book lays out the story of how Waikiki went from a self-sufficient agricultural area to a tourism mecca, detailing the price that was paid along the way.

Film

My favorite films made in Hawaii but about other places are these:

- **Donovan's Reef:** John Ford directed this 1963 John Wayne romantic comedy about two ex-navy men who remain on a South Seas island (played by Kauai) after World War II. "Guns" Donovan (Wayne) runs the local bar, while Doc Dedham (Jack Warden) has married a local princess. A former shipmate (Lee Marvin) arrives, followed by a high-society Bostonian (Elizabeth Allen).

o **Islands in the Stream:** Filmed on Kauai, this 1977 movie tells the story of Ernest Hemingway's last published novel. Set on the island of Bimini in the Caribbean, it is about artist Thomas Hudson's renewed relationship with his three young sons and former wife.

o **Jurassic Park:** Filmed on the islands of Kauai and Oahu, Steven Spielberg's 1993 megahit, which was billed as "an adventure 65 million years in the making," is the story of dinosaurs on the loose at the site of the world's only dinosaur farm and theme park, where creatures from the past are produced using harvested DNA.

o **The Karate Kid, Part II:** In one of those instances where the sequel is actually better than the original, this 1986 movie takes our hero Daniel LaRusso (Ralph Macchio) and his mentor, Mr. Miyagi (Pat Morita), to Miyagi's homeland, Okinawa, to visit his dying father and confront his old rival. An entire Okinawan village was re-created on Oahu's Windward Coast.

o **The Lost World: Jurassic Park:** In Steven Spielberg's 1997 follow-up to *Jurassic Park,* dinosaurs have been bred and then escaped following the abandonment of the project in the first installment. The sequel features much more Hawaiian scenery than the original.

o **None But the Brave:** Frank Sinatra directed and starred in this 1965 story of American and Japanese soldiers who, when stranded on a tiny Pacific island during World War II (filmed on Kauai), must make a temporary truce and cooperate to survive. This was the only film directed by Sinatra.

o **Raiders of the Lost Ark:** Filmed partly on Kauai, Steven Spielberg's 1981 film follows archaeologist Indiana Jones on a search for the Ark of the Covenant, which is also sought by the Nazis under orders from Hitler.

o **Six Days Seven Nights:** Ivan Reitman's 1998 adventure-comedy is about a New York magazine editor and a gruff pilot who are forced to put aside their dislike for each other in order to survive after crash-landing on a deserted South Seas island (filmed on Kauai). It stars Harrison Ford and Anne Heche.

o **South Pacific:** The 1958 motion-picture adaptation of the Rodgers and Hammerstein musical was filmed on Kauai. The film has an all-star cast, with Rossano Brazzi and Mitzi Gaynor in the lead roles. It was nominated for three Academy Awards but won only for best sound.

o **Waterworld:** Kevin Costner directed and starred in this 1995 film about a future in which the polar ice caps have melted, leaving most of the world's surface deep beneath the oceans. The survivors live poorly on the water's surface, dreaming of finding "dry land." Some of the water scenes were filmed

Elvis Presley's *Blue Hawaii.*

off Kauai. The final and most beautiful scenes in the movie were filmed in the Waipio Valley on the Big Island.

My favorite films made in Hawaii and about Hawaii are the following:

- o **Blue Hawaii:** Chad Gates (Elvis Presley), upon discharge from the Army, returns to Hawaii to enjoy life with his buddies and girlfriend, against the wishes of his parents, who want him to work for the family business. Elvis Presley, Joan Blackman, and Angela Lansbury make this 1961 film a classic, with great music and beautiful Hawaiian scenery from the early 1960s.

- o **50 First Dates:** This 2004 romantic comedy stars Drew Barrymore and Adam Sandler in a story about a young woman (Barrymore) who has lost her short-term memory in a car accident and who now relives each day as if it were October 13. She follows the same routine every day, until she meets Henry Roth (Sandler), who falls in love with her and seeks a way to forge a long-term relationship.

- o **From Here to Eternity:** Fred Zinnemann's 1953 multiple-Oscar winner, set in pre–World War II Hawaii, tells the story of several army soldiers stationed on Oahu on the eve of Pearl Harbor. The film won best picture, best supporting actor (Frank Sinatra), best supporting actress (Donna Reed), and five other awards.

- o **Hawaii:** George Roy Hill's 1966 adaptation of the James Michener novel features amazing island scenery and stars Julie Andrews, Max von Sydow, and Richard Harris. It is a great introduction to the early history of Hawaii.

- o **Molokai: The Story of Father Damien:** This 1999 film follows the life of Belgian priest Damien de Veuster from 1872, the year before his arrival in Kalaupapa, through his years ministering to the patients with Hansen's disease at Kalaupapa, until his death at the Molokai settlement in 1889.

- o **Pearl Harbor:** Michael Bay's 2001 film depicts the time before, during, and after the December 7, 1941, Japanese attack (with the best re-creation of the Pearl Harbor attack ever put on film) and tells the story of two best friends and the woman they both love.

- o **Picture Bride:** Japanese director Kayo Hatta presents this 1995 film about a Japanese woman who travels to Hawaii to marry a man she has never met, but only seen through photos and letters. She soon discovers that he is twice her age and that much turmoil awaits her in her new home. Beautifully filmed on the North Shore of Oahu and the Hamakua Coast of the Big Island, with a special appearance by Toshiro Mifune.

- o **Tora! Tora! Tora!:** This 1970 film tells the story of the Japanese attack on Pearl Harbor as seen from both the American and the Japanese perspectives.

A performer at the Masters of Hawaiian Slack-Key Guitar Concert Series.

Music

Hawaiian music ranges from traditional ancient chants and hula to slack-key guitar, to contemporary rock and a new genre, Jawaiian, a cross of reggae, Jamaican, and Hawaiian. To listen to Hawaiian music, check out Hawaiian 105 (www.hawaiian105.com). Below are my picks for Hawaiian music.

- o *Best of the Gabby Band,* by Gabby Pahinui (traditional Hawaiian)
- o *Gently Weeps,* by Jake Shimabukuro (contemporary Hawaiian)
- o *Hapa,* by Hapa (contemporary Hawaiian)
- o *Hawaiian Blossom,* by Raiatea Helm (traditional Hawaiian)
- o *Hawaiian Tradition,* by Amy Hanaiali'i Gilliom (traditional Hawaiian)
- o *Honolulu City Lights,* by Keola & Kapono Beamer (contemporary Hawaiian)
- o *Legends of Hawaiian Slack Key Guitar,* by various artists (a collection of slack-key guitar music and a 2007 Grammy winner)
- o *Masters of Hawaiian Slack Key, Vol. 1,* by various artists (a collection of slack-key guitar music and a 2006 Grammy winner)
- o *Na Leo Hawaii,* by the Master Chanters of Hawaii (chanting)
- o *Na Pua O Hawaii,* by Makaha Sons (contemporary Hawaiian)
- o *Wonderful World,* by Israel Kamakawiwo'ole (contemporary Hawaiian)

EATING & DRINKING IN HAWAII
Tried & True: Hawaii Regional Cuisine

Peter Merriman, a founding member of Hawaii Regional Cuisine (HRC) and a recipient of the James Beard Award for Best Chef: Northwest/Hawaii (along with George Mavrothalassitis of Chef Mavro Restaurant), describes the current trend in Hawaii as a refinement, a tweaking upward, of everything from fine dining to down-home local cooking. This means sesame- or nori-crusted fresh catch on plate-lunch menus, and huli-huli chicken at five-diamond eateries, paired with Beaujolais and leeks and gourmet long rice.

At the same time, says Merriman, HRC, the style of cooking that put Hawaii on the international culinary map, has become watered down, a buzzword: "A lot of restaurants are paying lip service."

As it is with things au courant, it is easy to make a claim but another thing to live up to it. As Merriman points out, HRC was never solely about technique; it is equally about ingredients and the chef's creativity and integrity. "We continue to get local inspiration," says Merriman. "We've never restricted ourselves." If there is a fabulous French or Thai dish, chefs like Merriman will prepare it with local ingredients and add a creative edge that makes it distinctively Hawaii Regional.

HRC was established in the mid-1980s in a culinary revolution that catapulted Hawaii into the global epicurean arena. The international training, creative vigor, fresh ingredients, and cross-cultural menus of the 12 original HRC chefs have made the islands a dining destination applauded nationwide. (In a tip of the toque to island tradition, *ahi*—a word ubiquitous in Hawaii—has replaced *tuna* on many chic New York menus.)

Here's a sampling of what you can expect to find on a Hawaii Regional menu: seared Hawaiian fish with lilikoi shrimp butter; taro-crab cakes; Pahoa corn cakes; Molokai sweet-potato or breadfruit vichyssoise; Ka'u orange sauce and Kahua Ranch lamb; fern shoots from Waipio Valley; Maui onion soup and Hawaiian bouillabaisse, with fresh snapper, Kona crab, and fresh aquacultured shrimp; blackened ahi summer rolls; herb-crusted onaga; and gourmet Waimanalo greens, picked that day. You may also encounter locally made cheeses, squash and taro risottos, Polynesian imu-baked foods, and guava-smoked meats. If there's pasta or risotto or rack of lamb on the menu, it could be nori (red algae) linguine with opihi (limpet) sauce, or risotto with local seafood served in taro cups, or rack of lamb in cabernet and hoisin sauce (fermented soybean, garlic, and spices). Watch for ponzu sauce, too; it's lemony and zesty, much more flavorful than the soy sauce it resembles.

Plate Lunches & More: Local Food

At the other end of the spectrum is the vast and endearing world of "local food." By that I mean plate lunches and poke, shave ice and saimin, bento lunches and manapua—cultural hybrids all.

Reflecting a polyglot population of many styles and ethnicities, Hawaii's idiosyncratic dining scene is eminently inclusive. Consider surfer chic: Barefoot in the sand, in a swimsuit, you chow down on a **plate lunch** ordered from a lunch wagon, consisting of fried mahimahi, "two scoops rice," macaroni salad, and a few leaves of green, typically julienned cabbage. (Generally, teriyaki beef and shoyu chicken are options.) Heavy gravy is often the condiment of choice, accompanied by a soft drink in a paper cup or straight out of the can. Like

A typical luau spread.

saimin—the local version of noodles in broth topped with scrambled eggs, green onions, and sometimes pork—the plate lunch is Hawaii's version of high camp.

But it was only a matter of time before the humble plate lunch became a culinary icon in Hawaii. These days, even the most chichi restaurant has a version of this modest island symbol (not at plate-lunch prices, of course), while vendors selling the real thing—carb-driven meals served from wagons—have lines that never end.

Because this is Hawaii, at least a few licks of poi—cooked, pounded taro (the traditional Hawaiian staple crop)—are a must. Other **native foods** include those from before and after Western contact, such as laulau (pork, chicken, or fish steamed in ti leaves), kalua pork (pork cooked in a Polynesian underground oven known here as an *imu*), lomi salmon (salted salmon with tomatoes and green onions), squid luau (cooked in coconut milk and taro tops), poke (cubed raw fish seasoned with onions and seaweed and the occasional sprinkling of roasted kukui nuts), haupia (creamy coconut pudding), and kulolo (steamed pudding of coconut, brown sugar, and taro).

Bento, another popular quick meal available throughout Hawaii, is a compact, boxed assortment of picnic fare usually consisting of neatly arranged sections of rice, pickled vegetables, and fried chicken, beef, or pork. Increasingly, however, the bento is becoming more health conscious, as in macrobiotic or vegetarian brown-rice bentos. A derivative of the modest lunch box for Japanese immigrants who once labored in the sugar and pineapple fields, bentos are dispensed everywhere, from department stores to corner delis and supermarkets.

Also from the plantations come **manapua,** a bready, doughy sphere with tasty fillings of sweetened pork or sweet beans. In the old days, the Chinese "manapua man" would make his rounds with bamboo containers balanced on a rod over his shoulders. Today you'll find white or whole-wheat manapua containing chicken, vegetables, curry, and other savory fillings.

The daintier Chinese delicacy **dim sum** is made of translucent wrappers filled with fresh seafood, pork hash, and vegetables, served for breakfast and lunch in Chinatown restaurants. The Hong Kong–style dumplings are ordered fresh and hot from bamboo steamers rolled on carts from table to table. Much like hailing a taxi in Manhattan, you have to be quick and loud for dim sum.

For dessert or a snack, particularly on Oahu's North Shore, the prevailing choice is **shave ice,** the Island version of a snow cone. Particularly on hot, humid days, long lines of shave-ice lovers gather for heaps of finely shaved ice topped with sweet tropical syrups. (The sweet-sour *li hing mui* flavor is a current favorite.) The fast-melting mounds, which require prompt, efficient consumption, are quite the local summer ritual for sweet tooths. Aficionados order shave ice with ice cream and sweetened adzuki beans plopped in the middle.

Ahi, Ono & Opakapaka: A Hawaiian Seafood Primer

The seafood in Hawaii has been described as the best in the world. And why not? Without a doubt, the islands' surrounding waters, including the waters of the remote northwestern Hawaiian Islands, and a growing aquaculture industry contribute to the high quality of the seafood here.

The reputable restaurants in Hawaii buy fresh fish daily at predawn auctions or from local fishermen. Some chefs even catch their ingredients

Giovanni's Shrimp Truck on Oahu.

themselves. "Still wiggling" and "just off the hook" are the ultimate terms for freshness in Hawaii.

Although some menus include the Western description for the fresh fish used, most often the local nomenclature is listed, turning dinner into a confusing, quasi-foreign experience for the uninitiated. To help familiarize you with the menu language of Hawaii, here's a basic glossary of Island fish:

ahi yellowfin or big-eye tuna, important for its use in sashimi and poke at sushi bars and in Hawaii Regional Cuisine

aku skipjack tuna, heavily used by local families in home cooking and poke

ehu red snapper, delicate and sumptuous, yet lesser known than opakapaka

hapuupuu grouper, a sea bass whose use is expanding

hebi spearfish, mildly flavored and frequently featured as the "catch of the day" in upscale restaurants

kajiki Pacific blue marlin, also called *au,* with a firm flesh and high fat content that make it a plausible substitute for tuna

kumu goatfish, a luxury item on Chinese and upscale menus, served *en papillote* (wrapped in parchment paper and baked) or steamed whole, Oriental style, with scallions, ginger, and garlic

mahimahi dolphin fish (the game fish, not the mammal) or dorado, a classic sweet, white-fleshed fish requiring vigilance among purists because it's often disguised as fresh when it's actually "fresh-frozen"—a big difference

monchong bigscale or sickle pomfret, an exotic, tasty fish, scarce but gaining a higher profile on Hawaiian Island menus

nairagi striped marlin, also called *au,* good as sashimi and in poke, and often substituted for ahi in raw-fish products

onaga   ruby snapper, a luxury fish, versatile, moist, and flaky

ono   wahoo, firmer and drier than the snappers, often served grilled and in sandwiches

opah   moonfish, rich and fatty, and versatile—cooked, raw, smoked, and broiled

opakapaka   pink snapper, light, flaky, and luxurious, suited for sashimi, poaching, sautéing, and baking; the best-known upscale fish

papio   jack trevally, light, firm, and flavorful, and favored in Island cookery

shutome   broadbill swordfish, of beeflike texture and rich flavor

tombo   albacore tuna, with a high fat content, suitable for grilling

uhu   parrotfish, most often encountered steamed, Chinese style

uku   gray snapper of clear, pale-pink flesh, delicately flavored and moist

ulua   large jack trevally, firm-fleshed and versatile

3

PLANNING YOUR TRIP TO HAWAII

Hawaii has so many places to explore, things to do, sights to see—it can be bewildering to plan your trip with so much vying for your attention. Where to start? That's where I come in. In the pages that follow, I've compiled everything you need to know to plan your ideal trip to Hawaii.

The first thing to do: Decide where you want to go. Read through each chapter (especially each chapter introduction) to see which islands fit the profile and offer the activities you're looking for. I strongly recommend that you **limit your island-hopping** to one island per week. If you decide to go to more than one in a week, be warned: You could spend much of your precious vacation time in airports and checking in and out of hotels. Not much fun!

My second tip is to **fly directly to the island of your choice;** doing so can save you a 2-hour layover in Honolulu and another plane ride. Oahu, the Big Island, Maui, and Kauai now all receive direct flights from the mainland; if you're heading to Molokai or Lanai, you'll have the easiest connections if you fly into Honolulu.

So let's get on with the process of planning your trip. Searching out the best deals and planning your dream vacation to Hawaii should be half the fun.

For additional help in planning your trip and for more on-the-ground resources in Hawaii, turn to chapter 11, "Fast Facts."

WHEN TO GO

Most visitors don't come to Hawaii when the weather's best in the islands; rather, they come when it's at its worst everywhere else. Thus, the **high season**—when prices are up and resorts are often booked to capacity—is generally from mid-December to March or mid-April. The last 2 weeks of December, in particular, are the prime time for travel to Hawaii. If you're planning a holiday trip, make your reservations as early as possible, expect crowds, and prepare to pay top dollar for accommodations, car rentals, and airfare.

The **off season,** when the best rates are available and the islands are less crowded, is spring (mid-Apr to mid-June) and fall (Sept to mid-Dec)—a paradox because these are the best seasons to be in Hawaii, in terms of reliably great weather. If you're looking to save money, or if you just want to avoid the crowds, this is the time to visit. Hotel rates and airfares tend to be significantly lower, and good packages are often available.

Note: If you plan to come to Hawaii between the last week in April and early May, be sure you book your accommodations, interisland air reservations, and car rentals in advance. In Japan, the last week of April is called **Golden Week** because three Japanese holidays take place one after the other. Waikiki is especially busy with Japanese tourists during this time, but the neighboring islands also see dramatic increases.

PREVIOUS PAGE: **Arriving in Hawaii.**

Due to the large number of families traveling in **summer** (June–Aug), you won't get the fantastic bargains of spring and fall. However, you'll still do much better on packages, airfare, and accommodations than you will in the winter months.

📎 Travel Tip

Your best bets for total ye___
Waikiki Beach and the Ko___
coast of Oahu, the Big Islan___
Coast, the south **(Kihei/Wai**___
(Lahaina/Kapalua) coasts of ___
Poipu Beach and the southwe___ __.
Kauai.

Climate

Because Hawaii lies at the edge of the tropical zone, it technically has only two seasons, both of them warm. There's a dry season that corresponds to **summer** (Apr–Oct) and a rainy season in **winter** (Nov–Mar). It rains every day somewhere in the islands any time of the year, but the rainy season sometimes brings enough gray weather to spoil your tanning opportunities. Fortunately, it seldom rains in one spot for more than 3 days straight.

The **year-round temperature** doesn't vary much. At the beach, the average daytime high in summer is 85°F (29°C), while the average daytime high in winter is 78°F (26°C); nighttime lows are usually about 10°F cooler. But how warm it is on any given day really depends on *where* you are on the island.

Each island has a leeward side (the side sheltered from the wind) and a windward side (the side that gets the wind's full force). The **leeward** sides (the west and south) are usually hot and dry, while the **windward** sides (east and north) are generally cooler and moist. When you want arid, sunbaked, desertlike weather, go leeward. When you want lush, wet, junglelike weather, go windward.

Hawaii is also full of **microclimates,** thanks to its interior valleys, coastal plains, and mountain peaks. Kauai's Mount Waialeale is the wettest spot on earth, yet Waimea Canyon, just a few miles away, is almost a desert. On the Big Island, Hilo is one of the wettest cities in the nation, with 180 inches of rainfall a year, but at Puako, only 60 miles away, it rains less than 6 inches a year. If you travel into the mountains, the climate can change from summer to winter in a

📎 Hey, No Smoking in Hawaii

Well, not *totally* no smoking, but Hawaii has one of the toughest laws against smoking in the U.S. It's against the law to smoke in public buildings, including airports, shopping malls, grocery stores, retail shops, buses, movie theaters, banks, convention facilities, and all government buildings and facilities. There is no smoking in restaurants, bars, and nightclubs. Most bed-and-breakfasts prohibit smoking indoors, and more and more hotels and resorts are becoming smoke-free even in public areas. Also, there is no smoking within 20 feet of a doorway, window, or ventilation intake (so no hanging around outside a bar to smoke—you must go 20 ft. away). Even some beaches have no-smoking policies (and at those that do allow smoking, you'd better pick up your butts and not use the sand as your own private ashtray—or else face stiff fines). Breathing fresh, clear air is "in," while smoking in Hawaii is "out."

of hours because it's cooler the higher you go. So if the weather doesn't
you, just go to the other side of the island—or head into the hills.

On rare occasions, the weather can be disastrous, as when Hurricane Iniki
crushed Kauai in September 1992 with 225-mph winds. Tsunamis have swept
Hilo and the south shore of Oahu. But those are extreme exceptions. Mostly, one
day follows another here in glorious, sunny procession, each quite like the other.

Average Temperature & Number of Rainy Days in Waikiki

	JAN	FEB	MAR	APR	MAY	JUNE	JULY	AUG	SEPT	OCT	NOV	DEC
HIGH (°F/°C)	80/27	80/27	81/27	82/28	84/29	86/30	87/31	88/31	88/31	86/30	84/29	81/27
LOW (°F/°C)	70/21	66/19	66/19	69/21	70/21	72/22	73/23	74/23	74/23	72/22	70/21	67/19
RAIN DAYS	10	9	9	9	7	6	7	6	7	9	9	10

Average Temperature & Number of Rainy Days in Hanalei, Kauai

	JAN	FEB	MAR	APR	MAY	JUNE	JULY	AUG	SEPT	OCT	NOV	DEC
HIGH (°F/°C)	79/26	80/27	80/27	82/28	84/29	86/30	88/31	88/31	87/31	86/30	83/28	80/27
LOW (°F/°C)	61/17	61/16	62/17	63/17	65/18	66/19	66/19	67/19	68/20	67/19	65/18	62/17
RAIN DAYS	8	5	6	3	3	2	8	2	3	3	4	7

Holidays

When Hawaii observes holidays (especially those over a long weekend), travel
between the islands increases, interisland airline seats are fully booked, rental
cars are at a premium, and hotels and restaurants are busier.

Federal, state, and county government offices are closed on all federal holidays; for a list, go to "Holidays" in chapter 11.

State and county offices are also closed on local holidays, including Prince
Kuhio Day (Mar 26), honoring the birthday of Hawaii's first delegate to the U.S.
Congress; King Kamehameha Day (June 11), a statewide holiday commemorat-
ing Kamehameha the Great, who united the islands and ruled from 1795 to
1819; and Admissions Day (third Fri in Aug), which honors the admittance of
Hawaii as the 50th state on August 21, 1959.

Other special days that are celebrated in Hawaii by many people, but
involve no closing of federal, state, and county offices are the Chinese New Year
(which can fall in Jan or Feb), Girls' Day (Mar 3), Buddha's Birthday (Apr 8),
Father Damien's Day (Apr 15), Boys' Day (May 5), Samoan Flag Day (in Aug),
Aloha Festivals (Sept–Oct), and Pearl Harbor Day (Dec 7).

Hawaii Calendar of Events

Please note that as with any schedule of upcoming events, the following information is subject to change; always confirm the details before you plan your trip around an event.

For an exhaustive list of events beyond those listed here, check http://events.frommers.com, where you'll find a searchable, up-to-the-minute roster of what's happening in cities all over the world.

JANUARY

PGA SBS Championship, Kapalua Resort, Maui. Top PGA golfers compete for $1 million. Call ✆ **808/669-2440** (www.kapaluamaui.com). Generally early January.

EA Sports Maui Invitational Basketball Tournament, Lahaina Civic Center, Lahaina. Top college teams vie in this annual preseason tournament. Call ✆ **847/850-1818** (www.mauiinvitational.com). Early January.

Pacific Islands Arts Festival at Thomas Square, across from Honolulu Academy of the Arts, Honolulu, Oahu. More than 100 artists and handicraft artisans, entertainment, food, and demonstrations fill the day. Admission is free. Call ✆ **808/696-6717.** Mid-January.

Ka Molokai Makahiki, Kaunakakai Town Baseball Park, Mitchell Pauole Center, Kaunakakai, Molokai. Makahiki, a traditional time of peace in ancient Hawaii, is re-created with performances by Hawaiian music groups and *halau* (hula schools), ancient Hawaiian games, a sporting competition, and Hawaiian crafts and food. It's a wonderful chance to experience the Hawaii of yesteryear. Call ✆ **800/800-6367** or 808/553-3876 (www.molokai-hawaii.com). Late January.

Wendy's Champions Skins ProAm Golf Tournament, Royal Kaanapali Golf Course. Several of PGA's most legendary professionals play alongside amateurs on Royal Kaanapali's Golf Course. Call ✆ **808/661-3271** (www.kaanapaliresort.com). Late January to early February.

Chinese New Year. Lahaina town rolls out the red carpet for this important event with a traditional lion dance at the historic Wo Hing Temple on Front Street, accompanied by fireworks, food booths, and a host of activities. Call ✆ **888/310-1117** or 808/667-9175. Also on Market Street in Wailuku; call ✆ **808/244-3888.** Chinese New Year can fall in January or February; in 2011, the year of the rabbit, it's February 3. In 2012, the year of the dragon, it's on January 23.

FEBRUARY

Narcissus Festival, Honolulu, Oahu. Taking place around the Chinese New Year, this cultural festival includes a queen pageant, cooking demonstrations, and a cultural fair. Call ✆ **808/533-3181.**

Waimea Town Celebration, Waimea, Kauai. This annual 2-day party on Kauai's west side celebrates the Hawaiian and multiethnic history of the town where Captain Cook first landed. This is the island's biggest event, drawing some 10,000 people. Top Hawaiian entertainers, sporting events, rodeo, and lots of food are on tap during the weekend celebration. Call ✆ **808/338-1332** (www.wkbpa.org/events.html). Weekend after Presidents' Day weekend.

Sand Castle Building Contest, Kailua Beach Park, Oahu. Students from the University of Hawaii School of Architecture compete against professional architects to see who can build the best, most unusual, and most outrageous sand sculpture. Call ✆ **808/956-3518.**

Whale Day Celebration, Kalama Park, Kihei. A daylong celebration in the park,

Daylight Saving Time

Since 1966, most of the United States has observed daylight saving time from the first Sunday in April to the last Sunday in October. In 2007, these dates changed, and now daylight saving time lasts from 2am on the second Sunday in March to 2am on the first Sunday in November. **Note that Hawaii does** *not*

observe daylight saving time. So when daylight saving time is in effect in most of the U.S., Hawaii is 3 hours behind the West Coast and 6 hours behind the East Coast. When the U.S. reverts to standard time in November, Hawaii is 2 hours behind the West Coast and 5 hours behind the East Coast.

with a parade of whales, entertainment, a crafts fair, games, and food. Call ☎ **808/249-8811** (www.visitmaui.com). Early or mid-February.

Punahou School Carnival, Punahou School, Honolulu, Oahu. This event has everything you can imagine in a school carnival, from high-speed rides to home-made jellies. All proceeds go to scholarship funds for Hawaii's most prestigious private high school. Call ☎ **808/944-5753.** Early to mid-February.

Buffalo's Big Board Classic, Makaha Beach, Oahu. This contest involves traditional Hawaiian surfing, longboarding, and canoe surfing. Call ☎ **808/951-7877.** Depending on surf conditions, it can be held in February or March.

MARCH

Ocean Arts Festival, Lahaina. The entire town of Lahaina celebrates the annual migration of Pacific humpback whales with this festival in Banyan Tree Park. Artists display their best ocean-themed art for sale, while Hawaiian musicians and hula troupes entertain. Enjoy marine-related activities, games, and a Creature Feature touch-pool exhibit for children. Call ☎ **888/310-1117** or 808/667-9194 (www.visitlahaina.com). Mid-March.

Kona Brewers Festival, King Kamehameha's Kona Beach Hotel Luau Grounds, Kailua-Kona, Big Island. This annual event features microbreweries from around the world, with beer tastings, food, and entertainment. Call

☎ **808/334-1133** (www.konabrewers festival.com). Mid-March.

St. Patrick's Day Parade, Waikiki (Fort DeRussy to Kapiolani Park), Oahu. Bag-pipers, bands, clowns, and marching groups parade through the heart of Waikiki, with lots of Irish-style celebrating all day. Call ☎ **808/536-4612** (O'Toole's Pub). March 17.

Kona Chocolate Festival, Kona, Big Island. A 3-day celebration of the chocolate (cacao) that is grown and produced in Hawaii. Days 1 and 2 are filled with symposiums and seminars on chocolate and its uses. Day 3 features a gala party with samples of chocolate creations by Big Island chefs, caterers, and ice-cream and candy makers. A chocoholic's dream! For information and tickets, call ☎ **808/324-4606** (www.kona chocolatefestival.com). Mid-March to early April.

Prince Kuhio Day Celebrations, all islands. On this state holiday, various festivals throughout Hawaii celebrate the birth of Jonah Kuhio Kalanianaole, who was born on March 26, 1871, and elected to Congress in 1902. Kauai, his birth-place, stages a huge celebration in Lihue; call ☎ **808/240-6369** for details. Molokai also hosts a 2-day celebration; call ☎ **808/553-3876** to learn more. March 26.

APRIL

East Maui Taro Festival, Hana, Maui. Taro, a Hawaiian staple food, is celebrated through music, hula, arts, crafts, and, of course, food. Call ✆ **808/264-3336** (www.tarofestival.org). Varying dates in April.

Buddha Day, Lahaina Jodo Mission, Lahaina, Maui. Each year on the first Saturday in April, this historic mission holds a flower festival pageant honoring the birth of Buddha. The first Saturday in April.

Celebration of the Arts, Ritz-Carlton Kapalua, Kapalua Resort, Maui. Contemporary and traditional artists give free hands-on lessons during this 4-day festival, which begins the Thursday before Easter. Call ✆ **808/669-6200** (www.celebrationofthearts.org). April 1–4, 2011; April 21–24, 2012.

Easter Sunrise Service, National Memorial Cemetery of the Pacific, Punchbowl Crater, Honolulu, Oahu. For a century, people have gathered at this famous cemetery for Easter sunrise services. Call ✆ **808/566-1430.** April 24, 2011 and April 8, 2012.

Merrie Monarch Hula Festival, Hilo, Big Island. Hawaii's biggest hula festival features 3 nights of modern (auana) and ancient (kahiko) dance competition in honor of King David Kalakaua, the "Merrie Monarch" who revived the dance. It takes place the week after Easter, but tickets sell out by January 30—reserve early. Call ✆ **808/935-9168** (www.merriemonarchfestival.org). April 24–30, 2011, and April 8–14, 2012.

MAY

Outrigger Canoe Season, all islands. From May to September, canoe paddlers across the state participate in outrigger canoe races nearly every weekend. Call ✆ **808/383-7798** (www.y2kanu.com) for this year's schedule of events.

Lei Day Celebrations, various locations on all islands. May Day is Lei Day in Hawaii, celebrated with lei-making contests, pageantry, arts and crafts, and the real highlight, a Brothers Cazimero concert at the Waikiki Shell (call

✆ **808/597-1888,** ext. 232, for the show). Call ✆ **808/692-5118** (www.honolulu.gov/parks/programs/leiday) for Oahu events. Call ✆ **808/886-1655** for Big Island events, ✆ **808/224-6042** for Maui events, or ✆ **808/245-6931** for Kauai events. May 1.

Maui Onion Festival, Whalers Village, Kaanapali. Everything you ever wanted to know about the sweetest onions in the world. Food, entertainment, tastings, and the Maui Onion cook-off. Call ✆ **808/661-4567** (www.whalersvillage.com). Early May.

World Fire-Knife Dance Championships & Samoa Festival, Polynesian Cultural Center, Laie, Oahu. Junior and adult fire-knife dancers from around the world converge on the center for one of the most amazing performances you'll ever see. Authentic Samoan food and cultural festivities round out the fun. Call ✆ **808/293-3333** (www.polynesianculturalcenter.com). Mid-May.

Lantern Floating Hawaii, Magic Island at Ala Moana Beach Park, Honolulu, Oahu. The Shinnyo-en Temple's ceremonial floating of some 700 lanterns takes place at sunset, representing an appeal for peace and harmony. Hula and music follow the ceremony. Call ✆ **808/947-2814** (www.lanternfloatinghawaii.com). Memorial Day weekend.

Memorial Day, National Memorial Cemetery of the Pacific, Punchbowl Crater, Honolulu, Oahu. The armed forces hold a ceremony recognizing those who died for their country, beginning at 9am. Call ✆ **808/532-3720.** Memorial Day (last Mon in May).

Molokai Ka Hula Piko Festival, Papohaku Beach Park, Kaluakoi, Molokai. This daylong celebration of the hula takes place in mid-May on the island where it was born. It features performances by hula schools, musicians, and singers from across Hawaii, as well as local food and Hawaiian crafts, including quilting, woodworking, feather work, and deer-horn scrimshaw. Call ✆ **800/800-6367** or 808/553-3876 (www.molokai events.com). Dates vary in May.

Da Kine Classic Windsurfing Event, Kanaha Beach Park, Kahului. This annual windsurfing slalom race takes place at Kanaha Beach Park, west of Kahului Airport in central Maui. Call ✆ **808/877-2111.** Early June.

King Kamehameha Celebration, all islands. This state holiday (officially June 11, but celebrated on different dates on each island) features a massive floral parade, *hoolaulea* (party), and much more. Call ✆ **808/586-0333** for Oahu and Kauai events, ✆ **808/886-1655** for Big Island events, ✆ **808/667-9194** for Maui events, or ✆ **808/553-3876** for Molokai events. Most events in 2011 will be held June 11–12; in 2012, either June 9–10 or June 16–17.

Great Waikoloa Food, Wine & Music Festival, Hilton Waikoloa Village, Big Island. One of the Big Island's best food-and-wine festivals features Hawaii's top chefs (and a few mainland chefs) showing off their culinary talents, wines from around the world, and an excellent jazz concert with fireworks. Not to be missed. Call ✆ **808/886-1234** (www.hilton waikoloavillage.com or www.dolphin days.com). Mid-June.

Maui Film Festival, Wailea Resort, Maui. Five days and nights of screenings of premieres and special films, along with traditional Hawaiian storytelling, chants, hula, and contemporary music. It begins the Wednesday before Father's Day. Call ✆ **808/572-3456** (www.mauifilm festival.com). June 15–19, 2011, and June 13–17, 2012.

King Kamehameha Hula Competition, Neal Blaisdell Center, Honolulu, Oahu. This is one of the top hula competitions in the world, with dancers from as far away as Japan. It's held the third weekend in June. Call ✆ **808/586-0333** (www.hawaii.gov/dags/king_

kamehameha_commission). Mid- to late June.

Flavors of Honolulu, Civic Center Grounds, Honolulu, Oahu. Formerly known as the "Taste of Honolulu," Hawaii's premier outdoor food festival features samples from 25 restaurants, entertainment, beer and wine tasting, cooking demos, and a gourmet market-place. Proceeds go to Abilities Unlimited. Call ✆ **808/532-2115** (www.abilities unlimitedhi.org). Late June.

Hawaiian Slack-Key Guitar Festival, Maui Arts & Cultural Center, Kahului, Maui. Great music performed by the best musicians in Hawaii. It's 5 hours long and free. Call ✆ **808/226-2697** (www.slackkeyfestival.com). Late June.

Kapalua Wine & Food Festival, Kapalua Resort, Maui. Famous wine and food experts and oenophiles gather at the Ritz-Carlton hotel for formal tastings, panel discussions, and samplings of new releases. Call ✆ **800/KAPALUA** (527-2582; www.kapaluaresort.com). June or mid-July.

Makawao Parade & Rodeo, Makawao, Maui. The annual parade and rodeo event has been taking place in this upcountry cowboy town for generations. See www.visitmaui.com. July 4.

Lanai Pineapple Festival, Lanai City, Lanai. This festival on the first Saturday in July celebrates Lanai's history of pine-apple plantations and ranching, including a pineapple-eating contest, a pineapple-cooking contest, entertainment, arts and crafts, food, and fire-works. Call ✆ **808/565-7600** (www.visitlanai.net).

Fourth of July Fireworks, Desiderio and Sills Field, Schofield Barracks, Oahu. A free daylong celebration, with entertainment, food, and games, ends with a spectacular fireworks show. Call ✆ **808/655-0110.**

Bon Dance & Lantern Ceremony, Lahaina, Maui. This colorful Buddhist ceremony honors the souls of the dead. Call ✆ **808/661-4304.** Usually early July.

Quiksilver Molokai to Oahu Paddleboard Race, starts on Molokai and finishes on Oahu. Some 70 participants from an international field journey to Molokai to compete in this 32-mile race, considered to be the world championship of long-distance paddleboard racing. The race begins at Kaluakoi Beach on Molokai at 7:30am and finishes at Maunaloa Bay on Oahu around 12:30pm. Call ✆ **808/638-8208.** Mid- to late July.

Ukulele Festival, Kapiolani Park Bandstand, Waikiki, Oahu. This free concert features a ukulele orchestra of some 600 students, ages 4 to 92. Hawaii's top musicians all pitch in. Call ✆ **808/732-3739** (www.roysakuma.net). Late July.

Queen Liliuokalani Keiki Hula Competition, Neal Blaisdell Center, Honolulu, Oahu. More than 500 *keiki* (children) representing 22 *halau* (hula schools) from the islands compete in this dance-fest. The event is broadcast a week later on KITV-TV. Call ✆ **808/521-6905.** Late July.

Hawaii State Farm Fair, Aloha Stadium, Honolulu, Oahu. The annual state fair is a great one: It features displays of Hawaii agricultural products (including orchids), educational and cultural exhibits, entertainment, and local-style food. Call ✆ **808/682-5767** (www.ekfernandez. com). Late July or early August.

Transpac Yacht Race. This international yacht race is held during July in odd-numbered years only (2011 and so on). Sailors from the United States, Japan, Australia, New Zealand, Europe, and Hawaii race from Long Beach to Honolulu. They then participate in a series of races around the state. Call ✆ **808/944-9666** (www.transpacificyc.org).

Hawaii International Jazz Festival, Hawaii Theatre, Honolulu, Oahu. This festival includes evening concerts and daily jam sessions, plus scholarship giveaways, the University of Southern California jazz band, and many popular jazz and blues artists. Call ✆ **808/941-9974.** Early August.

Hawaii State Windsurfing Championship, Kanaha Beach Park, Kahului, Maui. Top windsurfers compete. Call ✆ **808/877-2111.** Early August.

Tahiti Fete, War Memorial Gym, Wailuku, Maui. This annual festival includes Tahitian dance competition, arts and crafts, and food. Call ✆ **808/244-8088.**

Puukohola Heiau National Historic Site Anniversary Celebration, Kawaihae, Big Island. This is a weekend of Hawaiian crafts, workshops, and games. Call ✆ **808/882-7218.** Mid-August.

Duke's OceanFest Hoolaulea, Waikiki, Oahu. Nine days of water-oriented competitions and festivities celebrate the life of Duke Kahanamoku. Events include the Hawaii Paddleboard Championship, the Pro Surf Longboard contest, the International Tandem Surfing Championship, the Corona Extra Duke Volleyball Classic, a Surf Polo tournament, and a Hawaiian luau (the luau is $60 at the door). Call ✆ **808/545-4880** (www.dukefoundation. org). Mid-August.

Admissions Day, all islands. Hawaii became the 50th state on August 21, 1959. On the third Friday in August, the state takes a holiday (all state-related facilities are closed).

Hawaiian Slack-Key Guitar Festival Gabby Style, Queen Kapiolani Park Bandstand, Honolulu, Oahu. The best of Hawaii's folk music—slack-key guitar—performed by the best musicians in Hawaii. It takes place from noon to 6pm and is free. Call ✆ **808/226-2697**

(www.slackkeyfestival.com). Third Sunday in August.

Waikiki Roughwater Swim, Waikiki, Oahu. This popular 2½-mile, open-ocean swim goes from Sans Souci Beach to Duke Kahanamoku Beach in Waikiki. Early registration is encouraged, but last-minute entries on race day are allowed. Visit www.waikikiroughwaterswim.com for more info. Labor Day.

Queen Liliuokalani Canoe Race, Kailua-Kona to Honaunau, Big Island. It's the world's largest long-distance canoe race, with hundreds participating. Call ✆ **808/331-8849** (www.kaiopua.org). Labor Day weekend.

Parker Ranch Rodeo, Waimea, Big Island. This is a hot rodeo competition in the heart of cowboy country. Call ✆ **808/885-7311** (www.parkerranch.com). Labor Day weekend.

Hawaiian Slack-Key Guitar Festival, Sheraton Keauhou Bay Resort & Spa, Kona, Big Island. The best of Hawaii's folk music (slack-key guitar) performed by the best musicians in Hawaii. It's 5 hours long and free. Call ✆ **808/239-4336** (kahokuproductions@yahoo.com). Early September.

Aloha Festivals, various locations on all islands. Parades and other events celebrate Hawaiian culture and friendliness throughout the state. Call ✆ **808/589-1771** (www.alohafestivals.com).

Aloha Festivals' Poke Contest, Hapuna Beach Prince Hotel, Big Island. Top chefs from across Hawaii and the U.S. mainland, as well as local amateurs, compete in making this Hawaiian delicacy, poke (pronounced *po-kay*): chopped raw fish mixed with seaweed and spices. Here's your chance to sample poke at its best. Call ✆ **808/880-3424.**

A Taste of Lahaina, Lahaina Civic Center, Maui. Some 30,000 people show up to sample 40 signature entrees from Maui's premier chefs during this weekend festival, which includes cooking demonstrations, wine tastings, and live entertainment. The event begins Friday night with Maui Chefs Present, a dinner/cocktail party featuring about a dozen of Maui's best chefs. Call ✆ **888/310-1117** (www.visitmaui.com). Second weekend in September.

Maui County Fair, War Memorial Complex, Wailuku, Maui. The oldest county fair in Hawaii features a parade, amusement rides, live entertainment, and exhibits. Call ✆ **808/270-7626** (www.calendarmaui.com). Last weekend in September.

Emalani Festival, Kokee State Park, Kauai. This festival honors Her Majesty Queen Emma, an inveterate gardener and Hawaii's first environmental queen, who made a forest trek to Kokee with 100 friends in 1871. Call ✆ **808/245-3971.** Second Saturday in October.

Aloha Classic Wave Championships, Hookipa Beach Park, Maui. The top windsurfers in the world gather for this final event in the Pro Boardsailing World Tour. If you're on Maui, don't miss it—it's spectacular to watch. Call ✆ **808/298-3560.** Depending on weather, it can be held in October or November.

Ironman Triathlon World Championship, Kailua-Kona, Big Island. Some 1,500-plus world-class athletes run a full marathon, swim 2½ miles, and bike 112 miles on the Kona-Kohala Coast of the Big Island. Spectators can watch the action along the route for free. The best place to see the 7am start is along the seawall on Alii Drive, facing Kailua Bay; arrive before 5:30am to get a seat. The best place to see the bike-and-run portion is along Alii Drive (which will be closed to traffic; park on a side street and walk down). To watch the finishers come in, line up along Alii Drive from Holualoa Street to the finish at Palani Road/Alii Drive; the first finisher can arrive as early as 2:30pm, and the course closes at midnight. Call ✆ **808/329-0063** (www. ironman.com/worldchampionship). Sunday closest to the full moon in October.

Hana Hoohiwahiwa O Kaiulani, Sheraton Princess Kaiulani, Waikiki, Oahu. This hotel commemorates the birthday of its namesake, Princess Victoria Kaiulani, with a week of special activities: complimentary hula lessons, lei making, ukulele lessons, and more. The crowning touch is the Princess Kaiulani Keiki Hula Festival, which showcases performances by more than 200 *keiki* from *halau* on the island of Oahu. Admission is free. Call ✆ **808/ 931-4524.** Mid-October.

NOVEMBER

Hawaiian Slack-Key Guitar Festival, Kauai Marriott Resort, Lihue, Kauai. The best of Hawaii's folk music (slack-key guitar) performed by the best musicians in Hawaii. It's 5 hours long and free. Call ✆ **808/226-2697** (kahokuproductions@ yahoo.com). Mid-November.

Kona Coffee Cultural Festival, Kailua-Kona, Big Island. Celebrate the coffee harvest with a bean-picking contest, lei contests, song and dance, and the Miss Kona Coffee Pageant. Call ✆ **808/326-7820** (www.konacoffeefest.com). Events throughout November.

Hawaii International Film Festival, various locations throughout the state. This cinema festival with a cross-cultural spin features filmmakers from Asia, the Pacific Islands, and the United States. Call ✆ **808/550-8457** (www.hiff.org). First 2 weeks in November.

Invitational Wreath Exhibit, Volcano Art Center, Hawaii Volcanoes National Park, Big Island. Thirty-two artists, including painters, sculptors, glass artists, fiber artists, and potters, produce both whimsical and traditional "wreaths" for this exhibit. Park entrance fees apply. Call ✆ **866/967-7565** or 808/967-7565 (www.volcanoartcenter.org). Mid-November to early January.

Triple Crown of Surfing, North Shore, Oahu. The world's top professional surfers compete in events for more than $1 million in prize money. Call ✆ **808/739-3965** (www.triplecrownofsurfing.com). Held between mid-November and mid-December, whenever conditions are best.

DECEMBER

Na Mele O Maui, Kaanapali, Maui. A traditional Hawaiian song competition for children in kindergarten through 12th grade, held in the ballroom of one of the Kaanapali Resort hotels. Admission is $2. Call ✆ **808/661-3271** (www.kaanapali resort.com). First Friday in December.

Billabong Pro Maui, Honolua Bay at Kapalua Resort, Maui. The final Triple Crown women's surfing contest of the year, bringing together the best of the women's international surfing community. Call ✆ **808/669-2440** (www. kapalua.com). Early December.

Festival of Lights, all islands. On Oahu, the mayor throws the switch to light up the 40-foot-tall Norfolk pine and other trees in front of Honolulu Hale, while on Maui, marching bands, floats, and Santa roll down Lahaina's Front Street in an annual parade. Molokai celebrates with a host of activities in Kaunakakai; on Kauai, the lighting ceremony takes place in front of the former county building on Rice Street, in Lihue. Call ✆ **808/523-4385** on Oahu, ✆ **808/667-9175** on Maui, ✆ **808/552-2800** on Molokai, or ✆ **808/828-0014** on Kauai. Early December.

Old-Fashioned Holiday Celebration, Lahaina, Maui. This day of Christmas carolers, Santa Claus, live music and entertainment, a crafts fair, holiday baked goods, and activities for children takes place in the Banyan Tree Park on Front Street. Call ✆ **888/310-1117** (www. visitlahaina.com). Second Saturday in December.

Honolulu Marathon, Honolulu, Oahu. This is one of the largest marathons in the world, with more than 30,000 competitors. Call ☎ **808/734-7200** (www.honolulumarathon.org). Second Sunday in December.

Aloha Bowl, Aloha Stadium, Honolulu, Oahu. A Pac 10 team plays a Big 12 team in this nationally televised collegiate football classic. Call ☎ **808/483-2500.** Christmas Day.

First Light, Maui Arts & Cultural Center, Kahului, Maui. Major films are screened at this festival; past selections have included *The Lord of the Rings: Return of the King, Mystic River, The Aviator, Hotel Rwanda,* and many others. Not to be missed. Call ☎ **808/573-3456** (www.mauifilmfestival.com). Late December and early January.

WHAT TO PACK

Hawaii is very informal. Shorts, T-shirts, and tennis shoes will get you by at most restaurants and attractions; a casual dress or a polo shirt and khakis are fine even in the most expensive places. Jackets for men are required only in some of the fine-dining rooms of a very few ultraexclusive resorts, such as the Halekulani on Oahu, the Big Island's Mauna Kea Beach Hotel, and the Lodge at Koele on Lanai—and they'll cordially provide you with a jacket if you don't bring your own. Aloha wear is acceptable everywhere, so you may want to plan on buying an aloha shirt or a muumuu (a Hawaiian-style dress) while you're in the islands.

So bring T-shirts, shorts, long pants, a couple of bathing suits, a long-sleeve coverup (to throw on at the beach when you've had enough sun for the day), tennis shoes, rubber water shoes or flip-flops, and hiking boots and good socks if you plan on hiking.

The tropical sun poses the greatest threat to anyone who ventures into the great outdoors, so be sure to pack **sun protection:** a good pair of sunglasses, strong sunscreen, a light hat, and a canteen or water bottle if you'll be hiking—you'll easily dehydrate in the tropical heat, so figure on carrying 2 liters of water per day on any hike. Campers should bring water-purification tablets or devices. Also see "Health" and "Safety," later in this chapter.

One last thing: **It really can get cold in Hawaii.** If you plan to see the sunrise from the top of Maui's Haleakala Crater, venture into the Big Island's Hawaii Volcanoes National Park, or spend time in Kokee State Park on Kauai, bring a warm jacket; 40°F (4°C) upcountry temperatures, even in summer when it's 80°F (27°C) at the beach, are not uncommon. It's always a good idea to bring at least a windbreaker, a sweater, or a light jacket. And be sure to toss some **rain gear** into your suitcase if you'll be in Hawaii between November and March.

ENTRY REQUIREMENTS

Passports

Virtually every air traveler entering the U.S. is required to show a passport. All persons, including U.S. citizens, traveling by air between the United States and Canada, Mexico, Central and South America, the Caribbean, and Bermuda are required to present a valid passport. U.S. and Canadian citizens entering the U.S. at land and sea ports of entry from within the western hemisphere will need to present government-issued proof of citizenship, such as a birth certificate, along with a government-issued photo ID, such as a driver's license. A passport is not required for U.S. or Canadian citizens entering by land or sea, but you are highly encouraged to carry one.

For information on how to obtain a passport, see "Fast Facts," on p. 732.

Visas

For information on obtaining a visa, visit "Fast Facts," on p. 734.

The U.S. State Department has a **Visa Waiver Program (VWP)** allowing citizens of the following countries to enter the United States without a visa for stays of up to 90 days: Andorra, Australia, Austria, Belgium, Brunei, Denmark, Finland, France, Germany, Iceland, Ireland, Italy, Japan, Liechtenstein, Luxembourg, Monaco, the Netherlands, New Zealand, Norway, Portugal, San Marino, Singapore, Slovenia, Spain, Sweden, Switzerland, and the United Kingdom. Citizens of Czech Republic, Estonia, Hungary, Latvia, Lithuania, Malta, Republic of Korea, and Slovakia are soon to be admitted to the VWP. (**Note:** This list was accurate at press time; for the most up-to-date list of countries in the VWP, consult http://travel.state.gov/visa.) Even though a visa isn't necessary, in an effort to help U.S. officials check travelers against terror watch lists before they arrive at U.S. borders, visitors from VWP countries must register online through the Electronic System for Travel Authorization (ESTA) before boarding a plane or a boat to the U.S. Travelers will complete an electronic application providing basic personal and travel eligibility information. The Department of Homeland Security recommends filling out the form at least 3 days before traveling. Authorizations will be valid for up to 2 years or until the traveler's passport expires, whichever comes first. Currently, there is no fee for the online application. **Note:** Any passport issued on or after October 26, 2006, by a VWP country must be an **e-Passport** for VWP travelers to be eligible to enter the U.S. without a visa. Citizens of these nations also need to present a round-trip air or cruise ticket upon arrival. E-Passports contain computer chips capable of storing biometric information, such as the required digital photograph of the holder. If your passport doesn't have this feature, you can still travel without a visa if it is a valid passport issued before October 26, 2005, and includes a machine-readable zone, or between October 26, 2005, and October 25, 2006, and includes a digital photograph. For more information, go to **http://travel.state.gov/visa**. Canadian citizens may enter the United States without visas; they will need to show passports (if traveling by air) and proof of residence, however.

Citizens of all other countries must have (1) a valid passport that expires at least 6 months later than the scheduled end of their visit to the U.S., and (2) a tourist visa.

Customs

WHAT YOU CAN BRING INTO THE U.S.

Every visitor 21 years of age or older may bring in, free of duty, the following: (1) 1 liter of wine or hard liquor; (2) 200 cigarettes, 100 cigars (but not from Cuba), or 3 pounds of smoking tobacco; and (3) $100 worth of gifts. These exemptions are offered to travelers who spend at least 72 hours in the United States and who have not claimed them within the preceding 6 months. It is forbidden to bring into the country almost any meat products (including canned, fresh, and dried meat products such as bouillon, soup mixes, and so on). Generally, condiments including vinegars, oils, spices, coffee, tea, and some cheeses and baked goods are permitted. Avoid rice products, as rice can often harbor insects. Bringing fruits and vegetables is not advised, though not prohibited. Customs will allow produce depending on where you got it and where you're going after you arrive in the U.S. International visitors may carry in or out up to $10,000 in U.S. or foreign currency with no formalities; larger sums must be declared to U.S. Customs on entering or leaving, which includes filing form CM 4790. For details regarding U.S. Customs and Border Protection, consult your nearest U.S. embassy or consulate, or **U.S. Customs** (www.customs.gov).

WHAT YOU CAN TAKE HOME FROM HAWAII

You cannot take home fresh fruit, plants, or seeds (including some leis) unless they are sealed. You cannot seal and pack them yourself.

For information on what you're allowed to bring home, contact one of the following agencies:

U.S. Citizens: U.S. Customs & Border Protection (CBP), 1300 Pennsylvania Ave., NW, Washington, DC 20229 (✆ **877/287-8667;** www.cbp.gov).

Canadian Citizens: Canada Border Services Agency (✆ **800/461-9999** in Canada, or 204/983-3500; www.cbsa-asfc.gc.ca).

U.K. Citizens: HM Customs & Excise at ✆ **0845/010-9000** (from outside the U.K., 020/8929-0152), or consult their website at **www.hmce. gov.uk**.

Australian Citizens: Australian Customs Service at ✆ **1300/363-263,** or log on to **www.customs.gov.au**.

New Zealand Citizens: New Zealand Customs, The Customhouse, 17–21 Whitmore St., Box 2218, Wellington (✆ **04/473-6099** or 0800/428-786; **www.customs.govt.nz**).

Medical Requirements

Unless you're arriving from an area known to be suffering from an epidemic (particularly cholera or yellow fever), inoculations or vaccinations are not required for entry into the United States.

GETTING THERE & GETTING AROUND

Getting to Hawaii

BY PLANE

Most major U.S. and many international carriers fly to **Honolulu International Airport** (HNL), on Oahu. Some also offer direct flights to **Kona International Airport** (KOA), near Kailua-Kona on the Big Island; **Kahului Airport** (OGG), on Maui; and **Lihue Airport** (LIH), on Kauai. If you can fly directly to the island of your choice, you'll be spared a 2-hour layover in Honolulu and another plane ride. If you're heading to Molokai or Lanai, you'll have the easiest connections if you fly into Honolulu.

United Airlines offers the most frequent service from the U.S. mainland, with flights to Honolulu as well as nonstop service from Los Angeles and San Francisco to the Big Island, Maui, and Kauai. **Alaska Airlines** offers daily flights from Anchorage to Seattle to Maui from April to October, and twice-weekly flights on the same run from October 31 to April 25. **American Airlines** offers flights from Dallas, Chicago, San Francisco, San Jose, Los Angeles, and St. Louis to Honolulu, plus several direct flights to Maui and Kona.

Continental Airlines offers the only daily nonstop from the New York area (Newark) to Honolulu. **Delta Air Lines** flies nonstop from the West Coast and from Houston and Cincinnati. **Hawaiian Airlines** offers nonstop flights to Honolulu from several West Coast cities (including new service from San Diego), plus nonstop service from Los Angeles to Maui. **Northwest Airlines** has a daily nonstop from Detroit to Honolulu.

Airlines serving Hawaii from places other than the U.S. mainland include **Air Canada; Air New Zealand; Qantas Airways; Japan Air Lines; All Nippon Airways** (ANA); the Taiwan-based **China Airlines; Air Pacific,** which serves Fiji, Australia, New Zealand, and the South Pacific; **Korean Air;** and **Philippine Airlines. Hawaiian Airlines** also flies nonstop to Sydney, Tahiti, and American Samoa.

ARRIVING AT THE AIRPORT

IMMIGRATION & CUSTOMS CLEARANCE   International visitors arriving by air should cultivate patience and resignation before setting foot on U.S. soil. U.S. airports have considerably beefed up security clearances in the years since the terrorist attacks of September 11, and clearing Customs and Immigration can take as long as 2 hours.

AGRICULTURAL SCREENING AT THE AIRPORTS   At Honolulu International and the neighbor-island airports, baggage and passengers bound for the mainland must be screened by agricultural officials. Officials will confiscate local produce like fresh avocados, bananas, and mangoes, in the name of fruit-fly control. Pineapples, coconuts, and papayas inspected and certified for export; boxed flowers; leis without seeds; and processed foods (macadamia nuts, coffee, jams, dried fruit, and the like) will pass.

Getting Around Hawaii

For additional advice on travel within each island, see "Getting Around" in the individual island chapters that follow.

INTERISLAND FLIGHTS

Since September 11, 2001, the major interisland carriers have cut way back on the number of interisland flights. The airlines warn you to show up at least 90 minutes before your flight, and believe me, with all the security inspections, you will need all 90 minutes to catch your flight.

Hawaii has three major interisland carriers: **Hawaiian Airlines** (✆ 800/367-5320; www.hawaiianair.com); **go!** (✆ 888/I-FLY-GO-2 [435-9462]; www.iflygo.com); and **Mokulele Airlines** (✆ 808/426-7070; www.mokulele airlines.com).

Visitors to Molokai and Lanai have three commuter airlines to choose from: **Island Air** (✆ 800/323-3345; www.islandair.com), **Mokulele Airlines** (✆ 808/426-7070 or www.mokuleleairlines.com), or **Pacific Wings** (✆ 888/575-4546; www.pacificwings.com), which all serve Hawaii's small interisland airports on Maui, Molokai, and Lanai. However, I have to warn you that I have not had stellar service on Island Air and recommend that you book another carrier.

Cruising Through the Islands

If you're looking for a taste of several islands in a single week, consider **Norwegian Cruise Line** (*©* 800/327-7030; www.ncl.com), the only cruise line that operates year-round in Hawaii. NCL's 2,240-passenger ship *Pride of Aloha* circles the Hawaiian Islands, stopping on the Big Island, Maui, Kauai, and Oahu; some itineraries even go to Fanning Island in the Republic of Kiribati before returning to Honolulu. The disadvantage of a cruise is that you won't be able to see any of the islands in depth or at leisure; the advantage is that you can spend your days exploring the island where the ship is docked and your nights aboard ship sailing to the next port of call.

Some large airlines offer transatlantic or transpacific passengers special discount tickets under the name **Visit USA,** which allows mostly one-way travel from one U.S. destination to another at very low prices. Unavailable in the U.S., these discount tickets must be purchased abroad in conjunction with your international fare. This system is the easiest, fastest, cheapest way to see the country.

BY CAR

Hawaii has some of the lowest car-rental rates in the country. (An exception is the island of Lanai, where they're very expensive.) To rent a car in Hawaii, you must be at least 25 years of age and have a valid driver's license and credit card. *Note:* If you're visiting from abroad and plan to rent a car in the United States, keep in mind that foreign driver's licenses are usually recognized in the U.S., but you should get an international one if your home license is not in English.

At Honolulu International Airport and most neighbor-island airports, you'll find most major car-rental agencies, including **Alamo, Avis, Budget, Dollar, Enterprise, Hertz, National,** and **Thrifty.** For complete rental-agency contact information, see chapter 11. It's almost always cheaper to rent a car at the airport than in Waikiki or through your hotel (unless there's one already included in your package deal).

Rental cars are usually at a premium on Kauai, Molokai, and Lanai, and may be sold out on the neighbor islands on holiday weekends, so be sure to book well ahead.

INSURANCE   Hawaii is a no-fault state, which means that if you don't have collision-damage insurance, you are required to pay for all damages before you leave the state, whether or not the accident was your fault. Your personal car insurance may provide rental-car coverage; check before you leave home. Bring your insurance identification card if you decline the optional insurance, which usually costs from $12 to $20 a day. Obtain the name of your company's local claim representative before you go. Some credit card companies also provide collision-damage insurance for their customers; check with yours before you rent.

DRIVING RULES   Hawaii state law mandates that all car passengers must wear a **seat belt** and all infants must be strapped into a car seat. You'll pay a $50 fine if you don't buckle up. **Pedestrians** always have the right of way, even if they're not in the crosswalk. You can turn **right on red** after a full and complete stop, unless otherwise posted.

ROAD MAPS The best and most detailed maps for activities are published by **Franko Maps** (www.frankosmaps.com); they feature a host of island maps, plus a terrific *Hawaiian Reef Creatures Guide* for snorkelers curious about those fish they spot underwater. Free road maps are published by *This Week Magazine,* a visitor publication available on Oahu, the Big Island, Maui, and Kauai. For even greater detail, check out **Odyssey Publishing** (℘ 888/729-1074; www.hawaiimapsource.com), which has very detailed maps of East and West Hawaii, Maui, and Kauai.

Another good source is the University of Hawaii Press maps, which include a detailed network of island roads, large-scale insets of towns, historical and contemporary points of interest, parks, beaches, and hiking trails. If you can't find them in a bookstore near you, contact **University of Hawaii Press,** 2840 Kolowalu St., Honolulu, HI 96822 (℘ 888/847-7737; www.uhpress.hawaii.edu). For topographic and other maps of the islands, go to the **Hawaii Geographic Society,** 49 S. Hotel St., Honolulu, or contact P.O. Box 1698, Honolulu, HI 96806 (℘ 800/538-3950 or 808/538-3952).

MONEY & COSTS

THE VALUE OF US$ VS. OTHER POPULAR CURRENCIES

US$	C$	£	€	A$	NZ$
1.00	1.17	.65	.74	1.32	1.69

Frommer's lists exact prices in the local currency. The currency conversions quoted above were correct at press time. However, rates fluctuate, so before departing consult a currency exchange website such as **www.oanda.com/convert/classic** to check up-to-the-minute rates.

Why Oahu Is More Expensive

No, it's not your imagination—Oahu *is* more expensive than the other Hawaiian Islands. That's the result of the Hawaii State Legislature passing a bill allowing the City and County of Honolulu (which is the entire island of Oahu) to add an additional .5% tax onto the state general excise tax of 4%. Everything you buy on Oahu will have this tax, and so will your hotel bill. The funds from this additional tax are earmarked for mass transit for Oahu.

WHAT THINGS COST IN HAWAII	US$
Hamburger	6.00
Movie ticket (adult/child)	9.00/5.50
Taxi from Honolulu Airport to Waikiki	30.00
Entry to Bishop Museum (adult/child)	16.00/13.00
Entry to Hawaiian Water Adventure Park (adult/child)	35.00/25.00
Entry to Honolulu Zoo (adult/child)	8.00/1.00
Entry to Maui Ocean Center (adult/child)	25.00/18.50
Entry to Maui Tropical Plantation (adult/child)	14.00/5.00
Entry to Haleakala National Park	5.00
Old Lahaina Luau (adult/child)	96.00/65.00
20-ounce soft drink at convenience store	2.50
16-ounce apple juice	3.50
Cup of coffee	3.00
Moderately priced three-course dinner without alcohol	50.00
Moderately priced Waikiki hotel room (double)	125.00

ATMs

Nationwide, the easiest and best way to get cash away from home is from an ATM (automated teller machine), sometimes referred to as a "cash machine" or "cashpoint." ATMs are everywhere in Hawaii—at banks, supermarkets, Longs Drugs, and Honolulu International Airport, and in some resorts and shopping centers. The **Cirrus** (© **800/424-7787;** www.mastercard.com) and **PLUS** (© **800/843-7587;** www.visa.com) networks span the country; you can find them even in remote regions. Go to your bank card's website to find ATM locations at your destination. Be sure you know your daily withdrawal limit before you depart.

Note: Many banks impose a fee every time you use a card at another bank's ATM, and that fee is often higher for international transactions (up to $5 or more) than for domestic ones (where they're rarely more than $2). In addition, the bank from which you withdraw cash may charge its own fee. To compare banks' ATM fees within the U.S., use **www.bankrate.com**. Visitors from outside the U.S. should also find out whether their bank assesses a 1% to 3% fee on charges incurred abroad.

Credit Cards & Debit Cards

Credit cards are the most widely used form of payment in the United States: **Visa** (Barclaycard in Britain), **MasterCard** (Eurocard in Europe, Access in Britain, Chargex in Canada), **American Express, Diners Club,** and **Discover.** They also provide a convenient record of all your expenses and offer relatively good exchange rates. You can withdraw cash advances from your credit cards at banks or ATMs, but high fees make credit card cash advances a pricey way to get cash.

It's highly recommended that you travel with at least one major credit card. You must have a credit card to rent a car, and hotels and airlines usually require a credit card imprint as a deposit against expenses.

ATM cards with major credit card backing, known as **"debit cards,"** are now a commonly acceptable form of payment in most stores and restaurants. Debit cards draw money directly from your checking account. Some stores enable you to receive cash back on your debit card purchases as well. The same is true at most U.S. post offices.

Credit cards are accepted everywhere except TheBus (on Oahu), taxicabs (all islands), and some small restaurants and bed-and-breakfast accommodations.

HEALTH
Staying Healthy
INSECTS & SCORPIONS

Like any tropical climate, Hawaii is home to lots of bugs. Most of them won't harm you. However, watch out for mosquitoes, centipedes, and scorpions, which do sting and may cause anything from mild annoyance to severe swelling and pain.

MOSQUITOES These pesky insects are not native to Hawaii but arrived as larvae stowed away in water barrels on the ship *Wellington* in 1826, when it anchored in Lahaina. There's not a whole lot you can do about them, except to apply commercial repellent, which you can pick up at any drugstore.

CENTIPEDES These segmented bugs with a jillion legs come in two varieties: 6- to 8-inch-long brown ones and 2- to 3-inch-long blue guys. Both can really pack a wallop with their sting. Centipedes are generally found in damp, wet places, such as under woodpiles or compost heaps; wearing closed-toe shoes can help prevent stings. If you're stung, apply ice at once to prevent swelling. See a doctor if you experience extreme pain, swelling, nausea, or any other severe reaction.

SCORPIONS Rarely seen, scorpions are found in arid, warm regions; their stings can be serious. Campers in dry areas should always check their boots before putting them on and shake out sleeping bags and bed rolls. Symptoms of a scorpion sting include shortness of breath, hives, swelling, and nausea. In the unlikely event that you're stung, apply diluted household ammonia and cold compresses to the area of the sting and seek medical help immediately.

HIKING SAFETY

In addition to taking the appropriate precautions regarding Hawaii's bug population, hikers should always let someone know where they're heading, when they're going, and when they plan to return; too many hikers get lost in Hawaii because they don't let others know their basic plans. And make sure you know how strenuous the route and trail you will follow are—don't overestimate your ability.

Before you head out, always check weather conditions with the **National Weather Service** (© **808/973-4381** on Oahu; see individual island chapters

DON'T GET BURNED: smart tanning TIPS

Hawaii's Caucasian population has the highest incidence of malignant melanoma (deadly skin cancer) in the world. And nobody is completely safe from the sun's harmful rays: All skin types and races can burn. To ensure that your vacation won't be ruined by a painful sunburn, be sure to wear a strong sunscreen that protects against both UVA and UVB rays at all times (look for zinc oxide, benzophenone, oxybenzone, sulisobenzone, titanium dioxide, or avobenzone in the list of ingredients). Wear a wide-brimmed hat and sunglasses. Keep infants under 6 months out of the sun completely, and slather older babies and children with strong sunscreen frequently.

If you do get a burn, aloe vera, cool compresses, cold baths, and benzocaine can help with the pain. Stay out of the sun until the burn is completely gone.

for local weather information). Do not hike if rain or a storm is predicted; flash floods are common in Hawaii. Hike with a pal, never alone. Plan to finish your hike at least an hour before sunset; because Hawaii is so close to the equator, it does not have a twilight period, and thus it gets dark quickly after the sun sets. Wear hiking boots, a sun hat, clothes to protect you from the sun and from getting scratches, and high-SPF sunscreen on all exposed areas of skin. Take plenty of water, basic first aid, a snack, and a bag to pack out what you pack in. Stay on the trail. Watch your step. It's easy to slip off precipitous trails and into steep canyons. Many experienced hikers and boaters today pack a cellphone in case of emergency; just dial ✆ **911.**

VOG

The volcanic haze dubbed *vog* is caused by gases released when molten lava—from the continuous eruption of Kilauea volcano on the Big Island—pours into the ocean. Some people claim that long-term exposure to the hazy, smoglike air has caused bronchial ailments, but it's highly unlikely to cause you any harm in the course of your visit.

There actually is a vog season in Hawaii: the fall and winter months, when the trade winds that blow the fumes out to sea die down. The vog is felt not only on the Big Island, but also as far away as Maui and Oahu.

One more word of caution: If you're pregnant or have heart or breathing problems, you should avoid exposure to the sulfuric fumes that are ever present in and around the Big Island's Hawaii Volcanoes National Park.

OCEAN SAFETY

Because most people coming to Hawaii are unfamiliar with the ocean environment, they're often unaware of the natural hazards it holds. With just a few precautions, your ocean experience can be a safe and happy one. An excellent book is *All Stings Considered: First Aid and Medical Treatment of Hawaii's Marine Injuries,* by Craig Thomas and Susan Scott (University of Hawaii Press, 1997).

Note that sharks are not a big problem in Hawaii; in fact, they appear so infrequently that locals look forward to seeing them. Since records have been kept, starting in 1779, there have been only about 100 shark attacks in Hawaii, of which 40% have been fatal. Most attacks occurred after someone fell into the ocean from the shore or from a boat; in these cases, the sharks probably attacked after the person was dead. But here are the general rules for avoiding sharks: Don't swim at sunrise, at sunset, or where the water is murky due to stream run-off—sharks may mistake you for one of their usual meals. And don't swim where there are bloody fish in the water, as sharks become aggressive around blood.

SEASICKNESS   The waters in Hawaii can range from as calm as glass (off the Kona Coast on the Big Island) to downright frightening (in storm conditions); they usually fall somewhere in between. In general, expect rougher conditions in winter than in summer. Some 90% of the population tends toward seasickness. If you've never been out on a boat, or if you've been seasick in the past, you might want to heed the following suggestions:

o The day before you go out on the boat, avoid alcohol, caffeine, citrus and other acidic juices, and greasy, spicy, or hard-to-digest foods.

o Get a good night's sleep the night before.

o Take or use whatever seasickness prevention works best for you—medication, an acupressure wristband, ginger-root tea or capsules, or any combination. But do it *before* you board; once you set sail, it's generally too late.

o While you're on the boat, stay as low and as near the center of the boat as possible. Avoid the fumes (especially if it's a diesel boat); stay out in the fresh air and watch the horizon. Do not read.

o If you start to feel queasy, drink clear fluids like water, and eat something bland, such as a soda cracker.

STINGS   The most common stings in Hawaii come from jellyfish, particularly Portuguese man-of-war and box jellyfish. Since the poisons they inject are very different, you need to treat each type of sting differently.

A bluish-purple floating bubble with a long tail, the **Portuguese man-of-war** is responsible for some 6,500 stings a year on Oahu alone. These stings, although painful and a nuisance, are rarely harmful; fewer than 1 in 1,000 requires medical treatment. The best prevention is to watch for these floating bubbles as you snorkel (look for the hanging tentacles below the surface). Get out of the water if anyone near you spots these jellyfish.

Reactions to stings range from mild burning and reddening to severe welts and blisters. *All Stings Considered* recommends the following treatment: First, pick off any visible tentacles with a gloved hand, a stick, or anything handy; then rinse the sting with salt- or fresh water, and apply ice to prevent swelling and to help control pain. Avoid folk remedies like vinegar, baking soda, or urinating on the wound, which may actually cause further damage. Most Portuguese man-of-war stings will disappear by themselves within 15 to 20 minutes if you do nothing at all to treat them.

Everything You've Always Wanted to Know About Sharks

The Hawaii State Department of Land and Natural Resources has launched a website, **www.hawaiisharks.com,** that covers the biology, history, and culture of these carnivores. It also provides safety information and data on shark bites in Hawaii.

Enjoying the Ocean & Avoiding Mishaps

The Pacific Whale Foundation has a free brochure called *Enjoying Maui's Unique Ocean Environment* that introduces visitors to Hawaii's ocean, beaches, tide pools, and reefs. Although written for Maui (with maps showing Maui's beaches), it's a great general resource on how to stay safe around the ocean, with hints on how to assess weather before you jump into the water and the best ways to view marine wildlife. To get the brochure, call ✆ **808/244-8390** or visit www.pacificwhale.org.

Still, be sure to see a doctor if pain persists or a rash or other symptoms develop.

Transparent, square-shaped **box jellyfish** are nearly impossible to see in the water. Fortunately, they seem to follow a monthly cycle: 8 to 10 days after the full moon, they appear in the waters on the leeward side of each island and hang around for about 3 days. Also, they seem to sting more in the morning hours, when they're on or near the surface.

The stings can cause anything from no visible marks to hivelike welts, blisters, and pain lasting from 10 minutes to 8 hours. *All Stings Considered* recommends the following treatment: First, pour regular household vinegar on the sting; this will stop additional burning. Do not rub the area. Pick off any vinegar-soaked tentacles with a stick. For pain, apply an ice pack. Seek additional medical treatment if you experience shortness of breath, weakness, palpitations, muscle cramps, or any other severe symptoms. Most box-jellyfish stings disappear by themselves without any treatment.

PUNCTURES Most sea-related punctures come from stepping on or brushing against the needlelike spines of sea urchins (known locally as *wana*). Be careful when you're in the water; don't put your foot down (even if you have booties or fins on) if you can't clearly see the bottom. Waves can push you into wana in a surge zone in shallow water. The spines can even puncture a wet suit.

A sea urchin puncture can result in burning, aching, swelling, and discoloration (black or purple) around the area where the spines entered your skin. The best thing to do is to pull any protruding spines out. The body will absorb the spines within 24 hours to 3 weeks, or the remainder of the spines will work themselves out. Again, contrary to popular wisdom, do not urinate or pour vinegar on the embedded spines—this will not help.

CUTS All cuts obtained in the marine environment must be taken seriously because the high level of bacteria present in the water can quickly cause the cut to become infected. The best way to prevent cuts is to wear a wet suit, gloves, and reef shoes. Never touch coral; not only can you get cut, but you also can damage a living organism that took decades to grow.

The symptoms of a coral cut can range from a slight scratch to severe welts and blisters. *All Stings Considered* recommends gently pulling the edges of the skin open and removing any embedded coral or grains of sand with tweezers. Next, scrub the cut well with fresh water. If pressing a clean cloth against the wound doesn't stop the bleeding, or the edges of the injury are jagged or gaping, seek medical treatment.

What to Do If You Get Sick Away from Home

If you suffer from a chronic illness, consult your doctor before your departure. Pack prescription medications in your carry-on luggage, and carry them in their original containers, with pharmacy labels—otherwise, they won't make it through airport security. Visitors from outside the U.S. should carry generic names of prescription drugs. For U.S. travelers, most reliable healthcare plans provide coverage if you get sick away from home. Foreign visitors may have to pay all medical costs upfront and be reimbursed later. For information on traveler's insurance, trip-cancellation insurance, and medical insurance while traveling, please visit www.frommers.com/planning.

I list additional **emergency numbers** in "Fast Facts," p. 730. Also see "Fast Facts" in the individual island chapters for listings of local **doctors, dentists, hospitals,** and **emergency numbers.**

SAFETY
General Safety

Although tourist areas are generally safe, visitors should always stay alert, even in laid-back Hawaii (and especially in Waikiki). It's wise to ask the island tourist office if you're in doubt about which neighborhoods are safe. Avoid deserted areas, especially at night. Don't go into any city park at night unless there's an event that attracts crowds—for example, the Waikiki Shell concerts in Kapiolani Park. Generally speaking, you can feel safe in areas where there are many people and open establishments.

Avoid carrying valuables with you on the street, and don't display expensive cameras or electronic equipment. Hold on to your pocketbook, and place your billfold in an inside pocket. In theaters, restaurants, and other public places, keep your possessions in sight.

Oahu has seen a series of purse-snatching incidents, in which thieves in slow-moving cars or on foot have snatched handbags from female pedestrians. The Honolulu police department advises women to carry purses on the shoulder away from the street or, better yet, to wear the strap across the chest instead of on one shoulder. Women with clutch bags should hold them close to their chest.

Remember also that hotels are open to the public and that in a large property, security may not be able to screen everyone entering. Always lock your room door—don't assume that once inside your hotel, you're automatically safe.

Driving Safety

Recently, burglaries of tourists' rental cars in hotel parking structures and at beach parking lots have become more common. Park in well-lighted and well-traveled areas, if possible. Never leave any packages or valuables visible in the car. If someone attempts to rob you or steal your car, do not try to resist the thief or carjacker—report the incident to the police department immediately. Ask your rental agency about personal safety, and get written directions or a map with the route to your destination clearly marked.

What Is Illegal

Generally, Hawaii has the same laws as the mainland United States. Nudity is illegal in Hawaii. There are *no* legal nude beaches (I don't care what you have read). If you are nude on a beach (or anywhere) in Hawaii, you can be arrested.

Smoking marijuana also is illegal. Yes, there are lots of "stories" claiming that marijuana is grown in Hawaii, but the drug is illegal; if you attempt to buy it or light up, you can be arrested.

SPECIALIZED TRAVEL RESOURCES

In addition to the destination-specific resources listed below, visit Frommers. com for additional specialized travel resources.

Gay & Lesbian Travelers

Hawaii is known for its acceptance of all groups. The number of gay- or lesbian-specific accommodations on the islands is limited, but most properties welcome gays and lesbians like any other travelers.

Out in Honolulu (www.outinhonolulu.com) is a website with gay and lesbian news, blogs, features, shopping, classifieds, and other info.

For information on Kauai's gay community and related events, contact the **Kauai Gay/Lesbian/Bisexual/Transgender Audio Bulletin Board** (✆ 808/823-6248).

For the Big Island, Oahu, Maui, and Kauai, check out the website for **Out in Hawaii** (www.outinhawaii.com), which calls itself "Queer Resources and Information for The State of Hawaii," with vacation ideas, a calendar of events, information on Hawaii, and even a chat room.

For more gay and lesbian travel resources, visit frommers.com.

Travelers with Disabilities

Most disabilities shouldn't stop anyone from traveling in the U.S. Thanks to provisions in the Americans with Disabilities Act, most public places are required to comply with disability-friendly regulations. There are more options and resources out there than ever before.

Travelers with disabilities are made to feel very welcome in Hawaii. There are more than 2,000 ramped curbs in Oahu alone, hotels are usually equipped with wheelchair-accessible rooms, and tour companies provide many special services. The **Hawaii Center for Independent Living,** 414 Kauwili St., Ste. 102, Honolulu, HI 96817 (✆ 808/522-5400; fax 808/586-8129), can provide information.

The only travel agency in Hawaii specializing in needs for travelers with disabilities is **Access Aloha Travel** (✆ 800/480-1143; www.accessalohatravel. com), which can book anything, including rental vans (available on Maui and Oahu only), accommodations, tours, cruises, airfare, and anything else you can think of. For more details on wheelchair transportation and tours around the islands, see "Getting Around" in the individual island chapters.

The **America the Beautiful—National Park and Federal Recreational Lands Pass—Access Pass** (formerly the **Golden Access Passport**) gives visually impaired persons or persons with permanent disabilities (regardless of age) free lifetime entrance to federal recreation sites administered by the National Park Service, including the Fish and Wildlife Service, the Forest Service, the Bureau of Land Management, and the Bureau of Reclamation. This may include national parks, monuments, historic sites, recreation areas, and national wildlife refuges.

The America the Beautiful Access Pass can be obtained only in person at any NPS facility that charges an entrance fee. You need to show proof of medically determined disability. Besides free entry, the pass offers a 50% discount on some federal-use fees charged for such facilities as camping, swimming, parking, boat launching, and tours. For more information, go to www.nps.gov/fees_passes. htm or call the United States Geological Survey (USGS), which issues the passes, at ☎ **888/275-8747.**

For more on organizations that offer resources to travelers with disabilities, go to frommers.com.

Family Travel

Hawaii is paradise for children: beaches to run on, water to splash in, and unusual sights to see. To locate accommodations, restaurants, and attractions that are particularly child-friendly, refer to the "Kids" icon throughout this guide, and take a look at "The Best Places to Stay with the Kids," in chapter 1. Be sure to check out the "Especially for Kids" boxes in each island chapter for suggested family activities. And look for *Frommer's Hawaii with Kids* (Wiley Publishing, Inc.).

The larger hotels and resorts offer supervised programs for children and can refer you to qualified babysitters. By state law, hotels can accept only children ages 5 to 12 in supervised activities programs, but they often accommodate younger kids by simply hiring babysitters to watch over them. You can also contact **People Attentive to Children (PATCH),** which can refer you to babysitters who have taken a training course on childcare. On Oahu, call ☎ 808/839-1988; on the Big Island, call ☎ 808/329-7101 in Kona or ☎ 808/961-3169 in Hilo; on Maui, call ☎ 808/242-9232; on Kauai, call ☎ 808/246-0622; on Molokai and Lanai, call ☎ 800/498-4145; or visit www.patchhawaii.org.

Baby's Away (www.babysaway.com) rents cribs, strollers, highchairs, playpens, infant seats, and the like on Oahu (☎ 800/496-6386 or 808/222-6041), the Big Island (☎ 800/996-9030 or 808/987-9236), and Maui (☎ 800/942-9030 or 808/875-9030). The staff will deliver whatever you need to wherever you're staying and pick it up when you're done.

Recommended family-travel websites include **Family Travel Forum** (www.familytravelforum.com), a comprehensive site that offers customized trip planning; **Family Travel Network** (www.familytravelnetwork.com), an online magazine providing travel tips; and **TravelWithYourKids.com** (www.travelwith yourkids.com), a comprehensive site written by parents for parents offering sound advice for long-distance and international travel with children. For a list of more family-friendly travel resources, turn to the experts at frommers.com.

Senior Travel

Discounts for seniors are available at almost all of Hawaii's major attractions and occasionally at hotels and restaurants. The Outrigger hotel chain, for instance, offers travelers ages 50 and older a 20% discount off regular published rates—and an additional 5% off for members of AARP. Always ask when making hotel reservations or buying tickets. And always carry identification with proof of your age—it can really pay off.

The U.S. National Park Service offers an **America the Beautiful—National Park and Federal Recreational Lands Pass—Senior Pass** (formerly the **Golden Age Passport**), which gives seniors 62 years or older lifetime entrance to all properties administered by the National Park Service—national parks, monuments, historic sites, recreation areas, and national wildlife refuges—for a one-time processing fee of $10. The pass must be purchased in person at any NPS facility that charges an entrance fee. Besides free entry, the America the Beautiful Senior Pass offers a 50% discount on some federal-use fees charged for such facilities as camping, swimming, parking, boat launching, and tours. For more information, go to www.nps.gov/fees_passes.htm or call the United States Geological Survey (USGS), which issues the passes, at © **888/275-8747.**

Frommers.com offers more information and resources on travel for seniors.

SUSTAINABLE TOURISM

If there is one place on the planet that seems ideally suited for eco-tourism and sustainable travel, it's Hawaii, a place people visit because of the ecology—the ocean, the beach, the mountains, and the overall beauty of the place. It seems only natural that the maintenance of its environment would be a concern, both to the people who live there and the visitors who come to enjoy all that its eco-system has to offer.

In fact, Hawaii has a long history of environmental stewardship. The ancient Hawaiians not only knew about sustainability, but also practiced it in their daily lives. They had to! When the ancient Hawaiians occupied the islands, they did not have the luxury of "importing" goods from anywhere else. They had the land under their feet and the ocean to gain subsistence from, and those resources had to last not only for their own lifetime, but also for the lifetimes of generations to come. So these ancient people lived in harmony with the land and sea, and had a complex social structure that managed resources and forbade the taking of various resources during certain times of the year, to allow those resources to replenish themselves.

Now fast-forward to the 21st century. Today we, the current stewards of the islands of Hawaii, are just beginning to appreciate how wise and advanced the ancient Hawaiians were. In some ways, the state of Hawaii is a pioneer when it comes to the various ways it protects and saves its natural resources (for example, Hawaii is second only to California in the number of marine reserves in the National System of Marine Protected Areas). And yet in other ways, modern Hawaii still falls short of the ancient Hawaiians, whose unique system sustained, without imports, the entire population.

Ongoing Environmental Initiatives

The State of Hawaii has several excellent stewardship programs to preserve the ocean environment and its resources, such as Marine Life Conservation Districts (an ocean version of parks; Kealakekua, on the Big Island of Hawaii, and

Hanauma Bay, on Oahu, are two examples), Fishery Management Areas (where what you can take from the ocean is restricted), Fishery Replenishment Areas, and Estuarine Reserves. On land, there are corresponding programs to protect the environment, from the Soil and Water Conservation District to Watershed Reserves.

In the visitor industry, the majority of hotels have adopted green practices, not only to save the environment, but also to save them money. Nearly every hotel in the state will have a card in your room asking you to really consider if you need a new towel or if you can hang it up and use it one more day. Various statewide organizations have programs recognizing hotels which are helping the environment, such as the Green Business Awards Program, which recently awarded the Maui Price Hotel its top award for the steps the hotel took to modify equipment and work practices to reduce energy by more than 10%, reduce water consumption by some 10 million gallons, and increase recycling to 560 tons of their total 880 tons of annual waste.

Every island has recycling centers (varying from collection of recyclable bottles only to places that take everything). For a list of recycling centers close to where you will be staying, visit the website of the **Hawaii State Department of Health** (http://hi5deposit.com/redcenters.html).

Restaurants across the state are using more local products and produce than ever. Many proudly tell you that all of their products were grown, grazed, or caught within 100 miles of their restaurant. You can support this effort by ordering local (drink Kona coffee, not a coffee from Central America; eat local fish, not imported seafood). Ask the restaurant which items on its menu are grown or raised on the island, and then order the local items.

Below are some helpful hints travelers to Hawaii might want to keep in mind during their adventure to the islands so that their ecological footprint on Hawaii will be minimal.

WHAT VISITORS CAN DO IN & AROUND THE OCEAN

1. Do not touch anything in the ocean. In fact, unless you are standing on the sandy bottom where the waves roll into shore, try not to walk or stand on the ocean floor. The no-touch rule of thumb is not only for your protection—there are plenty of stinging, stabbing things out there that could turn your vacation into a nightmare—but also for the protection of the marine environment. Coral is composed of living things, which take years to grow, and a careless brush of your hand or foot could destroy them. Fragile habitats for marine critters can be damaged forever by your heavy foot.

2. Do not feed the fish, or any other marine creature. They have their own food and diet, and they can be irreparably harmed by your good intentions if you feed them "people food" or, even worse, some "fish food" you have purchased.

3. Leave the ocean and beach area cleaner than you found it. If you see trash in the ocean (plastic bags, bottles, and so on), remove it. You may have saved the life of a fish, turtle, marine mammal, or even seabird by removing that trash, which kills hundreds of marine inhabitants every year. The same thing is true of the beach: Pick up trash, even if it's not yours.

4. The beach is not an ashtray. Do not use the sand for your cigarette butts. How would you like someone using your living room carpet as his ashtray?

5. Look at, but don't approach, turtles or Hawaiian monk seals resting on the shoreline. The good news is that the number of turtles and Hawaiian monk seals on the main Hawaiian Islands is increasing. But while visitors may not know it, both are protected by law. You must stay 100 feet away from them. So take photos, but do not attempt to get close to the resting sea creatures (and no, they are not dead or injured, just resting).

6. If you plan to go fishing, practice catch and release. Let the fish live another day. Ask your charter-boat captain if they practice catch and release; if they say no, book with someone else.

7. If you are environmentally conscious, I do not recommend that you rent jet skis, which have a significant environmental impact.

WHAT VISITORS CAN DO ON LAND

1. Don't litter (this includes throwing a cigarette butt out of your car).

2. Before you go hiking, in addition to the safety tips outlined on p. 79, scrub your hiking shoes (especially the soles) to get rid of seeds and soil.

3. When hiking, carry a garbage bag so you can carry out everything you carried in, including your litter (and if you see other garbage on the trail, carry it out, too).

4. Stay on the trail. Not only is wandering off a trail dangerous to you (you can get lost, fall off overgrown cliffs, or get injured by stepping into a hidden hole), but you could also carry invasive species into the native forests.

5. Do not pick flowers or plants along your hike. Just leave the environment the way you found it.

TRANSPORTATION CONCERNS

RENTAL CARS   Most visitors coming to Hawaii seem to think "convertible" when they think of renting a car, or they think "SUV" for off-road adventures. If you're thinking "hybrid," you'll have to check your budget, because hybrids from car-rental agencies are not only hard to find, but also extremely expensive in Hawaii. Car-rental agencies do have a variety of cars to rent, though,

---

Volunteering on Vacation

If you are looking for a different type of experience during your next vacation to Hawaii, you might want to consider becoming a volunteer and leaving the islands a little nicer than when you arrived. People interested in volunteering at beach and ocean cleanups can contact the **University of Hawaii Sea Grant College Program** (✆ **808/397-2651,** ext. 256) or **Hawaii Wildlife Fund** (✆ **808/756-1808**). For ecovolunteering on land, contact **Malama Hawaii** (www.malamahawaii.org/get_involved/volunteer.php), a statewide organization dedicated to *malama* (taking care) of the culture and environment of Hawaii. At this site you will find a range of opportunities on various islands, such as weeding gardens and potting plants in botanical gardens, restoring taro patches, cleaning up mountain streams, bird-watching, and even hanging out at Waikiki Beach helping with a reef project.

One of the toughest questions in Hawaii is, "What is the carrying capacity of the islands?" How much can be built before Hawaii becomes overbuilt, or unable to support the increased infrastructure and increased population? How many people can Hawaii hold, and how many visitors, before the beaches are too crowded, the lifestyle is gone, and the islands have more concrete than open green spaces?

Along those same lines, the people of Hawaii are constantly debating cultural issues vs. social issues. For example, currently laws regarding ancient burial sites can stop, reroute, or delay construction projects ranging from roads to shopping centers. How much do we protect and preserve vs. how much do we allow new infrastructure or buildings to be built to meet modern wants and needs?

and you can make a point of selecting a car that gets the best gas mileage. Also, ask for a white car, because they use less energy to air-condition than a dark-colored car.

INTERISLAND TRANSPORTATION Now that the interisland ferry, Superferry, has declared bankruptcy, the only option for interisland travel between most islands is via air. There are two exceptions, however. If you're traveling between Maui and Lanai, you may want to consider taking the passenger-only Lanai Ferry. If you're traveling between Maui and Molokai, you can take the passenger-only Molokai Princess. Not only are these ferries cheaper than air travel, but their impact on the environment is less, especially when you consider that most airlines will route you from Maui to Honolulu, then from Honolulu on to either Molokai or Lanai.

Hawaiian Culture

One of Hawaii's most cherished resources is the Hawaiian culture. After years of ignoring it, it is flourishing more than ever today. Part of the Hawaii school system are the Hawaiian immersion schools, where all children (not just Hawaiians) can attend schools from kindergarten to college taught in the Hawaiian language. And cultural events in Hawaii are very popular. If you want to see the Merrie Monarch Hula Festival (p. 67), for example, which is the "Super Bowl of hula," where the top *halau* compete each year during the week after Easter, you had better get your tickets by the end of December—it's sold out by January 1.

If you want to support Hawaiian culture, plan to attend cultural events like Hawaiian music and dance performances (see "Hawaii Calendar of Events," p. 65).

Search out locally owned establishments (look for recommendations in this book). Attempt to buy souvenirs made in Hawaii by local residents (I have recommendations in the shopping sections of each island chapter).

If you visit a cultural site, like an ancient *heiau* (temple), the protocol calls for reverence. Be as respectful as you would at a cathedral or church. Never climb or sit on rock walls at a *heiau*. Never take anything from a *heiau,* even rocks, and never pick flowers there. You may see offerings of flowers or fruit—do not disturb them.

GENERAL RESOURCES FOR green travel

The following websites provide valuable wide-ranging information on sustainable travel. For a list of even more sustainable resources, as well as tips and explanations on how to travel greener, visit www.frommers.com/planning.

o **Responsible Travel** (www.responsible travel.com) is a great source of sustainable travel ideas; the site is run by a spokesperson for ethical tourism in the travel industry. **Sustainable Travel International** (www.sustainable travelinternational.org) promotes ethical tourism practices, and manages an extensive directory of sustainable properties and tour operators around the world.

o In the U.K., **Tourism Concern** (www. tourismconcern.org.uk) works to reduce social and environmental problems connected to tourism. The **Association of Independent Tour Operators (AITO;** www.aito.co.uk) is a group of specialist operators leading the field in making holidays sustainable.

o In Canada, **www.greenlivingonline. com** offers extensive content on how to travel sustainably, including a travel and transport section and profiles of the best green shops and services in Toronto, Vancouver, and Calgary.

o In Australia, the national body that sets guidelines and standards for eco-tourism is **Ecotourism Australia** (www.ecotourism.org.au). **The Green Directory** (www.thegreendirectory. com.au), **Green Pages** (www.the greenpages.com.au), and **Eco Directory** (www.ecodirectory.com.au) offer sustainable travel tips and directories of green businesses.

o **Carbonfund** (www.carbonfund.org), **TerraPass** (www.terrapass.org), and

Carbon Neutral (www.carbonneutral. org) provide info on "carbon offsetting," or offsetting the greenhouse gas emitted during flights.

o **Greenhotels** (www.greenhotels.com) recommends green-rated member hotels around the world that fulfill the company's stringent environmental requirements. **Environmentally Friendly Hotels** (www.environmentally friendlyhotels.com) offers more green accommodation ratings. The **Hotel Association of Canada** (www.hac greenhotels.com) has a Green Key Eco-Rating Program, which audits the environmental performance of Canadian hotels, motels, and resorts.

o **Sustain Lane** (www.sustainlane.com) lists sustainable eating and drinking choices around the U.S.; also visit **www.eatwellguide.org** for tips on eating sustainably in the U.S. and Canada.

o For information on animal-friendly issues throughout the world, visit **Tread Lightly** (www.treadlightly.org). For information about the ethics of swimming with dolphins, visit the **Whale and Dolphin Conservation Society** (www.wdcs.org).

o **Volunteer International** (www. volunteerinternational.org) has a list of questions to help you determine the intentions and the nature of a volunteer program. For general info on volunteer travel, visit **www. volunteerabroad.org** and **www. idealist.org**.

HOW TO FIT IN LIKE A LOCAL

Most visitors to Hawaii want to fit in, and be respectful of the local residents. The best way to do that is to be friendly and practice the same common courtesy that you do in your own neighborhood. If you smile and are polite to local residents, chances are they will smile back at you. There are a few things you might want to think about:

1. Be superpolite when driving. People in Hawaii do not use their car horn as a comment on other people's driving. Most Hawaii residents use their car horn only as a greeting to a friend.

2. Another driving comment: You may be on vacation, but not everyone here is, so check your rearview mirror. If you are impeding traffic by driving slowly, pull off the road. If you want to watch the sunset, pull off the road. If you have a long line of cars behind you, pull off the road. If you are traveling on Kauai, where there are lots of one-lane bridges, read up on Kauai bridge etiquette (p. 716).

3. Dress respectfully. Just because it's Hawaii and warm does not mean that it is acceptable to wear your swimwear into a restaurant. A good rule of thumb is to ask yourself this: Would I wear this outfit to a restaurant or retail store at home?

4. Remember Hawaii is part of the United States, and is, in fact, a state. A good way to alienate local residents is to say something like "I'm from the States," or "Back in the States, we do it this way."

SPECIAL-INTEREST TRIPS

If all you want is a fabulous beach and a perfectly mixed mai tai, then Hawaii has what you're looking for. But the islands' wealth of natural wonders is equally hard to resist; the year-round tropical climate and spectacular scenery tend to inspire almost everyone to get outside and explore.

If you don't have your own snorkel gear or other watersports equipment, or if you just don't feel like packing it, don't fret: Everything you'll need is available for rent in the islands. I discuss all kinds of places to rent or buy gear in the chapters that follow.

Setting Out on Your Own vs. Using an Outfitter

There are two ways to go: Plan all the details before you leave and either rent gear or schlep your stuff 2,500 miles across the Pacific, or go with an outfitter or a guide and let someone else worry about the details.

Experienced outdoors enthusiasts may head to coastal campgrounds or even trek to the 13,796-foot-high summit of Mauna Loa on their own. But in Hawaii, it's often preferable to go with a local guide who is familiar with the conditions at both sea level and summit peaks, knows the land and its flora and fauna in detail, and has all the gear you'll need. It's also good to go with a guide if time is an issue or if you have specialized interests. If you really want to see native birds, for instance, an experienced guide will take you directly to the best areas for sightings. And many forests and valleys in the interior of the islands are either on private property or in wilderness preserves accessible only on guided tours.

Outdoor Etiquette

Act locally, think globally, and carry out what you carry in. Find a trash container for all your litter (including cigarette butts; it's *very* bad form to throw them out of your car window or to use the beach as an ashtray). Observe KAPU (taboo) and NO TRESPASSING signs. Don't climb on ancient Hawaiian *heiau* (temple) walls or carry home rocks, all of which belong to the Hawaiian volcano goddess, Pele. Some say it's just a silly superstition, but each year the national and state park services get boxes of lava rocks in the mail that have been sent back to Hawaii by visitors who've experienced unusually bad luck.

The downside? If you go with a guide, plan on spending at least $100 a day per person. I've recommended the best local outfitters and tour-guide operators on each island in the chapters that follow.

But if you have the time, already own the gear, and love doing the research and planning, try exploring on your own. Each island chapter discusses the best spots to set out on your own, from the top offshore snorkel and dive spots to great daylong hikes, as well as the federal, state, and county agencies that can help you with hikes on public property; I also list references for spotting birds, plants, and sea life. I recommend that you always use the resources available to inquire about weather, trail, or surf conditions; water availability; and other conditions before you take off on your adventure.

For hikers, a great alternative to hiring a private guide is taking a guided hike offered by the **Nature Conservancy of Hawaii,** P.O. Box 96, Honolulu, HI 96759 (© **808/621-2008** on Oahu, 808/572-7849 on Maui, or 808/553-5236 on Molokai); or the **Hawaii Chapter of the Sierra Club,** P.O. Box 2577, Honolulu, HI 96813 (© **808/579-9802** on Oahu; www.hi.sierraclub.org). Both organizations offer guided hikes in preserves and special areas during the year, as well as day- to weeklong work trips to restore habitats and trails and to root out invasive plants. It might not sound like a dream vacation to everyone, but it's a chance to see the "real" Hawaii—including wilderness areas that are ordinarily off-limits.

All Nature Conservancy hikes and work trips are free (donations are appreciated). However, you must reserve a spot for yourself, and a deposit is required for guided hikes to ensure that you'll show up; your deposit is refunded when you do. The hikes are generally offered once a month on Maui, Molokai, and Lanai, and twice a month on Oahu. For all islands, call the Oahu office for reservations. Write for a schedule of guided hikes and other programs.

The Sierra Club offers weekly hikes on Oahu and Maui. They are led by certified Sierra Club volunteers and are classified as easy, moderate, or strenuous. These half- or all-day affairs cost $1 for Sierra Club members and $3 for nonmembers (bring exact change). For a copy of the club newsletter, which lists all outings and trail-repair work, send $2 to the address above.

Local eco-tourism opportunities are also discussed in the individual island chapters. For more information, contact the **Hawaii Ecotourism Association** (© **877/300-7058;** www.hawaiiecotourism.org).

Using Activities Desks to Book Your Island Fun

If you're unsure of which activity or which outfitter or guide is the right one for you and your family, you might want to consider booking through a discount activities center or activities desk. Not only will they save you money, but good activities centers should also be able to help you find, say, the snorkel cruise that's right for you, or the luau that's most suitable for both you *and* the kids.

Remember, however, that it's in the activities agent's best interest to sign you up with outfitters from which they earn the most commission. Some agents have no qualms about booking you into any activity if it means an extra buck for them. If an agent tries to push a particular outfitter or activity too hard, be skeptical. Conversely, they'll try to steer you away from outfitters who don't offer big commissions. For example, Trilogy, the company that offers Maui's most popular snorkel cruises to Lanai (and the only one with rights to land at Lanai's Hulopoe Beach), offers only minimum commissions to agents and does not allow agents to offer any discounts at all. As a result, most activities desks will automatically try to steer you away from Trilogy.

Another word of warning: Stay away from activities centers that offer discounts as fronts for timeshare sales presentations. Using a free or discounted snorkel cruise or luau tickets as bait, they'll suck you into a 90-minute presentation—and try to get you to buy into a Hawaii timeshare in the process. Because their business is timeshares, not activities, they won't be as interested, or as knowledgeable, about which activities might be right for you. These shady deals seem to be particularly rampant on Maui.

There are a number of very reliable local activities centers on each of the neighbor islands. On Maui, your best bet is **Tom Barefoot's Cashback Tours,** 250 Alamaha St., Kahului (© **800/895-2040** or 808/661-8889; www.tombarefoot.com). Tom offers a 10% discount on all tours, activities, and adventures if you pay using cash, a personal check, or traveler's checks. If you use a credit card, you'll get a 7% discount. On the Big Island, check out the **Activity Connection,** Bougainvillea Plaza, 75–5656 Kuakini Hwy., Ste. 102, Kailua-Kona (© **800/459-7156** or 808/329-1038), which offers up to 15% off on various island activities.

Finally, you can reserve activities yourself and save the commission by booking via the Internet. Most outfitters offer 10% to 25% off their prices if you book online.

Outdoor Activities A to Z

Here's a brief rundown of the many outdoor activities available in Hawaii. For my recommendations on the best places to go, the best shops for renting equipment, and the best outfitters to use, see the individual island chapters later in this book.

BIRDING

Many of Hawaii's tropical birds are found nowhere else on earth. There are curved-bill honeycreepers, black-winged red birds, and the rare o'o, whose yellow feathers Hawaiians once plucked to make royal capes. When you go birding, take along *A Field Guide to the Birds of Hawaii and the Tropical Pacific,* by H. Douglas

Pratt, Phillip L. Bruner, and Delwyn G. Berett (Princeton University Press, 1987).

Kauai and Molokai, in particular, are great places to go birding. On Kauai, large colonies of seabirds nest at Kilauea National Wildlife Refuge and along the Na Pali Coast. Be sure to take along a copy of *The Birds of Kauai,* by Jim Denny (University of Hawaii Press). The lush rainforest of Molokai's Kamakou Preserve is home to the Molokai thrush and Molokai creeper, which live only on this 30-mile-long island.

For more on birding, see p. 375 for the Big Island, p. 702 for Kauai, and p. 598 for the discussion of Molokai's Kamakou Preserve.

BOATING

Almost every type of nautical experience is available in the islands, from old-fashioned Polynesian outrigger canoes to America's Cup racing sloops to submarines. You'll find details on all these seafaring experiences in the individual island chapters that follow.

No matter which type of vessel you choose, be sure to see the Hawaiian Islands from offshore if you can afford it. It's easy to combine multiple activities into one cruise: Lots of snorkel boats double as sightseeing cruises and, in winter, whale-watching cruises. The main harbors for visitor activities are Kewalo Basin, Oahu; Honokohau, Kailua-Kona, and Kawaihae on the Big Island; Lahaina and Maalaea, Maui; Kaunakakai, Molokai; and Nawiliwili and Port Allen, Kauai.

BODY BOARDING (BOOGIE BOARDING) & BODYSURFING

Bodysurfing—riding the waves without a board, becoming one with the rolling water—is a way of life in Hawaii. Some bodysurfers just rely on hands to ride the waves; others use hand boards (flat, paddlelike gloves). For additional maneuverability, try a boogie board or body board (also known as belly boards or *paipo* boards). These 3-foot-long boards support the upper part of your body and are very maneuverable in the water. Both bodysurfing and body boarding require a pair of open-heeled swim fins to help propel you through the water. The equipment is inexpensive and easy to carry, and both sports can be practiced in the small, gentle waves. See the individual island chapters for details on where to rent boards and where to go.

CAMPING

Hawaii's year-round balmy climate makes camping a breeze. However, tropical campers should always be ready for rain, especially in Hawaii's wet winter season, but in the dry summer season as well. And remember to bring a good mosquito repellent. If you're heading to the top of Hawaii's volcanoes, you'll need a down mummy bag. If you plan to camp on the beach, bring a mosquito net and a rain poncho. Always be prepared to deal with contaminated water (purify it by boiling, through filtration, or by using iodine tablets) and the tropical sun (protect yourself with sunscreen, a hat, and a long-sleeved shirt). Also be sure to check out the "Health" section, earlier in this chapter, for hiking and camping tips.

There are many established campgrounds at beach parks, including Kauai's Anini Beach, Oahu's Malaekahana Beach, Maui's Waianapanapa Beach, and the Big Island's Hapuna Beach. Campgrounds are also located in the interior at

Maui's Haleakala National Park and the Big Island's Hawaii Volcanoes National Park, as well as at Kalalau Beach on Kauai's Na Pali Coast and in the cool uplands of Kokee State Park. See "Beaches" and "Hiking & Camping," in the individual island chapters, for the best places to camp.

Travel Tip

When planning sunset activities, be aware that Hawaii, like other places close to the equator, has a very short (5- to 10-min.) twilight period after the sun sets. After that, it's dark. If you hike out to watch the sunset, be sure you can make it back quickly, or else take a flashlight.

Hawaiian Trail and Mountain Club, P.O. Box 2238, Honolulu, HI 96804, offers an information packet on hiking and camping throughout the islands. Send $2 and a legal-size, self-addressed, stamped envelope for information. Another good source is the *Hiking/Camping Information Packet,* available from **Hawaii Geographic Maps and Books,** 49 S. Hotel St., Honolulu, HI 96813 (© **800/538-3950** or 808/538-3952), for $7. The **University of Hawaii Press,** 2840 Kolowalu St., Honolulu, HI 96822 (© **888/ 847-7737;** www.uhpress.hawaii.edu), has an excellent selection of hiking, backpacking, and bird-watching guides, especially *The Hiker's Guide to the Hawaiian Islands,* by Stuart M. Ball, Jr.

GOLF

Nowhere else on earth can you tee off to whale spouts, putt under rainbows, and play around a live volcano. Hawaii has some of the world's top-rated golf courses. But be forewarned: Each course features hellish natural hazards, like razor-sharp lava, gusty trade winds, an occasional wild pig, and the tropical heat. And greens fees tend to be very expensive. Still, golfers flock here from around the world and love every minute of it. See the individual island chapters for coverage of the resort courses worth splurging on (with details, where applicable, on money-saving twilight rates), as well as the best budget and municipal courses. Also check out "The Best Golf Courses," in chapter 1.

A few tips on golfing in Hawaii: There's generally wind—10 to 30 mph is not unusual between 10am and 2pm—so you may have to play two to three clubs up or down to compensate. Bring extra balls: The rough is thick, water hazards are everywhere, and the wind wreaks havoc with your game. On the greens, your putt will *always* break toward the ocean. Hit deeper and more aggressively in the sand because the type of sand used on most Hawaii courses is firmer and more compact than that used on mainland courses (lighter sand would blow away in the constant wind). And bring a camera—you'll kick yourself if you don't capture those spectacular views.

HIKING

Hiking in Hawaii is a breathtaking experience. The islands have hundreds of miles of trails, many of which reward you with a hidden beach, a private waterfall, an Edenlike valley, or simply an unforgettable view. However, rock climbers are out of luck: Most of Hawaii's volcanic cliffs are too steep and brittle to scale.

Hawaiian Trail and Mountain Club, P.O. Box 2238, Honolulu, HI 96804, offers an information packet on hiking and camping in Hawaii; to receive a copy, send $2 and a legal-size, self-addressed, stamped envelope. **Hawaii Geographic Maps and Books,** 49 S. Hotel St., Honolulu, HI 96813 (© **800/538-3950** or 808/538-3952), offers the *Hiking/Camping Information Packet* for $7. Also note that the **Hawaii State Department of Land and Natural Resources,** 1151 Punchbowl St., No. 131, Honolulu, HI 96809 (© **808/587-0300;** www.hawaii.gov), will send you free topographic trail maps.

The **Nature Conservancy of Hawaii** (© **808/537-4508** on Oahu, 808/572-7849 on Maui, or 808/553-5236 on Molokai; www.tnc.org/hawaii) and the **Hawaii Chapter of the Sierra Club,** P.O. Box 2577, Honolulu, HI 96803 (© **808/579-9802** on Oahu; www.hi.sierraclub.org), both offer guided hikes in preserves and special areas during the year. Also see the individual island chapters for complete details on the best hikes for all ability levels.

A couple of terrific books on hiking are *The Hiker's Guide to the Hawaiian Islands* and *The Hiker's Guide to Oahu,* both by Stuart M. Ball, Jr. (both from University of Hawaii Press).

Before you set out on the trail, see "Health," earlier in this chapter, for tips on hiking safety, as well as "What to Pack," at the beginning of this chapter.

HORSEBACK RIDING

One of the best ways to see Hawaii is on horseback; almost all islands offer riding opportunities for just about every age and level of experience. You can ride into Maui's Haleakala Crater, along Kauai's Mahaulepu Beach, or through Oahu's remote windward valleys on Kualoa Ranch, or you can gallop across the wide-open spaces of the Big Island's Parker Ranch, one of the largest privately owned ranches in the United States. See the individual island chapters for details. Be sure to bring a pair of jeans and closed-toe shoes to wear on your ride.

DON'T LEAVE HOME WITHOUT YOUR gold card

Almost any activity you can think of, from submarine rides to Polynesian luau, can be purchased at a discount by using the **Activities & Attractions Association of Hawaii Gold Card,** 355 Hukilike St., No. 202, Kahului, HI 96732 (© **800/398-9698** or 808/871-7947; fax 808/877-3104; www.hawaiifun.org). The Gold Card, accepted by members on all islands, offers a discount of 10% to 25% off activities and meals for up to four people. It's good for a year from the purchase date and costs $30.

Your Gold Card can lower the regular $149 price of a helicopter ride to only $119, saving you $120 for a group of four. And there are hundreds of activities to choose from: dinner cruises, horseback riding, watersports, and more—plus savings on rental cars, restaurants, and golf.

Contact Activities & Attractions to purchase your card. You then contact the outfitter, restaurant, rental-car agency, or other proprietor directly; supply your card number; and receive the discount.

KAYAKING

Hawaii is one of the world's most popular destinations for ocean kayaking. Beginners can paddle across a tropical lagoon to two uninhabited islets off Lanikai Beach on Oahu, while more experienced kayakers can take on Kauai's awesome Na Pali Coast. In summer, experts take advantage of the usually flat conditions on the north shore of Molokai, where the sea cliffs are the steepest on earth and the remote valleys can be reached only by sea. See "Watersports," in chapters 5 through 10, for local outfitters and tour guides.

SCUBA DIVING

Some people come to the islands solely to take the plunge into the tropical Pacific and explore the underwater world. Hawaii is one of the world's top-10 dive destinations, according to *Rodale's Scuba Diving Magazine*. Here you can see the great variety of tropical marine life (more than 100 endemic species found nowhere else on the planet), explore sea caves, and swim with sea turtles and monk seals in clear, tropical water. If you're not certified, try to take classes before you come to Hawaii so you don't waste time learning and can dive right in.

If you dive, **go early in the morning.** Trade winds often rough up the seas in the afternoon, especially on Maui, so most operators schedule early morning dives that end at noon. To organize a dive on your own, order *The Oahu Snorkelers and Shore Divers Guide,* by Francisco B. de Carvalho, from University of Hawaii Press.

Tip: It's usually worth the extra bucks to go with a good dive operator. Check "Scuba Diving" in the island chapters that follow; I've listed the operators that'll give you the most for your money.

SNORKELING

Snorkeling is one of Hawaii's main attractions, and almost anyone can do it. All you need is a mask, a snorkel, fins, and some basic swimming skills. In many places, all you have to do is wade into the water and look down at the magical underwater world.

If you've never snorkeled before, most resorts and excursion boats offer snorkeling equipment and lessons. You don't really need lessons, however; it's plenty easy to figure out for yourself, especially once you're at the beach, where everybody around you will be doing it. If you don't have your own gear, you can rent it from one of dozens of dive shops and activities booths, discussed in the individual island chapters.

While everyone heads for Oahu's Hanauma Bay—the perfect spot for first-timers—other favorite snorkel spots include Kee Beach on Kauai, Kahaluu Beach on the Big Island, Hulopoe Bay on Lanai, and Kapalua Bay on Maui. Although snorkeling is excellent on all the islands, the Big Island, with its recent lava formations and abrupt drop-offs, offers some particularly spectacular opportunities. Some of the best snorkel spots in the islands—notably, the Big Island's Kealakekua Bay and Molokini Crater just off Maui—are accessible only by boat; for tips on the islands' top snorkel boats, see "Watersports" in the chapters that follow.

Some snorkeling tips: Always snorkel with a buddy. Look up every once in a while to see where you are and see if there's any boat traffic. Don't touch anything; not only can you damage coral, but camouflaged fish and shells with poisonous spines may also surprise you. Always check with a dive shop, life-guards, or others on the beach about the area in which you plan to snorkel and ask if there are any dangerous conditions you should know about.

SPORT FISHING

Big-game fishing at its best is found off the Big Island of Hawaii at **Kailua-Kona,** where the deep blue waters offshore yield trophy marlin year-round. You can also try for spearfish, swordfish, various tuna, mahimahi (dorado), rainbow runners, wahoo, barracuda, trevallies, bonefish, and bottom fish like snappers and groupers. Each island offers deep-sea boat charters for good-eating fish like tuna, wahoo, and mahimahi. Visiting anglers currently need no license.

Charter fishing boats range widely both in size—from small 24-foot open skiffs to luxurious 50-foot-plus yachts—and in price—from about $100 per person to "share" a boat with other anglers for a half-day, to $900 a day to book an entire luxury sport-fishing yacht on an exclusive basis. Shop around. Prices vary according to the boat, the crowd, and the captain. See the individual island chapters for details. Also, many boat captains tag and release marlin or keep the fish for themselves (sorry, that's Hawaii style). If you want to eat your mahimahi for dinner or have your marlin mounted, tell the captain before you go.

Money-saving tip: Try contacting the charter-boat captain directly and bargaining. Many charter captains pay a 20% to 30% commission to charter-booking agencies and may be willing to give you a discount if you book directly.

SURFING

The ancient Hawaiian practice of *hee nalu* (wave sliding) is probably the sport most people picture when they think of Hawaii. Believe it or not, you too can do some wave sliding—just sign up at any of the numerous surfing schools located throughout the islands (listed in the relevant island chapters under "Surfing," in the "Watersports" section). On world-famous Waikiki Beach, just head over to one of the surf stands that line the sand; these guys say they can get anybody up and standing on a board. If you're already a big kahuna in surfing, check the island chapters for the best deals on rental equipment and the best places to hang ten.

TENNIS

Tennis is a popular sport in the islands. Each island chapter lists details on free municipal courts as well as the best deals on private courts. The etiquette at the free county courts is to play only 45 minutes if someone is waiting.

WHALE-WATCHING

Every winter, pods of Pacific humpback whales make the 3,000-mile swim from the chilly waters of Alaska to bask in Hawaii's summery shallows, fluking, spy hopping, spouting, breaching, and having an all-around swell time. About 1,500 to 3,000 humpback whales appear in Hawaiian waters each year.

Humpbacks are one of the world's oldest, most impressive inhabitants. Adults grow to be about 45 feet long and weigh a hefty 40 tons. Humpbacks are officially an endangered species; in 1992, the waters around Maui, Molokai, and Lanai were designated a Humpback Whale National Marine Sanctuary. Despite the world's newfound ecological awareness, humpbacks and their habitats and food resources are still under threat from whalers and pollution.

The season's first whale is usually spotted in November, but the best time to see humpback whales in Hawaii is **between January and April,** from any island. Just look out to sea. Each island also offers a variety of whale-watching cruises, which will bring you up close and personal with the mammoth mammals; see the individual island chapters for details.

Money-saving tip: Book a snorkeling cruise during the winter whale-watching months. The captain of the boat will often take you through the best local whale-watching areas on the way, and you'll get two activities for the price of one. It's well worth the money.

WINDSURFING

Maui is Hawaii's top windsurfing destination. World-class windsurfers head for Hookipa Beach, where the wind roars through Maui's isthmus and creates some of the best windsurfing conditions in the world. Funky Paia, a derelict sugar town saved from extinction by surfers, is now the world capital of big-wave board sailing. And along Maui's Hana Highway, there are lookouts where you can watch the pros flip off the lip of 10-foot waves and gain hang time in the air.

Others, especially beginners, set their sails for Oahu's Kailua Bay or Kauai's Anini Beach, where gentle onshore breezes make learning this sport a snap.

See the individual island chapters for outfitters and local instructors.

STAYING CONNECTED
Telephones

Generally, hotel surcharges on long-distance and local calls are astronomical, so you're better off using your **cellphone** or a **public pay telephone.** Many convenience groceries and packaging services sell **prepaid calling cards** in denominations up to $50; for international visitors, these can be the least expensive way to call home. Many public pay phones at airports now accept American Express, MasterCard, and Visa credit cards. **Local calls** made from pay phones in most locales cost 50¢ (no pennies, please).

All calls on-island are local calls; calls from one island to another via a land line are long distance and you must dial 1; then the Hawaii area code, 808; and then the phone number.

Most long-distance and international calls can be dialed directly from any phone. **For calls within the United States and to Canada,** dial 1 followed by the area code and the seven-digit number. **For other international calls,** dial 011 followed by the country code, city code, and number you are calling.

Calls to area codes **800, 888, 877,** and **866** are toll-free. However, calls to area codes **700** and **900** (chat lines, bulletin boards, "dating" services, and so on) can be very expensive—usually a charge of 95¢ to $3 or more per minute, and they sometimes have minimum charges that can run as high as $15 or more.

For **reversed-charge or collect calls,** and for person-to-person calls, dial the number 0 and then the area code and number; an operator will come on the line, and you should specify whether you are calling collect, person-to-person, or both. If your operator-assisted call is international, ask for the overseas operator.

For **local directory assistance** ("information"), dial 411; for long-distance information, dial 1, then the appropriate area code, and 555-1212.

Cellphones

Just because your cellphone works at home doesn't mean it'll work everywhere in the U.S. (thanks to our nation's fragmented cellphone system). It's a good bet that your phone will work in major cities, but take a look at your wireless company's coverage map on its website before heading out; T-Mobile, Sprint, and Nextel are particularly weak in rural areas. If you need to stay in touch at a destination where you know your phone won't work, **rent** a phone that does from **InTouch USA** (🕿 **800/872-7626;** www.intouchglobal.com) or a rental-car location, but be aware that you'll pay $1 a minute or more for airtime.

If you're not from the U.S., you'll be appalled at the poor reach of our **GSM (Global System for Mobile Communications) wireless network,** which is used by much of the rest of the world. Your phone will probably work in most major U.S. cities; it definitely won't work in many rural areas. To see where GSM phones work in the U.S., check out www.t-mobile.com/coverage/national_popup.asp. And you may or may not be able to send SMS (text messaging) home.

Internet/E-mail

WITHOUT YOUR OWN COMPUTER

To find cybercafes in your destination, check **www.cybercaptive.com** and **www.cybercafe.com**.

Most major airports have **Internet kiosks** that provide basic Web access for a per-minute fee that's usually higher than cybercafe prices. Check out copy shops like FedEx Office (formerly Kinkos), which offers computer stations with fully loaded software (as well as Wi-Fi).

WITH YOUR OWN COMPUTER

More and more hotels, resorts, airports, cafes, and retailers are going Wi-Fi (wireless fidelity), becoming "hotspots" that offer free high-speed Wi-Fi access or charge a small fee for usage. Wi-Fi is even found in campgrounds, RV parks, and entire towns. Most laptops sold today have built-in wireless capability. To find public Wi-Fi hotspots at your destination, go to **www.jiwire.com**; its Hotspot Finder holds the world's largest directory of public wireless hotspots.

For dial-up access, most business-class hotels in the U.S. offer dataports for laptop modems, and a few thousand hotels in the U.S. and Europe now offer free high-speed Internet access.

Wherever you go, bring a **connection kit** of the right power and phone adapters, a spare phone cord, and a spare Ethernet network cable—or find out whether your hotel supplies them to guests.

For information on electrical currency conversions, see "Electricity," in the "Fast Facts" chapter at the end of this book.

TIPS ON ACCOMMODATIONS

Hawaii offers all kinds of accommodations, from simple rooms in restored plantation homes and quaint cottages on the beach to luxurious oceanview condo units and opulent suites in beachfront resorts. Each type has its pluses and minuses, so before you book, make sure you know what you're getting into.

Types of Accommodations
HOTELS

In Hawaii, "hotel" can indicate a wide range of options, from few or no on-site amenities to enough extras to qualify as a miniresort. Generally, a hotel offers daily maid service and has a restaurant, on-site laundry facilities, a pool, and a sundries/convenience–type shop. Top hotels also have activities desks, concierge and valet services, room service, business centers, airport shuttles, bars and/or lounges, and perhaps a few more shops.

The advantages of staying in a hotel are privacy and convenience; the disadvantage is generally noise (either thin walls between rooms or loud music from a lobby lounge late into the night). Hotels are often a short walk from the beach rather than right on the beachfront (although there are exceptions).

RESORTS

In Hawaii, a resort offers everything a hotel does—and more. You can expect direct beach access, with beach cabanas and lounge chairs; pools and a Jacuzzi; a spa and fitness center; restaurants, bars, and lounges; a 24-hour front desk; concierge, valet, and bellhop services; room service (often 24-hr.); an activities desk; tennis and golf; ocean activities; a business center; kids' programs; and more.

Nickel-and-Dime Charges at High-Priced Hotels

Several upscale resorts in Hawaii engage in a practice that I find distasteful and dishonest: charging a so-called "resort fee." This daily fee is added to your bill for such "complimentary" items as a daily newspaper, local phone calls, and use of the fitness facilities—amenities that the resort has been happily providing free to its guests for years. In most cases, you do not have an option to decline the resort fee—in other words, this is a sneaky way to increase the nightly rate without telling you.

The advantages of a resort are that you have everything you could possibly want in the way of services and things to do; the disadvantage is that the price generally reflects this. And don't be misled by a name—just because a place is called "ABC Resort" doesn't mean it actually *is* a resort. Make sure you're getting what you pay for.

CONDOS

The roominess and convenience of a condo—which is usually a fully equipped, multiple-bedroom apartment—makes this a great choice for families. Condominium properties in Hawaii generally consist of several apartments set in either a single high-rise or a cluster of low-rise units. Condos usually have amenities such as some maid service (ranging from daily to weekly; it may or may not be included in your rate), a pool, and an on-site front desk or a live-in property manager. Condos tend to be clustered in resort areas. There are some very high-end condos, but most are quite affordable, especially if you're traveling in a group.

The advantages of a condo are privacy, space, and conveniences—which usually include a full kitchen, a washer and dryer, a private phone, and more. The downsides are the standard lack of an on-site restaurant and the density of the units (vs. the privacy of a single-unit vacation rental).

BED & BREAKFASTS

Hawaii has a wide range of places that call themselves B&Bs: everything from a traditional B&B—several bedrooms in a home, with breakfast served in the morning—to what is essentially a vacation rental on an owner's property that comes with fixings for you to make your own breakfast. Make sure that the B&B you're booking matches your own mental picture. Note that laundry facilities and private phones are not always available. I've reviewed lots of wonderful B&Bs in the island chapters that follow. If you have to share a bathroom, I've spelled it out in the listings; otherwise, you can assume that you will have your own.

The advantages of a traditional B&B are its individual style and congenial atmosphere, with a host who's often happy to act as your own private concierge. In addition, they're usually an affordable way to go. The disadvantages are lack of privacy, usually a set time for breakfast, few amenities, and generally no maid service. Also, B&B owners typically require a minimum stay of 2 or 3 nights, and it's often a drive to the beach.

B&B Etiquette

In Hawaii, it is traditional and customary to remove your shoes before entering anyone's home. The same is true at most bed-and-breakfast facilities. If this custom is unpleasant to you, a B&B may not be for you.

Hawaii also has a very strict no-smoking law (no smoking in public buildings, restaurants, bars, retail stores, and the like), and more and more hotels, resorts, condos, and vacation rentals generally do *not* allow smoking in the guest rooms (those hotels that still do allow smoking all have nonsmoking rooms available). The majority of bed-and-breakfast units already forbid smoking in the rooms. Be sure to check the policy of your accommodations before you book.

VACATION RENTALS

This is another great choice for families and for long-term stays. "Vacation rental" usually means that there will be no one on the property where you're staying. The actual accommodations can range from an apartment to an entire fully equipped house. Generally, vacation rentals allow you to settle in and make yourself at home for a while. They have kitchen facilities (at least a kitchenette), on-site laundry facilities, and a phone; some also come with such extras as a TV, VCR or DVD player, and stereo.

The advantages of a vacation rental are complete privacy, your own kitchen (which can save you money on meals), and lots of conveniences. The disadvantages are a lack of an on-site property manager and generally no maid service; often a minimum stay is required (sometimes as much as a week). If you book a vacation rental, be sure that you have a 24-hour contact to call if the toilet won't flush or you can't figure out how to turn on the air-conditioning.

Using a Booking Agency vs. Doing It Yourself

If you don't have the time to call several places yourself to make sure they offer the amenities you'd like, you might consider a booking agency.

A statewide booking agent for B&Bs is **Bed & Breakfast Hawaii** (② 800/733-1632 or 808/822-7771; fax 808/822-2723; www.bandb-hawaii.com), offering a range of accommodations from vacation homes to bed-and-breakfast inns, starting at $65 a night. For vacation rentals, contact **Hawaii Beachfront Vacation Homes** (② 808/247-3637; fax 808/235-2644). **Hawaii Condo Exchange** (② 800/442-0404; www.myhawaiibeachfront.com) acts as a consolidator for condo and vacation-rental properties.

GETTING MARRIED IN THE ISLANDS

Hawaii is a great place for a wedding. The islands exude romance and natural beauty, and after the ceremony, you're already on your honeymoon. And the members of your wedding party will most likely be delighted, since you've given them the perfect excuse for their own island vacation.

More than 20,000 marriages are performed annually on the islands, mostly on Oahu; nearly half are for couples from somewhere else. The booming wedding business has spawned more than 70 companies that can help you organize a long-distance event and stage an unforgettable wedding, Hawaiian style or your style. However, you can also plan your own island wedding, even from afar, and not spend a fortune doing it.

The Paperwork

The state of Hawaii has some very minimal procedures for obtaining a marriage license. The first thing you should do is contact the **Honolulu Marriage License Office,** State Department of Health Building, 1250 Punchbowl St., Honolulu, HI 96813 (② 808/586-4545; www.state.hi.us/doh/records/vr_marri. html), which is open Monday through Friday from 8am to 4pm. The office will no longer mail you the brochure *Getting Married;* you can download it from the website or contact a marriage-licensing agent closest to where you'll be staying in Hawaii (also listed on the website).

Once in Hawaii, the prospective bride and groom must go together to the marriage-licensing agent to get the license, which costs $60 and is good for 30 days. Both parties must be 15 years of age or older (couples 15–17 years old must have proof of age, written consent of both parents, and written approval of the judge of the family court) and not more closely related than first cousins. That's it.

Gay couples cannot marry in Hawaii. After a protracted legal battle and much discussion in the state legislature, the Hawaii Supreme Court ruled that the state will not issue marriage licenses to same-sex couples.

Planning the Wedding

DOING IT YOURSELF

The marriage-licensing agents, who range from employees of the governor's satellite office in Kona to private individuals, are usually friendly, helpful people who can steer you to a nondenominational minister or marriage performer who's licensed by the state of Hawaii. These marriage performers are great sources of information for budget weddings. They usually know wonderful places to have the ceremony for free or for a nominal fee. For the names and addresses of marriage-licensing agents on the Big Island, call ℂ **808/974-6008;** on Maui, ℂ **808/984-8210;** on Molokai, ℂ **808/553-3663;** on Lanai, ℂ **808/565-6411;** and on Kauai, ℂ **808/241-3498.**

If you don't want to use a wedding planner (see below), but you do want to make arrangements before you arrive in Hawaii, my best advice is to get a copy of the daily newspapers on the island where you want to have the wedding. People willing and qualified to conduct weddings advertise in the classifieds. They're great sources of information, as they know the best places to have the ceremony and can recommend caterers, florists, and everything else you'll need. If you want to have your wedding on the Kona/Waimea side of the Big Island, get *West Hawaii Today,* P.O. Box 789, Kailua-Kona, HI 96745 (ℂ 808/329-9311; www.westhawaiitoday.com); for the Hilo/Puna side, try the *Hawaii Tribune Herald,* P.O. Box 767, Hilo, HI 96720 (ℂ 808/935-6621; www.hilohawaiitribune.com). On Maui, get the *Maui News,* P.O. Box 550, Wailuku, HI 96793 (ℂ 808/244-3981; www.mauinews.com). On Kauai, try the *Garden Island,* 3137 Kuhio Hwy., Lihue, HI 96766 (ℂ 808/245-3681; www.kauaiworld.com). And on Oahu, check out the *Honolulu Advertiser,* P.O. Box 3110, Honolulu, HI 96802 (ℂ 808/525-8000; www.honoluluadvertiser.com); the *Honolulu Star Bulletin,* 7 Waterfront Plaza, Ste. 500, Honolulu, HI 96813 (ℂ 808/529-4700; www.honolulustarbulletin.com); and *MidWeek,* 45–525 Luluku Rd., Kaneohe, HI 96744 (ℂ 808/235-5881; www.midweek.com).

USING A WEDDING PLANNER

Wedding planners—many of whom are marriage-licensing agents as well—can arrange everything for you, from a small, private outdoor affair to a full-blown formal ceremony in a tropical setting. They charge anywhere from $225 to a small fortune—it all depends on what you want. On the Big Island, contact **Paradise Weddings Hawaii** (ℂ 800/428-5844 or 808/883-9067; www.paradiseweddings hawaii.com); on Maui, contact **First Class Weddings** (ℂ 800/262-8433 or

808/877-1411; www.firstclassweddings.com); on Kauai, try **Coconut Coast Weddings & Honeymoons** (✆ 800/585-5595 or 808/826-5557; www.kauai wedding.com); on Oahu, contact Rev. Toni Baran and Rev. Jerry Le Lesch at **Love Hawaii** (✆ 808/235-6966; www.lovehawaii.com), which offers wedding services starting at $95. **The Hawaii Visitors & Convention Bureau,** Waikiki Business Plaza, 2270 Kalakaua Ave., Ste. 801, Honolulu, HI 96815 (✆ **800/GO-HAWAII** [464-2924] or 808/923-1811; www.gohawaii.com) can provide contact information for other wedding coordinators, and many of the big resorts have their own coordinators on staff as well.

3

PLANNING YOUR TRIP TO HAWAII

Getting Married in the Islands

4

SUGGESTED HAWAII ITINERARIES

W hat should I do in Hawaii? This is the most common question that readers ask me. The purpose of this chapter is to give you my expert advice on the best things to see and do on each island, and how to do them so you can spend more time "doing" and less time "getting there."

First, here's the best advice I can give you: *Do not plan to see more than one island per week.* With the exception of the ferry between Maui and Lanai, getting from one island to another is an all-day affair once you figure in packing, checking out of and into hotels, driving to and from airports, and dealing with rental cars, not to mention time actually spent at the airport and on the flight. Don't waste a day of your vacation seeing our interisland air terminals.

Second, *don't max out your days.* This is Hawaii—allow some time to do nothing but relax. You most likely will arrive jet-lagged, so it's a good idea to ease into your vacation. In fact, exposure to sunlight can help reset your internal clock, so I include time at the beach on the first day of most of these itineraries.

Third, *if this is your first trip to Hawaii, think of it as a "scouting" trip.* Hawaii is too beautiful, too sensual, too enticing to see just once in a lifetime. You'll be back. You don't need to see and do everything on this trip.

Finally, keep in mind that the following itineraries are designed to appeal to a wide range of people. If you have a specific interest, such as golfing or scuba diving, check out chapter 1, "The Best of Hawaii," to plan your trip around your passion.

One last thing: You will need a car to get around the islands. Oahu has an adequate public transportation service, but even so, it's set up for residents, not tourists carrying coolers and beach toys (all carry-ons must fit under the bus seat). So plan to rent a car. But also plan to get out of the car as much as possible—to smell the sweet perfume of plumeria, to hear the sound of the wind through a bamboo forest, and to plunge into the gentle waters of the Pacific.

A WEEK ON OAHU

Oahu is so stunning that the *alii*, the kings of Hawaii, made it the capital of the island nation. Below, I've presumed that you are staying in Waikiki; if your hotel is in another location, be sure to factor in extra time for traveling.

DAY 1: Arriving & Seeing Waikiki Beach ★★

After you get off the plane, lather up in sunscreen and head for the most famous beach in the world—**Waikiki Beach** (p. 200). If you have kids in tow or you can't handle a whole afternoon in the intense sun, check out Hawaii's water world at the **Waikiki Aquarium** (p. 249), or gain insight into Waikiki's past on the **Waikiki Historic Trail** (p. 235), a 2-mile trail

FACING PAGE: **The Hana Highway.**

marked with bronzed surfboards. Be sure to catch the sunset (anywhere on Waikiki Beach will do), and get an early dinner.

DAY 2: Visiting Pearl Harbor ★★★ & Honolulu's Chinatown ★★★

Head to the **USS *Arizona* Memorial at Pearl Harbor** (p. 242). Get here as early as possible—by the afternoon, the lines are 2 hours long. While here, be sure to see the **USS *Missouri* Memorial** (p. 244) and the **USS *Bowfin* Submarine Museum & Park** (p. 243). On your way back, stop in **Chinatown** for lunch and a self-guided walking tour (p. 253). In the afternoon, take a nap or head for the beach at **Ala Moana Beach Park** (p. 200) or a shopping spree across the street at the **Ala Moana Center** (p. 133). Have dinner in Honolulu or the surrounding area.

A shrine in the Chinese Cultural Plaza in Chinatown.

DAY 3: Exploring the North Shore ★★★ & the Polynesian Cultural Center ★

Start your day with a drive to the **North Shore** (see "Central Oahu & the North Shore," on p. 274). If you're up early, have breakfast in the quaint town of **Haleiwa;** if not, at least stop and get a picnic lunch before you beach-hop down the coast of the North Shore and choose from some of the world's most beautiful beaches, like **Waimea Beach Park** (p. 206). After lunch, head for the **Polynesian Cultural Center,** in Laie (p. 273). Allow at least 2 hours to tour this mini-glimpse of the Pacific. Continue driving down the coast road to the small town of **Kailua.** Stay for dinner here to avoid the traffic back to Waikiki.

DAY 4: Snorkeling in Hanauma Bay ★★ & Visiting Sea Life Park

If it's not Tuesday (when the park is closed), head out in the morning for the spectacular snorkeling at **Hanauma Bay** (p. 202). If you have kids, wander down the coast to **Sea Life Park** (p. 248). Otherwise, continue beach-hopping down the coastline—check out **Sandy Beach** (p. 203) and **Makapuu Beach Park** (p. 203) to see which one appeals to you. Then turn back to take the Pali Highway home to Waikiki—and be sure to stop at the **Pali Lookout** (p. 250).

Oahu in 1 Week

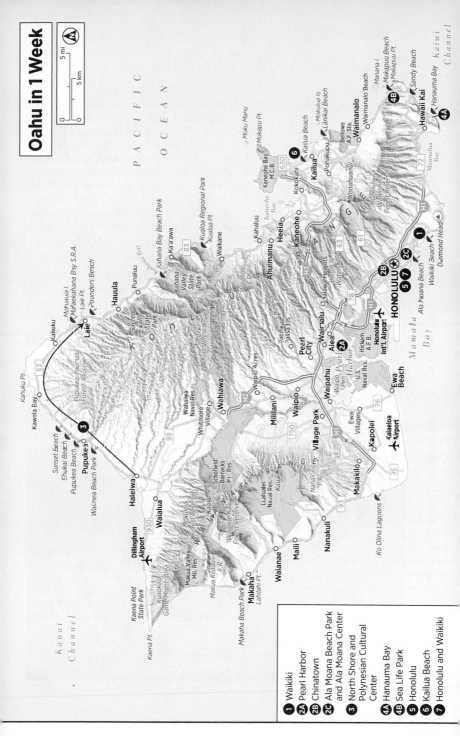

1 Waikiki
2A Pearl Harbor
2B Chinatown
2C Ala Moana Beach Park and Ala Moana Center
3 North Shore and Polynesian Cultural Center
4A Hanauma Bay
4B Sea Life Park
5 Honolulu
6 Kailua Beach
7 Honolulu and Waikiki

DAY 5: Hiking a Rainforest ★★, Glimpsing Historic Honolulu & Experiencing Hawaiian Culture

You could probably use a day out of the sun by now, so try a short hike into the rainforest, just a 15-minute drive from downtown Honolulu. Be sure to wear good hiking or trail shoes for the **Manoa Falls Trail** (p. 219), and bring mosquito repellent. Next, head for downtown Honolulu to see some of the city's historic sites, including the **Hawaii Maritime Center, Iolani Palace, Kawaiahao Church,** and **Mission Houses Museum** (coverage starts on p. 235). To see where you've been, go to the top of the **Aloha Tower,** at the Aloha Tower Marketplace, for a bird's-eye view of Honolulu. Grab lunch at the Marketplace or one of the nearby restaurants. Spend the afternoon at the **Bishop Museum** (p. 235) to immerse yourself in Hawaiian culture.

DAY 6: Relaxing at Kailua Beach ★★★

On your last full day on Oahu, travel over the Pali Highway to the windward side of the island and spend a day at **Kailua Beach** (p. 204)—but before you leave Waikiki, drop by **MAC 24-7** (p. 174) and pick up a picnic lunch. Kailua is the perfect beach on which to just relax or snorkel or try something different, such as kayaking or windsurfing. You can spend the entire day here, or you can take an afternoon hike at the **Hoomaluhia Botanical Garden** (p. 223).

DAY 7: Shopping & Museum-Hopping

Been having too much fun to shop for gifts for your friends back home? You can find a great selection of stores in Waikiki at the **Ala Moana Center** (p. 286), the **DFS Galleria** (p. 287), and the **Royal Hawaiian Shopping**

Hoomaluhia Botanical Garden.

Center (p. 288). If you're more interested in looking than buying, check out the **Honolulu Academy of Arts** (p. 250), **The Contemporary Museum** (p. 250), or the **Hawaii State Art Museum** (p. 251). On your way to the airport, be sure to stop at one of the **Maunakea Street lei shops** (p. 253) in Chinatown to buy a sweet-smelling souvenir of your trip.

A WEEK ON THE BIG ISLAND OF HAWAII

A week is barely enough time to see the entire Big Island; 2 weeks would be better. But if your schedule doesn't allow more time, this tour will let you see the highlights of this huge island (twice the size of the other islands combined). The itinerary is set up for those staying in Kailua-Kona or on the Kohala Coast; I suggest you also spend at least 2 nights in Volcano Village to enjoy Hawaii Volcanoes National Park.

DAY 1: Arriving & Making Beach Time

After you settle into your hotel, head for the beach: Snorkelers should go to **Kahaluu Beach Park** (p. 353), surfers to **White Sands Beach** (p. 354), privacy buffs to **Kekaha Kai State Park** (**Kona Coast State Park;** p. 354), beach aficionados can choose from **Anaehoomalu Bay (A-Bay), Hapuna Beach,** and **Kaunaoa Beach (Mauna Kea Beach),** depending on whether you want to snorkel, body board, or just relax (see reviews starting on p. 354 to help you decide). When the sun starts to wane, head for old Kailua-Kona town (coverage starts on p. 378) and wander through the **Hulihee Palace, Mokuaikaua Church,** and **Kamehameha's Compound at Kamakahonu Bay.** Find a spot on the pier or along the sea wall to watch the sunset, and then head for dinner in Kailua-Kona or Keauhou.

DAY 2: Enjoying a Morning Sail & Afternoon Drive to Hawaii Volcanoes National Park ★★★

Since you most likely will be up early on your first day in Hawaii (and still on mainland time), take advantage of it and book a morning sail/snorkel tour with **Fair Wind** (p. 360) to **Kealakekua Bay,** a marine-life preserve. After you return to Keauhou, start driving south. Great stops along the way are **Puuhonua O Honaunau National Historical Park** (p. 384), **South Point** (p. 408), and **Green Sand Beach (Papakolea Beach;** p. 357). Then head up **Mauna Kea** to **Hawaii Volcanoes National Park** (p. 368) and stay at one of the quaint B&Bs in the tiny village of **Volcano** (a list of recommended accommodations starts on p. 329).

DAY 3: Exploring an Active Volcano ★★★

The highlight of your trip most likely will be the incredible **Hawaii Volcanoes National Park** (p. 368). Your first stop should be the Kilauea Visitor Center; then you can explore **Halemaumau Crater, Thurston Lava Tube, Devastation Trail,** and the other sights in the crater. Find out from

Volcano art outside Kilauea General Store.

the rangers how to get to the current lava flow. In the afternoon, drive down to the current flow and walk out as far as the rangers will allow. Go eat a nice dinner in Volcano and return to the flow after dark, armed with a flashlight, water bottle, and jacket. Since you were here earlier during the day, the path to the volcano after dark will be familiar to you. Seeing the ribbon of red lava snake its way down the side of the mountain and then thunder into the ocean is a sight you will never forget. You are going to be tired after this full day, so I recommend spending another night in Volcano.

DAY 4: Touring Old Hawaii: Hilo Town ★★★, Akaka Falls ★★★, Waipio Valley ★★★ & Cowboy Country

It's just a 45-minute drive from Volcano to **Hilo** (coverage starts on p. 396), so plan to arrive early in the morning, grab a cup of joe at **Bears' Coffee** (p. 339), and wander through the old town, being sure to see **Banyan Drive, Liliuokalani Gardens, Lyman Museum & Mission House,** the **Pacific Tsunami Museum,** and one of the wonderful botanical gardens, such as **Nani Mau Gardens** (p. 399), **Hawaii Tropical Botanical Garden** (p. 392), or **World Botanical Gardens** (p. 393). Head up the Hamakua Coast, stopping at **Akaka Falls** (p. 392) and Honokaa for lunch. Afterward, be sure to see **Waipio Valley** (p. 394), the birthplace of Hawaii's kings, before heading for **Waimea** (p. 413). Spend some time in this cowboy town and at the **Parker Ranch Visitor Center & Museum** (p. 376). Spend the night along the Kohala Coast.

DAY 5: Stepping Back in Time on the Kohala Coast ★★★

Get an early start on your trip back in time. The first stop is just south of Kawaihae, at the **Puukohola Heiau National Historic Site** (p. 384), the temple Kamehameha built to the war god to ensure his success in battle.

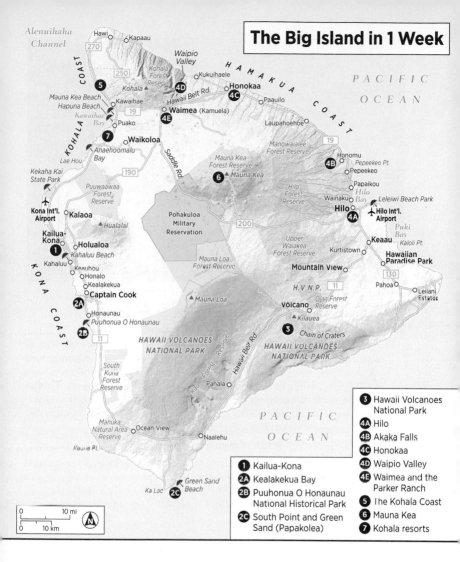

Alenuihaha Channel

Hawi   Kapaau

Waipio Valley

Kohala Forest Reserve

Kukuihaele

H A M A K U A

Honokaa

Hawaii Belt Rd.

Paauilo

Waimea (Kamuela)

Kohala

Mauna Kea Beach   Kawaihae

Hapuna Beach

Kawaihae Bay   Puako

C O A S T

K O H A L A   C O A S T

Laupahoehoe

P A C I F I C

O C E A N

Waikoloa

Anaehoomalu Bay

Lae Hou

Manowaialee Forest Reserve

Honomu

Pepeekeo Pt.

Pepeekeo

Kekaha Kai State Park

Puuwaawaa Forest Reserve

Mauna Kea Forest Reserve

Mauna Kea

Hilo Forest Reserve

Papaikou

Wainaku   Hilo Bay   Leleiwi Beach Park

Kona Int'l. Airport

Kalaoa

Hualalai

Pohakuloa Military Reservation

Hilo   Hilo Int'l. Airport

Kailua-Kona

Holualoa

Kahaluu Beach

Kahaluu

Keauhou

Honalo

Kealakekua

Captain Cook

Honaunau

Puuhonua O Honaunau

K O N A   C O A S T

Mauna Loa Forest Reserve

Mauna Loa

Upper Waiakea Forest Reserve

Kurtistown

Mountain View

Olaa Forest Reserve

Volcano

Kilauea

Keaau

Puki Bay   Kaloli Pt.

Hawaiian Paradise Park

Pahoa   Leilani Estates

H.V.N.P.

HAWAII VOLCANOES NATIONAL PARK

Kau Forest Reserve

Hawaii Belt Rd.

Chain of Craters

HAWAII VOLCANOES NATIONAL PARK

South Kona Forest Reserve

Pahala

Manuka Natural Area Reserve

Ocean View

Naalehu

Kaena Pt.

P A C I F I C

O C E A N

Green Sand Beach

Ka Lae

0   10 mi
0   10 km

3 Hawaii Volcanoes National Park
4A Hilo
4B Akaka Falls
4C Honokaa
4D Waipio Valley
4E Waimea and the Parker Ranch
5 The Kohala Coast
6 Mauna Kea
7 Kohala resorts

1 Kailua-Kona
2A Kealakekua Bay
2B Puuhonua O Honaunau National Historical Park
2C South Point and Green Sand (Papakolea)

Allow at least an hour here. Keep driving up Hwy. 270 to **Lapakahi State Historical Park** (p. 387) for a view of a typical 14th-century Hawaiian village and the **Mookini Luakini Heiau** (p. 387). Plan a lunch stop in Hawi or Kapaau at either **Bamboo** (p. 344) or **Kohala Rainbow Cafe,** and stop by the **Original King Kamehameha Statue** (p. 388) in Kapaau. The final stop on your northward journey is the **Pololu Valley Lookout** (p. 388). On your way back, in the late afternoon (the best time for viewing), be sure to stop at the **Puako Petroglyph Archaeological District** (p. 387). If it's Friday, make reservations at the **Kona Village Luau** (p. 419) for the perfect ending to your trip back in time.

The Pololu Valley Lookout.

DAY 6: Seeing Mauna Kea ★★★

Sleep in, have a lazy morning at the beach, and in the afternoon plan to explore Hawaii's tallest mountain (and dormant volcano), **Mauna Kea** (p. 389). You need a four-wheel-drive vehicle to climb to the top of the 13,796-foot Mauna Kea, so I recommend booking with the experts, **Mauna Kea Summit Adventures** (p. 394), for a 7- to 8-hour visit to this mountain, sacred to the Hawaiians and treasured by astronomers around the globe.

DAY 7: Relaxing & Shopping

Depending on how much time you have on your final day, I recommend either relaxing on the beach or being pampered at a spa. Spa-goers can choose from a range of terrific spas among the **Kohala resorts** (reviews begin on p. 318). Shoppers have lots of options—see my recommendations starting on p. 412.

A WEEK ON MAUI

I've outlined the highlights of Maui for those who have just 7 days and want to see everything. Two suggestions: First, spend 2 nights in Hana, a decision you will not regret, and second, take the Trilogy boat trip to Lanai for the day. I've designed this itinerary assuming you'll stay in West Maui for 5 days. If you are staying elsewhere (like Wailea or Kihei), allow extra driving time.

DAY 1: Arriving & Seeing Kapalua Beach ★★★

After checking into your hotel, head for **Kapalua Beach** (p. 501). After an hour or two in the sun, drive to **Lahaina** (p. 533) and spend a couple of hours walking the historic old town. Go to the **Old Lahaina Luau** (p. 564) at sunset to immerse yourself in Hawaiian culture.

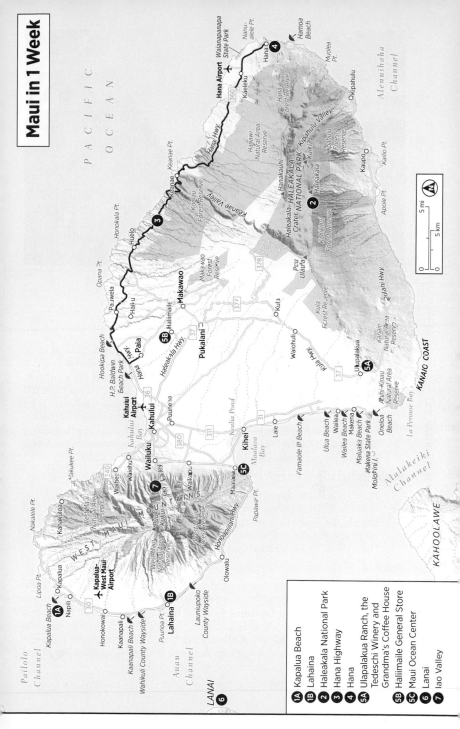

Maui in 1 Week

1A Kapalua Beach
1B Lahaina
2 Haleakala National Park
3 Hana Highway
4 Hana
5A Ulapalakua Ranch, the Tedeschi Winery and Grandma's Coffee House
5B Haliimaile General Store
5C Maui Ocean Center
6 Lanai
7 Iao Valley

Lahaina.

DAY 2: Going Up a 10,000-Foot Volcano & Down Again ★★★

You'll likely wake up early on your first day in Hawaii, so take advantage of it and head up to the 10,000-foot dormant volcano, **Haleakala.** You can **hike in the crater** (p. 519), **speed down the mountain on a bicycle** (p. 526), or just wander about the national park. You don't have to be at the top for sunrise; in fact, it has gotten so congested at sunrise that you may be too busy fighting the crowds to have an awe-inspiring experience. Instead, I suggest wandering up any time during the day. On your way back down, stop and tour **Upcountry Maui** (p. 543), particularly the communities of **Kula, Makawao,** and **Paia.** Plan for a sunset dinner in Paia or Kuau.

DAY 3: Driving the Hana Highway ★★★

Pack a lunch and spend the entire day driving the scenic **Hana Highway** (p. 544). Pull over often and get out to take photos, smell the flowers, and jump in the mountain-stream pools. Wave to everyone, move off the road for those speeding by, and breathe in Hawaii. Plan to spend at least 2 nights in Hana (hotel recommendations start on p. 464).

DAY 4: Spending a Day in Heavenly Hana ★★★

Take an early morning hike along the black sands of **Waianapanapa State Park** (p. 506); then explore the tiny town of **Hana** (p. 549). Be sure to see the **Hana Museum Cultural Center, Hasegawa General Store,** and **Hana Coast Gallery.** Get a picnic lunch and drive out to the Kipahulu end of Haleakala National Park at **Oheo Gulch** (p. 550). Hike to the waterfalls and swim in the pools. Splurge on dinner at the dining room at the **Hotel Hana-Maui** (p. 500). Spend another night in Hana.

Oheo Gulch.

DAY 5: Enjoying Wine, Food & (Hawaiian) Song

Check to see if the road past Hana is open (occasionally it is closed due to road conditions); if it is, continue driving around the island, past Kaupo and up to the **Ulupalakua Ranch** and the **Tedeschi Vineyards and Winery** (p. 543). Stop at **Grandma's Coffee House** (p. 496) for a cup of java and head down the mountain, with a stop for lunch at **Haliimaile General Store** (p. 495). Spend the afternoon at the **Maui Ocean Center,** in Maalaea (p. 535), checking out the sharks and other marine life. Plan a dinner in Lahaina and see the drama/dance/music show **Ulalena** (p. 565). If the road past Hana is closed, go back along the Hana Highway the way you came, stopping for lunch at Haliimaile, and then follow the rest of the itinerary from there.

DAY 6: Sailing to Lanai ★★★

Trilogy (p. 510) provides the best sailing/snorkeling trip in Hawaii, so don't miss it. You'll spend the day (breakfast and lunch included) sailing to Lanai, snorkeling, touring the island, and sailing back to Lahaina. Plus, you still have the afternoon free to shop or take a nap.

DAY 7: Relaxing & Shopping

Depending on how much time you have on your final day, you can decide to relax on the beach, get pampered in a spa, or shop for souvenirs. Spa-goers have a range of terrific spas to choose from, and shopping aficionados should check out some of my favorite stores (recommendations start on p. 552). If you have a late flight, you might want to check out **Iao Valley** (p. 531).

A WEEK ON MOLOKAI

The island of Molokai is for people trying to get away from everything or those looking for adventure. There are no direct flights from the mainland to Molokai, so you will have to fly into Honolulu and then take a commuter plane to Molokai.

DAY 1: Arriving & Stopping in Kaunakakai

If you're staying in a condo or vacation rental, head into **Kaunakakai** and stock up on groceries. While you're here, wander around the old two-street town and check out the stores. Be sure to stop at the **Kapuaiwa Coconut Grove/Kiowea Park** (p. 592) and watch the sunset.

DAY 2: Riding a Mule to Kalaupapa ★★★

Your internal clock will still be set to mainland time, so you should have no problem waking up early for the **Molokai Mule Ride** (p. 596). This adventure will take you through 26 switchbacks on a 1,600-foot cliff and give you a chance to tour the **Kalaupapa Peninsula,** where people suffering from leprosy lived for decades.

DAY 3: Heading for the Beach

Molokai has terrific beaches—and on weekdays they are generally empty! Depending on the time of year and the weather, great beaches for snorkeling are **Murphy Beach Park (Kumimi Beach Park;** p. 585) and **Sandy Beach** (p. 585) on the East End, and **Kapukahehu (Dixie Maru) Beach** (p. 587) on the West End. Pack a picnic lunch or stop by **Outpost Natural Foods** (p. 582), in Kaunakakai. Stay all day. Relax.

The Kalaupapa Peninsula.

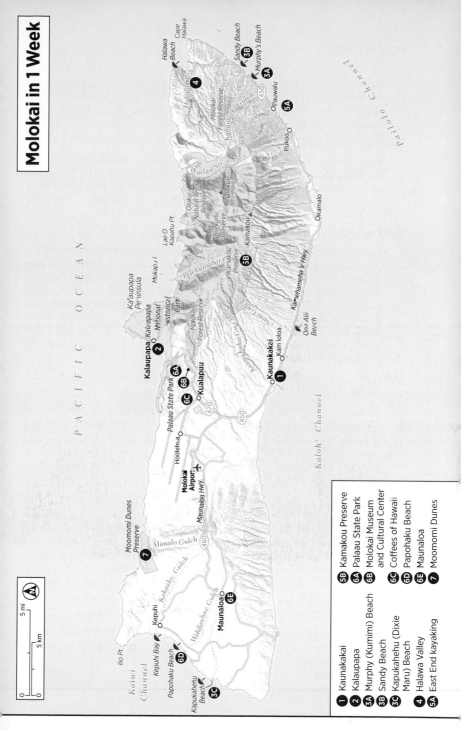

Molokai in 1 Week

1 Kaunakakai
2 Kalaupapa
3A Murphy (Kumimi) Beach
3B Sandy Beach
3C Kapukahehu (Dixie Maru) Beach
4 Halawa Valley
5A East End kayaking
5B Kamakou Preserve
6A Palaau State Park
6B Molokai Museum and Cultural Center
6C Coffees of Hawaii
6D Papohaku Beach
6E Maunaloa
7 Moomomi Dunes

DAY 4: Hiking in a Tropical Valley & Venturing into Paradise ★

After a day at the beach, you'll be ready for a hike into the tropical jungle of **Halawa Valley** (p. 599). Bring a picnic lunch for after the hike, and then spend the rest of the day on the beach at Halawa. Stop to see the **fish ponds** (p. 598) before you leave the East End.

DAY 5: Exploring the Outdoors ★

Spend a day kayaking, biking, or hiking. **Molokai Outdoors Activities** (p. 586) can set you up with kayaks, mountain bikes, or maps for hiking. My choice would be kayaking along the shallow waters of the East End. Hikers should check out **Pepeopae Trail** (p. 588) or the **Kamakou Preserve** (p. 598).

DAY 6: Touring the West End ★★

Since you've already seen the East End, spend a day exploring the rest of the island. Start out with a tour of the central part of Molokai by driving out to **Palaau State Park** (p. 594), which overlooks the Kalaupapa Peninsula, and then stop at the **Molokai Museum and Cultural Center** (p. 593) and take a coffee break at **Coffees of Hawaii Plantation Store and Espresso Bar** (p. 602). Next head to the 3-mile-long, white-sand **Papohaku Beach** (p. 584). After an hour or so at the beach, drive up to the cool air in Maunaloa town to see the best store on the island: the **Big Wind Kite Factory & Plantation Gallery** (p. 603).

DAY 7: Seeing Moomomi Dunes: Archaeology Heaven

Before your flight back, stop by the **Moomomi Dunes** (p. 597), located close to the Hoolehua Airport. This wild, sand-covered coast is a treasure trove for archaeologists. Buried in the mounds are ancient Hawaiian burial sites, fossils, Hawaiian artifacts, and even the bones of prehistoric birds. If you have time, take the 20-minute easy walk west to **Kawaaloa Bay,** the perfect place to say aloha to Molokai.

A WEEK ON LANAI

The smallest of all the Hawaiian Islands, Lanai was once a big pineapple plantation and is now home to two exclusive resorts, hundreds of years of history, and just one small town with some of the friendliest people you will ever meet. As with the island of Molokai, there are no direct flights from the mainland to Lanai. You will have to fly into Honolulu and then take a commuter plane to Lanai.

DAY 1: Arriving & Seeing Hulopoe Bay ★★

After you settle into your hotel, head for the best beach on the island: the marine preserve at **Hulopoe Bay** (p. 617). It's generally safe for swimming, the snorkeling is terrific, and the fish are so friendly you practically have to shoo them away.

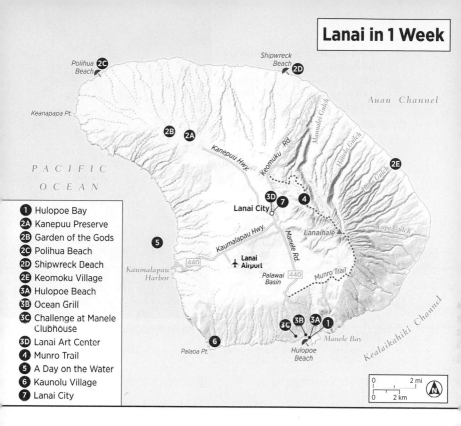

1. Hulopoe Bay
2A. Kanepuu Preserve
2B. Garden of the Gods
2C. Polihua Beach
2D. Shipwreck Beach
2E. Keomoku Village
3A. Hulopoe Beach
3B. Ocean Grill
3C. Challenge at Manele Clubhouse
3D. Lanai Art Center
4. Munro Trail
5. A Day on the Water
6. Kaunolu Village
7. Lanai City

DAY 2: Touring the Island in a Four-Wheel-Drive Vehicle

Lanai is a fantastic place to go four-wheeling. Generally you won't need a car if you're staying at one of the two resorts or at the Hotel Lanai (they provide shuttle service), so splurge and rent a four-wheel-drive vehicle for 2 or 3 days. Get a picnic lunch from **Pele's Other Garden** (p. 616) and head out of Lanai City to the **Kanepuu Preserve** (p. 626), a 590-acre dry-land forest. Next stop is **Garden of the Gods** (p. 623) and a picnic lunch at **Polihua Beach** (p. 617), Lanai's largest white-sand beach. The beach generally is not safe for swimming and can be windy, but it will probably be deserted and you'll have a great view of Molokai in the distance. After lunch, reverse directions and head to **Shipwreck Beach** (p. 617) and then on to **Keomoku Village** (p. 626).

DAY 3: Spending a Day at the Beach

Plan a lazy day at **Hulopoe Beach** (p. 617). Grab a book, watch the kids play in the surf, or take a long walk around the crescent-shaped bay. For lunch, wander over to the **Four Seasons Resort at Manele Bay** and sit poolside at the **Ocean Grill** (p. 614), or else head to the resort's **Challenge at Manele Clubhouse** (p. 615). In the afternoon, plan a nap or try your hand at some Island crafts at the **Lanai Art Center** (p. 628).

DAY 4: Hiking (or Driving) the Munro Trail

If it has not been raining and the ground is dry, do a little exploring. The adventurous can spend the day (allow at least 7 hr.) climbing to the top of Lanai on the **Munro Trail** (p. 623). The not-so-adventurous can take a four-wheel-drive vehicle. Soak in a hot tub on your return.

DAY 5: Enjoying a Day on the Water ★★

The Garden of the Gods.

Ring up **Trilogy Lanai Ocean Sports** (p. 618) and book a sailing/snorkeling, whale-watching, or scuba trip.

DAY 6: Horseback Riding & Taking a Trip Back in Time

Saddle up. Horse lovers should arrange a tour of Lanai through the **Stables at Koele** (p. 622) in the morning. Then plan a four-wheel-drive trip in the afternoon to the historic ruins of the old **Kaunolu Village** (p. 625), on the southwestern side of the island.

DAY 7: Biking & Shopping

The best way to get around the tiny village of Lanai City is via bicycle. Rent one from the **Four Seasons Resort Lanai, The Lodge at Koele** (p. 612), and ride (downhill) into town. Lanai City has some terrific boutiques that you'll find nowhere else (descriptions of my favorites start on p. 627).

A WEEK ON KAUAI

Hawaii's oldest island, ringed with white-sand beaches, is small and easy to circumnavigate in a week. But there are so many wonderful things to do and see that you may find yourself wishing you had more time.

DAY 1: Arriving & Making Beach Time

After settling into your hotel, head for the beach. If you're staying on the south side, **Poipu Beach** (p. 677) is your best bet; on the east in the Coconut Coast area, go to **Lydgate State Park** (p. 680); and if you're on the North Shore, try **Anini, Haena, Hanalei,** or **Kee beaches** (p. 680).

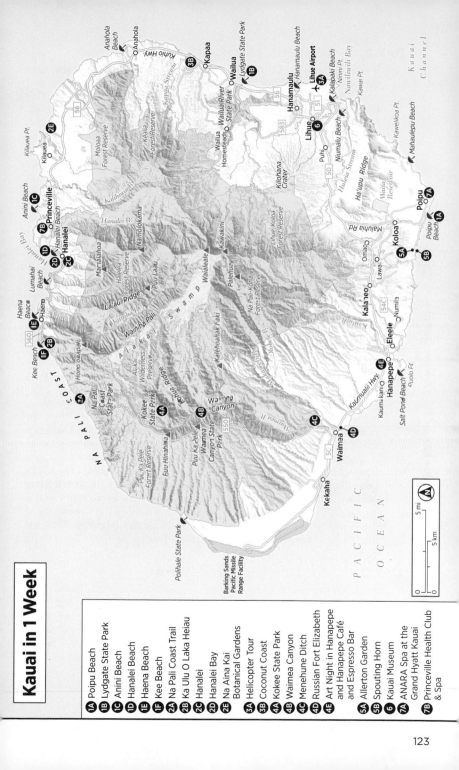

Kauai in 1 Week

1A Poipu Beach
1B Lydgate State Park
1C Anini Beach
1D Hanalei Beach
1E Haena Beach
1F Kee Beach
2A Na Pali Coast Trail
2B Ka Ulu O Laka Heiau
2C Hanalei
2D Hanalei Bay
2E Na Aina Kai
     Botanical Gardens
3A Helicopter Tour
3B Coconut Coast
4A Kokee State Park
4B Waimea Canyon
4C Menehune Ditch
4D Russian Fort Elizabeth
4E Art Night in Hanapepe
     and Hanapepe Café
     and Espresso Bar
5A Allerton Garden
5B Spouting Horn
6   Kauai Museum
7A ANARA Spa at the
     Grand Hyatt Kauai
7B Princeville Health Club
     & Spa

DAY 2: Touring the North Shore ★★

It rains often on the Garden Isle of Kauai, so on your first sunny day, head out for the **North Shore** (p. 680). Drive all the way to the end of the road to Kee Beach. Plan to hike a little on the famous Kalalau Trail in **Na Pali Coast State Park** (p. 697)—bring hiking shoes or closed-toe tennis shoes. A half-hour on the trail will give you an idea of the spectacular coastline. The hearty may want to hike all the way to **Hanakapiai Beach,** a 2-hour trip one-way. After your hike, take a look at **Ka Ulu O Laka Heiau** (p. 716) at Kee Beach. Head into **Hanalei** (p. 637) for lunch, and then drive down to **Hanalei Bay** (p. 681) for a quiet afternoon on the beach, or book a tour at **Na Aina Kai Botanical Gardens** (p. 717) to see one of Kauai's most beautiful (and whimsical) gardens. Plan to have dinner on the North Shore—my recommendations begin on p. 673.

DAY 3: Seeing Kauai from the Air on a Helicopter Tour ★★★

Book a **helicopter tour** (p. 710), but not until 10 or 11am at the earliest, to avoid the bumper-to-bumper commuter traffic. After your tour, head to the Coconut Coast area for lunch (my dining recommendations start on p. 670). Learn about Hawaiian history at **Wailua River State Park** (p. 712).

DAY 4: Hiking Kokee State Park ★★ & Waimea Canyon ★★★

Get an early start and drive up to the 4,640-acre **Kokee State Park** (p. 694), where you will find a range of trails to fit every ability. Birders, hikers, and sightseers will love wandering around this park. You can get lunch at the **Kokee Lodge Restaurant** (p. 696), open from 9am to 3:30pm. Be sure to stop by the **Kokee Natural History Museum** (p. 709), which is full of great information as well as trail maps. In the afternoon, stop at the "Grand Canyon of the Pacific," **Waimea Canyon** (p. 693), with more great hiking. After you've had your fill of hiking for the day, don't miss the **Kiki a Ola** (**Menehune Ditch;** p. 703) and the **Russian Fort Elizabeth State Historical Park** (p. 707) on your way out of Waimea town. *Tip:* Friday is a great day to plan this trip to Kokee and Waimea. Since you'll already be on the west side, you can attend Hanapepe's Friday **Art Night** (p. 726), and the terrific **Hanapepe Cafe & Espresso Bar** (p. 669) will be open for dinner.

DAY 5: Enjoying a Beach Day ★★

Kauai has the best beaches in Hawaii, so you should devote at least a day to them. Check out my beach recommendations, starting on p. 676. If you're not the type to just lie around, you can book a kayak or snorkel tour (water-sports options begin on p. 684—I particularly recommend a tour of the Na Pali Coast). If you've had enough sun to last awhile, reserve a tour at

Spouting Horn.

Allerton Garden of the National Tropical Botanical Garden (p. 705). On your way back from the garden, stop and marvel at the very unusual **Spouting Horn** (p. 706).

DAY 6: Getting out of the Rain (or Sun)

It's best to plan for at least one rainy day on Kauai, but my rainy-day suggestions are just as much fun even when it's not rainy. **Hawaii Movie Tours** (p. 714) takes you to some of the many spots on Kauai where films have been made. The **Kauai Museum,** in Lihue (p. 704), is filled with treasures. And shoppers will enjoy Kauai's many unique markets (my recommendations start on p. 718).

DAY 7: Indulging in a Spa Day

A treatment at a rejuvenating spa is a great way to end your trip. Kauai's best spa is the **ANARA Spa,** at the **Grand Hyatt Kauai Resort** (p. 644). In addition to the fabulous menu of treatments, it has a great area to relax, take a steam or a sauna, or just hang out in the hot tub. On the North Shore, try the **Princeville Health Club & Spa,** at the St. Regis Princeville (p. 656), which is small but very good.

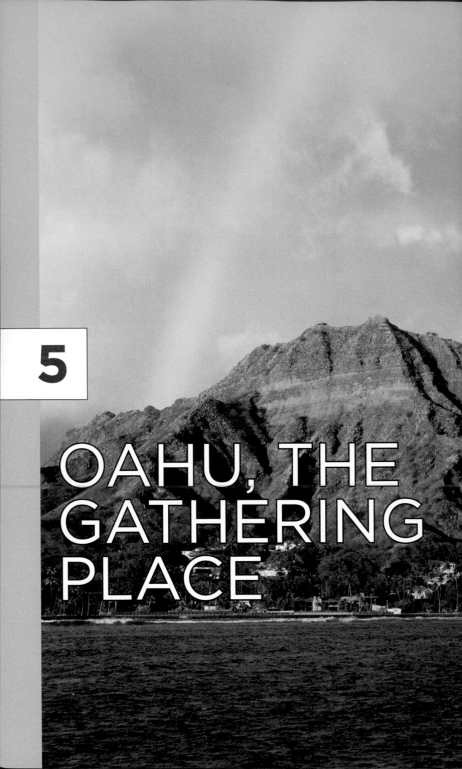

5

OAHU, THE GATHERING PLACE

A wise Hawaiian kahuna once told me that the islands are like children—each is special yet different, and each is to be loved for its individual qualities. One thing's for sure: You'll never find another island like Oahu, the commercial and population center of Hawaii.

Honolulu offers a fast-paced urban setting with Hawaii's hottest nightlife, its best shopping, and a huge array of restaurants. But the North Shore and the windward side of the island present a different face: miles of white-sand beaches and a slower, country way of life. If just the thought of rush-hour traffic, freeways, high-rise towers, and parking fees makes your back molars hurt, then either head for the North Shore or take the next plane out to a quieter neighbor island.

It's astounding to spend hours flying across the barren blue of the Pacific and then suddenly see the most remote big city on earth, a 26-mile-long metropolis of some 899,600 souls living in the middle of nowhere. Once on its streets, you'll find bright city lights, excellent restaurants, nightclubs, world-class shopping, a vibrant arts scene, and grand old hotels.

Nine out of 10 visitors to Hawaii—some five million people a year—stop on Oahu, and most of them end up along the canyonlike streets of Waikiki, Honolulu's well-known hotel district and its most densely populated neighborhood. Some days it seems as though the entire world is sunning itself on Waikiki's famous beach. Beyond Waikiki, Honolulu is clean and easy to enjoy. The city is coming of age for the 21st century: The old port town opened a new convention center in 1998 and is reshaping its waterfront, altering its skyline, opening new world-class hotels, and all the while trying to preserve its historic roots and revive its Polynesian heritage.

Out in the country, Oahu can be as down-home as a slack-key guitar. This is where you'll find a big blue sky, perfect waves, empty beaches, rainbows and waterfalls, sweet tropical flowers, and fiery Pacific sunsets. In fact, nowhere else within 60 minutes of a major American city can you snorkel in a crystal-clear lagoon, climb an old volcano, surf monster waves, kayak to a desert isle, picnic on a sandbar, soar in a glider over tide pools, skin-dive over a sunken airplane, bicycle through a rainforest, golf a championship course, and sail into the setting sun.

And in terms of weather, no other Hawaiian island has it as fine as Oahu. The Big Island is hotter, Kauai is wetter, Maui has more wind, and Molokai and Lanai are drier. But Oahu enjoys a kind of perpetual late spring, with light trade winds and 82°F (28°C) days almost year-round. In fact, the climate is supposed to be the best on the planet. Once you have that, the rest is easy.

FACING PAGE: **Waikiki Beach.**

ORIENTATION

Arriving

Honolulu is your gateway to the Hawaiian Islands; even though more and more transpacific flights are going directly to the neighbor islands these days, chances are still good that you'll touch down on Oahu first. **Honolulu International Airport** sits on the south shore of Oahu, west of downtown Honolulu and Waikiki near Pearl Harbor. Many major American and international carriers fly to Honolulu from the mainland; for a list of airlines, see chapter 11.

LANDING AT HONOLULU INTERNATIONAL AIRPORT

The airport at Honolulu is probably the most cosmopolitan spot in the Pacific, with passengers from every corner of the globe. You can walk or take the free airport shuttle from your arrival gate to the main terminal and baggage claim, on the ground level. After collecting your bags, unless you're getting on an interisland flight immediately, you'll exit to the palm-lined street, where uniformed attendants can either flag down a taxi or direct you to **TheBus** (for transportation information, see below). For Waikiki shuttles and rental-agency vans, cross the street to the center island and wait at the designated stop.

Passengers connecting to neighbor-island flights take the free shuttle or walk to the large interisland terminal serving Hawaiian Airlines or the more distant commuter terminal, which serves smaller carriers such as Island Air, go!Express, and PW Express. (For details on interisland flights, see "Getting Around," on p. 138.)

GETTING TO & FROM THE AIRPORT

BY RENTAL CAR   All major rental companies have cars available at the airport (see chapter 11). Rental-agency vans will pick you up curbside at the center island outside baggage claim and take you to their off-site lot.

BY TAXI   Taxis are abundant at the airport; an attendant will be happy to flag one down for you. Taxi fare is about $25 from Honolulu International to downtown Honolulu, about $35 to $40 to Waikiki. If you need to call a taxi, see "Getting Around," later in this chapter, for a list of cab companies.

BY AIRPORT SHUTTLE   Airport Waikiki Express (© 800/831-5541; http://hawaii.gov/hnl) offers 24-hour service every day of the year between the airport and all 350 hotels and condos in Waikiki. A one-way trip from the airport to Waikiki in one of the company's air-conditioned vans costs just $9 per person ($15 round-trip). You'll find the shuttle at street level, on the median, outside baggage claim. You can board with two pieces of luggage and a carry-on at no extra charge. Tips are welcome. For advance purchase of group tickets, call the number above.

BY BUS   TheBus (© 808/848-4500) nos. 19 and 20 (Waikiki Beach and Hotels) run from the airport to downtown Honolulu and Waikiki. The first bus from Waikiki to the airport leaves at 4:55am Monday through Friday and 5:10am Saturday and Sunday; the last bus departs the airport for Waikiki at 1:22am Monday through Friday, 1:24am Saturday and Sunday. There are two bus stops on the main terminal's upper level; a third is on the second level of the interisland terminal. You can board TheBus with a carry-on or

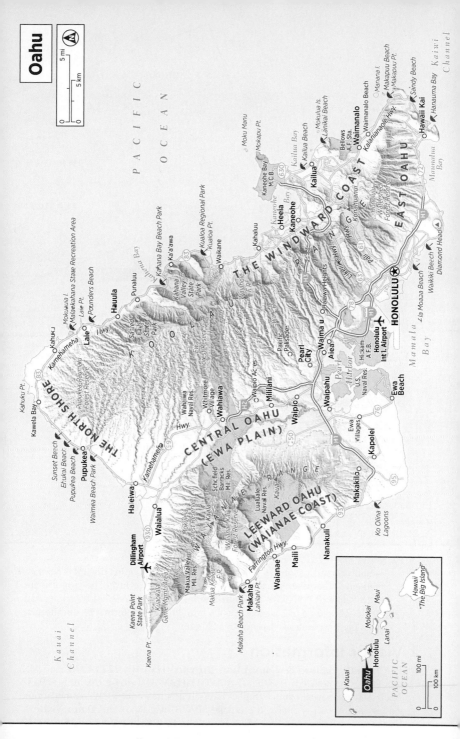

Oahu

5 mi
5 km

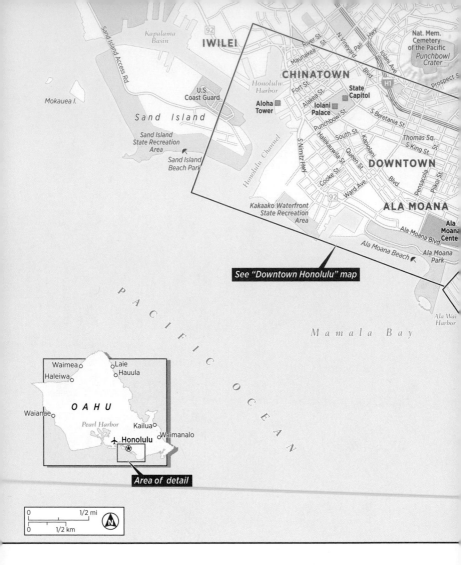

small suitcase, as long as it fits under the seat and doesn't disrupt other passengers; otherwise, you'll have to take a shuttle or taxi. The approximate travel time to Waikiki is an hour. The one-way fare is $2.50 for adults and $1 for children 6 to 17, exact change only. For more information on TheBus, see "Getting Around," later in this chapter.

Visitor Information

The **Hawaii Visitors & Convention Bureau (HVCB),** 2270 Kalakaua Ave., Ste. 801, Honolulu, HI 96815 (© **800/GO-HAWAII** [464-2924] or 808/923-1811; www.gohawaii.com), supplies free brochures, maps, accommodations guides, and *Islands of Aloha,* the official HVCB magazine. The **Oahu Visitors Bureau,** 733 Bishop St., Ste. 1520, Honolulu, HI 96813 (© **877/525-OAHU**

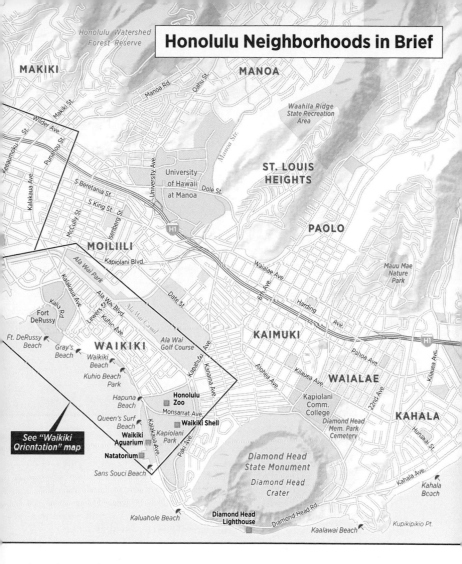

See "Waikiki Orientation" map

Honolulu Neighborhoods in Brief

[6248] or 808/524-0722; fax 808/521-1620; www.visit-oahu.com), distributes a free travel planner and map.

A number of free publications, such as **This Week Oahu,** are packed with money-saving coupons and good regional maps; look for them on racks at the airport and around town.

The Island in Brief

HONOLULU

Hawaii's largest city looks like any other big metropolitan center with tall buildings. In fact, some cynics refer to it as "Los Angeles West." But within Honolulu's boundaries, you'll find rainforests, deep canyons, valleys, waterfalls, a nearly

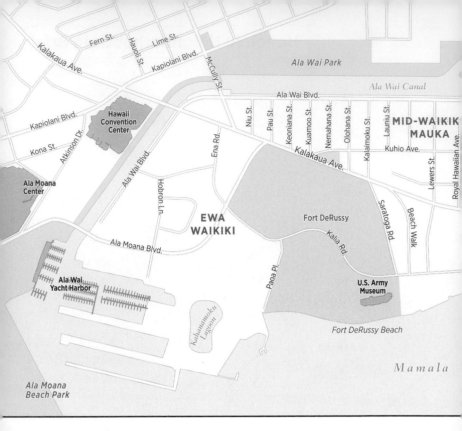

mile-high mountain range, coral reefs, and gold-sand beaches. The city proper—where most of Honolulu's residents live—is approximately 12 miles wide and 26 miles long, running east-west roughly between Diamond Head and Pearl Harbor. Within the city are seven hills laced by seven streams that run to Mamala Bay.

A plethora of neighborhoods surrounds the central area. These areas are generally quieter and more residential than Waikiki, but they're still within minutes of beaches, shopping, and all the activities Oahu has to offer.

WAIKIKI ★★★   Some say that Waikiki is past its prime—that everybody goes to Maui now. If it has fallen out of favor, you couldn't prove it by me. Waikiki is the very incarnation of Yogi Berra's comment about Toots Shor's famous New York restaurant: "Nobody goes there anymore. It's too crowded."

In 1875 when King Kalakaua played in Waikiki, it was "a hamlet of plain cottages . . . its excitements caused by the activity of insect tribes and the occasional fall of a coconut." The Merrie Monarch, who gave his name to Waikiki's main street, would love the scene today. Some five million tourists visit Oahu every year, and 9 out of 10 of them stay in Waikiki. This urban beach is where all the action is; it's backed by 175 high-rise hotels with more than 33,000 guest rooms and hundreds of bars and restaurants, all in a 1½-square-mile beach zone. Waikiki means honeymooners and sun seekers, bikinis and bare buns, a 'round-the-clock beach party every day of

Ala Wai Golf Course

Ala Wai Blvd.

Nohonani St.

Nahua St.

Walina St.

Kanekapolei St.

Kailuani Ave.

Seaside Ave.

Cleghorn St.

Ave.

Ave.

Pualani Wy.

Leahi Ave.

Paki Ave.

DIAMOND HEAD WAIKIKI

Kaiulani Ave.

Pr. Edward St.

Koa Ave.

Liliuokalani Ave.

Kealohilani Ave.

Ohua

Paoakalani

Kuhio Ave.

Cartwright Rd.

Lemon Rd.

Kapahulu Ave.

Honolulu Zoo

International Market Place

Kalakaua Ave.

MID-WAIKIKI, MAKAI

Waikiki Beach

Kuhio Beach Park

Munsarrat Ave.

Kalakaua Ave.

Kapiolani Park

Gray's Beach

Queen's Surf Beach

Bay

Waikiki Aquarium

To Diamond Head

Natatorium

0   1/4 mi
0   1/4 km

the year—and it's all because of a thin crescent of sand that was shipped over from Molokai. Staying in Waikiki puts you in the heart of it all, but also be aware that this is an on-the-go place with traffic noise 24 hours a day and its share of crime—and it's almost always crowded.

ALA MOANA ★★   A great beach as well as a famous shopping mall, Ala Moana is the retail and transportation heart of Honolulu, a place where you can both shop and suntan in one afternoon. All bus routes lead to the open-air **Ala Moana Center,** across the street from **Ala Moana Beach Park.** This 50-acre, 200-shop behemoth attracts 56 million customers a year (people fly up from Tahiti just to buy their Christmas gifts here). Every European designer from Armani to Vuitton is represented in Honolulu's answer to Beverly Hills' Rodeo Drive. For our purposes, the neighborhood called "Ala Moana" extends along Ala Moana Boulevard from Waikiki in the direction of Diamond Head to downtown Honolulu in the Ewa direction (west) and includes the **Ward Centre** and **Ward Warehouse** complexes, as well as **Restaurant Row.**

DOWNTOWN ★★   A tiny cluster of high-rises west of Waikiki, downtown Honolulu is the financial, business, and government center of Hawaii. On the waterfront stands the iconic 1926 Aloha Tower, now the centerpiece of a harborfront shopping and restaurant complex known as the **Aloha Tower**

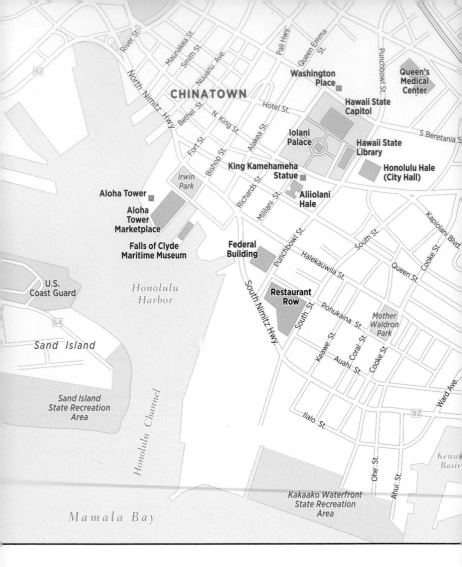

Marketplace. The whole history of Honolulu can be seen in just a few short blocks: Street vendors sell papayas from trucks on skyscraper-lined concrete canyons; joggers and BMWs rush by a lacy palace where U.S. Marines overthrew Hawaii's last queen and stole her kingdom; burly bus drivers sport fragrant white ginger flowers on their dashboards; Methodist churches look like Asian temples; and businessmen wear aloha shirts to billion-dollar meetings.

On the edge of downtown is the **Chinatown Historic District ★★★**, the oldest Chinatown in America and still one of Honolulu's liveliest neighborhoods, a nonstop pageant of people, sights, sounds, smells, and tastes—not all Chinese, now that Southeast Asians, including many Vietnamese,

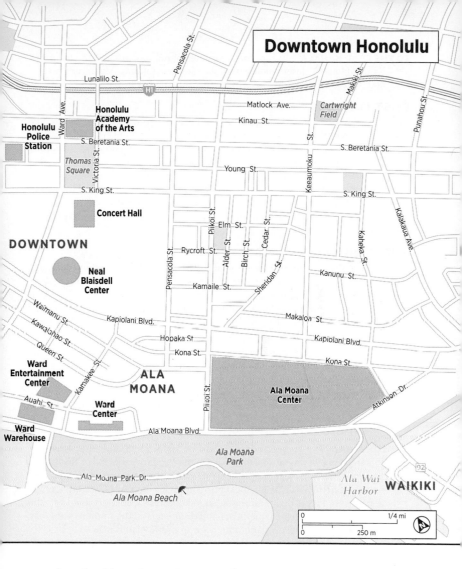

Downtown Honolulu

share the old storefronts. Go on Saturday morning, when everyone shops for fresh goods such as ginger root, fern shoots, and hogs' heads.

Among the historic buildings and Pan-Pacific corporate headquarters are a few hotels, geared mainly toward business travelers. Most visitors prefer the excitement of Waikiki or choose a quieter neighborhood outside the city.

MANOA VALLEY ★ First inhabited by white settlers, the Manoa Valley, above Waikiki, still has vintage *kamaaina* (native-born) homes, one of Hawaii's premier botanical gardens (the Lyon Arboretum), the ever-gushing Manoa Falls, and the 320-acre campus of the University of Hawaii, where 50,000 students hit the books when they're not on the beach.

TO THE EAST: KAHALA Except for the estates of millionaires and the luxurious Kahala Hotel & Resort (home of Hoku's, an outstanding beachfront restaurant), there's not much out this way that's of interest to visitors.

EAST OAHU

Beyond Kahala lies East Honolulu and suburban bedroom communities like Aina Haina, Niu Valley, and Hawaii Kai, among others, all linked by the Kalanianaole Highway and loaded with homes, condos, fast-food joints, and shopping malls. It looks like Southern California on a good day. There are only a few reasons to come here: to have dinner at **Roy's,** the original and still-outstanding Hawaii Regional Cuisine restaurant, in Hawaii Kai; to snorkel at **Hanauma Bay** or watch daredevil surfers at **Sandy Beach;** or to just enjoy the natural splendor of the lovely coastline, which might include a hike to **Makapuu Lighthouse.**

THE WINDWARD COAST

The windward side is the opposite side of the island from Waikiki. On this coast, trade winds blow cooling breezes over gorgeous beaches; rain squalls inspire lush, tropical vegetation; and miles of subdivisions dot the landscape. Bed-and-breakfasts, ranging from oceanfront estates to tiny cottages on quiet residential streets, are everywhere. Vacations here are spent enjoying ocean activities and exploring the surrounding areas. Waikiki is just a 15-minute drive away.

KAILUA ★ The biggest little beach town in Hawaii, Kailua sits at the foot of the sheer green Koolau mountain range, on a great bay with two of Hawaii's best beaches. The town itself is a funky low-rise cluster of timeworn shops and homes. Kailua has become the B&B capital of Hawaii; it's an affordable alternative to Waikiki, with rooms and vacation rentals starting at $60 a day. With the prevailing trade winds whipping up a cooling breeze, Kailua attracts windsurfers from around the world.

KANEOHE BAY ★ Helter-skelter suburbia sprawls around the edges of Kaneohe, one of the most scenic bays in the Pacific. A handful of B&Bs dots its edge. After you clear the trafficky maze of town, Oahu returns to its more natural state. This great bay beckons you to get out on the water; you can depart from Heeia Boat Harbor on snorkel or fishing charters and visit Ahu a Laka a, the sandbar that appears and disappears in the middle of the bay. From here, you'll have a panoramic view of the Koolau Range.

KUALOA/LAIE ★★ The upper-northeast shore is one of Oahu's most sacred places, an early Hawaiian landing spot where kings dipped their sails, cliffs hold ancient burial sites, and ghosts still march in the night. Sheer cliffs stab the reef-fringed seacoast, while old fish ponds are tucked along the two-lane coast road that winds past empty gold-sand beaches around beautiful Kahana Bay. Thousands "explore" the South Pacific at the **Polynesian Cultural Center,** in Laie, a Mormon settlement with its own Tabernacle Choir of sweet Samoan harmony.

THE NORTH SHORE ★★★

Here's the Hawaii of Hollywood—giant waves, surfers galore, tropical jungles, waterfalls, and mysterious Hawaiian temples. If you're looking for a quieter vacation that's closer to nature and filled with swimming, snorkeling, diving, and surfing, or just plain hanging out on some of the world's most beautiful beaches, the North Shore is your place. The artsy little beach town of **Haleiwa** ★★ and the surrounding shoreline seem a world away from Waikiki. The North Shore boasts good restaurants, shopping, and cultural activities—but they come with the quiet of country living. Bed-and-breakfasts are the most common accommodations, but there's one first-class hotel and some vacation rentals as well. Be forewarned: It's a long trip—nearly an hour's drive—to Honolulu and Waikiki, and it's about twice as rainy on the North Shore as in Honolulu.

CENTRAL OAHU: THE EWA PLAIN

Flanked by the Koolau and Waianae mountain ranges, the hot, sunbaked Ewa Plain runs up and down the center of Oahu. Once covered with sandalwood forests (hacked down for the China trade) and later the sugar cane and pineapple backbone of Hawaii, Ewa today sports a new crop: suburban houses stretching to the sea. But let your eye wander west to the Waianae Range and Mount Kaala, at 4,020 feet the highest summit on Oahu; up there in the misty rainforest, native birds thrive in the hummocky bog. In 1914, the U.S. Army pitched a tent camp on the plain; author James Jones would later call **Schofield Barracks** "the most beautiful army post in the world." Hollywood filmed Jones's *From Here to Eternity* here.

LEEWARD OAHU: THE WAIANAE COAST

The west coast of Oahu is a hot and dry place of dramatic beauty: white-sand beaches bordering the deep-blue ocean, steep verdant green cliffs, and miles of Mother Nature's wildness. Except for the luxurious JW Marriott Ihilani Resort & Spa, Roy's Restaurant at the Ko Olina Resort, and the Makaha Resort Golf Club, you'll find virtually no tourist services out here. The funky west-coast villages of Nanakuli, Waianae, and Makaha are the last stands of native Hawaiians. This side of Oahu is seldom visited, except by surfers bound for **Yokohama Bay** and those coming to see needle-nose **Kaena Point** (the island's westernmost outpost), which has a coastal wilderness park.

Finding Your Way Around, Oahu Style

Mainlanders sometimes find the directions given by locals a bit confusing. Seldom will you hear the terms *east, west, north,* and *south;* instead, islanders refer to directions as either **makai** (ma-*kae*), meaning toward the sea, or **mauka** (*mow*-kah), toward the mountains. In Honolulu, people use **Diamond Head** as a direction meaning to the east (in the direction of the world-famous crater called Diamond Head), and **Ewa** as a direction meaning to the west (toward the town called Ewa, on the other side of Pearl Harbor).

So if you ask a local for directions, this is what you're likely to hear: "Drive 2 blocks makai (toward the sea), and then turn Diamond Head (east) at the stoplight. Go 1 block, and turn mauka (toward the mountains). It's on the Ewa (western) side of the street."

GETTING AROUND

BY CAR   Oahu residents own more than 686,000 registered vehicles, but they have only 1,500 miles of mostly two-lane roads to use. That's 400 cars for every mile, a fact that becomes abundantly clear during morning and evening rush hours. You can avoid the gridlock by driving between 9am and 3pm or after 6pm.

All of the major car-rental firms have agencies on Oahu, at the airport and in Waikiki. For a complete listing, see chapter 11. For tips on insurance and driving rules in Hawaii, see p. 76.

BY BUS   One of the best deals anywhere, **TheBus** will take you around the whole island for $2.50. In fact, every day more than 260,000 people use the system's 68 lines and 4,000 bus stops. TheBus goes almost everywhere almost all the time. The most popular route is **no. 8,** which arrives every 10 minutes or so to shuttle people between Waikiki and Ala Moana Center (the ride takes 15–20 min.). The **no. 19** (Airport/Hickam), **no. 20** (Airport/Halawa Gate), **no. 47** (Waipahu), and **no. 58** (Waikiki/Ala Moana) also cover the same stretch. Waikiki service begins daily at 5am and runs until midnight; most buses run about every 15 minutes during the day and every 30 minutes in the evening.

The Circle Island–North Shore route is **no. 52** (Wahiawa/Circle Island); the Circle Island–South Shore route is **no. 55** (Kaneohe/Circle Island). Both routes leave Ala Moana Center every 30 minutes and take about 4½ hours to circle the island. Be aware that at Turtle Bay Resort, just outside Kahuku, the 52 becomes the 55 and returns to Honolulu via the coast, and the 55 becomes the 52 and returns to Honolulu on the inland route. (Translation: You have to get off and switch buses to complete your island tour.) There are express buses available to some areas (for example, **no. 54** to Pearl City, **no. 85** to Kailua, and **no. 85** to Kaneohe).

For more information on routes and schedules, call **TheBus** (*©* **808/848-5555,** or 808/296-1818 for recorded information) or check out **www.thebus.org**, which provides timetables and maps for all routes, plus directions to many local attractions and a list of upcoming events. Taking TheBus is often easier than parking your car.

BY TROLLEY   It's fun to ride the 34-seat, open-air, motorized **Waikiki Trolley** (*©* **800/824-8804** or 808/593-2822; www.waikikitrolley.com), which looks like a San Francisco cable car (see "Orientation Tours," on p. 232). The trolley loops around Waikiki and downtown Honolulu, stopping every 40 minutes at 12 key places like Iolani Palace, Chinatown, the State Capitol, the King Kamehameha Statue, the Mission Houses Museum, the Aloha Tower, the Honolulu Academy of Arts, the Hawaii Maritime Center, Fisherman's Wharf, and Restaurant Row. The driver provides commentary along the way. Stops on the new 2-hour, fully narrated Ocean Coast Line (the blue line) of the southeast side of Oahu include Sea Life Park, Diamond Head, and Waikiki Beach. A 1-day trolley pass—which costs $30 for adults, $20 for seniors over 62, and $13 for kids ages 4 to 11—allows you to jump on and off all day long (8:30am–11:35pm). Four-day passes cost

$52 for adults, $31 for seniors, and $20 for kids 4 to 11 (lower prices available online).

BY TAXI   Oahu's major cab companies offer 24-hour, islandwide, radio-dispatched service, with multilingual drivers and air-conditioned cars, limos, and vans, including vehicles equipped with wheelchair lifts (there's a $9 charge for wheelchairs). Fares are standard for all taxi firms; from the airport, expect to pay about $35 to $40 to Waikiki, about $20 to $35 to downtown, $60 and up to Kailua, $60 plus to Hawaii Kai, and about $90 to $125 to the North Shore (plus tip). Plus there is a $4.75 fee per piece of luggage.

For a flat fee of $25 to $30, **Star Taxi** ★ (© **800/671-2999** or 808/942-STAR [7827]; www.startaxihawaii.com) will take up to four passengers from the airport to Waikiki (with no extra charge for baggage); however, you must book in advance, then call Star the day before your arrival with your arrival time and flight number. After you pick up your luggage, call again for directions on where to meet your car.

For a metered cab, try **Charley's Taxi & Tours** (© 808/531-1333), **Elite Limousine Service** (© 808/735-2431), or **V.I.P. Transportation** (© 808/836-0317) **Robert's Taxi and Shuttle** (© 808/261-8555) serves windward Oahu, while **Hawaii Kai Hui/Koko Head Taxi** (© 808/396-6633) serves east Honolulu/southeast Oahu.

[Fast FACTS] OAHU

American Express   The Honolulu office is at 677 Ala Moana Blvd., 100 (© **808/585-3200**), and is open Monday through Friday from 8am to 5pm. There's also an office at **Hilton Hawaiian Village,** 2005 Kalia Rd. (© **808/947-2607** or 808/951-0644).

Dentists   If you need dental attention on Oahu, contact the **Hawaii Dental Association** (© **808/593-7956**). They prefer that you use their website, www.hawaiidental association.net, as they won't recommend any one dentist.

Doctors   **Straub Doctors on Call,** 2222 Kalakaua Ave., at Lewers Street, Honolulu (© **808/971-6000**), can dispatch a van if you need help getting to the main clinic or to any of its additional clinics at the Hilton Hawaiian Village and the Sheraton Princess.

Emergencies   Call © **911** for police, fire, and ambulance. For the **Poison Control Center,** call © **800/222-1222;** you will automatically be directed to the Poison Control Center for the area code of the phone you are calling from.

Hospitals   Hospitals offering 24-hour emergency care include **Queen's Medical Center,** 1301 Punchbowl St. (© 808/538-9011); **Kuakini Medical Center,** 347 Kuakini St. (© 808/536-2236); **Straub Clinic and Hospital,** 888 S. King St. (© 808/522-4000); **Moanalua Medical Center,** 3288 Moanalua Rd. (© 808/432-0000); **Kapiolani Medical Center for Women and Children,** 1319 Punahou St. (© 808/983-8633); and **Kapiolani Medical Center at Pali Momi,** 98–1079 Moanalua Rd. (© 808/486-6000).

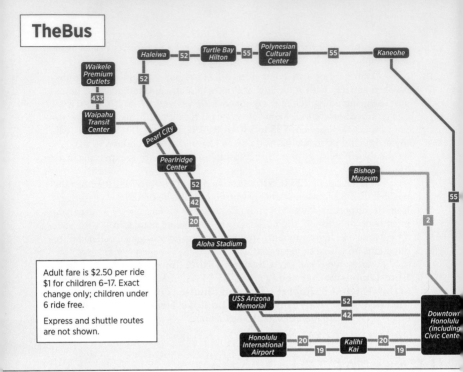

TheBus

Waikele Premium Outlets

433

Waipahu Transit Center

Haleiwa — 52 — Turtle Bay Hilton — 55 — Polynesian Cultural Center — 55 — Kaneohe

52

Pearl City

Pearlridge Center

52

42

20

Aloha Stadium

Bishop Museum

55

2

Adult fare is $2.50 per ride $1 for children 6–17. Exact change only; children under 6 ride free.

Express and shuttle routes are not shown.

USS Arizona Memorial — 52 — 42

Downtown Honolulu (including Civic Center

Honolulu International Airport — 20 — 19 — Kalihi Kai — 20 — 19

Getting There on TheBus:

Academy of Arts Take #2 bus (School/Middle St) to Beretania St. and Ward Ave.

Ala Moana Center Take bus #19 & #20 AIRPORT. Return via #19 WAIKIKI, or cross Ala Moana Blvd. for #20.

Bishop Museum Take #2 SCHOOL STREET. Get off at Kapalama St., cross School St., walk down Bernice St. Return to School St. and take #2 WAIKIKI.

Byodo-In Temple Take bus #2 to Hotel-Alakea St. (TRF) to #55 KANEOHE-KAHALUU. Get off at Valley of the Temple cemetery. Also #19 and #20 AIRPORT to King-Alakea St., (TRF) on Alakea St. to #55 KANEOHE-KAHALUU.

Circle Island Take a bus to ALA MOANA CENTER (TRF) to #52 WAHIAWA CIRCLE ISLAND or #55 KANEOHE CIRCLE ISLAND. This is a 4-hour bus ride.

Chinatown or Downtown Take any #2 bus going out of Waikiki to Hotel St. Return, take #2 WAIKIKI on Hotel St., or #19 or #20 on King St.

The Contemporary Museum & **Punchbowl (National Cemetery of the Pacific)** Take #2 bus (TRF) at Alapai St. to #15 MAKIKI-PACIFIC HGTS. Return, take #15 and get off at King St., area (TRF) #2 WAIKIKI.

Diamond Head Crater Take #22 HAWAII KAI-SEA LIFE PARK to the crater. Take a flashlight. Return to the same area and take #22 WAIKIKI.

Dole Plantation Take bus to ALA MOANA CENTER (TRF) to #52 WAHIAWA CIRCLE ISLAND.

Foster Botanical Garden Take #2 bus to Hotel-Riviera St. Walk to Vineyard Blvd. Return to Hotel St. Take #2 WAIKIKI, or take #4 NUUANU and get off at Nuuanu-Vineyard. Cross Nuuanu Ave. and walk one block to the gardens.

Hanauma Bay Take #22 Beach Bus.

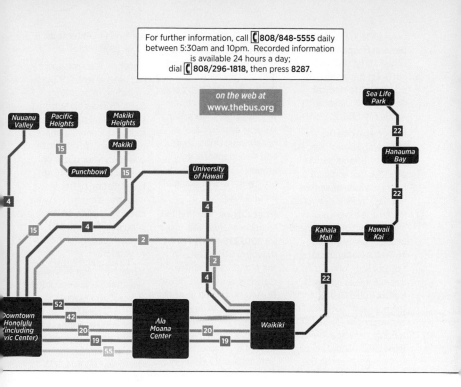

For further information, call ☎ **808/848-5555** daily between 5:30am and 10pm. Recorded information is available 24 hours a day; dial ☎ **808/296-1818**, then press **8287**.

on the web at
www.thebus.org

Aloha Tower Marketplace & **Hawaii Maritime Center** Take #19-#20 AIRPORT and get off at Alakea–Ala Moana. Cross the street to the Aloha Tower.

Honolulu Zoo Take any bus on Kuhio Ave. going DIAMOND HEAD direction to Kapahulu Ave.

Iolani Palace (also **State Capitol, Honolulu Hale, Kawaihao Church, Mission Houses, Queen's Hospital, King Kamehameha Statue, State Judiciary Bldg.**) Take any #2 bus and get off at Punchbowl and Beretania St. Walk to King St. Return #2 WAIKIKI on King St.

Kahala Mall Take #22 HAWAII KAI–SEA LIFE PARK to Kilauea Ave. Return, #22 WAIKIKI.

Pearl Harbor (*Arizona* **Memorial**) Take #20 AIRPORT. Get off across from Memorial, or take a bus to ALA MOANA CENTER (TRF) to #52.

Polynesian Cultural Center Take a bus to ALA MOANA CENTER (TRF) to #55 KANEOHE CIRCLE ISLAND. Bus ride takes 2 hours one-way.

Queen Emma's Summer Home Take #4 NUUANU, or board a bus to ALA MOANA CENTER (TRF) to #55 KANEOHE.

Sea Life Park Take #22 HAWAII KAI-SEA LIFE PARK. #22 will stop at Hanauma Bay en route to the park.

University of Hawaii Take #4 NUUANU. The bus will go to the University en route to Nuuanu.

Waimea Valley Audobon Center Take a bus to ALA MOANA CENTER (TRF) to #52 WAHIAWA CIRCLE ISLAND or #55 KANEOHE CIRCLE ISLAND.

Waikele Premium Outlets Take bus #42 from Waikiki to Wapahu Transit Center, then bus #433 to Waikele.

Central Oahu has **Wahiawa General Hospital,** 128 Lehua St. (🕿 808/621-8411). On the windward side is **Castle Medical Center,** 640 Ulukahiki St., Kailua (🕿 808/263-5500).

Internet Access ShakaNet, Hawaii's largest wireless Internet service provider, has completed the first phase of its free Wireless Waikiki network. Phase one covers a significant portion of Waikiki and includes an estimated 1,000 hotel rooms, portions of the Honolulu Zoo, Kapiolani Park, Queen's Beach, Kuhio Beach, and the adjacent shoreline. The boundaries of Phase I are roughly Kalakaua Avenue from Liliuokalani Avenue to Queen's Beach in the Diamond Head direction, and Liliuokalani Avenue/ Kuhio Avenue on the Ewa side, down Kuhio Avenue across Kapiolani Park to Monsarrat Avenue.

Newspapers The *Honolulu Advertiser* and *Honolulu Star-Bulletin* are Oahu's daily papers. *Pacific Business News* and *Honolulu Weekly* are weekly papers. *Honolulu Weekly,* available free at restaurants, clubs, shops, and newspaper racks around Oahu, is the best source for what's going on around town.

Post Office To find the location nearest you, call 🕿 **800/275-8777.** The downtown location is in the old U.S. Post Office, Customs, and Court House Building (referred to as the Old Federal Building) at 335 Merchant St., across from Iolani Palace and next to the Kamehameha Statue (bus: 2). Other branch offices can be found in Waikiki, at 330 Saratoga Ave. (Diamond Head side of Fort DeRussy; bus: 19 or 20), and in the

Ala Moana Center (bus: 8, 19, or 20).

Safety Recently there has been a series of purse-snatching incidents in Oahu. Thieves work from slow-moving cars or on foot. The Honolulu police department advises that you carry your purse on the shoulder away from the street or, better yet, wear the strap across your chest instead of on one shoulder. If you're carrying a clutch bag, hold it close to your chest.

Weather For National Weather Service recorded forecasts for Oahu, call 🕿 **808/973-4380** (this number has options for marine and surf reports); for elsewhere on the island, call 🕿 **808/973-4381.** For marine reports, call 🕿 **808/973-4382.** For surf reports, call 🕿 **808/ 973-4383.**

WHERE TO STAY

Before you reach for the phone to book a place to stay, consider when you'll be visiting. The high season, when hotels are full and rates are at their peak, is mid-December to March. The secondary high season, when rates are high but rooms are somewhat easier to come by, is June to September. The low seasons—when you can expect fewer tourists and better deals—are April to June and September to mid-December. (For more on Hawaii's travel seasons, see "When to Go," on p. 62.) No matter when you travel, you can often get the best rate at many of Waikiki's hotels by booking a package.

For a description of each neighborhood, see "The Island in Brief" (p. 131). It can help you decide where you'd like to base yourself.

Remember that hotel and room taxes of 14.25% (as of July 1, 2010) will be added to your bill (Oahu has a .005% additional tax that the other islands do not have). And don't forget about parking charges—at up to $28 a day in Waikiki, they can add up quickly.

BED & BREAKFASTS For a more intimate experience, try staying in a B&_ Accommodations on Oahu calling themselves bed-and-breakfasts vary from a room in a house (sometimes with a shared bathroom) to a vacation rental in a private cottage. Breakfast can be anything from coffee, pastries, and fruit to a home-cooked gourmet meal with just-caught fresh fish. Due to space limitations, I can include only a handful of Oahu's best B&Bs below; for a wider selection, check out *Frommer's Honolulu, Waikiki & Oahu,* or call one of the statewide booking agencies recommended in "Tips on Accommodations" (p. 101).

AIRPORT HOTELS If you're arriving late at night or leaving early in the morning, consider a hotel near the airport (just for a night—this is not the place to spend your whole vacation). **Best Western–The Plaza Hotel,** 3253 N. Nimitz Hwy., Honolulu (✆ **800/780-7234** or 808/836-3636; www.best western.com), has rooms from $129 (now charging $10 per day for parking); the **Ohana Honolulu Airport Hotel** (✆ **800/462-6262** or 808/836-0661; www.ohanahotels.com) has rooms from $99 ($10 per day for parking). Both offer free airport shuttle service.

Waikiki

EWA WAIKIKI

All the hotels listed below are located between the ocean and Kalakaua Avenue, and between Ala Wai Terrace in the Ewa (western) direction and Olohana Street and Fort DeRussy Park in the Diamond Head (eastern) direction.

Very Expensive

Outrigger Reef on the Beach ★★ Location, location, location! Waikiki's only condominium on the beach in Waikiki, the Outrigger is part of the well-respected chain in Hawaii that promises reliable, great accommodations at reasonable prices. The units range from studio (a hotel room with kitchen) to four bedroom units, most with ocean views, offering the amenities of a condominium (especially a kitchen) with the views of Waikiki Beach. This big hotel is right on Waikiki Beach, across from Fort DeRussy, with three towers of beautifully appointed rooms (completely remodeled in 2007–08), excellent service, and a myriad of activities, shops, and restaurants. The $100 million in renovations really was closer to a "rebuild" and the rooms were redesigned and upgraded (with 32-in. LCD TVs). The new porte-cochere, which resembles a traditional A-frame canoe longhouse, in fact houses a 100-year-old Hawaiian fishing canoe. Throughout the lobby are enough shops to qualify as a mini-mall. Off the lobby is an enormous swimming pool, with some 300 chaise lounges surrounding it, three whirlpool spas, and food and cocktail service within hailing distance. And, of course, beautiful Waikiki is in the backyard. The rooms have the usual well-designed, well-appointed Outrigger furnishings and decorations with great views and plenty of extra room for a couple of kids to bed down. Blackout drapes are a nice touch for jet-lagged travelers, as is a hospitality room (with showers) for early check-ins or late checkouts. The on-site Shorebird Beach Broiler is an immensely popular oceanside spot offering buffet breakfasts and broil-your-own dinners. A new restaurant, Kani Ka Pila Grille, offers great meals and terrific live Hawaiian entertainment.

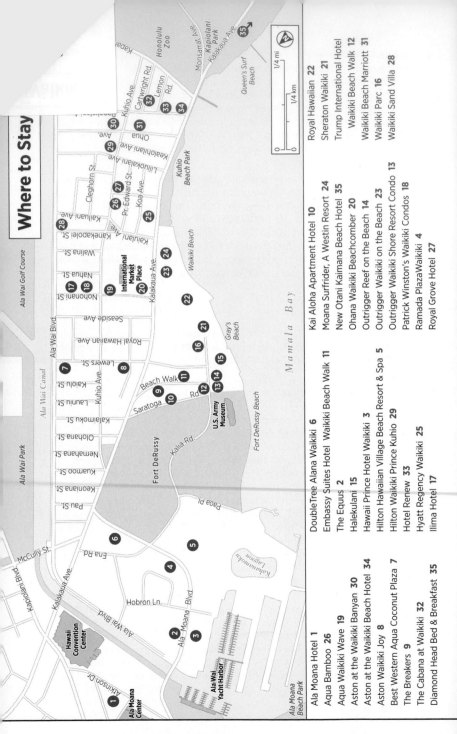

Where to Stay

Ala Moana Hotel 1
Aqua Bamboo 26
Aqua Waikiki Wave 19
Aston at the Waikiki Banyan 30
Aston at the Waikiki Beach Hotel 34
Aston Waikiki Joy 8
Best Western Aqua Coconut Plaza 7
The Breakers 9
The Cabana at Waikiki 32
Diamond Head Bed & Breakfast 35

DoubleTree Alana Waikiki 6
Embassy Suites Hotel Waikiki Beach Walk 11
The Equus 2
Halekulani 15
Hawaii Prince Hotel Waikiki 3
Hilton Hawaiian Village Beach Resort & Spa 5
Hilton Waikiki Prince Kuhio 29
Hotel Renew 33
Hyatt Regency Waikiki 25
Ilima Hotel 17

Kai Aloha Apartment Hotel 10
Moana Surfrider, A Westin Resort 24
New Otani Kaimana Beach Hotel 35
Ohana Waikiki Beachcomber 20
Outrigger Reef on the Beach 14
Outrigger Waikiki on the Beach 23
Outrigger Waikiki Shore Resort Condo 13
Patrick Winston's Waikiki Condos 18
Ramada PlazaWaikiki 4
Royal Grove Hotel 27

Royal Hawaiian 22
Sheraton Waikiki 21
Trump International Hotel
Waikiki Beach Walk 12
Waikiki Beach Marriott 31
Waikiki Parc 16
Waikiki Sand Villa 28

2169 Kalia Rd. (at Saratoga Rd.), Waikiki, HI 96815. ☎ **800/OUTRIGGER** (688-7444) or 808/923-3111. Fax 808/924-4957. www.outriggerreef.com. 639 units. $369–$679 hotel room double; $599–$1,299 1-bedroom double; $2,099–$2,299 2-bedroom double; $3,449 3-bedroom double; $4,599 4-bedroom double. Extra person (over 2 adults) $50 per person per night. Children 18 and under stay free in parent's room. AE, DC, DISC, MC, V. Valet parking only (no self-parking) $25. Bus: 19 or 20. **Amenities:** 2 restaurants; 2 bars; babysitting; outdoor pools. *In room:* A/C, TV, hair dryer, high-speed Internet access ($10 per day), kitchen.

Trump International Hotel Waikiki Beach Walk ★★★   Overlooking the Fort DeRussy Park—and from the upper floors, the beach of Waikiki—this 38-story, 464-unit high-rise is the latest hotel to open in this visitor destination area. It proudly bears the name of the U.S.'s most famous real estate developer, Donald Trump. This luxury hotel, made up of condominium units, has only one caveat: It is not on the beach. But it is across the street from the beach (well, across the street and behind another large condominium hotel). Plus, Trump offers a "beach attaché," sort of a beach butler to help carry your beach toys (or you can get a complimentary beach bag with cooler, drinks, towels, and reading material) from the hotel to the beach. They also offer a beach desk on the beach for renting lounge chairs, umbrellas, and so on. They will even take your order and deliver lunch, if you ask.

An exquisite spa, two restaurants (including **BLT Steak,** p. 170), and excellent concierge service make this property one of Waikiki's most luxurious accommodations. Just a few notes: There is a very small "plunge" pool on the property (families with kids, take note—this is not a pool for them). Although absolutely beautiful and luxurious, the property does not "feel" like Hawaii, but more like a luxury hotel in New York. If you are looking for a taste of the islands, this may not be your property.

223 Saratoga Rd. (at Kalia Rd.), Waikiki, HI 96815. ☎ **877/683-7401** or 808/683-7401. Fax 808/683-7788. www.trumpwaikikihotel.com. 464 units. $295–$725 studio; $525–$1,075 one-bedroom. AE, DC, DISC, MC, V. Valet parking $28. Bus: 19 or 20. **Amenities:** 2 restaurants (including **BLT,** p. 170); lounge; babysitting; concierge; fitness center; outdoor "plunge" pool; room service; spa. *In room:* A/C, TV, hair dryer, high-speed Internet access ($20 per day), kitchen.

Expensive

Hawaii Prince Hotel Waikiki ★★   For a vacation with a view and the feel of a palace, stay in this striking $150-million modern structure (actually, twin 33-story high-tech towers). The lobby is a mass of pink Italian marble with English slate accents; a grand piano sits in the midst of the raised seating area, where high tea is served every afternoon. Culinary options include two great restaurants, one with award-winning Japanese cuisine and one with Euro-Asian buffets, plus a lobby coffee bar in the morning and a wine bar in the afternoon. The outdoor pool is one of the few saltwater pools in Waikiki, with no chemicals or chlorine added. A glass elevator offers views of Honolulu and the Ala Wai Yacht Harbor. Guest rooms include floor-to-ceiling sliding-glass windows (sorry, no lanais). All of the comfortably appointed rooms are basically the same, but the higher the floor, the higher the price.

Following Japanese standards, the level of service is impeccable; no detail is ignored, and no request is too small. The location is perfect for shopping—Ala Moana Center is a 10-minute walk away—and Waikiki's beaches are just a 5-minute walk (both are also accessible via the hotel's own shuttle bus).

100 Holomoana St. (just across Ala Wai Canal Bridge, on the ocean side of Ala Moana Blvd.), Honolulu, HI 96815. ✆ **800/321-OAHU** (6248) or 808/956-1111. Fax 808/946-0811. www.prince resortshawaii.com. 521 units. $199–$249 double; from $379 suite. Extra person $60. Children 17 and under stay free in parent's room using existing bedding. AE, DC, DISC, MC, V. Valet parking $21; self-parking $15. Bus: 19 or 20. **Amenities:** 2 restaurants (see Prince Court, p. 173); outdoor bar; babysitting; concierge; fitness center; 27-hole golf club (40-min. drive away in Ewa Beach via hotel shuttle); Jacuzzi; outdoor pool; room service; spa. *In room:* A/C, TV, fridge, hair dryer, high-speed Internet access ($12 per day).

Hilton Hawaiian Village Beach Resort & Spa ★★ ☺ Sprawling over 20 acres, this is Waikiki's biggest resort—a minicity unto itself, so big it even has its own post office. If you're looking for a big resort "village" that has everything you need for a lively, activity-packed vacation, this is your place. You'll find tropical gardens dotted with exotic wildlife (flamingos, peacocks, and even tropical penguins), award-winning restaurants, 100 different shops, a secluded lagoon, two minigolf courses, and a gorgeous stretch of Waikiki Beach. The children's program, one of Waikiki's best, offers a wide range of educational and fun activities, and at three of the resort's restaurants, kids ages 4 and under eat free.

There's a wide choice of accommodations. Rooms, which range from simply lovely to ultradeluxe, are housed in five towers, each with its own restaurants and shopping. This division cuts down on the chaotic, impersonal feeling you can get from a resort this size. (Still, those seeking a more intimate experience might want to look elsewhere.) All rooms are large and beautifully furnished; if you can afford them, I highly recommend the ones in the Alii Tower, located right on the

✎ affordable parking IN WAIKIKI

It *is* possible to find affordable parking in Waikiki if you know where to look. I've divided up the parking in Waikiki into free or metered parking and carry-a-big-wallet parking.

FREE OR METERED PARKING:

o All side streets in Waikiki

o Ala Wai Boulevard along the Ala Wai Canal, 180 stalls

o Waikiki Zoo, 217 stalls

o Kuhio Avenue (at Lewers)—this 65-stall metered parking lot is the best secret in Waikiki

CARRY-A-BIG-WALLET PARKING:

o Hilton Hawaiian Village, 2005 Kalia Rd., free if you eat here (up to 6 hr.), not so free if you don't ($7 an hour)

o Ohana East, 150 Kaiulani Ave., 238 stalls, $6 per hour, maximum 5 hours

o Waikiki Beach Marriott, 2552 Kalakaua Ave. (entrance on Ohua Ave.), validated and reduced fee if you eat here, $4 per half-hour if you don't

o Sheraton Princess Kaiulani, 120 Kaiulani Ave., validated and reduced fee if you eat here; otherwise, $5 an hour

o Sheraton Waikiki and Royal Hawaiian, 2365 Kalakaua Ave., 4 hours free with validation from one of the resort's restaurants; otherwise, $5 per hour

o Hawaii Prince Hotel, 100 Holomoana St., $3 self-parking or $5 valet parking with validation from hotel restaurant; otherwise, $1 per hour up to 4 hours

ocean. Guests in these 348 amenity-laden rooms and suites get the royal treatment, including in-room registration, an exclusive health club and pool, and the
full attention of a multilingual staff. But if you opt for one of the more affordable
towers, you'll still be happy.

The **Mandara Spa ★★** is a state-of-the-art fitness center and traditional
body-treatment spa. A recently added 24-hour business center is located on the
ground floor of the Diamond Head tower. The latest addition is the $6-million
Ocean Crystal Chapel, Waikiki's only free-standing resort wedding chapel,
ready for couples to say "I do."

2005 Kalia Rd. (at Ala Moana Blvd.), Honolulu, HI 96815. ℂ **800/HILTONS** [445-8667] or 808/
949-4321. Fax 808/951-5458. www.hiltonhawaiianvillage.com. 2,860 units. $199–$610 double;
from $305 suite. Extra person (over 2 adults) $50 per person. Children 18 and under stay free in
parent's room. AE, DC, DISC, MC, V. Valet parking $30; self-parking $24. Bus: 19 or 20. **Amenities:** 16 restaurants (including Bali Steak & Seafood, p. 172); 5 bars; babysitting; year-round children's program; concierge; concierge-level rooms; fitness center w/high-tech equipment;
5 outdoor pools; room service; superplush Mandara Spa; watersports equipment rentals.
In room: A/C, TV, fridge, hair dryer, high-speed Internet access ($17 per day).

Moderate

DoubleTree Alana Hotel Waikiki ★ This boutique hotel is a welcome oasis
of beauty, comfort, and prompt service (operated by the Hilton Hawaiian Village). It's an intimate choice, offering the amenities of a much larger, more luxurious hotel at more affordable prices. The guest rooms last underwent a $2.9-million
renovation a few years ago, with new carpet, wallpaper, woven-palm-frond curtains, refinished and reupholstered furniture, 25-inch TVs, and "Sweet Dream"
pillow-top beds. Guests can enjoy wireless "g" Internet service throughout the
hotel and hard-wired DSL service on four floors. Some of the rooms are small but
make good use of space and offer all the amenities you'd expect from a more
expensive hotel. Many guests are business travelers who expect top-drawer service—and the Alana Waikiki delivers. The staff is attentive to detail and willing
to go to any lengths to make you happy. Waikiki Beach is a 10-minute walk away;
the convention center is about a 7-minute walk.

1956 Ala Moana Blvd. (on the Ewa side, near Kalakaua Ave.), Honolulu, HI 96815. ℂ **800/222-
TREE** (8733) or 808/941-7275. Fax 808/949-0996. www.doubletree.com. 317 units. From $134
double; from $189 suite. Extra person $40. Children 17 and under stay free in parent's room. AE,
DC, DISC, MC, V. Valet parking $27. Bus: 19 or 20. **Amenities:** Bar; concierge; poolside fitness
center; outdoor heated pool; room service. *In room:* A/C, TV, fridge, hair dryer, Wi-Fi ($10 per day
in room, free in lobby).

Ramada Plaza Waikiki Formerly the Holiday Inn Waikiki, located just 2
blocks from the beach, 2 blocks from Ala Moana Center, and a 7-minute walk
from the convention center, this Ramada Inn has a great location and offers the
chain's usual amenities for prices that are quite reasonable (for Waikiki, anyway).
Just 1 month before the change in management from Holiday Inn to Ramada in
2010, the property finished a 15-month, $3-million renovation, upgrading all the
guest rooms (all have the Serta Presidential Plush Suite mattress, usually found
at more expensive hotels). The 16-story property was built in 1969 and called the
Dynasty Hotel; in 1993 it became a Holiday Inn. Today the Ramada Plaza is the
highest tier of Ramada's three brands. All rooms, which have a modern Asian look
(60% of the guests are from Asia, including flight crews from China Airlines and

IT'S NOT YOUR FATHER'S waikiki

More big changes are in store for Waikiki. The Outrigger has completed its $500-million-plus Waikiki Beach Walk project (see "Waikiki Beach Walk" on p. 154), which seems to have inspired a host of renovations, upgrading, and rebranding of other properties in Waikiki. The upshot is that Waikiki is going through major changes, and in the next few years the world-famous resort area will be even more beautiful, with more upscale properties.

Hilton took over the moderately priced Radisson Waikiki Prince Kuhio (now the **Hilton Waikiki Prince Kuhio**) and put some $55 million into renovations. Most of it went into upgrading the rooms, which now feature 42-inch plasma-screen TVs that link to laptops, portable DVD players, and MP3 players. Also new is a 24-hour eatery, **MAC 24-7** (p. 174). Rates are fairly moderate (for Waikiki), from $169.

Aqua Hotels and Resorts, which specializes in boutique properties, upgraded and rebranded several off-the-beach properties in Waikiki. Its 10 hotels are divided into three levels (Elite, Moderate, and Lite), all offering such amenities as spas and fitness centers, daily continental breakfast, minikitchens, and free wireless and high-speed Internet in each room. **Aqua Waikiki Wave** (formerly the Coral Reef), which fits in Aqua's Moderate category, has rates starting at $94.

Not to be outdone, three of the five **Starwood** properties in Waikiki have nearly completed huge renovations:

o **Royal Hawaiian:** Just completed are renovations to all rooms and a new restaurant, Surf Lanai (which replaces the old Surf Room at the ocean's edge), a renovated pool/beachfront area, and the Monarch Room.

o **Moana Surfrider, A Westin Resort:** Rebranded in 2007 from a Sheraton to a Westin, this hotel has renovated the Banyan Wing and added a spa on the entire second floor.

o **Sheraton Waikiki:** Look for continued room renovations and upgrades, new lobby, new restaurants, and new pool.

Japan Airlines), come with either a king-size bed or two double beds. The property sits back from the street, so noise is at a minimum.

1830 Ala Moana Blvd. (btw. Hobron Lane and Kalia Rd.), Honolulu, HI 96815. ✆ **800/272-6232** or 808/955-1111. Fax 808/947-1799. www.ramadaplazawaikiki.com. 198 units. $129–$154 double; from $289 suite. Children 19 and under stay free in parent's room using existing bedding. AE, DISC, MC, V. Parking $15. Bus: 19 or 20. **Amenities:** Restaurant; fitness room; outdoor pool; room service. *In room:* A/C, TV, fridge, hair dryer, free high-speed Internet access.

Inexpensive

The Equus Formerly the Hawaii Polo Inn, and now owned by Aqua Hotels and Resorts, this small boutique hotel has been renovated and upgraded into a very comfortable inn within walking distance to the Ala Moana Center, Waikiki Beach, and the Hawaii Convention Center. The suites have microwaves and hot plates. A few years ago, management added more studio units (with kitchenette, two-burner stove, dishwasher, microwave, and such) next door at the Aqua Waikiki Marina. *Warning:* Ala Moana Boulevard is very noisy; ask for a room in the back or bring earplugs.

1696 Ala Moana Blvd. (btw. Hobron Lane and Ala Wai Canal), Honolulu, HI 96815. ℂ **866/406-2782** or 808/949-0061. Fax 808/949-4906. www.aquaresorts.com/aqua-equus. 68 units (all with shower only). $68–$119 double; $149–$229 suite; from $69 studio with kitchenette in Aqua Waikiki Marina next door. Extra person $50. Children 18 and under stay free in parent's room. AE, DISC, MC, V. Parking $19. Bus: 19 or 20. **Amenities:** Tiny outdoor wading pool. *In room:* A/C, TV, fridge, hair dryer, free Internet access, microwave.

MID-WAIKIKI, MAKAI

All the hotels listed below are between Kalakaua Avenue and the ocean, and between Fort DeRussy in the Ewa (western) direction and Kaiulani Street in the Diamond Head (eastern) direction.

Very Expensive

Embassy Suites Hotel–Waikiki Beach Walk ★★★ ☺   This ultraluxurious all-suite hotel chain, famous for its complimentary all-you-can-eat, cooked-to-order breakfast and evening manager's cocktail reception, opened in 2007 at one of the best locations in Waikiki. The beach is just a block away, and the hotel sits in the midst of the shops and restaurants of the newly opened **Waikiki Beach Walk** (p. 154). The amenities here are numerous: First there are the wonderful one- and two-bedroom suites, where you get a separate living room, flatscreen TV, phone in each bedroom and living room, wet bar, and lots of entertainment electronics to keep the teenagers happy. Suites also feature top-of-the-line furniture, Hawaiian decor such as bronze hula lamps, plush mattresses, expensive linens, granite bathroom counters, and views from every window. The two-towered property is connected via a huge lobby area (with sun deck, pool, waterfall, and covered terrace for those yummy breakfasts). At first glance, the prices may seem high, but when you consider the free breakfast, the evening reception, and all the amenities, it adds up to quite a deal for families.

201 Beachwalk St., Honolulu, HI 96815 ℂ **800/EMBASSY** (362-2779) or 808/921-2345. Fax 808/921-2343. www.waikikibeach.embassysuites.com. 421 suites. $239–$319 1-bedroom; $439–$600 2-bedroom. Extra person (over 2 in 1-bedroom) $60. Rates include "cooked to order" breakfast and cocktail party daily. AE, DC, DISC, MC, V. Parking $25. Bus: 19 or 20. **Amenities:** Nearby restaurants and bars; bike rentals; children's program in summer and at Christmas; 24-hr. concierge; 24-hour fitness center; outdoor pool and whirlpool spa; room service; watersports equipment rentals. *In room:* A/C, TV/DVD, CD/MP3 player, small fridge, hair dryer, microwave, free Wi-Fi.

Halekulani ★★★ ☺   Here's the ultimate heavenly Hawaii vacation. *Halekulani* translates as "house befitting heaven"—an apt description of this luxury resort. It's spread over 5 acres of prime Waikiki beachfront in five buildings that are connected by open courtyards and lush gardens. Upon arrival, you're immediately greeted and escorted to your room, where registration is handled in comfort and privacy.

There are so many things that set this luxury hotel apart from the others, the most important being the rooms: About 90% face the ocean, and they're big (averaging 620 sq. ft.), each with a separate sitting area and a large, furnished lanai. Each bathroom features a deep soaking tub, a separate glassed-in shower, and a marble basin. Recent renovations include total refurbishment of the rooms, new entertainment centers with DVD players, bedside control panels, wireless Internet service, and a new spa.

There's a great children's program during the summer and at Christmas. Other perks include complimentary tickets to any or all of the following: The Contemporary Museum (TCM), the Bishop Museum, the Honolulu Academy of Arts, and Ihilani Palace (a combined value of about $100 per person). The hotel's restaurants are outstanding, and the **House Without a Key** ★★ is surely one of the world's most romantic spots for sunset cocktails, light meals, and entertainment. You can't find a better location on Waikiki Beach or a more luxurious hotel.

2199 Kalia Rd. (at the ocean end of Lewers St.), Honolulu, HI 96815. © **800/367-2343** or 808/ 923-2311. Fax 808/926-8004. www.halekulani.com. 455 units. $460–$680 double; from $875 suite. Extra person $125. 1 child 16 or under stays free in parent's room using existing bedding; additional rollaway bed $40. Maximum 3 people per room. AE, DC, MC, V. Parking $22 (self- or valet).Bus: 19 or 20. **Amenities:** 3 superb restaurants (including La Mer, p. 170, and Orchids, p. 172); 2 bars (including Lewers Lounge, p. 295); babysitting; bike rentals; children's program in summer and at Christmas; 24-hr. concierge; fitness center; gorgeous outdoor pool; room service; spa; watersports equipment rentals. *In room:* A/C, TV/DVD, hair dryer, minibar, free Wi-Fi.

Moana Surfrider, a Westin Resort ★★ Recently, this wonderful momentous property, Waikiki's first hotel, which dates from 1901 and is listed on the National Register of Historic Places, completed renovations (including installing Westin's Heavenly Beds and flatscreen TVs); added the Westin Kids Club program; opened a new spa, which fills most of the second floor; and was rebranded a Westin (it used to be a Sheraton). It's hard to get a bad room here (even before the renovations): Most have ocean views, and all come with bedside controls, luxury amenities, and plush bathrobes. My pick is the Banyan Wing, whose historic rooms are a modern replica of the hotel's first rooms. They are small and don't have lanais, but they all carry that feeling of Hawaii of 1901, when steamship travel with big trunks was the only way to see the islands. Be sure to stop by the Historical Room and peruse Waikiki's past. Speaking of the past, when the hotel was built, it was considered an innovation in the travel industry because the Moana featured a private bathroom and a phone in each guest room—an unheard-of luxury in the early 20th century. Yesteryear lives on at this grand hotel, from the main entry through the original colonial porte-cochere to the highly polished front porch dotted with rocking chairs to the perfectly restored lobby with detailed millwork and intricate plasterwork. The female employees even wear traditional Victorian-era muumuu. The aloha spirit that pervades this classy and charming place is infectious.

One of the best reasons to stay here is the hotel's prime stretch of beach, with a lifeguard, beach chairs, towels, and any other service you desire. The Beach Bar and a poolside snack bar are located in an oceanfront courtyard centered on a 100-year-old banyan tree, where there's live music in the evenings.

2365 Kalakaua Ave. (ocean side of the street, across from Kaiulani St.), Honolulu, HI 96815. © **800/325-3535** or 808/922-3111. Fax 808/923-0308. www.moana-surfrider.com or www. starwoodhotelshawaii.com. 793 units. $235–$310 double; from $1,050 suite. Extra person and rollaway bed $85. Children 17 and under stay free in parent's room using existing bedding. AE, DC, DISC, MC, V. Valet parking $20; self-parking at sister property $20. Bus: 19 or 20. **Amenities:** 3 restaurants; bar; babysitting; children's program; concierge; nearby fitness room (about a 2-min. walk down the beach at the Sheraton Waikiki); outdoor pool; room service; watersports equipment rentals. *In room:* A/C, TV, fridge, hair dryer, high-speed Internet access ($13 per day).

Outrigger Waikiki on the Beach ★ ☺   The same value and quality that I've come to expect in every Outrigger hotel is definitely in evidence here, only multiplied by a factor of 10. Even the standard rooms in this 16-story oceanfront hotel are large and comfortable. In 2004, the Outrigger poured some $20 million into the guest rooms, upgrading the furniture and sprucing up the bathrooms with new granite counters, ceramic floor tiles, and lighted makeup mirrors. All units have huge closets, roomy bathrooms, and plenty of amenities, plus a spacious lanai; the price is entirely dependent on the view. Just added: free high-speed Internet access (most hotels charge at least $10 a day) and free calls to Hawaii and the U.S. mainland (very, very unusual for Waikiki). If money is no object, book the Deluxe Oceanfront units, which feature oversize Jacuzzi bathtubs that have an ocean view of Waikiki Beach. This hotel's prime beachfront location and loads of facilities help make it one of the chain's most attractive properties. Even if you aren't staying here, wander through the renovated lobby, filled with rare and historic Hawaiian artifacts (like a century-old canoe made of koa). And don't miss the **Hula Grill Waikiki** (p. 175).

2335 Kalakaua Ave. (btw. the Royal Hawaiian Shopping Center and the Moana Surfrider), Honolulu, HI 96815. ☏ **800/OUTRIGGER** (688-7444) or 808/923-0711. Fax 800/622-4852. www.outrigger.com. 525 units. $179 $509 double; from $699 suite. Extra person $50. Children 17 and under stay free in parent's room using existing bedding. Ask about package deals, like 5th night free or discount rates for seniors over 50. AE, DC, DISC, MC, V. Valet-only parking $25. Bus: 19 or 20. **Amenities:** 3 restaurants (including Hula Grill Waikiki, p. 175, and Duke's Waikiki, p. 174); 3 bars; showroom w/nightly entertainment; babysitting; year-round children's program; concierge; concierge-level rooms; fitness center; Jacuzzi; giant outdoor pool; room service; new Waikiki Plantation Spa; watersports equipment rentals. *In room:* A/C, TV, hair dryer, free high-speed Internet access, kitchenette (in some units).

Royal Hawaiian ★★   It's back. After a complete makeover, this flamingo pink oasis, hidden away among blooming gardens within the concrete jungle of Waikiki, was restored in 2009 to its reputation as a symbol of luxury. Built by Matson steamship lines, the Spanish/Moorish "Pink Palace" opened in 1927 on the same spot where Queen Kaahumanu had her summer palace—on one of the best stretches of Waikiki Beach. On your way into the hotel, you pass the lush gardens, with their spectacular banyan tree, and then step into the black terrazzo-marble lobby, which boasts hand-woven pink carpets and giant floral arrangements. In 2009, all rooms were renovated and a new swimming pool complex was added oceanside. Another plus: 24-hour medical services at the Princess Kaiulani nearby on the property. My heart was won over by the rooms in the Historic Wing, which contain carved wooden doors, four-poster canopy beds, flowered wallpaper, and period furniture. If you prefer the newer rooms, the latest decor is a la Tommy Bahama, with a tropical palm-tree motif.

One of Waikiki's best spas, **Abhasa** ★★ (☏ **808/922-8200;** www.abhasa.com), is located on the property. This contemporary spa, spread out over 7,000 square feet, concentrates on natural, organic treatments in a soothing atmosphere (the smell of eucalyptus wafts through the air), with everything from the latest aromatherapy thalassotherapy (soaking in a sweet-smelling hot bath of saltwater) to shiatsu massages. Its specialty is a cold-laser, antiaging treatment that promises to give you a refreshed, revitalized face in just 30 minutes.

A ROOM FOR EVERYONE IN waikiki: THE OUTRIGGER & OHANA HOTELS DYNASTY

Among the largest hotel chains in Waikiki, Outrigger and Ohana hotels offer excellent accommodations across the board. The Outrigger properties are more resort-oriented, with amenities like concierge service, children's programs, and a variety of restaurants and shops. The Outrigger resorts are priced higher than their sister hotels, in the Ohana brand. You'll be comfortable at any of the Outrigger outposts: **Outrigger Waikiki on the Beach** (see complete review, above), **Outrigger Reef on the Beach** (rooms from $169), and **Outrigger Waikiki Shore Resort Condo** (condominiums from $155). Plus, there are plenty of packages available for these properties. Ask about other deals, like a fifth night free, discount rates for seniors over 50, family plans (children 17 and under stay free in parent's room using existing bedding), and even romance and honeymoon packages. To ask about current offerings and make reservations at any of the Outrigger properties throughout the islands, contact **Outrigger Hotels & Resorts** (✆ **800/OUTRIGGER** [688-7444] or 808/942-7722; www.outrigger.com).

The Ohana Hotels, which are part of the Outrigger chain, offer moderately priced, well-appointed rooms in central locations, slightly less than the Outrigger resorts prices. The chain's price structure (from $149) is based entirely on location, room size, and amenities. Check the website, where "best available rates" start at $125 (a true bargain in Waikiki!). Ohana also offers other deals, including air and car-rental packages; for information, contact **Ohana Hotels & Resorts** (✆ **800/462-6262;** www.ohanahotels.com).

In the culinary department, the **Surf Lanai** has replaced the former Surf Room as the properties' oceanfront eatery featuring American cuisine (hamburgers), along with another beachfront restaurant, **Azure,** with Hawaii Regional Cuisine. The Royal Hawaiian luau is done in grand style on Monday nights. And the hotel's **Mai Tai Bar ★★** is one of the most popular places in Waikiki for its namesake drink, which supposedly originated here.

2259 Kalakaua Ave. (at Royal Hawaiian Ave., on the ocean side of the Royal Hawaiian Shopping Center), Honolulu, HI 96815. ✆ **800/325-3535** or 808/923-7311. Fax 808/924-7098. www. royal-hawaiian.com or www.starwoodhotelshawaii.com. 527 units. $350–$500 double; from $400 suite. Extra person $125. Ask about special packages. AE, DC, DISC, MC, V. Valet parking $33; self-parking at Sheraton Waikiki $26. Bus: 19 or 20. **Amenities:** 2 restaurants; landmark bar; babysitting; bike rentals; excellent year-round children's program; multilingual concierge desk; nearby fitness room (next door at the Sheraton Waikiki); preferential tee times at various golf courses; good-size outdoor pool; room service; excellent full-service spa (Abhasa); watersports equipment rentals. *In room:* A/C, TV, fridge, hair dryer, high-speed Internet access ($13 per day).

Sheraton Waikiki ★ ☺ Occupying two 30-story towers, this is by far the biggest of the four Starwood properties on the beach. The lobby is immense and filled with shops, travel desks, and people. Not surprisingly, this hotel hosts numerous conventions; if you're not comfortable with crowds and conventioneers, book elsewhere. However, size has its advantages: The Sheraton has everything from a fabulous kids' program, with a fee (boogie boarding, kite flying, nightly movies, and more), to historical walks and cooking demonstrations for Mom and Dad. Plus, you can "play and charge" at Starwood's other Waikiki's hotels.

It's hard to get a bad room here, and they all were completely renovated in 2009. A whopping 1,200 units have some sort of ocean view, and 650 rooms overlook Diamond Head. Accommodations are spacious, with big lanais to take in those magnificent vistas. In 2007, Sheraton updated all rooms with a clean, uncluttered look and added minimalist furniture, Sweet Sleeper Beds, big flatscreen TVs, high-speed Internet access ($14–$25 per day depending on speed), and new windows out of the bathroom wall over the sink to give a more expansive feel.

2255 Kalakaua Ave. (at Royal Hawaiian Ave., on the ocean side of the Royal Hawaiian Shopping Center and west of the Royal Hawaiian), Honolulu, HI 96815. ℂ **800/325-3535** or 808/922-4422. Fax 808/923-8785. www.sheraton.com or www.starwoodhotelshawaii.com. 1,852 units. $199–$245 double; from $340 suite. Extra person $90. Children 17 and under stay free in parent's room. AE, DC, DISC, MC, V. Valet parking $33; self-parking $25. Bus: 19 or 20. **Amenities:** 4 restaurants; 3 bars; nightclub; babysitting; bike rentals; children's program; concierge; fitness center; access to Makaha Golf Club's golf and tennis facilities (about 1 hr. away); 2 large outdoor pools, including one of the biggest and sunniest along the Waikiki beachfront; room service; watersports equipment rentals. In room: A/C, TV, fridge, hair dryer, high-speed Internet access ($14–$25 per day), minibar.

Expensive

Waikiki Parc ★★   Although not on Waikiki Beach, this property offers lots of bonuses: It has a terrific location, just 100 yards from the beach, and it's managed and run by the ultraluxury Halekulani Hotel, but at a more reasonable price. The compact, beautifully appointed rooms underwent complete renovation in 2006 with modern Hawaiian-Zen decor. Superfluous furniture was removed to make the rooms look more spacious, and wired Internet access was installed (the thick concrete walls and the density of Waikiki buildings make wireless reception practically impossible). All rooms have lanais with an ocean, mountain, or city view. Nice extras include adjustable floor-to-ceiling shutters for those who want to sleep in. The Parc features the same level of service that has made the Halekulani famous. A branch of internationally famous chef Nobu Matsuhisa's Nobu restaurant opened in 2007.

2233 Helumoa Rd. (at Lewers St.), Honolulu, HI 96815. ℂ **800/422-0450** or 808/921-7272. Fax 808/923-1336. www.waikikiparc.com. 297 units. $285–$415 double. Extra person $65. Children 17 and under stay free in parent's room. Ask about room and package deals that start at just $269 a night. AE, DC, MC, V. Self- or valet parking $20. Bus: 19 or 20. **Amenities:** 2 restaurants; babysitting; concierge; fitness center; 8th-floor pool deck; room service. In room: A/C, TV, fridge, hair dryer, high-speed Internet access ($10 per day).

Inexpensive

The Breakers ★ 🍴   Another great buy just a 2-minute walk to Waikiki Beach, the Breakers offers old-fashioned Hawaiian aloha, comfortable budget accommodations, and family-friendly prices. This two-story 1950s hotel has an accommodating staff and a loyal following. Its six buildings are set around a pool and a tropical garden blooming with brilliant red and yellow hibiscus; wooden jalousies and shoji doors further the tropical ambience. Each of the tastefully decorated, slightly oversize rooms comes with a lanai and a kitchenette. Every Wednesday

WAIKIKI beach walk

One of the biggest projects to take place in Waikiki in decades is the total renovation of an 8-acre area—bound by Saratoga Road, Kalakaua Avenue, Lewers Street, and Kalia Road—called the Waikiki Beach Walk. The project, by Outrigger Hotels & Resorts, cost some $460 million.

Phase one, completed in 2007, reconfigured the formerly very congested area (narrow streets, lots of delivery trucks double-parked, crowded sidewalks, and no vegetation) into an oasis of broad sidewalks, tropical foliage, water features, open space, and totally renovated hotels. Eleven hotels were razed, upgraded, or changed to suites or condos. Five hotels and one timeshare condominium remain. The bad news is that the near-oceanfront budget hotels, neighborhood eateries, and small independent shops have been replaced with luxury (higher-priced) properties and 90,000 square feet of swank shops and trendy restaurants to match, all linked through pedestrian bridges and connecting walkways.

Changes to the hotels in this area include:

- The 38-story **Trump International Hotel Waikiki Beach,** with 464 luxury condominium units, opened recently.

- Down the block, the 421-suite **Embassy Suites Hotel-Waikiki Beach Walk** also has opened.

- The former 480-room Ohana Reef Towers is now a 193-unit condominium

timeshare, operated by Outrigger and renamed **Wyndham Waikiki Beach Walk.**

- The Ohana Edgewater and Ohana Coral Seas were razed and replaced by the 90,000-square-foot **Waikiki Beach Walk** retail/entertainment complex. It features 40 retail shops, four major restaurants, a few smaller food and beverage places, and an open pedestrian plaza.

- The former Ohana Waikiki Village and the Ohana Waikiki Tower hotels, which had a total of 881 rooms, were demolished and replaced by **Embassy Suites Hotel–Waikiki Beach Walk** (reviewed earlier), which offers 421 suites.

- The **Outrigger Reef on the Beach** totally refurbished its 858 rooms.

- In the culinary world, some of Waikiki's top restaurants are located here: **La Mer** and **Orchids** at Halakulani, 2199 Kalia Rd., recently opened **BLT Steak,** at the Trump International, 223 Saratoga Rd., and **Roy's,** next door to Embassy Suites Hotel–Waikiki Beach Walk, 201 Beachwalk St.

and Friday, you're invited to a formal Japanese tea ceremony from 10am to noon at the Urasenke Tea House next door. One of the best things about the Breakers is the location—easy walking distance to numerous restaurants, shopping, and Waikiki Beach.

250 Beach Walk (btw. Kalakaua Ave. and Kalia Rd.), Honolulu, HI 96815. © **800/426-0494** or 808/923-3181. Fax 808/923-7174. www.breakers-hawaii.com. 64 units (all with shower only). $120–$130 double (extra person $20 per day); $185 garden suites double ($205 for 3, $225 for 4, and $245 for 5). AE, DC, MC, V. Limited free parking (just 7 stalls); additional parking across the

street $16 per day. Bus: 19 or 20. **Amenities:** Restaurant; poolside bar; grill; outdoor pool; free Wi-Fi in lobby and pool areas. *In room:* A/C, TV, hair dryer (on request), kitchenette.

Kai Aloha Apartment Hotel ✦ If you want to experience what Waikiki was like 40 years ago, stay here. This small apartment hotel just a block from the beach is reminiscent of the low-key hotels that used to line the blocks of Waikiki in the good old days. It offers one-bedroom apartments and studios, all furnished in modest rattan and colorful island prints. Each of the one-bedroom units has a bedroom with either a queen-size bed or two twins, a living room with a couch and two additional twins (Hawaiian houses of 40 years ago all had extra beds in the living room, called *punee,* for guests to sleep on), a full kitchen, a dining table, and even voice mail. These units are large enough to accommodate a rolla-way bed for a fifth person. Glass jalousies take advantage of the cooling trade winds, but there's also air-conditioning for very hot days. The studios have two twin beds, a kitchenette, a balcony, a Plexiglas roof in the bathroom (the forerun-ner of the skylight), and a screen door for ventilation. The units aren't exactly designer showrooms, but they do have a homey feel and provide daily maid ser-vice. You're sure to forgive the lack of aesthetics when you're presented with the bill. A large deck on the second floor is a great place to sip early morning coffee or watch the sun sink into the Pacific.

235 Saratoga Rd. (across from Fort DeRussy and Waikiki post office, btw. Kalakaua Ave. and Kalia Rd.), Honolulu, HI 96815. © **808/923-6723.** Fax 808/922-7592. www.kaialohahotel.com. 18 units. $85–$95 studio double; $90–$100 1-bedroom double. Extra person $20. 2-night mini-mum. AE, MC, V. Parking at separate pay lot across the street for $16. Bus: 19 or 20. *In room:* A/C, TV, computer with Internet access available in the office for guests, kitchenette.

MID-WAIKIKI, MAUKA

These mid-Waikiki hotels, on the mountain side of Kalakaua Avenue, are a little farther away from the beach than those listed above. All are between Kalakaua Avenue and Ala Wai Canal, and between Kalaimoku Street in the Ewa (western) direction and Kaiulani Street in the Diamond Head (eastern) direction.

Expensive

Ohana Waikiki Beachcomber Management of this high-rise property has been taken over by Ohana Hotels & Resorts. One of the best features of this property is the great location—a block from Waikiki Beach, across the street from the upscale Royal Hawaiian Shopping Center, and next door to bargain shopping at the International Market Place. The rooms feature Berber carpets, contemporary furniture, and voice mail. This is one of the few hotels in Waikiki with great nightlife—*The Magic of Polynesia,* a show with illusionist John Hiro-kawa, plays nightly.

2300 Kalakaua Ave. (at Duke's Lane), Honolulu, HI 96815. © **800/462-6262** or 808/922-4646. Fax 808/926-9973. www.ohanahotels.com. 492 units (all with shower only). $125–$279 double; from $399 suite. Extra person from $30. Check the website for special AAA and senior rates. AE, DC, DISC, MC, V. Parking $18. Bus: 19 or 20. **Amenities:** Poolside coffee shop in hotel and Jimmy Buffet's Restaurant next door; outdoor pool; free Wi-Fi in lobby. *In room:* A/C, TV, fridge, hair dryer, high-speed Internet access (free).

Moderate/Inexpensive

Aqua Waikiki Wave ★ 🎒 It's hard to believe that this sleek, modern oasis could emerge from the old Coral Reef—a wreck of a hotel. Aqua completely gutted the old place, spending $7.6 million in renovations. The result is a clean, hip decor with bright white walls, offset by the burnt-orange fabric on the bed headboard, which extends up to the ceiling. Potted plants and live orchids liven up the rooms, which have either two queen beds or a king (with comfy Serta mattresses). The 21st century has arrived at the Wave—guests here enjoy flatscreen TVs and free Wi-Fi and high-speed Internet access. The decades-old bathrooms have new plumbing, modern fixtures, and resurfaced tiles and tubs. The Wave is about a 10-minute walk from the beach and right next door to the International Market Place.

2299 Kuhio Ave. (at Duke's Lane), Honolulu, HI 96817. *(?)* **866/406-2782** or 808/922-1262. Fax 808/922-5048. www.aquaresorts.com. 247 units. $94–$115 double; from $135 suite. Extra person $25. AE, DISC, MC, V. Parking $20. Bus: 19 or 20. **Amenities:** 2 restaurants; babysitting; fitness room; outdoor pool; spa. *In room:* A/C, TV/DVD, fridge, hair dryer, free Wi-Fi.

Aston Waikiki Joy Hotel   Tucked away down a narrow path on a side street, this boutique hotel offers not only outstanding personal service, but also a Jacuzzi in every room. Complimentary continental breakfast is included in the price. The Italian marble–accented open-air lobby and the tropical veranda set the scene for the beautifully decorated guest rooms, each with a marble entry, tropical-island decor, and a lanai wide enough for you to sit and enjoy the views. Another plus: All rooms are soundproof. The suites are even more luxurious, with a king-size bed or two doubles, fridge, microwave, and wet bar. Executive suites come with two double beds and a kitchen with microwave and full fridge; the executive king suites add a separate living room and bedroom. Every unit comes with voice mail, as well as fax and modem hookups. There are, however, a couple of downsides: The 1960 hotel has had some renovations, such as new carpet and fresh paint, but you won't mistake it for a new hotel. The rack rates are on the high side, considering the 10- to 15-minute walk to the beach, and although there's an on-site sandwich/coffee shop, the food's nothing memorable.

320 Lewers St. (btw. Kuhio and Kalakaua aves.), Honolulu, HI 96815. *(?)* **877/997-6667** or 808/923-2300. Fax 808/924-4010. www.AstonHotels.com. 94 units. $97–$168 double; $131–$187 double club suite; $180–$257 junior suite with kitchen (sleeps up to 4); $215–$307 1-bedroom executive suite with kitchen (up to 4). Extra person $30 for certain rooms. Check the website for special deals and packages. Rates include continental breakfast. AE, DC, DISC, MC, V. Valet-only parking $19. Bus: 19 or 20. **Amenities:** Restaurant; bar (karaoke); concierge; minuscule outdoor pool w/dry sauna. *In room:* A/C, TV, hair dryer (fee), Internet access ($10), kitchenette (full kitchen in suites).

Best Western Aqua Coconut Waikiki   The good news is that this property, built in 1962, was totally renovated in 2007 into a fabulous boutique inn with modern decor and amenities (such as free high-speed Internet and flatscreen TVs in every room). Formerly the Coconut Plaza, it has been managed by a host of companies, from ResortQuest to Aqua. In 2008, Best Western took over and made it a very affordable and welcoming place to stay that's only a 10-minute walk to the beach.

450 Lewers St. (at Ala Wai Blvd.), Honolulu, HI 96815. *(?)* **808/923-8828.** Fax 808/923-3473. www.bestwesternhawaii.com/hotels/best-western-coconut-waikiki-hotel. 80 units. $119–$159 double; from $410 suite. Extra person $40. Rates include continental breakfast. AE, DC, MC, V. Valet parking $22. Bus: 19 or 20. **Amenities:** Tiny outdoor pool w/sun deck. *In room:* A/C, TV, fridge, hair dryer, free high-speed Internet, microwave.

Ilima Hotel   This was once a great value property, but alas, they have raised rates so high that that no longer is true. At these rates, you can do better. The Teruya brothers, former owners of Hawaii's Times Supermarket, wanted to offer comfortable accommodations that Hawaii residents could afford, and for years, they succeeded. One of Hawaii's small, well-located condo-style hotels, the 17-story, pale-pink Ilima (named for the native orange flower used in royal leis) used to offer value for your money. But then in 2010, they had a very large rate increase, and although the rooms are huge, and the location (near the International Market Place and the Royal Hawaiian Shopping Center; 2 blocks to Waikiki Beach) is great, prices have gotten too high for what you get. A tasteful koa-wood lobby lined with works by Hawaiian artists greets you upon arrival. The one-bedroom units now have Jacuzzi tubs. There are three sun decks, a dry sauna, and truly nice people staffing the front desk to help you enjoy your vacation. Another caveat: no ocean views.

445 Nohonani St. (near Ala Wai Blvd.), Honolulu, HI 96815. ⓒ **800/801-9366** or 808/923-1877. Fax 808/924-2617. www.ilima.com. 99 units. $188–$268 double; $230–$280 1-bedroom (rate for 4); $300–$350 2-bedroom (rate for 4, sleeps up to 6), $560–$600 3 bedroom (rate for 6, sleeps up to 8). Extra person $10. Discounts available for seniors and business travelers. AE, DC, DISC, MC, V. Limited free on-site parking, $18 across the street. Bus: 19 or 20. **Amenities:** Exercise room; outdoor pool w/sauna. *In room:* A/C, TV, hair dryer (fee), free high-speed Internet access in deluxe rooms (floors 10–16), kitchen.

Patrick Winston's Waikiki Condos 🛏   Looking for a condo priced to fit a tight budget, with a hefty dose of old-fashioned aloha thrown in? Try Patrick Winston's rentals, located on a quiet side street. When this five-story condominium hotel was built in 1981, Winston bought one unit; he has since acquired 24 more, spent hundreds of thousands of dollars on refurbishment, and put his spacious suites on the market at frugal prices. Staying here is like having a personal concierge: Winston has lots of terrific tips on where to eat, where to shop, and how to get the most for your money, and he can book any activity you want.

Three types of units are available: standard/budget rooms, one-bedroom suites, and ground-floor junior business suites. All have sofa beds, separate bedrooms, lanais with breakfast table and chairs, ceiling fans, and full kitchens; most have a washer and dryer. All are individually decorated. Eight units are "standard budget," which means the carpet has not been replaced or the walls need repainting, but they're otherwise a terrific deal for those looking for a condo unit at a penny-pinching price. Waikiki Beach is just a 10- to 15-minute walk away, shopping is a half-block away, and restaurants are within a 5- to 10-minute walk. This area of Waikiki is a little scary at night—not totally safe for a woman to be wandering about by herself. Also be aware there is *no* maid service (you are the maid) and there is a cleaning fee.

Hawaiian King Bldg., 417 Nohonani St., Ste. 409 (btw. Kuhio Ave. and Ala Wai Blvd.), Honolulu, HI 96815. ⓒ **800/545-1948** or 808/924-3332. Fax 808/922-3894. www.winstonswaikikicondos. com. 24 units (all with shower only). $125–$145 1-bedroom; $145–$165 business suite; $165–$185 1-bedroom with den. Extra person $10. Ask for the Frommer's readers' discount. Cleaning fee $75–$100. 7-night minimum. AE, DC, DISC, MC, V. Limited parking $14. Bus: 19 or 20. **Amenities:** Bar; babysitting; small outdoor pool surrounded by a tropical courtyard. *In room:* A/C, TV, hair dryer, kitchen.

DIAMOND HEAD WAIKIKI

You'll find all these hotels between Ala Wai Boulevard and the ocean, and between Kaiulani Street (1 block east of the International Market Place) and world-famous Diamond Head itself.

Very Expensive

Waikiki Beach Marriott Resort & Spa   This 1,310-room hotel, which was completely renovated in 2002 (to the tune of $60 million), has a lot to offer, including a terrific location just across the street from Waikiki Beach, great restaurants (including renowned Maui chef D. K. Kodama's **Sansei Seafood Restaurant & Sushi Bar,** p. 176, and **d.k Steakhouse,** p. 174), a terrific spa, and lots of nightly entertainment.

The 5¼-acre property has two towers (one 33 stories, the other 25 stories) and a long list of amenities to keep guests happy, from an espresso bar to an array of shops. The newly done rooms feature comfortable Island-style decor, marble floors, and granite counters in the bathroom. When it opened in 2002, it had moderate prices, but they've been creeping up every year. Don't pay the rack rates—you can do better elsewhere in Waikiki for that kind of money. But if you get a good deal, go for it. *Tip:* Check the website for specials; rooms sometimes go for half-price.

Even if you don't stay here, spa aficionados won't want to miss the **Spa Olakino & Salon** ★. Conceived and managed by Paul Brown, a well-known hairstylist with numerous salons in Hawaii, this boutique spa offers a unique experience: The spa looks directly out onto Waikiki Beach (technically, Kuhio Beach, at the far end of Waikiki). Comfy cushioned chairs allow you to sit and stare at the rolling surf of Waikiki before or after your treatment. The spa menu of treatments is one of the most enchanting I have seen. I recommend the Na La'au, which starts with a Hawaiian lomilomi massage (using traditional native Hawaiian plants like kukui-nut oil), then goes on to a noni-plant-and-ti-leaf body wrap, and concludes with a private steam room and shower.

2552 Kalakaua Ave. (entrance on Ohua Ave.), Honolulu, HI 96815. ℂ **800/367-5370** or 808/922-6611. Fax 808/921-5255. www.marriottwaikiki.com. 1,310 units. $370–$470 double; from $540 suite. Extra person $50. Children 17 and under stay free in parent's room using existing bedding. AE, DC, DISC, MC, V. Valet parking $33; self-parking $28. Bus: 19 or 20. **Amenities:** 5 restaurants (including Sansei Seafood Restaurant & Sushi Bar, p. 176, and d.k Steakhouse, p. 174); 2 bars; babysitting; concierge; fitness room; Jacuzzi; outdoor pool w/view of Waikiki; room service; spa. *In room:* A/C, TV, hair dryer, Wi-Fi ($15 per day).

Expensive

Hyatt Regency Waikiki ★   This is one of Waikiki's biggest hotels, a $100-million project sporting two 40-story towers and covering nearly an entire city block, just across the street from the Diamond Head end of Waikiki Beach. Some may love the location, but others will find this behemoth too big and impersonal—you can get lost just trying to find the registration desk. The huge second-floor lobby is decorated in koa and wraps around an atrium that rises *40 floors* from the ground level. It's filled with the squawks of parrots, tumbling waterfalls, and traffic noise from busy Kalakaua Avenue outside.

The guest rooms are spacious and luxuriously furnished. The deluxe ocean-view rooms overlooking Waikiki Beach are fabulous but can be noisy (traffic on

Kalakaua is constant). For a few dollars more (well, actually more than a few dollars), you can upgrade to the Regency Club floors, where the rooms are nicer; you'll also be entitled to an expedited check-in and entry to a private rooftop sun deck and Jacuzzi, as well as the Regency Club, which has concierge service all day and serves complimentary continental breakfast and afternoon pupu. The 10,000-square-foot, two-story luxury spa offers all the massage services, body treatments, and facials you can imagine. *Tip:* Check the website's "Aloha" rates, which can save you up to $100 per night.

2424 Kalakaua Ave. (at Kaiulani St., across the street from the beach), Honolulu, HI 96815. ☎ **800/492-8804** or 808/923-1234. Fax 808/926-3415. www.waikiki.hyatt.com. 1,230 units. $220–$539 double; $469–$569 Regency Club double; from $864 suite. Extra person $75 ($125 Regency Club). Children 17 and under stay free in parent's room using existing bedding. Check website for special packages. AE, DISC, MC, V. Valet parking $33; self-parking $28. Bus: 19 or 20. **Amenities:** 4 restaurants (including Ciao Mein, p. 173); elegant poolside bar; babysitting; children's program (fee; Fri–Sat evening in winter, daily in summer); concierge; concierge-level rooms; fitness room; Jacuzzi; outdoor pool w/view of Waikiki; room service; spa. *In room:* A/C, TV, fridge, hair dryer, high-speed Internet access ($10 per day).

Moderate

Aston at the Waikiki Banyan ☺ The one bedrooms here combine the homey comforts of a condo apartment with the amenities of a hotel. You'll get daily maid service, bellhop service, the assistance of the front desk, and much more, including an enormous sixth-floor recreation deck with a panoramic mountain view, complete with sauna, barbecue areas, snack bar, and children's play area—a great boon for families—plus there's a kids' library with games and terrific Hawaiian children's books. Kids 12 and under even get a toy when you check in. Your introduction to this complex is through the open-air lobby with impressive lacquer artwork, hand-carved and painted in Hong Kong. All units have a fully equipped full-size kitchen, a breakfast bar that opens to a comfortably furnished living room (with sofa bed), and a separate bedroom with two double beds or a queen-size bed. The one I stayed in had an old-fashioned air conditioner in the wall, but it did the job. Each apartment opens onto a fairly good-size lanai with chairs and a small table; there's a partial ocean view, with some buildings blocking the way.

201 Ohua Ave. (on mountain side, at Kuhio Ave.), Honolulu, HI 96815. ☎ **866/77-HAWAII** (774-2924) or 808/922-0555. Fax 808/922-0906. www.AstonHotels.com. 307 units. $128–$227 for up to 5. Check website for special rates and package deals. AE, DC, DISC, MC, V. Self-parking $10. Bus: 19 or 20. **Amenities:** Children's playground; huge outdoor pool; free tennis courts; 2 whirlpools; barbecue. *In room:* A/C, TV, hair dryer, free high-speed Internet access, kitchen.

Aston Waikiki Beach Hotel Rebranded from ResortQuest in 2009 and after a $30-million renovation, this property is once again managed by Aston. The location, directly across the street from the beach, couldn't be better, but the rooms couldn't be smaller—averaging 225 to 266 square feet (though 85% of them have ocean views). When ResortQuest took over management in 2006, it immediately got rid of the Hawaiian "kitschy nostalgia" theme (the horrible garish colors are gone, replaced with wooden baseboards and bamboo trim over floral carpet), installed 32-inch flatscreen TVs and bamboo dressers, and punched up the decor with bright floral headboards and accents. One of the good

5

Where to Stay

ideas that Aston has kept is the "Breakfast on the Beach" deal—you get a free breakfast, which you can pack up in an insulated carrying bag and walk across the street to eat. This is a full, hot breakfast, too, with several food stations offering everything from burritos (veggie, ham, or cheese), pastries, fruit, and cereals to a Japanese breakfast of miso, rice, and fish.

2570 Kalakaua Ave. (at Paoakalani St.), Honolulu, HI 96815. (C) **866/77-HAWAII** (774-2924), 800/877-7666, or 808/922-2511. Fax 808/923-3656. www.AstonHotels.com. 717 units. $135–$300 double; from $233 suite. Extra person $45. Check website for special rates and package deals. AE, DC, DISC, MC, V. Valet parking $27. Bus: 19 or 20. **Amenities:** 2 restaurants (including Tiki's Grill & Bar, p. 177); bar; outdoor pool. *In room:* A/C, TV, fridge, hair dryer, high-speed Internet access ($10).

Hilton Waikiki Prince Kuhio Hilton took over this 37-floor hotel, several long blocks from the beach and a couple of blocks from the zoo, in 2007. After spending $50 million on renovations, it has turned this formerly midpriced Radisson into a high-tech, 21st-century luxury property. The sleek, modern rooms all have high-speed Internet access (for a fee) and a flatscreen 42-inch high-def TV with multimedia monitor that you can use with a laptop, a game-station console, a camera, or an MP3 player. The contemporary furnishings include Hilton's comfy beds, and the bathrooms feature marble and natural stone and top-end amenities. All of the rooms are the same; the floor and the view determine the price (from the 18th floor and up, the mountain views overlooking the Ala Wai Canal are spectacular and not as pricey as the oceanview rooms). Hilton has added a 24-hour eatery, MAC 24-7 (p. 174), which comes in handy if you arrive late at night. *Note:* Be warned that the hotel is located about a 5-minute walk to the beach.

2500 Kuhio Ave. (at Liliuokalani Ave.), Honolulu, HI 96815. (C) **800-HILTONS** (445-8667) or 808/922-0811. Fax 808/921-5507. www.waikikiprincekuhio.hilton.com. 601 units. $169–$205 double; from $369 suite for 4. Extra person $40. AE, DC, DISC, MC, V. Valet-only parking $25. Bus: 19 or 20. **Amenities:** Restaurant; bar; concierge; concierge-level rooms; small fitness room; Jacuzzi; outdoor pool; room service. *In room:* A/C, TV, fridge, hair dryer, high-speed Internet access ($10 per day).

Hotel Renew ★★ Once upon a time, this now-70-room boutique hotel was one of the towers to the Aston Waikiki Beach Hotel (see above)—that was the "before." The "after" is an oasis of tranquillity and excellent taste in a sea of tired, aging Waikiki hotels. After several million dollars in renovations (every single surface was redone), the Hotel Renew offers a quiet, relaxing vacation just a block from the beach. Guests are seated at the front desk to check in while their luggage is whisked to their room. The new rooms are designed with a clean, Zenlike decor, with black and white walls, discreet lighting, and a hint of scented candles in the air (it reminds me of the W chain, but for a fraction of the price). But it's the high-tech electronics that won me over—a DVD player that projects onto a 6×4-foot screen (and can work with your laptop), a 42-inch high-definition flatscreen TV, complimentary high-speed Internet, a library of more than 500 movies, and even an iPod docking station. The final touch: a fresh flower lei when you depart to remember your sweet time here.

129 Paoakalani Ave. (at Lemon Rd.), Honolulu, HI 96815. (C) **888/485-7639** or 808/687-7700. Fax 808/687-7701. www.hotelrenew.com. 70 units. $128–$155 double. Extra person $50. Rates

include continental breakfast. AE, DISC, MC, V. Parking $22. Bus: 19 or 20. **Amenities:** Cafe and lounge; concierge; spa. *In room:* A/C, TV/DVD, CD player, fridge, hair dryer, free high-speed Internet access.

New Otani Kaimana Beach Hotel ★ 🎁 This is one of Waikiki's best-kept secrets: a boutique hotel nestled right on a lovely stretch of beach at the foot of Diamond Head, with Kapiolani Park just across the street. Robert Louis Stevenson's description of Sans Souci, the beach fronting the hotel, still holds true: "If anyone desires lovely scenery, pure air, clear sea water, good food, and heavenly sunsets, I recommend him cordially to the Sans Souci." The Waikiki-side guest rooms are teeny-tiny, with barely room for two, but they are tastefully decorated in pale pastels and open onto lanais with ocean and park views. A good budget buy is the parkview studio with kitchen (you can stock up on provisions from the on-site Mini-Mart, open until 11pm). *Tip:* Check the website for special deals.

Because the hotel overlooks Kapiolani Park, guests have easy access to activities such as golf, tennis, jogging, and bicycling; kayaking and snorkeling are available at the beach. The hotel also arranges for visitors to climb to the top of Diamond Head. The airy lobby opens onto the alfresco Hau Tree Lanai restaurant (p. 175) and features music nightly. The beachfront **Sunset Lanai Lounge ★** is great for cocktails and has live Hawaiian music at lunch on Friday.

2863 Kalakaua Ave. (ocean side of the street just Diamond Head of the Waikiki Aquarium, across from Kapiolani Park), Honolulu, HI 96815. (C) **800/356-8264** or 800/023-1555. Fax 808/922-9404. www.kaimana.com. 124 units. $175–$450 double; from $215 studio; from $325 junior suite; from $515 regular suite. Extra person $50. Children 12 and under stay free in parent's room using existing bedding. Check website for special packages. AE, DC, DISC, MC, V. Valet parking $18. Bus: 2 or 14. **Amenities:** 2 restaurants (including the Hau Tree Lanai, p. 175); beachfront bar; babysitting; concierge; fitness room; room service; watersports equipment rentals. *In room:* A/C, TV, dataport, hair dryer, high-speed Internet $12, kitchenette (in some units), minibar (on request).

Inexpensive

Aqua Bamboo and Spa ★ 🦺 Formerly a very neglected budget hotel just a couple of blocks from Waikiki Beach, Bamboo has been transformed into a contemporary condotel (a condominium/hotel) decorated with an Asian flair. The rooms are stylish and functional, with modern furniture, flatscreen TVs, marble bathrooms, and kitchenettes or kitchens. The location is good, too—it's within walking distance to numerous restaurants, shopping, and the Honolulu Zoo, and just 3 minutes to the beach. Because it's small, the staff gives guests personalized attention. When booking, be sure to reserve a parking space if you need one—the lot has a limited number of spaces.

2425 Kuhio Ave. (at Kaiulani Ave.), Honolulu, HI 96815. (C) **866/406-2782** or 808/922-7777. Fax 808/922-9473. www.aquaresorts.com. 90 units. $85–$159 double; $111–$179 studio double; from $170 1-bedroom; from $638 luxury 2-bedroom suite. Extra person $25. Rates include continental breakfast. AE, DISC, MC, V. Valet parking $10–$20. Bus: 19 or 20. **Amenities:** Concierge; fitness center; Jacuzzi; outdoor pool; sauna; spa. *In room:* A/C, TV, hair dryer, free high-speed Internet access, kitchenette or kitchen.

The Cabana at Waikiki Located on a quiet street in Waikiki, this boutique hotel is gay-friendly and features exquisitely decorated rooms. (Rooms were completely renovated in late 2008 and each has a kitchen.) Each has a king-size bed and pullout sofa bed or trundle bed, entertainment center with VCR and CD player, lanai, and well-equipped kitchen. The Cabana is within walking distance of gay nightclubs and the gay scene at Queen's Surf Beach.

2551 Cartwright Rd. (btw. Paoakalani and Kapahulu aves.), Honolulu, HI 96815. ℂ 877/902-2121 or 808/926-5555. Fax 808/926-5566. www.cabanavacationsuites.com. 15 units. $129–$229 double. Extra person $25. Check the website for rates as low as $99. AE, DC, DISC, MC, V. Parking $10. Bus: 19 or 20. **Amenities:** Concierge; complimentary access to nearby (about a 15-min. walk) fitness complex; free Internet access in lobby; Jacuzzi. *In room:* A/C, TV, hair dryer, kitchen, Wi-Fi ($5 per day).

Diamond Head Bed & Breakfast ★ 🎁   Hostess Joanne offers a quiet, relaxing place to stay on the far side of Kapiolani Park, away from the hustle and bustle of Waikiki. Staying here is like venturing back 50 years to a time when *kamaaina* (native-born) families built huge houses with airy rooms opening onto big lanais and tropical gardens. The house is filled with family heirlooms and Joanne's artwork. You can choose from three heirloom-furnished bedrooms (one contains the beyond-king-size carved-koa bed that once belonged to Princess Ruth, a member of Hawaii's royal family); or the Makai Suite, with two antique four-poster beds and a fabulous view; or Grampa's Apartment, a separate 500-square-foot apartment that really was built for Joanne's grandfather, with living room, separate bedroom, and bathroom.

3240 Noela Dr. (at Paki Ave., off Diamond Head Rd.), Honolulu, HI 96815. ℂ/fax **808/923-3360.** www.diamondheadbnb.com. 3 units. $130–$145 double. Extra person $20. Rates include full breakfast. 2-night minimum. No credit cards. Free parking. Bus: 2. *In room:* TV, fridge, hair dryer.

Royal Grove Hotel ★ 🐟   This is a great bargain for frugal travelers. You can't miss the Royal Grove—it's bright pink. Among Waikiki's canyons of corporate-owned high-rises, it's also a rarity in another way: It's a small, family-owned hotel. What you get here is old-fashioned aloha in cozy accommodations along the lines of Motel 6—basic and clean. For years, Frommer's readers have written about the aloha spirit of the Fong family; they love the potluck dinners and get-togethers the Fongs have organized so that their guests can get to know one another. And you can't do better for the price—this has to be *the* bargain of Waikiki. For $55 to $60 (about the same price a couple would pay to stay in a private room at the hostel in Waikiki), you get a clean room in the older Mauka Wing, with a double and a twin bed, plus a kitchenette with refrigerator and stove. I suggest spending a few dollars more on an air-conditioned room ($67–$70) to help drown out the street noise. Even the most expensive unit, a one-bedroom suite with three beds and kitchenette for $90 to $100, is half the price of similar accommodations elsewhere. At these rates, you won't mind that maid service is only twice a week. The hotel is built around a courtyard pool, and the beach is just a 3-minute walk away. All of Waikiki's attractions are within walking distance. *Tip:* If you book 7 nights or more from April to November, you'll get a discount on the already low rates.

151 Uluniu Ave. (btw. Prince Edward and Kuhio aves.), Honolulu, HI 96815. ℂ **808/923-7691.** Fax 808/922-7508. www.royalgrovehotel.com. 85 units. $55–$60 double (no A/C); $67–$70 standard double; $90–$100 standard 1-bedroom. Extra person $10. Children 5 and under stay free in parent's room. AE, DC, DISC, MC, V. Nearby parking $10. Bus: 19 or 20. **Amenities:** Pool. *In room:* A/C (in most rooms), TV, kitchen.

Waikiki Sand Villa   Budget travelers, take note: This very affordable hotel is located on the quieter side of Waikiki, across the street from the Ala Wai Canal. The 10-story tower has medium-size rooms, most with a double bed plus a single bed (convenient for families) and a lanai with great views of the green mountains. The adjacent three-story building features studio apartments with kitchenettes (fridge, stove, and microwave). For guests arriving early or catching a late flight, there's a luggage-storage area and a hospitality room (complete with shower) for late checkout.

2375 Ala Wai Blvd. (entrance on Kanekapolei Ave.), Honolulu, HI 96815. © **800/247-1903** or 808/922-4744. Fax 808/926-7587. www.waikikisandvillahotel.com. 214 units. $73–$110 double; $130 studio with kitchenette; from $230 suite. Extra person $28. Children 16 and under stay free in parent's room using existing bedding. Rates include continental breakfast served poolside every morning. AE, DC, DISC, MC, V. Valet-only parking $15 ($7.50 if you book directly with hotel). Bus: 19 or 20. **Amenities:** 70-ft. outdoor pool w/adjoining whirlpool spa. *In room:* A/C, TV w/Nintendo, fridge (in some units), free high-speed Internet access, kitchenette (in some units), microwave (in some units).

Honolulu Beyond Waikiki

ALA MOANA

Ala Moana Hotel   This former 1,152-room hotel (on 36 floors) recently went through a multimillion-dollar renovation that converted it into a condominium/hotel (sometimes called a condotel), in which the units are individually owned, but most are put back into the rental pool for guests. Renovations include redone suites and a new pool, sun deck, and fitness center/spa. It's run by the Outrigger/Ohana Resort group. The main advantage of staying here is its proximity to Waikiki, the downtown financial and business district, the new convention center, and Hawaii's largest mall, the Ala Moana Center. If you're headed for a convention at the convention center, this hotel is your best bet. The rooms vary in price according to size: The cheaper rooms are small, but all come with two double beds and all the amenities you'll need for a comfortable stay. The views of Waikiki and Honolulu from the upper floors are spectacular.

410 Atkinson Dr. (at Kona St., next to Ala Moana Center), Honolulu, HI 96814. © **800/367-6025** or 808/955-4811. Fax 808/944-6839. www.alamoanahotel.com. 1,152 units. $99–$159 double; from $249 suite. Extra person $40. Children 17 and under stay free in parent's room. AE, DC, DISC, MC, V. Valet parking $20; self-parking $15. Bus: 19 or 20. **Amenities:** 5 restaurants; 2 bars (including Rumours Nightclub, p. 294, plus a Polynesian show); concierge; small fitness room; large outdoor pool; limited room service. *In room:* A/C, TV, fridge, hair dryer, free high-speed Internet access.

Pagoda Hotel   This is where local residents from neighbor islands stay when they come to Honolulu. Close to shopping and downtown, the Pagoda has been serving Hawaii's island community for decades. This modest hotel has very plain (motel-like) rooms: clean and utilitarian, with no extra frills. Studios and one- and two-bedroom units have kitchenettes. Ask for a mountainview room to avoid the street noise. There's easy access to Waikiki via TheBus—the nearest stop is just half a block away. *Tip:* Check the website for "Hot Deals" from $95 and excellent rental-car packages.

1525 Rycroft St. (btw. Keeaumoku and Kaheka sts.), Honolulu, HI 96814. © **800/367-6060** or 808/923-4511. Fax 808/955-5067. www.pagodahotel.com. 361 units. From $88 double hotel room; from $140 studio w/kitchenette; from $95 1-bedroom double; from $153 2-bedroom double (sleeps up to 5); lowest rates Sun–Thurs. Extra person $35. Free cribs available. Ask about rental-car packages. AE, DC, DISC, MC, V. Parking $9. Bus: 5 or 6. **Amenities:** Restaurant; bar; babysitting; 2 outdoor pools. *In room:* A/C, TV, fridge, hair dryer, high-speed Internet access ($9 per day), kitchenette (in some units).

DOWNTOWN

Aston at the Executive Centre Hotel ★   Located in the heart of downtown, this is the perfect hotel for the business traveler. Not only is it close to the business and financial center of Honolulu, but the staff goes out of its way to meet every need. The hotel occupies the top 10 floors of a 40-story, multiuse, glass-walled tower. Every room is a spacious suite, with three phones, a whirlpool bathtub, and unobstructed views of the city, the mountains, and Honolulu Harbor. Executive suites add a full kitchen, washer/dryer, and VCR. The only downside is that the suites are privately owned, so quality is inconsistent—some are fantastic, but some need work.

1088 Bishop St. (at S. Hotel St.), Honolulu, HI 96813. © **866/77-HAWAII** (774-2924) or 808/539-3000. Fax 808/523-1088. www.AstonHotels.com. 114 units. $255–$276 suite; $306–$325 1-bedroom. No extra persons. Rates include continental breakfast. AE, DC, DISC, MC, V. Parking $22. Bus: 1, 2, 3, 9, or 12. **Amenities:** Restaurant; concierge; 24-hr. fitness center w/free weights and aerobic equipment; outdoor pool. *In room:* A/C, TV, hair dryer, free high-speed Internet access, kitchenette.

MANOA VALLEY

Manoa Valley Inn   The owners have done quite a bit of repair to the outside of this historic 1915 Gothic home, after being hit hard by the 2006 earthquake (the entire chimney collapsed, taking with it some of the exterior siding). Since then, they've cleaned up the damage (unfortunately, they could not replace the chimney), and the inn, listed on the National Register of Historic Places, is running smoothly again. Completely off the tourist trail, this oasis of peace and tranquillity is nestled on a quiet residential street near the University of Hawaii. It offers a charming venture into the past, with rooms filled with antiques, old-fashioned rose wallpaper, and king-size koa beds. The two top-floor rooms share a full bathroom; the others have private bathrooms.

2001 Vancouver Dr. (at University Ave.), Honolulu, HI 96822. © **808/947-6019.** Fax 808/946-6168. www.manoavalleyinn.com. 7 units, 2 with shared bathroom. $89–$99 double with shared bathroom; $145–$149 double with private bathroom (shower only). Rates include continental breakfast. MC, V. Free parking. Bus: 4 or 6. Children 8 and older preferred. *In room:* A/C (in some units), TV (in some units), free Wi-Fi (in some rooms).

TO THE EAST: KAHALA

Kahala Hotel & Resort ★★★ ☺   After 11 years under the helm of the Mandarin Oriental Group, this grand old hotel (which first opened in 1964) changed management in 2006. The new team, Landmark Hotels, immediately embarked on a $20-million upgrade of the hotel, removing the former 19th-century plantation look and replacing it with 21st-century "Kahala Chic," which resembles the stylish interiors of most of the multimillion-dollar homes in the surrounding area. Everything in the rooms is new: the custom-designed wall-to-wall carpeting, tropical ceiling fans, retro Island artwork, and two- or four-poster beds with comfy Stearns & Foster pillow-top mattresses made up with 310-thread-count Egyptian cotton linens. Accompanying the new look is state-of-the-art technology, including high-speed wireless Internet, 40-inch flatscreen TVs, iPod or MP3 player hookups, and cordless phones. The old girl is grand again!

The location alone makes this hotel worth recommending: Situated in one of Oahu's most prestigious residential areas, the Kahala offers the peace and serenity of a neighbor-island vacation, but with the conveniences of Waikiki just a 10-minute drive away. The lush, tropical grounds include an 800-foot crescent-shaped beach and a 26,000-square-foot lagoon (home to two bottle-nosed dolphins, sea turtles, and tropical fish).

Other extras that make this property outstanding: fabulous dining opportunities (**Hoku's,** p. 194), Hawaiian cultural programs, shuttle service to Waikiki and major shopping centers, free scuba lessons in the pool, daily dolphin-education talks by a trainer from Sea Life Park, and a great children's program. The recently added spa offers treatments such as massages, body scrubs, wraps, and other pampering therapies.

5000 Kahala Ave. (next to the Waialae Country Club), Honolulu, HI 96816. (℗ **800/367-2525** or 808/739-8888. Fax 808/739-8800. www.kahalaresort.com. 343 units. $515–$1,055 double; from $1,700 suite. Extra person $175. Children 17 and under stay free in parent's room. Check the website's "Specials & Packages" for discounts. AE, DC, DISC, MC, V. Parking $25. **Amenities:** 5 restaurants (including Hoku's); 4 bars (including Veranda, p. 295); babysitting; complimentary use of bikes; year-round children's program; concierge; great fitness center w/steam rooms, Jacuzzis, and dry sauna; nearby golf course; large outdoor pool; room service; tennis courts; watersports equipment rentals. *In room:* A/C, TV, hair dryer, minibar, Wi-Fi ($15 per day).

The Windward Coast

Note: Windward Coast accommodations are located on the "Eastern Oahu & the Windward Coast" map (p. 269).

KAILUA

Pat O'Malley of **Pat's Kailua Beach Properties,** 204 S. Kalaheo Ave., Kailua, HI 96734 (℗ **808/261-1653** or 808/262-4128; fax 808/261-0893; www.pats kailua.com), books a wide range of houses and cottages on or near Kailua Beach. Rates start at $100 a day for a studio cottage 33 feet from the beach and go up to $600 per day for a multimillion-dollar home right on the sand with room to sleep eight. All units are fully furnished, with everything from cooking utensils to telephone and TV, even washer/dryers.

Lanikai Tree House & Garden Studio ★ 🏠 This old-time bed-and-breakfast, a *kamaaina* home that reflects the Hawaii of yesteryear, is now into its second generation of owners. The 1,000-square-foot upstairs apartment, which easily accommodates four, is decorated in old Hawaii bungalow style. There's a king-size bed in one bedroom, twin beds in the other bedroom, a large living/dining room, a big bathroom, a kitchenette, and all the modern conveniences—DVD player, cordless phone with answering machine—plus oversize windows to let you enjoy wonderful views. Or you can follow the ginger- and ti-lined path to a 540-square-foot honeymooners' delight, a quaint studio with a huge patio, recently remodeled full-size kitchen, queen-size bed, and sitting area with DVD player, cordless phone, and answering machine. The units are stocked with breakfast fixings (bagels, juice, fruit, coffee, tea) and all the beach equipment you'll need (towels, mats, chairs, coolers, water jugs).

1277 Mokulua Dr. (btw. Onekea and Aala drives in Lanikai), Kailua, HI 96734. ☎ **808/261-7895** or 808/261-1059. www.lanikaibeachrentals.com/vacationrentalsoahu.htm. 2 units. $160 studio double; $175 apt double or $250 for 3 or 4. Cleaning fee $50–$75. Rates include starter breakfast items in fridge. 5-night minimum. MC, V. Free parking. Bus: 52, 55, or 56. **Amenities:** Washer/dryer, gas grill. *In room:* TV/DVD, hair dryer, free high-speed Internet access, kitchenette or kitchen.

Sheffield House ☺ If you're traveling with kids or need rooms for those with disabilities, here's your place in the suburbs of Kailua. Unlike many other B&Bs, Sheffield House welcomes children. The owners, Paul Sheffield and his wife, Rachel, have raised three kids, so they can help you with whatever you need to make your vacation comfortable. There are two units here, a one-bedroom and a studio (which is fully wheelchair-accessible), each with a private entry (through elaborately landscaped tropical gardens) and a full kitchen. The two units can be combined and rented as two-bedroom/two-bathroom accommodations.

131 Kuulei Rd. (at Kalaheo Dr.), Kailua, HI 96734. ☎/fax **808/262-0721.** www.hawaiisheffield house.com. 2 units. $105–$125 double studio (shower only); $125–$155 apt for 4; $230–$280 2-bedroom for 6. Extra person $20. Lower rates sometimes available, depending on the season. Cleaning fee $45. Rates include 1st day's continental breakfast. 3-night minimum. MC, V. Free parking. Bus: 56 or 57. *In room:* TV, kitchenette, free Wi-Fi.

KANEOHE

Alii Bluffs Windward Bed & Breakfast Located on a quiet residential street just 15 minutes from the beach, this traditional B&B is filled with antiques and collectibles, as well as the owners' original art. The guest wing has two rooms, one with a double bed and adjacent bathroom, the other with two extralong twins and a bathroom across the hall. The yard blooms with tropical plants, and the view of Kaneohe Bay from the pool area is breathtaking. Lots of extras make this place stand out from the crowd: daily maid service, a large continental breakfast served on the poolside lanai, afternoon tea, and sewing kits in the bathroom—they'll even lend you anything you need for the beach.

46–251 Ikiiki St. (off Kamehameha Hwy.), Kaneohe, HI 96744. ☎ **800/235-1151** or 808/235-1124. Fax 808/235-1124. www.hawaiiscene.com/aliibluffs. 2 units. $70–$80 double. Rates include continental breakfast. 3-night minimum. MC, V. Free parking. Bus: 55 or 65. Children must be 16 or older. **Amenities:** Outdoor pool. *In room:* Hair dryer, no phone.

Schrader's Windward Country Inn The ambience here is more motel than resort, but Schrader's offers a good alternative for families. The property is nestled in a tranquil, tropical setting on Kaneohe Bay, a 30-minute drive from Waikiki. The complex is made up of cottage-style motels and a collection of older homes. Cottages contain either a full kitchen or a kitchenette with refrigerator and microwave. There's also a picnic area with barbecue grills. Prices are based on the views; depending on how much you're willing to pay, you can look out over a Kahaluu fish pond, the Koolau Range, or Kaneohe Bay. Lots of watersports are available at an additional cost; don't miss the complimentary 2-hour boat cruise with snorkeling and kayaking. Evening activities include Hawaiian music night and karaoke night, both with free pupu (Hawaii-style appetizers). *Tip:* When booking, ask for a unit with a lanai; that way, you'll end up with at least a partial view of the bay.

47–039 Lihikai Dr. (off Kamehameha Hwy.), Kaneohe, HI 96744. © **800/735-5071** or 808/239-5711. Fax 808/239-6658. www.hawaiiscene.com/schrader. 20 units. $72–$143 1-bedroom double; $127–$215 2-bedroom for 4; $226–$358 3-bedroom for 6; $446–$501 4-bedroom for 8. Extra person $7.50. Rates include continental breakfast. 2-night minimum. AE, DC, DISC, MC, V. Free parking. Bus: 52, 55, or 56. **Amenities:** Outdoor pool; watersports equipment rentals. *In room:* TV, kitchenette.

The North Shore

The North Shore doesn't have many accommodations or an abundance of tourist facilities—some say that's its charm. **Team Real Estate,** 66–250 Kamehameha Hwy., Ste. D-103, Haleiwa, HI 96712 (© **800/982-8602** or 808/637-3507; fax 808/637-8881; www.teamrealestate.com), manages North Shore vacation rentals, ranging from affordable cottages to condos to oceanfront homes, at rates of $65 for a condo unit, $120 for a one-bedroom apartment, and $835 a night for an 11-bedroom oceanfront luxury home. Cleaning fees vary. A minimum stay of 1 week is required for some properties, but shorter stays are available as well.

Note: North Shore accommodations are located on the "Oahu's North Shore" map (p. 279).

VERY EXPENSIVE

Turtle Bay Resort ★★   This property recently underwent a massive $35-million renovation. When the resort was first built 36 years ago, there was hope that it would become a "gaming operation" (with Vegas-style gambling). That never materialized, but the dark interior, closed to the awe-inspiring view, remained. With the new renovations, the lobby is now open and airy, with floor-to-ceiling windows overlooking the dramatic ocean view. The resort is spectacular: an hour's drive from Waikiki, but eons away in its country feel. Sitting on 808 acres, this place is loaded with activities, including a stable that offers horseback riding, and 5 miles of shoreline with secluded white-sand coves. It's located on Kalaeokaunu Point ("Point of the Altar"), where ancient Hawaiians built a small altar to the fish gods (the altar's remains are now at the Bishop Museum).

All guest rooms have ocean views and balconies, marble floors and counters in the bathrooms, and comfy bedding. If you can afford it, book one of the separate beach cottages. Positioned right on the ocean (the views alone are worth the price), the 42 bungalows boast hardwood floors, poster beds with feather comforters, butler service, and separate check-in and private concierge (like a hotel within a hotel).

The biggest change here is the new Spa Luana, with six treatment rooms, a meditation waiting area, an outdoor workout area, plus a complete fitness center and a private elevator to the rooms on the second floor, reserved for guests getting spa treatments. The signature restaurant, **21 Degrees North** (p. 197), is so fabulous that people are driving from all over the island to eat here.

57–091 Kamehameha Hwy. (Hwy. 83), Kahuku, HI 96731. © **800/203-3650** or 808/293-6000. Fax 808/293-9147. www.turtlebayresort.com. 443 units. $186–$219 double; from $381 cottage; from $270 suite; from $1,090 villa. Extra person $50. Children 17 and under stay free in parent's room. Check website for special packages. Daily $25 resort fee for self-parking, Internet access, and more. AE, DC, DISC, MC, V. Bus: 52 or 55. **Amenities:** 4 restaurants (including 21 Degrees

North and Ola, p. 197); 2 bars, plus a poolside bar; babysitting; concierge; 36 holes of golf; 2 Jacuzzis; 2 outdoor heated pools (w/80-ft. water slide); room service; spa w/fitness center; 10 Plexipave tennis courts; watersports equipment rentals. *In room:* A/C, TV, fridge, hair dryer, high-speed Internet access.

MODERATE

Santa's by the Sea ★ 📫   This certainly must be where Santa Claus comes to vacation: St. Nick knows a bargain when he sees it. The location, price, and style make this a must-stay if you plan to see the North Shore. It's one of the few North Shore B&Bs right on the beach—and not just any beach, but the famous Banzai Pipeline. You can go from your bed to the sand in less than 30 seconds to watch the sun rise over the Pacific. The one-bedroom downstairs unit features finely crafted woodwork, bay windows, and a collection of unique Santa figurines and one-of-a-kind Christmas items. It may sound schlocky, but somehow it gives the apartment a country charm. Honeymooners, take note: There's lots of privacy here. The unit has its own entrance, a living room with VCR and stereo, and a full kitchen with everything a cook could need. There's also a barbecue area. Fruit, cereal, bread, coffee, tea, and juice are provided on the first morning, to get you started.

Ke Waena Rd. (off Kamehameha Hwy.), Haleiwa, HI 96712. ℂ **808/638-7837.** www.santasby thesea.com. 1 unit (shower only). $225 double. Extra person $10. Rates include breakfast items in fridge. 2-night minimum. AE, MC, V through PayPal. Free parking. Bus: 52 or 55. *In room:* A/C (in bedroom), TV/VCR, hair dryer, computer w/Internet access, kitchen.

INEXPENSIVE

Ke Iki Beach Bungalows   This collection of studio, one-bedroom, and two-bedroom cottages, located on a beautiful white-sand beach, has been totally renovated, to the tune of $1 million. Snuggled on a large lot with its own 200-foot stretch of beach between two legendary surf spots (Waimea Bay and Banzai Pipeline), the units are still reasonably priced—and if you can live without being right on the ocean, the garden units are very affordable for the location. All units have full kitchens and their own barbecue areas. Most units are compact, with very small bedrooms. But, hey, with the ocean right outside, just how much time are you going to spend indoors? The winter waves are too rough for most swimmers, but there's a large lava reef nearby with tide pools to explore and, on the other side, Shark's Cove, a relatively protected snorkeling area. Nearby are tennis courts and a jogging path. *Tip:* Stay on the beach side, where the views are well worth the extra bucks.

59–579 Ke Iki Rd. (off Kamehameha Hwy.), Haleiwa, HI 96712. ℂ **866/638-8229** or 808/638-8229. Fax 808/637-6100. www.keikibeach.com. 11 units. $160 double gardenview studio; $145 double gardenview 1-bedroom; $195–$215 double beachfront 1-bedroom; $175–$185 double gardenview 2-bedroom; $220–$230 double beachfront 2-bedroom. Extra person stays free. Cleaning fee $55–$100 per week *or* per visit (if less than a week). AE, MC, V. Free parking. Bus: 52. **Amenities:** Complimentary watersports equipment and bikes. *In room:* TV, CD player, kitchen.

Leeward Oahu: The Waianae Coast

JW Marriott Ihilani Resort & Spa at Ko Olina Resort ★★★ ☺   When the 640-acre Ko Olina Resort community opened, some 17 miles and 25 minutes west of Honolulu Airport (and worlds away from the tourist scene of Waikiki), critics wondered who would want to stay so far from the city. Lots of people, it turns out. Ihilani ("Heavenly Splendor") is nestled in a quiet location between the Pacific Ocean and the first of four man-made beach lagoons. Featuring a luxury spa and fitness center, plus tennis and one of Hawaii's premier golf courses, it's a haven of relaxation and well-being. The spa alone is reason enough to come here. Treatments include thalassotherapy, Vichy showers, Roman pools, and various kinds of massages. You can even have a fitness-and-relaxation program custom designed.

It's hard to get a bad room in the 15-story building—some 85% of the units enjoy lagoon or ocean views. Accommodations are spacious (680 sq. ft.) and luxuriously appointed, with huge lanais outfitted with very comfortable cushioned teak furniture. Luxurious marble bathrooms have deep soaking tubs, glass-enclosed showers, and many more amenities. Other extras include transportation to Waikiki and Ala Moana Center, a 3-mile coastal fitness trail, and a stretch of four white-sand beaches for ocean activities.

The Ihilani's children's program puts all others to shame, offering year-round outdoor adventures and indoor learning activities for toddlers and teens alike. There's a 125-gallon fish tank, an evening lounge for teen-themed parties, and more.

92–1001 Olani St., Kapolei, HI 96707. (C) **800/626-4446** or 808/679-0079. Fax 808/679-0080. www.ihilani.com. 387 units. $269–$464 double; from $665 suite. Extra person $50. Children 16 and under (maximum 2) stay free in parent's room using existing bedding. Ask about Paradise Plus package rates, which include a free car rental or daily breakfast for 2 starting at $369. AE, DC, DISC, MC, V. Parking $29. No bus service. Take H-1 west toward Pearl City/Ewa Beach; stay on H-1 until it becomes Hwy. 93 (Farrington Hwy.); look for the exit sign for Ko Olina Resort; turn right on Olani St. **Amenities:** 3 restaurants; 2 bars (w/nightly entertainment poolside); babysitting; excellent children's program; concierge; championship 18-hole Ko Olina Golf Course, designed by Ted Robinson; 2 outdoor pools; room service; world-class spa; tennis club w/pro shop; watersports equipment rentals. *In room:* A/C, TV, hair dryer, minibar, Wi-Fi ($13 per day).

WHERE TO DINE

On Oahu, the full range of dining choices includes chef-owned glamour restaurants, neighborhood eateries, fast-food joints, ethnic spots, and food courts in shopping malls. The recommendations below are organized by location, beginning with Waikiki, then neighborhoods west of Waikiki, neighborhoods east of Waikiki, and finally the Windward Coast and the North Shore.

Waikiki

VERY EXPENSIVE

Azure Restaurant ★★★ SEAFOOD   For a night of romance, this lantern-lit, oceanside restaurant offers fresh fish prepared with a mixture of French and Hawaiian influences and top-notch service at the Royal Hawaiian Hotel. Part of the recent $85-million renovation of the hotel, this exotic locale lets you dine in plush banquettes with comfy pillows or rent a beachfront cabana and have your own private dining area. Hawaii's fresh fish (most bought that morning from the Honolulu Fish Market) is the star of the menu. (Tasting menus and prix fixe menus are available.)

Royal Hawaiian Hotel, 2259 Kalakaua Ave., Honolulu, HI 96815. ℂ **808/823-7311.** www.royal-hawaiian.com. Reservations recommended. Entrees-only $32–$60; 3-course prix-fixe dinner $59. AE, DC, MC, V. Nightly 5:30–9pm.

BLT Steak ★★★ STEAKHOUSE   BLT Steak does not stand for bacon-lettuce-tomato Steak but for Bistro Laurent Tourondel, the French-trained chef who began his franchise of well-known steakhouses to big applause in New York City. This large (4,000-square-foot) restaurant sits on the ground floor of the newly opened (2010) Trump International Hotel, joining several other high-end, fabulous restaurants in the surrounding blocks (Nobu Waikiki at the Waikiki Parc, La Mer at the Halekulani, and Roy's on the ground floor of the Waikiki Embassy Suites). You can choose to sit inside the clubby steakhouse or dine alfresco with a view of traffic-clogged Kalia Road. The service is impeccable. And if you are a carnivore, this steakhouse is for you. The steaks, from Wagyu beef in the Midwest, are broiled at 1,700 degrees and finished with herb butter and an option of nine sauces (ranging from a tangy red-wine sauce to a dreamy Roquefort sauce). In true Steakhouse tradition, everything is a la carte—appetizers, meats, sides, and dessert. Don't turn your nose up at the sides; I could have made a meal of the creamed spinach with nutmeg, the leek-and-potatoes hash browns, or the jalapeño mashed potatoes (each $8). And, if you aren't too full, the desserts ($10 each) are divine, such as the crepe soufflé with passion fruit sauce or the warm chocolate tart with pistachio ice cream or the sticky toffee pudding with pecan ice cream. *Budget travelers note:* They serve a very large portion prix-fixe meal with appetizer, entree, side dish, and dessert for $60.

Trump International Hotel, 223 Saratoga Rd. ℂ **808/683-7440.** www.bltsteak.com. Reservations recommended. Entree-only $29–$42; prix-fixe dinner $60 for 3 courses. AE, DC, MC, V. Sun–Thurs 5:30–10pm; Fri–Sat 5:30–11pm.

La Mer ★★★ NEOCLASSIC FRENCH   This is the splurge restaurant of Hawaii, the oceanfront bastion of haute cuisine, where two of the state's finest chefs (George Mavrothalassitis and Philippe Padovani, each with his own eponymous restaurant now) quietly redefined fine dining in Hawaii. La Mer is romantic, elegant, and expensive; dress up not to be seen, but to match the ambience and food. It's the only AAA Five Diamond restaurant in the state, with a second-floor, open-sided room with views of Diamond Head and the sound of trade winds rustling the nearby coconut fronds. Michelin Award–winning chef Yves Garnier melds classical French influences with fresh Island ingredients. The former a la carte menu is now prix-fixe, ranging from two courses ($90) to five courses ($150). Winners include the signature crispy-skin filet of onaga with truffle jus, tomato confit, and fresh basil, and the delightful local fish baked in a rosemary-salt crust. The wine list, desserts, and service—formal without being stiff—complete the dining experience.

At the Halekulani, 2199 Kalia Rd. ℂ **808/923-2311.** www.halekulani.com. Reservations recommended. Jackets or long-sleeved shirts required for men. Prix-fixe menus $90 for 2 courses, $120 for 3 courses, $135 for 4 courses; $150 for "Ultimate" dinner. AE, DC, MC, V. Daily 6–10pm.

Michel's ★★ FRENCH/HAWAII REGIONAL   This room on the sand at Sans Souci Beach has windows that open to the ocean air. One side faces the sunset, with torches on the breakwater and a hula moon above the palm fronds; the entire Waikiki skyline is visible on the other. The live music (beginning at

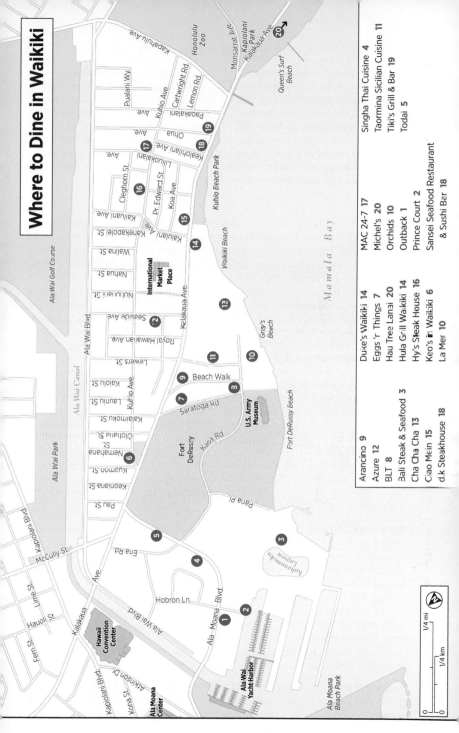

Where to Dine in Waikiki

Arancino **9**
Azure **12**
BLT **8**
Bali Steak & Seafood **3**
Cha Cha Cha **13**
Ciao Mein **15**
d.k Steakhouse **18**

Duke's Waikiki **14**
Eggs 'r' Things **7**
Hau Tree Lanai **20**
Hula Grill Waikiki **14**
Hy's Steak House **16**
Keo's in Waikiki **6**
La Mer **10**

MAC 24-7 **17**
Michel's **20**
Orchids **10**
Outback **1**
Prince Court **2**
Sansei Seafood Restaurant
& Sushi Bar **18**

Singha Thai Cuisine **4**
Taormina Sicilian Cuisine **11**
Tiki's Grill & Bar **19**
Todai **5**

You're not limited to the room-service menu in your hotel room; **Room Service in Paradise** (© 808/941-DINE [3463]; www.941-dine.com) delivers nearly a dozen different cuisines (from Pacific Rim to Italian to burgers) from oodles of restaurants right to your room. All you do is select a restaurant and order what you want (see the online menu or pick up one of its magazines in various Waikiki locations). You'll be charged for the food, plus a $8.25 to $9.25 delivery fee in Waikiki (more in outlying areas) and a tip for the driver. Best of all, you can pay with your credit card. Both lunch and dinner are available; you can call in advance and have your food delivered whenever you want.

6:30pm) attracts music lovers. All tables have an ocean view, and dining here is less stiff and more welcoming than in bygone years (jackets are no longer required for men). Chef Hardy Kintscher has added his touch to the classics (onion soup, steak tartare, chateaubriand, bouillabaisse) and prepares fresh seafood, vegetarian creations, and rack of lamb with restraint and creativity.

At the Colony Surf Condominiums, 2895 Kalakaua Ave. © 808/923-6552. www.michelshawaii.com. Reservations recommended. Collared shirts and long pants preferred for men; no shorts or beachwear permitted. Main courses $36–$50. AE, DC, MC, V. Daily 5:30–9pm.

EXPENSIVE

Bali Steak & Seafood ★★ CONTINENTAL/PACIFIC RIM   This is another memorable oceanfront dining room—pale and full of light, with a white grand piano at the entrance and sweeping views of the ocean (ask for a table by the window). The menu merges Island cooking styles and ingredients, as in the sugar cane–crusted scallops in a ponzu-infused sauce served with a warm pickled seaweed salad. Or try the wonderful surf and turf—Kona lobster tail, lobster mac 'n cheese with tomato butter sauce and filet mignon. The new menu features the signature orange miso–glazed Kona kampachi, as well as steaks seasoned with Kona sea salt and served with a variety of sauces from the classic Bernaise to Poha berry chutney. Leave room for the mouthwatering desserts.

At the Hilton Hawaiian Village, 2005 Kalia Rd. © 808/949-4321, ext. 43. Reservations recommended. Main courses $30–$65. AE, DC, DISC, MC, V. Tues–Sat 5:30–9:30pm.

Hy's Steak House AMERICAN   The atmosphere here is traditional steakhouse: dark, clubby, lots of leather, with the smell of good Scotch and filet mignon wafting through the air. It's a great choice for steak lovers with hefty pocketbooks or for those who have tired of Hawaii Regional Cuisine. Hy's has demonstrated admirable staying power in the cult of the low-fat, still scoring high among carnivores while offering ample alternatives, such as a grilled vegetable platter and excellent salads prepared tableside (the spinach and Caesar are textbook perfect). Garlic lovers swear by "Hy's Garlic Steak," a richly endowed filet with sliced mushrooms.

2440 Kuhio Ave. © 808/922-5555. www.hyshawaii.com. Reservations recommended. Main courses $28–$70 or market price. AE, DC, DISC, MC, V. Mon–Fri 6–10pm; Sat–Sun 5:30–10pm.

Orchids ★★ INTERNATIONAL/SEAFOOD   Orchids highlights elegant presentations of fresh local produce and seafood in a fantasy setting with consummate service. It's an extraordinary venue, and the food ranges from good to excellent. Blinding-white linens and a view of Diamond Head from the open oceanfront dining room will start you off with a smile. (The parade of oiled bodies traversing the sea wall is part of the entertainment.) At lunch, the seafood curry, though pricey, is a winner, as are the tagine of roasted vegetables and the niçoise salad with seared tuna. At dinner, onaga (ruby snapper) is steamed with ginger, Chinese parsley, shiitake mushrooms, and soy sauce, and then drizzled with hot sesame oil—delightful. The delicious moi, seared and served on shaved fennel with pearl onions, olives, and a Ka'u orange vinaigrette, blends Mediterranean and Asian. There are lamb, chicken, and beef entrees as well, and the desserts, especially the chocolate-hazelnut dacquoise and the Halekulani signature coconut cake, are extraordinary. *Tip:* Book weeks in advance for **Sunday brunch ★★★**, one of the best in Hawaii.

At the Halekulani, 2199 Kalia Rd. ℃ **808/923-2311.** Reservations recommended. Dinner main courses $26–$51; Sun brunch $55 adults, $29 children 5-12. AE, DC, MC, V. Mon–Sat 7:30–11am, 11:30am–2pm, and 6–10pm; Sun 9:30am–2:30pm and 6–10pm.

Prince Court ★ CONTEMPORARY ISLAND   Floor to-ceiling windows, sunny views of the harbor, and top-notch buffets are Prince Court's attractions, especially at lunch, when locals and visitors line up at the international buffet. The harbor view is particularly pleasing at sunset and on Friday nights, when fireworks light up the sky. Chef Khamtan Tanhchaleun keeps the menu fresh and the dining room busy. Friday through Sunday, diners can sample everything from local seafood and Hawaii Regional specialties (like melt-in-your-mouth ahi carpaccio) to excellent grilled and roasted meats. Desserts, too, are legendary, especially the custard-drenched bread pudding and the macadamia-nut pie.

At the Hawaii Prince Hotel Waikiki, 100 Holomoana St. ℃ **808/944-4494.** Reservations recommended. Dinner prix fixe and buffet $37–$57 (no a la carte for dinner); breakfast buffet $21; weekend brunch $37; luncheon buffet $25; seafood dinner buffet $45. AE, DC, MC, V. Daily 6–10:30am; Mon–Sat 11am–2pm; Sun brunch 10am–1pm; Mon–Thurs 6–9:30pm; Fri–Sun 5:30–9:30pm.

MODERATE

Arancino ITALIAN   When jaded Honolulu residents venture into Waikiki for dinner, it had better be good; Arancino is worth the hunt. Here's what you'll find: a cheerful cafe of Monet-yellow walls and tile floors, respectable pastas, wonderful pizzas, fabulous red-pepper salsa and rock-salt focaccia, we-try-harder service, and reasonable prices. The risotto changes daily. Don't miss the Gorgonzola-asparagus pizza if it's on the menu. The line on the sidewalk to get in is worth the wait.

255 Beach Walk. ℃ **808/923-5557.** Main courses $12–$35. AE, DC, DISC, MC, V. Daily 11:30am–2:30pm and 5–10pm.

Ciao Mein ITALIAN/CHINESE   Risotto with chopsticks, fried rice with a fork—such is the cross-cultural way of Ciao Mein, a decade and a half old and still going strong. The large, pleasant dining room; efficient service; surprisingly good Chinese food (especially for a hotel restaurant); and award-winning menu items have made this a haven for noodle lovers. The honey-walnut shrimp is a hit, the angel-hair pasta with spicy ginger-garlic shrimp is a big seller, and few who have tasted Ciao Mein's tiramisu (Tirami Su) will forget its creamy, ambrosial kick. The antipasto is Italian, and the seafood funn lasagna (as in chow

If your flight to Honolulu arrives late, you won't starve in Waikiki, thanks to the newly opened **MAC 24-7** (which stands for Modern American Cooking, 24 hr. a day, 7 days a week), at the **Hilton Waikiki Prince Kuhio,** 2500 Kuhio Ave., at Liliuokalani Avenue (🕾 808/921-5564). All day long, the menu has everything from breakfast, lunch, and dinner to snacks and desserts (though the bar stops pouring 4–6am). It's not just for late-night dining (although it comes in handy, as Waikiki eateries shut down by 10 or 11pm); it's also a great place to get picnic lunches during the day. The view from the floor-to-ceiling windows is of the landscaped gardens in the lobby, the interior is sophisticated but sparse in a Zenlike way, and the waitstaff is friendly and helpful. The comfort food is reasonably priced for Waikiki (most entrees are $13–$28), and the portion sizes can feed two or even three hungry people. My pick for best meal of the day is breakfast: The giant 6-inch buttery cinnamon roll ($6) will feed two, and the yummy wild-blueberry pancakes ($15) are supersized—you get three pancakes, each one 14 inches in diameter. Another must-try: the delicious meatloaf with garlic mashed potatoes and mushroom gravy ($18).

funn) is a form of what Ciao Mein calls "collision cuisine"—a mix of Chinese and Italian.

At the Hyatt Regency Waikiki, 2424 Kalakaua Ave. 🕾 **808/923-2426.** Reservations recommended. Main courses $21–$40; prix-fixe menu $47–$78. AE, DC, DISC, MC, V. Daily 6–10pm.

d.k Steakhouse ★ STEAK   Attention, carnivores: This place opened in 2004 to rave reviews, giving the national chains and the top local steakhouses a run for their money. Locally known chef D. K. Kodama (of Sansei Seafood Restaurant & Sushi Bar, p. 176, and Vino Italian Tapas & Wine Bar, p. 186) and Hawaii's top sommelier, Chuck Furuya, have created the ultimate steakhouse for the 21st century at very reasonable prices (especially for Waikiki). Purists will love the prime-grade and dry-aged (in-house for 10 days) New York strip and filet mignon, served either unadorned or with one of the following toppings: sauce au poivre with two types of peppercorn; or D. K.'s own sesame seed–miso sauce. The ultimate treat is the 22-ounce, bone-in rib-eye (aged for 15 days): Every bite has a melt-in-your-mouth richness that steak fans will remember forever. For the non-steak lovers, the menu also includes a fresh catch, lamb chops, and chicken. Come early and book a table on the lanai to watch the sun set on Waikiki Beach. The decor inside is romantic, too, with dim lighting and intimate wooden booths.

At the Waikiki Beach Marriott Resort, 2552 Kalakaua Ave., 3rd floor. 🕾 **808/931-6280.** www. dksteakhouse.com. Reservations recommended. Main courses $18–$80. AE, DISC, MC, V. Daily 5:30–10pm.

Duke's Waikiki ★ 🍴 STEAK/SEAFOOD   Hip, busy, and on the ocean—this is what dining in Waikiki should be. There's hardly a time when the open-air dining room isn't filled with good Hawaiian music. But just because Duke's is popular among singles, don't dismiss it as a pickup bar—its ambience is stellar. Named after fabled surfer Duke Kahanamoku, this casual, upbeat hot spot buzzes with diners and Hawaiian-music lovers throughout the day. Lunch and the Barefoot

Bar menu include pizza, sandwiches, burgers, salads, and appetizers su
mac-nut and crab wontons and the ever-popular grilled chicken quesadillas. 1
ner fare is steak and seafood, with decent marks for the fresh catch, prepared 1
your choice of five styles. There's live entertainment nightly from 4 to 6pm and
9:30pm to midnight, with no cover. Be prepared to fight the crowds if you come
at sunset.

At the Outrigger Waikiki on the Beach, 2335 Kalakaua Ave. ✆ 808/922-2268. www.dukes
waikiki.com. Reservations recommended for dinner. Main courses $20–$32; breakfast buffet $15.
AE, DC, DISC, MC, V. Daily 7am–midnight.

Hau Tree Lanai ★ PACIFIC RIM   This delightful Honolulu institution scores
higher on ambience than on food. The outdoor setting and earnest menu make it
a popular informal dining spot; an ancient hau tree provides shade and charm for
diners. A diverse parade of beachgoers at Sans Souci Beach (called "Dig Me"
Beach for its eye-candy sunbathers) is part of the scenery. Breakfast here is a
must: Choices include salmon Florentine, served with a fresh-baked scone; poi
pancakes; Belgian waffles, eggs Benedict; and the Hawaiian platter of miniature
poi pancakes, eggs, and a medley of Island sausages. Lunchtime offerings include
an assortment of burgers, sandwiches, salads, fish, and pasta. Dinner selections
are more ambitious and less reliable: fresh moonfish, red snapper, opakapaka,
ahi, and chef's specials, in preparations ranging from plain grilled to stuffed and
over-the-top rich.

At the New Otani Kaimana Beach Hotel, 2863 Kalakaua Ave. ✆ 808/921-7066. www.kaimana.
com. Reservations recommended. Breakfast $12–$16; lunch $13–$17; dinner $30–$39. AE, DC,
DISC, MC, V. Mon–Sat 7–10:45am, 11:45am–2pm, and 5:30–9pm; Sun 7–10:45am, noon–2pm, and
5:30–9pm. Late lunch in the open-air bar daily 2–4pm.

Hula Grill Waikiki ★★ 🍴 HAWAII REGIONAL   This beachside bistro is the
best place for breakfast in Waikiki: Not only does it have a terrific view of all of
Waikiki (clear to Diamond Head), but the food is fabulous and a great value.
Choose from a generous selection of pancakes (banana, mac-nut, pineapple,
even coconut) and eggs (from crab-cake eggs Benedict to a ham, bacon, and Portuguese sausage omelet). Come back for a romantic dinner   the restaurant is
decorated in a 1930s Hawaii waterfront-home theme, with touches like the ohia-
log bar, a hula-doll collection, slate floors, and lauhala-pine ceilings. Signature
dinner dishes include Hawaiian ceviche, fire-grilled ahi steak, and chili-roasted
tandoori opah (moonfish). Live Hawaiian music nightly from 7 to 9pm.

At the Outrigger Waikiki on the Beach, 2335 Kalakaua Ave. ✆ 808/923-HULA (4852). www.
hulapie.com. Reservations recommended for dinner. Breakfast $6–$14; main courses $17–$33.
AE, DC, MC, V. Daily 6:30–10:45am, 4:30–6pm (happy hour with light menu), and 5–10pm.

Keo's in Waikiki ★ THAI   With fresh spices and spirited dishes, Keo's arrived
in Waikiki with a splashy tropical ambience and a menu that locals and visitors
love. Owner Keo Sananikone grows his own herbs, fruits, and vegetables without
pesticides on his North Shore farm. Satay shrimp, basil-infused eggplant with
tofu, evil jungle prince (shrimp, chicken, or vegetables in a basil-coconut-chili
sauce), Thai garlic shrimp with mushrooms, pad Thai noodles, and the ever-
delectable panang, green, and yellow curries are among his abiding delights.

2028 Kuhio Ave. ✆ 808/951-9355. www.keosthaicuisine.com. Reservations recommended.
Main courses $13–$20; prix-fixe menu $30–$45. AE, DC, DISC, MC, V. Daily 4–10:30pm.

...estaurant at a time. ...wspaper food critic ...ay has put together **Hawaii Food Tours** to show you a side of Hawaii that you would not discover on your own. He offers three different tours, all with transportation from your Waikiki hotel in an air-conditioned van and all with running commentary on Hawaii's history, culture, and architecture. My favorite was the **Hole-in-the-Wall Tour,** a lunch tour from 10am to 2pm, for $99 per person, that includes a visit to at least six ethnic restaurants (plus a behind-the-scenes walking and tasting tour of Chinatown—yum, yum). The **Gourmet Trilogy Tour for Food & Wine Lovers** visits three restaurants for everything from champagne to a decadent dessert, at a price of $199 per person. For information and booking, call ✆ **800/ 715-2468** or 808/926-FOOD (3663), or go to www.hawaiifoodtours.com.

Sansei Seafood Restaurant & Sushi Bar ★★ SUSHI/PACIFIC RIM   Perpetual award-winner D. K. Kodama, who built Kapalua's Sansei into one of Maui's most popular eateries, has become something of a local legend with his exuberant brand of sushi and fusion cooking. Although some of the flavors (sweet Thai chili sauce with cilantro, for example) may be too fussy for sushi purists, there are ample choices. On the extensive menu, you'll see Sansei's award-winning trademark Asian rock-shrimp cake and Japanese calamari salad, as well as seared foie gras nigiri (lightly seared duck liver over sushi rice, accompanied by caramelized onion and ripe mango) or the wonderful hand roll with mango, blue crab, greens, and peanuts. More traditional selections range from very fresh yellowtail sushi to Japanese miso eggplant.

At the Waikiki Beach Marriott Resort, 2552 Kalakaua Ave., 3rd floor. ✆ **808/931-6286.** www. sanseihawaii.com. Reservations recommended. Sushi $8–$20; entrees $16–$43. AE, DISC, MC, V. Daily 5:30–10pm; Fri 10pm–2am karaoke.

Singha Thai Cuisine THAI   The Royal Thai dancers arch their graceful fingers nightly in classical Thai dance on the small center stage, but you may be too busy tucking into your blackened-ahi summer rolls to notice. Imaginative combination dinners and the use of local organic ingredients are among the special touches of this Thai-fusion restaurant. Complete dinners for two to five cover many tastes and are an ideal way for the uninitiated to sample the menu, which also shows the considerable influence of Hawaii Regional Cuisine. Some highlights: local fresh catch with Thai chili and light black-bean sauce; red, green, yellow, and vegetarian curries; spicy lemon grass soup with shrimp; and many seafood dishes. Such extensive use of fresh fish (mahimahi, ono, ahi, opakapaka, onaga, and uku) in traditional Thai preparations is unusual for a Thai restaurant. The entertainment and indoor-outdoor dining add to this first-class experience.

1910 Ala Moana Blvd. (at the Ala Moana end of Waikiki). ✆ **808/941-2898.** www.singhathai.com. Reservations recommended. Main courses $16–$32; complete dinners $35. AE, DC, DISC, MC, V. Daily 4–10pm.

Tiki's Grill & Bar AMERICAN/PACIFIC RIM   Located on the second floor of the Aston Waikiki Beach Hotel, overlooking Waikiki Beach (get an outside table on the lanai at sunset), this casual eatery is done up with lava-rock walls, palm-wood flooring, and fishnets hanging from the ceiling. A 30-foot volcano is the showpiece in the bar, where you can snack on pupu. The cuisine is good ol' American with a touch of Pacific Rim, apparent in all the fish dishes. Tiki's signature dish is king salmon glazed with lemon grass beurre blanc. Also high on the list is the ahi seared with Cajun spices and served with kalua-pig mashed potatoes. Save room for the chocolate lava flow, ice-cream cookie sandwich, and outstanding guava cheesecake. There's live Hawaiian music in the bar nightly at 6pm.

At the Aston Waikiki Beach Hotel, 2570 Kalakaua Ave. (at Paoakalani St.). ☏ **808/923-TIKI** (8454). www.tikisgrill.com. Main courses $12–$20 lunch, $22–$50 dinner. AE, DC, DISC, MC, V. Daily 10:30am–midnight.

INEXPENSIVE

Cha Cha Cha MEXICAN/CARIBBEAN   Its heroic margaritas, cheap happy-hour beer, pupu, excellent homemade chips, and all-around lovable menu make this a Waikiki treasure. From the beans to the salsa to the grilled Jamaican chicken, there's nothing wimpy about the flavors here. The lime, coconut, and Caribbean spices make Cha Cha Cha more than plain ol' Mex, adding zing to the fresh-fish burritos, the jerk chicken, and the grilled veggies in a spinach tortilla. Tacos, tamales, quesadillas, soups, enchiladas, chimichangas, and a host of spicy pork, chicken, and fish ensembles are real pleasers. Ask about the specials—they're likely to be wonderful. Blackened swordfish, shrimp fajitas, and home-made desserts (including a creamy toasted coconut custard you won't want to miss) are some of the highlights. The location, across from two of Waikiki's three movie theaters, makes it a choice spot for pre- and post-theater dining.

342 Seaside Ave. ☏ **808/923-7797.** Main courses $9–$13 breakfast; complete dinners $10–$19. DISC, MC, V. Daily 6–10am and 11:30am–11pm; happy hour daily 4–6pm and 9–11pm.

Eggs 'n Things ★★ BREAKFAST   After a fire burned down the old location, this new "eggs" has opened across from the Ft. DeRussy Park. You'll find the fluffiest omelets (which come with pancakes, potatoes, and toast) and melt-in-your-mouth waffles (piled high with fruit and whipped cream). Dinner/lunch is also available (chicken-fried steak, calamari fried steak and fresh ahi steak are the headliners). Prices are surprisingly reasonable, making this place worth standing in line for.

343 Saratoga Rd., Honolulu 96815. ☏ **808/949-0820.** www.eggsnthings.com. Breakfast entrees $7–$12. Lunch/dinner entrees $9.25–$13. DC, MC, V. Daily 6am–2pm and 5–10pm.

Taormina Sicilian Cuisine ★★ ITALIAN   An elegant slice of Italy in the midst of Waikiki offers lunch and dinner with recipes from Sicily's seaside town of Taormina. It's owned by Japanese WDI International Corporation, with a Japanese chef at the helm; the food is pure Sicilian, the atmosphere in the two-story restaurant serene, and the service efficient. The pastas are not soaked in heavy sauces but dressed in pure, extra-virgin olive oil with fresh vegetables or lightly grilled fish. Be sure to try the antipasti misti, which includes Palermo-style caponata, marinated sweet shrimp, baby octopus, and artichokes. Their speciality dish is *uni pasta* (sea urchin pasta). Save room for the *dolci* (dessert)—I'd recommend the cannoli with pistachio gelato. Reservations are a must.

227 Lewers St. (btw. Don Ho and Lewers sts.), Waikiki, HI 96815. ℂ **808/926-5050.** www.taorminarestaurant.com. Reservations required. Lunch entrees $14–$17; dinner entrees $16–$42. MC, V. Sun–Thurs 11am–10pm; Fri–Sat 11am–11pm.

Honolulu Beyond Waikiki

ALA MOANA & KAKAAKO

Expensive

Longhi's ITALIAN/MEDITERRANEAN   Bob Longhi, who opened Longhi's in Lahaina in 1976, is behind this swank, open-air restaurant with romantic sunset views of the ocean. It features the family's famous cooking in dishes like lobster Longhi over linguine, prawns Amaretto, and Ahi Torino (sushi-grade ahi in a macadamia-nut crust). Meals can be pricey, in part because everything comes a la carte, but the view is spectacular and the service is prompt. It's also a great place for breakfast (the French toast with a "touch" of Grand Marnier is wickedly divine, and the baked goods are delicious), with surprisingly moderate prices and that same terrific view. Lunch, which can get crowded, features yummy salads, sandwiches, pastas, and excellent fish entrees.

At the Ala Moana Center, 1450 Ala Moana Blvd. ℂ **808/947-9899.** www.longhis.com. Reservations recommended for dinner. Main courses $8.50–$21 breakfast; $12–$38 lunch; $17–$42 dinner. AE, DISC, MC, V. Mon–Fri 8am–10pm; Sat–Sun 7:45am–10pm.

Mariposa ★★ PACIFIC RIM/SOUTHWESTERN   Once you get past the gourmet-food department of the new Neiman Marcus, you'll be in Mariposa, a popular lunch spot in town. High ceilings and tables on the deck, with views of Ala Moana Park and its Art Deco bridges, add up to a pleasing ambience, with or without the shopping. You'll find cordial service, nearly a dozen reasonably priced wines by the glass, and a menu of Pacific and American specialties that include everything from seared scallops with Lilikoi butter, risotto, and sautéed beet greens to New York strip. Chef Mark Anthony Freiberg's creativity comes out in dishes like the Laksa seafood curry, which, unfortunately, is available only at lunch. Save room for my favorite dessert, the Valrhona chocolate fudge cake with raspberry compote—heaven on earth!

At Neiman Marcus, Ala Moana Center, 1450 Ala Moana Blvd. ℂ **808/951-3420.** www.neimanmarcushawaii.com. Reservations recommended. Main courses $14–$24 lunch, $27–$36 dinner. AE, MC, V. Mon–Sun 11am–9pm. Now doing prix-fixe lunches $25–$35, and dinners $55–$65.

The Pineapple Room ★★ HAWAII REGIONAL   Yes, it's in a Macy's department store, but the chef is Alan Wong, a culinary icon. The food is terrific, particularly anything with fresh fish or kalua pig (like the kalua-pig BLT). Wong conjures culinary masterpieces that will make you want to come back and try breakfast, lunch, and dinner. The room features an open kitchen with a lava-rock wall and abundant natural light, but the food takes center stage. The menu changes regularly, but keep an eye out for the fresh Big Island moi (served whole and steamed Chinese style), the crispy Asian slaw (with cilantro and mac nuts), the miso-glazed salmon, the black-pepper ahi with risotto, and pineapple barbecued baby back ribs (with garlic mashed potatoes and sautéed corn). Last time I was here, I salivated over the apple-curry glazed pork chop with pumpkin and mascarpone purée and mango chutney. Alan Wong is a culinary master.

At Macy's, 1450 Ala Moana Blvd. © **808/945-6573.** www.alanwongs.com. Reservations recommended for lunch and dinner. Main courses $16–$25 lunch; main courses $28–$38 dinner; sampling dinner $37–$45. AE, DC, MC, V. Mon–Fri 11am–8:30pm; Sat 11:30am–8:30pm; Sun 11:30am–3pm.

Sushi Sasabune ★★ 🎏 SUSHI   This elegant restaurant, tucked away among nondescript shops along a very busy street, is one of the marvels of the edible world. If you wish to order from the regular menu, by all means grab a table. But if you sit at the sushi bar, you must submit to the Japanese version of the *Seinfeld* Soup Nazi, otherwise known as *omakase:* You obey the chef and eat what's served, and God help you if you dip something in wasabi without permission. The payoff is that whatever you eat is freshly shipped in that day. Whether it's salmon from Nova Scotia, sea urchin from Japan, blue crab from Louisiana, or farmed oyster from Washington, chef Seiji Kumagawa's sushi comes with a strict protocol: Dip only with permission, and then with restraint. This is an extraordinary experience for sushi aficionados—a journey into new tastes, textures, and sensations. It's expensive but well worth it.

1417 S. King St. © **808/947-3800.** Reservations recommended. Sushi $5–$15; *omakase* can run $80–$100 per person. AE, DC, DISC, MC, V. Tues–Fri noon–2pm; Mon–Sat 5:30–10pm.

Moderate

Akasaka ★ JAPANESE/SUSHI   Akasaka is difficult to find, and once you do find it, you enter through a back door; but this cozy, casual, and always busy restaurant wins high marks for its sushi, sizzling tofu and scallops, miso-clam soup, and the overall quality of its cuisine. Highlights include the zesty spicy-tuna hand roll (*temaki*), scallop roll with flying-fish roe, yellowtail (*hamachi*), and soft-shell crab in season. Lunch and dinner specials help ease the bite of the bill; ordering noodles or other less expensive a la carte items can also reduce the cost considerably. The staff is efficient but not necessarily accommodating.

Map labels: Keehi Lagoon, Kapalama Mil. Res., Kapalama Basin, IWILEI, Sand Island Access Rd, Mokauea I., U.S. Coast Guard, Sand Island, Sand Island State Recreation Area, Sand Island Beach Park, Honolulu Harbor, Aloha Tower, Honolulu Channel, Kakaako Waterfront State Recreation Area, N. Vineyard Blvd, Foster Botanical Garden, Nat. Mem. Cemetery of the Pacific, Punchbowl Crater, CHINA-TOWN, Maunakea St., River St., Pali Hwy, Nuuanu Ave., Smith St., Fort St., Hotel St., Queen Emma St., Beretania St., State Capitol, Iolani Palace, DOWNTOWN, South St., S King St., S Beretania St., Thomas Sq., Punchbowl St., Halekauwila St., Cooke St., Ward Ave., Queen St., Kapiolani Blvd, Pensacola St., Piikoi St., Sheridan St., ALA MOANA, Ala Moana Center, Ala Moana Blvd., Ala Moana Beach, Ala Moana Park, Ala Wai Harbor, Ala Moana Blvd, Prospect St., Richards St., Alakea St., Auwaiolimu

Restaurant index (keyed to map):

1646B Kona St. ℂ **808/942-4466.** Reservations recommended. Main courses $12–$25 lunch, $15–$33 dinner; sushi $5–$16. AE, DC, DISC, MC, V. Mon–Sat 11am–2:30pm and 5pm–1am; Sun 5pm–1am.

Assaggio ★ ITALIAN   This wildly popular chain, until recently the toast of suburban Oahu (see p. 195 for the Kailua location), moved into the Ala Moana Center to a roar of approval and immediate success. Townies can now enjoy Assaggio's extensive, high-quality Italian offerings—at good prices. The lighter lunch menu features pasta dishes and entrees for around $16 or less. At dinner, a panoply of pastas and specialties streams out of the kitchen: at least nine chicken dishes, pastas ranging from mushroom and clam to linguine primavera, and eight veal choices. One of Assaggio's best features is its prodigious seafood

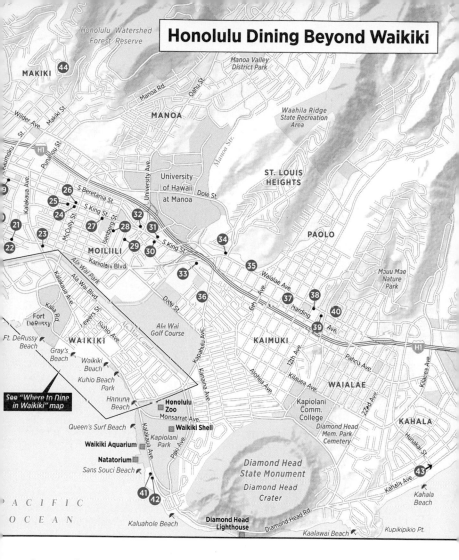

selection: shrimp, scallops, mussels, calamari, and fresh fish in many preparations, ranging from plain garlic and olive oil to spicy tomato and wine sauces.
Assaggio's excellent service paired with many entrees priced under $20 deserves
applause.

At the Ala Moana Center, 1450 Ala Moana Blvd. ℂ **808/942-3446.** Reservations recommended.
Main courses $10–$18 lunch, $16–$31 dinner. AE, DC, DISC, MC, V. Daily 11am–3pm and 4:30–
9:30pm (until 10pm Fri–Sat).

Kincaid's Fish, Chop, and Steakhouse ★ SEAFOOD/STEAK Kincaid's
always wins surveys for one thing or another—best place for a business lunch,
best seafood restaurant—because it pleases wide-ranging tastes and budgets.
Brisk service, a harbor view, and an extensive seafood menu keep the large dining

room full. Fresh-fish sandwiches, seafood chowders, and French onion soup top the menu. There's also a memorable rack-salted prime rib, pepper-crusted steak, and, if you can't make up your mind, a combo plate of center-cut filet mignon with Australian lobster tail. You might want to save room for the true-blue Key lime pie. Kincaid's is a popular happy-hour rendezvous, with inexpensive beer and appetizers.

At Ward Warehouse, 1050 Ala Moana Blvd. ✆ 808/591-2005. www.kincaids.com. Reservations recommended. Lunch $13–$21; dinner main courses $16–$40; 4–6pm 3-course dinner $25; half-price wine on Sun. AE, DC, DISC, MC, V. Daily 11am–10pm. Bar 11am–midnight.

Inexpensive

Angelo Pietro PIZZA/SPAGHETTI   This restaurant has a quirky take on Italian food that could come only from Japan. You can order raw potato salad with any of four dressings—shoyu, ginger, *ume* (plum), or sesame-miso—and chase it with one of more than four dozen spaghetti choices, with sauces and toppings ranging from several types of mushroom, shrimp, chicken, spinach, and sausage to squid ink and eggplant—everything is grist for the spaghetti mill at the hands of Angelo Pietro. Garlic lovers adore the crisp garlic chips that are heaped atop some of the selections.

1585 Kapiolani Blvd. ✆ 808/941-0555. www.angelopietro.com. Reservations recommended for groups of 5 or more, not accepted for smaller groups. Main courses $9–$15. AE, DC, DISC, MC, V. Sun–Thurs 11am–10pm; Fri–Sat 11am–11pm.

I ♥ Country Café INTERNATIONAL   Give yourself time to peruse the lengthy list of specials posted on the menu board, as well as the prodigious printed menu. Stand in line at the counter, place your order and pay, and find a Formica-topped table; or wait about 10 minutes for your takeout order to appear on a Styrofoam plate heaped with salad and other accompaniments. The small cafe is filled with families and people in terrific shape (athlete and bodybuilder types). The menu ranges from virtually fat-free vegetarian meals to local-style plate-lunch specials with plenty of gravy. If you're looking for something healthful, it's a good place to be virtuous.

At Ala Moana Plaza, 451 Piikoi St. ✆ 808/596-8108. Main courses $8–$12. AE, DC, DISC, MC, V. Daily 8am–9pm.

Kaka'ako Kitchen ★★ 🍴 GOURMET PLATE LUNCHES   This popular industrial-style plate-lunch haven is busier than ever since it moved to the trendy Ward Centre in 2000, with an expanded concept that includes dinner and breakfast service. It's owned by chef Russell Siu, of **3660 On the Rise** (p. 192). You'll get excellent home-style cooking served on Styrofoam plates in a warehouse ambience. The menu, which changes every 3 to 4 months, includes a seared ahi sandwich with *tobiko* (flying-fish roe) aioli, sandwiches, beef stew, five-spice shoyu chicken, the very popular meatloaf, and other multiethnic entrees, all at budget prices.

At Ward Centre, 1200 Ala Moana Blvd. ✆ 808/596-7488. Breakfast $5–$9; lunch and dinner main courses $7–$13. AE, MC, V. Mon–Thurs 8am–9pm; Fri–Sat 8am–10pm; Sun 8am–5pm.

Kua Aina ★ 🥪 AMERICAN   This popular branch of the ultimate sandwich shop (the original is a North Shore fixture) is in the Ward Centre area (near Borders and Starbucks). Phone in your order, if you can. During lunch and dinner hours, people wait patiently in long lines for the famous burgers and sandwiches: the beef burgers with heroic toppings, mahimahi with Ortega chili and cheese (a legend), grilled eggplant and peppers, roast turkey, tuna and avocado, roast beef and avocado, and about a dozen other selections. The sandwiches and fries are excellent, and the outdoor section with tables has grown (thank goodness). The takeout business is brisk.

At Ward Village, 1116 Auahi St. 📞 **808/591-9133.** Sandwiches and burgers $4.50–$9. MC, V. Daily 10:30am–9pm.

Panda Cuisine ★ DIM SUM/SEAFOOD/HONG KONG–STYLE CHINESE
This is dim sum heaven, not only for the selection, but also for the late-night (after 10pm) dim sum service, a rare thing for what is a morning and lunchtime tradition in Hong Kong. Panda's dim sum selection—spinach-scallop, chive, taro, shrimp, pork-hash, and some 50-plus others—is a real pleaser. *Tip:* The spinach-scallop and taro-puff varieties are a cut above. The reckless can spring for the live Maine lobster and Dungeness crab in season, or the king clam and steamed fresh fish, but the steaming bamboo carts yielding toothsome surprises are hard to resist. Noodles and sizzling platters make good accompaniments.

641 Keeaumoku St 📞 **808/947-1688.** Main courses $10–$30; dim sum $3–$5. MC, V. Daily 10:30am–2:30pm; Mon–Sat 5:30pm–12:30am; Sun 5:30am–10pm.

Shokudo ★ ▮▮ JAPANESE/SUSHI *Shokudo* means "dining room" in Japanese, and this large, beautifully designed but casual dining room is the first U.S. restaurant of this popular Japanese chain. It attracts local families and hip 20-somethings more than tourists. The eatery is a cross between an *izakaya* (Japanese pub where people eat appetizers and have a beer or two) and a sushi bar. The place is huge and looks even bigger with its high ceiling, tiered seating, and central bar. The food comes on small plates, so bring a crowd to taste several items. The 60-item menu (complete with vivid color photos and an English translation of the food, with detailed descriptions of each dish) includes appetizers, tofu, salad, fish and meat, rice, soup, sushi, sashimi, nabe, ishiyaki, noodles, and desserts. Here are my picks: deep-fried battered tofu ($7), grilled herb-spiced chicken ($12), garlic tuna seared on a hot plate ($14), and the honey toast dessert ($7.50), a sumo-size serving of soft, toasted bread drizzled with honey and topped with vanilla ice cream. The waitstaff is extremely knowledgeable, but service suffers during the busy dinner hours.

At the Ala Moana Pacific Center, 1585 Kapiolani Blvd. (at Kaheka St.). 📞 **808/941-3701.** Entrees $7.75–$23. MC, V. Sun–Thurs 11:30am–1am; Fri–Sat 11:30am–2am.

Side Street Inn ★ ▮▮ LOCAL After their own fancy kitchens have closed, some of Honolulu's top chefs head to this off-the-beaten-track neighborhood bar with TVs on the walls and a backroom with a dartboard and neon beer signs. Very camp. This small side street near Ala Moana Center is noted more for its seedy bars than for pesto-crusted ahi and gourmet Nalo greens, which makes Side Street Inn such a pleasant surprise. The grinds (that's local slang for "eats") are fabulous, with no pretensions and a spirited local feel. The barbecued baby back ribs in *lilikoi* (yellow passion fruit) sauce are tender, flavorful, and a steal at $17. My faves are the blackened ahi, pesto-crusted ahi, shrimp scampi, escargots, and tender fresh-steamed Manila clams in a wine-garlic broth. By the end of the meal, you'll be planning when to return.

1225 Hopaka St. ☎ **808/591-0253.** Reservations recommended for groups of 4 or more. Main courses $8–$30. AE, DC, MC, V. Daily 3pm–midnight. Bar 2pm–2am.

ALOHA TOWER MARKETPLACE

Chai's Island Bistro ★ PACIFIC RIM/ASIAN   This 200-seat restaurant has high ceilings, a good location (though not on the waterfront), indoor/outdoor seating, and a discreetly placed open kitchen. I give Chai's high marks for food but am less enthusiastic about service and ambience, especially at dinner, when the nightly entertainment, usually live music starting at 6:45pm, can be excruciatingly loud. (Also, dinner entree prices have risen significantly.) But the food is generally of high quality and creativity. The appetizer sampler for two appears on a boat-size platter—a feast of ahi katsu with yellow curry sauce and wasabi; macnut-crusted tiger prawns; and Alaskan king-crab cakes. The fusion dishes include steamed Asian-style moi and an ample selection of vegetarian options.

At the Aloha Tower Marketplace, 1 Aloha Tower Dr. ☎ **808/585-0011.** www.chaisislandbistro.com. Reservations recommended. Main courses $13–$32 lunch, $28–$48 dinner. AE, DC, MC, V. Tues–Fri 11am–10pm; Sat–Mon 4–10pm.

Don Ho's Island Grill HAWAIIAN/CONTEMPORARY ISLAND   This shrine to Don Ho, who passed away in 2007, mixes a number of nostalgic interior elements: koa paneling, thatched roof, split-bamboo ceilings, old pictures of Ho with celebrities, faux palm trees, and open sides looking out onto the harbor. It's kitschy and charming, down to the vinyl pareu-printed tablecloths and the flower behind the server's ear. The Hawaiian food served here is perfectly fine, but people come more for the atmosphere than for the cuisine.

At the Aloha Tower Marketplace, 1 Aloha Tower Dr. ☎ **808/528-0807.** www.donho.com. Reservations recommended. Main courses $8–$15 lunch, $8–$28 dinner. AE, DC, DISC, MC, V. Daily 10am–9pm.

Gordon Biersch Brewery Restaurant NEW AMERICAN/PACIFIC RIM   German-style lagers brewed on the premises would be enough of a draw, but the food is also a lure at Gordon Biersch, one of Honolulu's liveliest after-work hangouts. The lanai bar and the brewery bar—open until 1am on the weekends—are the brightest spots in the marketplace, teeming with downtown types who nosh on pot stickers, grilled steaks, baby back ribs, chicken pizza, garlic fries, and any number of American classics with deft cross-cultural touches. Fresh Pacific and Island seafood are particular highlights on the eclectic menu. Extensive renovations in 1999 created a stage area for live music, a popular weekend feature.

At the Aloha Tower Marketplace, 1 Aloha Tower Dr. ☎ **808/599-4877.** Reservations recommended. Main courses $10–$28. AE, DC, DISC, MC, V. Sun–Thurs 10am–midnight; Fri–Sat 10am–12:30am.

DOWNTOWN

Downtowners love the informal walk-in cafes lining one side of attractive **Bishop Square,** 1001 Bishop St. (at King St.), in the middle of the business district, where free entertainment is offered every Friday during lunch hour. The popular **Che Pasta** is a stalwart here, chic enough for business meetings and not too formal (or expensive) for a spontaneous rendezvous over pasta and minestrone. Some places in Bishop Square open for breakfast and lunch, others just for lunch, but most close when business offices empty.

Note: Keep in mind that **Restaurant Row** (Ala Moana Blvd., btw. Punchbowl and South sts.), which features several hot new establishments, offers free validated parking in the evening.

Duc's Bistro ★★ 🍴 FRENCH/VIETNAMESE   Surrounded by lei stands and marked by a cheery neon sign, this cozy 80-seater stands out at the mauka end of Maunakea in Chinatown. Narrow and quietly elegant, the restaurant has three components: the front room, looking out on Maunakea Street; the windowless back room; and the tiny bar. It has an edgy chic feel that's more like Manhattan than Honolulu, and the food is beautifully prepared and presented. Sauces for the meats hint of Grand Marnier (duck supreme), Bordeaux (New Zealand lamb chops), cognac (New York steak), and Pernod. From the seafood spring rolls with shrimp, taro, and mushrooms to the elegant French dishes, creative touches abound. There's live music nightly, and surprise vocalists and hula dancers are known to join in the fun.

1188 Maunakea St., Chinatown. ℂ **808/531-6325.** www.ducsbistro.com. Reservations recommended. Main dishes $12–$20. AE, DC, DISC, MC, V. Mon–Fri 11:30am–10pm; Mon–Sat 5–10pm.

Hiroshi Eurasian Tapas ★★ EURO-ASIAN   Part of the new trend in cuisine, tapas, or small plates, make up most of the menu here. Star chef Hiroshi Fukui opened this restaurant in 2004, along with Hawaii's only master sommelier, Chuck Furuya, and manager Cheryle Gomez. The result is fabulous, especially for foodies who want to nosh their way through the menu (the staff recommends three dishes per person). These small plates offer a range of tastes, from the foie gras sushi with a teriyaki glaze to the simple sizzling Koa kampachi carpaccio (with ginger, tomato, tofu, and ponzu vinaigrette) to the Portuguese sausage pot stickers (with sweet corn, garlic chili foam, and truffled ponzu sauce). Go with as many people as possible so you can sample more items. The menu also lists larger plates, like the dreamy crab-stuffed mahimahi, the catch of the day, and a steamed veal cheek. Try to hold out for the desserts: a delicious haupia lemon grass crème brûlée, a wicked chocolate cake with chocolate ooze, and a great panna cotta.

On Restaurant Row, 500 Ala Moana Blvd. ℂ **808/533-HIRO** (4476). www.hiroshihawaii.com. Reservations recommended. Tapas $8.50–$17, larger plates $22–$37. AE, DISC, MC, V. Daily 5:30–9:30pm.

Indigo Eurasian Cuisine ★★ EURO-ASIAN   Hardwood floors, red brick, wicker, high ceilings, and an overall feeling of Indochine luxury give Indigo a stylish edge. You can dine indoors or in a garden setting on menu offerings such as pot stickers, Buddhist *bao* buns, savory brochettes, ten thousand chili chicken, Asian-style noodles and dumplings, plum-glazed baby back ribs, and cleverly named offerings from both East and West. Chef Glenn Chu is popular, but many claim that Indigo is more style than flavor. I disagree—this is a great restaurant.

1121 Nuuanu Ave. ℂ **808/521-2900.** www.indigo-hawaii.com. Reservations recommended. Lunch buffet $16; dinner main dishes $22–$35. AE, DC, DISC, MC, V. Tues–Fri 11:30am–2pm; Tues–Thurs 6–9pm; Fri–Sat 6–10pm; martini time in the Green Room Tues–Fri 4–7pm.

Legend Seafood Restaurant ★ DIM SUM/SEAFOOD   It's like being in Hong Kong here, with a Chinese-speaking clientele poring over Chinese newspapers and the clatter of chopsticks punctuating conversations. Excellent dim sum comes in bamboo steamers that beckon seductively from carts. Although dining here is a form of assertiveness training (you must wave madly to catch the server's eye and then point to what you want), the system doesn't deter fans from returning. Among my favorites: deep-fried taro puffs, prawn dumplings, shrimp dim sum, vegetable dumplings, and the open-faced seafood omelets in a puff pastry (with shiitake, scallops, and a tofu product called *aburage*). Dim sum is served only at lunch, but dinnertime seafood dishes comfort sufficiently. Not a very elegant restaurant, but the food is serious and great.

At the Chinese Cultural Plaza, 100 N. Beretania St. (✆) **808/532-1868.** Reservations recommended for dinner. Most items under $17. AE, DC, MC, V. Mon–Fri 10:30am–2pm and 5:30–9pm; Sat–Sun 8am–2pm and 5:30–9pm.

Little Village Noodle House CHINESE   Don't let the decor throw you—the interior design here reminds me of a small French bistro in Provence. No matter, the food is "simple and healthy" (its motto) and authentic Chinese (Northern, Canton, and Hong Kong style). My picks are the Shanghai noodles with stir-fried veggies, the walnut shrimp, and the butterfish in black-bean sauce. The menu is eclectic and offers some interesting selections you don't often see. Not only is the service friendly (a rarity in Chinatown), but the waitstaff is quite knowledgeable about the dishes. Even more unique (for Chinatown), there's parking in the back! It's BYOB, but there's an excellent wine store just around the corner (the staff will point it out to you) that delivers to the restaurant.

1113 Smith St. (✆) **808/545-3008.** Most items under $15. AE, DISC, MC, V. Sun–Thurs 10:30am–10:30pm; Fri–Sat 10:30am–midnight.

To Chau ★★ 🍴 VIETNAMESE PHO   The two stars are strictly for the pho (noodle soup), which many think is the best in a city studded with pho houses. Ambience is nil: You'll have to stand in line, and service can be brusque. But that's all part of the charm of this no-nonsense Formica-style pho house, located in Chinatown. The anticipation is heightened by the view of diners relishing their steaming, long-awaited orders, visible through the windows as you wait your turn on the sidewalk. There are spring rolls and chicken and pork-chop plates, but I've never seen anyone order anything but pho. And what a soup it is! The broth is marvelously flavored with hints of cinnamon and spice. You can order it with several choices of meat, and it comes with a heaping platter of fresh bean sprouts, basil, hot green peppers, and an Asian green called *boke* (bo-*kay*). It's worth the wait, and so inexpensive.

1007 River St., Chinatown. (✆) **808/533-4549.** Reservations not accepted. Pho $6–$7.75. No credit cards. Daily 8:30am–2:30pm (or until the food runs out).

Vino Italian Tapas & Wine Bar ★ 🏛 ITALIAN   Two Japanese guys, D. K. Kodama (chef and owner of Sansei Seafood Restaurant & Sushi Bar, p. 176, and d.k Steakhouse, p. 174) and Chuck Furuya (Hawaii's top master sommelier), teamed up to create this culinary adventure for foodies. The cozy room, with murals of a vineyard and a kitchen with barrels of wine on the walls, makes you ready for the mouthwatering Italian creations by chef Tom Selman. The menu, similar to Vino on Maui, features tapas, or small plates. Signature dishes include grilled romaine salad with Gorgonzola and poached egg, tender crispy calamari, seared foie gras, and petite *osso buco*. Don't pass up the house-made gnocchi, the daily pizza, or any ravioli on the menu. Furuya has put together an amazing array of wines by the glass, dispensed from a custom-crafted 20-spigot wine cruvinet. The idea here is to enjoy great wines and be able to taste great Italian food.

On Restaurant Row, 500 Ala Moana Blvd. ℂ **808/524-8466.** Reservations recommended. Tapas $8–$23. AE, DISC, MC, V. Wed–Thurs 5:30–9:30pm; Fri–Sat 5:30–10:30pm.

Yanagi Sushi ★ JAPANESE/SUSHI   I love the late-night hours, the sushi bar, and the extensive choices of combination lunches and dinners. But I also love the a la carte Japanese menu, which covers everything from *chazuke* (a comfort food of rice with tea, salmon, seaweed, and other condiments) to *shabu-shabu* and other steaming earthenware-pot dishes. Complete dinners come with choices of sashimi, shrimp tempura, broiled salmon, New York steak, and many other possibilities. You can dine here affordably or extravagantly, on $11 noodles or a $36 lobster *nabe* (cooked in seasoned broth). Consistently crisp tempura and fine spicy-ahi hand rolls also make Yanagi worth remembering.

762 Kapiolani Blvd. ℂ **808/597-1525.** www.yanagisushi-hawaii.com. Reservations recommended. Main courses $8–$23; complete dinners $21–$26. AE, DC, DISC, MC, V. Daily 11am–2pm; Mon–Sat 5:30pm–2am; Sun 5:30–10pm.

KALIHI/SAND ISLAND

La Mariana AMERICAN   Just try to find a spot more evocative or nostalgic than this South Seas oasis at lagoon's edge in the bowels of industrial Honolulu, with carved Tikis, glass balls suspended in fishing nets, shell chandeliers, and old tables made from koa trees. In the back section, the entire ceiling is made of tree limbs. This unique, nearly 50-year-old restaurant is popular for lunch, sunset appetizers, and impromptu Friday- and Saturday-night singalongs at the piano bar, where a colorful crowd (including some Don Ho look-alikes) gathers to sing Hawaiian classics like a 1950s high-school glee club. It is delightful. The seared Cajun-style ahi is your best bet as an appetizer or entree; La Mariana is more about spirit and ambience than food.

50 Sand Island Rd. ℂ **808/848-2800.** Reservations recommended, especially on weekends. Main courses $6.50–$15 lunch, $10–$35 dinner. AE, MC, V. Daily 11am–9pm. Turn makai (toward the ocean) on Sand Island Rd. from Nimitz Hwy.; immediately after the first light on Sand Island, take a right and drive toward the ocean; it's not far from the airport.

Nico's at Pier 38 ★★ 🍴 FRESH FISH   Gourmet French cuisine produced Island-style in Styrofoam takeout containers at local plate-lunch prices—you can't get any better than this. French-born chef Nicolas "Nico" Chize has cooked at such upscale eateries as Michel's and the Bistro at Century Center, but his own tiny, oddly located eatery is so popular you'll have to stand in line during the crowded lunch hour (when you will see commercial fishermen, business executives, and a small smattering of tourists). My favorite is the *furikake* (a blend of Japanese seasonings) pan-seared ahi with the addictive ginger-garlic-cilantro dip, served with greens or macaroni salad for $9.20. There's also a wicked catch of the day (like grilled swordfish with a fennel-cream sauce), a double cheeseburger to die for, and a mean beef stew. Hearty breakfasts are served until 9:30am weekdays and 10:30am on Saturday. You can munch on your goodies at plastic tables under an awning at the edge of the pier.

Pier 38, 1133 N. Nimitz Hwy., Iwilei. ℂ **808/540-1377.** www.nicospier38.com. Reservations not accepted, but takeout orders accepted by phone. Main courses $6.55–$10. AE, DISC, MC, V. Mon–Fri 6:30am–5pm; Sat 6:30am–2:30pm.

Sam Choy's Breakfast, Lunch, Crab & Big Aloha Brewery ISLAND/SEAFOOD   This is a happy, carefree eatery—elegance and cholesterol be damned.

LOCAL chains & FAMILIAR NAMES

Todai, 1910 Ala Moana Blvd. (✆ **808/ 947-1000**), part of a string of Japanese seafood buffet restaurants with locations ranging from Dallas to Portland to the Beverly Center, is packing 'em in at the gateway to Waikiki with bountiful buffet of sushi (40 kinds), hot entrees (tempura, calamari, fresh fish, gyoza, king crab legs, teppanyaki), and delectable desserts. There's not much ambience, but no one cares; the food is terrific, the selection is impressive, the operation is as smooth as the green-tea cake, and the prices are eye-popping: Lunch is $15 on weekdays and $18 on weekends; dinner is $29 on weekdays and $30 on weekends.

Ala Moana Center's third floor is a mecca for dining and schmoozing. The open-air **Mai Tai Bar** is a popular watering hole. Next door are the boisterous **Bubba Gump Shrimp Company** (✆ **808/ 949-4867**) and the **California Pizza Kitchen** (✆ **808/941-7715**), which also maintains branches in Waikiki at 2284 Kalakaua Ave., next door to the Waikiki Beachcomber (✆ 808/924-2000); Kahala Mall, 4211 Waialae Ave. (✆ 808/7 37-9446); and Pearlridge, 98–1005 Moanalua Rd. (✆ 808/487-7741).

L & L Drive-Inn is a plate-lunch bonanza, with 45 locations in Hawaii—36 on Oahu alone. Meanwhile, **Zippy's Restaurants** ★, the maestros of quick meals, offer a surprisingly good selection of fresh seafood, saimin, chili, and local fare, plus the wholesome new low-fat, vegetarian "Shintani Cuisine" (based on the dietary principles of Hawaiian doctor Terry Shintani). Every restaurant (21 of them on Oahu, at last count) offers a daily Shintani special, and some locations (Kahala, Vineyard, Pearlridge, Kapolei, Waipio) sell cold Shintani items in 2-pound portions to take home and heat up. Call ✆ **808/973-0880** or www.zippys. com to find the location nearest you.

It's hard to spend more than $8 on the French and Vietnamese specials at the **Ba-Le Sandwich Shops:** pho, croissants as good as the espresso, and wonderful taro/tapioca desserts. Among Ba-Le's 20 locations are those at Ala Moana Center (✆ **808/944-4752**) and 333 Ward Ave. (✆ **808/591-0935**).

The ubiquitous **Boston's North End Pizza Bakery** (www.bostonspizzahawaii. com) chain claims an enthusiastic following with its reasonable prices and generous toppings. Boston's can be found in Kaimuki, Kaneohe, and Makakilo.

For Italian food, **Buca di Beppo** (✆ **808/591-0880**) is in the Ward Entertainment Center, 1030 Auahi St. Heaping plates of Italian food, enough to feed a hungry family, make this place quite popular, along with the reasonable prices. Reservations are a must.

In Waikiki, the local **Hard Rock Cafe** is currently located at 1837 Kapiolani Blvd., but be aware that it's scheduled to move to 280 Beachwalk Ave. by the end of 2010 (✆ **808/955-7383**). At the Ala Moana end of Waikiki, **Outback Steakhouse,** 1765 Ala Moana Blvd. (✆ **808/ 951-6274**), serves great steaks and is always full. In downtown's Restaurant Row, beef eaters can also chow down at swanky **Ruth's Chris Steak House,** 500 Ala Moana Blvd. (✆ **808/599-3860**).

Chef/restaurateur Sam Choy's crab house features great fun and gigantic meals (a Choy trademark). Imagine dining in an all-wood sampan (a type of boat, the centerpiece of the 11,000-sq.-ft. restaurant) and washing your hands in an oversize wok in the middle of the room. A 2,000-gallon tank containing a live assortment of crabs in season (Kona, Maryland, Samoan, Dungeness, Florida stone) lines the open kitchen. Clam chowder, seafood gumbos, oysters from the oyster bar, and assorted poke (marinated raw fish) are also offered at dinner, which comes complete with soup, salad, and entree. Children's menus are an attractive feature for families. Several varieties of Big Aloha beer, brewed on-site, go well with the crab and poke.

580 Nimitz Hwy., Iwilei. ☎ **808/545-7979.** www.samchoy.com. Reservations recommended for lunch and dinner. Main courses $8–$15 breakfast, $12–$36 lunch, $20–$47 dinner. AE, DC, DISC, MC, V. Sun–Thurs 7am–9:30pm; Fri–Sat 7am–10pm. Located in the Iwilei industrial area near Honolulu Harbor, across the street from Gentry Pacific Design Center.

MANOA VALLEY/MOILIILI/MAKIKI
Very Expensive
Alan Wong's Restaurant ★★★ HAWAII REGIONAL   Alan Wong is one of Hawaii's most popular chefs, as evidenced by the worshipful foodies who come from all over to wait for a table at this bustling eatery—which *Gourmet* magazine named the eighth best in the "Top 50 Best Restaurants in America." And deservedly so—the food here is brilliant and the menu irresistible. The 90-seat room has a glassed-in terrace and an open kitchen. Sensitive lighting and curly koa wall panels accent an unobtrusively pleasing environment—casual, but not too. The menu's cutting-edge offerings sizzle with the Asian flavors of lemon grass, sweet-and-sour, garlic, and wasabi, deftly molded with the fresh seafood and produce of the Islands. The California roll is a triumph, made with salmon roe, wasabi, and Kona lobster instead of rice, and served warm. I love the opihi (limpet) shooters, plum barbecued ribs, and fresh-fish preparations. But don't get attached to any one item—the menu changes daily. The only downside is this place can get very noisy.

1857 S. King St., 3rd floor. ☎ **808/949-2526.** www.alanwongs.com. Reservations recommended. Main courses $30–$50; 5-course sampling menu $75 ($105 with wine); chef's 7-course tasting menu $95 ($135 with wine). AE, DC, MC, V. Daily 5–10pm.

Chef Mavro Restaurant ★★★ PROVENÇAL/HAWAII REGIONAL   If you have only a single night on Oahu, this is the restaurant to go to. Chef/owner George Mavrothalassitis, a native of Provence (and winner of the 2003 James Beard Award for Best Chef for Hawaii and the Pacific Northwest), has fans all over the world who have admired his creativity since his days at Halekulani's La Mer and the Four Seasons Resort Wailea's Seasons. His restaurant resides in a convenient, nontouristy neighborhood in McCully. You can order prix fixe or a la carte, with or without wine pairings (which are dazzling). The list of signature items includes an award-winning onaga marinated with fennel and served with "Big Wave" tomatoes, vegetables a la grecque, and sauce raíte. Recently added: sautéed foie gras with five spice beets, pistachio financier, and grapefruit marmalade. Hints of Tahitian vanilla, lemon grass, ogo (a type of seaweed), rosemary, and Madras curry add exotic flavors to the French-inspired cooking and fresh Island ingredients. The desserts are extraordinary; his latest are lilikoi malasadas with pineapple-coconut ice cream and chocolate black and tan: chocolate, peanut butter, banana sauce, and Guinness froth. (Provence cuisine marries Hawaii produce). The split-level room is quietly cordial, and the menu changes monthly to highlight seasonal ingredients.

1969 S. King St. ☎ **808/944-4714.** www.chefmavro.com. Reservations recommended. Prix-fixe menu $69–$165 ($117–$250 with wine pairings). AE, DC, DISC, MC, V. Tues–Sun 6–9:30pm.

Moderate

Contemporary Museum Cafe ★ 🎁 HEALTHFUL GOURMET   The surroundings are an integral part of the dining experience at this tiny lunchtime cafe, part of an art museum nestled on the slopes of Tantalus amid carefully cultivated Asian gardens, with a breathtaking view of Diamond Head and priceless contemporary artwork displayed indoors and out. The menu is limited to sandwiches, soups, salads, and appetizers, but you won't leave disappointed: They're perfect lunchtime fare. Try the day's crostini, hummus and pita, grilled vegetable sandwich, or the Waldorf salad with grilled chicken. Crown your meal with flourless chocolate cake or fresh, locally made gelato. Try a Lauhala picnic for two ($30) to enjoy in the gardens.

At The Contemporary Museum (TCM), 2411 Makiki Heights Dr. ℂ **808/523-3362.** www.tcmhi.org. Reservations recommended. Main courses $7–$12. AE, MC, V. Tues–Sat 11:30am–2:30pm; Sun noon–2:30pm.

Maple Garden ASIAN   It hums like a top and rarely disappoints. Maple Garden is known for its garlic eggplant, Peking duck, and Chinaman's Hat, a version of mu shu pork, available in vegetarian form as well. Other hits: the crisp green beans, which are out of this world, and the braised scallops with Chinese mushrooms, sautéed spinach, and prawns in chili sauce. There are ample vegetarian selections and dozens of seafood entrees—everything from sea cucumbers and braised salmon to lobster with black-bean sauce. An ever-expanding visual feast adorns the dining room walls, which are covered with original drawings, sketches, and murals by noted artist John Young. The staff is unbelievably friendly, and service is top-notch.

909 Isenberg St. ℂ **808/941-6641.** Plates $9–$30; buffet $12 lunch, $16 dinner. MC, V. Daily 11am–2pm and 5:30–10pm.

Sushi King 🍴 JAPANESE/SUSHI   This is a top value for lovers of Japanese food. Brusque service can't deter the throngs that arrive for the excellent lunch specials. It's tricky to find, located in a small mini-mall (look for University Flower Shop). Don't pass up the jumbo platters—soup, pickles, California roll, and your choice of chicken teriyaki, beef teriyaki, shrimp and vegetable tempura, or calamari and vegetable tempura, all at arrestingly low prices. Other combination lunches offer generous choices that include sashimi, tempura, butterfish, fried oysters, and noodles hot and cold. Early-bird specials are offered daily from 5:30 to 7pm.

2700 S. King St. ℂ **808/947-2836.** Reservations recommended, especially for groups of 5 or more on weekends. Lunch $9–$17; dinner main courses $15–$23. AE, DC, DISC, MC, V. Daily 11:30am–2pm; Wed–Mon 5:30pm–2am; Tues 5:30–10pm.

Willows LOCAL   Food is not the headliner here; the ambience is. There just aren't many places in Hawaii anymore with this kind of tropical setting. Shoes click on hardwood floors in rooms surrounded by lush foliage and fountains fed by the natural springs of the area. The open-air dining rooms have private umbrella tables scattered about. Willows will never regain the charm and nostalgia of its early *kamaaina* days, but it has been beautifully restored, and the food is more than adequate, with some of the Hawaiian dishes (laulau, lomi salmon, poke) quite good. Everything is served buffet-style.

817 Hausten St. ℂ **808/952-9200.** www.willowshawaii.com. Reservations recommended. Lunch buffet $20 Mon–Fri, $25 Sat, $35 Sun; dinner buffet $35 daily. AE, DC, DISC, MC, V.

Mon–Fri 11am–2pm and 5:30–9pm; Sat–Sun 10am–2:30pm and 5–9pm. No neighborhood parking; valet parking $3; self-parking $4.

Inexpensive

Chiang Mai Thai Cuisine THAI   Chiang Mai made sticky rice famous in Honolulu, serving it in bamboo steamers with fish and exotic curries. Menu items include toothsome red, green, and yellow curries; the signature Cornish game hen in lemon grass and spices; and a garlic-infused green-papaya salad marinated in tamarind sauce. Spicy shrimp soup, eggplant with basil and tofu, and vegetarian green curry are favorites.

2239 S. King St. ℂ **808/941-1151.** www.808chiangmai.com. Reservations recommended for dinner. Main courses $7–$16. AE, DC, MC, V. Mon–Fri 11am–2pm; daily 5:30–9:30pm.

Jimbo's Restaurant ★ 🍴 JAPANESE   Jimbo's is the quintessential neighborhood restaurant—small, with a line of regulars outside who come for fantastic house-made noodles at affordable prices. A must for any noodle lover is the homemade udon in a flawless broth with a subtly smoky flavor, topped with shrimp tempura, chicken, eggs, vegetables, seaweed, roasted mochi, and a variety of accompaniments of your choice. Cold noodles (the Tanuki salad is wonderful!), stir-fried noodles, *donburi* (rice dishes), and combination dinners are other delights. The earthenware pot of noodles, with shiitake mushrooms, vegetables, and udon, plus a platter of tempura on the side, is the top-of-the-line combo. But my favorite is the *nabeyaki* (an earthenware pot of udon with tempura on top). Owner Jimbo Motojima, a perfectionist, uses only the finest ingredients from Japan.

1936 S. King St. ℂ **808/947-2211.** Reservations not accepted. Main courses $10–$20. AE, DC, MC, V. Daily 11am–2:45pm and 5–9;45pm (Fri–Sat 5–10:30pm).

Spices 🍴 SOUTHEAST ASIAN   Located in a small building near the university, this tiny Asian bistro specializes in tantalizing traditional dishes from Vietnam, Laos, Thailand, and Burma (now known as Myanmar) using local Hawaii ingredients. True to the restaurant's name, the smell of pungent spices greets you as you enter; the walls, painted in saffron orange, mustard yellow, and green basil, let you know that you are in for a treat. A cornucopia of Southeast Asian specialties (with plenty of vegetarian dishes) ranges from curries (green, yellow, Malaysian, and Laotian) to noodles (pad Thai) to soups. But the best are the homemade ice creams, with such unusual flavors as durian, pandanus, or chili/lemon grass.

2671 S. King St. (at University Ave.). ℂ **808/949-2679.** www.spiceshawaii.com. Curries $14–$18; rice and noodle dishes $13–$15. MC, V. Tues–Fri 11:30am–2pm and 5:30–9:30pm; Sat 5:30–9:30pm; Sun 5–9pm. Limited parking (about 8 stalls) behind the restaurant.

Well Bento 🍱 HEALTHFUL GOURMET   I wondered whether such healthy organic food—without the use of eggs, refined sugar, or dairy products—would be satisfying. Countless plate lunches later, I can report that Well Bento will make a guiltless gourmet out of even the fussiest palate. Each plate is aesthetically pleasing, wholesome, and tasty. Louisiana tempeh, salmon grilled over lava rocks or poached with shiitake mushrooms, Cajun-style chicken, and creative vegetarian selections ("plant-based plates") make this a place worth trying. Bean salad, cabbage and seaweed salads, and organic brown rice accompany each plate and are as decorative as they are delicious. This is a good picnic choice, as it's mostly takeout, with only a few seats available.

2570 S. Beretania St., 2nd floor. © **808/941-5261.** Plate lunches $9.50–$14. AE, MC, V. Mon–Sat 11am–8pm.

KAIMUKI/KAPAHULU
Expensive

Ninniku-Ya Garlic Restaurant EURO-ASIAN   This great restaurant is a paean to the stinking rose. Ninniku-Ya is located in a cozy old home, with tables in a split-level dining room and outdoors under venerable trees. The menu titillates with many garlic surprises. The seasonal specialties are fine, but the staples are quite wonderful. The four-mushroom pasta is sublime, the hot-stone filet mignon tender and tasty, and the garlic rice a meal in itself. Every garlic lover should experience the garlic toast and the roasted garlic with blue cheese. Everything contains garlic, even the house-made garlic gelato, but it doesn't overpower. Yes, I said garlic gelato—and it gets high marks from me. Look for the festive fairy lights lining the building.

3196 Waialae Ave. © **808/735-0784.** Reservations recommended. Main dishes $16–$38. AE, DC, DISC, MC, V. Tues–Sun 5:30–9pm.

3660 On the Rise ★★★ EURO-ISLAND   Ever since *Wine Spectator* gave this restaurant its Award of Excellence, this place has been packed, and with good reason. In his 200-seat restaurant, chef Russell Siu adds an Asian or local touch to the basics: rack of lamb with macadamia nuts, tempura catfish in ponzu (a Japanese sauce), and seared ahi salad with grilled shiitake mushrooms, a local favorite. The ahi katsu, wrapped in nori and fried medium rare, is a main attraction in the appetizer department. Diners rave over the warm chocolate souffle cake.

3660 Waialae Ave. © **808/737-1177.** www.3660.com. Reservations suggested. Main courses $19–$59; prix-fixe menu $40. AE, DC, DISC, MC, V. Tues–Sun 5:30–8:30pm.

Moderate

Genki Sushi ★ SUSHI   Take your place in line for a seat at one of the U-shaped counters, watching the freshly made sushi parade by on conveyor belts (usually two pieces per color-coded plate, priced inexpensively). The possibilities are dizzying: spicy tuna with scallions, ahi, scallops with mayonnaise, Canadian roll (like a California roll, except with salmon), sea urchin, sweet shrimp, surf clam, tuna salad, and so on. Genki starts with a Japanese culinary tradition and takes liberties with it, so don't be a purist. By the end of the meal, the piled-high plates are tallied up by color—and, presto, your bill appears. Combination platters are available for takeout.

900 Kapahulu Ave. © **808/735-7700.** A la carte sushi from $1.50 for 2 pieces; takeout combination platters $26–$46. AE, DC, DISC, MC, V. Sun–Thurs 11am–9pm; Fri–Sat 11am–10pm; takeout available daily 11am–9pm.

Town ★ 🎁 CONTEMPORARY ITALIAN   The latest hip restaurant along Waialae's miracle mile of "in" spots is a surprisingly delicious place to eat (generally the new hot spots tend more toward pretense than lip-smacking food). Ignore the high-tech metro atmosphere of highly polished concrete floors, stainless-steel tables, and incredibly uncomfortable chairs, and instead ask for a table out on the lanai (where the noise level will be bearable). The creative menu changes daily but promises "local first, organic whenever possible, with aloha always"— and delivers. On my last visit, I sampled the ahi tartare on risotto cakes and the fritto misto, an Italian tempura of scallops, celery, lemon, and white beans. Entrees range from braised lamb to excellent gnocchi to crispy moi (a highly prized Hawaiian fish). Desserts include buttermilk panna cotta and chocolate panini with bananas—yum. Lunches are along the lines of sandwiches, salads, and pastas; breakfast (frittata of the day, eggs, wonderful baked goods) is now available, too.

3435 Waialae Ave. (at 9th St.). ✆ **808/735-5900.** Reservations required for dinner. Main courses $5–$9.50 breakfast, $10–$15 lunch, $19–$26 dinner. AE, MC, V. Mon–Sat 7am–2pm and 5:30–9pm.

12th Avenue Grill ★ 🛉 RETRO-AMERICAN   Since the doors opened in 2004, this tiny (14 tables) upscale neighborhood diner is packed every night. Chef Kevin Hanney whips up gourmet versions of American classics, such as macaroni and cheese (with smoked Parmesan), and the restaurant's signature dish: brined, grilled center-cut pork chop with apple chutney and potato pancakes. A chalkboard menu lists the specials of the night (the smoked trout is a must). Diners are packed in close, so noise is a problem, but the food more than makes up for this one flaw. Whatever you order, leave room for desserts, done by Zachary Most. The fruit crisp of the day is a good bet. A full bar was recently added.

1145-C 12th Ave. (at Waialae Ave.). ✆ **808/732-9469.** www.12thavegrill.com. Reservations recommended. Small plates $6–$12; large plates $18–$32. MC, V. Mon–Thurs 5:30–9pm; Fri–Sat 5:30–10pm.

Inexpensive

Cafe Kaila ★★ COFFEE SHOP   Tucked in a strip mall next to the freeway is this hidden treasure: a European-style bistro or French-country cafe where breakfast is always served. Owner/Chef Chrissie "Kaila" Castillo dishes up all her favorites (do not miss the incredibly fluffy pancakes or the yummy frittata) in a relaxed atmosphere (including a trickling fountain). **Warning:** Because of the great food and budget prices, this place is packed at breakfast and lunch. I suggest going late for breakfast (after 9:30am) and lunch (after 1:30pm), so you won't have to wait for a table. Even if you do run into a long line, grab a latte and relax—the food is well worth the wait. Bring cash; they don't take credit cards.

Market City Shopping Center, 2919 Kapiolani Rd. (at Harding St.), Honolulu, HI 96826. ✆ **808/732-3330.** Breakfast and lunch entrees $9–$13. No credit cards. Mon–Fri 7am–5pm; Sat–Sun 8am–3pm.

Cafe Laufer ★ BAKERY/SANDWICH SHOP   This small, cheerful cafe has frilly decor and sublime pastries—from apple scones and Linzer tortes to fruit flan, decadent chocolate mousse, and carrot cake—to accompany the latte and espresso. Fans drop in for simple soups and deli sandwiches on fresh-baked breads; biscotti during coffee break; or hearty loaves of seven-grain, rye, pumpernickel, or French bread. The small but satisfying lunch menu includes soup-salad-sandwich specials for a song, a fabulous spinach salad with dried cranberries and Gorgonzola, and gourmet greens with mango-infused honey-mustard dressing. The orange-seared shrimp salad and the Chinese chicken salad are hits for the light eater; also excellent is the smoked Atlantic salmon with fresh pumpernickel bread and cream cheese, Maui onions, and capers. The special Saturday-night desserts draw a brisk post-movie business.

3565 Waialae Ave. ℂ **808/735-7717**. www.cafelaufer.com. Checks average $15 per person. AE, DC, DISC, MC, V. Sun and Wed–Thurs 10am–9pm; Fri–Sat 10am–10pm.

The Fat Greek ★★ 🍴 GREEK   Budget travelers take note: This tiny hole-in-the-wall with just counter service has wonderful Greek dishes at money-saving prices. Try the "Papa Special," New Zealand rack of lamb marinated in the "special" house sauce with rosemary and garlic plus potato wedges and a Greek salad for just $20, or *shawarma* (lamb and beef in a pita with tzatkiki sauce and salad for $10), or the daily specials from moussaka to kabobs to souvlakia. The atmosphere is either a blaring television in the enclosed dining area (next to the always busy takeout counter) or an open-air patio. Consider takeout. Also, parking is limited. I suggest going across the street to the City Mill lot and paying $2. Bring your own liquor (no corkage fee!).

3040 Waialae Ave. (at St. Louis Ave.), Honolulu, HI 96816. ℂ **808/734-0404**. www.thefatgreek.net. Entrees $8–$15. DC, DISC, MC, V. Daily 11am–10pm.

Hale Vietnam VIETNAMESE   Duck into this house of pho and brave the no-frills service for the steaming noodle soups, the house specialty. The stock is simmered for many hours and is accompanied by noodles, beef, chicken, and a platter of bean sprouts and fresh herbs. Approach the green chilies with caution. I love the chicken soup and shrimp vermicelli, as well as the seafood pho and spicy chicken with eggplant. Be advised that this restaurant, like most other Vietnamese eateries, uses MSG, and that the pho, although respectable, does not equal that of To Chau in Chinatown.

1140 12th Ave. ℂ **808/735-7581**. Reservations recommended for groups. Main courses $12–$28. AE, DISC, MC, V. Daily 10am–9:45pm.

TO THE EAST: KAHALA

Hoku's ★★★ HAWAII REGIONAL   Elegant without being stuffy, creative without being overwrought, the upscale dining room of the Kahala Hotel & Resort combines European finesse with an Island touch. This is fusion that really works. The ocean view, open kitchen, and astonishing bamboo floor are stellar features. Reflecting the restaurant's cross-cultural influences, the kitchen is equipped with a kiawe grill and Szechuan woks for the prawn, lobster, tofu, and other stir-fried specialties. The wok-fried whole fresh fish is worthy of a special occasion. The chef's daily selection of appetizers could include pan-seared Hudson Valley foie gras, sashimi, slow-braised pork belly, and other dainty tastings, and is a good choice for the curious. Salt-crusted rack of lamb, sesame ginger black cod, and the full range of East-West specialties appeal to many tastes. Sunday brunch is not to be missed. This is one of the few places in Hawaii that has a "dress code"—collared shirts with slacks or evening wear for men.

At the Kahala Hotel & Resort, 5000 Kahala Ave. ℂ **808/739-8780**. www.kahalaresort.com/dining/hoku.cfm. Reservations recommended. Collared shirts and long pants preferred for men. Main courses $30–$84; brunch $58 ($29 children 4–12). AE, DC, DISC, MC, V. Daily 5:30–10pm; Sun brunch 10:30am–2pm.

Olive Tree Cafe ★★ 🍴 GREEK/EASTERN MEDITERRANEAN   Bargain-priced delectables stream out of the tiny open kitchen here. Recently voted "Best

Restaurant in Hawaii Under $20" in a local survey, Olive Tree is every neighborhood's dream—a totally hip restaurant with divine Greek fare and friendly prices. There are umbrella tables outside and a few seats indoors; you order and pay at the counter. The mussel ceviche is broke-the-mouth fabulous, with lemon, lime, capers, herbs, and olive oil—a perfect blend of flavors. The tender chicken saffron, a frequent special, always elicits groans of pleasure, as does the robust and generous Greek salad. I also love the souvlakia, ranging from fresh fish to chicken and lamb, spruced up with the chef's homemade yogurt-dill sauce. A large group can dine here like sultans without breaking the bank and take in a movie next door, too. It's BYOB.

4614 Kilauea Ave., next to Kahala Mall. *C* **808/737-0303.** Main courses $10–$15. No credit cards. Daily 5–10pm.

East Oahu

Roy's Restaurant ★★★ EURO-ASIAN   This is the first of Roy Yamaguchi's six signature restaurants in Hawaii (he now has two dozen all over the world). It is still the flagship and many people's favorite, true to its Euro-Asian roots and Yamaguchi's winning formula: open kitchen, fresh ingredients, ethnic touches, and a good dose of nostalgia mingled with European techniques. The menu changes nightly, but you can generally count on individual pizzas, a varied appetizer menu (Szechuan-spiced baby back ribs, blackened ahi), a small pasta selection, and entrees such as garlic-mustard short ribs, hibachi-style salmon in ponzu sauce, and several types of fresh catch. One of Hawaii's most popular restaurants, Roy's is lit up at night with Tiki torches outside; the view from within is of scenic Maunalua Bay. Roy's is also renowned for its high-decibel style of dining—it's always full and noisy. There's live music Tuesday through Saturday evenings from 6:30 to 9:30pm.

Other Roy's restaurants in Hawaii are located in Ko Olina, Oahu; Poipu, Kauai; Waikoloa, Big Island; and Kihei and Napili, Maui.

6600 Kalanianaole Hwy., Hawaii Kai. *C* **808/396-7697.** www.roysrestaurant.com. Reservations recommended. Main courses $28–$45; 3-course prix-fixe $42. AE, DC, DISC, MC, V. Mon–Fri 5:30–9pm (Fri to 9:30pm); Sat 5–9:30pm; Sun 5–9pm.

The Windward Coast

Note: The following restaurants are located on the "Eastern Oahu & the Windward Coast" map (p. 269).

Assaggio ★ ITALIAN   This was the mother ship of the Assaggio empire before **Ala Moana** (p. 200) opened in 1999. The affordable prices, attentive service, and winning menu have attracted loyal fans throughout the years. The best-selling homemade hot antipasti has jumbo shrimp, fresh clams, mussels, and calamari in a sauce of cayenne pepper, white wine, and garlic. You can choose linguine, fettuccine, or ziti with 10 different sauces in small or regular portions, or any of nine chicken pastas (the chicken Assaggio, with garlic, peppers, and mushrooms, is especially flavorful). Equally impressive is the extensive list of seafood pastas, including the garlic and olive oil sauté. A plus: At dinner, servings come in two sizes and prices.

354 Uluniu St., Kailua. *C* **808/261-2772.** www.assaggiohi.com. Reservations recommended. Main courses $9–$11 lunch, $16–$20 dinner. AE, DC, DISC, MC, V. Daily 11:30am–2:30pm; Sun–Thurs 5–9:30pm; Fri–Sat 5–10pm.

Maybe it's a Hawaii thing, but the best, sweetest, juiciest shrimp you are ever going to eat will be from a shrimp truck on Oahu's North Shore. Several trucks line up around the entry to Haleiwa, just off the Kamehameha Highway, but here are my two favorites:

Giovanni's Original White Shrimp Truck (☎ 808/293-1839), which usually parks across the street from the Haleiwa Senior Housing (or McDonald's), claims to be the first shrimp truck to serve the delicious aquaculture shrimp farmed in the surrounding area. The menu is simple: spicy, garlic, or lemon-and-butter shrimp. Skip the lemon-and-butter (boring), and go for the garlic (my fave) or the spicy (but beware—it really packs a punch). The battered white truck has picnic tables under its awning, so you can munch away right there.

Holy Smokes: Hawaiian Meats and Seafood, the other truck parked in the same area, has a bit more extensive menu; in addition to the famous shrimp, it offers pork spare ribs ($10), smoked chicken ($9), and a steak plate ($12).

The trucks are usually in place before noon and stay until about sunset. Depending on how much shrimp you can down, expect to spend no more than $12 per person.

Buzz's Original Steak House STEAK/SEAFOOD   A Lanikai fixture for nearly a half-century, Buzz's is a few feet from Kailua Beach (windsurfing central), just past the bridge that leads into Lanikai. (Though it's on the beach, shirt and shoes are required.) A small deck, a varnished koa bar, rattan furniture, and wood walls covered with snapshots and surf pictures will put you immediately at ease. Buzz's has the perfect Gauguin-esque tropical ambience to go with its offerings: great burgers at lunch (including a terrific mushroom Gardenburger), fresh catch, superb artichoke appetizer, and steak-and-lobster combos, all much loved by fans. Dinner offerings are pricier but include Alaskan king crab legs (market price), prime rib, fresh fish, and wonderful items at the soup and salad bar. Bring cash—they do *not* take credit cards.

413 Kawailoa Rd., Lanikai. ☎ **808/261-4661.** www.buzzssteakhouse.com. Reservations required. Main courses $9–$15 lunch, $16–$36 dinner. No credit cards. Daily 11am–3pm and 4:30–9:30pm.

Lucy's Grill 'n Bar ★★ HAWAII REGIONAL   This is one of Kailua's most popular restaurants, not just because of the open-air bar and the outdoor lanai seating, but also thanks to the terrific food. The menu is eclectic Hawaii Regional Cuisine, with lots of choices and giant-size portions. The dress is casual, the clientele local. Be sure to order the spicy ahi tower with sushi rice, avocado, wasabi cream, and roasted nori to get you started. The fresh-fish and seafood items are wonderful, especially the Szechuan-spiced jumbo tiger prawns with black-bean cream and penne pasta, or the lemon grass–crusted scallops with yellow Thai curry. Save room for dessert: crème brûlée with Tahitian vanilla bean, dark-chocolate soufflé cake, or "damn fine" apple crisp—a la mode, of course.

33 Aulike St., Kailua. ☎ **808/230-8188.** Reservations recommended. Main courses $12–$30. MC, V. Daily 5–10pm. Now serving small and large plates.

The North Shore

Note: The following can be located on the "Oahu's North Shore" map (p. 279).

EXPENSIVE

21 Degrees North ★★★ PACIFIC RIM *Foodies, take note:* It is well worth the 45- to 60-minute drive from Waikiki to the North Shore to enjoy this impressive signature restaurant at Turtle Bay Resort (p. 227). Not only is it visually inspiring, with floor-to-ceiling windows overlooking the North Shore's famous rolling surf, but the food is also outstanding—chef John Armstrong makes contemporary Island cuisine fresh and interesting. The ever-changing menu takes Hawaiian dining to a new level, with such unusual combinations as crab-crusted Hawaiian sea bass with a lemon grass coulis, salmon with Molokai mashed sweet potatoes and an orange and soy glaze, and roasted Peking duck with a vanilla and plum sweet-and-sour glaze. Or try numerous creations with the five-course tasting menu.

At Turtle Bay Resort, 57-091 Kamehameha Hwy., Kahuku. ✆ **808/293-8811.** www.turtlebay resort.com. Reservations required. Main courses $28–$50; 5-course tasting menu $75 without wine, $105 with wine. AE, DC, DISC, MC, V. Tues–Sat 6–9:30pm.

MODERATE

Haleiwa Joe's AMERICAN/SEAFOOD Next to the Haleiwa bridge, with a great harbor and sunset view, Haleiwa Joe's serves up local seafood such as whole Hawaiian moi, opakapaka, ahi, and whatever comes in fresh that day. This harborside restaurant has indoor-outdoor seating and a surf-and-turf menu that could also include New York steak, coconut shrimp, and black-and-blue sashimi. Sandwiches and salads make it a great lunch stop, too. There are only two Haleiwa restaurants close to the ocean, and this is one of them.

66-011 Kamehameha Hwy., Haleiwa. ✆ **808/637-8005.** www.haleiwajoes.com. Reservations not accepted. Main courses $9–$18 lunch, $16–$30 dinner. MC, V. Mon–Thurs 11:30am–9:30pm (limited menu 4:15–5:30pm); Fri–Sat 11:30am–10pm (limited menu 4:15–5:30pm, bar until midnight); Sun 11:30am–9:30pm (limited menu 3:45–5pm).

Jameson's by the Sea SEAFOOD Duck into this roadside watering hole across the street from the ocean for cocktails, sashimi, and the celebrated salmon pâté, or for other hot and cold appetizers, salads, and sandwiches. The grilled crab-and-shrimp sandwich on sourdough is a perennial, and it's hard to go wrong with the fresh-fish sandwich of the day, grilled plain and simple. The dinner menu offers the usual surf-and-turf choices: fresh opakapaka ulua (Hawaiian jackfish), mahimahi, scallops in lemon butter and capers, lobster tail, and steaks.

62-540 Kamehameha Hwy., Haleiwa. ✆ **808/637-4336.** www.jamesonshawaii.com. Reservations recommended. Main courses $8–$20 lunch, $24–$45 dinner. AE, DC, DISC, MC, V. Mon–Fri 11am–9:30pm; Sat–Sun 9am–9:30pm.

Ola at Turtle Bay Resort ★★ 🍴 HAWAIIAN/SEAFOOD Even if you are staying in Waikiki, plan a day at the beach on the North Shore and eat here for dinner. You will not regret it. First, there's the location—literally on the sand next door to the **Turtle Bay Resort.** Second, the restaurant is an open-air (as in, no walls) beach pavilion, made from ironwood trees harvested from the surrounding area. The view is of lapping waves of the Pacific. The atmosphere when the Tiki torches are lit at sunset is very, very romantic. Best of all is the food! Chef Fred DeAngelo named his restaurant Ola, which means "alive" or "healthy" in Hawaiian, and he insists on only the freshest of ingredients. The menu is filled with creative selections (like the ahi and lobster poke served with a wonton spoon) and some of the best food you will eat in Hawaii. My favorites are the incredible slow-poached togarashi salmon with a sugar-cane crust, served with Okinawan sweet potato and locally grown corn; the Lawai'a fishermen's stew with lobster, shrimp, scallops, and fresh fish; and an unforgettable kiawe-smoked beef tenderloin.

At Turtle Bay Resort, 57–091 Kamehameha Hwy., Kahuku. ℂ 808/293-0801. www.olaislife. com. Reservations recommended for dinner. Main courses $10–$24 lunch, $19–$60 dinner. AE, DC, DISC, MC, V. Daily 11am–3pm and 5:30–10pm.

INEXPENSIVE

Cafe Haleiwa BREAKFAST/LUNCH/MEXICAN   Haleiwa's legendary breakfast joint is a big hit with surfers, urban gentry with weekend country homes, reclusive artists, and anyone who loves mahimahi plate lunches and heroic sandwiches. It's a wake-up-and-hit-the-beach kind of place, serving generous omelets with names like Off the Wall, Off the Lip, and Breakfast in a Barrel. Surf pictures line the walls, and the ambience is Formica-style casual. Hit the espresso bar for a caffeine fix.

66–460 Kamehameha Hwy., Haleiwa. ℂ 808/637-5516. Reservations not accepted. Main courses $7–$14. AE, MC, V. Daily 7am–1:45pm.

Cholos Homestyle Mexican II 🏅 MEXICAN   There's usually a wait at this popular North Shore eatery, where great home-style Mexican food is presented with so-so service. Still, this is the unhurried North Shore, and the biggest rush for most folks is getting to and from the beach. I recommend the spinach quesadilla, a generous serving filled with black beans, cheese, and fresh vegetables; the chicken-fajita plate; and the fish-taco plate, a steal at $9.25 (just $5.50 a la carte). There are tables and stools outdoors; indoors, it's dark and cavelike, with loud music and Mexican handicrafts all over the place.

At the North Shore Marketplace, 66–250 Kamehameha Hwy. ℂ 808/637-3059. Combination plates $9–$13. AE, DISC, MC, V. Daily 10:30am–9 or 9:30pm depending on business.

Kua Aina ★ 🏅 AMERICAN   "What's the name of that sandwich shop on the North Shore?" I hear that often. After 29 years at the same spot, Kua Aina moved a few years ago down the street and to a larger, 75-seat space. It's as busy as ever, and many diners get their burgers to go and head for the beach. Kua Aina's thin and spindly french fries, renowned islandwide, are the perfect accompaniment to the legendary burgers. Fat, moist, and homemade, the burgers can be ordered with avocado, bacon, and many other accompaniments, including Ortega chilies and cheese. The roast turkey, mahimahi, and tuna and avocado sandwiches are excellent alternatives. Kua Aina is unparalleled on the island and is a North Shore must, eclipsing its fancier competitors at lunch.

66–160 Kamehameha Hwy., Haleiwa. ℂ 808/637-6067. Sandwiches and burgers $7–$8.50. No credit cards. Daily 11am–8pm.

Paradise Found Cafe VEGETARIAN   A tiny cafe behind Celestial Natural Foods, Paradise Found requires a bit of a hunt, but stick with it. For more than a few townies, the North Shore sojourn begins at Paradise, the only pure vegetarian restaurant in these parts. Breakfasts feature the breakfast burrito (scrambled

eggs, veggies, and home fries wrapped in a tortilla) and the "nanna nutty" (peanut butter, banana, honey, granola, and cinnamon wrapped in a flour tortilla and grilled). The smoothies (especially the Waimea Shorebreak) are legendary, and the organic soups, fresh-pressed vegetable juices, sandwiches, and healthy plate lunches make a great launch to a Haleiwa day. Vegan substitutions are willingly made in place of dairy products.

66-443 Kamehameha Hwy., Haleiwa. (℃ **808/637-4540.** All items under $12. AE, MC, V. Mon-Sat 9am-5pm; Sun 9am-4pm.

Leeward Oahu: The Waianae Coast

Roy's Ko Olina ★★★ 🍴 EURO-ASIAN   The latest in the Roy's empire of excellent restaurants opened in 2004 at the Ko Olina Resort on the leeward coast of Oahu, some 16 years after the flagship restaurant (p. 195) first opened in Hawaii Kai. One of some nearly three dozen locations around the globe, Roy's Ko Olina perches in a peerless location overlooking the lagoon, waterfalls, and 18th hole of the Ko Olina Golf Club. You'll find Roy's famous display kitchen here, with floor-to-ceiling windows that showcase the view. Roy's usual high-decibel style of dining has been replaced by a relaxing, romantic atmosphere where you can have a conversation without shouting. The menu changes daily, but you can generally count on Roy's classics: blackened ahi, hibachi salmon, and Szechuan baby back ribs. Some great additions include Asian pesto–steamed fresh fish, cilantro-dusted papio (jack trevally), kiawe-grilled filet mignon, and roasted chicken with huli-huli sauce. Ko Olina is also open for lunch, and after that you can get appetizers at the bar. It's worth the drive for this incredible dining experience.

At the Ko Olina Resort, 92-1220 Aliinui Dr., Kapolei. (℃ **808/676-7697.** www.roysrestaurant. com. Reservations recommended. Lunch $17-$28; appetizers at the bar $11-$17; dinner entrees $22-$48. AE, DC, DISC, MC, V. Daily 11am-2pm and 5:30-9:30pm (appetizers only 2-5:30pm).

BEACHES
The Waikiki Coast
ALA MOANA BEACH PARK ★★

Gold-sand Ala Moana (by the sea), on sunny Mamala Bay, stretches for more than a mile along Honolulu's coast between downtown and Waikiki. This 76-acre midtown beach park, with spreading lawns shaded by banyans and palms, is one of the island's most popular playgrounds. It has a man-made beach, created in the 1930s by filling a coral reef with Waianae Coast sand, as well as its own lagoon, yacht harbor, tennis courts, music pavilion, bathhouses, picnic tables, and enough wide-open green spaces to accommodate four million visitors a year. The water is calm almost year-round, protected by black-lava rocks set offshore. There's a large parking lot as well as metered street parking.

WAIKIKI BEACH ★★★

No beach anywhere is so widely known or so universally sought after as this narrow, 1½-mile-long crescent of imported sand (from Molokai) at the foot of a string of high-rise hotels. Home to the world's longest-running beach party, Waikiki attracts nearly five million visitors a year from every corner of the planet. First-timers are amazed to discover how small Waikiki Beach actually is, but there's always a place for them under the tropical sun here.

Waikiki is actually a string of beaches that extends between **Sans Souci State Recreational Area,** near Diamond Head to the east, and **Duke Kahanamoku Beach,** in front of the Hilton Hawaiian Village to the west. Great stretches along Waikiki include **Kuhio Beach,** next to the Moana Surfrider, which provides the quickest access to the Waikiki shoreline; the stretch in front of the Royal Hawaiian Hotel known as **Grey's Beach,** which is canted so it catches the rays perfectly; and **Sans Souci,** the small, popular beach in front of the New Otani Kaimana Beach Hotel that's locally known as "Dig Me" Beach because of all the gorgeous bods who strut their stuff here.

Waikiki is fabulous for swimming, board surfing and bodysurfing, outrigger canoeing, diving, sailing, snorkeling, and pole fishing. Every imaginable type of marine equipment is available for rent here. Facilities include showers, lifeguards, restrooms, grills, picnic tables, and pavilions at the **Queen's Surf** end of the beach (at Kapiolani

Ala Moana Beach Park.

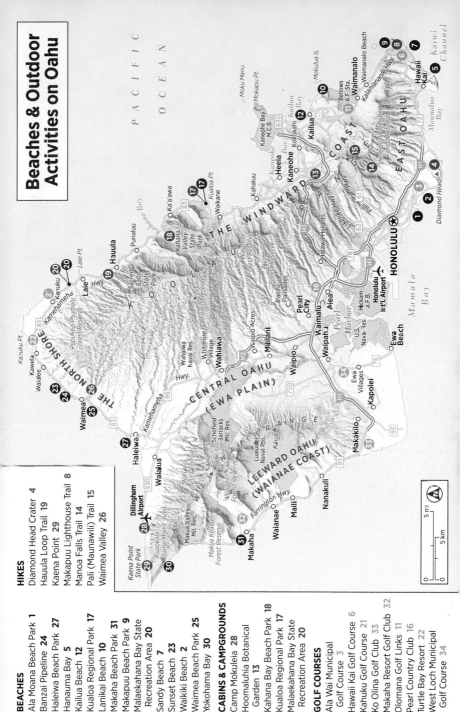

Beaches & Outdoor Activities on Oahu

BEACHES

Ala Moana Beach Park **1**
Banzai Pipeline **24**
Haleiwa Beach Park **27**
Hanauma Bay **5**
Kailua Beach **12**
Kualoa Regional Park **17**
Lanikai Beach **10**
Makaha Beach Park **31**
Makapuu Beach Park **9**
Malaekahana Bay State Recreation Area **20**
Sandy Beach **7**
Sunset Beach **23**
Waikiki Beach **2**
Waimea Beach Park **25**
Yokohama Bay **30**

CABINS & CAMPGROUNDS

Camp Mokuleia **28**
Hoomaluhia Botanical Garden **13**
Kahana Bay Beach Park **18**
Kualoa Regional Park **17**
Malaekahana Bay State Recreation Area **20**

GOLF COURSES

Ala Wai Municipal Golf Course **3**
Hawaii Kai Golf Course **6**
Kahuku Golf Course **21**
Ko Olina Golf Club **33**
Makaha Resort Golf Club **32**
Olomana Golf Links **11**
Pearl Country Club **16**
Turtle Bay Resort **22**
West Loch Municipal Golf Course **34**

HIKES

Diamond Head Crater **4**
Hauula Loop Trail **19**
Kaena Point **29**
Makapuu Lighthouse Trail **8**
Manoa Falls Trail **14**
Pali (Maunawili) Trail **15**
Waimea Valley **26**

201

Waikiki Beach.

Park, between the zoo and the aquarium). The best place to park is at Kapiolani Park, near Sans Souci.

East Oahu
HANAUMA BAY ★★

Oahu's most popular snorkeling spot is this volcanic crater with a broken sea wall; its small, curved, 2,000-foot gold-sand beach is packed elbow-to-elbow with people year-round. The bay's shallow shoreline water and abundant marine life are the main attractions, but this good-looking beach is also popular for sunbathing and people-watching. Serious divers shoot "the slot" (a passage through the reef) to get to Witch's Brew, a turbulent cove, and then brave strong currents in 70-foot depths at the bay mouth to see coral gardens, turtles, and even sharks. (**Divers:** Beware of the Molokai Express, a strong current.) You can snorkel in the safe, shallow (10-ft.) inner bay, which, along with the beach, is almost always crowded. Because Hanauma Bay is a conservation district, you cannot touch or take any marine life here. Feeding the fish is also prohibited.

A $13-million Marine Education Center features exhibits and a 7-minute video orienting visitors on this Marine Life Sanctuary. The 10,000-square-foot center includes a training room, a gift shop, public restrooms, a snack bar, and a staging area for the motorized tram, which, for a fee (50¢ for one ride, or $2 for an all-day pass), will take you down the steep road to the beach. Facilities include parking, restrooms, a pavilion, a grass volleyball court, lifeguards, barbecues, picnic tables, and food concessions. Alcohol is prohibited in the park; there is no smoking past the visitor center. Expect to pay $1 per vehicle to park plus an entrance fee of $5 per person (free for children 12 and under).

If you're driving, take Kalanianaole Highway to Koko Head Regional Park. Avoid the crowds by going early, about 8am, on a weekday morning; once the parking lot's full, you're out of luck. Alternatively, take TheBus to escape the parking problem: The Hanauma Bay Shuttle runs from Waikiki to Hanauma Bay every half-hour from 8:45am to 1pm; you can catch it at the Ala Moana Hotel, the Ilikai Hotel, or other city bus stops. It returns every hour from noon to 4pm. Hanauma Bay is closed on Tuesday so the fish can have a day off.

SANDY BEACH ★

Sandy Beach is one of the best bodysurfing beaches on Oahu; it's also one of the most dangerous. It's better to just stand and watch the daredevils literally risk their necks at this 1,200-foot-long gold-sand beach that's pounded by wild waves and haunted by a dangerous shore break and strong backwash. Weak swimmers and children should definitely stay out of the water here; Sandy Beach's heroic lifeguards make more rescues in a year than those at any other beach. Visitors, easily fooled by experienced bodysurfers who make it look easy, often fall victim to the bone-crunching waves. Lifeguards post flags to alert beachgoers to the day's surf: Green means safe, yellow means caution, and red indicates very dangerous water conditions.

Facilities include restrooms and parking. Go weekdays to avoid the crowds or weekends to catch the bodysurfers in action. From Waikiki, drive east on the H-1, which becomes Kalanianaole Highway; proceed past Hawaii Kai, up the hill to Hanauma Bay, past the Halona Blowhole, and along the coast. The next big gold beach on the right is Sandy Beach. TheBus no. 22 will also bring you here.

Hanauma Bay.

MAKAPUU BEACH PARK ★

Makapuu Beach, the most famous bodysurfing beach in Hawaii, is a beautiful 1,000-foot-long gold-sand beach cupped in the stark black Koolau cliffs on Oahu's easternmost point. Even if you never venture into the water, it's worth a visit just to enjoy the great natural beauty of this classic Hawaiian beach. (You've probably already seen it in countless TV shows, from *Hawaii Five-O* to *Magnum, P.I.*) In summer, the ocean here is as gentle as a Jacuzzi, and swimming and diving are perfect; come winter, however, Makapuu is a hit with expert bodysurfers, who come for big, pounding waves that are too dangerous for regular swimmers. Small boards—3 feet or less with no skeg (bottom fin)—are permitted; no regular board surfing is allowed.

Facilities include restrooms, lifeguards, barbecue grills, picnic tables, and parking. To get here, follow Kalanianaole Highway toward Waimanalo, or take TheBus no. 57 or 58.

Sandy Beach.

Makapuu Beach Park.

The Windward Coast

LANIKAI BEACH ★★

One of Hawaii's best spots for swimming, gold-sand Lanikai's crystal-clear lagoon is like a giant saltwater swimming pool that you're lucky enough to be able to share with the resident tropical fish and sea turtles. Too gorgeous to be real, this is one of Hawaii's postcard-perfect beaches: It's a mile long and thin in places, but the sand's as soft as talcum powder. Prevailing onshore trade winds make this an excellent place for sailing and windsurfing. Kayakers often paddle out to the two tiny offshore Mokulua islands, which are seabird sanctuaries. Because Lanikai is in a residential neighborhood, it's less crowded than other Oahu beaches, the perfect place to enjoy a quiet day. Sun worshipers should arrive in the morning, though, as the Koolau Range blocks the afternoon rays.

There are no facilities here, just off-street parking. From Waikiki, take the H-1 to the Pali Highway (Hwy. 61) through the Nuuanu Pali Tunnel to Kailua, where the Pali Highway becomes Kailua Road as it proceeds through town. At Kalaheo Avenue, turn right and follow the coast about 2 miles to Kailua Beach Park; just past it, turn left at the T intersection and drive uphill on Aalapapa Drive, a one-way street that loops back as Mokulua Drive. Park on Mokulua Drive and walk down any of the eight public-access lanes to the shore. Or take TheBus no. 56 or 57 (Kailua) and then transfer to the shuttle bus.

KAILUA BEACH ★★★

Windward Oahu's premier beach is a 2-mile-long, wide golden strand with dunes, palm trees, panoramic views, and offshore islets that are home to seabirds. The swimming is excellent, and the azure waters are usually decorated with bright sails; this is Oahu's premier windsurfing beach as well. It's also a favorite spot to sail catamarans, bodysurf the gentle waves, or paddle a kayak. Water conditions are quite safe, especially at the mouth of Kaelepulu Stream, where toddlers play in the freshwater shallows at the middle of the beach park. The water is usually about 78°F (26°C), the views are spectacular, and the setting, at the foot of the sheer green Koolau Range, is idyllic. Best of all, the crowds haven't found it yet.

The 35-acre beach park is intersected by a freshwater stream and watched over by lifeguards. Facilities include picnic tables, barbecues, restrooms, a volleyball court, a public boat ramp, free parking, and an open-air cafe. Kailua's new bike path weaves through the park, and windsurfer and kayak rentals are available as well. To get here, take Pali Highway (Hwy. 61) to Kailua, drive through town, turn right on Kalaheo Avenue, and go a mile until you see the beach on your left. Or take TheBus no. 56 or 57 into Kailua, and then the no. 70 shuttle.

KUALOA REGIONAL PARK ★★

This 150-acre coco palm–fringed peninsula is the biggest beach park on the windward side and one of Hawaii's most scenic. It's located on Kaneohe Bay's north shore, at the foot of the spiky Koolau Ridge. The park has a broad, grassy lawn and a long, narrow white-sand beach ideal for swimming, walking, beach-combing, kite flying, or just enjoying the natural beauty of this once-sacred Hawaiian shore, listed on the National Register of Historic Places. The waters are shallow and safe for swimming year-round (lifeguards are on duty). Offshore is Mokolii, the picturesque islet otherwise known as Chinaman's Hat. At low tide, you can swim or wade out to the island, which has a small sandy beach and is a bird preserve—so don't spook the red-footed boobies.

Lanikai Beach.

Kailua Beach.

Kualoa Regional Park.

The park is located on Kamehameha Highway (Hwy. 83) in Kualoa; you can get here via TheBus no. 55.

The North Shore

MALAEKAHANA BAY STATE RECREATION AREA ★★

This white-sand crescent, almost a mile long, lives up to just about everyone's image of the perfect Hawaii beach. It's excellent for swimming. On a weekday, you may be the only one here; but should some net fisherman—or kindred soul—intrude upon your delicious privacy, you can swim out to Goat Island (or wade across at low tide), a sanctuary for seabirds and turtles (so don't chase 'em, brah).

Facilities include restrooms, barbecue grills, picnic tables, outdoor showers, and parking. To get here, take Kamehameha Highway (Hwy. 83) 2 miles north of the Polynesian Cultural Center; as you enter the main gate, you'll come upon the wooded beach park. Or you can take TheBus no. 52.

WAIMEA BEACH PARK ★★

This deep, sandy bowl has gentle summer waves that are excellent for swimming, snorkeling, and bodysurfing. To one side of the bay is a huge rock that local kids like to climb up and dive from. In this placid scene, the only clues of what's to come in winter are those evacuation whistles on poles beside the road. But what a difference a season makes: Winter waves pound the narrow bay, sometimes rising to 50 feet high. When the surf's really up, very strong currents and shore breaks sweep the bay—and it seems like everyone on Oahu drives out to Waimea to get a look at the monster waves and those who ride them. Weekends are great for watching the surfers; to avoid the crowds, go on weekdays.

Facilities include lifeguards, restrooms, showers, parking, and nearby restaurants and shops in Haleiwa town. The beach is located on Kamehameha Highway (Hwy. 83); from Waikiki, you can take TheBus no. 52.

FROM LEFT: Malaekahana Bay State Recreation Area; Waimea Beach Park.

Leeward Oahu: The Waianae Coast

MAKAHA BEACH PARK ★★

When surf's up here, it's spectacular: Monstrous waves pound the beach. This is the original home of Hawaii's big-wave surfing championship; surfers today know it as the home of Buffalo's Big Board Surf Classic, where surfers ride the waves on 10-foot-long wooden boards in the old Hawaiian style of surfing. Nearly a mile long, this half-moon, gold-sand beach is tucked between 231-foot Lahilahi Point, which locals call Black Rock, and Kepuhi Point, a toe of the Waianae mountain

Makaha Beach Park.

FROMMER'S FAVORITE
oahu EXPERIENCES

Getting a Tan on Waikiki Beach. The best spot for catching the rays on the world-famous beach (p. 200) is in front of the big pink Royal Hawaiian Hotel—the beach here is set at the perfect angle for sunning. It's also a great spot for people-watching. Get here early; by midday, it's towel-to-towel.

Exploring Oahu's Rainforests. In the misty sunbeams, colorful birds flit among giant ferns and hanging vines, while towering tropical trees form a thick canopy that shelters all below in cool shadows. This emerald world is a true Eden. For the full experience, try Manoa Falls Trail (p. 219), a walk of about a mile that ends at a freshwater pool and waterfall.

Snorkeling the Glistening Waters of Hanauma Bay. This underwater park (p. 202), once a volcanic crater, is teeming with a rainbow of tropical fish. Bordered by a 2,000-foot gold-sand beach, the bay's shallow water (10 ft. in places) is perfect for neophyte snorkelers. Arrive early to beat the crowds—and don't forget that the bay is closed on Tuesday.

Hiking to the Top of Diamond Head Crater. Almost everyone can make this easy hike to the top of Hawaii's most famous landmark. The 1½-mile round-trip (p. 218) goes up to the top of the 750-foot volcanic cone, where you have a 360-degree view of Oahu. Allow an hour for the trip up and back, bring a buck for the entry fee, and don't forget your camera.

Heading to Waimea Bay When the Surf's Up. From November to March, monstrous waves—some 50 feet tall—roll into Waimea (p. 206). When they break on the shore, the ground actually shakes and everyone on the beach is covered with salt spray mist. The best surfers in the world paddle out to challenge these freight trains. It's amazing to see how small they appear in the lip of the giant waves. This is an experience you'll never forget—and the show won't cost you a dime.

Hearing the Sounds of History. The Royal Hawaiian Band, which has been performing since being commissioned by King Kamehameha III in 1836, plays every Friday at noon in front of the Iolani Palace and every Sunday at 2pm in the bandstand in Kapiolani Park. Both events are free.

Watching the Ancient Hawaiian Sport of Canoe Paddling. On weekday evenings and weekend days from February to September, hundreds of paddlers gather at Ala Wai Canal and practice taking traditional Hawaiian canoes out to sea. Find a comfortable spot at Ala Wai Park, next to the canal, and watch the canoe paddlers re-create this centuries-old sport.

Finding a Bargain at the Aloha Flea Market. Just 50¢ will get you into this all-day show at the Aloha Stadium

range. Summer is the best time to hit this beach—the waves are small, the sand is abundant, and the water is safe for swimming. Children hug the shore on the north side of the beach, near the lifeguard stand, while surfers dodge the rocks and divers seek an offshore channel full of big fish. *A caveat:* This is a "local" beach; you are welcome, of course, but you can expect "stink eye" (mild

parking lot, where more than 1,000 vendors sell everything from junk to jewels. Go early for the best deals. Open Wednesday, Saturday, and Sunday from 6am to 3pm.

Attending a Hawaiian-Language Church Service. Built in 1842, Kawaiahao Church (p. 240) is the Westminster Abbey of Hawaii; the vestibule is lined with portraits of the Hawaiian monarchy, many of whom were crowned in this very building. The coral church is a perfect setting to experience an all-Hawaiian service, complete with Hawaiian song. Hawaiian-language services are held every Sunday at 9am; admission is free (donations appreciated).

Visiting the Lei Sellers in Chinatown. There's a host of cultural sights and experiences to be had in Honolulu's Chinatown. Wander through this several-square-block area with its jumble of exotic shops offering herbs, Chinese groceries, and acupuncture services. Be sure to check out the lei sellers on Maunakea Street (near N. Hotel St.), where Hawaii's finest leis go for as little as $2.50. See p. 285 for more on shopping for leis; see p. 253 for a Chinatown walking tour.

Experiencing a Turning Point in America's History: The Bombing of Pearl Harbor. Standing on the deck of the USS *Arizona* Memorial at Pearl Harbor (p. 242), with the ship underneath, is an unforgettable experience. On that fateful day—December 7, 1941—the 608-foot

Arizona sank in just 9 minutes, killing 1,177 of the men onboard, after being bombed during the Japanese air raid that sent the U.S. to war. Go early; you'll wait 2 to 3 hours if you visit at midday. You must wear closed-toe shoes (no sandals allowed).

Watching the Sun Sink into the Pacific from a Hill Named after a Sweet Potato. Actually, it's more romantic than it sounds. Puu Ualakaa State Park (p. 251), at the end of Round Hill Drive, translates into "rolling sweet-potato hill." This majestic view of the sunset is not to be missed.

Ordering a Shave Ice in a Tropical Flavor You Can Hardly Pronounce. In Haleiwa, stop at Matsumoto Shave Ice (p. 277) for a snow cone with an exotic flavor poured over the top. Get the local favorite, the fruity *li hing mui*, or try one with sweet Japanese adzuki beans hidden inside. This taste of tropical paradise goes for just $1.

Listening to the Soothing Sounds of Hawaiian Music. Sit under the huge banyan tree at the Moana Surfrider's Banyan Veranda in Waikiki, order a cocktail, and sway to live Hawaiian music any night of the week. Another quintessential sunset oasis is the Halekulani's House Without a Key, a sophisticated oceanfront lounge with wonderful hula and steel-guitar music, a great view of Diamond Head, and the best mai tais on the island.

approbation) if you are not respectful of the beach and the local residents who use the facility all the time.

Facilities include restrooms, lifeguards, and parking. To get here, take the H-1 freeway to the end of the line, where it becomes Farrington Highway (Hwy. 93), and follow it to the beach; or you can take TheBus no. 51.

Yokohama Bay.

YOKOHAMA BAY ★

Where Farrington Highway (Hwy. 93) ends, the wilderness of Kaena Point State Park begins. It's a remote 853-acre coastline park of empty beaches, sand dunes, cliffs, and deep-blue water. This is the last sandy stretch of shore on the northwest coast of Oahu. Sometimes it's known as Keawalua Beach or Puau Beach, but everybody here calls it Yokohama, after the Japanese immigrants who came from that port city to work the cane fields and fished along this shoreline. When the surf's calm—mainly in summer—this is a good area for snorkeling, diving, swimming, shore fishing, and picnicking. When surf's up, board surfers and bodysurfers are out in droves; don't go in the water then unless you're an expert. There are no lifeguards or facilities, except at the park entrance, where there's a restroom and lifeguard stand. No bus service, either.

WATERSPORTS

If you want to rent beach toys (snorkeling equipment, boogie boards, surfboards, kayaks, and more), check out **Snorkel Bob's,** on the way to Hanauma Bay at 700 Kapahulu Ave. (at Date St.), Honolulu (✆ **808/735-7944;** www.snorkel bob.com); or **Aloha Beach Service,** in the Moana Surfrider, 2365 Kalakaua Ave., in Waikiki (✆ **808/922-3111,** ext. 2341). On Oahu's windward side, try **Kailua Sailboards & Kayaks,** 130 Kailua Rd., a block from Kailua Beach Park (✆ **808/262-2555;** www.kailuasailboards.com). On the North Shore, get equipment from **Surf-N-Sea,** 62–595 Kamehameha Hwy., Haleiwa (✆ **808/637-9887;** www.surfnsea.com).

For general advice on the activities listed below, see "Special-Interest Trips," in chapter 3.

Boating

A funny thing happens to people when they come to Hawaii: Maybe it's the salt air, the warm tropical nights, or the blue Hawaiian moonlight, but otherwise-rational people who have never set foot on a boat in their life suddenly want to go out to sea. You can opt for a "booze cruise," jammed with loud, rum-soaked strangers, or you can sail on one of these special yachts, all of which will take you out **whale-watching** in season (roughly Jan–Apr). For fishing charters, see "Sport Fishing," below.

Captain Bob's Adventure Cruises ★ See the majestic Windward Coast the way it should be seen—from a boat. Captain Bob will take you on a 4-hour lazy-day sail of Kaneohe Bay aboard his 42-foot catamaran, which skims across the almost always calm water above the shallow coral reef, lands at the disappearing sandbar Ahu o Laka, and takes you past two small islands to snorkel spots full of tropical fish and sometimes turtles. The color of the water alone is worth the price. This is an all-day affair: A shuttle will pick you up at your Waikiki hotel between 9 and 9:30am and bring you back at about 4pm.

Kaneohe Bay. ℭ **808/942-5077.** All-day cruise $88 adults, $73 children 3-14. Rates include all you-can-eat barbecue lunch and transportation from Waikiki hotels. No cruises Sun and holidays. Bus: 55 or 56.

Navatek I ★★ You've never been on a boat, you don't want to be on a boat, but here you are being dragged aboard one. Why are you boarding this weird-looking vessel? It guarantees that you'll be "seasick free," that's why. The 140-foot-long *Navatek I* isn't even a boat; it's actually a SWATH (Small Waterplane Area Twin Hull) vessel. That means the ship's superstructure—the part you ride on—rests on twin torpedo-like hulls that cut through the water so you don't bob like a cork and spill your mai tai. It's the smoothest ride on Mamala Bay. In fact, *Navatek I* is the only dinner cruise ship to receive U.S. Coast Guard certification to travel beyond Diamond Head.

Sunset dinner cruises leave Pier 6 (across from the Hawaii Maritime Center) nightly. If you have your heart set on seeing the city lights, take the Royal Sunset Dinner Cruise, which runs from 5 to 7:30pm. The best deal is the **lunch cruise,** with a full buffet and a great view of Oahu offshore. During **whale season** (roughly Jan–Apr), you get whales, to boot. The lunch cruise lasts from noon to 2:30pm. Both cruises include live Hawaiian music.

Aloha Tower Marketplace, Pier 6, c/o Hawaiian Cruises Ltd. ℭ **808/973-1311.** www.atlantis adventures.com/oahu.cfm. Dinner cruises $80 adults, $48 children 2-12; lunch cruises $74 adults, $38 children 2-11. Validated parking $3–$8 before 4:30pm, flat fee of $2 after 4:30pm. Bus: 8, 19, 20, 55, 56, or 57.

Wild Side Tours Picture this: You're floating in the calm waters off the Waianae coast, where your 42-foot sailing catamaran has just dropped you off. Below, in the reef, are turtles, and suddenly in the distance, you see spinner dolphins. Happens every day on the 4-hour tours operated by the Cullins family, which has swum in these waters for decades. In winter, you may spot humpback whales on the morning cruise, which also includes continental breakfast, snorkel gear, instruction, and a floatation device. The tour lasts from 8 to 11am; you'll check in at 7:30am.

Watersports

Waianae Boat Harbor, 87–1286 Farrington Hwy., Waianae. ☎ **808/306-7273.** www.sailhawaii. com. Morning sail/snorkel $115 for ages 6 and up (not recommended for younger children); sunset sail $95. MC, V. Bus: 19 or 20 to Ala Moana Center, then 40 or 40A.

Body Boarding (Boogie Boarding) & Bodysurfing

Good places to learn to body board are in the small waves of **Waikiki Beach** and **Kailua Beach** (both reviewed under "Beaches," earlier in this chapter), and **Bellows Field Beach Park,** off Kalanianaole Highway (Hwy. 72) in Waimanalo, which is open to the public on weekends (from noon Fri to midnight Sun and holidays). To get here, turn toward the ocean on Hughs Road, and then right on Tinker Road, which takes you to the park.

See the introduction to this section for a list of rental shops where you can get a boogie board.

Ocean Kayaking

For a wonderful adventure, rent a kayak, arrive at Lanikai Beach just as the sun is appearing, and paddle across the emerald lagoon to the pyramid-shaped islands called Mokulua—it's an experience you won't forget. Kayak equipment rental starts at $12 an hour for a single kayak and $25 an hour for a double kayak. In Waikiki, try **Prime Time Sports,** Fort DeRussy Beach (☎ **808/949-8952**). On the windward side, check out **Kailua Sailboards & Kayaks,** 130 Kailua Rd., a block from Kailua Beach Park (☎ **808/262-2555;** www.kailuasailboards.com), where single kayaks rent for $39 for a half-day and double kayaks rent for $55 for a half-day.

First-timers should go to Kailua Sailboards & Kayaks, which offers a guided tour with the novice in mind in a safe, protected environment. Prices, which start at $95 for adults and $81 for kids 8 to 13, include lunch, all equipment, and transportation from Waikiki hotels. Kayak lessons and self-guided trips are also available.

If you're staying on the North Shore, go to **Surf-N-Sea,** 62–595 Kamehameha Hwy., Haleiwa (☎ **808/637-9887;** www.surfnsea.com), where kayak rentals start at $10 an hour or $60 a day.

Scuba Diving

Oahu is a wonderful place to scuba dive, especially for those interested in wreck diving. One of the more famous wrecks in Hawaii is the *Mahi,* a 185-foot former minesweeper easily accessible just south of Waianae. Abundant marine life makes this a great place to shoot photos—schools of lemon butterflyfish and taape (blue-lined snapper) are so comfortable with divers and photographers that they practically pose. Eagle rays, green sea turtles, manta rays, and white-tipped sharks occasionally cruise by as well, and eels peer out from the wreck.

For nonwreck diving, one of the best dive spots in summer is **Kahuna Canyon.** In Hawaiian, *kahuna* means priest, wise man, or sorcerer; this massive amphitheater, located near Mokuleia, is a perfect example of something a sorcerer might conjure up. Walls rising from the ocean floor create the illusion of an underwater Grand Canyon. Inside the amphitheater, crabs, octopuses, slippers,

EXPERIENCING jaws: UP CLOSE & PERSONAL

You're 4 miles out from land, surrounded by open ocean. Suddenly, from out of the blue depths, a shape emerges: the sleek, pale shadow of a 6-foot-long gray reef shark, followed quickly by a couple of 10-foot-long Galapagos sharks. Within moments, you are surrounded by sharks on all sides. Do you panic? No, you paid $96 to be in the midst of these jaws of the deep. And, of course, you have a 6×6×10-foot aluminum shark cage separating you from all those teeth.

It happens every day at **North Shore Shark Adventures** (☎ 808/228-5900; www.hawaiisharkadventures.com), the dream of Capt. Joe Pavsek, who decided after some 30 years of surfing and diving to share the experience of seeing a shark with visitors. To make sure that the predators of the deep will show up for the viewing, Captain Pavsek heaves "chum," a not very appetizing concoction of fish trimmings and entrails, over the side of his 26-foot boat, *Kailolo*. After a few minutes, the sharks (generally gray reef, Galapagos, and sandbars, ranging 5–15 ft.) show up—sometimes just a few,

sometimes a couple dozen. Depending on the sea conditions and the weather, snorkelers can stay in the cage as long as they wish, with the sharks just inches away. The shark cage, connected to the boat with wire line, holds up to four snorkelers (it's comfortable with two but pretty snug at full capacity). You can also stay on the boat and view the sharks from a more respectable distance for just $60. The more adventurous, down in the cage with just thin aluminum separating them from the sharks, are sure to have an experience they won't forget.

and spiny lobsters abound (be aware that taking them in summer is illegal), and giant trevally, parrotfish, and unicorn fish congregate as well. Outside the amphitheater, you're likely to see an occasional shark in the distance.

Because Oahu's greatest dives are offshore, your best bet is to book a two-tank dive from a dive boat. Hawaii's oldest and largest outfitter is **Aaron's Dive Shop,** 307 Hahani St., Kailua (© **808/262-2333;** www.hawaii-scuba.com), which offers boat and beach dive excursions off the coast. The two-tank boat dives start at $115 per person if you have all your gear or $125 including gear, and transportation from the Kailua shop is provided. The beach dive off the North Shore in summer or the Waianae Coast in winter is the same price as a boat dive, including all gear and transportation, so Aaron's recommends the boat dive. They will do Waikiki hotel pickups at no additional charge.

In Waikiki, **Dive Oahu,** 1085 Ala Moana (© **808/922-3483;** www.dive oahu.com), offers dives from shipwrecks to dives in Waikiki for just $129 for a two-tank boat dive (friends or family members can tag along for just $35 each to snorkel). Captain Brian, who has been diving for a couple of decades, loves to help beginners feel comfortable, as well as show experienced scuba divers what the Waikiki coast has to offer.

On the North Shore, **Surf-N-Sea,** 62–595 Kamehameha Hwy., Haleiwa (© **808/637-9887;** www.surfnsea.com), has dive tours from the shore (starting at $75 for one tank) and from a boat ($140 for two tanks). Surf-N-Sea also rents equipment and can point you to the best dive sites in the area.

Snorkeling

Some of the best snorkeling in Oahu is at **Hanauma Bay ★★**. It's crowded—sometimes it seems there are more people than fish—but Hanauma has clear, warm, protected waters and an abundance of friendly reef fish, including Moorish idols, scores of butterflyfish, damselfish, and wrasses. Hanauma Bay has two

Snorkeling is great throughout Oahu, but especially at Hanauma Bay.

An Atlantis submarine.

reefs, an inner and an outer—the first for novices, the other for experts. The inner reef is calm and shallow (less than 10 ft.); in some places, you can just wade and put your face in the water. Go early: It's packed by 10am. And it's closed on Tuesdays. For details, see "Beaches," earlier in this chapter.

Braver snorkelers may want to head to **Shark's Cove,** on the North Shore just off Kamehameha Highway, between Haleiwa and Pupukea. Sounds risky, I know, but I've never seen or heard of any sharks in this cove, and in summer this big, lava-edged pool is one of Oahu's best snorkel spots. Waves splash over the natural lava grotto and cascade like waterfalls into the pool full of tropical fish. To the right of the cove are deep-sea caves to explore.

Sport Fishing

Kewalo Basin, located between the Honolulu International Airport and Waikiki, is the main location for charter fishing boats on Oahu. From Waikiki, take Kalakaua Avenue Ewa (west) beyond Ala Moana Center; Kewalo Basin is on the left, across from Ward Centre. Look for charter boats all in a row in their slips; when the fish are biting, the captains display the catch of the day in the afternoon. You can also take TheBus no. 19 or 20 (Airport).

The best sport-fishing booking desk in the state is **Sportfish Hawaii ★** (© **877/388-1376** or 808/396-2607; www.sportfishhawaii.com), which books boats on all the islands. These fishing vessels have been inspected and must meet rigorous criteria to guarantee that you will have a great time. Prices range from $812 to $1,300 for a full-day exclusive charter (you, plus five friends, get the entire boat to yourself), from $717 for a half-day exclusive, or from $191 for a full-day shared charter (you share the boat with five other people).

A bodyboarder attempting to catch a wave.

Submarine Dives

Here's your chance to play Jules Verne and experience the underwater world from the comfort of a submarine, which will take you on an adventure below the surface in high-tech comfort. The entire trip is narrated as you watch tropical fish and sunken ships just outside the sub; if swimming's not your thing, this is a great way to see Hawaii's spectacular sea life. Shuttle boats to the sub leave from the Hilton Hawaiian Village Pier. Call **Atlantis Submarines ★** (© **800/548-6262** or 808/973-9811; www.atlantisadventures.com/hawaii.cfm) to reserve. The cost is $106 for adults, $48 for kids 12 and under (children must be at least 36 in. tall). *Tip:* Book online for discount rates of $96 for adults and $44 for kids. *Warning:* Skip this if you suffer from claustrophobia.

Surfing

In summer, when the water's warm and there's a soft breeze in the air, the south swell comes up. It's surf season in Waikiki, the best place on Oahu to learn how to surf. For lessons, go early to **Aloha Beach Service,** next to the Moana Surfrider, 2365 Kalakaua Ave., Waikiki (© **808/922-3111**). The beach boys offer group lessons for $30 an hour; board rentals are $10 to $15 for the first hour and $5 for every hour after that. You must know how to swim.

On the North Shore, there's no excuse not to learn to surf: Hans Hedemann, a champion surfer for some 34 years, has opened the **Hans Hedemann Surf School** (© 808/924-7778; www.hhsurf.com) at Turtle Bay Resort. Hedemann himself gives private lessons—at $150 for an hour. (He has taught celebrities such as Cameron Diaz and Adam Sandler.) If the expenditure is beyond your budget, go for a $75 2-hour group lesson (maximum four people). The surf school has one other location, in Waikiki at the Park Shore Waikiki.

Surfboards are also available for rent on the North Shore at **Surf-N-Sea,** 62–595 Kamehameha Hwy., Haleiwa (© **800/899-7873;** www.surfnsea.com), for $5 to $7 an hour. Lessons go for $85 for 2 to 3 hours. For the best surf shops, where you can soak in the culture as well as pick up gear, see "Shopping A to Z" (p. 280).

On the windward side, call **Kimo's Surf Hut,** 776 Kailua Rd., in Kailua (© **808/262-1644;** www.kimossurfhut.com). Kimo and his wife, Ruth, couldn't be more friendly and helpful. In addition to surfboards for rent ($50 a day), Kimo has his own personal collection of vintage surfboards lovingly displayed on the walls of the shop. If you have the time, he will gladly tell you the pedigree and history of each board. Although Kimo doesn't offer formal surfing lessons, he'd be happy to give you pointers.

More experienced surfers should drop in on any surf shop around Oahu, or call the **Surf News Network Surfline** (© **808/596-SURF** [7873]) to get the latest surf conditions. **The Cliffs,** at the base of Diamond Head, is a good spot for advanced surfers; 4- to 6-foot waves churn here, allowing high-performance surfing.

If you're in Hawaii in winter and want to see the serious surfers catch the really big waves, bring your binoculars and grab a front-row seat on the beach near **Kalalua Point.** To get there from Waikiki, take the H-1 toward the North Shore, veering off at H-2, which becomes Kamehameha Highway (Hwy. 83). Keep going to the funky surf town of Haleiwa and Waimea Bay; the big waves will be on your left, just past Pupukea Beach Park.

Windsurfing & Kitesurfing

Windward Oahu's **Kailua Beach** is the home of pioneer windsurfer Robby Naish; it's also the best place to learn to windsurf. The oldest and most established windsurfing business in Hawaii is **Naish Hawaii/Naish Windsurfing Hawaii,** 155-A Hamakua Dr., Kailua (© **800/767-6068** or 808/262-6068; www.naish.com). The company offers everything: lessons, sales, rentals, repair, and free advice on where to go when the wind and waves are happening. Private 60-minute lessons start at $75 for one; you'll need about three lessons to be up and happening. They also have kitesurfing rentals (boards only) for $30 a day.

Kailua Sailboards & Kayaks, 130 Kailua Rd., a block from Kailua Beach Park (© **808/262-2555;** www.kailuasailboards.com), offers 2 hour small group windsurfing lessons ($129 per person, including all gear, plus lunch), private lessons for $109 an hour, and rentals of windsurfing equipment (from $59 for a half-day), as well as surfboards, snorkel gear, and ocean kayaks.

NATURE HIKES

People are often surprised to discover that the great outdoors is less than an hour away from downtown Honolulu. The island's 33 major hiking trails traverse razor-thin ridgebacks, deep waterfall valleys, and more. The best source of hiking information on Oahu is the state's **Na Ala Hele (Trails to Go On) Program** (© **808/973-9782;** www.hawaiitrails.org). The website has everything you need: detailed maps and descriptions of 40 trails in the state's Na Ala Hele, a hiking safety brochure, updates on the trails, hyperlinks to weather information, health warnings, info on native plants, how to volunteer for trail upkeep, and more.

The **Hawaiian Trail and Mountain Club,** P.O. Box 2238, Honolulu, HI 96804 (www.htmclub.org), offers regular hikes on Oahu. Bring a couple of bucks for the donation, your own lunch, and drinking water, and meet up with the club members at the scheduled location to join them on a hike. In addition, the club meets for Saturday and Sunday hikes at the Iolani Palace, at King Street between Richard and Punchbowl streets in downtown Honolulu. Generally they meet at 8am; look for a group of people dressed in hiking clothes and boots at the left rear of the palace.

Other organizations that offer regularly scheduled hikes are the **Sierra Club,** 1040 Richards St., Honolulu, HI 96813 (www.hi.sierraclub.org); the **Nature Conservancy,** 1116 Smith St., Ste. 201, Honolulu, HI 96817 (*©* **808/ 537-4508;** www.nature.org/wherewework/northamerica/states/hawaii); and the **Hawaii Nature Center,** 2131 Makiki Heights Dr. (*©* **888/955-0104;** www. hawaiinaturecenter.org).

Honolulu-Area Hikes
DIAMOND HEAD CRATER ★★★

This is a moderate but steep walk to the summit of Hawaii's most famous landmark. Kids love to look out from the top of the 760-foot volcanic cone, where they have 360-degree views of Oahu up the leeward coast from Waikiki. The 1.5-mile round-trip takes about 1½ hours, and the entry fee is $1.

Diamond Head was created by a volcanic explosion about half a million years ago. The Hawaiians called the crater *Leahi* (meaning the brow of the ahi, or tuna, referring to the shape of the crater). Diamond Head was considered a sacred spot; King Kamehameha offered human sacrifices at a *heiau* on the western slope. It wasn't until the 19th century that Mount Leahi got its current name:

The view from the Diamond Head lookout.

A group of sailors found what they thought were diamonds in the crater; it turned out they were just worthless calcite crystals, but the name stuck.

Before you begin your journey to the top of the crater, put on some decent shoes (rubber-soled tennies are fine) and pack a flashlight (you'll walk through several dark tunnels, which are not always lighted), binoculars (for better viewing at the top), water (very important), a hat to protect you from the sun, and a camera. You might want to put all your gear in a pack to leave your hands free for the climb. If you don't have a flashlight or your hotel can't lend you one, you can buy a small one for a few dollars as part of a Diamond Head "climber's kit" at the gift shop at the New Otani Kaimana Beach Hotel, on the Diamond Head end of Kalakaua Avenue, just past the Waikiki Aquarium and across from Kapiolani Park.

Go early, preferably just after the 6:30am opening, before the midday sun starts beating down. The hike to the summit starts at Monsarrat and 18th avenues on the crater's inland (or mauka) side. To get here, take TheBus no. 58 from the Ala Moana Center or drive to the intersection of Diamond Head Road and 18th Avenue. Follow the road through the tunnel (which is closed 6pm–6am) and park in the lot. From the trail head in the parking lot, you'll proceed along a paved walkway (with handrails) as you climb up the slope. You'll pass old World War I and II pillboxes, gun emplacements, and tunnels built as part of the Pacific defense network. Several steps take you up to the top observation post on Point Leahi. The views are incredible.

If you want to go with a guide, the Clean Air Team leads a guided hike to the top of Diamond Head the first Saturday of every month. The group gathers at 9am, near the front entrance to the Honolulu Zoo (at the Mahatma Gandhi statue). Hikers should bring a flashlight and a $10 fee. Each person will be given a bag and asked to help keep the trail clean by picking up litter. For more information, call ✆ **808/948-3299.**

MANOA FALLS TRAIL ★★

This easy .75-mile (one-way) hike is terrific for families; it takes less than an hour to reach idyllic Manoa Falls. The trail head, marked by a footbridge, is at the end of Manoa Road, past Lyon Arboretum. The staff at the arboretum prefers that hikers do not park in their lot, so the best place to park is in the residential area below Paradise Park; you can also get to the arboretum via TheBus no. 5. The often-muddy trail follows Waihi Stream and meanders through the forest reserve past guavas, mountain apples, and wild ginger. The forest is moist and humid and is inhabited by giant bloodthirsty mosquitoes, so bring repellent. If it has rained recently, stay on the trail and step carefully, as it can be very slippery (and it's a long way down if you slide off the side). The trail sometimes closes due to unsafe conditions; before you venture out, call ✆ **808/587-0300** to check whether it's open.

East Oahu Hikes

MAKAPUU LIGHTHOUSE TRAIL ★

You've seen this famous old lighthouse on episodes of *Magnum, P.I.* and *Hawaii Five-O.* No longer staffed by the Coast Guard (it's fully automated now), the lighthouse sits at the end of a precipitous cliff trail on an airy perch over the Windward Coast, Manana (Rabbit) Island, and the azure Pacific. It's about a

45-minute, 1-mile hike from Kalani-anaole Highway (Hwy. 72), along a paved road that begins across from Hawaii Kai Executive Golf Course and winds around the 646-foot-high sea bluff to the lighthouse lookout.

To get to the trail head from Waikiki, take Kalanianaole Highway (Hwy. 72) past Hanauma Bay and Sandy Beach to Makapuu Head, the southeastern tip of the island; you can also take TheBus no. 57 or 58. Look for a sign that says NO VEHICLES ALLOWED on a gate to the right, a few hundred yards past the entrance to the golf course. The trail isn't marked, but it's fairly obvious: Just follow the abandoned road that leads gradually uphill to a trail that wraps around Makapuu Point. It's a little precarious, but anyone in reasonably good shape can handle it.

Makapuu Lighthouse.

Blowhole alert: When the south swell is running, usually in summer, there are a couple of blowholes on the south side of Makapuu Head that put the famous Halona Blowhole to shame.

Windward Coast Hikes

HAUULA LOOP TRAIL ★

For one of the best views of the coast and the ocean, follow the Hauula Loop Trail on the windward side of the island. It's an easy 2.5-mile loop on a well-maintained path that passes through a whispering ironwood forest and a grove of tall Norfolk pines. The trip takes about 3 hours and gains some 600 feet in elevation.

To get to the trail, take TheBus no. 55 or follow Hwy. 83 to Hauula Beach Park. Turn toward the mountains on Hauula Homestead Road; when it forks to the left at Maakua Road, park on the side of the road. Walk along Maakua Road to the wide, grassy trail that begins the hike into the mountains. The climb is fairly steep for about 900 feet but turns into easier-on-the-calves switchbacks as you go up the ridge. Look down as you climb: You'll spot wildflowers and mushrooms among the matted needles. The trail continues up, crossing Waipilopilo Gulch, where you'll see several forms of native plant life. Eventually, you reach the top of the ridge, where the views are spectacular.

Camping is permitted along the trail, but it's difficult to find a place to pitch a tent on the steep slopes and in the dense forest growth. There are a few places along the ridge, however, that are wide enough for a tent. Contact the **Division of Forestry and Wildlife,** 1151 Punchbowl St., Honolulu, HI 96813 (© **808/ 587-0166;** www.dofaw.net), for information on camping permits.

PALI (MAUNAWILI) TRAIL ★

For a million-dollar view of the Windward Coast, take this 11-mile (one-way) foothill trail. The trail head is about 6 miles from downtown Honolulu, on the windward side of the Nuuanu Pali Tunnel, at the scenic lookout just beyond the hairpin turn of the Pali Highway (Hwy. 61). Just as you begin the turn, look for the scenic overlook sign, slow down, and pull off the highway into the parking lot (sorry, no bus service available).

The mostly flat, well-marked, easy-to-moderate trail goes through the forest on the lower slopes of the 3,000-foot Koolau mountain range and ends up in the backyard of the coastal Hawaiian village of Waimanalo. Go halfway to get the view and then return to your car, or have someone meet you in 'Nalo.

North Shore Hikes

WAIMEA VALLEY

For nearly 3 decades, 1,875-acre Waimea Valley, 59–864 Kamehameha Hwy., Haleiwa (© **808/638-7766;** www.waimeavalley.net), has lured visitors with activities from cliff diving and hula performances to kayaking and ATV tours. In 2008, the Office of Hawaiian Affairs took over and formed a new nonprofit corporation, Hiipaka, to run the park, with an emphasis on perpetuating and sharing the "living Hawaiian culture."

A visit here offers a lush walk into the past. The valley is packed with archaeological sites, including the 600-year-old Hale O Lono, a *heiau* dedicated to the Hawaiian god Lono, which you'll find to the left of the entrance. The botanical collection has 35 different gardens, including super-rare Hawaiian species such as the endangered *Kokia cookei* hibiscus. The valley is also home to fauna such as the endangered Hawaiian moorhen; look for a black bird with a red face cruising in the ponds. The 150-acre Arboretum and Botanical Garden contains more than 5,000 species of tropical plants. Walk through the gardens (take the paved paths or dirt trails) and wind up at 45-foot-high Waimea Falls—bring your bathing suit and you can dive into the cold, murky water. The public is

The Koolau mountain range near the Maunawili Kailua area of Oahu.

Nature Hikes

invited to hike the trails and spend a day in this quiet oasis. There are several free walking tours at 10am, 11am, 1pm, and 2pm. Plus there are cultural activities like lei making, kappa demonstrations, hula lessons, Hawaiian games and crafts, and music and storytelling throughout the day. The entrance fee is $13 for adults, $6 for children 4 to 12, and $6 for seniors (parking is free).

To Land's End: A Leeward Oahu Hike

KAENA POINT ★

At the very western tip of Oahu lie the dry, barren lands of Kaena Point State Park, 853 acres of jagged sea cliffs, deep gulches, sand dunes, endangered plant life, and a remote, wild, wind- and surf-battered coastline. *Kaena* means "red-hot" or "glowing" in Hawaiian; the name refers to the brilliant sunsets visible from the point.

Kaena Point.

Kaena is steeped in numerous legends. A popular one concerns the demigod Maui: Maui had a famous hook that he used to raise islands from the sea. He decided that he wanted to bring the islands of Oahu and Kauai closer together, so one day he threw his hook across the Kauai Channel and snagged Kauai (which is actually visible from Kaena Point on clear days). Using all his might, Maui was able to pull loose a huge boulder, which fell into the waters very close to the present lighthouse at Kaena. The rock is still called *Pohaku o Kauai* ("the rock from Kauai"). Like Black Rock in Kaanapali on Maui, Kaena is thought of as the point on Oahu from which souls depart.

To hike out to the departing place, take the clearly marked trail from the parking lot of Kaena Point State Park. The moderate 5-mile round-trip hike to the point will take a couple of hours. The trail along the cliff passes tide pools abundant in marine life and rugged protrusions of lava reaching out to the turbulent sea; seabirds circle overhead. Do *not* go off the trail; you might step on buried birds' eggs. There are no sandy beaches, and the water is nearly always turbulent here. In winter, when a big north swell is running, the waves at Kaena are the biggest in the state, averaging heights of 30 to 40 feet. Even when the water appears calm, offshore currents are powerful, so don't plan to swim. Go early in the morning to see the schools of porpoises that frequent the area just offshore.

To get to the trail head from Honolulu or Waikiki, take the H-1 west to its end; continue on Hwy. 93 past Makaha and follow Hwy. 930 to the end of the road. There's no bus service.

CAMPING & WILDERNESS CABINS

If you plan to camp, you must bring your own gear or buy it here—no one on Oahu rents gear. If you are bringing your own equipment, remember that you can't transport fuel (even in a canister) on the plane. Also, if your equipment runs on butane, don't bother bringing it—butane is very difficult to find here.

The best places to camp on Oahu are listed below. TheBus's Circle Island route can get you to or near all these sites, but remember: On TheBus, you're allowed only one bag, which has to fit under the seat. If you have more gear, you're going to have to drive or take a cab.

The Windward Coast

HOOMALUHIA BOTANICAL GARDEN ★

This little-known windward campground outside Kaneohe is a real treasure. It's hard to believe that it's just half an hour from downtown Honolulu. The name *Hoomaluhia,* or "peace and tranquillity," accurately describes this 400-acre botanical garden at the foot of the jagged Koolau Range. In this lush setting, gardens are devoted to plants specific to tropical America, native Hawaii, Polynesia, India, Sri Lanka, and Africa. A 32-acre lake sits in the middle of the scenic park (no swimming or boating allowed), and there are numerous hiking trails. The visitor center offers free guided walks Saturday at 10am and Sunday at 1pm (call the number below to register).

Facilities for this tent-camp area include restrooms, cold showers, dishwashing stations, picnic tables, and water. A public phone is available at the visitor center. Shopping and gas are available in Kaneohe, 2 miles away. Permits are

Hoomaluhia Botanical Garden.

free (although there is talk of changing that), but stays are limited to 3 nights (Fri–Sun only); the office is closed on Sunday. The gate is locked at 4pm and doesn't open again until 9am, so you're locked in for the night. To get a permit, you must apply in person. For inquiries and reservations, contact **Hoomaluhia Botanical Garden,** 45–680 Luluku Rd. (at Kamehameha Hwy.), Kaneohe, HI 96744 (℗ **808/233-7323;** www.co.honolulu.hi.us/parks/hbg/hmbg.htm). To get here from Waikiki, take H-1 to the Pali Highway (Hwy. 61); turn left on Kamehameha Highway (Hwy. 83); and at the fourth light, turn left on Luluku Road. TheBus nos. 55 and 56 stop nearby on Kamehameha Highway; from here, you have to walk 2 miles to the visitor center.

KAHANA BAY BEACH PARK ★★

Lying under Tahiti-like cliffs, with a beautiful gold-sand crescent beach framed by pine-needle casuarina trees, Kahana Bay Beach Park is a place of serene beauty. You can swim, bodysurf, fish, hike, and picnic, or just sit and listen to the trade winds whistle through the beach pines. Only tent and vehicle camping are allowed at this oceanside oasis.

Facilities include restrooms, picnic tables, drinking water, public phones, and a boat-launching ramp. *Note:* The restrooms are located at the north end of the beach, far away from the camping area, and there are no showers. There's an $18 fee for camping (per campsite per night), and you must get a permit. Permits are limited to 5 nights (Fri–Wed); contact the **Department of Land and Natural Resources,** State Parks Division, P.O. Box 621, Honolulu, HI 96809 (℗ **808/587-0300;** www.hawaiistateparks.org/camping/fees.cfm).

Kahana Bay Beach Park is located in the 52–222 block of Kamehameha Highway (Hwy. 83) in Kahana. From Waikiki, take the H-1 west to the Likelike Highway (Hwy. 63). Continue north on the Likelike, through the Wilson Tunnel, turning left on Hwy. 83; Kahana Bay is 13 miles down the road on the right. You can also get here via TheBus no. 55.

KUALOA REGIONAL PARK ★★

This park has a spectacular setting on a peninsula on Kaneohe Bay. The gold-sand beach is excellent for snorkeling, and fishing can be rewarding as well (see the "Beaches" section, earlier in this chapter).

There are two campgrounds. Campground A—located in a wooded area with a sandy beach and palm, ironwood, kamani, and monkeypod trees—is mainly used for groups. It does have a few sites for families, except during the summer (June–Aug), when the Department of Parks and Recreation conducts a children's camping program here. Campground B is on the main beach; it has fewer shade trees but a great view of Mokolii Island. Facilities at both sites include restrooms, showers, picnic tables, drinking fountains, and a public phone. Campground A also has sinks for washing dishes, a volleyball court, and a kitchen building. Gas and groceries are available in Kaaawa, 2½ miles away. The gate hours at Kualoa Regional Park are 7am to 8pm. Permits are free but limited to 3 to 5 days (no camping in Campground A Mon–Thurs; in Campground B, no camping Thurs). Contact the **Honolulu Department of Parks and Recreation Permits,** 650

S. King St., Honolulu, HI 96713 (© **808/768-3440;** www.honolulu.gov/parks/parkuse.htm), for information and permits. You must apply for a camping permit in person at any Satellite City Hall.

To get to the park, take the Likelike Highway (Hwy. 63); after the Wilson Tunnel, get in the right lane and turn off on Kahakili Highway (Hwy. 83). Or take TheBus no. 55.

The North Shore

CAMP MOKULEIA ★

The centerpiece of this 9-acre campground is a quiet, isolated beach on Oahu's North Shore, 4 miles from Kaena Point. Camping is available on the beach or in a grassy, wooded area. Activities include swimming, surfing, shore fishing, and beachcombing. This place makes a great getaway.

Facilities include tent camping, cabins, and lodge accommodations. The tent-camping site has portable chemical toilets, a water spigot, and outdoor showers; there are no picnic tables or barbecue grills, so come prepared. Tent camping is $15 per person, per night. The cabins sleep up to 22 people in bunk beds. Rates are $238 per night for the 14-bed cabin and $344 per night for the 22-bed cabin. Rooms at the lodge are $95 for a shared bathroom and $95 to $105 for a private bathroom. A studio cottage rents for $85 and sleeps two; a three-bedroom beach house goes for $225 and sleeps six. "Home cooked" meals can be had for $9 to $10. Many groups use the camp, but there's a real sense of privacy. Reservations are required; contact **Camp Mokuleia,** 68–72 Farrington Hwy., Waialua, HI 96791 (© **808/637-6241;** www.campmokuleia.com).

Camp Mokuleia is located on Farrington Highway, west of Haleiwa. From Waikiki, take the H-1 to the H-2 exit; stay on H-2 until the end. Where the road forks, bear left to Waialua on Hwy. 803, which turns into Hwy. 930 to Kaena Point. Look for the green fence on the right, where a small sign at the driveway reads CAMP MOKULEIA, EPISCOPAL CHURCH OF HAWAII.

MALAEKAHANA BAY STATE RECREATION AREA ★★

This is one of the most beautiful beach-camping areas in the state, with a mile-long, gold-sand beach on Oahu's North Shore (see "Beaches," earlier in this chapter, for details). There are two areas for tent camping. Facilities include picnic tables, restrooms, showers, sinks, drinking water, and a phone. For your safety, the park gate is closed between 6:45pm and 7am; vehicles cannot enter or exit during those hours. Groceries and gas are available in Laie and Kahuku, each less than a mile away.

Permits are $18 per campsite per night and are limited to 5 nights (Fri–Wed); they can be obtained at any state park office, including the **Department of Land and Natural Resources,** State Parks Division, P.O. Box 621, Honolulu, HI 96809 (© **808/587-0300;** www.hawaiistateparks.org).

The recreation area is located on Kamehameha Highway (Hwy. 83) between Laie and Kahuku. Take the H-2 to Hwy. 99 to Hwy. 83 (both roads are called Kamehameha Hwy.); continue on Hwy. 83 just past Kahuku. You can also get here via TheBus no. 55.

GOLF & OTHER OUTDOOR ACTIVITIES
Golf

Oahu has nearly three dozen golf courses, ranging from bare-bones municipal courses to exclusive country-club courses with membership fees running to six figures a year. Below are the best of a great bunch.

As you get to know Oahu's courses, you'll see that the windward courses play much differently than the leeward courses. On the windward side, the prevailing winds blow from the ocean to shore, and the grain direction of the greens tends to run the same way—from the ocean to the mountains. Leeward golf courses have the opposite tendency: The winds usually blow from the mountains to the ocean, with the grain direction of the greens corresponding.

Tips on beating the crowds and saving money: Oahu's golf courses tend to be crowded, so I suggest that you go midweek, if you can. Also, most island courses have twilight rates that offer substantial discounts if you're willing to tee off in the afternoon; these are included in the listings below, where applicable.

Transportation note: TheBus does not allow golf-club bags onboard, so if you want to use TheBus to get to a course, you're going to have to rent clubs there.

WAIKIKI

Ala Wai Municipal Golf Course The *Guinness Book of World Records* lists Ala Wai as the busiest golf course in the world; some 500 rounds a day are played on this 18-hole municipal course within walking distance of Waikiki's hotels. For years I've held off recommending this par-70, 6,020-yard course because it was so busy (tee times were taken by local retirees), but a recent scandal, involving phone-company employees tapping into the reservations system to get tee times, has shaken up the old system, and visitors now have a better chance of playing here. It's still a challenge to get a tee time, and the computerized tee reservations system for all of Oahu's municipal courses will allow you to book only 3 days in advance, but keep trying. Ala Wai has a flat layout bordered by the Ala Wai Canal on one side and the Manoa-Palolo Stream on the other. It's less windy than most Oahu courses, but pay attention to the 372-yard, par-4 1st hole, which demands a straight and long shot to the very tiny green. If you miss, you can make it up on the 478-yard, par-5 10th hole—the green is reachable in two, so with a two-putt, a birdie is within reach.

> **Insider Tip**
>
> For last-minute and discount tee times, call Stand-by Golf (© 888/645-2665; www.hawaiistandbygolf.com), which offers discounted tee times for same-day or next-day golfing. Call between 7am and 2:30pm and 6 to 10pm for a guaranteed tee time with up to a 30% discount off greens fees.

404 Kapahulu Ave., Waikiki. © **808/733-7387** for golf course, or 808/296-2000 for tee-time reservations. www.co.honolulu.hi.us/des/golf/alawai.htm. Greens fees $44; twilight rates $23; cart $19. From Waikiki, turn left on Kapahulu Ave.; the course is on the mauka side of Ala Wai Canal. Bus: 19, 20, or 22.

EAST OAHU

Hawaii Kai Golf Course   This is actually two golf courses in one. The par-72, 6,222-yard **Championship Course** is moderately challenging, with scenic vistas. The course is forgiving to high-handicap golfers, although it does have a few surprises. The par-55 **Executive Course** is fun for beginners and those just getting back in the game after a few years. The course has lots of hills and valleys, with no water hazards and only a few sand traps. Lockers are available.

8902 Kalanianaole Hwy., Honolulu. ℂ **808/395-2358.** www.hawaiikaigolf.com. Greens fees: Championship Course $100 Mon–Fri, $110 Sat–Sun, twilight rates $70; Executive Course $39 Mon–Fri, $44 Sat–Sun. Take H-1 east past Hawaii Kai; it's immediately past Sandy Beach on the left. Bus: 58.

THE WINDWARD COAST

Olomana Golf Links   Low-handicap golfers may not find this gorgeous course difficult, but the striking views of the craggy Koolau mountain ridge alone are worth the fees. The par-72, 6,326-yard course is popular with locals and visitors alike. The course starts off a bit hilly on the front 9 but flattens out by the back 9, where there are some tricky water hazards. The 1st hole, a 384-yard par-4 that tees downhill and approaches uphill, is definitely a warm-up. The next hole is a 160-yard par-3 that starts from an elevated tee to an elevated green over a severely banked V-shaped gully. Shoot long here—it's longer than you think, and short shots tend to roll all the way back down the fairway to the base of the gully. This course is very, very green; the rain gods bless it regularly with brief passing showers. You can spot the regular players here—they all carry umbrellas, wait patiently for the squalls to pass, and then resume play. Reservations are a must. Facilities include a driving range, practice greens, club rental, a pro shop, and a restaurant.

41-1801 Kalanianaole Hwy., Waimanalo. ℂ **808/259-7926.** www.olomanagolflinks.com. Greens fees $95; twilight fees $80. **Tip:** Rates go down on your 2nd and 3rd visits. Take H-1 to the Pali Hwy. (Hwy. 61); turn right on Kalanianaole Hwy.; after 5 miles, it will be on the left. Bus: 57.

THE NORTH SHORE

Kahuku Golf Course 🎁   This 9-hole budget golf course is a bit funky. There are no club rentals, no clubhouse, and no facilities other than a few pull carts that disappear with the first handful of golfers. But a round at this scenic oceanside course amid the tranquillity of the North Shore is quite an experience nonetheless. Duffers will love the ease of this recreational course, and weight watchers will be happy to walk the gently sloping greens. Don't forget to bring your camera for the views (especially at holes 3, 4, 7, and 8, which are right on the ocean). No reservations are taken; tee times are first-come, first-served, and with plenty of retirees happy to sit and wait, the competition is fierce for early tee times. Bring your own clubs and call ahead to check the weather. The cost for this experience? Under 12 bucks!

56-501 Kamehameha Hwy., Kahuku. ℂ **808/293-5842.** www.co.honolulu.hi.us/des/golf/kahuku. htm. Greens fees $12. Take H-1 west to H-2; follow H-2 through Wahiawa to Kamehameha Hwy. (Hwy. 99, then Hwy. 83); follow it to Kahuku.

Turtle Bay Resort ★   This North Shore resort is home to two of Hawaii's top golf courses. The 18-hole **Arnold Palmer Course** (formerly the Links at Kuilima) was designed by Arnold Palmer and Ed Seay. Now that the casuarina (ironwood) trees have matured, it's not as windy as it used to be, but this is still a challenging course. The front 9, with rolling terrain, only a few trees, and lots of wind, play like a British Isles course. The back 9 have narrower tree-lined fairways and water. The course circles Punahoolapa Marsh, a protected wetland for endangered Hawaiian waterfowl.

Another option is the par-71, 6,200-yard **George Fazio Course**—the only Fazio course in Hawaii. Larry Keil, pro at Turtle Bay, says that people like it because it's a more forgiving course, without all the water hazards and bunkers of the Palmer course. The 6th hole has two greens, so you can play the hole as a par-3 or a par-4. The toughest hole has to be the par-3, 176-yard 2nd hole, where you tee off across a lake with a mean crosswind. The most scenic hole is the 7th, where the ocean is on your left; in winter, you might get lucky and see some whales.

Facilities include a pro shop, driving range, putting and chipping green, and snack bar. Weekdays are best for tee times.

57–049 Kamehameha Hwy., Kahuku. (℗ **808/293-8574** or 808/293-9094. www.turtlebay resort.com. Greens fees: Palmer Course $175, $110 after 2pm; Fazio Course $125 before noon, $110 noon–2pm, $75 after 2pm, and, here's the deal: After 3pm you can walk the course for $15! Take H-1 west past Pearl City; when the freeway splits, take H-2 and follow the signs to Haleiwa; at Haleiwa, take Hwy. 83 to Turtle Bay Resort. Bus: 52 or 55.

CENTRAL OAHU

Pearl Country Club   Looking for a challenge? You'll find one at this popular public course, located just above Pearl City in Aiea. Sure, the 6,230-yard, par-72 looks harmless enough, and the views of Pearl Harbor and the USS *Arizona* Memorial are gorgeous, but around the 5th hole, you'll start to see what you're in

Pearl Country Club.

Ko Olina Golf Club.

for. That par-5, a blind 472-yard hole, doglegs seriously to the left (with a small margin of error between the tee and the steep out-of-bounds hillside on the entire left side of the fairway). A water hazard and a forest await your next two shots. Suddenly, this nice public course becomes not so nice. Oahu residents can't get enough of it, so don't even try to get a tee time on weekends. Stick to weekdays—Mondays are usually the best bet. Facilities include a driving range, practice greens, club rental, a pro shop, and a restaurant.

98-535 Kaonohi St., Aiea. ℂ **808/487-3802.** www.pearlcc.com. Greens fees $110 Mon–Fri, $120 Sat–Sun; after 3:30pm 9 holes are $45 weekdays, $50 weekends. Book at least a week in advance. Take H-1 past Pearl Harbor to Hwy. 78 (Moanalua Fwy.), exit 13A; stay in the left lane where Hwy. 78 becomes Hwy. 99 (Kamehameha Hwy.); turn right on Kaonohi St.; entrance is on the right. Bus: 32 (stops at Pearlridge Shopping Center at Kaonohi and Moanalua sts.; you'll have to walk about a half-mile uphill from here).

LEEWARD OAHU

Ko Olina Golf Club ★★★   *Golf Digest* named this par-72, 6,867-yard course one of "America's Top 75 Resort Courses" in 1992. The Ted Robinson–designed course has rolling fairways and elevated tee and water features. The signature hole—the 12th, a par 3—has an elevated tee that sits on a rock garden with a cascading waterfall. At the 18th hole, you'll see and hear water all around you— seven pools begin on the right side of the fairway and slope down to a lake. A waterfall is on your left off the elevated green. You'll have no choice but to play the left and approach the green over the water. Book in advance; this course is crowded all the time. Facilities include a driving range, locker rooms, a Jacuzzi, steam rooms, and a restaurant and bar. Lessons are available.

92-1220 Aliinui Dr., Kapolei. ℂ **808/676-5300.** www.koolinagolf.com. Greens fees $179 ($159 for Ihilani Resort guests); noon rates $149 ($129 for guests); twilight rates (after 1pm in winter and 2:30pm in summer) $109. Ask about transportation package from Waikiki hotels. Collared shirts

Biking on Oahu.

Riding horses along Kawela Bay.

requested for men and women. Take H-1 west until it becomes Hwy. 93 (Farrington Hwy.); turn off at the Ko Olina exit; take the exit road (Aliinui Dr.) into Ko Olina Resort; turn left into the clubhouse. No bus service.

Makaha Resort Golf Club ★★   This challenging course sits some 45 miles west of Honolulu, in Makaha Valley. Designed by William Bell, the par-72, 7,091-yard course meanders toward the ocean before turning and heading into the valley. Sheer volcanic walls tower 1,500 feet above the course, which is surrounded by swaying palm trees and neon-bright bougainvillea; an occasional peacock will even strut across the fairways. The beauty here could make it difficult to keep your mind on the game if it weren't for the course's many challenges: eight water hazards, 107 bunkers, and frequent brisk winds. This course is packed on weekends, so it's best to try weekdays. Facilities include a pro shop, bag storage, and a snack shop.

84–627 Makaha Valley Rd., Waianae. ✆ **808/695-9544.** www.makaharesort.net. Greens fees $160, twilight $130 (check for specials). Take H-1 west until it turns into Hwy. 93, which winds through the coastal towns of Nanakuli, Waianae, and Makaha. Turn right on Makaha Valley Rd. and follow it to the fork; the course is on the left. Bus: 51.

West Loch Municipal Golf Course   This par-72, 6,615-yard course located just 30 minutes from Waikiki, in Ewa Beach, offers golfers a challenge at bargain rates. The difficulties on this unusual municipal course, designed by Robin Nelson and Rodney Wright, are water (lots of hazards), constant trade winds, and narrow fairways. To help you out, the course features a "water" driving range (with a lake) to practice your drives. In addition to the driving range, West Loch has practice greens, a pro shop, and a restaurant.

91–1126 Okupe St., Ewa Beach. ✆ **808/675-6076.** www.co.honolulu.hi.us/des/golf/westloch. htm. Greens fees $45; 9 holes after 1pm $23; cart $19. Book 3 days in advance. Take H-1 west to the Hwy. 76 exit; stay in the left lane and turn left at West Loch Estates, just opposite St. Francis Medical Center. To park, take 2 immediate right turns. Bus: 50.

Biking

Bicycling is a great way to see Oahu; most streets here have bike lanes. For information on bikeways and maps, contact the **Honolulu City and County Bicycle Coordinator** (© 808/768-8335) or email csayers@honolulu.gov or go to www.honolulu.gov/dts/bikepage.htm.

If you're in Waikiki, you can rent a bike for as little as $10 for a half-day and $20 for 24 hours at **Big Kahuna Rentals,** 407 Seaside Ave. (© 888/451-5544 or 808/924-2736; www.bigkahunarentals.com/sntmainbikes.htm).

For a bike-and-hike adventure, call **Bike Hawaii** (© 877/683-7433 or 808/734-4214; www.bikehawaii.com), which has a variety of group tours, like its Mountain Biking Kaaawa Valley at Kualoa. This guided mountain bike tour follows dirt roads and single tracks meandering through the 1,000-acre Kaaawa Valley on Oahu's northeast shore, with stops at a reconstructed Hawaiian *hale* (house) and *kalo lo'i* (taro terrace) for some cultural narrative, plus an old military bunker that has been converted into a movie museum for films shot here (*Jurassic Park, Godzilla, Mighty Joe Young, Windtalkers,* and more). The 6-mile trip, which takes 2 to 3 hours of riding, includes van transportation from your hotel, bike, helmet, snacks, picnic lunch, water bottle, and guide; it's $110 for adults and $80 for children 13 and under.

If you'd like to join in on some club rides, contact the **Hawaii Bicycle League** (© 808/735-5756; www.hbl.org), which offers rides every weekend, as well as several annual events, plus great maps for bike outings. The league can also provide a schedule of upcoming rides, races, and outings.

Horseback Riding

You can gallop on the beach at the **Turtle Bay Resort,** 57–091 Kamehameha Hwy., Kahuku (© 808/293-8811; www.turtlebayresort.com; bus: 52 or 55), where 45-minute rides along sandy beaches with spectacular ocean views and through a forest of ironwood trees cost $65 for ages 7 and up (they must be at least 4 ft., 4 in. tall). Romantic evening rides are $105 per person. Private rides for up to 4 people are $110 per person.

Tennis

If you're staying in Waikiki, try the **Waikiki Tennis Court and Lessons,** at the Aqua Waikiki Marina, 1700 Ala Moana Blvd. (© 808/551-9438; bus: 19 or 20), which has one lighted court (daily 9am–9pm), with court rental for $25 per hour, racket rental for $5 person per day, private lessons for $60 per hour, and semiprivate lessons for $60 per hour for two or more.

If you're on the North Shore, head to the **Turtle Bay Resort,** 57–091 Kamehameha Hwy., Kahuku (© 808/293-8811; www.turtlebayresort.com; bus: 52 or 55), which has 10 courts, 4 of which are lit for night play. You must reserve the night courts in advance, as they're very popular. Court time costs $10 per person per hour (complimentary for guests); equipment rental and lessons are also available.

ORIENTATION TOURS
Guided Sightseeing Tours

If your time is limited, you might want to consider a guided tour. These tours are informative, can give you a good overview of Honolulu or Oahu in a limited amount of time, and are surprisingly entertaining.

E Noa Tours, 1141 Waimanu St., Ste. 105, Honolulu (© **800/824-8804** or 808/591-2561; www.enoa.com), offers a range of narrated tours, from island loops to explorations of historic Honolulu, on air-conditioned, 27-passenger minibuses. The Royal Circle Island Tour ($71 for adults, $58 for children 5–11, $50 for children 4 and under) stops at Diamond Head Crater, Hanauma Bay, Byodo-In Temple, Sunset Beach, Waimea Valley (admission included), and various beach sites along the way. Other tours go to Pearl Harbor/USS *Arizona* Memorial and the Polynesian Cultural Center.

Waikiki Trolley Tours ★, 1141 Waimanu St., Ste. 105, Honolulu (© **800/824-8804** or 808/596-2199; www.waikikitrolley.com), offers three fun tours of sightseeing, entertainment, dining, and shopping. These are a great way to get the lay of the land. You can get on and off the trolley as needed (trolleys come along every 2–20 min.). An all-day pass (8:30am–11:35pm) is $30 for adults, $20 for seniors, and $14 for children 4 to 11; a 4-day pass is $52 for adults, $31 for seniors, and $20 for children. For the same price, you can experience the 2-hour narrated Ocean Coast Line tour of the southeast side of Oahu, an easy way to see the stunning views.

Polynesian Adventure Tours, 1049 Kikowaena Place, Honolulu (© **800/622-3011** or 808/833-3000; www.polyad.com), offers several excursions. The all-day circle island tour starts at $74 for adults, $42 for children 3 to 11; and the half-day USS *Arizona* Memorial Excursion is $33 for adults and $22 for children.

For those who'd prefer a self-guided driving tour, **TourTalk Oahu** (© **877/585-7499;** www.tourtalkhawaii.com) offers a complete package of

⊙ A BIRD'S-EYE view

To understand why Oahu was the island of kings, you need to see it from the air. **Island Seaplane Service** ★★ (© **808/836-6273;** www.islandseaplane.com) operates flights departing from a floating dock in the protected waters of Keehi Lagoon in either a six-passenger DeHavilland Beaver or a four-passenger Cessna 206. There's nothing quite like feeling the slap of the waves as the plane skims across the water and then effortlessly lifts into the air.

The half-hour tour ($135) gives you aerial views of Waikiki Beach, Diamond Head Crater, Kahala's luxury estates, and the sparkling waters of Hanauma and Kaneohe bays; the 1-hour tour ($250) continues on to Chinaman's Hat, the Polynesian Cultural Center, and the rolling surf of the North Shore. The flight returns across the island, over Hawaii's historic wartime sites: Schofield Barracks and the Pearl Harbor memorials.

Capt. Pat Magie, company president, has logged more than 36,000 hours of flight time without an accident (29,000 hr. in seaplanes in Alaska, Canada, the Arctic, and the Caribbean) and holds the world record for seaplane hours.

Izumo Taishakyo Mission Culture Hall in Chinatown.

Ulupo Heiau.

2½-hour narrated CDs (or cassettes), driving instructions, and a 72-page booklet containing color maps, photos, cultural and historical information, and Hawaii facts for $25.

Waikiki & Honolulu Walking Tours

The **Hawaii Geographic Society** (© 800/538-3950; hawaiigeographic society@gmail.com) presents numerous interesting and unusual tours, such as "A Temple Tour," which includes Chinese, Japanese, Christian, and Jewish houses of worship; an archaeology tour in and around downtown Honolulu; and others. Each is led by an expert from the Hawaii Geographic Society and must have a minimum of three people; the cost is $15 per person. The society's brochure, *Historic Downtown Honolulu Walking Tour,* is a fascinating self-guided tour of the 200-year-old city center. If you'd like a copy, contact **Hawaii Geographic Maps and Books,** 49 S. Hotel St. (P.O. Box 1698), Honolulu, HI 96808, at **hawaiigeographicsociety@gmail.com**. The Society prefers that people contact them via email.

For a self-guided tour of the neighborhood, see the "Historic Honolulu" walking tour on p. 260.

Guided Eco-Tours

Oahu isn't just high-rises in Waikiki or urban sprawl in Honolulu, but extinct craters, hidden waterfalls, lush rainforests, forgotten coastlines, and rainbow-filled valleys. To experience the other side of Oahu, contact **Oahu Nature Tours** (© 808/924-2473; www.oahunaturetours.com). It offers a dozen different eco-tours, starting at $27 per person, and provides everything: expert guides (geologists, historians, archaeologists), round-trip transportation, entrance fees, bottled water, and use of day packs, binoculars, flashlights, and rain gear.

Specialty Tours

Below are a couple of little-known, off-the-beaten-path tours of unusual subjects that might pique your interest.

Hawaii Coffee Company ★★, 1555 Kalani St. (© **808/847-3600;** www.hicoffeeco.com), has an excellent behind-the-scenes tour of its LION and Royal Kona Coffee facility (as well as its Hawaiian Island Tea Company). You will be met in the retail/cafe area of the facility and taken through the 55,000-square-foot plant on a step-by-step tour of how Hawaii's oldest and largest coffee company processes and roasts its dozens of brands and types of coffee. Tea lovers will also get to experience the processing of tea. Allow 30 to 45 minutes for the tour, plus extra time to try the various coffees in the cafe. This is one of the best places in Oahu to stock up on a few bags of coffee or boxes of teas (not to mention the logo retail items). Not only are the prices competitive, but in November and December specialty Christmas coffee can be purchased only at this location. The free tours are given Monday to Thursday (call for current tour times and reservations). The E Noa Trolley no. 10 also stops here for the tour.

For a really different look at Honolulu and the island, **Oahu Ghost Tours** ★★ (© 877/597-7325; www.oahughosttours.com) offers a look at the supernatural side of this ancient place. Originally started by Glen Grant (1947–2003), who dedicated his life to exploring stories and sightings of the paranormal, the company has continued his investigations of ghosts, unusual sightings, and the unexplainable. The offerings include **Honolulu City Haunts,** a 2-mile walking tour of places where supernatural events are still happening today ($29 for adults, $22 for children 11 and under); **Sacred Spirits,** a 5-hour walking tour of the most sacred native Hawaiian spots on Oahu ($52 adults, $39 children); and the **Orbs of Oahu** driving tour, which circles the island, stopping at some of the "most haunted" locations ($49 adults, $37 children).

ROLLING THROUGH WAIKIKI ON A segway

One of my favorite ways to tour Waikiki is on a Segway Personal Transporter, the silly looking two-wheeled machine that looks like an old push lawn mower (big wheels and a long handle). But amazingly enough, within just a few minutes, you get the hang of this contraption, which works through a series of high-tech stabilization mechanisms that read the motion of your body to turn or go forward or backward, and is propelled forward through twisting of the hand throttle. It's lots of fun—think back to the first time you rode a bicycle, and the incredible freedom of zipping through space without walking. **Glide Ride Tours and Rentals,** located at the Aloha Tower, 1 Aloha Tower Dr. (© **808/941-3151;** www.segwayofhawaii.com), will instruct you on the Segway (the staff makes sure that you are fully competent before you leave their training area) and then take you on a 40-minute introduction tour for $89 per person. Their 2½-hour tour of Waikiki, Kapiolani Park, and Diamond Head starts from the Hilton Hawaiian Village for $110 per person. The Segway Intro Tour is open to kids 14 and older; all other tours have a minimum age of 16.

ATTRACTIONS IN & AROUND HONOLULU & WAIKIKI

Historic Honolulu

The Waikiki you see today bears no resemblance to the Waikiki of yesteryear, a place of vast taro fields extending from the ocean to deep into Manoa Valley, dotted with numerous fish ponds and gardens tended by thousands of people. This picture of old Waikiki can be recaptured by following the emerging **Waikiki Historic Trail** ★ (www.waikikihistorictrail.com), a meandering 2-mile walk with 20 bronze surfboard markers (standing 6 ft., 5 in. tall—you can't miss 'em), complete with descriptions and archival photos of the historic sites. The markers note everything from Waikiki's ancient fish ponds to the history of the Ala Wai Canal. The trail begins at Kuhio Beach and ends at the King Kalakaua statue, at the intersection of Kuhio and Kalakaua avenues.

Bishop Museum ★★★ ☺ Even if you don't have kids, this is a must-see. Not only does this museum have the world's greatest collection of natural and cultural artifacts from Hawaii and the Pacific, but it also added the terrific new 16,500-square-foot **Richard T. Mamiya Science Adventure Center,** specializing in volcanology, oceanography, and biodiversity. You'll become a kid again in this fun, interactive environment where you walk down a "Hawaiian origins" tunnel into the deep ocean zone, stopping along the way to play with all the cool, high-tech toys, and then explore the interior of a volcano and climb to the top to get a bird's-eye view of an erupting caldera (it looks like the real thing!).

The Bishop Museum was founded by a Hawaiian princess, Bernice Pauahi, who collected priceless artifacts and, in her will, instructed her husband, Charles Reed Bishop, to establish a Hawaiian museum "to enrich and delight" the people of Hawaii. The **Hawaiian Hall,** the original cut-stone building (built in 1889), recently underwent a massive $20-million renovation, bringing the old displays up-to-date with 21st century technology using computers, new lighting, surround sound, and prerecorded Hawaiian voices and chants to give the museumgoer the experience of being back in old Hawaii. Hawaii's story is told from the ground up, so to speak. The first floor shows what Hawaii was like before Westerners arrived; the next floor explains the importance to Hawaiians of land and nature; and the top floor has changing exhibits that center on issues relating to Hawaii. It's a great rainy-day diversion; plan to spend at least half a day here.

A bronze surfboard marker on the Waikiki Historic Trail.

Other buildings on the grounds are jampacked with acquisitions—from insect specimens and ceremonial spears to calabashes and old photos of topless hula dancers. A visit here will give you a good basis for understanding Hawaiian life and culture. You'll see the great feathered capes of kings,

Honolulu Attractions

See "Walking Tour: Historic Chinatown" map

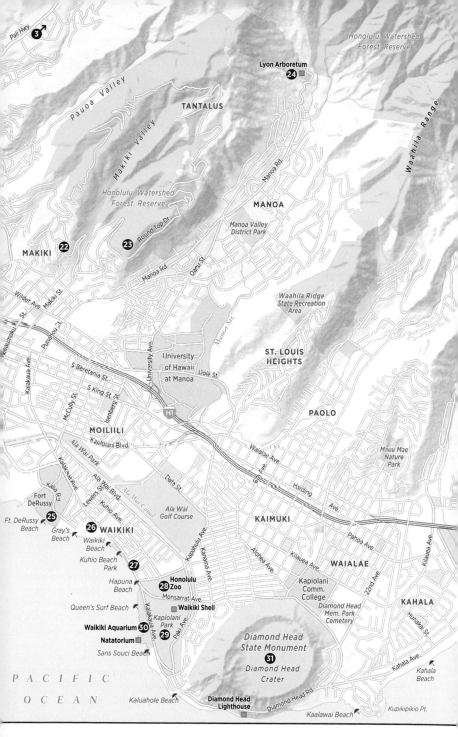

Pali Hwy. 3

Honolulu Watershed
Forest Reserve

Lyon Arboretum 24

Pauoa Valley

TANTALUS

Makiki Valley

Waahila Range

Honolulu Watershed
Forest Reserve

Manoa Rd.

MANOA

Manoa Valley
District Park

MAKIKI 22

Round Top Dr.

23

Oahu St.

Manoa Rd.

Manoa Str.

Waahila Ridge
State Recreation
Area

ST. LOUIS
HEIGHTS

Wilder Ave. Makiki St.

Nehoa St.

Punahou St.

University Ave.

S Beretania St.

S King St.

Isenberg St.

Dole St.

University
of Hawaii
at Manoa

PAOLO

Kalakaua Ave.

McCully St.

H1

MOILIILI

Kapiolani Blvd.

Waialae Ave.

Mauu Mae
Nature
Park

Ala Wai Park

Ala Wai Park

Date St.

Ala Wai Canal

Ala Wai
Golf Course

Harding Ave.

KAIMUKI

Kalia Rd.

Kalakaua Ave.

Ala Wai Blvd.

Lewers St.

Kuhio Ave.

Kapahulu Ave.

Kanaina Ave.

Pahoa Ave.

Fort
DeRussy

Ft. DeRussy
Beach 25

Gray's
Beach

26 WAIKIKI

Waikiki
Beach

Kuhio Beach
Park 27

Hapuna
Beach

28 Honolulu
Zoo

Monsarrat Ave.

Waikiki Shell

Kapiolani
Park

29

Aliohea Ave.

Kilauea Ave.

WAIALAE

Kapiolani
Comm.
College

Diamond Head
Mem. Park
Cemetery

22nd Ave.

Kilauea Ave.

KAHALA

Queen's Surf Beach

Waikiki Aquarium 30

Natatorium

Sans Souci Beach

Paki Ave.

Kalakaua Ave.

Diamond Head
State Monument

31

Diamond Head
Crater

Hunakai St.

Kahala Ave.

Kahala
Beach

PACIFIC

OCEAN

Kaluahole Beach

Diamond Head
Lighthouse

Diamond Head Rd.

Kaalawai Beach

Kupikipikio Pt.

The Hawaii Maritime Center.

the last grass shack in Hawaii, preindustrial Polynesian art, and even the skeleton of a 50-foot sperm whale.

Hula performances ★ take place Wednesday to Monday at 2pm—it's worth making time for this daily cultural event. The **Na Mea Makamae Tour,** at 10am, tells the story of the creation of the museum and the treasures of Hawaiian culture; the **Plants of Paradise Garden Tour** meets at 10:30am; and **Meet Me at the Hot Spot—Lava Melting Demonstration** is held at noon and 2pm. Personally, I would plan my trip around the shows in the planetarium: *The Sky Tonight* at 11:30am, *Explorers of Mauna Kea* at 1:30pm, and (my favorite) *Explorers of Polynesia* at 3:30pm daily.

1525 Bernice St., just off Kalihi St./Likelike Hwy. ☎ **808/847-3511.** www.bishopmuseum.org. Admission $18 adults, $15 seniors and children 4-12. Wed–Mon 9am–5pm. Bus: 2.

Hawaii Maritime Center ★ 📖 As we went to press, Bishop Museum, owner of the Hawaii Maritime Center, "temporarily" closed operations here "due to adverse economic conditions." Please call the Bishop Museum (☎ **808/846-3511**) to see if the Hawaii Maritime Center has reopened. If it has, it is well worth a couple of hours of your time to wander around and learn the story of Hawaii's rich maritime past, from the ancient journey of Polynesian voyagers to the nostalgic days of the *Lurline,* which once brought tourists from San Francisco on 4-day cruises. Inside the Hawaii Maritime Center's Kalakaua Boathouse, patterned after His Majesty King David Kalakaua's own canoe house, are more than 30 exhibits, including Matson cruise ships (which brought the first tourists to Waikiki), flying boats that delivered the mail, and the skeleton of a Pacific humpback whale that beached on Kahoolawe. Outside, the *Hokulea,* a double-hulled sailing canoe that in 1976 reenacted the Polynesian voyage of discovery, is moored next to the *Falls of Clyde,* a four-masted schooner that once ran tea from China to the west coast of the U.S. mainland.

ESPECIALLY FOR kids

Seeing an Erupting Volcano (p. 235) It looks like the real thing (only you're standing just a few feet away)—a roaring, molten-spewing, rock-launching volcano—and it's in the Bishop Museum. It's the new 16,500-square-foot Science Adventure Center (pictured below), specializing in volcanology, oceanography, and biodiversity. The kids will be spellbound playing with all the cool, high-tech toys; exploring the interior of a volcano; and climbing to the top to get a bird's-eye view of an erupting caldera.

Visiting the Honolulu Zoo (p. 247) Visit Africa in Hawaii at Waikiki's Kapiolani Park. The lions, giraffes, zebras, and elephants delight youngsters and parents alike. But the great new thrill is the Zoo by Twilight Tour—so kids can see what really goes bump in the night.

Shopping the Aloha Flea Market Most kids hate to shop. But the Aloha Flea Market, a giant outdoor bazaar at Aloha Stadium every Wednesday, Saturday, and Sunday, is more than shopping. It's an experience akin to a carnival, full of strange food, odd goods, and bold barkers. Nobody ever leaves this place empty-handed—or without having had lots of fun.

Flying a Kite at Kapiolani Park Great open expanses of green and constant trade winds make this urban park one of Hawaii's prime locations for kite flying. You can watch the pros fly dragon kites and stage kite-fighting contests, or join in the fun after checking out the convenient kite shop across the street in New Otani's arcade.

Spending a Day at Waimea Beach Park (p. 206) What many think is only a botanical garden tucked away on the North Shore is really a child's garden of delight. There are waterfalls and pools for swimming, and much more. Try kayaking the Waimea River or hiking through a junglelike forest.

Eating Shave Ice at Haleiwa (p. 277) No visit to Hawaii is complete without an authentic shave ice. You can find shave ice in all kinds of tropical flavors throughout the islands, but for some reason, it tastes better in this funky North Shore surf town.

Beating Bamboo Drums in a Fijian Village (p. 273) The Polynesian Cultural Center introduces kids to the games played by Polynesian and Melanesian children. The activities, which range from face painting to Hawaiian bowling, go on every day from 12:30 to 5:30pm.

The Aloha Flea Market.

Inside Iolani Palace.

Pier 7 (next to Aloha Tower), Honolulu Harbor. (C) **808/536-6373.** www.bishopmuseum.org/exhibits/hmc/hmc.html. Admission $8.50 adults, $7 seniors, $5.50 children 4–12. Daily 9am–5pm. Bus: 19 or 20.

Iolani Palace ★ If you want to really "understand" Hawaii, this 45-minute tour is well worth the time. The Iolani Palace was built by King David Kalakaua, who spared no expense. The 4-year project, completed in 1882, cost $360,000—and nearly bankrupted the Hawaiian kingdom. This four-story Italian Renaissance palace was the first electrified building in Honolulu (it had electricity before the White House and Buckingham Palace). Royals lived here for 11 years, until Queen Liliuokalani was deposed and the Hawaiian monarchy fell forever, in a palace coup led by U.S. Marines on January 17, 1893, at the demand of sugar planters and missionary descendants.

Cherished by latter-day royalists, the 10-room palace stands as an architectural statement of the monarchy period. Iolani attracts 60,000 visitors a year in groups of 15; everyone must don denim booties to scoot across the royal floors. Visitors may take a comprehensive **Grand Tour** ★, which offers a brief video about the history of the palace, a docent-guided tour of the interior, and a self-guided tour of the basement galleries; an **Audio Tour,** which provides guests with an audio wand for a tour through the first and second floors and concludes with a self-guided tour of the galleries; or the **Gallery Tour,** a self-guided tour of the basement galleries, complete with crown jewels, ancient feathered cloaks, the royal china, and more.

364 S. King St. (at Richards St.). (C) **800/532-1051** or 808/522-0832. www.iolanipalace.org. Grand Tour $20 adults, $5 children 5–12; Audio Tour $13 adults, $5 children 5–12; Gallery Tour $6 adults, $3 children 5–12. Tues–Sat 8:30am–2pm. Call ahead to reserve the Grand Tour. Children 4 and under not permitted. Extremely limited parking on palace grounds; try metered parking on the street. Bus: 2.

Kawaiahao Church ★ In 1842, Kawaiahao Church stood complete at last, the crowning achievement of missionaries and Hawaiians working together for the first time on a common project. Designed by Rev. Hiram Bingham and supervised by Kamehameha III, who ordered his people to help build it, the project took 5 years to complete. Workers quarried 14,000 coral blocks weighing 1,000 pounds each from the offshore reefs and cut timber in the forests for the beams.

This proud stone church, complete with bell tower and colonial colonnade, was the first permanent Western house of worship in the islands. It became the church of the Hawaiian royalty and remains in use today. Some fine portraits of Hawaiian royalty hang inside. I recommend seeing this edifice at the **Hawaiian-language services ★★** (which probably set old Rev. Bingham spinning in his grave), conducted on Sundays at 9am.

957 Punchbowl St. (at King St.). ✆ **808/522-1333.** Free admission (donations appreciated). Mon–Fri 8am–4:30pm; Sun services 9am. Bus: 2. Entrance on the side of church.

Mission Houses Museum American Protestant missionaries established their headquarters here in 1820. Today this museum tells the dramatic story of cultural change in 19th-century Hawaii. Included in the complex are a visitor center and three historic mission buildings, which have been restored and refurnished to reflect the daily life and work of the missionaries.

553 S. King St. (at Kawaiahao St.). ✆ **808/531-0481.** www.missionhouses.org. Admission $10 adults, $8 military personnel and seniors, $6 students and children 6 and over, free for children 5 and under. Tues–Sat 10am–4pm. Bus: 2.

Queen Emma Summer Palace Hanaiakamalama, the name of the country estate of Kamehameha IV and Queen Emma, was once in the secluded uplands of Nuuanu Valley. These days, it's adjacent to a six-lane highway full of speeding cars. This simple seven-room New England–style house, built in 1848 and restored by the Daughters of Hawaii, is worth about an hour of your time to see the interesting blend of Victorian furniture and hallmarks of Hawaiian royalty, including feather cloaks and *kahili,* the feathered standards that mark the presence of *alii* (royalty). Other royal treasures include a canoe-shaped cradle for Queen Emma's baby, Prince Albert, who died at the age of 4. (Kauai's ritzy Princeville Resort is named for the little prince.)

2913 Pali Hwy. (at Old Pali Rd.). ✆ **808/595-6291.** www.daughtersofhawaii.org. Admission $6 adults, $1 children 11 and under. Daily 9am–4pm. Bus: 4, 55, 56, 57, or 65.

FROM TOP: **Kawaiahao Church; royal portraits inside the Kawaiahao Church.**

241

Queen Emma Summer Palace.

Wartime Honolulu

USS Arizona Memorial at Pearl Harbor ★★★ On December 7, 1941, the USS *Arizona*, while moored here in Pearl Harbor, was bombed in a Japanese air raid. The 608-foot battleship sank in 9 minutes without firing a shot, taking 1,177 sailors and Marines to their deaths—and catapulting the United States into World War II.

Nobody who visits the memorial will ever forget it. The deck of the ship lies 6 feet below the surface of the sea. Oil still oozes slowly up from the Arizona's engine room and stains the harbor's calm, blue water; some say the ship still weeps for its lost crew. The memorial is a stark white 184-foot rectangle that spans the sunken hull of the ship; it was designed by Alfred Pries, a German architect interned on Sand Island during the war. It contains the ship's bell, recovered from the wreckage, and a shrine room with the names of the dead carved in stone.

Today, free U.S. Navy launches take visitors to the *Arizona*. Try to arrive at the visitor center, operated by the National Park Service, no later than 1:30pm to avoid the huge crowds; waits of 1 to 3 hours are common, and reservations are not accepted at this time. While you're waiting for the free shuttle to take you out to the ship, get the **Audio Tour** ★★★, which will make the trip even more meaningful. The tour (on an MP3 player) is about 2½ hours long, costs $5, and is worth every nickel. It's like having your own personal park ranger as your guide. The tape is narrated by Ernest Borgnine and features stories told by actual Pearl Harbor survivors—both American and Japanese. Plus, while you're waiting for

rainy DAYS

If the kids are bored on yet another rainy day, or your little darlings are lobster red from being in the sun (even after you told them to put more sunscreen on), take them directly to the **Hawaii Children's Discovery Center,** 111 Ohe St. (across from Kakaako Waterfront Park), Honolulu (✆ **808/524-5437;** www. discoverycenterhawaii.org). Perfect for ages 2 to 13, these 37,000 square feet of color, motion, and activities will entertain them for hours through hands-on exhibits and interactive stations. Where else can they play volleyball with a cyber-robot, or put on sparkling costumes from India, or dress up as a purple octopus, or write their names with backward letters while looking in a mirror? Lots of summer classes and activities are offered—from painting to playing with clay (most of them invite the parents to participate, too). Admission is $10, $6 for seniors, and free for kids under 1. Open Tuesday through Friday from 9am to 1pm, Saturday and Sunday from 10am to 3pm. From Waikiki, take TheBus no. 19 or 20; from Ala Moana Center, take no. 55, 56, or 57.

The USS *Arizona* Memorial at Pearl Harbor.　　　The USS *Bowfin* Submarine Museum & Park

the launch, the tour will take you step by step through the museum's personal mementos, photographs, and historic documents. You can pause the tour for the moving 20-minute film that precedes your trip to the ship. The tour continues on the launch, describing the shoreline and letting you know what's in store at the memorial itself. At the memorial, the tour gives you a mental picture of that fateful day, and the narration continues on your boat ride back. Allow a total of at least 4 hours for your visit.

Due to increased security measures, visitors cannot carry purses, handbags, fanny packs, backpacks, camera bags (though you can carry your camera or video camera with you), diaper bags, or other items that offer concealment on the boat. However, there is a storage facility where you can stash carry-on-size items (no bigger than 30×30×18 in.), for a fee. *Note:* You must wear **closed-toe shoes** (no sandals allowed). *A reminder to parents:* Baby strollers, baby carriages, and baby backpacks are not allowed in the theater, on the boat, or on the USS *Arizona* Memorial. All babies must be carried. *One last note:* Most unfortunately, the USS *Arizona* Memorial is a high-theft area—so leave your valuables at the hotel.

Pearl Harbor. © **808/422-0561** (recorded info) or 808/422-2771. www.nps.gov/usar. Free admission. Daily 7am–5pm (programs run 7:45am–3pm). Children 11 and under should be accompanied by an adult. Shirts and closed-toe shoes required; no swimsuits or flip-flops allowed (shorts are okay). Wheelchairs gladly accommodated. Drive west on H-1 past the airport; take the USS *Arizona* Memorial exit and follow the green-and-white signs; there's ample free parking. Bus: 20; or *Arizona* Memorial Shuttle Bus VIP (© **808/839-0911**), which picks up at Waikiki hotels 6:50am–1pm ($9 per person round-trip).

USS Bowfin Submarine Museum & Park ★

The USS *Bowfin* is one of only 15 World War II submarines still in existence today. You can go below deck of this famous submarine—nicknamed the "Pearl Harbor Avenger" for its successful attacks on the Japanese—and see how the 80-man crew lived during wartime.

You no longer have to run around Ford Island to get tickets to see the exhibits of Pearl Harbor. The new Visitors Center at the USS *Arizona* Memorial has a centralized ticketing office for the historic sites here. Entry to the USS *Arizona* Memorial is free, but you still must get a ticket. The centralized ticketing office will issue tickets for the USS *Bowfin* Submarine Museum, the USS *Missouri* Memorial, and the new Pacific Aviation Museum. These three exhibits require a fee; see below.

The *Bowfin* Museum has an impressive collection of submarine-related artifacts. The Waterfront Memorial honors submariners lost during World War II.

11 Arizona Memorial Dr. (next to the USS *Arizona* Memorial Visitor Center). ☎ **808/423-1341.** www.bowfin.org. Admission $10 adults, $7 active-duty military personnel and seniors, $4 children 4–12 (children 3 and under not permitted for safety reasons). Daily 7am–5pm. See USS *Arizona* Memorial, above, for driving, bus, and shuttle directions.

USS Missouri Memorial ★ On the deck of this 58,000-ton battleship (the last one the navy launched), World War II came to an end with the signing of the Japanese surrender on September 2, 1945. The *Missouri* was part of the force that carried out bombing raids over Tokyo and provided firepower in the battles of Iwo Jima and Okinawa. In 1955, the navy decommissioned the ship and placed it in mothballs at the Puget Sound Naval Shipyard, in Washington State. But the *Missouri* was modernized and called back into action in 1986, eventually being deployed in the Persian Gulf War, before retiring once again in 1992. Here it sat until another battle ensued, this time over who would get the right to keep this living legend. Hawaii won that battle and brought the ship to Pearl Harbor in 1998. The 887-foot ship is now open to visitors as a museum memorial.

If you have the time, take the tour, which begins with the shuttle ride, departing from the USS *Bowfin* Submarine Museum (see above). Guests are shuttled to Ford Island on military-style buses while listening to a 1940s-style radio program (complete with news clips, wartime commercials, and music). Once on the ship, guests watch an informational film and are then free to explore on their own or take a guided tour. Highlights of this massive (more than 200 ft. tall) battleship include the forecastle (or *fo'c's'le,* in navy talk), where the 30,000-pound anchors are "dropped" on 1,080 feet of anchor chain; the 16-inch guns (each 65 ft. long and weighing 116 tons), which can accurately fire a 2,700-pound shell some 23 miles in 50 seconds; and the spot where the Instrument of Surrender was signed as Douglas MacArthur, Chester Nimitz, and "Bull" Halsey looked on.

Battleship Row, Pearl Harbor. ☎ **877/MIGHTY-MO** (644-4896). www.ussmissouri.com. Admission $20 adults, $10 children 4–12, which includes one of 4 tours ranging from a guided tour to an audiovisual tour. The new Battle Station Tour (90 min.) is an additional $25 for adults and $12 for children. Daily 9am–5pm; guided tours 9:30am–4:30pm. Check in at the USS *Bowfin* Submarine Museum, next to the USS *Arizona* Memorial Visitor Center. Drive west on H-1 past the airport, take the USS *Arizona* Memorial exit, and follow the brown-and-white signs; there's ample free parking. Bus: 20 or 47.

Pacific Aviation Museum ★★   As part of the expanded historical exhibits on Pearl Harbor, this recently open museum features the aircraft used in World War II in a 42,000-square-foot seaplane hanger that was used in World War II, and survived the Japanese attack on Pearl Harbor. The tour begins with a film, and then you enter the museum, where you will find a Japanese Zero plane (used in the attack on Pearl Harbor), a P-40 fighter (the plane launched from Honolulu to fight the Japanese during the Pearl Harbor attack), a B-25B Mitchell (similar to the ones used in the Doolittle Raid in Japan in April 1942), a SBD Dauntless dive bomber (from the Battle of Midway), and an F4F Wildcat, featured in the Guadalcanal battle. But my favorite part is the opportunity to become a World War II pilot, sitting in the interactive cockpit of a Combat Flight Simulator. You get to take off and land on an aircraft carrier and engage in a dogfight with the enemy. Hanger 39, 319 Lexington Blvd., Ford Island (next to the Red & White Control Tower). *C* **808/441-1000.** www.pacificaviationmuseum.org. Daily 9am–5pm. Admission $15 adults, $8 children 4–12 (tickets online or at the USS *Arizona* Memorial at Pearl Harbor Visitors Center); guided behind-the-scenes tour $25 adults, $18 children 4–12. Directions from Waikiki: Head west on Ala Moana Blvd./Nimitz Hwy. Stay slightly left to take Interstate H-1 West ramp; merge onto H-1 West. Take exit 15A, Hwy. 99 W Arizona Memorial, Stadium. At 4th traffic light, turn left onto Kalaloa St. Arrive at Arizona Memorial Place. Turn left at 5th light, Ford Island Blvd. Drive over the new Adm. Clarey Bridge and Causeway. Enter the roundabout, turning 270 degrees to the left, and take 3rd exit onto O'Kane Pkwy. Drive south, paralleling Luke Field Runway. Turn left onto Enterprise St. at the Red & White Control Tower. Turn right into the Pacific Aviation Museum.

National Memorial Cemetery of the Pacific   The National Memorial Cemetery of the Pacific (also known as the Punchbowl) is an ash-and-lava tuff cone that exploded about 150,000 years ago—like Diamond Head, only smaller. Early Hawaiians called it Puowaina, or "hill of sacrifice." The old crater is a burial

The Hawaiian Railway.

Hawaii's Plantation Village.

ground for 35,000 victims of three American wars in Asia and the Pacific: World War II, Korea, and Vietnam. Among the graves, you'll find many unmarked ones with the date December 7, 1941, carved in stone. Some will be unknown forever; others are famous, like that of war correspondent Ernie Pyle, killed by a Japanese sniper in April 1945 on Okinawa; still others buried here are remembered only by family and surviving buddies. The white stone tablets known as the Courts of the Missing bear the names of 28,788 Americans missing in action in World War II.

Survivors come here often to reflect on the meaning of war and to remember those, like themselves, who stood in harm's way to win peace a half-century ago. Some fight back tears, remembering lost buddies, lost missions, and the sacrifices of those who died.

Punchbowl Crater, 2177 Puowaina Dr. (at the end of the road). *C* **808/541-1434.** Free admission. Daily 8am–5:30pm (Mar–Sept to 6:30pm). Bus: 15.

Just Beyond Pearl Harbor

Hawaiian Railway ☺   All aboard! This is a train ride back into history. Between 1890 and 1947, the chief mode of transportation for Oahu's sugar mills was the Oahu Railway and Land Co.'s narrow-gauge trains. The line carried not only equipment, raw sugar, and supplies, but also passengers from one side of the island to the other. You can relive those days every Sunday with a 1½-hour narrated ride through Ko Olina Resort and out to Makaha. As an added attraction, on the second Sunday of the month, you can ride on the nearly 100-year-old custom-built parlor-observation car belonging to Benjamin F. Dillingham, founder of the Oahu Railway and Land Co.; the fare is $20 (no kids 12 and under), and you must reserve in advance.

Ewa Station, Ewa Beach. *C* **808/681-5461.** www.hawaiianrailway.com. Admission $10 adults, $7 seniors and children 2–12. Departures Sun 1 and 3pm and weekdays by appointment. Take H-1 west to exit 5A; take Hwy. 76 south for 2½ miles to Tesoro Gas; turn right on Renton Rd. and drive 1½ miles to end of paved section. The station is on the left. Bus: C-Express to Kapalei, then transfer to no. 41, which goes through Ewa and drops you off outside the gate.

Hawaii's Plantation Village   The hour-long tour of this restored 50-acre village offers a glimpse back in time to when sugar planters shaped the land, economy, and culture of Hawaii. From 1852, when the first contract laborers arrived here from China, to 1947, when the plantation era ended, more than 400,000 men, women, and children from China, Japan, Portugal, Puerto Rico, Korea, and the Philippines came to work the sugar-cane fields. The "talk story" tour brings the old village alive with 30 faithfully restored camp houses, Chinese and Japanese temples, the Plantation Store, and even a sumo-wrestling ring.

Waipahu Cultural Garden Park, 94–695 Waipahu St. (at Waipahu Depot Rd.), Waipahu. *C* **808/ 677-0110.** www.hawaiiplantationvillage-info.com. Admission (including escorted tour) $13 adults, $10 seniors, $7 military personnel, $5 children 4–11. Mon–Sat 10am–2pm. Take H-1 west to Waikele-Waipahu exit (exit 7); get in the left lane on exit and turn left on Paiwa St.; at the 5th light, turn right onto Waipahu St.; after the 2nd light, turn left. Bus: 47.

Wet 'n' Wild ★ ☺   Formerly called the Hawaiian Waters Adventure Park, kids love this 29-acre water-theme amusement park, which opened in 1999 with some $14 million in attractions. Plan to spend the day. Highlights are a football-field-size wave pool for bodysurfing, two 65-foot-high free-fall slides, two water-toboggan bullet slides, inner-tube slides, body-flume slides, a continuous river for

FROM LEFT: The Foster Botanical Garden; the Honolulu Zoo.

floating inner tubes, and separate pools for adults, teens, and children In addition, there are restaurants, Hawaiian performances, and shops.

400 Farrington Hwy., Kapolei. ℂ **808/674-WAVE** (9283). www.hawaiiwetnwild.com. Admission $42 adults, $17 seniors, $32 children 3–11, free for children 2 and under. Parking $5. Hours vary, but generally the park is open Mon and Thurs–Fri 10:30am–3:30pm and 10:30am–4pm Sat Sun; closed Tues–Wed. Take H-1 west to exit 1 (Campbell Industrial Park). Make an immediate left to Farrington Hwy.; you will see the park on your left.

Fish, Flora & Fauna

Foster Botanical Garden ★★ 🎁 You could spend days in this unique historic garden, a leafy oasis amid the high-rises of downtown Honolulu. Combine a tour of the garden with a trip to Chinatown (just across the street) to maximize your time. The giant trees that tower over the main terrace were planted in the 1850s by William Hillebrand, a German physician and botanist, on royal land leased from Queen Emma. Today this 14-acre public garden, on the north side of Chinatown, is a living museum of plants, some rare and endangered, collected from the tropical regions of the world. Of special interest are 26 "Exceptional Trees" protected by state law, a large palm collection, a primitive cycad garden, and a hybrid orchid collection.

50 N. Vineyard Blvd. (at Nuuanu Ave.). ℂ **808/522-7066.** www.co.honolulu.hi.us/parks/hbg/fbg.htm. Admission $5 adults, $1 children 6–12. Daily 9am–4pm; guided tours Mon–Sat at 1pm (reservations recommended). Bus: 2, 4, or 13.

Honolulu Zoo ★ ☺ Nobody comes to Hawaii to see an Indian elephant or African lions and zebras, right? Wrong. This 43-acre municipal zoo in Waikiki attracts visitors in droves. If you've got kids, allot at least half a day. The highlight is the new African Savannah, a 10-acre exhibit with more than 40 African critters roaming around in the open. The zoo also has a rare Hawaiian nene goose, a Hawaiian pig, and mouflon sheep. (Only the goose, an evolved version of the

Canadian honker, is considered to be truly Hawaiian; the others were imported from Polynesia, India, and elsewhere.)

For a real treat, take the **Zoo by Twilight Tour** ★, which offers a rare behind-the-scenes look into the lives of the zoo's nocturnal residents. Tours are Friday and Saturday from 5:30 to 7:30pm; the cost is $14 for adults and $10 for children 4 to 12. Other great family programs include **Snooze in the Zoo,** in which you discover "who is roaring and who is snoring" during the night with pizza, tours, and campfire time with s'mores, plus breakfast and a morning stroll (check website for dates); and **Star Gazing at the Zoo,** an evening tour of the zoo that also explores the night sky above Hawaii with astronomer Dr. Michael Chauvin ($16 adults, $12 children).

Lyon Arboretum.

151 Kapahulu Ave. (btw. Paki and Kalakaua aves.), at entrance to Kapiolani Park. ℂ **808/971-7171.** www.honoluluzoo.org. Admission $12 adults, $3 children 6–12; family pass $25. Daily 9am–4:30pm. Zoo parking lot (entrance on Kapahulu Ave.) 25¢ per hour; free parking at Shell parking lot across the street on Monsarrat Ave. Bus: 2, 8, 19, 20, or 47.

Lyon Arboretum ★   The Lyon Arboretum dates from 1918, when the Hawaiian Sugar Planters Association wanted to demonstrate the value of watershed for reforestation. In 1953, it became part of the University of Hawaii, where they continued to expand the extensive collection of tropical plants. Six-story-tall breadfruit trees, yellow orchids no bigger than a bus token, ferns with fuzzy buds as big as a human head—these are just a few of the botanical wonders you'll find at the 194-acre arboretum. A whole different world opens up to you along the self-guided 20-minute hike through the arboretum to Inspiration Point. You'll pass more than 5,000 exotic tropical plants full of singing birds in this cultivated rainforest at the head of Manoa Valley.

3860 Manoa Rd. (near the top of the road). ℂ **808/988-0456.** www.hawaii.edu/lyonarboretum. Suggested donation $5. Mon–Fri 9am–4pm; Sat 9am–3pm. Bus: 5.

Sea Life Park ☺   This 62-acre ocean-theme park, located in East Oahu, is one of the island's top attractions. Admission fees, however, have been creeping up the past few years, and now I feel it is way overpriced (two adults and two children will run nearly $100, which is just not worth it). Yes, it does feature whales from Puget Sound, Atlantic bottle-nosed dolphins, California sea lions, and penguins going through their hoops to the delight of kids of all ages. If you do go, allow all day to take in the sights and see the shows (hey, at these prices, get your money's worth). There's also a Hawaiian reef tank full of tropical fish; a "touch" pool, where you can touch a real sea cucumber (commonly found in tide pools);

and a bird sanctuary, where you can see birds like the red-footed booby and the frigate bird. The chief curiosity, though, is the world's only "wholphin"—a cross between a false killer whale and an Atlantic bottle-nosed dolphin. Marine biologists operate an on-site recovery center for endangered marine life; during your visit, you may be able to see rehabilitated Hawaiian monk seals and seabirds.

41-202 Kalanianaole Hwy. (at Makapuu Point), Honolulu. © **808/259-7933.** www.sealifepark hawaii.com. Admission $31 adults, $21 children 4–12. Daily 10:30am–5pm. Parking $5. Shuttle buses from Waikiki $20 per person. Bus: 22 or 58.

Waikiki Aquarium ★★★ ☺   Do not miss this! Half of Hawaii's beauty is its underwater world; plan to spend at least 2 hours discovering it. Behold the chambered nautilus, nature's submarine and inspiration for Jules Verne's *20,000 Leagues Under the Sea.* You can see this tropical spiral-shelled cephalopod mollusk—the only living one born in captivity—any day of the week here. Its natural habitat is the deep waters of Micronesia, but aquarium director Bruce Carlson not only succeeded in trapping the pearly shelled creature in 1,500 feet of water (by dangling chunks of raw tuna), but also managed to breed this ancient relative of the octopus. There are plenty of other fish in this small but first-class aquarium, located on a live coral reef. The Hawaiian reef habitat features sharks, eels, a touch tank, and habitats for the endangered Hawaiian monk seal and green sea turtle. Recently added: a rotating biodiversity exhibit and interactive displays focusing on corals and coral reefs.

2777 Kalakaua Ave. (across from Kapiolani Park). © **808/923-9741.** www.waquarium.org. Admission $9 adults; $6 active military, seniors, and college students; $4 children 13–17; $2 children 5–12. Daily 9am–4:30pm. Bus: 2.

Other Natural Wonders & Spectacular Views

In addition to the attractions listed below, check out the hike to **Diamond Head Crater** (p. 218); almost everybody can handle it, and the 360-degree views from the top are fabulous.

Sea Life Park.

OAHU'S VIBRANT arts SCENE

Passionate art lovers should head straight to Hawaii's three top cultural resources: the Honolulu Academy of Arts, The Contemporary Museum (TCM), and the Hawaii State Art Museum.

The acclaimed **Honolulu Academy of Arts** ★★ (pictured far right), 900 S. Beretania St. (✆ **808/532-8700,** or 808/532-8701 for recording; www.honoluluacademy.org), is the state's only general fine arts museum. It boasts one of the top Asian art collections in the country; also on exhibit are American and European masters and prehistoric works of Mayan, Greek, and Hawaiian art. The museum's award-winning architecture is a paragon of graciousness, featuring magnificent courtyards, lily ponds, and sensitively designed galleries. Open Tuesday through Saturday from 10am to 4:30pm, Sunday from 1 to 5pm (the 2nd Thurs of each month until 9pm); tours are held at 10:15 and 11:30am and 1:30pm Tuesday through Saturday and 1:15pm on Sunday. Admission is $10 for adults and $5 for students, seniors, and military personnel; children 11 and under enter free. Cafe open Tuesday to Saturday 11:30am to 1:30pm, reservations 808/532-8734.

The Contemporary Museum.

The Contemporary Museum (pictured above), 2411 Makiki Heights Dr. (✆ **808/526-0232;** www.tcmhi.org)—set up on the slopes of Tantalus, one of Honolulu's upscale residential communities—is renowned for its 3 acres of Asian gardens (with reflecting pools, sun-drenched terraces, views of Diamond Head, and stone benches for quiet contemplation). Equally prominent is the

Nuuanu Pali Lookout ★  Gale-force winds sometimes howl through the mountain pass at this 1,186-foot-high perch guarded by 3,000-foot peaks, so hold on to your hat—and small children. But if you walk up from the parking lot to the precipice, you'll be rewarded with a view that'll blow you away. At the edge, the dizzying panorama of Oahu's windward side is breathtaking: Clouds low enough to pinch scoot by on trade winds; pinnacles of the *pali* (cliffs), green with ferns, often disappear in the mist. From on high, the tropical palette of green and blue runs down to the sea. Combine this 10-minute stop with a trip over the *pali* to the windward side. Parking is $3.

Near the summit of Pali Hwy. (Hwy. 61); take the Nuuanu Pali Lookout turnoff.

Nuuanu Valley Rain Forest 👪 It's not the same as a peaceful nature walk, but if time is short and hiking isn't your thing, Honolulu has a rainforest you can drive through. It's only a few minutes from downtown Honolulu in verdant Nuuanu Valley, where it rains nearly 300 inches a year. And it's easy to reach: As the Pali Highway leaves residential Nuuanu and begins its climb though the

The Honolulu Academy of Arts.

presence of contemporary Hawaii artists in the museum's programs and exhibitions. Open Tuesday through Saturday from 10am to 4pm, Sunday from noon to 4pm. A 1-day membership is $8 for adults, $6 for seniors and students, and free for children 12 and under. The third Thursday of each month is free. Ask about the daily docent-led tours, and check out the excellent cafe and shop.

The **Hawaii State Art Museum,** 250 S. Hotel St., at Richards Street (📞 **808/ 586-0900;** www.state.hi.us/sfca), housed in the original Royal Hawaiian Hotel, was built in 1872 during the reign of King Kamehameha V. All of the 360 works currently displayed were created by artists who live in Hawaii. The pieces were purchased by the state, thanks to a 1967 law that says that 1% of the cost of state buildings must be used to acquire works of art. Nearly 4 decades later, the state has amassed some 5,000 pieces. Open Tuesday through Saturday from 10am to 4pm; admission is free. Take the no. 2 bus from Waikiki. If you're driving, look for street (metered) parking.

forest, the last stoplight is the Nuuanu Pali Road turnoff; turn right for a jungle-y detour of about 2 miles under a thick canopy strung with liana vines, past giant bamboo that creaks in the wind, Norfolk pines, and wild shell ginger. The road rises and the vegetation clears as you drive, blinking in the bright light of day, past a small mountain reservoir. Soon the road rejoins the Pali Highway. Kailua is to the right and Honolulu to the left—but it can be a hair-raising turn. Instead, turn right, go a half-mile to the Nuuanu Pali Lookout (see above), stop for a panoramic view of Oahu's windward side, and return to the town-bound highway on the other side.

Take the Old Nuuanu Pali Rd. exit off Pali Hwy. (Hwy. 61).

Puu Ualakaa State Park ★ 📷

The best **sunset view** of Honolulu is from a 1,048-foot-high hill named for sweet potatoes. Actually, the poetic Hawaiian name means "rolling sweet-potato hill" and was named such because of how early planters used gravity to harvest their crop. The panorama is sweeping and

Nuuanu Valley Rain Forest.

majestic. On a clear day—which is almost always—you can see from Diamond Head to the Waianae Range, almost the length of Oahu. At night, several scenic overlooks provide romantic spots for young lovers who like to smooch under the stars with the city lights at their feet. It's a top-of-the-world experience—the view, that is.

At the end of Round Hill Dr. Daily 7am–6:45pm (to 7:45pm in summer). From Waikiki, take Ala Wai Blvd. to McCully St., turn right, and drive mauka (inland) beyond the H-1 on-ramps to Wilder St.; turn left and go to Makiki St.; turn right, and continue onward and upward about 3 miles.

More Museums

For details on Honolulu's three wonderful art museums, **The Contemporary Museum,** the **Honolulu Academy of Arts,** and the **Hawaii State Art Museum,** see "Oahu's Vibrant Arts Scene," above.

Aliiolani Hale   Don't be surprised if this place looks familiar: You probably saw it on *Magnum, P.I.* This gingerbread Italianate building, designed by Australian Thomas Rowe in Renaissance revival style, was built in 1874 and was originally intended to be a palace. Instead, Aliiolani Hale (chief unto heavens) became the Supreme Court and Parliament government building. Inside, there's a **Judiciary History Center ★**, which features a multimedia presentation, a restored historic

The Nuuanu Pali Lookout.

The view from Puu Ualakaa State Park.

Aliiolani Hale.

courtroom, and exhibits tracing Hawaii's transition from precontact Hawaiian law to Western law.

417 S. King St. (btw. Mililani and Punchbowl sts.). ℂ **808/539-4999.** www.jhchawaii.net. Free admission. Mon–Fri 9am–4pm for self-guided tours; reservations accepted for group tours only. Limited parking; metered parking on street. Bus: 1, 2, 3, 4, 8, 11, or 12.

U.S. Army Museum   This museum, a former military fort built in 1909 and used in defense of Honolulu and Pearl Harbor, houses military memorabilia ranging from ancient Hawaiian warfare items to modern-day, high-tech munitions. On the upper deck, the Corps of Engineers Pacific Regional Visitor Center shows how the corps works with the civilian community to manage water resources in an island environment.

Fort DeRussy Park, Waikiki. ℂ **808/438-2822.** Free admission. Tues–Sun 10am–4:30pm. Bus: 8.

WALKING TOUR 1: **HISTORIC CHINATOWN**

GETTING THERE:	**From Waikiki, take Ala Moana Boulevard and turn right on Smith Street; make a left on Beretania Street and a left again at Maunakea. The city parking garage (50¢ per half-hour) is on the Ewa (west) side of Maunakea Street, between North Hotel and North King streets. Bus: 2 or 20 toward downtown (get off on N. Hotel St., after Maunakea St.).**
START & FINISH:	**North Hotel and Maunakea streets.**
TIME:	**1 to 2 hours, depending on how much time you spend browsing.**
BEST TIMES:	**Daylight hours.**

Chinese laborers from the Guangdong Province first came to work on Hawaii's sugar and pineapple plantations in the 1850s. They quickly figured out that they would never get rich working in the fields; once their contracts were up, some started up small shops and restaurants in the area around River Street.

Chinatown was twice devastated by fire, once in 1886 and again in 1900. The second fire still intrigues historians. In December 1899, bubonic plague broke out in the area, and the Board of Health immediately quarantined its 7,000 Chinese and Japanese residents. But the plague continued to spread. On January 20, 1900, the board decided to burn down plague-infected homes, starting at the corner of Beretania Street and Nuuanu Avenue. But the fire department wasn't quite ready; a sudden wind quickly spread the flames from one wooden building to another in the densely built area, and soon Chinatown's entire 40 acres were leveled. Many historians believe that the "out-of-control" fire may have been purposely set to drive Chinese merchants—who were becoming economically powerful and controlled prime real estate—out of Honolulu. If this was indeed the case, it didn't work: The determined merchants built a new Chinatown in the same spot.

Chinatown reached its peak in the 1930s. In the days before air travel, visitors arrived here by cruise ship. Just a block up the street was the pier where they disembarked—and they often headed straight for the shops and restaurants of Chinatown, which mainlanders considered an exotic treat. In the 1940s, military personnel on leave flocked here looking for different kinds of exotic treats—in the form of pool halls, tattoo joints, and brothels.

Today Chinatown is again rising from the ashes. After deteriorating over the years into a tawdry district of seedy bars, drug dealing, and homeless squatters, the neighborhood recently underwent extensive urban renewal. There's still just enough sleaze on the fringes (a few peep shows and a couple of topless bars) to keep it from being some theme-park-style tourist attraction, but Chinatown is poised to relive its glory days.

It's not exactly a microcosm of China, however. What you'll find is a mix of Asian cultures, all packed into a small area where tangy spices rule the cuisine, open-air markets have kept out the mini-malls, and the way to good health is through acupuncture and herbalists. The jumble of streets comes alive every day with bustling residents and visitors from all over the world; with a cacophony of sounds, from the high-pitched bleating of vendors in the market to the lyrical dialects of the retired men "talking story" over a game of mah-jongg; and with brilliant reds, blues, and greens trimming buildings and goods everywhere you look. No trip to Honolulu is complete without a visit to this exotic historic district.

Start your walk on the Ewa (west) side of Maunakea Street at:

1   Hotel Street

During World War II, Hotel Street was synonymous with good times. Pool halls and beer parlors lined the blocks, and prostitutes were plentiful. Nowadays, the more nefarious establishments have been replaced with small shops, from art galleries to specialty boutiques, and urban professionals and recent immigrants look for bargains where the sailors once roamed.

Once you're done wandering through the shops, head to the intersection with Smith Street. On the Diamond Head (east) side of Smith, you'll notice stones in the sidewalk; they were taken from the sandalwood ships,

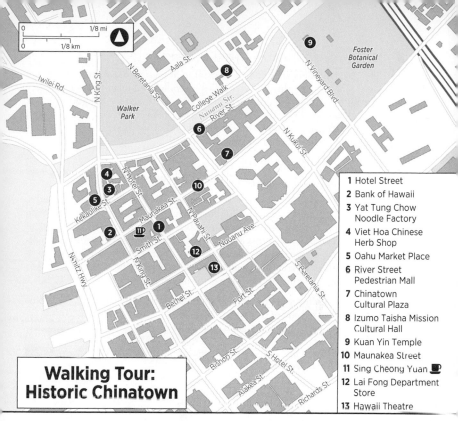

Walking Tour: Historic Chinatown

which came to Hawaii empty of cargo except for these stones, which were used as ballast on the trip over. The stones were removed and the ships' hulls were filled with sandalwood for the return to the mainland.

From Hotel Street, turn toward the ocean on Maunakea and proceed to the corner of King Street to the:

2 Bank of Hawaii

This unusual-looking bank is not the conservative edifice you'd expect—it's guarded by two fire-breathing-dragon statues.

Turn right onto King Street, where you'll pass the shops of various Chinese herbalists. Stop at 150 N. King St., where you'll find the:

The Bank of Hawaii.

3 Yat Tung Chow Noodle Factory

The delicious, delicate noodles that star in numerous Asian dishes are made here, ranging from threadlike noodles (literally no thicker than embroidery thread) to fat udon. There aren't any tours of the factory, but you can look through the window, past the white cloud of flour that hangs in the air, and watch as dough is fed into rollers at one end of the noodle machines; perfectly cut noodles emerge at the other end.

Proceed to 162 N. King St., to the:

4 Viet Hoa Chinese Herb Shop

Here Chinese herbalists act as both doctors and dispensers of herbs. Patients come in and tell the herbalist what ails them; the herbalist then decides which of the myriad herbs to mix together. Usually, there's a wall of tiny drawers all labeled in Chinese characters; the herbalist quickly pulls from the drawers various objects that range from dried flowers and ground-up roots to such exotics as mashed antelope antler. The patient then takes the concoction home to brew into a strong tea.

Cross to the south side of King Street, where, just west of Kekaulike Street, you'll come to the most-visited part of Chinatown, the open-air market known as:

5 Oahu Market Place

Those interested in Asian cooking will find all the necessary ingredients here, including pigs' heads, poultry (some still squawking), fresh octopuses, salted jellyfish, pungent fish sauce, fresh herbs, and thousand-year-old eggs. The friendly vendors are happy to explain their wares and give instructions on how to prepare these exotic treats. The market, which has been at this spot since 1904, is divided into meats, poultry, fish, vegetables, and fruits. Past the open market are several grocery stores with fresh produce on display on the sidewalk. You're bound to spot some goodies here that you're not used to seeing at your local supermarket.

Oahu Market Place.

Follow King down to River Street and turn right toward the mountains. A range of inexpensive restaurants lines River Street from King to Beretania. You can get the best Vietnamese and Filipino food in town in these blocks, but go early—lines for lunch start at 11:15am. Beyond Beretania Street is the:

6 River Street Pedestrian Mall

Here River Street ends and the pedestrian mall begins with the **statue of Chinese revolutionary leader Sun Yat-sen.** The wide mall, which

Bargaining: A Way of Life in Chinatown

In Chinatown, nearly every purchase—from chicken's feet to an 18-karat-gold necklace—is made by bargaining. It's the way of life for most Asian countries—and part of the fun and charm of shopping in Chinatown.

The main rule of thumb when negotiating a price is **respect**. The customer must have respect for the merchant and understand that he's in business to make money. This respect is coupled with the understanding that the customer does not want to be taken advantage of and would like the best deal possible.

Keep in mind two rules when bargaining: **cash** and **volume**. Don't even begin haggling if you're not planning to pay cash. The second you pull out a credit card (if the merchant or vendor will even accept it), all deals are off. And remember, the more you buy, the better the deal the merchant will extend to you.

Significant savings can be realized for high-ticket items like jewelry. The price of gold in Chinatown is based on the posted price of the tael (a unit of weight slightly more than an ounce), which is listed for 14-, 18-, and 24-karat gold, plus the value of the labor. There's no negotiating on the tael price, but the cost of the labor is where the bargaining begins.

---

borders the Nuuanu Stream, is lined with shade trees, park benches, and tables where seniors gather to play mah-jongg and checkers. There are plenty of takeout restaurants nearby if you'd like to eat lunch outdoors. If you're up early (5:30am in summer and 6am in winter), you'll see seniors practicing tai chi.

Along the River Street Mall, extending nearly a block over to Maunakea Street, is the:

7 Chinatown Cultural Plaza

This modern complex is filled with shops featuring everything from tailors to calligraphers (most somewhat more expensive than their streetside counterparts), as well as numerous restaurants—a great idea, but in reality, people seem to prefer wandering Chinatown's crowded streets to venturing into a modern mall. A couple of interesting shops here specialize in Asian magazines; there's also a small post office tucked away in a corner of the plaza, for those who want to mail cards home with the "Chinatown" postmark. The best feature of the plaza is the **Moongate Stage** in the center, the site of many cultural presentations, especially around the Chinese New Year.

Continue up the River Street Mall and cross the Nuuanu Stream via the bridge at Kukui Street, which will bring you to the:

8 Izumo Taisha Mission Cultural Hall

This small wooden Shinto shrine, built in 1923, houses a male deity (look for the X-shaped crosses on the top). Members of the faith ring the bell out front as an act of purification when they come to pray. Inside the temple is a 100-pound sack of rice, symbolizing good health. During World War II, the shrine was confiscated by the city of Honolulu and wasn't returned to the congregation until 1962.

Kuan Yin Temple.

If temples interest you, walk a block toward the mountains to Vineyard Boulevard; cross back over Nuuanu Stream, past the entrance of Foster Botanical Garden, to:

9 Kuan Yin Temple

This Buddhist temple, painted in a brilliant red with a green ceramic-tiled roof, is dedicated to Kuan Yin Bodhisattva, the goddess of mercy, whose statue towers in the prayer hall. The aroma of burning incense is your clue that the temple is still a house of worship, not an exhibit, so enter with respect and leave your shoes outside. You may see people burning paper "money" for prosperity and good luck, or leaving flowers and fruits at the altar (gifts to the goddess). A common offering is the pomelo, a grapefruit-like fruit that's a fertility symbol as well as a gift, indicating a request for the blessing of children.

Continue down Vineyard and then turn right (toward the ocean) on:

10 Maunakea Street

Between Beretania and King streets are numerous **lei shops** (with lei makers working away right on the premises). The air is heavy with the aroma of flowers being woven into beautiful treasures. Not only is this the best place in all of Hawaii to get a deal on leis, but the size, color, and design of the leis made here are exceptional. Wander through the shops before you decide which lei you want.

11 Take a Break

Sing Cheng Yuan ★ ☺ ☕. Grab Asian pastries (my picks: moon cakes and almond cookies) at this tempting shop, which also has a wide selection of dried and sugared candies (ginger, pineapple, and lotus root) that you can eat as you stroll or give as an exotic gift to friends back home. 1027 Maunakea St. (near King St.), ✆ **808/531-6688.** Daily 6am–4:30pm. $.

Near the waterfront, in downtown Honolulu, local residents love Restaurant Row, a block-long complex of restaurants, but it's off the beaten path for most visitors—too bad. My advice? Don't miss it. Come here for dinner (my favs are Hiroshi Eurasian Tapa, p. 185, and Vino, p. 186) and a movie (Restaurant Row 9 Theater) at night, when the crowds are smaller. Avoid lunchtime, when nearby office buildings seem to empty out and workers flock to the variety of eateries here (which range from gourmet Hawaiian Regional cuisine to burger joints).

Turn left on King Street and walk in the Diamond Head (east) direction to:

12 Lai Fong Department Store

Before you enter this classic Chinatown store, take a moment to notice the sidewalks on Nuuanu, which are made of granite blocks used as ballast in ships that brought tea from China to Hawaii in the 1800s. This old store, owned by the same family for more than 80 years, sells everything from precious antiques to god-awful knickknacks to rare Hawaiian postcards from

Hawaii Theatre.

THE aloha TOWER

One of the reasons that the word *aloha* is synonymous with Hawaii is because of the Aloha Tower. Built in 1926 (for the then-outrageous sum of $160,000), this 184-foot, 10-story tower (until 1959, the tallest structure in Hawaii) has clocks on all four of its sides with the word *aloha* under each clock. Aloha, which has come to mean both "hello" and "farewell," was the first thing steamship passengers saw when they entered Honolulu Harbor. In the days when tourists arrived by steamer, "boat days" were a very big occasion. The Royal Hawaiian Band was on hand to play, crowds gathered, flower leis were freely given, and Honolulu came to a standstill to greet the visitors.

Go up the elevator inside the Aloha Tower to the 10th-floor **observation deck** for a bird's-eye view that encompasses Diamond Head and Waikiki, the downtown and Chinatown areas, and the harbor coastline to the airport. On the ocean side you can see the harbor mouth, Sand Island, the Honolulu reef runway, and the

Pearl Harbor entrance channel. No charge to see the view; the Aloha Tower is open daily from 9am to 5pm.

the early 1900s—but it has built its reputation on its fabulous selection of Chinese silks, brocades, and custom dresses.

At Pauahi Street, turn toward Diamond Head and walk up to Bethel Street and the:

13 Hawaii Theatre

This restored 1920 Art Deco theater is a work of art in itself. It hosts a variety of programs, from the Hawaii International Film Festival to beauty pageants (see "Oahu After Dark," on p. 292, for more information).

Turn right onto Bethel and walk toward the ocean. Turn right again onto Hotel Street, which will lead you back to where you started.

WALKING TOUR 2: HISTORIC HONOLULU

GETTING THERE: **From Waikiki, take Ala Moana Boulevard in the Ewa direction. Ala Moana Boulevard ends at Nimitz Highway. Turn right on the next street on your right (Alakea St.). Park in the garage across from St. Andrews Church after you cross Beretania Street. Bus: 1, 2, 3, 4, 11, 12, or 50.**

START & FINISH:	**St. Andrew's Church, Beretania and Alakea streets.**
TIME:	**2 to 3 hours, depending on how long you linger in museums.**
BEST TIMES:	**Wednesday through Saturday, daytime, when the Iolani Palace has tours.**

The 1800s were a turbulent time in Hawaii. By the end of the 1790s, Kamehameha the Great had united all the islands. Foreigners then began arriving by ship—first explorers, then merchants, and then, in 1820, missionaries. The rulers of Hawaii were hard-pressed to keep up. By 1840, it was clear that the capital had shifted from Lahaina, where the Kingdom of Hawaii was actually centered, to Honolulu, where the majority of commerce and trade was taking place. In 1848, the Great Mahele (division) enabled commoners and eventually foreigners to own crown land, and in two generations, more than 80% of all private lands had shifted to foreign ownership. With the introduction of sugar as a crop, the foreigners prospered, and in time they put more and more pressures on the government.

By 1872, the monarchy had run through the Kamehameha line and, in 1873, David Kalakaua was elected to the throne. Known as the "Merrie Monarch," Kalakaua redefined the monarchy by going on a world tour, building Iolani Palace, having a European-style coronation, and throwing extravagant parties. By the end of the 1800s, however, the foreign sugar growers and merchants had become extremely powerful in Hawaii. With the assistance of the U.S. Marines, they orchestrated the overthrow of Queen Liliuokalani, Hawaii's last reigning monarch, in 1893. The United States declared Hawaii a territory in 1898.

You can witness the remnants of these turbulent years in just a few short blocks.

Cross the street from the garage and venture back to 1858 when you enter:

1 St. Andrew's Church

The Hawaiian monarchs were greatly influenced by the royals in Europe. When King Kamehameha IV saw the grandeur of the Church of England, he decided to build his own cathedral. He and Queen Emma founded the Anglican Church of Hawaii in 1858. The king, however, didn't live to see the church completed; he died on St. Andrew's Day, 4 years before King Kamehameha V oversaw the laying of the cornerstone in 1867. The church was named St. Andrew's in honor of King Kamehameha IV's death. This French-Gothic structure was shipped in pieces from England and reassembled here. Even if you aren't fond of visiting churches, you have to see the floor-to-eaves handblown stained-glass window that faces the setting sun. In the glass is a mural of Rev. Thomas Staley, the first bishop in Hawaii; King Kamehameha IV; and Queen Emma. There's also an excellent thrift shop on the grounds with some real bargains;

St. Andrew's Church.

open Monday, Wednesday, and Friday from 9:30am to 4pm and Saturday from 9am to 1pm.

Next, walk down Beretania Street in the Diamond Head direction to the gates of:

2 Washington Place

Once the residence of the governor of Hawaii (sorry, no tours; just peek through the iron fence), it occupies a distinguished place in Hawaii's history. The Greek Revival–style home, built in 1842 by a U.S. sea captain named John Dominis, got its name from the U.S. ambassador who once stayed here and told so many stories about President George Washington that people starting calling the home Washington Place. The sea captain's son, also named John, married a beautiful Hawaiian princess, Lydia Kapaakea, who later became Hawaii's last queen, Liliuokalani. When the queen was overthrown by U.S. businessmen in 1893, she moved out of Iolani Palace and into her husband's inherited home, Washington Place, where she lived until her death in 1917. On the left side of the building, near the sidewalk, is a plaque inscribed with the words to one of the most popular songs written by Queen Liliuokalani, "Aloha Oe" ("Farewell to Thee").

Cross the street and walk to the front of the Hawaii State Capitol, where you'll find the:

3 Father Damien Statue

The people of Hawaii have never forgotten the sacrifice this Belgian priest made to help the sufferers of leprosy when he volunteered to work with them in exile on the Kalaupapa Peninsula on the island of Molokai. After 16 years of service, Father Damien died of leprosy, at the age of 49. The statue is frequently draped in leis in recognition of Father Damien's humanitarian work.

Behind the Father Damien Statue is the:

4 Hawaii State Capitol

Here's where Hawaii's state legislators work from mid-January to the end of April every year. This is not your typical white dome structure, but rather a building symbolic of Hawaii. Unfortunately, it symbolizes more of Hawaii than the architect and the state legislature probably bargained for. The building's unusual design has palm tree–shaped pillars, two cone-shaped chambers (representing volcanoes) for the legislative bodies, and, in the inner courtyard, a 600,000-tile mosaic of the sea (Aquarius) created by a local artist. A reflecting pool (representing the sea) surrounds the entire structure. Like a lot of things in Hawaii, it was a great idea, but no one considered the logistics. The reflecting pond also draws brackish water, which rusts the hardware; when it rains, water pours into the rotunda, dampening government business; and the Aquarius floor mosaic was so damaged by the elements that it became a hazard. In the 1990s, the entire building (built in 1969) was closed for a couple of years for renovations, forcing the legislature to set up temporary quarters in several buildings. It's open again, and you are welcome to go into the rotunda and see the woven hangings and murals at the entrance, or take the elevator up to the fifth floor for a spectacular view of the city's historic center.

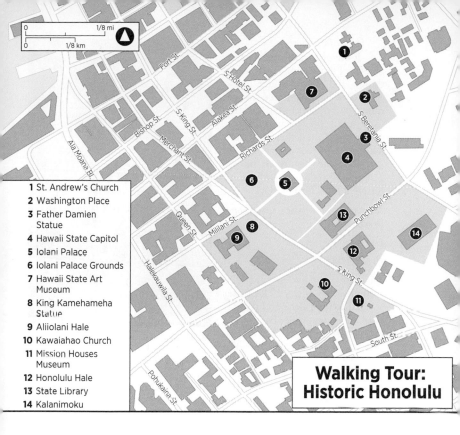

Walking Tour: Historic Honolulu

Walk down Richards Street toward the ocean and stop at:

5 Iolani Palace

Hawaii is the only state in the U.S. to have not one, but two royal palaces: one in Kona, where the royals went during the summer, and Iolani Palace (*Iolani* means "royal hawk"). Don't miss the opportunity to see this grande dame of historic buildings. Admission is $20 for adults, $5 for children 5 to 13. Guided tours are offered Tuesday through Saturday from 9am to 2:15pm; call ☏ **808/522-0832** to reserve in advance, as spots are limited.

In ancient times, a *heiau* stood in this area. When it became clear to King Kamehameha III that the capital should be transferred from Lahaina to Honolulu, he moved to a modest building here in 1845. The construction of the palace was undertaken by King David Kalakaua and was begun in 1879; it was finished 3 years later at a cost of $350,000. The king spared no expense: You can still see the glass and ironwork imported from San Francisco, and the palace had all the modern conveniences for its time. Electric lights were installed 4 years before the White House had them, and every bedroom had its own full bathroom with hot and cold running water, copper-lined tub, flush toilet, and bidet. The king had a telephone line from the palace to his boathouse on the water a year after Alexander Graham Bell introduced it to the world.

It was also in this palace that Queen Liliuokalani was overthrown and placed under house arrest for 9 months. Later, the territorial and then the state government used the palace until it outgrew it. When the legislature left in 1968, the palace was in shambles and has since undergone a $7-million overhaul to restore it to its former glory.

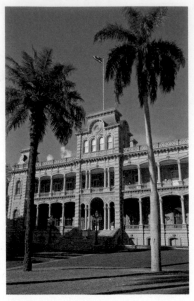

Iolani Palace.

After you visit the palace, spend some time on the:

6 Iolani Palace Grounds

You can wander around the grounds at no charge. The ticket window to the palace and the gift shop are in the former barracks of the Royal Household Guards. The domed pavilion on the grounds was originally built as a Coronation Stand by King Kalakaua (9 years after he took the throne, he decided to have a formal European-style coronation ceremony in which he crowned himself and his queen, Kapiolani). Later he used it as a **Royal Bandstand** for concerts (King Kalakaua, along with Henri Berger, the first Royal Hawaiian Bandmaster, wrote "Hawaii Pono'i," the state anthem). Today the Royal Bandstand is still used for concerts by the Royal Hawaiian Band. The more modern building on the grounds is the **State Archives,** built in 1953, which hold records, documents, and photos of Hawaii's people and its history.

From the palace grounds, turn in the Ewa direction, cross Richards Street, and walk to the corner of Richards and Hotel streets to the:

7 Hawaii State Art Museum

Opened in 2002, the Hawaii State Art Museum is housed in the original Royal Hawaiian Hotel built in 1872, during the reign of King Kamehameha V. All of the 360 works currently displayed were created by artists who live in Hawaii. The pieces were purchased by the state, thanks to a 1967 law that says that 1% of the cost of state buildings will be used to acquire works of art. Nearly 4 decades later, the state has amassed some 5,000 pieces. The current exhibit depicts Hawaii and its history, culture, and ideals, through a variety of media.

Walk makai down Richards Street and turn left (toward Diamond Head) on South King Street to the:

8 King Kamehameha Statue

At the juncture of King, Merchant, and Mililani streets stands a replica of the man who united the Hawaiian Islands. The striking black-and-gold bronze statue is magnificent. The best day to see the statue is on June 11 (King Kamehameha Day), when it is covered with leis in honor of Hawaii's favorite son.

King Kamehameha statue.

The statue of Kamehameha I was cast by Thomas Gould in 1880 in Paris. However, it was lost at sea somewhere near the Falkland Islands. Subsequently, the insurance money was used to pay for a second statue, but in the meantime, the original statue was recovered. The original was eventually sent to the town of Kapaau on the Big Island, the birthplace of Kamehameha, and the second statue was placed in Honolulu in 1883, as part of King David Kalakaua's coronation ceremony. A third statue (all three are very different, but they were supposedly all cast from the same mold) was sent to Washington, D.C., when Hawaii became a state in 1959.

Right behind the King Kamehameha Statue is:

9 Aliiolani Hale

The name translates to "House of Heavenly Kings." This distinctive building, with a clock tower, now houses the State Judiciary Building. King Kamehameha V originally wanted to build a palace here and commissioned the Australian architect Thomas Rowe in 1872. However, it ended up as the first major government building for the Hawaiian monarchy. Kamehameha V didn't live to see it completed, and King David Kalakaua dedicated the building in 1874. Ironically, less than 20 years later, on January 17, 1893, Stanford Dole, backed by other prominent sugar planters, stood on the steps to this building and proclaimed the overthrow of the Hawaiian monarchy and the establishment of a provisional government. Self-guided tours are available Monday through Friday from 9am to 4pm.

Walk toward Diamond Head on King Street; at the corner of King and Punchbowl, stop in at the:

10 Kawaiahao Church

When the missionaries came to Hawaii, the first thing they did was build churches. Four thatched-grass churches (one measured 54×22 ft. and could seat 300 people on lauhala mats; the last thatched church held 4,500 people) had been built on this site through 1837 before Rev. Hiram Bingham began building what he considered a "real" church—a New England–style congregational structure with Gothic influences. Between 1837 and 1842, the construction of the church required some 14,000 giant coral slabs (some weighing more than 1,000 lb.). Hawaiian divers ravaged the reefs, digging out huge chunks of coral and causing irreparable environmental damage.

Kawaiahao is Hawaii's oldest church, and it has been the site of numerous historic events, such as a speech made by King Kamehameha III in 1843, an excerpt from which became Hawaii's state motto (*"Ua mau ke ea o ka aina i ka pono,"* which translates as "The life of the land is preserved in righteousness").

The clock tower in the church, which was donated by King Kamehameha III and installed in 1850, continues to tick today. The church is open Monday through Saturday from 8am to 4pm; you'll find it to be very cool in temperature. Don't sit in the pews in the back, marked with kahili feathers and velvet cushions; they are still reserved for the descendants of royalty. Sunday service (in Hawaiian) is at 9am.

Cross the street, and you'll see the:

11 Mission Houses Museum

On the corner of King and Kawaiahao streets stand the original buildings of the Sandwich Islands Mission Headquarters: the **Frame House** (built in 1821), the **Chamberlain House** (1831), and the **Printing Office** (1841). The complex is open Tuesday through Saturday from 10am to 4pm; admission is $10 for adults, $8 for seniors and military personnel, and $6 for students and children 6 and older. The tours are often led by descendants of the original missionaries to Hawaii.

Believe it or not, the missionaries brought their own prefab house along with them when they came around Cape Horn from Boston in 1819. The Frame House was designed for New England winters and had small windows (it must have been stiflingly hot inside). Finished in 1921 (the interior frame was left behind and didn't arrive until Christmas 1920), it is Hawaii's oldest wooden structure. The Chamberlain House, built in 1931, was used by the missionaries as a storehouse.

The missionaries believed that the best way to spread the Lord's message to the Hawaiians was to learn their language, and then to print literature for them to read. So it was the missionaries who gave the Hawaiians a written language. The Printing House on the grounds was where the lead-type Ramage press (brought from New England, of course) was used to print the Hawaiian Bible.

Cross King Street and walk in the Ewa direction to the corner of Punchbowl and King to:

12 Honolulu Hale

The **Honolulu City Hall,** built in 1927, was designed by Honolulu's most famous architect, C. W. Dickey. His Spanish mission–style building has an open-air courtyard, which is used for art exhibits and concerts. Open Monday through Friday.

Honolulu Hale.

Cross Punchbowl Street and walk mauka to the:

13 State Library

Anything you want to know about Hawaii and the Pacific can be found here, the main branch of the state's library system. Located in a restored historic building, it has an open garden courtyard in the middle, great for stopping for a rest on your walk.

Head mauka up Punchbowl to the corner of Punchbowl and Beretania streets, where you'll see:

14 Kalanimoku

This beautiful name, "Ship of Heaven," has been given to this dour state office building. Here you can get information from the Department of Land and Natural Resources on hiking and camping in state parks.

Retrace your steps in the Ewa direction down Beretania to Alakea back to the parking garage.

BEYOND HONOLULU: EXPLORING THE ISLAND BY CAR

The moment always arrives—usually after a couple of days at the beach, snorkeling in the warm blue green waters of Hanauma Bay, enjoying sundown mai tais—when a certain curiosity kicks in about the rest of Oahu, largely unknown to most visitors. It's time to find the rental car in the hotel garage and set out around the island. You can also explore Oahu using **TheBus** (see "Getting Around," on p. 138).

Oahu's Southeast Coast

From the high-rises of Waikiki, venture down Kalakaua Avenue through tree-lined Kapiolani Park to take a look at a different side of Oahu, the arid south shore. The landscape here is more moonscape, with prickly cactuses onshore and, in winter, spouting whales cavorting in the water. Some call it the South Shore, others Sandy's (after the mile-long beach here), but Hawaiians call it **Ka Iwi,** which means "the bone"—no doubt because of all the bone-cracking shore breaks along this popular body-boarding coastline. The beaches here are long, wide, and popular with local daredevils.

To get to this coast, follow Kalakaua Avenue past the multitiered Dillingham Fountain and around the bend in the road, which now becomes Poni Moi Road. Make a right on Diamond Head Road and begin the climb up the side of the old crater. At the top are several lookout points, so if the official Diamond Head Lookout is jammed with cars, try one of the other lookouts just down the road. The view of the rolling waves is spectacular; take the time to pull over.

Diamond Head Road rolls downhill into the ritzy community of **Kahala.** At the V in the road at the triangular Fort Ruger Park, veer to your right and continue on the palm tree–lined Kahala Avenue. Make a left on Hunakai Street, then a right on Kilauea Avenue, and look for the sign H-1 WEST—WAIMANALO. Turn right at the sign, although you won't get on the H-1 freeway; instead, get on the Kalanianaole Highway, a four-lane highway interrupted every few blocks by a stoplight. This is the suburban bedroom community to Honolulu, marked by malls on the left and beach parks on the right.

One of these parks is **Hanauma Bay ★★** (p. 202); you'll see the turnoff on the right when you're about half an hour from Waikiki. This marine preserve is a great place to stop for a swim; you'll find the friendliest fish on the island here. *A reminder:* The beach park is closed on Tuesday.

Around mile marker 11, the jagged lava coast itself spouts sea foam at the **Halona Blowhole.** Look out to sea from Halona over Sandy Beach and across the 26-mile gulf to neighboring Molokai and the faint triangular

Halona Blowhole.

shadow of Lanai on the far horizon. **Sandy Beach** (p. 203) is Oahu's most dangerous beach; it's the only one with an ambulance always standing by to whisk injured wave catchers to the hospital. Body boarders just love it.

The coast looks raw and empty along this stretch, but the road weaves past old Hawaiian fish ponds and the famous formation known as **Pele's Chair,** just off Kalanianaole Highway (Hwy. 72) above Queen's Beach. From a distance, the lava-rock outcropping looks like a mighty throne; it's believed to be the fire goddess's last resting place on Oahu before she flew off to continue her work on other islands.

Ahead lies 647-foot-high **Makapuu Point,** with a lighthouse that once signaled safe passage for steamship passengers arriving from San Francisco. The automated light now brightens Oahu's south coast for passing tankers, fishing boats, and sailors. You can take a short hike up here for a spectacular vista (p. 219).

Turn the corner at Makapuu and you're on Oahu's windward side, where cooling trade winds propel windsurfers across turquoise bays; the waves at **Makapuu Beach Park** (p. 203) are perfect for bodysurfing.

Ahead, the coastal vista is a profusion of fluted green mountains and strange peaks, edged by golden beaches and the blue, blue Pacific. The 3,000-foot-high sheer green Koolau mountains plunge almost straight down, presenting an irresistible jumping-off spot for hang glider pilots, who catch the thermals on hourslong rides.

Winding up the coast, Kalanianaole Highway (Hwy. 72) leads through rural **Waimanalo,** a country beach town of nurseries and stables, fresh-fruit stands, and some of the island's best conch- and triton-shell specimens at roadside stands. Nearly 4 miles long, **Waimanalo Beach** is Oahu's longest beach and the most popular for bodysurfing. Take a swim here or head on to **Kailua Beach ★★** (p. 204), one of Hawaii's best.

If it's still early in the day, you can head up the lush, green Windward Coast by turning right at the Castle Junction, where Hwy. 72 meets Hwy. 61 (which is called Kailua Rd. on the makai, or seaward, side of the junction, and Kalanianaole Hwy. on the mauka, or inland, side of the junction), and continuing down

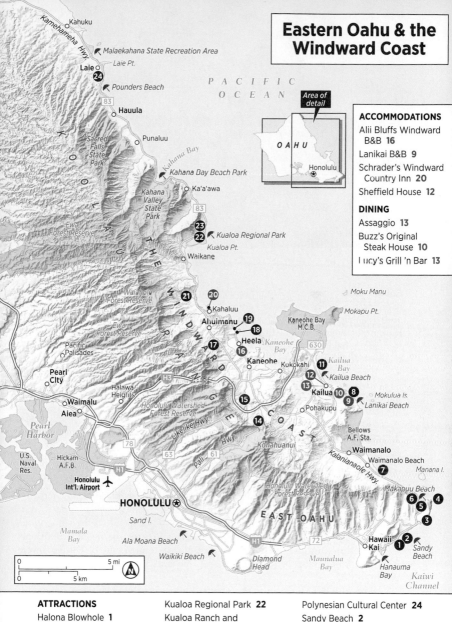

Eastern Oahu & the Windward Coast

ACCOMMODATIONS
Alii Bluffs Windward B&B **16**
Lanikai B&B **9**
Schrader's Windward Country Inn **20**
Sheffield House **12**

DINING
Assaggio **13**
Buzz's Original Steak House **10**
Lucy's Grill 'n Bar **13**

ATTRACTIONS

Halona Blowhole **1**	Kualoa Regional Park **22**	Polynesian Cultural Center **24**
Heeia Pier **19**	Kualoa Ranch and Activity Club **23**	Sandy Beach **2**
Heeia State Park/ Heeia Fish Pond **18**	Lanikai Beach **8**	Sea Life Park **6**
Hoomaluhia Botanical Gardens **15**	Makapuu Beach Park **5**	Senator Fong's Plantation & Gardens **21**
Kailua Beach **11**	Makapuu Point **4**	Valley of the Temples **17**
	Nuuanu Pali Lookout **14**	Waimanalo Beach **7**
	Pele's Chair **3**	

Pele's Chair.

Kailua Road (Hwy. 61). After Kailua Road crosses the Kaelepulu Stream, the name of the road changes to Kuulei Road. When Kuulei Road ends, turn left onto Kalaheo Avenue, which becomes Kaneohe Bay Drive after it crosses the Kawainui Channel. Follow this scenic drive around the peninsula until you get to Kamehameha Highway (Hwy. 83); turn right and continue on Kamehameha Highway for a scenic drive along the ocean.

If you're in a hurry to get back to Waikiki, turn left at Castle Junction and head over the Pali Highway (Hwy. 61), which becomes Bishop Street in Honolulu and ends at Ala Moana. Turn left for Waikiki; it's the second beach on the right.

The Windward Coast

From the **Nuuanu Pali Lookout ★**, near the summit of the Pali Highway (Hwy. 61), you get the first hint of the other side of Oahu, a region so green and lovely that it could be an island sibling of Tahiti. With its many beaches and bays, the scenic 30-mile Windward Coast parallels the corduroy-ridged, nearly perpendicular cliffs of the Koolau Range, which separates the windward side of the island from Honolulu and the rest of Oahu. As you descend on the serpentine Pali Highway beneath often-gushing waterfalls, you'll see the nearly 1,000-foot spike of **Olomana,** the bold pinnacle that always reminds me of Devils Tower National Monument in Wyoming, and, beyond, the Hawaiian village of **Waimanalo.**

From the Pali Highway, to the right is Kailua, Hawaii's biggest beach town, with more than 50,000 residents and two special beaches, **Kailua Beach** (p. 204) and **Lanikai Beach** (p. 204). Funky little Kailua is lined with million-dollar houses next to tar paper shacks, antiques shops, and bed-and-breakfasts. Although the Pali Highway (Hwy. 61) proceeds directly to the coast, it undergoes two name changes, becoming first Kalanianaole Highway—from the intersection of Kamehameha Highway (Hwy. 83)—and then Kailua Road as it heads into Kailua town; but the road remains Hwy. 61 the whole way. Kailua Road ends at the T intersection at Kalaheo Drive, which follows the coast in a northerly and southerly direction. Turn right on South Kalaheo Drive to get to Kailua Beach and Lanikai Beach. No signs point the way, but you can't miss them.

If you spend a day at the beach here, stick around for sunset, when the sun sinks behind the Koolau Range and tints the clouds pink and orange. After a hard day at the beach, you'll work up an appetite, and Kailua has several great inexpensive restaurants (see p. 195 for a few ideas).

If you want to skip the beaches this time, turn left on North Kalaheo Drive, which becomes Kaneohe Bay Drive as it skirts Kaneohe Bay and leads back to Kamehameha Highway (Hwy. 83), which then passes through Kaneohe. The suburban maze of Kaneohe is one giant strip mall of retail excess that mars one of the Pacific's most picturesque bays. After you've cleared this obstacle, the place begins to look like Hawaii again.

Incredibly scenic Kaneohe Bay is spiked with islets and lined with gold-sand beach parks like **Kualoa Regional Park** (p. 224), a favorite picnic spot. The bay has a barrier reef and four tiny islets, one of which is known as Moku o loe, or Coconut Island. Don't be surprised if it looks familiar—it appeared in *Gilligan's Island*.

At Heeia State Park is **Heeia Fish Pond,** which ancient Hawaiians built by enclosing natural bays with rocks to trap fish on the incoming tide. The 88-acre fish pond, which is made of lava rock and had four watchtowers to observe fish movement and several sluice gates along the 5,000-foot-long wall, is now in the process of being restored.

Stop by the **Heeia Pier,** which juts onto Kaneohe Bay. You can take a snorkel cruise here or sail out to a sandbar in the middle of the bay for an incredible view of Oahu that most people, even those who live here, never see. If it's Tuesday or Thursday through Sunday between 7am and 4pm, stop in at the **Deli on Heeia Kea Pier** (© **808/235-2192**), serving fishermen, sailors, and kayakers the town's best omelets and plate lunches since 1979.

Everyone calls it **Chinaman's Hat,** but the tiny island off the eastern shore of Kualoa Regional Park is really named **Mokolii.** It's a sacred *puu honua,* or place of refuge, like the restored Puu Honua Honaunau on the Big Island of Hawaii. Excavations have unearthed evidence that this area was the home of ancient *alii* (royalty). Early Hawaiians believed that Mokolii ("fin of the lizard") is all that remains of a *mo'o,* or lizard, slain by Pele's sister, Hiiaka, and hurled into the sea. At low tide you can swim out to the island, but keep watch on the changing tide, which can sweep you out to sea. The islet has a small sandy beach and is a bird preserve, so don't spook the red-footed boobies.

Little polyvoweled beach towns like **Kahaluu, Kaaawa, Punaluu,** and **Hauula** pop up along the coast, offering passersby shell shops and art galleries to explore. Famed hula photographer **Kim Taylor Reece** lives on this coast; his gallery at 53–866 Kamehameha Hwy., near Sacred Falls (© **808/293-2000;** www.kimtaylorreece.com), is open Thursday through Saturday from noon to 5pm. You'll also see working cattle ranches, fishermen's wharves, and roadside fruit and flower stands vending ice-cold coconuts (to drink) and tree-ripened mangoes, papayas, and apple bananas (short bananas with an apple aftertaste).

Sugar, once the sole industry of this region, is gone. But **Kahuku,** the former sugar-plantation town, has found new life as a small aquaculture community with prawn farms that supply island restaurants.

From here, continue along Kamehameha Highway (Hwy. 83) to the North Shore.

5

OAHU, THE GATHERING PLACE

Beyond Honolulu

Heeia Fish Pond.

A Laysan Albatross.

ATTRACTIONS ALONG THE WINDWARD COAST

The attractions below are arranged geographically as you drive up the coast from south to north.

Hoomaluhia Botanical Garden ★   This 400-acre botanical garden at the foot of the steepled Koolau Range is the perfect place for a picnic. Its name means "a peaceful refuge," and that's exactly what the Army Corps of Engineers created when they installed a flood-control project here, which resulted in a 32-acre freshwater lake and garden. Just unfold a beach mat, lie back, and watch the clouds race across the rippled cliffs of the majestic Koolau mountains. This is one of the few public places on Oahu that provides a close-up view of the steepled cliffs. The park has hiking trails and—best of all—the island's only free inland campground (p. 223). If you like hiking and nature, plan to spend at least a half-day here. Be prepared for rain, mud, and mosquitoes.

45–680 Luluku Rd., Kaneohe. ℂ **808/233-7323.** www.co.honolulu.hi.us/parks/hbg/hmbg.htm. Free admission. Daily 9am–4pm. Guided nature hikes Sat 10am and Sun 1pm. Take H-1 to the Pali Hwy. (Hwy. 61); turn left on Kamehameha Hwy. (Hwy. 83); at the 4th light, turn left onto Luluku Rd. Bus: 55 or 56 will stop on Kamehameha Hwy.; it's a 2-mile walk to the visitor center.

Valley of the Temples   This famous cemetery in a cleft of the *pali* is stalked by wild peacocks and about 700 curious people a day, who pay to see the 9-foot meditation Buddha, acres of ponds full of more than 10,000 Japanese koi carp, and a replica of Japan's 900-year-old Byodo-in Temple of Equality. The original, made of wood, stands in Uji, on the outskirts of Kyoto; the Hawaiian version, made of concrete, was erected in 1968 to commemorate the 100th anniversary of the arrival of the first Japanese immigrants to Hawaii. It's not the same as seeing the original, but it's worth a detour. A 3-ton brass temple bell brings good luck to those who can ring it—although the gongs do jar the Zenlike serenity of this little bit of Japan. If you are in a rush, you can sail through here in an hour, but you'll probably want to stay longer.

47–200 Kahekili Hwy. (across the street from Temple Valley Shopping Center), Kaneohe. © **808/239-8811.** Admission $3 adults, $2 children 11 and under and seniors 65 and over. Daily 9am–5pm. Take the H-1 to the Likelike Hwy. (Hwy. 63); after the Wilson Tunnel, get in the right lane and take the Kahekili Hwy. (Hwy. 63); at the 6th traffic light is the entrance to the cemetery (on the left). Bus: 65.

Senator Fong's Plantation & Gardens   Sen. Hiram Fong, the first Chinese American elected to the U.S. Senate, served 17 years before retiring to this 725-acre tropical garden years ago. This land originally belonged to King Lunalilo; Senator Fong purchased it in 1950. The landscape you see today is relatively the same as what early Polynesians saw hundreds of years ago, with forests of kukui, hala, koa, and *ohia-'ai* (mountain apple). Ti and pili grass still cover the slopes. It's definitely worth an hour—if you haven't already seen enough flora to last a lifetime.

47–285 Pulama Rd., Kaneohe. © **808/239-6775.** www.fonggarden.net. Admission $15 adults, $13 seniors, $9 children 5–12. Daily 10am–2pm; guided walking tours daily 10:30am and 1pm. Take the H-1 to the Likelike Hwy. (Hwy. 63); turn left at Kahekili Hwy. (Hwy. 83); continue to Kaneohe and turn left on Pulama Rd. Bus: 55; it's a 1-mile walk uphill from the stop.

Kualoa Ranch and Activity Club   This once-working ranch now has various adventure packages covering numerous activities on its 4,000 acres. Options include horseback riding, ATV rides, ranch tours, and more.

49–560 Kamehameha Hwy., Kaaawa. © **800/231-7321** or 808/237-7321. www.kualoa.com. Reservations required. Various packages available; single activities $21–$93. Daily 8am–3pm. Take H-1 to the Likelike Hwy. (Hwy. 63), turn left at Kahekili Hwy. (Hwy. 83), and continue to Kaaawa. Bus: 52.

Polynesian Cultural Center ★ ☺   Even if you never leave Hawaii, you can still experience the natural beauty and culture of the vast Pacific in a single day

Valley of the Temples.

at the Polynesian Cultural Center, a kind of living museum of Polynesia. Here you can see firsthand the lifestyles, songs, dance, costumes, and architecture of seven Pacific islands or archipelagos—Fiji, New Zealand, Marquesas, Samoa, Tahiti, Tonga, and Hawaii—in the re-created villages scattered throughout the 42-acre lagoon park. A recent $1.1-million renovation project remodeled the front entrance and added an exhibit on the story of the Polynesian immigration.

You "travel" through this museum by foot or in a canoe on a man-made freshwater lagoon. Each village is "inhabited" by native students from Polynesia who attend Hawaii's Brigham Young University. The park, which is operated by the Mormon Church, also features a variety of stage shows celebrating the music, dance, history, and culture of Polynesia. There's a luau every evening. Because a visit can take up to 8 hours, it's a good idea to arrive before 2pm.

Just beyond the center is the Hawaii Temple of the Church of Jesus Christ of Latter-day Saints, which is built of volcanic rock and concrete in the form of a Greek cross, and includes reflecting pools, formal gardens, and royal palms. Completed in 1919, it was the first Mormon temple built outside the continental United States. An optional tour of the Temple Visitors Center, as well as neighboring Brigham Young University Hawaii, is included in the package admission prices.

55–370 Kamehameha Hwy., Laie. ✆ **800/367-7060,** 808/293-3333, or 808/923-2911. www. polynesia.com. Various packages available for $45–$225 adults, $35–$175 children 3–11. Mon-Sat noon–9pm. Take H-1 to Pali Hwy. (Hwy. 61) and turn left on Kamehameha Hwy. (Hwy. 83). Bus: 55. Polynesian Cultural Center coaches $19 round-trip; call numbers above to book.

Central Oahu & the North Shore

If you can afford the splurge, rent a bright, shiny convertible—the perfect car for Oahu because you can tan as you go—and head for the North Shore and Hawaii's surf city: **Haleiwa ★**, a quaint sugar-plantation town designated a historic site. A collection of faded clapboard stores with a picturesque harbor, Haleiwa has evolved into a surfer outpost and major roadside attraction with art galleries, restaurants, and shops that sell hand-decorated clothing, jewelry, and sports gear (see "Shopping A to Z," below).

Getting here is half the fun. You have two choices: The first is to meander north along the lush Windward Coast, through country hamlets with roadside stands selling mangoes, bright tropical pareu, fresh corn, and pond-raised prawns. Attractions along that route are discussed in the previous section.

The second choice is to cruise up the H-2 through Oahu's broad and fertile central valley, past Pearl Harbor and the Schofield Barracks of *From Here to Eternity* fame, and on through the red-earthed heart of the island, where pineapple and sugar-cane fields stretch from the Koolau to the Waianae mountains, until the sea reappears on the horizon. If you take this route, the tough part is getting on and off the H-1 freeway from Waikiki, which is done by way of convoluted routing on neighborhood streets. Try McCully Street off Ala Wai Boulevard, which is always crowded but usually the most direct route.

Once you're on H-1, stay to the right side; the freeway tends to divide abruptly. Keep following the signs for the H-1 (it separates off to Hwy. 78 at the airport and reunites later; either way will get you there), and then the H-1/H-2. Leave the H-1 where the two highways divide; take the H-2 up the middle of the island, heading north toward the town of Wahiawa. That's what the sign will say—not North Shore or Haleiwa, but Wahiawa.

Central & Leeward Oahu

ATTRACTIONS

Dole Pineapple Plantation **2**

Hawaii's Plantation Village **6**

Hawaiian Railway **7**

Hawaiian Waters Adventure Park **8**

Kaena Point State Park **1**

Kukaniloko Birthing Stones **3**

Tropic Lightning Museum **4**

U.S. Army Schofield Barracks **4**

ACCOMMODATIONS

J. W. Marriott Ihilani Resort & Spa **9**

DINING

Roy's Ko Olina **10**

SHOPPING

Waikele Premium Outlets **5**

The H-2 runs out and becomes a two-lane country road about 18 miles outside downtown Honolulu, near Schofield Barracks (see below). The highway becomes Kamehameha Highway (Hwy. 99 and later Hwy. 83) at Wahiawa. Just past Wahiawa, about a half-hour out of Honolulu, the **Dole Pineapple Plantation,** 64–1550 Kamehameha Hwy. (© 808/621-8408; www.dole-plantation. com; daily 9am–6pm; bus: 52), offers a rest stop with pineapples, pineapple history, pineapple trinkets, and pineapple juice. This agricultural exhibit/retail area features a maze kids will love to wander through, open daily from 9am to 5:30pm ($6 for adults, $4 for children 4–12). The Pineapple Express is a single-engine diesel locomotive with four cars that takes a 22-minute tour around 2¼ miles of the plantation's grounds, with an educational spiel on the legacy of the pineapple and agriculture in Hawaii. The first tour departs at 9am, and the last tour gets back to the station at 5pm. It costs $8 for adults and $6 for children 4 to 12. The latest attraction is the Plantation Garden Tour, a self-guided tour through the various crops that have been grown on Oahu's North Shore. That costs $4 for adults and $3.50 for children.

"Kam" Highway, as everyone calls it, will be your road for most of the rest of the trip to Haleiwa, on the North Shore.

CENTRAL OAHU ATTRACTIONS

On the central plains of Oahu, tract homes and malls with factory-outlet stores are now spreading across abandoned sugar-cane fields, where sandalwood forests used to stand at the foot of Mount Kaala, the mighty summit of Oahu. Hawaiian chiefs once sent commoners into thick sandalwood forests to cut down trees, which were then sold to China traders for small fortunes. The scantily clad natives caught cold in the cool uplands, and many died.

On these plains in 1908, the U.S. Army pitched a tent that later became a fort. And on December 7, 1941, Japanese pilots came screaming through Kolekole Pass to shoot up the barracks at Schofield, sending soldiers running for cover, and then flew on to sink ships at Pearl Harbor.

U.S. Army Schofield Barracks & Tropic Lightning Museum James Jones, author of *From Here to Eternity,* called Schofield Barracks "the most beautiful army post the U.S. has or ever had." The *Honolulu Star Bulletin* called it a country club. More than a million soldiers have called Schofield Barracks home. With its broad, palm-lined boulevards and Art Deco buildings, this old army cavalry post is still the largest operated by the U.S. Army outside the continental United States. And it's still one of the best places to be a soldier.

You can no longer visit the barracks themselves, but the history of Schofield Barracks and the 25th Infantry Division is told in the small **Tropic Lightning Museum.** Displays range from a 1917 bunker exhibit to a replica of Vietnam's infamous Cu Chi tunnels.

Schofield Barracks, Bldg. 361, Waianae Ave. © 808/655-0438. www.25idl.army.mil/tropic%20 lightning%20museum/index.html. Free admission. Tues–Sat 10am–4pm. Bus: 52 to Wahiawa; transfer at California Ave. to no. 72, Schofield Barracks Shuttle.

Kukaniloko Birthing Stones This is the most sacred site in central Oahu. Two rows of 18 lava rocks once flanked a central birthing stone, where women of ancient Hawaii gave birth to potential *alii* (royalty). The rocks, according to Hawaiian belief, held the power to ease the labor pains of childbirth. Birth rituals involved 48 chiefs who pounded drums to announce the arrival of newborns likely to become chiefs. Children born here were taken to the now-destroyed Holonopahu Heiau in the pineapple field, where chiefs ceremoniously cut the umbilical cord.

Used by Oahu's *alii* for generations of births, the *pohaku* (rocks), many in bowl-like shapes, now lie strewn in a grove of trees that stands in a pineapple field here. Some think the site may also have served ancient astronomers—like a Hawaiian Stonehenge. Petroglyphs of human forms and circles appear on some of the stones. The Wahiawa Hawaiian Civic Club recently erected two interpretive signs, one explaining why this was chosen as a birth site and the other telling how the stones were used to aid in the birth process.

The Kukanlloko Birthing Stones.

Off Kamehameha Hwy. btw. Wahiawa and Haleiwa, on Plantation Rd. opposite the road to Whitmore Village.

SURF CITY: HALEIWA

Only 28 miles from Waikiki is Haleiwa, the funky former sugar plantation town that's now the world capital of big-wave surfing. This beach town really comes alive in winter, when waves rise up, light rain falls, and temperatures dip into the 70s (low to mid-20s Celsius); then, it seems, every surfer in the world is here to see and be seen.

Officially designated a historic cultural and scenic district, Haleiwa thrives in a time warp recalling the early 20th century, when it was founded by sugar baron Benjamin Dillingham, who built a 30-mile railroad to link his Honolulu and North Shore plantations in 1899. He opened a Victorian hotel overlooking Kaiaka Bay and named it Haleiwa, or "house of the Iwa," the tropical seabird often seen here. The hotel and railroad are gone, but the town of Haleiwa, which was rediscovered in the late 1960s by hippies, resonates with rare rustic charm. Tofu, not taro, is a staple in the local diet. Arts and crafts, boutiques, and burger stands line both sides of the town. There's also a busy fishing harbor full of charter boats and captains who hunt the Kauai Channel daily for tuna, mahimahi, and marlin. The bartenders at **Jameson's by the Sea ★**, 62–540 Kamehameha Hwy. (© **808/637-6272**), make the best mai tais on the North Shore; they use the original recipe by Trader Vic Bergeron.

Once in Haleiwa, the hot and thirsty traveler should report directly to the nearest shave-ice stand, like **Matsumoto Shave Ice ★★**, 66–087 Kamehameha Hwy. (© **808/637-4827**). For 40 years, this small, humble shop operated by the Matsumoto family has served a popular rendition of the Hawaii-style snow cone flavored with tropical tastes. The cooling treat is also available at neighboring stores, some of which still shave the ice with a hand-crank device.

Just down the road are some of the fabled shrines of surfing—**Waimea Beach, Banzai Pipeline, Sunset Beach**—where some of the world's largest waves, reaching 20 feet and more, rise up between November and January. They draw professional surfers as well as reckless daredevils and hordes of onlookers, who jump in their cars and head north when word goes out that "surf's up." Don't forget your binoculars. For more details on North Shore beaches, see p. 206.

North Shore Surf and Cultural Museum Even if you've never set foot on a surfboard, you'll want to visit Oahu's only surf museum to learn the history of this Hawaiian sport of kings. This collection of memorabilia traces the evolution of surfboards from an enormous, weathered redwood board made in the 1930s for Turkey Love, one of Waikiki's legendary beach boys, to the modern-day equivalent—a light, sleek, racy foam-and-fiberglass board made for big-wave surfer Mark Foo, who drowned while surfing in California in 1994. Other items include classic 1950s surf-meet posters, 1960s surf-music album covers, old beach-movie posters with Frankie Avalon and Sandra Dee, early black-and-white photos by legendary surf photographer LeRoy Grannis, and trophies won by surfing's greatest. Curator Steve Gould is working on a new exhibit of surfing in the ancient Hawaiian culture, complete with Hawaiian artifacts.

At the North Shore Marketplace, 66–250 Kamehameha Hwy. (behind Kentucky Fried Chicken), Haleiwa. ✆ **808/637-8888.** www. captainrick.com/surf_museum.htm. Free admission. Tues–Sun noon–6pm (unless the surf is up).

MORE NORTH SHORE ATTRACTIONS

Puu o Mahuka Heiau ★ 📷 Go around sundown to feel the *mana* (sacred spirit) of this Hawaiian place. The largest sacrificial temple on Oahu, it's associated with the great Kaopulu-pulu, who sought peace between Oahu and Kauai. This prescient kahuna predicted that the island would be overrun by strangers from a distant land. In 1794, three of Capt. George Vancouver's men of the *Daedalus* were sacrificed here. In 1819, the year before New England missionaries landed in Hawaii, King Kamehameha II ordered all idols here to be destroyed.

A national historic landmark, this 18th-century *heiau,* known as the "hill of escape," sits on a 300-foot bluff overlooking Waimea Bay and 25 miles of Oahu's wave-lashed north coast—all the way to Kaena Point, where the Waianae Range ends in a spirit leap to the other world. The *heiau* appears as a

FROM TOP: The Puu o Mahuka Heiau; an Hawaiian moorhen.

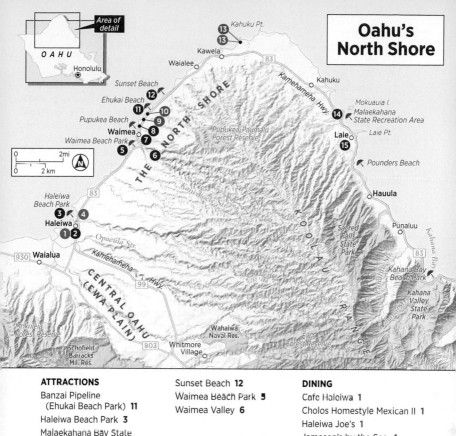

Oahu's North Shore

ATTRACTIONS

Banzai Pipeline
 (Ehukai Beach Park) **11**

Haleiwa Beach Park **3**

Malaekahana Bay State
 Recreation Area **14**

North Shore Surf and
 Cultural Museum **2**

Polynesian Cultural Center **15**

Puu o Mahuka Heiau **7**

Shark's Cove,
 Pupukea Beach Park **8**

Sunset Beach **12**

Waimea Beach Park **5**

Waimea Valley **6**

ACCOMMODATIONS

Ke Iki Beach Bungalows **9**

Santa's by the Sea **10**

Turtle Bay Resort **13**

DINING

Cafe Haleiwa **1**

Cholos Homestyle Mexican II **1**

Haleiwa Joe's **1**

Jameson's by the Sea **4**

Kua Aina **1**

Matsumoto Shave Ice **1**

Ola at Turtle Bay Resort **13**

Paradise Found Cafe **1**

Shrimp trucks **1**

21 Degrees North **13**

---

huge rectangle of rocks twice as big as a football field, with an altar often covered by the flower and fruit offerings left by native Hawaiians.

1 mile past Waimea Bay. Take Pupukea Rd. mauka (inland) off Kamehameha Hwy. at Foodland, and drive 1 mile up a switchback road. Bus: 52, then walk up Pupukea Rd.

Waimea Valley ★ ☺   For nearly 3 decades, this 1,875-acre park has lured visitors with activities from cliff diving and hula performances to kayaking and ATV tours. In 2008, the Office of Hawaiian Affairs took over and formed a new nonprofit corporation, Hiipaka, to run the park, with an emphasis on perpetuating and sharing the "living Hawaiian culture." A visit here offers a lush walk into the past. The valley is packed with archaeological sites, including the 600-year-old Hale O Lono, a *heiau* dedicated to the Hawaiian god Lono, which you'll find to the left of the entrance. The botanical collection has 35 different gardens, including super-rare Hawaiian species such as the endangered *Kokia cookei* hibiscus. The valley is also home to fauna such as the endangered Hawaiian moorhen; look for a black bird with a red face cruising in the ponds. The 150-acre Arboretum and Botanical Garden contains more than 5,000 species of tropical plants. Walk through the gardens (take the paved paths or dirt trails) and wind up at 45-foot-high Waimea Falls—bring your bathing suit and you can dive into the cold, murky water. The public is invited to hike the trails and spend a day in this quiet oasis. There are several free walking tours, at 10am, 11am, 1pm, and 2pm, plus cultural activities like lei making, kappa demonstrations, hula lessons, Hawaiian games and crafts, and music and storytelling.

59–864 Kamehameha Hwy. (✆) **808/638-7766.** www.waimeavalley.net. Admission $13 adults, $6 seniors and children 4–12. Daily 9am–5pm. Bus: 52.

SHOPPING A TO Z

Shopping competes with golf, surfing, and sightseeing as a bona fide Honolulu activity. And why not? The proliferation of top-notch made-in-Hawaii products, the vitality of the local crafts scene, and the unquenchable thirst for mementos of the islands lend respectability to shopping here.

Oahu is also a haven for mall mavens. More than 1,000 stores occupy the 11 major shopping centers on this island. From souvenir T-shirts to high fashion, posh European to down-home local, avant-garde to unspeakably tacky, Oahu's offerings are wide ranging indeed. But you must sometimes wade through oceans of schlock to arrive at the mother lode. Nestled amid the Louis Vuitton, Chanel, and Tiffany boutiques on Waikiki's Kalakaua Avenue are plenty of tacky booths hawking air-brushed T-shirts, gold by the inch, and tasteless aloha shirts.

The section that follows is not about finding cheap souvenirs or tony items from designer fashion chains; you can find these on your own. Rather, I offer a guide to finding those special treasures that lie somewhere in between.

Shopping in & Around Honolulu & Waikiki

ALOHA WEAR

One of Hawaii's lasting afflictions is the penchant tourists have for wearing loud, matching aloha shirts and muumuu. I applaud such visitors' good intentions (to act local), but no local resident would be caught dead in such a get-up. Muumuu and aloha shirts are wonderful, but the real thing is what island folks wear on Aloha Friday (every Fri), to the Brothers Cazimero Lei Day Concert (every May 1), or to work (where allowed). It's what they wear at home and to special parties where the invitation reads "Aloha Attire."

Aside from the vintage 1930s to 1950s Hawaiian wear found in collectibles shops and at swap meets, my favorite contemporary aloha-wear designer is Hawaii's **Tori Richard.** Another Hawaii-shirt icon is the **Tommy Bahama** line, which never calls its shirts "aloha shirts" but claims, instead, a Caribbean influence. The up-and-coming **Tiki** brand, quirky and distinctive, shows elements that hearken back to 1950s bowling shirts and Jimmy Dean charisma.

The best aloha shirts are pricey these days, going for $80 to $125. For the vintage look, **Avanti** (www.avantishirts.com) has a corner on the market with its stunning line of silk shirts and dresses in authentic patterns from the 1930s to 1950s. These shirts ($60–$105) boast all the qualities of a vintage silky, but without the high price or the web-thin fragility of an authentic antique. The dresses and other styles are the epitome of comfort and nostalgic good looks. The line is distributed in better boutiques and department stores throughout Hawaii.

Also popular is **Kahala Sportswear,** a well-known local company established in 1936. Kahala has faithfully reproduced, with astounding success, the linoleum-block prints of noted Maui artist Avi Kiriaty and the designs of other contemporary artists. Kahala is sold in department stores, surf shops, and stylish boutiques throughout Hawaii and the mainland.

Reyn Spooner is another source of attractive aloha shirts and muumuu in traditional and contemporary styles, with stores in the Ala Moana Center, Kahala Mall, and Sheraton Waikiki.

Well-known muumuu labels in Hawaii include **Mamo Howell,** with a boutique in Ward Warehouse, and **Princess Kaiulani** and **Bete** for the dressier muu, sold along with many other lines at Macy's and other department stores. The **Hilo Hattie** store in Ala Moana (✆ **808/973-3266;** www.hilohattie.com) is a gold mine of affordable aloha wear. Hilo Hattie's also offers free daily shuttle service from Waikiki to its retail outlet on Nimitz Highway (✆ **808/535-6500**). You'll find macadamia nuts, Hawaii coffees, and other souvenirs at these Hilo Hattie's stores.

ANTIQUES & COLLECTIBLES

Antique Alley   This narrow shop is chockablock with the passionate collections of several vendors, with an expanded assortment of old Hawaiian artifacts and surfing and hula nostalgia. The showcases include estate jewelry, antique silver, Hawaiian bottles, collectible toys, pottery, cameras, Depression glass, linens, plantation photos and ephemera, and a wide selection of nostalgic items from Hawaii and across America. At the rear is a small, attractive selection of Soiree clothing, made by Julie Lauster, including antique kimonos and obis. 1347 Kapiolani Blvd., behind Mattress Outlet. ✆ **808/941-8551.**

Bailey's Antiques & Aloha Shirts   Thousands of vintage, secondhand, and nearly new aloha shirts and other collectibles fill this eclectic emporium. It looks as though the owners regularly scour Hollywood movie costume departments for oddball gowns, feather boas, fur stoles, leather jackets, 1930s dresses, and scads of other garments from periods past. Bailey's has one of the largest vintage aloha-shirt collections in Honolulu, with prices ranging from inexpensive to sky-high. Old Levi's jeans, mandarin jackets, vintage vases, household items, shawls, purses, and an eye-popping assortment of bark-cloth fabrics (the real thing, not repros) are among the mementos in this monumental collection. 517 Kapahulu Ave. ✆ **808/734-7628.**

T. Fujii Japanese Antiques   This is a long-standing icon in Hawaii's antiques world and an impeccable source for ukiyo-e prints, scrolls, obis, Imari porcelain, tansu, tea-ceremony bowls, and screens, as well as contemporary ceramics from Mashiko and Kasama, with prices from $25 to $18,000. 1016 Kapahulu Ave. ✆ **808/732-7860.**

Store times vary; call in advance to make sure they are open.

BOOKSTORES

Barnes & Noble   With more than 150,000 titles, a respectable music department, and strong Hawaiiana, fiction, and new-release departments, as well as a popular coffee bar, Barnes & Noble has become the second home of Honolulu's casual readers and bibliophiles. In the Kahala Mall, 4211 Waialae Ave. ☏ **808/737-3323.**

Borders Borders is a beehive of literary activity, with weekly signings, prominent local and mainland musicians at least monthly, and special events almost daily that make this chain a major Honolulu attraction. There are two Borders on Oahu: Ward Centre, 1200 Ala Moana Blvd. (☏ 808/591-8995); and Waikele Center, 94–821 Lumiaina St. (☏ **808/676-6699**).

Rainbow Books & Records A little weird but totally lovable, especially among students and eccentrics (and insatiable readers), Rainbow Books is notable for its selection of popular fiction, records, and Hawaii-themed books, secondhand and reduced. It's about the size of a large closet, but you'll be surprised by what you'll find. 1010 University Ave. (at S. King St., next to Bank of Hawaii). ☏ **808/955-7994.**

EDIBLES

In addition to the stores listed below, I recommend **Executive Chef,** in the Ward Warehouse (☏ **808/596-2433**), and **Islands' Best** (☏ **808/949-5345**), in the Ala Moana Center. Both shops contain wide-ranging selections that include Hawaii's specialty food items.

If you're looking for a bakery, **Saint-Germain,** in Shirokiya at Ala Moana Center (☏ **808/955-1711**), and near Times Supermarket, 1296 S. Beretania St. (☏ **808/593-8711**), sells baguettes, country loaves, and oddball delicacies such as mini mushroom-and-spinach pizzas. The reigning queen of bakers, though, is **Cafe Laufer,** 3565 Waialae Ave. (☏ **808/735-7717;** p. 193). Nearby, old-timers still line up at **Sconees,** 1117 12th Ave. (☏ **808/734-4024**), formerly Bea's Pies, for the fantastic scones, pumpkin-custard pies, and Danishes. And don't forget **Cake Works,** 2820 S. King St. (☏ **808/946-4333**), a great place for quality cakes and European pastries.

Asian Grocery Asian Grocery supplies many of Honolulu's Thai, Vietnamese, Chinese, Indonesian, and Filipino restaurants with authentic spices, herbs, rice, noodles, produce, sauces, and adventurous ingredients. Browse among

fish **MARKETS**

Tamashiro Market, 802 N. King St., Kalihi (☏ **808/841-8047**), is the grandfather of fish markets and the ace in the hole for home chefs with bouillabaisse or paella in mind. A separate counter sells seaweed salad, prepared poke, Filipino and Puerto Rican ti-wrapped steamed rice, and dozens of other ethnic foods.

Neighbor islanders have been known to drive directly from the airport to **Yama's Fish Market,** 2332 Young St., Moiliili (☏ **808/941-9994**), for one of the best plate lunches in town. But Yama's is also known for its inexpensive fresh fish, tasty poke, and lomi salmon. Chilled beer, boiled peanuts, and fresh ahi sliced into sashimi are popular for local-style gatherings, sunset beach parties, and festive *pau hana* (after-work) celebrations. New standouts include a fabulous assortment of chocolate biscotti and chocolate-chip cookies, sweet-potato and custard mochi, and a *haupia* (coconut-pudding) pie layered with bright-purple Okinawa sweet potato.

the kaffir-lime leaves, tamarind and fish pastes, red and green chilies, curries, chutneys, lotus leaves, gingko nuts, jasmine and basmati rice, and shelf upon shelf of medium to hot sauces. 1319 S. Beretania St. (C) **808/593-8440.**

Don Quijote   Stands offering takeout sushi, Korean *kalbi,* pizza, Chinese food, flowers, Mrs. Fields cookies, and other items for self and home surround this huge emporium. Inside you'll find household products, a pharmacy, and inexpensive clothing, but it's the prepared foods and produce that excel. The fresh-seafood section is one of Honolulu's best, not far from where regulars line up for the bento lunches and individually wrapped sushi. When Kau navel oranges, macadamia nuts, Kona coffee, Chinese taro, and other Hawaii products are on sale, savvy locals arrive in droves to take advantage of the high quality and good value. Additional branches are at 345 Hahani St., Kailua ((C) **808/266-4400**); 850 Kam Hwy., Pearl City ((C) **808/453-5509**); and 94–144 Farrington Hwy., Waipahu ((C) **808/678-6800**). 801 Kaheka St. (C) **808/973-4800.**

Fujioka's Wine Merchants   Oenophiles flock here for a mouthwatering selection of single-malt Scotches, excellent Italian wines, and affordable, farm-raised caviar—food and libations for all occasions. Everyday wines, special-occasion wines, and esoteric wines are priced lower here than at most places. The wine-tasting bar at the rear of the store is a new attraction. At the Market City Shopping Center, 2919 Kapiolani Blvd., lower level. (C) **808/739-9463.**

Honolulu Chocolate Co.   Life's greatest pleasures are dispensed here with abandon: expensive gourmet chocolates made in Honolulu, Italian and Hawaiian biscotti, boulder-size turtles, truffles, chocolate-covered coffee beans, and jumbo apricots in white and dark chocolate, to name a few. You pay dearly for them, but the dark-chocolate-dipped macadamia nut clusters are beyond compare. At the Ward Centre, 1200 Ala Moana Blvd. (C) **808/591-2997.**

It's Chili in Hawaii   This is *the* oasis for chili-heads, a house of heat with endorphins aplenty and good food to accompany the hot sauces from around the world, including a fabulous selection of made-in-Hawaii products. Scoville units (measurements of heat in food) are the topic of the day in this shop, lined with thousands of bottles of hot sauces, salsas, and other chili-based products. Not everything is scorching, however; some items, like Dave's Soyabi and the limu-habanero sauce called Makai, are everyday flavor enhancers that can be used on rice, salads, meats, and pasta. If you're eating in, the fresh-frozen tamales, in several varieties (including meatless), are now in regular supply. 2080 S. King St., Ste. 105 (near McCully St., across the street from McDonald's). (C) **808/945-7070.**

Mauna Kea Marketplace Food Court   Hungry patrons line up for everything from pizza and plate lunches to quick, authentic, and inexpensive Vietnamese, Thai, Italian, Chinese, Japanese, and Filipino dishes. The best seafood fried rice comes from the woks of **Malee Thai/Vietnamese Cuisine**—it's perfectly flavored, with morsels of fish, squid, and shrimp. **Tandoori Chicken Cafe** serves a fount of Indian culinary pleasures, from curries and jasmine-chicken rice balls to spiced rounds of curried potatoes and a wonderful lentil dal. **Masa's** serves bento and Japanese dishes, such as miso eggplant, that are famous. You'll find the best dessert around at **Pho Lau,** which serves haupia (coconut pudding), tapioca, and taro in individual baskets made of pandanus. Join in the spirit of discovery at the produce stalls (pungent odors, fish heads, and chicken feet on counters—not for the squeamish). Vendors sell everything from fresh ahi and whole snapper to yams and taro, seaweed, and fruits and vegetables. 1120 Maunakea St., Chinatown. ☎ **808/524-3409.**

People's Open Markets Truck farmers from all over the island bring their produce to Oahu's neighborhoods in regularly scheduled, city-sponsored open markets, held Monday through Saturday at various locations. Among the tables of ong choy, choi sum, Okinawan spinach, opal basil, papayas, mangoes, seaweed, and fresh fish, you'll find homemade banana bread, Chinese pomelo (like large grapefruit), fresh fiddleheads (fern shoots) when available, and colorful, bountiful harvests from land and sea. Various sites around town; call to find the open market nearest you. ☎ **808/522-7088.** www. co.honolulu.hi.us/parks/programs/pom.

One of Oahu's People's Open Markets.

R. Field Wine Co. Foodland has won countless new converts since Richard Field—oenophile, gourmet, and cigar aficionado—moved his wine shop here. The thriving gourmet store offers gemlike vine-ripened tomatoes and juicy clementines, sparkling bags of Nalo gourmet greens, designer cheeses, caviar, Langenstein Farms macadamia nuts, vegetarian and salmon mousses, vinegars, and all manner of epicurean delights, including wines and single-malt Scotches. The warm, just-baked breads (rosemary–olive oil, whole-wheat, organic wheat, and others) baked on the premises with dough flown in from Los Angeles's famous La Brea Bakery are a huge hit. At the Foodland Super Market, 1460 S. Beretania St. ☎ **808/596-9463.**

Sushi Company It's not easy to find premium-grade *hamachi* (yellowtail), ahi, *ikura* (salmon roe), *ika* (cuttlefish), and other top-grade fresh ingredients in anything but a bona fide sit-down sushi bar. But here it is, a small sparkling gem of a

---

Health Food Stores

In the university district, **Down to Earth,** 2525 S. King St., Moiliili (☎ **808/947-7678**), sells organic vegetables and vegetarian bulk foods, with good prices, a strong selection of supplements and herbs, and a vegetarian juice-and-sandwich bar. But my favorite is nearby **Kokua Market,** 2643 S. King St. (☎ **808/941-1922**), a health food cooperative and Honolulu's best source for organic vegetables. It also has an excellent variety of cheeses; pastas and bulk grains; sandwiches, salads, and prepared foods; organic wines; and an expanded vitamin section.

Tiny but powerful, with a loyal clientele, **House of Health,** 1541 S. Beretania St. (☎ **808/955-6168**), has competitive prices and a wide selection of health food supplements. There's no produce, but there are frozen vegetarian foods, bulk grains, and healthful snacks.

sushi maker that sells fast-food sushi of non-fast-food quality, at great prices. Order ahead or wait while they make it. The combinations range from mini sets (27 pieces) to large-variety sets (43–51 pieces), ideal for picnics and potlucks. Sushi Company has one small two-person table; most of the business is takeout. 1111 McCully St. (at Young St.). ✆ **808/947-5411.**

FLOWERS & LEIS

At most lei shops, simple leis sell for $12 and up, deluxe leis for $25 and up. For a special-occasion designer bouquet or lei, you can't do better than Michael Miyashiro of **Rainforest Plantes et Fleurs** (Kilohana Sq., on Kapahulu Ave.; ✆ 808/738-0999). He's an ecologically aware, highly gifted lei maker—his leis are pricey but worth it. He custom-designs the lei for the person and occasion. Order by phone or stop by the Ward Warehouse, where his tiny shop is an oasis of green and beauty. Upon request, Miyashiro's leis will come in ti-leaf bundles called *pu'olo,* custom gift baskets (in woven green coconut baskets), and special arrangements. You can even request the card sentiments in Hawaiian, with English translations.

The other primary sources for flowers and leis are the shops lining the streets of Moiliili and Chinatown. Moiliili favorites include **Rudy's Flowers,** at Isenberg and South King streets (✆ 808/944-8844), a local institution with the best prices on roses, Micronesian ginger lei, and a variety of cut blooms. Across the street, **Flowers for a Friend,** 2739 S. King St. (✆ 808/955-4227), has good prices on leis, floral arrangements, and cut flowers. Nearby, **Flowers by Jr. and Lou,** 2652 S. King St. (✆ 808/941-2022), offers calla lilies, Gerbera daisies, a riot of potted orchids, and the full range of cut flowers along with its lei selection.

In Chinatown, lei vendors line Beretania and Maunakea streets, and the fragrances of their wares mix with the earthy scents of incense and ethnic foods. My top picks are **Lita's Leis,** 59 N. Beretania St. (✆ 808/521-9065), which has fresh puakenikeni, gardenias that last, and a supply of fresh and reasonable leis; **Lin's Lei Shop,** 1017-A Maunakea St. (✆ 808/537-4112), with creatively fashioned, unusual leis; and **Cindy's Lei Shoppe,** 1034 Maunakea St. (✆ 808/536-6538), with terrific sources for unusual leis such as feather dendrobiums, firecracker combinations, and everyday favorites like ginger, tuberose, orchid, and pikake. "Curb service" is available with phone orders. Just give them your car's color and model, and you can pick up your lei curbside—a great convenience on this busy street.

HAWAIIANA & GIFT ITEMS

My top recommendations are the **Academy Shop,** at the Honolulu Academy of Arts, 900 S. Beretania St. (✆ 808/523-8703), and the **Contemporary Museum Shop,** 2411 Makiki Heights Rd. (✆ 808/523-3447), two of the finest shopping stops on Oahu and worth a special trip whether or not you want to see the museums themselves. (And you will want to see the museums, especially the recently expanded Honolulu Academy of Arts.) The Academy Shop offers art books, jewelry, basketry, ethnic fabrics, native crafts from all over the world, posters and books, and fiber vessels and accessories. The Contemporary Museum Shop focuses on arts and crafts such as avant-garde jewelry, cards and stationery, books, home accessories, and gift items made by artists from Hawaii and across the country. I love the glammy selection of jewelry and novelties, such as the twisted-wire wall hangings.

Hula Supply Center   Hawaiiana meets kitsch in this shop's marvelous selection of Day-Glo cellophane skirts, bamboo nose flutes, T-shirts, hula drums, shell leis, feathered rattle gourds, lauhala accessories, fiber mats, and a wide assortment of pareu fabrics. Although hula dancers shop here for their dance accouterments, it's not all serious shopping. This is fertile ground for souvenirs and memorabilia of Hawaii, rooted somewhere between irreverent humor and cultural integrity. 2338 S. King St. (at Isenberg St.), Moiliili. 🕿 **808/941-5379.**

Native Books & Beautiful Things 🎁   This *hui* (association) of artists and craftspeople is a browser's paradise featuring a variety of Hawaiian items from musical instruments to calabashes, jewelry, leis, and books. You'll find contemporary Hawaiian clothing; handmade koa journals; Hawaii-themed home accessories; lauhala handbags and accessories; jams, jellies, and food products; etched glass; hand-painted fabrics and clothing; stone poi pounders; and other high-quality gift items. Some of Hawaii's finest artists in all craft media have their works available here on a regular basis, and the Hawaiian-book selection is tops. At the Ward Warehouse, 1050 Ala Moana Blvd. 🕿 **808/596-8885.**

Nohea Gallery   A fine showcase for contemporary Hawaii art, Nohea celebrates the islands with thoughtful, attractive selections like pit-fired raku, finely turned wood vessels, jewelry, handblown glass, paintings, prints, fabrics (including Hawaiian-quilt cushions), and furniture. Nohea's selection is always evolving and growing, with 90% of the works by Hawaii artists. At the Ward Warehouse, 1050 Ala Moana Blvd. (🕿 **808/596-0074**); and at the Moana Surfrider, 2365 Kalakaua Ave. (🕿 **808/923-6644**). www.noheagallery.com.

Shop Pacifica   Local crafts, lauhala and Cook Island woven coconut, Hawaiian music tapes and CDs, pareu, and a vast selection of Hawaii-themed books anchor this gift shop. Hawaiian-quilt-cushion kits, jewelry, glassware, seed and Niihau shell leis, cookbooks, and many other gift possibilities will keep you occupied in between stargazing in the planetarium and pondering the shells and antiquities of the esteemed historical museum. At the Bishop Museum, 1525 Bernice St. 🕿 **808/848-4158.**

SHOPPING CENTERS

Ala Moana Center   Nearly 400 shops and restaurants sprawl over several blocks (and 1.8 million sq. ft. of store space), catering to every imaginable need, from over-the-top upscale (**Tiffany, Chanel, St. John**) to mainstream chains such as **Gap** and **Banana Republic.** Many of the shops here are the familiar names of mainland chains, such as **DKNY, Old Navy,** and **J. Crew on the Island.** The three-story, superluxe **Neiman Marcus,** which opened in 1998, was a bold move in Hawaii's troubled economy and has retained its position as the shrine of the fashionistas. But there are practical touches in the center, too, such as banks, a foreign-exchange service (**Travelex**), a post office, several optical companies (including 1-hr. service by **LensCrafters**), a **Foodland Super Market,** a branch of **Longs Drugs,** and a handful of photo-processing services. The smaller, locally owned stores are scattered among the behemoths, mostly on the ground floor. Department stores such as **Macy's** sell fashion, food, cosmetics, shoes, and household needs. Need shoes? They're a kick at **Nordstrom,** and **Walking Co.** has first-rate comfort styles by Mephisto, Ecco, and Naot.

A good stop for gifts is **Islands' Best,** which spills over with Hawaiian-made foodstuffs, ceramics, fragrances, and more. **Splash! Hawaii** is a reliable source for women's swimwear. For aloha shirts and men's swimwear, try **Macy's, Town & Country Surf, Reyn's,** or the terminally hip **Hawaiian Island Creations.** Lovers of Polynesian wear and pareu shouldn't miss **Tahiti Imports.** The **food court** is abuzz with dozens of stalls purveying Cajun food, ramen, pizza, plate lunches, vegetarian fare, green tea and fruit freezes (like frozen yogurt), panini, and countless other treats. Open Monday through Saturday from 9:30am to 9pm, Sunday from 10am to 7pm. 1450 Ala Moana Blvd., Honolulu. © **808/ 955-9517.** www.alamoanacenter.com. Bus: 8, 19, or 20. Various shuttle services also stop here. For Waikiki Trolley information, see "Getting Around" (p. 138).

Aloha Tower Marketplace The refurbished Aloha Tower, once the tallest structure in Honolulu, still stands high over the Marketplace complex. Dining and shopping prospects abound: **Aloha Tower Collections** gift shop, **Hawaiian Ukulele Company, Sunglass King, Don Ho's Island Grill, Chai's Island Bistro,** and **Gordon Biersch Brewery Restaurant** (p. 184). There is a perpetual parking shortage here, and if you do manage to find a parking spot, the rates are sky high. Take the trolley if you can. Retail shops are open Monday through Saturday from 9am to 9pm, Sunday from 9am to 6pm; dining and entertainment are generally open daily from 8am to midnight. 1 Aloha Tower Dr., on the waterfront between piers 8 and 11, Honolulu Harbor. © **808/528-5700,** or 808/566-2333 for entertainment hotline. www.alohatower.com. Various trolleys stop here; for a direct ride from Waikiki, take the free Hilo Hattie trolley or the Waikiki Red Line Trolley, which continues on to Hilo Hattie's in Iwilei.

DFS Galleria "Boat days" is the theme at this newly renovated (to the tune of $65 million) Waikiki emporium, a three-floor extravaganza of shops ranging from the superluxe (like **Givenchy** and **Coach**) to the very touristy. Fragrances and cosmetics make a big splash at **DFS.** There are some great Hawaii food products, ranging from the incomparable **Big Island Candies** shortbread cookies to a spate of coffees and preserves. There are multitudes of aloha shirts and T-shirts, a virtual golf course, surf and skate equipment, a terrific Hawaiian-music department, and a labyrinth of fashionable stores once you get past the Waikiki Walk. **Starbucks** serves up a host of Hawaiian coffees. *Warning:* Some sections are duty-free and, therefore, restricted to international travelers only. Open daily from 9am to 11pm. 330 Royal Hawaiian Ave. (corner of Kalakaua and Royal Hawaiian aves.), Waikiki. © **808/931-2655.** www.dfsgalleria.com.

Kahala Mall Chic, manageable, and unfrenzied, Kahala Mall is home to some of Honolulu's best shops. Located east of Waikiki in the posh neighborhood of Kahala, the mall has everything from a small **Macy's** to chain stores such as **Banana Republic**—nearly 100 specialty shops (including dozens of eateries and eight movie theaters) in an enclosed, air-conditioned area. **Starbucks** serves up hot java, and smoothie lovers form long lines at **Jamba Juice.** For specialty stores, my picks of the mall's best and brightest are the **Compleat Kitchen;** the **Paperie,** with an impressive selection of stationery, cards, napkins, and paper goods; and the sprawling **Whole Foods Market.** Open Monday through Saturday from 10am to 9pm, Sunday from 10am to 5pm. 4211 Waialae Ave., Kahala. © **808/732-7736.** www.kahalamallcenter.com.

Royal Hawaiian Shopping Center

After 2 years and $84 million in renovations, a larger, more upscale shopping center opened in 2007 with 110 stores, restaurants, and entertainment on four levels. The open-air mall even has a garden grove of 70 coconut trees with a pond, an artesian fountain, a stream running through, and a performance area. The most exciting addition is the $15-million, 760-seat theater, with moving stages and acrobatic rigging. After the show, half of the theater's seating retracts to create a nightclub that can hold up to 1,000 people. *Upscale* is the operative word here. Although there are drugstores, lei stands, restaurants, and food kiosks, the

Hula lessons at the Royal Hawaiian Center.

most conspicuous stores are the designer boutiques (**Bvlgari, Ferrari,** and more) that cater largely to visitors from Japan. Open daily from 10am to 10pm. 2201 Kalakaua Ave., Honolulu. © **808/922-0588.** www.royalhawaiiancenter.com.

Waikele Premium Outlets   Just say the word *Waikele* and my eyes glaze over. So many shops, so little time! There are two sections to this sprawling discount shopping mecca: the **Waikele Premium Outlets,** some 51 retailers offering designer and name-brand merchandise, and the **Waikele Value Center** across the street, with another 25 stores more practical than fashion oriented (**Eagle Hardware, Sports Authority**). The 64-acre complex has made discount shopping a travel pursuit in itself, with tours for visitor groups and carloads of neighbor islanders and Oahu residents making pilgrimages from all corners of the state. They come to hunt down bargains on everything from perfumes, luggage, and hardware to sporting goods, fashions, vitamins, and china. Examples: **Saks Fifth Avenue, Anne Klein, Banana Republic,** and the ultrachic **Barneys.** Open Monday through Friday from 9am to 9pm, Sunday from 10am to 6pm. 94-790 Lumiaina St., Waikele (about 20 miles from Waikiki). © **808/676-5656.** www. premiumoutlets.com. Take H-1 west toward Waianae and turn off at exit 7. Bus: 42 from Waikiki to Waipahu Transit Center, then 433 from Transit Center to Waikele. To find out which companies offer shopping tours with Waikiki pickups, call the Information Center at © **808/ 678-0786.**

Ward Centre   Although it has a high turnover and a changeable profile, Ward Centre is a standout for its concentration of restaurants and shops. **Kakaako Kitchen** is as popular as ever, with lanai views of the sprawling **Pier 1 Imports** across the street. **Borders** is action central, bustling with browsers. Ward Centre's shops also include **Crazy Shirts Factory Outlet** for T-shirts, **Honolulu Chocolate Co.** (see "Edibles," earlier in this chapter). **Nordstrom Rack** and **Office Depot** have sprouted in a new development area that also includes a 16-theater movie megaplex. All these establishments are part of developer Victoria Ward's Kakaako projects, which take up several blocks in this area: Ward Centre, Ward Farmers Market, Ward Village, Ward Gateway Center, and Ward

Warehouse. Open Monday through Saturday from 10am to 9pm, Sunday from 10am to 5pm. 1200 Ala Moana Blvd. ℂ **808/591-8411.** www.victoriaward.com.

Ward Entertainment Center   This large, multiblock complex includes Ward Centre, mentioned above, and Ward Warehouse, mentioned below, at the corner of Auahi and Kamakee streets. The complex has undergone enormous expansion, beginning with a new 16-movie megaplex and a retail-and-restaurant complex, with eateries like **Dave & Buster's** (with virtual golf, games, interactive entertainment, bars, and a restaurant), **Buca di Beppo, Wahoo's Fish Taco,** and **Cold Stone Creamery.** Open Monday through Saturday from 10am to 10pm, Sunday from 10am to 9pm. Auahi and Kamakee sts. ℂ **808/591-8411.** www.victoria ward.com.

Ward Warehouse   Older than its sister property, Ward Centre, and endowed with an endearing patina, Ward Warehouse remains a popular stop for dining and shopping. **Native Books & Beautiful Things** and the **Nohea Gallery** (see "Hawaiiana & Gift Items," above, for both) are excellent sources for quality Hawaii-made arts and crafts. Other recommended stops include **C. June Shoes** for designer footwear and **Mamo Howell** for distinctive aloha wear. Open Monday through Saturday from 10am to 9pm, Sunday from 10am to 5pm. 1050 Ala Moana Blvd. ℂ **808/591-8411.** www.victoriaward.com.

SURF & SPORTS

The surf-and-sports shops scattered throughout Honolulu are a highly competitive lot, with each trying to capture your interest (and dollars). The top sources for sports gear and accessories in town are **McCully Bicycle & Sporting Goods,** 2124 S. King St. (ℂ **808/955-6329**), with everything from bikes and fishing gear to athletic shoes and accessories, along with a stunning selection of sunglasses; and **The Bike Shop,** 1149 S. King St., near Piikoi Street (ℂ **808/ 596-0588**), excellent for cycling and backpacking equipment for all levels, with major camping lines such as North Face, MSR, and Kelty. It's a must-stop for avid cyclists coming to Oahu, as it's the hub of cycling news on the island. The **Sports Authority,** at 333 Ward Ave. (ℂ **808/596-0166**) and at Waikele Center (ℂ **808/677-9933**), is a discount megaoutlet offering clothing, bicycles, and equipment.

Surf shops, centers of fashion as well as definers of daring, include **Local Motion,** in Waikiki, Waikele Premium Outlets (see above), and in the Windward Mall (ℂ **808/263-7873**). Local Motion is the icon of surfers and skateboarders, both professionals and wannabes; the shop offers surfboards, T-shirts, aloha and casual wear, boogie boards, and countless accessories for life in the sun. Hawaiian Island Creations is another supercool surf shop offering sunglasses, surf wear, and accessories galore.

Shopping in Windward Oahu

Windward Oahu's largest shopping complex is **Windward Mall,** 46–056 Kamehameha Hwy., in Kaneohe (ℂ **808/235-1143;** www.windwardmall.com), open Monday through Saturday from 10am to 9pm and Sunday from 10am to 5pm. The 100 stores and services at this standard suburban mall include **Macy's** and **Sears,** health stores, airline counters, surf shops, **LensCrafters,** and a 10-screen theater complex. A small food court serves pizza, Chinese fare, tacos, and other morsels.

All of the listings below can be found in the town of **Kailua,** whose shopping nexus is formed by **Longs Drugs** and **Macy's** department store, located side by side on Kailua Road. The *malassada* mecca of Oahu is **Agnes Portuguese Bake Shop,** 46 Hoolai St. (© **808/262-5367**). Malassadas are sugary Portuguese dumplings, like doughnuts without holes. With its abundance of free parking and a menu of homemade soups, artisan breads, and unique pastries, Agnes is a Kailua treasure.

Alii Antiques of Kailua II   Abandon all restraint, particularly if you have a weakness for vintage Hawaiiana. Koa lamps and rattan furniture from the 1930s and 1940s, hula nodders, rare 1940s koa tables, Roseville vases, Don Blanding dinnerware, and a breathtaking array of vintage etched-glass vases and trays are some of the items in this unforgettable shop. Across the street, the owner's wife runs **Alii Antiques of Kailua,** which is chockablock with jewelry, clothing, Bauer and Fiesta Ware, linens, Bakelite bracelets, and floor-to-ceiling collectibles. 9-A Maluniu Ave., Kailua. © **808/261-1705.**

BookEnds   BookEnds is the quintessential neighborhood bookstore, run by a pro who buys good books and knows how to find the ones she doesn't have. There are more than 60,000 titles here, new and used, from *Celtic Mandalas* to the full roster of current bestsellers. Volumes on childcare, cooking, and self-improvement; a hefty periodicals section; and mainstream and offbeat titles are among the treasures to be found. 600 Kailua Rd., Kailua. © **808/261-1996.**

Heritage Antiques & Gifts   This Kailua landmark is known for its selection of Tiffany-style lamps ($200–$2,000). The mind-boggling inventory also includes European, Asian, American, local, and Pacific Island collectibles. The shop is fun, the people are friendly, and the selection is diverse enough to appeal to the casual as well as serious collector. Glassware, china, and estate, costume, and fine jewelry are among the items of note. Heritage has its own jeweler who does custom designs and repairs, plus a stable of woodworkers who turn out custommade koa rockers and hutches to complement the selection of antique furniture. 670 Kailua Rd. © **808/261-8700.**

Shopping on the North Shore: Haleiwa

Like Hilo on the Big Island and Maui's upcountry Makawao, Haleiwa means serious shopping for those who know that the unhurried pace of rural life can conceal vast material treasures. Ask the legions of townies who drive an hour each way just to stock up on wine and clothes at Haleiwa stores. (Of course, a cooler is de rigueur for perishables.) Below are some Haleiwa highlights.

ARTS, CRAFTS & GIFT ITEMS

Haleiwa's shops and galleries display a combination of marine art, watercolors, sculptures, and a plethora of crafts trying to masquerade (quite transparently) as fine art. This is the town for gifts, fashions, and surf stuff—mostly casual, despite some very high price tags. **Haleiwa Gallery** (© **808/637-3368**), next door to the North Shore Marketplace, displays a lot of local art of the nonmarine variety, and some of it is very appealing.

   Global Creations Interiors, 66–079 Kamehameha Hwy. (© **808/637-1505**), offers casual clothes as well as international imports for the home, including Balinese bamboo furniture and colorful Yucatán hammocks. There are gifts and crafts by 115 local potters, painters, and artists of other media.

North Shore Glass Blowers, in the North Shore Marketplace (© 808/637-4853), is an art-glass studio featuring the work of Tracy and Denise Jacob. Additional glass art can be found in the same shopping center at **Oceans in Glass** (© 808/637-3366), which has sculptures of dolphins, sea turtles, humpback whales, sharks, and colorful reef fish. You can watch as local artists create these beautiful sculptures in their studios within the gallery.

EDIBLES

Haleiwa is best known for its roadside shave-ice stands: the famous **Matsumoto Shave Ice ★★**, 66–087 Kamehameha Hwy. (© 808/637-4827), with the perennial queue snaking along Kamehameha Highway, and nearby **Aoki's.** Shave ice is the popular island version of a snow cone, topped with your choice of syrups, such as strawberry, rainbow, root beer, vanilla, or passion fruit. For a real exotic treat, order the *li hing mui* flavor. Aficionados get it with a scoop of ice cream and sweetened black adzuki beans nestled in the middle.

Tiny, funky **Celestial Natural Foods,** 66–443 Kamehameha Hwy. (© 808/637-6729), is the health foodies' Grand Central for everything from wooden spine massagers to health supplements, produce, cosmetics, and bulk foods.

FASHION

Although Haleiwa used to be an incense-infused surfer outpost where zoris and tank tops were the regional uniform and the Beach Boys and Ravi Shankar the music of the day, today it's one of the top shopping destinations for those with unconventional tastes. Specialty shops abound.

Top-drawer **Silver Moon Emporium,** in the North Shore Marketplace, 66–250 Kamehameha Hwy. (© 808/637-7710), features the terrific finds of owner Lucie Talbot-Holu. Exquisite clothing and handbags, reasonably priced footwear, hats straight out of *Vogue,* jewelry, scarves, and a full gamut of other treasures pepper the attractive boutique. The entire line of chic Brighton accessories—shoes, handbags, fragrance, belts, and jewelry—is a prized addition.

In addition to Silver Moon, highlights of the prominent North Shore Marketplace include **Patagonia** (© 808/637-1245), for high-quality surf, swim, hiking, kayaking, and all-around adventure wear; **North Shore Swimwear** (© 808/637-6859), for excellent mix-and-match bikinis and one-piece suits, custom ordered or off the rack; and **Jungle Gems** (© 808/637-6609), the mother lode of gemstones, crystals, silver, and beadwork.

Nearby **Oogenesis Boutique,** 66–249 Kamehameha Hwy. (© 808/637-4422), in the southern part of Haleiwa, features a storefront lined with vintage-looking dresses that flutter prettily in the North Shore breeze.

SURF SHOPS

Haleiwa's ubiquitous surf shops are the best on earth, surfers say. At the top of the heap is **Northshore Boardriders Club,** in the North Shore Marketplace, 66–250 Kamehameha Hwy. (© 808/637-5026), the mecca of the board-riding elite, with sleek, fast, elegant, and top-of-the-line boards designed by North Shore legends such as longboard shapers Barry Kanaiaupuni, John Carper, Jeff Bushman, and Pat Rawson. The store is also a testing ground for the newest and hottest trends in surf wear put out by retail giant Quicksilver.

Raging Isle Sports, also in the North Shore Marketplace (© 808/637-7707), is the surf-and-cycle center of the area, with everything from wet suits and surfboards to surf gear and clothing for men, women, and children. The adjoining surfboard factory puts out custom-built boards of high renown. There's also a large inventory of mountain bikes for rent.

A longtime favorite among old-timers is the newly expanded **Surf & Sea Surf Sail & Dive Shop,** 62–595 Kamehameha Hwy. (© 808/637-9887), a flamboyant roadside structure just over the bridge, with old wood floors and a tangle of surf- and swimwear, T-shirts, surfboards, boogie boards, fins, watches, sunglasses, and more; you can also rent surf and snorkel equipment here.

Tropical Rush, 62–620-A Kamehameha Hwy. (© 808/637-8886), has a huge inventory of surf and swim gear: surfboards, longboards, body boards, Sector 9 skateboards, and slippers and swimwear for men and women. T-shirts, hats, sunglasses, and visors are among the scads of cool gear, and you can rent equipment and arrange surf lessons, too.

OAHU AFTER DARK

Nightlife in Hawaii begins at sunset, when all eyes turn westward to see how the day will end. Sunset viewers always seem to bond in the mutual enjoyment of a natural spectacle. People in Hawaii are fortunate to have an environment that encourages this cultural ritual.

On Friday and Saturday at 6:30pm in winter and at 7pm in summer, as the sun casts its golden glow on the beach, **Kuhio Beach,** where Kalakaua Avenue intersects with Kaiulani, eases into evening with hula dancing and a torch-lighting ceremony. This is a thoroughly delightful, free weekend offering. Start off earlier with a picnic basket and walk along the oceanside path fronting Queen's Surf, near the Waikiki Aquarium. (You can park along Kapiolani Park or near the zoo.) There are few more pleasing spots in Waikiki than the benches at water's edge at this Diamond Head end of Kalakaua Avenue. A short walk across the intersection of Kalakaua and Kapahulu avenues, where the sea wall and daring boogie boarders attract hordes of spectators, takes you to the Duke Kahanamoku statue on Kuhio Beach and the nearby Wizard Stones. Here you can view the torch-lighting and hula, and gear up for the strolling musicians who amble down Kalakaua Avenue every Friday from 8 to 10pm. The musicians begin at Beachwalk Avenue at the Ewa (western) end of Waikiki and end up at the statue.

The Bar Scene

ON THE BEACH Waikiki's beachfront bars offer many possibilities, from the **Mai Tai Bar** (© 808/923-7311) at the Royal Hawaiian (p. 151), a few feet from the sand, to the unfailingly enchanting **House Without a Key** (© 808/923-2311) at the Halekulani

The Duke Kahanamoku statue on Kuhio Beach.

(p. 149), where the breathtaking **Kanoelehua Miller** dances hula to the riffs of Hawaiian steel-pedal guitar under a century-old kiawe tree with the sunset and ocean glowing behind her—a romantic, evocative, nostalgic scene. It doesn't hurt, either, that the Halekulani happens to make the best mai tais in the world. This place has the after-dinner hours covered, too, with light jazz by local artists from 8:30pm to 12:30am nightly (see "Live Blues, R & B, Jazz & Pop," below).

Another great bar for watching the sun sink into the Pacific is **Duke's Waikiki** (② 808/922-2268; www.dukeswaikiki.com), in the Outrigger Waikiki on the Beach (p. 151). The outside Barefoot Bar is perfect for sipping a tropical drink, watching the waves and sunset, and listening to music. It can get crowded, so get here early. Hawaii sunset music is usually from 4 to 6pm on weekends, and there's live entertainment nightly from 9:30pm to midnight.

ALOHA TOWER MARKETPLACE   The landmark Aloha Tower at Honolulu Harbor, once Oahu's tallest building, has always occupied Honolulu's prime downtown location—on the water, at a naturally sheltered bay, near the business and civic center of Honolulu. Since its construction, the Aloha Tower Marketplace, 1 Aloha Tower Dr. (on the waterfront between piers 8 and 11; ② 808/528-5700), has gained popularity as an entertainment and nightlife spot, with more than 100 shops and restaurants, including several venues for Honolulu's leading musical groups.

At the recently expanded **Gordon Biersch Brewery Restaurant** (p. 184), where a new stage area was added, diners swing to jazz, blues, and island riffs. Most notable, however, are **Don Ho's Island Grill** (p. 184) and **Chai's Island Bistro,** Honolulu's hottest nightspots (see "Hawaiian Music," below, for more on Chai's).

DOWNTOWN   The downtown scene is awakening from a long slumber, thanks to the performances at the Hawaii Theatre and the popular Nuuanu Avenue block parties, courtesy of some tenacious entrepreneurs who want everyone to love Nuuanu as much as they do. **Hanks Café,** on Nuuanu Avenue between Hotel and King streets (② 808/526-1410), is a tiny, kitschy, friendly pub with live music nightly, open-mic nights, and special events that attract great talent and a supportive crowd. On some nights, the music spills out into the streets and it's so packed you have to press your nose against the window to see what you're missing. At the makai end of Nuuanu, toward the pier, **Murphy's Bar & Grill** (② 808/531-0422) is a popular downtown ale house and media haunt that has kept Irish eyes smiling for years.

The Club Scene

The nightclub scene in Waikiki and Honolulu is just as hot as the sun-kissed beaches during the day. It's more laid-back than in big cities like New York, dress is casual (though no slippers, tank tops, or athletic wear), and there's no point to even showing up until midnight.

Twice the size of the Wave and filled with dancing, darts, pool, and a sports bar with huge TVs is the **Pipeline,** 805 Pohukaina St., in Kakaako (② 808/589-1999; www.pipelinecafehawaii.com). Patrons here tend to be young (you can get in at 18 years old, but some events specify 21 and over) and dressed to go clubbing. The cover is generally $7 to $10; concerts are around $20 to $30.

The 20-something crowd, visitors, and military personnel head to **Moose McGillycuddy's,** 310 Lewers St., in Waikiki (© **808/923-0751;** www.moosemcgillycuddys.com). Downstairs is a cafe serving breakfast, lunch, and dinner; upstairs is a happening entertainment and dance club. Tuesday is $1 drink night, but with a $5 cover (it's the busiest night of the week).

At the edge of Chinatown is something straight out of 1940s film noir: **Indigo's,** 1121 Nuuanu Ave. (© **808/521-2900;** www.indigo-hawaii.com), which serves sizzling food during the day, turns to cool jazz in the early evening, and progresses to late-night DJs spinning Top 40, disco, rock, funk, and more.

Another Chinatown "in" spot is **thirtyninehotel,** 39 N. Hotel St., between Smith Street and Nuuanu Avenue (© **808/599-2552;** www.thirtyninehotel. com), where live jazz and visiting and resident DJs rock all night (but during the day, it morphs into an art gallery, open Tues–Sat 4–9pm, featuring contemporary local artists). The door is unmarked, with only the address to tell you where you are. Enter and walk up the stairs to the second floor. The cover is $8.

Next door to thirtyninehotel is **Bar 35,** 35 N. Hotel St. (© **808/537-3535**), whose claim to fame is its 110 beers available, plus wine, cocktails, and even pizzas. You must be 21 to enter (strictly enforced).

Rumours Nightclub, in the lobby of the Ala Moana Hotel, 410 Atkinson Dr. (© **808/955-4811**), is the disco of choice for those who remember Paul McCartney as something other than Stella's father. The theme changes by the month, but generally, it's Salsa on Thursdays; the "Big Chill" '60s, '70s, and '80s music on Friday; and the "Little Chill" on Saturday. A spacious dance floor, a good sound system, and Top 40 music draw a mix of generations.

Hawaiian Music

Oahu has several key spots for Hawaiian music. The **Brothers Cazimero** remain one of Hawaii's most gifted duos (Robert on bass, Roland on 12-string guitar), appearing every Wednesday at 7pm at a leading venue for Hawaiian entertainment, **Chai's Island Bistro,** in the Aloha Tower Marketplace (© **808/585-0011;** www.chaisislandbistro.com). Also at Chai's: Robert Cazimero plays by himself on the piano every Tuesday at 7pm, and **Jerry Santos** and **Hula** perform on Monday at 7pm. If you're here on May 1, Lei Day, try to make it to the special concert the Brothers Caz give every year at the **Waikiki Shell.** Locals dress up in their leis and best aloha shirts, the air smells like pikake and pakalana, and you might even see the moon rise over Diamond Head.

The **Hilton Hawaiian Village** (© **808/949-4321**) has live music nightly at the Tapa Bar and at the Tropics Bar and Grill. Plus every Friday night is the King's Jubilee with fireworks starting at 7pm. The Waikiki Styke Luau also features Hawaiian entertainment with dinner 5 nights a week (Sun–Thurs) for $95.

Nearby, the Moana Surfrider offers a nightly program of live Hawaiian music and piano in its **Banyan Veranda** (© **808/922-3111**), which surrounds an islet-size canopy of banyan tree and roots where Robert Louis Stevenson loved to linger. The Banyan Veranda serves afternoon tea, a sunset buffet, and cocktails.

My best advice for lovers of Hawaiian music is to scan the local dailies or the *Honolulu Weekly* (www.honoluluweekly.com) to see if and where the following Hawaiian entertainers are appearing: **Kekuhi Kanahele,** an accomplished,

A performance at the Banyan Veranda.

award-winning chanter and *kahiko* (ancient hula) dancer; **Ho'okena,** a symphonically rich quintet featuring **Manu Boyd,** one of the most prolific songwriters and chanters in Hawaii; **Keali'i Reichel,** premier chanter, dancer, and award-winning recording artist; **Robbie Kahakalau,** another award-winning musician; **Kapena,** for contemporary Hawaiian music; **Na Leo Pilimehana,** a trio of angelic Hawaiian singers; the **Makaha Sons of Niihau,** pioneers in the Hawaiian cultural renaissance; **Fiji,** the stage name of artist George Veikoso, one of the most popular entertainers in Hawaii, with a unique blend of Hawaiian, Fijian, and other Polynesian music; and slack-key guitar master **Raymond Kane.**

For the best in hula, check the dailies for *halau* (hula school) fundraisers, which are always authentic, enriching, and local to the core. Consider the gods beneficent if you happen to be here when the hula halau of **Frank Kawaikapuo-kalani Hewett** is holding its annual fundraiser. It's a rousing, inspired family effort that always features the best in ancient and contemporary Hawaiian music.

Live Blues, R & B, Jazz & Pop

The blues are alive and well in Hawaii, with quality acts (both local and from the mainland) drawing enthusiastic crowds. Past performers include **Junior Wells, Willie & Lobo,** and **War,** with surprise appearances by the likes of **Bonnie Raitt.** The best-loved Oahu venue is **Anna Bannana's,** 2440 S. Beretania St., between University Avenue and Isenberg Street (© **808/946-5190**), still rocking after 30 years in the business, with reggae, blues, and rock—plus video games and darts.

To find out what's happening in the jazz scene while you're in town, check out www.honolulujazzscene.net. Jazz lovers should watch for the **Great Hawaiian Jazz Blowout,** every March at Mid-Pacific Institute's Bakken Hall, at the south end of Honolulu, near Diamond Head. **Duc's Bistro** (© **808/531-6325;** p. 185), downtown, has live jazz on Friday and Saturday. Thursday, vocalist Mihana Souza performs Hawaiian music.

Tops in taste and ambience is the perennially alluring **Lewers Lounge,** in the Halekulani, 2199 Kalia Rd. (© **808/923-2311;** www.halekulani.com). Recent renovations (including comfy intimate seating around the pillars) make this a great spot for contemporary jazz Wednesday through Saturday from 8:30pm to midnight, and with expert mixologist Dale DeGroff (the "king of cocktails") now the hotel's director of beverages, the drinks are better than ever. Be sure to try the Hpnotiq Liqueur, a blend of premium vodka, cognac, and fruit juices from France.

Outside Waikiki, the **Veranda,** at the Kahala Hotel & Resort, 5000 Kahala Ave. (© **808/739-8888;** www.kahalaresort.com), is a popular spot for the over-40 crowd, with nightly jazz music and a dance floor.

Around town, watch for **Sandy Tsukiyama,** a gifted singer (Brazilian, Latin, jazz) and one of Honolulu's great assets, and jazz singers **Rachel Gonzales** and **Loretta Ables Sayre.** Other groups in jazz, blues, and R & B include **Blue Budda, Bongo Tribe, Secondhand Smoke, Bluzilla, Piranha Brothers,** and the **Greg Pai Trio.**

Showroom Acts & Revues

Showroom acts that have maintained a following include *The Magic of Polynesia* (© 808/971-4321; www.magicofpolynesia.com), a show with illusionist **John Hirokana** nightly at the Waikiki Beachcomber Hotel at 7pm (dinner show $72–$118 adults, $48–$58 children 4–11; show only $45 adults, $28 children 4–11). This was also the home of Hawaiian entertainer Don Ho, who passed away in 2007.

Across Kalakaua Avenue at the **Outrigger Waikiki on the Beach,** you can catch the nightclub act of the **Society of Seven** (© 877/877-1222; www.societyofseven.com), a blend of skits, Broadway hits, popular music, and costumed musical acts that's into its third decade—no small feat for performers. Shows are Wednesday through Saturday at 7pm (dinner show $75 adults and children, show only $43 adults, $25 ages 2–20).

Still sizzling in the Polynesian revue world is the Sheraton Princess Kaiulani's **Creation—A Polynesian Odyssey** (© 808/922-5811), in the hotel's second-floor Ainahau Showroom. Produced by Tihati, the state's largest entertainment company, the show is a theatrical journey of fire dancing, special effects, illusions, hula, and dances from Hawaii and the South Pacific. Shows are Tuesday, Thursday, Friday, Saturday, and Sunday (dinner show starts at $95 adults, $71 children 5–12; cocktail show $55 adults).

GET down WITH ARTAFTERDARK

On the last Friday of every month (except Nov–Dec), the place to be after the sun goes down is **ARTafterDARK,** a *pau hana* (after-work) mixer in the **Honolulu Academy of Arts,** 900 S. Beretania St., that brings residents and visitors together around a theme combining art with food, music, and dancing. In addition to the exhibits in the gallery, ARTafterDARK features visual and live performances. Previous themes have ranged from "Plant Rice"—with rice and sake tastings, rice dishes, Asian beers, live Asian fusion music, and a tour of the *Art of Rice* exhibit—to "'80s Night," "Turkish Delights," "Cool Nights, Hot Jazz and Blues," and "Havana Heat."

The entrance fee is $10. The party gets going around 6pm and lasts till 10pm. The crowd ranges from 20s to 50s, and the dress is everything from jeans and T-shirts to designer cocktail-party attire. For more information, call © **808/532-8700** or go to www.artafterdark.org.

The best in comedy is **Andy Bumatai,** who performs local stand-up sketches that will have you not only understanding local residents, but also screaming with laughter. Another excellent comic is **Frank De Lima.** If he's playing anywhere on Oahu, it's worth the drive to see this comic genius, who sings, dances, and performs routines that will have you laughing until your sides hurt.

The Performing Arts

"Aloha shirt to Armani" is how I describe the night scene in Honolulu—mostly casual, but with ample opportunity to part with your flip-flops and dress up.

Audiences have grooved to the beat of off-Broadway percussion hit Stomp and have enjoyed the talent of Tap Dogs, Momix, the Jim Nabors Christmas show, the Hawaii International Jazz Festival, the American Repertory Dance Company, barbershop quartets, and John Ka'imikaua's halau—all at the **Hawaii Theatre,** 1130 Bethel St., downtown (© **808/528-0506;** www.hawaiitheatre. com). The theater is still basking in its renaissance following a 4-year, $22-million renovation. The neoclassical Beaux Arts landmark features a 1922 dome, 1,400 plush seats, a hydraulically elevated organ, breathtaking murals, and gilt galore, all working to create an atmosphere that's making the theater a leading multipurpose center for the performing arts.

The **Honolulu Symphony Orchestra** (www.honolulusymphony.com) has booked some of its performances at the new theater, but it still performs at the Waikiki Shell and the **Neal Blaisdell Concert Hall** (© **808/591-2211;** www. blaisdellcenter.com). Meanwhile, the highly successful **Hawaii Opera Theatre,** in its 41st season (past hits have included *La Bohème, Carmen,* and *Aïda*), still draws fans to the Neal Blaisdell Concert Hall, as do Hawaii's four ballet companies: **Hawaii Ballet Theatre, Ballet Hawaii, Hawaii State Ballet,** and **Honolulu Dance Theatre.** Contemporary performances by **Dances We Dance** and the **Iona Pear Dance Company,** a strikingly creative group performing Butoh (a contemporary dance form that originated in Japan), are worth tracking down if you love the avant-garde.

HAWAII, THE BIG ISLAND

T

he Big Island of Hawaii—the island that lends its name to the entire 1,500-mile-long Hawaiian archipelago—is where Mother Nature pulled out all the stops. Simply put, it's spectacular.

The Big Island has it all: fiery volcanoes and sparkling waterfalls, black-lava deserts and snowcapped mountain peaks, tropical rainforests and alpine meadows, a glacial lake and miles of golden, black, and even green-sand beaches. The Big Island has an unmatched diversity of terrain and climate. A 50-mile drive will take you from snowy winter to sultry summer, passing through spring or fall along the way. The island looks like the inside of a barbecue pit on one side and a lush jungle on the other.

The Big Island is the largest island in the Hawaiian chain (4,038 sq. miles—about the size of Connecticut), the youngest (800,000 years), and the least populated (with 30 people per sq. mile). It has the highest peaks in the Pacific, the most volcanoes of any Hawaiian island, and the newest land on earth.

Five volcanoes—one still erupting—have created this continental island, which is growing bigger daily. At its heart is snowcapped Mauna Kea, the world's tallest sea mountain (measured from the ocean floor), complete with its own glacial lake. Mauna Kea's nearest neighbor is Mauna Loa (or "Long Mountain"), creator of one-sixth of the island; it's the largest volcano on earth, rising 30,000 feet out of the ocean floor (of course, you can see only the 13,796 ft. that are above sea level). Kilauea's eruptions make the Big Island bigger every day—and, if you're lucky, you can stand just a few feet away and watch it do its work.

Steeped in tradition and shrouded in the primal mist of creation, the Big Island radiates what the Hawaiians call *mana*, a sense of spirituality that's still apparent in the acres of petroglyphs etched in the black lava, the numerous *heiau* (temples), the burial caves scattered in the cliffs, the sacred shrines both on land and in the sea, and even the sound the wind makes as it blows across the desolate lava fields.

The Big Island is not for everyone, however. It refuses to fit the stereotype of a tropical island. Some tourists are taken aback at the sight of stark fields of lava or black-sand beaches. You must remember that it's *big* (expect to do lots of driving). And you may have to go out of your way if you're looking for traditional tropical beauty, such as a quintessential white-sand beach.

On the other hand, if you're into watersports, this is paradise. The two tall volcanoes mean the water on the leeward side is calm 350 days a year. The underwater landscape of caves, cliffs, and tunnels attracts a stunning array of colorful marine life. The island's west coast is one of the best destinations in the world for big-game fishing. And its miles of remote coastline are a kayaker's dream of caves, secluded coves, and crescent-shaped beaches reachable only by sea.

On land, hikers, bikers, and horseback riders can head up and down a volcano, across beaches, into remote valleys, and through rainforests without seeing another soul. Bird-watchers are rewarded with sightings of the rare, rapidly dwindling native birds of Hawaii. Golfers can find nirvana on a wide variety of courses.

FACING PAGE: **Kilauea Volcano.**

This is the least-explored island in the Hawaiian chain, but if you're looking to get away from it all and back to nature in its most primal state, that might be the best thing about it. Where else can you witness fiery creation and swim with dolphins, ponder the stars from the world's tallest mountain and catch a blue marlin, downhill-ski and surf the waves in a single day? You can do all this and more on only one island in the world: the Big Island of Hawaii.

ORIENTATION

Most people arrive on the Big Island at Kona International Airport, on the island's west coast. From the airport, Kilauea volcano is to the right (counterclockwise), and the ritzy Kohala Coast is to the left (clockwise). (If you land in Hilo, of course, the volcano is clockwise and Kohala is counterclockwise.)

Arriving

The Big Island has two major airports for jet traffic between the islands, in Kona and Hilo.

The **Kona International Airport** receives direct overseas flights from Japan on **Japan Airlines** (℃ 800/525-3663; www.jal.co.jp/en) and from Vancouver on **Air Canada** (℃ 888/247-2262; www.aircanada.com). Carriers from the mainland include **American Airlines** (℃ 800/433-7300; www.aa.com), with flights from Los Angeles; **Delta Air Lines** (℃ 800/221-1212; www.delta. com), with nonstop flights from Salt Lake City (originating in Atlanta); **Northwest Airlines** (℃ 800/225-2525; www.nwa.com), with flights from Seattle; **US Airways/American West** (℃ 800/428-4322; www.usairways.com), with flights from Phoenix; and **United Airlines** (℃ 800/241-6522; www.united. com), with nonstop flights from Denver, Los Angeles, and San Francisco, and a direct flight from Chicago.

The **Hilo International Airport** used to have a direct flight from Oakland via ATA, but with the demise of that airline, it is now served only by interisland carriers.

If you cannot get a direct flight to the Big Island, you'll have to pick up an interisland flight in Honolulu. **Hawaiian Airlines** (℃ 800/367-5320; www.hawaiianair.com) and **go!** (℃ 888/I-FLY-GO-2 [435-9462]; www.iflygo. com) offer jet service to both Big Island airports.

All major rental companies have cars available at both airports; see chapter 11 for a full list. Also see "Getting There & Getting Around" (p. 74) for details on interisland travel, insurance, and driving in Hawaii. For shuttle services from the Kona Airport, see "Getting Around," later in this chapter.

Visitor Information

The **Big Island Visitors Bureau** (℃ 800/648-2441; www.bigisland.org) has two offices on the Big Island: one at 250 Keawe St., Hilo, HI 96720 (℃ **808/961-5797;** fax 808/961-2126) and the other at 65–1158 Mamalahoa Hwy., Ste. 37-B, Kamuela, HI 96743 (℃ **808/885-1655**).

On the west side of the island, there are two additional sources to contact for information: the **Kohala Coast Resort Association,** 68–1310 Mauna Lani Dr., Ste. 101, Kohala Coast, HI 96743 (℃ **800/318-3637** or 808/885-6414; fax 808/ 885-6145; www.kohalacoastresorts.com); and **Destination Kona Coast,** P.O. Box 2850, Kailua-Kona, HI 96745 (℃ **808/329-6748;** fax 808/328-0614). The

The Big Island

Alenuihaha Channel

PACIFIC OCEAN

NORTH KOHALA

KOHALA COAST

HAMAKUA COAST

KONA COAST

HAWAII VOLCANOES NATIONAL PARK

KAU DESERT

PUNA REGION

H.V.N.P.

Hawi
Kapaau
Waipio Valley
Kukuihaele
Honokaa
Paauilo
Kohala Forest Reserve
Kohala
Kawaihae
Hawaii Belt Rd.
Waimea (Kamuela)
Kawaihae Bay
Puako
Walkoloa
Anaehoomalu Bay
Lae Hou
Kekaha Kai State Park
Puuwaawaa Forest Reserve
Kona Int'l. Airport
Kalaoa
Kailua-Kona
Holualoa
Kahaluu
Kahaluu Reach
Keauhou
Honalo
Kealakekua
Captain Cook
Honaunau
Saddle Rd.
Mauna Kea Forest Reserve
Mauna Kea
Pohakuloa Military Reservation
Mauna Loa Forest Reserve
Mauna Loa
Upper Waiakea Forest Reserve
Kau Forest Reserve
Hawaii Belt Rd.
Manowaialee Forest Reserve
Laupahoehoe
Homomu
Pepeeken Pt.
Pepeekeo
Papaikou
Hilo Forest Reserve
Wainaku
Hilo Bay
Leleiwi Beach Park
Hilo
Hilo Int'l. Airport
Puki Bay
Kaloli Pt.
Keaau
Maunaloa Macadamia Nut Factory
Kurtistown
Hawaiian Paradise Park
Mountain View
Pahoa
Iliani Estates
Vulcano
Olaa Forest Reserve
Kilauea
Chain of Craters
Pahala
Manuka Natural Area Reserve
Ocean View
Naalehu
Kauna Pt.
Ka Lae
Green Sand Beach

Pololu Valley Lookout
Waipio Valley Lookout
Pacific Ocean

South Kona Forest Reserve

Inset map

Kauai
Oahu
Honolulu
Molokai
Lanai
Maui

0 — 100 mi
0 — 100 km

PACIFIC OCEAN

Hawaii "The Big Island"

0 — 10 mi
0 — 10 km

N

Kailua-Kona.

Big Island's best free tourist publications are *This Week,* the *Beach and Activity Guide,* and *101 Things to Do on Hawaii the Big Island.* All three offer lots of useful information, as well as discount coupons on a variety of island adventures. Copies are easy to find all around the island.

The Island in Brief

THE KONA COAST ★★   Kona is synonymous with great coffee and big fish—both of which are found in abundance along this 70-mile-long stretch of black-lava-covered coast.

A collection of tiny communities devoted to farming and fishing along the sun-baked leeward side of the island, the Kona Coast has an amazingly diverse geography and climate for such a compact area. The oceanfront town of **Kailua-Kona,** a quaint fishing village that now caters more to tourists than to boat captains, is its commercial center. The lands of Kona range from stark, black, dry coastal desert to cool, cloudy upcountry where glossy green coffee, macadamia nuts, tropical fruit, and a riotous profusion of flowers covers the steep, jagged slopes. Among the coffee fields, you'll find the funky, artsy village of **Holualoa.** Higher yet in elevation are native forests of giant trees filled with tiny, colorful birds, some perilously close to extinction. About 7 miles south of Kailua-Kona, bordering the ocean, is the resort area of **Keauhou,** a suburban-like series of upscale condominiums, a shopping center, and million-dollar homes.

Kona means "leeward side" in Hawaiian—and that means full-on sun every day of the year. This is an affordable vacation spot: An ample selection of midpriced condo units, peppered with a few older hotels and B&Bs, lines the shore, which is mostly rocky lava reef, interrupted by an occasional pocket beach. Here, too, stand two world-class resorts: Kona Village, the site of one of the best luau in the islands, and the Four Seasons at Hualalai, one of Hawaii's luxury retreats.

Away from the bright lights of the town of Kailua lies the rural **South Kona Coast,** home to coffee farmers, macadamia-nut growers, and people escaping to the country. The serrated South Kona Coast is indented with numerous bays, from **Kealakekua,** a marine-life preserve that's the island's best diving spot, down to **Honaunau,** where a national historical park recalls the days of old Hawaii. Accommodations in this area are mainly B&Bs. This coast is a great place to stay if you want to get away from crowds and experience peaceful country living. You'll be within driving distance of beaches and the sights of Kailua.

THE KOHALA COAST ★★   Fringes of palms and flowers, brilliant blankets of emerald green, and an occasional flash of white buildings are your only clues from the road that this black-lava coast north of Kona is more than bleak and barren. But, oh, is it! Down by the sea, pleasure domes rise like palaces no Hawaiian king ever imagined. This is where the Lear-jet set escapes to play in world-class beachfront hotels set like jewels in the golden sand. But you don't have to be a billionaire to visit the Waikoloa, Mauna Lani, and Mauna Kea resorts: The fabulous beaches and abundant historic sites are open to the public, with parking and other facilities, including restaurants, golf courses, and shopping, provided by the resorts.

NORTH KOHALA ★★   Seven sugar mills once shipped enough sugar from three harbors on this knob of land to sweeten all the coffee in San Francisco. **Hawi,** the region's hub and home to the Kohala Sugar Co., was a flourishing town. Today Hawi's quaint, 3-block-long strip of sun-faded, false-fronted

Holualoa.

buildings and 1920s vintage shops lives on as a minor tourist stop in one of Hawaii's most scenic rural regions, located at the northernmost reaches of the island. Hidden in the oceanfront rolling hills lies the **Hawaii Island Retreat** (p. 320), one of Hawaii's most luxurious and relaxing boutique hotels with a fabulous spa. North Kohala is most famous as the birthplace of King Kamehameha the Great; a statue commemorates the royal site. It's also home to the islands' most sacred site, the 1,500-year-old **Mookini Heiau.**

WAIMEA (KAMUELA) ★★   This old upcountry cow town on the northern road between the coasts is set in lovely country: rolling green pastures, wide-open spaces dotted by *puu* (hills), and real cowpokes who ride mammoth **Parker Ranch,** Hawaii's largest working ranch. The town is also headquarters for the **Keck Telescope,** the largest and most powerful in the world. Waimea is home to several affordable B&Bs, and Merriman's restaurant is a popular foodie outpost at Opelo Plaza.

THE HAMAKUA COAST ★★   This emerald coast, a 52-mile stretch from Honokaa to Hilo on the island's windward northeast side, was once planted with sugar cane; it now blooms with flowers, macadamia nuts, papayas, and marijuana, also known as *pakalolo* (still Hawaii's number-one cash crop). Resort-free and nearly without beaches, the Hamakua Coast still has a few major destinations. Picture-perfect **Waipio Valley** has impossibly steep sides, taro patches, a green riot of wild plants, and a winding stream leading to a broad, black-sand beach; and the historic plantation town of **Honokaa** is making a comeback as the B&B capital on the coastal trail. **Akaka Falls** and **Laupahoehoe Beach Park** are also worth seeking out.

HILO ★★   When the sun shines in Hilo, it's one of the most beautiful tropical cities in the Pacific. Being here is an entirely different kind of island experience: Hawaii's largest metropolis after Honolulu is a quaint, misty, flower-filled city of Victorian houses overlooking a half-moon bay, with a restored historic downtown and a clear view of Mauna Loa's often snow-capped peak. Hilo catches everyone's eye until it rains—it rains a lot in Hilo, and when it rains, it pours.

Hilo is one of America's wettest towns, with 128 inches of rain annually. It's ideal for growing ferns, orchids, and anthuriums, but not for catching a few rays. But there's lots to see and do in Hilo, so grab your umbrella. The rain is warm (the temperature seldom dips below 70°F/21°C), and there's usually a rainbow afterward.

Hilo's oversize airport and hotels are remnants of a dream: The city wanted to be Hawaii's

Keck Observatory.

Hilo.

major port of entry. That didn't happen, but the facilities here are excellent. Hilo is also Hawaii's best bargain for budget travelers. It has plenty of hotel rooms—most of the year, that is. Hilo's magic moment comes in spring, the week after Easter, when hula *halau* (schools) arrive for the annual **Merrie Monarch Hula Festival** hula competition (see "Hawaii Calendar of Events," on p. 65). This is a full-on Hawaiian spectacle and a wonderful cultural event. Plan ahead if you want to go: Tickets are sold out by the first week in January, and the hotels within 30 miles are usually booked solid.

The Merrie Monarch Hula Festival.

Hilo is also the gateway to Hawaii Volcanoes National Park; it's just an hour's drive up-slope.

HAWAII VOLCANOES NATIONAL PARK ★★★ This is America's most exciting national park, where a live volcano called Kilauea erupts daily. If you're lucky, it will be a spectacular sight. At other times, you may not be able to see the molten lava at all, but there's always a lot to see and learn. Ideally, you should plan to spend 3 days at the park exploring the trails, watching the volcano, visiting the rainforest, and just enjoying this spectacular place.

But even if you have only a day, get here—it's worth the trip. Bring your sweats or jacket (honest!); it's cool up here, especially at night.

If you plan to dally in the park, plan to stay in the sleepy hamlet of **Volcano Village,** just outside the national park entrance. Several terrifically cozy B&Bs, some with fireplaces, hide under tree ferns in this cool mountain hideaway. The tiny highland community (elevation 4,000 ft.), first settled by Japanese immigrants, is now inhabited by artists, soul-searchers, and others who like the crisp air of Hawaii's high country. It has just enough civilization to sustain a good life: a few stores, a handful of eateries, a gas station, and a golf course.

KA LAE: SOUTH POINT ★★   This is the Plymouth Rock of Hawaii, where the first Polynesians arrived in seagoing canoes, probably from the Marquesas Islands or Tahiti, around A.D. 500. You'll feel like you're at the end of the world on this lonely, windswept place, the southernmost point of the United States (a geographic claim that belonged to Key West, Florida, before Hawaii became a state in 1959). Hawaii ends in a sharp, black-lava point. Bold 500-foot cliffs stand against the blue sea to the west and shelter the old fishing village of Waiahukini, which was populated from A.D. 750 until the 1860s. Ancient canoe moorings, shelter caves, and *heiau* (temples) poke through windblown pili grass. The east coast curves inland to reveal a green-sand beach, a world-famous anomaly that's accessible only by foot or four-wheel-drive. For most, the only reason to venture down to the southern tip is to experience the empty vista of land's end.

Everything in **Naalehu** and **Waiohinu,** the two wide spots in the road that pass for towns at South Point, claims to be the southernmost this or that. Except for a monkeypod tree planted by Mark Twain in 1866, there's not much else to crow about. There is, thankfully, a gas station, along with a couple of places to eat, a fruit stand, and a few B&Bs. These end-of-the-world towns are just about as far removed from the real world as you can get.

The Sunday Farmer's Market at Volcano Village.

A monkeypod tree.

Ka Lae.

GETTING AROUND

BY CAR You'll need a rental car on the Big Island; not having one will really limit you. All major car-rental firms have agencies at the airports and at the Kohala Coast resorts; for a complete list, see chapter 11. For tips on insurance and driving rules, see "Getting There & Getting Around" (p. 74).

There are more than 480 miles of paved road on the Big Island. The highway that circles the island is called the **Hawaii Belt Road.** On the Kona side of the island, you have two choices: the scenic "upper" road, **Mamalahoa Highway** (Hwy. 190), or the speedier "lower" road, **Queen Kaahumanu Highway** (Hwy. 19). The road that links east to west is called **Saddle Road** (Hwy. 200). Saddle Road looks like a shortcut from Kona to Hilo, but it usually doesn't make for a shorter trip. It's rough, narrow, and plagued by bad weather; as a result, most rental-car agencies forbid you from taking their cars on it.

BY TAXI Taxis are readily available at both Kona and Hilo airports. In Kailua-Kona, call **Kona Airport Taxi** (① 808/329-7779). In Hilo, call **Ace-1** (① 808/935-8303). Taxis will take you wherever you want to go on the Big Island, but it's prohibitively expensive to use them for long distances.

BY BUS & SHUTTLE For transportation from the Kona Airport, there are shuttle services that will come when you call them. Door-to-door service is provided by **SpeediShuttle** (① 808/329-5433; www.speedishuttle.com). Some sample per-person rates from the airport: $28 to Kailua-Kona, $27 to the Four Seasons, and $55 to the Mauna Lani Resort.

The islandwide bus system, the **Hele-On Bus** (① 808/961-8744; www.heleonbus.org), offers the best deal on the island—it's free—but, unfortunately, does not serve either airport. The recently created Kokua Zone allows riders in West Hawaii to travel from as far south as Ocean View to as far north as Kawaihae for free; in East Hawaii, riders can ride free from Pahoa to Hilo. Visitors can pick up the free, air-conditioned bus from the Kohala hotels and ride south to shopping destinations like Costco, Lanihau Center, Kmart, Wal-Mart, and Keauhou Shopping Center. The Hele-On Bus also stops at the Kona Community Hospital and provides wheelchair access.

In the Keauhou Resort area, there's a free, open-air, 44-seat **Keauhou Resort Trolley,** with stops at Keauhou Bay, Sheraton Keauhou Bay Resort & Spa, Kona Country Club, Keauhou Shopping Center, Outrigger Keauhou Beach Resort, and Kahaluu Beach Park. In addition, three times a day the trolley travels round-trip, via Alii Drive to Kailua Village, stopping at White Sands Beach on the way. For information, contact the concierge at either the Sheraton Keauhou Bay Resort & Spa (✆ 808/930-4900) or the Outrigger Keauhou Beach Resort (✆ 808/322-3411).

[FastFACTS] THE BIG ISLAND

American Express The office on the Big Island has closed. To report lost or stolen traveler's checks, call ✆ 800/221-7282.

Dentists In an emergency, contact **Dr. Craig C. Kimura** at Kamuela Office Center (✆ 808/885-5947). In Kona, call **Dr. Frank Sayre** at Frame 10 Center, behind Lanihau Shopping Center on Palani Road (✆ 808/329-8067).

Doctors In Hilo, the **Hilo Medical Center** is at 1190 Waianuenue Ave. (✆ 808/974-4700); on the Kona side, call **Hualalai Urgent Care,** 75-1028 Henry St., across the street from Safeway (✆ 808/327-HELP [4357]). Closed on Sunday.

Emergencies For ambulance, fire, and rescue services, dial ✆ 911. The **Poison Control Center** hot line is ✆ 800/222-1222 (will route you to a center based on the area code of the phone you are calling from, but all centers can help).

Hospitals Hospitals offering 24-hour urgent-care facilities include the **Hilo Medical Center,** 1190 Waianuenue Ave., Hilo (✆ 808/974-4700); **North Hawaii Community Hospital,** Waimea (✆ 808/885-4444); and **Kona Community Hospital,** on the Kona Coast in Kealakekua (✆ 808/322-9311).

Internet Access The cheapest access is at the

Hawaii Public Library, www.librarieshawaii.org (for your closest location and more info on reserving a computer).

Police Dial ✆ 911 in case of emergency; otherwise, call the **Hawaii Police Department** at ✆ 808/935-3311 islandwide.

Post Office All calls to the U.S. Postal Service can be directed to ✆ 800/275-8777. There are local branches in Hilo at 1299 Kekuanaoa Ave., in Kailua-Kona at 74-5577 Palani Rd., and in Waimea on Lindsey Road.

Weather For conditions on the Big Island, call ✆ 808/961-5582. For marine forecasts, call ✆ 808/935-9883.

WHERE TO STAY

Before you reach for the phone to reserve your accommodations, refer to "Tips on Accommodations" (p. 101) to make sure you book the kind of place you want. Also remember that the Big Island is really big; see "The Island in Brief," earlier in this chapter, to decide where to base yourself.

Remember to add Hawaii's 12.42% in taxes to your final bill. In the listings below, all rooms come with a full private bathroom (with tub or shower) and free parking unless otherwise noted.

For additional information on bed-and-breakfasts, contact the **Hawaii Island B&B Association,** P.O. Box 1890, Honokaa, HI 96727 (no phone; www.stayhawaii.com). If you would like to go "on the road," contact **Island RV & Safari Activities** (📞 **800/406-4555** or 808/334-0464; www.islandrv.com). It offers weekly rentals of a 21-foot class-C motor home, which sleeps up to four, for $2,200. Included in the package are airport pickup, all linens, barbecue grill, all park registration fee permits, your last night in a hotel (Royal Kona Resort), and help with planning your itinerary and booking activities.

The Kona Coast

IN & AROUND KAILUA-KONA

For a detailed map of central Kailua Kona, see p. 311.

Very Expensive

Four Seasons Resort Hualalai at Historic Kaupulehu ★★★ ☺ This is a great place to relax in the lap of luxury. Low-rise clusters of oceanview villas nestle between the sea and the greens of a new golf course. The Four Seasons has no concrete corridors and no massive central building—it looks like a two-story town house project, clustered around three seaside swimming pools and a snorkeling pond. Guest rooms are furnished in Pacific tropical style: light gold walls, hand-knotted rugs over clay-colored slate, and rattan-and-bamboo settees. The ground-level rooms have bathrooms with private outdoor gardens—surrounded by black lava rock and a bamboo roof—so you can shower under the tropical sun or nighttime stars. All units have new flatscreen TVs.

If you can afford it, this is the place to be pampered—sit back and relax as the pool attendants bring you ice-cold water, chilled towels, and fresh-fruit kabobs. Other pluses include a Hawaiian history and cultural interpretive center, complimentary scuba lessons, a complimentary valet, twice-daily maid service, and a multilingual concierge. The spa has been selected by *Condé Nast Traveler* magazine as the world's best resort spa. One of the five pools is a saltwater pond carved out of black-lava rock with reef fish swimming about. The new Lava Lounge offers exotic martinis, entertainment, and the best view for watching the sun sink into the Pacific.

Your kids will be pampered, too—the complimentary Kids for All Seasons program features plenty of activities to keep the little ones busy. The resort also offers children's menus in all restaurants, a game room, videos, complimentary infant gear (cribs, highchairs, and so on), and more.

72-100 Kaupulehu Dr., Kailua-Kona, HI 96745. 📞 **888/340-5662** or 808/325-8000. Fax 808/325-8053. www.fourseasons.com/hualalai. 243 units. $595–$1,035 double; from $1,300 suite. Extra person $170. Children 18 and under stay free in parent's room (maximum occupancy 3 people; couples with more than 1 child must get 2 rooms). Valet parking $20 per day. AE, DC, DISC, MC, V. **Amenities:** 3 restaurants (including Pahu i'a, p. 333; and Beach Tree Bar & Grill,

p. 333); 2 bars (w/nightly entertainment ranging from contemporary Hawaiian to pianist); baby-sitting; complimentary year-round children's program; concierge; complete fitness center; 18-hole Jack Nicklaus signature golf course exclusively for guests and residents; 5 exquisite out-door pools (including a giant infinity pool and a lap pool); room service; award-winning spa; 8 tennis courts (4 lit for night play); watersports equipment rentals; 6 whirlpools. *In room:* A/C, TV/DVD, fridge, hair dryer, wired Internet or Wi-Fi ($14 per day).

Kona Village Resort ★ ☺   This fabulous resort, which had begun to fall into disrepair in the past few years, was recently sold (to computer magnate Michael Dell), and it appears that the new owners are pouring much-needed funds into maintenance of this oceanside Polynesian village. Since 1965, those seeking a great escape have crossed the black-lava fields to find refuge at this exclusive, one-of-a-kind haven by the sea with its wonderful dark-sand beach. Unfortu-nately, longtime guests of the Village have noted a remarkable decline in the once-sterling aloha service. Veteran employees still have that gracious welcoming attitude, but the newer employees (who are quickly becoming a majority) don't seem able to match the high standards that made the resort famous. Dining ser-vice is rushed and, in some cases, practically nonexistent for a luxury resort.

But yes, that blissful languor still settles in as you surrender to the peaceful, low-key atmosphere here. The resort resembles an eclectic Polynesian village, with historic sites and beaches. Make sure you request one of the "renovated" thatched-roof, island-style bungalows—and, if money is no object, ask for one of my favorite bungalows, the Lava Tahitians, each of which has a hot tub on the deck overlooking the ocean. The Village is no longer located on a secluded cove (guests at the nearby Four Seasons can now walk the beach) and will likely get even more crowded—houses and condos are scheduled to be built. On the plus side, however: The room rate includes breakfast, lunch, and dinner—the luau here is fabulous—plus all snorkeling equipment, other beach toys, and sched-uled activities throughout the day for kids and teens (there's even a special dinner seating for kids so parents can have a quiet meal alone). They now have a "Bed & Breakfast" option, room and breakfast only, starting at $410.

P.O. Box 1299, Kailua-Kona, HI 96745. ☎ **800/367-5290** or 808/325-5555. Fax 808/325-5124. www.konavillage.com. 125 units. $555–$1,180 double. Extra person $250 per adult (13 and up), $185 per child 10–12, $140 per child 5–9. Children 4 and under stay free in parent's room. Pack-ages available. Rates include all meals (including luau) for 2 adults, tennis, watersports, and wal-king tours. AE, DC, MC, V. **Amenities:** 2 restaurants (plus Wed and Fri luau, p. 419); 3 bars (w/live entertainment most nights); babysitting; extensive children's program (especially in summer, when it extends past dinnertime); concierge; fitness room; Internet access; 2 Jacuzzis; 2 outdoor pools; tennis courts; complimentary use of watersports equipment. *In room:* Fridge, hair dryer, no phone.

Expensive
Outrigger Royal Sea Cliff ☺   Families will love these luxuriously appointed apartments and their affordable rates. The architecturally striking, five-story white buildings that make up this resort/condo complex, 2 miles from Kailua-Kona, are stepped back from the ocean for maximum views and privacy. (The downside is that there's no ocean swimming here, but the waves are near enough to lull you to sleep, and there's a decent swimming beach about a mile away.) Atrium gardens and hanging bougainvillea soften the look. The spacious units are furnished in tropical rattan with a full kitchen; a washer/dryer; and a large, sunny lanai. There are barbecue and picnic facilities for oceanfront dining.

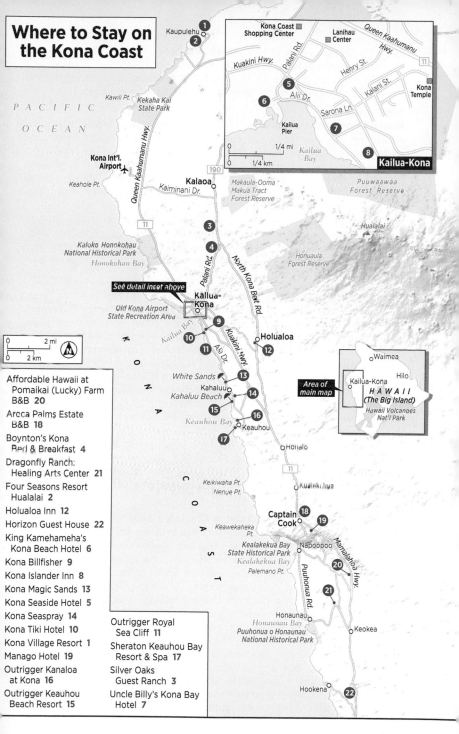

Where to Stay on the Kona Coast

Kaupulehu ❶ ❷

PACIFIC OCEAN

Kawili Pt. Kekaha Kai State Park

Kona Int'l. Airport

Keahole Pt.

Kaiminani Dr.

Kalaoa

190

Makaula-Ooma Makua Tract Forest Reserve

Puuwaawaa Forest Reserve

Queen Kaahumanu Hwy.

11

Hualalai

Kaloko Honokohau National Historical Park
Honokohau Bay

Palani Rd.

❸
❹

North Kona Belt Rd.

Honuaula Forest Reserve

See detail inset above

Kailua-Kona

Old Kona Airport State Recreation Area

Kailua Bay

❾
❿
⓫

Kuakini Hwy.

Holualoa
⓬

Alii Dr.

White Sands ⓭
Kahaluu
Kahaluu Beach ⓮
⓯
⓰
Keauhou Bay ⓱ Keauhou

Area of main map

Kailua-Kona

Waimea
Hilo

HAWAII (The Big Island)

Hawaii Volcanoes Nat'l Park

Honalo

11

Kuakini Hwy.

Keikiwaha Pt.
Nenue Pt.

Captain Cook ⓲ ⓳

Keawekaheka Pt.

Kealakekua Bay State Historical Park
Kealakekua Bay
Palemano Pt.

Napoopoo

Mamalahoa Hwy.

⓴

㉑

Honaunau
Honaunau Bay
Puuhonua o Honaunau National Historical Park

Puuhonua Rd.

Keokea

Hookena ㉒

Kailua-Kona (detail inset)

Kona Coast Shopping Center
Lanihau Center

Kuakini Hwy.

Palani Rd.

Henry St.

Queen Kaahumanu Hwy.

11

❺
❻

Alii Dr.

Kalani St.

Kona Temple

Sarona Ln.

Kailua Pier
❼

Kailua Bay

❽

Kailua-Kona

0 1/4 mi
0 1/4 km

Listings

Affordable Hawaii at Pomaikai (Lucky) Farm B&B **20**

Areca Palms Estate B&B **18**

Boynton's Kona Bed & Breakfast **4**

Dragonfly Ranch: Healing Arts Center **21**

Four Seasons Resort Hualalai **2**

Holualoa Inn **12**

Horizon Guest House **22**

King Kamehameha's Kona Beach Hotel **6**

Kona Billfisher **9**

Kona Islander Inn **8**

Kona Magic Sands **13**

Kona Seaside Hotel **5**

Kona Seaspray **14**

Kona Tiki Hotel **10**

Kona Village Resort **1**

Manago Hotel **19**

Outrigger Kanaloa at Kona **16**

Outrigger Keauhou Beach Resort **15**

Outrigger Royal Sea Cliff **11**

Sheraton Keauhou Bay Resort & Spa **17**

Silver Oaks Guest Ranch **3**

Uncle Billy's Kona Bay Hotel **7**

75–6040 Alii Dr., Kailua-Kona, HI 96740. ℂ **800/688-7444** or 808/329-8021. Fax 808/326-1887. www.outrigger.com. 148 units. From $109 studio double; $125–$325 1-bedroom apt for 4; $145–$365 2-bedroom apt for 6. AE, DC, DISC, MC, V. **Amenities:** Jacuzzi; 2 outdoor pools; complimentary tennis courts; Wi-Fi in lobby. *In room:* A/C, TV, hair dryer, kitchen.

Moderate

King Kamehameha's Kona Beach Hotel   The location is terrific: downtown Kailua-Kona, right on the ocean. This 30-plus-year-old hotel offers views of an ancient banyan tree, the Kailua Pier, or sparkling Kailua Bay. The hotel's own small gold-sand beach is right out the front door. The restaurant is forgettable, but you're within walking distance of dozens of other options. As we went to press, the hotel was in the process of completing a total renovation of the property, including plumbing and LCD flatscreen TVs.

75–5660 Palani Rd., Kailua-Kona, HI 96740. ℂ **800/367-2111** or 808/329-2911. Fax 808/922-8061. www.konabeachhotel.com. 460 units. $125–$269 up to 4 people. AE, DC, DISC, MC, V. Parking $10. **Amenities:** Restaurant; outdoor bar w/Hawaiian entertainment; Jacuzzi; outdoor pool; room service; 4 tennis courts; watersports equipment rentals. *In room:* A/C, TV, fridge, hair dryer, free Wi-Fi.

Silver Oaks Guest Ranch ★★ 👜   Book this place! This is a true "guest ranch," consisting of two cottages spread over a 10-acre working ranch complete with friendly horses (no riding, just petting), the cutest Nigerian dwarf goats, chickens, and wild turkeys. The ranch sits at 1,300 feet, where the temperatures are in the 70s (low to middle 20s Celsius) year-round. The views are spectacular, some 40 miles of coastline from the ocean to Mauna Loa, yet the place is just 5 miles from the airport and 5 miles from downtown Kailua-Kona. Hosts Amy and Rick Decker have impeccable taste, and each unit is uniquely decorated. You'll get breakfast items (cereal, milk, yogurt, coffee, fruit, and bread) for your first day. They have a closet full of beach gear for guests, not to mention books, videos, binoculars, and even a couple of backpacks.

Reservations c/o 75–1027 Henry St., Ste. 310, Kailua-Kona, HI 96740. ℂ **808/325-2000.** Fax 808/325-2200. www.silveroaksranch.com. 3 units, plus additional space available for large groups. $125–$200 double. Extra person $20. 5-night minimum. MC, V. **Amenities:** Jacuzzi; outdoor pool. *In room:* TV/VCR, high-speed Internet access, kitchen or kitchenette.

Inexpensive

Boynton's Kona Bed & Breakfast ★ ☺   Just 3 miles from Kailua-Kona, but up in the cooler, rolling hills, is this quaint two-bedroom B&B, perfect for a family vacation. The house is perched at 1,000 feet in a quiet country neighborhood; guests can enjoy views of the coastline from the lanai. A private entrance leads into the full kitchen, which is stocked with breakfast fixings (including eggs, cereals, muffins, and juice). You have a choice of a two-bedroom unit, with complete kitchen and a hot tub outdoors, or a one-bedroom unit, with a small kitchenette and spacious lanai outside.

The two-bedroom unit has one bedroom that looks out on tropical greenery, while the other has an ocean view. The second unit, which is just one-bedroom, and perfect for a couple, is located next door. This one-bedroom unit has a large lanai (with a dining table and a terrific panoramic ocean view), a sleeper bed in the living room, and a small kitchenette (refrigerator, electric teapot, coffeemaker, and a microwave), great for a couple who wants to eat out but would like a hot cup of coffee or tea in the morning. King bed in separate bedroom. Hosts

Peter and Tracy Boynton have lovingly created a little bit of heaven here, complete with a hot tub on the deck outside. The beach is just a 5-minute drive away.

74-4920-A Palani Rd., Kailua-Kona, HI 96740. ✆ **808/329-4178.** Fax 808/326-1510. www.kona bandb.com. 2 units. $90 double 1-bedroom, $120 double 2-bedroom. Extra person $15. 3-night minimum. No credit cards. **Amenities:** Hot tub. *In room:* TV, hair dryer, kitchenette (1-bedroom), kitchen (2-bedroom), free Wi-Fi.

Kona Billfisher ☺ The pluses here: It's within walking distance of downtown Kailua-Kona, and the big, blue Pacific is just across the street. (The ocean here is not good for swimming or snorkeling, but there's an on-site pool, and you can swim at the Kailua Pier, just a mile away.) The property is very well maintained. Each unit comes with a full kitchen and a balcony, and features new furnishings and king-size beds. The one-bedroom units have sliding-glass doors that allow you to close off the living room and make it into another private bedroom, so for the price of a one-bedroom unit, you can have a two-bedroom—a real deal and a great setup for families. Other on-site facilities include a barbecue area.

Alii Dr. (across from the Royal Kona Resort), Kailua-Kona, HI 96740. Reservations c/o Hawaii Resort Management, P.O. Box 39, Kailua-Kona, HI 96745. ✆ **800/244-4752** or 808/329-3333. Fax 808/326-4137. www.konahawaii.com. 60 units. High season $150 1-bedroom, $165 2-bedroom; low season $115 1-bedroom, $135 2-bedroom. Cleaning fee $35–$45. 3-night minimum. DC, DISC, MC, V. **Amenities:** Outdoor pool. *In room:* TV, kitchen.

Kona Islander Inn 🗝 This is the most affordable place to stay in the downtown Kailua-Kona area. These plantation-style, three-story buildings are surrounded by lush palm-tree-lined gardens with torch-lit pathways that make it hard to believe you're smack-dab in the middle of downtown. The central location—across the street from the historic Kona Inn Shops—is convenient but can be noisy. Built in 1962, the complex is showing some signs of age, but the units were recently outfitted with new appliances, new bedspreads and curtains, and a fresh coat of paint. The studios are small, but extras like lanais and kitchenettes outfitted with microwaves, minifridges, and coffeemakers make up for the lack of space.

75-5776 Kuakini Hwy. (south of Hualalai Rd.), Kailua-Kona, HI 96740. Reservations c/o Hawaii Resort Management, P.O. Box 39, Kailua-Kona, HI 96745. ✆ **800/244-4752** or 808/329-3333. Fax 808/326-4137. www.konahawaii.com. 80 units. $80–$115 double. DC, DISC, MC, V. **Amenities:** Hot tub; outdoor pool. *In room:* A/C, TV, kitchenette.

Kona Magic Sands ★ 🗝 If you want to stay right on the ocean without spending a fortune, this is the place to do it—it's one of the best oceanfront deals you'll find on a Kona condo, and the only one with a beach for swimming and snorkeling right next door. Every unit in this older complex has a lanai that steps out over the ocean, and sunset views that you'll dream about long after you return home. These studio units aren't luxurious; they're small (two people max) and cozy, great for people who want to be lulled to sleep by the sound of the waves crashing on the shore. Each consists of one long, narrow room with a small kitchen at one end and the lanai at the other, with a living room/dining room/bedroom combo in between.

77–6452 Alii Dr. (next to Magic Sands Beach Park), Kailua-Kona, HI 96740. Reservations c/o Hawaii Resort Management, P.O. Box 39, Kailua-Kona, HI 96745. ✆ **800/244-4752** or 808/329-3333. Fax 808/326-4137. www.konahawaii.com. 37 units (all with shower only). $115–$159 double. Cleaning fee $85. 3-night minimum. DC, DISC, MC, V. **Amenities:** Excellent restaurant; bar; oceanfront outdoor pool. *In room:* TV, high-speed Internet, kitchen.

Kona Seaside Hotel   Located in the heart of Kailua-Kona, the Kona Seaside is just steps away from Kailua Bay and Kailua-Kona's shopping, restaurants, and historic sites. The rooms are large and comfy (even if they don't have fancy soaps and extra amenities), but they can be noisy (ask for one away from the road). You may want to splurge on one of the 14 units with kitchenettes.

75–5646 Palani Rd. (at Kuakini Hwy.), Kailua-Kona, HI 96740. © **800/560-5558** or 808/329-2455. Fax 808/329-6157. www.sand-seaside.com. 225 units. $110–$130 double. Extra person $15. Children 11 and under stay free in parent's room. Check the website for specials starting at $79. AE, DC, MC, V. Parking $5. **Amenities:** Restaurant; bar; 2 small outdoor pools. *In room:* A/C, TV, fridge, kitchenette (in some units).

Kona Tiki Hotel ★★ 🎁   It's hard to believe that places like this still exist. The Kona Tiki, located right on the ocean, away from the hustle and bustle of downtown Kailua-Kona, is one of the best budget deals in Hawaii. All of the rooms are tastefully decorated and feature queen-size beds, ceiling fans, and private lanais overlooking the water. Although it's called a hotel, this small, family-run operation is more like a large B&B, with lots of aloha and plenty of friendly conversation at the morning breakfast buffet around the pool. The staff is helpful in planning activities. There are no TVs or phones in the rooms, but there's a pay phone in the lobby. If a double with a kitchenette is available, grab it—the extra few bucks will save you a bundle in food costs. Book way in advance.

75–5968 Alii Dr. (about a mile from downtown Kailua-Kona), Kailua-Kona, HI 96740. © **808/329-1425.** Fax 808/327-9402. www.konatiki.com. 15 units. $72–$86 double; $96 double w/kitchenette. Extra person $11 per adult, $6 per child 2–12. Rates include continental breakfast. 3-night minimum. No credit cards. **Amenities:** Outdoor pool. *In room:* Fridge, kitchenette (in some units), no phone.

Uncle Billy's Kona Bay Hotel   An institution in Kona, Uncle Billy's is where visitors from the other islands stay. A thatched roof hangs over the lobby area, and a Polynesian longhouse restaurant is next door. The rooms are old but comfortable and come with large lanais; most also have minifridges (request one at booking), and 16 are condo-style units with kitchenettes. This budget hotel is a good place to sleep, but don't expect new carpeting or fancy soap in the bathroom. It can be noisy at night when big groups book in; avoid Labor Day weekend, when all the canoe paddlers in the state want to stay here and rehash the race into the wee morning hours.

75–5739 Alii Dr., Kailua-Kona, HI 96740. © **800/367-5102** or 808/961-5818. Fax 808/935-7903. www.unclebilly.com. 139 units. $119–$129 double. Extra person $20. Children 18 and under stay free in parent's room. Check the website for specials starting at $75. AE, DC, DISC, MC, V. **Amenities:** Restaurant; bar (w/Hawaiian entertainment); 2 outdoor pools (1 just for children); watersports equipment rentals. *In room:* A/C, TV, fridge, hair dryer (in some units), kitchenette (in some units).

UPCOUNTRY KONA: HOLUALOA
Expensive
Holualoa Inn ★★ 🎁   The quiet, secluded setting of this B&B—30 pastoral acres just off the main drag of the artsy village of Holualoa, 1,350 feet above Kailua-Kona—provides stunning panoramic views of the entire coast. Recently sold to Sandy Hazen, a local Kona coffee farmer, this contemporary 7,000-square-foot Hawaiian home has six private suites and window-walls that roll back to embrace the gardens and views. Sandy rejuvenated the guest rooms with new

furnishings, upgraded bathrooms, and lauhala matting on the ceilings. Plus, the inn now has a chef cooking your gourmet breakfast. Cows graze on the bucolic pastures below the garden Jacuzzi and pool, and the 30-acre estate includes 3,000 coffee trees, which are the source of the morning brew. The inn offers a gas grill for a romantic dinner beside the pool, a telescope for stargazing, and a billiard table. It's a 15-minute drive down the hill to busy Kailua-Kona and about 20 minutes to the beach, but the pool has a stunning view of Kailua-Kona and the sparkling Pacific below.

76–5932 Mamalahoa Hwy. (P.O. Box 222), Holualoa, HI 96725. © **800/392-1812** or 808/324-1121. Fax 808/322-2472. www.holualoainn.com. 6 units (1 with shower only) $286–$320 double. Rates include full breakfast. AE, DC, DISC, MC, V. On Mamalahoa Hwy., just after the Holualoa post office, look for Paul's Place General Store; the next driveway is the inn. Children must be 13 or older. **Amenities:** Jacuzzi; huge outdoor pool. *In room:* Hair dryer, no phone, free Wi-Fi.

KEAUHOU
Expensive
Sheraton Keauhou Bay Resort & Spa ★ ☺ The Sheraton Keauhou Bay Resort offers an incredible view of Keauhou Bay. Large, modern rooms include Sheraton's Sweet Sleeper Beds, with a cushy mattress top, a featherweight duvet, and five pillows to choose from. The mammoth freshwater pool is tucked in around tropical gardens and splashing waterfalls, with its own small man-made beach, the island's largest water slide, bubbling whirlpool spas, and a children's play area. Speaking of kids, there's a children's center and program on the property and plenty to keep the little ones occupied (water activities, cultural games, arts and crafts, video games, and so on). Plus, the Sheraton has a golf course next door, on-site tennis courts, and a shopping center (with restaurants) close by.

78–128 Ehukai St., Kailua-Kona, HI 96740. © **888/488-3535** or 808/930-4900. Fax 808/930-4800. www.sheratonkeauhou.com. 522 units. $159–$219 double; from $950 suite. Extra person $60. Children 18 and under stay free in parent's room using existing bedding. AE, DC, DISC, MC, V. Valet parking $16; self-parking $10. **Amenities:** 2 restaurants (luau Mon nights, p 419); bar; babysitting; basketball court; year-round children's program; concierge; fitness center; 36-hole golf course nearby w/preferred guest rate; multilevel pool w/200 ft. water slide; room service; spa; 2 tennis courts; sand volleyball court; whirlpool. *In room:* A/C, TV, fridge, hair dryer, Wi-Fi ($13 per day).

Moderate
Kona Seaspray ★ 🏄 The Kona Seaspray has a couple of great things going for it: location and price. It's just across from the Kahaluu Beach Park, possibly the best snorkeling area in Kona. The rates are a great deal when you consider that the one-bedroom apartments easily sleep four and the two-bedroom units can sleep six. It's under new ownership, and all units are undergoing renovations that include upgraded furniture and new carpets. Every unit has a full kitchen, lanai, and fabulous ocean view. Golf and tennis are nearby; there's also a barbecue area. This is the place to book if you are going to spend a lot of time lounging around, or if you need the extra space.

78–6671 Alii Dr., Kailua-Kona, HI 96740. Reservations c/o Johnson Resort Properties, 78–6665 Alii Dr., Kailua-Kona, HI 96740. © **808/322-2403.** Fax 808/322-0105. www.konaseaspray.com. 12 units. $135–$175 1-bedroom double; $149–$190 2-bedroom/2-bathroom. Extra person $20. Cleaning fee $55–$75. 3-night minimum. AE, DISC, MC, V. **Amenities:** Gorgeous outdoor pool w/waterfall; whirlpool hot tub. *In room:* TV/VCR, full-size fridge, hair dryer, full kitchen, Wi-Fi.

Outrigger Kanaloa at Kona ★★ ☺ These big, comfortable, well-managed, and spacious vacation condos, on 16 landscaped acres, border the rocky coast beside Keauhou Bay, 6 miles south of Kailua-Kona. They're exceptional units, ideal for families, with comforts such as huge bathrooms with whirlpool bathtubs, dressing rooms, and bidets. In addition, the spacious lanais, tropical decor, and many appliances make for free and easy living. It's easy to stock up on supplies at the supermarket at the new mall just up the hill.

78–261 Manukai St., Kailua-Kona, HI 96740. ℂ **800/959-5662** or 808/322-9625. Fax 808/322-3818. www.outrigger.com. 76 units. $135–$159 1-bedroom apt. (sleeps up to 4); $155–$215 2-bedroom apt. (up to 6). AE, DC, DISC, MC, V. **Amenities:** Restaurant; oceanside bar; babysitting; concierge; 3 Jacuzzis; 3 outdoor pools (1 for adults only); 2 tennis courts (lit for night play). *In room:* TV, hair dryer, high-speed Internet, kitchen.

Outrigger Keauhou Beach Resort ★ ✦ Located on 10 acres, this former Ohana Keauhou Beach Hotel, still owned by the same company, has been upgraded to the more upscale Outrigger brand. The setting is perfect, on a large reef system (where sea turtles come ashore for a brief nap) and next door to one of Kona's best white-sand beaches, Kahaluu. Lush tropical gardens of native plants and flowers surround the hotel, and it's just a mile from the Kona Country Club's 36 holes of golf. The rooms are small (you could fit a crib in there, but a family of four should get two rooms); the oceanview units are well worth the extra money. The main dining room serves fresh local produce, meats, and fish, and you also have the option of other restaurants and shopping at the nearby Keauhou Shopping Center, just a 2-minute drive away.

78–6740 Alii Dr., Kailua-Kona, HI 96740. ℂ **800/959-5662** or 808/322-3441. Fax 808/322-3117. www.outrigger.com. 309 units. $126–$186 double; from $329 suite. Extra person $50. AE, DC, DISC, MC, V. Parking $8 per day. **Amenities:** 2 restaurants; 4 bars; concierge; fitness center; 36-hole golf course nearby; outdoor pool; room service; spa; 6 tennis courts (2 lit for night play); whirlpool. *In room:* A/C, TV, fridge, hair dryer, high-speed Internet access.

SOUTH KONA

Expensive

Horizon Guest House ★★ 🏠 If you're planning to stay in South Kona, get on the phone right now and book this place—it's the Hawaiian hideaway of your dreams. Host Clem Classen spent 2 years researching the elements of a perfect B&B, and the Horizon Guest House is the result. Its 40 acres of pastureland are located at an altitude of 1,100 feet. You can see 25 miles of coastline, from Kealakekua to just about South Point, yet you cannot see another structure or hear any sounds of civilization. The carefully thought out individual units (all under one roof but positioned at an angle to one another so you don't see any other units) are filled with incredible Hawaiian furnishings, including hand-quilted Hawaiian bedspreads, and boast private lanais with coastline views. The property features barbecue facilities, gardens everywhere, an outdoor shower, and plenty of beach toys. Clem whips up a gourmet breakfast in the main house, which also features a media room with library, video collection, TV (which you can take to your room if you use headphones so you won't disturb other guests), DVD player, VCR, and cordless phone. At first glance, the rates may seem high, but once you're ensconced on the unique property, I think you'll agree it's worth every penny.

P.O. Box 268, Honaunau, HI 96726. ℂ **888/328-8301** or 808/328-2540. Fax 808/328-8707. www.horizonguesthouse.com. 4 units. $250–$350 double based on 1–3 nights. Rates include full gourmet breakfast. MC, V. Located 21 miles south of Kailua-Kona on Hwy. 11, just before mile marker 100. Children must be 14 or older. **Amenities:** Jacuzzi perfectly placed to watch the sunset behind Kealakekua Bay; large outdoor pool worthy of a big resort; Wi-Fi. *In room:* Fridge, hair dryer, no phone.

Inexpensive

Affordable Hawaii at Pomaikai (Lucky) Farm Bed & Breakfast 🔥 True
to its name, Affordable Hawaii offers an inexpensive perch from which to explore the South Kona Coast. This century-old 4-acre farm is overflowing with macadamia nuts, coffee, avocados as big as footballs, tropical fruits, and even *jaboticaba,* an exotic fruit that makes a zingy jam and local wine. The least expensive room is inside the old farmhouse (hey, at $90 a night, this is a deal!). The Greenhouse wing has two rooms with wooden floors, big windows, and private entrances. The most unusual accommodation is the old coffee barn, updated into a rustic room for two with a raised queen-size bed, a fabulous view of the coastline, and an outdoor shower. Guests can use a common kitchen with a refrigerator, microwave, hot plate, and barbecue grill.

83–5465 Mamalahoa Hwy (south of Kailua-Kona, after mile marker 107), Captain Cook, HI 96704. ℂ **800/325-6427** or 808/328-2112. Fax 808/328-2112. www.luckyfarm.com. 4 units. $90–$140 double. Extra person $10 ($5 per child 5 and under). Rates include full farm breakfast. 2-night minimum. AE, DISC, MC, V. **Amenities:** Wi-Fi. *In room:* No phone.

Areca Palms Estate Bed & Breakfast ★ 🎁 Everything about this upcoun-
try B&B is impeccable: the landscaping, the furnishings, the fresh flowers in every room—even breakfast is served with attention to every detail. This charming cedar home, surrounded by immaculate parklike landscaping, sits above the Captain Cook–Kealakekua area, close to beaches, shopping, and restaurants. Guests enjoy watching the sun sink into the ocean from the large lanai or gazing at the starry sky as they soak in the hot tub. Hosts Janice and Steve Glass serve memorable breakfasts (orange-oatmeal quiche, tropical stuffed French toast, tree-ripened banana cakes), offer daily maid service, provide guests with beach equipment, and gladly help with reservations for activities and dinner.

P.O. Box 489, Captain Cook, HI 96704. ℂ **800/545-4390** or 808/323-2276. Fax 808/323-3749. www.konabedandbreakfast.com. 4 units. $115–$145 double. Extra person $30. Rates include full breakfast. 2-night minimum. No credit cards. From Hwy. 11, make a left at the Pacific Island Tire dealer (after mile marker 111) and follow the signs. **Amenities:** Outdoor Jacuzzi; guest phone. *In room:* TV, hair dryer, no phone, free Wi-Fi.

Dragonfly Ranch: Healing Arts Center Some may find the Dragonfly
Ranch too rustic. But if you want to enjoy Hawaii's tropical outdoors and you're thrilled by the island's most unique architecture—structures that bring the outdoors inside—this may be the place for you. Cabins range from one room (with screens only, no drapes) to suites; you might describe the style as "early hippie." Breakfast includes healthy hot cereal such as amaranth, quinoa, and oatmeal with assorted toppings (toasted pecans, sunflower seeds, walnuts, raisins, and golden flaxseed); fresh homegrown organic fruit (apple bananas and strawberry papayas); wheat-free granola and waffles; and sprouted grain bread. The location is ideal, with Puuhonua O Honaunau National Historical Park right down the road and five bays offering great swimming and diving just minutes away. The

place itself, with free-standing cabins tucked away on 2 acres of fruit trees and exotic flowers, truly is a tropical fantasy.

P.O. Box 675 (19 miles south of Kailua-Kona on Hwy. 160), Honaunau, HI 96726. © **808/328-2159.** Fax 808/328-9570. www.dragonflyranch.com. 5 units (4 w/ private bathroom, 1 w/ shower only). $100–$250 double; $300 3-bedroom cottage for 4 persons. Extra person $20. Rates include continental breakfast. 3-night minimum. MC, V. From Hwy. 11, turn onto Hwy. 160 (the road to Puuhonua O Honaunau National Historical Park), btw. mile markers 103 and 104; after 1½ miles, look for the Dragonfly Ranch mailbox. **Amenities:** Babysitting; watersports equipment rentals; yoga studio & fitness room. *In room:* TV, fridge, hair dryer, kitchenette (in some units), free Wi-Fi.

Manago Hotel ♨ If you want to experience the history and culture of the 50th state, the Manago Hotel may be the place for you. This living relic is still operated by the third generation of the same Japanese family who opened it in 1917. It offers clean accommodations, tasty home cooking, and generous helpings of aloha, all at budget prices. The older rooms (with community bathrooms) are ultraspartan—strictly for desperate budget travelers. The rooms with private bathrooms in the new wing are still pretty sparse (freshly painted walls with no decoration and no TV), but they're spotlessly clean and surrounded by Japanese gardens with a koi pond. The rates increase as you go up; the third-floor units have the most spectacular views of the Kona coastline. Adventuresome travelers might want to try the Japanese rooms with tatami mats to sleep on and *furo* (deep hot tubs) in each room to soak in. By the end of your stay, you may leave with new friends—the Manago family is very friendly.

P.O. Box 145, Captain Cook, HI 96704. © **808/323-2642.** Fax 808/323-3451. www.managohotel.com. 63 units (some with shared bathroom). $33 double with shared bathroom; $59–$64 double with private bathroom; $78 double Japanese room with small *furo* tub and private bathroom. Extra person $3. DISC, MC, V. **Amenities:** Restaurant (Manago Hotel Restaurant, p. 340); bar. *In room:* No phone.

The Kohala Coast
VERY EXPENSIVE

The Fairmont Orchid Hawaii ★★★ ☺ Located on 32 acres of oceanfront property, the Orchid is the place for watersports nuts, cultural explorers, families with children, or anyone who just wants to lie back and soak up the sun. This elegant beach resort takes full advantage of the spectacular ocean views and historic sites on its grounds. The sports facilities here are extensive, and there's an excellent Hawaiiana program: The "beach boys" demonstrate how to do everything from creating drums from the trunks of coconut trees to paddling a Hawaiian canoe to strumming a ukulele.

All rooms in this luxury hotel underwent complete renovation in 2006 (to the tune of $9.3 million) and sport new carpets, paint, artwork, lanai furniture, and amenities. Every unit has a big lanai, sitting area, and marble bathroom with double vanity and separate shower. I recommend spending a few dollars more to book a room on the Fairmont Gold Floor, which offers personalized service, complimentary Internet access, a lounge (serving continental breakfast, finger sandwiches in the afternoon, and appetizers in the evening), and exquisite ocean views. The Spa Without Walls allows you to book a massage just about anywhere on the property—overlooking the ocean, nestled deep in the lush vegetation, or in the privacy of your room.

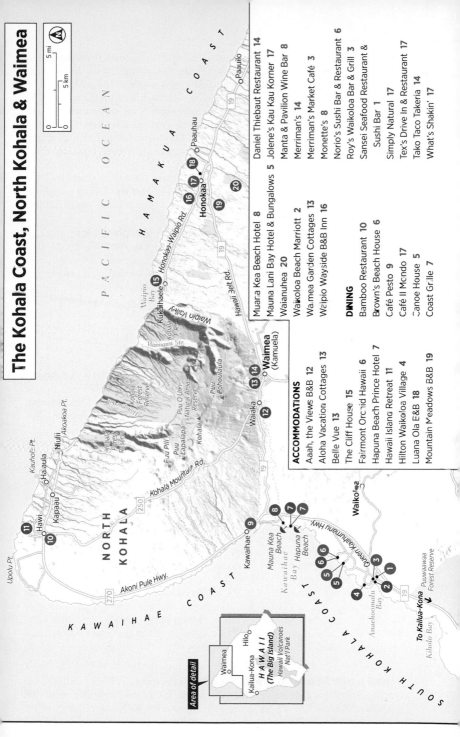

The Kohala Coast, North Kohala & Waimea

ACCOMMODATIONS

Aaah, the Views B&B **12**
Aloha Vacation Cottages **13**
Belle Vue **13**
The Cliff House **15**
Fairmont Orchid Hawaii **6**
Hapuna Beach Prince Hotel **7**
Hawaii Island Retreat **11**
Hilton Waikoloa Village **4**
Luana Ola E&B **18**
Mountain Meadows B&B **19**
Muara Kea Beach Hotel **8**
Mauna Lani Bay Hotel & Bungalows **5**
Waianuhea **20**
Waikoloa Beach Marriott **2**
Wamea Garden Cottages **13**
Waipio Wayside B&B Inn **16**

DINING

Bamboo Restaurant **10**
Brown's Beach House **6**
Café Pesto **9**
Café Il Mcndo **17**
Canoe House **5**
Coast Grille **7**
Daniel Thiebaut Restaurant **14**
Jolene's Kau Kau Korner **17**
Manta & Pavilion Wine Bar **8**
Merriman's **14**
Merriman's Market Café **3**
Monette's **8**
Norio's Sushi Bar & Restaurant **6**
Roy's Waikoloa Bar & Grill **3**
Sansei Seafood Restaurant & Sushi Bar **1**
Simply Natural **17**
Tex's Drive In & Restaurant **17**
Tako Taco Takeria **14**
What's Shakin' **17**

319

The Orchid's four restaurants are all wonderful, with a casual, relaxed atmosphere. The award-winning Norio's Sushi Bar & Restaurant has expanded, with three sushi chefs chopping, rolling, and performing magic at the sushi bar. The recently opened luau and Polynesian revue (see "Gathering of the Kings," p. 419) is making a big splash, with everything from fire-knife dancing performances to culinary creations from Samoa, Tahiti, and New Zealand. The Keiki Aloha program, for kids 5 to 12, features watersports, Hawaiian cultural activities, and other supervised adventures. Some special money-saving family packages are also available.

I applaud the Fairmont Orchid for dropping the obnoxious "resort fee" and allowing guests to pay for the extra services they want. *Hot tip:* Before you arrive, sign up online for the Fairmont President's Club (which is free)—you'll get lots of benefits, including free Internet access.

At the Mauna Lani Resort, 1 N. Kaniku Dr., Kohala Coast, HI 96743. © **800/845-9905** or 808/885-2000. Fax 808/885-5778. www.fairmont.com/orchid. 540 units. $369–$619 double; $589–$669 Gold Floor double; from $789 suite. Extra person $75. Children 17 and under stay free in parent's room. AE, DC, DISC, MC, V. Valet parking $22; self-parking $17. **Amenities:** 4 restaurants (including Norio's Sushi Bar & Restaurant, p. 342, and Brown's Beach House, p. 341); 5 bars (Tues–Sat entertainment at Brown's Beach House); luau and Polynesian revue; babysitting; bike rentals; year-round children's program; concierge; concierge-level rooms; well-equipped fitness center; 2 championship golf courses; large outdoor pool; room service; outstanding spa; 10 award-winning Plexipave tennis courts (7 lit for night play); watersports equipment rentals; 2 lava-rock whirlpools. *In room:* A/C, TV, hair dryer, high-speed Internet access.

Hapuna Beach Prince Hotel ★★ This hotel enjoys one of the best locations on the Kohala Coast, adjacent to the magnificent white sands of Hapuna Beach. The Hapuna Beach Prince is more formal than other hotels on the Kohala Coast; guests, many from Japan, dress up here, some in the latest Tokyo fashions. You won't feel comfortable parading around in your T-shirt and flip-flops.

Accommodations are comfortable, all attuned to the fabulous ocean view and the sea breezes. Although the rooms are small for a luxury hotel, the sprawling grounds make up for it (some guests, however, complain about the long walk from the lobby to their rooms). Service is friendly and caring. There is also a wealth of amenities on the property, from the 18-hole championship golf course (designed by Arnold Palmer and Ed Seay, and reserved for guests and residents) to the state-of-the-art fitness center and world-class Paul Brown Salon & Spa, one of the state's top salons.

At the Mauna Kea Resort, 62–100 Kaunaoa Dr., Kohala Coast, HI 96743. © **800/882-6060** or 808/880-1111. Fax 808/880-3112. www.princeresortshawaii.com. 350 units. $294–$725 double; from $679 suite. Extra person $60. Children 17 and under stay free in parent's room using existing bedding. Check website for deals. AE, DC, MC, V. Valet parking $20; self-parking $15. **Amenities:** 3 restaurants (including the Coast Grille, p. 342); 2 bars (including an open-air beachfront bar w/ live evening entertainment on the weekends); babysitting; year-round Keiki Club children's program; concierge; fitness center; golf course; Jacuzzi; huge outdoor pool; room service; spa; 13 tennis courts; watersports equipment rentals. *In room:* A/C, TV, fridge, hair dryer, Wi-Fi ($11 per day).

Hawaii Island Retreat ★★★ Hidden in the rolling Hills of North Kohala is a 50-acre palatial estate overlooking the ocean. It's the perfect spot to relax and rejuvenate. Created by the local town doctor and his wife, the property offers accommodations in an eco-friendly, sumptuous boutique hotel or in the nearby luxury yurts, with a full spa and yoga and fitness classes. Both include an opulent breakfast. The entire property is self-sufficient down to the organic food grown on-site. Each of the large rooms in the main hotel is decorated with turn-of-the-20th-century Hawaiian furniture and has a private lanai. The individual yurts, nestled in an iron-tree grove, are surprisingly spacious with a private toilet (showers are shared). The yurts are located next door to the spa massage treatment area, fitness center, sauna, and infinity pool. For those on a budget, the yurts allow more affordable accommodations, with all the amenities of the breakfast, spa, and fitness classes. All inclusive, custom packages (meals, spa treatments, and fitness classes) are available. This is the place to come if you are looking for a vacation to restore your energy. The property is honeycombed with hiking trails down to the ocean, and the atmosphere is steeped in Hawaiian culture.

54–250 Maluhia Rd., P.O. Box 189, Hawi, HI 96719. ℂ **808/889-6336.** www.hawaiiislandretreat. com. 10 rooms in hotel; 7 yurts. $300–$450 double in hotel; $175 double yurts. Rates include breakfast; other meals available for a fee. DISC, MC, V. Parking free. **Amenities:** Outdoor pool; spa; free Wi-Fi in public areas; yoga. In room: CD player.

Mauna Kea Beach Hotel ★★★   The phoenix has risen! Totally renovated and back in business, this grande dame of Hawaii resorts closed for 2 years for extensive renovations due to the 2006 earthquake. The resort is better than ever—the renovations allowed management to bring this wonderful icon into the 21st century. They took three hotel rooms and converted them into just two hotel rooms with spacious bathrooms (with a shower with a view in the deluxe units, huge soaking tubs, and a separate sink/dressing area with two separate sinks). Also added in the rooms: a giant walk-in closet, 44-inch flatscreen TV, lots of plugs to charge your computer, an iPod docking station, one-switch light controls both at the bed and at the entry door, and a coffeemaker.

This resort dates from the early 1960s. Laurance S. Rockefeller was sailing around Hawaii when he spotted a perfect crescent of gold sand and dropped anchor. In 1965, he built the Mauna Kea on the spot. Since then, several luxury hotels have been added to the area, but Mauna Kea's beach out front tops them all, and the loyal old-money guests keep coming back to savor the relaxed clubby ambience, remote setting, world-class golf, and old Hawaii ways. Rooms are huge by today's standards, with breathtaking views from the large lanais—plus the hotel is positioned to catch the cooling trade winds. The two championship golf courses—the famous Mauna Kea course, designed by Robert Trent Jones, Sr., and the Hapuna course, designed by Arnold Palmer—are both award winners.

At the Mauna Kea Resort, 62–100 Mauna Kea Beach Dr., Kohala Coast, HI 96743. ℂ **866/977-4589** or 808/882-7222. Fax 808/880-3112. www.princeresortshawaii.com. 310 units. $315–$900 double; from $1,010 suite. Extra person $75. AE, DC, MC, V. Valet parking $20; self-parking $15. **Amenities:** 4 restaurants; 3 bars w/live music on weekends; babysitting; children's program; concierge; excellent fitness center; 2 championship golf courses; Jacuzzi; large outdoor pool; room service; spa; 13-court oceanside tennis complex; watersports equipment rentals. In room: A/C, TV, fridge, hair dryer, Wi-Fi ($11).

Mauna Lani Bay Hotel & Bungalows ★★ ☺   Burned out? In need of tranquillity and gorgeous surroundings? Look no further. Sandy beaches and lava tide pools are the focus of this serene seaside resort, where gracious hospitality is dispensed in a historic setting. From the lounge chairs on the pristine beach to the turndown service at night, everything here is done impeccably. Louvered doors open onto the plush guest rooms, which are outfitted in natural tones with teak accents, each with a lanai. They're arranged to capture maximum ocean views, and they surround interior atrium gardens and pools in which endangered baby sea turtles are raised. A shoreline trail leads across the whole 3,200-acre resort, giving you an intimate glimpse into the ancient past, when people lived in lava caves and tended the large complex of fish ponds.

The hotel offers a very complete children's program, plus kid-friendly restaurants, but in addition, this is simply a great place for kids to explore. The saltwater stream that meanders through the hotel and onto the property outside is filled with reef fish and even a shark. The fish ponds are a great educational experience for *keiki*, and the beach has plenty of room for the youngsters to run and play. Next door to the resort are ancient Hawaiian petroglyph fields, where older kids can learn about Hawaii's past.

The Sports & Fitness Club (one of the best on the island) was just renovated, and the Shops at Mauna Lani recently opened with great retail-therapy opportunities and several food options.

At the Mauna Lani Resort, 68–1400 Mauna Lani Dr., Kohala Coast, HI 96743. ℂ **800/367-2323** or 808/885-6622. Fax 808/885-1484. www.panpacific.com/maunalanibay or www.maunalani. com. 342 units. $370–$915 double; from $850 suite; $3,300–$7,000 bungalow (sleeps up to 4). Extra person $75. AE, DC, DISC, MC, V. Valet parking $21. **Amenities:** 5 excellent restaurants (including CanoeHouse, p. 341); bar (w/live music nightly); babysitting; bike rentals; concierge; year-round children's program; full-service fitness facility; 2 celebrated 18-hole championship golf courses; Jacuzzi; large outdoor pool; room service; 10 Plexipave tennis courts; watersports equipment rentals. *In room:* A/C, TV, CD player, fridge, hair dryer, high-speed Internet access.

EXPENSIVE

Hilton Waikoloa Village ★ ☺   This hotel is a fantasy world all its own, perfect for those who love Vegas and Disneyland. Its high-rise towers are connected by silver-bullet trams, boats, and museum-like walkways lined with $7 million in Asian/Pacific reproductions. The kids will love it, but Mom and Dad may get a little weary waiting for the tram or boat to take them to breakfast (sometimes a 20-min. ordeal or a mile-long walk). The 62 acres feature tropical gardens, cascading waterfalls, exotic wildlife, exaggerated architecture, a 175-foot water slide twisting into a 1-acre pool, hidden grottoes, and man-made lagoons, including a dolphin lagoon (Dolphin Quest allows families to swim with the dolphins for a fee).

The contemporary guest rooms are spacious and luxurious, with built-in platform beds, lanais, and loads of amenities, from spacious dressing areas to a second phone line in all units. All rooms and bathrooms have recently undergone renovations from top to bottom, including new drapes, new beds and bedding, bigger televisions, and new carpet and tile. With nine restaurants to choose from, you'll never lack for culinary options, and golfers can try out the two championship golf courses, one designed by Robert Trent Jones, Jr., and the other by Tom Weiskopf.

Even if you aren't staying here, drop by for the Kohala Sports Club & Spa, one of the best spas on the Kohala Coast, with 25,000 square feet of treatment rooms, saunas, whirlpools, and a host of treatments, including acupuncture and Eastern medicine practices—there's even an astrologer on staff!

69–425 Waikoloa Beach Dr., Waikoloa, HI 96738. ℂ **800/HILTONS** [445-8667] or 808/886-1234. Fax 808/886-2900. www.hiltonwaikoloavillage.com. 1,240 units. $219–$284 double; $289–$319 tower deluxe double; from $539 suite. Extra person $50. Children 18 and under stay free in parent's room. AE, DC, DISC, MC, V. Valet parking $21; self-parking $15. **Amenities:** 5 restaurants; 9 bars (many w/entertainment); babysitting; bike rentals; fabulous children's program; concierge; concierge-level rooms; 2 18-hole golf courses; Jacuzzi; 3 huge outdoor pools (w/waterfalls, slides, whirlpools, and an adults-only pool); room service; excellent spa w/cardio machines, weights, and a multitude of services; 8 tennis courts; watersports equipment rentals. *In room:* A/C, TV, hair dryer, high-speed Internet ($20 per day), minibar/fridge.

Waikoloa Beach Marriott Resort & Spa ★ This resort has always had one outstanding attribute: an excellent location on Anaehoomalu Bay (or A-Bay, as the locals call it), one of the best ocean-sports bays on the Kohala Coast. The gentle sloping beach has everything: swimming, snorkeling, diving, kayaking, windsurfing, and even old royal fish ponds. Now Marriott has made big, big changes here. It has gutted all the guest rooms (back down to the bare concrete) and redesigned them, adding 27-inch flatscreen TVs, putting in glass lanai railings (which actually glow at sunset), and topping everything off with Marriott's very comfy Revive beds. The property still isn't as posh as other luxury hotels along the Kohala Coast, but it also isn't nearly as expensive. The size and layout of the guest rooms remain the same— perfectly nice, but not luxurious. Families might want to book the deluxe units, which are oversized. A new adults-only infinity pool was added in 2006, and the Mandara Spa was expanded to 5,000 square feet on two levels. The main dining room, Hawaii Calls, was also expanded, with a new patio area and a new menu. Guests may use the two championship golf courses at the adjacent Hilton Waikoloa Village.

69–275 Waikoloa Beach Dr., Waikoloa, HI 96738. *©* **888/236-2427** or 808/886-6789. Fax 808/866-3601. www.marriotthawaii.com. 555 units. $199–$324 double; from $500 suite. Extra person $45. Children 17 and under stay free in parent's room. Daily $20 resort fee for overnight self-parking, half-day snorkel rental for 2, free local calls, and Internet access. AE, DC, DISC, MC, V. Valet parking $21. **Amenities:** 2 restaurants; bar; babysitting; concierge; fitness center; Jacuzzi; outdoor pools (including a huge pool w/water slide and separate children's pool); room service; full-service Mandara Spa; 2 tennis courts; watersports equipment rentals; Hawaiian cultural activities, including petroglyphs tour and evening luau. *In room:* A/C, TV, fridge, hair dryer, high-speed Internet access.

Waimea

Note: You'll find Waimea accommodations on the map on p. 319.

MODERATE

Aaah, the Views Bed & Breakfast ★ 🦪
This quiet B&B, just 15 minutes from the fabulous beaches of the Kohala Coast and 5 minutes from the cowboy town of Waimea, lives up to its name—each of the two units has huge picture windows from which you can watch the sun rise or set, or gaze out over green pastureland to the slopes of Mauna Kea. One unit is a studio apartment, complete with kitchen. The second unit is a two-bedroom, one-bathroom with kitchenette that can sleep up to six people. New owners Erika and Derek Stuart recently took over this B&B and have added a new deck to the streamside property. Rooms have a phone with free long distance to the mainland.

P.O. Box 6593, Kamuela, HI 96743. *©* **808/885-3455.** Fax 808/885-4031. www.aaahtheviews. com. 2 units. $165–$185 double. Extra person $20. Rates include continental breakfast. 2-night minimum. MC, V. *In room:* TV/VCR, hair dryer, kitchenette, Wi-Fi.

Waimea Gardens Cottages ★★ 🎁 Imagine rolling hills on pastoral ranch land. Then add a babbling stream and two cozy Hawaiian cottages. Complete the picture with mountain views, and you have Waimea Gardens Cottages. One unit has the feel of an old English country cottage, with oak floors, a fireplace, and French doors opening onto a spacious brick patio. The other is a remodeled century-old Hawaiian wash house, filled with antiques, eucalyptus-wood floors, and a full kitchen. Extra touches keep guests returning again and again: plush English robes, sandalwood soaps in the bathroom, mints next to the bed, and fresh flowers throughout. Hosts Barbara and Charlie Campbell live on the spacious property. They have added a studio with kitchenette, attached to the main house, with a private entrance.

P.O. Box 563 (off Mamalahoa Hwy., 2 miles west of Waimea town center), Kamuela, HI 96743. ℂ **808/885-8550.** Fax 808/885-0473. www.waimeagardens.com. 3 units. $150–$180 double. Extra person $50 ages 12 and over, $25 children. Rates include breakfast treats in the refrigerator. 3-night minimum. No credit cards. *In room:* TV/VCR, hair dryer, kitchen, whirlpool bathtub (in 1 unit), fireplace (in 1 unit).

INEXPENSIVE

Aloha Vacation Cottages ★ 🎁 You'll find these two rental units in a residential area in the cool climate of Waimea. The small, intimate guesthouse has a full kitchen, a separate bedroom, a washer/dryer, and all the comforts of home, including a selection of pillows and a mattress with an adjustable "comfort level" on each side. The larger stand-alone cottage has all the same amenities, plus more space. Guests are greeted with a fruit basket; barbecue facilities are available. The cottages are on the "dry" side of Waimea, about a 10- to 15-minute drive to the beach and just a few minutes to the restaurants of Waimea.

P.O. Box 1395, Kamuela, HI 96743. ℂ **877/875-1722** or 808/885-6535. www.alohavacation cottages.com. 2 units. $120–$150 double. Extra person $20. 5-night minimum. Credit cards through PayPal. *In room:* TV/VCR, hair dryer, free high-speed Internet access and computer.

Belle Vue ★ This two-story vacation rental has a truly beautiful view. Sitting in the hills overlooking Waimea and surrounded by manicured gardens, the charming home is just 15 minutes from the Kohala Coast beaches. The penthouse unit is a large cathedral-ceilinged studio apartment with a kitchenette, huge bedroom, luxurious bathroom, and view of Mauna Loa and Mauna Kea mountains down to the Pacific Ocean. The one-bedroom apartment has a kitchenette and a sofa bed. Each unit has a separate entrance. The rates include breakfast fixings (toast, juice, fruit, cereal, coffee) inside the kitchenettes.

1351 Konokohau Rd., off Opelo Rd. (P.O. Box 1295), Kamuela, HI 96743. ℂ **800/772-5044** or tel/ fax 808/885-7732. www.hawaii-bellevue.com. 2 units. $95–$175 double. Extra person $25. 2-night minimum. AE, MC, V. *In room:* TV, hair dryer, kitchenette, Wi-Fi.

The Hamakua Coast

In addition to those listed below, another B&B in this area, in Ahualoa, a mountain community a short drive from Waipio, is **Mountain Meadow Ranch Bed & Breakfast,** 46–3895 Kapuna Rd., Honokaa, HI 96727 (ℂ **808/775-9376;** www.mountainmeadowranch.com), offering both a private cottage ($150 for four) and rooms in a house ($115 double).

Note: You'll find the following accommodations on the map on p. 319.

EXPENSIVE

Waianuhea ★★ 📖 Located in the rural rolling hills above Honokaa, totally off the grid, and nestled in seven beautifully landscaped acres (with a lily pond, fruit trees, a vegetable garden, and a bucolic horse pasture) lies this oasis of luxury and relaxation. Just off a narrow country road, the two-story inn features five posh guest rooms with soaking tubs, gas or wood stoves, phones, and flatscreen satellite TVs, all on photovoltaic solar power. Splurge a little and ask for the Malamalama suite, with a cherrywood sleigh bed, an extralarge soaking tub, a glass-enclosed shower, and a separate living room. The inn's sumptuous main room has highly polished wood floors, a rock fireplace, and custom Italian sofas, while the Great Room has wraparound glass windows with multicolored glass balloons hanging from the ceiling. Other amenities include nightly wine tasting (featuring different wines every month) with gourmet hors d'oeuvres, a guest kitchenette stocked with a range of goodies (enough to make a meal), and beverages at surprisingly reasonable prices. Complete multicourse gourmet breakfasts are served every morning.

45-3503 Kahana Dr. (P.O. Box 185), Honokaa, HI 96727. © **888/775-2577** or 808/775-1118. Fax 888/296-6302. www.waianuhea.com 5 units. $195–$400 double. Rates include full breakfast. AE, MC, V. **Amenities:** Outdoor hot tub; guest kitchenette. *In room:* TV/DVD, hair dryer.

MODERATE

The Cliff House ★★ 📖 Perched on the cliffs above the ocean is this romantic two-bedroom getaway, surrounded by horse pastures and million-dollar views. A large deck takes in the ocean vista, where whales frolic offshore in winter. Impeccably decorated (the owner also owns Waipio Valley Artworks), the unit features a very well-equipped kitchen with access to a barbecue, two large bedrooms, and a full bathroom. Lots of little touches make this property stand out from the others: an answering machine for the phone, a pair of binoculars, a chess set, and even an umbrella for the rain squalls. Four people could comfortably share this unit.

P.O. Box 5070, Kukuihaele, HI 96727. © **800/492-4746** or 808/775-0005. Fax 808/775-0058. www.cliffhousehawaii.com. 1 unit. $199 double. Extra person $35. 2-night minimum. MC, V. *In room:* TV/VCR, CD player, hair dryer, high-speed Internet access, kitchen, microwave.

INEXPENSIVE

Luana Ola B&B Cottages ★ 📖 These off-the-beaten-path, plantation-style, open-room cottages hearken back to the romantic 1940s. Furnished in rattan and wicker, each features a kitchenette and sleeps up to four. One unit has a spectacular ocean view; although the ocean view from the other unit isn't as panoramic, a satellite TV helps make up for it. Hostess Marsha Tokareff leaves all the fixings for a continental breakfast (fruit, pastries, and coffee) in your kitchen so you can get up at your leisure. The cottages are within walking distance to Honokaa town, yet far enough away to feel the peace and quiet of this bucolic area.

P.O. Box 1967, Honokaa, HI 96727. © **800/357-7727** or 808/775-1150. www.island-hawaii.com. 2 units. $115 double. Extra person $15. Rates include coffee, tea, and fresh fruit. 2-night minimum. MC, V. *In room:* TV, CD player, hair dryer, kitchenette, Wi-Fi.

Waipio Wayside Bed & Breakfast Inn ★★ 📖 Jackie Horne's restored Hamakua Sugar supervisor's home, built in 1938, sits nestled among fruit trees, surrounded by sweet-smelling ginger, fragile orchids, and blooming birds of paradise. The comfortable house, done in old Hawaii style, abounds with thoughtful touches, such as the help-yourself tea-and-snacks bar with 26 kinds of tea. A sunny lanai with hammocks overlooks a yard lush with banana, lemon, lime, tangerine, and avocado trees; the cliffside gazebo has views of the ocean 600 feet below. There are five vintage rooms to choose from. My favorite is the master bedroom suite (dubbed the Birds Eye Room), with double doors that open onto the deck; I also love the Library Room, which has an ocean view, hundreds of books, and a skylight in the shower. There's a shared living room with a TV (including VCR and DVD player). Jackie's friendly hospitality and excellent breakfasts round out the experience.

P.O. Box 840, Honokaa, HI 96727. (📞 **800/833-8849** or 808/775-0275. www.waipiowayside. com. 5 units. $99–$190 double. Extra person $25. Rates include full organic tropical breakfast with coffee, fruit (sunrise papayas, mangoes, tangerines), granola, yogurt, and muffins. 3-night minimum. MC, V. Located on Hwy. 240, 2 miles from the Honokaa post office; look on the right for a long white picket fence and sign on the ocean side of the road; the 2nd driveway is the parking lot. **Amenities:** TV/VCR/DVD in living room; concierge; Wi-Fi throughout the Inn.

Hilo

Just outside Hilo is a terrific bed-and-breakfast called **Lihi Kai,** 30 Kahoa St., Hilo, HI 96720 (📞 **808/935-7865**), a beautifully designed house with mahogany floors, perched on the edge of a cliff with a wide-angle view of Hilo Bay. Double rooms start at $78 a night.

Note: You'll find these accommodations on the "Hilo" map on p. 397.

EXPENSIVE

The Palms Cliff House Inn ★★ 🎁 This inn is a 15-minute drive north of Hilo town, at Honomu (where Akaka Falls is located). Perched on the side of a cliff, the grand old Victorian-style inn is surrounded by manicured lawns and macadamia nut, lemon, banana, lime, orange, avocado, papaya, star fruit, breadfruit, grapefruit, and mango trees. Eight oversize suites, filled with antiques and equipped with DVD players, fireplaces, and private lanais, all overlook the ocean. Four rooms have private Jacuzzis; other extras on the property include yoga classes, hula lessons, high tea, and private massages and other spa treatments. A gourmet hot breakfast (entrees range from banana/mac-nut pancakes to asparagus/sweet-potato quiche) is served on the wraparound lanai overlooking the rolling surf. A magnificent getaway.

P.O. Box 189, Honomu, 96728. (📞 **866/963-6076** or 808/963-6076. Fax 808/963-6316. www. palmscliffhouse.com. 8 units. $199–$349 double. Rates include full gourmet breakfast. AE, DC, DISC, MC, V. **Amenities:** Hot tub. *In room:* A/C (in upper units), TV/DVD, fridge, hair dryer, Jacuzzi (in some units).

MODERATE

Shipman House Bed & Breakfast Inn ★★ 🎁 Built in 1900, the Shipman House is on both the national and state registers of historic places. This Victorian mansion has been totally restored by Barbara Andersen, the great-granddaughter of the original owner, and her husband, Gary. Despite the home's historic appearance, Barbara has made sure that its conveniences are strictly 21st century, including full bathrooms with all the amenities. All five guest bedrooms are large, with 10- to 12-foot ceilings and touches like heirloom furnishings and hand-woven lauhala mats. Wake up to a large continental breakfast buffet (with fresh fruit from the garden). On Wednesday evenings, guests can join in with the hula class practicing on the lanai. The owners have recently added lei making and other cultural activities.

131 Kaiulani St., Hilo, HI 96720. ℂ **800/627-8447** or 808/934-8002. Fax 808/934-8002. www. hilo-hawaii.com. 5 units. $219–$249 double. Extra person $35. Rates include continental breakfast. 2-night minimum. AE, MC, V. From Hwy. 19, take Waianuenue Ave.; turn right on Kaiulani St. and go 1 block over the wooden bridge; look for the large house on the left. *In room:* Small fridge, no phone, Wi-Fi.

INEXPENSIVE

The Bay House ★ 🎁 Overlooking Hilo Bay, this B&B offers immaculate rooms (each with oak floors, king-size bed, sofa, private bathroom, and ocean-view lanai) at reasonable prices. A continental breakfast of tropical fruit, pastries, and Kona coffee is set out every morning in a common area (which also has a refrigerator, toaster, and microwave for guests' use); you can take all you want to eat back to your lanai and watch the sun rise over Hilo Bay. In the evening, relax in the cliffside Jacuzzi as the stars come out.

42 Pukihae St., Hilo, HI 96720. ℂ **888/235-8195** or tel/fax 808/961-6311. www.bayhousehawaii. com. 3 units. $150 double (no 3rd person in units). Rates include continental breakfast. AE, MC, V. **Amenities:** Hot tub. *In room:* TV, hair dryer, Wi-Fi.

Dolphin Bay Hotel ★ 🖋 This two-story, motel-like building, 4 blocks from downtown, is a clean, family-run property that offers good value in a quiet garden setting. Ripe star fruit hang from the trees, flowers abound, and there's a jungle-like trail by a stream. The tidy concrete-block apartments are small and often breezeless, but they're equipped with table fans and jalousie windows. Rooms are brightly painted and outfitted with rattan furniture and Hawaiian prints. There are no phones in the units, but there's one in the lobby. You're welcome to all the papayas and bananas you can eat.

333 Iliahi St., Hilo, HI 96720. ℂ **808/935-1466.** Fax 808/935-1523. www.dolphinbayhilo.com. 18 units. $109–$110 studio double; $149 1-bedroom apt. double; $159 2-bedroom apt. double. Extra person $10. Savings for multiple nights. MC, V. From Hwy. 19, turn mauka (toward the mountains) on Hwy. 200 (Waianuenue St.), and then right on Puueo St.; go over the bridge and turn left on Iliahi St. **Amenities:** Concierge. *In room:* TV, hair dryer (on request), high-speed Internet access, kitchenette, no phone.

Hale Kai Hawaii ★ 🖋 An eye-popping view of the ocean runs the entire length of this house; you can sit on the wide deck and watch the surfers slide down the waves. All guest rooms have that fabulous ocean view through sliding-glass doors. There's one suite, with a living room, kitchenette, and separate bedroom. Guests have access to a pool, hot tub, and small common area with fridge, telephone, and library. Breakfast is a treat, with entrees like homemade mac-nut waffles or double-cheese soufflé. New owners Maria Macias and Ricardo Zepeda have breathed new life into this B&B. The rooms are now all painted in vibrant tropical colors, Maria has improved the landscaping, and they've installed privacy barriers between the rooms.

111 Honolii Pali, Hilo, HI 96720. ℂ **808/935-6330.** Fax 808/935-8439. www.halekaihawaii.com. 4 units. $145–$155 double; $165 suite. Extra person $30. Rates include gourmet breakfast. 2-night minimum. MC, V. **Amenities:** Jacuzzi, oceanfront outdoor pool. *In room:* TV, no phone, free Wi-Fi.

Hilo Seaside Hotel This family-operated hotel is located across Hilo Bay on historic Banyan Drive. Surrounded by lush tropical gardens and a spring pond filled with Japanese carp, this place isn't fancy, but it's great for those on a budget. The rooms were updated and repainted in 2006. The location is terrific for exploring East Hawaii: It's a 45-minute scenic drive to Hawaii Volcanoes National Park, a few minutes by car to downtown, and close to a 9-hole golf course and tennis courts.

126 Banyan Dr. (off Hwy. 19), Hilo, HI 96720. ℭ **800/560-5557** or 808/935-0821. Fax 808/969-9195. www.hiloseasidehotel.com. 135 units. $100–$130 double. Extra person $15. Check website for deals. AE, DC, MC, V. **Amenities:** Restaurant; bar; 9-hole golf course nearby; outdoor pool. *In room:* A/C, TV, fridge, hair dryer (in some units, on request).

The Inn at Kulaniapia Falls ★ 🎒 The view from this off-the-beaten-track inn is worth the price alone: the 120-foot Kulaniapia Waterfall in one direction and the entire town of Hilo sprawled out 850 feet below in another direction. This is *the* place for a romantic getaway. In addition to luxury accommodations in the well-appointed rooms (with balconies), you'll enjoy a royal breakfast with egg dishes, fresh fruit grown on the 22-acre property, and just-baked breads. Wander along the 2-mile pathways that follow the Waiau River (check out the exotic bamboo garden) or swim at the base of the waterfall in the 300-foot pond. In addition to the Inn, they've added a couple of very beautiful guesthouses. It's just 15 minutes from Hilo, but you'll feel a zillion miles away from everything in the peaceful surroundings of a 2,000-acre macadamia-nut grove.

P.O. Box 11338, Hilo, HI 96720. ℭ **866/935-6789** or 808/935-6789. www.waterfall.net. 10 units. $119–$139 rooms in Inn double; $185 cottage double. Extra person $25. Rates include full breakfast. AE, MC, V. **Amenities:** Hot tub; high-speed Internet access. *In room:* TV in some rooms.

The Old Hawaiian Bed & Breakfast 🍴 Bargain hunters, take note: This old plantation house from the 1930s has been renovated and offers great room rates that include breakfast. Located on the Wailuku River, the house features a large lanai, where guests have use of a phone, refrigerator, and microwave. The rooms range from tiny to large (the latter with its own sitting area, sunken bathtub, and separate shower). All have their own private entrances and private bathrooms. Hosts Stewart and Lory Hunter prepare a beautiful breakfast of fruit cup, fruit smoothie, juice, coffee or tea, and two types of homemade bread (you'll want seconds of Lory's mac-nut scones). The Hunters happily help guests with sightseeing plans, too.

1492 Wailuku Dr., Hilo, HI 96720. ℭ **877/961-2816** or 808/961-2816. www.thebigislandvacation. com. 3 units. $80–$110 double. Extra person $10. 2-night minimum. MC, V. *In room:* Hair dryer, Wi-Fi.

Uncle Billy's Hilo Bay Hotel Uncle Billy's is one of the least expensive places to stay along Hilo's hotel row, Banyan Drive. This oceanfront budget hotel boasts a dynamite location. You enter via a tiny lobby, gussied up Polynesian-style; it's slightly overdone, with sagging fishnets and tapa (bark cloth) on the walls. The guest rooms are simple: bed, TV, phone, closet, and bathroom—that's about it. The walls seem paper thin, and it can get very noisy at night (you may want to bring earplugs), but at these rates, you're still getting your money's worth.

87 Banyan Dr. (off Hwy. 19), Hilo, HI 96720. ℭ **800/367-5102** or 808/935-0861. Fax 808/935-7903. www.unclebilly.com. 144 units. $104–$129 double; $119 studio with kitchenette. Extra person $20. Children 18 and under stay free in parent's room. Check the website for specials starting

at $73, car/room packages, and senior rates. Rates include continental breakfast buffet. AE, DC, DISC, MC, V. **Amenities:** Restaurant; bar w/nightly live entertainment; oceanfront pool. *In room:* A/C, TV, fridge (in some units), hair dryer (in some units), kitchenette (in some units).

Hawaii Volcanoes National Park

As a result of Hawaii Volcanoes being officially designated a national park in 1916, a village has popped up at its front door. Volcano Village isn't so much a town as a wide spot in Old Volcano Road, with two general stores, a handful of restaurants, a post office, a coffee shop, a new firehouse, and a winery.

Except for Volcano House (see below), which is within the national park, all of the accommodations in this section are in Volcano Village. It gets cool here at night—Volcano Village is located at 3,700 feet—so a fireplace might be an attractive amenity. It also rains a lot in Volcano—100 inches a year—which makes everything grow *Jack and the Beanstalk* style.

I recommend spending at least 3 days to really see and enjoy the park. The best way to do this is to rent a cottage or house, and the best rental agency is **Hawaii Volcano Vacations** ★★, P.O. Box 913, Volcano, HI 96785 (℗ **800/709-0907** or 808/967-7271; www.hawaiivolcanovacations.com). Manager Joey Gutierrez selects only the top cottages, cabins, and houses in Volcano and makes sure they're perfect for you. Her reasonably priced units range from $99 to $200, and each one is outfitted with a full kitchen, plus an outdoor grill, cooler, flashlight, umbrella, and fresh flowers for your arrival. Many of them are great options for families traveling with kids.

EXPENSIVE

The Inn at Volcano Formerly called Chalet Kilauea, this is the most expensive B&B in Volcano. It has a storybook, enchanting quality to it. The least expensive room is decorated in memorabilia from the owners' extensive travels to eastern and southern Africa. Other units include the Jade Room (with collectibles from the Far East), the Continental Suite (with Victorian decor), the Treehouse Suite, and a separate cabin located next door to the Inn. I found some rooms, although exquisitely decorated, not very practical for things like hanging clothes, storing toiletries, and so on.

P.O. Box 998, Volcano, HI 96785. ℗ **800/937-7786** or 808/967-7786. Fax 808/967-8660. www. volcano-hawaii.com. 5 units. $185–$399 double. Extra person $25. Rates include continental breakfast and afternoon tea. AE, DC, DISC, MC, V. **Amenities:** Hot tub; 3 of the rooms share a fridge, microwave, and coffeemaker on the porch. *In room:* TV/DVD, fridge (in some units), microwave (in some units), free Wi-Fi.

MODERATE

The **Volcano Teapot Cottage** (℗ **808/967-7112;** www.volcanoteapot.com) is a quaint 1914 two-bedroom cottage, decorated with one-of-a-kind antiques, and complete with hot tub in the forest out back ($195 double).

Kilauea Lodge & Restaurant ★ This popular roadside lodge, built in 1938 as a YMCA camp, sits on 10 wooded and landscaped acres. Its rooms offer heating systems and towel warmers, beautiful art on the walls, fresh flowers, and, in some, fireplaces. In addition to the Lodge, there are two cottages available: a 1929 two-bedroom cottage with a fireplace and a full kitchen, just a couple of blocks down the street, and a two-bedroom with full kitchen on the sixth fairway of the Volcano Golf Course. A full gourmet breakfast is served to guests at the restaurant.

P.O. Box 116 (1 block off Hwy. 11 on Old Volcano Rd.), Volcano, HI 96785. ✆ **808/967-7366.** Fax 808/967-7367. www.kilauealodge.com. 14 units. $170–$225 double room; $185–$300 cottage. Extra person $20. Rates include full breakfast. AE, MC, V. **Amenities:** Restaurant; hot tub.

INEXPENSIVE

On the way to the park is **Bed & Breakfast Mountain View** (✆ **888/698-9896** or 808/968-6868; www.bbmtview.com), a 7,000-square-foot home overlooking a 10,000-square-foot fish pond with teahouse, spa, and patio; rooms start at $90 (2-night minimum). The **Log Cabin** (✆ **808/735-9191;** www.crubinstein.com/cabin.html) is a century-old ohia-log cabin for the young at heart ($125 for two, $150 for four, and $200 for six).

Hale Ohia Cottages ★ 🏠   Take a step back in time to the 1930s. Here you'll have a choice of suites, each with private entrance. There are also four guest cottages, ranging from one bedroom to three. The surrounding botanical gardens contribute to the overall tranquil ambience of the estate. They were groomed in the 1930s by a resident Japanese gardener, who worked with the natural volcanic terrain but gently tamed the flora into soothing shapes and designs. The lush grounds are just a mile from Hawaii Volcanoes National Park. The latest addition is a romantic, cozy cottage with fireplace, hot tub, and unusual bedroom made from a 1930s redwood water tank.

P.O. Box 758 (Hale Ohia Rd., off Hwy. 11), Volcano, HI 96785. ✆ **800/455-3803** or 808/967-7986. Fax 808/985-8887. www.haleohia.com. 10 units. $105–$189 double. Extra person $20. Rates include continental breakfast. MC, V. *In room:* Fridge, hair dryer, no phone, Wi-Fi (some units).

Volcano Hale 🍃   If you're on a tight budget, check into this charming 1912 historic home offering comfortable, clean, quiet rooms, all with shared bathrooms. The restored house sits on beautifully landscaped grounds and has new carpeting throughout, plus new furnishings in the common area. The bedrooms are tiny but clean and inviting. The common rooms include a living room with TV/VCR, a reading room, and a sunroom.

P.O. Box 998 (19–4178 Wright Rd., off Hwy. 11), Volcano, HI 96785. ✆ **800/937-7786** or 808/967-7786. Fax 808/967-8660. www.volcano-hawaii.com. 6 units (none with private bathroom). $69–$89 double. Extra person $25. Rates include continental breakfast. AE, DC, DISC, MC, V. From Hwy. 11, turn north onto Wright Rd.; go 1 mile to the Inn at Volcano on the right, where you'll check in. **Amenities:** Free Wi-Fi at the office. *In room:* No phone.

Volcano House   As we went to press, the Volcano House was currently closed for renovations and not expected to reopen until mid-2011. The property has a great location—inside the boundaries of the national park—and that's about all. This mountain lodge, which evolved out of a grass lean-to in 1865, is Hawaii's oldest visitor accommodations. It stands on the edge of Halemaumau's bubbling crater, and although the view of the crater is still an awesome sight, don't expect the Ritz here—rooms are very plain and heated with volcanic steam. *Tip:* Book only if you can get one of the rooms facing the volcano; if they are filled, don't bother—you can do better elsewhere.

P.O. Box 53, Hawaii Volcanoes National Park, HI 96718. ✆ **808/967-7321.** Fax 808/967-8429. www.volcanohousehotel.com. 42 units. Call for room rates, not available as we went to press. Plus one-time $10 park entrance fee. AE, DC, DISC, MC, V. **Amenities:** Restaurant w/great view; bar.

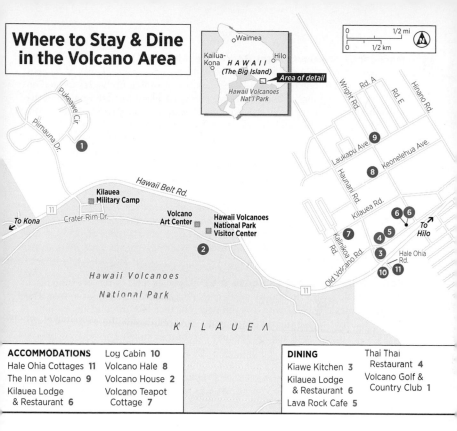

Where to Stay & Dine in the Volcano Area

HAWAII (The Big Island)

Kailua-Kona

Waimea

Hilo

Area of detail

Hawaii Volcanoes Nat'l Park

Kilauea Military Camp

Hawaii Belt Rd.

Crater Rim Dr.

To Kona

Volcano Art Center

Hawaii Volcanoes National Park Visitor Center

Hawaii Volcanoes

National Park

KILAUEA

Pukeawe Cir.

Piimauna Dr.

Wright Rd.

Rd. A.

Rd. E

Hinano Rd.

Laukapu Ave.

Haunani Rd.

Keonelehua Ave.

Kilauea Rd.

Kalinikoa Rd.

Old Volcano Rd.

Hale Ohia Rd.

To Hilo

ACCOMMODATIONS	
Hale Ohia Cottages **11**	Log Cabin **10**
The Inn at Volcano **9**	Volcano Hale **8**
Kilauea Lodge & Restaurant **6**	Volcano House **2**
	Volcano Teapot Cottage **7**

DINING	
Kiawe Kitchen **3**	Thai Thai Restaurant **4**
Kilauea Lodge & Restaurant **6**	Volcano Golf & Country Club **1**
Lava Rock Cafe **5**	

South Point

Bougainvillea Bed & Breakfast ★ 🎁   Don and Martie Jean Nitsche bought this 3-acre property in the Hawaiian Rancho subdivision of Ocean View and had a *Field of Dreams* experience: They decided that if they built a bed-and-breakfast, people would come. Where some people saw just lava, the Nitsches saw the ancient Hawaiian path that went from the mountain to the sea. So they built. And out of the lava came gardens—colorful bougainvillea, a pineapple patch, and a fish pond to add to the pool and hot tub. Word got out. Martie's breakfast—her secret-recipe banana and mac-nut pancakes, sausage, fruit, and coffee—drew people from all over. Things got so good, they had to add more rooms (all with their own private entrances) and expand the living room (complete with TV, VCR, and video library) and dining room. Guests usually take their breakfast plates out to the lanai, which boasts ocean views. Or they wander over to the pavilion, located next to the pool, which has a big barbecue area (with a kitchenette), a games area (darts, Ping-Pong, and so on), satellite TV, some exercise equipment, even a horseshoe pit. You can borrow snorkeling gear, beach mats, coolers, and other beach equipment. Massage and acupuncture available.

P.O. Box 6045, Ocean View, HI 96737. ℂ **800/688-1763** or 808/929-7089. Fax 808/929-7089. www.bougainvilleabedandbreakfast.com. 4 units. $89 double. Extra person $15. Rates include full breakfast. AE, DC, DISC, MC, V. **Amenities:** Concierge; hot tub; big outdoor pool. *In room:* TV/VCR, hair dryer, no phone, Wi-Fi.

Macadamia Meadows Farm Bed & Breakfast ★ ☺   Near the southern-most point in the United States and just 45 minutes from Hawaii Volcanoes National Park lies one of the Big Island's most welcoming B&Bs. It's located on an 8-acre working macadamia-nut farm, in a great place for stargazing, and the warmth and hospitality of host Charlene Cowan is unsurpassed. Because the owner has children herself, the entire property is very kid-friendly. In addition to exploring the groves of mac-nut trees, children can swim in the pool or play tennis. Charlene also has puzzles, games, and other rainy-day items to entertain youngsters. All rooms have private entrances and are immaculately clean; two of the units can be reserved together as a two-bedroom suite. Ask Charlene about the free orchid tours.

94–6263 Kamoa Rd., Waiohinu, HI 96772. Reservations c/o P.O. Box 756, Naalehu, HI 96772. ⓒ **888/929-8118** or 808/929-8097. Fax 808/929-8097. www.macadamiameadows.com. 5 units. $119–$135 double. Extra person $15 per adult, $10 per child 17 and under. Rates include continental breakfast. AE, DISC, MC, V. **Amenities:** Resort-size outdoor pool; tennis courts. *In room:* TV, fridge, microwave, no phone.

South Point Banyan Tree House ★ 🎁   Couples looking for an exotic place to nest should try this treehouse nestled inside a huge Chinese banyan tree. The cottage comes complete with see-through roof that lets the outside in, plus a comfy, just-for-two hot tub on the wraparound deck. Inside there's a queen-size bed and a kitchen with microwave and two-burner stove. The scent of ginger brings you sweet dreams at night, and the twitter of birds greets you in the morning.

At Hwy. 11 and Pinao St., Waiohinu, HI 96772. ⓒ **808/217-2504** or 808/929-8515. www.south pointbth.com. 1 unit. $100 double. 2-night minimum. No credit cards. **Amenities:** Hot tub; outside grill. *In room:* TV/VCR, CD player, kitchen.

WHERE TO DINE

So many restaurants, so little time. What's a traveler to do? The Big Island's delicious dilemma is its daunting size and abundant offerings. Its gastronomic environment—the fruitful marriage of creative chefs, good soil, and rich cultural traditions—has made this island as much a culinary destination as a recreational one. And from the Kona Coffee Festival to the Aloha Festival's Poke Recipe Contest, the Big Island is host to extraordinary world-renowned culinary events.

The Big Island's volcanic soil produces fine tomatoes, lettuces, beets, beans, fruit, and basic herbs and vegetables that were once difficult to find locally. Southeast Asian fruit, such as mangosteen and rambutan, are beginning to appear in markets, along with the sweet white pineapple that is by now a well-established Big Island crop. Along with the lamb and beef from Big Island ranches and seafood from local fishermen, this fresh produce forms the backbone of ethnic cookery and Hawaii Regional Cuisine.

Kailua-Kona is teeming with restaurants for all pocketbooks, while the haute cuisine of the island is concentrated in the Kohala Coast resorts. Waimea, also known as Kamuela, is a thriving upcountry community, a haven for yuppies, techies, and retirees who know a good place when they see one. In Hawi, North Kohala, expect bakeries, neighborhood diners, and one tropical-chic restaurant that's worth a special trip. In Hilo in East Hawaii, you'll find pockets of trendiness among the precious old Japanese and ethnic restaurants that provide honest, tasty, and affordable meals in unpretentious surroundings.

In the listings below, reservations are not necessary unless otherwise noted. *Warning:* Big Island restaurants, especially along the Kona Coast, seem to have a chronic shortage of waitstaff. Come prepared for a leisurely meal; sit and enjoy the warm moonlit night, sip a liquid libation, and realize time is relative here.

The Kona Coast

IN & AROUND KAILUA-KONA, HOLUALOA & KEAUHOU

Note: Pahu i'a and Beach Tree Bar & Grill are located north of Kailua-Kona in the Four Seasons Resort Hualalai, 6 miles north of the Kona Airport and just south of the Kohala Coast.

Very Expensive

Pahu i'a ★★★ CONTEMPORARY PACIFIC RIM   You can't find a better oceanfront location on the Big Island (maybe in the entire state)—Pahu i'a sits just feet from the lapping waves. A small bridge of natural logs leads to this enchanting oceanfront dining room, where views on three sides expand on the aquatic theme (*pahu i'a* is Hawaiian for "aquarium," and there's a large one at the entrance). The cuisine highlights fresh produce and seafood from the island— and even from the resort's own aquaculture ponds, which teem with shrimp and moi (threadfin), a rich Island fish. The day begins with the coast's most elegant breakfast buffet, featuring excellent omelets, meats, fresh fruit, and regional specialties. At dinner, part of the menu changes daily and always includes several fresh seafood preparations; prosciutto wrapped kampachi; dry-aged prime New York steak; and butter-poached Hawaiian lobster. From ambience to execution to presentation, Pahu i'a is top-drawer. On Saturday, the Surf, Sand, and Stars feast offers an array of buffet-style items from fresh fish to grilled New York sirloin. Live music 6 to 9pm nightly.

At the Four Seasons Resort Hualalai, Queen Kaahumanu Hwy., Kaupulehu-Kona. *☎* **808/325-8000.** Reservations recommended. Breakfast buffet $34; dinner main courses $17–$60; Surf, Sand, and Stars buffet $85 adults, $43 kids 5–12. AE, DC, DISC, MC, V. Daily 6:30–11:30am (buffet 7–10:30am) and 5:30–8:30pm.

Expensive

Beach Tree Bar & Grill ★★★ CASUAL GOURMET   Here's an example of outstanding cuisine in a perfect setting—without being fancy, fussy, or prohibitively expensive. The bar on the sand is a sunset paradise, and the seafood, and grilled items at the casual outdoor restaurant (a few feet from the bar) are in a class of their own—simple, excellent, and imaginatively prepared. The menu, which varies, includes items from Italian dishes to grilled fresh fish, even vegetarian specialties. An added attraction is entertainment from 6 to 9pm nightly.

At the Four Seasons Resort Hualalai, Queen Kaahumanu Hwy., Kaupulehu-Kona. *☎* **808/325-8000.** Reservations recommended. Main courses $17–$30 lunch, $18–$40 dinner. AE, DC, DISC, MC, V. Daily 11:30am–8:30pm.

Huggo's ★ PACIFIC RIM/SEAFOOD   At the main Huggo's dining room, fresh seafood remains the signature, as does the coral-strewn beach with tide pools just beyond the wooden deck. The tables are so close to the water, you can see the entire curve of Kailua Bay. Feast on sautéed mahimahi, steamed clams, seared ahi, or *imu*-style chicken cooked in ti leaves. At lunch, specialties include kalua-chicken quesadillas, brick-oven pizzas, and sandwiches ranging from hot turkey to prime rib and fresh fish.

Huggo's on the Rocks ★ is a thatched-bar fantasy that's *really* on the rocks. This mound of thatch, rock, and grassy-sandy ground, right next to Huggo's, is a sunset-lover's nirvana. At sundown, this thatched-bar fantasy is packed with people sipping mai tais and noshing on salads, poke, sandwiches, plate lunches, sashimi, and fish and chips. At lunchtime, the new menu ranges from a spicy grilled mahimahi taco plate to a huge burger with barbecue sauce. From 6 to 11am, this same location turns into the **Java on the Rocks** ★★ espresso bar, which is *not* to be missed—sip Kona coffee, enjoy your eggs, and watch the waves roll onto the shore.

75-5828 Kahakai Rd., Kailua-Kona. ✆ **808/329-1493.** www.huggos.com. Reservations recommended. Main courses $11–$25 at Huggo's on the Rocks, $20–$37 at Huggo's. AE, MC, V. Daily 6–11am, 11:30am–2:30pm, and 5:30–11pm.

Kona Inn Restaurant ★ AMERICAN/SEAFOOD   This is touristy, but it can be a very pleasant experience, especially when the sun is setting. The wide-ranging menu and fresh seafood in the open-air oceanfront setting will remind you why you have come to Kailua-Kona. The large, open room and panoramic view of the Kailua shoreline are the most attractive features, especially for sunset cocktails and appetizers. It's a huge menu—everything from nachos and chicken Caesar salad to sandwiches, pasta, stir-fried dishes, and the highlight: the fresh fish served Cajun-style or broiled and basted in lemon butter. Watch for the daily specials on the less expensive Cafe Grill menu (coconut shrimp, stuffed mushrooms, fish and chips, and so on).

At the Kona Inn Shopping Village, 75-5744 Alii Dr., Kailua-Kona. ✆ **808/329-4455.** www. konainnrestaurant.com. Reservations recommended for dinner. Main courses $18–$37; Cafe Grill $7–$18. AE, MC, V. Dinner menu daily 5–9pm (mid-Apr to mid-Dec 5:30–9pm); Cafe Grill menu daily 11:30am–9pm.

La Bourgogne ★★★ 🍴 CLASSIC FRENCH   An intimate spot with 10 tables, La Bourgogne serves classic French fare with simple, skillful elegance. Baked Brie in puff pastry is a taste treat, and the fresh Maine lobster salad, served on a bed of greens with mango slices and a passion-fruit vinaigrette, is a master stroke. Other offerings include classic onion soup, fresh catch of the day, *osso buco,* and New Zealand mussels steamed in apple cider, thyme, shallots, and cognac. The roast duck breast with raspberries and pine nuts is exactly the kind of dish that characterizes La Bourgogne—done to perfection, presented attractively, and with an unbeatable match of flavors and textures. Classically trained chef Ron Gallaher expresses his allegiance to *la cuisine française* down to the last morsel of flourless chocolate cake and lemon tartlette. Don't be disappointed—book way in advance!

77-6400 Nalani St. (3 miles south of Kailua-Kona), Kailua-Kona. ✆ **808/329-6711.** Reservations recommended. Main courses $28–$39. AE, DC, DISC, MC, V. Tues–Sat 6–10pm.

Moderate

Jackie Rey's Ohana Grill ★★ 🍴 ECLECTIC   This off-the-beaten-path eatery is hard to categorize: part sports bar, part family restaurant, part music/dancing (salsa, country and western), part neighborhood cafe. No matter what you call it, you'll get great food at wallet-pleasing prices. Locals pile in at lunch for burgers, fish tacos, and mac-nut basil chicken sandwich, or the daily Blue Plate Special for $12. On weekdays, a happy-hour crowd downs a few brews and pupu (appetizers). Starting at 5pm, families with kids in tow show up for the delicious

Where to Dine on the Kona Coast

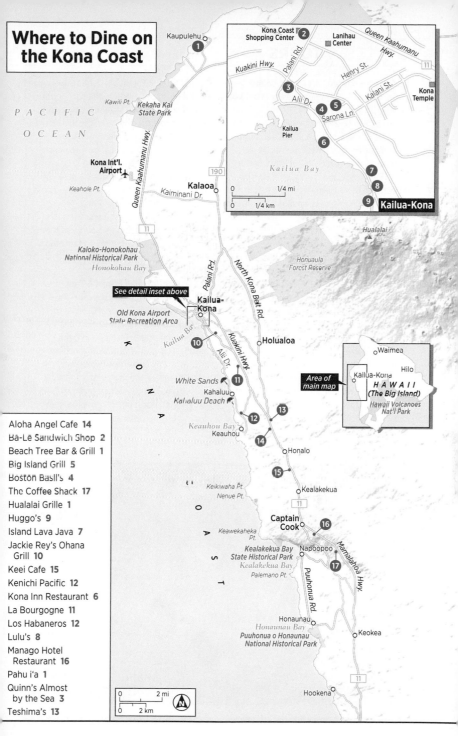

Kailua-Kona

tasty TOURS

Kona Joe Coffee Farm & Chocolate Company, 79–7346 Mamalahoa Hwy., between mile markers 113 and 114, in Kealakekua (*📞* **808/322-2100;** www.konajoe.com), home of the world's first trellised coffee farm, offers guided tours at its 20-acre estate in the "Gold Belt of Kona Coffee."

The tours begin with an excursion through the well-manicured fields of the unique coffee plants on a patented trellis technology developed by Joe Alban. When he began farming in 1997, Alban wanted a unique, top-of-the-line coffee, so he turned to his brother, John, who is a graduate of the viticulture and oenology program at the University of California, Davis. Joe planted 5 acres of coffee in the traditional way and 5 acres of trellised coffee. The trellised coffee had a harvest of 35% more berries, which produced a sweeter, fuller-bodied coffee. With lots of pruning and uniform sun exposure, Kona Joe coffee was awarded the "Best New Roasted Coffee" blue ribbon by the Specialty Coffee Association in 2001, and a local newspaper gave Kona Joe the "People's Choice Award for Best Coffee" in 2006.

In the 10,000-square-foot visitor center on the plantation, the tour continues with live demonstrations on roasting, sorting, brewing, and panning. At the end, you'll get a sample of Kona Joe Coffee and the brownies, truffles, and chocolate-covered coffee beans (yum, yum!) also sold here. Tours are given on request, daily from 9am to 4pm, and cost $15 adults and $7.50 children.

Attention, foodies: If you want to enjoy the full agricultural bounty of the Big Island, consider joining a **Merriman's Farm Visits & Dinner** tour, offered Monday through Thursday afternoons in partnership with **Hawaii Forest & Trail.** The half-day adventure takes you behind the scenes of Hawaii Regional Cuisine, to the Big Island's finest and most picturesque small-batch farms, where the emphasis is on sustainable agriculture. Your tour will culminate with a four-course feast at the restaurant. Tours run daily from 2:30 to 7:30pm and cost $155 per person. For more information, visit www.merrimanshawaii.com.

blackened ahi tuna and scallops, grilled pork chops, seafood pasta, and beef short ribs with a ko-chu-jang glaze.

75-5995 Kuakini Hwy., Kailua-Kona. (C) **808/327-0209.** www.jackiereys.com. Reservations recommended for dinner. Main courses $9–$17 lunch, $22–$30 dinner; pupu menu $7.50–$17. MC, V. Mon–Fri 11am–9pm; Sat–Sun 5–9pm.

Kenichi Pacific ★★★ 🍴 PACIFIC RIM/SUSHI   Hidden in the Keauhou Shopping Center is this gem of a restaurant, decorated in muted tones and with understated furnishings, featuring both Pacific Rim fusion cuisine and a sushi bar. The fantastic food and efficient service will leave you smiling. The appetizer menu is so tempting (ginger-marinated squid, blackened tuna, Dungeness crab cakes, fresh lobster summer rolls), you might just want to graze from one dish to the next. Entrees include fresh catch of the day; macadamia-crusted lamb accompanied by taro risotto; ono tataki; lemon grass ahi; and bamboo salmon. If you love duck, don't miss Kenichi's duck confit, which has Chinese five-spice cured duck leg with celeriac purée, ali'i mushrooms, pea tendrils, red-pepper coulis, and balsamic reduction. Leave room for the warm flourless molten cake with Kona coffee–chip ice cream.

At the Keauhou Shopping Center, 78-6831 Alii Dr., Keauhou. (C) **808/322-6400.** www.kenichi restaurants.com. Reservations recommended for dinner. Main courses $19–$32. AE, DC, DISC, MC, V. Tues–Fri 11:30am–1:30pm; daily 5–9:30pm.

Inexpensive

Ba-Le Sandwich Shop 🍴 FRENCH-VIETNAMESE SANDWICHES & BAKERY   This statewide chain specializes in "fast" French-Vietnamese sandwiches, Vietnamese rice and noodle entrees, and bakery items. It's a nondescript place in a local shopping center, but with great deals like sandwiches on home-made French rolls from just $4, this family-run restaurant is the perfect place to stop before heading for the beach.

At the Kona Coast Shopping Center, 74-5588 Palani Rd., Kailua-Kona. (C) **808/327-1212.** Entrees $9.50–$15; sandwiches $4–$7.50. MC, V. Mon–Sat 10am–9pm; Sun 11am–7pm.

Big Island Grill 🍴 AMERICAN   One of the best-kept secrets among local residents is the Big Island Grill, where you get huge servings of home cooking at 1970s prices. The place is always packed, from the first cup of coffee at breakfast to the last bite of dessert at night. In 2007, Chef Bruce Gould sold the restaurant to a family who has kept the staff and recipes of this localized American cuisine. This is a place to take the family for dinner (excellent fresh salmon, generous salads, and the world's tastiest mashed potatoes) without having to go into debt. *Warning:* You'll likely have to wait (no reservations), and once you finally land a table, service can sometimes be slow. Relax, it's Hawaii.

75-5702 Kuakini Hwy., Kailua-Kona. (C) **808/326-1153.** Reservations not accepted. Main courses breakfast $4.75–$20, lunch $8–$19, dinner $8.75–$23. AE, MC, V. Mon–Sat 6–9pm.

Boston Basil's ★ PIZZA/ITALIAN   Longtime pizzeria Basil's became Boston Basil's in 2007 and grew up. Yes, it still has delicious pizza, but its Italian food now shines. Two dining rooms seat 100 in a garlic-infused atmosphere where prices are low, considering the location across the street from the ocean on Alii Drive. Shrimp pesto and the original barbecue-chicken pizza are long-standing favorites, as is the artichoke-olive-caper version, a Greek-Italian hybrid. The menu has recently expanded to include sandwiches and burgers. Very popular with the 20-something crowd as well as hungry visitors drawn in by the wonderful aroma wafting out into the street.

75-5707 Alii Dr., Kailua-Kona. ℂ **808/326-7836.** Individual pizzas $14–$17; main courses $13–$24. MC, V. Sun–Fri 11am–9pm; Sat 11am–9:30pm.

Island Lava Java ★ 🍴 AMERICAN Perched directly across the street from the ocean with an unimpaired view of the water activities in Kailua Bay, this inexpensive outdoor coffee shop started as a small espresso joint with a few pastries a few years ago. Eventually it added lunch and then dinner. Today Lava Java is the "in" place to sip espresso drinks, chow down on good food, and enjoy the ocean view. A handful of tables ring the small shop outside, and a few more tiny tables are located inside at this counter-service-only restaurant. The breakfast menu features stacks of pancakes and eggs in various preparations, such as in a massive omelet, wrapped in a tortilla, or on an English muffin or bagel. The lunch menu is big on sandwiches, burgers, and salads. Dinners can be small (sandwiches or salads) or big (New York steak with all the trimmings, veggie lasagna, fresh fish). Be sure to come with a laid-back attitude; service can be slow or forgetful (I once had to reorder a couple of times because the counter person kept getting my order wrong), but the price and the view more than make up for it.

75-5799 Alii Dr., Kailua-Kona. ℂ **808/327-2161.** www.islandlavajavakona.com. Breakfast items $4.75–$14; lunch items $10–$15; dinner items $9–$22. AE, DISC, MC, V. Daily 6am–9:30pm.

Los Habaneros 🍴 MEXICAN There's no leisurely dining at this small eatery—just great, fast Mexican food at budget prices. You order at one counter and pick up at another. Habaneros starts off the day with huevos rancheros and other egg dishes, such as a chorizo-egg burrito. Lunch and dinner items include burritos (the fish with black bean is my favorite), soft and hard tacos (the veggie is surprisingly tasty and filling), nachos, tostadas, quesadillas, enchiladas, and daily specials—like Friday night's shrimp Vallarta. Bring cash.

At the Keauhou Shopping Center, 78–6831 Alii Dr., Keauhou. ℂ **808/324-HOTT** [4688]. All items under $11. No credit cards. Mon–Sat 9am–9pm.

Lulu's AMERICAN As is often the case with popular joints, Lulu's has fallen prey to the deadly sin of self-importance. Service is brisk and can be downright rude. The place is casual, noisy, and corny (black-velvet paintings at the entrance), but it's undeniably popular, with open-air dining, ocean views, and a sports bar atmosphere. Other elements include Capiz-shell lamps, clamshell sconces, and hula-girl replicas. The offerings include appetizers, sandwiches, salads, burgers, fresh-fish tacos, and fresh fish and meats in the evening.

At the Coconut Grove Market Place, 75–5819 Alii Dr., Kailua-Kona. ℂ **808/331-2633.** www.lulus hawaii.com. Reservations not accepted. Main courses $10–$16. AE, DC, DISC, MC, V. Mon–Fri 10:30am–10pm; Sat–Sun 8am–10pm. Bar until 2am.

Quinn's Almost by the Sea ★ STEAK/SEAFOOD Late-night noshers, take note: This is one of the few places you can grab a bite in Kona after 9pm. Quinn's, located at the northern gateway to town, has a nautical/sports bar atmosphere and offers casual alfresco dining on a garden lanai, with an air-conditioned, non-smoking area also available. The menu is surf-and-turf basic: burgers, sandwiches, and a limited dinner menu of dependably good fresh fish, filet mignon,

KONA coffee CRAZE!

Coffeehouses are booming on the Big Island—this is, after all, the home of Kona coffee, with dozens of vendors competing for your loyalty and dollars.

Most of the farms are concentrated in the North and South Kona districts, where coffee remains a viable industry. Notable among them is the **Kona Blue Sky Coffee Company,** in Holualoa (© **877/322-1700** or 808/322-1700; www.konabluesky coffee.com), which handles its own beans exclusively. The Christian Twigg-Smith family and staff grow, handpick, sun dry, roast, grind, and sell their coffee on a 400-acre estate. You can buy coffee on the farm itself and see the operation from field to final product. You can also find Blue Sky at the Waikoloa Beach Marriott Resort and at KTA Super Stores in Kailua-Kona and Keauhou. Open Monday through Saturday 9am to 3pm.

Also in Holualoa, 10 minutes above Kailua-Kona, **Holualoa Kona Coffee Company** (© **800/334-0348** or 808/322-9937; www.konalea.com) purveys organic Kona from its own farm and other growers. Not only can you buy premium, unadulterated Kona coffee here, but you also can witness the hulling, sorting, roasting, and packaging of beans on a farm tour Monday through Friday from 7:30am to 4pm.

Some other coffees to watch for: **Bong Brothers** (© **808/328-9289;** www.bongbrothers.com) thrives with its coffees, roadside fruit stand, and natural-foods deli that sells smoothies and healthful foods. Aficionados know that **Langenstein Farms** (© **808/938-4739;** www.kona-coffee.com/konastore), a name associated with quality and integrity, distributes excellent Kona coffee and distinctively tasty macadamia nuts in the town of Honaunau. There are also great tours of the farm; just call ahead to set one up. **Rooster Farms,** also in Honaunau (© **808/328-9173;** www.roosterfarms.com), enjoys an excellent reputation for the quality of its organic coffee beans.

A good bet in Hilo is **Bears' Coffee,** 106 Keawe St. (© **808/935-0708**), the quintessential sidewalk coffeehouse and a local stalwart. Regulars love to start their day here, with coffee and specialties such as souffléd eggs, cooked light and fluffy in the espresso machine and served in a croissant. It's a great lunchtime spot as well, and a dinner menu was recently added.

and a few shrimp dishes. There are eight burger selections and, when available, fresh ahi or ono sandwiches.

75-5655A Palani Rd., Kailua-Kona. © **808/329-3822.** Main courses $7–$25. DISC, MC, V. Daily 11am–11pm.

SOUTH KONA

Moderate

Aloha Angel Cafe ISLAND   The former Aloha Cafe is under new management, but it has kept the trademark large servings, heroic burgers and sandwiches, and a home-style menu for vegetarians and carnivores alike. Breakfast and lunch are served on the veranda that wraps around the old Aloha Theatre, with sweeping views down from the coffee fields to the shoreline. Dinner is served in the tiny dining room (which, sadly, has no view); space is limited, so phone ahead to ensure that you get a table. The cheaper daytime staples include omelets, burritos, tostadas, quesadillas, and home-baked goods (breakfast is served all day). Most of the produce is organic, and fresh-squeezed orange juice and fresh-fruit smoothies are served daily. Sandwiches, from turkey to tofu-avocado and a wonderful fresh ahi, are heaped with vegetables on tasty whole-wheat buns. Unfortunately, dinner is served only when an event (community theater or dance performance) is happening at the Aloha Theater.

79–7384 Mamalahoa Hwy. (Hwy. 11), Kainaliu. 𝄐 **808/322-3383.** Reservations recommended for event-night dinner. Main courses $7–$15 breakfast, $10–$15 lunch. AE, MC, V. Daily 7:30am–2:30pm (dinner 5:30–7:30pm when an event is scheduled for the Aloha Theater).

Keei Cafe ✋ MEDITERRANEAN/LATIN AMERICAN/ISLAND   When this bistro cafe opened in a former fish market in Keei, it was fabulous in every respect—delicious food at frugal prices, friendly service, and quirky decor. The restaurant became so popular, it moved a few years ago to a new location with hardwood floors, first-class artwork, and a view of the coast. It got really big, really fast, and can't seem to keep up with the rapid growth. The first thing that went was seating people on time. On my last visit, I waited more than an hour for a 7:30pm reservation (the staff was unapologetic). Now the food, once the draw, is no longer dependably good. I'm including the restaurant in this guide because it's so popular, but I can no longer recommend it—not only because of the not-up-to-par food and the slow service, but more because of the cavalier attitude: The owners are making money (right now) and don't really care how they treat their clientele.

79–7511 Mamalahoa Hwy. (Hwy. 11, by mile marker 113), Kealakekua. 𝄐 **808/322-9992.** Main courses $9–$12 lunch, $15–$25 dinner. No credit cards. Tues–Fri 10:30am–2pm and 5–9pm; Sat 5–9pm.

Inexpensive

The Coffee Shack ★★ ☺ COFFEEHOUSE/DELI   Great food, crisp air, and a sweeping ocean view make the Coffee Shack one of South Kona's great finds. It's an informal place with counter service, pool chairs, and white trellises on the deck, which is framed by ferns, palms, and banana and avocado trees. The fare is equally inviting: French toast made with homemade luau bread, lemon bars and carrot cake, and eggs Benedict with a delectable hollandaise. At lunch, you'll find an assortment of imported beers, excellent sandwiches on home-baked breads, and fresh, hearty salads made with organic lettuces. Let the kids order peanut-butter-and-jelly or grilled-cheese sandwiches while you head for the smoked Alaskan salmon sandwich or the hot, authentic Reuben.

Hwy. 11, 1 mile south of Captain Cook. 𝄐 **808/328-9555.** www.coffeeshack.com. Most items under $11; pizzas $11–$14. DISC, MC, V. Daily 7:30am–3pm.

Manago Hotel Restaurant 𝄐 AMERICAN   The dining room of the decades-old Manago Hotel is a local legend, greatly loved for its unpretentious, tasty food at bargain prices. At breakfast, $6 buys you eggs, bacon, papaya, rice, and coffee. At lunch or dinner, you can dine on a 12-ounce T-bone, fried ahi, opelu, or the house specialty, pork chops—the restaurant serves nearly 1,500 pounds monthly. When the akule or opelu are running, count on a rush by the regular customers. This place is nothing fancy, and lots of things are fried, but the local folks would riot if anything were to change after so many years.

At the Manago Hotel, Hwy. 11, Captain Cook. 𝄐 **808/323-2642.** Reservations recommended for dinner. Main courses $8.50–$15. DISC, MC, V. Tues–Sun 7–9am, 11am–2pm, and 5–7:30pm.

Teshima's JAPANESE/AMERICAN   This is local style all the way. Shizuko Teshima has a strong following among those who have made her miso soup and sukiyaki an integral part of their lives. The early-morning crowd starts gathering for omelets or Japanese breakfasts (soup, rice, and fish) while it's still dark outside. As the day progresses, the orders pour in for shrimp tempura and sukiyaki. By dinner, no. 3 teishoku trays—miso soup, sashimi, sukiyaki, shrimp, pickles, and other delights—are streaming out of the kitchen. Other combinations include steak and shrimp tempura, beef teriyaki and shrimp tempura, and the deep-sea trio of shrimp tempura, fried fish, and sashimi.

Hwy. 11, Honalo. © **808/322-9140.** Reservations recommended. Complete dinners $24 and under. No credit cards. Daily 6:30am–2pm and 5–9pm.

The Kohala Coast

Note: You'll find the following restaurants on "The Kohala Coast, North Kohala & Waimea" map (p. 319).

VERY EXPENSIVE

Brown's Beach House ★★ BIG ISLAND   The nearby lagoon takes on the pink orange glow of sunset, while torches flicker among the coconut trees. With white tablecloths, candles, and seating near the lagoon, this is a spectacular setting, complemented by a menu that keeps getting better by the year. The chef de cuisine, Thepthikone Keosavang, from Dubai, serves Big Island cuisine with a flair that includes unusual dishes like grilled Walu with lemon balm emulsion, wok-charred filet with cabernet reduction, grilled coriander snapper with lilikoi vinaigrette, and pineapple pork tenderloin with a Waipi'o taro crisp. Next door is **Brown's Deli,** with freshly made breads, pastries, and espresso coffees for breakfast, and pizza, salads, and sandwiches for lunch and dinner.

At the Fairmont Orchid, Mauna Lani Resort, 1 N. Kaniku Dr. © **808/885-2000.** www.fairmont. com/orchid. Reservations recommended for dinner. Main courses $32–$50 dinner; from $10 in the deli. AE, DC, DISC, MC, V. Daily 6:30am–5pm deli and 5:30–9:30pm Beach House.

CanoeHouse ★★ HAWAII REGIONAL   The setting is as gorgeous as ever, but this is not the same restaurant as it was when Alan Wong was the chef and the food coming out of the kitchen was nothing short of extraordinary. However, Wong didn't take the ambience with him, and the legendary sunset views remain, along with a koa canoe hanging from the ceiling in the open-air dining room. (*Tip:* Reserve a table outside and go at sunset to get the real flavor of this incredible setting.) The menu, which changes seasonally, includes great fish items (blackened ahi and scallops, sweet-sour chili prawns and scallops, and fresh fish cooked a variety of ways), meats (Mongolian-barbecued rack of lamb, Big Island goat cheese and potato ravioli with Hilo corn and a balsamic glaze and pan-roasted chicken with pineapple and fingerling potatoes), and even vegetarian items. Save room for dessert!

At the Mauna Lani Bay Hotel & Bungalows, Mauna Lani Resort, 68-1400 Mauna Lani Dr. © **808/881-7911.** Reservations recommended. Main courses $32–$46. AE, DC, DISC, MC, V. Summer daily 6–9pm; winter daily 5:30–9pm.

Manta & Pavilion Wine Bar ★★★ HAWAIIAN REGIONAL   The view alone is enough to draw you into Mauna Kea Beach Hotel's casual-but-elegant restaurant. That ocean vista is just the beginning. The added value here is the incredible cuisine of Executive Chef George Gomes and the attraction of their "enomatic" wine system (which allows them to pour one glass at a time). This is "the" place to have breakfast on a sunny deck overlooking the ocean as lazy waves roll in. Choose either the breakfast buffet ($32) with numerous items (including made-to-order omelets and waffles). Off the a la carte menu, I recommend the homemade Portuguese sweet-bread French toast with wild poha jam ($17) or the Hamakua three-egg omelet with feta cheese, spinach, mushrooms, and olives ($24). The atmosphere changes when the sun sets for dinner. A variety of wines by the glass are offered. Dinner, which Chef Gomes calls Kohala Cuisine, features fresh ingredients found within a 20-mile radius of the restaurant. This ranges from Big Island grass-fed beef to locally raised rack of lamb to just-caught Hawaiian fish. Personally, I could make a meal on the creative appetizers, such as Hawaii Island goat-cheese ravioli with local lobster and smoked bacon ($15), Hawaiian shrimp tempura with local fern shoots, green papaya and chili water aioli ($16), or roasted organic baby beets ($13).

Mauna Kea Beach Hotel, 62–100 Mauna Kea Beach Dr., Kohala Coast, HI 96743. 𝒞 **808/882-5810.** www.princeresortshawaii.com/mauna-kea-beach-hotel/big-island-restaurants.php. Reservations recommended. Main courses dinner $35–$45, breakfast $16–$26; Sunday brunch $48 adults, $24 children 11 and under. AE, DISC, MC, V. Breakfast daily 6:30am–11am; Sunday brunch 11:30am–2pm; dinner Tues–Sat 6–9pm.

Monettes ★★★ FISH/STEAK   The Mauna Kea's top restaurant was designed by the Monette brothers, owners of the award-winning Flagstaff House Restaurant in Boulder, Colorado, in the mode of the new, "modern" steakhouse. Luxury dining with eye-popping ocean views and outstanding service describe this top-notch restaurant, a must for any foodie. The a la cart menu changes daily but always features fresh island fish (like potato-crusted mahimahi or prosciutto-wrapped ono) and a variety of steaks, not to mention some creative fare like short ribs in a coconut brown ale or pineapple-braised port cheeks.

Mauna Kea Beach Hotel, 62–100 Mauna Kea Beach Dr., Kohala Coast, HI 96743. 𝒞 **808/443-2853.** www.princeresortshawaii.com/mauna-kea-beach-hotel/hawaii-fine-dining.php. Reservations required. Main courses $25–$56. AE, DISC, MC, V. Thurs–Mon 5:30–10pm.

EXPENSIVE

Coast Grille ★★ STEAK/SEAFOOD/HAWAII REGIONAL   It's a 3-minute walk from the main lobby to the open-air Grille, but the view along the way is nothing to complain about and will help you work up an appetite. The split-level dining room has banquettes and wicker furniture, open-air seating, and an oyster bar that's famous. The extensive seafood selection includes poke, clams, and fresh oysters from all over the world, as well as fresh seafood from local waters, served in multicultural preparations.

At the Hapuna Beach Prince Hotel, Mauna Kea Resort, 62–100 Kaunaoa Dr. 𝒞 **808/880-1111.** www.hapunabeachprincehotel.com. Reservations recommended. Main courses $15–$30. AE, DISC, MC, V. Sat–Thurs 6–9pm.

Norio's Sushi Bar & Restaurant ★ JAPANESE/SUSHI   This new upscale sushi bar and restaurant at the Fairmont Orchid features master sushi chef Norio Yamamoto, who trained in Tokyo and most recently worked at the sushi bar at the Ritz-Carlton Kapalua on Maui. His menu reflects a reverence for traditional Japanese delicacies such as sushi and tempura dishes, plus a few signature items like *kushi katsu* (a panko-fried pork loin and onion skewer served with sesame-katsu sauce) and *sukiyaki* (thinly sliced beef and vegetables). Also on the menu are a selection of sakes, Japanese beers, and green teas. Sushi lovers can sit at the newly expanded 15-seat sushi bar to watch the master and his team of three at work.

At the Fairmont Orchid, Mauna Lani Resort, 1 N. Kaniku Dr. ☎ **808/885-2000.** www.fairmont. com/orchid. Reservations recommended. Main courses $28–$44. AE, DC, DISC, MC, V. Thurs–Mon 5:30–9pm.

Roy's Waikoloa Bar & Grill ★★★ PACIFIC RIM/EURO-ASIAN   Don't let the resort-mall location fool you—Roy's Waikoloa has several distinctive and inviting features, such as a golf-course view, large windows overlooking a 10-acre lake, and the East-West cuisine and upbeat service that are Roy Yamaguchi signatures. This is a clone of his Oahu restaurant, offering favorites like Szechuan baby back ribs, blackened Island ahi, hibachi-style salmon, and six other types of fresh fish prepared charred, steamed, or seared, and topped with exotic sauces such as shiitake-miso and gingered lime-chile butter. Yamaguchi's tireless exploration of local ingredients and world traditions produces food that keeps him at Hawaii's culinary cutting edge. ***Be warned:*** Roy's is always packed (make reservations!) and noisy, but the food is always great and the service is excellent. Menu changes daily.

At Kings' Shops, Waikoloa Beach Resort, 69–250 Waikoloa Beach Dr. ☎ **808/886-4321.** www. roysrestaurant.com. Reservations recommended. Main courses $28–$42. AE, DC, DISC, MC, V. Daily 5–9:30pm.

Sansei Seafood Restaurant & Sushi Bar ★★★ SUSHI/PACIFIC RIM   In 2007, award-winning chef D. K. Kodama opened a branch of his popular Sansei (also on Maui and Oahu) on the Big Island. The very classy restaurant offers an extensive menu of Japanese and East-West delicacies. Part fusion, part Hawaii Regional Cuisine, Sansei is tirelessly creative, with a menu that scores higher with adventurous palates than with purists (although there are endless traditional choices as well). Options include panko-crusted ahi sashimi, miso garlic prawns, noodle dishes, Asian shrimp cakes, and sauces that surprise, in creative combinations such as ginger-lime chile butter and cilantro pesto. But there's simpler fare as well, such as shrimp tempura, noodles, and wok-tossed upcountry vegetables. Desserts are not to be missed. If it's autumn, don't pass up the Granny Smith apple tart with vanilla ice cream and homemade caramel sauce. In other seasons, opt for tempura-fried ice cream with chocolate sauce. There's karaoke on Friday nights from 10pm to 2am. ***Money-saving tip:*** Eat early: Specials like a 25% discount are offered between 5:30 and 6pm.

At Queens' MarketPlace, Waikoloa Beach Resort, 69–191 Waikoloa Beach Dr. ☎ **808/886-6286.** www.sanseihawaii.com. Reservations recommended. Main courses $18–$50; sushi $5–$17. AE, DISC, MC, V. Daily 5:30–10pm (Fri–Sat karaoke and sushi until 1am).

MODERATE

Cafe Pesto ★★ MEDITERRANEAN/ITALIAN   Fans drive miles for the gourmet pizzas, calzones, and fresh organic greens grown from Kealakekua to Kamuela. The herb-infused Italian pies are adorned with lobster from the aquaculture farms on Keahole Point, shiitake mushrooms from a few miles mauka (inland), and fresh fish, shrimp, and crab. Seared poke with spinach, Santa Fe chicken pasta, and local seafood risotto are other favorites.

At the Kawaihae Shopping Center, at Kawaihae Harbor, Pule Hwy. and Kawaihae Rd. ℭ **808/882-1071**. www.cafepesto.com. Main courses $11–$17 lunch, $18–$37 dinner, $9–$21 pizza. AE, DC, DISC, MC, V. Daily 11am–9pm.

Merriman's Market Cafe ★ MEDITERRANEAN/DELI   Peter Merriman, who has long reigned as king of Hawaii Regional Cuisine with Merriman's restaurant in Waimea, has opened this tiny "market cafe" featuring cuisines of the Mediterranean made with fresh local produce, house-made sausages, artisan-style breads, and great cheese and wines. This is a fun place for lunch or a light dinner. The 3,000-square-foot restaurant and deli features full-service indoor and outdoor dining in a casual atmosphere. Lunch ranges from salads to sandwiches; dinner features small-plate dishes, pizzas, and entrees from grilled fish to large salads.

At Kings' Shops, Waikoloa Beach Resort, 69–250 Waikoloa Beach Dr. ℭ **808/886-1700**. www.merrimanshawaii.com. Main courses: $10–$17 lunch specials, $19–$28 all day. AE, MC, V. Daily 11:30am–9:30pm.

North Kohala

Note: You'll find the following restaurant on "The Kohala Coast, North Kohala & Waimea" map (p. 319).

MODERATE

Bamboo ★★ 🍴 PACIFIC RIM   Serving fresh fish and Asian specialties in a historic building, Hawaii's self-professed "tropical saloon" is a major attraction on the island's northern coastline. The exotic interior is a nod to nostalgia, with high wicker chairs from Waikiki's historic Moana Hotel, works by local artists, and old Matson liner menus accenting the bamboo-lined walls. The fare, Island favorites in sophisticated presentations, is a match for all this style: *imu*-smoked pork quesadillas, fish prepared several ways, sesame-nori-crusted or tequila-lime shrimp, and selections of pork, beef, and chicken. There are even some local faves, such as fried noodles served vegetarian, with chicken, or with shrimp. Produce from nearby gardens and fish fresh off the chef's own hook are among the highlights. Hawaiian music wafts through Bamboo from 6pm to closing on Saturdays and some Friday nights.

Hwy. 270, Hawi. ℭ **808/889-5555**. www.bamboorestaurant.info. Reservations recommended. Main courses $10–$20 lunch, $8–$35 dinner (full- and half-size portions available at dinner). MC, V. Tues–Sat 11:30am–2:30pm and 6–8pm; Sun brunch 11:30am–2:30pm.

Waimea

Note: You'll find the following restaurants on "The Kohala Coast, North Kohala & Waimea" map (p. 319).

EXPENSIVE

Daniel Thiebaut Restaurant ★★ FRENCH/ASIAN   Come here for Sunday brunch. This restaurant features Big Island products (Kamuela Pride beef, Kahua Ranch lettuces, Hirabara Farms field greens, herbs and greens from Adaptations in South Kona) as interpreted by the French-trained Thiebaut, formerly executive chef at Mauna Kea Beach Resort. Brunch is just as fabulous as the fancy Kohala resorts at half the price. Dinner highlights include Hunan-style rack of lamb, wok-fried scallops, vegetarian specials (such as crispy avocado spring rolls

Tropical Dreams of Ice Cream

Tropical Dreams ice creams has spread out over the island but got its start in North Kohala. Across the street from Bamboo, **Kohala Coffee Mill and Tropical Dreams Ice Cream,** Hwy. 270, Hawi (✆ 808/889-5577), serves upscale ice creams along with sandwiches, pastries, and a selection of Island coffees. The Tahitian vanilla and litchi ice creams are local legends. Jams, jellies, herb vinegars, Hawaiian honey, herbal salts, and macadamia-nut oils are among the gift items for sale. It's open Monday through Friday from 6am to 6pm, and Saturday and Sunday from 7am to 5:30pm. For other Tropical Dreams outlets, check www.tropicaldreamsicecream.com.

with a smoked-tomato coulis), and fresh fish. The recently remodeled restaurant is full of intimate enclaves and has a gaily lit plantation-style veranda. In recent years, unfortunately, the quality of this once-sterling restaurant has varied wildly. If chef Daniel is in, you will most likely get an excellent meal, but if he is not cooking that night, service may suffer. My other complaints are the alarming rise in prices and simultaneous decrease in the amount of food on your plate.

At the Historic Yellow Bldg., 65-1259 Kawaihae Rd. ✆ **808/887-2200.** www.danielthiebaut.com. Reservations recommended. Main courses $10–$18 lunch, $25–$50 dinner; Sun brunch $24 adults, $12 children 5–11, free for children 4 and under. AE, DISC, MC, V. Mon–Fri 11:30am–3:30pm; Sun brunch 10am–2pm; daily 3:30–9pm.

Merriman's ★★ HAWAII REGIONAL   Merriman's is peerless. Although founder/owner/chef Peter Merriman now commutes between the Big Island and Maui, where he runs the Hula Grill, he manages to maintain the sizzle that has made Merriman's a premier Hawaii attraction. Order anything from Chinese short ribs to grilled shrimp and asparagus for lunch; at dinner, choose from the signature wok-charred ahi, Szechuan pepper–rubbed New York steak, lamb from nearby Kahua Ranch, and a noteworthy vegetarian selection. Among my favorites are the Caesar salad with sashimi, baked local goat cheese in pastry, and the steamed Opakapaka with macadamia nut spaetzle and pineapple cinnamon sauce. Kalua-pig quesadillas and the famous platters of seafood and meats are among the many reasons this is still the best, and busiest, dining spot in Waimea.

At the Opelo Plaza, Hwy. 19. ✆ **808/885-6822.** www.merrimanshawaii.com. Reservations recommended. Main courses $9–$18 lunch, $23–$46 dinner (market prices for ranch lamb and ahi). AE, MC, V. Mon–Fri 11:30am–1:30pm; daily 5:30–9pm.

INEXPENSIVE

Tako Taco Taqueria MEXICAN   Once a tiny hole in the wall with the most delicious (and healthy) Mexican food, Tako Taco recently moved to the other side of Waimea into bigger quarters and added margaritas, beer, and wine to the menu. Alas, the food is not what it once was. There's plenty of room to eat in, or you can take out. Most items fall between $9 and $12. There are plenty of vegetarian selections as well. If the Mexican wedding cookies or chocolate-chip cookies are available, grab one (they're huge and only 75¢–$1.25 each).

64-1066 Mamalahoa Hwy. ✆ **808/887-1717.** www.takotaco.com. All items $17 and under. AE, MC, V. Daily 11am–8:30pm.

The Hamakua Coast

INEXPENSIVE

Cafe Il Mondo ★ PIZZA/ESPRESSO BAR   A tiny cafe with a big spirit has taken over the Andrade Building in the heart of Honokaa. Tropical watercolors and local art, the irresistible aromas of garlic sauces and pizzas, and a 1924 koa bar meld gracefully in Sergio and Dena Ramirez's tribute to the Old World. A classical and flamenco guitarist, Sergio occasionally plays solo guitar in his restaurant while contented diners tuck into the stone-oven-baked pizzas. Try the Sergio—pesto pizza with marinated artichokes and mushrooms—or one of the calzones. Sandwiches come cradled in fresh-baked French, onion, or rustic buns. There's fresh soup daily, roasted chicken, and other specials; all greens are local and organic.

Mamane St., Honokaa. ✆ **808/775-7711.** Pizzas $12–$23; sandwiches $7–$8; pastas $13–$15. No credit cards. Mon–Sat 11am–8pm.

Jolene's Kau Kau Korner AMERICAN/LOCAL   This place is nothing fancy, but it's homey and friendly, with eight tables and windows overlooking a scene much like an old Western town but for the cars. Choose from saimin, stir-fried tempeh with vegetables, sandwiches (including a good vegetarian tempeh burger), plate lunches (mahimahi, fried chicken, shrimp, beef stew), and familiar selections of local food.

At Mamane St. and Lehua, Honokaa. ✆ **808/775-9498.** Plate lunches $9–$25. No credit cards. Tues and Thurs–Sun 10:30am–3pm; Mon and Wed 10:30am–8pm.

Simply Natural ★ 🍴 HEALTH FOOD/SANDWICH SHOP   Simply Natural is a superb find on Honokaa's main street. I love this charming deli with its friendly staff, wholesome food, and vintage interior. It offers a counter and a few small tables with bright tablecloths and fresh anthuriums. Don't be fooled by the unpretentiousness of the place. The wholesome menu features flavorful items (saimin bowls, tuna melts), and breakfast delights that include taro-banana pancakes. Top it off with a smoothie: The mango-pineapple-banana-strawberry version is sublime.

Mamane St., Honokaa. ✆ **808/775-0119.** www.hawaiisimplynatural.com. Deli items $5–$9. No credit cards. Mon–Sat 8am–3:30pm.

Tex Drive-In & Restaurant AMERICAN/LOCAL   When Ada Pulin-Lamme bought the old Tex Drive-In, she made significant changes, such as improving upon an ages-old recipe for Portuguese *malasadas,* a cakelike doughnut without a hole. Tex sells tens of thousands of these sugar-rolled morsels a month, including ones filled with pineapple/papaya preserves, pepper jelly, or Bavarian cream. The menu has a local flavor and features ethnic specialties: Korean chicken, teriyaki meat, kalua pork with cabbage, Filipino specials, and a new addition, Tex wraps served with homemade sweet-potato chips. With its gift shop and visitor center, Tex is a roadside attraction and a local hangout; residents have been gathering here over early-morning coffee and breakfast for decades.

Hwy. 19, Honokaa. ✆ **808/775-0598.** www.texdrivein.com. Main courses $4–$12. MC, V. Daily 6am–8pm.

What's Shakin' ★ 🍹 HEALTH FOOD   Look for the cheerful yellow-and-white plantation-style wooden house with a green roof, 2 miles north of the Hawaii Tropical Botanical Garden. Many of the bananas and papayas from Patsy and Tim Withers's 20-acre farm end up here, in fresh-fruit smoothies like the

Papaya Paradise, an ambrosial blend of pineapples, coconuts, papayas, and bananas. If you're in the mood for something more substantial, try the chicken tamale with homemade salsa, the taro burger with their homegrown avocado, or one of the wraps. There are several lunch specials daily, and every plate arrives with fresh fruit and a green salad topped with Patsy's Oriental sesame dressing. You can sit outdoors in the garden and enjoy the staggering ocean view.

27-999 Old Mamalahoa Hwy. (on the 4-mile scenic drive), Pepeekeo. © **808/964-3080.** Most items under $9.50; smoothies $6.50. MC, V. Daily 10am–5pm.

Hilo

Note: You'll find the following restaurants on the "Hilo" map on p. 397.

EXPENSIVE

Pescatore ★ SOUTHERN ITALIAN   In a town of ethnic eateries and casual mom-and-pop diners, this is a special-occasion restaurant, dressier and pricier than most Hilo choices. It's ornate, especially for Hilo, with gilded frames on antique paintings, chairs of vintage velvet, koa walls, and a tile floor. The fresh

A lunch FOR ALL FIVE SENSES

Hidden in the tall eucalyptus trees outside the old plantation community of Paauilo lies the **Hawaiian Vanilla Company,** on Paauilo Mauka Road (© **877/ 771-1771** or 808/776-1771; www.hawaiian vanilla.com). Located next to a gulch, surrounded by wild coffee, guava, loquat, and avocado trees, the company hosts one of the truly sensuous experiences on the Big Island—a multicourse Vanilla Luncheon. Before you even enter the huge Vanilla Gallery and Kitchen, you will be embraced by the heavenly sent of vanilla. You'll see vanilla orchid vines and, if you're truly lucky, the elusive blossoms. One of the real treats is listening to owner Jim Reddekopp's presentation (and video) on how vanilla is grown, how it's used in the meal you will be eating, and just about everything else you ever wanted to know about this magical orchid and bean. The four-course, 2-hour **Hawaiian Vanilla Luncheon** is held Wednesday through Friday from 12:30 to 2:30pm (reservations required); the cost is $36 and it's worth every penny. Check out the retail store, where myriad vanilla products, from beans to extracts, teas to lotions, are for sale. You can also arrange to do a **Vanilla Tasting,** which occurs Monday through Saturday at 10am and lasts until 10:45 or 11am; the cost is $25 per person (reservations required). Recently they added a cafe with light fare (Mon–Sat 11am–3pm; gift shop 10am–5pm).

catch is offered in several preparations, including reduced-cream and Parmesan or capers and wine. The paper-thin ahi carpaccio is garnished with capers, red onion, garlic, lemon, olive oil, and shaved Parmesan—and it's superb. Chicken, veal, and fish Marsala; a rich and garlicky scampi Alfredo; and the *fra diavolo* (a spicy seafood marinara) are among the dinner offerings, which come with soup or salad. Lighter fare, such as simple pasta marinara and chicken Parmesan, prevails at lunch. Breakfast is terrific, too.

235 Keawe St. ℭ **808/969-9090.** Reservations recommended for dinner. Main courses $7–$11 breakfast, $9–$15 lunch, $16–$38 dinner. AE, DC, DISC, MC, V. Mon–Fri 11am–5pm and 5:30–9pm; Sat 9am–5pm and 5:30–9pm; Sun 7:30–5pm and 5:30–9pm.

MODERATE

Hilo Bay Café ★★ 🏨 PACIFIC RIM *Foodie alert:* In the midst of a suburban shopping mall is this upscale, elegant eatery. It was created by the people from the Island Naturals Market & Deli, located on the other side of the shopping center. When you enter, the cascade of orchids on the marble bar is the first thing you see. Mellow jazz wafts from speakers, and plush chairs at low tables fill out the room. The creative menu ranges from lamb *osso buco* with brown butter mashed potatoes to sautéed fresh catch to seared scallops with wasabi cream and green tea soba. Lunch features salads (such as seared ahi Caesar), sandwiches (think sun-dried tomato, spinach, and Gorgonzola chicken salad), and entrees (such as flaky-crust vegetarian potpie, slow-cooked pork barbecue ribs, and crispy fish and chips). There are also a terrific wine list and great martinis. Don't miss eating here.

At the Waiakea Center, 315 Makaala St. ℭ **808/935-4939.** www.hilobaycafe.com. Reservations recommended for dinner. Main courses $9–$16 lunch, $9–$27 dinner. AE, DISC, MC, V. Mon–Sat 11am–9pm; Sun 5–9pm.

Nihon Restaurant & Cultural Center ★ 🍴 JAPANESE This restaurant offers a beautiful view of Hilo Bay on one side and the soothing green sprawl of Liliuokalani Gardens on the other. This is a magnificent part of Hilo that's often overlooked because of its distance from the central business district. The menu features steak-and-seafood combination dinners and selections from the sushi bar, including the innovative poke and lomi-salmon hand rolls. The Businessman's Lunch, a terrific deal, comes with sushi, potato salad, soup, vegetables, and two choices from the following: butterfish, shrimp tempura, sashimi,

---

🍟 BET YOU CAN'T eat JUST ONE

Hawaii Island Gourmet Products, which, under the brand Atebara Chips, has been making potato, taro, and shrimp chips in Hilo for 70 years, recently added a couple of new products that you just cannot miss: sweet-potato chips and the delicious taro, and regular potato chips covered in chocolate (the first-place winner at the Taste of Hilo). You can find them at most stores and major resorts on the Big Island, or contact the company directly (ℭ **808/969-9600;** www.hawaiichips. com). *Warning:* As we say in Hawaii, these chips are so *ono* (delicious), you will be mail-ordering more when you get home.

chicken, and other morsels. This isn't inexpensive dining, but the value is sky-high, with a presentation that matches the serenity of the room and its stunning view of the bay.

123 Lihiwai St., overlooking Liliuokalani Gardens and Hilo Bay. ✆ **808/969-1133.** Reservations recommended. Main courses $12–$20 lunch, $16–$26 dinner; combination dinners $22. AE, DC, DISC, MC, V. Mon–Sat 11am–1:15pm and 5–8pm.

Ocean Sushi Deli ★ 🎁 SUSHI   At Hilo's nexus of affordable sushi, local-style specials stretch purist boundaries but are so much fun: lomi salmon, oyster nigiri, opihi nigiri, unagi-avocado hand roll, ahi-poke roll, and special new rolls that use thin sheets of tofu skins and cooked egg. For traditionalists, there are ample shrimp, salmon, hamachi, clam, and other sushi delights—a long menu of them, including sukiyaki and *shabu-shabu* (you cook your own ingredients in a heavy pot).

250 Keawe St. ✆ **808/961-6625.** Sushi boxes $4.75–$13; sushi family platters $20–$50. MC, V. Mon–Sat 10am–2pm and 5–9pm.

Queen's Court Restaurant AMERICAN/BUFFET   Many of those with a "not me!" attitude toward buffets have been disarmed by the Hilo Hawaiian's generous and well-rounded offerings at budget-friendly prices. A la carte menu items are offered Monday through Thursday, but it's the seafood buffet on the weekends that draw throngs of local families.

At the Hilo Hawaiian Hotel, 71 Banyan Dr. ✆ **808/935-9361.** www.castleresorts.com. Reservations recommended. Fri–Sun seafood buffet $36. AE, DC, DISC, MC, V. Daily 6:30–9am, 11:30am–5pm, and 5:30–9pm.

Restaurant Miwa ★ JAPANESE/SUSHI   Come to the Hilo Shopping Center to discover sensational seafood in a quintessential neighborhood sushi bar. This self-contained slice of Japan is a pleasant surprise in an otherwise unremarkable mall. *Shabu-shabu* (you cook your own ingredients in a heavy pot), tempura, fresh catch, and a full sushi selection are among the offerings. At dinner, you can splurge on the steak and lobster combination without dressing up. The *haupia* (coconut pudding) cream cheese pie is a Miwa signature; blueberry cream cheese is the alternative.

At the Hilo Shopping Center, 1261 Kilauea Ave. ✆ **808/961-4454.** Reservations recommended. Main courses $9–$21 lunch (most items $10–$15), $12–$40 dinner. AE, DC, DISC, MC, V. Mon–Sat 11am–2pm and 5–9pm; Sun 5–9pm. Closed 3rd Sun of the month.

Seaside Restaurant ★★ STEAK/SEAFOOD   This is a casual local favorite, a Hilo signature with a character all its own. The restaurant has large windows overlooking glassy ponds—from which your dinner of mullet and *aholehole* (a silvery mountain bass) is fished out shortly before you arrive (you can't get much fresher than that!). Colin Nakagawa and his family cook the fish in two unadorned styles: fried or steamed in ti leaves with lemon juice and onions. Daily specials include steamed opakapaka, onaga (snapper), steak and lobster, paniolo-style prime rib, salmon encrusted with a nori-wasabi sprinkle, New York steak, and shrimp. Very fresh sushi is available daily. *Note:* If you want fish from the pond, *you must call ahead.* The outdoor tables are fabulous at dusk, when the light reflects on the water with an otherworldly glow.

1790 Kalanianaole Ave. ✆ **808/935-8825.** www.seasiderestaurant.com. Reservations recommended. Main courses $14–$33. AE, DC, MC, V. Tues–Thurs and Sun 5–8:30pm; Fri–Sat 5–9pm.

INEXPENSIVE

Cafe Pesto ★★ PIZZA/PACIFIC RIM   Cafe Pesto's Italian brick oven burns many bushels of ohia and kiawe wood to turn out its toothsome pizzas, topped with fresh organic herbs and island-grown produce. It's difficult to resist the wild-mushroom-and-artichoke pizza or the chipotle-and-tomato-drenched Southwestern. But go with the Four Seasons, dripping with prosciutto, bell peppers, and mushrooms—it won't disappoint. Some of my other favorites are the Milolii, a crab-shrimp-mushroom sandwich with basil pesto; the chili-grilled shrimp pizza; and the flash-seared poke and spinach salad. The restaurant's high-ceilinged 1912 room looks out over Hilo's bay.

At the S. Hata Bldg., 308 Kamehameha Ave. ℂ 808/969-6640. www.cafepesto.com. Pizzas $9–$21, main courses $11–$17 lunch, $18–$27 dinner. AE, DC, DISC, MC, V. Sun–Thurs 11am–9pm; Fri-Sat 11am–10pm.

Ken's House of Pancakes AMERICAN/LOCAL   The only 24-hour coffee shop on the Big Island, Ken's fulfills basic dining needs simply and efficiently, with a good dose of local color. Lighter servings and a concession toward health-conscious meals and salads have been added to the menu, a clever antidote to the numerous pies available. Omelets, pancakes, French toast made with Portuguese sweet bread, saimin, sandwiches, and soup stream out of the busy kitchen. Other affordable selections include fried chicken, steak, prime rib, and grilled fish. Tuesday is taco night, Wednesday is prime-rib night, Thursday is Hawaiian-plate night, and Sunday is all-you-can-eat-spaghetti night. Very local, very Hilo.

1730 Kamehameha Ave. ℂ 808/935-8711. http://kenshouseofpancakes-hilohi.com. Most items under $12. AE, DC, DISC, MC, V. Daily 24 hr.

Miyo's JAPANESE   Often cited by local publications as the island's best Japanese restaurant, Miyo's offers home-cooked, healthy food (no MSG) served in an open-air room on Wailoa Pond, where curving footpaths and greenery fill the horizon. Sliding shoji doors bordering the dining area are left open so you can take in the view, which includes Mauna Kea on clear days. The sesame chicken (deep-fried and boneless with a spine-tingling sesame sauce) is a bestseller, but the entire menu is appealing. For vegetarians, there are specials such as vegetable tempura, vegetarian *shabu-shabu* (cooked in a chafing dish at your table, then dipped in a special sauce), and noodle and seaweed dishes. Other choices include mouthwatering sashimi, beef teriyaki, fried oysters, tempura, ahi *donburi* (seasoned and steamed in a bowl of rice), sukiyaki, and generous combination dinners. All orders are served with rice, soup, and pickled vegetables. The miso soup is a wonder, and the ahi-tempura plate is one of Hilo's best buys. Special diets (low sodium, sugarless) are cheerfully accommodated.

At the Waiakea Villas Hotel, 400 Hualani St. ℂ 808/935-2273. Lunch main courses $7–$14, combinations $12–$15; dinner main courses $9–$16, combinations $13–$17. MC, V. Mon–Sat 11am–2pm and 5:30–8:30pm.

Naung Mai 🍴 THAI   This quintessential hole in the wall has gained an extra room, but even with 26 seats, it fills up quickly. In a short time, Naung Mai has gained the respect of Hilo residents for its curries and pad Thai—and for its use of fresh local ingredients. The flavors are assertive, the produce comes straight from the Hilo Farmers Market, and the prices are good. The four curries—green, red, yellow, and Mussaman (Thai Muslim)—go with the jasmine, brown, white, and sticky rice. The pad Thai rice noodles, served with tofu and fresh vegetables, come with a choice of chicken, pork, or shrimp, and are sprinkled with fresh peanuts. You can order your curry Thai-spicy (incendiary) or American-spicy (moderately hot), but even mild, the flavors are outstanding. Chefs Sukanya Heideman and Siriporn Elkins also make wonderful spring rolls and a Tom Yum spicy soup that is legendary. Lunch specials are a steal. Naung Mai is obscured behind the Garden Exchange, so it may take some seeking out.

86 Kilauea Ave. ✆ **808/934-7540.** www.naungmaithai.com. Reservations recommended. Main dishes $11–$16. MC, V. Daily 11am–9pm.

Nori's Saimin & Snacks ★ 🎁 SAIMIN/NOODLES   Like Naung Mai, Nori's requires some searching out, but it's worth it. Unmarked and not visible from the street, it's located across from the Hilo Lanes bowling alley, down a short driveway into an obscure parking lot. You'll wonder what you're doing here, but stroll into the tiny noodle house with the neon sign of chopsticks and a bowl, grab a plywood booth or Formica table, and prepare to enjoy the best saimin on the island. Saimin comes fried or in a savory homemade broth—the key to its success—with various embellishments, from seaweed to wonton dumplings. Ramen, soba, udon, and *mundoo* (a Korean noodle soup) are among the 16 varieties of noodle soups. The barbecued chicken and beef sticks are smoky and marvelous. Plate lunches (teriyaki beef, ahi, Korean short ribs) and sandwiches give diners ample choices from morning to late night, though noodles are the stars. The "big plate" dinners feature ahi, barbecued beef, fried noodles, kalbi ribs, and salad—not for junior appetites. The desserts at Nori's are also legendary, with the signature haupia and sweet-potato pies flying out the door almost as fast as the famous chocolate-mochi cookies and cakes.

688 Kinoole St. ✆ **808/935-9133.** Most items under $12; "big plate" dinners (for 2) $22. AE, DC, MC, V. Mon–Thurs 10:30am–11pm; Fri–Sat 10:30am–midnight; Sun 10:30am–10pm.

Royal Siam Thai Restaurant ★ THAI   A popular neighborhood restaurant, the Royal Siam serves consistently good Thai curries in a simple room just off the sidewalk. Fresh herbs and vegetables from the owner's gardens add an extra zip to the platters of noodles, soups, curries, and specialties, which pour out of the kitchen in clouds of spicy fragrance. The Buddha Rama, a wonderful concoction of spinach, chicken, and peanut sauce, is a scene stealer and a personal favorite. The Thai garlic chicken, in sweet basil with garlic and coconut milk, is equally superb.

70 Mamo St. ✆ **808/961-6100.** Main courses $7–$13. AE, DC, DISC, MC, V. Mon–Sat 11am–2pm and 5–8:30pm; Sun 5–8:30pm.

Hawaii Volcanoes National Park

Note: You'll find the following restaurants on the "Where to Stay & Dine in the Volcano Area" map (p. 331).

EXPENSIVE

Kiawe Kitchen PIZZA/MEDITERRANEAN   Although it has a somewhat limited menu, this small eatery is a great place to stop for hot soup or fresh salad after viewing the volcano; it has recently added a full bar. The pizza is excellent (all fresh ingredients) but pricey; I recommend the insalata caprese and a bowl of soup for lunch. Dinners include lamb (both rack and shank), pasta dishes, a vegetarian item, and usually beef. The menu changes daily (whatever they can get fresh that day). There's an interesting beer list (all from Hawaii) and yummy espresso drinks (including Kona coffees). You can eat on the lanai or inside the restaurant.

19–4005 Haunani Rd. (off Hwy. 11, Volcano Village exit). *©* **808/967-7711.** Main courses $10–$16 lunch, $15–$34 dinner. MC, V. Daily 11am–2:30pm and 5:30–8:30pm.

Kilauea Lodge & Restaurant ★ CONTINENTAL   Diners travel long distances to escape from the crisp upland air into the warmth of this high-ceilinged lodge. The decor is a cross between chalet-cozy and volcano-rugged; the sofa in front of the 1938 fireplace is especially inviting when a fire is roaring. The European cooking is a fine culinary act. Favorites include the fresh catch, hasenpffer, potato-leek soup (all flavor and no cream), and Alsatian soup. All dinners come with soup or salad and a loaf of freshly baked bread.

19–3948 Old Volcano Rd. (1 block off Hwy. 11, Volcano Village exit). *©* **808/967-7366.** www. kilaualodge.com. Reservations recommended. Main courses $7–$13 breakfast, $8–$11 lunch, $20–$47 dinner. AE, MC, V. Daily 7:30am–2pm; 5–9pm.

INEXPENSIVE

Lava Rock Cafe ★ ECLECTIC/LOCAL   Volcano Village's newest favorite spot is a cheerful, airy oasis with tables and booths indoors and semioutdoors, under a clear corrugated-plastic ceiling. The cross-cultural menu includes everything from chow fun to fajitas. The choices include three-egg omelets and pancakes with wonderful house-made lilikoi butter, teriyaki beef and chicken, fresh catch, T-bone steak, steak-and-shrimp combos, and serious desserts (like mango cheesecake). The lunchtime winners are the "seismic sandwiches" (which the cafe will pack for hikers), chili, quarter-pound burgers, salads, plate lunches, and "volcanic" heavies such as southern-fried chicken and grilled meats.

19–3972 Old Volcano Rd. (1 block off Hwy. 11, Volcano Village exit), next to Kilauea Kreations. *©* **808/967-8526.** Main courses $7–$11 breakfast, $8–$12 lunch, $9–$20 dinner. MC, V. Sun 7:30am–4pm; Mon 7:30am–5pm; Tues–Sat 7:30am–9pm.

Thai Thai Restaurant THAI   Volcano's first Thai restaurant adds warming curries to the chill of upcountry life. The menu features spicy curries (five types, rich with coconut milk and spices), satays, coconut-rich soups, noodles and rice, and sweet-and-sour stir-fries of fish, vegetables, beef, cashew chicken, and garlic shrimp. A big hit is the green-papaya salad made with tomatoes, crunchy green beans, green onions, and a heap of raw and roasted peanuts—a full symphony of color, aroma, texture, and flavor.

19–4084 Old Volcano Rd. (1 block off Hwy. 11, Volcano Village exit). *©* **808/967-7969.** Main courses $15–$26. AE, DISC, MC, V. Thurs–Tues noon–9pm.

Volcano Golf & Country Club AMERICAN/LOCAL   One of the first two eateries in the area, this golf-course clubhouse has a reputation as a low-key purveyor of local specialties. The food ranges from okay to good, while the room—looking out over a fairway—is cordial. It's not as clichéd as it sounds, especially when the mists are rolling in and the greens and grays assume an eye-popping intensity; I've even seen nene geese from my table. In the typically cool Volcano air, local favorites such as chicken or fish sandwiches, hamburgers, pastas, saimin, and Hawaiian stew with rice become especially comforting. Also featured are stir-fry and teriyaki beef or chicken.

Pii Mauna Dr., off Hwy. 11 (mile marker 30). ✆ **808/967-8228.** www.volcanogolfshop.com. Reservations recommended for large groups. Breakfast items under $10; lunch items under $13. AE, DC, DISC, MC, V. Daily 8am–3pm.

South Point/Naalehu

MODERATE

South Side Shaka Restaurant ☺ AMERICAN/LOCAL   You can't miss the Shaka sign from the highway. This welcome addition to the Naalehu restaurant scene has white tile floors, long tables, an espresso machine, and a friendly, casual atmosphere. The serviceable menu of plate lunches and American fare will seem like gourmet cuisine after a long drive through the Kau Desert. The servings are humongous, and the prices are kind to your wallet. Locals come for the plate lunches, sandwiches (the Shaka burger is very popular), and honey-dipped fried chicken, and for the fresh catch at dinner—grilled, deep-fried, or prepared in a special panko crust. In fact, the new owner, a former fish wholesaler, is now focusing more on fresh fish.

95–5673 Mamalahoa Hwy. (Hwy. 11), Naalehu. ✆ **808/929-7404.** www.shakarestaurant.com. Main courses $5–$13 lunch, $11–$22 dinner. MC, V. Daily 11am–9pm.

BEACHES

Too young geologically to have many great beaches, the Big Island instead has a collection of unusual ones: brand-new black-sand beaches, green-sand beaches, salt-and-pepper beaches, and even a rare (for this island) white-sand beach.

The Kona Coast

KAHALUU BEACH PARK ★★

This is the most popular beach on the Kona Coast; these reef-protected lagoons attract 1,000 people a day almost year-round. Kahaluu is the best all-around

beach on Alii Drive, with coconut trees lining a narrow salt-and-pepper sand shore that gently slopes to turquoise pools. The schools of brilliantly colored tropical fish that weave in and out of the reef make this a great place to snorkel. In summer, it's also an ideal spot for children and beginning snorkelers; the water is so shallow that you can just stand up if you feel uncomfortable. But in winter, there's a rip current when high surf rolls in; look for the lifeguard warnings. Kahaluu isn't the biggest beach on the island, but it's one of the best equipped, with off-road parking, beach-gear rentals, a covered pavilion, restrooms, barbecue pits, and a food concession. It gets crowded, so come early to stake out a spot.

Kahaluu Beach Park.

Kekaha Kai State Park.

White Sands Beach.

KEKAHA KAI STATE PARK (KONA COAST STATE PARK) ★

This beach is about 2 miles north of the Kona Airport on Queen Kaahumanu Highway; turn left at a sign pointing improbably down a bumpy road. You won't need a four-wheel-drive vehicle to make it down here—just drive slowly and watch out for potholes. At the end you'll find 5 miles of shoreline with a half-dozen long, curving beaches and a big cove on Mahaiula Bay, as well as archaeological and historical sites. The series of well-protected coves is excellent for swimming, and there's great snorkeling and diving offshore; the big winter waves attract surfers. Facilities include restrooms, picnic tables, and barbecue pits; you'll have to bring your own drinking water. The beach is open daily from 8am to 8pm (the closing time is strictly enforced, and there's no overnight camping).

WHITE SANDS BEACH ★

Don't blink as you cruise Alii Drive, or you'll miss White Sands Beach. This small white-sand pocket beach about 4½ miles south of Kailua-Kona is sometimes called Disappearing Beach because it does just that, especially at high tide or during storms. It vanished completely when Hurricane Iniki hit in 1991, but it's now back in place (at least, it was the last time I looked). On calm days, the water is perfect for swimming and snorkeling. Locals use the elementary waves to teach their children how to surf and boogie board. In winter, the waves swell to expert levels, attracting surfers and spectators. Facilities include restrooms, showers, lifeguards, and a small parking lot.

The Kohala Coast

ANAEHOOMALU BAY (A-BAY) ★★

The Big Island makes up for its dearth of beaches with a few spectacular ones, like Anaehoomalu, or A-Bay, as the locals call it. This popular gold-sand beach, fringed

Beaches & Outdoor Activities on the Big Island

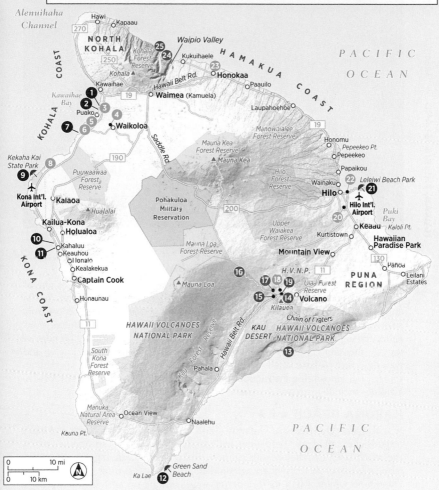

BEACHES

Anaehoomalu Bay (A-Bay) **7**

Green Sand (Papakolea) Beach **12**

Hapuna Beach **2**

Kahuluu Beach Park **11**

Kaunaoa (Mauna Kea) Beach **1**

Kekaha Kai State Park **9**

Leleiwi Beach Park **21**

White Sands Beach **10**

CABINS & CAMPGROUNDS

Halape Shelter **13**

Kilauea Military Camp **19**

Namakani Paio Campground **15**

Waimanu Valley Campground **25**

HIKES

Kilauea Caldera Trails **14**
  Devastation Trail
  Halemaumau Trail
  Kilauea Iki Trail

Kipuka Puaulu (Bird Park) Trail **17**

Mauna Loa Trail **16**

Waimanu Valley's Muliwai Trail **24**

GOLF COURSES

Hamakua Country Club **23**

Hapuna Golf Course **3**

Hilo Municipal Golf Course **20**

Hualalai Golf Course **8**

Mauna Kea Golf Course **3**

Mauna Lani Francis I'i Brown Championship Courses **5**

Naniloa Country Club **22**

Volcano Golf and Country Club **18**

Waikoloa Beach Golf Course **6**

Waikoloa Kings' Golf Course **6**

Waikoloa Village Golf Course **4**

Kiteboarding off Anaehoomalu Bay.

by a grove of palms and backed by royal fish ponds still full of mullet, is one of Hawaii's most beautiful. It fronts the Waikoloa Beach Marriott Resort and is enjoyed by guests and locals alike (it's busier in summer, but doesn't ever get truly crowded). The beach slopes gently from shallow to deep water; swimming, snorkeling, diving, kayaking, and windsurfing are all excellent here. At the far edge of the bay, snorkelers and divers can watch endangered green sea turtles line up and wait their turn to have small fish clean them. Equipment rental and snorkeling, scuba, and windsurfing instruction are available at the north end of the beach. Facilities include restrooms, showers, picnic tables, and plenty of parking.

HAPUNA BEACH ★★★

Just off Queen Kaahumanu Highway, south of the Hapuna Beach Prince Hotel, lies this crescent of gold sand—big, wide, and a half-mile long. In summer, when the beach is widest, the ocean is calmest, and the crowds are biggest, this is the island's best beach for swimming, snorkeling, and bodysurfing. But beware of Hapuna in winter, when its thundering waves, strong rip currents, and lack of lifeguards can be dangerous. Facilities include A-frame cabins for camping, pavilions, restrooms, showers, and plenty of parking.

KAUNAOA BEACH (MAUNA KEA BEACH) ★★★

Everyone calls this gold-sand beach Mauna Kea Beach (it's at the foot of Mauna Kea Beach Hotel), but its real name is Hawaiian for "native dodder," a lacy, yellow-orange vine that once thrived on the shore. A coconut grove sweeps around this golden crescent, where the water is calm and protected by two black-lava points. The sandy bottom slopes gently into the bay, which often fills with tropical fish, sea turtles, and manta rays, especially at night, when the hotel lights flood the shore. Swimming is excellent year-round, except in rare winter storms. Snorkelers prefer the rocky points, where fish thrive in the surge. Facilities include restrooms, showers, and ample parking, but there are no lifeguards.

Hilo

LELEIWI BEACH PARK ★

Hilo's beaches may be few, but Leleiwi is one of Hawaii's most beautiful. This unusual cove of palm-fringed black-lava tide pools fed by freshwater springs and rippled by gentle waves is a photographer's delight—and the perfect place to take a plunge. In winter, big waves can splash these ponds, but the shallow pools are generally free of currents and ideal for families with children, especially in the protected inlets at the center of the park. Leleiwi often attracts endangered sea turtles, making this one of Hawaii's most popular snorkeling spots. The beach is 4 miles out of town on Kalanianaole Avenue. Facilities include restrooms, showers, lifeguards, picnic pavilions, and paved walkways. There's also a marine-life exhibit here.

South Point

GREEN SAND BEACH (PAPAKOLEA BEACH) ★

Hawaii's famous green-sand beach is located at the base of Puu o Mahana, an old cinder cone spilling into the sea. The place has its problems: It's difficult to reach; the open bay is often rough; there are no facilities, fresh water, or shade from the relentless sun; and howling winds scour the point. Nevertheless, each year the unusual green sands attract thousands of oglers, who follow a well-worn four-wheel-drive-only road for 2½ miles to the top of a cliff, which you have to climb down to reach the beach. The sand is crushed olivine, a green semiprecious mineral found in eruptive rocks and meteorites.

To get to Green Sand Beach from the boat ramp at South Point, follow the four-wheel-drive trail, even if you have a four-wheel-drive vehicle, you may want to walk because the trail is very, very bad in parts. Make sure you have

Kaunaoa Beach.

FROM TOP: **Leleiwi Beach Park; Green Sand Beach.**

appropriate closed-toe footwear: tennis shoes or hiking boots. The trail is relatively flat, but you're usually walking into the wind as you head toward the beach. The beginning of the trail is lava. After the first 10 to 15 minutes of walking, the lava disappears and the trail begins to cross pastureland. After about 30 to 40 minutes more, you'll see an eroded cinder cone by the water; continue to the edge, and there lie the green sands below.

The best way to reach the beach is to go over the edge from the cinder cone. (It looks like walking around the south side of the cone would be easier, but it's not.) From the cinder cone, go over the overhang of the rock, and you'll see a trail.

Going down to the beach is very difficult and treacherous, as you'll be able to see from the top. You'll have to make it over and around big lava boulders, dropping down 4 to 5 feet from boulder to boulder in certain spots. And don't forget that you'll have to climb back up. Look before you start; if you have any hesitation, don't go down (you get a pretty good view from the top, anyway).

Warning: When you get to the beach, watch the waves for about 15 minutes and make sure they don't break over the entire beach. If you walk on the beach, always keep one eye on the ocean and stick close to the rock wall. There can be strong rip currents here, and it's imperative to avoid them. Allow a minimum of 2 to 3 hours for this entire excursion.

WATERSPORTS

If you want to rent beach toys, like snorkel gear or boogie boards, the beach concessions at all the big resorts, as well as tour desks and dive shops, offer equipment rentals and sometimes lessons for beginners. The cheapest place to get great rental equipment is **Snorkel Bob's,** in the parking lot of Huggo's restaurant at 75–5831 Kahakai Rd., at Alii Drive, Kailua-Kona (𝄐 **808/329-0770;** www.snorkelbob.com), and in the New Industrial Area, 73–4976 Kamanu St. (𝄐 **808/329-0771**).

For general advice on the activities listed below, see "Special-Interest Trips," in chapter 3.

Boating

For fishing charters, see "Sport Fishing: The Hunt for Granders," on p. 366.

Body Glove Cruises ★★   The *Body Glove,* a 65-foot catamaran that carries up to 149 passengers, runs an adventurous sail-snorkel-dive cruise at a reasonable price. You'll be greeted with fresh Kona coffee, fruit, and breakfast pastries; you'll then sail north of Kailua to Pawai Bay, a marine preserve where you can snorkel, scuba dive, swim, or just hang out on the deck for a couple of hours. After a buffet deli lunch spread, you might want to take the plunge off the boat's waterslide or diving board before heading back to Kailua Pier. The boat departs daily from the pier at 9am and returns at 1:30pm. The only thing you need to bring is a towel; snorkeling equipment (and scuba equipment, if you choose to dive) is provided. *Money-saving tip:* The afternoon trip is cheaper. Check website for discounts.

Kailua Pier. 𝄐 **800/551-8911** or 808/326-7122. www.bodyglovehawaii.com. Morning cruises $120 adults, $78 children 6–12, free for children 5 and under; afternoon cruises (May–Nov) $78 adults, $58 children 6–12, free for children 5 and under; extra $64 for certified scuba divers with own equipment; $74 without own equipment; extra $84 for introductory scuba. Whale-watching cruises (Dec–Apr) $78 adults, $58 children 6–12, free for children 5 and under.

Captain Dan McSweeney's Year-Round Whale-Watching Adventures ★★★   Hawaii's most impressive visitors—45-foot humpback whales — return to the waters off Kona every winter. Capt. Dan McSweeney, a whale researcher for more than 25 years, works daily with the whales, so he has no problem finding them. Frequently, he drops an underwater microphone into the water so you can listen to their songs, or uses an underwater video camera to show you what's going on. In humpback season—roughly December through April—Dan makes two 3-hour trips daily. From July 1 to December 20, he schedules one morning trip on Tuesday, Thursday, and Saturday to look for pilot, sperm, false killer, melon-headed, pygmy killer, and beaked whales. Captain Dan guarantees a sighting, or he'll take you out again for free. No cruises in May and June.

Honokohau Harbor. 𝄐 **888/942-5376** or 808/322-0028. www.ilovewhales.com. Whale-watching cruises $80 adults, $70 children 10 and under.

Captain Zodiac   If you'd prefer to take a **snorkel cruise to Kealakekua Bay** in a small boat, go in Captain Zodiac's 16-passenger, 24-foot inflatable rubber life raft. The boat takes you on a wild ride 14 miles down the Kona Coast to Kealakekua, where you'll spend about an hour snorkeling in the bay and then enjoy snacks and beverages at the picnic snorkel site. Trips are twice daily, from 8am to 12:15pm and from 12:45 to 5pm. *Warning:* Pregnant women and those with bad backs should avoid this often-bumpy ride.

Gentry's Marina, Honokohau Harbor. ☏ **808/329-3199.** www.captainzodiac.com. 4-hr. snorkel cruises $93 adults, $78 children 3–12; 3-hr. whale-watching cruises $65 adults, $59 children 4–12. Book online for better rates.

Fair Wind Snorkeling & Diving Adventures ★★★ ☺   One of the best ways to snorkel Kealakekua Bay, the marine-life preserve that's one of the top snorkel spots in Hawaii, is on Fair Wind's half-day **sail-and-snorkel cruise to Kealakekua Bay.** The company recently added the *Hula Kai*, the latest (state-of-the-art) 55-foot foil-assist catamaran (the first on the Big Island), which offers an upscale experience and a faster, smoother ride on a boat full of luxury. I

FROMMER'S FAVORITE BIG ISLAND
experiences

Creeping Up to the Ooze (p. 305). Since Kilauea's ongoing eruption began in 1983, lava has been bubbling and oozing in a mild-mannered way that lets you walk right up to the creeping flow for an up-close encounter.

Going Underwater at Kealakekua Bay (p. 365). The islands have lots of extraordinary snorkel and dive sites, but none is so easily accessible as mile-wide Kealakekua Bay, an uncrowded marine preserve on the South Kona Coast. Here you can swim with dolphins, sea turtles, octopuses, and every species of tropical fish that calls Hawaii's waters home.

Discovering Old Hawaii at Puuhonua O Honaunau National Historical Park (p. 384). Protected by a huge rock wall, this sacred Honaunau site was once a refuge for ancient Hawaiian warriors. Today you can walk the consecrated grounds and glimpse a former way of life in a partially restored 16th-century village, complete with thatched huts, canoes, forbidding idols, and a temple that holds the bones of 23 Hawaiian chiefs.

Stargazing from Mauna Kea (p. 389). A jacket, a beach mat, and binoculars are all you need to see every star and planet in this ultraclean atmosphere, where the visibility is so good that 11 nations have

set up telescopes (two of them the biggest in the world) to probe deep space.

Watching for Whales (p. 381). Humpback whales pass through waters off the Kona Coast every December through April. To spot them from shore, head down to the Natural Energy Laboratory of Hawaii Authority, just south of Kona Airport, and keep your eyes peeled as you walk the shoreline. To get here, follow Queen Kaahumanu Highway (Hwy. 19) toward the airport; 6 miles outside of town, look for the sign NATURAL ENERGY LAB and turn left. Just after the road takes a sharp turn to the right, there's a small paved parking area with restrooms; a beach trail is on the ocean side of the lot.

Savoring a Cup of Kona Coffee. It's just one of those things you have to do while you're on the Big Island. For a truly authentic cup of java, head upcountry to **Holuakoa Café,** on Mamalahoa Highway (Hwy. 180) in Holualoa (☏ **808/322-2233**), where you can sip a cup of java and look out over the coffee fields.

Hanging Out in Waipio Valley (p. 394). Pack a picnic and head for this gorgeously lush valley that time forgot. Delve deep into the jungle on foot, comb the black-sand beach, or just laze

recommend the *Hula Kai* 5-hour snorkel-and-dive morning cruise, which includes a light breakfast, a gourmet barbecue lunch, two snorkeling sites, a guided tour, and optional scuba diving ($155 adults; minimum age 18). The *Fair Wind II* 60-foot catamaran, which holds up to 100 passengers, offers a morning cruise that leaves from Keauhou Bay at 9am and returns at 1:30pm; it includes a light breakfast, lunch, snorkel gear, and lessons ($125 adults, $75 kids 4–12, $29 toddlers). The afternoon deluxe cruise (summer only) runs from 2 to 6:30pm and includes a barbecue lunch, sailing, snorkeling, and equipment ($109 adults, $69 kids 4–12, free for kids 3 and under). Also on the *Fair Wind II* is a shorter (and

the day away by a babbling stream, the tail end of a 1,000-foot waterfall.

Chasing Rainbows at Akaka Falls
(p. 392). When the light is right, a perfect prism is formed and a rainbow leaps out of this spectacular 442-foot waterfall, about an 11-mile drive from Hilo. Take time to roam through the surrounding rainforest, where you're sure to have close encounters with exotic birds, aromatic plumeria trees, and shocking red-torch ginger.

Gawking at the Day's Catch in Honokohau Harbor.
Every afternoon between 4 and 5pm, local fishermen pull into the fuel dock to weigh in their big-game fish: 1,000-pound blue marlins, 150-pound yellowfin tunas, and plenty of scale-tipping mahimahi, ono (also known as wahoo), and others. Sit in the

bleachers and check out these magnificent creatures.

Hunting for Petroglyphs (p. 387).
The majority of Hawaii's ancient rock carvings are found in the 233-acre Puako Petroglyph Archaeological District, near Mauna Lani Resort. The best time to go looking is in the cool early morning or late afternoon. There are more than 3,000 petroglyphs in this area alone—see how many you can spot.

Shopping at the Hilo Farmers Market
(p. 417). For a handful of dollars, you can buy a pound of rambutan (a sweet Indonesian fruit), a bouquet of tropical orchids, or a couple of tasty foot-long Hawaiian laulau (pork, chicken, or fish steamed in ti leaves). But be sure to arrive early (the market opens at sunrise)—many of the 60 or so vendors quickly sell out.

cheaper) sail-and-snorkel cruise for $75 adults and $45 children—there's no lunch, just fruit and a snack plus snorkeling equipment.

78–7130 Kaleiopapa St., Kailua-Kona. ✆ **800/677-9461** or 808/322-2788. www.fair-wind.com. Snorkel cruises $65–$139 adults, $39–$59 children 4–12; prices vary depending on cruise.

Kamanu Charters ★★   This sleek catamaran, 36 feet long and 22 feet wide, provides a laid-back sail-and-snorkel cruise from Honokohau Harbor to Pawai Bay. The 3½-hour trip includes a tropical lunch (deli sandwiches, chips, fresh fruit, and beverages), snorkeling gear, and personalized instruction for first-time snorkelers. The *Kamanu* sails daily (weather permitting) at 9am and 12:30pm; it can hold up to 24 people.

Honokohau Harbor. ✆ **800/348-3091** or 808/329-2021. www.kamanu.com. Sail-and-snorkel cruises $90 adults, $50 children 12 and under.

Body Boarding (Boogie Boarding) & Bodysurfing

On the Kona side of the island, the best beaches for body boarding and bodysurfing are **Hapuna Beach, White Sands Beach,** and **Kekaha Kai State Park** (Kona Coast State Park). On the east side, try **Leleiwi Beach.**

Ocean Kayaking

Imagine sitting at sea level, eye to eye with a turtle, a dolphin, or even a whale—it's possible in an oceangoing kayak. Anyone can kayak in calm waters: Just get in, find your balance, and paddle. After a few minutes of instruction and a little practice in a calm area (like the lagoon in front of **King Kamehameha's Kona Beach Hotel**), you'll be ready to explore. Beginners can practice their skills in **Kailua Bay** and **Kealakekua Bay;** intermediates might try paddling from **Honokohau Harbor** to **Kekaha Kai State Park;** and the **Hamakua Coast** is a challenge for experienced kayakers.

What's SUP?

Easier than surfing, but more challenging than canoeing or kayaking, stand-up paddling (or SUP, for short) is the newest way to get out on the water. You stand facing the front of a long, wide, thick surfboard and paddle your way around with a long outrigger canoe paddle. If you've never surfed before, it'll take at least an hour to get the hang of it. To try your hand (and feet) at this core-strengthening workout, make sure to go early in the morning, when the water is calmest; if you wait until afternoon, you'll have to deal with choppy waves.

Most ocean activities centers offer stand-up paddling instruction and rentals. If the one closest to your hotel does not, try **Hawaiian Ocean Sports,** on A-Bay in front of the Waikoloa Beach Marriott (✆**808/886-6666** ext. 101; www.hawaiianoceansports.com). They'll give you a free lesson with your first rental ($31.25 for a half hour or $60 for an hour). South of town, contact **Kona Boys,** 79-8539 Mamalahoa Hwy., Kealakekua (✆ **808/328-1234;** www.konaboys.com). Rental boards are $25/hour or $67 for the day; lessons are $150 for a 90-minute private or $75 for a group of 2–4.

You can rent one- and two-person kayaks (and other ocean toys) from **Aloha Kayak ★★★** (© **877/322-1444** or 808/322-2868; www.alohakayak.com). Half-day rates are $25 for a single and $45 for a double; full-day rates are $35 for a single and $60 for a double. Aloha Kayak also has a unique tour from Keauhou Bay and the Captain Cook Monument, with Hawaiian guides showing you sea caves and snorkeling areas full of fish and turtles. The tours last either 4 hours ($119–$129 adults, $60–$65 children 11 and under) or 6 hours ($159 adults, $80 children 11 and under) and include all equipment, beverages, snorkeling gear, and snacks.

Parasailing

Get a bird's-eye view of Hawaii's pristine waters with **UFO Parasail** (© **888/ 359-4836** or 808/325-5836; www.ufoparasail.net), which offers parasail rides daily from 8am to 2pm from Kailua Pier. The cost is $65 for the standard flight of 7 minutes of air time at 600 feet, and $75 for a deluxe 10-minute ride at 1,200 feet. You can go up alone or with a friend; no experience is necessary. *Tip:* Take the early-bird special at 8am (when the light is fantastic and the price is right) for just $60 for 600 feet, or $70 for 1,200 feet.

Scuba Diving

The Big Island's leeward coast offers some of the best diving in the world; the water is calm, warm, and clear. Want to swim with fast-moving game fish? Try **Ulua Cave** at the north end of the Kohala Coast. There are nearly two dozen dive operators on the west side of the Big Island, plus a couple in Hilo. They offer everything from scuba-certification courses to guided boat dives.

"This is not your mother or father's dive shop," says new owner Simon Key, of **BottomTime Hawaii,** in the Old Industrial area, 74–5467 Luhia St., Kailua-Kona (© **866/GO-DIVEN** [463-4836] or 808/331-1858; www.bottomtime hawaii.com). "This is a dive shop for today's diver." Key claims what sets Bottom-Time apart is its willingness to take its 34-foot catamaran (complete with showers, TV, and restrooms) to unusual dive sites, and "not those sites just 2 minutes from the mouth of the harbor." BottomTime also offers introductory dives in enriched air (Nitrox) for an additional $10; two-tank dives for $120 to $130.

One of Kona's oldest dive shops, **Jack's Diving Locker,** 75–5813 Alii Dr. (© **800/345-4807** or 808/329-7585; www. jacksdivinglocker.com), recently purchased another longtime dive shop, Kona Coast Divers, and combined the two businesses into one. Plus, it expanded its former 600-square-foot retail store into

Night-diving with manta rays.

an 8,000-square-foot dive center with swimming pool (featuring underwater viewing windows), classrooms, full-service rentals, and full-service sports-diving and technical-diving facility. It offers the classic two-tank dive for $125 and a two-tank manta ray night dive for $145.

HOT-LAVA DIVES   Hilo's **Nautilus Dive Center,** 382 Kamehameha Ave., between Open Market and the Shell gas station (© **808/935-6939;** www. nautilusdivehilo.com), offers a very unusual opportunity for advanced divers: diving where the lava flows into the ocean. "Sometimes you can feel the pressure from the sound waves as the lava explodes," owner Bill De Rooy says. "Sometimes you have perfect visibility to the color show of your life." As we went to press, these hot-lava dives were on hold (an unstable collapse of a recent lava field sent 20 acres of lava into the ocean; fortunately, no one was injured). Call to see if the dives have resumed.

NIGHT DIVES WITH MANTA RAYS ★★   A little less risky—but still something you'll never forget—is swimming with manta rays on a night dive. These giant, harmless creatures, with wingspans that reach up to 14 feet, glide gracefully through the water to feed on simple plankton. **Jack's Diving Locker,** 75–5819 Alii Dr. (© **800/345-4807** or 808/329-7585; www.jacks divinglocker.com), offers its "Manta Ray Madness" for $145 for a two-tank dive and $95 for snorkelers. Everyone from beginners through experts will love this dive. Jack's cannot guarantee that these wild creatures will show up every night, but does boast a more than 90% sightings record.

If Jack's is booked, try **Sandwich Isle Divers,** 75–5729 Alii Dr., in the back of the Kona Marketplace (© **888/743-3483** or 808/329-9188; www.sandwichisledivers.com). It offers two-tank nighttime manta dives for $165 (including equipment), or $140 if you have your own gear.

WEEKLONG DIVES   If you're looking for an all-diving vacation, you might think about spending a week on the 80-foot *Kona Aggressor II* ★ (© **800/344-5662** or 808/329-8182; www.aggressor.com), a live-aboard dive boat that promises to provide unlimited underwater exploration, including day and night dives, along 85 miles of the Big Island's coastline. You might spot harmless 70-foot whale sharks, plus not-so-harmless tiger and hammerhead sharks, as well as dolphins, whales, monk seals, and sea turtles. Ten divers are accommodated in five staterooms. Guided dives are available, but as long as you're certified, just log in with the dive master and you're free to follow the limits of your dive computer. It's $2,635 for 7 days (without gear), double occupancy, which includes excellent accommodations and all meals. Rental gear, from cameras (starting at $100 a week) to B.C./Reg ($120) to computers ($125), is available.

Snorkeling

If you come to Hawaii and don't snorkel, you'll miss half the fun. The year-round calm waters along the Kona and Kohala coasts are home to spectacular marine life. Some of the best snorkeling areas on the Kona-Kohala coasts include **Hapuna Beach Cove,** at the foot of the Hapuna Beach Prince Hotel, a secluded little cove where you can snorkel with schools of yellow tangs, needlefish, and green sea turtles. But if you've never snorkeled in your life, **Kahaluu Beach Park** is the best place to start. Just wade in and look down at the schools of fish in the bay's black-lava tide pools. Another "hidden" snorkeling spot is off the rocks north of the boat-launch ramp at **Honaunau Bay.** Other great snorkel sites include **White Sands Beach, Kekaha Kai State Park,** and **Hookena, Honaunau, Puako,** and **Spencer** beach parks.

In addition to **Snorkel Bob's,** mentioned in the intro to this section, you can rent gear from **Jack's Diving Locker ★,** Coconut Grove Marketplace and Honokohau Marina, Kailua-Kona (② **808/329-8802;** www.jacksdiving locker.com).

SNORKELING CRUISES TO KEALAKEKUA BAY ★★★ Probably the best snorkeling for all levels can be found in **Kealakekua Bay.** The calm waters of this underwater preserve teem with a wealth of marine life. Coral heads, lava tubes, and underwater caves all provide an excellent habitat for Hawaii's vast array of tropical fish, making mile-wide Kealakekua the Big Island's best accessible spot for snorkeling and diving. Without looking very hard, you can see octopuses, free-swimming moray eels, parrotfish, and goat fish, once in a while, a pod of spinner dolphins streaks across the bay. Kealakekua is reachable only by boat; in addition to **Fair Wind** (p. 360) and **Captain Zodiac** (p. 359), check out **Sea Quest Snorkeling and Rafting Adventures** (② **808/329-RAFT** [7238]; www.seaquesthawaii. com), which offers unique coastal adventures through sea caves and lava tubes on the Kona Coast, as well as snorkeling plunges into the ocean at the historic Place of Refuge in Honaunau and at the Captain Cook Monument at Kealakekua. The six-passenger, rigid-hull, inflatable rafts can go where larger boats can't. The 4-hour morning tour is $92 for adults and $75 for children, while the 3-hour afternoon tour goes for $72 for adults and $62 for children. During whale season, there's a 3-hour whale-watching cruise for $56 for adults and children. Children 5 and under, pregnant women, and people with bad backs are not allowed.

Snuba

If you're not quite ready to make the commitment to scuba but you want more time underwater than snorkeling allows, **Big Island Snuba Tours** (② **808/ 326-7446;** www.snubabig island.com) may be the answer. Just like in scuba, the diver wears a regulator and mask; however, the tank floats on the surface on a raft and is connected to the diver's regulator by a

Snuba.

hose that allows the diver to go 20 to 25 feet down. You need only 15 minutes of instruction before you're ready to go. Snuba can actually be easier than snorkeling, as the water is calmer beneath the surface. It costs $89 for a 1½-hour dive from the beach, $145 for one dive from a boat, and $170 for two dives from a boat; children must be at least 8 years old.

Sport Fishing: The Hunt for Granders ★★

If you want to catch fish, it doesn't get any better than the Kona Coast, known internationally as the marlin capital of the world. Big-game fish, including gigantic blue marlin and other Pacific billfish, tuna, mahimahi, sailfish, swordfish, ono (also known as wahoo), and giant trevallies (ulua), roam the waters here. When anglers catch marlin that weigh 1,000 pounds or more, they call them *granders;* there's even a "wall of fame" on Kailua-Kona's Waterfront Row, honoring 40 anglers who've nailed more than 20 tons of fighting fish.

Nearly 100 charter boats with professional captains and crew offer fishing charters out of **Keauhou, Kawaihae, Honokohau,** and **Kailua Bay harbors.** If you're not an expert angler, the best way to arrange a charter is through a booking agency like the **Charter Desk at Honokohau Marina** (𝄢 888/566-2487 or 808/326-1800; www.charterdesk.com) or **Charter Services Hawaii** (𝄢 800/ 567-2650 or 808/334-1881; www.konazone.com). Either one will sort through the more than 40 types of vessels, fishing specialties, and personalities to match you with the right boat. Prices range from $750 to $3,500 or so for a full-day exclusive charter (you and up to five of your friends have the entire boat to yourselves), or for $95 you can share a boat with others and rotate your turn at pulling in the big one.

Serious sport fishers should call the boats directly. They include *Anxious* (𝄢 808/326-1229; www.alohazone.com), *Marlin Magic* (𝄢 808/325-7138; www.marlinmagic.com), and *Ihu Nui* (𝄢 808/325-1513; www.ihunui.com). If you aren't into hooking a 1,000-pound marlin or 200-pound tuna and just want to go out to catch some smaller fish and have fun, I recommend **Reel Action Light Tackle Sportfishing** ★★ (𝄢 808/325-6811; www.charternet.com/flyfish/hawaii.html). Light-tackle anglers and saltwater fly fishermen should contact *Sea Genie II* ★★ (𝄢 808/325-5355; www.seageniesportfishing.com), which has helped several anglers set world records. All of the above outfitters operate out of Honokohau Harbor.

Most big-game charter boats carry six passengers max, and the boats supply all equipment, bait, tackle, and lures. No license is required. Many captains now tag and release marlins; other fish caught belong to the boat (not to you, but to the charter)—that's Island style. If you want to eat your catch or have your trophy marlin mounted, arrange it with the captain before you go.

Submarine Dives

This is the stuff movies are made of: venturing 100 feet below the sea in a high-tech 65-foot submarine. On a 1-hour trip, you'll be able to explore a 25-acre coral reef that's teeming with schools of colorful tropical fish. Look closely and you might catch glimpses of moray eels—or even a shark—in and around the reef. On selected trips, you'll watch as divers swim among these aquatic creatures, luring them to the view ports for face-to-face observation. Call **Atlantis Submarines** ★, 75–5669 Alii Dr. (across the street from Kailua Pier), Kailua-Kona (𝄢 800/548-6262; www.atlantisadventures.com). Trips leave daily between 10am and 1pm. The cost is $99 for adults and $45 for children 11 and under (book on their website for a discount). *Note:* The ride is safe for everyone, but skip it if you suffer from claustrophobia.

Surfing

Most surfing off the Big Island is for the experienced only. As a general rule, the beaches on the north and west shores of the island get northern swells in winter, while those on the south and east shores get southern swells in summer. Experienced surfers should check out the waves at **Pine Trees** (north of Kailua-Kona), **Lyman's** (off Alii Dr. in Kailua-Kona), and **Banyan's** (also off Alii Dr.); reliable spots on the east side of the island include **Honolii Point** (outside Hilo), **Hilo Bay Front Park,** and **Keaukaha Beach Park.** But there are a few sites where beginners can catch a wave, too: You might want to try **Kahaluu Beach Park,** where the waves are manageable most of the year, other surfers are around to give you pointers, and there's a lifeguard onshore.

Ocean Eco Tours (© **808/324-SURF** [7873]; www.oceanecotours. com), owned and operated by veteran surfers, is one of the few companies on the Big Island that teaches surfing. Private lessons cost $150 per person (including all equipment) and usually last a minimum of 2 hours; 2- to 3-hour group lessons go for $95 (also including all equipment), with a maximum of four students. Both teachers love this ancient Hawaiian sport, and their enthusiasm is contagious. The minimum age is 8, and you must be a fairly good swimmer.

Your only Big Island choice for surfboard rentals is **Pacific Vibrations,** 75–5702 Likana Lane (just off Alii Dr., across from the pier), Kailua-Kona (© **808/ 329-4140**), where shortboards go for $15 and longboards for $20 per day.

HIKING & CAMPING

For information on camping and hiking, contact **Hawaii Volcanoes National Park,** P.O. Box 52, Hawaii National Park, HI 96718 (© 808/985-6000; www. nps.gov/havo); **Puuhonua O Honaunau National Historical Park,** Honaunau, HI 96726 (© 808/328-2288; www.nps.gov/puho); the **State Division of Forestry and Wildlife,** 19 E. Kawili St., Hilo, HI 96720 (© 808/974-4221; www.hawaii.gov/dlnr/dofaw); the **State Division of Parks,** P.O. Box 936, Hilo, HI 96721 (© 808/974-6200; www.hawaiistateparks.org); the **County Department of Parks and Recreation,** 101 Pauahi St., Ste. 6, Hilo, HI 96720 (© 808/961-8311; www.hawaii-county.com; parks_recreation@co.hawaii.hi.us); or the **Hawaii Sierra Club** (© 808/538-6616; www.hi.sierraclub.org/Hawaii/ excomm.html).

Camping equipment is *not* available for rent on the Big Island. Plan to bring your own or buy it at the **Hilo Surplus Store,** 148 Mamo St., Hilo (© **808/ 935-6398**).

GUIDED DAY HIKES   A guided day hike is a great way to discover natural Hawaii without having to sleep under a tree to do it. Call the following outfitters ahead of time (before you arrive) for a schedule of trips; they fill up quickly.

A longtime resident of Hawaii, Dr. Hugh Montgomery of **Hawaiian Walkways** ★, Honokaa (© **800/457-7759** or 808/775-0372; www.hawaiian walkways.com), formerly named "Tour Operator of the Year" by the Hawaii Ecotourism Association of Hawaii, offers a variety of options, ranging from excursions that skirt the rim of immense valleys to hikes through the clouds on the volcano. Hikes range from $99 to $169 for adults, $99 to $119 for kids. Custom hikes are available for one to four hikers for $600. Prices include food, beverages, and equipment.

Naturalist and educator Rob Pacheco of **Hawaii Forest & Trail ★★**, 74–5035-B Queen Kaahumanu Hwy. (behind the Chevron station), Kailua-Kona (© **800/464-1993** or 808/331-8505; www.hawaii-forest.com), offers day trips to some of the island's most remote, pristine areas, some of which he has exclusive access to. Rob's fully trained staff narrates the entire trip, offering extensive natural, geological, and cultural commentary (and more than a little humor). Tours are limited to 10 people and are highly personalized to meet the group's interests and abilities. Options include waterfall adventures, rainforest discovery hikes, birding tours, volcanoes, and even an off-road adventure in a 6×6 Pinzgauer Scrambler that allows you to explore hard-to-reach places. Each tour involves 3 to 4 hours of easy-to-moderate walking, over terrain manageable by anyone in average physical condition. Half-day trips, including snacks, beverages, water, and gear, are from $115 adults, and $89 to $119 for children ages 8 to 12. Full-day adventures (8–11 hr.) are $169 to $185 adults and $199 to $139 children.

GUIDED NIGHT HIKES For an off-the-beaten-track experience, **Arnott's Lodge,** 98 Apapane Rd., Hilo (© **808/969-7097;** www.arnottslodge.com), offers a daylong tour of Hawaii Volcanoes National Park, followed by a night lava hike right up to the fiery flow. The 9½-hour tour leaves the lodge at noon and spends most of the afternoon in the park. The lava hike (a 4-hr., somewhat strenuous round-trip hike) takes place as the sun is setting, so you can see the glow of the flow both during and after sunset. The cost is $85 to $110.

Hawaii Volcanoes National Park ★★★

This national park is a wilderness wonderland. Miles of trails not only lace the lava, but also cross deserts, rainforests, beaches, and, in winter, snow at 13,650 feet. Trail maps (highly recommended) are sold at park headquarters. Check conditions before you head out. Come prepared for sun, rain, and hard wind any time of year. Always wear sunscreen and bring plenty of drinking water.

For complete coverage of the national park, see p. 401. *Warning:* If you have heart or respiratory problems or if you're pregnant, don't attempt any hike in the park; the fumes will bother you.

TRAILS IN THE PARK

KILAUEA IKI TRAIL You'll experience the work of the volcano goddess, Pele, firsthand on this hike. The 4-mile trail begins at the visitor center, descends through a forest of ferns into still-fuming Kilauea Iki Crater, and then crosses the crater floor past the vent where a 1959 lava blast shot a fountain of fire 1,900 feet into the air for 36 days. Allow 2 hours for this fair-to-moderate hike.

HALEMAUMAU TRAIL This moderate 3.5-mile hike starts at the visitor center, goes down 500 feet to the floor of Kilauea Crater, crosses the crater, and ends at Halemaumau Overlook.

DEVASTATION TRAIL Up on the rim of Kilauea Iki Crater, you can see what an erupting volcano did to a once-flourishing ohia forest. The scorched earth with its ghostly tree skeletons stands in sharp contrast to the rest of the lush forest. Everyone can take this .5-mile hike on a paved path across the eerie bed of black cinders. The trail head is on Crater Rim Road at Puu Puai Overlook.

Devastation Trail.

KIPUKA PUAULU (BIRD PARK) TRAIL This easy 1.5-mile, hour-long hike lets you see native Hawaiian flora and fauna in a little oasis of living nature in a field of lava. For some reason, the once red-hot lava skirted this miniforest and let it survive. At the trail head on Mauna Loa Road, there's a display of plants and birds you'll see on the walk. Go early in the morning or in the evening (or, even better, just after a rain) to see native birds like the apapane (a small, bright-red bird with black wings and tail) and the *iiwi* (larger and orange-vermilion colored, with a curved orange bill). Native trees along the trail include giant ohia, koa, soapberry, kolea, and mamani.

MAUNA LOA TRAIL Probably the most challenging hike in Hawaii, this trail goes 7.5 miles from the lookout to a cabin at 10,035 feet and then 12 more miles up to the primitive Mauna Loa summit cabin at 13,250 feet, where the climate is subarctic and overnight temperatures are below freezing year-round. This 4-day round-trip requires advance planning, great physical condition, and registration at the visitor center. Call ✆ **808/985-6000** for maps and details. The trail head begins where Mauna Loa Road ends, 14 miles north of Hwy. 11.

CAMPGROUNDS & WILDERNESS CABINS IN THE PARK

The only park campground accessible by car is **Namakani Paio,** which has a pavilion with picnic tables and a fireplace (no wood is provided). Tent camping is free; no reservations are required. Stays are limited to 7 days per year. Backpack camping at hiker shelters and cabins is available on a first-come, shared basis, but you must register at the visitor center.

Kilauea Military Camp (www.kmc-volcano.com), a mile from the visitor center, is a rest-and-recreation camp for active and retired military personnel. Facilities include 75 one- to three-bedroom cabins with fireplaces (some with a Jacuzzi), cafeteria, bowling alley, bar, general store, weight room, and tennis and basketball courts. Rates are based on rank, ranging from $72 to $240 a night. Call ✆ **808/967-8333** on the Big Island, or 808/438-6707 on Oahu.

The following cabins and campgrounds are the best of what the park and surrounding area have to offer:

HALAPE SHELTER This backcountry site, about 7 miles from the nearest road, is the place for those who want to get away from it all and enjoy their own private white-sand beach. The small, three-sided stone shelter, with a roof but no floor, can accommodate two people comfortably, but four's a crowd. You could pitch a tent inside, but if the weather is nice, you're better off setting up outside. There's a catchment water tank, but check with rangers on the water situation before hiking in (sometimes they don't have accurate information on the water level; bring extra water just in case). The only other facility is a pit toilet. Go on weekdays if you're really looking for an escape. It's free to stay here, but you're limited to 3 nights. Permits are available at the visitor center on a first-come, first-served basis, no earlier than noon on the day before your trip. For more information, call (**808/985-6000.**

NAMAKANI PAIO CAMPGROUNDS & CABINS Just 5 miles west of the park entrance is a tall eucalyptus forest where you can pitch a tent in an open grassy field. The trail to Kilauea Crater is just a half-mile away. No permit is needed, but stays are limited to 7 days. Facilities include pavilions with barbecues and a fireplace, picnic tables, outdoor dish-washing areas, restrooms, and drinking water. There are also 10 cabins that accommodate up to four people each. Every cabin has a covered picnic table at the entrance and a fireplace with a grill. Toilets, sinks, and hot showers are available in a separate building. You can get groceries and gas in the town of Volcano, 4 miles away. Make cabin reservations through **Volcano House,** P.O. Box 53, Hawaii National Park, HI 96718 ((**808/967-7321**); the cost is $40 per night for two adults (and two children), $48 for three adults, and $56 for four adults. As we went to press, the campgrounds and cabins were currently closed for renovations, expected to reopen in 2011.

Waimanu Valley's Muliwai Trail

This difficult 2- to 3-day backpacking adventure—only for the hardy—takes you to a hidden valley some call Eden, with virgin waterfalls and pools and spectacular views. The trail, which goes from sea level to 1,350 feet and down to the sea again, takes more than 9 hours to hike in and more than 10 hours to hike out. Be prepared for clouds of bloodthirsty mosquitoes, and look out for wild pigs. If it's raining, forget it: You'll have 13 streams to cross before you reach the rim of Waimanu Valley, and rain means flash floods.

You must get permission to camp in Waimanu Valley from the **Division of Forestry and Wildlife,** 19 E. Kawili St., Hilo, HI 96720 ((**808/974-4221**). Permits to the nine designated campsites are assigned by number. They're free, but you're limited to a 7-day stay. Facilities are limited to two composting pit toilets. The best water in the valley is from the stream on the western wall, a 15-minute walk up a trail from the beach. All water must be treated before drinking. The water from the Waimanu Stream drains from a swamp, so skip it. Be sure to pack out what you take in.

For information on Muliwai Trail, visit the Na Ala Hele website at www. hawaiitrails.org. To get to the trail head, take Hwy. 19 to the turnoff for Honokaa; drive 9½ miles to the Waipio Valley Lookout. Unless you have four-wheel-drive, this is where your hike begins. Walk down the road and wade the Wailoa Stream; then cross the beach and go to the northwest wall. The trail starts here and goes up the valley floor, past a swamp, and into a forest before beginning a series of switchbacks that parallel the coastline. These switchbacks go up and down about 14 gulches. At the ninth gulch, about two-thirds of the way along the trail, is a shelter. After the shelter, the trail descends into Waimanu Valley, which looks like a smaller version of Waipio Valley but without signs of human intrusion.

GOLF & OTHER OUTDOOR ACTIVITIES

Golf

For last-minute and discount tee times, call **Stand-by Golf** (© 888/645-2665 or 808/322-BOOK [2665]; www.standbygolf.com) between 7am and 2:30pm and 6 and 10pm. Stand-by Golf offers discounted (10%–40% off), guaranteed tee times for same-day or next-day golfing.

If your game's a little rusty, head for the **Swing Zone,** 74–5562 Makala Blvd. (at Kuikuni Hwy., by the Old Airport Park), Kailua-Kona (© **808/329-6909**). The driving range has 27 mats and 10 grass tee spaces, the practice putting green and chipping area is free with a bucket of balls (60 balls for $7 [for mat] or $9 [for grass]), and the pro shop sells limited supplies (rental clubs are available, too, for just $2.75 each or $11 a set). For $7, including a putter and a ball, you can play a round on the 18-hole, all-grass putting course built in the shape of the Big Island.

In addition to the courses below, I love the fabulous **Hualalai Golf Course** ★★★ at the Four Seasons Resort Hualalai (p. 309). Unfortunately, it's open only to resort guests—but for committed golfers, this Jack Nicklaus–designed championship course is reason enough to pay the sky high rates.

THE KOHALA COAST

Hapuna Golf Course ★★★   Since its opening in 1992, this 18-hole championship course has been named the most environmentally sensitive course by *Golf* magazine, as well as "Course of the Future" by the U.S. Golf Association. Designed by Arnold Palmer and Ed Seay, this 6,027-yard, links-style course extends from the shoreline to 700 feet above sea level, with views of the pastoral Kohala Mountains and the Kohala coastline. The elevation changes on the course keep it challenging (and windy at the higher elevations). There are a few elevated tee boxes and only 40 bunkers. Facilities include putting greens, driving ranges, lockers, showers, a pro shop, and restaurants.

At the Hapuna Beach Prince Hotel, Mauna Kea Resort, off Hwy. 19 (near mile marker 69). © **808/880-3000.** www.princeresortshawaii.com. Greens fees $135 ($95 for resort guests), $75 after 1pm.

Mauna Kea Golf Course ★★★   This breathtakingly beautiful, par-72, 7,114-yard championship course, designed by Robert Trent Jones, Jr., is consistently rated one of the top golf courses in the United States. The signature 3rd hole is 175 yards long; the Pacific Ocean and shoreline cliffs stand between the tee and the green, giving every golfer, from beginner to pro, a real challenge. Another par-3 that confounds duffers is the 11th hole, which drops 100 feet from tee to green and plays down to the ocean, into the steady trade winds. When the trades are blowing, 181 yards might as well be 1,000 yards. Book ahead; the course is very popular, especially for early weekend tee times. **Note:** As we went to press,

Mauna Kea's greens, tees, fairways, and rough had just been replaced with new hybrids of turf that can be groomed for the skill levels of both resort and professional golfers, and the bunkers were restored to their original configuration.

At the Mauna Kea Beach Hotel, Mauna Kea Resort, off Hwy. 19 (near mile marker 68). © **808/882-5400.** www.princeresortshawaii.com. Greens fees $250, $155 after 1:30pm.

Mauna Lani Francis H. I'i Brown Championship Courses ★★★ The **South Course,** a 7,029-yard par-72, has an unforgettable ocean hole: the downhill, 221-yard, par-3 7th, which is bordered by the sea, a salt-and-pepper sand dune, and lush kiawe trees. The **North Course** may not have the drama of the oceanfront holes, but because it was built on older lava flows, the more extensive indigenous vegetation gives the course a Scottish feel. The hole that's cursed the most is the 140-yard, par-3 17th: It's absolutely beautiful but plays right into the surrounding lava field. Facilities include two driving ranges, a golf shop (with teaching pros), a restaurant, and putting greens.

At the Mauna Lani Resort, Mauna Lani Dr., off Hwy. 19 (20 miles north of Kona Airport). © **808/885-6655.** www.maunalani.com. Greens fees $260 ($160 for resort guests).

Waikoloa Beach Golf Course ★ This pristine 18-hole, par-70 course certainly reflects the motto of designer Robert Trent Jones, Jr.: "Hard par, easy bogey." Most golfers remember the par-5, 505-yard 12th hole, a sharp dogleg left with bunkers in the corner and an elevated tee surrounded by lava. Facilities include a golf shop, restaurant, and driving range.

At the Waikoloa Beach Resort, 1020 Keana Place (adjacent to the Waikoloa Beach Marriott Resort and the Hilton Waikoloa Village). © **877/WAIKOLOA** [924-5656] or 808/886-6060. www.waikoloabeachresort.com. Greens fees $195 ($130 for resort guests), $105 after 11:30am, $95 after 1:30pm.

Mauna Kea Golf Course.

IMPROVE YOUR golf GAME IN 2½ HOURS

Darrin Gee's Spirit of Golf Academy ★★★, P.O. Box 2308, Kohala (📞 **866/ GOLF-433** [465-3433] or 808/887-6800; www.spiritofgolfhawaii.com), has developed a program for the inner, mental game of golf that will improve your score in just 2½ hours, whether you're a beginner or you've been swinging clubs for years. Unlike the majority of golf schools, which focus on the mechanics of the golf swing, for just $250 you will learn how to improve your mental game, using Gee's Seven Principles of Golf, which means learning how to increase your focus and concentration, how to relax under pressure, and how to play to your potential. The small clinics (four players to one instructor) are available at championship golf courses on the Big Island. *Tip:* Book online for a 20% discount.

Waikoloa Kings' Golf Course ★   This sister course to the Waikoloa Beach Golf Course is about 500 yards longer. Designed by Tom Weiskopf and Jay Morrish, the 18-hole links-style tract features a double green at the 3rd and 6th holes, and several carefully placed bunkers that often come into play due to the ever-present trade winds. Facilities include a pro shop and showers.

At the Waikoloa Beach Resort, 600 Waikoloa Beach Dr. (adjacent to the Waikoloa Beach Marriott Resort and the Hilton Waikoloa Village). 📞 **877/WAIKOLOA** [924-5656] or 808/886-7888. www.waikoloabeachresort.com. Greens fees $195 ($130 for resort guests), $105 after 11:30am, $95 after 1:30pm.

Waikoloa Village Golf Course   This semiprivate 18-hole course, with a par-72 for each of the three sets of tees, is hidden in the town of Waikoloa and usually overshadowed by the glamour resort courses along the Kohala Coast. Not only is it a beautiful course with great views, but it also offers some great golfing. The wind can play havoc with your game here (like most Hawaii golf courses). Robert Trent Jones, Jr., designed this challenging course, inserting his trademark sand traps, slick greens, and great fairways. I'm particularly fond of the 18th hole: This par-5, 490-yard thriller doglegs to the left, and the last 75 yards up to the green are water, water, water. Enjoy the fabulous views of Mauna Kea and Mauna Loa, and—on a very clear day—Maui's Haleakala in the distance.

Waikoloa Rd., off Hwy. 19 (18 miles north of Kona Airport), Waikoloa Village. 📞 **808/883-9621.** www.waikoloa.org/golf. Greens fees $80. Turn left at the Waikoloa sign; it's about 6 miles up, on the left.

THE HAMAKUA COAST

Hamakua Country Club 🏌   As you approach the sugar town of Honokaa, you can't miss this funky 9-hole course, built in the 1920s on a very steep hill overlooking the ocean. It's a par-33, 2,520-yard course. Architect Frank Anderson managed to squeeze in 9 holes by crisscrossing holes across fairways—you may never see a layout like this again. But the best part about Hamakua is the price: just $20 for 18 holes (you play the 9-hole course twice). The course is open to nonmembers on weekdays only. You don't need a tee time; just show up, and if no one's around, drop your $20 in the box and head out. Carts aren't allowed because of the steep hills.

On the ocean side of Hwy. 19 (41 miles from Hilo), Honokaa. ☎ **808/775-7244.** Greens fees $20 for 18 holes (you play the 9-hole course twice).

HILO

Hilo Municipal Golf Course   This is a great course for the casual golfer: It's flat, scenic, and often fun. *Warning:* Don't go after a heavy rain (especially in winter), when the fairways can get really soggy and play can slow way down. The rain does keep the course green and beautiful, though. Wonderful trees (monkeypods, coconuts, eucalyptus, banyans) dot the grounds, and the views—of Mauna Kea on one side and Hilo Bay on the other—are breathtaking. There are four sets of tees, with a par-71 from all; the back tees give you 6,325 yards of play. Getting a tee time can be a challenge; weekdays are your best bet.

340 Haihai St. (btw. Kinoole and Iwalani sts.). ☎ **808/959-7711.** Greens fees $29 Mon–Fri, $34 Sat–Sun and holidays. From Hilo, take Hwy. 11 toward Volcano; turn right at Puainako St. (at Prince Kuhio Plaza), left on Kinoole, and then right on Haihai St.

Naniloa Country Club   At first glance, this semiprivate 9-hole course looks pretty flat and short, but once you get beyond the 1st hole—a wide, straightforward 330-yard par-4—things get challenging. The tree-lined fairways require straight drives, and the huge lake on the 2nd and 5th holes is sure to haunt you. This course is very popular with locals and visitors alike. Rental clubs are available.

120 Banyan Dr. (at the intersection of Hwy. 11 and Hwy. 19). ☎ **808/935-3000.** Greens fees $15 walking for 18 holes, $54 with cart; $8 after 4pm.

VOLCANO VILLAGE

Volcano Golf & Country Club   Located at an altitude of 4,200 feet, this public course got its start in 1922, when the Blackshear family put in a green using old tomato cans for the holes. It now has three sets of tees to choose from, all with a par of 72. The course is unusually landscaped, making use of the pine and ohia trees scattered throughout. It's considered challenging by locals. Some tips from the regulars: Because the course is at such a high altitude, the ball travels farther than you're probably used to, so club down. If you hit the ball off the fairway, take the stroke—you don't want to look for your ball in the forest and undergrowth. Also, play a pitch-and-run game—the greens are slick.

Hwy. 11, on the right side, just after the entrance to Hawaii Volcanoes National Park. ☎ **808/967-7331.** www.volcanogolfshop.com. Greens fees $70; $57 after noon.

Biking

For mountain bike and cross-training bike rentals in Kona, go to **Hawaiian Pedals ★**, Kona Inn Shopping Village, Alii Drive, Kailua-Kona (☎ **808/329-2294**), and **Hawaiian Pedals Bike Works,** Hale Hana Centre, 74–5583 Luhia St., Kailua-Kona (☎ **808/326-2453;** www.hawaiianpedals.com); both have a huge selection of bikes: mountain bikes and hybrids ($20 a day), and racing bikes and front-suspension mountain bikes ($60 a day). Bike racks go for $5 a day, and you pay only for the days you actually use it (the honor system): If you have the bike for a week but use it for only 2 days, you'll be charged just $10. The folks at the shops are friendly and knowledgeable about cycling routes all over the Big Island.

GUIDED BIKE TOURS   Check out **Kona Coast Cycling** (☎ **877/592-BIKE** [2453] or 808/327-1133; www.cyclekona.com), which offers half-day (3–4 hr.) and full-day (4–6 hr.) bicycling tours, ranging from a casual ride to intense mountain biking at its best to 6-day bike tours of the Big Island. The locations are diverse, from the rolling hills of a Kona coffee farm to awesome views of the Waipio Valley Lookout. Most tours include round-trip transportation from hotels, van support, tour guide, helmet, gloves, water, snacks, and lunch on the full-day trips. Prices range from $125 to $145 for the day tours and $2,200 to $2,700 for the 6- to 8-day tours (includes airport pickup, accommodations, breakfast and lunch, bicycle, helmet, and tour guide). The **Hilo Bike Company,** 318 E. Kawili St., Hilo, HI 96720 (© **808/961-4452**), carries John Alford's book *Mountain Biking the Hawaiian Islands,* which includes maps and descriptions of rides for all of the islands.

The endangered Tiwi (scarlet honeycreeper).

Birding

Native Hawaiian birds are few—and dwindling. But Hawaii still offers extraordinary birding for anyone nimble enough to traverse tough, mucky landscape. And the best birding is on the Big Island; birders the world over come here hoping to see three Hawaiian birds, in particular: the akiapolaau, a woodpecker wannabe with a war club–like head; the nukupuu, an elusive little yellow bird with a curved beak, one of the crown jewels of Hawaiian birding; and the alala, a critically endangered Hawaiian crow that's now almost impossible to see in the wild.

If you don't know an apapane from a nukupuu, go with someone who does. Contact **Hawaii Forest & Trail,** 74–5035-B Queen Kaahumanu Hwy. (behind the Chevron station), Kailua-Kona (© **800/464-1993** or 808/331-8505; www.hawaii-forest.com), to sign up for the **Rainforest & Dryforest Adventure ★★**, led by naturalist Rob Pacheco. On this tour, you'll venture into pristine rainforest to see rare and endangered Hawaiian birds. The guide will also point out Hawaii's unique botany and evolution. The full-day (11-hr.) tour costs $179 and includes a midmorning snack with coffee, lunch, beverages, day pack, binoculars, walking stick, and rain gear.

If you want to head out on your own, good spots to see native Hawaiian and other birds include the following:

HAWAII VOLCANOES NATIONAL PARK   The best places for accomplished birders to go on their own are the ohia forests of this national park, usually at sunrise or sunset, when the little forest birds seem to be most active. The Hawaiian nene goose can be spotted at the park's Kipuka Nene Campground, a favorite nesting habitat. Geese and pheasants sometimes appear on the Volcano Golf Course in the afternoon.

HAKALAU FOREST NATIONAL WILDLIFE REFUGE   The first national wildlife refuge established solely for forest bird management is on the eastern slope of Mauna Kea above the Hamakua Coast. It's open for birding on Saturday, Sunday, and state holidays, using the public access road only. You must call ahead of time to get the gate combinations of the locked gates and to register. Every visitor to Upper Maulua is required to have a reservation. Reservations can be made by calling the Hakalau Forest NWR office (© 808/443-2300) between 8am and 4pm Monday through Friday at least 1 week prior to entry. Visitors will be asked to provide (1) their telephone number; (2) the number of people in their group; (3) the license plate numbers(s) of the vehicle(s) to be used; and (4) a description of the vehicle(s) to be used. A four-wheel-drive vehicle is required for the 50-mile trip, which takes almost 2 hours each way from Hilo or Kona. More information is available at www.fws.gov/hakalauforest. As we went to press, the Big Island was in the midst of a major drought and the area was currently closed.

HILO PONDS   Ducks, coots, herons (night and great blue), cattle egrets, and even Canada and snow geese fly into these popular coastal wetlands in Hilo, near the airport. Take Kalanianaole Highway about 3 miles east, past the industrial port facilities to Loko Waka Pond and Waiakea Pond.

Horseback Riding

Kohala Naalapa ★, on Kohala Mountain Road (Hwy. 250), mile marker 11 (ask for directions to the stables at the security-guard station; © 808/889-0022; www.naalapastables.com), offers unforgettable journeys into the rolling hills of Kahua and Kohala ranches, past ancient Hawaiian ruins, through lush pastures with grazing sheep and cows, and along mountaintops with panoramic coastal views. The horses and various riding areas are suited to everyone from first-timers to experienced equestrians. There are two trips a day: a 2½-hour tour at 8:30am for $89 and a 1½-hour tour at 1pm for $68. No kids 7 and under, pregnant riders, or riders over 230 pounds permitted.

Experienced riders should sign up for a trip with **Kings' Trail Rides, Tack, and Gift Shop ★★**, Hwy. 11 at mile marker 111, Kealakekua (© 808/323-2388; www.konacowboy.com). These 4-hour trips, with 2 hours of riding, are limited to four people. You'll head down the mountain along Monument Trail to the Captain Cook Monument in Kealakekua Bay, where you'll stop for lunch and an hour of snorkeling. The price ($135) includes lunch and gear.

To see Waipio Valley on horseback, call **Waipio Naalapa Trail Rides ★** (© 808/775-0419; www.naalapastables.com). The 2½-hour tours of this gorgeous tropical valley depart daily at 9:30am and 1pm (don't forget your camera). The guides are well versed in Hawaiian history and provide running commentary as you move through this historic place. The cost is $89 for adults. No kids 7 and under, pregnant riders, or riders over 230 pounds permitted.

Visitors can explore **Parker Ranch** (© 808/887-1046; www.parkerranch.com) and its vast 175,000-acre working cattle ranch. You'll learn firsthand about the ranch, its history, and its variety of plant life, and you may even catch glimpses of pheasant, francolins, or wild pigs. Rides (suitable for beginners) are available daily at 8:15am, and 12:15pm, and last 2 hours. Kids must be at least 7 years old. Riders will feel like Hawaiian *paniolo* (cowboys) as they ride through stone corrals where up to 5,000 Hereford cattle were rounded up after being brought

Horseback riding at Parker Ranch.

down from the slopes of Mauna Kea. A visit to the racetrack where Parker Ranch thoroughbreds were trained and still hold the record for speed is included in the excursion. The rides all begin at the Blacksmith Shop on Pukalani Road.

Tennis

You can play for free at any Hawaii County tennis court; for a detailed list of all courts on the island, contact **Hawaii County Department of Parks and Recreation,** 101 Pauahi St., Ste. 6, Hilo, HI 96720 (② **808/961-8311;** www. hawaii-county.com/parks/parks.htm). The best courts in Hilo are at the Hoolulu Tennis Stadium, located next to the Civic Auditorium on Manono Street (② **808/ 961-8720,** ext. 28). Most resorts in the Kona and Kohala areas do not allow nonguests to use their tennis facilities.

SEEING THE SIGHTS
The Kona Coast

GUIDED WALKING TOURS The **Kona Historical Society** (② 808/323-3222; www.konahistorical.org) hosts two historical walking tours in the Kona region. All walks must be booked in advance; call for reservations and departure locations. The 75-minute **Historic Kailua Village Walking Tour ★** (② 808/938-8825; www.konahistorical.org) is the most comprehensive tour of the Kona Coast. It takes you all around Kailua-Kona, from King Kamehameha's last seat of government to the summer palace of the Hawaiian royal family and beyond, with lots of Hawaiian history along the way. Tickets are $15 for adults, $10 for children 5 to 12, and include a 24-page booklet with more than 40 archival photographs of Kailua village. The self-guided **Kona Coffee Living History Tour** takes you through the everyday life of a Japanese family on the Uchida Coffee Farm during the

EXPERIENCE HOW THE LOCALS
live (and eat!)

"Go local for a day" is the mantra of **Home Tours Hawaii** ★★★ (℗ **877/ 325-5772** or 808/325-5772; www.home tourshawaii.com), which features chef Ann Sutherland, who was born, raised, and earned her sterling reputation as a gourmet chef in Hawaii. She invites visitors to experience what it's like to live (and, most important, eat) in Hawaii for a day. Chef Ann and her partner, Pat, pick you up in an air-conditioned van and then escort you to various private homes in the Kona region (from an upscale, multimillion-dollar oceanfront home to a handmade cottage in the middle of a

coffee plantation to a luxury estate) with a progressive brunch, prepared using local products, at each home you visit. Chef Ann is a funny storyteller who entertains you with history and trivia as you drive from one home to the next. Don't be too shocked when you hear the astronomical prices of real estate in Hawaii. You won't want to miss this insider's look at how residents live in Hawaii. Chef Ann's mouthwatering masterpieces are worth the price alone. The 4-hour tour, with transportation, brunch, and a gift bag of local products to take home with you, is $125.

1920s to 1940s. Interact with costumed interpreters as they go about life on a coffee farm. The tour is offered Monday through Thursday on the hour from 10am to 1pm, for $20 adults and $5 kids 5 to 12. Meet at the Kona Historical Society office, 81–6551 Mamalahoa Hwy. (next to Kona Specialty Meats), across from mile marker 110, Kealakekua. *Budget Tip:* Mondays are two for the price of one admission for the Kona Coffee tour.

SELF-GUIDED DRIVING TOURS   **Big Island Audio Tour** (℗ 808/896-4275), a self-guided audio tour on CD, features 36 tracks of information, including directions to the well-known sights plus tracks on beaches, short hikes, side trips, and information on Hawaiian language, history, and culture. The cost is $20.

If you're interested in seeing how your morning cup of joe goes from beans to brew, get a copy of the **Coffee Country Driving Tour.** This self-guided drive will take you farm by farm through Kona's famous coffee country; it also features a fascinating history of the area, the lowdown on coffee-making lingo, some insider tips on how to make a great cup, and even a recipe for Kona-coffee macadamia-nut chocolate-chunk pie (goes great with a cup of java). The free brochure is available at the **Big Island Visitors Bureau,** 250 Keawe St., Hilo, HI 96720 (℗ **808/961-5797;** www. bigisland.org).

IN & AROUND KAILUA-KONA ★★★

Ellison S. Onizuka Space Center ☺   This small museum has a real moon rock and memorabilia in honor of Big Island–born astronaut Ellison Onizuka, who died in the 1986 *Challenger* space shuttle disaster. Displays include a gravity well, which illustrates orbital motion, and an interactive rocket-propulsion exhibit, where you can launch your own miniature space shuttle.

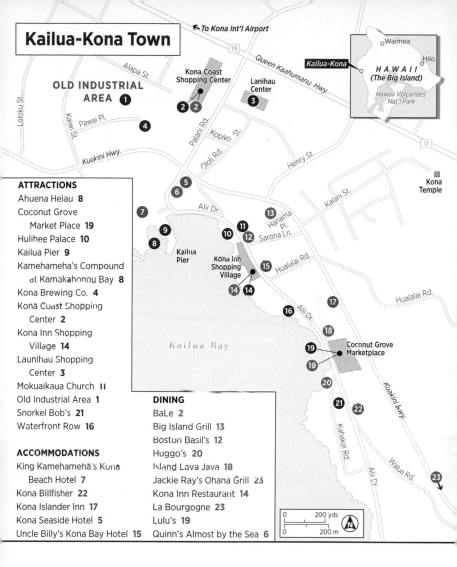

Kailua-Kona Town

← To Kona Int'l Airport

OLD INDUSTRIAL AREA ❶

Kona Coast Shopping Center

Lanihau Center

HAWAII (The Big Island)

Waimea • Hilo •
Kailua-Kona

Hawaii Volcanoes Nat'l Park

Kona Temple

Kailua Pier

Kailua Bay

Coconut Grove Marketplace

ATTRACTIONS
Ahuena Heiau **8**
Coconut Grove Market Place **19**
Hulihee Palace **10**
Kailua Pier **9**
Kamehameha's Compound at Kamakahonu Bay **8**
Kona Brewing Co. **4**
Kona Coast Shopping Center **2**
Kona Inn Shopping Village **14**
Lanihau Shopping Center **3**
Mokuaikaua Church **11**
Old Industrial Area **1**
Snorkel Bob's **21**
Waterfront Row **16**

ACCOMMODATIONS
King Kamehameha's Kona Beach Hotel **7**
Kona Billfisher **22**
Kona Islander Inn **17**
Kona Seaside Hotel **5**
Uncle Billy's Kona Bay Hotel **15**

DINING
BaLe **2**
Big Island Grill **13**
Boston Basil's **12**
Huggo's **20**
Island Lava Java **18**
Jackie Ray's Ohana Grill **23**
Kona Inn Restaurant **14**
La Bourgogne **23**
Lulu's **19**
Quinn's Almost by the Sea **6**

0   200 yds
0   200 m

At Kona International Airport, Kailua-Kona. ☏ **808/329-3441.** www.hawaiimuseums.org/mc/ishawaii_astronaut.htm. Admission $3 adults, $1 children 18 and under. Daily 8:30am–4:30pm. Parking in airport lot $2 per hour.

Hulihee Palace ★★   This two-story New England–style mansion of lava rock and coral mortar, built in 1838 by the Big Island's governor, John Adams Kuakini, overlooks the harbor at Kailua-Kona. The largest, most elegant residence on the island when it was erected, Hulihee became a home to Hawaii's royalty, making it the other royal palace in the United States (the most famous being Oahu's Iolani Palace). Now run by Daughters of Hawaii, it features many 19th-century mementos and gorgeous koa furniture. You'll get lots of background and royal lore on the guided tour (no photography allowed). There was some damage to this historic structure in the 2006 earthquake, but by the time you read this, all is scheduled to be repaired.

The palace hosts 12 free **Hawaiian music and hula concerts** a year, each dedicated to a Hawaiian monarch, at 4pm, generally on the third Sunday of the month (except June and Dec, when the performances are held in conjunction with King Kamehameha Day and Christmas). Call for dates.

Across the street is **Mokuaikaua Church** (© 808/329-1589), the oldest Christian church in Hawaii. It's constructed of lava stones, but its architecture is New England style all the way. The 112-foot steeple is still the tallest man-made structure in Kailua-Kona.

75–5718 Alii Dr., Kailua-Kona. © **808/329-1877.** www.daughtersofhawaii.com. Admission $6 adults, $4 seniors, $1 children. Wed–Sat 10am–3pm. Tours held throughout the day (arrive at least 1 hr. before closing).

Kailua Pier   This is action central for water adventures. Fishing charters, snorkel cruises, and party boats all come and go here. Stop by around 4pm, when the captains weigh in with the catch of the day, usually huge marlin—the record-setters often come in here. It's also a great place to watch the sunset.
On the waterfront outside Honokohau Harbor, Kailua-Kona.

Kamehameha's Compound at Kamakahonu Bay ★★   On the ocean side of the Kona Beach Hotel is a restored area of deep spiritual meaning to Hawaiians. This was the spot that King Kamehameha the Great chose to retreat to in 1812 after conquering the Hawaiian Islands. He stayed until his death in 1819. The king built a temple, **Ahuena Heiau,** and used it as a gathering place for his *kahuna* (priests) to counsel him on governing his people in times of peace. It was on this sacred ground in 1820 that Kamehameha's son Liholiho, as king, sat down to eat with his mother, Keopuolani, and Kamehameha's principal queen,

Hulihee Palace.

Mokuaikaua Church.

Kailua Pier.

Kaahumanu, thus breaking the ancient *kapu* (taboo) against eating with women; this act established a new order in the Hawaiian kingdom. The temple grounds are now just a third of their original size, but they're still impressive. You're free to wander the grounds, envisioning the days when King Kamehameha appealed to the gods to help him rule with the spirit of humanity's highest nature.

On the grounds of King Kamehameha's Kona Beach Hotel, 75-5660 Palani Rd., Kailua-Kona. ☎ **808/329-2911.** www.konabeachhotel.com/history.cfm. Free admission. Guided tours Mon–Fri at 1:30pm.

Kona Brewing Co. & Pub   This microbrewery is the first of its kind on the Big Island. Spoon and Pops, a father-and-son duo from Oregon, brought their brewing talents here and now produce about 25 barrels (about 124,000 gal.) per year. Drop by anytime during their business hours and take a quick, informal tour of the brewery, after which you get to taste the product. A brewpub on the property serves gourmet pizza, salads, and fresh-brewed Hawaiian ales.

75-5629 Kuakini Hwy. (entry on Pawai Place), Kailua-Kona. ☎ **808/334-BREW** [2739]. www.konabrewingco.com. Free tours and tastings. Tours daily 10:30am and 3pm. Turn north on Kuakini Hwy. (from Palani Rd.) and drive approximately ½ mile to the 1st stop sign, Kaiwi St., and turn right. Take the 1st right on Pawai Place and follow it until it ends at the brewery parking lot. Watch for directional signs along the way.

Natural Energy Laboratory of Hawaii Authority (NELHA)   Technology buffs should consider a visit to NELHA, where the hot tropical sun, in combination with a complex pumping system that brings 42°F (6°C) ocean water from 2,000 feet deep up to land, is used to develop innovations in agriculture, aquaculture, and ocean conservation. The interesting 75-minute tour takes in all areas of the high-tech ocean science and technology park, including the seawater delivery system, the energy-conversion process, and some of the park's more interesting tenants, from Maine lobsters to giant clams.

73-4460 Queen Kaahumanu Hwy. (at mile marker 94), Kailua-Kona. ☎ **808/329-8073.** www.nelha.org. Public presentation tours $18 adults, $15 seniors, free for children 8 and under. Mon–Thurs 10am–11:30am; reservations required.

UPCOUNTRY KONA: HOLUALOA ★★

On the slope of Hualalai volcano above Kailua-Kona sits the small village of Holualoa, which attracts travelers weary of super-resorts. Here you'll find a little art and culture—and shade.

This funky upcountry town, centered on two-lane Mamalahoa Highway, is nestled amid a lush, tropical landscape where avocados grow as big as footballs. Little more than a wide spot in the road, Holualoa is a cluster of brightly painted, tin-roofed plantation shacks enjoying a revival as B&Bs, art galleries, and quaint shops (see "Shops & Galleries," later in this chapter, for details). In 2 blocks, it manages to pack in two first-rate galleries, a frame shop, a potter, a glassworks, a goldsmith, an old-fashioned general store, a vintage 1930s gas station, a tiny post office, a Catholic church, and the **Kona Hotel,** a hot-pink clapboard structure that looks like a Western movie set—you're welcome to peek in, and you should.

The cool up-slope village is the best place in Hawaii for a coffee break. That's because Holualoa is in the heart of the coffee belt, a 20-mile-long strip at an elevation of between 1,000 and 1,400 feet, where all the Kona coffee in the world is grown in the rich volcanic soil of the cool uplands (see "Kona Coffee Craze!" on p. 339). Everyone's backyard seems to teem with glossy green leaves and ruby-red cherries (which contain the seeds, or beans, used to make coffee), and the air smells like an espresso bar. **Holuakoa Café,** on Mamalahoa Highway (Hwy. 180) in Holualoa (✆ **808/322-2233**), is a great place to get a freshly brewed cup and a bite to eat.

To reach Holualoa, follow narrow, winding Hualalai Road up the hill from Hwy. 19; it's about a 15-minute drive.

SOUTH KONA ★★★

Kona Historical Society Museum ★★ This well-organized museum is housed in the historic Greenwell Store, built in 1875 by Henry Nicholas Greenwell out of native stone. Antiques, artifacts, and photos tell the story of this fabled coast. The museum is filled with items that were common to everyday life here when coffee growing and cattle raising were the main industries. Stocked with accurate reproductions of goods that filled the shelves and hung from the ceiling joists, the store offers a glimpse of the past, complete with storekeepers dressed in period costumes, offering visitors St. Jacobs Oil to cure their arthritis or rheumatism. Before you leave, the shopkeeper may share some gossip about local people and events.

The Historical Society has another project in the works: the Kona Heritage Ranch, an outdoor museum on the daily life of a rancher in 1890, which will be located next door to the Greenwell Store. As part of the project, the society has created a replica of an 1890 Portuguese stone oven, the first of several structures and programs planned for the Kona Heritage Ranch. Portuguese from the Azores or Madeira started coming to Kona in the 1870s to help develop and manage dairies, a key phase of the ranching industry in Hawaii. The outdoor hive-type oven, made with cemented stone, was a constant presence wherever the Portuguese dairymen (and sugar-industry workers) settled. They brought with them both their knowledge of dairying on tropical islands and their love of freshly baked stone-oven bread. An informal group gathers every Thursday to learn about wood-fired baking techniques.

Serious history buffs should sign up for one of the museum's walking tours (see "Guided Walking Tours," on p. 377).

Hwy. 11, btw. mile markers 111 and 112, Kealakekua. ☎ **808/323-3222** or 808/323-2006. www.
konahistorical.org. Free admission (donations accepted); admission to Greenwell Store $7 adults,
$3 children 5–12. Mon–Thurs 10am–2pm. Parking on grassy area next to Kona Specialty Meats
parking lot.

Kula Kai Caverns & Lava Tubes ★★ 🎁

Before you trudge up to Pele's vol-
canic eruption, take a look at her underground handiwork. Ric Elhard and Rose
Herrera have explored and mapped out the labyrinth of lava tubes and caves,
carved out over the past 1,000 years or so, that crisscross their property on the
southwest rift zone on the slopes of Mauna Loa near South Point. Options
range from an easy half-hour tour on a well-lit underground route to a more
adventuresome 2-hour caving trip (recommended minimum age is 8). Helmets,
lights, gloves, and kneepads are all included. Sturdy shoes are recommended
for caving.

Off Hwy. 11, btw. mile markers 78 and 79, Ocean View. ☎ **808/929-7539.** www.kulakaicaverns.
com. Half-hour tour $15 adults, $10 children 6–12; 2- to 3-hr. tour $95 per person. Reservations
required.

The Painted Church ★ 🎁

Oh, those Belgian priests—what a talented lot. In
the late 1800s, Father John Berchman Velghe borrowed a page from Michelan-
gelo and painted biblical scenes inside St. Benedict's Catholic Church so the
illiterate Hawaiians could visualize the white man's version of creation.

84-5140 Painted Church Rd., Capt. Cook. ☎ **808/328-2227.** www.thepaintedchurch.org. Turn
off Hwy. 11 (toward the ocean) at about the 104 mile marker onto Rte. 160. Go on about a mile to

Kula Kai Caverns & Lava Tubes.

The Painted Church.

Idols at Puuhonua O Honaunau National Historical Park.

the 1st turnoff to the right. Watch for the King Kamehameha sign opposite. Continue along a narrow, winding road about ¼ mile to sign and turn right.

Puuhonua O Honaunau National Historical Park ★★★ With its fierce, haunting idols, this sacred site on the black-lava Kona Coast certainly looks forbidding. To ancient Hawaiians, however, Puuhonua O Honaunau served as a 16th-century place of refuge, providing sanctuary for defeated warriors and *kapu* (taboo) violators. A great rock wall—1,000 feet long, 10 feet high, and 17 feet thick—defines the refuge where Hawaiians found safety. On the wall's north end is Hale O Keawe Heiau, which holds the bones of 23 Hawaiian chiefs. Other archaeological finds include burial sites, old trails, and a portion of an ancient village. On a self-guided tour of the 180-acre site—which has been restored to its precontact state—you can see and learn about reconstructed thatched huts, canoes, and idols, and feel the *mana* (power) of old Hawaii.

A cultural festival, usually held in June, allows you to join in games, learn crafts, sample Hawaiian food, see traditional hula, and experience life in precontact Hawaii. Every Labor Day weekend, one of Hawaii's major outrigger canoe races starts here and ends in Kailua-Kona. Call for details on both events.

Hwy. 160 (off Hwy. 11 at mile marker 104), Honaunau. ℂ **808/328-2288.** www.nps.gov/puho. Admission $5 per vehicle, good for 7 days. Visitor center daily 8am–5:30pm; park daily 7am–7pm. From Hwy. 11, it's 3½ miles to the park entrance.

The Kohala Coast ★★★

Puukohola Heiau National Historic Site ★★★ This seacoast temple, called "the hill of the whale," is the single most imposing and dramatic structure of the ancient Hawaiians. It was built by Kamehameha I from 1790 to 1791. The *heiau* stands 224 feet long by 100 feet wide, with three narrow terraces on the seaside and an amphitheater to view canoes. Kamehameha built this temple after a prophet told him he would conquer and unite the islands if he did so; 4 years

Walking Through Thurston Lava Tube at Hawaii Volcanoes National Park (p. 368) It's scary, it's spooky, and most kids love it. You hike downhill through a rainforest full of little chittering native birds to enter this huge, silent black hole full of drips, cobwebs, and tree roots that stretch underground for almost a half-mile.

Snorkeling Kahaluu Beach Park (p. 364) The shallow, calm waters off Kahaluu Beach are the perfect place to take kids snorkeling. The waters are protected by a barrier reef, and the abundance of fish will keep the kids' attention. You can pick up a fish identification card at any dive shop and make a game out of seeing how many fish the kids can find.

Riding a Submarine into the Underwater World (p. 366) The huge viewing windows on Atlantis's 48-passenger sub will have the kids enthralled as the high-tech craft leaves the surface and plunges 120 feet down through the mysterious Neptunian waters. The trip isn't too long—just an hour—and there are plenty of reef fish and prehistoric-looking corals to hold the young ones' attention.

Launching Your Own Space Shuttle (p. 378) Okay, it's a model of a space shuttle, but it's still a real blast. The Ellison S. Onizuka Space Center has dozens of interactive displays to thrill budding young astronauts, such as a hands-on experience with gyroscopic stabilization. Great video clips of astronauts working and living in space may inspire your kids as well.

Hunting for Petroglyphs (p. 387) There's plenty of space to run around and discover ancient stone carvings at either the Puako Petroglyph Archaeological District (at Mauna Lani Resort) or the Kings' Trail (by the Waikoloa Beach Marriott Resort). And finding the petroglyphs is only part of the game—once you find them, you have to guess what the designs mean.

Watching the Volcano (p. 401) Any kid who doesn't get a kick out of watching a live volcano set the night on fire has been watching too much television. Take snacks, bottled water, flashlights, and sturdy shoes, and follow the ranger's instructions on where to view the lava safely.

Swimming with Dolphins (p. 322) Would your kids like to swim with, touch, and even kiss a real live bottlenose dolphin, without ever going out into open water? If so, then **Dolphin Quest** (www.dolphinquest.com) is for you. Kids as young as 5 can participate in several dolphin-encounter programs ($210–$250, or $1,350 for the whole family), while those 10 and up can become trainer for a day ($650 per child). There's even a 10-minute meet-and-greet with a dolphin for tots age 2 to 4 (at a pricey $80 for parent and child). You don't need to be a guest at the Hilton Waikoloa Village to take advantage of this unique opportunity to interact with marine life.

---

later, he fulfilled his kingly goal. The site also includes an interactive visitor center, the house of John Young (a trusted advisor of Kamehameha), and, offshore, the submerged ruins of Hale O Ka Puni, a shrine dedicated to the shark gods.

Hwy. 270, near Kawaihae Harbor. (✆ **808/882-7218.** www.nps.gov/puhe. Free admission. Prearranged tours are free. Daily 7:45am–4:30pm. The visitor center is on Hwy. 270; the *heiau* is a short walk away. The trail is closed when it's too windy, so call ahead if you're in doubt.

Into Another Dimension

What could be better than 3-D? How about 4-D? The 24-seat **Great 4-D Movie Ride** at the Shops at Mauna Lani features films that not only look life-like, they sound and feel like you're a part of the action, with surround sound, full-range motion seats, and blown air and water spray for an experience that will trip all your senses. At press time, screenings included SpongeBob Squarepants, National Geographic Sea Monsters, and Alien Safari; call ℗ 786/320-8884 or visit www.shops atmaunalani.com for updated titles and show times. Tickets are $5 before 5pm and $7 after.

ANCIENT HAWAIIAN FISH PONDS

Like their Polynesian forebears, Hawaiians were among the first aquaculturists on the planet. Scientists still marvel at the ways they used the brackish ponds along the shoreline to stock and harvest fish. There are actually two different types of ancient fish ponds (or *loko i'a*). Closed ponds, located inshore, were closed off from the ocean. Open ponds used rock walls as a barrier to the ocean and sluice gates that connected the ponds to the ocean. The gates were woven vines, with just enough room for juvenile fish to swim in at high tide while keeping the bigger, fatter fish from swimming out. Generally, the Hawaiians kept and raised mullet, milkfish, and shrimp in these open ponds; juvenile manini, papio, eels, and barracuda occasionally found their way in, too.

The **Kalahuipuaa Fish Ponds,** at Mauna Lani Resort (℗ **808/885-6622**), are great examples of both types of ponds in a lush tropical setting. South of the Mauna Lani Resort are **Kuualii** and **Kahapapa Fish Ponds,** at the Waikoloa Beach Marriott Resort (℗ **808/886-6789**). Both resorts have taken great pains to restore the ponds to their original states and to preserve them for future generations; call ahead to arrange a free guided tour.

Puukohola Heiau National Historic Site.

Kohala Coast Petroglyphs.

KOHALA COAST PETROGLYPHS

The Hawaiian petroglyphs are a great enigma of the Pacific—no one knows who made them or why. They appear at 135 sites on six inhabited islands, but most of them are found on the Big Island.

At first glance, the huge slate of pahoehoe looks like any other smooth black slate of lava on the seacoast of the Big Island—until gradually, in slanting rays of the sun, a wonderful cast of characters leaps to life before your eyes. You might see dancers and paddlers, fishermen and chiefs, and hundreds of marchers all in a row. Pictures of the tools of daily life are everywhere: fishhooks, spears, poi pounders, canoes. The most common representations are family groups. There are also post–European contact petroglyphs of ships, anchors, horses, and guns.

The largest concentration of these stone symbols in the Pacific lies within the 233-acre **Puako Petroglyph Archaeological District ★**, near Mauna Lani Resort. A total of 3,000 designs have been identified. The 1.5-mile **Malama Trail** starts north of Mauna Lani Resort; take Hwy. 19 to the resort turnoff and drive toward the coast on North Kaniku Drive, which ends at a parking lot; the trail head is marked by a sign and interpretive kiosk. Go in the early morning or late afternoon, when it's cool.

The **Kings' Shops** (✆ 808/886-8811), at the Waikoloa Beach Resort, offers a free 1-hour tour of the surrounding petroglyphs Thursday through Sunday at 10:30am. Register in advance.

Warning: The petroglyphs are thousands of years old and easily destroyed. Do not walk on them or attempt to take a rubbing (there's a special area in the Puako Preserve for doing so). The best way to capture a petroglyph is with a photo in the late afternoon, when the shadows are long.

North Kohala ★★★

Lapakahi State Historical Park ★ ☺ This 14th-century fishing village, on a hot, dry, dusty stretch of coast, offers a glimpse into the lifestyle of the ancients. Lapakahi is the best-preserved fishing village in Hawaii. Take the self-guided 1-mile loop trail past stone platforms, fish shrines, rock shelters, salt pans, and restored *hale* (houses) to a coral-sand beach and the deep-blue sea (good snorkeling). Wear good hiking shoes or tennies; it's a hearty 45-minute walk. Go early in the morning or late in the afternoon to beat the heat.

Hwy. 270, Mahukona. ✆ **808/327-4958.** www.hawaiistateparks.org/parks/hawaii/Index. cfm?park_id=50. Free admission. Daily 8am–4pm. Guided tours by appointment.

Mookini Luakini Heiau ★★ 📷 The 1,500-year-old Mookini Heiau, once used by kings to pray and offer human sacrifices, is Hawaii's oldest, largest, and most sacred religious site (and now a national historic landmark). The massive three-story stone temple, dedicated to Ku, the Hawaiian god of war, was erected in A.D. 480; each stone is said to have been passed hand to hand from Pololu Valley, 14 miles away, by 18,000 men who worked from sunset to sunrise. Kamehameha, born nearby under Halley's Comet, sought spiritual guidance here before embarking on his campaign to unite Hawaii. You can see the temple only by appointment. Contact the Mookini Preservation Foundation, on Oahu (✆ **808/373-8000**).

On the north shore, near Upolu Point Airport.

Pua Mau Place.

Original King Kamehameha Statue ★★ Here stands King Kamehameha the Great, right arm outstretched, left arm holding a spear, as if guarding the seniors who have turned a century-old New England–style courthouse into an airy center for their golden years. The center is worth a stop just to meet the town elders, who are quick to point out the local sights, hand you a free *Guide to Historic North Kohala,* and give you a brief tour of the courthouse, whose walls are covered with the faces of innocent-looking local boys killed in World War II, Korea, and Vietnam.

But the statue's the main attraction here. There's one just like it in Honolulu, across the street from Iolani Palace, but this is the original: an 8-foot, 6-inch bronze by Thomas R. Gould, a Boston sculptor. It was cast in Europe in 1880 but was lost at sea on its way to Hawaii. A sea captain eventually recovered the statue, which was placed here, near Kamehameha's Kohala birthplace, in 1912.

Kamehameha was born in 1750, became ruler of Hawaii in 1810, and died in Kailua-Kona in 1819. His burial site remains a mystery.

Hwy. 270, Kapaau.

Pololu Valley Lookout ★★★ At this end-of-the-road scenic lookout, you can gaze at the vertical jade-green cliffs of the Hamakua Coast and two islets offshore. The view may look familiar once you get here—it often appears on travel posters. Linger if you can; adventurous travelers can take a switchback trail (a good 45-min. hike) to a secluded black-sand beach at the mouth of a wild valley once planted in taro; bring water and bug spray.

At the end of Hwy. 270, Makapala.

Pua Mau Place ☺ Perched on the sun-kissed western slopes of the Kohala Mountains and dotted with deep, craggy ravines is one of Hawaii's most unusual botanical gardens, Pua Mau Place, a 45-acre oasis with breathtaking views of both the ocean and the majestic mountains. It's dedicated to plants that are "ever blooming," an expansive collection of continuously flowering tropical flowers, trees, and shrubs. The gardens also have an aviary of exotic birds and a unique hibiscus maze planted with some 200 varieties of hibiscus. This is a great place for families; children are invited to feed the birds in the aviary. Visitors can take the self-guided tour (along with a booklet filled with the names and descriptions of all the plants) along mulched pathways meandering through the gardens, where every plant is clearly marked.

10 Ala Kahua Dr., Kawaihae. © **808/882-0888.** www.puamau.com. Admission $10 adults, $8 seniors and students, free for children 12 and under. Daily 9am–4pm. Located off Hwy. 270 on Ala Kahua Dr. (in Kohala Estates), just north of Kawaihae. Turn at mile marker 6, ½ mile up the hill to the gate at a lava-rock wall.

Waimea (Kamuela) ★★★

Kamuela Museum It takes only about an hour to explore tiny Kamuela Museum. Its eclectic collection includes an early Hawaiian dogtooth death cup, a piece of rope used on the *Apollo* mission, and ancient artifacts from the royal family.

At the junction of Hwy. 19 and Hwy. 250, Waimea. © **808/885-4724.** www.hawaiimuseums.org/mc/ishawaii_kamuela.htm. Admission $5 adults, $2 children 11 and under. Daily 8am–5pm.

Mauna Kea ★★★

The summit of Mauna Kea, the world's tallest mountain if measured from its base on the ocean floor, is the best place on earth for astronomical observations because its mid-Pacific site is near the equator and because it enjoys clear, pollution-free skies and pitch-black nights with no urban light to interfere. That's why Mauna Kea is home to the world's largest telescope—but the stargazing from here is fantastic even with the naked eye.

SETTING OUT You'll need a four-wheel-drive vehicle to climb to the peak, **Observatory Hill.** A standard car will get you as far as the visitor center, but check your rental agreement before you go; some agencies prohibit you from taking your car on the Saddle Road, which is narrow and rutted, and has a soft shoulder.

SAFETY TIPS Always check the weather and Mauna Kea road conditions before you head out (© **808/961-5582**). Dress warmly; the temperatures drop into the 30s Fahrenheit (around 0°C) after dark. Drink as much liquid as possible, avoiding alcohol and coffee, in the 36 hours surrounding your trip to avoid dehydration. Don't go within 24 hours of scuba diving—you could get the bends. The day before you go, avoid gas-producing foods, such as beans, cabbage, onions, soft drinks, or starches. If you smoke, take a break for 48 hours beforehand to allow the carbon monoxide in your bloodstream

---

📎 **Everything You've Always Wanted to Know About Mauna Kea**

One of the best books on Mauna Kea, written by Onizuka Visitor Information Station manager David Byrne and Big Island writer Leslie Lang, is *Mauna Kea: A Guide to Hawaii's Sacred Mountain,* published by Watermark Publishing (© 866/900-BOOK [2665]; www.books hawaii.net). The book ($18) covers everything from the cultural history of the sacred mountain to her natural history, even great insights on the scientific value of the dormant volcano. Plus, the authors give valuable tips on how to make the most of your visit to truly one of the wonders of the world.

Mauna Kea.

to dissipate—you need all the oxygen you can get. Wear dark sunglasses to avoid snow blindness, and use lots of sunscreen and lip balm. Pregnant women and anyone 12 and under or with a heart condition or lung ailment are advised to stay below. Once you're at the top, don't overexert yourself; it's bad for your heart. Take it easy up here.

ACCESS POINTS & VISITOR CENTERS   It's about an hour from Hilo or Waimea to the visitor center and another 30 to 45 minutes from here to the summit. Take the Saddle Road (Hwy. 200) from Hwy. 190; it's about 19 miles to Mauna Kea State Recreation Area, a good place to stop and stretch your legs. Go another 9 miles to the unmarked Summit Road turnoff, at mile marker 28 (about 9,300 ft.), across from the Hunter's Check-in Station. People usually start getting lightheaded after the 9,600-foot marker (about 6¼ miles up the Summit Rd.), the site of the last comfort zone and the **Onizuka Visitor Information Station** (✆ **808/961-2180;** www.ifa. hawaii.edu/info/vis). Named in memory of Hawaii's fallen astronaut, a native of the Big Island and a victim of the *Challenger* explosion, the center is open daily from 9am to 10pm.

TOURS & PROGRAMS   If you'd rather not go it alone to the top, you can caravan up as part of a **free summit tour,** offered Saturday and Sunday at 1pm from the visitor center (returns at 5pm). You must be 16 or older and in good health (no cardiopulmonary problems), not be pregnant, and have a four-wheel-drive vehicle. The tours explain the development of the facilities on Mauna Kea and include a walking tour of an observatory at 13,796 feet. Call ✆ **808/961-2180** if you'd like to participate.

Every night from 6 to 10pm, you can do some serious **stargazing** from the Onizuka Visitor Information Station. There's a free lecture at 6pm, followed by a video, a question-and-answer session, and your chance to peer through 11-, 14-, and 16-inch telescopes. Bring a snack and, if you've got them, your own telescope or binoculars, along with a flashlight with a red filter. Dress for 30° to 40°F (−1° to 4°C) temperatures, but call ✆ **808/961-5582** for the weather report first. Families are welcome.

At the **Keck Telescope Control Center,** 65–1120 Mamalahoa Hwy. (Hwy. 19), across from the North Hawaii Community Hospital, Waimea (© 808/885-7887; www.keckobservatory.org), you can see a model of the world's largest telescope, which sits atop Mauna Kea. The center is open Monday through Friday from 8am to 4:30pm. A 12-minute video explains the Keck's search for objects in deep space.

The **W. M. Keck Observatory** at the summit does not offer tours, but it does provide a visitor gallery with a 12-minute video, informational panels on the observatory layout and science results, two public restrooms, and a viewing area with partial views of the Keck telescope and dome. Gallery hours are Monday through Friday from 10am to 4pm.

MAKING THE CLIMB If you're heading up on your own, stop at the visitor center for about a half-hour to get acquainted with the altitude. Walk around, eat a banana, and drink some water before you press onward and upward in low gear, engine whining. It takes about 30 to 45 minutes to get to the top from here. The trip is a mere 6 miles, but you climb from 9,000 to nearly 14,000 feet.

AT THE SUMMIT Up here, 11 nations, including Japan, France, and Canada, have set up infrared telescopes to look into deep space. Among them sits the **Keck Telescope,** the world's largest. Developed by the University of California and the California Institute of Technology, it's eight stories high, weighs 150 tons, and has a 33-foot-diameter mirror made of 36 perfectly attuned hexagon mirrors, like a fly's eye, rather than one conventional lens.

Also at the summit, up a narrow footpath, is a cairn of rocks; from it, you can see across the Pacific Ocean in a 360-degree view that's beyond words and pictures. When it's socked in, you get a surreal look at the summits of

Lake Waiau, located inside the cinder cone just below the summit of Mauna Kea.

Mauna Loa and Maui's Haleakala poking through the puffy white cumulus clouds beneath your feet.

Inside a cinder cone just below the summit is **Lake Waiau,** the only glacial lake in the mid-Pacific and, at 13,020 feet above sea level, one of the highest lakes in the world. The lake never dries up, even though it gets only 15 inches of rain a year and sits in porous lava where there are no springs. Nobody quite knows what to make of this, but scientists suspect the lake is replenished by snowmelt and permafrost from submerged lava tubes. You can't see the lake from Summit Road; you must take a brief high-altitude hike. But it's easy: On the final approach to the summit area, upon regaining the blacktop road, go about 600 feet to the major switchback and make a hard right turn. Park on the shoulder of the road (which is at 13,200 ft.). No sign points the way, but there's an obvious .5-mile trail that goes down to the lake about 200 feet across the lava. Follow the base of the big cinder cone on your left; you should have the summit of Mauna Loa in view directly ahead as you walk.

The Hamakua Coast ★★★

The sugar industry's rich 117-year history, along the scenic 45-mile coastline from Hilo to Hamakua, comes alive in the interpretive *Hilo-Hamakua Heritage Coast* drive guide found on the **Hawaii Island Economic Development Board's** website, 117 Kiawe St., Hilo, HI 96720 (© **808/935-2180;** http://hiedb.org/our-areas-of-focus/tourism, info@hiedb.org). The downloadable guide not only points out the historic sites and museums, scenic photo opportunities, restaurants and stores, and even restrooms along the Hawaii Belt Road (Hwy. 19), but also has corresponding brown-and-white points-of-interest signs on the highway. Visitor centers anchored at either end in Hilo and in Hamakua offer additional information on the area.

NATURAL WONDERS ALONG THE COAST

Akaka Falls ★★★   See one of Hawaii's most scenic waterfalls via an easy 1-mile paved loop through a rainforest, past bamboo and ginger, and down to an observation point. You'll have a perfect view of 442-foot Akaka and nearby Kahuna Falls, which is a mere 100-footer. Keep your eyes peeled for rainbows. The noise you hear is the sound of coqui frogs, an alien frog from Puerto Rico that has become a pest on the Big Island.

On Hwy. 19, Honomu (8 miles north of Hilo). Turn left at Honomu and head 3½ miles inland on Akaka Falls Rd. (Hwy. 220).

Hawaii Tropical Botanical Garden ★★   More than 1,800 species of tropical plants thrive in this little-known Eden by the sea. The 40-acre garden, nestled between the crashing surf and a thundering waterfall, has the world's largest selection of tropical plants growing in a natural environment, including torch gingers (which tower on 12-ft. stalks), a banyan canyon, an orchid garden, a banana grove, a bromeliad hill, and a golden bamboo grove, which rattles like a jungle drum in the trade winds. Some endangered Hawaiian specimens, such as the rare *Gardenia remyi,* are flourishing in this habitat. The gardens are seldom crowded; you can wander around by yourself all day.

Off Hwy. 19 on the 4-mile Scenic Route (8 miles north of Hilo), Onomea Bay. *C* **808/964-5233.** www.htbg.com. Admission $15 adults, $5 children 6–16, free for children 5 and under. Daily 9am–5pm.

Laupahoehoe Beach Park ★   This idyllic place holds a grim reminder of nature's fury. In 1946, a tidal wave swept across the village that once stood on this lava-leaf (that's what *laupahoehoe* means) peninsula and claimed the lives of 20 students and four teachers. A memorial in this pretty little park recalls the tragedy. The land here ends in black sea stacks that resemble tombstones. It's not a place for swimming, but the views are spectacular.

Off Hwy. 19, Laupahoehoe Point exit.

World Botanical Gardens ★★   Just north of Hilo is Hawaii's largest botanical garden, with some 5,000 species. When the fruits are in season, the staff hands out free chilled juices. One of the most spectacular sights is the .25-mile rainforest walk (wheelchair accessible), along a stream on a flower-lined path to the viewing area of the three-tiered, 300 foot Umauma Falls. Parents will appreciate the large children's maze, where the "prize" is a playing field near the exit. The mock-orange hedge, which defines the various paths in the maze, is only 5 feet tall, so most parents can peer over the edge to keep an eye on their *keiki*. Other terrific walks include the "rainbow walk," through an ethnobotanical garden, and one through a wellness garden with medicinal Hawaiian plants. There's also an arboretum. Still under construction as we went to press is a phylogenetic garden with plants and trees arranged in roughly the same sequence in which they first appeared on earth.

Off Hwy. 19 near mile marker 16, Umauma. *C* **808/963-5427.** www.worldbotanicalgardens. com. Admission $13 adults, $6 teens 13–19, $3 children 5–12, free for children 4 and under. Guided tours $33 adults, $23 teens, $13 children. Daily 9am–5pm.

Akaka Falls.

EXPERIENCING WHERE THE gods LIVE

"The ancient Hawaiians thought of the top of Mauna Kea as heaven, or at least where the gods and goddesses lived," according to Monte "Pat" Wright, owner and chief guide of **Mauna Kea Summit Adventures.** Wright, the first guide to take people up to the top of Mauna Kea, the world's tallest mountain when measured from the base and an astonishing 13,796 feet when measured from sea level, says he fell in love with this often-snowcapped peak the first time he saw it.

Mauna Kea Summit Adventures offers a luxurious trip to the top of the world. The 7- to 8-hour adventure begins midafternoon, when guests are picked up along the Kona-Kohala coasts in a $65,000 custom four-wheel-drive turbo-diesel van. As the passengers make the drive up the mountain, the extensively trained guide discusses the geography, geology, natural history, and Hawaiian culture along the way.

The first stop is at the Onizuka Visitor Information Station, at 9,000 feet, where guests can stretch, get acclimatized to the altitude, and eat dinner. As they gear up with Mauna Kea Summit Adventures' heavy arctic-style hooded parkas and gloves (the average temperature on the mountain is 30°F/–1°C), the guide describes why the world's largest telescopes (pictured at right) are located on Mauna Kea and also tells stories about the lifestyle of astronomers who live for a clear night sky.

After a dinner of gourmet sandwiches, vegetarian onion soup, and hot chocolate, coffee, or tea, everyone climbs back into the van for the half-hour ride to the summit. As the sun sinks into the Pacific nearly 14,000 feet below, the guide points out the various world-renowned telescopes as they rotate into position for the night viewing.

After the last trace of sunset colors has disappeared from the sky, the tour

HONOKAA ★★★

Honokaa is worth a visit to see the remnants of plantation life, when sugar was king. This is a real place that hasn't yet been boutiqued into a shopping mall; it looks as if someone has kept it in a bell jar since 1920. There's a real barbershop, a real Filipino store, some good shopping (see "Shops & Galleries," later in this chapter), and a hotel with creaky floorboards that dishes up hearty food. The town also serves as the gateway to spectacular **Waipio Valley** (see below).

Honokaa has no attractions, per se, but you might want to check out the **Katsu Goto Memorial,** next to the library at the Hilo end of town. Katsu Goto, one of the first indentured Japanese immigrants, arrived in Honokaa in the late 1800s to work on the sugar plantations. He learned English, quit the plantation, and aided his fellow immigrants in labor disputes with American planters. On October 23, 1889, he was hanged from a lamppost in Honokaa, a victim of local-style justice.

THE END OF THE ROAD: WAIPIO VALLEY ★★★

Long ago, this lush, tropical place was the valley of kings, who called it the valley of "curving water" (which is what *Waipio* means). From the black-sand bay at its mouth, Waipio sweeps 6 miles between sheer, cathedral-like walls that reach

again descends down to midmountain, where the climate is more agreeable, for stargazing. Each tour has Celestron Celestar 8 deluxe telescopes, which are capable of 30X to 175X magnification and gather up to 500 times more light than the unaided eye.

Wright advises people to book the adventure early in their vacation. "Although we do cancel about 25 trips a year due to weather, we want to be able to accommodate everyone," he says. If

guests book at the beginning of their holiday and the trip is canceled due to weather, then Mauna Kea Summit Adventures will attempt to reschedule another day.

Note that the summit's low oxygen level (40% less oxygen than at sea level) and the diminished air pressure (also 40% less air pressure than at sea level) can be a serious problem for people with heart or lung problems or for scuba divers who have been diving in the previous 24 hours. Pregnant women, children 12 and under, and obese people should not travel to the summit due to the decreased oxygen. Because the roads to the summit are bumpy, anyone with a bad back might want to opt out, too.

The cost for this celestial adventure is $200 including tax (15% off if you book online 2 weeks in advance). For more information, call ✆ **888/322-2366** or 808/322-2366, or go to www.maunakea.com.

almost a mile high. Once 40,000 Hawaiians lived here, amid taro, red bananas, and wild guavas in an area etched by streams and waterfalls. Only about 50 Hawaiians live in the valley today, tending taro, fishing, and soaking up the ambience of this old Hawaiian place.

The sacred valley is steeped in myth and legend. Many of the ancient royals are buried here; some believe they rise up to become Marchers of the Night, whose chants reverberate through the valley. The caskets of Hawaiian chiefs Liloa and Lono Ika Makahiki, stolen from the Bishop Museum, are believed to have been brought here by Hawaiians.

To get to Waipio Valley, take Hwy. 19 from Hilo to Honokaa, and then Hwy. 240 to the **Waipio Valley Lookout ★★★**, a grassy park on the edge of Waipio Valley's sheer cliffs with splendid views of the wild oasis below. This is a great place for a picnic; you can sit at old redwood picnic tables and watch the white combers race along the black-sand beach at the mouth of the valley. From the lookout, you can hike down into the valley.

Warning: Do not attempt to drive your rental car down into the valley (even if you see someone else doing it). The problem is not so much going down as coming back up. Every day, rental cars have to be "rescued" and towed back up to the top, at great expense to the driver. Instead, hop on the **Waipio Valley**

Co-*key,* Co-*key:* What Is That Noise?

That loud noise you hear after dark, especially on the eastern side of the Big Island, is the cry of the male coqui frog looking for a mate. A native of Puerto Rico, where the frogs are kept in check by snakes, the coqui frog came to Hawaii in some plant material, found no natural enemies, and spread across the Big Island (and Maui). A chorus of several hundred coqui frogs is deafening (up to 163 decibels, or the noise level of a jet engine from 100 ft.). In some places, like Akaka Falls, there are so many frogs that they are now chirping during daylight hours.

Shuttle (© 808/775-7121 for reservations) for a 90- to 120-minute guided tour, offered Monday through Saturday from 9am to 3pm. Get your tickets at **Waipio Valley Artworks,** on Hwy. 240, 2 miles from the lookout (© 808/775-0958; www.waipiovalleyartworks.com). Tickets are $55 for adults, $28 for kids 12 and under.

You can also explore the valley with **Waipio Valley Wagon Tours** (© 808/775-9518; www.waipiovalleywagontours.com), which offers narrated 90-minute historical rides by mule-drawn surrey. Tours are offered daily at 10:30am, 12:30pm, and 2:30pm. It costs $55 for adults, $50 for seniors, and $25 for children 4 to 12; call for reservations.

If you want to spend more than a day in the valley, plan ahead. A few simple B&Bs are situated on the ridge overlooking the valley and require advance reservations (see p. 324 for listings).

Hilo ★★★

Contact or stop by the **Downtown Hilo Improvement Association,** 329 Kamehameha Ave., Hilo, HI 96720 (© 808/935-8850; www.downtownhilo. com), for a copy of its very informative self-guided walking tour of Hilo, which focuses on 18 historic sites dating from the 1870s to the present.

ON THE WATERFRONT

Old banyan trees shade **Banyan Drive ★★**, the lane that curves along the waterfront to the Hilo Bay hotels. Most of the trees were planted in the mid-1930s by memorable visitors like Cecil B. DeMille (who was here in 1933 filming *Four Frightened People*), Babe Ruth (his tree is in front of the Hilo Hawaiian Hotel), King George V, Amelia Earhart, and other celebrities whose fleeting fame didn't last as long as the trees themselves.

It's worth a stop along Banyan Drive—especially if the coast is clear and the summit of Mauna Kea is free of clouds—to make the short walk across the concrete-arch bridge in front of the Naniloa Hotel to **Coconut Island ★**, if only to gain a panoramic sense of the place.

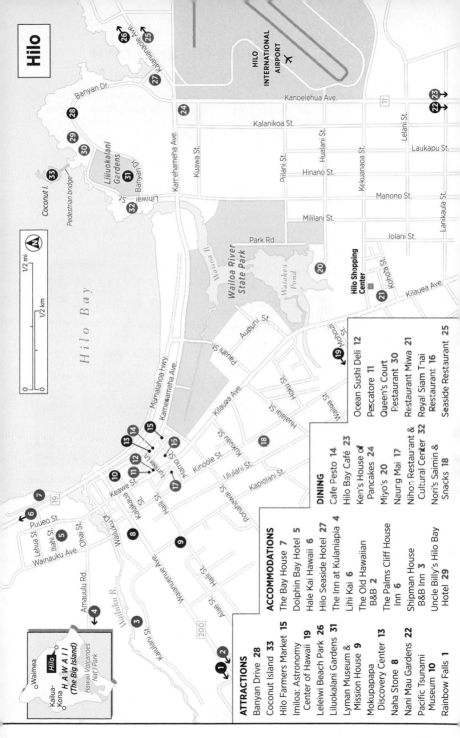

Hilo

ATTRACTIONS
Banyan Drive **28**
Coconut Island **33**
Hilo Farmers Market **15**
Imiloa: Astronomy
  Center of Hawaii **19**
Leleiwi Beach Park **26**
Liliuokalani Gardens **31**
Lyman Museum &
  Mission House **9**
Mokupapapa
  Discovery Center **13**
Naha Stone **8**
Nani Mau Gardens **22**
Pacific Tsunami
  Museum **10**
Rainbow Falls **1**

ACCOMMODATIONS
The Bay House **7**
Dolphin Bay Hotel **5**
Hale Kai Hawaii **6**
Hilo Seaside Hotel **27**
The Inn at Kulaniapia **4**
Lihi Kai **6**
The Old Hawaiian
  B&B **2**
The Palms Cliff House
  Inn **6**
Shipman House
  B&B Inn **3**
Uncle Billy's Hilo Bay
  Hotel **29**

DINING
Cafe Pesto **14**
Hilo Bay Café **23**
Ken's House of
  Pancakes **24**
Miyo's **20**
Naurg Mai **17**
Nihon Restaurant &
  Cultural Center **32**
Nori's Saimin &
  Snacks **18**
Ocean Sushi Deli **12**
Pescatore **11**
Queen's Court
  Restaurant **30**
Restaurant Miwa **21**
Royal Siam Thai
  Restaurant **16**
Seaside Restaurant **25**

imiloa: EXPLORING THE UNKNOWN

Absolutely do *not* miss the recently opened **Imiloa: Astronomy Center of Hawaii ★★★**. The 300 exhibits in the 12,000-square-foot gallery make the connection between the Hawaiian culture and its explorers, who "discovered" the Hawaiian Islands, and the astronomers who explore the heavens from the observatories atop Mauna Kea. *Imiloa,* which means "explorer" or "seeker of profound truth," is the perfect name for this architecturally stunning center, located on 9 landscaped acres overlooking Hilo Bay in the University of Hawaii at Hilo Science and Technology Park campus, 600 Imiloa Place (✆ 808/969-9703; www.imiloa hawaii.org). Plan to spend at least a couple of hours here; a half-day would be better, to allow time to browse the excellent interactive exhibits as well as take in one of the planetarium shows, which boast a state-of-the-art digital projection system. Open Tuesday through Sunday from 9am to 4pm; admission is $18 for adults and $9.50 for children 4 to 12.

'Imiloa Astronomy Center of Hawai'i University of Hawai'i at Hilo

Also along Banyan Drive is **Liliuokalani Gardens ★★**, the largest formal Japanese garden this side of Tokyo. This 30-acre park, named for Hawaii's last monarch, Queen Liliuokalani, is as pretty as a postcard, with bonsai, carp ponds, pagodas, and a moon-gate bridge. Admission is free; open 24 hours.

OTHER HILO SIGHTS

Lyman Museum & Mission House ★ ☺   The oldest wood-frame house on the island was built in 1839 by David and Sarah Lyman, a missionary couple who arrived from New England in 1832. This hybrid combined New England- and Hawaiian-style architecture and is built of hand-hewn koa planks and native timbers. Here the Lymans received such guests as Mark Twain and Hawaii's monarchs. The well-preserved house is the best example of missionary life and times in Hawaii. You'll find lots of artifacts from the 19th century, including furniture and clothing from the Lymans and one of the first mirrors in Hilo.

The **Earth Heritage Gallery,** in the complex next door, continues the story of the islands with geology and volcanology exhibits, a mineral-rock collection that's rated one of the best in the country, and a section on local flora and fauna. The **Island Heritage Gallery** features displays on Hawaiian culture, including a replica of a grass *hale,* as well as on other cultures transplanted to Hawaii's shores. A special gallery features changing exhibits on the history, art, and culture of Hawaii.

276 Haili St. (at Kapiolani St.). ℂ **808/935-5021.** www.lymanmuseum.org. Admission $10 adults, $8 seniors over 60, $3 children 6–17, $21 per family. Mon–Sat 10am–4:30pm. Tours at 11am and 2pm.

Maunaloa Macadamia Nut Factory   Explore this unique factory to learn how Hawaii's favorite nut is grown and processed. And, of course, you'll want to try a few samples.

Macadamia Nut Rd., off Hwy. 11 (8 miles from Hilo). ℂ **888/628-6256** or 808/966-8618. www.maunaloa.com. Free admission; self-guided factory tours. Daily 8:30am–5pm. From Hwy. 11, turn on Macadamia Nut Rd.; go 3 miles down the road to the factory.

Mokupapapa: Discovery Center for Hawaii's Remote Coral Reefs ☺ ✦
This 4,000-square-foot center is perfect for children, who can explore the Northwest Hawaiian Islands coral reef ecosystem. Through interactive displays, engaging three-dimensional models, and an immersion theater, the kids can learn natural science, culture, and history while having a great time. A 2,500-gallon saltwater aquarium provides a habitat for a collection of fish from the Northwest Hawaiian Islands reefs. Lots of fun at a terrific price: free!

308 Kamehameha Ave., Ste. 109. ℂ **808/933-8195.** www.hawaiireef.noaa.gov. Free admission. Tues–Sat 9am–4pm.

The Naha Stone.

Naha Stone   This 2½-ton stone was used as a test of royal strength. Ancient legend said that whoever could move the stone would conquer and unite the islands. As a 14-year-old boy, King Kamehameha the Great moved the stone—and later fulfilled his destiny. The Pinao stone, next to it, once guarded an ancient temple.

In front of the Hilo Public Library, 300 Waianuenue Ave.

Nani Mau Gardens ★   Just outside Hilo is Nani Mau ("forever beautiful"), where Makato Nitahara, who turned a 20-acre papaya patch into a tropical garden, claims to have every flowering plant in Hawaii. His collection includes more than 2,000 varieties, from fragile hibiscus, whose blooms last only a day, to durable red anthuriums imported from South America. There are also Japanese gardens, an orchid walkway, a botanical museum, a house full of butterflies, and a restaurant that's open for lunch.

421 Makalika St. ℂ **808/959-3500.** www.nanimau.com. Admission $10 adults, $5 children 4–10. Tram tours $7 extra for adults, $5 extra for children. Daily 10:30am–3pm. Go 3 miles south of Hilo Airport on Hwy. 11, turn on Makalika St., and continue ¾ mile.

Pacific Tsunami Museum ★   The most interesting artifacts here are not the exhibits, but the volunteers who survived Hawaii's most deadly "walls of water" in 1946 and 1960, both of which reshaped the town of Hilo. Visitors can listen to their stories of terror and view a range of exhibits, from interactive computers to a display on what happens when a local earthquake triggers a seismic wave, as it did in 1975 during the Big Island's last tsunami.

130 Kamehameha Ave. ℂ **808/935-0926.** www.tsunami.org. Admission $8 adults, $7 seniors, $4 children 6-17. Mon–Sat 9am–4pm.

Rainbow Falls.

Panaewa Rainforest Zoo ★ ☺ This 12-acre zoo, nestled in the heart of the Panaewa Forest Reserve south of Hilo, is the only outdoor rainforest zoo in the United States. Some 50 species of animals from rainforests around the globe call Panaewa home—including several endangered Hawaiian birds. All of them are exhibited in a natural setting. This is one of the few zoos where you can observe Sumatran tigers, Brazilian tapirs, and the rare pygmy hippopotamus, an endangered "mini-hippo" found in western Africa.

Stainback Hwy. (off Hwy. 11). ℂ **808/959-7224.** www.hilozoo.com. Free admission. Daily 9am–4pm. Petting zoo Sat 1:30–2:30pm; tiger feeding daily 3:30pm.

Rainbow Falls ★ 📷   Go in the morning, around 9 or 10am, just as the sun comes over the mango trees, to see Rainbow Falls at its best. The 80-foot falls spill into a big round natural pool surrounded by wild ginger. According to legend, Hina, the mother of Maui, lives in the cave behind the falls. Unfortunately, swimming in the pool is no longer allowed.

West on Waianuenue Ave., past Kaumana Dr.

📎 A Desert Crossing

If you follow Hwy. 11 counterclockwise from Kona to the Volcano, you'll get a preview of what lies ahead in the national park: hot, scorched, quake-shaken, bubbling-up new/dead land. This is the great Kau Desert, layer upon layer of lava flows, fine ash, and fallout. As you traverse the desert, you cross the Great Crack and the Southwest Rift Zone, a major fault zone that looks like a giant groove in the earth, before you reach Kilauea Volcano.

Hawaii Volcanoes National Park ★★★

Yellowstone, Yosemite, and other national parks are spectacular, no doubt about it. But in my opinion, they're all ho-hum compared to this one: Here nothing less than the miracle of creation is the daily attraction.

In the 19th century, before tourism became Hawaii's middle name, the islands' singular attraction for visitors wasn't the beach, but the volcano. From the world over, curious spectators gathered on the rim of Kilauea's Halemaumau crater to see one of the greatest wonders of the globe. Nearly a century after it was named a national park (in 1916), Hawaii Volcanoes remains the state's premier natural attraction.

Hawaii Volcanoes has the only rainforest in the U.S. National Park system—and it's the only park that's home to an active volcano. Most people drive through the park (it has 50 miles of good roads, some of them often covered by lava flows) and call it a day. But it takes at least 3 days to explore the whole park, including such oddities as **Halemaumau Crater ★★★**, a still-fuming pit of steam and sulfur; the intestinal-looking **Thurston Lava Tube ★★★**; **Devastation Trail ★★★**, a short hike through a desolated area destroyed by lava; and, finally, the end of **Chain of Craters Road ★★★**, where lava regularly spills across the man-made two lane blacktop to create its own red-hot freeway to the sea. In addition to some of the world's weirdest landscapes, the park has hiking trails, rainforests, campgrounds, a historic old hotel on the crater's rim, and that spectacular, still-erupting volcano.

NOTES ON THE ERUPTING VOLCANO Volcanologists refer to Hawaii's volcanic eruptions as "quiet" eruptions because gases escape slowly instead of building up and exploding violently all at once. Hawaii's eruptions produce slow-moving, oozing lava that provides excellent, safe viewing most of the time.

Even so, the volcano has still caused its share of destruction. Since the current eruption of Kilauea began on January 3, 1983, lava has covered some 16,000 acres of lowland and rainforest, threatening rare hawks, honeycreeper birds, spiders, and bats, while destroying power and telephone lines and eliminating water service possibly forever. Some areas have been mantled repeatedly and are now buried underneath 80 feet of lava. At last count, the lava flow had destroyed nearly 200 homes and businesses, wiped out Kaimu Black Sand Beach (once Hawaii's most photographed beach) and Queen's Bath, obliterated entire towns and subdivisions (Kalapana, Royal Gardens, Kalapana Gardens, and Kapaahu Homesteads), and buried natural and historic landmarks (a 12th-c. *heiau,* the century-old Kalapana Mauna Kea Church, Wahaulu Visitor Center, and thousands of archaeological artifacts and sites). The cost of the destruction—so far—is estimated at $100 million. But how do you price the destruction of a 700-year-old temple or a 100-year-old church?

However, Kilauea hasn't just destroyed parts of the island; it has also added to it—more than 560 acres of new land. The volume of erupted lava over the past 2 decades measures nearly 2 billion cubic yards—enough new rock to pave a two-lane highway 1.25 million miles long, circling the earth some 50 times. Or, as a spokesperson for the park puts it: "Every 5 days, there is enough lava coming out of Kilauea volcano's eruption to place a thin veneer over Washington, D.C.—all 63 square miles."

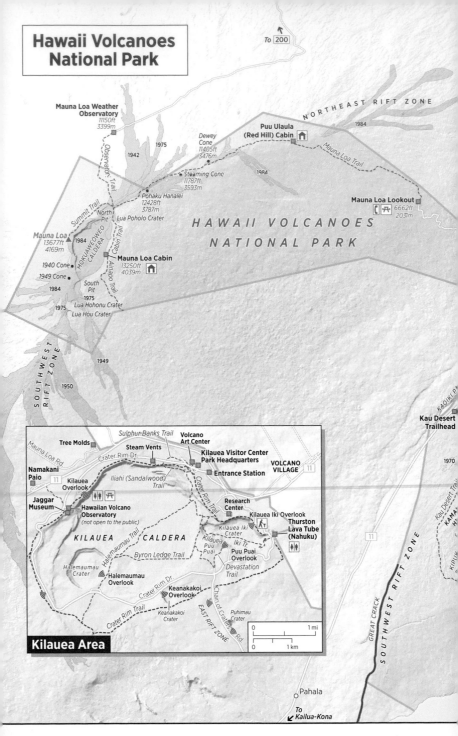

Hawaii Volcanoes National Park

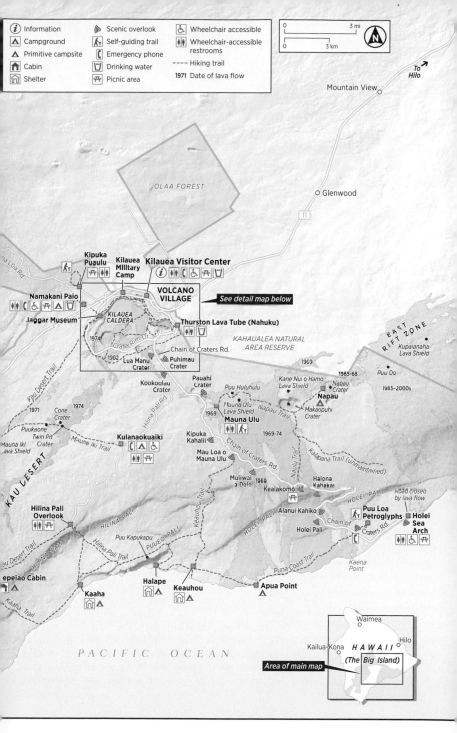

Legend

- (i) Information
- ⛺ Campground
- ⛺ Primitive campsite
- 🏠 Cabin
- 🏠 Shelter
- 👁 Scenic overlook
- 🥾 Self-guiding trail
- 📞 Emergency phone
- 🚰 Drinking water
- 🌲 Picnic area
- ♿ Wheelchair accessible
- 🚻 Wheelchair-accessible restrooms
- ---- Hiking trail
- 1971 Date of lava flow

0 _____ 3 mi
0 _____ 3 km

To Hilo

Mountain View

OLAA FOREST

Glenwood

11

Kipuka Puaulu

Kilauea Military Camp

Kilauea Visitor Center

VOLCANO VILLAGE

See detail map below

Namakani Paio

Jaggar Museum

KILAUEA CALDERA

Thurston Lava Tube (Nahuku)

KAHAUALEA NATURAL AREA RESERVE

EAST RIFT ZONE

Kupaianaha Lava Shield

1974

Crater Rim Dr.

Chain of Craters Rd.

1969

1965-68

Puu Oo

1983-2000s

1902

Lua Manu Crater

Puhimau Crater

Kookoolau Crater

Pauahi Crater

Puu Huluhulu

Kane Nui o Hamo Lava Shield

Napau Crater

Kau Desert Trail

1971

1974

Cone Crater

Puukaone Twin Pit Crater

Mauna Iki Lava Shield

Mauna Iki Trail

Kulanaokuaiki

Mauna Ulu Lava Shield

1969

Mauna Ulu

Napau Trail

Makaopuhi Crater

Napau

KAU DESERT

Kipuka Kahalii

Mau Loa o Mauna Ulu

Chain of Craters Rd.

1969-74

Kalapana Trail (unmaintained)

Muliwai a Dolo

1969

Kealakomo

Halona Kahakai

Hilina Pali Overlook

HILINA PALI

Puu Kapukapu

Keauhou Trail

HOLEI PALI

Alanui Kahiko

Holei Pali

Road closed by lava flow.

Puu Loa Petroglyphs

Holei Sea Arch

Chain of Craters Rd.

PUUEO PALI

Hilina Pali Trail

HOLEI PALI

Puna Coast Trail

Kaena Point

...epeiao Cabin

Kaaha

Kaaha Trail

Halape

Keauhou

Apua Point

PACIFIC OCEAN

Waimea

Hilo

Kailua-Kona

HAWAII (The Big Island)

Area of main map

Hawaii Volcanoes National Park.

The most prominent vent of the eruption has been Puu Oo, a 760-foot-high cinder-and-spatter cone. The most recent flow—the one you'll be able to see, if you're lucky—follows a 7-mile-long tube from the Puu Oo vent area to the sea. This lava flow has extended the Big Island's shoreline seaward and added hundreds of acres of new land along the steep southern slopes. Periodically, the new land proves unstable, falls under its own weight, and slides into the ocean. (These areas of ground gained and lost are not included in the tally of new acreage—only the land that sticks counts.)

Scientists are also keeping an eye on Mauna Loa, which has been swelling since its last eruption in 1983. If there's a new eruption, there could be a fast-moving flow down the southwest side of the island, possibly into South Kona or Kau.

WHAT YOU'RE LIKELY TO SEE   With luck, the volcano will still be streaming rivers of red lava when you visit the park, but a continuous eruption of this length (more than 2 decades) is setting new ground, so to speak. Kilauea continues to perplex volcanologists because most major eruptions in the past have ended abruptly after only several months.

But neither Mother Nature nor Madame Pele (the volcano goddess) runs on a schedule. The volcano could be shooting fountains of lava hundreds of feet into the air on the day you arrive, or it could be completely quiet—there are no guarantees. On many days, the lava flows right by accessible roads, and you can get as close as the heat will allow; sometimes, however, the flow is in underground tubes where you can't see it, or miles away from the nearest access point, visible only in the distance. Always ask the park rangers for advice before you set out on any lava-viewing expeditions.

VOLCANO VOCABULARY   The volcano has its own unique, poetic vocabulary that describes in Hawaiian what cannot be said so well in English. The lava that looks like swirls of chocolate cake frosting is called **pahoehoe** (pa-*hoy-hoy*); it results from a fast-moving flow that curls artistically as it moves. The big, blocky, jumbled lava that looks like a chopped-up parking lot is called **aa** (ah-ah); it's caused by lava that moves slowly, pulling apart as it overruns itself.

Newer words include **vog,** which is volcanic smog made of volcanic gases and smoke from forests set on fire by aa and pahoehoe. **Laze** results when sulfuric acid hits the water and vaporizes, and mixes with chlorine to become, as any chemistry student knows, hydrochloric acid. Both vog and laze sting your eyes and can cause respiratory illness; don't expose yourself to either for too long. Anyone with heart or breathing trouble, as well as women who are pregnant, should avoid both vog and laze.

JUST THE FACTS

WHEN TO GO   The best time to go is when Kilauea is really pumping. If you're lucky, you'll be in the park when the volcano is active and there's a fountain of lava; mostly, the lava runs like a red river downslope into the sea. If you're on another part of the island and hear a TV news bulletin that the volcano is acting up, head to Hilo to see the spectacle. You won't be sorry—and your favorite beach will still be there when you get back.

ACCESS POINTS   Hawaii Volcanoes National Park is 29 miles from Hilo, on Hawaii Belt Road (Hwy. 11). If you're staying in Kailua-Kona, it's 100 miles, or about a 2½-hour drive, to the park. At press time, admission was still $10 per vehicle, but the park was proposing to double that to $20 per car; once you pay the fee, you can come and go as often as you want for 7 days. Hikers and bicyclists pay $5; bikes are allowed only on roads and paved trails.

VISITOR CENTERS & INFORMATION   Contact **Hawaii Volcanoes National Park,** P.O. Box 52, Hawaii Volcanoes National Park, HI 96718 (© **808/985-6000;** www.nps.gov/havo). The **Kilauea Visitor Center** is at the entrance to the park, just off Hwy. 11; it's open daily from 7:45am to 5pm.

ERUPTION UPDATES   Everything you wanted to know about Hawaii's volcanoes, from what's going on with the current eruptions to where the next eruption is likely to be, is now available on the Hawaiian Volcano Observatory's new website, http://volcanoes.usgs.gov/hvo/activity/kilaueastatus.php. The site is divided into areas on Kilauea (the currently erupting volcano), Mauna Loa (which last erupted in 1984), and Hawaii's other volcanoes. Each

---

A Volcano-Visiting Tip

Thanks to its higher elevation and windward (rainier) location, this neck of the woods is always colder than it is at the beach. If you're coming from the Kona side of the island in summer, expect it to be at least 10° to 20° cooler at the volcano; bring a sweater or light jacket. In the winter months, expect temperatures to be in the 40s or 50s (single digits to midteens Celsius), and dress accordingly. Always have rain gear on hand, especially in winter.

section provides photos, maps, eruption summaries, and historical information.

You can also get the latest on volcanic activity in the park by calling the park's **24-hour hot line** (© **808/985-6000**). Updates on volcanic activity are posted daily on the bulletin board at the visitor center.

HIKING & CAMPING IN THE PARK   Hawaii Volcanoes National Park offers a wealth of hiking and camping possibilities. See "Hiking & Camping," p. 367, for details.

ACCOMMODATIONS IN & AROUND THE PARK   If camping isn't your thing, don't worry. There's a hotel, **Volcano House** (p. 330), within the park boundary, on the rim of Halemaumau Crater. Volcano Village, just outside the park, has plenty of comfortable and convenient hotels and restaurants; see p. 329 for hotel listings and p. 332 for restaurant listings. *Note:* The Volcano House hotel and Namakanipaio Cabins will be closed until 2011, due to seismic retrofitting, fire suppression upgrades, and rehabilitation of the interior of the facility.

SEEING THE HIGHLIGHTS

Your first stop should be **Kilauea Visitor Center** ★★, a rustic structure in a shady grove of trees just inside the entrance to the park. Here you can get up-to-the-minute reports on the volcano's activity, learn how volcanoes work, see a film showing blasts from the past, get information on hiking and camping, and pick up the obligatory postcards.

Filled with a new understanding of volcanology and the volcano goddess, Pele, you should get a look at **Kilauea Caldera** ★★★, a 2½-mile-wide, 500-foot-deep hole. The caldera used to be a bubbling pit of fountaining lava; today you can still see wisps of steam that might, while you're standing there, turn into something more.

Now get out on the road and drive by the **Sulphur Banks** ★, which smell like rotten eggs, and the **Steam Vents** ★★★, where trails of smoke, once molten lava, rise from within the inner reaches of the earth. This is one of the places where you feel that the volcano is really alive.

Stop at the **Thomas A. Jaggar Museum** ★★★ (daily 8:30am–7:30pm; free admission) for a good look at Halemaumau Crater, which is a half-mile across and 1,000 feet deep. On a clear day, you might also see Mauna Loa, 20 miles to the west. The museum shows video from days when the volcano was really spewing, explains the Pele legend in murals, and monitors earthquakes (a precursor of eruptions) on a seismograph.

When you've seen the museum, drive around the caldera to the south side, park your car, and take the short walk to the edge of **Halemaumau Crater** ★★★, past stinky sulfur banks and steam vents, to stand at the overlook and stare in awe at this once-fuming old fire pit, which still generates ferocious heat out of vestigial vents.

If you feel the need to cool off, go to the **Thurston Lava Tube** ★★★, the coolest place in the park. You'll hike down into a natural bowl in the earth, a forest preserve the lava didn't touch—full of native birds and giant tree ferns. Then you'll see a black hole in the earth; step in. It's all drippy and cool here, with bare roots hanging down. You can either resurface into the bright daylight or, if you have a flashlight, poke on deeper into the tube, which goes for another ½ mile or so.

If you're still game for a good hike, try **Kilauea Iki Trail ★**, a 4-mile, 2-hour hike across the floor of the crater, which became a bubbling pool of lava in 1959 and sent fountains of lava 1,900 feet in the air, completely devastating a nearby ohia forest and leaving another popular hike ominously known as **Devastation Trail ★★★**. This .5-mile walk is a startling look at the powers of a volcanic eruption on the environment. (See "Hiking & Camping," on p. 367, for details on these and other park hikes.)

Check out ancient Hawaiian art at the **Puu Loa Petroglyphs ★**, around mile marker 15 down Chain of Craters Road. Look for the stack of rocks on the road. A brief .5-mile walk will bring you to a circular boardwalk where you can see thousands of mysterious Hawaiian petroglyphs carved in stone. (*Warning:* It's very easy to destroy these ancient works of art. Do not leave the boardwalk, and do not walk on or around the petroglyphs. Rubbings of petroglyphs will destroy them; the best way to capture them is by taking a photo.) This area, Puu Loa, was a sacred place for generations. Fathers came here to bury their newborns' umbilical cords in the numerous small holes in the lava, thus ensuring a long life for the child.

THE VOLCANO AFTER DARK   If the volcano is erupting, be sure to see it after dark. Brilliant red lava snakes down the side of the mountain and pours into the sea, creating a vivid display you'll never forget. About 1½ hours before sunset, head out of the park and back down Volcano Highway (Hwy. 11). Turn onto Hwy. 130 at Keaau; go past Pahoa to the end of the road. (The drive takes the better part of an hour.) From here (depending on the flow), it's about a mile walk over sharp crusted lava; park rangers will tell you how to get to the best viewing locations, or you can call ahead (© **808/985-6000**) to check where the current eruption is and how to get there. Be forewarned that the flow changes constantly and, on some days, may be too far from the road to hike, in which case you'll have to be content with seeing it from a distance. Be sure to heed the rangers: In the past, a handful of hikers who ignored these directions died en route; new lava can be unstable and break off without warning. Take water, a flashlight, and your camera, and wear sturdy shoes.

A BIRD'S-EYE VIEW   The best way to see Kilauea's bubbling caldera is from on high, in a helicopter. This bird's-eye view puts the enormity of it all into perspective. I recommend **Blue Hawaiian Helicopters ★★★** (© **800/745-BLUE** [2583] or 808/886-1768; www.bluehawaiian.com), a professionally run, locally based company with an excellent safety record; comfortable, top-of-the-line copters; and pilots who are extremely knowledgeable about everything from volcanology to Hawaii lore. The company flies out of both Hilo and Waikoloa (Hilo is cheaper because it's closer). From Hilo, the 45-minute **Circle of Fire Tour ★★** takes you over the boiling volcano and then on to a bird's-eye view of the destruction the lava has caused as well as of remote beaches ($210 per person, 15% discount online). From Waikoloa, the 2-hour **Big Island Spectacular ★★★** stars the volcano, tropical valleys, Hamakua Coast waterfalls, and the Kohala Mountains (from $531, or 15% off online, but worth every penny).

6 South Point: Land's End ★★★

At the end of 11 miles of bad road that peters out at Kaulana Bay, in the lee of a jagged, black-lava point, you'll find Land's End—the tail end of the United States. From the tip (beware of the big waves that lash the shore if you walk out there), the nearest continental landfall is Antarctica, 7,500 miles away.

It's a 2½-mile four-wheel-drive trip and a hike down a cliff from South Point to the anomaly known as **Green Sand Beach** ★, described on p. 357 in the "Beaches" section of this chapter.

Back on the Mamalahoa Highway (Hwy. 11), about 20 miles east, is the small town of Pahoa; turn off the highway and travel about 5 miles through this once-thriving sugar plantation and beyond to the **Wood Valley Temple & Retreat Center** ★ (© 808/928-8539; www.nechung.org), also known as Nechung Dorje Drayang Ling ("Island of Melodious Sound"). It's an oasis of tranquillity tucked into the rainforest. Built by Japanese sugar-cane workers, the temple, retreat center, and surrounding gardens were rededicated by the Dalai Lama in 1980 to serve as a spiritual center for Tibetan Buddhism. You can walk the beautiful grounds, attend services, and breathe in the quiet mindfulness of this serene area.

SHOPS & GALLERIES

While chefs and farmers tout this island as fertile ground for crops and food, artists point to its primal, volcanic energy as a boost to their creative endeavors. Art communities and galleries are sprinkled across the Big Island, in villages like Holualoa and Volcano, where fine works in pottery, wood-turning, handmade glass, and other two- and three-dimensional media are sold in serene settings.

Although the visual arts are flourishing on this island, the line between shop and gallery can often be too fine to determine. Too many self-proclaimed "galleries" sell schlock or a mixture of arts, crafts, and tacky souvenirs. T-shirts and Kona coffee mugs are a souvenir staple in many so-called galleries.

The galleries and shops below offer a broad mix in many media. Items for the home, jewelry and accessories, vintage Hawaiiana, and accouterments at various prices and for various tastes can make great gifts to go, as can locally made food products such as preserves, cookies, flowers, Kona coffee, and macadamia nuts. You'll find that bowls made of rare native woods such as koa are especially abundant on the Big Island. This is an area in which politics and art intersect: Although reforestation efforts are underway to plant new koa trees, the decline of old-growth forests is causing many artists to turn to equally beautiful, and more environmentally sensitive, alternative woods.

The Kona Coast
IN & AROUND KAILUA-KONA

Kailua-Kona's shopping prospects pour out into the streets in a festival atmosphere of T-shirts, trinkets, and dime-a-dozen souvenirs, with Alii Drive at the center of this activity. But the **Coconut Grove Market Place,** on Alii Drive, across the street from the sea wall, has changed that image and added some great new shops around a sand volleyball court.

Shopping stalwarts in Kona are the **Kona Square,** across from **King Kamehameha's Kona Beach Hotel;** the hotel's shopping mall, with close to two dozen shops; and the **Kona Inn Shopping Village,** on Alii Drive. All include the usual assortment of T-shirt shops. One highlight is **Alii Gardens Marketplace** at the southern end of Kailua-Kona, a pleasant, tented outdoor marketplace with fresh fruit, flowers, imports, local crafts, and a wonderful selection of orchid plants. There's cheesy stuff here, too, but somehow it's less noticeable outdoors.

The newly opened **Kona International Market,** 74–5533 Luhia St. (near Kaiwi St.), in the Old Industrial Area, is a great idea, a series of small open-air shops in a large pavilion with food vendors, similar to Waikiki's International Market. Unfortunately, with just a few exceptions, I find this "market" disappointing. I searched all the vendors looking for something made in Hawaii, and with very few exceptions (some jewelry), most of the trinkets sold here were not from the Big Island, and not even from Hawaii, and prices were not that attractive.

Honolua Surf Co. This shop targets the surf-and-sun enthusiast with good things for good times: towels, flip-flops, body boards, sunglasses, swimsuits, and everything else you need for ocean and shore action. Quiksilver, Tommy Bahama, Roxy, Billabong, and Kahala are among the top menswear labels here, but I also like the quirky, colorful Toes on the Nose. Also popular is the full line of products with the Honolua Surf Co. label, including T-shirts, hats, bags, dresses, sweatshirts, aloha shirts, and swimwear. At the Kona Inn Shopping Village, 75-5744 Alii Dr. ✆ **808/329-1001.** www.honoluasurf.com.

Edibles & Everyday Things

The Big Island's **green markets** are notable for the quality of produce and the abundance of Island specialties at better-than-usual prices. Look for the cheerful green kiosks at the **Alii Gardens Marketplace,** 75–6129 Alii Dr. (at the south end), where local farmers and artists set up their wares Wednesday to Sunday, from 9am to 5pm. This is not your garden-variety marketplace; some vendors are permanent, some drive over from Hilo, and the owners have planted shade trees and foliage to make the 5-acre plot a Kona landmark. There are 40 to 50 vendors on any given day, selling jewelry, woodcrafts, produce, macadamia nuts, orchids, and—my favorite—the fresh juices of Kay Reeves, owner of Wau, who gets up before dawn to make her sensational lilikoi and lime juices. Kona Blue Sky Coffee is also here, as is Lynn Cappell, a fine painter of island landscapes, and Laura de Rosa's sensational A'ala Dreams lotions and oils.

Java junkies jump-start their day at **Island Lava Java** (✆ **808/327-2161**), the hot new magnet for coffee lovers at the Coconut Grove Market Place, on Alii Drive. At the other end of Kailua-Kona, in the New Industrial Area, between Costco and Home Depot, the handmade candies of the **Kailua Candy Company,** 73-5612 Kauhola St. (✆ **808/329-2522,** or 800/622-2462 for orders), also beckon, especially the macadamia-nut clusters with ground ginger or the legendary macadamia-nut *honu* (turtle). Other products include truffles, pure Kona coffee, shortbread cookies, toffee, T-shirts, mugs, mustards, and other gift items.

Kona Wine Market, in the **Kona Commons Shopping Center,** 74-5450 Makala Blvd., Kailua Kona (✆ **808/329-9400**), has a noteworthy selection, including some esoteric vintages, at prices you'll love. This is a wine lover's store, with selections from California, Europe, and points beyond, as well as gift baskets, cheeses, cigars, oils and vinegars, specialty pastas and condiments, Riedel glassware, and friendly, knowledgeable service.

For everyday grocery needs, **KTA Super Stores** (in the Kona Coast Shopping Center, at Palani Rd. and the Queen Kaahumanu Hwy., and in the Keauhou Shopping Center, on Alii Dr.) are always my first choice. Through its Mountain Apple brand, KTA sells hundreds of top-notch local products—from Kona smoked marlin and Hilo-grown rainbow trout to cookies, breads, jams and jellies, taro chips, and *kulolo,* the decadently dense taro-coconut steamed pudding—by dozens of local vendors. The fresh-fish department is always an adventure; if anything esoteric is running, such as the flashy red aweoweo, it's sure to be on KTA's counters, along with a large spread of prepared foods for sunset picnics and barbecues.

My other favorite is **Kona Natural Foods,** at the Crossroads Shopping Center, 75–1027 Henry St. (© **808/329-2296**). It's been upgraded from a health food store to a full-on healthful supermarket. And it's the only full-service natural-food store for miles, selling bulk grains and cereals, vitamins, snacks, fresh-fruit smoothies, and sandwiches and salads from its takeout deli. Organic greens, grown in the South Kona area, are a small but strong feature of the produce section.

UPCOUNTRY KONA: HOLUALOA

Charming Holualoa, 1,400 feet and 10 minutes above Kailua-Kona at the top of Hualalai Road, is a place for strong espresso, leisurely gallery hopping, and nostalgic explorations across several cultural and time zones. One narrow road takes you across generations and cultures. **Paul's Place** is Holualoa's only all-purpose general store, a time warp tucked between frame shops, galleries, and studios.

Prominent Holualoa artists include the jewelry maker/sculptor Sam Rosen, who years ago set the pace for found-object art and today makes beautiful pieces at the rear of Chestnut Gallery; the furniture maker and wood sculptor Gerald Ben; the printmaker Nora Yamanoha; the glass artist Wilfred Yamazawa; the sculptor Cal Hashimoto; and Hiroki and Setsuko Morinoue of Studio 7 gallery. All galleries listed are on the main street, Mamalahoa Highway, and all are within walking distance of one another.

Dovetail Gallery & Design   Located behind the old historic post office, Dovetail features contemporary and abstract art, as well as the works of high-end, fine craftsmen and furniture makers. But the gallery's custom woodworking shop separates it from all the other galleries lining the Mamalahoa Highway. It features top craftsmen and the design work of Gerald Ben, who not only is a skilled ceramist, but also has been a custom woodworker for 22 years. His expertise is designing furniture and wood accessories for his clients, who include collectors, homeowners, interior designers, and architects. 76-5942 Mamalahoa Hwy. © **808/322-4046.**

Holualoa Gallery   Owners Matthew and Mary Lovein show their own work as well as the work of selected Hawaii artists in this roadside gallery in Holualoa. Sculptures, paintings, koa furniture, fused-glass bowls, raku ceramics, and creations in paper, bronze, metal, and glass are among the gallery's offerings. 76-5921 Mamalahoa Hwy. © **808/322-8484.** www.lovein.com.

Kimura Lauhala Shop   Everyone loves Kimura and the masterpieces of weaving that spill out of the tiny shop. It's lined with lauhala, from rolled-up mats and wide-brimmed hats to tote bags, coasters, and coin purses. The fragrant, resilient fiber, woven from the spiny leaves of the *hala* (pandanus) tree, is smooth to the touch and becomes softer with use. Lauhala also varies in color, according to region and growing conditions. Although Kimura employs a covey of local weavers who use the renowned hala leaves of Kona, some South Pacific imports bolster the supply. 77-996 Mamalahoa Hwy., at Hualalai Rd. *C* **808/324-0053.**

Studio 7 🎁 Some of Hawaii's most respected artists, among them gallery owners Setsuko and Hiroki Morinoue, exhibit their works in this serenely beautiful studio. Smooth pebbles, stark woods, and a garden setting provide the backdrop for Hiroki's paintings and prints, and Setsuko's pottery, paper collages, and wall pieces. The Main Gallery houses multimedia art; the Print Gallery, sculptural pieces and two-dimensional works; and the Ceramic Gallery, the works of Clayton Amemiya, Chiu Leong, and Gerald Ben. This is the hub of the Holualoa art community; activities include workshops, classes, and special events by visiting artists. 76-5920 Mamalahoa Hwy. *C* **808/324-1335.**

SOUTH KONA

In Kealakekua, the **Kamigaki Market,** on Hwy. 11 (Mamalahoa Hwy.), is a reliable source of food items, especially for regional specialties such as macadamia nuts and Kona coffee.

In Honaunau, farther south, keep an eye out for the **Bong Brothers Store,** on Hwy. 11 between mile markers 103 and 104 (www.bongbrothers.com), and its eye-catching selections of fresh local fruit—from cherimoya (in season) to star fruit and white Sugarloaf pineapples. The Bongs are known for their deli items, produce, and Kona coffee fresh from their own roasting room, but I think their black, very hip Bong Brothers and Bong Sistah T-shirts are the find of the region. The juice bar offers homemade soups and smoothies made with fresh local fruit.

In the town of Captain Cook, look for the big BANANA BREAD sign (you can't miss it) across the street from the fire station on Hwy. 11, and you'll come across the **Captain Cook Baking Company,** which bakes excellent banana bread with macadamia nuts, under the Auntie Helen's label. The bread is made with Big Island bananas and macadamia-nut honey, and baked right here in the kitchen. This bakery/sandwich shop also sells Lilikoi Gold passion butter, cheesecake brownies, and submarine sandwiches on its own house-made breads.

Antiques & Orchids Beverly Napolitan and her husband took over Captain Cook's oldest building (built in 1906) and filled it with an eclectic array of antiques, collectibles, and fresh orchids. There are a few vintage Hawaiian items, lots of teacups, raspberry-colored walls, linens, old kimonos, celadon, etched

---

📎 **Farmers Market, Fruit Stands & Espresso Bar**

South Kona, one of the best growing regions on the Big Island, has a weekly **Farmers Market** every Saturday from 8am to noon at the **Keauhou Shopping Center** parking lot, near Ace Hardware. It's a true farmers market, selling only produce grown on the Big Island.

Another great vegetable and fruit stand down south is the **South Kona Fruit Stand,** 84-4770 Mamalahoa Hwy. (between mile markers 103 and 104), Captain Cook (*C* **808/328-8547**), which sells some of the most unusual tropical produce from the Big Island.

glass and crystal lamps, and even a Queen Liliuokalani lanai sofa from the 1800s. You can't miss this green building with white trim, on the mauka side of the highway in Captain Cook. Hwy. 11, Captain Cook. © **808/323-9851.**

Kimura Store 🎁 This old-fashioned general store is one of those places you'll be glad you found—a store with spirit and character, plus everything you need and don't need. You'll see Hawaii's finest selection of yardage, enough cookware for a multicourse dinner, aspirin, Shiseido cosmetics, and an eye-popping assortment of buttons, zippers, and quilting materials. Irene Kimura, the family matriarch, who presided over the store for more than 60 years until she passed away recently, said she quit counting the fabric bolts at 8,000 but estimated there were more than 10,000. Kimura's is the spot for pareu and Hawaiian fabrics, brocades, silks, and offbeat gift items, such as Japanese china and *tabi,* the comfortable cloth footwear. Hwy. 11, Kainaliu. © **808/322-3771.**

The Kohala Coast

Harbor Gallery ★★ Formerly Kohala Kollection, this two-story gallery has made a seamless transition, remaining a big draw next to Cafe Pesto in this industrial harbor area of Kawaihae. Frances Dennis's painted Island scenes on canvas are among the works by more than 150 artists, primarily from the Big Island. The range is vast—from jewelry to basketry, ceramics to heirloom-quality koa furniture. At the Kawaihae Shopping Center, Hwy. 270, just north of Hwy. 19, Kawaihae. © **808/882-1510.**

RESORT SHOPPING

Most Kohala Coast shops are concentrated in and around the resorts, listed below.

HILTON WAIKOLOA VILLAGE Among the hotel's shops, **Sandal Tree** carries footwear with style and kick: Italian sandals at non-Italian prices, designer pumps, and other footwear to carry you from dockside to dance floor.

KINGS' SHOPS These stores are located at the entrance to the Waikoloa Beach Resort. A recent find here is **Walking in Paradise** (© **808/886-2600**). The footwear—much of it made in France (Mephisto, Arche)—can be expensive, but it's worthwhile for anyone seeking comfort while exploring the harsh lava terrain of this island or the pedestrian culture of Kailua-Kona's Alii Drive. Toward the mauka (mountainside) end is **Noa Noa,** filled with exotic artifacts from Java and Borneo, plus tropical clothing for easy-going life on the Pacific Rim. At **Under the Koa Tree,** some of the island's finest artists display their prints, woodcrafts, and paintings. For snacks, ice, sunscreen, wine, postcards, newspapers, and everyday essentials, there's the **Whalers General Store,** and for dining on the run, a small food court with pizza, plate lunches, and the **Jungle Edge Coffee** for a steaming cup of brew.

QUEENS' MARKETPLACE The recently opened Queens' MarketPlace, located across the street from the Kings' Shops, offers a range of shops, from Giggles, Lids, Blue Ginger, Reyn's, and Local Motion to eateries like Sansei Seafood Restaurant & Sushi Bar, Charley's Thai Cuisine, Queens' Deli, and Starbucks to the Island Gourmet Market.

HUALALAI RESORT The **Kaupulehu Store,** in the Four Seasons Resort Hualalai, is a perfect blend of high quality and cultural integrity. Located within the award-winning Kaupulehu Cultural Center, the store carries items made in Hawaii: handmade paper, hand-painted silks, seed leis, greeting cards, koa bowls, wreaths, John Kelly prints, and a selection of Hawaii-themed books. The **Hualalai Sports Club & Spa,** in the same resort, has a winning retail section of beauty and treatment products, including Hana Naia aromatherapy oils. The selection includes mango and jasmine perfumes, Bulgarian rose water, and herbal lotions and potions.

MAUNA LANI RESORT   The recently opened **Shops at Mauna Lani** is a high-end cluster of well-known name stores and a sprinkling of local, homegrown places such as terrific restaurants: shops include Lahaina Galleries, Caché, Kohala Goldsmiths, Tori Richard, and Foodland Farms market. Chain eateries include Ruth's Chris Steak House, Tommy Bahama's Tropical Cafe, and Marble Slab ice cream.

North Kohala

Ackerman Gallery   Crafts and fine arts are housed in two separate galleries a few blocks apart. Artist Gary Ackerman and his wife, Yesan, display gifts, crafts, and the works of award-winning Big Island artists, including Ackerman's own Impressionistic paintings. There are Kelly Dunn's hand-turned Norfolk pine bowls, Jer Houston's heirloom-quality koa-and-ebony desks, and Wilfred Yamazawa's handblown-glass perfume bottles and sculptures. Primitive artifacts, Asian antiques, jewelry, and Cal Hashimoto's bamboo sculptures are also among the discoveries here. The crafts-and-gifts gallery, across from the King Kamehameha Statue, has recently doubled in size; it features gift ideas in all media and price ranges. Hwy. 270 (across from the Kamehameha Statue; also 3 blocks away, on the opposite side of the street), Kapaau. ✆ **808/889-5971.** www.ackermangalleries.com.

As Hawi Turns   You never know what you'll find in this whimsical, delightful shop of women's clothing and accessories. The windows might be filled with painted paper lanterns in the shapes of stars, or retro-painted switch plates, or kicky straw hats paired with bias-cut silk dresses and quirky jewelry. This is the perfect place to pamper yourself with such fripperies as tatami zoris and flamboyant accessories for a colorful, tropical life. Hwy. 270 (Akoni Pule Hwy.), Hawi. ✆ **808/ 889-5023.**

Elements   John Flynn designs jewelry, and his wife, Prakash, assembles fountains and other treasures, and together they've filled their quiet gallery with an assortment of arts and crafts from the Big Island. The lauhala accessories, jewelry, and fountains—simple bowls filled with smooth gemstones such as amethyst and rose quartz—make great gifts and accessories. Hwy. 270 (Akoni Pule Hwy.), Kapaau. ✆ **808/889-0760.**

Waimea

Waimea is lei country as well as the island's breadbasket, so look for protea, vegetables, vine-ripened tomatoes, and tuberose stalks here at reasonable prices. Mainstays include **Honopua Farm** and **Hufford's Farm,** side by side, selling freshly cut flowers and organic vegetables.

Small and sublime, the **Waimea Farmers Market,** Hwy. 19, at mile marker 55 on the Hamakua side of Waimea town (on the lawn in front of the Department of Hawaiian Home Lands, West Hawaii office), draws a loyal crowd from 7am to noon on Saturday. At the other end of Waimea, the **Parker School**

Farmers Market, held Saturday from 7:30am to noon, is smaller and more subdued, but with choice items as well. The Kalopa macadamia nuts are the sweetest and tastiest I've ever had.

Hilo's wonderful **Dan De Luz Woods** has a branch at 64–1013 Mamalahoa Hwy., in front of the True Value hardware store. Other shops in Waimea range from the small roadside storefronts lining Hwy. 19 and Hwy. 190, which intersect in the middle of town, to complexes such as the **Waimea Center,** where you'll find the trusty old **KTA Super Store,** the one-stop shop for all your basic necessities, plus a glorious profusion of interesting local foods. Across the street, with its upscale galleries and shops, **Parker Square** will likely be your most rewarding stop.

Bentley's Home & Garden Collection   To its lavish list of glassware, linens, chenille throws, home fragrances, stuffed animals, and Wild West gift wraps, Bentley's has added casual country clothing in linens and cottons. Dresses, sweaters, raffia hats, top-drawer Western shirts, handbags, and woven shoes adorn this fragrant, gardenlike shop. At Parker Sq., Hwy. 19. ℂ **808/885-5565.**

Gallery of Great Things   Here's an eye-popping assemblage of local art and Pacific Rim artifacts. Browse under the watchful gaze of an antique Tongan war club (not for sale) and authentic rhinoceros- and deer-horn blowguns from Borneo, among the plethora of treasures from Polynesia, Micronesia, and Indonesia. You'll find jewelry, glassware, photographs, greeting cards, fiber baskets, and hand-turned bowls of beautifully grained woods. Photos by Victoria McCormick, the sketches of Kathy Long, feather masks by Beth McCormick, and the paintings of Yvonne Cheng are among the treasures by local artists. There are a few pieces of etched glass and vintage clothing, too, along with a small, gorgeous collection of antique kimonos. At Parker Sq., Hwy. 19. ℂ **808/885-7706.** www.galleryof greatthingshawaii.com.

Sweet Wind   Because the owner loves beauty and harmonious things, you'll find chimes, carved dolphins, crystals, geodes, incense (an excellent selection), beads, jewelry, gems, essential oils, and thoughtfully selected books worth more than a casual glance. The books cover self-help, health, metaphysics, Hawaiian spirituality, yoga, meditation, and other topics for wholesome living. At Parker Sq., Hwy. 19. ℂ **808/885-0562.**

Waimea General Store   This charming, unpretentious country store offers a superb assortment of Hawaii-themed books, soaps and toiletries, cookbooks and kitchen accessories, candles, linens, greeting cards, dolls, Japanese hapi coats, Island teas, rare kiawe honey, preserves, cookies, and countless gift items, from the practical to the whimsical. At Parker Sq., Hwy. 19. ℂ **808/885-4479.**

The Hamakua Coast

HONOKAA

Honokaa Market Place   I've noticed a proliferation of Balinese imports (not a good sign) mingling with the old and new Hawaiiana. The eclectic selection of Hawaiian, Asian, and Indonesian handicrafts includes wood crafts, Hawaiian prints, and Hawaiian quilts, from wall hangings and pillows to full-size quilts, plus a few pieces of jewelry. 45-3321 Mamane St. ℂ **808/775-8255.**

Honokaa Trading Company   "Rustic, tacky, rare—there's something for everyone," says owner Grace Walker. Every inch of this labyrinthine

2,200-square-foot bazaar is occupied by antiques and collectibles, new and used goods, and countless treasures. You'll find plantation memorabilia, Hawaiiana, bark-cloth fabrics from the 1940s, rhinestone jewelry and rattan furniture from the 1930s, vintage ukuleles, Depression glass, dinnerware from Honolulu's landmark Willows restaurant, koa lamps, Francis Oda airbrush paintings, vintage kimonos, and linens. It's an unbelievable conglomeration, with surprises in every corner. Vigilant collectors make regular forays here to scoop up the 1950s ivory jewelry and John Kelly prints. Mamane St. © **808/775-0808.**

Taro Patch Gifts   Taro Patch carries an eclectic assortment of Hawaiian music tapes and CDs, switch plates printed with Hawaiian labels, Kau coffee, local jams and jellies, soaps, pareu, books, ceramics, sushi candles, essential oils, and sportswear, such as Hawaiian-print cowboy shirts. 45–3599 Mamane St. © **808/775-7228.** www.taropatchgifts.com.

THE END OF THE ROAD: WAIPIO VALLEY

Waipio Valley Artworks 🎁   Housed in an old wooden building at the end of the road before the Waipio Valley, this gallery/boutique offers treasures for the home. The focus here is strictly local, with a strong emphasis on woodwork—one of the largest selections, if not the largest, in the state. A recent expansion has brought more chests and tables and gift items by Big Island artists. All the luminaries of wood turning have works here: Jack Straka, Robert Butts, Scott Hare, Kevin Parks. Their bowls, rocking chairs, and jewelry boxes exhibit flawless craftsmanship and richly burnished grains. More affordable are the pens and hair accessories. Deli sandwiches and Tropical Dreams ice cream are served in the expanded cafe. 48–5416 Kukuihaele Rd., Kukuihaele. © **808/775-0958.** www.waipiovalleyartworks.com.

Hilo

Shopping in Hilo is centered on the **Kaikoo Mall,** 777 Kilauea Ave., near the state and county buildings; the **Prince Kuhio Plaza,** 111 E. Puainako St., just off Hwy. 11 on the road north to Volcano, where you'll find a supermarket, drugstore, Macy's, and other standards; the **Bayfront** area downtown, where the hippest new businesses have taken up residence in the historic buildings lining Kamehameha Avenue; and the new **Waiakea Plaza,** where the big-box retailers (Ross, OfficeMax, Borders, Wal-Mart) have moved in. For practical needs, there's a **KTA Super Store** at 323 Keawe St. and another at 50 E. Puainako St.

Basically Books   This bookstore, affectionately called "the map shop," is a sanctuary for lovers of books, maps, and the environment. It has expanded its selection of Hawaii-themed gift items while maintaining the engaging selection of printed materials covering geology, history, topography, botany, mythology, and more. Get your bearings by browsing among the nautical charts, U.S. Geological Survey maps, street maps, raised relief maps, atlases, compasses, and books on travel, natural history, music, spirituality, and much more. This bountiful source of information, specializing in Hawaii and the Pacific, will enhance any visit to the islands. 160 Kamehameha Ave. © **808/961-0144.** www.basicallybooks.com.

Dragon Mama 🎁   For a dreamy stop in Hilo, head for this haven of all-natural comforters, cushions, futons, meditation pillows, hemp yarns and shirts, antique kimonos and obi, tatami mats sold by the panel, and all manner of comforts in the elegantly spare Japanese aesthetic. The bolts of lavish silks and pure, crisp cottons, sold by the yard, can be used for clothing or interior decorating. Dragon Mama also offers custom sewing, and you know she's good: She sewed the futon and bedding for the Dalai Lama when he visited the island a few years ago. 266 Kamehameha Ave. (C) 808/934-9081. www.dragonmama.com.

Hana Hou 🎁 Michele Zane-Faridi has done a superlative job of assembling, designing, and collecting objects of beauty that evoke old and new Hawaii. If you are looking for Hawaiian lauhala weaving, this is the place for mats, hats, purses, place mats, slippers, and even tissue-box covers. But that's not all: Vintage shirts, china, books, dresses, jewelry, handbags, accessories, Mundorff prints, 1940s sheet music, and fabrics are displayed in surprising corners. The feathered leis and collectibles—such as vintage silver-and-ivory jewelry by Ming—disappear quickly. 164 Kamehameha Ave. (C) 808/935-4555.

Hawaiian Force Artist Craig Neff and his wife, Luana, hang their shingle at the original location of Sig Zane Designs (good karma), where they sell wonderful bold T-shirt dresses, mamaki tea they gather themselves, lauhala fans and trivets, surf wear, aloha shirts, and jewelry made of opihi and Niihau shells. Everything here is Hawaiian, most of it made or designed by the Neffs. Their handsome two-tone T-shirt dresses are a Hawaiian Force signature, ideal for island living, and very popular. 140 Kilauea Ave. (C) 808/934-7171. www.hawaiianforce.com.

Sig Zane Designs 🎁 My favorite stop in Hilo, Sig Zane Designs evokes such loyalty that people make special trips from the outer islands for this inspired line of authentic Hawaiian wear. The spirit of this place complements the high aesthetic standards; everyone involved is completely immersed in Hawaiian culture and dance. The partnership of Zane and his wife, the revered hula master Nalani Kanaka'ole, is stunningly creative. The shop is awash in gleaming woods, lauhala mats, and clothing and accessories—handmade house slippers, aloha shirts, pareu, muumuu, T-shirts, and high-quality crafts. They all center on the Sig Zane fabric designs. These bedcovers, cushions, fabrics, clothing, and custom-ordered upholstery will bring the rainforest into your room. To add to the delight, Sig and his staff take time to talk story and explain the significance of the images, or simply chat about Hilo, hula, and Hawaiian culture. 122 Kamehameha Ave. (C) 808/935-7077. www.sigzane.com.

EDIBLES

Abundant Life Natural Foods Stock up here on healthful snacks, organic produce, vitamins and supplements, bulk grains, baked goods, and the latest in health foods. There's a sound selection of natural remedies and herbal body, face, and hair products. The takeout deli makes fresh-fruit smoothies and sprout- and

---

📎 A Special Arts Center & Gallery

Part gallery, part retail store, and part consortium of the arts, the **East Hawaii Cultural Center**, 141 Kalakaua St., across from Kalakaua Park ((C) 808/961-5711; www.ehcc.org), is run by volunteers in the visual and performing arts. Keep it in mind for gifts of Hawaii, or if you have any questions regarding the **Hawaii Concert Society, Hilo Community Players, Big Island Dance Council,** or **Big Island Art Guild.** The art gallery and gift shop exhibit locally made cards, jewelry, books, sculptures, and wood objects, including museum-quality works.

Hilo Farmers Market.

nutrient-rich sandwiches and salads. Seniors get a 10% discount. 292 Kamehameha Ave. ✆ 808/935-7411.

Big Island Candies Abandon all restraint: The chocolate-dipped shortbread and macadamia nuts, not to mention the free samples, will make it very hard to be sensible. Owner Alan Ikawa has turned cookie making into a spectator sport. Large viewing windows allow you to watch the hand-dipping from huge vats of chocolate while the aroma of butter fills the room. Ikawa uses eggs straight from a nearby farm, pure butter, Hawaiian cane sugar, no preservatives, and premium chocolate. Gift boxes are carted interisland—or shipped all over the country—in staggering volumes. The Hawaiian Da-Kine line is irrepressibly local: mochi crunch, fortune cookies, animal crackers, and other morsels—all dipped in chocolate. By far the best are the shortbread cookies, dipped in chocolate, peanut butter, and white chocolate. If you get thirsty, there's a juice-and-smoothie bar. Outside are picnic tables on the manicured grounds. 585 Hinano St. ✆ **800/935-5510** or 808/935-8890. www.bigislandcandies.com.

Hilo Farmers Market 🎒 This has grown into the state's best farmers market, embodying what I love most in Hawaii: local color, good soil and weather, the mixing of cultures, and new adventures in taste. More than 120 vendors from around the island bring their flowers, produce, and baked goods to this teeming corner of Hilo every Wednesday and Saturday from sunrise to 4pm. Because many of the vendors sell out quickly, go as early as you can. Expect to find a stunning assortment: homegrown oyster mushrooms from Kona; the creamy, sweet, queenly Indonesian fruit called mangosteen; warm breads, from focaccia to walnut; an array of flowers; fresh aquacultured seaweed; corn from Pahoa; Waimea strawberries; taro and taro products; foot-long, miso-flavored, and traditional Hawaiian laulau; made-from-scratch tamales; and fabulous ethnic vegetables. The selection changes by the week, but it's always reasonable, fresh, and appealing, with a good cross-section of the island's specialties. Although it's open daily, Wednesday and Saturday are the days when all the vendors are there. Kamehameha Ave. at Mamo St. ✆ **808/933-1000.**

Hawaii Volcanoes National Park

Kilauea Kreations This is the quilting center of Volcano, a co-op made up of local Volcano artists and crafters who create quilts, jewelry, feather leis, ceramics, baskets, and fiber arts. Gift items made by Volcano artists are also sold here, but it's the quilts and quilting materials that distinguish the shop. Starter kits are available for beginners. I also like the Hawaiian seed leis and items made of lauhala, as well as the locally made soaps and bath products and the greeting cards, picture frames, and candles. Old Volcano Rd. ✆ **808/967-8090.**

Volcano Art Center The Volcano Island's frontier spirit and raw, primal energy have spawned a close-knit community of artists, and the Volcano Art Center (VAC) is the hub of the island's arts activity. Housed in the original 1877

Volcano House, VAC is a not-for-profit art-education center that offers exhibits and shows that change monthly, as well as workshops and retail space. Marian Berger watercolors of endangered birds, Dietrich Varez oils and block prints, Avi Kiriaty oils, Kelly Dunn and Jack Straka woods, Brad Lewis photography, Harry Wishard paintings, Ira Ono goddess masks, and Mike Riley furnishings are among the works you'll see. Of the 300 artists represented, 90% come from the Big Island. The fine crafts include baskets, jewelry, mixed-media pieces, stone and wood carvings, and the wood diaries of Jesus Sanchez, a third-generation Vatican bookbinder who has turned his skills to the island's woods. At Hawaii Volcanoes National Park. ☎ **808-967-7565.** www.volcanoartcenter.org.

Volcano Store Walk up the wooden steps into a wonderland of flowers and local specialties. Tangy lilikoi butter (transportable, and worth a special trip) and flamboyant sprays of cymbidiums, tuberoses, dendrobiums, anthuriums, hanging plants, mixed bouquets, and calla lilies make a breathtaking assemblage in the enclosed front porch. Volcano residents are lucky to have these blooms at such prices. The flowers can also be shipped (orders are taken by phone); Marie and Ronald Onouye and their staff pack them meticulously (and if mainland weather is too humid or frosty for reliable shipping, they'll let you know). Produce, stone cookies (as in hard-as-stone) from Mountain View, Hilo taro chips, bottled water (a necessity in Volcano), local *poha* (gooseberry) jam, and bowls of chili rice (a local favorite) round out the selection. Even if you're just visiting the park for the day, it's worth turning off to stop for gas here; kindly clerks will give directions. At Huanani Rd. and Old Volcano Rd. ☎ **808/967-7210.**

Volcano Winery Lift a glass of Volcano Blush or Macadamia Nut Honey and toast Pele at this boutique winery, where the local wines are made from tropical honey (no grapes) and tropical fruit blends (half-grape and half-fruit). It's open daily from 10am to 5:30pm; tastings are free. Plans are in the works to expand the winery to accommodate tours. You can order wines online. Pii Mauna Dr., off Hwy. 11 at mile marker 30, all the way to the end. ☎ **808/967-7772.** www.volcanowinery.com.

STUDIO VISITS

Adding to the vitality of the Volcano arts environment are the studio visits offered by the **Volcano Village Art Studios** (this is offered once a year, usually around Thanksgiving). Several respected artists in various media open their studios to the public by appointment. Artists in the hui include **Ira Ono** (☎ 808/967-7261), who makes masks, water containers, fountains, paste-paper journals, garden vessels, and goddesses out of clay and found objects; and sculptor **Randy Takaki** (☎ 808/985-8756), who works in wood, metal, and ceramics.

THE BIG ISLAND AFTER DARK

Jokes abound about neighbor-island nightlife being an oxymoron, but there are a few pockets of entertainment here, largely in the Kailua-Kona and Kohala Coast resorts. Your best bet is to check the local newspapers—*Honolulu Advertiser* and *West Hawaii Today*—for special shows, such as fundraisers, that are held at local venues. Other than that, regular entertainment in the local clubs usually consists of mellow Hawaiian music at sunset, small hula groups, or jazz trios.

Some of the island's best events are held at the **Kahilu Theatre,** in Waimea (☎ 808/885-6888; www.kahilutheatre.org), so be on the lookout for

The Kona Village Luau.

any mention of it during your stay. Hula, the top Hawaiian music groups from all over Hawaii, drama, and all aspects of the performing arts use Kahilu as a venue.

Big Island Luau

Kona Village Luau ★★★ 📷

The longest continuously running luau on the island is still the best—a combination of an authentic Polynesian venue with a menu that works, impressive entertainment, and the spirit of old Hawaii. The feast begins with a ceremony in a sandy kiawe grove, where the pig is unearthed after a full day of cooking in a rock-heated underground oven. In the open-air dining room, next to prehistoric lagoons and tropical gardens, you'll sample a Polynesian buffet: *poisson cru,* poi, laulau (butterfish, seasoned pork, and taro leaves cooked in ti leaves), lomi salmon, squid luau (cooked taro leaves with steamed octopus and coconut milk), ahi poke, opihi (fresh limpets), coconut pudding, taro chips, sweet potatoes, chicken long rice, steamed breadfruit, and the shredded *kalua* pig. The Polynesian revue, a fast-moving, mesmerizing tour of South Pacific cultures, manages—miraculously—to avoid being clichéd or corny. At the Kona Village Resort. ℅ 808/325-5555. www.konavillage.com. Reservations required. Part of the Full American Plan for Kona Village guests; for nonguests, $98 adults, $67 children 6–12, $40 children 3–5. AE, DC, MC, V. Wed and Fri 5pm.

Gathering of the Kings The Fairmont Orchid's Polynesian show—a series of traditional dances and music, blended with modern choreography, island rhythms, and high-tech lighting and set design—tells the story of the Polynesians' journey across the Pacific to Hawaii. It features the culture and arts of the islands of Samoa, Tahiti, New Zealand, and Hawaii. Complementing the show, the luau also highlights the cuisine of these Pacific islands. At the Fairmont Orchid, Mauna Lani Resort, 1 N. Kaniku Dr. ℅ **808/329-8111.** www.islandbreezeluau.com/gotk. Reservations required. Show and luau $99 adults, $65 children 6–12, free for children 5 and under. AE, MC, V. Sat 4:30pm.

Firenesia If you are unable to get into the luau at Kona Village, the Sheraton Keauhou Bay Resort's is my second pick. The food is fine, but you really come here for the show, created by Island Breeze Productions. Filled with lavish theatrics woven into Hawaiian chants, legends, hula, and acrobatic performing arts, this is definitely not your tired Polynesian revue. At the Sheraton-Keauhou Bay Resort, 78–128 Ehukai St. ℅ **808/930-4828.** www.sheratonkeauhou.com. Reservations required. Show and luau $80 adults, $50 children 5–12. AE, MC, V. Mon 5:30pm.

Kailua-Kona

A host of bars and restaurants feature dancing and live music when the sun goes down, all of them on Alii Drive in Kailua-Kona. Starting from the south end of Alii Drive, **Huggo's on the Rocks** (℅ **808/329-1493**) has dancing and live

AN evening UNDER THE STARS

This is one of those unique Hawaii experiences that you will remember long after your tan has faded. Perched from the vantage point of 3,200 feet on the slopes of the Kohala Mountains, **"An Evening at Kahua Ranch"** is a night under the stars with wonderful food, great entertainment, fun activities, and storytelling around a traditional campfire.

The evening begins when you are picked up at your hotel. As you relax in the air-conditioned van, enjoying the scenic coastline, your guide spins stories about this historic area. Arriving at the 8,500-acre working cattle ranch, you are personally greeted by the ranch owner, John Richards. When the sun starts to sink into the Pacific, beer, wine, and soft drinks are served as John talks about how cattle ranching came to Hawaii and how they manage the ranch in the 21st century. A traditional ranch-style barbecue of sirloin steak, chicken, locally grown potatoes, Waimea corn on the cob, baked beans, Big Island green salad, Kona coffee, and dessert is served shortly after sunset.

After dinner, the fun and games begin: Local entertainers pull out guitars, line dancing gets going on the dance floor, and several *paniolo* (cowboy) activities take place. You can choose from learning how to rope, playing a game of horseshoes, or trying your hand at branding (a cedar shingle, yours to take home as a souvenir). When the stars come out, look through an 8-inch telescope to gaze into the moon or search for distant planets. A campfire gets started, and the ranch's cowboys come over and start telling stories as you toast marshmallows for old-fashioned s'mores over a crackling campfire.

The entire experience, including transportation, dinner, and entertainment, is only $145 per person, children half-price. For more information, call ☏ **808/987-2108** or go to www.evening-at-kahua.com. Ask about discounts.

You may have so much fun that you'll want to come back to see the working cattle ranch during the day. The best way to experience ranching in Hawaii is to see the ranch like the cowboys do: on an ATV. Each guest on the **ATV Adventure at Kahua Ranch** (www.kahuaranch.com) is given a top-of-the-line Kawasaki 360 4x4; helmet, gloves, and goggles; and a safety-oriented training session. Although it is a guided tour, with a guide for every six guests, it is not a single-file/stay-on-the-road type of ATV experience. You travel across rangelands and cattle pastures of the 8,500-acre ranch, from the Kehena rainforest to the Pohakuloa desert and from 2,500 to 4,500 feet. Novices have the assurance of a guide to watch over their safety, while experienced riders have the freedom to ride the rolling hills. Cost is $105 for adults and $50 for children 8 to 15.

music nightly, and next door at **Huggo's** restaurant, there's jazz and blues and a piano bar.

Across the street in the Coconut Grove Market Place, **Lulu's** (✆ **808/321-2633**) draws a 20-something crowd with music and dancing Friday and Saturday until 1am.

If you're in the mood for a few laughs, the **Big Island Comedy Club** usually has a live performance once a week of stand-up comedians on tour. Performances are at the Royal Kona Resort; for information, call ✆ **808/329-4368.**

The Kohala Coast

Evening entertainment here usually takes the form of a luau or indistinctive lounge music at scenic resort bars with scintillating sunset views. But newcomer Waikoloa Beach Marriott's **Clipper Lounge** is a bright new venue for local musicians, with live music some nights from 8 to 10pm; call first, at ✆ **808/886-6789.**

The Wednesday and Friday luau at the **Kona Village Resort** (see above) is the best choice on the island. Otherwise, the resort roundup includes the Hilton Waikoloa Village's **Legends of the Pacific** (✆ **808/886-1234**) Tuesday and Friday and Sunday dinner show ($99 adults, $89 seniors, $51 children 5–12). The Hilton's newly opened **Malolo Lounge** also has nightly live entertainment of Hawaiian music (6–9pm).

If you get a chance to see the **Lim Family,** don't miss them. Immensely talented in hula and song, members of the family perform Thursday through Saturday nights in the intimate setting of the Mauna Lani Bay Hotel's **Atrium Bar** (✆ **808/885-6622**).

Just beyond the resorts lies a great music spot—the **Blue Dragon,** 61–3616 Kawaihae Rd., Kawaihae (✆ **808/882-7771**), where you can enjoy an eclectic mix of music (jazz, rock, swing, Hawaiian, and even big-band music) Wednesday through Saturday.

Hilo

Hilo's most notable events are special or annual occasions such as the **Merrie Monarch Hula Festival,** the state's largest, which continues for a week after Easter Sunday. The festivities include hula competitions from all over the world, demonstrations, and crafts fairs. A staggering spirit of pageantry takes over the entire town. Tickets are always hard to come by; call ✆ **808/935-9168** well ahead of time, and see the "Hawaii Calendar of Events" (p. 65) for further information.

A special new venue is the old **Palace Theater,** 38 Haili St. (✆ **808/934-7010;** www.hilopalace.com), restored and back in action thanks to the diligent Friends of the Palace Theater. The neoclassical wonder first opened in 1925, was last restored in 1940, and has reopened for first-run movies while restoration continues. Film festivals, art movies, hula, community events, concerts (including the Slack Key Guitar Festival), and all manner of special entertainment take place here.

OLD-STYLE HAWAIIAN entertainment

The plaintive drone of the conch shell pierces the air, calling all to assemble. A sizzling orange sun sinks slowly toward the cobalt waters of the Pacific. In the distance, the majestic mountain, Mauna Kea, reflects the waning sun's light with a fiery red that fades to a hazy purple and finally to an inky black as a voluptuous full moon dramatically rises over its shoulder.

It's **Twilight at Kalahuipua'a,** a monthly Hawaiian cultural celebration that includes storytelling, singing, and dancing on the oceanside grassy lawn at Mauna Lani Resort (© 808/885-6622). These full-moon events, created by Daniel Akaka, Jr., who is Mauna Lani Resort's director of cultural affairs, hearken back to another time in Hawaii, when family and neighbors gathered to sing, dance, and "talk story."

Each month, the guests, ranging from the ultra-well-known in the world of Hawaiian entertainment to the virtually unknown local *kupuna* (elder), gather to perpetuate the traditional folk art of storytelling, with plenty of music and dance thrown in.

Twilight at Kalahuipua'a, always set on a Saturday closest to the full moon, really gets underway at least an hour before the 5:30pm start, when people from across the island and guests staying at the hotel begin arriving. They carry picnic baskets, mats, coolers, babies, and cameras. A sort of oceanside, premusic tailgate party takes place with *kamaaina* (local resident) families sharing their plate lunches, sushi, and beverages with visitors, who have catered lunches, packaged sandwiches, and taro chips, in a truly old-fashioned demonstration of aloha.

Volcano Village

Tucked into the rainforest of Volcano Village is the **Volcano Art Center's Niaulani Campus** in Volcano Village (© **808/967-8222;** www.volcanoartcenter.org). The name Niaulani, which means "brushed by the heavens" or "billowing heavens," actually describes the way the clouds and fog move through the rainforest. The new 4,400-square-foot administration building houses an intimate great room with a fireplace, sofas, and large windows looking out to the fern forest outside. Check local listings for the free events, ranging from cultural talks to music and dance performances.

7

MAUI, THE VALLEY ISLE

M

aui meets all the criteria for a tropical paradise: swaying palm trees bordering perfect white-sand coves, free-falling waterfalls etching the faces of mountains, voluptuous jungles bursting with bright color and bird song, and moonlight sparkling on calm, turquoise seas.

And everybody, it seems, knows it. Next to Waikiki, Maui is Hawaii's most popular destination, welcoming 2.5 million people each year to its sunny shores. As soon as you arrive at Kahului Airport, a huge banner will tell you that readers of *Condé Nast Traveler* voted Maui the best island *in the world*—and they've done so more than 13 years running. *Travel + Leisure*'s readers also ranked Maui as their favorite island and top travel destination.

Maui has become *the* hip travel destination. Indeed, sometimes it feels a little too well known—especially when you're stuck in bumper-to-bumper traffic or the wall-to-wall boat jam at Maui's popular snorkeling-diving atoll, Molokini Crater. However, the congestion here pales in comparison to big-city Honolulu; Maui is really just a casual collection of small towns. Once you move beyond the resort areas, you'll find a slower, more peaceful way of life, where car horns are used only to greet friends, posted store hours mean nothing if the surf's up, and taking time to watch the sunset is part of the daily routine.

Warm and friendly Maui has an easygoing lifestyle that's perfect for relaxing. But Maui also has an underlying energy that can nudge devout sunbathers right off the beach. People get inspired to do things they might not do otherwise, like rise before dawn to catch the sunrise over Haleakala Crater and then mount a bicycle to coast 37 miles down to sea level; head out to sea on a kayak to look for wintering humpback whales; or swim in the clear pool of a waterfall.

The island of Maui is the result of a marriage of two shield volcanoes, 10,023-foot-high Haleakala and 5,788-foot-high Puu Kukui, that spilled enough lava between them to create a valley—and inspire the island's nickname, the Valley Isle. Thanks to this unusual makeup, Maui packs a lot of nature in and around its landscape. The 727-square-mile island has two peaks more than a mile high, thousands of waterfalls, 120 miles of shoreline, and more than 80 golden-sand beaches. Its microclimates offer distinct variations on the tropical-island theme: The island's as lush as an equatorial rainforest in Hana, as dry as the Arizona desert in Makena, as hot as Mexico in Lahaina, and as cool and misty as Oregon up in Kula.

ORIENTATION
Arriving

If you think of the island of Maui as the shape of a person's head and shoulders, you'll probably arrive near its neck, at **Kahului Airport.**

PREVIOUS PAGE: **Keanae Town.**

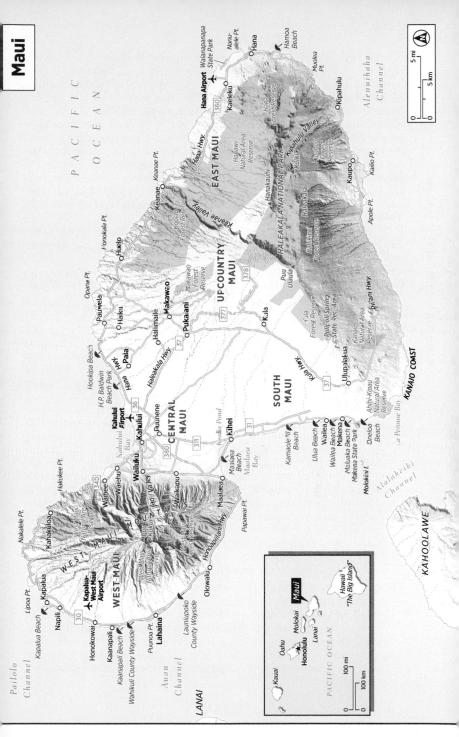

Maui

PACIFIC OCEAN

Nanualele Pt.

Waianapanapa State Park

Hana Airport ✈ Hana

Hamoa Beach

Hana Hwy. 360

Kaeleku

Muolea Pt.

Kipahulu

EAST MAUI

Haleakala National Park

Haiawi Natural Area Reserve

Hana Forest Reserve

Kipahulu Valley

Kipahulu Forest Reserve

Kulki

Kaupo

Koolau Forest Reserve

Hanakauhi

Hanakauhi

Keanae

Keanae Pt.

Keanae Valley

Kailio Pt.

Honokala Pt.

Opana Pt.

Huelo

378

UPCOUNTRY MAUI

Puu Ulaula

Kula Forest Reserve

Kailiini Forest Reserve

Apole Pt.

Pauwela

Olaha

Haliimaile

Makawao

Makawao Forest Reserve

57

Kula

Polipoli Spring State Rec. Area

Piilani Hwy.

Kanaio Natural Area Reserve

Haiku

Puka'ani

Hookipa Beach

H.P. Baldwin Beach Park

Hana Hwy.

Paia

Haleakala Hwy. 37

Ulupalakua

Kahului Airport ✈

Kahului

Puunene

SOUTH MAUI

Kula Hwy. 37

Ahihi-Kinau Natural Area Reserve

La Perouse Bay

KANAIO COAST

CENTRAL MAUI

380

311

Keaila Pond

Kihei

31

Kamaole III Beach

Ulua Beach

Wailea

Wailea Beach

Makena

Maluaka Beach

Makena State Park

Oneloa Beach

Wailuku

Waiehu

340

Waikapu

Iao Valley

WEST MAUI MOUNTAINS

Maalaea Beach

Maalaea Bay

Molokini I.

Alalakeiki Channel

KAHOOLAWE

Waihee

Hakakee Pt.

Waihee Ridge Reserve

West Maui Natural Area Reserve

West Maui Forest Reserve

Honoapiilani Hwy.

Maalaea

Papawai Pt.

Nakalele Pt.

Kahakuloa

WEST MAUI MOUNTAINS

Olowalu

Launiupoko County Wayside

Lipoa Pt.

Kapalua

Kapalua Beach

Napili

Honokowai

Kapalua-West Maui Airport ✈

Kaanapali

Kaanapali Beach

Wahikuli County Wayside

Puunoa Pt.

Lahaina

WEST MAUI

30

PACIFIC OCEAN

Paiolo Channel

LANAI

Auau Channel

Kauai

Oahu

Honolulu

Molokai

Maui

Lanai

Hawaii "The Big Island"

PACIFIC OCEAN

100 mi

100 km

N

5 mi

5 km

Alenuihaha Channel

Try to fly directly to Maui—otherwise, you will be stuck with flying into Honolulu, with the likelihood of a 2-hour layover between flights. As of press time, these airlines fly directly from the U.S. mainland to Maui: **United Airlines** (✆ **800/241-6522;** www.united.com) has nonstop service from Chicago, Los Angeles, and San Francisco; **Hawaiian Airlines** (✆ **800/367-5320;** www.hawaiianair.com) offers direct flights from Seattle, Portland, and San Diego; **Alaska Airlines** (✆ **800/252/7522;** www.alaskaair.com) has nonstop flights from Seattle and twice-weekly seasonal service from Anchorage; **American Airlines** (✆ **800/433-7300;** www.aa.com) has direct service from Los Angeles and Dallas; **Delta Air Lines** (✆ **800/221-1212;** www.delta.com) flies direct from Los Angeles and Salt Lake City; **Northwest Airlines** (✆ **800/221-1212;** www.nwa.com) travels from Seattle; and **US Airways/American West** (✆ **800/428-4322;** www.usairways.com) flies from Phoenix.

Direct flights from Canada are available on **Air Canada** (✆ **888/247-2262;** www.aircanada.com) and **West Jet** (✆ **888/937-8538;** www.westjet.com), which both fly from Vancouver.

The other major carriers fly to Honolulu, where you'll have to pick up an interisland flight to Maui. **Hawaiian Airlines** (✆ **800/367-5320** or 808/838-1555; www.hawaiianair.com); **Mokulele Airlines** (✆ **808/426-7070** or www.mokuleleairlines.com); and **go!** (✆ **888/I-FLY-GO-2** [435-9462]; www.iflygo.com) offer jet service from Honolulu and the other neighbor islands.

LANDING AT KAHULUI   If there's a long wait at baggage claim, step over to the state-operated **Visitor Information Center** and pick up brochures and the latest issue of *This Week Maui,* which features great regional maps of the islands. After collecting your bags, proceed to the rental-car pickup area (at the ocean end, to your right as you stand with your back to the terminal, behind the rental-car desks) and wait for the appropriate rental-agency shuttle van to take you a half-mile away to the rental-car checkout desk. All of the major rental companies, listed in chapter 11, have branches at Kahului. For tips on insurance and driving rules in Hawaii, see "Getting There & Getting Around" (p. 74).

If you're not renting a car, the cheapest way to get to your hotel is via **SpeediShuttle** (✆ **800/977/2605** or 808/661-6667; www.speedishuttle.com), which can take you between Kahului Airport and all the major resorts between 6am and 11pm daily. Rates vary, but figure on $39 for one person one-way to Wailea, $54 one-way to Kaanapali, and $74 one-way to Kapalua. Be sure to call ahead to arrange pickup.

If possible, avoid landing between 3 and 6pm, when Maui's working stiffs are "*pau* work" (finished with work) and a major traffic jam occurs.

AVOIDING KAHULUI   If you're planning to stay at any of the hotels in Kapalua or at the Kaanapali resorts, you might consider flying **Island Air** (✆ **800/323-3345;** www.islandair.com) or **Mokulele Airlines** (✆ **808/426-7070;** www.mokuleleairlines.com) from Honolulu to **Kapalua—West Maui Airport.** From this airport, it's only a 10- to 15-minute drive to most hotels in West Maui, as opposed to an hour from Kahului. However, my experience with Island Air has not been stellar; they've left me stranded midroute not once, but twice.

Visitor Information

The **Maui Visitors Bureau** is at 1727 Wili Pa Loop, Wailuku, Maui, HI 96793
(*C* **800/525-MAUI** [6284] or 808/244-3530; fax 808/244-1337; www.visit
maui.com). To get here from the airport, go right on Hwy. 36 (Hana Hwy.) to
Kaahumanu Avenue (Hwy. 32); follow it past Maui Community College and
Wailuku War Memorial Park onto East Main Street in Wailuku. At North Market
Street, turn right and then right again on Mill Street; go left on Imi Kala Street
and left again onto Wili Pa Loop.

The Island in Brief

CENTRAL MAUI

Maui's main airport lies in this flat, windy corridor between Maui's two volcanoes, and this is where most of the island's population lives. You'll find good shopping and dining bargains here, as well as the heart of the business community
and the local government.

KAHULUI   This is "Dream City," home to thousands of former sugar-cane workers whose dream in life was to own their own home away from the sugar
plantation. There's wonderful shopping here (especially at discount stores),
but this is not a place to spend your vacation.

WAILUKU   Wailuku is like a time capsule, with its faded wooden storefronts, old
plantation homes, shops straight out of the 1950s, and relaxed way of life.
While most people race through on their way to see the natural beauty of
Iao Valley, this quaint little town is worth a brief visit, if only to see a real
place where real people actually appear to be working at something other
than a suntan. This is the county seat, so you'll see people in suits on important missions in the tropical heat. The town has a spectacular view of Hale
akala Crater, great budget restaurants, some interesting bungalow
architecture, a Frank Lloyd Wright building, a wonderful historic B&B, and
the always-endearing Bailey House Museum.

Wailuku.

427

WEST MAUI

This is the fabled Maui you see on postcards. Jagged peaks, green velvet valleys, a wilderness full of native species—the majestic West Maui Mountains are the epitome of earthly paradise. The beaches here are some of the islands' best. And it's no secret: This stretch of coastline along Maui's "forehead," from Kapalua to the historic port of Lahaina, is the island's most bustling resort area (with South Maui close behind). Expect a few mainland-style traffic jams.

If you want to book into a resort or condo on this coast, first consider what community you'd like to base yourself in. Starting at the southern end of West Maui and moving northward, the coastal communities look like this:

LAHAINA This old seaport is a tame version of its former self, a raucous whaling town where sailors swaggered ashore in search of women and grog. Today, the village teems with restaurants, T-shirt shops, and galleries, and parts of it are downright tacky, but there's still lots of real history to be found. Lahaina is a great place to stay; accommodations include a few old hotels (such as the newly restored 1901 Pioneer Inn on the harbor), quaint bed-and-breakfasts, and a handful of oceanfront condos.

KAANAPALI ★ Farther north along the West Maui coast is Hawaii's first master-planned family resort. Pricey mid-rise hotels line nearly 3 miles of gold-sand beach; they're linked by a landscaped parkway and a walking path along the sand. Golf greens wrap around the slope between beachfront and hillside properties. **Whalers Village**—a seaside mall with 48 shops and restaurants, plus the best little whale museum in Hawaii—and other restaurants are easy to reach on foot along the oceanfront walkway or by resort shuttle, which also serves the small West Maui airport just to the north. Shuttles also go to Lahaina (see above), 3 miles to the south, for shopping, dining, entertainment, and boat tours. Kaanapali is popular with meeting groups and families—especially those with teenagers, who like all the action.

HONOKOWAI, KAHANA & NAPILI In the building binge of the 1970s, condominiums sprouted along this gorgeous coastline like mushrooms after a rain. Today, these older oceanside units offer excellent bargains for astute travelers. The great location—along sandy beaches, within minutes of both the Kapalua and Kaanapali resort areas, and close enough to the goings-on in Lahaina town—makes this area an accommodations heaven for the budget-minded.

In **Honokowai** and **Mahinahina,** you'll find mostly older units that tend to be cheaper. There's not much shopping here (mostly convenience stores), but you'll have easy access to the shops and restaurants of Kaanapali.

Kahana is a little more upscale than Honokowai and Mahinahina. Most of its condos are big high-rise types, newer than those immediately to the south. You'll find a nice selection of shops and restaurants (including the Maui branch of Roy's) in the area, and Kapalua–West Maui Airport is nearby.

Napili is a much-sought-after area for condo seekers: It's quiet; has great beaches, restaurants, and shops; and is close to Kapalua. Units are generally more expensive here (although I've found a few hidden gems at affordable prices).

KAPALUA ★★   North beyond Kaanapali and the shopping centers of Napili and Kahana, the road starts to climb and the vista opens up to fields of golden-green pineapple and manicured golf fairways. A country lane lined with Pacific pines that leads toward the sea brings you to Kapalua. It's the very exclusive domain of the luxurious Ritz-Carlton hotel and expensive condos and villas, set on one of Hawaii's best white-sand beaches, next to two bays that are marine-life preserves (with fabulous surfing in winter).

Even if you don't stay here, you're welcome to come and enjoy Kapalua. The fancy hotel here provides public parking and beach access. The resort has an art school where you can learn local crafts, as well as three golf courses, historic features, swanky condos and homes (many available for vacation rental at astronomical prices), and wide-open spaces that include a rainforest preserve—all open to the general public.

SOUTH MAUI

This is the hottest, sunniest, driest, most popular coastline on Maui for sun lovers—Arizona by the sea. Rain rarely falls here, and temperatures stick around 85°F (29°C) year-round. On this former scrubland from Maalaea to Makena, where cacti once grew wild and cows grazed, there are now four distinctive areas—Maalaea, Kihei, Wailea, and Makena—and a surprising amount of traffic.

MAALAEA   If West Maui is the island's head, Maalaea is just under the chin. This windy, oceanfront village centers on the small boat harbor (with a general store and a couple of restaurants) and the **Maui Ocean Center ★★**, an aquarium/ocean complex. Visitors staying here should be aware that it's almost always very windy. All the wind from the Pacific is funneled between the West Maui Mountains and Haleakala, and comes out in Maalaea.

KIHEI   Kihei is less a proper town than a nearly continuous series of condos and mini-malls lining South Kihei Road. This is Maui's best vacation bargain. Budget travelers swarm like sun-seeking geckos over the eight sandy beaches along this scalloped, condo-packed 7-mile stretch of coast. Kihei is neither charming nor quaint; what it lacks in aesthetics, though, it more than makes up for in sunshine, affordability, and convenience. If you want a latte in the morning, the beach in the afternoon, and Hawaii Regional Cuisine in the evening—all at budget prices—head to Kihei.

WAILEA ★★   Just 3 decades ago, this was wall-to-wall scrub kiawe trees, but now Wailea is a manicured oasis of multimillion-dollar resort hotels along 2 miles of palm-fringed gold coast. Wailea has warm, clear water full of tropical fish; year-round golden sunshine and clear blue skies; and hedonistic pleasure palaces on 1,500 acres of black-lava shore indented by five beautiful beaches. Amazing what a billion dollars can do.

This is the playground of the stretch-limo set. The planned resort development—practically a well-heeled town—has a shopping village, three prized golf courses of its own and three more in close range, and a tennis complex. A growing number of large homes sprawl over the upper hillside, some offering excellent bed-and-breakfast units at reasonable prices. The resorts along this fantasy coast are spectacular, to say the least. Next door to the Four Seasons, the most elegant, is the Grand Wailea Resort Hotel & Spa, a public display of ego by Tokyo mogul Takeshi Sekiguchi, who dropped $600 million in 1991 to create his own minicity. Stop in and take a look—it's so gauche you've gotta see it.

Appealing natural features include the coastal trail, a 3-mile round-trip path along the oceanfront with pleasing views everywhere you look. The trail's south end borders an extensive garden of native coastal plants, as well as the ruins of ancient lava-rock houses juxtaposed with elegant oceanfront condos. But the chief attractions, of course, are those five outstanding beaches (the best is Wailea).

MAKENA ★★   Suddenly, the road enters raw wilderness. After Wailea's overdone density, the thorny landscape is a welcome relief. Although beautiful, this is an end-of-the-road kind of place: It's a long drive from Makena to anywhere on Maui. If you're looking for an activity-filled vacation, you might want to try somewhere else, or you'll spend most of your vacation in the car. But if you want a quiet, relaxing respite, where the biggest trip of the day is from your bed to the beach, Makena is the place.

Beyond Makena, you'll discover Haleakala's last lava flow, which ran to the sea in 1790; the bay named for French explorer La Pérouse; and a chunky lava trail known as the King's Highway, which leads around Maui's empty south shore past ruins and fish camps. Puu Olai stands like Maui's Diamond Head on the shore, where a sunken crater shelters tropical fish, and empty golden-sand beaches stand at the end of dirt roads.

UPCOUNTRY MAUI

After a few days at the beach, you'll probably notice the 10,000-foot mountain in the middle of Maui. The slopes of Haleakala ("House of the Sun") are home to cowboys, growers, and other country people who wave at you as you drive by. They're all up here enjoying the crisp air, emerald pastures, eucalyptus, and flower farms of this tropical Olympus—there's even a misty California redwood grove. You can see a thousand tropical sunsets reflected in the windows of houses old and new, strung along a road that runs like a loose hound from Makawao to Kula, where the road leads up to the crater and **Haleakala National Park** ★★★. The rumpled, two-lane blacktop of Hwy. 37 narrows on the other side of Tedeschi Winery, where wine grapes and wild elk flourish on the Ulupalakua Ranch, the biggest on Maui. A stay upcountry is usually affordable and a nice contrast to the sizzling beaches and busy resorts below.

Makena.

Haleakala.

MAKAWAO ★★ Until recently, this small, two-street upcountry town was little more than a post office, gas station, feed store, bakery, and restaurant/bar serving the cowboys and farmers living in the surrounding community; the hitching posts outside storefronts were really used to tie up horses. As the population of Maui started expanding in the 1970s, a health food store sprang up, followed by boutiques, a chiropractic clinic, and a host of health-conscious restaurants. The result is an eclectic amalgam of old *paniolo* (cowboy) Hawaii and the baby-boomer trends of transplanted mainlanders. **Hui No'Eau Visual Arts Center** ★, Hawaii's premier arts collective, is definitely worth a peek. The only accommodations here are reasonably priced bed-and-breakfasts, perfect for those who enjoy great views and don't mind slightly chilly nights.

KULA A feeling of pastoral remoteness prevails in this upcountry community of old flower farms, humble cottages, and new suburban ranch houses with million-dollar views that take in the ocean, the isthmus, the West Maui Mountains, and, at night, the lights that run along the gold coast like a string of pearls from Maalaea to Puu Olai. Everything flourishes at a cool 3,000 feet (bring a jacket), just below the cloud line, along a winding road on the way up to Haleakala National Park. Everyone here grows something—Maui onions, carnations, orchids, and proteas—and B&Bs cater to guests seeking cool tropic nights, panoramic views, and a rural upland escape. Here you'll find the true peace and quiet that only rural farming country can offer—yet you're still just 30 to 40 minutes away from the beach and an hour's drive from Lahaina.

EAST MAUI

ON THE ROAD TO HANA ★★★ When old sugar towns die, they usually fade away in rust and red dirt. Not **Paia** ★★. The tangled spaghetti of electrical, phone, and cable wires hanging overhead symbolizes the town's ability to adapt to the times—it may look messy, but it works. Here, trendy restaurants, eclectic boutiques, and high-tech windsurf shops stand next door to a ma-and-pa grocery, a fish market, and stores that have been serving customers since plantation days. Hippies took over in the 1970s; although their macrobiotic restaurants and old-style artists' co-ops have made way for Hawaii Regional Cuisine and galleries featuring the works of renowned international artists, Paia still manages to maintain a pleasant granola vibe. The town's main attraction, though, is **Hookipa Beach Park** ★, where the wind that roars through the isthmus of Maui brings windsurfers from around the world. A few B&Bs are located just outside Paia in the tiny community of **Kuau.**

Ten minutes down the road from Paia and up the hill from the Hana Highway—the connector road to the entire east side of Maui—is **Haiku.** Once a pineapple-plantation village, complete with a cannery (now a shopping complex), Haiku offers vacation rentals and B&Bs in a quiet, pastoral setting: the perfect base for those who want to get off the beaten path and experience the quieter side of Maui, but don't want to feel too removed (the beach is only 10 min. away).

About 15 to 20 minutes past Haiku is the largely unknown community of **Huelo ★**. Every day, thousands of cars whiz by on the road to Hana; most barely glance at the double row of mailboxes overseen by a fading Hawaii Visitors Bureau sign. But down the gunmetal road lies a hidden Hawaii—a Hawaii of an earlier time, where Mother Nature is still sensual and wild, where ocean waves pummel soaring lava cliffs, and where an indescribable sense

Paia.

of serenity prevails. Huelo isn't for everyone, but those who hunger for a place still largely untouched by "progress" should check into a B&B or vacation rental here.

HANA ★★★   Set between an emerald rainforest and the blue Pacific is a village probably best defined by what it lacks: golf courses, shopping malls, and McDonald's. Except for a gas station and a bank with an ATM, you'll find little of what passes for progress here. Instead, you'll discover the simple joys of fragrant tropical flowers, the sweet taste of backyard bananas and papayas, and the easy calm and unabashed small-town aloha spirit of old Hawaii. What saved "Heavenly" Hana from the inevitable march of progress? The 52-mile Hana Highway, which winds around 600 curves and crosses more than 50 one-lane bridges on its way from Kahului. You can go to Hana for the day—it's 3 hours (and a half-century) from Kihei and Lahaina—but 3 days are better.

GETTING AROUND

BY CAR   The only way to really see Maui is by rental car; there's no islandwide public transit. All of the major car-rental firms have agencies on Maui; for a complete listing, see chapter 11. For tips on insurance and driving rules in Hawaii, see "Getting There & Getting Around" (p. 74).

Maui has only a handful of major roads, and you can expect to encounter a traffic jam or two in the major resort areas. Two of the roads follow the coastline around the two volcanoes that form the island, Haleakala and Puu Kukui (the West Maui Mountains), one road goes up to Haleakala's summit, one road goes to Hana, one goes to Wailea, and one goes to Lahaina. It sounds simple, right? Well, it isn't because the names of the few roads change en route. Study a map before you set out.

A traffic advisory: Be alert on the Honoapiilani Highway (Hwy. 30) en route to Lahaina because drivers who spot whales in the channel between Maui and Lanai often slam on the brakes and cause major tie-ups and accidents. Since this is the only main road connecting the west side to the rest of the island, if there is an accident, flooding, a rock slide, or any other road hazard, traffic can back up for 1 to 8 hours (no joking)—plan accordingly.

If you get into trouble on Maui's highways, look for the flashing blue strobe lights on 12-foot poles; at the base are emergency solar-powered call boxes (programmed to dial 911 as soon as you pick up the handset). There are 29 emergency call boxes on the island's busiest highways and remote areas, including along the Hana and Haleakala highways and on the north end of the island in the remote community of Kahakuloa.

BY MOTORCYCLE Feel the wind on your face and smell the salt air as you tour the island on a Harley, available for rent from **Cycle City Maui,** 150 Dairy Rd., Kahului, or 602 Front St., Lahaina (📞 **808/877-7433;** www.mauicar sandbikes.com). Rentals start at $79 for 3 hours or $129 a day (8:30am–5pm weekdays and 10am–3pm weekends).

BY TAXI & SHUTTLE **Alii Taxi** (📞 808/661-3688) offers 24-hour service islandwide. You can also call **Kihei Taxi** (📞 808/879-3000), **Islandwide Taxi & Tours** (📞 808/874-TAXI [8294]), or **Sunshine Cabs of Maui** (📞 808/879-2220) if you need a ride.

Maui Public Transit is a public/private partnership that has convenient, economical, and air-conditioned shuttle buses on 11 routes, all operated by Roberts Hawaii (📞 **808/871-4838;** www.mauicounty.gov/bus). These routes are funded by the County of Maui and provide service in and between various Central, West, South, and Upcountry Maui communities (including the airport). All routes operate daily. The routes go from as far south as Wailea up to as far north as Kapalua. Fares are $1 for most routes, and Kahului and Wailuku Loop and the Lahaina Villager routes are free.

[Fast FACTS] MAUI

American Express Offices are located in South Maui at the **Grand Wailea Resort** (📞 **808/875-4526**), and in West Maui at the **Westin Maui Resort** at Kaanapali Beach (📞 **808/661-7155**).

Dentists Emergency dental care is available at **Kihei Dental Center,** 1847 S. Kihei Rd., Kihei (📞 **808/874-8401**), or at **Aloha Lahaina Dentists,** 134 Luakini St. (in the Maui Medical Group Building),

Lahaina (📞 **808/661-4005**).

Doctors The **West Maui Healthcare Center,** Whalers Village, 2435 Kaanapali Pkwy., Ste. H-7 (near Leilani's on the Beach),

Kaanapali (☎ **808/667-9721**), is open 365 days a year until 10pm nightly; no appointment is necessary. In Kihei, call **Urgent Care Maui,** 1325 S. Kihei Rd., Ste. 103 (at Lipoa St., across from Star Market), Kihei (☎ **808/879-7781**), open daily from 6am to midnight.

Emergencies Call ☎ **911** for police, fire, and ambulance service. District stations are located in Lahaina (☎ **808/661-4441**) and in Hana (☎ **808/248-8311**).

Hospitals In Central Maui, **Maui Memorial Hospital** is at 221 Mahalani, Wailuku (☎ **808/244-9056**). East Maui's **Hana Medical Center** is on the Hana Highway (☎ **808/248-8924**). In Upcountry Maui, **Kula Hospital** is at 204 Kula Hwy., Kula (☎ **808/878-1221**).

Internet Access Every major hotel and even many small B&Bs have Internet access. Many of them offer high-speed wireless; check ahead of time, and check the charges, which can be exorbitant. The best Internet deal in Hawaii is the service at the public libraries (to find the location nearest you, check www.publiclibraries.com/hawaii.htm), which offer free access if you have a library card, which you can purchase for $10 for 3 months. Other Internet access: Try **The Coffee Store,** 5095 Napilihau St., #108-B, Napili (☎ **808/669-4170**), open daily from 6am to 6pm; **Lighthouse Maui Café,** 70 E. Kaahumanu Ave., Kahului (☎ **808/871-0875**), open Monday through Thursday and Saturday from 9am to 6pm, Friday from 9am to

8pm, and Sunday from 10am to 4pm; and **Blue Moon Café,** located off Kihei Road, behind the Tesoro Gas Station, at 362 Huku Lii Place, Kihei (☎ **808/874-8600**), open daily from 7am to 8pm.

Post Office To find the nearest post office, call ☎ **800/ASK-USPS** (275-8777). In Lahaina, there are branches at the Lahaina Civic Center, 1760 Honoapiilani Hwy., and at the Lahaina Shopping Center, 132 Papalaua St. In Kahului, there's a branch at 138 S. Puunene Ave., and in Kihei, there's one at 1254 S. Kihei Rd.

Weather For the current weather, call ☎ **808/871-5054;** for Haleakala National Park weather, call ☎ **808/572-9306;** for marine weather and surf and wave conditions, call ☎ **808/877-3477.**

WHERE TO STAY

Maui has accommodations to fit every kind of vacation, from deluxe oceanfront resorts to reasonably priced condos to historic bed-and-breakfasts. Before you book, be sure to read "The Island in Brief," earlier in this chapter, which will help you settle on a location. Also check out "Tips on Accommodations" (p. 101).

Remember that Hawaii's 11.42% accommodations tax will be added to your final bill. Parking is free unless otherwise noted. Also, if you're booking a stay at an upscale hotel, be sure to ask if there is a "resort fee" ($12–$17 a day) tacked onto your bill.

For an even wider selection of places to stay, check out *Frommer's Maui.*

Central Maui

If you're arriving late at night or you have an early-morning flight out, the best choice near Kahului Airport is the **Maui Beach Hotel,** 170 Kaahumanu Ave., Kahului, HI 96732 (☎ **800/367-5004** or 808/877-0051; fax 808/871-5797; http://castleresorts.com/MBH). The nondescript, motel-like rooms (the standard room is so small, you can barely walk around the queen-size bed) start at $117 and include free airport shuttle service (6am–9pm only). It's okay for a night, but it's not a place to spend your entire vacation.

WAILUKU

Happy Valley Hale 🎣 The Kong family, owners of Nona Lani Cottages in Kihei (p. 456), has with loving care turned this old plantation home into a tiny oasis in the midst of an economically challenged area. Keep in mind these are budget accommodations—really an alternative to a youth hostel. However, the place is immaculately clean, and the Kongs have made extensive renovations. The four bedrooms—each with twin beds, small fridge, dresser, and closet—share two bathrooms. It's like staying in a family home, with a shared kitchen (no stove, but microwave, griddle, coffeemaker, and so on) and common room with TV. The front yard sports a barbecue and picnic area. The only drawback is that Happy Valley is not exactly a resort area—public housing is just across the street. But for those on extremely tight budgets, it's a good option.

332 N. Market St., Wailuku, HI 96793. ✆ **800/733-2688** or 808/870-9100. www.nonalanicottages. com. 4 units. $33 per bed in shared room; $65 double private room; $99 triple private room. 3-night minimum. MC, V. **Amenities:** Shared kitchen. *In room:* Small fridge, kitchen in cottages, no phone.

Old Wailuku Inn at Ulupono ★★ 🏨 This 1924 former plantation manager's home, lovingly restored by innkeepers Janice and Thomas Fairbanks and their daughter Shelly, offers a genuine old Hawaii experience. The theme is Hawaii of the 1920s and 1930s, with decor, design, and landscaping to match. The spacious rooms are gorgeously outfitted with exotic ohia-wood floors, high ceilings, and traditional Hawaiian quilts. The mammoth bathrooms (some with claw-foot tubs, others with Jacuzzis) have plush towels and earth-friendly toiletries on hand. The owners recently added the Vagabond House, a modern three-room complex in the inn's lavishly landscaped backyard. These rooms are decorated in Island designer Sig Zane's floral prints with rare framed prints of indigenous Hawaiian flowers, plus plenty of modern amenities (including an ultraluxurious multihead shower). You'll feel right at home lounging on the living room sofa or in an old wicker chair on the enclosed lanai, where a full gourmet breakfast is served in the morning. The inn is located in the historic area of Wailuku, just a few minutes' walk from the Maui County Seat Government Building, the courthouse, and a wonderful stretch of antiques shops.

2199 Kahookele St. (at High St., across from the Wailuku School), Wailuku, HI 96732. ✆ **800/ 305-4899** or 808/244-5897. Fax 808/242-9600. www.mauiinn.com. 10 units. $165–$195 double. Rates include full breakfast. 2-night minimum. MC, V. **Amenities:** Jacuzzi. *In room:* A/C, TV/VCR, high-speed Internet access.

West Maui

In addition to the following choices, you may want to consider the oceanfront condos at **Lahaina Shores Beach Resort,** 475 Front St. (✆ **800/642-6284;** www.lahainashores.com). Rates are $218 to $290 studio double; $266 to $355 one-bedroom double; from $355 one-bedroom penthouse double. Value-priced **Old Lahaina House,** P.O. Box 10355 (✆ **800/847-0761** or 808/667-4663; fax 808/667-5615; www.oldlahaina.com), features comfy twin- and king-bedded doubles for just $89 to $139; it's about a 2-minute walk to the water just across Front Street.

LAHAINA

Expensive

Outrigger Aina Nalu ★   Set on 9 acres in the middle of Lahaina, this property was totally rebuilt, renovated, and remodeled in 2005. Then the units were sold off to private owners and put into a rental pool. The result is a brand-new first-class property, with all the latest appliances, new furniture, and 21st-century conveniences. The property is on a quiet side street (a rarity in Lahaina) and within walking distance of restaurants, shops, attractions, and the beach (just 3 blocks away). All of the good-size rooms, decorated in tropical-island style, are comfortable and quiet. The complex includes a sun deck and pool, a barbecue, and a picnic area. The aloha-friendly staff will take the time to answer all of your questions.

660 Wainee St. (btw. Dickenson and Prison sts.), Lahaina, HI 96761. © **800/OUTRIGGER** (688-7444) or 808/667-9766. Fax 808/661-3733. www.outrigger.com. 197 units. $119–$139 studio with kitchenette; $165–$185 1-bedroom with kitchen (sleeps up to 4); $165–$185 2-bedroom with 1 bathroom and kitchen (sleeps 6); $175–$195 2-bedroom with 2 bathrooms and kitchen (sleeps 6). AE, DC, DISC, MC, V. Parking $15. **Amenities:** Outdoor pool; whirlpool. *In room:* A/C, TV/DVD, high-speed Internet access, kitchenette (in studio), full kitchen (in 1- and 2-bedroom units).

The Plantation Inn ★★ 🛏   Attention, romance-seeking couples: Look no further. This charming Victorian-style inn, located a couple of blocks from the water, looks like it's been here 100 years or more, but it's actually of 1990s vintage—an artful deception. The rooms are romantic to the max, tastefully done with period furniture, hardwood floors, stained glass, and ceiling fans. There are four-poster canopy beds in some rooms, brass beds and wicker in others. All units are soundproof (a plus in Lahaina) and come with a private lanai; the suites have kitchenettes. The rooms wrap around the large pool and deck. Breakfast is served around the pool and in an elegant pavilion lounge. Also on the property is an outstanding French restaurant (guests get a discount).

174 Lahainaluna Rd. (btw. Wainee and Luakini sts., 1 block from Hwy. 30), Lahaina, HI 96761. © **800/433-6815** or 808/667-9225. Fax 808/667-9293. www.theplantationinn.com. 19 units (some with shower only). $159–$245 double; from $239 suite. Extra person $30. Check the website for great package deals. Rates include full breakfast. AE, DC, DISC, MC, V. **Amenities:** Acclaimed restaurant and bar (Gerard's, p. 475); concierge; Jacuzzi; large outdoor pool. *In room:* A/C, TV/DVD, hair dryer, kitchenette (in suites), Wi-Fi.

Puamana   These 28 acres of town houses set right on the water are ideal for those who want to be able to retreat from the crowds and cacophony of downtown Lahaina into the serene quiet of an elegant neighborhood. "Private" and "peaceful" are apt descriptions for this complex: Each unit is a privately owned individual home, with no neighbors above or below. Most are exquisitely decorated, and all come with full kitchen, lanai, barbecue, and at least two bathrooms. Puamana was once a private estate in the 1920s, part of the sugar plantations that dominated Lahaina; the plantation manager's house has been converted into a clubhouse with an oceanfront lanai, library, card room, sauna, table-tennis tables, and office. I've found the best rates by booking through Klahani Travel (see below for contact information), but its office is not on-site, which has caused some problems with guests getting assistance. If you'd rather book directly with the Puamana association office, contact Puamana Community

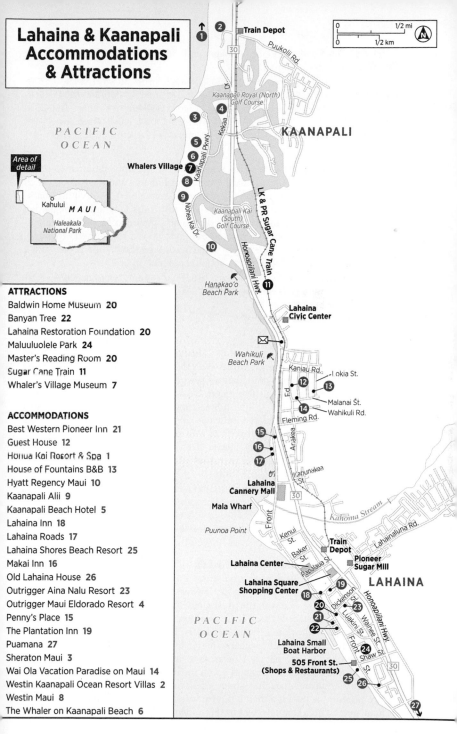

Lahaina & Kaanapali Accommodations & Attractions

PACIFIC
OCEAN

Area of detail

Kahului
MAUI
Haleakala
National Park

KAANAPALI

Train Depot

Puukolii Rd.

Kaanapali Royal (North)
Golf Course

Kekaa

Whalers Village

Kaanapali Pkwy

Nohea Ka Dr.

Kaanapali Kai
(South)
Golf Course

Honoapiilani Hwy.

LK & PR Sugar Cane Train

Hanakao'o
Beach Park

Lahaina
Civic Center

Wahikuli
Beach Park

Kaniau Rd.

Iokia St.

Rd.

Malanai St.

Wahikuli Rd.

Fleming Rd.

Arakea

Lahaina
Cannery Mall

Mala Wharf

Puunoa Point

Wahunakea St.

Kahoma Stream

Lahainaluna Rd.

Front

Kenui St.

Baker St.

Papalaua St.

Train
Depot

Pioneer
Sugar Mill

Lahaina Center

Lahaina Square
Shopping Center

Dickenson
St.

Liekin St.

Wainee St.

Honoapiilani Hwy.

LAHAINA

PACIFIC
OCEAN

Lahaina Small
Boat Harbor

505 Front St.
(Shops & Restaurants)

Front St.

Shaw St.

ATTRACTIONS

Baldwin Home Museum **20**
Banyan Tree **22**
Lahaina Restoration Foundation **20**
Maluuluolele Park **24**
Master's Reading Room **20**
Sugar Cane Train **11**
Whaler's Village Museum **7**

ACCOMMODATIONS

Best Western Pioneer Inn **21**
Guest House **12**
Honua Kai Resort & Spa **1**
House of Fountains B&B **13**
Hyatt Regency Maui **10**
Kaanapali Alii **9**
Kaanapali Beach Hotel **5**
Lahaina Inn **18**
Lahaina Roads **17**
Lahaina Shores Beach Resort **25**
Makai Inn **16**
Old Lahaina House **26**
Outrigger Aina Nalu Resort **23**
Outrigger Maui Eldorado Resort **4**
Penny's Place **15**
The Plantation Inn **19**
Puamana **27**
Sheraton Maui **3**
Wai Ola Vacation Paradise on Maui **14**
Westin Kaanapali Ocean Resort Villas **2**
Westin Maui **8**
The Whaler on Kaanapali Beach **6**

0   1/2 mi
0   1/2 km

Association, 34 Puailima Place, Lahaina, HI 96761 (© **808/661-3423;** fax 808/667-0398; info@Puamana.info).

Front St. (at the extreme southern end of Lahaina, ½ mile from downtown), Lahaina, HI 96761. Reservations c/o Klahani Travel, 159 Halelo St., Lahaina, HI 96761. © **800/669-6284** or 808/ 667-2712. Fax 808/661-5875. www.klahani.com. 40 units. $140–$250 1-bedroom; $160–$350 2-bedroom; $350–$500 3-bedroom. 3-night minimum. AE, DISC, MC, V. **Amenities:** 3 pools (1 for adults only); Jacuzzi; tennis court. *In room:* TV, hair dryer, kitchen.

Moderate

Best Western Pioneer Inn   This hotel is a two-story plantation-style structure with big verandas that overlook the streets of Lahaina and the harbor, which is just 50 feet away. All rooms have been totally remodeled, with vintage bathrooms and new curtains and carpets. The quietest units face either the garden courtyard—devoted to refined outdoor dining accompanied by live (but quiet) music—or the square-block-size banyan tree next door. I recommend room no. 31, over the banyan court, with a view of the ocean and the harbor. If you want a front-row seat for all the Front Street action, book no. 36 or 49.

658 Wharf St. (in front of Lahaina Pier), Lahaina, HI 96761. © **800/457-5457** or 808/661-3636. Fax 808/667-5708. www.pioneerinnmaui.com. 34 units. $145–$205 double; from $185 suite. Extra person (12 or over) $20. AE, DC, DISC, MC, V. Parking included in room rates. **Amenities:** Restaurant (good for breakfast); bar w/live music; outdoor pool. *In room:* A/C, TV, fridge, hair dryer, high-speed Internet access.

Guest House ★★ 🎁   This is one of Lahaina's great bed-and-breakfast deals: a charming house with more amenities than the expensive Kaanapali hotels just down the road. The roomy home features parquet floors and floor-to-ceiling windows; its swimming pool—surrounded by a deck and comfortable lounge chairs—is larger than some at high-priced condos. Every unit has a quiet lanai and a romantic Jacuzzi. The large, fully equipped kitchen is available for guests' use. Scuba divers are welcome here (and well taken care of, with places to wash and store their gear). The Guest House also operates Trinity Tours and offers discounts on car rentals and other island activities. Tennis courts are nearby, and the nearest beach is about a block away.

1620 Ainakea Rd. (off Fleming Rd., north of Lahaina town), Lahaina, HI 96761. © **800/621-8942** or 808/661-8085. Fax 808/661-1896. www.mauiguesthouse.com. 4 units. $149 single; $169 double. Extra person $15. Rates include expanded continental breakfast. MC, V. Take Fleming Rd. off Hwy. 30; turn left on Ainakea; it's 2 blocks down. **Amenities:** Concierge; huge outdoor pool; free use of watersports equipment. *In room:* A/C, TV/VCR/DVD, fridge, Jacuzzi, Wi-Fi.

House of Fountains Bed & Breakfast 🎁   This 7,000-square-foot contemporary home, in a quiet residential subdivision at the north end of town, is popular with visitors from around the world. Hostess Daniela Atay keeps the place immaculate; in 2002, she won the prestigious "Most Hawaiian Accommodation" award from the Hawaii Visitors & Convention Bureau. The oversize rooms are fresh and quiet, with white ceramic-tile floors, handmade koa furniture, Hawaiian quilt bedspreads, and a Hawaiiana theme; the four downstairs rooms all open onto flower-filled private patios. Guests share a fully equipped kitchen and barbecue area, and are welcome to curl up on the living room sofa with a book from the library. The nearest beach is about a 5-minute drive away; tennis courts are nearby. Around the pool is a thatch hut for weekly hula performances, an *imu* pit for luau, and an area that's perfect for Hawaiian weddings.

1579 Lokia St. (off Fleming Rd., north of Lahaina town), Lahaina, HI 96761. © **800/789-6865** or 808/667-2121. Fax 808/667-2120. www.alohahouse.com. 6 units (all with shower only). $150–$170 double (2 people per room). Rates include full breakfast. AE, MC, V. From Hwy. 30, take the Fleming Rd. exit; turn left on Ainakea; after 2 blocks, turn right on Malanai St.; go 3 blocks, and turn left onto Lokia St. **Amenities:** Jacuzzi; outdoor pool. *In room:* A/C, TV/VCR, fridge, hair dryer, Wi-Fi.

Lahaina Inn ★   If you like old hotels that have genuine historic touches, you'll love this place. As in many older hotels, some of these antiques-stuffed rooms are small; if that's a problem for you, ask for a larger unit. All come with private bathrooms and lanais. The best room in the house is no. 7, which overlooks the beach, the town, and the island of Lanai. There's an excellent, though unaffiliated, restaurant in the same building (Lahaina Grill, p. 475) and a bar downstairs.

127 Lahainaluna Rd. (near Front St.), Lahaina, HI 96761. © **800/669-3444** or 808/661-0577. Fax 808/667-9480. www.lahainainn.com. 12 units (most with shower only). $160–$180 double; from $205 suite. AE, MC, V. Next-door parking $7 per day. **Amenities:** Bar; concierge; Wi-Fi. *In room:* A/C, hair dryer.

Lahaina Roads 🏄   If you dream of an oceanfront condo but your budget is on the slim side, here's your place. This condominium complex offers small, reasonably priced units in an older building located in the quiet part of Lahaina, away from the noisy, crowded downtown area, overlooking the boats in the Mala Wharf roadstead (a protected place to anchor near the shore). The compact units have full kitchens and soundproof walls—a real plus. The bedrooms face the road, while the living rooms and lanais overlook the ocean and the island of Lanai. The building is about 35 years old but well maintained. The only drawbacks are no air-conditioning (it can be boiling hot in Lahaina) and no laundry facilities.

1403 Front St. (1 block north of Lahaina Cannery Mall), Lahaina, HI 96761. Reservations c/o Klahani Travel, 159 Halelo St., Lahaina, HI 96761. © **800/669-MAUI** (6284) or 808/667-2712. Fax 808/661-5875. www.klahani.com. 5 units. $150 1-bedroom (sleeps up to 4). 3-night minimum. AE, DISC, MC, V. **Amenities:** Oceanside outdoor pool. *In room:* TV, hair dryer, kitchen.

Wai Ola Vacation Paradise on Maui ★ 🎁   Just 2 blocks from the beach, in a quiet residential development behind a tall concrete wall, lies this lovely retreat, with shade trees, sitting areas, gardens, a pool, an ocean mural, and a range of accommodations. You can book a small studio, a couple of suites inside the home, a separate honeymoon cottage, a one-bedroom apartment, or the entire 5,000-square-foot house. Hosts Kim and Jim Wicker will gladly provide any information you need to make your vacation fabulous. Every unit has a welcome fruit basket when you arrive, plus coffee beans for the coffeemaker. Kim often surprises her guests with "a little something" from her kitchen, like cheesecake or heavenly brownies. You'll also find a deck, barbecue facilities, free wireless Internet, and an outdoor wet bar on the property; a great beach and tennis courts are nearby.

1565 Kuuipo St. (P.O. Box 12580), Lahaina, HI 96761. © **800/492-4652** or 808/661-7901. Fax 808/661-1119. www.waiola.com. 4 units. $169–$235 studio; from $179 suite; from $209 1-bedroom honeymoon cottage for 2. AE, DISC, MC, V. **Amenities:** Jacuzzi; outdoor pool; free use of watersports equipment. *In room:* A/C, TV/DVD/VCR, hair dryer, kitchenette, Wi-Fi.

Inexpensive

Makai Inn 🍃 *Budget travelers, take note:* Here's a small apartment complex located right on the water (okay, no white-sand beach out front, but what do you want at these eye-popping prices?). You can take a 10-minute stroll from this quiet neighborhood to the closest white-sand beach, or walk 20 minutes to the center of Lahaina town. The units are small (400 sq. ft.) but clean and have full kitchens, views of the ocean (from most units), and separate bedrooms. There are no phones or TVs, but there's a public phone by the office. In the middle of the complex is a tropical garden. I recommend the Ginger Hideaway unit, which has windows on two sides overlooking the ocean, for just $156. Families will like the Pineapple Suite, the only two-bedroom unit (800 sq. ft.), also priced at $156.

1415 Front St., Lahaina, HI 96761. ✆ **808/662-3200.** Fax 808/661-9027. www.makaiinn.net. 18 units. $105–$180 double. Extra person $15. AE, MC, V. *In room:* Kitchen, no phone, Wi-Fi.

Penny's Place in Paradise 🏠 No attention to detail has been spared in this Victorian-style bed-and-breakfast, just 50 feet from the water with a fabulous view from the front porch of Molokai and Lanai. Each of the four rooms is uniquely decorated, with themes ranging from contemporary Hawaiian to formal Victorian. Guests are welcome to use the balcony kitchenette (fridge, microwave, toaster, coffeemaker, and ice machine). Only the location is a problem—Penny's is located in a small island bounded by Honoapiilani Highway on one side and busy Front Street on the other. The house is soundproof, and air-conditioning in each room drowns out the noise inside. Penny recently enclosed the outdoor lanai area, so you can enjoy your breakfast without the highway noise.

1440 Front St., Lahaina, HI 96761. ✆ **888/329-0777** or 808/661-1068. Fax 808/667-7102. www. pennysplace.net. 4 units. $98–$147 double. Rates include continental breakfast Mon–Sat. 3-night minimum. DISC, MC, V. *In room:* A/C, TV, DVD, Wi-Fi.

KAANAPALI

If you stay at one of Starwood's Maui properties (Sheraton Maui Resort, Westin Maui Resort & Spa, or the Westin Kaanapali Ocean Resort Villas), there is complimentary shuttle service to Lahaina and back.

Note: You'll find Kaanapali hotels on the "Lahaina & Kaanapali Accommodations & Attractions" map (p. 437).

Very Expensive

Hyatt Regency Maui Resort & Spa ★★ ☺ Spa-goers will love this resort. Hawaii's first oceanfront spa, the Spa Moana, opened here in 2000 with some 20,000 square feet of facilities, including an exercise floor with an ocean view, 15 treatment rooms, sauna and steam rooms, and a huge menu of massages, body treatments, and therapies. Book your treatment before you leave home—this place is popular.

The management has poured some $19 million in renovations into this fantasy resort, the southernmost of the Kaanapali beachfront properties. It certainly has lots of imaginative touches: a collection of exotic species (pink flamingos, unhappy-looking penguins, and an assortment of loud parrots and macaws in the lobby), nine waterfalls, and an eclectic Asian and Pacific art collection. This huge place covers some 40 acres; even if you don't stay here, you might want to walk through the expansive tree-filled atrium and the parklike grounds, which contain a ½-acre outdoor pool with a 150-foot lava-tube slide, a cocktail bar under the falls, a "honeymooners' cave," and a swinging rope bridge. There's even a kids-only pool with its own beach and fountains.

The rooms, spread out among three towers, are pleasantly outfitted with an array of amenities and have very comfortable separate sitting areas and private lanais with eye-popping views. The latest, most comfortable bedding is now standard in every room (you will sleep like a baby in these fluffy feather beds). Two Regency Club floors offer a private concierge, complimentary breakfast, sunset cocktails, and snacks.

Families will appreciate Camp Hyatt, a year-round program offering young guests a range of activities, from "Olympic Games" to a scavenger hunt. There's also a game room for kids with video games, pool, Ping-Pong, and air hockey.

200 Nohea Kai Dr., Lahaina, HI 96761 📞 **800/233-1234** or 808/661-1234. Fax 808/667-4498. www.maui.hyatt.com. 806 units. $311–$485 double; $461–$785 Regency Club double; from $1,000 suite. Extra person $75 ($125 in Regency Club rooms). Children 18 and under stay free in parent's room using existing bedding. Packages available. Daily $15 resort fee for access to Moana Athletic Club, local newspaper delivery, local and toll-free calls, and 1-hr. tennis-court time per day. AE, DC, DISC, MC, V. Valet parking $12; free self-parking. **Amenities:** 5 restaurants (including Son'z Maui at Swan Court, p. 402); 2 bars; babysitting; year-round children's program ($70 full day, $45 half-day per child); concierge; concierge-level rooms; 36-hole golf course; health club w/weight room; Jacuzzi; ½-acre outdoor pool; room service; state-of-the-art spa; 6 tennis courts; watersports equipment rentals. *In room:* A/C, TV, fridge, hair dryer, high-speed Internet access ($10 per day), minibar.

Kaanapali Alii ★★ ☺ These luxurious oceanfront condominiums sit on 8 landscaped acres right on Kaanapali Beach. Kaanapali Alii combines the amenities of a luxury hotel (including a 24 hr. front desk) with the conveniences of a condominium. Each of the one-bedroom (1,500-sq.-ft.) and two-bedroom (1,900-sq.-ft.) units is impeccably decorated and comes with all the comforts of home (fully equipped kitchen, washer/dryer, lanai, two full bathrooms) and then some (room service, daily maid service, complimentary local newspaper) The views from each unit include not only the ocean, but also the island of Lanai in the distance. The beachside recreation area includes a swimming pool, a separate children's pool, a whirlpool, gas barbecue grills and picnic areas, exercise rooms, saunas, and tennis courts. You can even take yoga classes on the lawn.

50 Nohea Kai Dr., Lahaina, HI 96761. 📞 **866/664-6410** or 808/667-1400. Fax 808/661-5686. www.kaanapali-alii.com. 264 units. $295–$480 1-bedroom for 4; $390–$897 2-bedroom for 6. Check for Internet specials or call. AE, MC, V. Free parking. **Amenities:** Poolside cafe; 2 outdoor pools; babysitting; children's program (seasonally at the Westin next door for a fee); concierge; fitness center; nearby golf course; Jacuzzi; room service; 3 lighted tennis courts; watersports equipment rentals. *In room:* A/C, TV/DVD, hair dryer, high-speed Internet ($11 per day), kitchen.

Sheraton Maui Resort and Spa ★★ ☺ Terrific facilities for families and fitness buffs and a premier beach location make this beautiful resort an all-around great place to stay. The grande dame of Kaanapali Beach is built into the side of a cliff on the curving, white-sand cove next to Black Rock (a lava formation that rises 80 ft. above the beach), where there's excellent snorkeling. The resort comprises six buildings of six stories or less, set in well-established tropical gardens. The lobby has been elevated to take advantage of panoramic views, and a lagoonlike pool features lava-rock waterways, wooden bridges, and an open-air whirlpool. Cliff divers swan-dive off the torch-lit lava-rock headland in a traditional sunset ceremony—a sight to see. And the views of Kaanapali Beach, with Lanai and Molokai in the distance, are some of the best around.

The new emphasis is on family appeal, with a class of rooms dedicated to those traveling with kids. Every unit is outfitted with amenities galore, right down to toothbrushes and toothpaste. The kids will love the new 32-inch flatscreen TVs. Other pluses include the Sweet Sleeper Bed, a private balcony, and a "no hassle" check-in policy: The valet takes you and your luggage straight to your room.

2605 Kaanapali Pkwy., Lahaina, HI 96761. ✆ **866/716-8109** or 808/661-0031. Fax 808/661-0458. www.sheraton-maui.com. 510 units. $230–$515 double; from $560 suite. Extra person $80. Children 17 and under stay free in parent's room using existing bedding. Daily $26 resort fee for in-room Internet access, self-parking, local calls, and credit card calls up to 60 min. AE, DC, DISC, MC, V. Valet parking $5; free self-parking. **Amenities:** 2 restaurants; 1 poolside bar; indoor lounge; babysitting; children's program (at the Westin); lobby and poolside concierge; fitness center; 36-hole golf course; Jacuzzi; lagoon-style pool; room service; day spa; 3 tennis courts; watersports equipment rentals; weekly luau. *In room:* A/C, TV, PlayStation, fridge, hair dryer, high-speed Internet access.

The Westin Ka'anapali Ocean Resort Villas ★★ ☺

Not to be confused with the other Westin in Kaanapali (see Westin Maui Resort & Spa, below), this oceanfront condominium project is located at the very serene north end of Kaanapali. It features full kitchens with marble counters, large living rooms, spacious bedrooms, and whirlpool tubs in all guest rooms. The privately owned units are all managed by the Westin Resort people who maintain top standards, from the kitchen appliances to the comfy beds. The units range from 440-square-foot studios with complete kitchen to 960-square-foot one-bedroom units (with pull-out couch for the kids). In addition to all the amenities of the Kaanapali Resort (golf course, tennis courts, restaurant, and shops), the Westin also has three restaurants on property, plus a general store and a fresh food market. And don't miss the terrific Heavenly Spa.

6 Kai Ala Dr., Kaanapali Resort, HI 96761. ✆ **866/716-8112** or 808/667-3200. Fax 808/667-3201. www.westinkaanapali.com. 1,021 units. $380–$770 double studio; $540–$1,184 double 1-bedroom. Extra person $75. Shuttle services to Lahaina. AE, DC, DISC, MC, V. Valet parking $9; self-parking $7. **Amenities:** 3 restaurants; 2 bars; babysitting; children's program; concierge; 36-hole golf course; health club; Jacuzzi; 3 outdoor pools (separate children's pool); room service; sauna, spa; tennis courts. *In room:* A/C, TV, hair dryer, high-speed Internet access, complete kitchen.

Westin Maui Resort & Spa ★★★ ☺

This 758-room hotel recently refurbished its Ocean Tower with new carpeting, wallpaper, furniture, and flatscreen TVs. I love the fabulous pillow-top Westin Heavenly Beds, with your choice of five different pillows. If that doesn't give you sweet dreams, nothing will. The "aquatic playground"—an 87,000-square-foot pool area with five free-form heated pools joined by swim-through grottoes, waterfalls, and a 128-foot-long water slide—sets this resort apart from its peers along lovely Kaanapali Beach. This is the Disney World of water-park resorts, and your kids will be in water-hog heaven. The fantasy theme extends from the estatelike grounds into the interior's public spaces, which are filled with the shriek of tropical birds and the splash of waterfalls. The oversize architecture, requisite colonnade, and $2-million art collection make a pleasing backdrop for all the action. Most of the rooms in the two

11-story towers overlook the aquatic playground, the ocean, and the island of Lanai in the distance. *Note:* The Westin no longer allows smoking in its guest rooms and suites.

2365 Kaanapali Pkwy., Lahaina, HI 96761. © **866/716-8112** or 808/667-2525. Fax 808/661-5764. www.westinmaui.com. 758 units. $329–$800 double; from $800 suite (Starwood members receive a 35% discount). Extra person $75. Daily $25 resort fee for local calls, use of fitness center and spa, a souvenir shopping bag, a 4×6-in. photo, shuttle services to golf and tennis facilities, in-room high-speed Internet access, self-parking, and local newspaper delivery. AE, DC, DISC, MC, V. Valet parking $10; free self-parking. **Amenities:** 4 restaurants; 3 bars; babysitting; bike rental; children's program; concierge; 36-hole golf course; health club and spa; Jacuzzi; 5 free-form outdoor pools; room service; tennis courts; watersports equipment rentals. *In room:* A/C, TV, fridge, hair dryer, high-speed Internet access, minibar.

Expensive

Honua Kai Resort & Spa ★★   This new North Kaanapali Beach resort, on 38 acres facing the ocean, features luxury condominium units, ranging from 590-square-foot studios to 2,800-square-foot three-bedroom units, with top-of-the-line appliances, lanais, and ocean views. The property has a full-service restaurant (Duke's Beach House) plus a deli with takeout. If you are looking for a relaxing vacation for your family, this is the place.

130 Kai Malina Pkwy., North Kaanapali Beach, Hi 96761. © **800/877-7654** or 808/662-2800. Fax 808/667-5544. www.honua-kai-maui.com. 628 units. $175–$250 studio double; $225–$295 1-bedroom (up to 4 people); $350–$525 2-bedroom (up to 6 people); $550–$975 3-bedroom (up to 8 people). AE, DC, DISC, MC, V. $25 daily resort fee for unlimited local calls, fitness center, pool and beach services, resort charging privileges, in-room and resortwide Internet access, daily housekeeping, and parking. **Amenities:** Restaurant; deli; bar; nearby 36-hole golf course; 5 outdoor pools; 5 barbecue areas; nearby tennis courts; whirlpool. *In room:* A/C, TV/DVD, full kitchen.

The Whaler on Kaanapali Beach ★   In the heart of Kaanapali, right on the world-famous beach, lies this oasis of elegance, privacy, and luxury. The relaxing atmosphere strikes you as soon as you enter the open-air lobby, where light reflects off the dazzling koi in the meditative lily pond. No expense has been spared on these gorgeous accommodations; every unit boasts a full kitchen, washer/dryer, marble bathroom, 10-foot beamed ceilings, and blue-tiled lanai—and spectacular views of Kaanapali's gentle waves or the humpback peaks of the West Maui Mountains. Next door is Whalers Village, with numerous restaurants, bars, and shops; there's a barbecue area available to guests; and Kaanapali Golf Club's 36 holes are across the street.

2481 Kaanapali Pkwy. (next to Whalers Village), Lahaina, HI 96761. © **877/997-6667** or 808/661-4861. Fax 808/661-8315. www.resortquesthawaii.com. 360 units. $176–$224 studio double; $198–$283 1-bedroom (up to 4 people); $260–$429 2-bedroom (up to 6 people). Check website for specials. 2-night minimum. AE, DC, DISC, MC, V. Parking $12 per day. **Amenities:** Concierge; refurbished fitness room; Jacuzzi; outdoor pool; Hina Mana Salon & Spa; tennis courts. *In room:* A/C, TV/VCR/DVD, hair dryer, free high-speed Internet access, kitchen.

Moderate

Kaanapali Beach Hotel ★ ✦   It's older and less high-tech than its upscale neighbors, but the Kaanapali Beach Hotel has an irresistible local style and a real Hawaiian warmth that's missing from many other Maui properties. Three low-rise wings, bordering a fabulous stretch of beach, are set around a wide, grassy lawn with coco palms and a whale-shaped pool. The spacious, spotless motel-like rooms are done in wicker and rattan, with Hawaiian-style bedspreads and a lanai facing the courtyard and the beach. The beachfront rooms are separated from the water only by Kaanapali's landscaped walking trail.

Old Hawaii values and customs are always close at hand, and the service is some of the friendliest around. Tiki torches, hula, and Hawaiian music create a festive atmosphere every night in the expansive courtyard. As part of the hotel's extensive Hawaiiana program, you can learn to cut pineapple, weave lauhala, and even dance the hula. The children's program is complimentary. There's also an arts-and-crafts fair 4 days a week, a morning welcome reception Monday through Saturday, and a farewell lei ceremony when you depart.

2525 Kaanapali Pkwy., Lahaina, HI 96761. ☎ **800/262-8450** or 808/661-0011. Fax 808/667-5978. www.kbhmaui.com. 430 units. $225–$355 double; from $295 suite. Extra person $30. Car, golf, bed-and-breakfast, and romance packages available, as well as senior discounts. AE, DC, DISC, MC, V. Valet parking $11; self-parking $9. **Amenities:** 2 restaurants; poolside bar (where you can get a mean piña colada); babysitting; children's program; concierge/guest services; 36-hole golf course nearby; outdoor pool; access to tennis courts; watersports equipment rentals. *In room:* A/C, TV, fridge, high-speed Internet $10 per day.

Outrigger Maui Eldorado ★ ☺ These spacious condominium units—each with full kitchen, washer/dryer, and daily maid service—were built at a time when land in Kaanapali was cheap, contractors took pride in their work, and visitors expected spacious units with views from every window. You'll find it hard to believe that this was one of Kaanapali's first properties in the late 1960s; this first-class choice still looks like new. The Outrigger chain has managed to keep prices reasonable, especially in spring and fall. This is a great choice for families, with its big units, grassy areas that are perfect for running off excess energy, and a beachfront (with beach cabanas and a barbecue area) that's usually safe for swimming. Tennis courts are nearby.

2661 Kekaa Dr., Lahaina, HI 96761. ☎ **888/339-8585** or 808/661-0021. Fax 808/667-7039. www.outrigger.com. 204 units (87 managed by Outrigger). $129–$149 studio double; $169–$179 1-bedroom (up to 4); $199–$219 2-bedroom (up to 6). Numerous packages available, including 5th night free, rental-car deals, senior rates, and more. AE, DC, DISC, MC, V. Parking $7. **Amenities:** Concierge/activities desk; 36-hole golf course; 3 outdoor pools. *In room:* A/C, TV, fridge, hair dryer, high-speed Internet, kitchen.

HONOKOWAI, KAHANA & NAPILI
Expensive
Napili Kai Beach Resort ★★ 🎁 This comfortable oceanfront complex lies just south of the Bay Club restaurant in Kapalua, nestled in a small white-sand cove. The one- and two-story units, with double-hipped Hawaii-style roofs, face a gold-sand beach that's safe for swimming. Many units have a view of the Pacific, with Molokai and Lanai in the distance. Those who prefer air-conditioning should book into the Honolua Building, where you'll get a room set back from the shore around a grassy, parklike lawn and pool. Every unit (except eight hotel rooms) has a fully stocked kitchenette with full-size fridge, cooktop, microwave, toaster oven, washer/dryer, and coffeemaker; some have dishwashers. On-site pluses include daily maid service; two shuffleboard courts; barbecue areas; complimentary morning coffee at the beach pagoda; free afternoon tea; weekly lei

Where to Stay & Dine in West Maui

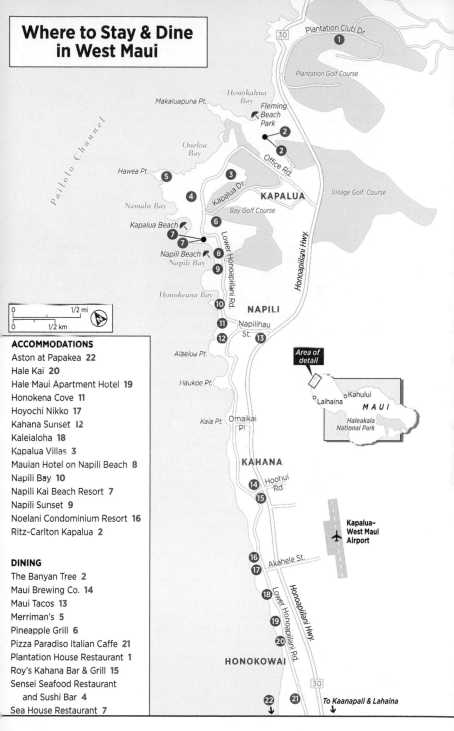

ACCOMMODATIONS

Aston at Papakea **22**
Hale Kai **20**
Hale Maui Apartment Hotel **19**
Honokena Cove **11**
Hoyochi Nikko **17**
Kahana Sunset **12**
Kaleialoha **18**
Kapalua Villas **3**
Mauian Hotel on Napili Beach **8**
Napili Bay **10**
Napili Kai Beach Resort **7**
Napili Sunset **9**
Noelani Condominium Resort **16**
Ritz-Carlton Kapalua **2**

DINING

The Banyan Tree **2**
Maui Brewing Co. **14**
Maui Tacos **13**
Merriman's **5**
Pineapple Grill **6**
Pizza Paradiso Italian Caffe **21**
Plantation House Restaurant **1**
Roy's Kahana Bar & Grill **15**
Sensei Seafood Restaurant
    and Sushi Bar **4**
Sea House Restaurant **7**

making, hula lessons, and horticultural tours; and a free weekly mai tai party. There are three nearby championship golf courses and excellent tennis courts at next-door Kapalua Resort.

5900 Honoapiilani Rd. (at the extreme north end of Napili, next to Kapalua), Lahaina, HI 96761. © **800/367-5030** or 808/669-6271. Fax 808/669-5740. www.napilikai.com. 162 units. $240–$345 hotel room double; $310–$455 studio double (sleeps 3–4); $475–$670 1-bedroom suite (sleeps up to 5); $685–$995 2-bedroom suite (sleeps up to 7). Packages available. AE, DISC, MC, V. **Amenities:** Restaurant (Sea House Restaurant, p. 486); bar; babysitting; free children's activities at Easter, June 15–Aug 31, and at Christmas; concierge; good-size fitness room; 2 18-hole putting greens (w/free use of golf putters); Jacuzzi; 4 outdoor pools; tennis courts nearby (and complimentary use of tennis rackets); complimentary watersports equipment. *In room:* A/C (in most units), TV/DVD, fridge, hair dryer, high-speed Internet access, kitchenette (in most units).

Moderate

Aston at Papakea Resort 🏖 Just a mile down the beach from Kaanapali lie these low-rise buildings, surrounded by manicured, landscaped grounds and ocean views galore. Palm trees and tropical plants dot the property, a putting green wraps around two kidney-shaped pools, and a footbridge arches over a lily pond brimming with carp. Each pool has its own private cabana with sauna, Jacuzzi, and barbecue grills; a poolside shop rents snorkel gear for exploring the offshore reefs. All units have dishwashers, big lanais, and washer/dryers. The studios have pull-down beds to maximize space. Definitely a good value.

3543 Lower Honoapiilani Rd. (in Honokowai), Lahaina, HI 96761. © **877/997-6667** or 808/669-4848. Fax 808/665-0662. www.astonhotels.com. 364 units. $141–$229 studio double; $157–$273 1-bedroom (sleeps up to 4); $187–$395 2-bedroom (sleeps up to 6). AE, DISC, MC, V. **Amenities:** 2 Jacuzzis; 2 outdoor pools; 3 tennis courts; watersports equipment rental. *In room:* A/C, TV/VCR, kitchen, Wi-Fi.

Hale Kai ★ ☺ This small two-story condo complex is ideally located, right on the beach and next door to a county park—a great location for those traveling with kids. Shops, restaurants, and ocean activities are all within a 6-mile radius. The units are older but in excellent shape and come with well-equipped kitchens (with dishwasher, disposal, microwave, and blender) and louvered windows that open to the trade winds. Lots of guests clamor for the oceanfront pool units, but I find the parkview units cooler, and they still have ocean views (upstairs units also have cathedral ceilings). This place fills up fast, so book early.

3691 Lower Honoapiilani Rd. (in Honokowai), Lahaina, HI 96761. © **800/446-7307** or 808/669-6333. Fax 888/831-0122. www.halekai.com. 40 units. $160 1-bedroom double; $210 2-bedroom (sleeps up to 4); $350 3-bedroom (sleeps up to 6). Extra person $10. 5-night minimum. MC, V. **Amenities:** Concierge; outdoor pool. *In room:* TV/VCR, hair dryer, high-speed Internet access, kitchen.

Honokeana Cove 🏖 These large, secluded units—cozily set around a pool in a lush tropical setting—have fabulous views of Honokeana Cove. The beach here isn't sandy (it's composed of smooth round rocks), but the water just offshore is excellent for snorkeling (turtles have been spotted here) and for whale-watching in winter. The well-appointed units all come with full kitchens and lanais. Amenities include barbecues and deck chairs. The management holds weekly pupu parties so you can meet the other guests. All in all, a well-priced option in an expensive neighborhood.

5255 Lower Honoapiilani Rd. (in Napili), Lahaina, HI 96761. ☏ **800/237-4948** or 808/669-6441. Fax 808/669-8777. www.honokeana-cove.com. 33 units. $189–$205 1-bedroom; $218–$305 2-bedroom (sleeps up to 4); $310 3-bedroom. Extra person $10–$15. 3- to 5-night minimum (Christmas/New Years 7- to 14-night). MC, V. **Amenities:** Concierge; outdoor pool. *In room:* TV/VCR, kitchen, Wi-Fi ($7 per day and $3 setup).

Kahana Sunset ★★ ☺   Lying in the crook of a sharp horseshoe curve on Lower Honoapiilani Road is this series of wooden condo units, stair-stepping down the side of a hill to a postcard-perfect white-sand beach. The unique location, nestled between the coastline and the road above, makes this a very private place to stay. In the midst of the buildings sits a grassy lawn with a small pool and Jacuzzi; down by the sandy beach are gazebos and picnic areas. The units feature full kitchens (complete with dishwashers), washer/dryers, large lanais with terrific views, sleeper sofas, and daily maid service. This is a great complex for families: The beach is safe for swimming, the grassy area is away from traffic, there's a barbecue area, and the units are roomy. The two-bedroom units have parking just outside.

4909 Lower Honoapiilani Hwy. (at the northern end of Kahana, almost in Napili), Lahaina, HI 96761. Reservations c/o Premier Properties, P.O. Box 10219, Lahaina, HI 96761. ☏ **800/669-1488** or 808/669-8700. Fax 808/669-4466. www.kahanasunset.com. 79 units. $165–$290 1-bedroom (sleeps up to 4); $225–$465 2-bedroom (sleeps up to 6). 2-night minimum. AE, MC, V. From Hwy. 30, turn makai (toward the ocean) at the Napili Plaza (Napilihau St.), and then left on Lower Honoapiilani Rd. **Amenities:** Concierge; 2 outdoor pools (1 for children). *In room:* TV/DVD/VCR, high-speed Internet access, kitchen (in some units).

Mauian Hotel on Napili Beach ★   The Mauian is perched above a beautiful half-mile-long white-sand beach with great swimming and snorkeling; there's a pool with lounges, umbrellas, and tables on the sun deck; and the verdant grounds burst with tropical color. The rooms feature hardwood floors, Indonesian-style furniture, and big lanais with great views. Thoughtful touches include fresh flowers, plus chilled champagne for guests celebrating a special occasion. There are no phones or TVs in the rooms (this place really is about getting away from it all), but the large *ohana* (family) room does have a TV with a VCR and an extensive library if you need entertainment. There's a barbecue area, great restaurants are just a 5-minute walk away, and Kapalua Resort is up the street. The nightly sunsets off the beach are spectacular.

5441 Lower Honoapiilani Rd. (in Napili), Lahaina, HI 96761. ☏ **800/367-5034** or 808/669-6205. Fax 808/669-0129. www.mauian.com. 44 units. $150–$165 double room; $165–$280 double studio (sleeps up to 4). Extra person $10. Children 4 and under stay free in parent's room. AE, DISC, MC, V. **Amenities:** Golf course nearby; outdoor pool; shuffleboard court; tennis courts nearby; free Wi-Fi in family room. *In room:* Fridge, kitchen (most units), no phone.

Napili Sunset 🍃   Housed in three buildings (two on the ocean, one across the street) and located just down the street from Napili Bay (see below), these clean, older, well-maintained units offer good value. At first glance, the plain two-story structures don't look like much, but the location, the bargain prices, and the friendly staff are the real hidden treasures here. In addition to daily maid service, the units all have full kitchens (with dishwashers), ceiling fans (no air-conditioning), sofa beds, small dining rooms, and small bedrooms. The studio units are located in the building off the beach and a few steps up a slight hill; they're a good size, with a full kitchen and either a sofa bed or a Murphy bed, and they overlook the small pool and garden. The one- and two-bedroom units are all on the beach (the downstairs units have lanais that lead right to the sand). The staff makes sure each unit has the basics (paper towels, dishwasher soap, coffee filters, condiments) to get your stay off to a good start. There are restaurants within walking distance. The beach—one of Maui's best—can get a little crowded.

46 Hui Rd. (in Napili), Lahaina, HI 96761. © **800/447-9229** or 808/669-8083. Fax 808/669-2730. www.napilisunset.com. 42 units. $135–$398 studio double, $239–$310 1-bedroom double (sleeps 5–6), $245–$419 2-bedroom (sleeps up to 7). Extra person $15. Children 2 and under stay free in parent's room. Check website for specials. MC, V. **Amenities:** Small outdoor pool. *In room:* TV, kitchen, Wi-Fi.

Noelani Condominium Resort ★★ ☺ This oceanfront condo is a great value, whether you stay in a studio or a three-bedroom unit (ideal for large families). Everything is first class, from the furnishings to the oceanfront location. Though it's on the water, there's no sandy beach here (despite the photos posted on the website)—but right next door is a sandy cove at the county park. There's good snorkeling off the cove, which is frequented by spinner dolphins and turtles in summer and humpback whales in winter. All units feature complete kitchens, entertainment centers, and spectacular views (all except the studio units also have their own washer/dryers and dishwashers). My favorites are in the Anthurium Building, where the condos have oceanfront lanais just 20 feet from the water. Frugal travelers will love the deluxe studios in the Orchid Building, with great ocean views. Guests are invited to a continental breakfast orientation on their first day and mai tai parties at night; there are also oceanfront barbecue grills for guest use. *Money-saving tip:* Save 5% by booking online.

4095 Lower Honoapiilani Rd. (in Kahana), Lahaina, HI 96761. © **800/367-6030** or 808/669-8374. Fax 808/669-7904. www.noelani-condo-resort.com. 45 units. $125–$175 studio double; $175–$197 1-bedroom (sleeps up to 4); $245–$290 2-bedroom (sleeps up to 6); $330–$357 3-bedroom (sleeps up to 8). Extra person $20. Children 17 and under stay free in parent's room. Packages for honeymooners, seniors, and AAA members available. Rates include continental breakfast on 1st morning. 3-night minimum. AE, MC, V. **Amenities:** Concierge; access to nearby health club; oceanfront Jacuzzi; 2 freshwater pools (1 heated for night swimming). *In room:* TV/VCR, hair dryer, high-speed Internet access, kitchen.

Inexpensive

In addition to the choices below, consider **Hale Maui Apartment Hotel** (© **808/669-6312;** fax 808/669-1302; www.maui.net/~halemaui), a wonderful tiny place run by Hans and Eva Zimmerman and their daughter, Marika, whose spirit is 100% aloha. The one-bedroom suites, which were remodeled with new furniture in 2008, start at around $115 for a double, and come with ceiling fans, private lanais, and complete kitchens. There's no pool, but a private path leads to a great swimming beach.

Another option is **Hoyochi Nikko,** 3901 Lower Honoapiilani Rd. (in Honokowai), Lahaina, HI 96761 (© **800/487-6002,** ext. 1, or 808/669-0089, ext. 1; fax 808/669-3937; www.mauilodging.com), which has 17 older (but well-maintained) one-bedroom units (and a few one-bedroom units with separate loft) sharing 180 feet of oceanfront ($130–$190 one-bedroom double). Surcharge for less than 10 nights.

Kaleialoha   This condo complex for the budget-minded has recently been upgraded, with new paint, bedspreads, and drapes in each apartment. Each one-bedroom unit has a sofa bed in the living room, which allows you to comfortably sleep four. All of the Island-style units feature fully equipped kitchens, with everything from dishwashers to washer/dryers (the only thing not supplied is beach towels, so bring your own). There's great ocean swimming just off the rock wall (no sandy beach); a protective reef mows waves down and allows even timid swimmers to relax.

3785 Lower Honoapiilani Rd. (in Honokowai), Lahaina, HI 96761. (℃ **800/222-8688** or 808/669-8197. Fax 808/669-2502. www.mauicondosoceanfront.com. 18 units. $99–$250 1-bedroom double. Extra person $10. Children 3 and under stay free in parent's room. Cleaning fee $95 for less than 7-night stay. 3- to 5-night minimum. DISC, MC, V. **Amenities:** Concierge; outdoor pool. *In room:* TV/DVD, high-speed Internet access, kitchen.

Napili Bay 🏨   One of Maui's best secret bargains is this small two-story complex right on Napili's beautiful half-mile white-sand beach. It's perfect for a romantic getaway: The atmosphere is comfortable and relaxing, the ocean lulls you to sleep at night, and birdsong wakes you in the morning. The beach here is one of the best on the coast, with great swimming and snorkeling—people staying at much more expensive resorts down the road frequently come here. The studio apartments are definitely small, but they pack in everything you need to feel at home, from a full kitchen to a comfortable queen-size bed, plus a roomy lanai that's great for watching the sun set over the Pacific. There's no air-conditioning, but louvered windows and ceiling fans keep the units fairly cool during the day. There are lots of restaurants and a convenience store within walking distance, and you're about 10 to 15 minutes away from Lahaina and some great golf courses.

33 Hui Dr. (off Lower Honoapiilani Hwy., in Napili), Lahaina, HI 96761. (℃ **877/877-5758** or 808/930/1830. www.alohacondos.com. 28 units. $120–$325 double. Cleaning fee $85–$110. 1- to 3-night minimum. AE, DC, MC, V. *In room:* TV, high-speed Internet access (most units), kitchen.

KAPALUA

If you're interested in a luxurious condo or town house, consider **Kapalua Villas** ((℃ **800/545-0018** or 808/669-8088; www.kapaluavillas.com). The palatial units dotting the oceanfront cliffs and fairways of this idyllic coast are a (relative) bargain, especially if you're traveling with a group. In 2009 the locally respected Outrigger chain of resorts took over the management of this property. The one-bedroom condos go for $299 to $449; two-bedrooms for $399 to $659; three-bedrooms from $599, plus a $25 daily recreation fee (which covers parking; unlimited local, national, and international calls; high-speed Internet access; use of in-villa safe; delivery of newspaper Mon–Fri; use of computer at Kapalua Resort Center; access to Ritz-Carlton pools and pool towels; access to Ritz Carlton Spa; preferred guest rates at the Kapalua Golf Courses and tennis courts; and resortwide charging privileges). Numerous package deals (which include golf, tennis, honeymoon amenities, and car) can save you even more money.

   Note: You'll find the following hotels on the "Where to Stay & Dine in West Maui" map (p. 445).

Very Expensive

Ritz-Carlton Kapalua ★★★ ☺ This Ritz is a complete universe, one of those resorts where you can happily sit by the ocean with a book for 2 whole weeks and never leave the grounds. It rises proudly on a knoll, in a singularly spectacular setting between the rainforest and the sea. During construction, the burial sites of hundreds of ancient Hawaiians were discovered in the sand, so the hotel was moved inland to avoid disrupting the graves. The setback gives the hotel a commanding view of Molokai.

In 2008, the Ritz reopened after an extensive $160-million renovation that transformed the place into an even more elegant property, with a focus on a Hawaiian (vs. the former European) theme. All guest rooms now have the latest technology, including flatscreen TVs, DVD players, iPod docking stations, and wireless Internet access (included in the resort fee). Marble bathrooms and private lanais are other nice touches. The penthouse floor has been converted into Residential Suites (with kitchens, living rooms, and separate bedrooms), available for guests. If you can afford it, stay on the **Club Level** ★★★—it offers the best amenities in the state, from French-roast coffee in the morning to a buffet at lunch, from cookies in the afternoon to pupu and drinks at sunset.

Other transformations include upgrades to the signature 10,000-square-foot, three-tiered pool; a new children's pool; an Ambassadors of the Environment Education Center (by Jean-Michel Cousteau); and a new 17,500-square-foot Waihua Spa, with 15 treatment rooms, saunas, whirlpool with lava-stone walls, and fitness center. Your children will enjoy the Ritz Kids program's wide variety of activities, plus the weekly "Ritz Kids Night Out" that allows parents to spend a quiet evening alone.

1 Ritz-Carlton Dr., Kapalua, HI 96761. ✆ **800/262-8440** or 808/669-6200. Fax 808/669-1566. www.ritzcarlton.com. 463 units. $299–$750 double; $595–$895 Club Level double; from $545 suite; from $995 Club Level suite; residential suites from $545 1-bedroom, $875 2-bedroom. Extra person $50 ($150 in Club Level rooms). Wedding/honeymoon, golf, and other packages available. Daily $20 resort fee for use of fitness center, steam room, and sauna; selected wellness classes; Aloha Friday festivities; cultural-history tours; in-room Wi-Fi; self-parking; resort shuttle service; morning coffee at the Lobby Lounge; preferred tee times; 9-hole putting green; tennis and basketball courts; and games of boccie ball on the lawn. AE, DC, DISC, MC, V. Valet parking $18; free self-parking. **Amenities:** 6 restaurants (including the Banyan Tree, p. 487); 4 bars (including 1 serving drinks and light fare next to the beach); babysitting; bike rentals; children's program; concierge; concierge-level rooms (some of Hawaii's best); fitness room; access to the Kapalua Resort's 3 championship golf courses (each w/its own pro shop), golf academy, and deluxe tennis complex; 2 outdoor hot tubs; outdoor pool; room service; spa; watersports equipment rentals. *In room:* A/C, TV, hair dryer, Wi-Fi.

South Maui

I recommend two booking agencies that rent a host of condominiums and vacation homes in the Kihei/Wailea/Maalaea area: **Kihei Maui Vacations** (✆ **800/541-6284** or 808/879-7581; www.kmvmaui.com) and **Condominium Rentals Hawaii** (✆ **800/367-5242** or 808/879-2778; www.crhmaui.com).

KIHEI

Alert: A new trend has sprouted up in South Maui, especially in the Kihei area—properties (especially condominiums) have started adding a booking fee ($25–$35). Most of the time, this is nonrefundable. The reasons for this fee seems to

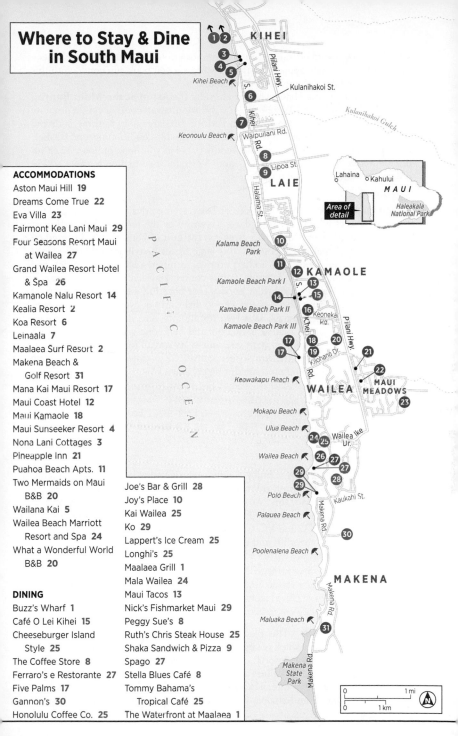

Where to Stay & Dine in South Maui

ACCOMMODATIONS

Aston Maui Hill **19**
Dreams Come True **22**
Eva Villa **23**
Fairmont Kea Lani Maui **29**
Four Seasons Resort Maui at Wailea **27**
Grand Wailea Resort Hotel & Spa **26**
Kamaole Nalu Resort **14**
Kealia Resort **2**
Koa Resort **6**
Leinaala **7**
Maalaea Surf Resort **2**
Makena Beach & Golf Resort **31**
Mana Kai Maui Resort **17**
Maui Coast Hotel **12**
Maui Kamaole **18**
Maui Sunseeker Resort **4**
Nona Lani Cottages **3**
Pineapple Inn **21**
Puahoa Beach Apts. **11**
Two Mermaids on Maui B&B **20**
Wailana Kai **5**
Wailea Beach Marriott Resort and Spa **24**
What a Wonderful World B&B **20**

DINING

Buzz's Wharf **1**
Café O Lei Kihei **15**
Cheeseburger Island Style **25**
The Coffee Store **8**
Ferraro's e Restorante **27**
Five Palms **17**
Gannon's **30**
Honolulu Coffee Co. **25**
Joe's Bar & Grill **28**
Joy's Place **10**
Kai Wailea **25**
Ko **29**
Lappert's Ice Cream **25**
Longhi's **25**
Maalaea Grill **1**
Mala Wailea **24**
Maui Tacos **13**
Nick's Fishmarket Maui **29**
Peggy Sue's **8**
Ruth's Chris Steak House **25**
Shaka Sandwich & Pizza **9**
Spago **27**
Stella Blues Café **8**
Tommy Bahama's Tropical Café **25**
The Waterfront at Maalaea **1**

451

stem from depressed economy (oh great, times are bad so charge your clients a new fee!). I am totally opposed to this new fee—if you book at a condo with this fee and are unhappy about it, let them know.

In addition to the choices below, consider the **Aston at the Maui Banyan** (✆ **877/997-6667** or 808/924-2924; www.astonhawaii.com), a condo property across the street from Kamaole Beach Park II. The large one- to three-bedroom units are very nicely done and feature full kitchens, air-conditioning, and washer/ dryers. Rates start at $189 for hotel rooms ($171 if you book online), $223 for one-bedroom units ($200 online), and $280 for two-bedroom units ($252 online); be sure to ask about packages.

Expensive

Aston Maui Hill ★   If you can't decide between the privacy of a condo and the conveniences of a hotel, try this place. Managed by the respected ResortQuest (formerly Aston) chain, Maui Hill gives you the best of both worlds. Located on a hill above the heat of Kihei town, this large Spanish-style resort (with stucco buildings, red-tile roofs, and arched entries) combines all the amenities and activities of a hotel—pool, hot tub, tennis courts, Hawaiiana classes, maid service, and more—with large luxury condos that have full kitchens and plenty of privacy. Nearly all units have ocean views, dishwashers, washer/dryers, queen-size sofa beds, and big lanais. Beaches, restaurants, and shops are within easy walking distance; a golf course is nearby; and barbecue grills are provided for guests' use. The management here goes out of its way to make sure your stay is perfect. *Note:* Some of the units have converted to timeshares, although no timeshare salesperson bothered me during my stay.

2881 S. Kihei Rd. (across from Kamaole Park III, btw. Keonekai St. and Kilohana Dr.), Kihei, HI 96753. ✆ **877/997-6667** or 808/879-6321. Fax 808/879-8945. www.astonhotels.com. 140 units. $240–$255 1-bedroom ($180–$191 if you book online); $289–$320 2-bedroom (from $217 online); $479 3-bedroom (from $431 online). AE, DC, DISC, MC, V. **Amenities:** Concierge; putting green; Jacuzzi; outdoor pool; tennis courts. *In room:* A/C, TV/VCR, hair dryer, high-speed Internet access, kitchen.

Maalaea Surf Resort ★   Enjoy a quiet, relaxing vacation on this well-landscaped property, with a beautiful white-sand beach right outside. Located at the quiet end of Kihei Road, this two-story complex sprawls across 5 acres of lush tropical gardens. The luxury town houses all have ocean views, big kitchens (with dishwashers), cable TV, and VCRs. Amenities include maid service (Mon–Sat), shuffleboard, barbecue grills, and discounts on tee times at nearby golf courses; restaurants and shops are within a 5-minute drive.

12 S. Kihei Rd. (at S. Kihei Rd. and Hwy. 350), Kihei, HI 96753. ✆ **800/423-7953** or 808/879-1267. Fax 808/874-2884. www.maalaeasurfresort.com. 34 units. $285–$335 1-bedroom (sleeps up to 4); $380–$450 2-bedroom (sleeps up to 6). MC, V. **Amenities:** Concierge; 2 outdoor pools; 2 tennis courts. *In room:* A/C, TV/VCR/DVD, hair dryer, high-speed Internet access, kitchen.

Maui Coast Hotel ★   This place stands out as one of the only moderately priced hotels in Kihei (which is largely full of affordable condo complexes rather than traditional hotels or resorts). That's big news—especially on Maui, where luxury abounds. The Extra Value Package gives you a rental car for just a few dollars more than your room rate. The other chief advantage of this hotel is its location, about a block from Kamaole Beach Park I, with plenty of bars, restaurants, and shopping within walking distance, plus a golf course nearby. Guest rooms offer extras such as sitting areas, whirlpool tubs, ceiling fans, and private lanais.

2259 S. Kihei Rd. (1 block from Kamaole Beach Park I), Kihei, HI 96753. ℂ **800/895-6284** or 808/874-6284. Fax 808/875-4731. www.mauicoasthotel.com. 265 units. $179 double; from $199 suite; $245 1-bedroom (sleeps up to 4). Children 17 and under stay free in parent's room using existing bedding. Packages available. Rollaway bed $30. AE, DC, DISC, MC, V. **Amenities:** Restaurant; pool bar w/nightly entertainment; concierge; fitness room; outdoor pool (plus children's wading pool); room service; 2 lighted tennis courts. *In room:* A/C, TV, fridge, hair dryer, high-speed Internet access ($10).

Moderate

The **Kihei Beach Resorts,** 36 S. Kihei Rd., Kihei, HI 96753 (ℂ **800/367-6034** or 808/879-2744; fax 808/875-0306; www.kiheibeachresort.com), has spacious condos right on the beach. The downside is the constant traffic noise from Kihei Road. Rates are $155 to $200 for a one-bedroom double, $260 to $295 for a two-bedroom (sleeps four); there's a 4- to 10-night minimum and a $10 charge per extra person.

Eva Villa ★ ★ 🏠 True to its name, this three-unit bed-and-breakfast is located on a ½ acre of lushly landscaped property at the top of the Maui Meadows subdivision. From the rooftop viewing lanai, guests have a spectacular view of the sunset behind Kahoolawe and Lanai, and in the distance the West Maui Mountains complete the 360-degree view. Hosts Rick and Dale Pounds have done everything to make this one of Maui's classiest vacation rentals. From the continental breakfast stocked in the unit's kitchen (fresh fruit, juice, bread, muffins, jam, coffee, and tea) to the decor of the suites, from the heated pool and Jacuzzi to the individual barbecue facilities, this is a great place to stay. The location couldn't be better—just a few minutes' drive to Kihei's sunny beaches, restaurants in Kihei and Wailea, six golf courses, and plenty of tennis and shopping. All units are a roomy 600 square feet. The separate cottage has a living room, full kitchen, bedroom, and washer/dryer; the poolside studio is a one-room unit with a huge kitchen; and the poolside suite has two bedrooms and a kitchenette. You can't go wrong booking here.

815 Kumulani Dr., Kihei, HI 96753. ℂ **800/884-1845** or 808/874-6407. Fax 808/874-6407. www.mauibnb.com. 3 units. $135–$175 double. 4-night minimum. No credit cards. **Amenities:** Barbeque grill, Jacuzzi; heated outdoor pool. *In room:* AC, TV/DVD, CD player, kitchen or kitchenette, Wi-Fi.

Kamaole Nalu Resort This six-story condominium complex is located between two beach parks, Kamaole I and Kamaole II, and right across the street from a shopping complex. Units have fabulous ocean views, large living rooms, and private lanais; the kitchens are a bit small but come fully equipped. I recommend no. 306 for its wonderful bird's-eye view. The property also has an oceanside pool and great barbecue facilities. Restaurants, bars, a golf course, and tennis courts are nearby; shopping is across the street. *Warning:* Because the building is right on Kihei Road, it can be noisy.

2450 S. Kihei Rd. (btw. Kanani and Keonekai roads, next to Kamaole Beach Park II), Kihei, HI 96753. ℂ **800/767-1497** or 808/879-1006. Fax 808/879-8693. www.kamaolenalu.com. 28 units. High season $250–$350 double; low season $190–$275 double. Extra person $20. Children 12 and under stay free in parent's room using existing bedding. $30 booking fee. 5-night minimum (2 weeks over Christmas and New Year's). MC, V. **Amenities:** Outdoor pool. *In room:* TV, hair dryer, high-speed Internet access, kitchen.

Kealia Resort 🐚   This oceanfront property at the northern end of Kihei is well maintained and nicely furnished—and the prices are excellent. As tempting as the lower-priced units may sound, don't give in: They face noisy Kihei Road and are near a major junction, so big trucks downshifting can be especially loud at night. Instead, go for one of the oceanview units, which all have full kitchens and private lanais. The grounds face a 5-mile stretch of white-sand beach. The management goes out of its way to provide opportunities for guests to meet; social gatherings include free coffee-and-doughnut get-togethers every Friday morning and pupu parties on Wednesdays.

191 N. Kihei Rd. (north of Hwy. 31, at the Maalaea end of Kihei), Kihei, HI 96753. ✆ **800/265-0686** or 808/280-1192. Fax 808/875-1540. www.kealiaresort.com. 51 units. $115–$130 studio double; $150–$190 1-bedroom double; $215–$250 2-bedroom (sleeps up to 4). Children 12 and under stay free in parent's room. $25 reservation fee. 4-night minimum (10 nights Dec. 15–Jan. 10). Cleaning fees $65–$95. AE, MC, V. **Amenities:** Outdoor pool. *In room:* TV, hair dryer, high-speed Internet access (some units), kitchen.

Leinaala ★   From Kihei Road, you can't see Leinaala amid the jumble of buildings, but this oceanfront boutique condo offers excellent accommodations at moderate prices. The building is set back from the water, with a county park—an oasis of green grass and tennis courts—in between. A golf course is nearby. The units are compact but filled with everything you need: a full kitchen, sofa bed, and oceanview lanai. (Hideaway beds are available if you need one.)

998 S. Kihei Rd., Kihei, HI 96753. ✆ **800/822-4409.** Fax 808/874-6144. www.mauicondo.com. 24 units. $132–$190 1-bedroom double; $168–$240 2-bedroom (sleeps up to 4). Check for Internet specials. $35 reservation fee. 4-night minimum. AE, MC, V. **Amenities:** Outdoor pool. *In room:* A/C, TV, high-speed Internet access ($10), kitchen.

Mana Kai Maui Resort ★ ☺   This eight-story complex, situated on a beautiful white-sand cove, is an unusual combination of hotel and condominium. The hotel rooms, which account for half of the total number of units, are small but nicely furnished. Families should consider the condo units, which feature full kitchens and open living rooms with sliding-glass doors that lead to small lanais overlooking the sandy beach and ocean. The building is more than 30 years old, and although some units are totally upgraded and look great, some still have that dreaded avocado-green carpet—but they're all clean and comfortable. One of the best snorkeling beaches on the coast is just steps away; a golf course and tennis courts are nearby.

2960 S. Kihei Rd. (btw. Kilohana and Keonekai roads, at the Wailea end of Kihei), Kihei, HI 96753. ✆ **800/367-5242** or 808/879-2778. Fax 808/879-7825. www.crhmaui.com. 105 units. $125–$185 hotel room double; $205–$365 1-bedroom (sleeps up to 4); $240–$430 2-bedroom (sleeps up to 6). Extra person $12. $30 reservation fee. 4-night minimum at Christmas. AE, MC, V. **Amenities:** Restaurant (Five Palms, p. 489); bar; concierge; outdoor pool. *In room:* A/C (in hotel rooms only), TV, fridge, high-speed Internet access (in condo units), kitchen (in condo units).

Maui Kamaole   You'll find this condo complex right across the street from the Kihei Public Boat Ramp and beautiful Kamaole Beach Park III, which is great for swimming, snorkeling, and beachcombing. Each roomy, fully furnished unit comes with a private lanai, two bathrooms (even in the one-bedroom units), and an all-electric kitchen. The one-bedroom units—which can comfortably accommodate four—are quite a deal, especially if you're traveling in low season. The grounds are nicely landscaped and offer barbecues. Restaurants and bars are within walking distance; a golf course and tennis courts are also nearby.

2777 S. Kihei Rd. (btw. Keonekai and Kilohana roads, at the Wailea end of Kihei), Kihei, HI 96753. © **800/822-4409** or 808/879-5445. Fax 808/874-6144. www.mauikamaole.com. 62 out of the 210 units are in the rental pool. $205–$280 1-bedroom (sleeps up to 4); $265–$350 2-bedroom (sleeps up to 6). $35 reservation fee. ($100 cleaning fee for less than 4 nights). AE, MC, V. **Amenities:** Jacuzzi; 2 outdoor pools; tennis courts. *In room:* A/C, TV, fridge (in some units), high-speed Internet access ($10), kitchen.

Maui Sunseeker 🏳️‍🌈 This former budget property, located just across the street from a terrific white-sand beach, has a new management team that "welcomes all, but caters primarily to gay and lesbian travelers." They've spiffed up the studio and one-bedroom units by adding custom furniture, air-conditioning, and other amenities not usually seen at small properties (like high-speed Internet access and concierge services). The redone units have been tastefully decorated. The one-bedrooms, which have a pullout sofa in the living room and new appliances in the kitchen, are a deal during low season. All units have private ocean-view lanais and the beach just a few steps away, plus there's a gas barbecue for guests' use. The new owners of Maui Sunseeker also bought the apartment complex next door. They revamped everything, put slate in the bathrooms and new tile on the floor, bought new furniture, and repainted. The units are small, but the lanais are large and the price is right—and there's even a rooftop lanai where you can sit in the hot tub and enjoy great ocean views.

551 S. Kihei Rd. (P.O. Box 276), Kihei, HI 96753. © **800/532-6284** or 808/879-1261. Fax 808/874-3877. www.mauisunseeker.com. 16 units. $105–$185 hotel room double; $110–$195 studio double; $125–$235 junior suite double; $145–$215 premium junior suite double; $145–$265 1-bedroom double; $275–$395 penthouse apt. Extra person $45. AE, DISC, MC, V. **Amenities:** Concierge; hot tub. *In room:* A/C, TV/VCR, hair dryer, kitchen or kitchenette, free Wi-Fi.

Inexpensive

In addition to the choices below, also check out **Luana Kai Resort,** 940 S. Kihei Rd., Kihei, HI 96753 (© **800/669-1127** or 808/879-1268; fax 808/879-1455; www.luanakai.com). This older condo complex has 113 units ($109–$179 one-bedroom; $129–$229 two-bedroom; $249–$299 three-bedroom; 4- to 7-night minimum).

Kihei Kai Resort, 61 N. Kihei Rd., Kihei, HI 96753 (© **888/778-7717** or 808/891-0780; fax 808/891-9403; www.kiheikai.com), has one-bedroom apartments ($125–$190 double; 4- to 7-night minimum) that are ideal for families.

Dreams Come True on Maui ✦ This bed-and-breakfast (where "you are never just renting a room") was a dream come true for hosts Tom Croly and Denise McKinnon, who, after several years of vacationing in Maui, opened this three-unit property in 2002. It's centrally located in the Maui Meadows subdivision, just a few minutes' drive to golf courses, tennis courts, white-sand beaches, shopping, and restaurants in Kihei and Wailea. The one-bedroom oceanview cottage has its own gourmet kitchen, two TVs, a washer/dryer, a computer with high-speed Internet access, and wraparound decks. Also available are two rooms in the house (one with king-size bed, one with queen-size), each with TV, private entrance, kitchenette, use of washer/dryer, and lots of other amenities not usually found in B&Bs. Guests are invited to use the centrally located oceanview deck; the house living room, which has a computer with high-speed Internet connection; and an outdoor cooking area with barbecue grill, sink, and microwave. Every guest is given personal concierge treatment, from the lowdown on good snorkeling to a tour of the property. In the evenings, Tom shows movies on an 8-foot-wide movie screen and frequently helps guests transfer their digital images to a CD so they can go out and shoot more photos of Maui. The owners recently acquired a one- and two-bedroom condo, across the street from the beach, which they rent for $135 to $169 a night.

3259 Akala Dr., Kihei, HI 96753. *℃* **877/782-9628** or 808/879-7099. Fax 808/879-7099. www. dreamscometrueonmaui.com. 3 units. $89–$109 room double (3- to 4-night minimum); $135–$169 cottage double (6-night minimum; extra person $15). Room rates include continental breakfast (except in cottage). MC, V. **Amenities:** Concierge service. *In room:* A/C ($3–$5 per day), TV/VCR, CD player, fridge, hair dryer, kitchen or kitchenette.

Koa Resort ★ ☺ Located just across the street from the ocean, Koa Resort comprises five two-story wooden buildings on more than 5½ acres of landscaped grounds. The spacious, privately owned one-, two-, and three-bedroom units are decorated with care and come fully equipped, right down to the dishwasher and disposal in the kitchens. The larger condos have both showers and tubs; the smaller units have showers only. All feature large lanais, ceiling fans, and washer/dryers. For maximum peace and quiet, ask for a unit far from Kihei Road. Bars, restaurants, and a golf course are nearby.

811 S. Kihei Rd. (btw. Kulanihakoi St. and Namauu Place), Kihei, HI 96753. Reservations c/o Bello Realty, P.O. Box 1776, Kihei, HI 96753. *℃* **800/541-3060** or 808/879-3328. Fax 808/875-1483. www.bellomaui.com. 54 units (some with shower only). High season $115–$120 1-bedroom, $120–$145 2-bedroom, $180–$275 3-bedroom; low season $99 1-bedroom, $100–$125 2-bedroom, $160–$240 3-bedroom. MC, V. **Amenities:** 18-hole putting green; Jacuzzi; outdoor pool; 2 tennis courts. *In room:* TV, high-speed Internet access (most units), kitchen.

Nona Lani Cottages ★ 🎁 Picture this: a grassy expanse dotted with eight cottages tucked among palm, fruit, and sweet-smelling flower trees, right across the street from a white-sand beach. This is one of the great hidden deals in Kihei. The cottages are tiny but probably contain everything you'll need: a small but complete kitchen, twin beds that double as couches in the living room, a separate bedroom with a queen-size bed, and a lanai with table and chairs. The cottages were renovated in 2002 with new ceramic flooring. The real attraction, however, is the garden setting next to the beach. There are no phones in the cabins, but there's a public one by the registration/check-in area. There's also a barbecue area. Your hosts, the industrious Kong family, also run Happy Valley Hale (p. 435), hostel accommodations on the other side of the island in Happy Valley, next to Wailuku.

455 S. Kihei Rd. (just south of Hwy. 31), P.O. Box 655, Kihei, HI 96753. *℃* **800/733-2688** or 808/879-2497. www.nonalanicottages.com. 11 units. $120–$150 cottage double. Extra person $15. 7-night minimum in high season. No credit cards. *In room:* A/C, TV, kitchen, no phone.

Pineapple Inn Maui ★★ 🎁 Just opened in late 2004, this charming inn (four rooms, plus a two-bedroom cottage) is not only an exquisite find, but also a terrific value. Located in the residential Maui Meadows area, with panoramic ocean views, the two-story inn is expertly landscaped, with a lily pond in the front and a giant saltwater pool and Jacuzzi overlooking the ocean. Each of the expertly decorated, soundproof rooms (you won't hear the traffic from nearby Piilani Hwy.) has a private lanai with incredible view, plus a small kitchenette (fridge, coffeemaker, toaster, and microwave) that's stocked with juice, pastries, and drinks on your arrival. There's also a darling two-bedroom, one-bathroom cottage (wood floors, beautiful artwork) that's landscaped for maximum privacy and has a full kitchen (even a dishwasher), separate bedrooms, phone and answering machine, and private lanai. There's a barbecue area for guests.

3170 Akala Dr., Kihei, HI 96753. ℂ **877/212-MAUI** (6284) or 808/298-4403. www.pineappleinn maui.com. 5 units. $139–$149 double; $215 cottage for 4. 3-night minimum for rooms, 6-night minimum for cottage. No credit cards. **Amenities:** Jacuzzi; large saltwater pool. *In room:* A/C, TV/ VCR, hair dryer, kitchenette or kitchen, no phone (in rooms), Wi-Fi.

Punahoa Beach Apartments ★ 🌶 Book this place! I can't put it any more simply than that. The location—off noisy, traffic-ridden Kihei Road, on a quiet side street with ocean frontage—is fabulous. A grassy lawn rolls about 50 feet down to the beach, where there's great snorkeling just offshore and a popular surfing spot next door; shopping and restaurants are all within walking distance. All of the beautifully decorated units in this small four-story building have fully equipped kitchens and lanais with great ocean views. Rooms go quickly in winter, so reserve early.

2142 Ililili Rd. (off S. Kihei Rd., 300 ft. from Kamaole Beach I), Kihei, HI 96753. ℂ **800/564-4380** or 808/879-2720. Fax 808/875-9147. www.punahoabeach.com. 13 units. $132–$159 studio double; $164–$244 1-bedroom double; $204–$274 2-bedroom double; $199–$269 1-bedroom penthouse. Extra person $15. $35 reservation fee. 5-night minimum. AE, MC, V. *In room:* AC (some units), TV, fridge, Internet access, kitchen.

Two Mermaids on Maui B&B ★ 🎁 The two mermaids, Juddee and Miranda, both avid scuba divers, offer a friendly B&B, professionally decorated with brilliant colors and hand-painted art of the island. It sits in a quiet neighborhood just a 10-minute walk from the beach. My favorite unit is the Ocean Ohana, a large one-bedroom apartment (with the option of a separate connecting bedroom), complete with kitchenette, huge private deck, private entry, and your own giant hot tub. Equally cute is the Poolside Suite, with private entry next to the outdoor pool. This studio (with the option of a separate connecting bedroom) is a living room during the day; at night it converts to a bedroom with a pull-down bed. Continental breakfast, with some of the best homemade bread on the island, is placed on your doorstep every morning (so you can sleep in). Amenities include guitars in every unit, a range of complimentary beach equipment, microwave popcorn, and a barbecue area. Juddee is a licensed minister who can perform weddings.

2840 Umalu Place, Kihei, HI 96753. ℂ **800/598-9550** or 808/874-8687. Fax 808/875-1833. www. twomermaids.com. 2 units. $115 studio double; $140 double 1-bedroom apt; $175–$200 2-bedroom double. Rates include continental breakfast. 3-night minimum. No credit cards, but will do credit cards through PayPal. **Amenities:** Babysitting; golf nearby; hot tub; outdoor pool; tennis courts nearby. *In room:* TV, DVD (on request), hair dryer, kitchenette, Wi-Fi.

Wailana Kai ★ 🌶 Bello Realty, which searches out the best deals in Kihei, has added this renovated two-story apartment building to its collection. Located at the end of a cul-de-sac street, and just a 1-minute walk to the beach, the property was totally renovated in 2004 with two types of units: standard (perfectly acceptable and clean, with new paint, furniture, and so on) and deluxe (the ones I recommend, for only a few dollars more). One-bedroom units currently start at $90—this deal will not last long. Once they get a reputation, the prices most likely will go up. All units have full kitchens and concrete soundproof walls, and the second floor has ocean views. There's also a barbecue area for guests.

34 Wailana Place, Kihei, HI 96753. Reservations c/o Bello Realty, P.O. Box 1776, Kihei, HI 96753. ℂ **800/541-3060** or 808/879-3328. Fax 808/875-1483. www.bellomaui.com. 10 units. $110–$120 1-bedroom; $115–$150 2-bedroom. MC, V. **Amenities:** Outdoor pool. *In room:* TV/VCR, high-speed Internet access (in some units), kitchen.

What a Wonderful World B&B ★ 🗝 I couldn't believe what I'd discovered here: an impeccably done B&B with a great location, excellent rates, and thought and care put into every room. Hostess Eva Tantillo has not only a full-service travel agency, but also a master's degree—along with several years of experience—in hotel management. The result? One of Maui's finest bed-and-breakfasts, centrally located in Kihei (a half-mile from Kamaole II Beach Park, 5 min. from Wailea golf courses, and convenient to shopping and restaurants). Choose from one of four units: the master suite (with a barbecue grill on the lanai), a studio apartment, or two one-bedroom apartments. Eva serves an expanded continental breakfast on her lanai, which boasts views of white-sand beaches, the West Maui Mountains, and Haleakala. You're also welcome to use the communal barbecue.

2828 Umalu Place (off Keonekai St., near Hwy. 31), Kihei, HI 96753. ℂ **800/943-5804** or 808/879-9103. Fax 808/879-5340. www.amauibedandbreakfast.com. 4 units. $89–$150 double. Children 11 and under stay free in parent's room. Rates include breakfast. AE, MC, V. **Amenities:** Hot tub. *In room:* TV, fridge, hair dryer, kitchen (in apartment units), Wi-Fi.

WAILEA

For a complete selection of condo units throughout Wailea and Makena, contact **Destination Resorts Hawaii** (ℂ **866/384-1366** or 808/891-6200; fax 808/874-3554; www.drhmaui.com). Its luxury units include studio doubles starting at $275, one-bedroom doubles from $275, two-bedrooms from $350, and three-bedrooms from $475. At most properties, those rates include free long-distance calls, high-speed Internet access, and parking; one property, the Polo Beach Club, is completely nonsmoking (indoors and out). Children 11 and under stay free; minimum stays vary by property.

Note: You'll find the following hotels on the "Where to Stay & Dine in South Maui" map (p. 451).

Very Expensive

The Fairmont Kea Lani Maui ★★★ At first glance, this blinding-white complex of arches and turrets may look a bit out of place in tropical Hawaii (it's a close architectural cousin of Las Hadas, the *Arabian Nights* fantasy resort in Manzanillo, Mexico). But once you enter the flower-filled lobby and see the big blue Pacific outside, there's no doubt you're in Hawaii.

It's not cheap, but for the price of a hotel room in other luxury resorts, you get an entire suite here—plus a few extras. Each unit in the all-suite hotel has a kitchenette (with microwave and coffeemaker), a living room with entertainment center and sofa bed (great if you have the kids in tow), a wet bar, an oversize marble bathroom (with separate shower big enough for a party), a spacious bedroom, and a large lanai that overlooks the pools, lawns, and white-sand beach.

Add to all that complimentary yoga classes, a Hawaiian cultural canoe experience, and free transportation within the Wailea Resort area. The small boutique **Spa Kea Lani** offers the latest in body work in intimate, relaxing surroundings—not to be missed, even if you're staying elsewhere.

The rich and famous stay in the villas—2,000-square-foot two- and three-bedroom fantasy beach bungalows, each with its own plunge pool and gourmet kitchen and includes a luxury car rental. *Hot Tip:* If you join the President's Club, which is free, there is *no* charge for the Internet access.

4100 Wailea Alanui Dr., Wailea, HI 96753. © **866/540-4456** or 808/875-4100. Fax 808/875-1200. www.fairmont.com/kealani. 450 units. $369–$1,100 suite (sleeps up to 4); from $1,300 villa. AE, DC, DISC, MC, V. Valet parking $20; free self-parking. **Amenities:** 4 restaurants (including Nick's Fishmarket Maui, p. 493), plus gourmet bakery and deli; 3 bars (w/sunset cocktails and entertainment at the Caffè Ciao Restaurant); babysitting; year-round children's program; concierge; fine 24-hr. fitness center; nearby Wailea Golf Club's 3 18-hole championship golf courses, as well as the Makena and Elleair golf courses; 2 large swimming lagoons connected by a 140-ft. water slide and swim-up bar, plus an adults-only pool; room service; excellent full-service spa; use of Wailea Tennis Center's 11 courts (3 lit for night play) and pro shop; watersports equipment rentals; 2 whirlpools. *In room:* A/C, TV/DVD/VCR, CD player, hair dryer, high-speed Internet access ($14 per day), kitchenette, microwave.

Four Seasons Resort Maui at Wailea ★★★ ☺

If money's no object, this is the place to spend it. It's hard to beat this modern version of a Hawaiian palace by the sea, with a relaxing, casual atmosphere. Although it sits on a glorious beach between two other hotels, you won't feel like you're on resort row: The Four Seasons inhabits its own world, thanks to an open courtyard of pools and gardens. Amenities are first-rate here, including outstanding restaurants and an excellent spa. This may also be the most kid-friendly resort on the island: There's a complete activities program for *keiki* (that is, kids; complimentary, of course), plus other perks like milk and cookies on arrival, kids' menus in all restaurants, free infant gear (cribs, strollers, and even toilet-seat locks), and a game room (video games, foosball, and more).

The spacious (about 600-sq.-ft.) guest rooms feature furnished lanais, nearly all with ocean views, that are great for watching whales in winter and sunsets year-round. The grand bathrooms contain deep marble tubs and showers for two. Service is attentive but not cloying. At the pool, guests lounge in casbahlike tents, pampered with iced Evian and chilled towels. And you'll never see a housekeeping cart in the hall: The cleaning staff works in teams, so they're as unobtrusive as possible and in and out of your room in minutes.

The fabulous spa offers facial treatments and products by Kate Somerville Skin Health Experts, a pioneer in the fields of paramedical esthetics and medi-based skin care (with a list of prominent clients from L.A., including Felicity Huffman, Paris Hilton, Jessica Alba, Eva Mendes, and others). The spa also has an incredible menu of treatments ranging from traditional Hawaiian to craniosacral to ayurvedic massage, offered in 13 treatment rooms and three oceanside *hale* (huts).

The ritzy neighborhood surrounding the hotel is home to great restaurants and shopping, the Wailea Tennis Center (known as Wimbledon West), and six golf courses—not to mention that great beach, with gentle waves and islands framing the view on either side.

3900 Wailea Alanui Dr., Wailea, HI 96753. ✆ **800/311-0630** or 808/874-8000. Fax 808/874-2244. www.fourseasons.com/maui. 380 units. $425–$970 double; $1,120–$1,220 Club Floor double; from $1,025 suite. Extra person $100 ($300 in Club Floor rooms). Children 17 and under stay free in parent's room. Packages available. AE, DC, MC, V. Valet parking $20. **Amenities:** 3 restaurants (including Spago, p. 493, and Bar e Ristorante, p. 493); 3 bars (w/nightly entertainment); babysitting; free use of bicycles; fabulous year-round children's' program; one of Maui's best concierge desks; concierge-level rooms; putting green and use of Wailea Golf Club's 3 18-hole championship golf courses, as well as the nearby Makena and Elleair golf courses; health club; 3 fabulous outdoor pools; room service; excellent spa; 2 on-site tennis courts (lit for night play); use of Wailea Tennis Center's 11 courts (3 lit for night play); beach pavilion w/watersports equipment rentals; 2 whirlpools (1 for adults only). *In room:* A/C, TV, fridge, hair dryer, minibar, Wi-Fi ($13 per day except Club Level).

Grand Wailea Resort Hotel & Spa ★★★ *Spa aficionados, take note:*

Hawaii's largest (50,000-sq.-ft.) and most elaborate spa is located here, with every kind of body treatment you can imagine. Treatments include use of the numerous baths, hot tubs, mineral pools, saunas, steam rooms, and other relaxation amenities in the his-and-hers spa area.

Built at the pinnacle of Hawaii's brief fling with fantasy megaresorts, the Grand Wailea is extremely popular with families, incentive groups, and conventions; it's the grand prize in Hawaii vacation contests and the dream of many honeymooners. It has a Japanese restaurant decorated with real rocks hewn from the slopes of Mount Fuji; 10,000 tropical plants in the lobby; an intricate pool system with slides, waterfalls, rapids, and a water-powered elevator to take you up to the top; a restaurant in a man-made tide pool; a floating New England–style wedding chapel; and nothing but oceanview, amenity-filled guest rooms. It's all crowned with a $30-million collection of original art, much of it created expressly for the hotel by Hawaii artists and sculptors. Though minimalists may be put off, there's no denying that the Grand Wailea is plush, professional, and pampering, with all the diversions you could imagine. Oh, and did I mention the fantastic beach out front?

Note: All rooms and suites are now nonsmoking. The former smoking rooms have undergone a thorough cleaning and have been deodorized. Smoking is limited to the private lanais outside the rooms.

3850 Wailea Alanui Dr., Wailea, HI 96753. ✆ **800/888-6100** or 808/875-1234. Fax 808/874-2442. www.grandwailea.com. 780 units. $429–$925 double; from $1,100 suite; from $729 Napua Club Room (in Napua Tower). Daily $25 resort fee for lei greeting on arrival, welcome drink, local calls, use of spa, admission to scuba-diving clinics and water aerobics, art and garden tours, nightly turndown service, in-room high-speed Internet access, self-parking, and shuttle service to Wailea area. Extra person $50 ($100 in Napua Tower). AE, DC, DISC, MC, V. Valet parking $20; free self-parking. **Amenities:** 6 restaurants; 7 bars (including a nightclub w/laser-light shows); babysitting; children's program; concierge; concierge-level rooms; complete fitness center; use of Wailea Golf Club's 3 18-hole championship golf courses, as well as the nearby Makena and Elleair golf courses; Jacuzzi; 2,000-ft.-long Activity Pool, featuring a swim/ride through mountains and grottoes; room service; Hawaii's largest spa; use of Wailea Tennis Center's 11 courts (3 lit for night play) and pro shop; watersports equipment rentals. *In room:* A/C, TV, fridge (fee of $25 per stay), hair dryer, high-speed Internet access, kitchenette, minibar.

Expensive

Wailea Beach Marriott Resort & Spa ★★ This classic, open-air, 1970s-style hotel in a tropical garden by the sea gives you a sense of what Maui was like before the big resort boom. It was the first resort built in Wailea (in 1976), and it remains the most Hawaiian of them all. Airy and comfortable, with touches of Hawaiian art throughout and a terrific aquarium that stretches forever behind the front desk, it just feels right. What's truly special about this hotel is how it fits into its environment without overwhelming it. Eight buildings, all low-rise except for an eight-story tower, are spread along 22 gracious acres of lawns and gardens spiked by coco palms, with lots of open space and a half-mile of oceanfront property on a point between Wailea and Ulua beaches. The vast, parklike expanses are a luxury on this now-crowded coast.

The small Mandara Spa offers a long list of treatments, from relaxing massages to aroma wraps to rejuvenating facials in a very Zen atmosphere. My only criticism is the lack (at this time) of a shower facility in the spa.

3700 Wailea Alanui Dr., Wailea, HI 96753. (ℰ **800/367-2960** or 808/879-1922. Fax 808/874-8331. www.waileamarriott.com. 545 units. $299–$735 double; from $400 suite. Extra person $40. Packages available. Daily $25 resort fee for local calls, discounts on luau and snorkel-gear rental, and free kids' meals with purchase of adult entree. AE, DC, DISC, MC, V. Valet parking $18; self-parking $15. **Amenities:** 2 restaurants; 2 bars; babysitting; concierge; fitness center; use of Wailea Golf Club's 3 18-hole championship golf courses; outdoor pools (including 1 for kids only); room service; full-service Mandara Spa w/steam rooms and whirlpools; use of Wailea Tennis Center's 11 courts (3 lit for night play) and pro shop; watersports equipment rentals. *In room:* A/C, TV, hair dryer, high-speed Internet access ($14).

MAKENA

Very Expensive

Makena Beach and Golf Resort ★★   If you're looking for a vacation in a beautiful, tranquil spot with a golden-sand beach, here's your place. But if you plan to tour Maui, you might try another hotel. The Makena Beach Resort is at the end of the road, far, far away from anything else on the island, so sightseeing in other areas would require a lot of driving.

Originally owned and built by the exclusive Prince Resorts, the property was designed for the Japanese market. In 2009, Benchmark Hospitality took over the management. In Hawaii, Benchmark did wonders with the Turtle Bay Resort on Oahu, so we expect that they will also bring this property up to luxury standards. The location, on one of Maui's best beaches, is beautiful, and the interior atrium, filled with tropical plants and a koi-filled waterfall stream, is gorgeous.

5400 Makena Alanui, Makena, HI 96753. (ℰ **800/321-6284** or 808/874-1111. Fax 808/879-8763. www.makenaresortmaui.com. 310 units. $425–$600 double; from $560 suite. Extra person $60. Packages available. AE, DC, MC, V. **Amenities:** 4 restaurants; 2 bars (w/local Hawaiian music nightly); babysitting; children's program; concierge; fitness room; 36-hole golf course (designed by Robert Trent Jones, Jr.); Jacuzzi; 2 outdoor pools (1 for adults, 1 for children); room service; 6 Plexipave tennis courts (2 lit for night play); watersports equipment rentals. *In room:* A/C, TV, fridge, hair dryer, high-speed Internet access.

Upcountry Maui

You'll find it cool and peaceful up here; be sure to bring a sweater.

MAKAWAO

Here you'll be (relatively) close to Haleakala National Park; Makawao is approximately 90 minutes from the entrance to the park at the 7,000-foot level (from there it's another 3,000 ft. and 30–45 min. to get to the top). Accommodations in Kula are the only ones closer to the park.

If you'd like your own private cottage, consider **Peace of Maui,** 1290 Haliimaile Rd. (just outside Haliimaile town), Haliimaile, HI 96768 (© **888/475-5045** or 808/572-5045; www.peaceofmaui.com), which has a full kitchen, two bedrooms, a day bed, and a large deck. The cottage goes for $150 ($75 cleaning fee) and children are welcome. The owners also have rooms in the main house (with shared bathroom and kitchen facilities) from $70 double.

Aloha Cottage ★★ 🎁 Hidden in the secluded rolling hills of Olinda on a 5-acre parcel of manicured, landscaped tropical foliage features a tropical cottage, designed and decorated by hosts Ron and Ranjana Serle. The Thai Tree House resembles an upscale Thai home with high vaulted ceilings, teak floors, and a king-size cherrywood bed in the center of the room. The private deck and private soaking tub make this a very romantic lodging. In fact, Ranjana can arrange weddings, prepare a private dinner, set up personal massages, and even organize a private yoga session for two.

1879 Olinda Rd., Makawao, HI 96765. © **888/328-3330** or 808/573-8555. Fax 808/573-2551. www.alohacottage.com. 1 cottage. $245 double. 3-night minimum preferred. MC, V. *In room:* TV/VCR, CD player, hair dryer, kitchen.

Banyan Tree House ★ 🎁 Huge monkeypod trees (complete with swing and hammock) extend their branches over this 2½-acre property like a giant green canopy. The restored 1920s plantation manager's house is decorated with Hawaiian furniture from the 1930s. The house can accommodate a big family or a group of friends; it has three spacious bedrooms and three private marble bathrooms. A fireplace stands at one end of the huge living room, a large lanai runs the entire length of the house, and the hardwood floors shine throughout. The four smaller guest cottages have been totally renovated and also feature hardwood floors and marble bathrooms. Floor plans vary; one has one queen-size bed, the others have two beds (a mix of queen-size, doubles, and twins). The quiet neighborhood and old Hawaii ambience give this place a comfortable, easygoing atmosphere. Restaurants and shops are just minutes away in Makawao, and the beach is a 15-minute drive—but this place is so relaxing that you may want to do nothing but lie in a hammock and watch the clouds float by. A recent addition is a yoga/meditation center on the property.

3265 Baldwin Ave. (next to Veterans' Cemetery, less than a mile below Makawao), Makawao, HI 96768. © **808/572-9021.** Fax 808/573-5072. www.banyantreehouse.com. 7 units. $165–$175 double room in house; $145–$190 cottage for 2. Extra person $25. Children 12 and under stay in parent's room for $10. Cleaning fee $20. AE, DC, DISC, MC, V. **Amenities:** Babysitting; Jacuzzi; outdoor pool. *In room:* TV (in some cottages), kitchen or kitchenette, Wi-Fi.

Hale Ho'okipa Inn Makawao ★ 🎁 Step back in time at this 1924 plantation-style home, rescued by owner Cherie Attix in 1996 and restored to its original charm (and listed on the State and National Historic Registers). Cherie lovingly refurbished the old wooden floors, filled the rooms with furniture from the 1920s, and hung works by local artists on the walls. The result is a charming, serene place to stay, just a 5-minute walk from the shops and restaurants of Makawao, 15 minutes from beaches, and an hour's drive from the top of Haleakala. The guest rooms have separate outside entrances and private bathrooms. The house's front and back porches are wonderful spots for sipping tea and watching the sun set. The Kona Wing is a two-bedroom suite with private bathroom and use of the kitchen.

Upcountry & East Maui

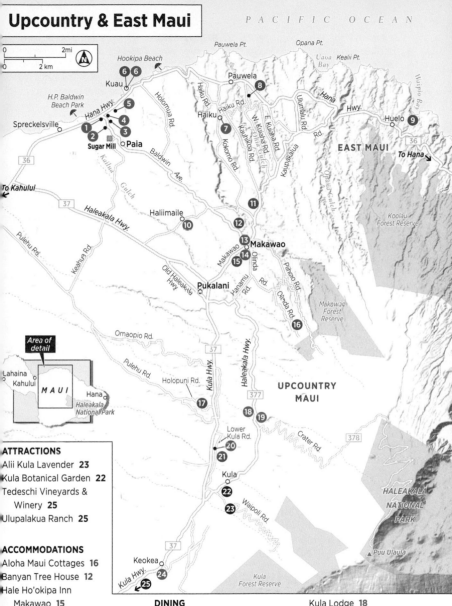

PACIFIC OCEAN

0 ——— 2mi
0 ——— 2 km

Hookipa Beach
Kuau
H.P. Baldwin Beach Park
Spreckelsville
Sugar Mill
Paia

Pauwela Pt.
Opana Pt.
Uaoa Bay
Kealii Pt.
Pauwela
Haiku
Hana Hwy.
Huelo

EAST MAUI
To Hana

To Kahului

Haleakala Hwy.
Haliimaile
Makawao
Pukalani

Koolau Forest Reserve

Makawao Forest Reserve

Area of detail
Lahaina
Kahului
MAUI
Hana
Haleakala National Park

Omaopio Rd.
Pulehu Rd.
Holopuni Rd.
Kula Hwy.

UPCOUNTRY MAUI

Lower Kula Rd.
Crater Rd.

Kula

HALEAKALA NATIONAL PARK
Puu Ulaula

Keokea
Kula Hwy.
Kula Forest Reserve

ATTRACTIONS
Alii Kula Lavender **23**
Kula Botanical Garden **22**
Tedeschi Vineyards & Winery **25**
Ulupalakua Ranch **25**

ACCOMMODATIONS
Aloha Maui Cottages **16**
Banyan Tree House **12**
Hale Hoʻokipa Inn Makawao **15**
Huelo Point Flower Farm **9**
The Inn at Mama's Fish House **6**
Kula Cottage **21**
Kula View B&B **17**
Maui Dream Cottage **8**
Peace of Maui **12**
Piilaloha B&B Cottage **11**

DINING
Cafe 808 **20**
Café des Amis **2**
Casanova Italian Restaurant **14**
Charlie's Restaurant **5**
Colleen's at the Cannery **7**
Grandma's Coffee House **24**
Haliimaile General Store **10**

Kula Lodge **18**
Kula Sandalwoods Restaurant **19**
Mama's Fish House **6**
Market Fresh Bistro **13**
Milagros Food Co. **4**
Moana Bakery & Café **3**
Paia Fish Market **1**

32 Pakani Place, Makawao, HI 96768. ☎ **877/572-6698** or ☎/fax 808/572-6698. www.maui-bed-and-breakfast.com. 4 units (2 with shower only). $125–$180 double. Extra person $20. Rates include continental breakfast. MC, V. From Haleakala Hwy., turn left on Makawao Ave., and turn right on the 5th street on the right off Makawao Ave. (Pakani Place); it's the 2nd-to-last house on the right (green house with white picket fence and water tower). *In room:* A/C, TV, hair dryer, Wi-Fi.

KULA (AT THE BASE OF HALEAKALA NATIONAL PARK)

Lodgings in Kula are the closest option to the entrance of Haleakala National Park (about 60 min. away).

Inexpensive

In addition to the options below, consider **Gildersleeve's Bed & Breakfast,** formerly known as Elaine's Upcountry Guest Rooms (☎ **808/878-6623**). The warm and welcoming hosts rent three rooms in their spacious pole house ($85 double; 3-night minimum).

Kula Cottage ★ 🎁 I can't imagine having a less-than-fantastic vacation here. Tucked away on a quiet street amid a large grove of blooming papaya and banana trees, Cecilia and Larry Gilbert's romantic honeymoon cottage is very private—it even has its own driveway and carport. The 700-square-foot cottage has a full kitchen (complete with dishwasher) and three huge closets that offer enough storage space for you to move in permanently. The lanai is outfitted with a gas barbecue and an umbrella-covered table and chairs. Cecilia delivers a continental breakfast daily. Groceries and a small takeout lunch counter are within walking distance; it's a 30-minute drive to the beach.

40 Puakea Place (off Lower Kula Rd.), Kula, HI 96790. ☎ **808/878-2043** or 808/871-6230. Fax 808/871-9187. www.kulacottage.com. 1 unit. $110 double. Extra person $15. Rate includes continental breakfast. 3-night minimum. No credit cards. *In room:* TV, kitchen.

Kula View Bed & Breakfast 🎁 Hostess and gardener extraordinaire Susan Kauai has this cute private suite (with its own deck and private entrance) upstairs in her home. The roomy studio has a huge deck with a panoramic view of Haleakala. Inside, there's a reading area with a comfy lounge chair and an eating area with table and chairs, toaster oven, coffeemaker, and electric teakettle. Susan serves breakfast in your suite (or will pack a picnic breakfast if you are out early) of tasty breads or muffins, fruit, juice, and tea and coffee. She has plenty of warm jackets, sweaters, and blankets you can borrow if you plan to make the trip to the top of Haleakala. Be sure to take a stroll through her magical garden.

P.O. Box 322, Kula, HI 96790. ☎ **808/878-6736.** 1 suite. $125 double. Rates include continental breakfast. 2-night minimum. No credit cards. *In room:* Fridge.

East Maui: On the Road to Hana

In addition to the choices below, consider the off-the-beaten-path **Tea House Cottage** (☎ **800/215-6130** or 808/572-5610; www.mauiteahouse.com) in Twin Falls. Get away from it all in a secluded jungle in a cottage powered by alternative energy (no utility poles!). Your private cottage has two decks, a screened lanai, a bedroom, a small kitchen, and a unique bathhouse. Rates of $135 single (2-night minimum) and $150 double (2-night minimum) include taxes and complimentary breakfast. Owner Ann DeWeese is on the property and can provide any helpful tips you need during your vacation. Discounts available for 4 or more nights.

Note: You'll find the accommodations in this section on the "Upcountry & East Maui" map (p. 505).

PAIA
Expensive

Paia Inn   I really wanted to love this inn. It's not on the ocean, but in the funky village of Paia. But the main problems here are that the rooms are tiny (almost claustrophobic), and noisy (not only from the street outside, but also from other guest rooms). Combined with very expensive rack rates, and virtually no parking, I'd suggest if you want to stay in this area, you can find better deals (see below). This boutique (only five rooms) inn opened in 2009 in the middle of the tiny town of Paia. The Inn features bamboo wood floors and a common living room area where guests can gather (which can be a problem late at night if you want to sleep and the other guests want to talk and listen to music). Each of the guest rooms has 500-thread-count sheets, tiny travertine bathrooms, high-definition flatscreen TV, complimentary wireless high-speed Internet, iPod docking station, and very limited space to unpack your clothes. There is complimentary coffee and tea with muffins and scones every morning

93 Hana Hwy., Paia, HI 96779. ✆ **800/721-4000** or 808/579-6000. 5 rooms. $189–$500 double, includes free coffee or tea and muffins and scones every morning. AE, MC, V. **Amenities:** Bicycle, surfboard, and stand-up paddleboard rentals; concierge; room service. *In room:* A/C, flatscreen TV, fridge, high-speed Internet access, MP3 docking station, Wi-Fi.

KUAU
Moderate

The Inn at Mama's Fish House ★★   The fabulous location (nestled in a coconut grove on secluded Kuau Beach), beautifully decorated interior (with rattan furniture and works by Hawaiian artists), and extras (gas barbecue, 27-in. TVs, and beach toys) make this place a gem for those seeking a centrally located vacation rental. All this, and the fabulous Mama's Fish House restaurant is just next door. The one-bedrooms are nestled in a tropical jungle (red ginger surrounds the garden patio), while the two-bedrooms face the beach. All have wood or terra-cotta floors, kitchenettes or complete kitchens (some even have dishwashers), sofa beds, and laundry facilities.

799 Poho Place (off the Hana Hwy. in Kuau), Paia, HI 96779. ✆ **800/860-HULA** (4852) or 808/579-9764. Fax 808/579-8594. www.mamasfishhouse.com. 12 units. $175 garden studio double; $225 1-bedroom (sleeps up to 4); $275–$575 2-bedroom (sleeps up to 6); $575 beachfront cottages and Junior Suite from $325. 3-night minimum in Dec and Jan. AE, DISC, MC, V. **Amenities:** Restaurant. *In room:* A/C, TV/VCR, hair dryer, kitchen, Wi-Fi.

HAIKU
Moderate

Pilialoha B&B Cottage ★   The minute you arrive at this split-level country cottage, set on a large lot with half-century-old eucalyptus trees, you'll see owner Machiko Heyde's artistry at work. Just in front of the quaint cottage (which is great for couples but can sleep up to five) is a garden blooming with some 200 varieties of roses. You'll find more of Machiko's handiwork inside. There's a queen-size bed in the master bedroom, a twin bed in a small adjoining room, and a queen-size sofa bed in the living room. A large lanai extends from the master bedroom. There's a great movie collection for rainy days or cool country nights, plus complimentary beach toys and snorkel equipment. If you plan on an early-morning ride to the top of Haleakala, Machiko will make sure you go with a thermos of coffee and her homemade bread.

2512 Kaupakalua Rd. (½ mile from Kokomo intersection), Haiku, HI 96708. © **808/572-1440.** 1 unit. $150 double. Extra person $30. 3-night minimum. No credit cards. *In room:* TV, kitchenette, Wi-Fi.

Inexpensive

Maui Dream Cottage   Essentially a vacation rental, this country estate is located atop a hill overlooking the ocean. The grounds are dotted with fruit trees (bananas, papayas, and avocados, all free for the picking), and the front lawn is comfortably equipped with a double hammock, chaise lounges, and table and chairs. One cottage has two bedrooms, the other just one (plus a sofa bed in the living room). They're both very well maintained and comfortably outfitted with furniture that's attractive but casual. The Haiku location is quiet and restful, and offers the opportunity to see how real islanders live. However, you'll have to drive a good 20 to 25 minutes to restaurants in Makawao or Paia. Hookipa Beach is about a 20-minute drive, and Baldwin Beach (good swimming) is 25 minutes away.

265 W. Kuiaha Rd. (1 block from Pauwela Cafe), Haiku, HI 96708. © **808/575-9079.** Fax 808/575-9477. www.mauidreamcottage.com. 1 unit (with shower only). $770 per week double. Extra person $10. 7-night minimum. MC, V. *In room:* TV, kitchen, Wi-Fi.

HUELO

Expensive

Huelo Point Flower Farm ★   Here's a little Eden by the sea on a spectacular, remote, 300-foot sea cliff near a waterfall stream. This estate overlooking Waipio Bay has two guest cottages, a guesthouse, and a main house available for rent. The studio-size Gazebo Cottage has three glass walls that make the most of the oceanfront location, a koa-wood captain's bed, a private oceanside patio, a private hot tub, and a half-bathroom with outdoor shower. The two-bedroom main house contains an exercise room, a fireplace, a sunken Roman bath, cathedral ceilings, and other extras. On the property is a natural pool with a waterfall and an oceanfront hot tub. You're welcome to pick fruit, vegetables, and flowers from the extensive garden. Homemade scones, tree-ripened papayas, and fresh-roasted coffee start your day. The secluded location, off the crooked road to Hana, is just a half-hour from Kahului, or about 20 minutes from Paia's shops and restaurants.

P.O. Box 791808 (off Hana Hwy., btw. mile markers 3 and 4), Paia, HI 96779. © **808/572-1850.** www.mauiflowerfarm.com. 3 units. $350 cottage double; $450 guesthouse double; $600 main house for 4. Extra person $35–$40. 2-night minimum. AE, MC, V. **Amenities:** 3 Jacuzzis; outdoor pool. *In room:* TV, hair dryer, kitchenette or kitchen.

At the End of the Road in East Maui: Hana

Note: You'll find Hana accommodations on the map on p. 551.

VERY EXPENSIVE

Hotel Hana-Maui ★★★ ☺   This hotel sits on 66 rolling seaside acres and offers a wellness center, two pools, and access to one of the best beaches in Hana. This is the atmosphere, the landscape, and the culture of old Hawaii set in 21st-century accommodations. Every unit is excellent, but my favorites are the Sea Ranch Cottages (especially nos. 215–218 for the best views), where individual duplex bungalows look out over the craggy shoreline to the rolling surf. You step out of the oversize, airy units (with floor-to-ceiling sliding doors) onto a huge lanai with views that will stay with you long after your tan has faded. These comfy units have been totally redecorated with every amenity you can think of, and you won't be nickel-and-dimed for things like coffee and water—everything provided, from the homemade banana bread to the bottled water, is complimentary. Cathedral ceilings, a plush feather bed, a giant soaking tub, Hawaiian artwork, bamboo floors—this is luxury. The white-sand beach (just a 5-min. shuttle away), top-notch wellness center with some of the best massage therapists in Hawaii, and numerous activities (horseback riding, mountain biking, tennis, pitch-and-putt golf) all add up to make this one of the top resorts in the state. There's no TV in the rooms, but the Club Room has a giant-screen TV, plus VCR and Internet access. I highly recommend this little slice of paradise.

5031 Hana Hwy. (P.O. Box 9), Hana, HI 96713. ℂ **800/321-HANA** (4262) or 808/248-8211. Fax 808/248-7202. www.hotelhanamaui.com. 66 units. $495 Bay Cottage double; $595–$1,075 Sea Ranch Cottage double; $1,800 3-bedroom suite for 6; from $4,000 2-bedroom Plantation House. Extra person $140. AE, DC, DISC, MC, V. **Amenities:** Restaurant (w/Hawaiian entertainment Fri); bar (entertainment 5 times a week); babysitting; concierge; fitness center; complimentary use of 3-hole practice golf courses (complimentary use of clubs); 2 outdoor pools; room service; full-service spa; tennis courts. *In room:* Hair dryer, kitchenette.

MODERATE

Bamboo Inn   This inn shares the same historic site as the Hana Hale Inn, and guests have full access to Hana Hale Inn's ancient fishponds and cave. There's access to a nearby rocky beach, which isn't good for swimming but makes a wonderful place to watch the sunset. All accommodations include fully equipped kitchens, bathrooms, bedrooms, living/dining areas, and private lanais. The oceanfront Bamboo Inn contains three units (two studios and a convertible one- or two-bedroom unit).

P.O. Box 374, Hana, HI 96713. ℂ **808/248-7718.** www.bambooinn.com. 3 units. $175–$240 double. Extra person $15. Rates include continental breakfast. 2-night minimum. MC, V. **Amenities:** Jacuzzi; Wi-Fi. *In room:* TV/DVD, Jacuzzi, kitchen.

Ekena ★   Just one glance at the 360-degree view, and you can see why hosts Robin and Gaylord gave up their careers on the mainland and moved here. This 8½-acre piece of paradise in rural Hana boasts ocean and rainforest vistas; the floor-to-ceiling glass doors in the spacious Hawaiian-style pole house bring the outside in. The elegant two-story home is exquisitely furnished, from the comfortable U-shaped couch that invites you to relax and take in the view to the top-of-the-line mattress on the king-size bed. The kitchen is fully equipped with high-tech conveniences (guests have made complete holiday meals here). Only one floor (and one two-bedroom unit) is rented at any given time to ensure privacy. The grounds are impeccably groomed and dotted with tropical plants and fruit trees. Hiking trails into the rainforest start right on the property, and beaches and waterfalls are just minutes away. Robin places fresh flowers in every room and makes sure you're comfortable; after that, she's available to answer questions, but she also respects your privacy.

P.O. Box 728 (off Hana Hwy., above Hana Airport), Hana, HI 96713. © **808/248-7047.** Fax 808/248-7853. www.ekenamaui.com. 2 units. $225 for 2; $295–$400 for 4. 3-night minimum. MC, V. Children must be 14 or over. *In room:* TV/DVD, CD player, kitchen, free Wi-Fi.

Hamoa Bay Bungalow ★ 🎁

Down a country lane guarded by two Balinese statues stands a little bit of Indonesia in Hawaii: a carefully crafted bungalow and an Asian-inspired two-bedroom house overlooking Hamoa Bay. This enchanting retreat is just 2 miles beyond Hasegawa General Store on the way to Kipahulu. It sits on 4 verdant acres within walking distance of Hamoa Beach (which James Michener considered one of the most beautiful in the Pacific). The 600-square-foot Balinese-style cottage is distinctly tropical, with elephant-bamboo furniture from Indonesia, batik prints, a king-size bed, a full kitchen, and a screened porch with hot tub and shower. Hidden from the cottage is a 1,300-square-foot home with a soaking tub and private outdoor stone shower. It offers an elephant-bamboo king-size bed in one room, a queen-size bed in another, a screened-in sleeping porch, a full kitchen, and wonderful ocean views.

P.O. Box 773, Hana, HI 96713. © **808/248-7884.** Fax 808/248-7853. 2 units. $225 cottage (sleeps only 2); $285 house for 2; $395 house for 4. 3-night minimum. MC, V. **Amenities:** Hot tub. *In room:* TV/DVD, CD player, kitchen, Wi-Fi in the house only.

Hana Hale Inn 🎁

Hana Hale Inn sits on a historic site with ancient fishponds and a cave mentioned in ancient chants. Host John takes excellent care of the ponds (you're welcome to watch him feed the fish at 5pm daily) and is fiercely protective of the hidden cave ("It's not a tourist attraction, but a sacred spot"). There's access to a nearby rocky beach, which isn't good for swimming but makes a wonderful place to watch the sunset. All accommodations include fully equipped kitchens, bathrooms, bedrooms, living/dining areas, and private lanais. Next to the fishpond, the Royal Lodge, a 2,600-square-foot architectural masterpiece built entirely of Philippine mahogany, has large skylights the entire length of the house and can be rented as a house or two separate units. The cottages range from the separate two-level Tree House Cottage (with Jacuzzi for two, a Balinese bamboo bed, small kitchen/living area, and deck upstairs) to the Pond View Bungalow (with private outdoor Jacuzzi and shower).

P.O. Box 374, Hana, HI 96713. © **808/248-7641.** www.hanahaleinn.com. 5 units. $160–$260 double. Extra person $15. 2-night minimum. MC, V. *In room:* TV/DVD, Jacuzzi (in all but 1 unit), kitchen.

Hana Kai Maui Resort

Hana's only vacation condo complex, Hana Kai offers studio and one-bedroom units overlooking Hana Bay. All units have large kitchens and private lanais. Each of the one-bedroom units has a sliding door that separates the bedroom from the living room, plus a sofa bed that sleeps two additional guests. Ask for a corner unit with wraparound ocean views.

1533 Uakea Rd. (P.O. Box 38), Hana, HI 96713. © **800/346-2772** or 808/248-8426. Fax 808/248-7482. www.hanakaimaui.com. 17 units. $185–$235 studio double; $210–$260 1-bedroom (sleeps up to 4); $450 2-bedroom. Extra person $15. Children 6 and under stay free in parent's room. $20 service fee for fewer than 3 nights. MC, V. *In room:* Kitchen, free Wi-Fi.

Hana Oceanfront Cottages ★★ Just across the street from Hamoa Bay, Hana's premier white-sand beach, lie these two plantation-style units, impeccably decorated in old Hawaii decor and outfitted with everything you should need during your vacation. My favorite unit is the romantic cottage, complete with old-fashioned front porch where you can sit and watch the ocean; a separate bedroom (with a bamboo sleigh bed), plus pullout sofa for extra guests; top-notch kitchen appliances; and comfy living room. The 1,000-square-foot vacation suite, located downstairs from hosts Dan and Sandi's home (but totally soundproof), has an elegant master bedroom with polished bamboo flooring, a spacious bathroom with custom hand-painted tile, and a fully appointed gourmet kitchen. Outside are a 320-square-foot lanai and a barbecue area. The units sit on the road facing Hana's most popular beach, so there is traffic during the day. At night the traffic disappears, the stars come out, and the sound of the ocean lulls you to sleep.

P.O. Box 843, Hana, HI 96713. © **808/248-7558.** Fax 808/248-8034. 2 units. $250–$275 double. 3-night minimum. MC, V. **Amenities:** Barbecue area. *In room:* TV/VCR/DVD, stereo/CD player, hair dryer, kitchen.

Heavenly Hana Inn ★★ 🎁 This place on the Hana Highway, just a stone's throw from the center of Hana town, is a little bit of heaven, where no attention to detail has been spared. Each suite has a sitting room with futon and couch, polished hardwood floors, and separate bedroom with a raised platform bed (with an excellent, firm mattress). The black-marble bathrooms have huge tubs. Flowers are everywhere, ceiling fans keep the rooms cool, and the delicious gourmet breakfast—worth splurging for—is served in an art-filled setting. The grounds are done in Japanese style with a bamboo fence, tiny bridges over a meandering stream, and Japanese gardens.

P.O. Box 790, Hana, HI 96713. ©/fax **808/248-8442.** 3 units. $350–$600 suite. Full gourmet breakfast available for $16 per person. 2-night minimum. AE, DISC, MC, V. Children must be 15 or older. *In room:* TV, no phone.

INEXPENSIVE

Mrs. Nakamura has been renting her **Aloha Cottages** (© **808/248-8420**) since the 1970s. Located in residential areas near Hana Bay, these five budget rentals are simply but adequately furnished, varying in size from a roomy studio with kitchenette to a three-bedroom, two-bathroom unit. They're all fully equipped, clean, and fairly well kept. Rates run from $75 to $105 double (rate includes the taxes). Not all units have TVs, and none have phones, but Mrs. N. is happy to take messages.

Baby Pigs Crossing Bed & Breakfast ★ 🎁 If you're looking for a quiet, romantic little cottage, nestled away from it all in old Hawaii but close enough to Hana to drive in for dinner, this is your place. International artist Arabella Gail Ark (formerly known as Gail Bakutis) has created a lovely retreat on her 1-acre parcel of land, which is landscaped in a "fragrance" garden carefully planted with Hawaii's best sweet-smelling plants. The separate guesthouse, with an ocean view from the lanai, is professionally decorated with comfort in mind, from the very cozy rattan furniture to the king-size sofa bed. There's a separate bedroom with a queen-size bed and a small but utilitarian kitchenette. But the surprise is the unique bathroom with glass ceiling and walls (with privacy curtains), which opens onto a garden area.

P.O. Box 667, Hana, HI 96713. ☎ **808/248-8890.** Fax 808/248-4865. www.mauibandb.com. 1 unit. $250 double for 1 night ($225 per night for 2 nights; $200 per night for 3 nights). AE, MC, V. *In room:* TV/VCR, kitchenette.

Hana's Tradewind Cottages ★ 🍴 ☺

Nestled among the ginger and helico-nias on a 5-acre flower farm are two separate cottages, each with carport, barbe-cue, private hot tub, ceiling fans, and sofa bed. The studio cottage sleeps up to four; a bamboo shoji blind separates the sleeping area (with queen-size bed) from the sofa bed in the living room. The Tradewinds cottage has two bedrooms (with a queen-size bed in one room and two twins in the other), one bathroom (shower only), and a huge front porch. The atmosphere is quiet and relaxing, and hostess Rebecca Buckley, who has been in business for a decade, welcomes families. You can use the laundry facilities if staying 3 or more nights.

135 Alalele Place (the airport road), P.O. Box 385, Hana, HI 96713. ☎ **800/327-8097** or 808/248-8980. Fax 808/248-7735. www.hanamaui.net. 2 units. $175 studio double; $175 2-bedroom dou-ble. Extra person $15. 2-night minimum. AE, DISC, MC, V. *In room:* TV, kitchen, no phone, Wi-Fi.

Joe's Rentals 🍴

This is as close to a hostel as you can get in Hana. Joe's is a large, rambling house located just spitting distance from Hana Bay. Seven spar-tan but immaculately clean bedrooms share showers and bathrooms; one has private facilities. All guests are welcome to use the large living room with TV and adjoining communal kitchen (free coffee available all day). Other amenities include a rec room, barbecue, and owner Ed Hill himself. He'll tell you the long story about the name if you ask, and can also talk about what to do and see in Hana all day if you let him.

4870 Uakea Rd. (P.O. Box 746), Hana, HI 96713. ☎ **808/248-7033.** www.joesrentals.com. 8 units (7 with shared bathroom). $50 double with shared bathroom; $60 double with private bathroom. Extra person $10. MC. V. **Amenities:** TV; kitchen. *In room:* No phone.

Waianapanapa State Park Cabins 🍴

These 12 rustic cabins are the best lodging deal on Maui. Everyone knows it, too—so make your reservations early (up to 6 months in advance). The cabins are warm and dry, and come complete with kitchen, living room, bedroom, and bathroom with hot shower; furnishings include linens, towels, dishes, and very basic cooking and eating utensils. Don't expect luxury—this is a step above camping, albeit in a beautiful tropical jungle setting. The key attraction at this 120-acre state beach park is the unusual horse-shoe-shaped black-sand beach on Pailoa Bay, popular for shore fishing, snorkel-ing, and swimming. There's an on-site caretaker, along with restrooms, showers, picnic tables, shoreline hiking trails, and historic sites. Bring mosquito protec-tion—this is the jungle, after all.

Off Hana Hwy. Reservations c/o State Parks Division, 54 S. High St., Room 101, Wailuku, HI 96793. ☎ **808/984-8109.** 10 units. $45 for 4 (sleeps up to 6). Extra person $5. 5-night maxi-mum. No credit cards. *In room:* Kitchen, no phone.

WHERE TO DINE

With soaring visitor statistics and a glamorous image, the Valley Isle is fertile ground for Hawaii's famous enterprising chefs (like Roy Yamaguchi from Roy's, Gerard Reversade of Gerard's, James McDonald of I'O and Pacific'O, Peter Mer-riman of Hula Grill, Mark Ellman of Maui Tacos and Mala Ocean Tavern, D. K.

Kodama of Sansei Seafood Restaurant & Sushi Bar, and Beverly Gannon of Hali-imaile General Store and Joe's), as well as an international name or two (Wolf-gang Puck of Spago). There are even a few newcomers who are cooking up a storm and getting a well-deserved following (Jennifer Nguyen of A Saigon Cafe, Dana Pastula of Cafe O'Lei and Maalaea Grill, and Don Ritchey of Moana Bak-ery & Cafe).

In this dizzying scenario, some things haven't changed: You can still dine well at Lahaina's open-air waterfront watering holes, where the view counts for 50% of the experience. There are still budget eateries, but not many; Maui's old-fashioned, multigenerational mom-and-pop diners are disappearing, eclipsed by the flashy newcomers, or clinging to the edge of existence in the older neighbor-hoods of Central Maui, like lovable Wailuku. Although you'll have to work harder to find them in the resort areas, you won't have to go far to find creative cuisine, pleasing style, and stellar dining experiences.

In the listings below, reservations are not necessary unless otherwise noted.

Central Maui

The **Queen Kaahumanu Center** (www.queenkaahumanucenter.com), the structure that looks like a white *Star Wars* umbrella in Kahului, at 275 Kaahu-manu Ave. (a 10-min. drive from Kahului Airport on Hwy. 32), has a very popular food court. Eateries include **Edo Japan,** whose flat Benihana-like grill dispenses marvelous, flavorful teppanyaki; **Panda Express,** which serves tasty Chinese food; and **Alexander's Fish and Chips,** a great place for fast takeout. Outside of the food court, but still in the shopping center, are **Ruby's,** dishing out burg-ers, fries, and shakes; and **Starbucks.** There's also a branch of **Maui Tacos** (p. 486). When you leave Kaahumanu Center, take a moment to gaze at the West Maui Mountains to your left from the parking lot.

MODERATE

Bistro Casanova ★ 🍴 MEDITERRANEAN   From the same group which brought interesting and delicious Italian food to Casanova Italian Restaurant and Deli in Makawao, this cosmopolitan bistro sits the heart of Kahului serving tapas, pastas, steaks, and seafood for lunch and dinner. The space, located in a Kahului office complex, formerly housing The Manana Garage restaurant, has been totally renovated and now sports a nautical theme (everything in blue) with a great outdoor dining area. Packed with a business crowd at lunch and a more relaxed atmosphere at dinner (where mainly local residents dine), Bistro Casa-nova offers some interesting items such as sweet and savory crepes, quinoa sal-ads, and Maui-raised beef, in addition to traditional Italian pastas, a tasty *osso buco,* and fresh fish.

33 Lono Ave., Kahului. ☎ **808/873-3650.** www.casanovamaui.com. Lunch entrees $7–$14; din-ner entrees $12–$36. AE, DISC, MC, V. Mon 11am–2:30pm; Tues–Sat 11am–2:30pm and 5–9:30pm.

Class Act ★ GLOBAL   Part of a program run by the distinguished Food Ser-vice Department of Maui Community College, now housed in a new state-of-the-art, $15-million culinary facility (with floor-to-ceiling windows at one end, exhibition kitchen at the other end), Class Act is a "classroom" restaurant with a huge following. Student chefs show their stuff with a flourish and pull out all the stops to give you a dining experience you will long remember. Linen, china, serv-ers in ties and white shirts, and a four-course lunch make this a unique value.

The appetizer, soup, salad, and dessert are set, but you can choose between the regular entrees and a heart-healthy main course prepared in the culinary tradition of the week. The menu roams the globe, with highlights of Italy, Mexico, Maui, Napa Valley, France, New Orleans, and other locales. The filet mignon of French week is popular, as are the New Orleans gumbo and Cajun shrimp, the sesame-crusted mahimahi on taro-leaf pasta, the polenta flan with eggplant, and the bean and green-chili chilaquile.

At Maui Community College, 310 Kaahumanu Ave., Wailuku. ☎ **808/984-3280.** www.maui culinary.com/academy/class_act.cfm. Reservations recommended. 4-course lunch $30. MC, V. Wed and Fri 11am–12:30pm (last seating). Closed June–Aug for summer vacation and parts of Dec and Jan. Menu and cuisine type change weekly.

Ichiban 🎁 JAPANESE/SUSHI   What a find: an informal neighborhood restaurant that serves inexpensive, home-cooked Japanese food *and* good sushi at realistic prices. Local residents consider Ichiban a staple for breakfast, lunch, or dinner and a haven of comforts: egg-white omelets; great saimin; combination plates of teriyaki chicken, teriyaki meat, *tonkatsu* (pork cutlet), rice, and pickled cabbage; chicken yakitori; and sushi—everything from unagi and scallop to California roll. The sushi items may not be cheap, but like the specials, such as steamed opakapaka, they're a good value. I love the tempura, miso soup, and spicy-ahi hand roll.

At the Kahului Shopping Center, 47 Kaahumanu Ave., Kahului. ☎ **808/871-6977.** Main courses $6–$7 breakfast, $10–$13 lunch (combination plates $13), $10–$30 dinner (combination dinner $15, dinner specials from $10). AE, DC, MC, V. Mon–Fri 7am–2pm and 5–9pm; Sat 10:30am–2pm and 5–9pm. Closed 2 weeks around Christmas and New Year's.

Marco's Grill & Deli ITALIAN   Located in the thick of Central Maui, where the roads to Upcountry, West, and South Maui converge, Marco's is popular among area residents for its homemade Italian fare and friendly informality. Everything—from the meatballs, sausages, and burgers to the sauces, salad dressings, and raviolis—is made in-house. The 35 different choices of hot and cold sandwiches and entrees are served all day; some favorites include vodka rigatoni with imported prosciutto and simple pasta with marinara sauce. The antipasto salad and roasted peppers are taste treats, but the meatballs and Italian sausage are famous in Central Maui. This is one of those comfortable neighborhood fixtures favored by all generations. It also has a full bar.

At the Dairy Center, 395 Dairy Rd., Kahului. ☎ **808/877-4446.** Main courses $6–$33. AE, DISC, MC, V. Daily 7:30am–10pm.

A Saigon Cafe ★★ 🎁 VIETNAMESE   Jennifer Nguyen has stuck to her guns and steadfastly refused to erect a sign, but diners find their way here anyway. That's how good the food is. Fans drive from all over the island for her crisp spiced Dungeness crab, steamed opakapaka with ginger and garlic, and wok-cooked Vietnamese specials tangy with spices, herbs, and lemon grass. There are a dozen different soups, cold and hot noodles (including the popular beef noodle soup called *pho*), and chicken and shrimp cooked in a clay pot. You can create your own Vietnamese "burritos" from a platter of tofu, noodles, and vegetables that you wrap in rice paper and dip in garlic sauce. Among my favorites are the shrimp lemon grass, savory and refreshing, and the tofu curry, swimming in herbs and vegetables straight from the garden. The Nhung Dam—a hearty spread of

ROSELANI: MAUI'S BEST ice cream

For the culinary highlight of your trip to Maui, try **Roselani Ice Cream,** Maui's only made-from-scratch, old-fashioned ice cream. In fact, be sure to try it early in your trip so you can eat your way through this little bit of heaven at restaurants and scooping parlors, or get your own stash at grocery stores. There are more than 40 flavors, divided into two brands under the Roselani label: the Premium Parlour Flavors (ranging from the traditional vanilla to the unique black cherry, cappuccino chip, fresh-brewed coffee, and choco-cookie crunch) and the Tropics (with delicious varieties like the best-selling haupia, made from coconut and macadamia nut, or the popular chocolate macadamia nut, Kona mud pie, mango and cream, coconut pineapple, and luau fudge pie). Each rich, creamy flavor contains 12% to 16% butterfat. For a list of hotels, restaurants, ice-cream parlors, and grocery stores that carry Roselani, either call Maui Soda & Ice Works at ✆ **808/244-7951** or check online at www.roselani.com.

basil, cucumbers, mint, romaine, bean sprouts, pickled carrots, turnips, and vermicelli, wrapped in rice paper and dipped in a legendary sauce—is cooked at your table.

1792 Main St., Wailuku. ✆ **808/243-9560.** Main courses $6.50–$21. MC, V. Daily 10am–9:30pm. Heading into Wailuku from Kahului, go over the bridge and take the 1st right onto Central Ave.; then take the 1st right on Nani St. At the next stop sign, look for the building with the neon sign that says OPEN.

INEXPENSIVE

A. K.'s Café ★★ 🍴 HEALTHFUL/PLATE LUNCHES   Chef Elaine Rothermel has a winner with this tiny cafe in the industrial district of Wailuku. It may be slightly off the tourist path, but it is well worth the effort to find this delicious eatery, with creative cuisine coming out of the kitchen—most dishes healthy, and a few dishes for those who just want to enjoy good food (forget the calories). Prices are so eye-poppingly cheap, you might find yourself wandering back here during your vacation. Lunches feature everything from grilled chicken with Thai sauce to fish tacos, from hamburger steak to seared ahi sandwich with tempura eggplant. Dinner specials include chicken Marsala over noodles, crab cakes with papaya beurre blanc, tofu Napoleon with ginger-basil sauce, and Hunan lamb chops. Plenty of heart-healthy options to choose from (low in sugar, salt, and fat).

1237 Lower Main St., Wailuku. ✆ **808/244-8774.** www.akscafe.com. Plate lunches $7.50–$16; dinners $14–$18. MC, V. Tues–Fri 11am–1:30pm; Tues–Sat 5:30–8:30pm. Live Hawaiian music Fri nights.

Down to Earth 🍴 ORGANIC HEALTH FOOD   If you are looking for a healthy alternative to fast foods, here's your place. Healthful organic ingredients, 90% vegan, appear in scrumptious salads, lasagna, chili, curries, and dozens of tasty dishes, presented at hot and cold serve-yourself stations. Stools line the counters in the simple dining area, where a few tables are available for those who don't want takeout. The food is great: millet cakes, mock tofu chicken, curried tofu, and Greek salad, nearly everything organic and tasty, with herb-tamari marinades and pleasing condiments such as currants or raisins, apples, and cashews.

(The fabulous tofu curry has apples, raw cashews, and raisins.) The food is sold by the pound, but you can buy a hearty, wholesome plate for $7. Vitamin supplements, health food products, fresh produce, and cosmetics fill the rest of the store.

305 Dairy Rd., Kahului. ✆ **808/877-2661.** www.downtoearth.org. Self-serve hot buffet and salad bar and deli; sandwiches $8, food sold by the pound, average $7–$9 for a plate. AE, MC, V. Mon–Sat 7am–7:45pm; Sun 8am–6:45pm.

Main Street Bistro ⚑ AMERICAN   Formerly Who's the Boss restaurant and, before that, Iao Café, this popular eatery, located on the main street of Wailuku, is now owned by chef Tom Selman, well known in culinary circles on Maui. He was formerly the chef de cuisine at Lahaina Grill and was also corporate chef for the Sansei/Vino restaurants. Main Street Bistro is open only for lunch, but Selman has added a *pau hana* (after-work) menu of tapas like crispy crab and shrimp gau gee, minihamburgers, and barbecued ribs. He calls his cuisine "refined comfort food," with signature items that include onion rings with house-made smoky ketchup, roasted Chinese chicken salad, "mother's roast beef sandwich" (served open-faced on a French roll), Southern-fried chicken, Maryland-style crab cake, and a roasted veggie sandwich. The chef will happily customize any menu item for those who prefer low-calorie, low-fat, or low-carbohydrate options. Daily specials range from grilled steak to Asian risotto with shrimp, crab, and veggies.

2051 Main St., Wailuku. ✆ **808/244-6816.** www.msbmaui.com. Main courses $7–$13 lunch; tapas $5–$23; daily specials $9–$17. MC, V. Mon–Fri 11am–7pm; tapas menu 3–7pm. Live music Fri evenings.

Restaurant Matsu JAPANESE/LOCAL   Customers have come from Hana (more than 50 miles away) just for Matsu's California rolls, while regulars line up for the cold saimin (julienned cucumber, egg, Chinese-style sweet pork, and red ginger on noodles) and for the bento plates (various assemblages of chicken, teriyaki beef, fish, and rice). The nigiri sushi items are popular, especially among the don't-dally lunch crowd. The katsu pork and chicken, breaded and deep-fried, are other specialties of this casual Formica-style diner. I love the tempura udon and the saimin, steaming mounds of wide and fine noodles swimming in homemade broths and topped with condiments. The daily specials are a changing lineup of home-cooked classics: oxtail soup, roast pork with gravy, teriyaki ahi, miso butterfish, and breaded mahimahi.

161 Alamaha St., Kahului. ✆ **808/871-0822.** Most items under $8. MC, V. Mon–Thurs 10am–3pm and 5–7:30pm; Fri 10am–3pm and 5–8pm.

Sam Sato's NOODLES/PLATE LUNCHES   Sam Sato's is a Maui institution, not only for its noodles (saimin, dry noodles, chow fun), but also for its flaky baked *manju,* a pastry filled with sweetened lima beans or adzuki beans. Sam opened his family eatery in 1933, and his daughter, Lynne Toma, makes the broth from scratch. The saimin and the dry noodles, with broth that comes in a separate bowl, are big sellers. Eat at the counter, with well-worn wooden stools and homemade salt and pepper shakers. Try the plate lunch with two barbecued meat sticks, two scoops of rice, and macaroni salad. The peach, apple, coconut, and pineapple turnovers fly out the door, as do takeout noodles. *Tip:* If you want them to hold the MSG, be sure to make your request early.

At the Millyard, 1750 Wili Pa Loop, Wailuku. ✆ **808/244-7124.** Plate lunches $7–$7.50. No credit cards. Mon–Sat 7am–2pm (2–4pm they do takeout of preordered items).

West Maui

LAHAINA

There's a **Maui Tacos** (p. 486) in Lahaina Square (© **808/661-8883**). Maui's branch of the **Hard Rock Cafe** is at 900 Front St., in Lahaina (© **808/ 667-7400**).

Very Expensive

The Feast at Lele ★★ POLYNESIAN   The owners of the Old Lahaina Luau (see "A Night to Remember: Luau, Maui Style," on p. 564) have teamed up with the culinary prowess of chef James McDonald (I'O and Pacific'O), placed it in a perfect outdoor oceanfront setting, and added the exquisite dancers of the Old Lahaina Luau. The result: a culinary and cultural experience that sizzles. As if the sunset weren't heady enough, dances from Hawaii, New Zealand, Tahiti, and Samoa are presented, up close and personal, in full costumed splendor. Chanting, singing, drumming, dancing, the swish of ti-leaf skirts, the scent of plumeria—it's a full adventure, even for the most jaded luau aficionado. Guests sit at white-clothed, candlelit tables set on the sand (unlike the luau, where seating is en masse) and dine on entrees from each island: *imu*-roasted kalua pig from Hawaii, Maori fishcake from New Zealand, poisson cru from Tahiti, and beef with breadfruit from Samoa. Particularly mesmerizing is the evening's opening: A softly lit canoe carries three people ashore to the sound of conch shells.

505 Front St. © **866/244-5353** or 808/667-5353. www.feastatlele.com. Reservations required. Set 5-course menu (including all beverages) $110 adults, $80 children 2–12. AE, MC, V. Apr–Sept daily 6–9pm; Oct–Mar daily 5:30–8:30pm.

Lahaina Grill ★★ NEW AMERICAN   Despite David Paul Johnson's departure, this Lahaina hot spot has maintained its popularity. It's still filled with chic, tanned diners in stylish aloha shirts, and there's still attitude aplenty at the entrance. The signature items remain: tequila shrimp and firecracker rice, Kona coffee–roasted rack of lamb, Maui onion–crusted seared ahi, and kalua-duck quesadilla. As always, a special custom-designed chef's table can be arranged with 72-hour notice for larger parties. The ambience—black-and-white tile floors, pressed-tin ceilings, eclectic 1890s decor—is striking, and the bar, despite not having an ocean view, is the busiest spot in Lahaina.

127 Lahainaluna Rd. © **808/667-5117.** www.lahainagrill.com. Reservations required. Main courses $33–$52. AE, DC, DISC, MC, V. Daily 6–10pm. Bar daily 6–10pm (earlier if it's slow).

Expensive

Gerard's ★★★ 🏅 FRENCH   The charm of Gerard's—soft lighting, excellent service, Edith Piaf on the sound system—is matched by a menu of uncompromising standards. After more than 2 decades in Lahaina, Gerard Reversade never runs out of creative offerings, yet stays true to his French roots. Roasted opakapaka with star anise, fennel fondue, and hints of orange and ginger is a stellar entree on a menu of winners. The Pacific bouillabaisse with local fish and lobster promises ecstasy, and the spinach salad with scallops is among the finest I've tasted. Gerard's has an excellent appetizer menu, with shiitake and oyster mushrooms in puff pastry, fresh ahi and smoked salmon carpaccio, and a very rich, highly touted escargot ragout with burgundy butter and garlic cream. The restaurant is a frequent winner of the *Wine Spectator* Award of Excellence, as well as the *Wine Enthusiast* 2006 Award of Distinction.

At the Plantation Inn, 174 Lahainaluna Rd. ℂ **808/661-8939.** www.gerardsmaui.com. Reservations recommended. Main courses $33–$54. AE, DC, DISC, MC, V. Daily 6–9pm.

I'o ★ PACIFIC RIM   I'O is a fantasy of sleek curves and etched glass, co-owned by chef James McDonald. He offers an impressive selection of appetizers (his strong suit) and some lavish Asian-Polynesian interpretations of seafood, such as his "rainbow catch"—fresh fish of the day topped with lemon grass pesto, tomatoes, truffle oil, and goat-cheese fondue sauce—or his "scallops ala bondage"—scallops wrapped in sage and jalapeño bacon, served with roasted Japanese eggplant and a ponzu-cream sauce. Unless you're sold on a particular entree, my advice is to go heavy on the superb appetizers, especially the blackened-ahi tower (a tower of ahi, avocado, fruit, and tomatoes), the shredded pork in a quesadilla with pepper-jack cheese, or the silken purse: wontons stuffed with roasted peppers, mushrooms, spinach, macadamia nuts, and tofu over a tomato coulis with creamy basil-yogurt purée. Chef McDonald also owns Pacific'O Restaurant (reviewed below) and is the chef for the Feast at Lele (reviewed above).

505 Front St. ℂ **808/661-8422.** www.iomaui.com. Reservations recommended. Main courses $32–$39. AE, DC, DISC, MC, V. Daily 5:50–9pm.

Pacific'O Restaurant ★ CONTEMPORARY PACIFIC RIM   You can't get any closer to the ocean than the tables here, which are literally on the beach. With good food complementing this sensational setting, foodies and aesthetes have much to enjoy. The split-level dining starts near the entrance, with a long bar (where you can also order lunch or dinner) and a few tables along the railing. Steps lead down to the outdoor tables, where the award-winning seafood dishes come to you with the backdrop of Lanai across the channel. Favorites include the fresh island catch dusted in Indian spices topped with a subtle coconut Wana (sea urchin), or sashimi blocks of fresh fish wrapped in a sheet of dry seaweed, quickly fried medium rare tempura-style, with white miso dressing and lime basil sauce. If you like seafood, sunsets, and touches of India and Indonesia in your fresh-from-the-sea dining choices, you should be happy here.

505 Front St. ℂ **808/667-4341.** www.pacificomaui.com. Reservations recommended. Main courses $13–$16 lunch, $32–$40 dinner. AE, DC, MC, V. Daily 11:30am–4pm and 5:30–9pm.

Moderate

David Paul's Island Grill ★★ NEW ISLAND CUISINE   He's back. One of Hawaii's top chefs, David Paul, opened a new restaurant in Lahaina introducing his "new island cooking," a combination of his latest American cuisine combined with his years in the island and using island products: items like slow-braised roasts, seared fresh fish, macadamia-nut-smoked and fire-grilled meals, brick-pressed chicken, and olive-oil-poached Keahole lobster. Although his menu changes daily, my picks are the roasted island snapper in Parmesan broth with sautéed upcountry field greens and house-cured pork shoulder, or the pot roast scented with five Chinese spices, or the grilled pork chops with shiitake reduction and lobster cream. The location, in the Lahaina Center, has plenty of parking and Chef David has an exhibit kitchen, so you can watch all the action. The Lanai Lounge has cocktails and a "tasting" menu of "small plate" versions of his entrees. Great wine deals too: 50 to 60 wines by the glass, most $10 or less.

Lahaina Center, 900 Front St., Ste. A-101, Lahaina. ℂ **808/662-3000.** www.davidpaulsisland grill.com. Main courses $20–$47; "9 item" tasting menu $40–$45. AE, DC, DISC, MC, V. Daily 5–9:30pm. Lounge 5pm–midnight.

Where to Dine in Lahaina & Kaanapali

PACIFIC OCEAN

Train Depot

Puukolii Rd.

Kaanapali Royal (North) Golf Course

KAANAPALI

Whalers Village 3

Kaanapali Kai (South) Golf Course

LK & PR Sugar Cane Train

Honoapiilani Hwy.

Hanakao'o Beach Park

Lahaina Civic Center

Wahikuli Beach Park

Kaniau Rd.

Lokia St.

Molahai St.

Wahikuli Rd.

Fleming Rd.

Anatea

Kapunakea St.

Lahaina Cannery Mall

Mala Wharf

Puunoa Point

Kahoma Stream

Lahainaluna Rd.

Front

Kenui St.

Baker St.

Train Depot

Papalaua St.

Pioneer Sugar Mill

LAHAINA

Lahaina Center

Dickenson St.

Wainee St.

Honoapiilani Hwy.

Luakini St.

Lahaina Small Boat Harbor

PACIFIC OCEAN

505 Front St. (Shops & Restaurants)

Shaw St.

Area of detail

Kahului   **MAUI**

Haleakala National Park

Aloha Mixed Plate **6**
Beachside Grill and Leilani's
   on the Beach **3**
Cane and Taro **3**
Cheeseburger in Paradise **13**
Cilantro: Fresh Mexican Grill **9**
CJ's Deli & Diner **2**
David Paul's Island Grill **7**
Duke's Beach House **1**
The Feast at Lele **19**
Gerard's **16**
Hard Rock Cafe **8**
I'o **19**
Kimo's **11**
Lahaina Coolers **17**
Lahaina Fish Co. **12**
Lahaina Grill **14**
Mala An Ocean Tavern **5**
Maui Sunrise Café **15**
Maui Swiss Cafe **18**
Maui Taco **10**
Nikki's Pizza **3**
Pacific 'O Restaurant **19**
Penne Pasta Café **17**
Son'z Maui at Swan Court **4**
Ulamalu **4**

The Ultimate Cookies

Looking for the ultimate taste treat to bring the folks back home? Try mouth-watering **Broke da Mouth Cookies,** 190 Alamaha St., Kahului (© 808/873-9255), open Monday through Friday from 6am to 7pm, Saturday from 7am to 5pm (get here early before the locals buy everything up). These terrific cookies range from chocolate mac-nut, oatmeal raisin, and shortbread to almond, peanut butter, and coconut crunch. While you're here, take a look at the other goodies—the sweet-potato haupia pie is to die for, and the *lilikoi* (passion fruit) cake will make your taste buds stand up and applaud.

Kimo's STEAK/SEAFOOD   Kimo's has a loyal following that keeps it from falling into the faceless morass of waterfront restaurants serving surf and turf with great sunset views. It's a formula restaurant (sibling to Leilani's on the Beach and Hula Grill) that works not only because of its oceanfront patio and upstairs dining room, but also because, for the price, there are some satisfying choices. It's always crowded, buzzing with people on a deck offering views of Molokai, Lanai, and Kahoolawe. Burgers and sandwiches are affordable and consistent, and the fresh catch in sweet-basil glaze is a top seller. The waistline-defying hula pie—macadamia-nut ice cream in a chocolate-wafer crust with fudge and whipped cream—originated here.

845 Front St. © **808/661-4811.** www.kimosmaui.com. Reservations recommended for dinner. Main courses $8–$13 lunch, $18–$35 dinner. AE, DC, DISC, MC, V. Daily 11am–3:30pm and 5–10pm. Bar 11am–12:30am; light menu 3:30–5pm.

Lahaina Fish Company SEAFOOD   The open-air dining room is literally over the water, with flickering torches after sunset and an affordable menu that covers the seafood-pasta basics. Head to an oceanside table and order a cheeseburger, chicken burger, fish burger, generous basket of peel-and-eat shrimp, or sashimi—lingering is highly recommended. The light lunch/grill menu offers appetizers (sashimi, seared ahi, spring rolls, and pot stickers), salads, and soups. The restaurant has spiffed up its dinner selections to include hand-carved steaks, several pasta choices, and local fare such as stir-fry dishes, teriyaki chicken, and luau-style ribs. The specialty, though, remains the fresh seafood: Four types of fresh fish are offered nightly, in three preparations. Pacific Rim specials include fresh ahi, seared spicy or cooked in a sweet ginger-soy sauce.

831 Front St. © **808/661-3472.** www.lahainafishcompany.com. Main courses $9–$15 lunch, $10–$30 dinner. AE, MC, V. Daily 11am–10pm.

Mala Ocean Tavern ★ ★ 🔸 LOCAL/SEAFOOD   Perched right on the ocean, this tiny "tavern" is the brainchild of Mark and Judy Ellman, owners of Maui Tacos and Penne Pasta Café. Their philosophy is healthy, organically grown food and fresh fish used to make intriguing dishes. The atmosphere could not be more enticing, with just a handful of tables out on the oceanfront lanai and several more tables in the warmly decorated interior. The staff is helpful and efficient, and the food is outstanding. If you're in the mood, ask for the exotic martini menu. You can opt for "tavern food" like an ahi burger or a cheeseburger, or one of the tempting salads (the beet and Kula goat cheese is divine), or something off the "big plate" menu (like wok-fried fresh fish or hoisin-glazed baby back ribs). Don't miss the weekend brunches (I recommend the "killer" French toast). This is a popular place, so avoid prime lunch and dinner hours.

1307 Front St. (across from the Lahaina Cannery Mall's Safeway grocery store). 🄯 **808/667-9394.** www.malaoceantavern.com. Main courses $13–$24 lunch, $17–$40 dinner; brunch $8–$16. AE, DISC, MC, V. Mon–Fri 11am–9:30pm; Sat–Sun 9am–9pm "or so."

Inexpensive
Aloha Mixed Plate ★ 🔸 PLATE LUNCHES/BEACHSIDE GRILL   Look for the festive turquoise-and-yellow, plantation-style front with the red corrugated-iron roof and adorable bar, tiny and busy, directly across from the Lahaina Cannery Mall. Grab a picnic table at ocean's edge, in the shade of large kiawe and milo trees, where you can watch the bobbing sailboats and two islands on the near horizon. (On the upper level, there are umbrellas and plumeria trees—just as charming.) Then tuck into inexpensive mahimahi, *kalua* pig and cabbage, shoyu chicken, teriyaki beef, and other local plate-lunch specials, all at budget-friendly prices, served with macaroni salad and rice. The shoyu chicken is the best I've had, fork-tender and tasty, and the spicy chicken drumettes come from a fabled family recipe. (The best sellers are the coconut prawns and Aloha Mixed Plate of shoyu chicken, teriyaki beef, and mahimahi.) I don't know of anywhere else where you can order a mai tai with a plate lunch and enjoy table service with an ocean view.

1285 Front St. 🄯 **808/661-3322.** www.alohamixedplate.com. Main courses $5–$14. MC, V. Daily 10:30am–10pm.

Cheeseburger in Paradise AMERICAN   Wildly successful, always crowded, highly visible, and very noisy (especially when live music plays in the evenings), Cheeseburger is a shrine to the American classic. The home of three-napkin cheeseburgers with attitude, this is burger country, tropical style, with everything from tofu and Gardenburgers to the biggest, juiciest beef and chicken burgers, served on whole-wheat and sesame buns baked fresh daily. There are good reasons why the two-story green-and-white building next to the sea wall is always packed: good value, good grinds, and a great ocean view. The Cheeseburger in Paradise—a hefty hunk with jack and cheddar cheeses, sautéed onions, lettuce, fresh tomatoes, and Thousand Island dressing—is a paean to the basics. You can build your own burger by adding sautéed mushrooms, bacon, grilled Ortega chilies, and other condiments for an extra charge. Onion rings, chili-cheese fries, and cold beer complete the carefree fantasy.

811 Front St. 🄯 **808/661-4855.** www.cheeseburgerland.com. Burgers $9–$16. AE, DISC, MC, V. Daily 8am–10pm.

Are you the type of visitor who feels you haven't "experienced" a destination unless you've hit the restaurants where the local residents eat? Or do you enjoy National Public Radio's "Road Food," or any of the Food Network's on-the-road culinary shows? Then sign up for **Tour da Food ★★★** (*(C)* **808/242-8383;** www.tourdafood.com). Pastry chef (and food writer, restaurant publicist, and cookbook author) Bonnie Friedman takes foodies off the tourist path to discover the culinary treasures—from snack shacks to restaurants to markets and manufacturers—that make up Maui's unique cuisine. You will laugh your way across the island with Bonnie's wonderful commentary about Maui's multicultural food options and its colorful history—and you'll also eat some of the island's most yummy food (which you never would have discovered on your own). Check out her website to read about the different tours (from breakfast at an old inn to "lunch like a local" to "plate lunch and picnic with poke"); prices begin at $280 per couple, which includes transportation, a main meal, snacks, an island traditional dessert, a bag of goodies to take home, and Bonnie's personal list of under-the-radar eating places. *Tip:* Book this tour early in your trip so that you have time to follow Bonnie's terrific suggestions of places to eat on Maui. (Best to book at least 1 week in advance.)

Cilantro: Fresh Mexican Grill ★ 🎒 ☺ MEXICAN   This is Maui's best bet for fabulous Mexican food at frugal prices (and winner of the Taste of Lahaina Award each of the past 3 years). And, believe it or not, this fast-food restaurant serves fresh, healthy food. The chef and owner is Paris Nabavi, creator of Maui's Pizza Paradiso Italian Kitchen. He wanted the "challenge of something different," so he took off to Mexico to find out how the Mexicans used to cook in "the old days." He's back on Maui with this unbelievably delicious eatery where everything is made from scratch. Even the corn tortillas are handmade daily. Signature dishes include the citrus-and-herb-marinated chipotle rotisserie chicken, the veggie Mariposa salad, the popular mother clucker flautas, and lip-smacking "al pastor" style adobo pork. All this at budget-pleasing prices. It's a great place to take the kids; Los Niños menu items are under $4.75.

170 Papalaua Ave. *(C)* **808/667-5444.** www.cilantrogrill.com. Entrees $8–$14. MC, V. Daily 11am–10pm.

Lahaina Coolers ★ AMERICAN/INTERNATIONAL   A huge marlin hangs above the bar, epic wave shots and wall sconces made of surfboard fins fill the walls, and open windows line three sides of this ultracasual indoor/outdoor restaurant. This is a great breakfast joint, with feta-cheese Mediterranean omelets, huevos rancheros, and fried rice made with jasmine rice, Kula vegetables, and Portuguese sausage. There are three types of eggs Benedict: the classic, a vegetarian version (with Kula vegetables—excellent), and the Local, with Kailua pork and sweetbread. At lunch, burgers rule and the sandwiches, from grilled portobellos to the classic tuna melt, are ideal for casual Lahaina. The pasta, made fresh daily, is prepared Asian style (with chicken and spicy Thai peanut sauce), with pesto, or vegetarian (in a spicy Creole sauce). Pizzas, fresh catch, steak, and enchiladas round out the entrees. Everything can be prepared vegetarian upon request.

180 Dickenson St. ℂ **808/661-7082.** www.lahainacoolers.com. Main courses $9–$12 breakfast, $10–$16 lunch, $18–$27 dinner. AE, DC, DISC, MC, V. Daily 8am–1am.

Maui Sunrise Café 🏄 GOURMET DELI/CAFE   If you want to know where to find the best breakfasts or the most filling lunches on a budget, follow the surfers to this teeny-tiny cafe located on Front Street, next door to the library. Eat in the patio garden out back or take your lunch to the beach. You'll find huge breakfasts, delicious gourmet sandwiches, and filling lunch plates all at bargain prices. It's tough to find a parking spot nearby (and you can't park at the library), but you'll probably want a brisk walk after eating here anyway.

693A Front St. ℂ **808/661-8558.** Breakfast items under $10; lunch items $7–$12. No credit cards. Daily 6am–4:30pm.

Maui Swiss Cafe SANDWICHES/PIZZA   Newly renovated and double its original size (which was tiny), Swiss Cafe now has 12 Internet stations and continues to serve excellent sandwiches and continental breakfast. Having gone from a sandwich-and-pizza shop to a European-style sidewalk Internet cafe, it still serves $7.50 lunch specials and two scoops of Roselani ice cream for $4 (and sometimes the ice cream is free with the lunch special). Top-quality breads baked fresh daily, Dijon mustard, good Swiss cheese, and keen attention to sandwich fillings and pizza toppings make this a very special sandwich shop. The new Swiss owner, Rolf Egli, bought the cafe from Dominique Martin 2 years ago, and has maintained the European flavor in this corner of Lahaina, down to the menus printed in English and German and the Swiss breakfast of sliced ham, cheese, hard-boiled egg, and freshly baked croissant. ***Tip:*** The "signature melt" sandwiches, with imported Emmenthal cheese baked on an Italian Parmesan crust, are something to watch for, and there are excellent vegetarian and turkey sandwiches as well.

640 Front St. ℂ **808/661-6776.** www.swisscafe.net. Sandwiches and 8-in. pizzas $6–$8. AE, DISC, MC, V. Daily 9am–6pm.

Penne Pasta Café ★ 🏠 ITALIAN/MEDITERRANEAN   Bargain hunters head for this neighborhood cafe, under the helm of chef Mark Ellman (of Maui Tacos and Mala fame). It features delicious Italian and Mediterranean cuisine. You'll get a sit-down meal at takeout prices, and *mama mia!*– those are big plates of pasta, pizzas, salads, and sandwiches. So, what's the catch? No waitstaff. You order at the counter and the manager delivers your order to your table. Favorites include the *molto bene* linguine pesto, baked penne, and pizza with olives, capers, basil, and roasted pepper. Wine (from $6.50 a glass) and beer are available, too.

180 Dickenson St. ℂ **808/661-6633.** www.pennepastacafe.com. Basic menu items under $10; specials up to $15. AE, DISC, MC, V. Mon–Fri 11am–9:30pm; Sat–Sun 5–9:30pm.

Kaanapali

Whalers Village, 2435 Kaanapali Pkwy. (www.whalersvillage.com/restaurants. htm), has a food court where you can buy pizza, Chinese, ice cream, sandwiches and wraps, and fast-food burgers at serve-yourself counters and courtyard tables. It's an inexpensive alternative and a quick, handy stop for shoppers and Kaanapali beachgoers.

EXPENSIVE

Son'z Maui at Swan Court ★★★ CONTEMPORARY EUROPEAN/ HAWAII REGIONAL   For 30 years, the Swan Court was *the* dining experience at the Hyatt Regency Maui Resort. When Tri-Star Restaurant Group CEO Aaron Placourakis (who also owns Nick's Fishmarket Maui, p. 493) took over this restaurant, he and executive chef Geno Sarmiento knew they wanted to hit a home run every night with the cuisine. The restaurant already had perhaps the most romantic location in Maui, overlooking a man-made lagoon with white and black swans swimming by and the rolling surf of the Pacific in the distance. Now the combination of the culinary team's creative dishes, fresh local ingredients (Kula corn and strawberries, Ono Farms avocados, Hana hearts of palm, Maui Cattle Company beef, fresh Hawaiian fish, and sweet Maui onions), top-notch service, and relaxing atmosphere makes this one of Maui's best restaurants. My personal picks from the very tempting menu are the Maui Surfing Goat Cheese ravioli appetizer (with Kula corn, edamame, Hamakua mushrooms, prosciutto, and a sherry-vinegar pan sauce) and, for a main course, either the Hawaiian opakapaka piccata (with artichokes, capers, Lisbon lemon, sweet-potato hash browns, and tomato purée) or the seared scallops BLT (with bacon and poached cherry tomatoes in a Caesar-salad emulsion, served with truffled potato chips). A beautiful breakfast buffet is also served.

At the Hyatt Regency Maui Resort, 200 Nohea Kai Dr. © **808/661-1234.** Reservations necessary for dinner. Entrees $31–$50. AE, DC, DISC, MC, V. Daily 5:30–10pm.

MODERATE

Beachside Grill/Leilani's on the Beach STEAK/SEAFOOD   The Beachside Grill is the informal, less-expensive room downstairs on the beach, where folks wander in off the sand for a frothy beer and a beachside burger. Leilani's is the dinner-only room, with more expensive but still not outrageously priced steak and seafood offerings. At Leilani's, you can order everything from fresh fish to filet mignon to fried coconut prawns. All of this, of course, comes with an ocean view. There's live music Friday, Saturday, and Sunday from 3 to 5:30pm.

At Whalers Village, 2435 Kaanapali Pkwy. © **808/661-4495.** www.leilanis.com. Reservations suggested for dinner. Lunch and dinner at Beachside Grill $9–$19; dinner at Leilani's $19–$33. AE, DC, DISC, MC, V. Beachside Grill daily 11am–11pm; Leilani's daily 5–9:30pm.

Cane & Taro ★ ASIAN   Another winner in Chef D. K. Kodama's growing list of fabulous restaurants (Sansei Seafood Restaurant & Sushi Bar on Maui, Oahu, and the Big Island, and d.k Steakhouse, Hiroshi and Vino on Oahu), Cane & Taro, opened in 2009. This is a departure from the well-known chef's creative sushi, steaks, and tapas (although you can find his best sellers on the menu here) into a hybrid Asian-pasta-steaks-seafood eatery located in the Whalers Village Shopping Center. Housed in the former Rusty Harpoon Restaurant location, great ocean views greet diners. The fantastic panorama quickly becomes secondary when the meal arrives. Serving breakfast (including five variations on eggs benedict), lunch (ranging from a build-your-own charbroiled hamburger to a Vietnamese chicken sandwich to a crab and shrimp cake sandwich) and dinner. Lunch and dinner feature the Chef's award-winning items like rock shrimp dynamite (crispy tempura rock shrimp with a masago aioli and unagi glaze), crunchy noodle crab and shrimp cake (with ginger lime chili and cilantro pesto)

THE tiki TERRACE

Bravo to the Kaanapali Beach Hotel for the low-salt, employee-tested Native Hawaiian diet served in its **Tiki Terrace Restaurant,** 2525 Kaanapali Pkwy. (*C* **808/667-0124**). The Hawaiian Combination features the healthy, traditional diet of fresh fish (you can also order it with chicken breast) and taro greens, flavored with herbs and spices. Fresh mild limu (seaweed) adds some natural saltiness, and you can always add your own salt and pepper to taste. The Native Hawaiian menu also includes a salad made from pohole fern shoots from Keanae Valley marinated with sweet Maui onions and seaweed and served with ginger-tomato dressing. (With their freshness, pleasing crunch, and mild flavor, fern shoots are one of the most underused greens of Hawaii.) Entree choices are accompanied by steamed sweet potato, taro, and fresh poi made on the premises. The dessert is half a chilled Hana papaya with lemon, grilled bananas, and pineapple slices. The cost for the Hawaiian Combination is $23.

The use of fresh local ingredients is a noteworthy touch in the a la carte menu as well. My favorites are the baked crab and shrimp with artichoke hearts and the coconut shrimp. Try Chef Muromoto's signature Sesame Shoyu dressing on the Kula greens salad—it's a house favorite. The a la carte menu entrees are headed up by the Huki Hukilau, a combination of fresh catch, jumbo prawn, and baby lobster tail. The menu also includes steak, ribs, teriyaki grilled chicken, and rack of lamb.

The dining room is old-fashioned Hawaii, not fancy, with tables on a terrace ringed with plumeria and palm trees. Nightly entertainment is a hula show from 6:30 to 7:30pm and music for dancing under the stars until 9pm.

The regular Tiki Terrace breakfast menu presents all the old favorites along with the opportunity to sample Hawaiian food in a familiar context: taro hash browns; three-egg lomi salmon omelet with sweet-potato home fries; a fruit plate of banana baked in ti leaf with lehua honey and macadamia nuts, served with yogurt; and French toast made with taro bread. There are even Hawaiian taro pancakes, and they're wonderful. The Hawaiian Sunday Champagne Brunch ($37; 9am–1pm) features more than 50 items on the buffet, plus stir-fry, carving, and omelet stations, along with Belgian waffles and great desserts, all accompanied by Hawaiian music.

The hotel also serves guests a complimentary Ohana Welcome Breakfast on their first morning at 8am Monday through Saturday, with live music, hula, a buffet breakfast, and advice on how to make the most of a Maui vacation. The hotel's staff greets guests, then takes to the stage for one of their specialties – singing and dancing hulas. Then they are off to work while guests enjoy a tour of hotel events and island activities.

The emphasis on Hawaiian food is only one part of a pervasive spirit of aloha that distinguishes this hotel. Reservations are recommended. Dinner is served daily from 6 to 9pm.

and Kona coffee baby back ribs (roasted with coffee-mango barbecue sauce and served with a smoked tomato slaw), as well as pastas (including kid's portions), sushi rolls, sashimi, fish, chicken, and steaks. The new restaurant is always packed; get reservations for dinner.

CHEF MCDONALD HAS A farm, E-I-E-I-O

Here's your chance to see where those delicious greens, sweet basil, and wonderful tropical fruits that make up your dinner at **Pacific'O** and **I'O** restaurants come from. **James McDonald** was the first chef in the state to own and operate a farm for the purpose of supplying his own restaurants. Your visit to **O'o Farm** begins with hot apple cider and pastries. The tour is led by a culinary specialist who helps you handpick items for your lunch. At the end of the tour, lunch is served. The cost is $50 per person. For more information, call © **808/667-4341** or go to www.oofarm.com.

Whaler's Village, 2435 Kaanapali Pkwy., Kaanapali. © **808/662-0668.** www.dkrestaurants.com. Reservations for dinner recommended. Lunch entrees $10–$14; dinner entrees $10–$37. AE, DC, DISC, MC, V. Daily 8am–10pm.

Duke's Beach House ★★ PACIFIC RIM   Perched on the side of the ocean, facing the beautiful Kaanapali Beach, and housed in what appears to be an open-air plantation home, the latest of TS Restaurants (Kimo's and Leilani's on Maui, Keoki's on Kauai, and Hula Grill in Waikiki, plus more restaurants on the Mainland) opened in late 2009. It has a fabulous beachfront location with great decor (the authentic memorabilia of Hawaii's Duke Kahanamoku, who was an award-winning Olympic swimmer, famous surfer, movie star, and unofficial Hawaii Ambassador of Aloha). More important, the food is fabulous. Following the new "localvore" tradition, the staff is committed to a "farm to fork" dining experience and stresses that ingredients are obtained locally on Maui. Breakfast features a host of eggs, pancakes, and even a "beach boy burrito (with eggs, sausage, bacon, potatoes, chipotle cream, and avocado salsa); lunch is creative salads, sandwiches, burgers, and fresh fish. Dinner features steaks, fish, chicken, and a seafood risotto. Leave room for the hula pie (Oreo cookie crust, topped with macadamia nut ice cream, hot fudge, and whipped cream).
Honua Kai Resort & Spa, 130 Kai Malina Pkwy., North Kaanapali Beach. © **808/662-2900.** www.dukesmaui.com. Breakfast items $6.25–$12; lunch entrees $10–$14; dinner entrees $18–$29. AE, MC, V. Daily 7am–8pm.

Umalu ★ PACIFIC RIM   This is the kind of restaurant that visitors dream about. Located oceanside, next to the Hyatt Regency Maui's pool with a great view of the islands of Molokai and Lanai in the distance, you will be happy way before you get your first exotic cocktail. Umalu translates into "the shade cast by a cliff" and that is a great description of the relaxed atmosphere of this outdoor restaurant (with plenty of huge umbrellas for shade). Lunch is very casual, with interesting sandwiches like the Maui Waui–style fish tacos with beer-battered mahimahi on warm flour tortillas; or the chicken sandwich with jalapeño jack cheese, crispy bacon, and avocado; or the angus burger (a half-pound grilled burger), as well as pizzas (from a sausage or pepperoni to a veggie to a ham-pineapple and Maui onion pie). By dinner, the atmosphere is still open-air but more upscale, with prime rib, seared ahi steaks, and sesame-orange chicken stir-fry, plus pizza, burgers, and sandwiches.

Hyatt Regency Maui Resort & Spa, 200 Nohea Kai Dr., Kaanapali. ℂ **808/661-1234.** Lunch entrees $10–$19; dinner entrees $16–$41. AE, DC, MC, V. Daily 11am–9:30pm. Live entertainment every evening.

INEXPENSIVE

CJ's Deli & Diner ★ 𝓮 AMERICAN/DELI   If you're staying in Kaanapali, this restaurant is within walking distance from your resort; if you're not staying in Kaanapali, it's worth the drive to sample the "comfort food" (as they call it) at this hip, happening eatery with prices so low you won't believe you're still on Maui. A huge billboard menu hangs from the yellow-and-gold textured wall, and highly polished wooden floors give the roadside eatery a homey feeling. You can eat in or take out (you can even get a "chef-to-go" to come to your accommodations and cook for you), the atmosphere is friendly, and there's a computer with high-speed Internet connection to keep the techies humming. Huge, delicious breakfasts are served from 7 to 11am (check out the $5.95 early-bird special of two eggs, bacon or sausage, rice, and coffee). There's a wide selection of egg dishes, plus pancakes and waffles, and don't forget the tempting delights from the bakery. Lunch ranges from deli sandwiches and burgers to pot roast, ribs, and fish dishes. If you are on your way to Hana or up to the top of Haleakala, stop by and get a box lunch. CJ's even has a menu for the kids.

At the Fairway Shops at Kaanapali, 2580 Kekaa Dr. (just off the Honoapiilani Hwy.), Kaanapali. ℂ **808/667-0968.** www.cjsmaui.com. Breakfast items $4–$9.50; lunch items $8.50–$15; Hana Lunch Box and Air Travel Lunch Box $12 each. AE, MC, V. Daily 7am–8pm.

Nikki's Pizza PIZZA   Formerly Pizza Paradiso, Nikki's has a full menu of pastas, pizzas, and desserts, including smoothies, coffee, and ice cream. This is a welcome addition to the Kaanapali scene, where casual is king and good food doesn't have to be fancy. The pizzas reflect a simple and effective formula that has won acclaim through the years: good crust, true-blue sauces, and toppings loyal to tradition but with just enough edge for those who want it. Create your own pizza with roasted eggplant, mushrooms, anchovies, artichoke hearts, sausage, and a slew of other toppings. Nikki's offers some heroic choices, from the veggie to the Hawaiian (ham and Maui pineapple) to the Sopranos (roasted chicken, artichoke hearts, sun-dried tomatoes).

At Whalers Village, 2435 Kaanapali Pkwy. ℂ **808/667-0333.** Gourmet pizza $4–$5 by the slice; whole pizzas $18–$28. AE, DISC, MC, V. Daily 8am–9pm.

Honokowai, Kahana & Napili

Note: You'll find the restaurants in this section on the "Where to Stay & Dine in West Maui" map (p. 445).

MODERATE

Maui Brewing Co. SEAFOOD/STEAK   This restaurant consists of a bar, a retail section, and tables. The small retail section sells fresh seafood, while the sit-down menu covers basic tastes: salads, fish and chips, fresh-fish sandwiches, cheeseburgers, and beer—lots of it. At dinner, count on heavier meats and the fresh catch of the day (maybe ahi, mahimahi, or ono), with rotisserie items such as grilled chicken, steaks, and duck. The late-night menu offers shrimp, cheese fries, quesadillas, and lighter fare.

At the Kahana Gateway Shopping Center, 4405 Honoapiilani Hwy. © **808/669-3474.** www. mauibrewingco.com. Reservations recommended for dinner. Main courses $11–$29. AE, DC, DISC, MC, V. Daily 11am–9:30pm; late-night menu 9:30pm–midnight; Sun brunch 8am–11pm during football season (Sept–Jan).

Roy's Kahana Bar & Grill ★★ EURO-ASIAN   Despite the lack of dramatic view and an upstairs location in a shopping mall, Roy's remains crowded and extremely popular for one reason: fabulous food on a frequently changing menu. It bustles with young, hip, impeccably trained servers. Menu highlights include Szechuan barbecue–grilled ahi steak, basil-seared opakapaka with wild mushroom and asparagus risotto, and glazed honey-mustard short ribs. You could make a meal of the incredibly creative appetizers, such as Roy's original Kai-style ahi, crab cakes, lobster and shrimp pot stickers, crispy shrimp and pork lumpia, or lemon grass–poached pear salad. Large picture windows open up Roy's Kahana but don't quell the noise, another tireless trait long ago established by Roy's Restaurant in Honolulu, the flagship of Yamaguchi's burgeoning empire.

At the Kahana Gateway Shopping Center, 4405 Honoapiilani Hwy. © **808/669-6999.** www. roysrestaurant.com. Reservations strongly recommended. Main courses $30–$46. AE, DC, DISC, MC, V. Daily 5:30–9:30pm.

Sea House Restaurant ASIAN/PACIFIC RIM   The Sea House is not glamorous, famous, or hip, but it's worth mentioning for its spectacular view of Napili Bay. The Napili Kai Beach Resort, where the Sea House is located, is a charming throwback to the days when hotels blended in with their surroundings, had lush tropical foliage, and were sprawling rather than vertical. Dinner entrees range from taro-crusted sea bass with green papaya salad to seafood cioppino to mustard and poha berry–crusted rack of lamb. There's even a menu for the *keiki,* with items such as hamburgers and chicken nuggets.

At the Napili Kai Beach Resort, 5900 Honoapiilani Hwy. © **808/669-1500.** Reservations required for dinner. Main courses $6–$12 breakfast, $11–$16 lunch, $26–$39 dinner; appetizer menu $9–$14. AE, DISC, MC, V. Daily 7am–9pm.

INEXPENSIVE

Maui Tacos MEXICAN   Mark Ellman's Maui Tacos chain has grown faster than you can say "Haleakala." Ellman put gourmet Mexican on paper plates and on the island's culinary map long before Maui became known as Hawaii's center for salsa and chimichangas. Barely more than a takeout counter with a few tables, this and the six other Maui Tacos in Hawaii (five on Maui alone) are popular with hungry surfers, discerning diners, burrito buffs, and Hollywood glitterati, like Sharon Stone, whose picture adorns a wall or two. Choices include excellent fresh-fish tacos (garlicky and flavorful), chimichangas, and mouth-breaking compositions such as the Hookipa (a personal favorite): a "surf burrito" of fresh fish, black beans, and salsa. The spinach burrito contains four kinds of beans, rice, and potatoes—it's a knockout, requiring a siesta afterward. Expect good food but not very fast service. Other locations are at Lahaina Square, Lahaina (© **808/661-8883**); Kamaole Beach Center, Kihei (© **808/879-5005**); Napili Plaza, Napili (© **808/665-0222**); Piilani Village Shopping Center, Kihei (© **808/875-9340**); and Kaahumanu Center, Kahului (© **808/871-7726**).

At Napili Plaza, 5095 Napili Hau St. © **808/665-0222.** www.mauitacos.com. All items $3–$10. AE, DISC, MC, V. Daily 10:30am–7:30pm.

Pizza Paradiso Italian Kitchen PIZZA/ITALIAN   Order at the counter (pastas, gourmet pizza whole or by the slice, panini, salads, and desserts) and find a seat at one of the few tables. The pasta sauces—marinara, pescatore, Alfredo, Florentine, and pesto, with options and add-ons—are as popular as the pizzas (which took "best pizza" in the 2005 *Maui News* reader poll). The Massimo, a pesto sauce with artichoke hearts, sun-dried tomatoes, and capers, comes with a choice of chicken, shrimp, or clams, and is so good it was a Taste of Lahaina winner. Recent additions to the menu include gyros, souvlakia, hummus, and cheese-steak sandwiches. Take out, dine in, or delivery (free!)—this is a hot spot in the neighborhood.

At the Honokowai Marketplace, 3350 Lower Honoapiilani Rd. ℭ **808/667-2929.** www.pizza paradiso.com. Pastas $10–$11; pizzas $16–$28. MC, V. Daily 10am–9pm.

Kapalua

Note: You'll find the restaurants in this section on the "Where to Stay & Dine in West Maui" map (p. 445).

VERY EXPENSIVE

The Banyan Tree ★★ ASIAN-INSPIRED   The most recent chef de cuisine, in a long line of outstanding chefs chosen from the stables of the Ritz-Carlton resorts around the globe, is Ryan Urig. His distinctive menu includes Kona lobster with ginger-carrot risotto; chorizo crusted opah; and grilled lamb loin. They are currently doing what they call their "50/50 Menu," a three-course dinner for $50 and a bottle of selected wine for $50. The atmosphere is extremely romantic, overlooking the ocean with the island of Molokai in the distance—get reservations for sunset.

At the Ritz-Carlton Kapalua, 1 Ritz-Carlton Dr. ℭ **808/669-6200.** Reservations recommended. Main courses $38–$65. AE, DC, DISC, MC, V. Tues–Sat 5:30–9:30pm.

Merriman's ★★★ PACIFIC RIM   This is probably the most beautiful location for a restaurant in the state. On a point jetting out into the ocean, overlooking Kapalua Bay on one side and the island of Molokai in the distance, the former location of the Kapalua Bay Club, well-known local Chef Peter Merriman (Merriman's Waimea on the Big Island, Merriman's Market Café on the Big Island, and Merriman's Poipu in Kauai), who is a James Beard award-winning chef, opened this spectacular restaurant in 2008. His fantastic menu (which has received rave reviews from major food publication), where he pioneered the "farm to table" concept of serving only fresh products from local farmers, fishermen, and ranchers, is on display here with Haleakala Ranch–raised lamb, his well-known wok-charred ahi (served with pumpkin puree and tangerine-green peppercorn jus), and even locally gown fresh-vegetable potpie for the vegetarians. To really experience Merriman's culinary genius, order the pupu (appetizer) taster. The night I dined, the taster (which changes daily) included fresh fish and avocado, local kalua pig with sweet onion quesadilla, baked local goat cheese with beet chutney and herbed tartines, and ahi sushi with miso-marinated calamari salad. *Insiders' tip:* Book your reservation for sunset to really experience this incredible vista. If sunset tables are booked, come for sunset anyway and sit on the large open-air patio, located out on the point, and enjoy a cocktail and an appetizer.

One Bay Club Place, Kapalua Resort. ℂ **808/669-6400.** www.merrimanshawaii.com. Reservations recommended. Dinner entrees $24–$44. AE, MC, V. Daily 5:30–9pm; Point Bar menu daily 5–9pm.

EXPENSIVE

Pineapple Grill ★★★ PACIFIC ISLAND   If you had only a single night to eat on the island of Maui, this would be the place to go. Up-and-coming young chef Ryan Luckey (a local Lahaina boy) has taken the helm and is winning high praise from both critics and the local residents who flock here nightly. My picks on this creative menu would be ahi steak crusted with pistachios and wasabi peas (served with coconut-scented "forbidden" rice, Makawao mushrooms, and wasabi-soy butter), candied macadamia-crusted roast mahimahi (in a poha berry beurre blanc), or the wonderful lemon porcini–dusted Monchong (served with mashed potatoes and tomato lomi-lomi). An excellent list of wine pairings by the glass is available. Save room for the Maui gold-pineapple upside-down cake (with Whaler dark-rum sauce and Maui-made Roselani gourmet mac-nut ice cream). There are lots of tasty sandwiches and salads at lunch. Plus, it's all served in a very Mauilike atmosphere, overlooking the rolling hills of the Kapalua golf course out to the Pacific Ocean.

At the Kapalua Golf Club Bay Course, 200 Kapalua Dr. ℂ **808/669-9600.** www.pineapplekapalua.com. Reservations recommended for dinner. Main courses $10–$18 lunch, $25–$50 dinner. AE, MC, V. Daily 11am–2:30pm, 2:30–5:30pm (grill menu), and 5:30–10pm.

Plantation House Restaurant ★★ SEAFOOD/HAWAIIAN-MEDITERRANEAN   With its teak tables, fireplace, and open sides, Plantation House gets stellar marks for atmosphere. The 360-degree view from high among the resort's pine-studded hills takes in Molokai and Lanai, the ocean, the rolling fairways and greens, the northwestern flanks of the West Maui Mountains, and the daily sunset spectacular. Readers of the *Maui News* have deemed this the island's "Best Ambience"—a big honor on an island of wonderful views. It's the best place for breakfast in West Maui, hands down, and one of my top choices for dinner. The eggs Mediterranean makes a superb start to your day, and at lunch, sandwiches (open-faced smoked turkey, roasted vegetable, and goat-cheese wrap) and salads rule. When the sun sets, the menu expands to marvelous starters such as polenta and scampi-style shrimp, crab cakes, and Kula and Mediterranean salads. The menu changes constantly but may include fresh fish prepared several ways— among them, Mediterranean (on roasted Maui onions with couscous), Venice (pressed in panko, with a golden-raisin/pine nut butter), Maui (pistachio-crusted), Plantation (with sautéed crab and lemon beurre blanc), and Italy (pepper-dusted with olives and caper salsa). Don't forget the numerous vegetarian entrees and wonderful Australian lamb, New Zealand lobster, and a Tuscan-style rib-eye steak you'll long remember.

At the Kapalua Golf Club Plantation Course, 2000 Plantation Club Dr. ℂ **808/669-6299.** www.theplantationhouse.com. Reservations recommended. Main courses $7.75–$15 breakfast, $12–$18 lunch, $20–$42 dinner. AE, DC, MC, V. Daily 8am–3pm and 5:30–9pm (6–9pm May 1–Sept 30).

Sansei Seafood Restaurant & Sushi Bar ★★ PACIFIC RIM/SUSHI   Perpetual award-winner Sansei offers an extensive menu of Japanese and East-West delicacies. Part fusion, part Hawaii Regional Cuisine, Sansei is tirelessly creative, with a menu that scores higher with adventurous palates than with purists (although there are endless traditional choices as well). If you don't like cilantro, watch out for those complex mango/crab-salad rolls. Other choices include panko-crusted ahi sashimi, sashimi trio, ahi carpaccio, noodle dishes, lobster, Asian shrimp cakes, and sauces that surprise, in creative combinations such as ginger-lime chili butter and cilantro pesto. But there's simpler fare as well, such as shrimp tempura, noodles, and wok-tossed upcountry vegetables. Desserts are not to be missed. If it's autumn, don't pass up the Granny Smith apple tart with vanilla ice cream and homemade caramel sauce. In other seasons, opt for tempura-fried ice cream with chocolate sauce. There's karaoke Thursday to Saturday nights from 10pm to 1am. *Money-saving tip:* Eat early; all food is 25% off between 5:30 and 6pm. Also at Kihei Town Center, Kihei (✆ 808/879-0004).

600 Office Rd. ✆ **808/669-6286.** www.sanseihawaii.com. Reservations recommended. Main courses $19–$43. AE, DISC, MC, V. Daily 5:30–10pm. Also at Kihei Town Center, Kihei (✆ **808/879-0004**).

South Maui
KIHEI/MAALAEA

There's a branch of **Maui Tacos** at Kamaole Beach Center, in Kihei (✆ **808/879-5005**).

Note: You'll find the Kihei restaurants in this section on the "Where to Stay & Dine in South Maui" map (p. 451).

Expensive

Buzz's Wharf AMERICAN   Buzz's is another formula restaurant that offers a superb view, substantial sandwiches, meaty french fries, and surf-and-turf fare—in a word, satisfying but not sensational. Still, this bright, airy dining room makes a fine way station for whale-watching over a cold beer and a mahimahi sandwich with fries. Some diners opt for several appetizers (stuffed mushrooms, steamer clams, clam chowder, onion soup) and a salad, and then splurge on dessert. Buzz's prize-winning Tahitian Baked Papaya is a warm, fragrant melding of fresh papaya with vanilla and coconut—the pride of the house.

50 Hauoli St., Maalaea Harbor. ✆ **808/244-5426.** www.buzzswharf.com. Reservations recommended. Main courses $11–$25 lunch, $21–$38 dinner. AE, DC, DISC, MC, V. Daily 11am–9pm.

Five Palms ★ PACIFIC RIM   This is the best lunch spot in Kihei—open air, with tables a few feet from the beach and up-close-and-personal views of Kahoolawe and Molokini. You'll have to walk through a nondescript parking area and the modest entrance of the Mana Kai Maui Resort to reach this unpretentious place. It features a menu of breakfast and lunch items served from 8am to 2:30pm, so if you're jet-lagged and your stomach isn't on Hawaiian time, you can get a crab omelet at 2 in the afternoon or a juicy Kobe beef hamburger at 8 in the morning. At dinner, with the torches lit on the beach and the main dining room open, the ambience shifts to evening romantic but still casual. Just-caught fish is the star of the dinner menu.

At the Mana Kai Maui Resort, 2960 S. Kihei Rd., Kihei. ✆ **808/879-2607.** www.fivepalmsrestaurant. com. Reservations recommended for dinner. Main courses $8–$20 breakfast and lunch, $28–$45 dinner. AE, DC, MC, V. Daily 8am–2:30pm and 5–9pm; pupu menu daily 2–7pm.

The Waterfront at Maalaea ★★ SEAFOOD   The family-owned Waterfront has won many prestigious awards for wine excellence, service, and seafood, but its biggest boost is word of mouth. Loyal diners rave about the friendly staff and seafood, fresh off the boat in nearby Maalaea Harbor and prepared with care. The bay and harbor view is one you'll never forget, especially at sunset. There are nine choices of preparations for the several varieties of fresh Hawaiian fish, ranging from *en papillote* (baked in buttered parchment) to Southwestern (smoked chili and cilantro butter) to Island-style (sautéed, broiled, poached, or baked and paired with tiger prawns). Other choices: Kula onion soup, an excellent Caesar salad, the signature lobster chowder, and grilled eggplant layered with Maui onions, tomatoes, and spinach, served with red-pepper coulis and feta ravioli. Like the seafood, it's superb.

50 Hauoli St., Maalaea Harbor. ✆ **808/244-9028.** www.waterfrontrestaurant.net. Reservations recommended. Main courses $21–$46. AE, DC, DISC, MC, V. Daily 5pm–closing (last seating at 8:30pm).

Moderate

Cafe O'Lei Kihei ★★ STEAK/SEAFOOD   Chefs Michael and Dana Pastula have had a host of Cafe O'Lei restaurants on Maui (in Makawao, Lahaina, Maalaea, and Napili), and I've loved every one of them. Their latest is in an out-of-the-way location, the unattractive Rainbow Mall. Never mind—you come here for the food, not the view (which is of congested Kihei Rd. and a small bit of ocean between the fence of high-rise condos across the street). Inside, the open and airy room has floor-to-ceiling windows, hardwood floors, a big circular bar in the middle, and, on one side, an exhibition kitchen. The atmosphere is relaxing and inviting. The food is, as usual, not only outstanding, but also a real bargain. You can't beat lunch with fresh fish, rice, and salad for under $9 (arrive early, as the locals are well aware of this wonderful gem and will book all the tables in advance). Dinners range from fresh fish to prime rib, mac-nut-crusted chicken breast to roast duck, and even a mushroom-asparagus-pine-nut linguine for the vegetarians. Save room for dessert, such as pineapple upside-down cake or a fudge-brownie sundae (yum, yum).

2439 S. Kihei Rd., Kihei. ✆ **808/891-1368.** www.cafeoleirestaurants.com. Reservations recommended. Main courses $7–$13 lunch, $17–$35 dinner. AE, DC, DISC, MC, V. Tues–Sun 10:30am–3:30pm and 5–9pm.

Stella Blues Cafe ★ AMERICAN   Stella Blues gets going at breakfast and continues through to dinner with something for everyone—vegetarians, kids, pasta and sandwich lovers, hefty steak eaters, and sensible diners who go for the inexpensive salad of fresh Maui greens. Grateful Dead posters line the walls, and a covey of gleaming motorcycles is invariably parked outside. It's loud and lively, irreverent and unpretentious. Sandwiches are the highlight, ranging from the half-pound Maui beef Company Blues burger to grilled chicken to the Kalua pork and cabbage plate lunch. Mountain-size salads are popular, as are large coffee shakes with mounds of whipped cream. Daily specials include fresh seafood and other surprises—all home-style cooking, made from scratch, down to the pesto mayonnaise and herb bread. At dinner, selections are geared toward good-value family dining, from affordable full dinners to pastas and burgers.

At the Azeka Place II Shopping Center, 1279 S. Kihei Rd., Kihei. ℂ **808/874-3779.** www.stella blues.com. Main courses $6–$13 breakfast, $9–$15 lunch, $15–$28 dinner. AE, DC, DISC, MC, V. Daily 7:30am–11pm.

Inexpensive

The Coffee Store COFFEEHOUSE   This simple, classic coffeehouse for caffeine connoisseurs serves two dozen types of coffee and coffee drinks, from mochas and lattes to cappuccinos, espressos, and toddies. Breakfast items include smoothies, lox and bagels, quiches, granola, and assorted pastries. Salads and sandwiches (tuna, turkey, ham, grilled veggie panini) also move briskly from the takeout counter. The turkey-and-veggie wraps are a local legend. There are only a few small tables, and they fill up fast, often with musicians and artists who've spent the previous evening entertaining at the Wailea and Kihei resorts.

At the Azeka Place II Shopping Center, 1279 S. Kihei Rd., Kihei. ℂ **808/875-4244.** www.maui coffee.com. All items under $10. AE, MC, V. Mon–Sat 6am–6pm; Sun 6am–5pm.

Joy's Place 🗡 HEALTHY DELI/SANDWICHES   If you're in Kihei and look-ing for a healthy, delicious lunch at a rock-bottom price, it's worth hunting around for Joy's Place. This tiny hole in the wall has humongous sandwiches (turkey and avocado, tuna salad), wheat-free wraps, fresh salads, hot items (falafel burger, veggie burger), soups, and desserts. Most items are organic. There are a few places to sit inside, but the beach is just a 2-minute walk away.

In the Island Surf Bldg., 1993 S. Kihei Rd. (entrance on Auhana St.). ℂ **808/879-9258.** All items under $12. AE, DC, DISC, MC, V. Mon–Sat 8am–3pm.

Peggy Sue's AMERICAN   Just for a moment, forget that diet and take a leap. This 1950s-style diner has oodles of charm and is a swell place to spring for the best chocolate malt on the island. You'll also find sodas, shakes, floats, egg creams, milkshakes, and scoops of made-on-Maui Roselani gourmet ice cream. Old-fashioned soda-shop stools, an Elvis Presley Boulevard sign, and jukeboxes on every Formica table serve as a backdrop for the famous burgers (and veggie burgers), brushed with teriyaki sauce and served with all the goodies. The fries are great, too.

At the Azeka Place II Shopping Center, 1279 S. Kihei Rd., Kihei. ℂ **808/875-8944.** Burgers (with fries) $9.45–$12; plate lunches $7–$9. AE, DISC, MC, V. Mon–Thurs 11am–9pm; Fri–Sun 11am–10pm.

Shaka Sandwich & Pizza PIZZA   How many "best pizzas" are there on Maui? It depends on which shore you're on, the west or the south. At this south-shore old-timer, which recently moved to a new (and much larger) location, they're still serving those award-winning pizzas, New York–style heroes, Philly cheese steaks, calzones, salads, and homemade garlic bread. Shaka uses fresh Maui produce, long-simmered sauces, and homemade Italian bread. Choose thin or Sicilian thick crust with gourmet toppings: Maui onions, spinach, anchovies, jalapeños, and a spate of other vegetables. Try the white pizza; with the perfectly balanced flavors of olive oil, garlic, and cheese, you won't even miss the tomato sauce. My favorite, the spinach pizza (with olive oil, spinach, garlic, and mozzarella), is a real treat.

1770 S. Kihei Rd., Kihei. ℂ **808/874-0331.** www.shakapizza.com. Sandwiches $7–$15; pizzas $18–$27. MC, V. Sun–Thurs 10:30am–9pm; Fri–Sat 10:30am–10pm.

WAILEA

The **Shops at Wailea** (www.shopsatwailea.com), with a sprawling location between the Grand Wailea Resort and Outrigger Wailea Resort, has added a spate of new shops and restaurants to this stretch of South Maui. Five restaurants and dozens of shops, most of them upscale, are among the new tenants of this complex. **Ruth's Chris Steak House** is here, as well as **Tommy Bahama's Tropical Cafe & Emporium, Honolulu Coffee Company, Kai Wailea, Longhi's,** and **Lappert's Ice Cream.**

Note: You'll find the restaurants in this section on the "Where to Stay & Dine in South Maui" map (p. 451).

Very Expensive

Ko ★★★ GOURMET PLANTATION CUISINE   The concept behind this successful restaurant in the Fairmont Kea Lani is pure genius—taking the various ethnic cuisine from Maui's old plantation days (Hawaiian, Filipino, Portuguese, Korean, Puerto Rican, and European) and cooking them up in a gourmet fashion. Quicker than you can say "humuhumukununukuapua'a" (Hawaii's state fish), you have a culinary success. Many of the recipes they use come from old family recipes handed down from the sugar cane plantation days. The word "ko" means cane, as in sugar cane, back to the old plantation days when the sugar cane plantations had "camp" housing for each ethnic group. There would be a Japanese camp, a Filipino camp, and so forth, and each group had its own cuisine. Here are some wonderful taste treats you are going to find only here—so don't miss them—including ahi (which is tuna) "on the rocks," where the server brings you chunks of fresh ahi and you cook them on hot ishiyaki stone to the desired doneness (from barely seared on the outside to fully cooked). Then you dip the ahi into the orange-ginger miso sauce. Other suggestions are Filipino lumpia (a sort of spring roll with green papaya, shrimp, and pork, or else chicken and mushroom, which you dip into a spicy sauce), *paniolo* rib-eye steak with fern shoots, and Korean-style spicy chicken served with Maui lavender honey and wonderful Portuguese bean soup.

Fairmont Kea Lani, 4100 Wailea Alanui Dr., Wailea. ℂ **808/875-4100.** www.fairmont.com. Reservations recommended. Entrees $21–$50. AE, DC, DISC, MC, V. Daily 5:30–10pm.

Longhi's ★ ITALIAN   Unfortunately, the ocean view is now blocked by yet another high-rise, but Longhi's open-air room and its trademark black-and-white checkered floor still make a great backdrop to start the day. Breakfasts here are worth waking up for: perfect baguettes, fresh-baked cinnamon rolls (one is enough for two people), and eggs Benedict or Florentine. Lunch is either an Italian banquet (ahi torino, prawns amaretto, and a wide variety of pastas) or fresh salads and sandwiches. Dinner is where Longhi's shines, with a long list of fresh-made pasta dishes, seafood platters, and beef and chicken dishes (filet mignon with basil, veal scaloppine). Leave room for the daily dessert specials.

At the Shops at Wailea, 3750 Wailea Alanui Dr., Wailea. ℂ **808/891-8883.** www.longhis.com. Reservations recommended for dinner. Breakfast items $8.50–$21; lunch items $9–$38; dinner main courses $17–$120. AE, DC, DISC, MC, V. Mon–Fri 8am–10pm; Sat–Sun 7:30am–10pm.

Mala Wailea ★★★ HAWAIIAN REGIONAL CUISINE/SEAFOOD   This upscale version of **Mala Ocean Tavern** in Lahaina (p. 479) now occupies the prime restaurant location at the Wailea Beach Marriott Resort & Spa. Serving breakfast and dinner, this is not to be missed as a food experience. Created by Chef Mark Ellman, one of the original founders of the Hawaiian Regional Cuisine movement (his other restaurants on Maui include Maui Tacos, Penne Pasta Café, and Mala Ocean Tavern), this is a great place to enjoy island food in a casual atmosphere. Chef Ellman has created a menu that rivals the spectacular ocean view for your attention: Balinese stir-fry with fresh island fish, or ginger garlic black-bean sauce over a whole wok-fried fish or hoisin-glazed baby back ribs. Or you can choose from the lighter "tavern" menu of ahi burger, fresh island fish sandwich, or Kobe beef cheeseburger. Breakfast features both ala carte fare (don't miss the "killer" French toast or the chilaquile—salsa, corn tortillas, eggs, sour cream, and feta cheese) and a full (more than full) buffet.

Wailea Beach Marriott Resort & Spa, 3700 Wailea Alanui Dr., Wailea. ℂ **808/875-9394.** www.malaoceantavern.com. Reservations recommended. Breakfast buffet $27; dinner entrees $19–$39. AE, DC, DISC, MC, V. Mon–Sat 6:30am–9:30pm; Sun 6:30am–9pm.

Nick's Fishmarket Maui ★★ SEAFOOD Here's the place to bring your sweetie to enjoy the moon rise and the sweet smell of the stephanotis growing on the terrace. Fans love this classic seafood restaurant that sticks to the tried and true. The few detractors complain that the food is too old-style (ca. 1970s), but most agree that there is a high degree of professionalism in both service and preparation. The Greek Maui Wowie salad gets my vote as one of the top salads in Hawaii. The rest of the menu features great fresh fish like opakapaka (one of the signature dishes), seared opah, and Hawaiian spiny lobster. For the non–fish eaters, rack of lamb, roasted chicken, and dry-aged New York steak offer ample choices for diners enjoying the fantasy setting on the South Maui shoreline.

At the Fairmont Kea Lani Maui, 4100 Wailea Alanui Dr. ℂ **808/879-7224.** www.tristarrestaurants.com. Reservations recommended. Main courses $30–$120. AE, DC, DISC, MC, V. Daily 5:30–9:45pm.

Spago ★★ HAWAIIAN/CALIFORNIA/PACIFIC REGIONAL California meets Hawaii in this contemporary eatery featuring fresh, local Hawaii ingredients prepared under the culinary watch of master chef Wolfgang Puck. The room, formerly Seasons Dining Room, has been stunningly transformed into a sleek modern layout using stone and wood in the open-air setting overlooking the Pacific. The cuisine lives up to Puck's reputation of tweaking traditional Hawaiian dishes with his own brand of cutting-edge innovations. The menu changes daily and can feature Hawaiian Moi steamed Hong Kong style; pineapple grilled mahimahi; grilled Chinois-style lamb chops; and roast Cantonese duck with pineapple and papaya. The wine and beverage list is well thought out and extensive. Make reservations as soon as you land on the island (if not before); this place is popular. And bring plenty of cash or your platinum card.

At the Four Seasons Resort Maui at Wailea, 3900 Wailea Alanui Dr. ℂ **808/879-2999.** www.fourseasons.com/maui. Reservations required. Main courses $39–$68. AE, DC, DISC, MC, V. Daily 6–9:30pm; bar with pupu daily 6–11pm.

Expensive

Ferraro's Bar e Ristorante ★ ITALIAN This was a master stroke for the Four Seasons: authentic Italian fare in a casual outdoor tropical setting, with a drop-dead-gorgeous view of the ocean and the West Maui Mountains. Ferraro's is not inexpensive, but the food is first rate. Lunch in the open-air restaurant features fabulous salads (my pick is the seared Hawaiian tuna and Niçoise salad), sandwiches (from a chicken pita to pizza), and some Hawaiian classics (try the Kalua pork quesadillas). At dinner, the romantic setting, with the sound of the ocean waves, makes for a memorable evening. The fish selection is noteworthy: fennel scented ahi with herb gnocchi, baby spinach, and tomato essence; or roasted sea bass, pepper cress butter sauce, and toasted pine nuts. Make room for dessert; my favorite is the fruit and marsala zabaione tart with vanilla-bean ice cream.

At the Four Seasons Resort Maui at Wailea, 3900 Wailea Alanui Dr. ✆ **808/874-8000.** www. fourseasons.com/maui. Reservations recommended. Main courses $19–$25 lunch, $30–$52 dinner. AE, DC, DISC, MC, V. Daily 11am–5:30pm, 4–9pm (pupu menu), and 6–9pm.

Moderate

Gannon's—A Pacific View Restaurant ★★ LOCAL/AMERICAN   Award-winning chef Bev Gannon has taken over the former Sea Watch restaurant, perched high on a hill, overlooking the Wailea Golf Course and the spectacular ocean view with Molokini in the distance. Chef Gannon (Haliimaile General Store and Joe's on Maui plus Lanai City Grille on Lanai) is known for her American home cooking with a regional twist, in this case—a Hawaiian twist, as in miso-glazed black cod with Asian slaw and wasabi mashed potatoes, or her ahi scaloppini with lemon capers and an eggplant terrine, or her venison loin with Parmesan risotto with smoked corn nage. The restaurant serves breakfast (don't miss the smoked salmon pâté with Maui onions, sliced tomato, cream cheese, and bagel or the Hawaiian sweet-bread French toast), lunch (the lobster salad with butter lettuce, jicama, zucchini, fresh corn, truffle vinaigrette and lemon crème fraîche is a must-try), and dinner. *Insider's tip:* Get dinner reservations that are timed to watch the sunset.

Wailea Golf Course, 100 Wailea Golf Club Dr., Wailea Resort. ✆ **808/875-8080.** www.bevgannon restaurants.com. Dinner reservations recommended. Breakfast entrees $10–$14; lunch entrees $10–$19; dinner entrees $26–$38. AE, DC, DISC, MC, V. Daily 8:30am–9pm.

Joe's ★★ AMERICAN/GRILL   The 270-degree view spans the golf course, tennis courts, ocean, and Haleakala—a worthy setting for Beverly Gannon's style of American home cooking with a regional twist. The hearty staples include excellent mashed potatoes, lobster, fresh fish, and filet mignon, but the meatloaf (a whole loaf, like Mom used to make) seems to upstage them all. The Tuscan white-bean soup is superb, and the grilled pork chop, homemade applesauce, and warm potato salad with bacon vinaigrette is American home cooking at its best. Daily specials could be grilled ahi with white-truffle Yukon gold mashed potatoes or sautéed mahimahi with shrimp bisque and sautéed spinach. If chocolate cake is on the menu, you should definitely spring for it.

At the Wailea Tennis Club, 131 Wailea Ike Place. ✆ **808/875-7767.** www.bevgannonrestaurants. com. Reservations recommended. Main courses $12–$42. AE, DC, DISC, MC, V. Daily 5:30–9pm.

Upcountry Maui

Note: You'll find the restaurants in this section on the "Upcountry & East Maui" map (p. 463).

HALIIMAILE (ON THE WAY TO UPCOUNTRY MAUI)

Haliimaile General Store ★★★ HAWAII REGIONAL/AMERICAN   For more than a decade, Bev Gannon, one of the original Hawaii Regional Cuisine chefs, has been going strong at her foodie haven in the pineapple fields. You'll dine at tables set on old wood floors under high ceilings (sound ricochets fiercely here), in a peach-colored room emblazoned with works by local artists. The food, a blend of eclectic American with ethnic touches, puts an innovative spin on Hawaii Regional Cuisine. Even the fresh-catch sandwich on the lunch menu is anything but prosaic. Sip the lilikoi lemonade and nibble the sashimi napoleon or the house salad (Island greens with mandarin oranges, onions, toasted walnuts, and blue cheese crumble); all are notable items on a menu that bridges Hawaii and Gannon's Texas roots.

900 Haliimaile Rd. ⓒ **808/572-2666.** www.haliimailegeneralstore.com. Reservations recommended. Main courses $14–$22 lunch, $24–$42 dinner. AE, DC, MC, V. Mon–Fri 11am–2:30pm; daily 5:30–9:30pm.

MAKAWAO & PUKALANI

Casanova Italian Restaurant ★ ITALIAN   Look for the tiny veranda with a few stools, always full, in front of a deli at Makawao's busiest intersection—that's the most visible part of the Casanova restaurant and lounge. Makawao's nightlife center contains a stage, dance floor, restaurant, and bar—and food to love and remember. This is pasta heaven; try the spaghetti *fra diavolo* or the spinach gnocchi in a fresh tomato-Gorgonzola sauce. Other options include a huge pizza selection, grilled lamb chops in an Italian mushroom marinade, lots more pasta dishes, and luscious desserts. My personal picks on a stellar menu: garlic spinach topped with Parmesan and pine nuts, and tiramisu, the best on the island.

1188 Makawao Ave. ⓒ **808/572-0220.** www.casanovamaui.com. Reservations recommended for dinner. Lunch items $8–$18; dinner main courses $22–$36; 12-in. pizzas $12–$20; pastas $12–$18 AE, DC, DISC, MC, V. Mon–Sat 11:30am–2pm and 5:30–9:30pm; Sun 5:30–9:30pm. Dancing Wed and Fri–Sat 10pm–1:30am. Lounge daily 5:30pm–1:30am (closing time varies depending on entertainment). Deli daily 7:30am–5:30pm. Check their website for the schedule of top entertainment, like Willie K and his band.

Market Fresh Bistro ★★ 🍴 LOCAL/MEDITERRAN   Attention foodies: Plan to eat dinner here at least once during your stay on Maui. Yes, it is a long drive from a resort area and, yes, parking is on the street and you may have to walk a block or two, but Chef Justin Pardo (formerly of the Union Square Café, New York City, and the Wailea Grand on Maui) is a culinary genius and he uses 80% to 90% local products and is having fun creating menus at this off-the-beaten-path restaurant, hidden in a mini-mall complex, behind the Makawao Steak House. You will be well rewarded for your efforts to get here. The menu changes daily, but here's a sample of the Chef's wonderful creations: an appetizer of pan-seared sea scallops with a watermelon curried gazpacho or a spice crested duck breast in a port-wine marinade with local figs and a local microgreen salad. Entrees range from taro-crusted fish with roasted carrots and asparagus in a fennel-saffron tomato jus, to a pork loin, wrapped in applewood-smoked bacon, with sweet potatoes and mushrooms, or a free-range chicken croquette with Maui onion and manchezo cheese with organic eggplant and smoked paprika tomato chutney. If you have time, call ahead for their once- or twice-a-month farm dinners, featuring the best from local farmers in a four-course dinner, plus dessert, for $50.

3620 Baldwin Ave., Makawao. ℂ **808/572-4877.** Reservations recommended for dinner. Dinner entrees $29–$30. MC, V. Mon–Wed 8am–11am and 11:30am–4pm; Thurs–Sat 8–11am, 11:30am–3pm, and 6–8:30pm; Sun 9am–2:30pm.

KULA (AT THE BASE OF HALEAKALA NATIONAL PARK)

Cafe 808 AMERICAN/LOCAL   Despite its out-of-the-way location (or perhaps because of it), Cafe 808 has become the universal favorite among upcountry residents of all ages. The breakfast coffee group, the lunchtime crowd, and dinner regulars all know it's the place for tasty home-style cooking with no pretensions: famous burgers (teriyaki, hamburger, cheeseburger, veggie burger, mahimahi, taro), roast pork, smoked turkey, and a huge selection of local-style specials. Regulars rave about the chicken katsu, saimin, and beef stew. The few tables are sprinkled around a room with linoleum floors, hardwood benches, plastic patio chairs, and old-fashioned booths—rough around the edges in a pleasing way, and very camp.

Lower Kula Rd., past Holy Ghost Church, across from Morihara Store. ℂ **808/878-6874.** Burgers from $5; main courses $8–$12. MC, V. Daily 6am–8:30pm.

Grandma's Coffee House COFFEEHOUSE/AMERICAN   Alfred Franco's grandmother started what is now a fifth-generation coffee business back in 1918, when she was 16 years old. Today this tiny wooden coffeehouse, still fueled by homegrown Haleakala coffee beans, is the quintessential roadside oasis. Grandma's offers espresso, hot and cold coffees, home-baked pastries, inexpensive pasta, sandwiches (including sensational avocado veggie burgers), homemade soups, fresh juices, and local plate-lunch specials that change daily. Rotating specials include Hawaiian beef stew, ginger chicken, chicken curry, lentil soup, and sandwiches piled high with Kula vegetables. The coffee is legendary, but the real standouts are the lemon squares and the pumpkin bread.

At the end of Hwy. 37, Keokea (about 6 miles before the Tedeschi Vineyards in Ulupalakua). ℂ **808/878-2140.** www.grandmascoffee.com. Most items under $9.50. DISC, MC, V. Daily 7am–5pm.

Kula Lodge ★ HAWAII REGIONAL/AMERICAN   Don't let the dinner prices scare you; the Kula Lodge is equally enjoyable, if not more so, at breakfast and lunch, when the prices are lower and the views through the picture windows have an eye-popping intensity. The million-dollar vista spans the flanks of Haleakala, rolling 3,200 feet down to Central Maui, the ocean, and the West Maui Mountains. The Kula Lodge has always been known for its breakfasts: fabulous eggs Benedict, including a vegetarian version with Kula onions, shiitake mushrooms, and scallions; legendary banana/mac-nut pancakes; and a highly recommended tofu scramble with green onions, Kula vegetables, and garlic chives. If possible, go for sunset cocktails and watch the colors change into deep end-of-day hues. When darkness descends, a roaring fire and lodge atmosphere add to the coziness of the room. The dinner menu features "small plates" of Thai summer rolls, seared ahi, and other starters. Fresh catch with a choice of preparations and sauces leads the seafood attractions, but there's also pasta, rack of lamb, filet mignon, and free-range chicken breast.

15200 Haleakala Hwy. (Hwy. 377). ℭ **808/878-2517.** www.kulalodge.com. Reservations recommended for dinner. Breakfast $10–$18; lunch $12–$22; dinner $25–$35. AE, DC, DISC, MC, V. Daily 7am–9pm.

Kula Sandalwoods Restaurant ★ AMERICAN   Chef Eleanor Loui, a graduate of the Culinary Institute of America, makes hollandaise sauce every morning from fresh upcountry egg yolks, sweet butter, and Meyer lemons, which her family grows in the yard above the restaurant. This is Kula cuisine, with produce from the backyard and everything made from scratch, including French toast with home-baked Portuguese sweetbread; hotcakes or Belgian waffles with fresh fruit; open-faced country omelets; hamburgers drenched in a special cheese sauce made with grated sharp cheddar; a killer kalua-pork sandwich; a grilled ono sandwich; and an outstanding veggie burger. The grilled chicken-steak sandwich is marvelous, served with soup of the day and Kula mixed greens. Dine in the gazebo or on the terrace, with dazzling views in all directions—including, in the spring, a yard dusted with lavender jacaranda flowers and a hillside ablaze with fields of orange akulikuli blossoms.

15427 Haleakala Hwy. (Hwy. 377). ℭ **808/878-3523.** www.kulasandalwoods.com. Breakfast $8–$14; lunch $9–$14; Sun brunch $7–$14. MC, V. Mon–Fri 7:30am–3pm; Sun 7:30–11:30am.

East Maui

Note: You'll find the restaurants in this section on the "Upcountry & East Maui" map (p. 463).

PAIA

Cafe des Amis ★★ 🍴 CREPES/MEDITERRANEAN/INDIAN   This tiny eatery is a hidden delight: healthy and tasty breakfasts, lunches, and dinners that are easy on the wallet. Crepes are the star here, and they are popular: spinach with feta cheese, shrimp curry with coconut milk, and dozens more choices, including breakfast crepes and dessert crepes (like banana and chocolate or strawberries and cream). Equally popular are the Greek salads and smoothies. Dinners feature authentic Indian curries (served with rice, mango chutney, and tomato chutney), such as a vegetable curry with spinach, carrots, cauliflower, and potato with Tamil spices and tomato. You'll also find the best coffee in Paia here.

42 Baldwin Ave. ℭ **808/579-6323.** Breakfast crepes $9–$10; lunch crepes $9–$11; dinner entrees $12–$17. MC, V. Daily 8:30am–8:30pm.

Charley's Restaurant ★ AMERICAN/MEXICAN   Although Charley's (named after Charley P. Woofer, a Great Dane) serves three meals a day, breakfast is really the time to come here. Located in downtown Paia, Charley's is a cross between a 1960s hippie hangout, a windsurfers' power-breakfast spot, and a honky-tonk bar that gets going after dark. Before you head out to Hana, stop at Charley's for a larger-than-life breakfast (eggs, potatoes, toast, and coffee cost about $7). There are plenty of espresso drinks, but the regular coffee is excellent. Lunch is burgers, sandwiches, calzones, and pizza (after 2pm). Dinner is grilled fish and steak—hearty, but nothing exciting. You'll see all walks of life here, from visitors on their way to Hana at 7am to buff windsurfers chowing down at noon to Willie Nelson on his way to the bar to play a tune. Their new chef is experimenting with smoked brisket and ribs, a variety of pasta dishes, fresh fish, and meatloaf.

142 Hana Hwy. ℂ **808/579-8085.** www.charleysmaui.com. Breakfast items $7.75–$13; lunch items $8.50–$14; dinner main courses $13–$22. AE, DISC, MC, V. Daily 7am–10pm; food served at the bar until 10pm.

Milagros Food Company ★ SOUTHWESTERN/SEAFOOD   Milagros has gained a following with its great home-style cooking, upbeat atmosphere, and highly touted margaritas. Sit outdoors and watch the parade of Willie Nelson look-alikes ambling by as you tuck into the ahi creation of the evening, a combination of southwestern and Pacific Rim styles and flavors accompanied by fresh veggies and Kula greens. For breakfast, I recommend the Popeye spinach omelet or the huevos rancheros. Lunch ranges from ahi burgers to honey and mac-nut grilled salmon salad. For dinner, options include a grilled ahi burrito, seafood enchiladas, New York strip steak, shrimp pasta, and sometimes Chesapeake Bay crab cakes. I love Paia's tie-dyes, beads, and hippie flavor, and this is the front-row seat for it all. Watch for happy hour, with cheap and fabulous margaritas.

Hana Hwy. and Baldwin Ave. ℂ **808/579-8755.** Breakfast items $7–$10; lunch items $10–$13; dinner main courses $13–$20. AE, MC, V. Daily 8am–10pm.

Moana Bakery & Cafe ★★ LOCAL/EURO-ASIAN   Moana gets high marks for its stylish concrete floors, high ceilings, booths and cafe tables, and fabulous food. Don Ritchey, formerly a chef at Haliimaile General Store, has created the perfect Paia eatery, a casual bakery/cafe that highlights his stellar skills. All the bases are covered: saimin, omelets, wraps, pancakes, and fresh-baked goods in the morning; soups, sandwiches, pasta, and satisfying salads for lunch; and, at dinner, varied selections with Asian and European influences and fresh Island ingredients. The lemon grass grilled prawns with green-papaya salad are an explosion of flavors and textures; the roasted vegetable napoleon is gourmet fare; and the Thai red curry with coconut milk, served over vegetables, seafood, or tofu, comes atop jasmine rice with crisp rice noodles and fresh sprouts to cool the fire. Ritchey's Thai-style curries are richly spiced and intense. I also vouch for his special gift with fish: The nori-sesame-crusted mahimahi with miso-garlic tapioca pearls is cooked, like the curry, to perfection. There's live jazz Wednesday nights.

71 Baldwin Ave. ℂ **808/579-9999.** Reservations recommended for dinner. Breakfast items $7–$12; lunch items $9–$17; dinner main courses $22–$34. MC, V. Tues–Sat 8am–9pm; Sun–Mon 8am–2:30pm and 4–9pm. Sun and Mon after 4pm serving Indian cuisine only; sushi after noon daily.

Paia Fish Market SEAFOOD   This is a true fish market, with fresh fish to take home and cooked seafood, salads, pastas, fajitas, and quesadillas to take out or enjoy at the few picnic tables inside the restaurant. It's an appealing selection: Cajun-style fresh catch, fresh-fish specials (usually ahi or salmon), fresh-fish tacos and quesadillas, and seafood and chicken pastas. You can also order hamburgers, cheeseburgers, fish and chips (or shrimp and chips), and wonderful lunch and dinner plates, cheap and tasty. Photos of the number-one sport here, windsurfing, adorn the walls.

110 Hana Hwy. ℂ **808/579-8030.** www.paiafishmarket.com. Lunch and dinner $8.50–$19. DISC, MC, V. Daily 11am–9:30pm.

HAIKU

Colleen's at the Cannery ★★ 🏠 ECLECTIC   Way, way, way off the beaten path lies this fabulous find in the rural Haiku Cannery Marketplace. Once through the doors, you'll swear you've dropped down in the middle of a hot, chic boutique restaurant in SoHo in Manhattan (only, when you look around at the patrons, they are pure Haiku upcountry residents). It's worth the drive to enjoy Colleen's fabulous culinary creations, like a wild-mushroom ravioli with sautéed portobello mushrooms, tomatoes, herbs, and a roasted-pepper coulis for $17 (not New York City prices); pan-seared ahi for $21; or filet mignon with a side salad for $30. Colleen also serves up smaller meals, such as burgers and fish and chips. Breakfast includes wonderful omelets ($11) and mouthwatering French toast made with Colleen's own homemade bread ($7.75). Lunch stars baguette sandwiches, wraps, salads, and burgers and fries. I only wish Colleen's would take reservations.

At the Haiku Cannery Marketplace, 810 Haiku Rd. ✆ **808/575-9211.** www.colleensinhaiku.com. Reservations not accepted. Breakfast $6.50–$14; lunch $8–15; dinner entrees $10–$33. AE, DISC, MC, V. Daily 6am–10pm.

ON THE ROAD TO HANA

Mama's Fish House ★★★ SEAFOOD   Okay, it's expensive (maybe the most expensive seafood house on Maui), but if you love fish, this is the place for you. The restaurant's entrance, a cove with windsurfers, tide pools, white sand, and a canoe resting under palm trees, is a South Seas fantasy worthy of Gauguin. The interior features curved lauhala-lined ceilings, walls of split bamboo, lavish arrangements of tropical blooms, and picture windows to let in the view. With servers wearing Polynesian prints and flowers behind their ears, and the sun setting in Kuau Cove, Mama's mood is hard to beat. The fish is fresh (the fishermen are even credited by name on the menu) and prepared either Hawaiian-style, with tropical fruit or baked in a crust of macadamia nuts and vanilla beans, or in a number of dishes involving ferns, seaweed, Maui onions, and roasted kukui nut. My favorite is mahimahi laulau with luau leaves (taro greens) and Maui onions, baked in ti leaves and served with kalua pig and Hanalei poi. You can get deep-water ahi seared with coconut and lime, or perhaps the ono "caught by Keith Nakamura along the 40-fathom ledge near Hana" in Hana ginger teriyaki with mac nuts and crisp Maui onion. Other special touches include the use of Molokai sweet potato, organic lettuces, Haiku bananas, and fresh coconut, which evoke the mood and tastes of old Hawaii.

799 Poho Place, just off the Hana Hwy., Kuau. ✆ **808/579-8488.** Reservations recommended for lunch, required for dinner. Main courses $27–$54 lunch, $27–$57 dinner. AE, DC, DISC, MC, V. Daily 11am–9pm (last seating).

HANA
Moderate
Hana Ranch Restaurant ✋AMERICAN   Part of the Hotel Hana-Maui operation, the Hana Ranch Restaurant is the informal alternative to the hotel's dining room for lunch. The menu is burgers and chicken and fish sandwiches. There are indoor tables as well as two outdoor pavilions that offer distant ocean views. At the adjoining takeout stand, fast-food classics prevail: teriyaki plate lunch, mahimahi sandwich, cheeseburgers, hot dogs, and ice cream.

Hana Hwy. ✆ **808/270-5280.** www.hotelhanamaui.com. Main courses $14–$18 lunch and dinner. AE, DISC, MC, V. Daily 11:30am–8pm; happy hour 4–7pm; takeout counter daily 11am–4pm.

Hotel Hana-Maui ★★★ LOCAL/ECLECTIC   Although the restaurant's official name is Ka'uiki, everyone in Hana just calls it the Hotel Hana-Maui. Names don't mean much out in this quaint Hawaiian village; in fact, not even Passport Resorts' executive chef, John Cox, who is in charge of developing the daily menu, can put his finger on the delicious type of cuisine served in the open, airy dining room. "I call it cuisine inspired by eastern Maui," he says, pointing to the ingredients-driven menu: the fresh fish caught by local fishermen, the produce brought in by nearby farmers, the fruits that are in season. The result is true Hawaiian food, grown right on the island. Breakfast features eggs Benedict with local fish, wilted Okinawa spinach and roasted tomato hollandaise, kalua pig hash and eggs, or local papaya with yogurt and homemade granola. Lunch ranges from Maui Cattle Company burgers to just-caught fish sandwiches. Dinner, which changes daily, can include fresh lettuce for salads (Kula-grown baby romaine with Gruyère crostini and sherry-thyme vinaigrette, or baby greens with Kula citrus, local radishes, and kalamata olives); a range of soups (such as a chilled Kula cucumber soup); and entrees like seared rare Hana-caught ahi with smoked bacon, forest mushrooms, and wilted greens, or oven-roasted chicken breast with crispy polenta, Nihiku bush beans, and mole sauce. Try the three- or four-course tasting menu or, even better, the Chef's Table.

Hana Hwy. ✆ **808/248-8212.** Reservations recommended for Fri–Sat dinner. Main courses $18–$23 breakfast, $26–$33 dinner. AE, DISC, MC, V. Daily 7:30–10:30am and 6–9pm; Fri 6–9pm Hawaiian show and buffet $50, 11 and under $35.

BEACHES

For beach toys and equipment, head to **Snorkel Bob's** (www.snorkelbob.com), which rents snorkel gear, boogie boards, and other ocean toys at four locations: Dickenson and Wainee streets, Lahaina (✆ **808/662-0104**); Napili Village, 5425-C Lower Honoapiilani Hwy., Napili (✆ **808/669-9603**); in North Kihei at Azeka Place II, 1279 S. Kihei Rd. #310 (✆ **808/875-6188**); and in South Kihei/Wailea at Kamaole Beach Center, 2411 S. Kihei Rd. (✆ **808/879-7449**). All locations are open daily from 8am to 5pm. If you're island-hopping, you can rent from a Snorkel Bob's location on one island and return to a branch on another.

West Maui
KAANAPALI BEACH ★
Four-mile-long Kaanapali is one of Maui's best beaches, with grainy gold sand as far as the eye can see. The

Kaanapali Beach.

Kapalua Beach.

beach parallels the sea channel through most of its length, and a paved walk links hotels and condos, open-air restaurants, and the Whalers Village shopping center. Because Kaanapali is so long and broad, and because most hotels have adjacent swimming pools, the beach is crowded only in pockets—there's plenty of room to find seclusion. Summertime swimming is excellent. The best snorkeling is around Black Rock, in front of the Sheraton, where the water is clear, calm, and populated with clouds of tropical fish.

Facilities include outdoor showers; you can also use the restrooms at the hotel pools. Various beach-activities vendors line up in front of the hotels. Parking is a problem, though. There are two public entrances: At the south end, turn off Honoapiilani Highway into the Kaanapali Resort and pay for parking here; or continue on Honoapiilani Highway, turn off at the last Kaanapali exit at the stoplight near the Maui Kaanapali Villas, and park next to the beach signs indicating public access.

KAPALUA BEACH ★★★

The beach cove that fronts the Coconut Grove Villas is the stuff of dreams: a golden crescent bordered by two palm-studded points. The sandy bottom slopes gently to deep water at the bay mouth; the water's so clear that you can see it turn to green and then deep blue. Protected from strong winds and currents by the lava-rock promontories, Kapalua's calm waters are ideal for swimmers of all ages and abilities, and the bay is big enough to paddle a kayak around in without getting into the more challenging channel that separates Maui from Molokai. Waves come in just right for riding, and fish hang out by the rocks, making it great for snorkeling.

The beach is accessible from the hotel on one end, which provides shaded sun chairs and a beach-activities center for its guests, and a public access way on

501

the other. It isn't so wide that you burn your feet getting in or out of the water, and the inland side is edged by a shady path and cool lawns. Outdoor showers are stationed at both ends. Parking is limited to about 30 spaces in a small lot off Lower Honoapiilani Road, by Napili Kai Beach Resort, so arrive early. Next door is a nice but pricey oceanfront restaurant, Kapalua's Bay Club. Facilities include showers, restrooms, lifeguards, a rental shack, and plenty of shade.

South Maui

Wailea's beaches may seem off-limits, hidden from plain view as they are by an intimidating wall of luxury resorts, but they're all open to the public by law. Look for the SHORELINE ACCESS signs along Wailea Alanui Drive, the resort's main boulevard.

Kamaole III Beach Park.

KAMAOLE III BEACH PARK ★

Three beach parks—Kamaole I, II, and III—stand like golden jewels in the front yard of the funky seaside town of Kihei, which, all of a sudden, is sprawling like suburban blight. The beaches are the best thing about Kihei; these three are popular with local residents and visitors alike because they're easily accessible. On weekends, they're jampacked with fishermen, picnickers, swimmers, and snorkelers. The most popular is Kamaole III, or "Kam-3." It's the biggest of the three beaches, with wide pockets of gold sand, and the only one with a children's playground and a grassy lawn. Swimming is safe here, but scattered lava rocks are toe-stubbers at the waterline, and parents should make sure kids don't venture too far out because the bottom slopes off quickly. Both the north and south shores are rocky fingers with a surge big enough to attract fish and snorkelers; the winter waves appeal to bodysurfers. Kam-3 is also a wonderful place to watch the sunset. Facilities include restrooms, showers, picnic tables, barbecue grills, and lifeguards. There's plenty of parking on South Kihei Road across from the Maui Parkshore condos.

ULUA BEACH ★

One of the most popular beaches in Wailea, Ulua is a long, wide, crescent-shaped gold-sand beach between two rocky points. When the ocean's calm, Ulua offers Wailea's best snorkeling; when it's rough, the waves are excellent for body-surfers. The ocean bottom is shallow and gently slopes down to deeper waters, making swimming generally safe. The beach is usually occupied by guests of nearby resorts. In high season (Christmas–Mar and June–Aug), it's carpeted with beach towels and packed with sunbathers like sardines in cocoa butter. Facilities include showers and restrooms. Beach equipment is available for rent at the nearby Wailea Ocean Activity Center. Look for the blue SHORELINE ACCESS sign

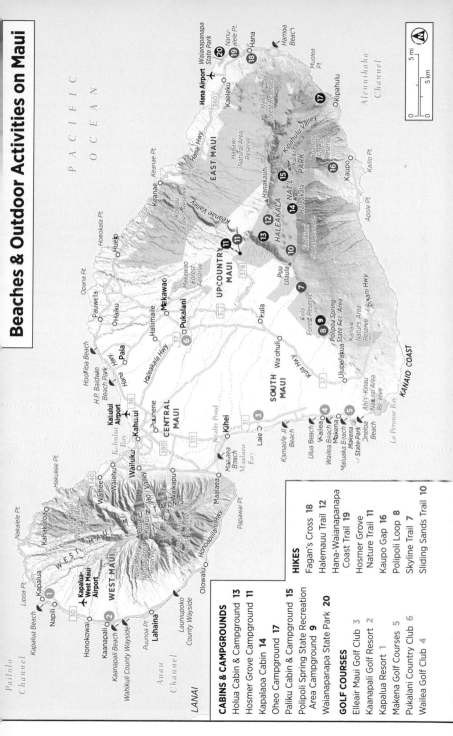

Beaches & Outdoor Activities on Maui

CABINS & CAMPGROUNDS

Holua Cabin & Campground **13**
Hosmer Grove Campground **11**
Kapalaoa Cabin **14**
Oheo Campground **17**
Paliku Cabin & Campground **15**
Polipoli Spring State Recreation
Area Campground **9**
Waianapanapa State Park **20**

GOLF COURSES

Elleair Maui Golf Club **3**
Kaanapali Golf Resort **2**
Kapalua Resort **1**
Makena Golf Courses **5**
Pukalani Country Club **6**
Wailea Golf Club **4**

HIKES

Fagan's Cross **18**
Halemauu Trail **12**
Hana-Waianapanapa
Coast Trail **19**
Hosmer Grove
Nature Trail **11**
Kaupo Gap **16**
Polipoli Loop **8**
Skyline Trail **7**
Sliding Sands Trail **10**

on South Kihei Road, near the Renaissance Wailea Beach Resort; a tiny parking lot is nearby.

WAILEA BEACH ★

Wailea is the best golden-sand crescent on Maui's sun-baked southwestern coast. One of five beaches within Wailea Resort, Wailea is big, wide, and protected on both sides by black-lava points. It's the front yard of the Four Seasons Resort and the Grand Wailea Resort, Maui's most elegant and outrageous beach hotels, respectively. From the beach, the view out to sea is magnificent, framed by neighboring Kahoolawe and Lanai and the tiny crescent of Molokini, probably the most popular snorkel spot in these parts. The clear waters tumble to shore in waves just the right size for gentle riding, with or without a board. From shore, you can see Pacific humpback whales in season (Dec–Apr) and unreal sunsets nightly. Facilities include restrooms, outdoor showers, and limited free parking at the blue SHORELINE ACCESS sign, which points toward Wailea Alanui Drive.

MALUAKA BEACH (MAKENA BEACH) ★

On the southern end of Maui's resort coast, development falls off dramatically, leaving a wild, dry countryside of green kiawe trees. The Maui Prince sits in isolated splendor, sharing Makena Resort's 1,800 acres with only a couple of first-rate golf courses and a necklace of perfect beaches. The strand nearest the hotel is Maluaka Beach, often called Makena, notable for its beauty and its views of Molokini Crater, the offshore islet, and Kahoolawe, the so-called "target" island (it was used as a bombing target from 1945 to the early 1990s). This is a short, wide, palm-fringed crescent of golden, grainy sand set between two black-lava points and bounded by big sand dunes topped by a grassy knoll. The swimming in this mostly calm bay is considered the best on Makena Bay, which is bordered on the south by Puu Olai Cinder Cone and historic Keawalai Congregational

Ulua Beach.

Wailea Beach.

Maluaka (Makena) Beach.

Church. The waters around Makena Landing, at the north end of the bay, are particularly good for snorkeling. Facilities include restrooms, showers, a landscaped park, lifeguards, and roadside parking. Along Makena Alanui, look for the SHORELINE ACCESS sign near the hotel, turn right, and head down to the shore.

ONELOA BEACH (BIG BEACH) ★★

Oneloa, meaning "long sand" in Hawaiian, is one of the most popular beaches on Maui. Locals call it "Big Beach"—it's 3,300 feet long and more than 100 feet wide. Mauians come here to swim, fish, sunbathe, surf, and enjoy the view of Kahoolawe and Lanai. Snorkeling is good around the north end, at the foot of Puu Olai, a 360-foot cinder cone. During storms, however, big waves lash the shore, and a strong rip current sweeps the sharp drop-off, posing a danger for inexperienced open-ocean swimmers. There are no facilities except for portable toilets, but there's plenty of parking. To get here, drive past the Maui Prince Hotel to the second dirt road, which leads through a kiawe thicket to the beach.

On the other side of Puu Olai is **Little Beach,** a small pocket beach where assorted nudists work on their all-over tans, to the chagrin of uptight authorities. You can get a nasty sunburn and a lewd-conduct ticket too.

Upcountry & East Maui

HOOKIPA BEACH PARK ★

Two miles past Paia, on the Hana Highway, is one of the most famous windsurfing sites in the world. Because of its hard, constant wind and endless waves, Hookipa attracts top windsurfers and wave jumpers from around the globe. Surfers and fishermen also enjoy this small gold-sand beach at the foot of a grassy cliff, which provides a natural amphitheater for spectators. Except when competitions are being held, weekdays are the best times to watch the daredevils fly over the waves. When waves are flat, snorkelers and divers explore the reef. Facilities include restrooms, showers, pavilions, picnic tables, barbecues, and parking.

FROMMER'S FAVORITE maui EXPERIENCES

Greeting the Rising Sun from atop Haleakala (p. 538). Bundle up, fill a thermos with hot java, and drive up the 37 miles from sea level to 10,000 feet to witness the birth of yet another day. Breathing in the rarefied air and watching the first rays of light streak across the sky makes the Haleakala sunrise a mystical experience.

Watching for Whales (p. 516). No need to head out in a boat—in winter you can see these majestic mammals breach and spy-hop from shore. One of the best places is scenic McGregor Point, at mile marker 9 along Honoapiilani Highway, just outside Maalaea in South Maui. The humpbacks arrive as early as November, but the majority travel through Maui's waters from mid-December to mid-April.

Snorkeling off Makena Landing (p. 504). Calm waters and an abundance of marine life make Makena Bay one of Hawaii's best places to swim with the fishes. Don a mask and snorkel to paddle with turtles, watch clouds of butterflyfish flitter past, and search for tiny damselfish in the coral.

Taking a Dip in the Seven Sacred Pools (p. 550). There are actually more than

seven of these fern-shrouded waterfall pools, and they're all beautiful. They spill seaward at Oheo Gulch, on the rainy eastern flanks of Haleakala. Some people try to swim in the pools nearest the ocean; if you do, keep an eye on the sky overhead so that a sudden cloudburst doesn't send you cascading out to sea.

Venturing Back in Time in a Historical Port Town (p. 533). In the 1800s, when whaling was at its height, seafarers swarmed into Lahaina and missionaries fought to stem the spread of their sinful influence. It was a wild time, and this tiny town was an exciting place. The Lahaina Restoration Foundation, in the Master's Reading Room on Front and Dickenson streets, provides a free map that will let you discover those wild whaling days for yourself.

Watching Windsurfers Ride the Waves at Hookipa (p. 517). Just off the Hana Highway past Paia is Hookipa Beach, known the world over as a windsurfing mecca. The great waves and consistent wind draw top windsurfers from around the globe. Watch spellbound as these colorful sailboarders ride, sail, and pirouette over the waves, turning into the wind and flipping into the air while

WAIANAPANAPA STATE PARK ★

Four miles before Hana, off the Hana Highway, is this beach park, which takes its name from the legend of the Waianapanapa Cave, where Chief Kaakea, a jealous and cruel man, suspected his wife, Popoalaea, of having an affair. Popoalaea left her husband and hid herself in a chamber of the Waianapanapa Cave. She and her attendant ventured out only at night for food. Nevertheless, a few days later, Kaakea was passing by the area and saw the shadow of the servant. Knowing he had found his wife's hiding place, Kaakea entered the cave and killed her. During certain times of the year, the water in the tide pool turns red, commemorating Popoalaea's death. (Scientists claim, less imaginatively, that the water turns red due to the presence of small red shrimp.)

Waianapanapa State Park's 120 acres contain 12 cabins (p. 470), a caretaker's residence, a beach park, picnic tables, barbecue grills, restrooms, showers, a parking lot, a shoreline hiking trail, and a black-sand beach (actually, small

rotating 360 degrees. It's the best free show in town.

Exploring Iao Valley (p. 531). When the sun strikes Iao Valley (pictured here) in the West Maui Mountains, an almost-ethereal light sends rays out in all directions. This really may be Eden.

Walking the Shoreline Trail at Waianap-anapa (p. 523). A 6-mile trail follows the shoreline, bordered on one side by lava cliffs and a forest of lauhala trees, on the other by the open ocean. As you go, you'll pass an ancient *heiau* (temple), some fascinating caves, a pretty cool blowhole, jungly native Hawaiian plants, and the ever-changing sea.

Heading to Kula to Bid the Sun Aloha. Harold Rice Park, just off Kula Highway, is the perfect vantage point for watching the sun set over the entire island: down the side of Haleakala, out across the isthmus, and over to the West Maui Mountains, with Molokai and Lanai in the distance. As the sun sinks in the sky, the light shifts from bright yellow to mellow red. Once the sun drops below the horizon, the sky puts on its own Technicolor show in a dazzling array of colors.

Experiencing Art Night in Lahaina (p. 555). Every Friday after the sun goes down, most of the town's galleries open their doors, serve pupu and refreshments, and hope you'll wander in. This is a fun, festive way to see what's going on in Maui's creative community. You may even be able to meet the artists; many are on hand to talk about their works.

black pebbles). This is a wonderful area for shoreline hikes (bring insect repellent—the mosquitoes are plentiful) and picnicking. Swimming is generally unsafe, though, due to strong waves and rip currents. Because Waianapanapa is crowded on weekends with local residents and their families, as well as tourists, weekdays are generally a better bet.

HAMOA BEACH ★

This half-moon-shaped, gray-sand beach (a mix of coral and lava) in a truly tropical setting is a favorite of sunbathers seeking rest and refuge. The Hotel Hana-Maui maintains the beach and acts as though it's private, which it isn't—so just march down the lava-rock steps and grab a spot on the sand. James Michener called it "a beach so perfectly formed that I wonder at its comparative obscurity." The 100-foot-wide beach is three football fields long and sits below 30-foot black-lava sea cliffs. Surf on this unprotected beach breaks offshore and rolls in, making it a popular surfing and bodysurfing area. Hamoa is often swept by powerful rip currents, so be careful. The calm left side is best for snorkeling in summer. The hotel has numerous facilities for guests; there are outdoor showers and restrooms for nonguests. Parking is limited. Look for the Hamoa Beach turnoff from Hana Highway.

WATERSPORTS

Snorkel Bob's (www.snorkelbob.com) rents snorkel gear, boogie boards, and other ocean toys at their locations: Dickenson and Wainee streets, Lahaina (© **808/662-0104**); Napili Village, 5425-C Lower Honoapiilani Hwy., Napili (© **808/669-9603**); in North Kihei at Azeka Place II, 1279 S. Kihei Rd. #310 (© **808/875-6188**); and in South Kihei/Wailea at Kamaole Beach Center, 2411 S. Kihei Rd. (© **808/879-7449**). All locations are open daily from 8am to 5pm. If you're island-hopping, you can rent from a Snorkel Bob's location on one island and return to a branch on another.

Boss Frog's Dive and Surf Shops (www.bossfrog.com) has eight locations for rental and other gear: Napili, 5059 Napilihau St. (© **808/669-4949**); Kahana Manor Shops, 4310 Lower Honoapiilani Rd., Kahana (© **808/669-6700**); Kaanapali, 3636 Lower Honoapiilani Rd. (© **808/665-1200**); Lahaina Cannery Mall, 1221 Honoapiilani Hwy. (© **808/661-5995**); 150 Lahainaluna Rd., in Lahaina (© **808/661-3333**); Longs Drugs Shopping Center, 1215 Kihei Rd., in North Kihei (© **808/891-0077**); Dolphin Plaza, 2395 S. Kihei Rd., behind Pizza Hut, in South Kihei (© **808/875-4477**); and 1770 S. Kihei Rd., Shaka Pizza Building (© **808/874-5225**).

Boating

Maui is big on snorkel cruises. The crescent-shaped islet called **Molokini** is one of the best snorkel and scuba spots in Hawaii. Trips to the island of **Lanai** (see

Oneloa Beach (Big Beach).   Hookipa Beach Park.

FROM LEFT: Waiʻanapanapa State Park; Hamoa Beach.

chapter 9) are also popular for a day of snorkeling. Always remember to bring a towel, a swimsuit, sunscreen, and a hat on a snorkel cruise; everything else is usually included. If you'd like to go a little deeper than snorkeling allows, consider trying **snuba,** a shallow-water diving system in which you are connected by a 20-foot air hose to an air tank that floats on a raft at the water's surface. Most of these snorkel boats offer it for an additional cost; it's usually around $50 for a half-hour or so. No certification is required for snuba. For fishing charters, see "Sport Fishing," later in this section.

Maui Classic Charters ★★   Maui Classic Charters offers morning and afternoon **snorkel-sail cruises to Molokini** on *Four Winds II,* a 55-foot glass-bottom catamaran. Rates for the morning sail are $89 adults and $59 children 3 to 12; in the afternoon, $42 adults and $30 children (book online to save 15%) *Four Winds* trips include continental breakfast and a hot lunch (lunch is optional on the afternoon cruise); complimentary beer, wine, and soda; snorkeling gear and instruction; and sport fishing along the way. Those looking for speed should book a trip on the state-of-the-art catamaran *Maui Magic.* A 5-hour snorkel journey to both Molokini and La Pérouse costs $112 adults and $92 children 5 to 12, including continental breakfast; barbecue lunch; beer, wine, and soda; snorkel gear; and instruction. During whale season (Dec 22–Apr 22), the *Four Winds* has a 3½-hour **whale-watch cruise** that goes for $42 adults and $30 children 3 to 12 (including beverages).

Maalaea Harbor, slip 55 and slip 80. (℃) **800/736-5740** or 808/879-8188. www.mauicharters. com. Prices vary depending on cruise.

Pacific Whale Foundation   This not-for-profit foundation supports its whale research by offering **whale-watch cruises** and **snorkel tours,** some to Molokini and Lanai. There are numerous daily trips to choose from, offered from December through May, out of both Lahaina and Maalaea harbors.

300 Ma'alaea Rd., Ste. 211, Wailuku. (℃) **800/942-5311** or 808/879-8811. www.pacificwhale.org. Trips from $20 adults, $17 children 7–12, free for ages 6 and under (1 free child per paying adult). They have stores at 612 Front St., Lahaina, and at the Harbor Shops at Ma'alaea.

Pride of Maui For a high-speed, action-packed snorkel-sail experience, consider the *Pride of Maui*. These 5-hour **snorkel cruises to Molokini** also stop at Turtle Bay and Makena; the cost is $90 for ages 13 and up ($80 if you book online) and $56 for children 3 to 12 ($50 online). Rates include continental breakfast, barbecue lunch, beverages and open bar, gear, and instruction. Other options include an afternoon Molokini cruise ($42 for ages 13 and up, $27 for children 3–12, with discounts online), an evening sunset cruise ($70 for ages 13 and up, $27 for children 3–12), and, during whale season, a whale-watching cruise ($42 for ages 13 and up, $30 for children 3–12). (**Tip:** Book on their website for $33 adults and $27 children.)

Maalaea Harbor. ☎ **877/TO-PRIDE** (867-7433) or 808/875-0955. www.prideofmaui.com. Prices vary depending on cruise.

Scuba diving.

Scotch Mist Sailing Charters This 50-foot Santa Cruz sailboat offers 2-hour sailing adventures. Prices include snorkel gear, juice, fresh fruit, beer, wine (on some cruises), and soda. Sunset sails are also available.

Lahaina Harbor, slip 2. ☎ **808/661-0386.** www.scotchmistsailingcharters.com. Sailing trips $50; sail and snorkel $90; whale-watching trips $50.

Trilogy ★★★ ☺ Trilogy offers my favorite **snorkel-sail trips.** Hop aboard one of the fleet of custom-built catamarans, from 54 to 64 feet long, for a 9-mile sail from Lahaina Harbor to **Lanai's Hulopoe Beach,** a terrific marine preserve, for a fun-filled day of sailing, snorkeling, swimming, and **whale-watching** (in season, of course). This is the only cruise that offers a personalized ground tour of the island and the only one with rights to take you to Hulopoe Beach. The full-day trip costs $189 for adults and $95 for children 3 to 12. Ask about overnighters to Lanai, too.

Trilogy also offers snorkel-sail trips to **Molokini,** one of Hawaii's best snorkel spots. This half-day trip leaves from Maalaea Harbor and costs $110 for adults, $55 for kids 3 to 12, including breakfast and a barbecue lunch. Other options include a late-morning half-day snorkel-sail off Kaanapali Beach for the same price, plus a host of other trips.

These are the most expensive sail-snorkel cruises on Maui, but they're worth every penny. The crews are fun and knowledgeable, and the boats comfortable and well equipped. All trips include breakfast (Mom's homemade cinnamon buns) and a very good barbecue lunch (onboard on the half-day trip, on land on the Lanai trip). Note, however, that you will be required to wear a flotation device no matter how good your swimming skills are; if this bothers you, go with another outfitter.

(C) **888/225-MAUI** (6284) or 808/TRILOGY (874-5649). www.sailtrilogy.com. Prices and departure points vary depending on cruise.

You can travel across the seas by ferry from Maui's Lahaina Harbor to Molokai's Kaunakakai Wharf on the *Molokai Princess* ((C) **877/500-6284** or 808/667-6165; www.mauiprincess.com). The 100-foot yacht, certified for 149 passengers, is fitted with the latest generation of gyroscopic stabilizers, making the ride smoother. The ferry makes the 90-minute journey from Lahaina to Kaunakakai daily; the round-trip cost is $101 for adults and $50 for children 3 to 12. Or you can choose to tour the island on one of two package options: Cruise-Drive, which includes round-trip passage and a rental car for $207 for the driver, $92 per additional adult passenger, and $46 for children; or the Alii Tour, which is a guided tour in an air-conditioned van plus lunch for $207 per adult and $142 per child.

DAY CRUISES TO LANAI

You can also get to the island of Lanai by booking a trip with **Trilogy** (see above).

Expeditions Lahaina/Lanai Passenger Ferry ★ 🔥 The cheapest way to reach Lanai is the ferry, which runs five times a day, 365 days a year. It leaves Lahaina at 6:45am, 9:15am, 12:45pm, 3:15pm, and 5:45pm; the return ferry from Lanai's Manele Bay leaves at 8am, 10:30am, 2pm, 4:30pm, and 6:45pm. The 9-mile channel crossing takes between 45 minutes and an hour, depending on sea conditions. Reservations are strongly recommended. Baggage is limited to two checked bags and one carry-on. Call **Lanai City Service** ((C) **800/800-4000** or 808/565-7227) to arrange a car rental or bus ride when you arrive.

Ferries depart from Lahaina Harbor; office: 658 Front St., Ste. 127, Lahaina. (C) **800/695-2624** or 808/661-3756. www.go-lanai.com. Round-trip fares from Maui to Lanai $60 adults, $40 children 2–11.

Body Boarding (Boogie Boarding) & Bodysurfing

In winter, Maui's best bodysurfing spot is **Mokuleia Beach,** known locally as Slaughterhouse because of the cattle slaughterhouse that once stood here, not because of the waves—although these waves are for expert bodysurfers only. Take Honoapiilani Highway just past Kapalua Resort; various trails will take you down to the pocket beach. Good body boarding can be found at **Baldwin Beach Park,** just outside Paia. Storms from the south bring fair bodysurfing conditions and great body boarding to the lee side of Maui: **Oneloa Beach** (or Big Beach) in Makena, **Ulua Beach** and **Kamaole III Beach Park** in Kihei, and **Kapalua Beach** are all good choices.

Ocean Kayaking

Gliding silently over the water, propelled by a paddle, seeing Maui from the sea the way the early Hawaiians did—that's what ocean kayaking is all about. One of Maui's best kayak routes is along the **Kihei Coast,** where there's easy access to calm water. Mornings are always best; the wind comes up around 11am, making seas choppy and paddling difficult.

For beginners, my favorite kayak-tour operator is **Makena Kayak & Tours** ★ (© 808/879-8426; www.makenakayaks.com). Professional guide Dino Ventura leads a 2½-hour trip from Makena Landing and loves taking first-timers over the secluded coral reefs and into remote coves. His wonderful tour will be a highlight of your vacation. This outfitter has kept its low price of $55, which includes refreshments and snorkel and kayak equipment; the 4-hour tour costs $85, including lunch.

South Pacific Kayaks, 2439 S. Kihei Rd., Kihei (© 800/776-2326 or 808/875-4848; www.mauikayak.com), is Maui's oldest kayak-tour company. Its experts lead ocean-kayak trips that include lessons, a guided tour, and snorkeling. Tours run from 2½ to 5 hours and range in price from $65 to $99.

Ocean Rafting

If you're semiadventurous and looking for a more intimate experience with the sea, try ocean rafting. The inflatable rafts hold 6 to 24 passengers. Tours usually include snorkeling and coastal cruising. One of the best (and most reasonable) outfitters is **Hawaii Ocean Rafting** (© 888/677-RAFT [7238] or 808/667-2191; www.hawaiioceanrafting.com), which operates out of Lahaina Harbor. The best deal is the 5-hour morning tour, which is $74 for adults and $53 for children 5 to 12 (book online and save $11); it includes three snorkeling stops and time spent searching for dolphins, plus continental breakfast and midmorning snacks.

Scuba Diving

Everyone dives **Molokini,** a marine-life park and one of Hawaii's top dive spots. This crescent-shaped crater has three tiers of diving: a 35-foot plateau inside the crater basin (used by beginning divers and snorkelers), a wall sloping to 70 feet just beyond the inside plateau, and a sheer wall on the outside and backside of the crater that plunges 350 feet. This underwater park is very popular, thanks to calm, clear, protected waters and an abundance of marine life, from manta rays to clouds of yellow butterflyfish.

Stop by any location of **Maui Dive Shop** ★ (www.mauidiveshop.com), Maui's largest diving retailer, with everything from rentals to scuba diving instruction to dive-boat charters, for a free copy of the 24-page *Maui Dive Guide.* Inside are maps of and details on the 20 best shoreline and offshore dives and snorkel sites, each ranked for beginner, intermediate, or advanced snorkelers/divers. Maui Dive Shop has branches in Kihei at Azeka Place II Shopping Center, 1455 S. Kihei Rd. (© 808/879-3388), Kamaole Shopping Center (© 808/879-1533), and Shops at Wailea (© 808/875-9904); in Lahaina at **Lahaina Gateway Mall,** 315 Keawe St., Ste. F101 (© 808/661-5388); and in the Hon-okowai Marketplace, 118 Lower Honoapiilani Hwy., Shop 4 and 5 (© 808/661-6166). Other locations include Whalers Village, 2435 Kaanapali Pkwy., Ste.-N, Kaanapali (© 808/661-5117); Maalaea Harbor Village, 300 Maalaea Rd. #225, Maalaea (© 808/244-5514); and Kahana Gateway, 4405 Honoapiilani Hwy., Ste. 204, Kahana (© 808/669-3800).

For personalized diving, **Ed Robinson's Diving Adventures** ★ (© 800/635-1273 or 808/879-3584; www.mauiscuba.com) is the only Maui company rated one of *Scuba Diver* magazine's top-five best dive operators for 7 years straight. Ed, a widely published underwater photographer, offers specialized charters for small groups. Two-tank dives are $130; his dive boats depart from Kihei Boat Ramp.

If Ed is booked, call **Mike Severns Diving** (© **808/879-6596;** www. mikeseverndiving.com) for small (maximum 12 people, divided into two groups of 6), personal diving tours on a 38-foot Munson/Hammerhead boat with freshwater shower. Mike and his wife, Pauline Fiene-Severns, are both biologists who make diving in Hawaii educational as well as fun (they have a spectacular underwater photography book, *Molokini Island*). In their 25 years of operation, they have been accident free. Two-tank dives are $145, including equipment rental, or $130 if you bring all your own equipment.

Snorkeling

Snorkel Bob's (www.snorkelbob.com) will rent you everything you need; see the introduction to this section for locations. Also see "Scuba Diving," above, for information on **Maui Dive Shop's** free booklet on great snorkeling sites.

Snorkeling on Maui is easy—there are so many great spots where you can just wade in the water with a face mask and look down to see the tropical fish. Mornings are best; local winds kick in around noon. Maui's best snorkeling spots include **Kapalua Beach;** along the Kihei coastline, especially at **Kamaole Beach Park III;** and along the Wailea coastline, particularly at **Ulua Beach.** For an off-the-beaten-track experience, head south to **Makena Beach,** where the bay is filled with clouds of tropical fish, and, on weekdays, the waters are virtually empty.

The snorkeling at **Black Rock at Kaanapali ★** is worth the inflated rates at the parking lots that buffer this beach. The prominent craggy cliff at the Sheraton Maui Resort doesn't just end when it plunges into the ocean. Underwater, the sheer wall continues, creating one of the west side's best snorkeling areas: Turtles, rays, and a variety of snappers and goatfish cruise along the sandy bottom. In the crevices, ledges, and holes of the rock wall, you can find eels, shrimp, lobster, and a range of rainbowed tropical fish.

Some snorkel tips: Always go with a buddy. Look up every once in a while to see where you are, how far offshore you are, and whether there's any boat traffic. Don't touch anything; not only can you damage coral, but camouflaged fish and shells with poisonous spines also might surprise you. Always check with a dive shop, lifeguards, and others on the beach about the area in which you plan to snorkel: Are there any dangerous conditions you should know about? What are the current surf, tide, and weather conditions? If you're not a good swimmer, wear a life jacket or other flotation device, which you can rent at most places offering watersports gear.

When the whales aren't around, **Capt. Steve's Rafting Excursions** (© **808/667-5565;** www.captainsteves.com) offers 7-hour snorkel trips from Mala Wharf in Lahaina to the waters around **Lanai** (you don't actually land on the island). Discounted online rates of $124 for adults and $89 for children 12 and under include breakfast, lunch, snorkel gear, and wet suits.

Two truly terrific snorkel spots are difficult to get to but worth the effort, as they're home to Hawaii's tropical marine life at its best:

Molokini ★★ This sunken crater sits like a crescent moon fallen from the sky, almost midway between Maui and the uninhabited island of Kahoolawe. Molokini stands like a scoop against the tide and serves, on its concave side, as a natural sanctuary and marine-life preserve for tropical fish. Snorkelers commute daily in a fleet of dive boats. Molokini is accessible only by boat; see "Boating," above, for outfitters that can take you here. Expect crowds in high season.

Ahihi-Kinau Natural Preserve ★★   In Ahihi Bay, you can't miss this 2,000-acre preserve in the lee of Cape Kinau, on Maui's rugged south coast, where, in 1790, Haleakala spilled red-hot lava that ran to the sea. Fishing is strictly forbidden here, and the fish know it; they're everywhere in this series of rocky coves and black-lava tide pools. To get here, drive south of Makena past Puu Olai to Ahihi Bay, where the road turns to gravel (and sometimes seems like it will disappear under the waves). At Cape Kinau, three four-wheel-drive trails lead across the lava flow; take the shortest one, nearest La Pérouse Bay. If you have a standard car, drive as far as you can, park, and walk the remainder of the way. Après-snorkel, check out La Pérouse Bay on the south side of Cape Kinau, where the French admiral La Pérouse became the first European to set foot on Maui. A lava-rock pyramid known as Pérouse Monument marks the spot. **Note:** The Hawaii State Department of Land and Natural Resources has temporarily restricted access to portions of the popular and heavily used reserve until July 31, 2012. Visit http://hawaii.gov/dlnr/dofaw/nars/reserves/maui/ahihikinau for more information and a downloadable brochure on the subject.

AN EXPERT SHARES HIS SECRETS:
maui's best dives

Ed Robinson, of Ed Robinson's Diving Adventures (see above), knows what makes a great dive. Here are some of his favorites on Maui:

Hawaiian Reef   This area off the Kihei-Wailea Coast is so named because it hosts a good cross section of Hawaiian topography and marine life. Diving to depths of 85 feet, you'll see everything from lava formations and coral reef to sand and rubble, plus a diverse range of both shallow and deepwater creatures. It's clear why this area was so popular with ancient Hawaiian fishermen: Large helmet shells, a healthy garden of antler coral heads, and big schools of snapper are common.

Third Tank   Located off Makena Beach at 80 feet, this World War II tank is one of the most picturesque artificial reefs you're likely to see around Maui. It acts like a fish magnet: Because it's the only large solid object in the area, any fish or invertebrate looking for a safe home comes here. Surrounding the tank is a cloak of schooling snapper and goatfish just waiting for a photographer with a wide-angle lens. Despite its small size, the Third Tank is loaded with more marine life per square inch than any site off Maui.

Molokini Crater   The backside is always done as a live boat-drift dive. The vertical wall plummets from more than 150 feet above sea level to around 250 feet below. Looking down to unseen depths gives you a feeling for the vastness of the open ocean. Pelagic fish and sharks are often sighted, and living coral perches on the wall, which is home to lobsters, crabs, and a number of photogenic black-coral trees at 50 feet.

There are actually two great dive sites around Molokini Crater. Named after common chub or rudderfish, **Enenue Side** gently slopes from the

Sport Fishing

Marlin, tuna, ono, and mahimahi await the baited hook in Maui's coastal and channel waters. No license is required; just book a sport-fishing vessel out of Lahaina or Maalaea harbors. Most charter boats that troll for big-game fish carry six passengers max.

The best way to book a sport-fishing charter is through the experts; the top booking desk in the state is **Sportfish Hawaii ★** (℃ **877/388-1376** or 808/396-2607; www.sportfishhawaii.com), which books boats on all the islands. These fishing vessels have been inspected and must meet rigorous criteria to guarantee that you'll have a great time. Prices range from $990 to $1,100 for a full-day exclusive charter (you, plus five friends, get the entire boat to yourself); it's $599 for a half-day exclusive.

Submarine Dives

Plunging 100 feet below the surface of the sea in a state-of-the-art, high-tech submarine is a great way to experience Maui's magnificent underwater world,

surface to about 60 feet and then drops rapidly to deeper waters. The shallower area is an easy dive, with lots of tame butterflyfish. It's also the home of Morgan Bentjaw, one of our friendliest moray eels. Enenue Side is often done as a live boat-drift dive to extend the range of the tour. Diving depths vary. Divers usually do a 50-foot dive, but on occasion, advanced divers drop to the 130-foot level to visit the rare boarfish and the shark condos.

Almost every kind of fish found in Hawaii can be seen in the crystalline waters of **Reef's End.** It's an extension of the rim of the crater, which runs for about 600 feet underwater, barely breaking the surface. Reef's End is shallow enough for novice snorkelers and exciting enough for experienced divers. The end and outside of this shoal drop off in dramatic terraces to beyond diving range. In deeper waters, there are shark ledges at varying depths and dozens of eels (some of which are tame), including

moray, dragon, snowflake, and garden eels. The shallower inner side is home to Garbanzo, one of the largest and first eels to be tamed. The reef is covered with cauliflower coral; in bright sunlight, it's one of the most dramatic underwater scenes in Hawaii.

La Pérouse Pinnacle In the middle of scenic La Pérouse Bay, site of Haleakala's most recent lava flow, is a pinnacle rising from the 60-foot bottom to about 10 feet below the surface. Getting to the dive site is half the fun: The scenery above water is as exciting as that below the surface. Underwater, you'll enjoy a very diversified dive. Clouds of damselfish and triggerfish will greet you on the surface. Divers can approach even the timid bird wrasse. There are more porcupine puffers here than anywhere else, as well as schools of goatfish and fields of healthy finger coral. La Pérouse is good for snorkeling and long, shallow second dives.

especially if you're not a swimmer. **Atlantis Submarines ★**, 658 Front St., Lahaina (🕐 **800/548-6262** or 808/667-2224; www.goatlantis.com), offers trips out of Lahaina Harbor every hour on the hour from 9am to 2pm; prices are $99 for adults and $45 for children 11 and under (children must be at least 3 ft. tall). Book online and save 10%. Allow 2 hours for this underwater adventure. *Warning:* This is not a good choice if you're claustrophobic.

Surfing

Expert surfers visit Maui in winter, when the surf's really up. The best surfing beaches include **Honolua Bay,** north of the Kapalua Resort (the third bay past the Ritz-Carlton Kapalua, off the Honoapiilani Hwy., or Hwy. 30); **Lahaina Harbor** (in summer, there'll be waves just off the channel entrance with a south swell); **Maalaea Beach,** just outside the break wall of the Maalaea Harbor (a clean, world-class left); and **Hookipa Beach,** where surfers get the waves until noon (after that—in a carefully worked-out compromise to share this prized surf spot—the windsurfers take over).

Always wanted to learn to surf but didn't know whom to ask? Tide and Kiva Rivers, two local boys (actually twins) who have been surfing since they could walk, operate **Rivers to the Sea** (🕐 **808/280-8795** or 280-6236; www.rivers tothesea.com), one of the best surfing schools on Maui. Rates are $75 each for a 2-hour class for a group of three or more, $220 for a couple for a 2-hour class, and $160 to $200 for a 2-hour private lesson. All lessons include equipment. The instructor decides where the lesson will take place based on the client's ability and where the surf is on that day. Tide, who has been surfing for over 25 years, says he has beginners standing up in their first lesson.

If they are booked, try **Nancy Emerson School of Surfing,** 358 Papa Place, Ste. F, Kahului (🕐 **808/244-SURF** [7873] or 808/662-4445; www.surf clinics.com). Nancy has been surfing since 1961 and has even been a stunt performer for various movies such as *Waterworld.* She's pioneered a new instructional technique called "Learn to Surf in One Lesson" (you can, really). It's $78 per person for a 2-hour group lesson; private 2-hour classes are $165.

Whale-Watching

The humpback is the star of the annual whale-watching season, which usually runs from about January to April (though it can begin as early as Dec and last until May). You can often see them from shore: Just look out to sea. There's no best time of day, but it seems that when the sea is glassy and there's no wind, the whales appear. Once you see one, keep watching in the same vicinity; they may stay down for 20 minutes. Bring a book. And binoculars, if you can.

Some good whale-watching spots on Maui include the following:

MCGREGOR POINT   On the way to Lahaina, there's a scenic lookout at mile marker 9 (just before you get to the Lahaina Tunnel); it's a good viewpoint to scan for whales.

OLOWALU REEF   Along the straight part of Honoapiilani Highway, between McGregor Point and Olowalu, you'll sometimes see whales leap out of the water. Their appearance can bring traffic to a screeching halt: People abandon their cars and run down to the sea to watch, causing a major traffic jam. If you stop, pull off the road so others may pass.

WAILEA BEACH MARRIOTT RESORT   On the Wailea coastal walk, stop at this resort to look for whales through the telescope installed as a public service by the Hawaii Island Humpback Whale National Marine Sanctuary.

PUU OLAI   It's a tough climb up this coastal landmark near the Maui Prince Hotel, but you're likely to be well rewarded: This is the island's best spot for offshore whale-watching. On the 360-foot cinder cone overlooking Makena Beach, you'll be at the right elevation to see Pacific humpbacks as they dodge Molokini and cruise up Alalakeiki Channel between Maui and Kahoolawe. If you don't see one, you'll at least have a whale of a view.

WHALE-WATCHING CRUISES   For a closer look, take a whale-watching cruise. Just about all of Hawaii's snorkel and dive boats become whale-watching boats in season; some of them even carry professional naturalists onboard so you'll know what you're seeing. For the best options, see "Boating," earlier in this section.

WHALE-WATCHING BY KAYAK & RAFT   Seeing a humpback whale from an ocean kayak or raft is awesome. **Capt. Steve's Rafting Excursions** (© **808/667-5565;** www.captainsteves.com) offers 2-hour whale-watching excursions out of Lahaina Harbor from $39 for adults, $29 for children 5 to 12. *Tip:* Save $10 by booking the early-bird adventure, which leaves at 7:30am.

Windsurfing

Maui has Hawaii's best windsurfing beaches. In winter, windsurfers from around the world flock to the town of **Paia** to ride the waves; **Hookipa Beach,** known all over the globe for its brisk winds and excellent waves, is the site of several world-championship contests. **Kanaha Beach,** west of Kahului Airport, also has dependable winds. When the winds turn northerly, **Kihei** is the spot to be; some days, you can spot whales in the distance behind the windsurfers. The northern end of Kihei is best: **Ohukai Park,** the first beach as you enter South Kihei Road from the northern end, has not only good winds, but also parking, a long strip of grass to assemble your gear, and good access to the water. Experienced windsurfers here are found in front of the **Maui Sunset** condo, 1032 S. Kihei Rd., near Waipuilani Street (a block north of McDonald's), which has great windsurfing conditions but a very shallow reef (not good for beginners).

    Hawaiian Island Surf & Sport, 415 Dairy Rd., Kahului (© **800/231-6958** or 808/871-4981; www.hawaiianisland.com), offers lessons (from $89), rentals, and repairs. Other shops that offer rentals and lessons are **Hawaiian Sailboarding Techniques,** 425 Koloa St., Kahului (© **800/968-5423** or 808/871-5423; www.hstwindsurfing.com), with 2½-hour lessons from $79; and **Maui Windsurf Co.,** 22 Hana Hwy., Kahului (© **800/872-0999** or 808/877-4816; www.maui-windsurf.com), which has complete equipment rental (board, sail, rig harness, and roof rack) from $49, plus 2½-hour lessons ranging from $60 to $99.

    For daily reports on wind and surf conditions, call the **Wind and Surf Report** at © **808/877-3611.**

HIKING & CAMPING

In the past 3 decades, Maui has grown from a rural island to a fast-paced resort destination, but its natural beauty remains largely inviolate; there are still many places that can be explored only on foot. Those interested in seeing the back-country—complete with virgin waterfalls, remote wilderness trails, and quiet, meditative settings—should head for Haleakala's upcountry or the tropical Hana Coast.

Camping on Maui can be extreme (inside a volcano) or benign (by the sea in Hana). It can be wet, cold, and rainy; or hot, dry, and windy—often all on the same day. If you're heading for Haleakala, remember that U.S. astronauts trained for the moon inside the volcano; bring survival gear. You'll need your swimsuit and rain gear if you're bound for Waianapanapa. Bring your own gear, as there are no places to rent camping equipment on Maui.

For more information on Maui camping and hiking trails, and to obtain free maps, contact **Haleakala National Park,** P.O. Box 369, Makawao, HI 96768 (© 808/572-4400; www.nps.gov/hale); or the **State Division of Forestry and Wildlife,** 54 S. High St., Wailuku, HI 96793 (© 808/984-8100; www. hawaiistateparks.org). For information on trails, hikes, camping, and permits for state parks, contact the **Hawaii State Department of Land and Natural Resources,** State Parks Division, P.O. Box 621, Honolulu, HI 96809 (© 808/587-0300; www.hawaiistateparks.org/camping/fees.cfm); note that you can get information from the website but cannot obtain permits there. For Maui County Parks, contact the **Maui County Department of Parks and Recreation,** 200 S. High St., Wailuku, HI 96793 (© 808/270-7230; www. co.maui.hi.us/departments/Parks).

Guided Hikes   If you'd like a knowledgeable guide to accompany you on a hike, call **Maui Hiking Safaris ★** (© 888/445-3963 or 808/573-0168; www.mauihikingsafaris.com). Owner Randy Warner takes visitors on half- and full-day hikes into valleys, rainforests, and coastal areas. Randy's been hiking around Maui for more than 25 years and is wise in the ways of Hawaiian history, native flora and fauna, and volcanology. His rates are $59 to $79 for a half-day and $105 to $139 for a full day, which include day packs, rain parkas, snacks, water, and, on full-day hikes, sandwiches.

Maui's oldest hiking-guide company is **Hike Maui ★** (© 808/879-5270; www.hikemaui.com), headed by Ken Schmitt, who pioneered guided hikes on the Valley Isle. Hike Maui offers five different hikes a day, ranging from an easy 1-mile, 3-hour hike to a waterfall ($75), to a strenuous full-day hike in Haleakala Crater ($150). All prices include equipment and transportation.

Venture into the lush West Maui Mountains with an experienced guide on one of the numerous hikes offered by **Maui Eco-Adventures** (© 877/661-7720 or 808/661-7720; www.ecomaui.com). I love the Rainforest/Waterfall Hike: After a continental breakfast, you'll hike by streams and waterfalls, through native trees and plants, and on to breathtaking vistas. The tour includes a picnic lunch, swims in secluded pools, and memorable photo ops. The 6-hour excursion costs $125 per person, including meals, a fanny pack with bottled water, and rain gear, if necessary. No children 12 and under are allowed. For those more "on vacation," an easier jaunt costs just $85.

For information on hikes given by the **Hawaii Sierra Club on Maui,** call © 808/573-4147 or go to www.hi.sierraclub.org.

zipping **OVER THE FOREST CANOPY**

For those looking for a different perspective of Haleakala, try **Skyline Eco-Adventures' Zipline Haleakala Tour** (☎ 808/878-8400; www.skylinehawaii.com), which blends a short hike through a eucalyptus forest with four "zipline" crossings. During the zipline crossing, you'll be outfitted with a seat harness and connected to a cable, then launched from a 70-foot-high platform to "zip" along the cable suspended over the slopes of Haleakala. From this viewpoint, you fly over treetops, valleys, gulches, and waterfalls at 10 to 35 mph. These bird's-eye tours operate daily and take riders from ages 10 and up, weighing between 80 and 260 pounds. The cost is $80, if you book on their website.

Haleakala National Park ★★★

For complete coverage of the national park, see p. 538.

HIKING INTO THE WILDERNESS AREA: SLIDING SANDS & HALEMAUU TRAILS

Hiking into Maui's dormant volcano is the best way to see it. The terrain inside the wilderness area of the volcano, which ranges from burnt-red cinder cones to ebony-black lava flows, is simply spectacular. There are some 27 miles of hiking trails, two camping sites, and three cabins.

Entrance to Haleakala National Park is $10 per car. The rangers offer free guided hikes, usually Monday and Thursday, which are a great way to learn about the unusual flora and geological formations here. Wear sturdy shoes and be prepared for wind, rain, and intense sun. Bring water and a hat. Additional options include full-moon hikes and star program hikes. **Always call at least a month in advance:** The hikes and briefing sessions may be canceled, so check first. For details, call the park at ☎ 808/572-4400 or visit www.nps.gov/hale.

Try to arrange to stay at least 1 night in the park; 2 or 3 nights will allow you more time to explore the fascinating interior of the volcano (see below for details on the cabins and campgrounds in the wilderness area of the valley). If you want to venture out on your own, the best route takes in two trails: into the crater along **Sliding Sands Trail,** which begins on the rim at 9,800 feet and descends into the belly of the beast, to the valley floor at 6,600 feet; and back out along **Halemauu Trail.** Hardy hikers can consider making the 11-mile, one-way descent, which takes 9 hours, and the equally long return ascent in a day. The rest of us can extend this steep hike to 2 days. The descending and ascending trails aren't loops; the trail heads are miles (and several thousand feet in elevation) apart, so you'll need to make transportation arrangements in advance. Before you set out, stop at park headquarters to get camping and hiking updates.

The trail head for Sliding Sands is well marked and the trail is easy to follow over lava flows and cinders. As you descend, look around: The view is breathtaking. In the afternoon, waves of clouds flow into the Kaupo and Koolau gaps. Vegetation is spare to nonexistent at the top, but the closer you get to the valley floor, the more growth you'll see: bracken ferns, pili grass, shrubs, even flowers. On the floor, the trail travels across rough lava flows, passing by rare silversword plants, volcanic vents, and multicolored cinder cones.

The Halemauu Trail goes over red and black lava and past vegetation, like evening primrose, as it begins its ascent up the valley wall. Occasionally, riders on horseback use this trail. The proper etiquette is to step aside and stand quietly next to the trail as the horses pass.

Some shorter and easier hiking options include the .5-mile walk down the **Hosmer Grove Nature Trail,** or just the first mile or two down **Sliding Sands Trail,** which gives you a hint of what lies ahead. (Even this short hike is exhausting at the high altitude.) A good day hike is **Halemauu Trail** to Holua Cabin and back, an 8-mile, half-day trip.

CABINS & CAMPGROUNDS IN THE WILDERNESS AREA

Most people stay at one of two tent campgrounds, unless they get lucky and win the lottery—the lottery, that is, for one of the three wilderness cabins. For more information, contact **Haleakala National Park,** P.O. Box 369, Makawao, HI 96768 (☎ **808/572-4400;** www.nps.gov/hale).

CABINS It can get really cold and windy down in the valley, so try for a cabin. They're warm, protected from the elements, and reasonably priced. Each has 12 padded bunks (but no bedding; bring your own), a table, chairs, cooking utensils, a two-burner propane stove, and a wood-burning stove with firewood (you may also have a few cockroaches). The cabins are spaced so that each one is an easy walk from the other: Holua cabin is on the Halemauu Trail, Kapalaoa cabin on Sliding Sands Trail, and Paliku cabin on the eastern end by the Kaupo Gap. The rates are $75 a night if you book more than 3 weeks in advance or $60 a night if you book less than 3 weeks in advance.

The cabins are so popular, requests for cabins must be made 3 months in advance (be sure to request alternate dates). You can request all three cabins at once; you're limited to 2 nights in one cabin and 3 nights total within the wilderness per month. At their website, www.fhnp.org/wcr, you'll find the rules and regs and the online application.

CAMPGROUNDS If you don't win the cabin lottery, all is not lost—there are three tent-camping sites that can accommodate you: two in the wilderness and one just outside at Hosmer Grove. There is no charge for tent camping.

Hosmer Grove, located at 6,800 feet, is a small, open, grassy area surrounded by a forest. Trees protect campers from the winds, but nights still get very cold; sometimes there's ice on the ground up here. This is the best place to spend the night in a tent if you want to see the Haleakala sunrise. Come up the day before, enjoy the park, take a day hike, and then turn in early. The enclosed-glass summit building opens at sunrise for those who come to greet the dawn—a welcome windbreak. Facilities at Hosmer Grove include a covered pavilion with picnic tables and grills, chemical toilets, and drinking water. No permits are needed, and there's no charge—but you can stay for only 3 nights in a 30-day period.

The two tent-camping areas inside the volcano are **Holua,** just off Halemauu at 6,920 feet; and **Paliku,** just before the Kaupo Gap at the eastern end of the valley, at 6,380 feet. Facilities at both campgrounds are limited to pit toilets and nonpotable catchment water. Water at Holua is limited, especially in summer. No open fires are allowed inside the volcano, so bring a stove if you plan to cook. Tent camping is restricted to the signed area. No camping is allowed in the horse pasture. The inviting grassy lawn in front of the cabin is off-limits. Camping is free but limited to 2 consecutive nights, and no more than 3 nights a month inside the volcano. Permits are issued at park headquarters daily from 8am to 3pm, on a first-come, first-served basis on the day you plan to camp. Occupancy is limited to 25 people in each campground.

HIKING & CAMPING AT KIPAHULU (NEAR HANA)

In the East Maui section of Haleakala National Park, you can set up at **Oheo Campground,** a first-come, first-served, drive-in campground with tent sites for 100 near the ocean. It has a few tables, barbecue grills, and chemical toilets. No permit is required, but there's a 3-night limit. No food or drinking water is available, so bring your own. Bring a tent as well—it rains 75 inches a year here. Contact **Kipahulu Ranger Station,** Haleakala National Park, HI 96713 (✆ **808/248-7375;** www.nps.gov/hale/planyourvisit/wilderness-camping.htm), for information.

HIKING FROM THE SUMMIT   If you hike from the crater rim down **Kaupo Gap** to the ocean, more than 20 miles away, you'll pass through several climate zones. On a clear day, you can see every island except Kauai on the trip down.

APPROACHING KIPAHULU FROM HANA   If you drive to Kipahulu, you'll have to approach it from the Hana Highway because it's not accessible from the summit. From the ranger station, it's a short hike above the famous **Oheo Gulch** (which was misnamed the Seven Sacred Pools in the 1940s) to two spectacular waterfalls. The first, **Makahiku Falls,** is easily reached from the central parking area; the trail head begins near the ranger station. Pipiwai Trail leads you up to the road and beyond for .5 miles to the overlook. If you hike another 1.5 miles up the trail across two bridges and through a bamboo forest, you reach **Waimoku Falls.** It's a good uphill hike, but press on to avoid the pool's crowd. In hard rain, streams swell quickly. Always be aware of your surroundings.

GUIDED HIKES   The rangers at Kipahulu conduct a 1-mile hike to the **Bamboo Forest ★** at 9:30am daily; and a 4-mile round-trip hike to **Waimoku Falls** on Saturday at 9:30am. All programs and hikes begin at the ranger station; they may be canceled, so check in advance by contacting the **Kipahulu Ranger Station,** Haleakala National Park, HI 96713 (✆ **808/248-7375;** www.nps.gov/hale).

Polipoli Spring State Recreation Area ★

At this state recreation area, part of the 21,000-acre Kula and Kahikinui forest reserves on the slope of Haleakala, it's hard to believe that you're in Hawaii. First of all, it's cold, even in summer, because the elevation is 5,300 to 6,200 feet. Second, this former forest of native koa, ohia, and mamane, which was over-logged in the 1800s, was reforested in the 1930s with introduced species: pine, Monterey cypress, ash, sugi, red alder, redwood, and several varieties of eucalyptus. The result is a cool area, with muted sunlight filtered by towering trees.

There's a campground at the recreation area at 6,300 feet. Permits and reservations are required, fees are $5 per campsite per night, and your stay must be limited to 5 nights. One 10-bunk cabin is available for $45 a night for one to four guests ($5 for each additional guest); it has a cold shower and a gas stove, but no electricity or drinking water (bring your own). To reserve, contact the **State Parks Division,** 54 S. High St., Room 101, Wailuku, HI 96793 (© **808/984-8109;** www.hawaiistateparks.org/camping/fees.cfm).

SKYLINE TRAIL

This is some hike—strenuous but worth every step if you like seeing the big picture. It's 8 miles, all downhill, with a dazzling 100-mile view of the islands dotting the blue Pacific, plus the West Maui Mountains, which seem like a separate island.

The trail is just outside Haleakala National Park at Polipoli Spring State Recreation Area; however, you access it by going through the national park to the summit. It starts just beyond the Puu Ulaula summit building on the south side of Science City and follows the southwest rift zone of Haleakala from its lunar-like cinder cones to a cool redwood grove. The trail drops 3,800 feet on a 4-hour hike to the recreation area in the 12,000-acre Kahikinui Forest Reserve. If you'd rather drive, you'll need a four-wheel-drive vehicle.

POLIPOLI LOOP

One of the most unusual hiking experiences in the state is this easy 3.5-mile hike, which takes about 3 hours; dress warmly for it. Take the Haleakala Highway (Hwy. 37) to Keokea and turn right onto Hwy. 337; after less than a half-mile, turn on Waipoli Road, which climbs swiftly. After 10 miles, Waipoli Road ends at the Polipoli Spring State Recreation Area campgrounds. The well-marked trail head is next to the parking lot, near a stand of Monterey cypress; the tree-lined trail offers the best view of the island.

Polipoli Loop is really a network of three trails: Haleakala Ridge, Plum Trail, and Redwood Trail. After .5 mile of meandering through groves of eucalyptus, blackwood, swamp mahogany, and hybrid cypress, you'll join the Haleakala Ridge Trail, which, about a mile in, joins with the Plum Trail (named for the plums that ripen in June–July). This trail passes through massive redwoods and by an old Conservation Corps bunkhouse and a run-down cabin before joining up with the Redwood Trail, which climbs through Mexican pine, tropical ash, Port Orford cedar, and, of course, redwood.

Kanaha Beach Park Camping

One of the few Maui County camping facilities on the island is at Kanaha Beach Park, located next to the Kahului Airport. The county has two separate areas for camping: 7 tent sites on the beach and an additional 10 tent sites inland. This well-used park is a favorite of windsurfers, who take advantage of the strong winds that roar across this end of the island. Facilities include a paved parking lot, portable toilets, outdoor showers, barbecue grills, and picnic tables. Camping is open 5 days a week (closed Tues–Wed) and limited to no more than 3 consecutive days. Permits, which are $5 per adult and $2 per child per night, can be obtained from the **Maui County Parks and Recreation Department,** 700 Halia Nakoa St., Unit 2, Wailuku, HI 96793 (© **808/243-7389;** www.mauimapp.com/information/campingcounty.htm). The 17 sites book up quickly; reserve your dates far in advance (the county will accept reservations a year in advance).

Waianapanapa State Park ★★

Tucked in a tropical jungle on the outskirts of the little coastal town of Hana is this state park, a black-sand beach set in an emerald forest.

The **Hana-Waianapanapa Coast Trail** is an easy 6-mile hike that takes you back in time. Allow 4 hours to walk along this relatively flat trail, which parallels the sea, along lava cliffs and a forest of lauhala trees. The best time to take the hike is either early morning or late afternoon, when the light on the lava and surf makes for great photos. Midday is the worst time; not only is it hot (lava intensifies the heat), but there's also no shade or potable water available.

There's no formal trail head; join the route at any point along the Waianapanapa Campground and go in either direction. Along the trail, you'll see remains of an ancient *heiau*, stands of lauhala trees, caves, a blowhole, and a remarkable plant, naupaka, which flourishes along the beach. Upon close inspection, you'll see that the naupaka have only half-blossoms; according to Hawaiian legend, a similar plant living in the mountains has the other half of the blossoms. One ancient explanation is that the two plants represent never-to-be reunited lovers: As the story goes, the couple bickered so much that the gods, fed up with their incessant quarreling, banished one lover to the mountain and the other to the sea.

Waianapanapa has 12 cabins and a tent campground. Go for the cabins (reviewed on p. 470), as it rains torrentially here, sometimes turning the campground into a mud-wrestling arena; the fee is $45 a night. Tent camping is $5 per night but limited to 5 nights in a 30-day period. Permits are available from the **State Parks Division,** 54 S. High St., Room 101, Wailuku, HI 96793 (© **808/984-8109;** www.hawaiistateparks.org/camping/fees.cfm). Facilities include restrooms, outdoor showers, drinking water, and picnic tables.

Hana: The Hike to Fagan's Cross

This 3-mile hike to the cross erected in memory of Paul Fagan, the founder of Hana Ranch and Hotel Hana-Maui, offers spectacular views of the Hana Coast, particularly at sunset. The uphill trail starts across Hana Highway

The Kaenae Lookout.

Fagan's Cross.

from the Hotel Hana-Maui. Enter the pastures at your own risk; they're often occupied by glaring bulls with sharp horns and cows with new calves. Watch your step as you ascend this steep hill on a jeep trail across open pastures to the cross and the breathtaking view.

GOLF & OTHER OUTDOOR ACTIVITIES

Golf

For last-minute and discount tee times, call **Stand-by Golf** (℃ 888/645-2665; www.mauiclubrentals.com/standBy.htm), which offers savings of up to 50% off greens fees, plus guaranteed tee times for same-day or next-day golfing. **Golf Club Rentals** (℃ 808/665-0800; www.mauiclubrentals.com) has custom-built clubs for men, women, and juniors (both right- and left-handed), which can be delivered islandwide; the rates are $25 a day for steel clubs, or $30 a day for a full graphite set.

WEST MAUI

Kaanapali Golf Resort ★   Both courses at Kaanapali offer a challenge to all golfers, from high handicappers to near-pros. The par-71, nearly 6,700-yard **Royal Kaanapali Course** is a true Robert Trent Jones, Sr., design: an abundance of wide bunkers; several long, stretched-out tees; and the largest, most contoured greens on Maui. The par-70, 6,400-yard **Kaanapali Kai** is an Arthur Jack Snyder design; although shorter than the North Course, it requires more accuracy on the narrow, hilly fairways. Facilities include a driving range, putting course, and clubhouse with dining. You'll have a better chance of getting a tee time on weekdays.

Off Hwy. 30, Kaanapali. ℃ **808/661-3691.** www.kaanapali-golf.com. Greens fees: Royal Kaanapali Course $235 ($190 for Kaanapali guests), twilight rates $120; Kaanapali Kai Course $195 ($150 for Kaanapali guests), twilight rates $95. At the 1st stoplight in Kaanapali, turn onto Kaanapali Pkwy.; the 1st building on your right is the clubhouse.

Kapalua Resort ★★★   The views from these two championship courses are worth the greens fees alone. The par-72, 6,761-yard **Bay Course** (℃ 808/669-8820) was designed by Arnold Palmer and Ed Seay. This course is a bit forgiving, with its wide fairways; the greens, however, are difficult to read. The often-photographed 5th overlooks a small ocean cove; even the pros have trouble with this rocky par-3, 205-yard hole. The **Plantation Course** (℃ 808/669-8877), site of the PGA Mercedes-Benz Championship, is a Ben Crenshaw/Bill Coore design. This 6,547-yard, par-73 course, set on a rolling hillside, is excellent for developing your low shots and precise chipping. Facilities for all three courses include locker rooms, a driving range, and excellent dining. Weekdays are your best bet for tee times.

Off Hwy. 30, Kapalua. ℃ **877/KAPALUA** (527-2582). www.kapaluamaui.com. Greens fees: Bay Course $220 ($183 for hotel guests), midday $176, twilight rates $138; Plantation Course $298 ($218 for guests), midday $238, twilight rates $150.

SOUTH MAUI

Elleair Maui Golf Club　Sitting in the foothills of Haleakala, just high enough to afford spectacular ocean vistas from every hole, Elleair (formerly Silversword Golf Club) is a course for golfers who love the views as much as the fairways and greens. It's very forgiving. *Just one caveat:* Go in the morning. Not only is it cooler, but, more important, it's also less windy. In the afternoon, the winds bluster down Haleakala with great gusto. This is a fun course to play, with some challenging holes; the par-5 2nd hole is a virtual minefield of bunkers, and the par-5 8th hole shoots over a swale and then uphill.

1345 Piilani Hwy. (near Lipoa St. turnoff), Kihei. © **808/874-0777.** www.elleairmauigolfclub.com. Greens fees $120; twilight rate $95.

Makena Golf Courses ★★　Here you'll find 36 holes of "Mr. Hawaii Golf"—Robert Trent Jones, Jr.—at its best. Add to that spectacular views: Molokini islet looms in the background, humpback whales gambol offshore in winter, and the tropical sunsets are spectacular. The par-72, 6,876-yard **South Course** has a couple of holes you'll never forget. The view from the par-4 15th, which shoots from an elevated tee 183 yards downhill to the Pacific, is magnificent. The 16th hole has a two-tiered green that's blind from the tee 383 yards away (that is, if you make it past the gully off the fairway). The par 72, 6,823-yard **North Course** is more difficult and more spectacular. The 13th hole, located partway up the mountain, has a view that makes most golfers stop and stare. The next hole is even more memorable: a 200-foot drop between tee and green. Facilities at Makena include a clubhouse, a driving range, two putting greens, a pro shop, lockers, and lessons. Beware of weekend crowds.

On Makena Alanui Dr., just past the Maui Prince Hotel. © **808/879-3344.** www.makenagolf.com. Greens fees $129 and $99 after noon ($99 and $79 for Makena Resort guests); twilight rate $60.

Wailea Golf Club ★★　There are three courses to choose from at Wailea. The **Blue Course,** a par-72, 6,758-yard course designed by Arthur Jack Snyder and dotted with bunkers and water hazards, is for duffers and pros alike. The wide fairways appeal to beginners, while the undulating terrain makes it a course everyone can enjoy. A little more difficult is the par-72, 7,078-yard championship **Gold Course,** with narrow fairways, several tricky dogleg holes, and the classic Robert Trent Jones, Jr., challenges: natural hazards, like lava-rock walls, and native Hawaiian grasses. The **Emerald Course,** also designed by Robert Trent Jones, Jr., is Wailea's newest, with tropical landscaping and a player-friendly design. With 54 holes to play, getting a tee time is slightly easier on weekends than at other resorts, but weekdays are still best (the Emerald Course is usually the toughest to book). Facilities include two pro shops, restaurants, locker rooms, and a complete golf training facility.

Wailea Alanui Dr. (off Wailea Iki Dr.), Wailea. © **888/328-MAUI** (6284) or 808/875-7450. www.waileagolf.com. Greens fees $225 ($190–$199 for resort guests), twilight rate $90.

UPCOUNTRY MAUI

Pukalani Country Club　This cool par-72, 6,962-yard course at 1,100 feet offers a break from the resorts' high greens fees, and it's really fun to play. The 3rd hole offers golfers two different options: a tough (especially into the wind) iron shot from the tee, across a gully (yuck!) to the green; or a shot down the side of the gully across a second green into sand traps below. (Most people choose to shoot down the side of the gully; it's actually easier than shooting across a ravine.) High handicappers will love this course, and more experienced players can make it more challenging by playing from the back tees. Facilities include club and shoe rentals, practice areas, lockers, a pro shop, and a restaurant.

360 Pukalani St., Pukalani. ℂ **808/572-1314.** www.pukalanigolf.com. Greens fees for 18 holes (including cart) $79 before 11am, $74 11am–2pm, $60 after 1pm, $27 after 2:30pm. Take the Hana Hwy. (Hwy. 36) to Haleakala Hwy. (Hwy. 37) to the Pukalani exit; turn right onto Pukalani St. and go 2 blocks.

Biking

Cruising Haleakala ★　It's not even close to dawn, but here you are, rubbing your eyes awake, riding in a van up the long, dark road to the top of Maui's dormant volcano. It's colder than you ever thought possible for a tropical island. The air is thin. The place is crowded, packed with people. You stomp your chilly feet while you wait, sipping hot coffee. Then comes the sun, exploding over the yawning Haleakala Crater, big enough to swallow Manhattan—a moment you won't soon forget. Now you know why Hawaiians named the crater the House of the Sun. But there's no time to linger: Decked out in your screaming-yellow parka, you mount your mechanical steed and test its most important feature, the brakes—because you're about to coast 37 miles down a 10,000-foot volcano.

Cruising down Haleakala, from the lunarlike landscape at the top past flower farms, pineapple fields, and eucalyptus groves, is quite an experience—and just about anybody can do it. This is a safe trip that requires some stamina in the colder, wetter winter months but is fun for everyone in the warmer months—the key word being *warmer*. In winter and the rainy season, conditions can be harsh, especially on the top, with below-freezing temperatures and 40-mph winds.

Maui's oldest downhill company is **Maui Downhill ★** (ℂ **800/535-BIKE** [2453] or 808/871-2155; www.mauidownhill.com), which offers a sunrise safari bike tour, including continental breakfast and a stop for lunch (not hosted), starting at $129 ($89 if booked online). If it's all booked up, try **Maui Mountain Cruisers** (ℂ **800/232-6284** or 808/871-6014; www.mauimountaincruisers. com), which has sunrise and midday trips for $170 ($135 if booked on the website). **Mountain Riders Bike Tours** (ℂ **800/706-7700** or 808/242-9739; www.mountainriders.com) offers sunrise rides for $150 ($120 if booked online) and midday trips for $130 ($104 online). All rates include hotel pickup, transport to the top, bicycle, safety equipment, and continental breakfast (there is a stop for food down the mountain that guests pay for themselves). Wear layers of warm clothing—there may be a 30°F (17°C) change in temperature from the top of the mountain to the ocean. Generally, tour groups will not take riders 11 and under, but younger children can ride along in the van that accompanies the groups, as can pregnant women.

If you want to avoid the crowds and go down the mountain at your own pace, call **Haleakala Bike Company** (ℂ **888/922-2453;** www.bikemaui. com), which will outfit you with the latest gear and take you up Haleakala.

Note: Not all tours go to the summit. If you want to start your bike ride at the summit, be sure to confirm. The cheapest trip starts at around the 6,500-foot

MORATORIUM ON bike tours IN HALEAKALA NATIONAL PARK

The National Park Service has issued a moratorium on commercial bicycle tours inside Haleakala National Park due to a September 26, 2007, death of a tourist who lost control of her bicycle and struck a van inside the park.

Some operators of Haleakala's "downhill bike tours" have circumvented this moratorium by staging their bicycle tours outside the park's boundaries. There are also a handful of companies who have "road-based" tour permits, which allows them to transport their clients within the park boundaries by van, but does not allow their clients to bike inside the park. If you want to see the sunrise from the Haleakala Crater, be sure to ask your tour operator if it has a road-based permit; otherwise, you will not be able to get inside the park.

The moratorium does not affect private citizens riding their bikes inside the park boundaries. For information on bikeways and maps, get a copy of the *Maui County Bicycle Map*, which has details on road suitability, climate, trade winds, mileage, elevation changes, bike shops, safety tips, and various bicycling routes. The map is available at bike shops all over the island. A great book for mountain bikers who want to venture out on their own is John Alford's *Mountain Biking the Hawaiian Islands*, published by Ohana Publishing (www.bikehawaii.com).

level (about two-thirds up the mountain). After making sure you are secure on the bike, they will let you ride down by yourself at your own pace. Trips range from $70 to $115; bicycle rentals (from $35 a day) are also available if you'd like to tour other parts of Maui on your own.

Horseback Riding

Maui offers spectacular adventure rides through rugged ranchlands, into tropical forests, and to remote swimming holes. I recommend riding with **Mendes Ranch & Trail Rides ★**, 3530 Kahekili Hwy., 4 miles past Wailuku (𝄯 **808/244-7320**; www.mendesranch.com). The 300-acre Mendes Ranch is a real-life working cowboy ranch that has the essential elements of an earthly paradise—rainbows, waterfalls, palm trees, coral-sand beaches, lagoons, tide pools, a rainforest, and its own volcanic peak (more than a mile high). Allan Mendes, a third-generation wrangler, will take you from the edge of the rainforest out to the sea. On the way, you'll cross tree-studded meadows where Texas longhorns sit in the shade and pass a dusty corral. Allan keeps close watch, turning often in his saddle to make sure everyone is happy. He points out flora and fauna and fields questions, but generally just lets you soak up Maui's natural splendor in golden silence. A 2-hour morning or afternoon ride costs $110; add on a barbecue lunch at the corral for an additional $20.

Another one of my favorites is **Piiholo Ranch,** in Makawao (𝄯 **866/572-5544** or 808/357-5544; www.piiholo.com). A working cattle ranch owned by the *kamaaina* (longtime resident) Baldwin family, it offers horseback-riding adventures with a variety of options to suit your ability; rates start at $120 for a 2-hour country ride through a working cattle ranch.

If you're out in Hana, don't pass up **Maui Horseback Tours at Maui Stables ★★**, a mile past Oheo Gulch in Kipahulu (© 808/248-7799; www.mauistables.com). It offers two rides daily (9:30am and 1pm) through the mountains above Kipahulu Valley—and you get a fantastic historical and cultural tour through the unspoiled landscape, to boot. It is an experience you will not forget. Both rides are $150. If you enjoy your ride, remember to kiss your horse and tip your guide.

For horse lovers looking for the ultimate, check out Frank Levinson's **Maui Horse Whisperer Experience** (© 808/572-6211; www.mauihorses.com), which includes a seminar on the language of the horse. Prices are $200 for half-day and $300 for full-day workshops. No horse aficionado should pass it up.

HALEAKALA ON HORSEBACK If you'd like to ride down into Haleakala's crater, contact **Pony Express Tours ★** (© 808/667-2200 or 878-6698; www.ponyexpresstours.com), which leads a variety of rides down to the crater floor and back up, from $182 per person. Shorter 1- and 2-hour rides are also offered at Haleakala Ranch, located on the beautiful lower slopes of the volcano, for $95 to $110. If you book via the website, you get 10% off. Pony Express provides well-trained horses and experienced guides, and accommodates all riding levels. You must be at least 10 years old, weigh no more than 230 pounds, and wear long pants and closed-toe shoes.

Tennis

Maui has excellent public tennis courts; all are free and available from daylight to sunset (a few are even lit for night play until 10pm). For a complete list of public courts, call **Maui County Parks and Recreation** (© 808/243-7230). The courts are available on a first-come, first-served basis; when someone's waiting, limit your play to 45 minutes. Most public courts do require a wait and are not conveniently located near the major resort areas, so most visitors are likely to play at their own hotels for a fee. The exceptions to this are in Kihei (which has courts in Kalama Park on South Kihei Rd., and in Waipualani Park on West Waipualani Rd., behind the Maui Sunset condo), in Lahaina (which has courts in Malu'uou o lele Park, at Front and Shaw sts.), and in Hana (which has courts in Hana Park, on the Hana Hwy.).

Private tennis courts are available at most resorts and hotels on the island. The **Kapalua Tennis Garden and Village Tennis Center,** Kapalua Resort (© 808/669-5677; www.kapaluamaui.com), is home to the Kapalua Open, which features the largest purse in the state, on Labor Day weekend. Court rentals are $15 per person for nonresort guests. The staff will match you up with a partner if you need one. In Wailea, try the **Wailea Tennis Club,** 131 Wailea Iki Place (© 808/879-1958; www.waileatennis.com), with 11 Plexipave courts. Court fees are $14 per person for resort guests and $16 per person for nonguests.

SEEING THE SIGHTS
Central Maui

Central Maui isn't exactly tourist central; this is where real people live. Most likely, you'll land here and head directly to the beach. However, there are a few sights worth checking out if you feel like a respite from the sun and surf.

Taking a Submarine Ride Atlantis Submarines (p. 516) takes you and the kids down into the shallow coastal waters off Lahaina in a real sub, where you'll see plenty of fish (and maybe even a shark!). They'll love it, and you'll stay dry the entire time. Allow about 2 hours for the trip.

Riding the Sugar Cane Train (pictured above) Small kids love this ride, as do train buffs of all ages. A steam engine pulls open-passenger cars of the Lahaina/Kaanapali and Pacific Railroad on a 30-minute, 12-mile round-trip through sugar cane fields between Lahaina and Kaanapali while the conductor sings and calls out the landmarks. Along the way, you can see the hidden parts of Kaanapali and the islands of Molokai and Lanai beyond. Tickets are $23 for adults, $16 for kids 3 to 12; call ℭ **808/661-0080** or visit www.sugar-canetrain.com for details.

Tour of the Stars After sunset, the stars over Kaanapali shine big and bright because the tropical sky is almost pollutant free and no big-city lights interfere with the cosmic view. Amateur astronomers can probe the Milky Way, see the rings of Saturn and Jupiter's moons, and scan the Sea of Tranquillity in a 60-minute star search on the world's first recreational computer-driven telescope. It all takes place nightly at the **Hyatt Regency Maui Resort,** 200 Nohea Kai Dr. (ℭ **808/661-1234**), weather permitting. The cost for hotel guests is $26 for adults and $16 for children 12 and under; nonguests pay $32 for adults and $21 for children.

Seeing Sharks, Stingrays & Starfish Hawaii's largest aquarium, the **Maui Ocean Center** (ℭ **808/270-7000;** p. 535), has a range of sea critters—from tiger sharks to tiny starfish—that are sure to fascinate kids of all ages. At this 5-acre facility in Maalaea, visitors can take a virtual walk from the beach down to the ocean depths via the three dozen tanks, countless exhibits, and 100-foot-long main oceanarium.

Getting a Dragonfly's View Kids will think this is too much fun to be educational. Don a face mask and get the dizzying perspective of what a dragonfly sees as it flies over a mountain stream, or watch the tiny *oopu* fish climb up a stream at the **Hawaii Nature Center** (ℭ **808/244-6500;** p. 532) in beautiful Iao Valley, where you'll find some 30 hands-on, interactive exhibits and displays of Hawaii's natural history.

KAHULUI

Under the airport flight path, next to Maui's busiest intersection and across from Costco and Kmart in Kahului's new business park, is a most unlikely place: the **Kanaha Wildlife Sanctuary,** Haleakala Highway Extension and Hana Highway (ℭ **808/984-8100**). Look for the parking area off Haleakala Highway Extension (behind the mall, across the Hana Hwy. from Cutter Automotive), and you'll find a 50-foot trail that meanders along the shore to a shade shelter and lookout. Look for the sign proclaiming this the permanent home of the endangered black-neck Hawaiian stilt, whose population is now down to about 1,000. Naturalists say this is a good place to see endangered Hawaiian koloa ducks, stilts, coots, and other migrating shorebirds. For a quieter, more natural-looking wildlife preserve, see the **Kealia Pond National Wildlife Preserve** in Kihei (p. 536).

WAILUKU & WAIKAPU

Wailuku, the historic gateway to Iao Valley, is worth a visit for a little antiquing and a visit to the **Bailey House Museum ★**, 2375-A Main St. (© **808/244-3326;** www.mauimuseum.org). Missionary and sugar planter Edward Bailey's 1833 home—an architectural hybrid of stones laid by Hawaiian craftsmen and timbers joined in a display of Yankee ingenuity—is a treasure-trove of Hawaiiana. Inside you'll find an eclectic collection, from precontact artifacts like scary temple images, dogtooth necklaces, and a rare lei made of tree-snail shells to latter-day relics like Duke Kahanamoku's 1919 redwood surfboard and a koa-wood table given to President Ulysses S. Grant, who had to refuse it because he couldn't accept gifts from foreign countries. There's also a gallery devoted to a few of Bailey's landscapes, painted from 1866 to 1896, which capture on canvas a Maui I can only imagine today. It's open Monday through Saturday from 10am to 4pm; admission is $7 for adults, $5 for seniors, and $2 for children 7 to 12.

About 3 miles south of Wailuku lies the tiny one-street village of Waikapu, which has two attractions that are worth a peek. Relive Maui's past by taking a 40-minute narrated tram ride around fields of pineapple, sugar cane, and papaya trees at **Maui Tropical Plantation,** 1670 Honoapiilani Hwy. (© **800/451-6805** or 808/244-7643; www.mauitropicalplantation.com), a real working plantation open daily from 9am to 5pm. A shop sells fresh and dried fruit, and a restaurant serves lunch. Admission is free; the tram tours, which start at 10am and leave about every 45 minutes, are $14 for adults, $5 for kids 3 to 12.

Kanaha Wildlife Sanctuary.

The Bailey House Museum.

Flying High: Helicopter Rides

Only a helicopter can bring you face to face with volcanoes, waterfalls, and remote places like Maui's little-known Wall of Tears, up near the summit of Puu Kukui in the West Maui Mountains. Today's pilots are part Hawaiian historian, part DJ, part amusement-ride operator, and part tour guide, telling you about Hawaii's flora, fauna, history, and culture. **Blue Hawaiian Helicopters** ★★★ (© 800/745-BLUE [2583] or 808/871-8844; www.blue hawaiian.com) is the Cadillac of helicopter-tour companies. It has the latest high-tech, environmentally friendly (and quiet) Eco-Star helicopters, specially designed for air-tour operators. Flight times range from 30 to 100 minutes and cost $206 to $413. *Tip:* Book on the website for substantial savings, where rates start at $139!

IAO VALLEY ★

A couple of miles north of Wailuku, where the little plantation houses stop and the road climbs ever higher, Maui's true nature begins to reveal itself. The transition from suburban sprawl to raw nature is so abrupt that most people who drive up into the valley don't realize they're suddenly in a rainforest. The moist, cool air and the shade are a welcome comfort after the hot tropic sun. This is Iao Valley, a 6¼-acre state park whose great nature, history, and beauty have been enjoyed by millions of people from around the world for more than a century. Iao ("Supreme Light") Valley, 10 miles long and encompassing 4,000 acres, is the eroded volcanic caldera of the West Maui Mountains. The head of the valley is a broad circular amphitheater where four major streams converge into Iao Stream. At the back of the amphitheater is rain-drenched Puu Kukui, the West Maui Mountains' highest point. No other Hawaiian valley lets you go from seacoast to rainforest so easily. This peaceful valley, full of tropical plants, rainbows, waterfalls, swimming holes, and hiking trails, is a place of solitude, reflection, and escape for residents and visitors alike.

To get here from Wailuku, take Main Street to Iao Valley Road to the entrance to the state park.

Two paved walkways loop into the massive green amphitheater, across the bridge of Iao Valley Stream, and along the stream itself. This paved .35-mile loop is Maui's easiest hike—you can take your grandmother on this one. The leisurely walk will allow you to enjoy lovely views of Iao Needle and the lush vegetation. Others often proceed beyond the state park border and take two trails deeper into the valley, but the trails enter private land, and NO TRESPASSING signs are posted.

The feature known as **Iao Needle** is an erosional remnant consisting of basalt dikes. This phallic rock juts an impressive 2,250 feet above sea level. Youngsters play in **Iao Stream,** a peaceful brook that belies its bloody history. In 1790, King Kamehameha the Great and his men engaged in the battle of Iao Valley to gain control of Maui. When the battle ended, so many bodies blocked Iao Stream that the battle site was named Kepaniwai, or "damming of the waters." An architectural heritage park of Hawaiian, Japanese, Chinese, Filipino, and New England–style houses stands in harmony by Iao Stream at **Kepaniwai Heritage Garden.** This is a good picnic spot, with plenty of tables and benches. You can see ferns, banana trees, and other native and exotic plants in the **Iao Valley Botanic Garden** along the stream.

WHEN TO GO The park is open daily from 7am to 7pm. Go early in the morning or late in the afternoon, when the sun's rays slant into the valley and create a mystical mood. You can bring a picnic and spend the day, but be prepared at any time for one of the frequent tropical cloudbursts that soak the valley and swell both waterfalls and streams.

Iao Needle.

INFORMATION & VISITOR CENTERS For information, contact **Iao Valley State Park,** State Parks and Recreation, 54 S. High St., Room 101, Wailuku, HI 96793 (© 808/984-8100). The **Hawaii Nature Center,** 875 Iao Valley Rd. (© 808/244-6500; www.hawaiinaturecenter.org), home to the Iao Valley Nature Center, features interactive exhibits and displays relating the story of Hawaiian natural history; it's an important stop for all who want to explore Iao Valley. Hours are daily from 10am to 4pm; admission is $6 for adults and $4 for children 4 to 12. **Rainforest Walks** are led Monday through Friday at 11:30am and 1:30pm, Saturday and Sunday at 11am and 2pm. Wear closed-toe shoes suitable for an uneven trail. The cost, which includes a visit to the museum, is $30 for adults and $20 for children 5 and older (younger children not allowed). Book in advance.

THE SCENIC ROUTE TO WEST MAUI: THE KAHEKILI HIGHWAY

The usual road to West Maui from Wailuku is the Honoapiilani Highway, which takes you south across the isthmus to Maalaea and then around to Lahaina, Kaanapali, and Kapalua. But those wanting a back-to-nature driving experience should go the other way, along the **Kahekili Highway** (Hwy. 340)—though *highway* is a bit of a misnomer for this paved but somewhat precarious road.

Drive north from Wailuku to Waiehu and onto this road named for King Kahekili, who built houses out of the skulls of his enemies. The true wild nature of Maui is on full display here. The narrow and winding road weaves for 20 miles along an ancient Hawaiian coastal footpath to Honokohau Bay, at the island's northernmost tip, past blowholes, sea stacks, seabird rookeries, and the imposing 636-foot Kahakuloa headland. On the land side, you'll pass high cliffs, deep valleys dotted with plantation houses, cattle grazing on green plateaus, old wooden churches, taro fields, and houses hung with fishing nets. It's slow going (you can drive only about 10 mph along the road), but it's probably the most beautiful drive in Maui. Your rental-car company might try to deter you, and you shouldn't go if it's been raining, but otherwise it's not really a hard drive and the views are spectacular.

At Honokohau, pick up Hwy. 30 and continue on to the West Maui resorts; the first one you'll reach is Kapalua (see below).

West Maui

For a map of attractions in Lahaina and Kaanapali, see p. 437.

HISTORIC LAHAINA

Back when "there was no God west of the Horn," Lahaina was the capital of Hawaii and the Pacific's wildest port. Today it's a milder version of its old self—mostly a hustle-bustle of whale art, timeshares, and "Just Got Lei'd" T-shirts. I'm not sure the rowdy whalers would be pleased. But if you look hard, you'll still find the historic port town they loved, filled with the kind of history that inspired James Michener to write his best-selling epic novel *Hawaii*.

Baldwin Home Museum ★   The oldest house in Lahaina, this coral-and-rock structure was built in 1834 by Rev. Dwight Baldwin, a doctor with the fourth company of American missionaries to sail round the Horn to Hawaii. Like many missionaries, he came to Hawaii to do good—and did very well for himself. After 17 years of service, Baldwin was granted 2,600 acres in Kapalua for farming and grazing. His ranch manager experimented with what Hawaiians called *hala-kahiki*, or pineapple, on a 4-acre plot; the rest is history. The house looks as if Baldwin has just stepped out for a minute to tend a sick neighbor down the street.

Next door is the **Master's Reading Room,** Maui's oldest building (included with museum admission). This became visiting sea captains' favorite hangout once the missionaries closed down all of Lahaina's grog shops and banned prostitution. By 1844, when hotels and bars started reopening, it lost its appeal. It's now the headquarters of the **Lahaina Restoration Foundation** (*©* **808/661-3262**; www.lahainarestoration.org), a plucky band of historians who try to keep this town alive and antique at the same time. Stop in and pick up a self-guided walking-tour map, which will take you to Lahaina's most historic sites.

120 Dickenson St. (at Front St.). *©* **808/661-3262.** www.lahainarestoration.org. Admission $3 adults, $2 seniors; $5 per couple. Daily 10am–4pm.

The Baldwin Home Museum.

Banyan Tree   Of all the banyan trees in Hawaii, this is the greatest of all—so big that you can't get it all in your camera's viewfinder. It was only 8 feet tall when it was planted in 1873 by Maui Sheriff William O. Smith to mark the 50th anniversary of Lahaina's first Christian mission. Today the big old banyan from India is more than 50 feet tall, has 12 major trunks, and shades two-thirds of an acre in Courthouse Square.

At the Courthouse Bldg., 649 Wharf St.

Maluuluolele Park   At first glance, this Front Street park appears to be only a hot, dry, dusty softball field. But under home plate is an edge of Mokuula, where a royal compound once stood more than 100 years ago, now buried under tons of red dirt and sand. Here, Prince Kauikeaolui, who ascended the throne as King Kamehameha III when he was only 10, lived with the love of his life, his sister, Princess Nahienaena. Missionaries took a dim view of incest, which was acceptable to Hawaiian nobles in order to preserve the royal bloodline. Torn between love for her brother and the new Christian morality, Nahienaena grew despondent and died at the age of 21. King Kamehameha III, who reigned for 29 years—longer than any other Hawaiian monarch—presided over Hawaii as it went from kingdom to constitutional monarchy, and as power over the islands began to shift from island nobles to missionaries, merchants, and sugar planters. Kamehameha died in 1854; he was 39. In 1918, his royal compound, containing a mausoleum and artifacts of the kingdom, was demolished and covered with dirt to create a public park. The baseball team from Lahainaluna School, the first American school founded by missionaries west of the Rockies, now plays games on the site of this royal place, still considered sacred to many Hawaiians.

Front and Shaw sts.

A WHALE OF A PLACE IN KAANAPALI

If you haven't seen a real whale yet, go to **Whalers Village,** 2435 Kaanapali Pkwy., an oceanfront shopping center that has adopted the whale as its mascot. You can't miss it: A huge, almost life-size metal sculpture of a mother whale and two nursing calves greets you. A few more steps, and you're met by the looming, bleached-white skeleton of a 40-foot sperm whale; it's pretty impressive.

On the second floor of the mall is the **Whalers Village Museum** (© 808/661-5992), which celebrates the "Golden Era of Whaling" from 1825 to 1860. Harpoons and scrimshaw are on display; the museum has even re-created the cramped quarters of a whaler's seagoing vessel. It's open daily from 9:30am to 10pm; admission is free.

KAPALUA

For generations, West Maui meant one thing: pineapple. Hawaii's only pineapple cannery today, **Maui Pineapple Co.,** offers tours of its plantation through the Kapalua Resort Activity Center (© 808/665-5491; www.kapalua.com/adventures/on-resort-adventures). Real plantation workers lead the 2½-hour tours. You'll learn about the history of West Maui, facts about growing and harvesting pineapple, and lots of trivia about plantation life; you can even pick your own pineapple. The tours, which depart from the Kapalua Villas Reception Center, 500 Office Rd., are offered daily except for the signature tour, which is offered only on Fridays, and the picnic tour, which is Monday through Thursday. The Express Tour costs $45 for adults, $40 for children ages 2 to 11; the Picnic Tour with lunch is $63 for adults, $55 for children ages 2 to 11; and the signature tour with a restaurant lunch is $70 for adults, $65 for children ages 2 to 11.

South Maui

MAALAEA

Maui Ocean Center ★★★ ☺   This 5-acre facility houses the largest aquarium in the state and features one of Hawaii's largest predators: the tiger shark. As you walk past the three dozen or so tanks and countless exhibits, you'll slowly descend from the "beach" to the deepest part of the ocean, without ever getting wet. Start at the surge pool, where you'll see shallow-water marine life like spiny urchins and cauliflower coral; then move on to the reef tanks, turtle pool, touch pool (with starfish and urchins), and eagle ray pool before reaching the star of the show: the 100-foot-long, 600,000-gallon main tank featuring tiger, gray, and white-tip sharks, as well as tuna, surgeonfish, triggerfish, and numerous others. The most phenomenal thing about this tank is that the walkway goes right through it, so you're surrounded on three sides by marine creatures. A very cool place, and well worth the time. Some new additions are a hammerhead exhibit, where juvenile scalloped hammerhead sharks are on display, and the Shark Dive Maui Program, where certified scuba divers plunge into the aquarium with sharks, stingrays, and tropical fish (yes, you, too, can dive with sharks), while friends and family watch safely from the other side of the glass.

At the Maalaea Harbor Village, 192 Maalaea Rd. (the triangle btw. Honoapiilani Hwy. and Maalaea Rd.). ☏ **808/270-7000.** www.mauioceancenter.com. Admission $26 adults, $23 seniors, $19 children 3–12. Daily 9am–5pm (to 6pm July–Aug).

Kihei

Capt. George Vancouver "discovered" Kihei in 1778, when it was only a collection of fishermen's grass shacks on the hot, dry, dusty coast (hard to believe, eh?). A **totem pole** stands today where he's believed to have landed, across from the Aston

The banyan tree at the courthouse.   Whalers Village.

Maui Ocean Center.

The Kihei totem pole.

Maui Lu Resort, 575 S. Kihei Rd. Vancouver sailed on to "discover" British Columbia, where a great international city and harbor now bear his name.

West of the junction of Piilani Highway (Hwy. 31) and Mokulele Highway (Hwy. 350) is **Kealia Pond National Wildlife Preserve** (© 808/ 875-1582), a 700-acre U.S. Fish and Wildlife wetland preserve where endangered Hawaiian stilts, coots, and ducks hang out and splash. These ponds work two ways: as bird preserves and as sedimentation basins that keep the coral reefs from silting from runoff. You can take a self-guided tour along a boardwalk dotted with interpretive signs and shade shelters, through sand dunes, and around ponds to Maalaea Harbor. The boardwalk starts at the outlet of Kealia Pond on the ocean side of North Kihei Road (near mile marker 2 on Piilani Hwy.). Among the Hawaiian water birds seen here are the black-crowned high heron, Hawaiian coot, Hawaiian duck, and Hawaiian stilt. There are also shorebirds like sanderlings, Pacific golden plovers, ruddy turnstones, and wandering tattlers. From July to December, the hawksbill turtle comes ashore here to lay its eggs.

WAILEA

The best way to explore this golden resort coast is to rise with the sun and head for Wailea's 1.5-mile **coastal nature trail ★**, stretching between the Fairmont Kea Lani and the kiawe thicket just beyond the Renaissance Wailea. It's a great morning walk on a serpentine path that meanders uphill and down past native plants, old Hawaiian habitats, and a billion dollars' worth of luxury hotels. You can pick up the trail at any of the resorts or from clearly marked SHORELINE ACCESS points along the coast. The best time to go is when you first wake up; by midmorning, the coastal trail is too often clogged with pushy joggers, and it grows crowded with beachgoers as the day wears on. As the path crosses several bold black-lava points, it affords new vistas of islands and ocean; benches allow you to pause and contemplate the view across Alalakeiki Channel, where you may see jumping whales in season. Sunset is another good time to hit the trail.

MAKENA

A few miles south of Wailea, the manicured coast turns to wilderness; now you're in Makena. Once cattle were driven down the slope from upland ranches, lashed to rafts, and sent into the water to swim to boats that waited to take them to market. Now **Makena Landing ★** is the best place to launch kayaks bound for La Pérouse Bay and Ahihi-Kinau Natural Preserve.

From the landing, go south on Makena Road; on the right is **Keawalai Congregational Church** (© **808/879-5557**), built in 1855, with walls 3 feet thick. Surrounded by ti leaves, which by Hawaiian custom provide protection, and built of lava rock with coral used as mortar, this church sits on its own cove with a gold-sand beach. It always attracts a Sunday crowd for its 9:30am Hawaiian-language service.

Keawalai Congregational Church.

La Pérouse Monument.

A little farther south on the coast is **La Pérouse Monument,** a pyramid of lava rocks that marks the spot where French explorer Adm. Comte de la Pérouse set foot on Maui in 1786. The first Westerner to "discover" the island, he described the "burning climate" of the leeward coast, observed several fishing villages near Kihei, and sailed on into oblivion, never to be seen again; some believe he may have been eaten by cannibals in what is now Vanuatu. To get here, drive south past Puu Olai to Ahihi Bay, where the road turns to gravel. Go another 2 miles along the coast to La Pérouse Bay; the monument sits amid a clearing in black lava at the end of the dirt road. As we went to press, the Hawaii State Department of Land and Natural Resources was in the process of proposing to temporarily restrict access to portions of the popular and heavily used reserve for 2 years. To find out if the area is open, call the Hawaii State Department of Land and Natural Resources office, © **808/984-8103.**

House of the Sun: Haleakala National Park ★★★

At once forbidding and compelling, Haleakala ("House of the Sun") National Park is Maui's main natural attraction. More than 1.3 million people a year go up the 10,023-foot-high mountain to peer down into the crater of the world's largest dormant volcano. (Haleakala is officially considered active, even though it has not rumbled since 1790.) That hole would hold Manhattan.

But there's more to do here than stare into a big black hole: Just going up the mountain is an experience. Where else on the planet can you climb from sea level to 10,000 feet in just 37 miles, or a 2-hour drive? The snaky road passes through big, puffy cumulus clouds to offer magnificent views of the isthmus of Maui, the West Maui Mountains, and the Pacific Ocean.

Many drive up to the summit in predawn darkness to watch the **sunrise over Haleakala ★★**; others coast down the 37-mile road from the summit on a bicycle with special brakes (see "Biking," on p. 526). Hardy adventurers hike and camp inside the crater's wilderness (see "Hiking & Camping," on p. 518). Those bound for the interior should bring their survival gear, for the terrain is raw, rugged, and punishing—not unlike the moon.

> ### Impressions
>
> *There are few enough places in the world that belong entirely to themselves. The human passion to carry all things everywhere, so that every place is home, seems well on its way to homogenizing our planet, save for the odd unreachable corner. Haleakala Crater is one of those corners.*
>
> —Barbara Kingsolver, the *New York Times*

JUST THE FACTS

Haleakala National Park extends from the summit of Mount Haleakala down the volcano's southeast flank to Maui's eastern coast, beyond Hana. There are actually two separate and distinct destinations within the park: **Haleakala Summit** and **Kipahulu** (see "Tropical Haleakala: Oheo Gulch at Kipahulu," on p. 550). The summit gets all the publicity, but the Kipahulu coast draws crowds, too—it's lush, green, and tropical, and home to Oheo Gulch (also known as Seven Sacred Pools). No road links the summit and the coast; you have to approach them separately, and you need at least a day to see each place.

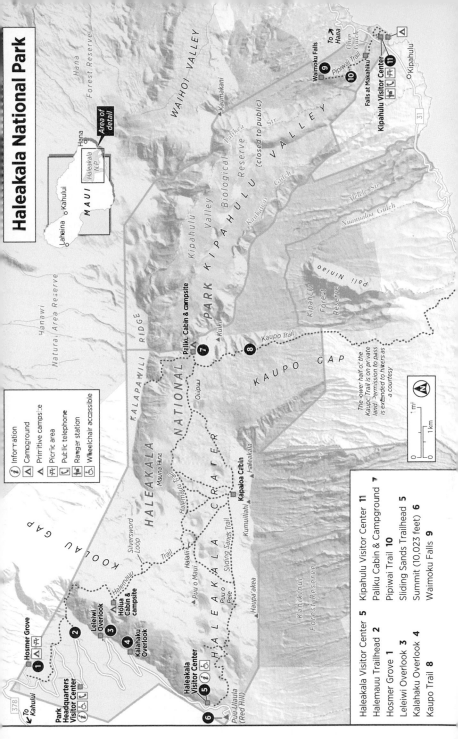

Haleakala National Park

Legend:
- ⓘ Information
- ⚠ Campground
- ⚠ Primitive campsite
- 🏕 Picnic area
- ☎ Public telephone
- 🏠 Ranger station
- ♿ Wheelchair accessible

Area of detail

MAUI — Lahaina ○ Kahului — Hana — Haleakala N.P.

Hana Forest Reserve

WAIHOI VALLEY

Kaumakani ▲

KIPAHULU VALLEY

Palikea Str.

Kipahulu Valley

Kipahulu Biological Reserve (closed to public)

Kukui Gulch

Keakiawai Gulch

Alelele Str.

Nuanualoa Gulch

PARK

Pali Ninao

Kipahulu Forest Reserve

9 Waimoku Falls
10 Pipiwai Trail
Falls at Makahiku
Oheo Gulch
To ↗ Hana
11 Kipahulu Visitor Center
31 ○Kipahulu

HALEAKALA RIDGE

KALAPAWILI RIDGE

Oilipu

7 Paliku Cabin & campsite
▲ Kuiki

8 Kaupo Trail

KAUPO GAP

The lower half of the Kaupo Trail is on private land. Permission to pass is extended to hikers as a courtesy

NATIONAL

HALEAKALA CRATER

Halemauu Trail

Mauna Hina

Silversword Loop

Halali

Sliding Sands Trail

Puu o Maui ▲
Puu o Pele ▲
Haupa'akea ▲

Kumuiliahi ▲
Haleakala ▲
Kapaloa Cabin

Kahikinui Forest Reserve

KOOLAU GAP

Hosmer Grove
1 ⚠ 🏕

Park Headquarters Visitor Center ⓘ ♿ ☎ 🏠

2
Leleiwi Overlook
3 ♿
Hōlua Cabin & campsite
4 Kalahaku Overlook

5 Haleakala Visitor Center ⓘ ♿
6 ◄ Puu Ulaula (Red Hill)

378 To ◄ Kahului

Haleakala Visitor Center **5**
Halemauu Trailhead **2**
Hosmer Grove **1**
Leleiwi Overlook **3**
Kalahaku Overlook **4**
Kaupo Trail **8**

Kipahulu Visitor Center **11**
Paliku Cabin & Campground **7**
Pipiwai Trail **10**
Sliding Sands Trailhead **5**
Summit (10,023 feet) **6**
Waimoku Falls **9**

N

0   1 mi
0   1 km

WHEN TO GO   At the 10,023-foot summit, weather changes fast. With wind chill, temperatures can be freezing any time of year. Summer can be dry and warm; winter can be wet, windy, and cold. Before you go, get current weather conditions from the park (© **808/572-4400**) or the **National Weather Service** (© **808/871-5054**). From sunrise to noon, the light is weak, but the view is usually free of clouds. The best time for photos is in the afternoon, when the sun lights the crater and clouds are few. Go on full-moon nights for spectacular viewing. *A note of caution:* This is Mother Nature, not Disneyland, so there are no guarantees or schedules. Especially in winter, some mornings may be misty or rainy, and sunrise viewing may be obscured. It's the luck of the draw.

ACCESS POINTS   **Haleakala Summit** is 37 miles, or a 1½- to 2-hour drive, from Kahului. To get here, take Hwy. 37 to Hwy. 377 to Hwy. 378. For details on the drive, see "The Drive to the Summit," below. Pukalani is the last town for water, food, and gas.

The **Kipahulu** section of Haleakala National Park is on Maui's east end near Hana, 60 miles from Kahului on Hwy. 36 (Hana Hwy.). Due to traffic and rough road conditions, plan on 4 hours for the one-way drive. For complete information, see "The Road to Hana" (p. 544) and "Tropical Haleakala: Oheo Gulch at Kipahulu" (p. 550).

At both entrances to the park, the admission fee is $5 per person or $10 per car, good for a week of unlimited entry.

INFORMATION, VISITOR CENTERS & RANGER PROGRAMS   For information before you go, contact **Haleakala National Park,** Box 369, Makawao, HI 96768 (© **808/572-4400;** www.nps.gov/hale).

One mile from the park entrance, at 7,000 feet, is **Haleakala National Park Headquarters** (© **808/572-4400**), open daily from 7:30am to 4pm. Stop here to pick up information on park programs and activities, get camping permits, and, occasionally, see a Hawaiian nene bird. Restrooms, a pay phone, and drinking water are available.

The **Haleakala Visitor Center,** open daily from sunrise to 3pm, is near the summit, 11 miles past the park entrance. It offers a panoramic view of the volcanic landscape, with photos identifying the various features, and exhibits that explain the area's history, ecology, geology, and volcanology. Park staff members are often on hand to answer questions. Restrooms and water are available.

Rangers offer excellent, informative, and free naturalist talks at 9:30, 10:30, and 11:30am daily in the summit building. For information on hiking and camping possibilities, including wilderness cabins and campgrounds, see "Hiking & Camping" (p. 518).

THE DRIVE TO THE SUMMIT

If you look on a Maui map, almost in the middle of the part that resembles a torso, there's a black wiggly line that looks like this: WWWWW. That's **Hwy. 378,** also known as **Haleakala Crater Road**—one of the fastest-ascending roads in the world. This grand corniche has at least 33 switchbacks; passes through numerous climate zones; goes under, in, and out of clouds; takes you past rare silversword plants and endangered Hawaiian geese sailing through the clear, thin air; and offers a view that extends for more than 100 miles.

Going to the summit takes 1½ to 2 hours from Kahului. No matter where you start out, you'll follow Hwy. 37 (Haleakala Hwy.) to Pukalani, where you'll

The sunrise over Haleakala.

Kipahulu.

pick up Hwy. 377 (aka Haleakala Hwy.), which you'll take to Hwy. 378. Along the way, expect fog, rain, and wind. You may encounter stray cattle and downhill bicyclists. Fill up your gas tank before you go—the only gas available is 27 miles below the summit at Pukalani. There are no facilities beyond the ranger stations—not even a coffee urn in sight. Bring your own food and water.

Remember, you're entering a high-altitude wilderness area. Some people get dizzy due to the lack of oxygen; you might also suffer from lightheadedness, shortness of breath, nausea, severe headaches, flatulence, or dehydration. People with asthma, pregnant women, heavy smokers, and those with heart conditions should be especially careful in the rarefied air. Bring water and a jacket or a blanket, especially if you go up for sunrise. Or you might want to go up to the summit for sunset, which is also spectacular.

At the **park entrance,** you'll pay an entrance fee of $10 per car (or $2 for a bicycle). About a mile from the entrance is **park headquarters,** where an endangered **nene,** or Hawaiian goose, may greet you with its unique call. With its black face, buff cheeks, and partially webbed feet, the gray-brown bird looks like a small Canada goose with zebra stripes; it brays out "nay-nay" (thus its name), doesn't migrate, and prefers lava beds to lakes. More than 25,000 nene once inhabited Hawaii, but habitat destruction and predators (hunters, pigs, feral cats and dogs, and mongooses) nearly caused their extinction. By 1951, there were only 30 left. Now protected as Hawaii's state bird, the wild nene on Haleakala number fewer than 250—the species remains endangered.

Beyond headquarters are **two scenic overlooks** on the way to the summit; stop at Leleiwi on the way up and Kalahaku on the way back down, if only to get out, stretch, and get accustomed to the heights. Take a deep breath, look around, and pop your ears. If you feel dizzy or drowsy, or get a sudden headache, consider turning around and going back down.

The Leleiwi Overlook.

Leleiwi Overlook ★ is just beyond mile marker 17. From the parking area, a short trail leads you to a panoramic view of the lunarlike crater. When the clouds are low and the sun is in the right place, usually around sunset, you may experience a phenomenon known as the "Specter of the Brocken"—you can see a reflection of your shadow, ringed by a rainbow, in the clouds below. It's an optical illusion caused by a rare combination of sun, shadow, and fog that occurs in only three places on the planet: Haleakala, Scotland, and Germany.

Two miles farther along is **Kalahaku Overlook ★**, the best place to see a rare **silversword.** You can turn into this overlook only when you are descending from the top. The silversword is the punk of the plant world, its silvery bayonets displaying tiny purple bouquets—like a spacey artichoke with attitude. This botanical wonder proved irresistible to humans, who gathered them in gunnysacks for Chinese potions and British specimen collections, and just for the sheer thrill of having something so rare. Silverswords grow only in Hawaii, take from 4 to 50 years to bloom, and then, usually between May and October, send up a 1- to 6-foot stalk with a purple bouquet of sunflower-like blooms. They're very rare, so don't even think about taking one home.

Silversword.

Continue on, and you'll quickly reach the **Haleakala Visitor Center,** which offers spectacular views. You'll feel as if you're at the edge of the earth, but the actual summit's a little farther on, at **Puu Ulaula Overlook ★★★** (also known as Red Hill), the volcano's highest point, where you'll find a cluster of buildings officially known as Haleakala Observatories, but unofficially called **Science City.** If you go up for sunrise, the building at Puu Ulaula Overlook, a triangle of glass that serves as a windbreak, is the best viewing

Kula Botanical Garden.

spot. After the daily miracle of sunrise—the sun seems to rise out of the vast ocean—you can see all the way across Alenuihaha Channel to the often-snowcapped summit of Mauna Kea on the Big Island.

Upcountry Maui

Come upcountry and discover a different side of Maui: On the slopes of Haleakala, cowboys, planters, and other country people make their homes in serene, neighborly communities like **Makawao** and **Kula,** a world away from the bustling beach resorts. Even if you can't spare a day or two in the cool, upcountry air, there are some sights that are worth a look on your way to or from the crater. Shoppers and gallery hoppers might want to spend more time here; see "Shops & Galleries" (p. 552) for details.

Kula Botanical Garden ★ You can take a self-guided, informative, leisurely stroll through more than 700 native and exotic plants—including three unique collections of orchids, proteas, and bromeliads—at this 5-acre garden. It offers a good overview of Hawaii's exotic flora in one small, cool place.

Hwy. 377, south of Haleakala Crater Rd. (Hwy. 378), ½ mile from Hwy. 37. ✆ **808/878-1715.** www.kulabotanicalgarden.com Admission $10 adults, $3 children 6–12. Daily 9am–4pm.

Tedeschi Vineyards and Winery ★ On the southern shoulder of Haleakala is **Ulupalakua Ranch,** a 20,000-acre spread once owned by legendary sea captain James Makee, celebrated in the Hawaiian song and dance *Hula O Makee.* Wounded in a Honolulu waterfront brawl in 1843, Makee moved to Maui and bought Ulupalakua. He renamed it Rose Ranch, planted sugar as a cash crop, and grew rich. Still in operation, the ranch is now home to Maui's only winery, established in 1974 by Napa vintner Emil Tedeschi, who began growing California and European grapes here and producing serious still and sparkling wines, plus a silly wine made of pineapple juice. The rustic grounds are the perfect place for a picnic. Pack a basket before you go, but don't BYOB: There's plenty of great wine to enjoy at Tedeschi. Settle in under the sprawling camphor tree, pop the cork on a blanc de blancs, and toast your good fortune in being here.

Off Hwy. 37 (Kula Hwy.). ✆ **808/878-6058.** www.mauiwine.com. Free tastings daily 9am–5pm. Free tours at 10:30am, 1:30pm, and 3pm.

East Maui & Heavenly Hana

Hana is Paradise on Earth—or just about as close as you can get to it, anyway. In and around Hana, you'll find a lush tropical rainforest dotted with cascading waterfalls and sparkling blue pools, skirted by red- and black-sand beaches.

The road to Hana.

THE ROAD TO HANA ★★★

Top down, sunscreen on, radio tuned to a little Hawaiian music on a Maui morning—it's time to head out to Hana along the Hana Highway (Hwy. 36), a wiggle of a road that runs along Maui's northeastern shore. The drive takes at least 3 hours from Lahaina or Kihei—but take all day. Going to Hana is about the journey, not the destination.

There are wilder roads, steeper roads, and more dangerous roads, but in all of Hawaii, no road is more celebrated than this one. It winds 50 miles past taro patches, magnificent seascapes, waterfall pools, botanical gardens, and verdant rainforests, and ends at one of Hawaii's most beautiful tropical places.

The outside world discovered the little village of Hana in 1926, when the narrow coastal road, carved by pickax-wielding convicts, opened. The mud-and-gravel road, often subject to landslides and washouts, was paved in 1962, when tourist traffic began to increase; it now sees 1,000 cars and dozens of vans a day, according to storekeeper Harry Hasegawa. That translates into half a million people a year, which is way too many. Go at the wrong time, and you'll be stuck in a bumper-to-bumper rental-car parade—peak traffic hours are midmorning and midafternoon year-round, especially on weekends.

In the rush to "do" Hana in a day, most visitors spin around town in 10 minutes and wonder what all the fuss is about. It takes time to take in Hana, play in the waterfalls, sniff the tropical flowers, hike to bamboo forests, and view the spectacular scenery. Stay overnight if you can, and meander back in a day or two. If you really must do the Hana Highway in a day, go just before sunrise and return after sunset.

Tips: Practice aloha. Give way at one-lane bridges, wave at oncoming motorists, let the big guys in 4×4s have the right of way—it's just common sense, brah. If the guy behind you blinks his lights, let him pass. And don't honk your horn—in Hawaii, it's considered rude.

THE JOURNEY BEGINS IN PAIA Before you even start out, fill up your gas tank. Gas in Paia is expensive, and it's the last place for gas until you get to Hana, some 54 bridges and 600 hairpin turns down the road.

Paia ★★ was once a thriving sugar-mill town. The mill is still here, but the population shifted to Kahului in the 1950s when subdivisions opened there, leaving Paia to shrivel up and die. But the town refused to give up, and it has proven its ability to adapt to the times. Now chic eateries and trendy shops stand next door to the old ma-and-pa establishments. Plan to be here early, around 7am, when **Charley's** ★, 142 Hana Hwy. (© **808/579-9453**), opens. Enjoy a big, hearty breakfast for a reasonable price.

WINDSURFING MECCA Just before mile marker 9 is **Hookipa Beach Park** ★, where top-ranked windsurfers come to test themselves against the forces of nature: thunderous surf and forceful wind. On nearly every windy day after noon (the board surfers have the waves in the morning), you can watch dozens of windsurfers twirling and dancing in the wind like colored butterflies. To watch them, do not stop on the highway, but go past the park and turn left at the entrance on the far side of the beach. You can either park on the high grassy bluff or drive down to the sandy beach and park alongside the pavilion. Facilities include restrooms, a shower, picnic tables, and a barbecue area.

INTO THE COUNTRY Past Hookipa Beach, the road winds down into **Maliko Gulch** at mile marker 10. At the bottom of the gulch, look for the road on your right, which will take you out to **Maliko Bay.** Take the first right, which goes under the bridge and past a rodeo arena and on to the rocky beach. There are no facilities here except a boat-launch ramp. In the 1940s, Maliko had a thriving community at the mouth of the bay, but its residents rebuilt farther inland after a strong tidal wave wiped it out.

Windsurfers at Hookipa Beach Park.

Twin Falls.

Back on the Hana Highway, for the next few miles, you'll pass through the rural area of **Haiku,** where you'll see banana patches, forests of guavas and palms, and avocados. Just before mile marker 15 is the **Maui Grown Market and Deli** (✆ **808/572-1693**), a good stop for drinks or snacks for the ride.

At mile marker 16, the curves begin, one right after another. Slow down and enjoy the view of bucolic rolling hills, mango trees, and vibrant ferns. After mile marker 16, the road is still called the Hana Highway, but the number changes from Hwy. 36 to Hwy. 360, and the mile markers go back to 0.

A GREAT PLUNGE ALONG THE WAY A dip in a waterfall pool is everybody's tropical-island fantasy. A great place to stop is **Twin Falls ★**, at mile marker 2. Just before the wide, concrete bridge, pull over on the mountain side and park. There is a NO TRESPASSING sign on the gate. Although you will see several cars parked in the area and a steady line of people going up to the falls, be aware that this is private property and trespassing is illegal in Hawaii. If you decide that you want to "risk it," you will walk about 3 to 5 minutes to the waterfall and pool, or continue on another 10 to 15 minutes to the second, larger waterfall and pool (don't go in if it has been raining).

HIDDEN HUELO Just before mile marker 4 on a blind curve, look for a double row of mailboxes on the left side by the pay phone. Down the road lies a hidden Hawaii of an earlier time, where an indescribable sense of serenity prevails. Hemmed in by Waipo and Hoalua bays is the remote community of **Huelo ★**. This fertile area once supported a population of 75,000; today only a few hundred live among the scattered homes here, where a handful of B&Bs and exquisite vacation rentals cater to a trickle of travelers (see p. 466 for my recommendation).

○ STOP & SMELL THE lavender

While in the upcountry Kula region, stop by **Alii Kula Lavender,** 1100 Waipoli Rd., Kula (✆ **808/878-3004;** www.aliikula lavender.com), which grows several varieties of lavender so one type of lavender will always be in bloom. On the 30-minute Lavender Garden Walking Tour (daily at 9:30am, 10:30am, 11:30am, 1pm, and 2:30pm for $12 per person), you're served lavender herb tea with a lavender scone and given a garden and studio tour. Be sure to stop by the store and look over the culinary products (lavender seasonings, dressings, scones, honey, jelly, and teas), bath and body goodies (lotions, soaps, bubble baths), aromatherapy (oil, candles, eye pillows), and other items (T-shirts, gift baskets, and dried lavender).

Huelo.

Kaulanapueo Church.

The only reason Huelo is even marked is the historic 1853 **Kaulanapueo Church.** Reminiscent of New England architecture, this coral-and-cement church, topped with a plantation-green steeple and a gray tin roof, is still in use, although services are held just once or twice a month. It still has the same austere interior of 1853: straight-backed benches, a no-nonsense platform for the minister, and no distractions on the walls to tempt you away from paying attention to the sermon. Next to the church is a small graveyard, a personal history of this village in concrete and stone

KOOLAU FOREST RESERVE   After Huelo, the vegetation seems more lush, as though Mother Nature had poured Miracle-Gro on everything. This is the edge of the **Koolau Forest Reserve.** *Koolau* means "windward," and this certainly is one of the greatest examples of a lush windward area: The coastline here gets about 60 to 80 inches of rain a year, as well as runoff from the 200 to 300 inches that falls farther up the mountain. You'll see trees laden with guavas, as well as mangoes, java plums, and avocados the size of softballs. The spiny, long-leafed plants are hala trees, which the Hawaiians used for weaving baskets, mats, and even canoe sails.

From here on out, there's a waterfall (and one-lane bridge) around nearly every turn in the road, so drive slowly and be prepared to stop and yield to oncoming cars.

DANGEROUS CURVES   About a half-mile after mile marker 6, there's a sharp U-curve in the road, going uphill. The road is practically one-lane here, with a brick wall on one side and virtually no maneuvering room. Sound your horn at the start of the U-curve to let approaching cars know you're coming. Take this curve, as well as the few more coming up in the next several miles, very slowly.

Just before mile marker 7 is a forest of waving **bamboo.** The sight is so spectacular that drivers are often tempted to take their eyes off the road. Be very cautious. Wait until just after mile marker 7, at the **Kaaiea Bridge** and stream below, to pull over and take a closer look at the hand-hewn stone walls. Then turn around to see the vista of bamboo.

547

A GREAT FAMILY HIKE At mile marker 9, there's a small state wayside area with restrooms, picnic tables, and a barbecue area. The sign says KOOLAU FOREST RESERVE, but the real attraction here is the **Waikamoi Ridge Trail ★**, an easy .75-mile loop. The start of the trail is just behind the QUIET TREES AT WORK sign. The well-marked trail meanders through eucalyptus, ferns, and hala trees.

SAFETY WARNING I used to recommend another waterfall, **Puohokamoa Falls,** at mile marker 11, but not anymore. Unfortunately, what was once a great thing has been overrun by hordes of not-so-polite tourists. You will see cars parking on the already dangerous, barely two-lane Hana Highway half a mile before the waterfall. Slow down after the 10-mile marker. As you get close to the 11-mile marker, the highway becomes a congested one-lane road due to visitors parking on this narrow stretch. Don't add to the congestion by trying to park: There are plenty of other great waterfalls; just drive slowly and safely through this area.

CAN'T-MISS PHOTO OPS Just past mile marker 12 is the **Kaumahina State Wayside Park ★**. This is not only a good pit stop (restrooms are available) and a wonderful place for a picnic (with tables and a barbecue area), but also a great vista point. The view of the rugged coastline makes an excellent shot—you can see all the way down to the jutting Keanae Peninsula.

Another mile and a couple of bends in the road, and you'll enter the Honomanu Valley, with its beautiful bay. To get to the **Honomanu Bay County Beach Park ★**, look for the turnoff on your left, just after mile marker 14, as you begin your ascent up the other side of the valley. The rutted dirt-and-cinder road takes you down to the rocky black-sand beach. There are no facilities here. Because of the strong rip currents offshore, swimming is best in the stream inland from the ocean. You'll consider the drive down worthwhile as you stand on the beach, well away from the ocean, and turn to look back on the steep cliffs covered with vegetation.

Koolau Forest Reserve.

Keanae.

KEANAE PENINSULA & ARBORETUM At mile marker 17, the old Hawaiian village of **Keanae ★★** stands out against the Pacific like a place time forgot. Here, on an old lava flow graced by an 1860 stone church and swaying palms, is one of the last coastal enclaves of native Hawaiians. They still grow taro in patches and pound it into poi, the staple of the old Hawaiian diet; and they still pluck opihi (limpet) from tide pools along the jagged coast and cast throw-nets at schools of fish.

At nearby **Keanae Arboretum,** Hawaii's botanical world is divided into three parts: native forest, introduced forest, and traditional Hawaiian plants, food, and medicine. You can swim in the pools of Piinaau Stream or press on along a mile-long trail into Keanae Valley, where a lovely tropical rainforest waits at the end.

WAIANAPANAPA STATE PARK ★★ On the outskirts of Hana, the shiny black-sand beach appears like a vivid dream, with bright-green jungle foliage on three sides and cobalt-blue water lapping at its feet. The 120-acre state park on an ancient lava flow includes sea cliffs, lava tubes, arches, and that beach—plus a dozen rustic cabins. See p. 470 for a review of the cabins. Also see "Beaches" and "Hiking & Camping," earlier in this chapter.

HANA ★★★

Green, tropical Hana, which some call heavenly, is a destination all its own, a small coastal village in a rainforest inhabited by 2,500 people, many part-Hawaiian. Beautiful Hana enjoys more than 90 inches of rain a year—more than enough to keep the scenery lush. Banyans, bamboo, breadfruit trees—everything seems larger than life, especially the flowers, like wild ginger and plumeria. Several roadside stands offer exotic blooms for $1 a bunch. Just "put money in box." It's the Hana honor system.

The last unspoiled Hawaiian town on Maui is, oddly enough, the home of Maui's first resort, which opened in 1946. Paul Fagan, owner of the San Francisco Seals baseball team, bought an old inn and turned it into the **Hotel Hana-Maui,** which gave Hana its first and, as it turns out, last taste of tourism. Others have tried to open hotels and golf courses and resorts, but Hana, which is interested in remaining Hana, always politely refuses. There are a few B&Bs here, though; see p. 466 for reviews.

A wood-frame 1871 building that served as the old Hana District Police Station now holds the **Hana Cultural Center & Museum,** 4974 Uakea Rd. (© **808/248-8622;** www.hookele.com/hccm). The center tells the history of the area, with some excellent artifacts, memorabilia, and photographs. Also stop in at **Hasegawa General Store,** a Maui institution.

On the green hills above Hana stands a 30-foot-high white cross made of lava rock. The cross was erected by citizens in memory of Paul Fagan, who helped keep the town alive. The 3-mile hike up to **Fagan's Cross** provides a gorgeous view of the Hana coast, especially at sunset, when Fagan himself liked to climb this hill (see p. 523 for details).

Most day-trippers to Hana miss the most unusual natural attraction of all: **Red Sand Beach ★**, officially named Kaihalulu Beach, which means "roaring sea." It's truly a sight to see. It's on the ocean side of Kauiki Hill, just south of Hana Bay, in a wild, natural setting in a pocket cove. Kauiki, a 390-foot-high volcanic cinder cone, lost its seaward wall to erosion and spilled red cinders everywhere, creating the red sands. To get here, walk south on Uakea Road, past the Hotel Hana-Maui to the end of the parking lot for Sea Ranch Cottages. Turn left, cross an open field past an old cemetery, and follow a well-worn path down a narrow cliff trail. In this private, romantic setting, some beachgoers shed their clothes, so try not to be offended.

TROPICAL HALEAKALA: OHEO GULCH AT KIPAHULU

If you're thinking about heading out to the so-called Seven Sacred Pools, out past Hana at the Kipahulu end of Haleakala National Park, let's clear this up right now: There are more than seven pools—about 24, actually—and *all* water in Hawaii is considered sacred. It's all a PR campaign that has spun out of control. Folks here call it by its rightful name, **Oheo**

Red Sand (Kaihalulu) Beach.

Gulch ★★★, and visitors sometimes refer to it as Kipahulu, which is actually the name of the area where Oheo Gulch is located. No matter what you call it, it's beautiful. This dazzling series of pools and cataracts is so popular that it has its own roadside parking lot.

From the ranger station, it's just a short hike above the famous Oheo Gulch to two spectacular **waterfalls.** Check with park rangers before hiking up to or swimming in the pools, and always keep an eye on the water in the streams. The sky can be sunny near the coast, but flood waters travel 6 miles down from the Kipahulu Valley, and the water level can rise 4 feet in less than 10 minutes. It's not a good idea to swim in the pools in winter.

Makahiku Falls is easily reached from the central parking area; the trail head begins near the ranger station. **Pipiwai Trail** leads up to the road and beyond for .5 mile to the overlook. If you hike another 1.5 miles up the trail across two bridges and through a bamboo forest, you reach **Waimoku Falls.** It's a hard uphill hike, but press on to avoid the pool's crowd.

ACCESS POINTS   Even though Oheo is part of Haleakala National Park, you cannot drive here from the summit. Oheo is about 30 to 50 minutes beyond Hana town, along Hwy. 31. The fee to enter is $5 per person or $10 per car. The Hwy. 31 bridge passes over some of the pools near the ocean; the others, plus magnificent 400-foot Waimoku Falls, are uphill, via an often-muddy but rewarding hour-long hike; see "Hiking & Camping at Kipahulu (Near Hana)," on p. 521. Expect showers on the Kipahulu coast.

VISITOR CENTER   The **Kipahulu Ranger** Station (© **808/248-7375**) is staffed from 9am to 5pm daily. Restrooms are available, but there's no drinking water. Here you'll find park-safety information, exhibits, and books. Rangers offer a variety of walks and hikes year-round; check at the station

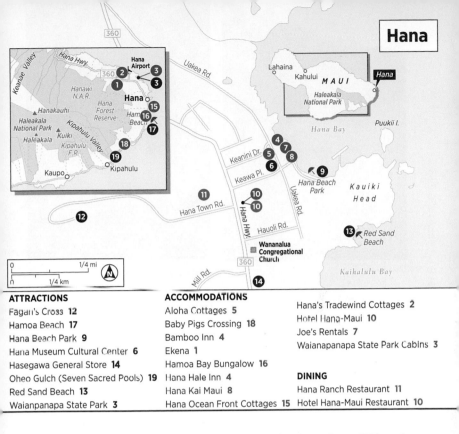

Hana

MAUI

Lahaina • Kahului

Hana

Haleakala National Park

Hana Bay

Puukii I.

Kauiki Head

Red Sand Beach

Kaihalulu Bay

Wananalua Congregational Church

Hasegawa General Store **14**

0   1/4 mi
0   1/4 km

ATTRACTIONS
Fagan's Cross **12**
Hamoa Beach **17**
Hana Beach Park **9**
Hana Museum Cultural Center **6**
Hasegawa General Store **14**
Oheo Gulch (Seven Sacred Pools) **19**
Red Sand Beach **13**
Waianpanapa State Park **3**

ACCOMMODATIONS
Aloha Cottages **5**
Baby Pigs Crossing **18**
Bamboo Inn **4**
Ekena **1**
Hamoa Bay Bungalow **16**
Hana Hale Inn **4**
Hana Kai Maui **8**
Hana Ocean Front Cottages **15**

Hana's Tradewind Cottages **2**
Hotel Hana-Maui **10**
Joe's Rentals **7**
Waianapanapa State Park Cabins **3**

DINING
Hana Ranch Restaurant **11**
Hotel Hana-Maui Restaurant **10**

for current activities. Tent camping is permitted in the park; see "Hiking & Camping at Kipahulu (Near Hana)," on p. 521, for details.

BEYOND OHEO GULCH

A mile past Oheo Gulch on the ocean side of the road is **Lindbergh's Grave.** First to fly across the Atlantic Ocean, Charles A. Lindbergh found peace in the Pacific; he settled in Hana, where he died of cancer in 1974. The famous aviator is buried under river stones in a seaside graveyard behind the 1857 **Palapala Hoomau Congregational Church.**

Those of you who are continuing on around Maui to the fishing village of **Kaupo** and beyond should be warned that Kaupo Road, or Old Piilani Highway (Hwy. 31), is rough and unpaved, often full of potholes and ruts. There are no goods or services until you reach **Ulupalakua Ranch,** where there's a winery, a general store, and a gas station, which is likely to be closed. Before you attempt this journey, ask around about road conditions, or call the **Maui Public Works Department** (© 808/248-8254) or the **Police Department** (© 808/248-8311). This road frequently washes out in the rain. Most rental-car companies forbid you from taking their cars on this road (they don't want to trek all the way out here to get you if your car breaks down), so you'd really be better off retracing your route back through Hana. But if conditions are good, it can be a pretty drive in the spring (it tends to be dry and boring in summer).

Oheo Gulch.

Charles Lindbergh's Grave.

SHOPS & GALLERIES

The island of Maui is a shopaholic's dream as well as an arts center, with a large number of resident artists who show their works in dozens of galleries and countless gift shops. Maui is also the queen of specialty products, an agricultural cornucopia that includes Kula onions, upcountry proteas, Kaanapali coffee, world-renowned potato chips, and many other tasty treats that are shipped worldwide.

As with any popular visitor destination, you'll have to wade through bad art and mountains of trinkets, particularly in Lahaina and Kihei, where touristy boutiques line the streets between rare pockets of treasures. If you shop in South or West Maui, expect to pay resort prices, clear down to a bottle of Evian or sunscreen.

There are two upscale resort shopping malls: the Shops at Wailea in South Maui and Whalers Village in Kaanapali. The 16-acre Shops at Wailea features more than 50 shops and numerous restaurants, everything from an ABC store to Louis Vuitton and Gap. Similarly, Whalers Village has a variety of shopping and restaurant activity concentrated in a single oceanfront complex.

Central Maui is home to some first-rate boutiques: Wailuku, a quaint 1930-ish type of town, has its own antiques alleys, a handful of cafes and ethnic restaurants, and a yummy bakery. The Kaahumanu Center, in neighboring Kahului, is *the* retail outlet for the island.

Upcountry, Makawao's boutiques are worth seeking out, despite some attitude and high prices. The charm of shopping on Maui has always rested in the small, independent shops and galleries that crop up in surprising places.

Central Maui

KAHULUI

Kahului's best shopping is concentrated in two places. The formerly rough-around-the-edges **Maui Mall**, 70 E. Kaahumanu Ave. (© **808/877-7559;** www.mauimall.com), is the place of everyday retail, from **Longs Drugs** and

Whole Foods to **Tasaka Guri Guri** (the decades-old purveyor of inimitable icy treats that are neither ice cream nor shave ice, but something in between) and Kahului's largest movie theater, a 12-screen megaplex that features current releases as well as art-house films.

Queen Kaahumanu Center, 275 Kaahumanu Ave. (© **808/877-3369;** www.queenkaahumanucenter.com), a 10-minute drive from the Kahului Airport on Hwy. 32, offers more than 100 shops, restaurants, and theaters. It covers all the bases, from arts and crafts to a **Foodland** and everything in between: a thriving food court; the island's best beauty supply, **Lisa's Beauty Supply & Salon** (© **808/877-6463**), and its sister store for cosmetics, **Madison Avenue Day Spa and Boutique** (© **808/873-0880**); mall standards like **Sunglass Hut, Radio Shack,** and **Local Motion** (surf- and beachwear); and standard department stores like **Macy's** and **Sears.** Its second-floor Plantation District offers home furnishings, accessories, and gifts.

COST LESS IMPORTS Natural fibers are ubiquitous in this newly expanded corner of the Maui Mall, three times larger than before. Home accessories include lauhala, bamboo blinds, grassy floor and window coverings, shoji-style lamps, burlap yardage, baskets, Balinese cushions, Asian imports, and top-of-the-line, made-on-Maui soaps and handicrafts. Japanese folk curtains, called *noreng,* are among the diverse items you'll find here; it's a good source of tropical and Asian home decor. At the Maui Mall. © **808/877-0300.** www.costlessimports-online.com.

MAUI SWAP MEET After 17 years on a parcel of land next to the Kahului post office, the popular Maui Swap Meet finally outgrew its home. In November 2008, it moved to the Maui Community College campus, in Kahului, where there is room enough for 300 vendors and plenty of parking. Every Saturday from 7am to 1pm, vendors spread out their wares in booths and under tarps, in a festival-like atmosphere that is pure Maui with a touch of kitsch. The colorful Maui specialties include vegetables from Kula and Keanae, fresh taro, plants, proteas, crafts, household items, homemade ethnic foods, and baked goods, including some fabulous fruit breads. Now students at the community college sell artwork and ceramics, and the culinary-arts program has prepared food for sale. Between the cheap Balinese imports and New Age crystals and incense, you may find some vintage John Kelly prints and 1930s collectibles. Admission is 50¢, and if you go early while the vendors are setting up, no one will turn you away. At Maui Community College, in an area bounded by Kahului Beach Rd. and Wahine Pio Ave. (access via Wahine Pio Ave). © **808/877-3100.**

WAILUKU

Wailuku's attractive vintage architecture, numerous antiques shops, and mom-and-pop eateries imbue the town with a charm noticeably absent in the resort areas of West, South, and Upcountry Maui. There is no plastic aloha in Wailuku. Of course, there's junk, but a stroll along Main and Market streets usually turns up a treasure or two. It's a mixed bag, but a treasure hunt, too.

Bailey House Museum Shop For made-in-Hawaii items, Bailey House is a must-stop. It offers a thoroughly enjoyable browse through authoritative Hawaiiana, in a building that's one of the finest examples of missionary architecture, dating from 1833. Gracious gardens, rare paintings of early Maui, wonderful programs in Hawaiian arts and culture, and a restored hand-hewn koa canoe await visitors. The shop, a small space of discriminating taste, packs a wallop with its selection of remarkable gift items, from Hawaiian music to exquisite woods, traditional Hawaiian games to pareu and books. Prints by the legendary Hawaii artist Madge Tennent, lauhala hats hanging in midair, hand-sewn pheasant hatbands, jams and jellies, Maui cookbooks, and an occasional Hawaiian quilt are some of the treasures to be found here. At the Bailey House Museum, 2375-A Main St. ✆ 808/244-3326.

Bird of Paradise Unique Antiques   Owner Joe Myhand loves furniture, old Matson liner menus, blue willow china, kimonos for children, and anything nostalgic that happens to be Hawaiian. The furniture in the strongly Hawaiian collection ranges from 1940s rattan to wicker and old koa—those items tailor-made for informal Island living and leisurely moments on the lanai. Myhand also collects bottles and mails his license plates all over the world. The collection ebbs and flows with his finds, keeping buyers waiting in the wings for his Depression glass, California pottery from the 1930s and 1940s, old dinnerware, perfume bottles, vintage aloha shirts, and vintage Hawaiian music on cassettes. N. Market St. ✆ 808/242-7699.

Brown-Kobayashi   Graceful living is the theme here. Prices range from a few dollars to the thousands in this 750-square-foot treasure-trove. The owners have added a fabulous selection of antique stone garden pieces that mingle quietly with Asian antiques and old and new French, European, and Hawaiian objects. Although the collection is eclectic, there is a strong cohesive aesthetic that sets Brown-Kobayashi apart from other Maui antiques stores. Japanese kimonos and obi, Bakelite and Peking glass beads, breathtaking Japanese lacquerware, cricket carriers, and cloisonné are among the delights here. Exotic and precious Chinese woods (purple sandalwood and huanghuali) glow discreetly from quiet corners, and an occasional monarchy-style lidded milo bowl comes in and flies out. 38 N. Market St. ✆ 808/242-0804.

Gottling Ltd.   Karl Gottling's shop specializes in Asian antique furniture, but you can also find smaller carvings, precious stones, jewelry, netsuke, opium weights, and finds in all sizes. I saw a 17th-century Buddha sitting serenely next to a 150-year-old Chinese cabinet. Ming Dynasty ceramics, carved wooden apples ($15), and a Persian rug ($65,000) give you an idea of the range of possibilities here. 34 N. Market St. ✆ 808/244-7779.

Sandell 🎁   Since the early 1970s, artist, illustrator, and cartoonist David Sandell has been commenting on Maui through his artwork. Don't miss the opportunity to stop by this shop and "talk story" with the talented artist, who watched Maui go from undiscovered to discovered. His work—from original oils to prints to T-shirts—makes excellent souvenirs to take home. 133 Market St. ✆ 808/249-2456 or 808/249-0234.

CENTRAL MAUI EDIBLES

Down to Earth Natural Foods, 305 Dairy Rd. (✆ **808/877-2661**), has a bountiful salad bar, sandwiches and smoothies, fresh organic produce, vitamins and supplements, fresh baked goods, chips and snacks, whole grains, and more.

Maui's produce has long been a source of pride for islanders. On Tuesday, Wednesday, and Friday from 7am to 3pm, the **Ohana Farmers Market,** at Queen Kaahumanu Shopping Center (✆ **808/878-3189**), is where you'll find a

MAUI'S OWN: OCEAN vodka

If you're looking for a souvenir of your fabulous Maui trip to take home or a unique gift for friends, Maui has its own vodka, called OCEAN Vodka. Produced by Hawaii Sea Spirits, this ultra-premium brand is made with water that comes from 3,000 feet beneath the ocean off the Kona coast of the Big Island. The deep-sea water is harvested by KOYO USA, producers of MaHaLo Hawaii Deep Sea Water. The desalinated water has become widely popular in Japan, where people swear it has provided beneficial health effects (so far, no scientific studies have backed up this claim). The MaHaLo water is shipped to Maui, where it is blended with organic corn and rye to produce this one-of-a-kind vodka. Available at restaurants, bars, hotels, and retail shops (for a complete list, see www.oceanvodka.com).

fresh, inexpensive selection of Maui-grown fruit, vegetables, flowers, and plants. Crafts and gourmet foods add to the event, and the large monkeypod trees provide welcome shade.

In the northern section of Wailuku, **Takamiya Market,** 359 N. Market St. (© **808/244-3404**), is much loved by local folks and visitors with adventurous palates, who often drive all the way from Kihei to stock up on picnic fare and mouthwatering ethnic foods for sunset gatherings. Unpretentious home-cooked foods from East and West are prepared daily and served on plastic-foam plates. From the chilled-fish counter come fresh sashimi and poke, and among the renowned assortment of prepared foods are mounds of shoyu chicken, tender fried squid, roast pork, kalua pork, laulau, Chinese noodles, fiddlehead ferns, and Western comfort foods such as corn bread and potato salad.

West Maui

LAHAINA

Lahaina's merchants and art galleries go all out from 7 to 9pm every Friday, when **Art Night ★** brings an extra measure of hospitality and community spirit. The Art Night openings are usually marked with live entertainment and refreshments, plus a livelier-than-usual street scene.

If you're in Lahaina on the second or last Thursday of the month, stroll by the front lawn of the **Baldwin Home Museum,** 120 Dickenson St. (at Front St.), for a splendid look at the craft of lei making (you can even buy the results).

Lahaina's Art Night.

What was formerly a big, belching pineapple cannery is now a maze of shops and restaurants at the northern end of Lahaina town, known as the **Lahaina Cannery Mall,** 1221 Honoapiilani Hwy. (© **808/661-5304; www.lahainacannerymall.com**). At the recently expanded food court, **L & L Drive-Inn** sells plate lunches near Greek, piboo, Vietnamese, and Japanese food at various booths. There's also a **Longs Drugs** and a 24-hour **Safeway** for groceries.

The Old **Lahaina Center,** 900 Front St. (© **808/667-9216**), is fairly new and still a work in progress. It's located north of Lahaina's most congested strip, where Front Street begins. Across the street from the center, the sea wall is a much-sought-after front-row seat to the sunset. There's plenty of free validated parking and easy access to more than 30 shops, a salon, restaurants, a nightclub, and a four-plex movie-theater complex. **Ruth's Chris Steak House** has opened its doors here, and the **Hard Rock Cafe** serves lunch and dinner and offers live music nightly except weekends. Among the shopping stops: **Hilo Hattie** (a dizzying emporium of aloha wear), **ABC Discount Store,** and a dozen other recreational, dining, and entertainment options.

A welcome touch of Hawaiiana at the Lahaina Center is the conversion of 10,000 square feet of parking space into the re-creation of a traditional Hawaiian village, called **Hale Kahiko.** With the commercialization of modern Lahaina, it's easy to forget that it was once the capital of the Hawaiian kingdom and a significant historic site. Hale Kahiko features three main *hale:* a sleeping house, the men's dining house, and the crafts house, where women pounded lauhala for mats and baskets. Construction of the houses consumed 10,000 feet of ohia wood from the island, 20 tons of pili grass, and more than 4 miles of hand-woven coconut sennit for the lashings. Artifacts, weapons, a canoe, and indigenous trees are among the authentic touches in this village; you can take a free guided tour daily between 9am and 6pm.

Lahaina Arts Society Galleries   With its membership of more than 185 Maui artists, the nonprofit Lahaina Arts Society is an excellent community resource. Changing monthly exhibits in the Banyan Tree and Old Jail galleries offer a good look at the island's artistic well: two-dimensional art, fiber art, ceramics, sculpture, prints, jewelry, and more. In the shade of the humongous banyan tree in the square across from Pioneer Inn, "Art in the Park" fairs are offered every second and fourth weekend of the month. 648 Wharf St. © **808/661-3228.**

Lei Spa Maui   The Lei Spa Maui has expanded to include two massage rooms and shower facilities, adding facials and other therapies to this day spa's menu. It's a good sign that 95% of the beauty and bath products sold are made on Maui, and that includes Hawaiian Botanical Pikake shower gel, kukui and macadamia-nut oils, Hawaiian potpourris, mud masks with Hawaiian seaweed, and a spate of rejuvenating potions for hair and skin. Aromatherapy body oils and perfumes are popular, as are the handmade soaps and fragrances of torch ginger, plumeria, coconut, tuberose, and sandalwood. Scented candles in coconut shells, inexpensive and fragrant, make great gifts. 505 Front St. © **808/661-1178.**

Maggie Coulombe 🎁   A haute couture store with the unique designs of Maggie Coulombe in the midst of Lahaina. You'll find Maggie's latest couture, jersey, linen, pareu, and shoes, plus accessories, jewelry, purses, and a few surprises. 505 Front St. © **808/662-0696.** www.maggiecoulombe.com.

The view from the sea wall across from the Lahaina Center.

Hale Kahiko.

Old Lahaina Book Emporium   What a bookstore! Chockablock with used books in stacks, on shelves, on counters, and in the aisles, this place is a browser's dream. More than 25,000 quality used books are lovingly housed in this shop, where owner JoAnn Carroll treats both books and customers well. Prices are low, and the selection is diverse, everything from *Li'l Abner* to *Genius and Lust*, old *Mad* magazines, *Aphrodisiac Cookery, Bhagavad-Gita, A History of Bicycles,* and *The Cockroach Combat Manual.* The store is 95% used books and 100% delight. Specialties include Hawaiiana, fiction, mystery, sci-fi, and military history, with substantial selections in cookbooks, children's books, and philosophy/religion. You could pay as little as $2 for a quality read, or a whole lot more for that rare first edition. Books on tape, videos, the classics, and old guitar magazines are among the treasures of this two-story emporium. 834 Front St. © **808/661-1399.** www.oldlahainabookemporium.com.

Village Galleries in Lahaina   The nearly 30-year-old Village Galleries is the oldest continuously running gallery on Maui, and it's esteemed as one of the few galleries with consistently high standards. Art collectors know this as a respectable showcase for regional artists; the selection of mostly original two- and three-dimensional art offers a good look at the quality of work originating on the island. The newer contemporary gallery offers colorful gift items and jewelry. An additional location is at the Ritz-Carlton Kapalua, 1 Ritz-Carlton Dr. (© **808/669-1800**). 120 and 180 Dickenson St. © **808/661-4402** or 808/661-5559.

KAANAPALI

On a recent trip, I was somewhat disappointed with upscale **Whalers Village,** 2435 Kaanapali Pkwy. (© **808/661-4567;** www.whalersvillage.com). Although it offers everything from whale blubber to Prada and Ferragamo, it's short on local shops, and parking at the nearby lot is expensive. The complex is home to the **Whalers Village Museum,** with its interactive exhibits, 40-foot sperm-whale skeleton, and sand castles on perpetual display, but shoppers come for the designer thrills and beachfront dining.

The always wonderful **Lahaina Printsellers** has a selection of antique prints, maps, paintings, and engravings, including 18th- to 20th-century cartography, all of which offer great browsing and gift potential. You can find award-winning, expanded **Reyn's** for aloha wear, and **Cinnamon Girl,** a hit in Honolulu for its matching mother-daughter clothing. Once you've stood under the authentic whale skeleton at the Whalers Village Museum, you can blow a bundle at **Coach, Louis Vuitton,** or any of the more than 60 shops and restaurants that have sprouted in this open-air shopping center. The posh Euro trend continues; despite obvious efforts to offer more of a balance between Island-made and designer goods, it's still open season for the chain luxury boutiques. Whalers Village is open daily from 9:30am to 10pm.

Sandal Tree   It's unusual for a resort shop to draw local customers on a regular basis, but the Sandal Tree attracts a flock of footwear fanatics who come here from throughout the islands for rubber thongs and Top-Siders, sandals and dressy pumps, athletic shoes and hats, designer footwear, and much more. Sandal Tree also carries a generous selection of Mephisto and Arche comfort sandals, Donald Pliner, Anne Klein, Charles Jourdan, and beachwear and casual footwear for all tastes. Accessories range from fashionable knapsacks to avant-garde geometrical handbags—for town and country, day and evening, kids, women, and men. Prices are realistic, too. Also at the Hyatt Regency Maui Resort, 200 Nohea Kai Dr., Kaanapali. At Whalers Village, 2435 Kaanapali Pkwy. ✆ **808/667-5330.**

Totally Hawaiian Gift Gallery   This gallery makes a good browse for its selection of Niihau shell jewelry, excellent Hawaiian CDs, Norfolk pine bowls, and Hawaiian quilt kits. Hawaiian quilt patterns sewn in Asia (at least they're honest about it) are labor-intensive, less expensive, and attractive, although not totally Hawaiian. Hawaiian-quilt-patterned gift wraps and tiles, perfumes and soaps, handcrafted dolls, and koa accessories are of good quality, and the artists, such as Kelly Dunn (Norfolk wood bowls), Jerry Kermode (wood), and Pat Coito (wood), are among the tops in their fields. At Whalers Village, 2435 Kaanapali Pkwy. ✆ **808/667-4070.** www.totallyhawaiian.com.

HONOKOWAI, KAHANA & NAPILI

Those driving north of Kaanapali toward Kapalua will notice the **Honokowai Marketplace,** on Lower Honoapiilani Road, only minutes before the Kapalua Airport. It houses restaurants and coffee shops, a dry cleaner, the flagship **Star Market,** a few clothing stores, and the sprawling **Hawaiian Interiors.**

Nearby **Kahana Gateway** is an unimpressive mall built to serve the condominium community that has sprawled along the coastline between Honokowai and Kapalua. If you need women's swimsuits, however, **Rainbow Beach Swimwear** is a find. It carries a selection of suits for all shapes, at lower-than-resort prices, slashed even further during the frequent sales. **Hutton's Fine Jewelry** offers high-end jewelry from designers around the country (lots of platinum and diamonds), reflecting discerning taste for those who can afford it. Tahitian black pearls and jade (some hundreds of years old, all certified) are among Hutton's specialties.

KAPALUA

Honolua Store   Walk on the old wood floors peppered with holes from golf shoes and find your everyday essentials: bottled water, stationery, mailing tape, jackets, chips, wine, soft drinks, paper products, fresh fruit and produce, and aisles of notions and necessities. With picnic tables on the veranda and a takeout counter offering deli items—more than a dozen types of sandwiches, salads, and budget-friendly breakfasts—there are always long lines of customers. Golfers and surfers love to come here for the morning paper and coffee. 502 Office Rd. (next to the Ritz-Carlton Kapalua). ℰ **808/669-6128.**

Village Galleries   Maui's finest artists exhibit their works here and in the other two Village Galleries in Lahaina. Take heart, art lovers: There's no clichéd marine art here. Translucent, delicately turned bowls of Norfolk pine gleam in the light, and George Allan, Betty Hay Freeland, Fred KenKnight, and Pamela Andelin are included in the pantheon of respected artists represented in the tiny gallery. Watercolors, oils, sculptures, handblown glass, Niihau shell leis, jewelry, and other media are represented. The Ritz-Carlton's monthly Artist-in-Residence program features gallery artists in demonstrations and special hands-on workshops—free, including materials. At the Ritz-Carlton Kapalua, 1 Ritz-Carlton Dr. ℰ **808/669-1800.**

South Maui

KIHEI

Kihei is one long strip of strip malls. Most of the shopping here is concentrated in the **Azeka Place Shopping Center** on South Kihei Road. Across the street, **Azeka Place II** houses several prominent attractions, including **The Coffee Store** (p. 491) and a cluster of specialty shops with everything from children's clothes to shoes, sunglasses, and swimwear.

WAILEA

Grand Wailea Shops   The sprawling Grand Wailea Resort is known for its long arcade of shops and galleries tailored to hefty pocketbooks. However, gift items in all price ranges can be found at Na Hoku, Pineapple Patch, Tradewinds Boutique, Quiksilver, and Napua Gallery, which houses the private collection of the resort owner. Ki'i Gallery is luminous with studio glass and exquisitely turned woods. At the Grand Wailea Resort, 3850 Wailea Alanui Dr. ℰ **808/875-1234.**

Ki'i Gallery   Some of the works are large and lavish, such as the Toland Sand prisms for just under $5,000 and the John Stokes handblown glass. Those who love glass in all forms, from handblown vessels to jewelry, will love a browse through Ki'i. I found Pat Kazi's work in porcelain and found objects, such as the mermaid in a teacup, inspired by fairy tales and mythology, both fantastic and compelling. The gallery is devoted to glass and original paintings and drawings; roughly half of the artists are from Hawaii. Grand Wailea Resort (ℰ **808/874-3059**) and the Shops at Wailea (ℰ **808/874-1181**).

Shops at Wailea   This is the big shopping boost that resort-goers have been awaiting for years. The high-end shops sell expensive souvenirs, gifts, clothing, and accessories for a life of perpetual vacations. Chains still rule (Gap, Louis Vuitton, Banana Republic, Tiffany, Crazy Shirts, Honolua Surf Co.), but there is still fertile ground for the inveterate shopper in the nearly 60 shops in the complex. **Martin & MacArthur** (furniture and gift gallery) has landed in Wailea as part of a retail mix that is similar to Whalers Village. One store of particular note is **CY Maui** (ℰ **808/891-0782**). Women who like washable, flowing clothing in silks, rayons, and natural fibers will love this place, formerly the popular Manikin in Kahului. If you don't find what you want on the racks of simple bias-cut designs, you can have it made from the bolts of stupendous fabrics lining the shop. Except for a few hand-painted silks, everything is washable. 3750 Wailea Alanui. ℂ **808/891-6770.**

Upcountry Maui

MAKAWAO

Besides being a shopper's paradise, Makawao is the home of the island's most prominent arts organization, the **Hui No'eau Visual Arts Center,** 2841 Baldwin Ave. (ℂ **808/572-6560;** www.huinoeau.com). Designed in 1917 by C. W. Dickey, one of Hawaii's most prominent architects, the two-story, Mediterranean-style stucco home that houses the center is located on a sprawling 9-acre estate called Kaluanui. Its tree-lined driveway features two of Maui's largest hybrid Cook and Norfolk Island pines. A legacy of Maui's prominent *kamaaina* (old-timers), Harry and Ethel Baldwin, the estate became an arts center in 1976. Visiting artists offer lectures, classes, and demonstrations, all at reasonable prices, in basketry, jewelry making, ceramics, painting, and other media. Classes on Hawaiian art, culture, and history are also available. Call ahead for schedules and details. The exhibits here are drawn from a wide range of disciplines and multicultural sources, and include both contemporary and traditional art from established and emerging artists. The gift shop, featuring many one-of-a-kind works by local artists and artisans, is worth a stop. Hours are Monday through Saturday from 10am to 4pm.

Collections This longtime Makawao attraction is showing renewed vigor after more than 2 decades on Baldwin Avenue. It's one of my favorite Makawao stops, full of gift items and spirited clothing reflecting the ease and color of island living. Its selection of sportswear, soaps, jewelry, candles, and tasteful, marvelous miscellany reflects good sense and style. Dresses (including up-to-the-moment Citron in cross-cultural and vintage-looking prints), separates, home and bath accessories, sweaters, and other good things make this a Makawao must. 3677 Baldwin Ave. ℂ **808/572-0781.**

Gecko Trading Co. Boutique The selection in this tiny boutique is eclectic and always changing: One day it's mesh T-shirts in a dragon motif, the next it's Provence soaps and antique lapis jewelry. I've seen everything from handmade crocheted bags from New York to hammered-tin candleholders from Mexico. The prices are reasonable, the service is friendly, and it's more homey than glammy—not as self-conscious as some of the other local boutiques. 3621 Baldwin Ave. ℂ **808/572-0249.**

Holiday & Co. Attractive women's clothing in natural fibers hangs from racks, while jewelry to go with it beckons from the counter. Recent finds include elegant fiber evening bags, luxurious bath gels, easygoing dresses and separates, Dansko clogs, shawls, soaps, aloha shirts, books, picture frames, and jewelry. 3681 Baldwin Ave. ℂ **808/572-1470.**

Hot Island Glassblowing Studio & Gallery You can watch the artist transform molten glass into works of art and utility in this studio at the Makawao Courtyard, where an award-winning family of glass blowers built their own furnaces. It's fascinating to watch the shapes emerge from glass melted at 2,300°F (1,260°C). The colorful works displayed range from small paperweights to large vessels. Four to five artists participate in the demonstrations, which begin when the furnace is heated, about a half-hour before the studio opens at 9am. 3620 Baldwin Ave. (☎) **808/572-4527.**

Hurricane This boutique carries clothing, gifts, accessories, and books that are two steps ahead of the competition. Tommy Bahama aloha shirts and aloha print dresses; Sigrid Olsen's knitted shells, cardigans, and extraordinary silk tank dresses; hats; work by local artists; a notable selection of fragrances for men and women; and hard-to-find, eccentric books and home accessories are part of the Hurricane appeal. 3639 Baldwin Ave. (☎) **808/572-5076.**

The Mercantile The jewelry, home accessories (especially the Tiffany-style glass-and-shell lamps), dinnerware, Italian linens, plantation-style furniture, and clothing here are a salute to the good life. There's exquisite bedding, rugs, hand-carved armoires, slipcovers, and a large selection of Kiehl's products. The clothing—comfortable cottons and upscale European linens—is for men and women, as are the soaps, which include Maui Herbal Soap products and some unusual finds from France. Maui-made jams, honey, soaps, ceramics, and Jurlique organic facial and body products are among the new winners. 3673 Baldwin Ave. (☎) **808/572-1407.**

Sherri Reeve Gallery & Gifts If you want to take a little bit of the beauty of Maui home with you, stop by this open-air gallery. Artist Sherri Reeve grew up in Hawaii (the local phone book featured her art on the cover one year), and she has captured the vibrant color and feel of the islands. You can find everything from inexpensive cards, hand-painted tiles, and T-shirts to original works and limited editions. 3669 Baldwin Ave. (☎) **808/572-8931.** www.sreeve.com.

Viewpoints Gallery Maui's only fine-arts cooperative showcases the work of 20 established artists in an airy, attractive gallery located in a restored theater with a courtyard, glass blowing studio, and restaurants. The gallery features two-dimensional art, jewelry, fiber art, stained glass, paper, sculpture, and other media. This is a fine example of what can happen in a collectively supportive artistic environment. 3620 Baldwin Ave. (☎) **808/572-5979.**

FRESH FLOWERS IN KULA

Like anthuriums on the Big Island, proteas are a Maui trademark and an abundant crop on Haleakala's rich volcanic slopes. They also travel well, dry beautifully, and can be shipped worldwide with ease. Among Maui's most prominent sources is **Sunrise Protea** (☎ **808/876-0200;** www.sunriseprotea.com), in Kula. It offers a walk-through garden and gift shops, friendly service, and a larger-than-usual selection. Freshly cut flowers arrive from the fields on Tuesday and Friday afternoons. You can order individual blooms, baskets, arrangements, or wreaths for shipping all over the world. (Next door, the Sunrise Country Market offers fresh local fruits, snacks, and sandwiches, with picnic tables for lingering.)

    Proteas of Hawaii (☎ **808/878-2533;** www.proteasofhawaii.com), another reliable source, offers regular walking tours of the University of Hawaii Extension Service gardens across the street in Kula.

    Outside of Kula, the Saturday-morning **Maui Swap Meet** (p. 553 is among the best and least expensive places for tropical flowers of every stripe.

UPCOUNTRY EDIBLES

Working folks in Makawao pick up spaghetti and lasagna, sandwiches, salads, and changing specials from the **Rodeo General Store,** 3661 Baldwin Ave. (℃ **808/572-7841**). At the far end of the store is the oenophile's bonanza, a superior wine selection housed in its own temperature-controlled cave.

In the more than 6 decades that the **T. Komoda Store and Bakery,** 3674 Baldwin Ave. (℃ **808/572-7261**), has spent in this spot, untold numbers have creaked over the wooden floors to pick up Komoda's famous cream puffs. Old-timers know to come early or they'll be sold out. Then the cinnamon rolls, doughnuts, pies, and chocolate cake take over. Pastries are just the beginning; poi, macadamia-nut candies and cookies, and small bunches of local fruit keep the customers coming.

East Maui

PAIA

Hemp House   Clothing and accessories made of hemp, a sturdy and sensible fiber, are finally making their way into the mainstream. The Hemp House has as complete a selection as you can expect to see in Hawaii, with "denim" hemp jeans, lightweight linenlike trousers, dresses, shirts, and a full range of sensible, easy-care wear. 16 Baldwin Ave. ℃ **808/579-8880.**

Maui Crafts Guild   The old wooden storefront at the gateway to Paia houses crafts of high quality and in all price ranges, from pit-fired raku to bowls of Norfolk pine and other Maui woods, fashioned by Maui hands. Artist-owned and operated, the guild claims 25 members who live and work on Maui. Basketry, hand-painted fabrics, jewelry, beadwork, traditional Hawaiian stonework, pressed flowers, fused glass, stained glass, copper sculpture, banana-bark paintings, and pottery of all styles are displayed in the two-story gift gallery. Upstairs, sculptor Arthur Dennis Williams shows his breathtaking work in wood, bronze, and stone. Everything can be shipped. **Aloha Bead Co.** (℃ **808/579-9709**), in the back of the gallery, is a treasure-trove for bead workers. 43 Hana Hwy. ℃ **808/579-9697.** www.mauicraftsguild.com.

Maui Hands   Maui hands have made 90% of the items in this shop/gallery. Because it's a consignment shop, you'll find Hawaii-made handicrafts and prices that aren't inflated. The selection includes paintings, prints, jewelry, glass marbles, native-wood bowls, and tchotchkes for every budget. This is an ideal stop for made-on-Maui products and crafts of good quality. 84 Hana Hwy., in Paia. ℃ **808/579-9245.**

Moonbow Tropics   If you're looking for a tasteful aloha shirt, go to Moonbow. The selection consists of a few carefully culled racks of the top labels in aloha wear, in fabrics ranging from the finest silks and linens to Egyptian cotton and spun rayons. Silk pants, silk shorts, vintage-print neckwear, and an upgraded women's selection hang on colorful racks. The jewelry pieces, ranging from tanzanite to topaz, rubies to moonstones, are mounted in unique settings made on-site. 36 Baldwin Ave. ℃ **808/579-8592.** www.moonbowtropics.com.

HANA

Hana Coast Gallery 🎁   This gallery is a good reason to go to Hana: It's an aesthetic and cultural experience that informs as it enlightens. Tucked away in the posh hideaway Hotel Hana-Maui, the gallery is known for its high level of curatorship and commitment to the cultural art of Hawaii. There are no jumping whales or dolphins here—and except for a section of European and Asian masters, the 3,000-square-foot gallery is devoted entirely to Hawaii artists, whose sculptures, paintings, prints, feather work, stonework, and carvings are featured in displays that are so natural, they could well exist in someone's home. Director/curator Patrick Robinson has expanded the selection of koa-wood furniture in response to the ongoing revival of the American Crafts Movement with a Hawaiian/Japanese influence. Stellar artists Tai Lake from the Big Island and Randall Watkins from Maui are among those represented. Connoisseurs of hand-turned bowls will find the crème de la crème of the genre here: J. Kelly Dunn, Ron Kent, Todd Campbell, Ed Perrira, and Gary Stevens. You won't find a better selection elsewhere under one roof. The award-winning gallery has won accolades from the top travel and arts magazines in the country (*Travel + Leisure*, *Arts & Antiques*) and has steered clear of trendiness and unfortunate tastes. At the Hotel Hana-Maui. *©* 808/248-8636. www.hanacoast.com.

Hasegawa General Store Established in 1910, immortalized in song since 1961, burned to the ground in 1990, and back in business in 1991, this legendary store is indefatigable and more colorful than ever in its fourth generation in business. The aisles are choked with merchandise: coffee specially roasted and blended for the store, Ono Farms organic dried fruit, fishing equipment, every tape and CD that mentions Hana, the best books on Hana to be found, T-shirts, beach and garden essentials, baseball caps, film, baby food, napkins, and other necessities for the Hana life. Hana Hwy. *©* 808/248-8231.

MAUI AFTER DARK

The island's most prestigious entertainment venue is the $32-million **Maui Arts & Cultural Center,** in Kahului (*©* 808/242-7469; www.mauiarts.org). Bonnie Raitt has performed here, as have B. B. King, Hiroshima, Pearl Jam, Ziggy Marley, Lou Rawls, the American Indian Dance Theatre, Jonny Lang, and Tony Bennett, not to mention Keali'i Reichel and the finest in local and Hawaii talent. The center is as precious to Maui as the Met is to New York, with a visual-arts gallery, an outdoor amphitheater, offices, rehearsal space, a 300-seat theater for experimental performances, and a 1,200-seat main theater. Whether it's hula, the Iona Pear Dance Company, Willie Nelson, or the Maui Symphony Orchestra, only the best appear here. The center's activities are well publicized locally, so check the *Maui News* or ask your hotel concierge what's going on during your visit.

Hana Nightlife

Nightlife in Hana is pretty sparse. The only exception is the **Hotel Hana-Maui** (*©* 808/248-8211), which features Hawaiian music in the Paniolo Lounge Wednesday through Sunday from 7 to 9:30pm, and hosts a dinner hula show every Friday from 7 to 7:45pm in the Main Dining Room.

HAWAIIAN MUSIC The best of Hawaiian music can be heard every Wednesday night at the Napili Kai Beach Resort's indoor amphitheater, thanks to the **Masters of Hawaiian Slack Key Guitar Series** (*©* 888/669-3858; www.slackkey.com). The weekly shows present a side of Hawaii that few visitors ever get to see. Host George Kahumoku, Jr., introduces a new slack-key master every week. Not only is there incredible Hawaiian music and singing, but George and his guest also "talk story" about old Hawaii, music, and Hawaiian culture. Not to be missed.

Except for **Casanova** in Makawao and **Maui Brews** in Lahaina, nightlife options on this island are limited. The major hotels generally have lobby lounges offering Hawaiian music, soft jazz, or hula shows beginning at sunset. If **Hapa, Willie K. and Amy Gilliom,** or the soloist **Keali'i Reichel** are playing anywhere on their native island, don't miss them; they're among the finest Hawaiian musicians around today.

A NIGHT TO REMEMBER: luau, MAUI STYLE

Most of the larger hotels in Maui's major resorts offer luau on a regular basis. You'll pay about $75 to $90 to attend one. To protect yourself from disappointment, don't expect it to be a homegrown affair prepared in the traditional Hawaiian way. There are, however, commercial luau that capture the romance and spirit of the luau with quality food and entertainment in outdoor settings.

Maui's best choice is indisputably the nightly **Old Lahaina Luau ★★** (© **800/248-5828** or 808/667-1998; www.oldlahainaluau.com). Located just oceanside of the Lahaina Cannery, the Old Lahaina Luau maintains its high standards in food and entertainment—and

enjoys an oceanfront setting that is peerless. Local craftspeople display their wares only a few feet from the ocean. Seating is provided on lauhala mats for those who wish to dine as the traditional Hawaiians did, but there are tables for everyone else. There's no fire dancing in the program, but you won't miss it (for that, go to the Feast at Lele, p. 475). This luau offers a healthy balance of entertainment, showmanship, authentic high-quality food, educational value, and sheer romantic beauty. (No watered-down mai tais, either; these are the real thing.)

The luau begins at sunset and features Tahitian and Hawaiian entertainment, including ancient hula, hula from the missionary era, modern hula, and an intelligent narrative on the dance's rocky course of survival into modern times. The entertainment is riveting, even for jaded locals. The food, which is served from an open-air thatched structure, is as much Pacific Rim as authentically Hawaiian: *imu*-roasted kalua pig, baked mahimahi in Maui onion cream sauce, guava chicken, teriyaki sirloin steak, lomi salmon, poi, dried fish, poke, Hawaiian sweet potato, sautéed vegetables, seafood salad, and the ultimate taste treat, taro leaves with coconut milk. The cost is $92 for adults, $62 for children 12 and under.

West Maui

The buzz in West Maui is all about **Ulalena ★**, Maui Theatre, 878 Front St., Lahaina (**℃ 877/688-4800** or 808/661-9913; www.ulalena.com), a riveting evening of entertainment that weaves Hawaiian mythology with drama, dance, and state-of-the-art multimedia capabilities in a brand-new multimillion-dollar theater. Polynesian dance, original music, acrobatics, and chant, performed by a local and international cast, combine to create an evocative experience that often leaves the audience speechless. It's interactive, with dancers coming down the aisles, drummers and musicians in surprising corners, and mind-boggling stage and lighting effects that draw the audience in. Some special moments: the goddesses dancing on the moon, the white sail of the first Europeans, the wrath of the volcano goddess, Pele, the labors of the fieldworker immigrants. The story unfolds seamlessly; at the end, you'll be shocked to realize that not a single word of dialogue was spoken. Performances are given Saturday through Tuesday. Tickets are $60 to $79 for adults, $40 to $59 for children 12 and under.

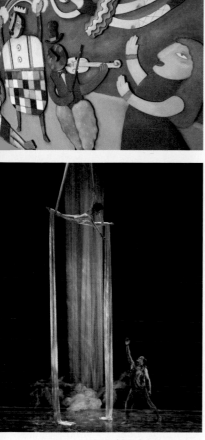

FROM TOP: **The Maui Arts & Cultural Center; Ulalena.**

A very different type of live entertainment is **Warren & Annabelle's,** 900 Front St., Lahaina (**℃ 808/667-6244;** www.warrenandannabelles. com), a magic/comedy cocktail show with illusionist Warren Gibson and "Annabelle," a ghost from the 1800s who plays the grand piano (even taking requests from the audience) as Warren dazzles you with his sleight-of-hand magic. Appetizers, desserts, and cocktails are available (either as a package or a la carte). Check-in is at 5 and 7:30pm. The show-only price is $56; the show plus gourmet appetizers and dessert costs $95. You must be 21 to attend.

The **Kaanapali Beach Hotel** has a wonderful show called **Kupanaha** (**℃ 808/661-0011;** www.kupanaha.com) that is perfect for the entire family. It features the renowned magicians Jody and Kathleen Baran and their entire family, including child-prodigy magicians Katrina and Crystal. The dinner show includes magic, illusions, and the story of the Hawaii fire goddess, Pele, presented through hula and chant performed by the children of the Kano'eau Dance Academy. The shows are Tuesday through Saturday; tickets are $79 to $89 for adults, and $39 to $89 for children 6 to 12. Prices include dinner (entree choices include Island fish, roasted stuffed chicken, steak and shrimp, and a vegetarian dish, with a children's menu available).

Maui Brews, 900 Front St., Lahaina (© **808/667-7794**), draws the late-night crowd to its corner of the Lahaina Center with swing, salsa, reggae, and jams. There's live music nights Wednesday and Saturday. Hours are daily from 11:30am, with happy hour from 3 to 6pm and nightclub hours from 9pm to 1:30am.

You won't have to ask what's going on at **Cheeseburger in Paradise,** 811 Front St., Lahaina (© **808/661-4855**), the two-story green-and-white building at the corner of Front and Lahainaluna streets. Just go outside and you'll hear it. Loud, live, and lively tropical rock blasts into the streets and out to sea nightly from 4:30 to 11pm.

Other venues for music in West Maui include the following:

○ **Lahaina Pizza,** 730 Front St., Lahaina (© **808/661-0700**), offers live music from 6:30 to 8:30pm Thursday through Saturday nights.

○ **Hula Grill,** in Whalers Village, Kaanapali (© **808/667-6636**), has live music (usually Hawaiian) from 3 to 5pm and again from 6:30 to 8:30pm nightly.

○ **Kimo's,** 845 Front St., Lahaina (© **808/661-4811**), has live musicians at various times; call for details.

○ **Leilani's on the Beach,** in Whalers Village, Kaanapali (© **808/661-4495**), has live music from 3 to 5pm Friday through Sunday; the styles range from contemporary Hawaiian to rock.

○ **Maui Brewing Co.,** in the Kahana Gateway Shopping Center, Kahana (© **808/669-3474**), has live music Wednesday and Saturday nights from 9:30pm to 12:30am.

○ **Moose McGillycuddy's,** 844 Front St., Lahaina (© **808/667-7758**), offers a DJ some nights from 5:30 to 8:30pm; the schedule varies, so call for details.

○ **Pineapple Grill,** 200 Kapalua Dr., Kapalua (© **808/669-9600**), features Hawaiian music on Friday and jazz on Saturday from 7 to 10pm.

○ **Pioneer Inn,** 658 Wharf St., Lahaina (© **808/661-3636**), offers a variety of live music Tuesday and Wednesday nights starting at 6pm.

○ **Sansei Seafood Restaurant & Sushi Bar,** 600 Office Rd., Kapalua (© **808/669-6286**), has karaoke on Thursday and Friday from 10pm to 1am.

○ **Sea House Restaurant,** at the Napili Kai Beach Resort, Napili (© **808/669-1500**), has live music from 7 to 9pm nightly.

South Maui

The Kihei, Wailea, and Maalaea areas in South Maui also feature music in a variety of locations:

○ **Capischi,** at the Diamond Resort, 555 Kaukahi St., Wailea (© **808/879-2224**), has live music Friday and Saturday from 7 to 10pm.

○ **Kahale's Beach Club,** 36 Keala Place, Kihei (© **808/875-7711**), offers a potpourri of live music nightly at 6:30pm; call for details.

- **Life's a Beach,** 1913 S. Kihei Rd., Kihei (© 808/891-8010), has nightly live music; call for times.

- **Lobby Lounge,** at the Four Seasons Resort Maui at Wailea (© 808/874-8000), features nightly live music from 5 to 11pm.

- **Lulu's,** 1945 S. Kihei Rd., Kihei (© 808/879-9944), offers entertainment most nights; call for schedule, cover charges, and times.

- **Mulligan's on the Blue,** 100 Kaukahi St., Wailea (© 808/874-1131), has live music nightly. Call for times and cover or check it out at www.mulligans ontheblue.com.

- **Sansei Seafood Restaurant & Sushi Bar,** in Kihei Town Center (© 808/879-0004), has karaoke Thursday through Saturday from 10pm to 1am.

- **South Shore Tiki Lounge,** 1913 S. Kihei Rd., Kihei (© 808/874-6444), has live music Wednesday through Monday from 4 to 6pm, and dancing from 10pm to 2am.

- **Sports Page Bar,** 2411 S. Kihei Rd., Kihei (© 808/879-0602), has live music or a DJ Friday and Saturday nights starting at 9pm.

Upcountry Maui

Upcountry in Makawao, the party never ends at **Casanova,** 1188 Makawao Ave. (© 808/572-0220), the popular Italian ristorante where the good times roll with the pasta. The newly renovated bar area has large booths, all the better for socializing around the stage and dance floor. If a big-name mainland band is resting up on Maui following a sold-out concert on Oahu, you may find its members setting up for an impromptu night here. DJs take over on Wednesday (ladies' night); on Friday and Saturday, live entertainment or a DJ draws fun-lovers from

---

WATCH FOR THE green flash

If you're gathered in a crowd on Maui watching a sunset, you may hear someone call out: "Green flash!" If you're lucky, you may get to see it yourself.

The romantic version of the story is that the green flash happens when the sun kisses the ocean good night (honeymooners love this version). The scientific version is not quite as dreamy: Light bends as it goes around the curve of the earth. When the sun dips beneath the horizon, it is at the far end of the spectrum. So this refraction of the sun's light, coupled with the atmosphere on the extreme angle of the sunset on the horizon, causes only the color green to be seen in the color spectrum just before the light disappears.

Here's how to view the green flash: First, it has to be a clear day, with no clouds or haze on the horizon. Second, the sun has to set on the ocean (if it sets behind an island, you won't see the flash). Keep checking the sun as it drops (try not to look directly into the sun; just glance at it to assess its position). If the conditions are ideal, just as the sun drops into the blue water, a "flash" or laserlike beam of green will appear to shoot out for an instant.

even the most remote reaches of the island. Entertainment starts at 10pm and continues to 1:30am (check the website, www.casanovamaui.com, for schedules and cover charges). Expect good blues, rock 'n' roll, reggae, jazz, Hawaiian, and the top names in local and visiting entertainment. Elvin Bishop, the local duo Hapa, Los Lobos, and many others have taken Casanova's stage. The cover is usually $5 to $10. Go Sunday afternoons, from 2:30 to 5:30pm, for excellent live jazz.

Paia & Central Maui

In central Maui, **Café Marc Aurel,** 28 N. Market St., Wailuku (© **808/244-0852;** www.cafemarcaurel.com), is the place for a range of eclectic music, from folk to Hawaiian to ethnic, and even some open-mic nights; call for information. The **Kahului Ale House,** 355 E. Kamehameha Ave., Kahului (© **808/877-9001;** www.alehouse.net), has live music Monday through Thursday, live DJs Friday to Sunday. Times vary; call or check the website for schedule and cover charges.

In Paia, **Charley's Restaurant,** 142 Hana Hwy. (© **808/579-8085**), features an eclectic selection of music from country and western (Willie Nelson has been seen sitting in) to fusion/reggae to rock 'n' roll; call for details. Also in Paia, the **Moana Bakery & Cafe,** 71 Baldwin Ave. (© **808/579-9999**), has everything from Hawaiian music to cool jazz to sizzling Latin to swing; call for details.

8

MOLOKAI, THE MOST HAWAIIAN ISLE

Born of volcanic eruptions 1.5 million years ago, Molokai remains a time capsule on the dawn of the 21st century. It has no deluxe resorts, no stoplights, and no buildings taller than a coconut tree. Molokai is the least developed, most "Hawaiian" of all the islands, making it especially attractive to adventure travelers and peace seekers.

Molokai lives up to its reputation as the most Hawaiian place chiefly through its lineage; there are more people here of Hawaiian blood than anywhere else. This slipper-shaped island was the cradle of Hawaiian dance (it's the birthplace of the hula) and the ancient science of aquaculture. An aura of ancient mysticism clings to the land, and the old ways still govern life. The residents survive by taking fish from the sea and hunting wild pigs and axis deer on the range. Some folks still catch fish for dinner by throwing nets and trolling the reef.

Modern Hawaii's high-rise hotels, shopping centers, and other trappings of tourism haven't been able to gain a foothold here. The lone low-rise resort on the island, Kaluakoi—a now-closed, empty hotel built 30 years ago—was Molokai's token attempt at contemporary tourism. The only "new" developments since Kaluakoi were the Molokai Ranch's eco-tourism project of upscale "camping" in semipermanent "tentalows" (a combination of a bungalow and a tent) and a 22-room lodge on the 65,000-acre ranch—both of which closed in 2008 when the Molokai Ranch shut down all operations.

Not everyone will love Molokai. The slow-paced, simple life of the people and the absence of contemporary landmarks attract those in search of the "real" Hawaii. I once received a letter from a New York City resident who claimed that any "big-city resident" would "blanche" at the lack of "sophistication." But that is exactly the charm of Molokai. This is a place where Mother Nature is wild and uninhibited, with very little intrusion by man. Forget sophistication; this is one of the few spots on the planet where one can stand in awe of the island's diverse natural wonders: Hawaii's highest waterfall and greatest collection of fish ponds; the world's tallest sea cliffs; sand dunes, coral reefs, rainforests, and hidden coves; and gloriously empty beaches.

EXPLORING THE "MOST HAWAIIAN" ISLE

Only 38 miles from end to end and just 10 miles wide, Molokai stands like a big green wedge in the blue Pacific. It has an east side, a west side, a backside, and a topside. This long, narrow island is like yin and yang: One side is a flat, austere, arid desert; the other is a lush, green, tropical Eden. Three volcanic eruptions formed Molokai; the last produced the island's "thumb"—a peninsula jutting out of the steep cliffs of the north shore, like a punctuation mark on the island's geological story.

PREVIOUS PAGE: **Kapuaiwa Coconut Grove/Kiowea Park.**

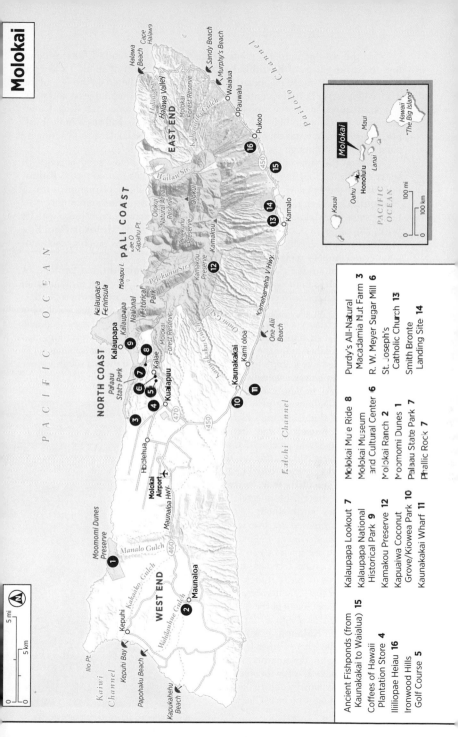

Molokai

PACIFIC OCEAN

Ilio Pt.

Kaiwi Channel

Kepuhi Bay
Kepuhi

Papohaku Beach

Kapukahehu Beach

WEST END

Kaluakoi Gulch

Wailuma Gulch

Manalo Gulch

Moomomi Dunes Preserve **1**

Maunaloa **2**

Maunaloa HWY.

Molokai Airport

Hoolehua

460

NORTH COAST

Moomomi Dunes Preserve

Palaau State Park

Kalaupapa Peninsula

Kalaupapa

Kalaupapa National Historical Park

Kualapuu

Kalae

470

450

Kaunakakai

Kamiloa

One Alii Beach

PALI COAST

Mokuai. Kapuhi Pt.
Lae O Kapahu Pt.

Oloku Natural Area Reserve

Olokui

Wailau Str.

Pelekunu Preserve

Pelekunu Str.

Kamakou Preserve

Kamakou

Kamalo

Kamehameha V Hwy.

Ualapue Gulch

Kawela Gulch

Molokai Forest Reserve

EAST END

Kalaupapa National Historical Park

Molokai Forest Reserve

Halawa Valley

Halawa Beach

Cape Halawa

Sandy Beach

Murphy's Beach

Waialua

Pauwalu

Pukoo

450

Kamalo

Pailolo Channel

l a n a i

PACIFIC OCEAN

Kauai

Oahu
Honolulu

Molokai

Lanai

Maui

Hawaii
"The Big Island"

0   100 mi
0   100 km

0   5 mi
0   5 km

N

571

Ancient Fishponds (from Kaunakakai to Waialua) **15**

Coffees of Hawaii Plantation Store **4**

Iliiliopae Heiau **16**

Ironwood Hills Golf Course **5**

Kalaupapa Lookout **7**

Kalaupapa National Historical Park **9**

Kamakou Preserve **12**

Kapuaiwa Coconut Grove/Kiowea Park **10**

Kaunakakai Wharf **11**

Molokai Mule Ride **8**

Molokai Museum and Cultural Center **6**

Molokai Ranch **2**

Moomomi Dunes **1**

Palaau State Park **7**

Phallic Rock **7**

Purdy's All-Natural Macadamia Nut Farm **3**

R. W. Meyer Sugar Mill **6**

St. Joseph's Catholic Church **13**

Smith Bronte Landing Site **14**

On the red-dirt southern plain, where most of the island's 7,000 residents live, the rustic village of **Kaunakakai** ★ looks like the set of an old Hollywood Western, with sun-faded clapboard houses and horses tethered on the side of the road. Mile marker 0, in the center of town, divides the island into east and west.

Eastbound, along the **coastal highway ★★★** named for King Kamehameha V, are Gauguin-like, palm-shaded cottages set on small coves or near fish ponds; spectacular vistas that take in Maui, Lanai, and Kahoolawe; and a fringing coral reef visible through the crystal-clear waves.

Out on the sun-scorched West End, overlooking a gold-sand beach with water usually too rough to swim in, is the island's lone destination resort, **Kaluakoi** (where the hotel is currently closed). The old hilltop plantation town of **Maunaloa** has been razed and rebuilt as a gentrified plantation community, now fading since the Molokai Ranch closed down the expensive country lodge with its pricey dining room. Cowboys no longer ride the range of **Molokai Ranch,** a 60,000-acre spread, which was closed in 2008 along with the ranch's accommodations and outdoor-recreation activities.

Elsewhere around the island, in hamlets like **Kualapuu,** old farmhouses with pickup trucks in the yards and sleepy dogs under the shade trees stand amid row crops of papaya, coffee, and corn—just like farm towns in Anywhere, U.S.A.

But that's not all there is. The "backside" of Molokai is a rugged wilderness of spectacular beauty. On the outskirts of **Kaunakakai,** the land rises gradually from sea-level fish ponds to cool uplands and the Molokai Forest, long ago stripped of sandalwood for the China trade. All that remains is an indentation in the earth shaped like a ship's hull, a crude matrix that gave them a rough idea of when they'd cut enough sandalwood to fill a ship (it's identified on good maps as *Luanamokuiliahi,* or Sandalwood Boat).

The land inclines sharply to the lofty mountains and the nearly mile-high summit of Mount Kamakou, and then ends abruptly with emerald-green cliffs, which plunge into a lurid aquamarine sea dotted with tiny deserted islets. These breathtaking 3,250-foot **sea cliffs ★★**, the highest in the world, stretch 14 majestic miles along Molokai's north shore, laced by waterfalls and creased by five valleys—Halawa, Papalaua, Wailau, Pelekunu, and Waikolu—once occupied by early Hawaiians who built stone terraces and used waterfalls to irrigate taro patches.

Long after the sea cliffs were formed, a tiny volcano erupted out of the sea at their feet and spread lava into a flat, leaflike peninsula called **Kalaupapa ★★★**—the 1860s leper exile where Father Damien de Veuster of Belgium devoted his life to caring for the afflicted. A few people remain in the remote colony by choice, keeping it tidy for the visitors who arrive daily.

A sign offering advice to Molokai's visitors.

WHAT A VISIT TO MOLOKAI IS REALLY LIKE

There's plenty of aloha on Molokai, but the so-called "friendly island" remains ambivalent about vacationers. One of the least-visited Hawaiian islands, Molokai welcomes about 80,000 visitors annually on its own take-it-or-leave-it terms and makes few concessions beyond that of gracious host; it never wants to attract too big of a crowd, anyway. A sign at the airport offers the first clue: SLOW DOWN, YOU ON MOLOKAI NOW—wisdom to heed on this island, where life proceeds at its own pace.

Rugged, red-dirt Molokai isn't for everyone, but those who like to explore remote places and seek their own adventures should love it. The best of the island can be seen only on foot, bicycle, mule, horseback, kayak, or boat. The sea cliffs are accessible only by sea in summer, when the Pacific is calm, or via a 10-mile trek through the Wailau Valley—an adventure only a handful of hardy hikers attempt each year. The great **Kamakou Preserve** is open just once a month, by special arrangement with the Nature Conservancy. Even **Moomomi,** which holds bony relics of prehistoric flightless birds and other creatures, requires a guide to divulge the secrets of the dunes.

Those in search of nightlife have come to the wrong place; Molokai shuts down after sunset. The only public diversions are softball games under the lights of Mitchell Pauole Field, movies at Maunaloa, and the few restaurants that stay open after dark, often serving local brew and pizza.

The "friendly" island may enchant you as the "real" Hawaii of your dreams. On the other hand, you may leave shaking your head, never to return. Regardless of how you approach Molokai, remember my advice: Take it slow.

ORIENTATION
Arriving

BY PLANE   Molokai has two airports, but you'll most likely fly into **Hoolehua Airport,** which everyone just calls the Molokai Airport. It's on a dusty plain about 6 miles from Kaunakakai town. Twin-engine planes offer daily service.

Pacific Wings (© **888/866-5022** or 808/873-0877; www.pacific wings.com) has several daily nonstop flights between Molokai and Honolulu (Oahu), and daily flights between Molokai and Kahului (Maui). **go!Express** (© **888/I-FLY-GO-2** [435-9462]; www.iflygo.com) provides service from Kona (the Big Island), Kahului (Maui), and Honolulu (Oahu) to Molokai. Currently, go!Express offers the best rates and deals among Hawaii's air carriers.

In general, go!Express and PW Express flights are substantially cheaper than those on the twin-engine planes flown by **Island Air** (© **800/323-3345** from the mainland, or 800/652-6541 interisland; www.islandair.com). And I must warn you that I have gotten less than sterling service from Island Air, which has left me stranded midroute—not once, but twice!

George's Aviation (© **866/834-2120,** 808/834-2120 from Honolulu, or 808/893-2120 from Maui; www.georgesaviation.com) has commuter flights on Monday, Friday, and Sunday from Honolulu and Maui to Molokai.

BY BOAT   You can travel across the seas by ferry from Maui's Lahaina Harbor to Molokai's Kaunakakai Wharf on the ***Molokai Princess*** (© **877/500-6284** or 808/667-6165; www.mauiprincess.com). The 100-foot yacht, certified for 149 passengers, is fitted with the latest generation of gyroscopic stabilizers, making the ride smoother. The ferry makes the 1-hour-and-45-minute journey from Lahaina to Kaunakakai daily; as we went to press, a one-way ticket cost $42 plus a fuel surcharge of $12 for a total of $54 adults (half-price for kids ages 3 to 12; kids 2 and under ride free). Be sure to check what the current fuel charge is before you go. Or you can choose to tour the island from two package options: Cruise-Drive, which includes round-trip passage and a rental car; or the Alii Tour, which is a guided tour in an air-conditioned van plus lunch.

Visitor Information

Contact the **Molokai Visitors Association,** P.O. Box 960, Kaunakakai, HI 96748 (© **800/800-6367** from the U.S. mainland and Canada, 800/553-0404 interisland, or 808/553-3876; www.molokai-hawaii.com), or stop by its office in the Moore Center, 2 Kamoi St., Ste. 200, Kaunakakai. The staff can give you all the information you need on what to see and do while you're on Molokai.

The Island in Brief

KAUNAKAKAI ★

Dusty vehicles—mostly pickup trucks—are parked diagonally along Ala Malama Street. You're in Kaunakakai, the closest thing Molokai has to a business district. Friendly Isle Realty and Friendly Isle Travel offer islanders dream homes and vacations; Rabang's Filipino Food posts bad checks in the window; antlered deer-head trophies guard the grocery aisles at Misaki's Market; and Kanemitsu's, the town's legendary bakery, churns out fresh loaves of onion-cheese bread daily.

Once an ancient canoe landing, Kaunakakai was the royal summer residence of King Kamehameha V. The port town bustled when pineapple and sugar were king. With its Old West–style storefronts laid out in a 3-block grid on a flat, dusty plain, Kaunakakai is a town from the past. At the end of Wharf Road is Molokai Wharf, a picturesque place to fish, photograph, and just hang out.

Kaunakakai is the dividing point between the lush, green East End and the dry, arid West End. On the west side of town stands a cactus, while on the east side of town there's thick, green vegetation.

THE NORTH COAST ★★

Upland from Kaunakakai, the land tilts skyward and turns green, with scented plumeria in yards and glossy coffee trees all in a row, until it blooms into a true forest—and then abruptly ends at a great precipice, falling 3,250 feet to the sea. The green sea cliffs are creased with five V-shaped crevices so deep that light is seldom seen (to paraphrase a Hawaiian poet). The north coast is a remote, forbidding place, with a solitary peninsula—**Kalaupapa ★★★**—that was once the home for exiled lepers (it's now a national historical park). This region is easy on the eyes but difficult to visit. It lies at a cool elevation, and frequent rain squalls blow in from the ocean. In summer, the ocean is calm, providing great opportunities for kayaking, fishing, and swimming, but during the rest of the year, giant waves come rolling onto the shores.

Kalaupapa peninsula leper colony.

THE WEST END ★

This end of the island, once home to **Molokai Ranch,** is miles of stark desert terrain bordered by the most beautiful white-sand beaches in Hawaii. The rugged rolling land slopes down to Molokai's only destination resort, **Kaluakoi,** a cul-de-sac of condos clustered around a 3-decade-old seafront hotel (which closed in 2001 and was still closed when we went to press) near 3-mile-long Papohaku, the island's biggest beach. On the way to Kaluakoi, you'll find **Maunaloa,** a 1920s-era pineapple-plantation town that's now a ghost town since the Molokai Ranch closed all of its operations in 2008, including the upscale lodge, a triplex theater, restaurants, and some shops. The West End is dry, dry, dry. It hardly ever rains, but when it does (usually in the winter), expect a downpour and lots of red mud.

THE EAST END ★★★

The area east of Kaunakakai becomes lush, green, and tropical, with golden pocket beaches and a handful of cottages and condos that are popular with thrifty travelers. With this voluptuous landscape comes rain. However, most storms are brief (15-min.) affairs. Winter is Hawaii's rainy season, so expect more rain from January to March, but even then, the storms are usually brief and the sun comes back out.

Beyond Kaunakakai, the two-lane road curves along the coast past piggeries, palm groves, a 20-mile string of fish ponds, an ancient *heiau* (temple), Damien-built churches, and a few contemporary condos by the sea. The road ends in the glorious **Halawa Valley ★**, one of Hawaii's most beautiful valleys.

Fast Facts Molokai

Molokai is part of Maui County. For **local emergencies,** call ✆ **911.** For non-emergencies, call the **police** at ✆ **808/553-5355,** the **fire department** at ✆ **808/553-5601,** or **Molokai General Hospital,** in Kaunakakai, at ✆ **808/553-5331.**

Downtown Kaunakakai has a **post office** (✆ **808/553-5845**) and several banks, including the **Bank of Hawaii** (✆ **808/553-3273**), which has a 24-hour ATM.

GETTING AROUND

Getting around Molokai isn't easy if you don't have a rental car, and rental cars are often hard to find here. On holiday weekends (see "When to Go," on p. 62), car-rental agencies simply run out of cars. Book before you go. There's no municipal transit or shuttle service, but a 24-hour taxi service is available (see below).

CAR-RENTAL AGENCIES   Rental cars are available from **Alamo** (© **877/222-9075;** www.alamo.com), located at the Molokai Airport. **National** has a rental desk at the Hotel Molokai (© **877/222-9058** or 808/553-3596; www.nationalcar.com).

TAXI & TOUR SERVICES   **Molokai Off-Road Tours & Taxi** (© **808/553-3369;** www.molokai.com/offroad) offers regular taxi service as well as an airport shuttle ($29 for one or two people one-way to Kaunakakai).

WHERE TO STAY

Molokai is Hawaii's most affordable island, especially for accommodations. And because the island's restaurants are few, most hotel rooms and condo units come with kitchens, which can save you a bundle on dining costs. The downside is that there aren't too many options—mostly B&Bs, condos, and a few quaint ocean-front vacation rentals. Hardy souls can pitch their own tent at the beach or in the cool upland forest (see "Hiking & Camping," p. 588).

I've listed my top picks below; for additional options, contact **Molokai Vacation Rentals,** P.O. Box 1979, Kaunakakai, HI 96748 (© **800/367-2984** or 808/553-8334; fax 808/553-3783; www.molokai-vacation-rental.com). *Note:* Taxes of 11.42% will be added to your hotel bill. Parking is free.

Kaunakakai

MODERATE

Hotel Molokai ★ ☺   Since the 2008 closing of the Lodge at Molokai Ranch, this nostalgic Hawaiian motel-like complex has been the only hotel on the island. The modest accommodations comprise a series of modified A-frame units, nestled under coco palms along a gray-sand beach that has a great view of Lanai but isn't good for swimming. In 2006, the entire hotel underwent a $1-million renovation, from repaving the parking lot to redoing the kitchen. All rooms have been upgraded and look clean and new, but they aren't fancy—this is still a modest budget hotel. Be sure to ask for a room with a ceiling fan; most units have a lanai. The mattresses are on the soft side, the sheets thin, and the bath towels rough, but you're on Molokai. The front desk is open only from 7am to 9pm; late check-ins or visitors with problems have to go to security.

Kamehameha V Hwy. (P.O. Box 1020), Kaunakakai, HI 96748. © **877/553-5347** or 808/553-5347. Fax 800/477-2329. www.hotelmolokai.com. 54 units. $159–$179; $199 with kitchen; from $249 double suite. Extra bed/crib $25. AE, DISC, MC, V. **Amenities:** Fairly good and reasonably priced restaurant w/bar; babysitting; bike rentals; outdoor pool; watersports equipment rentals. *In room:* A/C, TV, fridge, hair dryer, Internet for $10 a day, kitchenette (in some rooms).

Molokai Shores ☺   Basic units with kitchens and large lanais face a small gold-sand beach in this quiet complex of three-story Polynesian-style buildings, less than a mile from Kaunakakai. Alas, the beach is mostly for show (offshore, it's shallow mud flats underfoot), fishing, or launching kayaks, but the pool and

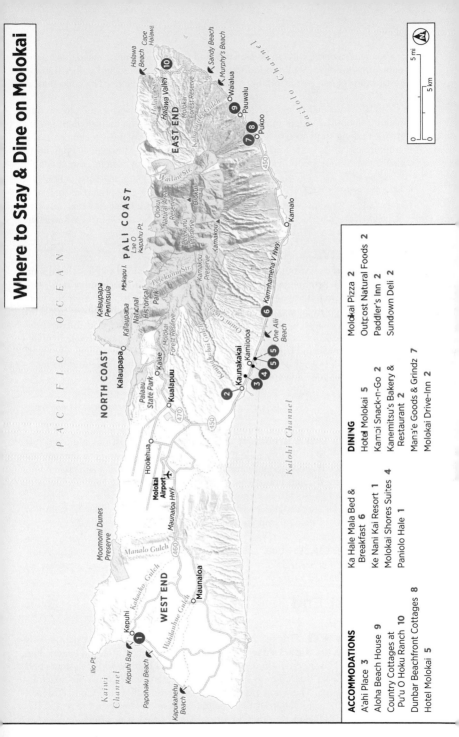

Where to Stay & Dine on Molokai

ACCOMMODATIONS

A'ahi Place **3**
Aloha Beach House **9**
Country Cottages at
Pu'u O Hoku Ranch **10**
Dunbar Beachfront Cottages **8**
Hotel Molokai **5**

Ka Hale Mala Bed &
Breakfast **6**
Ke Nani Kai Resort **1**
Molokai Shores Suites **4**
Paniolo Hale **1**

DINING

Hotel Molokai **5**
Kamoi Snack-n-Go **2**
Kanemitsu's Bakery &
Restaurant **2**
Mana'e Goods & Grindz **7**
Molokai Drive-Inn **2**

Molokai Pizza **2**
Outpost Natural Foods **2**
Paddler's Inn **2**
Sundown Deli **2**

577

barbecue area come with an ocean view, and the spacious units make this a good choice for families. Well-tended gardens, spreading lawns, and palms frame a restful view of fish ponds, offshore reefs, and neighbor islands. The central location is a plus.

There's no daily maid service here, and I have received some letters complaining about the lack of maintenance and cleanliness; the management swears that it's taking steps to correct these deficiencies. On my most recent visit, the grounds and units I saw were clean and well maintained. However, keep in mind that these condos are individually owned and managed by various companies.

Kamehameha V Hwy. (P.O. Box 1037), Kaunakakai, HI 96748. *C* **800/367-5004** or 808/553-5954. Fax 808/553-5954. www.castleresorts.com. 102 units. $169–$199 1-bedroom apt (sleeps up to 4); $250 2-bedroom apt (up to 6). Discounted rates for weekly and extended stays, plus corporate, military, and senior discounts and Internet-only specials. AE, DISC, MC, V. **Amenities:** Putting green. *In room:* TV, kitchen, free Wi-Fi.

INEXPENSIVE

A'ahi Place ✦ Just outside of Kaunakakai and up a small hill lies this dream vacation cottage, complete with a wicker sitting area, a kitchen, and two full-size beds in the bedroom. Two lanais make great places to just sit and enjoy the stars at night. The entire property is surrounded by tropical plants, flowers, and fruit trees. You can choose to forgo breakfast or for $10 more per night (for two people) get all the fixings for a continental breakfast (homegrown Molokai coffee, fresh baked goods, and fruit from the property) stocked in the kitchen. For those who seek a quiet vacation to unplug and unwind, this is the place. And for those who wish to explore Molokai, the central location is perfect.

P.O. Box 2006, Kaunakakai, HI 96748. *C* **808/553-8033.** www.molokai.com/aahi. 1 unit. $75–$85 double. Extra person $20. Continental breakfast $10 extra. 3-night minimum. No credit cards. *In room:* Kitchen, no phone.

Ka Hale Mala Bed & Breakfast ✦ In a subdivision just outside town (off Kamehameha V Hwy., before mile marker 5) is this large four-room unit, with a private entrance through the garden and a Jacuzzi just outside. Inside you'll find rattan furnishings, room enough to sleep four, and a full kitchen. The helpful owners meet all guests at the airport like long-lost relatives, provide a couple of bikes as well as snorkel and picnic gear, and happily share their homegrown organic produce; I recommend paying the extra $5 each for breakfast here.

7 Kamakana Place (P.O. Box 1582), Kaunakakai, HI 96748 (off Kamehameha V Hwy., before mile marker 5). *C*/fax **808/553-9009.** www.molokai-bnb.com. 1 unit. $80 double without breakfast, $90 double with breakfast. Extra person $15 without breakfast, $20 with breakfast. No credit cards. **Amenities:** Jacuzzi. *In room:* TV, kitchen.

The West End

MODERATE

Paniolo Hale ★ 🎁 Tucked into a verdant garden on the dry West End, this condo complex has the advantage of being next door to a white-sand beach. The two-story, old Hawaii ranch-house design is airy and homey, with oak floors and folding-glass doors that open to huge screened verandas. All units are spacious and well equipped. The whole place overlooks the Kaluakoi Golf Course (which closed in 2008), a green barrier that separates these condos from the rest of the rapidly fading Kaluakoi Resort. Out front, Kepuhi Beach is a scenic place for walkers and beachcombers, but the seas are too hazardous for most swimmers. A pool, paddle tennis, and barbecue facilities are on the property, which adjoins open grassland countryside.

As with most condominiums in a rental pool, the quality and upkeep of the individually owned units can vary widely. When booking, spend some time talking with the friendly people at Molokai Vacation Rentals so that you get a top-quality condo that has been renovated recently.

Lio Place (next door to Kaluakoi Resort), Kaluakoi, HI 96770. Reservations c/o Molokai Vacation Properties, P.O. Box 1979, Kaunakakai, HI 96748. ℃ **800/367-2984** or 808/553-8334. Fax 808/553-3783. www.molokai-vacation-rental.com. 77 units. $120–$150 double studio; $135–$195 1-bedroom apt (sleeps up to 4); $275 3-bedroom apt (sleeps up to 6). $65–$150 cleaning fee. 3-night minimum; 1-week minimum Dec 16–Jan 3. AE, MC, V. **Amenities:** Nearby golf course; outdoor pool. *In room:* TV, kitchen.

INEXPENSIVE

Ke Nani Kai Resort ★ ☺ These large apartments are set up for full-time living with real kitchens, attractive furnishings, and breezy lanais. There's a huge pool, a volleyball court, and tennis courts. These condos are farther from the sea than other local accommodations, but are still just a brief walk to the beach. The two-story buildings are surrounded by parking and garden areas. The only downside: Maid service is only every third day.

In the Kaluakoi Resort development, Kaluakoi Rd., off Hwy. 460 (P.O. Box 289), Maunaloa, HI 96770. Reservations c/o Molokai Vacation Properties, P.O. Box 1979, Kaunakakai, HI 96748. ℃ **800/367-2984** or 808/553-8334. Fax 808/553-3783. www.molokai-vacation-rental.com. 100 units. $105–$135 1-bedroom apt (sleeps up to 4); $125–$185 2-bedroom apt (sleeps up to 6). $75–$95 cleaning fee. 3-night minimum. AE, DC, DISC, MC, V. **Amenities:** Golf course; Jacuzzi; outdoor pool; 2 tennis courts. *In room:* TV, high-speed Internet, kitchen.

The East End

MODERATE

Aloha Beach House ★★ 🏠 ☺ This Hawaiian-style beach house sits right on the white-sand beach of Waialua in the lush East End. Perfect for families, the impeccably decorated two-bedroom, 1,600-square-foot property has a huge, airy living/dining/kitchen area that opens onto an old-fashioned porch for meals or just sitting in the comfy chairs and watching the clouds roll by. The place is fully equipped, from the complete kitchen (including a dishwasher) to a VCR (plus a library of videos) to all the beach toys you can think of. It's located close to Mana'e Goods and Grindz (p. 582).

Kamehameha V Hwy., just after mile marker 19. Reservations c/o The Rietows, P.O. Box 79, Kilauea, HI 96754. ℃ **888/828-1008** or 808/828-1100. Fax 808/828-2199. www.molokaivacation. com. 1 unit. $230–$290 double. One-time cleaning fee $175. Extra person $20 plus additional cleaning fee. 2-night minimum. No credit cards. *In room:* TV, kitchen.

Country Cottage at Pu'u O Hoku Ranch ★ ☺ *Pu'u o Hoku* ("Star Hill") Ranch, which spreads across 14,000 acres of pasture and forests, is the last place to stay before Halawa Valley—it's at least an hour's drive from Kaunakakai along the shoreline. Two acres of tropically landscaped property circle the ranch's rustic cottage, which boasts breathtaking views of rolling hills and the Pacific. The wooden cottage features comfortable country furniture, a full kitchen, two bedrooms (one with a double bed, one with two twins), two bathrooms, and a separate dining room on the enclosed lanai. Stargaze at night, watch the sunrise in the morning, and hike, swim, or play croquet in the afternoon. For larger parties, there's also a four-bedroom, three-bathroom house (sleeps up to eight) on the property. Kids will have plenty of room to run around and explore.

Kamehameha V Hwy., at mile marker 25. Reservations c/o P.O. Box 1889, Kaunakakai, HI 96748. ✆ **808/558-8109.** Fax 808/558-8100. www.puuohoku.com. 2 units. $140 double. Extra person $20. $75 cleaning fee. 2-night minimum. MC, V. *In room:* TV/VCR (available on request), kitchen.

Dunbar Beachfront Cottages ★★ ☺ This is one of the most peaceful, comfortable, and elegant properties on Molokai's East End, and the setting is simply stunning. Each of these two green-and-white plantation-style cottages sits on its own secluded beach (good for swimming)—you'll feel like you're on your own private island. Both cottages have ceiling fans, comfortable tropical furniture, large furnished decks (perfect for whale-watching in winter), and views of Maui, Lanai, and Kahoolawe across the channel.

Kamehameha V Hwy., past mile marker 18. Reservations c/o Matt and Genesis Dunbar, HC01 Box 738, Kaunakakai, HI 96748. ✆ **800/673-0520** or 808/558-8153. www.molokai-beach front-cottages.com. 2 units. $170 cottage (sleeps up to 4). One-time $75 cleaning fee. 3-night minimum. No credit cards. *In room:* TV, kitchen.

WHERE TO DINE

The good news is that you won't find long lines at overbooked, self-important restaurants. But when it comes to dining, Molokai is not nirvana.

A lot of people like it that way and acknowledge that the island's character is unchangeably rugged and natural. Molokai has retained its glacial pace of change. Its culinary offerings are dominated by mom-and-pop eateries, most of them fast-food or takeout places, and many of them with a home-cooked touch. Personally, I like the unpretentiousness of Molokai; it's an oasis in a state where plastic aloha abounds. But sybarites, foodies, and pampered oenophiles had best lower their expectations upon arrival, or turn around and leave the island's natural beauty to nature lovers.

You'll even find a certain defiant stance against the trappings of modernity. Although some of the best produce in Hawaii is grown on this island, you're not likely to find much of it served in its restaurants, other than in the takeout items at Outpost Natural Foods, or at the Molokai Pizza Cafe (one of the most pleasing eateries on the island) and the Hotel Molokai. The rest of the time, content yourself with ethnic or diner fare—or by cooking for yourself. The many visitors who stay in condos find that it doesn't take long to sniff out the best sources of produce, groceries, and fresh fish to fire up at home when the island's other dining options are exhausted. The "Edibles" sections under "Shopping" (later in this chapter) will point you to the places where you can pick up foodstuffs for your own Island-style feast.

Molokai's restaurants are inexpensive or moderately priced, and several of them do not accept credit cards. Regardless of where you eat, you certainly won't have to dress up. In most cases, I've listed just the town rather than the street address because, as you'll see, street addresses are as meaningless on this island as fancy cars and sequins. Reservations are not accepted unless otherwise noted.

Note: You'll find the restaurants reviewed in this chapter on the "Where to Stay & Dine on Molokai" map (p. 577).

Kaunakakai

INEXPENSIVE

Hotel Molokai Hula Shores ★ AMERICAN/ISLAND   Set on the ocean, with a view of Lanai, torches flickering under palm trees, and tiny fairy lights lining the room and the neighboring pool area, the Hotel Molokai's dining room evokes the romance of a South Seas fantasy. It's a casual room and, since its 1999 reopening, provides the only nightlife in Kaunakakai (see "Molokai After Dark," p. 604) and the most pleasing ambience on the island. Lunch choices consist of the basics; most promising are salads and sandwiches, from roast beef to grilled mahimahi. As the sun sets and the torches are lit for dinner, the menu turns to heavier meats, ribs, fish, and pasta. Try the fresh catch, kalbi ribs, barbecued pork ribs and shrimp plate, New York steak, or lip-smacking coconut shrimp. Temper your expectations of culinary excellence, and you're sure to enjoy a pleasing dinner in an atmosphere that's unequaled on the island.

On Kamehameha V Hwy. © **808/553-5347**. Reservations recommended for dinner. Main courses $9–$15 lunch, $15–$25 dinner. AE, DC, MC, V. Daily 7am–2pm and 6–9pm. Bar until 10:30pm.

Kamoi Snack-N-Go ICE CREAM/SNACKS   The Kamoi specialty: sweets and icy treats. Ice cream made by Dave's on Oahu comes in flavors such as green tea, litchi sherbet, *ube* (made from Okinawan sweet potato), haupia, mango, and many others. Lines form for the cones, shakes, sundaes, and popular Icee floats served at this tiny snack shop. If the ice cream doesn't tempt you, browse the aisles full of candies. It's takeout only (no tables).

In Kamoi Professional Center. © **808/553-3742**. Ice cream $2.25–$3.75; sundaes $4–$5. MC, V. Mon–Fri 11am–9pm; Sat 9am–9pm; Sun noon–9pm.

Kanemitsu's Bakery & Restaurant ★ BAKERY/DELI   Morning, noon, and night, this local legend fills the Kaunakakai air with the sweet smells of baking. Taro lavosh is the hot seller, joining Molokai bread—developed in 1935 in a cast-iron, kiawe-fired oven—as a Kanemitsu signature. Flavors range from apricot-pineapple to coconut or strawberry, but the white, wheat, cheese, sweet, and onion-cheese breads are classics. The bread mixes offer a way to take Molokai home. In the adjoining coffee shop/deli, the hamburgers and egg-salad sandwiches are popular and cheap.

Kanemitsu's has a life after dark, too. Whenever anyone on Molokai mentions "hot bread," he's talking about the hot-bread run at Kanemitsu's, the surreal late-night ritual for die-hard bread lovers. Those in the know line up at the bakery's back door beginning at 10pm, when the bread is whisked hot out of the oven and into waiting hands. You can order your fresh bread with butter, jelly, cinnamon, or cream cheese, and the bakers will cut the hot loaves down the middle and slather on the works so it melts in the bread. The cream cheese and jelly bread makes a fine substitute for dessert.

79 Ala Malama St. © **808/553-5855**. Most items less than $5.50. AE, MC, V. Restaurant Wed–Mon 5:30am–noon; bakery Wed–Mon 5:30am–5pm.

Molokai Drive-Inn AMERICAN/TAKEOUT   It is a greasy spoon, but it's one of the rare drive-up places with fresh akule (mackerel) and ahi (when available), plus fried saimin at budget-friendly prices. The honey-dipped fried chicken is a favorite among residents, who also come here for the floats, shakes, and other artery-clogging choices. But don't expect much in terms of ambience: This is a fast-food takeout counter, and it doesn't pretend to be otherwise.

Kaunakakai. ☏ **808/553-5655.** Most items under $11. No credit cards. Mon–Thurs 6am–10pm; Fri–Sun 6:30am–10:30pm.

Molokai Pizza Cafe ★ PIZZA   This gathering place serves excellent pizzas and sandwiches that have made it a Kaunakakai staple as well as one of my favorite eateries on the island. The best sellers are the Molokai (pepperoni and cheese), the Big Island (pepperoni, ham, mushroom, Italian sausage, bacon, and vegetables), and the Molokini (plain cheese slices). My personal fave is the vegetarian Maui pizza. Pasta, sandwiches, and new "gourmet" hamburgers on home-made buns round out the menu. Sunday is prime-rib day; Wednesday is Mexican. Coin-operated cars and a toy airplane follow the children's theme, but adults should feel equally at home with the very popular barbecued baby back ribs and the fresh-fish dinners.

At the Kahua Center, on the old Wharf Rd. ☏ **808/553-3288.** Large pizzas $17–$29. No credit cards. Sun 11am–10pm; Mon–Thurs 10am–10pm; Fri–Sat 10am–11pm.

Outpost Natural Foods ★ VEGETARIAN   The freshest food on the island is served at the counter of this health food store, around the corner from the main drag on the ocean side of Kaunakakai town. The tiny store abounds in Molokai papayas, bananas, herbs, potatoes, watermelon, and other local produce. The salads, burritos, tempeh sandwiches, and mock chicken, turkey, and meatloaf served at the lunch counter are testament to the fact that vegetarian food need not be boring. A must for health-conscious diners and shoppers.

70 Makaena Place. ☏ **808/553-3377.** Entrees $6–$10. AE, DISC, MC, V. Mon–Thurs 9am–6pm; Fri 9am–4pm; Sun 10am–5pm.

Paddlers' Inn AMERICAN/LOCAL   If you want to meet local residents, come to this friendly diner. Breakfast features specials like homemade sausage sauce and biscuits. At lunch, it's filled with hungry folks grinding on ⅓-pound all-beef burgers or plate lunches. Vegetarians will find a few items here, but not a lot. Call ahead for dinner specials; at press time, Wednesday evenings (5–7pm) featured a New York steak and shrimp special for just $17. Later on, the small cafe becomes a hot spot for Molokai entertainment (p. 604).

10 Mohala St. ☏ **808/553-5256.** Breakfast $5–$12; lunch $8–$15; dinner entrees $10–$30. AE, DC, DISC, MC, V. Daily 7am–9pm. Bar until 11pm.

Sundown Deli ★ DELI   From "gourmet saimin" to spinach pie, Sundown's offerings are home-cooked and healthful, with daily specials that include vegetarian lasagna and club sandwiches. Grab a sandwich (smoked turkey, chicken salad) or salad (Caesar, Oriental, stuffed tomato) or the daily soup (clam chowder, Portuguese bean). T-shirts and snacks are also sold in this tiny cafe, but most of the business is takeout. They are now doing picnic box lunches that you can take with you.

145 Puali St. (across the street from Veteran's Memorial Park). ☏ **808/553-3713.** Sandwiches, soups, and salads $3.95–$7.50. AE, MC, V. Mon–Fri 7:30am–3:30pm.

The East End

INEXPENSIVE

Mana'e Goods and Grindz ★ AMERICAN   Formerly the Neighborhood Store, this place has a new name, but it's still the same quick-stop market/lunch counter. It's nothing fancy, and that's what I love about it. Near mile marker 16 in the Pukoo area en route to the East End, this tiny store appears like a mirage, complete with a large parking area and picnic tables. The place serves omelets, Portuguese sausage, and other breakfast specials (brunch is very popular); it then segues into sandwiches, salads, and varied lunch offerings, served on paper plates with plastic utensils. Favorites include the mahimahi plate lunch, and the chicken katsu. There are daily specials, ethnic dishes, like the Mexican plate, and some vegetarian options, as well as a killer veggie burger, saimin, and legendary desserts. Made-on-Maui Roselani ice cream is a featured attraction in the store. A Molokai treasure, this is the only grocery store on the East End (see the shopping review on p. 603).

Pukoo. ℂ **808/558-8498.** Most items less than $10. MC, V. Store: Mon–Fri 6:30am–6pm, Sat–Sun 6:30am–5pm; food service: Mon–Tues and Thurs–Fri 9am–5pm, Wed 9am–3pm, Sat–Sun 7am–5pm.

BEACHES

With imposing sea cliffs on one side and lazy fish ponds on the other, Molokai has little room for beaches along its 106-mile coast. Still, a big gold-sand beach flourishes on the West End, and you'll find tiny pocket beaches on the East End. The emptiness of Molokai's beaches is both a blessing and a curse: The seclusion means no lifeguards on any of the beaches. To locate them, see the "Molokai" map (p. 571).

One Alii Beach Park.

Kepuhi Beach.

Kaunakakai
ONE ALII BEACH PARK

This thin strip of sand, once reserved for the *alii* (chiefs), is the oldest public beach park on Molokai. You'll find One Alii Beach Park (*One* is pronounced "*o*-nay," not "won") by a coconut grove on the outskirts of Kaunakakai. Safe for swimmers of all ages and abilities, it's often crowded with families on weekends, but it can be all yours on weekdays. Facilities include outdoor showers, restrooms, and free parking.

The West End
KEPUHI BEACH

Sunbathers like this picturesque golden strand's semiprivate grassy dunes—they're seldom, if ever, crowded. Beachcombers often find what they're looking for here, but swimmers have to dodge lava rocks and risk riptides. There are no facilities or lifeguards, but cold drinks and restrooms are handy at the resort.

PAPOHAKU BEACH ★★

Nearly 3 miles long and 300 feet wide, gold-sand Papohaku Beach is one of the biggest in Hawaii (17-mile-long Polihale Beach on Kauai is the biggest). It's great for walking, beachcombing, picnics, and sunset watching year-round. The big surf and riptides make swimming risky except in summer, when the waters are calmer. Go early in the day, when the tropic sun is less fierce and the winds are calm. The beach is so vast that you may never see another soul. Facilities include outdoor showers, restrooms, picnic grounds, and free parking.

Papohaku Beach.

Halawa Beach Park.

Murphy Beach Park (Kumimi Beach Park).

The East End

HALAWA BEACH PARK ★

At the foot of scenic Halawa Valley is this beautiful black-sand beach with a palm-fringed lagoon, a wave-lashed island offshore, and a distant view of the West Maui Mountains across the Pailolo Channel. The swimming is safe in the shallows close to shore, but where the waterfall stream meets the sea, the ocean is often murky and unnerving. A winter swell creases the mouth of Halawa Valley on the north side of the bay and attracts a crowd of local surfers. Facilities are minimal; bring your own water. To get here, take King Kamehameha V Highway (Hwy. 450) east to the end.

MURPHY BEACH PARK (KUMIMI BEACH PARK)

In 1970, the Molokai Jaycees wanted to create a sandy beach park with a good swimming area for the children of the East End. They chose a section known as Kumimi Beach, which was owned by the Pu'u o Hoku Ranch. The beach was a dump—literally. The ranch owner, George Murphy, gave his permission to use the site as a park, and the Jaycees cleaned it up and built three small pavilions, with picnic tables and barbecue grills. Officially, the park is called the George Murphy Beach Park (or just Murphy Beach Park), but some old-timers still call it Kumimi Beach, and, just to make things really confusing, some people call it Jaycees Park.

It's a small park shaded by ironwood trees that line a white-sand beach. This is generally a very safe swimming area, and on calm days snorkeling and diving are great outside the reef. Fishermen also come here to look for papio and other Island fish.

SANDY BEACH ★

Molokai's most popular swimming beach—ideal for families with small kids—is a roadside pocket of gold sand protected by a reef, with a great view of Maui and Lanai. You'll find it off the King Kamehameha V Highway (Hwy. 450) at mile marker 20. There are no facilities—just you, the sun, the sand, and the surf.

Sandy Beach.

WATERSPORTS

Molokai Fish & Dive, Kaunakakai (© **808/553-5926;** www.molokaifishand dive.com), rents snorkeling gear, fishing gear, and even ice chests. This is also a hot spot for fishing news and tips on what's running where.

For general advice on the activities listed below, see "Special-Interest Trips," in chapter 3.

Body Boarding (Boogie Boarding) & Bodysurfing

Molokai has only three beaches that offer ridable waves for body boarding and bodysurfing: Papohaku, Kepuhi, and Halawa. Even these beaches are only for experienced bodysurfers, due to the strength of the rip currents and under-tows. You can rent boogie boards with fins for just $5 a day or $20 a week at **Molokai Outdoors Activities** (© **877/553-4477** or 808/553-4477; www. molokai-outdoors.com).

Ocean Kayaking

During the summer, when the waters on the north shore are calm, Molokai offers some of the most spectacular kayaking in Hawaii. However, most of Molokai is for the experienced kayaker only. You must be adept in paddling through open ocean swells and rough waves. **Molokai Outdoors Activities** (© **877/553-4477** or 808/553-4477; www.molokai-outdoors.com) has a "downwinder" tour: See 6 miles of Molokai's reef as you paddle downwind ($89, plus $10 for lunch). It also rents kayaks starting at $26 a day.

Scuba Diving

Want to see turtles or manta rays up close? How about sharks? Molokai resident Bill Kapuni has been diving the waters around the island his entire life; he'll be

MOLOKAI'S BEST snorkel spots

Most Molokai beaches are too dangerous for snorkeling in winter, when big waves and strong currents are generated by storms that sweep down from Alaska. From mid-September to April, stick to Murphy Beach Park (also known as Kumimi Beach Park) on the East End. In summer, roughly May to mid-September, the Pacific Ocean turns into a flat lake, and the whole west coast of Molokai opens up for snorkeling. Mike Holmes, of Molokai Ranch & Fun Hogs Hawaii, says the best spots are as follows:

Kawaikiunui, Ilio Point & Pohaku Moiliili (West End): These are all special places seldom seen by even those who live on Molokai. You can reach Kawaikiunui and Pohaku Moiliili on foot after a long, hot, dusty ride in a four-wheel-drive vehicle, but it's much easier and quicker to go by sea. See above for places to rent a kayak and get advice. It's about 2 miles as the crow flies from Pohaku Moiliili to Ilio Point.

Kapukahehu (Dixie Maru) Beach (West End): This gold-sand family beach is well protected, and the reef is close and shallow. The name Dixie Maru comes from a

1920s Japanese fishing boat stranded off the rocky shore. One of the Molokai Ranch cowboys hung the wrecked boat's nameplate on a gate by Kapukahehu Beach, and the name stuck. To get here, take Kaluakoi Road to the end of the pavement, and then follow the footpath 300 feet to the beach.

Murphy (Kumimi) Beach Park ★ (East End): This beach is located between mile markers 20 and 21, off Kamehameha V Highway. The reef here is easily reachable, and the waters are calm year-round.

happy to show you whatever you're brave enough to encounter. You can book him through **Molokai Fish & Dive** (☎ 808/553-5926; www.molokaifishanddive.com), which offers scuba diving trips from $135 (two-tank dive) to $275 (three-tank dive).

Snorkeling

When the waters are calm, Molokai offers excellent snorkeling; you'll see a wide range of butterflyfish, tangs, and angelfish. Good snorkeling can be found—when conditions are right—at many of Molokai's beaches (see "Molokai's Best Snorkel Spots," below). **Molokai Fish & Dive,** Kaunakakai (☎ 808/553-5926; www.molokaifishanddive.com), rents mask, snorkel, and fins for $10 for 24 hours.

For snorkeling tours on a boat, Walter Naki of **Molokai Action Adventures** (☎ 808/558-8184) offers leisurely snorkeling, diving, and swimming trips in his 21-foot Boston whaler for $50 per person for a 4- to 6-hour custom tour.

Sport Fishing

Molokai's waters can provide prime sporting opportunities, whether you're looking for big-game sport fishing or bottom fishing. I recommend going with Captain Clay of **Hallelujah Hou Fishing** (☎ 808/336-1870; www.hallelujahhoufishing.com), who leads light-tackle guided fishing trips on his 24-foot power catamaran. The price is $395 to $495 for up to four adults for a half-day. He provides all tackle and bottled water; you bring the sunscreen. If you catch something, he'll even filet it for dinner. *A warning:* There is no "head" (toilet) on the boat.

When customers are scarce, Capt. Joe Reich goes commercial fishing, so he always knows where the fish are biting. He runs **Alyce C Sportfishing,** out of Kaunakakai Harbor (© **808/558-8377;** ace@aloha.net). A full day for up to six people is $550, three-quarters of a day is $500, and half a day is $450. You can usually persuade him to take a whale-watching cruise during the winter months.

For fly-fishing or light-tackle reef-fish trolling, contact Walter Naki at **Molokai Action Adventures** (© **808/558-8184**). A full-day trip in his 21-foot Boston whaler, for up to four people, goes for $400.

Molokai Fish & Dive, Kaunakakai (© **808/553-5926;** www.molokaifish anddive.com), has fishing tours for $400 for a half-day, $600 for a full day.

For deep-sea fishing, contact **Fun Hogs Hawaii,** which books through Molokai Outdoors Activities (see below). Excursions for six passengers on a fully equipped, 27-foot sport fishing vessel cost $365 for six passengers for 4 hours, $417 for 6 hours, and $521 for 8 hours.

Surfing

Depending on the time of year and the wave conditions, Molokai can offer some great surfing for the beginner as well as the expert. **Molokai Outdoors Activities** (© **877/553-4477** or 808/553-4477; www.molokai-outdoors.com) not only knows where the waves are but rents soft surfboards for $19 a day. Good surfing spots include Kaunakakai Wharf in town, Hale O Lono Beach and Papohaku Beach on the West End, and Halawa Beach on the East End.

HIKING & CAMPING
Hiking
THE PEPEOPAE TRAIL ★★

Molokai's most awesome hike is the Pepeopae Trail, which takes you back a few million years. On the cloud-draped trail (actually a boardwalk across the bog), you'll see mosses, sedges, native violets, knee-high ancient ohia, and lichens that evolved in total isolation over eons. Eerie intermittent mists blowing in and out will give you an idea of this island at its creation.

The narrow boardwalk, built by volunteers, protects the bog and keeps you out of the primal ooze. Don't venture off it; you could damage this fragile environment or get lost. The 3-mile round-trip takes about 90 minutes to hike—but first you have to drive about 20 miles from Kaunakakai, deep into the Molokai Forest Reserve on a four-wheel-drive road. Plan a full day for this outing. Better yet, go on a guided nature hike with the **Nature Conservancy of Hawaii,** which guards this unusual ecosystem. For information, write to the Nature Conservancy at 1116 Smith St., Ste. 201, Honolulu, HI 96817. No permit is required for this easy hike. Call ahead (© **808/553-5236;** www.nature.org) to check on the condition of the ungraded, red-dirt road that leads to the trail head and to let people know that you'll be up here. *Warning:* Don't try this with a regular rental car.

To get here, take Hwy. 460 west from Kaunakakai for 3½ miles and turn right before the Maunawainui Bridge onto the unmarked Molokai Forest Reserve Road (sorry, there aren't any road signs). The pavement ends at the cemetery; continue on the dirt road. After about 2 to 2½ miles, you'll see a sign telling you that you are now in the Molokai Forest Reserve. At the Waikolu Lookout and picnic area, which is just over 9 miles on the Molokai Forest Reserve Road, sign in at the box near the entrance. Continue on the road for another 5 miles to a fork in the road with the sign PUU KOLEKOLE pointing to the right side of the fork. Do not turn right; instead, continue straight at the fork, which leads to the clearly marked trail head. The drive will take about 45 minutes.

THE TRAIL TO KALAUPAPA ★★

This hike to the site of Molokai's famous leper colony is like going down a switch-back staircase with what seems like a million steps. You don't always see the breathtaking view because you're too busy watching your step. It's easier going down (surprise!)—in about an hour, you'll go 2½ miles, from 2,000 feet to sea level. The trip up sometimes takes twice as long. The trail head starts on the mauka (inland) side of Hwy. 470, just past the Mule Barn. Check in here at 7:30am, get a permit, and go before the mule train departs. You must be 16 or older (it's an old state law that kept kids out of the leper colony) and should be in good shape. Wear good hiking boots or sneakers.

THE WEST END

Molokai Outdoors Activities (© **877/553-4477** or 808/553-4477; www.molokai-outdoors.com) offers an all-day (6- to 8-hr.) Halawa Cultural Hike full of historical information on East Molokai. The hike is rated intermediate to advanced, with a distance of 2.2 miles. It has two river crossings and some rocky areas along the trails, with possible fallen trees after a storm. The cost is $78 per person and includes a picnic lunch. **Molokai Fish & Dive** (© **808/553-5926;** www.molokaifishanddive.com) offers a hike into Halawa Valley (p. 600) for $75.

Camping

Bring your own camping equipment, as none is available for rent on the island.

AT THE BEACH

One of the best year-round places to camp on Molokai is **Papohaku Beach Park ★**, on the island's West End. This drive-up seaside site makes a great get-away. Facilities include restrooms, drinking water, outdoor showers, barbecue grills, and picnic tables. Groceries and gas are available in Maunaloa, 6 miles away. Kaluakoi Resort is a mile away. Get camping permits by contacting **Maui County Parks Department,** P.O. Box 526, Kaunakakai, HI 96748 (© **808/553-3204;** www.co.maui.hi.us). Camping is limited to 3 days, but if nobody else has applied, the time limit is waived. The cost is $3 a person per night, Monday to Thursday, and $8 Friday to Sunday.

IN AN IRONWOOD FOREST

At the end of Hwy. 470 is the 234-acre piney woods known as **Palaau State Park ★★**, home to the Kalaupapa Lookout (the best vantage point for seeing the historic leper colony if you're not hiking or riding a mule in). It's airy and cool in the park's ironwood forest, where many love to camp at the designated state campground. Camping fees for Hawaii State Parks are $5 per campsite per night, and you'll need a permit from the **State Division of Parks** (© **808/567-6618;** www.hawaiistateparks.org/camping/maui.cfm). For more on the park, see p. 594.

FROMMER'S FAVORITE molokai EXPERIENCES

Riding a Mule into a Leper Colony: Don't pass up the opportunity to see this hauntingly beautiful peninsula. **Buzzy Sproat's** mules (p. 596) go up and down the 3-mile Kalaupapa Trail to Molokai's famous leper colony. The views are breathtaking: You'll see the world's highest sea cliffs (over 300 stories tall) and waterfalls plunging thousands of feet into the ocean. If you're afraid of heights, catch the views from the Kalaupapa Lookout.

Venturing into the Garden of Eden: Drive the 30 miles along Molokai's East End. Take your time. Stop to smell the flowers and pick guavas by the side of the road. Pull over for a swim. Wave at every car you pass and every person you see. At the end of the road, stand on the beach at Halawa Valley and see Hawaii as it must have looked in A.D. 650, when the first people arrived on the islands.

Celebrating the Ancient Hula: Hula is the heartbeat of Hawaiian culture, and Molokai is its birthplace. Although most visitors to Hawaii never get to experience the real thing, it's possible to see it here—once a year, on the third Saturday in May, when Molokai celebrates the birth of the hula at its **Ka Hula Piko Festival.** The daylong affair includes dance,

music, food, and crafts. For details, contact the Moloka`i Visitor Association (© **800/800-6367** or 808/553-3876; www.molokai-hawaii.com).

Strolling the Sands at Papohaku: Go early, when the tropical sun isn't so fierce, and stroll this 3-mile stretch of unspoiled golden sand on Molokai's West End. It's one of the longest beaches in Hawaii. The big surf and riptides make swimming somewhat risky, but Papohaku is perfect for walking, beachcombing, and, in the evening, sunset watching.

Traveling Back in Time on the Pepeopae Trail: This awesome hike takes you through the **Molokai Forest Reserve** (p. 588) and back a few million years in time. Along the misty trail (actually a boardwalk across the bog), expect close encounters of the botanical kind: mosses, sedges, violets, lichens, and knee-high ancient ohia.

Soaking in the Warm Waters off Sandy Beach: On the East End, about 20 miles outside Kaunakakai—just before the road starts to climb to Halawa Valley—lies a small pocket of white sand known as Sandy Beach. Submerging yourself here in the warm, calm waters (an outer reef protects the cove) is a sensuous experience par excellence.

GOLF & OTHER OUTDOOR ACTIVITIES

Golf

Golfing on Molokai is challenging and fun, tee times are open, and the rates are lower than your score will be. **Ironwood Hills Golf Course,** off Kalae Highway (© **808/567-6000**), is located just before the Molokai Mule Ride Mule

Snorkeling among Clouds of Butterfly-fish: The calm waters off Murphy (Kumimi) Beach, on the East End, are perfect for snorkelers. Just don your gear and head to the reef, where you'll find lots of exotic tropical fish, including long-nosed butterflyfish, saddle wrasses, and convict tangs.

Kayaking along the North Shore: This is the Hawaii of your dreams: waterfalls thundering down sheer cliffs, remote sand beaches, miles of tropical vegetation, and the wind whispering in your ear. The best times to go are late March and early April, or in summer, especially August to September, when the normally galloping ocean lies down flat.

Watching the Sunset from a Coconut Grove: Kapuaiwa Coconut Grove/Kiowea Park (p. 592), off Maunaloa Highway (Hwy. 460), is a perfect place to watch the sunset. The sky behind the coconut trees fills with a kaleidoscope of colors as the sun sinks into the Pacific. Be careful where you sit, though: Falling coconuts could have you seeing stars well before dusk.

Sampling the Local Brew: Saunter up to the Espresso Bar at the **Coffees of Hawaii Plantation Store** (p. 602), in Kualapuu, for a fresh cup of java made from beans that were grown, processed, and packed on this 450-acre plantation. While you sip, survey the vast collection of native crafts.

Tasting Aloha at a Macadamia Nut Farm: It could be the owner, Tuddie Purdy, and his friendly disposition that make the macadamia nuts here taste so good. Or it could be his years of practice in growing, harvesting, and shelling them on his 1½-acre farm. Either way, Purdy produces a perfect crop. See how he does it on a short, free tour of **Purdy's All-Natural Macadamia Nut Farm** (p. 592), in Hoolehua, just a nut's throw from the airport.

Talking Story with the Locals: The number-one favorite pastime of most islanders is "talking story," or exchanging experiences and knowledge. You can probably find residents more than willing to share their wisdom with you while fishing from the wharf at Kaunakakai, hanging out at **Molokai Fish & Dive** (p. 601), or having coffee at any of the island's restaurants.

Posting a Nut: Why send a picturesque postcard to your friends and family back home when you can send a coconut? The **Hoolehua Post Office** (p. 592) will supply the coconuts if you'll supply the postage fee of $9 to $13.

Barn, on the road to the Lookout. Built in 1929 by Del Monte Plantation for its executives, it's one of the oldest courses in the state. This unusual course, which sits in the cool air at 1,200 feet, delights with its rich foliage, open fairways, and spectacular views of the rest of the island. *Tip:* After teeing off on the 6th hole, just take whatever clubs you need in order to finish playing the hole and a driver for the 7th hole, and park your bag under a tree. The climb to the 7th hole is steep—you'll be glad that you're carrying only a few clubs. Greens fees are $31 for 18 holes.

Biking

Molokai is a great place to see by bicycle. The roads are not very busy, and there are great places to pull off the road and take a quick dip. **Molokai Bicycle,** 80 Mohala St., Kaunakakai (© 808/553-3931; www.bikehawaii.com/molokaibi cycle), offers bike rentals for $18 a day, or $80 a week, including helmet and lock. Owner Phillip Kikukawa is a schoolteacher, so call him in late afternoon when he's in the shop.

Tennis

The only two courts on Molokai are located at the **Mitchell Pauole Center,** in Kaunakakai (© 808/553-5141). Both are lit for night play and are available free on a first-come, first-served basis, with a 45-minute time limit if someone is waiting. You can also rent tennis rackets ($5 a day, $24 a week) and balls ($3 a day, $12 a week) from **Molokai Outdoors Activities** (© 877/553-4477 or 808/553-4477; www.molokai-outdoors.com).

SEEING THE SIGHTS

Note: You'll find the following attractions on the "Molokai" map (p. 571).

In & Around Kaunakakai

Kapuaiwa Coconut Grove/Kiowea Park ★ ☺   This royal grove—1,000 coconut trees on 10 acres planted in 1863 by the island's high chief Kapuaiwa (later King Kamehameha V)—is a major roadside attraction. The shoreline park is a favorite subject of sunset photographers and visitors, who delight in a hand-lettered sign that warns: DANGER: FALLING COCONUTS. In its backyard, across the highway, stands Church Row: seven churches, each a different denomination— clear evidence of the missionary impact on Hawaii.

Along Maunaloa Hwy. (Hwy. 460), 2 miles west of Kaunakakai.

Post-A-Nut ★   The postmaster on Molokai will help you say "Aloha" with a Molokai coconut. Just write a message on the coconut with a felt-tip pen, and she'll send it via U.S. mail. Coconuts are free, but postage averages $9 to $13 for a mainland-bound coconut.

Hoolehua Post Office, Puu Peelua Ave. (Hwy. 480), near Maunaloa Hwy. (Hwy. 460). © **808/567-6144.** Mon–Fri 8:30am–noon and 12:30–4pm.

Purdy's All-Natural Macadamia Nut Farm (Na Hua O'Ka Aina) ★ 🎁   The Purdys have made buying macadamia nuts an entertainment event, offering tours of the homestead and giving lively demonstrations of nutshell cracking in the shade of their towering trees. The tour of the 70-year-old nut farm explains the growth, bearing, harvesting, and shelling processes.

Lihi Pali Ave. (behind Molokai High School), Hoolehua. © **808/567-6601.** www.molokai-aloha. com/macnuts. Free admission. Mon–Fri 9:30am–3:30pm; Sat 10am–2pm. Closed on holidays.

The North Coast

Even if you don't get a chance to see Hawaii's most dramatic coast in its entirety— not many people do—you shouldn't miss the opportunity to glimpse it from the **Kalaupapa Lookout,** at Palaau State Park. On the way, there are a few diversions (arranged here in geographical order).

Coffees of Hawaii.

Kalaupapa Lookout.

EN ROUTE TO THE NORTH COAST

Coffees of Hawaii The defunct Del Monte pineapple town of Kualapuu is rising again—only this time, coffee is the catch, not pineapple. Located in the cool foothills, Coffees of Hawaii has planted coffee beans on 600 acres of former pineapple land. The plantation irrigates the plants with a high-tech, continuous water-and-fertilizer drip system. You can see it all on the self-guided walking tour or the Morning Espresso Tour, which is led by a guide from the plantation and gives you a tour of the sorting facility and processing procedures. The less physically motivated should try the Mule Drawn Wagon tour, great for a family. The 2-hour tour is led by a guide and two mules (Moana and Leila or Lilo and Loke) through the coffee fields and around the reservoir. The Plantation Store sells arts and crafts from Molokai. Stop by the Espresso Bar for a Mocha Mama, an intoxicating blend of coffee, ice cream, and chocolate that will keep you going all day—maybe even all night.

1630 Farrington Ave. (near the junction of Hwy. 470), Kualapuu. © **877/322-FARM** (3276) or 808/567-9490, ext. 26. www.coffeesofhawaii.com/plantations/molokai. Mon–Fri 7am–5pm; Sat 8am–8pm; Sun 8am–5pm. Self-guided tour free. Morning Espresso Tour Mon–Fri 11am; $25 adults, $10 kids 5–10, free for kids 4 and under. Mule Drawn Wagon Tour Tues and Fri 8am and 1pm; $40 adults, $12 kids 5–10, free for kids 4 and under.

Molokai Museum and Cultural Center En route to the California Gold Rush in 1849, Rudolph W. Meyer (a German professor) came to Molokai, married the high chieftess Kalama, and began to operate a small sugar plantation near his home. Now on the National Register of Historic Places, this restored 1878 sugar mill, with its century-old steam engine, mule-driven cane crusher, copper clarifiers, and redwood evaporating pan (all in working order), is the last of its kind in Hawaii. The mill also houses a museum that traces the history of sugar growing on Molokai and has special events, such as wine tastings, taro festivals, an annual music festival, and occasional classes in ukulele making, loom weaving, and sewing. Call for a schedule.

Meyer Sugar Mill, Hwy. 470 (just after the turnoff for the Ironwood Hills Golf Course and 2 miles below Kalaupapa Overlook), Kalae. © **808/567-6436.** Admission $3.50 adults, $1 children and students. Mon–Sat 10am–2pm.

Flying a Kite (p. 603): Not only can you get a guaranteed-to-fly kite at the **Big Wind Kite Factory** (✆ **808/552-2634**) in Maunaloa (pictured here), but kite designer Jonathan Socher also offers free kite-flying classes to kids, who'll learn how to make their kites soar, swoop, and, most important, stay in the air for more than 5 minutes.

Spending the Day at Murphy (Kumimi) Beach Park (p. 587): Just beyond Waialua on the East End is this small wayside park that's perfect for kids. You'll find safe swimming conditions, plenty of shade from the ironwood trees, and small pavilions with picnic tables and barbecue grills.

Palaau State Park ★   This 234-acre piney-woods park, 8 miles out of Kaunakakai, doesn't look like much until you get out of the car and take a hike, which literally puts you between a rock and a hard place. Go right, and you end up on the edge of Molokai's magnificent sea cliffs, with its panoramic view of the well-known Kalaupapa leper colony; go left, and you come face to face with a stone phallus.

If you have no plans to scale the cliffs by mule or on foot (see "Hiking & Camping," p. 588), the **Kalaupapa Lookout ★★★** is the only place from which to see the former place of exile. The trail is marked, and historic photos and interpretive signs will explain what you're seeing.

It's airy and cool in the ironwood forest, where camping is free at the designated state campground. You'll need a permit from the **State Division of Parks** (✆ **808/567-6618;** www.hawaiistateparks.org/camping/maui.cfm). Not many people seem to camp here, perhaps because of the legend associated with the

Phallic Rock.

Phallic Rock ★. Six feet high and pointed at an angle that means business, Molokai's famous Phallic Rock is a legendary fertility tool—according to Hawaiian legend, a woman who wishes to become pregnant need only spend the night near the rock and . . . *voilà!*

Phallic Rock is at the end of a well-worn uphill path that passes an ironwood grove and several other rocks that vaguely resemble sexual body parts. No mistaking the big guy, though. It supposedly belonged to

Nanahoa, a demigod who quarreled with his wife, Kawahuna, over a pretty girl. In the tussle, Kawahuna was thrown over the cliff, and both husband and wife were turned to stone. Of all the phallic rocks in Hawaii and the Pacific, this is the one to see. It's featured on a postcard with a tiny, awestruck Japanese woman standing next to it.

At the end of Hwy. 470.

THE LEGACY OF FATHER DAMIEN: KALAUPAPA NATIONAL HISTORICAL PARK ★★★

Kalaupapa, an old tongue of lava that sticks out to form a peninsula, became infamous because of man's inhumanity to victims of a formerly incurable contagious disease.

King Kamehameha V sent the first lepers—nine men and three women—into exile on January 6, 1866. By 1874, more than 11,000 lepers had been dispatched to die in one of the world's most beautiful—and lonely—places. They called it Kalaupapa, "The Place of the Living Dead."

Leprosy is actually one of the world's least contagious diseases, transmitted only by direct, repetitive contact over a long period. It's caused by a bacterium, *Mycobacterium leprae,* that attacks the nerves, skin, and eyes, and is found mainly, but not exclusively, in tropical regions. American scientists found a cure for the disease in the 1940s.

Before science intervened, there was Father Damien. Born to wealth in Belgium, Joseph de Veuster traded a life of excess for exile among lepers, devoting himself to caring for the afflicted at Kalaupapa. Horrified by the conditions in the leper colony, Father Damien worked at Kalaupapa for 11 years, building houses, schools, and churches, and giving hope to his patients. He died on April 15, 1889, in Kalaupapa, of leprosy. He was 49.

A hero nominated·for Catholic sainthood, Father Damien is buried not in his tomb next to Molokai's St. Philomena Church, but in his native Belgium. Well, most of him anyway. His hand was recently returned to Molokai and was reinterred at Kalaupapa as a relic of his martyrdom.

This small peninsula, at the base of ramparts that rise like temples against the Pacific, is the final resting place of possibly more than 11,000 souls. The sand dunes are littered with grave markers, sorted by the religious affiliation—Catholic, Protestant, Buddhist—of those who died here. But so many are buried in unmarked graves that no accurate census of the dead exists.

Kalaupapa is now a national historical park (✆ **808/567-6802;** www.nps. gov/kala) and one of Hawaii's richest archaeological preserves, with sites that date from A.D. 1000. About 60 former patients chose to remain in this tidy village, where statues of angels stand in the yards of the whitewashed houses. The original name for their former affliction, leprosy, was officially banned in Hawaii by the state legislature in 1981. The name used now is "Hansen's disease," for Dr. Gerhard Hansen of Norway, who discovered the bacterium in 1873.

Kalaupapa welcomes visitors who arrive on foot, by mule, or by small plane. Father Damien's St. Philomena Church, built in 1872, is open to visitors, who can see it from a yellow school bus driven by resident tour guide Richard Marks, an ex-seaman and sheriff who survived the disease. You won't be able to roam freely, and you'll be allowed to enter only the museum, the crafts shop, and the church.

Mule Rides to Kalaupapa ★★★   The first turn's a gasp, and it's all downhill from there. You can close your eyes and hold on for dear life, or slip the reins over the pommel and sit back, letting the mule do the walking down the precipitous path to Kalaupapa National Historical Park.

Even if you have only a day to spend on Molokai, spend it on a mule. This is a once-in-a-lifetime ride. The cliffs are taller than a 300-story skyscraper, but Buzzy Sproat's mules go safely up and down the narrow 3-mile trail daily, rain or shine. Starting at the top of the nearly perpendicular ridge (1,600 ft. high), the sure-footed mules step down the muddy trail, pausing often on the 26 switchbacks to calculate their next move—and always, it seems to me, veering a little too close to the edge. Each switchback is numbered; by the time you get to number four, you'll catch your breath, put the mule on cruise control, and begin to enjoy Hawaii's most awesome trail ride.

The mule tours are offered once a day Monday through Saturday; the park is closed on Sunday. Tours start at 8am and last until about 3:30pm. It costs $175 per person for the all-day adventure, which includes the round-trip mule ride, a guided tour of the settlement, a visit to Father Damien's church and tomb, lunch at Kalawao, and souvenirs. Book in advance, as these tours often fill up. To go, you must be at least 16 years old and physically fit, and weigh less than 250 pounds. Contact **Molokai Mule Ride** ★★★, 100 Kalae Hwy., Ste. 104, on Hwy. 470, 5 miles north of Hwy. 460 (𝓒 **800/567-7550** or 808/567-6088, 8am–10pm; www.muleride.com). Advance reservations (at least 2 weeks ahead) are required.

It's possible to see Kalaupapa as a day trip from Honolulu or Maui. Molokai Mule Ride (see above) offers a package from Honolulu that includes pickup at Kalaupapa airport, a tour of the town of Kalaupapa, mule tour, entry permits, Historical Park tour, and a picnic lunch for $319 per person, two-person minimum. If you are flying in from Maui, it might be possible to charter a shuttle to the top of the path down through **Molokai Fish & Dive,** 𝓒 **808/553-5926.**

Father Damien's grave outside St. Philomena Church.

The mule ride to Kalaupapa.

Another option from Maui is to take the ***Molokai Princess* ferry** to Molokai (℡ **800/275-6969** or 808/667-6165; www.mauiprincess.com), where you are met and transported by van to the top of the 1,700-foot sea cliffs. Here you hike down the 3-mile trail to the Kalaupapa National Historic Park; at the park, you are met by Damien Tours and given a van tour of the peninsula. This trip requires hiking down and back up the 1,700-foot cliffs, where you are picked up by the van and returned to the ferry dock for the trip back to Maui. This fabulous experience really should be undertaken only by the physically fit (it will take about an hour hiking down and another 90 min. to hike back up). Because of the ferry schedule, you will have to spend the night on Molokai. Cost for the ferry is $109, plus an additional $277 for transportation from the ferry dock to the top of the sea cliffs and return, tour, and lunch.

The West End

MAUNALOA

In the first and only attempt at urban renewal on Molokai, the 1920s-era pineapple-plantation town of Maunaloa has become a ghost town ever since the Molokai Ranch closed all of its operations in 2008 (including the movie theater, restaurant, lodge, and some shops).

ON THE NORTHWEST SHORE: MOOMOMI DUNES

Undisturbed for centuries, the Moomomi Dunes, on Molokai's northwest shore, are a unique treasure chest of great scientific value. The area may look like just a pile of sand as you fly over on the final approach to Hoolehua Airport, but Moomomi Dunes is much more than that. Archaeologists have found adz quarries, ancient Hawaiian burial sites, and shelter caves; botanists have identified five endangered plant species; and marine biologists are finding evidence that endangered green sea turtles are coming out from the waters once again to lay eggs here. The greatest discovery, however, belongs to Smithsonian Institute ornithologists, who have found bones of prehistoric birds—some of them flightless—that existed nowhere else on earth.

Accessible by jeep trails that thread downhill to the shore, this wild coast is buffeted by strong afternoon breezes. It's hot, dry, and windy, so take water, sunscreen, and a windbreaker. At Kawaaloa Bay, a 20-minute walk to the west, there's a broad golden beach that you can have all to yourself. (***Warning:*** Due to the rough seas, stay out of the water.) Within the dunes, there's a 920-acre preserve accessible via monthly guided nature tours led by the **Nature Conservancy of Hawaii;** call ℡ **808/553-5236** or 808/524-0779 for an exact schedule and details.

To get here, take Hwy. 460 (Maunaloa Hwy.) from Kaunakakai; turn right onto Hwy. 470, and follow it to Kualapuu. At Kualapuu, turn left on Hwy. 480 and go through Hoolehua Village; it's 3 miles to the bay.

The East End

The East End is a cool and inviting green place that's worth a drive to the end of King Kamehameha V Highway (Hwy. 450). Unfortunately, the trail that leads into the area's greatest natural attraction, Halawa Valley, is now off-limits.

KAMAKOU PRESERVE

It's hard to believe, but close to the nearly mile-high summit here, it rains more than 80 inches a year—enough to qualify as a rainforest. The Molokai Forest, as it was historically known, is the source of 60% of Molokai's water. Nearly 3,000 acres, from the summit to the lowland forests of eucalyptus and pine, are now held by the Nature Conservancy, which has identified 219 Hawaiian plants that grow here exclusively. The preserve is also the last stand of the endangered *olomao* (Molokai thrush) and *kawawahie* (Molokai creeper).

To get to the preserve, take the Molokai Forest Reserve Road from Kaunakakai. It's a 45-minute four-wheel-drive trip on a dirt trail to Waikolu Lookout Campground; from here, you can venture into the wilderness preserve on foot across a boardwalk on a 1½-hour hike (see "The Pepeopae Trail," p. 588). For more information, contact the **Nature Conservancy** (© **808/553-5236;** www.nature.org).

EN ROUTE TO HALAWA VALLEY

No visit to Molokai is complete without at least a passing glance at the island's **ancient fish ponds,** a singular achievement in Pacific aquaculture. With their hunger for fresh fish and lack of ice and refrigeration, Hawaiians perfected aquaculture in A.D. 1400, before Christopher Columbus "discovered" America. They built gated, U-shaped stone and coral walls on the shore to catch fish on the incoming tide; they would then raise them in captivity. The result: a constant, ready supply of fresh fish.

The ponds, which stretch for 20 miles along Molokai's south shore and are visible from Kamehameha V Highway (Hwy. 450), offer insight into the island's ancient population. It took something like a thousand people to tend a single fish pond, and more than 60 ponds once existed on this coast. Some are silted in by red-dirt runoff from south-coast gulches; others are in use by folks who raise fish and seaweed.

Alii Fish Pond.

St. Joseph's Catholic Church.

The largest, 54-acre **Keawa Nui Pond,** is surrounded by a 3-foot-high, 2,000-foot-long stone wall. **Alii Fish Pond,** reserved for kings, is visible through the coconut groves at One Alii Beach Park (p. 584). From the road, you can see **Kalokoeli Pond,** 6 miles east of Kaunakakai on the highway.

Our Lady of Sorrows Catholic Church, one of five built by Father Damien on Molokai and the first outside Kalaupapa, sits across the highway from a fish pond. Park in the church lot (except on Sun) for a closer look.

St. Joseph's Catholic Church The afternoon sun strikes St. Joseph's Church with such a bold ray of light that it looks as if God is about to perform a miracle. This little 1876 wood-frame church is one of four Father Damien built "topside" on Molokai. Restored in 1971, the church stands beside a seaside cemetery, where feral cats play under the gaze of a Damien statue amid gravestones decorated with flower leis.

King Kamehameha V Hwy. (Hwy. 450), just after mile marker 10.

Smith Bronte Landing Site In 1927, Charles Lindbergh soloed across the Atlantic Ocean in a plane called *The Spirit of St. Louis* and became an American hero. That same year, Ernie Smith and Emory B. Bronte took off from Oakland, California, on July 14, in a single-engine Travelair aircraft named *The City of Oakland,* headed across the Pacific Ocean for Honolulu, 2,397 miles away. The next day, after running out of fuel, they crash-landed upside down in a kiawe thicket on Molokai, but emerged unhurt to become the first civilians to fly to Hawaii from the U.S. mainland. The 25-hour, 2-minute flight landed Smith and Bronte a place in aviation history—and on a roadside marker on Molokai.

King Kamehameha V Hwy. (Hwy. 450), at mile marker 11, on the makai (ocean) side.

HALAWA VALLEY ★

Of the five great valleys of Molokai, only Halawa—with its two waterfalls, golden beach, sleepy lagoon, great surf, and offshore island—is easily accessible. Unfortunately, the trail through fertile Halawa Valley, which was inhabited for centuries, and on to the 250-foot Moaula Falls has been closed for some time. There is one operator who conducts hikes to the falls (see "Halawa Valley: A Hike Back in History," below).

You can spend a day at the county beach park (described under "Beaches," earlier in this chapter), but do not venture into the valley on your own. In a kind of 21st-century *kapu,* the private landowners in the valley, worried about slip-and-fall lawsuits, have posted NO TRESPASSING signs on their properties.

halawa valley: **A HIKE BACK IN HISTORY**

"There are things on Molokai, sacred things, that you may not be able to see or may not hear, but they are there," says Pilipo Solotario, who was born and raised in Halawa Valley and survived the 1946 tsunami that barreled into the ancient valley. "As Hawaiians, we respect these things." Solotario feels it is important that visitors learn about the history and culture of Molokai; that is part of the secret of appreciating the island.

"I see my role, and I'm nearly 70 years old, as educating people, outsiders, on our culture, our history," he said at the beginning of this cultural hike into his family property in Halawa Valley. "To really appreciate Molokai, you need to understand and know things so that you are *pono,* you are right with the land and don't disrespect the culture. Then you see the real Molokai."

Solotario and his family, who own the land in the valley, are the only people allowed to hike into Halawa. They lead daily tours, which begin at the county park pavilion, with a history of the valley, a discussion of Hawaiian culture, and a display of the fruits, trees, and other flora you will see. Along the hike, Solotario stops to point out historical and cultural aspects, including chanting in Hawaiian before entering a sacred *heiau.* At the waterfalls, visitors can swim in the brisk water. Cost for the 4-hour tour is $69. Book through **Molokai Fish & Dive** (✆ **808/553-5926;** www.molokaifish anddive.com). Bring insect repellent, water, a snack, and a swimsuit. Don't forget your camera.

Note that if you venture away from the county park into the valley on your own, you will be trespassing and can be prosecuted.

To get to Halawa Valley, drive north from Kaunakakai on Hwy. 450 for 30 miles along the coast to the end of the road, which descends into the valley past Jersalema Hou Church. If you'd just like a glimpse of the valley on your way to the beach, there's a scenic overlook along the road: After Pu'u o Hoku Ranch at mile marker 25, the narrow two-lane road widens at a hairpin curve, and you'll find the overlook on your right; it's 2 miles more to the valley floor.

SHOPPING

Kaunakakai

For food shopping, there are several good options—and because many visitors stay in condos, knowing the grocery stores is especially important. Other than that, serious shoppers will be disappointed, unless they love kites or native-wood vessels. The following are Kaunakakai's notable stores.

Bamboo Pantry　It's hard to believe this creative kitchenware, cutlery, and specialty-foods store is located in the heart of Kaunakakai. It has everything from dishes, woven baskets, and glassware to high-end cookware and gourmet food. 107 Ala Malama St., Kaunakakai. ✆ **808/553-3300.**

Imamura Store　Wilfred Imamura, whose mother founded this store, recalls the old railroad track that stretched from the pier to a spot across the street. "We brought our household things from the pier on a hand-pumped vehicle," he recalls. His store, appropriately, is a leap into the past. Rubber boots, Hawaiian print tablecloths, ukulele cases, plastic slippers, and even coconut bikini tops line the shelves. But it's not all nostalgia: The Molokai T-shirts, jeans, and palaka shorts are of good quality and inexpensive, and the pareu fabrics are a find. In Kaunakakai. ✆ **808/553-5615.**

Molokai Drugs　David Mikami, whose father-in-law founded this pharmacy in 1935, has made this more than a drugstore. It's a friendly stop full of life's basic necessities, with generous amenities such as a phone and a restroom for passersby. Here you'll find the best selection of guidebooks, books about Molokai, and maps, as well as paperbacks, cassette players, flip-flops, and every imaginable essential. The Mikamis are a household name on the island, not only because of their pharmacy, but also because the family has shown exceptional kindness to the often economically strapped Molokaians. At the Kamoi Professional Center. ✆ **808/553-5790.**

Molokai Fish & Dive　Here you'll find the island's largest selection of T-shirts and souvenirs, crammed in among fishing, snorkeling, and outdoor gear that you can rent or buy. Find your way around the fish nets, boogie boards, bamboo rakes, beach towels, juices and soft drinks, disposable cameras, and staggering miscellany of this store. The selection of Molokai books and souvenirs is extensive. The staff is happy to point out the best snorkeling spots of the day. In Kaunakakai. ✆ **808/553-5926.** www.molokaifishanddive.com.

Molokai Surf　This wooden building houses Molokai Surf and its selection of skateboards, surf shorts, sweatshirts, sunglasses, T-shirts, footwear, boogie boards, backpacks, and a broad range of clothing and accessories for life in the surf and sun. 130 Kamehameha V Hwy., Kaunakakai. ✆ **808/553-5093.**

Take's Variety Store　If you need luggage tags, buzz saws, toys, candy, cloth dolls, canned goods, canteens, camping equipment, hardware, batteries, candles, fishing supplies—whew!—and other products for work and play, this variety store is the answer. You may suffer from claustrophobia in the crowded, dusty aisles, but Take's carries everything. In Kaunakakai. ✆ **808/553-5442.**

EDIBLES

For fresh-baked goods, see **Kanemitsu's Bakery & Restaurant** (p. 581).

Friendly Market Center   You can't miss this salmon-colored storefront on the main drag of "downtown" Kaunakakai, where people of all generations can be found just talking story. Friendly's carries everything from local poi to Glenlivet. Blue-corn tortilla chips, soy milk, and Kumu Farms macadamia nut pesto, the island's stellar gourmet food, are among the items that surpass standard grocery-store fare. In Kaunakakai. (C) **808/553-5595.**

Misaki's Grocery and Dry Goods   Established in 1922, this third-generation local legend is one of Kaunakakai's two grocery stores. Some of its notable items: fresh luau leaves (taro greens), fresh okra, Boca Burgers, large Korean chestnuts in season, gorgeous bananas, and an ATM. The fish section includes akule and ahi, fresh and dried. Liquor, stationery, candies, and paper products round out the selection in this full-service grocery. In Kaunakakai. (C) **808/553-5505.**

Molokai Wines & Spirits   This is your best bet on the island for a decent bottle of wine. The shop offers 200 labels, including Caymus, Silver Oak, Joseph Phelps, Heitz, and Bonny Doon. The snack options include imported cheeses, salami, and Carr's biscuits. In Kaunakakai. (C) **808/553-5009.**

En Route to the North Coast

Coffees of Hawaii Plantation Store and Espresso Bar   This is a fairly slick—for Molokai—combination coffee bar, store, and gallery. Sold here are the Malulani Estate and Muleskinner coffees that are grown on the 500-acre plantation surrounding the shop (see p. 593 for plantation tours). The gift items are

THE PERFECT MOLOKAI souvenir

It's small, it's easy to pack and take back home, and it's made only on Molokai: It's Molokai salt. The Hawaii Kai Corporation (www.hawaiikaico.com) has two product lines featuring Molokai salt: the gourmet **Soul of the Sea** and the **Palm Island Premium.** Soul of the Sea salt is hand-harvested from some of the cleanest ocean water in the state, hand-processed, and hand-packed on Molokai. It comes in three varietals: Papohaku White, Kilauea Black, and Haleakala Red. While making Soul of the Sea salt, Hawaii Kai Corporation got a byproduct it calls Ocean Essence, which it blends with Molokai salt to restore trace minerals lost in the heating process. The result is Palm Island Premium, which comes in White Silver, Red Gold, Black Lava, and Bamboo Jade. The newest line is **Hawaii Kai Gourmet,** which comes in white, red, black, and green blends.

worth a look: pikake and plumeria soaps from Kauai, pure beeswax candles from Maui, koa bookmarks and hair sticks, pottery, and baskets. Hwy. 480 (near Hwy. 470), Kualapuu. ✆ **800/709-BEAN** (2326) or 808/567-9023.

Molokai Museum Gift Shop   This restored 1878 sugar mill sits 1,500 feet above the town of Kualapuu. It's a considerable drive from town, but a good cause for those who'd like to support the museum and the handful of local artisans who sell their crafts, fabrics, cookbooks, quilt sets, and other gift items in the tiny shop. There's also a modest selection of cards, T-shirts, coloring books, and, at Christmas, handmade ornaments made of lauhala and koa. Meyer Sugar Mill, Hwy. 470 (just after the turnoff for the Ironwood Hills Golf Course and 2 miles below Kalaupapa Overlook), Kalae. ✆ **808/567-6436.**

EDIBLES

Kualapuu Market   This market, in its third generation, is a stone's throw from the Coffees of Hawaii store. It's a scaled-down, one-stop shop with wine, food, and necessities—and a surprisingly presentable, albeit small, assortment of produce, from Molokai sweet potatoes to Ka'u navel oranges in season. The shelves are filled with canned goods, propane, rope, hoses, paper products, and baking goods, reflecting the rural lifestyle of the area. In Kualapuu. ✆ **808/567-6243.**

The West End

Big Wind Kite Factory & Plantation Gallery ★★   Jonathan and Daphne Socher have combined their interests in a kite factory/import shop that dominates the commercial landscape of Maunaloa, whose naturally windy conditions make it ideal for kite flying classes (offered free when conditions are right). The adjoining gallery features local handicrafts such as milo-wood bowls, locally made T-shirts, sandblasted glassware, lauhala baskets, and Hawaiian-music CDs. There are also many Balinese handicrafts, from jewelry to clothing and fabrics. In Maunaloa. ✆ **808/552-2364.**

A Touch of Molokai ★   Even though the Kaluakoi Hotel is closed, this fabulous shop remains open. It is well worth the drive. The surf shorts and aloha shirts sold here are better than the norm, with attractive, up-to-date choices by Jams, Quiksilver, and other brands. Tencel dresses, South Pacific shell necklaces (up to $400), and a magnificent hand-turned milo bowl also caught my attention. Most impressive are the wiliwili, kamani, and soap-berry leis and a handsome array of lauhala bags, all made on Molokai. At Kaluakoi Hotel & Golf Club. ✆ **808/552-0133.**

The East End

EDIBLES

Mana'e Goods and Grindz   Formerly the Neighborhood Store 'N Counter, this is the only grocery on the East End. Come here for batteries, film, aspirin, cookies, beer, Molokai produce, candies, paper products, and other sundries. There's good food pouring out of the kitchen at the breakfast and lunch counter, too. See p. 582 for a restaurant review. In Pukoo. ✆ **808/558-8498.**

MOLOKAI AFTER DARK

Hotel Molokai, in Kaunakakai (© 808/553-5347; www.hotelmolokai.com), offers live entertainment by local musicians poolside and in the dining room every night. On Friday from 4 to 6pm is Aloha Fridays Night, when the musicians of Molokai who have been performing here for decades show you why people love their music and hula. With its South Seas ambience and poolside setting, it has become the island's premier venue for local and visiting entertainers. The **Paddlers' Inn** (© 808/553-5256), also in Kaunakakai, recently has become a nightspot for live Hawaii music, comedy acts, and other entertainment. Call for what's coming up.

LANAI, A DIFFERENT KIND OF PARADISE

Lanai is not an easy place to reach. There are no direct flights from the mainland. It's almost as if this quiet, gentle oasis—known, paradoxically, for both its small-town feel and its celebrity appeal—demands that its visitors go to great lengths to get here in order to ensure that they will appreciate it.

Lanai (pronounced Lah-*nigh*-ee), the nation's biggest defunct pineapple patch, now claims to be one of the world's top tropical destinations. It's a bold claim because so little is here; Lanai has even fewer dining and accommodations choices than Molokai. There are no stoplights and barely 30 miles of paved road. This almost virgin island is unspoiled by what passes for progress, except for a tiny 1920s-era plantation village—and, of course, the village's fancy new arrivals: two first-class luxury hotels where room rates average $400-plus a night.

As soon as you arrive on Lanai, you'll feel the small-town coziness. People wave to every car, residents stop to "talk story" with their friends, fishing and working in the garden are considered priorities in life, and leaving the keys in your car's ignition is standard practice.

For generations, Lanai was little more than a small village, owned and operated by the pineapple company, surrounded by acres of pineapple fields. The few visitors to the island were either relatives of the residents or occasional weekend hunters. Life in the 1960s was pretty much the same as in the 1930s. But all that changed in 1990, when the Lodge at Koele, a 102-room hotel resembling an opulent English Tudor mansion, opened its doors, followed a year later by the 250-room Manele Bay, a Mediterranean-style luxury resort overlooking Hulopoe Bay. Overnight, the isolated island was transformed: Corporate jets streamed into tiny Lanai Airport, former plantation workers were retrained in the art of serving gourmet meals, and the population of 2,500 swelled with transient visitors and outsiders coming to work in the island's new hospitality industry. Microsoft billionaire Bill Gates chose the island for his lavish wedding, booking all of its hotel rooms to fend off the press—and uncomplicated Lanai went on the map as a vacation spot for the rich and powerful.

But this island is also a place where people come looking for dramatic beauty, quiet, solitude, and an experience with nature. The sojourners who find their way to Lanai seek out the dramatic views, the tropical fusion of stars at night, and the chance to be alone with the elements.

They also come for the wealth of activities: snorkeling and swimming in the marine preserve known as Hulopoe Bay, hiking on 100 miles of remote trails, talking story with the friendly locals, and beachcombing and whale-watching along stretches of otherwise deserted sand. For the adventurous, there's horseback riding in the forest, scuba diving in caves, playing golf on courses with stunning ocean views, or renting a four-wheel-drive vehicle for the day and discovering wild plains where spotted deer run free.

PREVIOUS PAGE: **Manele Bay Harbor.**

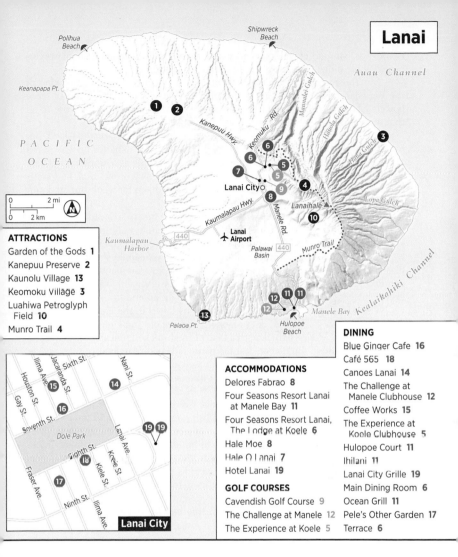

Lanai

Polihua Beach

Shipwreck Beach

Auau Channel

Keanapapa Pt.

Kanepuu Hwy.

Keomuku Rd.

Maunalei Gulch

Hauola Gulch

Waia Gulch

① **②**

⑥

⑥

⑦ **⑤**

③

⑤

④

Lopa Gulch

PACIFIC OCEAN

Lanai City ○

⑧ **⑨**

Kaumalapau Hwy.

Manele Rd.

Lanaihale ▲

⑩

0 ——— 2 mi
0 ——— 2 km

Kaumalapau Harbor

`440`

✈ **Lanai Airport**

Palawai Basin

`440`

Munro Trail

Kealaikahiki Channel

⑫ **⑪** **⑪**

⑫

Manele Bay

⑬

Palaoa Pt.

Hulopoe Beach

ATTRACTIONS

Garden of the Gods **1**
Kanepuu Preserve **2**
Kaunolu Village **13**
Keomoku Village **3**
Luahiwa Petroglyph Field **10**
Munro Trail **4**

Lanai City (inset map)

Sixth St.
Ilima Ave.
Jacaranda St.
Nani St.
Houston St.
Gay St.
Seventh St.
⑮
⑯
⑭
Dole Park
Lanai Ave.
⑲ **⑲**
Eighth St.
Koele St.
Kiele St.
⑱
Fraser Ave.
⑰
Ninth St.
Ilima Ave.
Lanai City

ACCOMMODATIONS

Delores Fabrao **8**
Four Seasons Resort Lanai at Manele Bay **11**
Four Seasons Resort Lanai, The Lodge at Koele **6**
Hale Moe **8**
Hale O Lanai **7**
Hotel Lanai **19**

GOLF COURSES

Cavendish Golf Course **9**
The Challenge at Manele **12**
The Experience at Koele **5**

DINING

Blue Ginger Cafe **16**
Café 565 **18**
Canoes Lanai **14**
The Challenge at Manele Clubhouse **12**
Coffee Works **15**
The Experience at Koele Clubhouse **5**
Hulopoe Court **11**
Ihilani **11**
Lanai City Grille **19**
Main Dining Room **6**
Ocean Grill **11**
Pele's Other Garden **17**
Terrace **6**

In a single decade, a plain red-dirt pineapple patch has become one of Hawaii's top fantasy destinations. But the real Lanai is a multifaceted place that's so much more than a luxury resort—and it's the traveler who comes to discover the island's natural wonders, local lifestyle, and other inherent joys who's bound to have the most genuine island experience.

The Pineapple Island's Unusual Past

This old shield volcano in the rain shadow of Maui has a history of resisting change in a big way. Early Polynesians, fierce Hawaiian kings, European explorers, 20th-century farmers—the island has seen them all and sent most of them packing, empty-handed and broken. The ancient Hawaiians believed that the island was haunted by spirits so wily and vicious that no human could survive here. People didn't settle here until around A.D. 1400.

But those spirits never really went away, it seems. In 1778, the king of the Big Island, Kalaniopuu, invaded Lanai in what was called "the war of loose bowels." His men slaughtered every warrior, cut down trees, and set fire to all that was left except a bitter fern whose roots gave them all dysentery.

In 1802, Wu Tsin made the first attempt to harvest a crop on the island, but he ultimately abandoned his cane fields and went away. Charles Gay acquired 600 acres at public auction to experiment with pineapple as a crop, but a 3-year drought left him bankrupt. Others tried in vain to grow cotton, sisal, and sugar beets; they started a dairy and a piggery and raised sheep for wool. But all enterprises failed, mostly for lack of water.

Harry Baldwin, a missionary's grandson, was the first to succeed on Lanai. He bought Lanai for $588,000 in 1917, developed a 20-mile water pipeline between Koele and Manele, and sold the island 5 years later to Jim Dole for $1.1 million.

Dole planted and irrigated 18,000 acres of pineapple, built Lanai City, blasted out a harbor, and turned the island into a fancy fruit plantation. For a half-century, he enjoyed great success. Even Dole was ultimately vanquished, however: Cheaper pineapple production in Asia brought an end to Lanai's heyday.

The island still resembles old photographs taken in the glory days of Dole. Any minute now, you half expect to look up and see old Jim Dole himself rattling up the road in a Model-T truck with a load of fresh-picked pineapples. Only now, there's a new lord of the manor, and his name is David Murdock.

Of all who have looked at Lanai with a gleam in their eye, nobody has succeeded quite like Murdock, a self-made billionaire who acquired the island in a merger more than a decade ago. About 97% of it is now his private holding.

Murdock spent $400 million to build two grand hotels on the island: the Lodge at Koele, which resembles an English country retreat, and the Four Seasons Resort Lanai at Manele Bay, a green tile-roofed Mediterranean palazzo by the sea. Murdock recycled the former field hands into waitstaff, even summoning a London butler to school the natives in the fine art of service, and carved a pair of daunting golf courses, one in the island's interior and the other along the wave-lashed coast. He then set out to attract tourists by touting Lanai as "the private island."

Murdock is now trying to make all this pay for itself by selling vacation homes and condos, all in the million-dollar range, next door to the two resorts.

The redevelopment of this tiny rock should have been a pushover for the big-time tycoon, but island-style politics have continually thwarted his schemes. GO SLOW, a sun-faded sign at Dole's old maintenance shed once said. Murdock might have heeded the warning because his grandiose plans are taking twice as long to accomplish as he had expected. Lanai is under the political thumb of many who believe that the island's precious water supply shouldn't all be diverted to championship golf courses and Jacuzzis, and there remains opposition from Lanaians for Sensible Growth, who advocate affordable housing, alternative water systems, and civic improvements that benefit residents.

Lanai residents might have lived in a rural setting, but they certainly haven't been isolated. Having watched the other islands in Hawaii attempt the balancing act of economic growth and the maintenance of an island lifestyle, the residents of Lanai are cautiously welcoming visitors, but at a pace that is still easy for this former plantation community to digest.

ORIENTATION
Arriving

BY PLANE No matter where you're coming from, you'll have to make a connection in Honolulu (on Oahu) or Kahului (on Maui), where you can catch a plane for the 25-minute flight to Lanai's airport. You'll touch down in Puuwai Basin, once the world's largest pineapple plantation; it's about 10 minutes by car to Lanai City and 25 minutes to Manele Bay.

Commuter airlines offering service to Lanai are **Go Airlines** (© **888/435-9462;** www.iflygo.com) and **Island Air** (© **800/323-3345** from the mainland, 800/652-6541 interisland, or 808/565-6744; www.island air.com), with daily flights from Honolulu. I must tell you, however, that I have gotten less than sterling service from Island Air, which has left me stranded midroute—not once, but twice!

BY BOAT A round-trip on **Expeditions Lahaina/Lanai Passenger Ferry** (© **808/661-3756**) takes you between Maui and Lanai for $30 adults and $20 children, each way. The ferry runs five times a day, 365 days a year, between Lahaina (on Maui) and Lanai's Manele Bay harbor. The 9-mile channel crossing takes 45 minutes to an hour, depending on sea conditions. Reservations are strongly recommended; call or book online. Baggage is limited to two checked bags and one carry-on.

Visitor Information

Lanai Visitors Bureau, P.O. Box 631436, Lanai City, HI 96763, or 431 Seventh St., Suite A, Lanai City (© **800/947-4774** or 808/565-7600; fax 808/565-9316; www.visitlanai.net), and the **Hawaii Visitors & Convention Bureau** (© **800/GO-HAWAII** [464-2924] or 808/923-1811; www.gohawaii.com) provide brochures, maps, and island guides.

The Island in Brief

Inhabited Lanai is divided into three parts—Lanai City, Koele, and Manele—and two distinct climate zones: hot and dry, and cool and misty.

Lanai City (pop. 3,200) sits at the heart of the island at 1,645 feet above sea level. It's the only place on the island where you'll find services. Built in 1924, this plantation village is a tidy grid of quaint tin-roofed cottages in bright pastels, with tropical gardens of banana, lilikoi, and papaya. Many of the residents are Filipino immigrants who once worked the pineapple fields. Their clapboard homes, now worth $500,000 or more (for a 1,000-sq.-ft. home, built in 1935, on a tiny 5,000-sq.-ft. lot), are excellent examples of historic preservation; the whole town looks like it's been kept under a bell jar.

Around Dole Park, a charming village square lined with towering Norfolk and Cook Island pines, plantation buildings house general stores selling basic necessities, a post office (where people stop to chat), two banks, three restaurants, an art gallery, an art center, a whimsical shop, and a coffee shop that outshines any Starbucks. A victim of "progress" was the local one-room police station with a jail that consisted of three blue-and-white wooden outhouse-size cells with padlocks. It's now a block from the square with "modern facilities," including regulation-size jail cells.

In the nearby cool upland district of **Koele** is the Lodge at Koele (now managed by the Four Seasons Resort), standing alone on a knoll overlooking pastures and the sea at the edge of a pine forest, like a grand European manor.

The other bastion of indulgence, the Four Seasons Resort Lanai at Manele Bay, is on the sunny southwestern tip of the island at **Manele.** You'll get more of what you expect from Hawaii here—beaches, swaying palms, mai tais, and the like.

Fast Facts Lanai

Lanai is part of Maui County. In case of **emergencies,** call the police, fire department, or ambulance services at © **911,** or the **Poison Control Center** at © **800/362-3585.** For nonemergencies, call the police at © **808/565-6428.**

Lanai City.

For emergency dental care, call **Dr. Nora Harmsen** (© **808/565-6418**). If you need a doctor, contact the **Straub Lanai Family Health Center** (© **808/565-6423**) or the **Lanai Community Hospital** (© **808/565-8450**).

For a weather report, call the **National Weather Service** at © **808/565-6033.**

GETTING AROUND

With so few paved roads here, you'll need a four-wheel-drive vehicle if you plan to explore the island's remote shores, its interior, or the summit of Mount Lanaihale. Even if you have only a day on Lanai, rent one and see the island. Both standard cars and four-wheel-drive vehicles are available at the **Dollar Rent-A-Car** desk at **Lanai City Service/Lanai Plantation Store,** 1036 Lanai Ave. (© **800/588-7808** for Dollar reservations, or 808/565-7227 for Lanai City Service). Expect to pay about $139 a day for a four-wheel-drive jeep.

Warning: Gas is expensive on Lanai, and those four-wheel-drive vehicles get terrible mileage. Because everything in Lanai City is within walking distance, it makes sense to rent a jeep only for the days you want to explore the island.

Though it's fun to rent a car and explore the island, it is possible to stay here and get to the beach without one. The two big resort hotels run shuttle vans to the Four Seasons Resort Lanai at Manele Bay; from there, you can walk to Hulopoe Beach. When you want to return, you just catch the hourly shuttle (it may run on the half-hour from Four Seasons Resort Lanai at Manele Bay) back to Lanai City. The shuttle picks up at Hotel Lanai as well and will take guests to town, the airport, and the golf courses. There is a one-time charge of $45 per person for Four Seasons guests and $35 per person for Hotel Lanai guests.

If you're staying elsewhere, you can walk to everything in Lanai City. Or you can most likely get a ride back up to Lanai City with a local resident from the airport. Whether or not you rent a car, sooner or later you'll find yourself at Lanai

City Service/Lanai Plantation Store. This all-in-one grocery store, gas station, rental-car agency, and souvenir shop serves as the island's Grand Central Terminal—you can pick up information, directions, maps, and all the local gossip here.

WHERE TO STAY

The majority of the accommodations are located "in the village," as residents call Lanai City. Above the village is the luxurious Lodge at Koele (now managed by Four Seasons), while down the hill at Hulopoe Bay are two options: the equally luxurious Four Seasons Resort Lanai at Manele Bay or tent camping under the stars at the park.

In addition to the choices listed below, consider a vacation-home rental like **Hale O Lanai,** in Lanai City (✆ **808/247-3637;** www.myhawaiibeachfront.com), which has a fully equipped two-bedroom vacation rental that sleeps up to six; rates range from $115 to $135 plus a $45 to $65 cleaning fee.

Don't forget to add 12.42% in taxes to all accommodations bills. Parking is free.

Expensive

Four Seasons Resort Lanai at Manele Bay ★★★   The well-known luxury hotel chain Four Seasons took over management of this 236-unit oceanside resort after a $50-million makeover. Every Four Seasons resort is spectacular, but this one really stands out. Located on a sun-washed southern bluff overlooking Hulopoe Beach, one of Hawaii's best stretches of golden sand, this U-shaped hotel steps down the hillside to the pool and the beach, and then fans out in oceanfront wings separated by gardens with lush flora, man-made waterfalls, lotus ponds, and streams. On the other side, it's bordered by golf greens. The place is a real oasis against the dry Arizona-like heat of Lanai's south coast.

Designed as a traditional luxury beachfront hotel, it features open, airy rooms, each with a breathtaking view of the big blue Pacific. Murals depicting scenes from Hawaiian history, sea charts, potted palms, soft camel-hued club chairs, and hand-woven kilim rugs fill the lobby. Redone in the clean, crisp style of an elegant Hawaiian resort, the oversize guest rooms have 40-inch flatscreen LCD TVs, huge marble bathrooms, and semiprivate lanais. This resort is much less formal than the Lodge at Koele up the hill and attracts more families. Speaking of families, in addition to the "Kids for All Seasons" child-care programs, the hotel features a teen center with video games, computers, a small pool table, and a 54-inch TV.

The new spa facility offers a variety of massages, facials, wraps, and scrubs (don't miss the signature Ali'i banana-coconut scrub). In addition, the Four Seasons has added a 1,500-square-foot fitness center (with one of the best ocean views in the resort) that has the latest cardiovascular and strength-training equipment, free weights, and a wood-floored studio for classes (spinning, yoga, Pilates, and meditation).

1 Manele Bay Rd., P.O. Box 631380, Lanai City, HI 96763. ✆ **800/321-4666** or 808/565-2000. Fax 808/565-2483. www.fourseasons.com/lanai. 236 units. $295–$795 double; from $1,000 suite. Extra person $100. Children 17 and under stay free in parent's room. Numerous packages available. AE, DC, MC, V. Airport shuttle $45 round-trip. **Amenities:** 4 restaurants (Ihilani, p. 613; Hulopoe Court, p. 614; Ocean Grill, p. 614; and the Challenge at Manele Clubhouse, p. 615); bar; babysitting; children's program; concierge; fitness center w/classes; golf at the Jack

Nicklaus–designed Challenge at Manele; Jacuzzi; outdoor pool; room service; spa; tennis courts; complimentary snorkeling equipment. *In room:* A/C, TV/DVD, hair dryer, minibar, Wi-Fi ($13 per day).

Four Seasons Resort Lanai, The Lodge at Koele ★★★ The luxury resort chain Four Seasons has come to Lanai. After some $50 million in renovations, the Four Seasons took over the management of the former Lodge at Koele. This inn, which resembles a grand English country estate, was built in 1991 and needed the makeover—the new look is spectacular. All 102 guest rooms were totally redone, a game room was added, the grounds have been spruced up, and a pagoda imported from China has been constructed on the sprawling English gardens' grounds (not my taste, but I'm sure it will be the backdrop for hundreds of wedding photos).

Inside, heavy timbers, beamed ceilings, and the two huge stone fireplaces of the Great Hall complete the look. Overstuffed furniture sits invitingly around the fireplaces, richly patterned rugs adorn the floor, and museum-quality art hangs on the walls. The guest rooms continue the English theme with four-poster beds, sitting areas (complete with window seats), formal writing desks, and bathrooms with oversize tubs. All rooms now have new carpeting and furniture, glass bathroom partitions, signature Four Seasons beds, 42-inch LCD flatscreen televisions, and high-speed Internet access.

The Four Seasons also retrained the staff to their level of excellent service. Don't expect the "sophisticated" service you'd get in most Four Seasons around the world—most of the staff have lived on Lanai for generations. Instead, you'll find a charming display of aloha spirit and a strong desire to make sure your vacation is perfect.

Before you reach for the phone, understand that this hotel is not located at the beach (see the Manele Bay resort, above), but rather in the cool mist of the mountains, on 21 acres at 1,700 feet above sea level, 8 miles inland from any beach. In the winter, temperatures can drop into the 50s (don't worry, the rooms have heat as well as air-conditioning). Most guests here are looking for relaxation: sitting on the rattan chairs on the porch, reading, watching the turkeys mosey across the manicured lawns, strolling through the Japanese hillside garden, or watching the sun sink into the Pacific.

There are plenty of activities here and at the sister resort down the hill, Manele, so you'll get the best of both hotels. Other pluses include a complimentary shuttle to the golf courses, beach, and Four Seasons Resort Lanai at Manele Bay; complimentary coffee and tea in the lobby; formal afternoon tea; and twice-daily maid service. Guests can take advantage of the croquet lawns, horseback riding, hiking trails, and garden walks.

1 Keomoku Hwy., P.O. Box 631380, Lanai City, HI 96763. ✆ **800/321-4666** or 808/565-4000. Fax 808/565-4561. www.fourseasons.com/lanai. 102 units. $295–$565 double; from $750 suite. Extra person $100. Children 17 and under stay free in parent's room. Numerous packages available. AE, DC, MC, V. Airport shuttle $45 round-trip. **Amenities:** 2 restaurants (including the Main Dining Room, p. 614, and Terrace, p. 615); bar; babysitting; bike rentals; children's program; concierge; fitness room; golf at Greg Norman–designed Experience at Koele (p. 622); Jacuzzi; outdoor pool; room service; tennis courts; complimentary snorkeling equipment at Four Seasons Resort Lanai at Manele Bay. *In room:* A/C TV/DVD, fridge, hair dryer, minibar, Wi-Fi ($13 per day).

Moderate

Hotel Lanai ★ ☺   This hotel lacks the facilities of the two resorts described above, but it's perfect for families and other vacationers who can't afford to spend $345 to $445 (and up) a night. In fact, if you're looking for the old-fashioned aloha that Lanai City is famous for, this is the place to stay. Built in the 1920s for VIP plantation guests, this clapboard plantation-era relic has retained its quaint character and lives on as a country inn.

In 2005, the entire hotel underwent renovations—repainting, remodeling, and a general sprucing up. The guest rooms, although extremely small, are clean and newly outfitted with Hawaiian quilts, wood furniture, and ceiling fans (but no air-conditioning or TVs). The most popular are the lanai units, which feature a shared lanai with the room next door. All rooms have private shower-only bathrooms. The one-bedroom cottage, with a TV and bathtub, is perfect for a small family.

The hotel serves as a down-home crossroads where total strangers meet local folks on the lanai to drink beer and talk story or play the ukulele and sing into the dark, tropical night. Often a curious visitor in search of an authentic experience will join the party and discover Lanai's very Hawaiian heart. Guests have the use of the shuttle to the Lodge at Koele, the Four Seasons Resort Lanai at Manele Bay, the golf courses (at which they get the same lower rates given to guests at the two resorts), and the beach, for a one-time fee of $35.

828 Lanai Ave. (P.O. Box 630520), Lanai City, HI 96763. ⓒ **800/795-7211** or 808/565-7211. Fax 808/565-6450. www.hotellanai.com. 11 units. $99–$149 double; $179 cottage double. Extra person $50. Rates include continental breakfast. AF, MC, V. Unlimited shuttle service for entire stay $35. **Amenities:** Excellent restaurant (Lanai City Grille, p. 615); intimate bar; access to 2 resort golf courses on the island; nearby tennis courts; complimentary snorkeling equipment.

WHERE TO DINE

Lanai is a curious mix of innocence and sophistication, with strong cross-cultural elements that liven up its culinary offerings. You can dine like a sultan on this island, but be prepared for high prices. The tony hotel restaurants require deep pockets, and there are only a handful of other options.

Note: You'll find the restaurants reviewed in this chapter on the map on p. 607.

Very Expensive

Ihilani ★★★ ITALIAN   A number of top Hawaii chefs (such as Philippe Padovani and Edwin Goto) have added bits of their own style to the inspiring menu, which melds Mediterranean with island cuisine. The result is one of Lanai's top gourmet restaurants. Padovani and Goto have been gone for a while. Padovani has his own restaurant on Oahu. The latest incarnation of this classy, formal restaurant, overlooking the resort and the ocean beyond, is traditional Italian cuisine. Try the perfect homemade gnocchi or the lobster risotto. My other favorites include the *osso buco,* duck and root vegetable orecchette, and shutome alla puttanesca with artichoke purée and a spicy tomato-and-caper sauce. Be sure to leave room for the scrumptious desserts.

At the Four Seasons Resort Lanai at Manele Bay. ✆ **808/565-2296.** www.fourseasons.com/
manelebay/dining. Reservations strongly recommended. Resort attire recommended. Set menu
$61 for 2 courses with dessert, $69 for 3 courses, $81 for 3 courses and dessert. AE, DC, MC, V.
Tues–Sat 6–9:30pm.

Main Dining Room ★★★ NEW AMERICAN The former Formal Dining
Room has been revamped under the Four Seasons management and has a new
menu. However, they did retain the relaxing setting, with a roaring fire, bountiful
sprays of orchids, sienna-colored walls, and a team of waitstaff serving in hushed
voices. The menu highlights American favorites. The appetizers are so tempting,
you could make a meal from the variety of choices: seared diver scallops with
sweet spring pea blini, foie gras and black-truffle parfait, and lava rock–seared
Lanai venison. The entrees vary according to the season; when I dined here, the
menu included Maui lavender honey–roasted duck breast, mustard-and-herb-
roasted rack of lamb, and a buttered poached lobster from the Big Island. The
service is impeccable, the atmosphere relaxing. But don't forget your platinum
credit card—you'll need it.

At the Four Seasons Resort Lanai, The Lodge at Koele. ✆ **808/565-4580.** www.fourseasons.
com/koele/dining. Reservations required. Resort attire recommended; collared shirts and
closed-toe footwear requested for men. Main courses $43–$59. AE, DC, MC, V. Fri–Tues 6–9:30pm.

Expensive

Hulopoe Court ★★ HAWAII REGIONAL This is the Manele Bay's informal dining room. It serves one of the best breakfast buffets I've seen in Hawaii,
with everything from an omelet station to breakfast meats, daily pancakes, potatoes, rice, and local tropical fruit. The dinner menu showcases the culinary influences in the islands, Pacific Islands, Chinese, Portuguese, and Japanese, with
dishes like steamed onaga with pork lau lau, Kung Pau chicken, shrimp with Piri
Piri sauce and oven-baked miso cod.

At the Four Seasons Resort Lanai at Manele Bay. ✆ **808/565-2290.** www.fourseasons.com/
manelebay/dining. Reservations recommended for dinner. Resort attire recommended. Breakfast main courses $17–$24, buffet $30–$34; dinner main courses $20–$33. AE, DC, MC, V. Daily
7–11am and Sat–Wed 6–9:30pm.

Ocean Grill ★ SEAFOOD The former Pool Grille has been remodeled and
expanded, and is now open for lunch and dinner. Located just off the pool, the
casual, open-air, Hawaii-style bistro serves interesting lunches like wraps and
sandwiches (such as a veggie panini with mushrooms, red bell peppers, mozzarella cheese, zucchini), a great selection of salads (including a yummy smoked
scallop and pink grapefruit, arugula and spinach), and a range of entrees such as
kalua pork and cheese quesadilla or mahimahi fish and chips. At dinner, watch
the sun set and the stars come out as you dine on fresh local fish, steak, free-
range chicken, or small-plate entrees such as Hawaiian kampachi, crab cakes,
lobster, and red-curry chowder. Don't be in a hurry as service here can be
s-l-o-w.

At the Four Seasons Resort Lanai at Manele Bay. ✆ **808/565-2092.** www.fourseasons.com/
manelebay/dining. Main courses $12–$21 lunch, $32–$49 dinner. AE, MC, V. Sun–Mon and Thurs–
Fri 11am–5pm and 5:30–9pm.

Terrace ★★ AMERICAN   Located next to the Main Dining Room in the Lodge at Koele, between the 35-foot-high Great Hall and a wall of glass looking out over prim English gardens, this wonderful spot is the Lodge's "casual" dining room. The Terrace is far from your typical hotel restaurant—the menu may be fancy for comfort food, but it does, indeed, comfort. Hearty breakfasts of waffles and cereals, fresh pineapple from the nearby Palawai Basin, Paniola rancheros, and traditional eggs Benedict make a grand start to the day. Dinner choices include flank steak, meatloaf, roasted pork loin, fresh fish of the day, and a vegetarian selection (ricotta and local mushroom risotto with basil and truffle oils).

At the Four Seasons Resort Lanai, The Lodge at Koele. ✆ **808/565-4580.** www.fourseasons. com/koele/dining. Reservations recommended. Resort attire recommended. Full breakfast $16–$40; lunch $14–$21; dinner main courses $23–$40. AE, DC, MC, V. Daily 7–11am, 11am–2pm, and 6–9:30pm.

Moderate

The Challenge at Manele Clubhouse ★ PACIFIC RIM   The view from the alfresco tables here may be the best on the island, encompassing Kahoolawe, Haleakala (on Maui), and, on an especially clear day, the peaks of Mauna Kea and Mauna Loa on the Big Island. You can lunch on salads and sandwiches (Asian tuna salad with grilled ahi, turkey club sandwich, clubhouse burgers with caramelized onions and cheese) or on more substantial entrees, ranging from fish and chips to kalbi beef. The clubhouse is casual, the view of the ocean is awe inspiring, and it's a great gathering place.

At the Challenge at Manele Golf Course. ✆ **808/565-2230.** www.fourseasons.com/manelebay/ dining. Reservations recommended. Main courses $11–$20. AE, DC, MC, V. Daily 11am–3pm.

The Experience at Koele Clubhouse AMERICAN   This tiny eatery overlooks the verdant, rolling hills of the Experience at Koele Golf Course. Most of your fellow diners will have just finished a round of golf; you can join them at one of a handful of tables inside or on the lanai overlooking the pastoral view. Soups, salads, and oversized sandwiches rule here, everything from a delicious portobello mushroom on toasted focaccia bread to open-faced chicken salad (with a yummy mango-avocado salsa), smoked turkey club, or charbroiled cheddar burger.

At the Experience at Koele Golf Course. ✆ **808/565-4605.** www.fourseasons.com/koele/ dining. Main courses $10–$20. AE, DC, MC, V. Wed–Sun 10am–3pm.

Lanai City Grille ★★ CAJUN/COUNTRY   Celebrated Maui chef Bev Gannon (Haliimaile General Store, Joe's Restaurant) redesigned the menu in this cute eatery, where the decor consists of pine-paneled walls, chintz curtains, and a fireplace. The menu sticks to whatever is in season and fresh that day, from the fish and seafood to meats and rotisserie chicken.

At the Hotel Lanai, 828 Lanai Ave., Lanai City. ✆ **808/565-7211.** www.hotellanai.com. Main courses $23–$40. AE, MC, V. Wed–Sun 5–9pm.

Inexpensive

Blue Ginger Cafe COFFEE SHOP   Famous for its mahimahi sandwiches and inexpensive omelets, Blue Ginger is a very local, very casual, and very reasonably priced alternative to Lanai's fancy hotel restaurants. The four tables on the front porch face the cool Norfolk pines of Dole Park and are always filled with locals who talk story from morning to night. The offerings are solid, no-nonsense, everyday fare: fried saimin (no MSG), very popular burgers on homemade buns, and mahimahi with capers and mushrooms. Blue Ginger also serves a tasty French toast made with homemade bread and a surprisingly good stir-fried vegetable dish.

409 Seventh St. (at Ilima St.), Lanai City. ☎ **808/565-6363.** Breakfast and lunch items under $15; dinner main courses under $17. No credit cards. Mon and Thurs–Fri 6am–8pm; Tues–Wed 6am–2pm; Sat–Sun 6:30am–8pm.

Canoes Lanai LOCAL   This ma-and-pa eatery may have changed its name (it used to be Tanigawa's), but it remains the landmark that it's been since the 1920s. In those days, the tiny storefront sold canned goods and cigarettes; the 10 tables, hamburgers, and Filipino food came later. This hole in the wall is a local institution, with a reputation for serving local-style breakfasts. The fare—fried rice, omelets, short stack, and simple ham and eggs—is more greasy spoon than gourmet, but it's definitely budget friendly.

419 Seventh St., Lanai City. ☎ **808/565-6537.** Reservations not accepted. Breakfast items under $9; sandwiches $4–$8; burgers $3–$7. No credit cards. Daily 6:30am–1pm.

Coffee Works ★ COFFEEHOUSE   Oahu's popular Ward Warehouse coffeehouse has opened a new branch on Lanai, with a menu of espresso drinks, ice cream (including local brands), and a small selection of pastries. It's Lanai City's new gathering place, a tiny cafe with tables and benches on a pleasing wooden deck just a stone's throw from Dole Park. Formerly a plantation house, the structure fits in with the surrounding plantation homes in the heart of Lanai City. There are some nice gift items available, including T-shirts, tea infusers, teapots, cookies, and gourmet coffees.

604 Ilima St., Lanai City (across from the post office). ☎ **808/565-6962.** Most items under $8. AE, DC, DISC, MC, V. Mon–Sat 7am–1:30pm.

Pele's Other Garden ★★ DELI/BISTRO   This popular eatery has added a patio with umbrella tables and expanded the kitchen in the back, so there's a lot more seating than there used to be—and a fuller menu to match. Owners Mark and Barbara have turned this small sandwich shop into a full-scale deli and bistro. Daily soup and menu specials, excellent pizza, fresh organic produce, and special items such as top-quality black-bean burritos make Pele's Other Garden a Lanai City must. Sandwiches are made as wraps or with whole-wheat, rye, sourdough, or French bread, all baked on the island and delivered fresh daily. In the evening, you can dine on china at cloth-covered tables, and the menu expands to include pastas (bow-tie pasta with butterflied garlic shrimp, fettuccine with smoked salmon), pizza, and salads. Beer and wines by the glass (from $4.25) and a full bar were recently added.

Dole Park, 811 Houston St., Lanai City. ☎ **888/764-3354** or 808/565-9628. www.pelesother garden.com. Main courses $7.50–$12 lunch, $17–$20 dinner; pizza from $9. AE, DISC, MC, V. Mon–Fri 11am–3pm and Mon–Sat 5–8pm (bar menu 4:30–6:30pm).

BEACHES

If you like big, wide, empty, gold-sand beaches and crystal-clear, cobalt-blue water full of bright tropical fish—and who doesn't?—go to Lanai. With 18 miles of sandy shoreline, Lanai has some of Hawaii's least crowded and most interesting beaches.

Hulopoe Beach ★★★

In 1997, Dr. Stephen Leatherman of the University of Maryland (a professional beach surveyor who's also known as "Dr. Beach") ranked Hulopoe the best beach in the United States. It's easy to see why. This palm-fringed, gold-sand beach is bordered by black-lava fingers, protecting swimmers from ocean currents. In summer, Hulopoe is perfect for swimming, snorkeling, or just lolling about; the water temperature is usually in the mid-70s (mid-20s Celsius). Swimming is usually safe, except when swells kick up in winter. The bay at the foot of the Four Seasons Resort Lanai at Manele Bay is a protected marine preserve, with schools of colorful fish and spinner dolphins. Humpback whales cruise by here in winter. Hulopoe is also Lanai's premier beach park, with a grassy lawn, picnic tables, barbecue grills, restrooms, showers, and ample parking. You can camp here, too.

Hulopoe Beach.

HULOPOE'S TIDE POOLS   Some of the best lava-rock tide pools in Hawaii are found along the south shore of Hulopoe Bay. These miniature SeaWorlds are full of strange creatures such as asteroids (sea stars) and holothurians (sea cucumbers), not to mention spaghetti worms, Barber Pole shrimp, and Hawaii's favorite local delicacy, the opihi, a tasty morsel also known as the limpet. Youngsters enjoy swimming in the enlarged tide pool at the eastern edge of the bay. When you explore tide pools, do so at low tide. Never turn your back on the waves. Wear tennis shoes or reef walkers, as wet rocks are slippery. Collecting specimens in this marine preserve is forbidden, so don't take any souvenirs home.

Polihua Beach ★

So many sea turtles once hauled themselves out of the water to lay their eggs in the sunbaked sand on Lanai's northwestern shore that Hawaiians named the beach here *Polihua,* or "egg nest." Although the endangered green sea turtles are making a comeback, they're seldom seen here now. You're more likely to spot an offshore whale (in season) or the perennial litter that washes up onto this deserted beach at the end of Polihua Road, a 4-mile jeep trail. This strand is ideal for beachcombing (those little green-glass Japanese fishing-net floats often show up here), fishing, or just being alone. There are no facilities except fishermen's huts and driftwood shelters. Bring water and sunscreen. Beware of the strong currents, which make the water unsafe for swimming.

Shipwreck Beach ★

This 8-mile-long windswept strand on Lanai's northeastern shore—named for the rusty ship *Liberty* stuck on the coral reef—is a sailor's nightmare and a beachcomber's dream. The strong currents yield all sorts of flotsam, from Japanese handblown-glass fish floats and rare pelagic paper nautilus shells to lots of junk. This is also a great place to spot whales from December to April, when the Pacific humpbacks cruise in from Alaska. The road to the beach is paved most of the way, but you really need a four-wheel-drive to get down here.

WATERSPORTS

Lanai has Hawaii's best water clarity because it lacks major development, it has low rainfall and runoff, and its coast is washed clean daily by the sea current (known as "The Way to Tahiti"). But the strong sea currents pose a threat to swimmers, and there are few good surf breaks. Most of the aquatic adventures—swimming, snorkeling, scuba diving—are centered on the somewhat protected south shore, around Hulopoe Bay.

The only outfitter for watersports is **Trilogy Lanai Ocean Sports ★★★** (✆ **888/MAUI-800** [628-4800]; www.visitlanai.com).

Sailing & Snorkeling

Trilogy Lanai Ocean Sports (see above), which has built a well-deserved reputation as the leader in sailing/snorkeling cruises in Hawaii, offers both a morning and an afternoon **snorkel sailing trip** onboard its luxury custom sailing catamarans or its 32-foot jet-drive rigid aluminum-inflatable vessel. The trips along Lanai's protected coastline sail past hundreds of spinner dolphins and into some of the best snorkeling sites in the world for $203 (half-price for children 3–15) and include lunch, sodas, snorkel gear, and instruction.

If you just want to snorkel on your own, Hulopoe is Lanai's best snorkeling spot. Fish are abundant in the marine-life conservation area. Try the lava-rock points at either end of the beach and around the lava pools.

Polihua Beach.

Shipwreck Beach.

The cargo ship *Liberty*, off the coast of Shipwreck Beach.

Scuba Diving

Two of Hawaii's best-known dive spots are found in Lanai's clear waters, just off the south shore: **Cathedrals I** and **II,** so named because the sun lights up an underwater grotto like a magnificent church. **Trilogy Lanai Ocean Sports** (see above for contact information) offers several kinds of sailing, diving, and snorkeling trips on catamarans and from its new 32-foot high-tech jet-drive ocean raft. It has its own version of "sunrise services" at the Cathedrals—not only is this the best time of day to dive this incredible area, but there are virtually no other dive boats in the water at this time. Cost is $169 to $199 for a two-tank dive, $79 for nondivers. Beach dives are available for $95 (one-tank dive) for certified divers and $95 for an introductory dive for noncertified divers.

Sport Fishing

Spinning Dolphin Charters of Lanai (© **808/565-7676;** www.sportfishing lanai.com) offers sport fishing on a 42-foot Hatteras boat. It will take up to six passengers for $700 for 4 hours ($110 for each additional hour), or you can share a boat for $150 each for 4 hours.

Surfing

If you've ever wanted to learn how to surf, let instructor Nick Palumbo, a surfing champion, take you on a four-wheel-drive surfing safari to a secluded surf spot. He'll have you up and riding the waves in no time. His **Lanai Surf School & Surf Safari** (© **808/565-7258;** www.lanaisurfsafari.com) offers a package that includes a 2½-hour lesson with surfboard, four-wheel-drive transportation, refreshments, and "a really good time" for $175 per person.

Whale-Watching

During whale season, from December to April, **Trilogy Lanai Ocean Sports** (see above for contact information) takes passengers out on its 26-passenger,

FROMMER'S FAVORITE lanai EXPERIENCES

Snorkeling Hulopoe Beach. Crystal-clear waters teem with brilliant tropical fish off one of Hawaii's best beaches. There are tide pools to explore, waves to play in, and other surprises—like a pod of spinner dolphins that often makes a splashy entrance.

Exploring the Garden of the Gods. Eroded by wind, rain, and time, these geologic badlands (p. 623, pictured here) are worth visiting at sunrise or sunset, when the low light plays tricks on the land—and your mind.

Hiking the Munro Trail. The 11-mile Munro Trail (p. 623) is a lofty, rigorous hike along the rim of an old volcano. You'll get great views of the nearby islands. Take a four-wheel-drive vehicle if you want to spend more time on top of the island.

Four-Wheeling It. Four-wheeling is a way of life on Lanai because there are only 30 miles of pavement on the whole island. Plenty of rugged trails lead to deserted beaches, abandoned villages, and valleys filled with wild game.

Camping Under the Stars. The campsites (below) at Hulopoe Beach Park are about as close to the heavens as you can get. The crashing surf will lull you to sleep at night, and chirping birds will wake you in the morning. If you're into roughing it, this is a great way to experience Lanai.

Watching the Whales at Polihua Beach. Located on the north shore, this beach—which gets its name from the turtles that nest here—is a great place to watch for whales during the winter months.

rigid-hulled inflatable boat, a 32-foot jet-drive Zodiac named *Manele Kai,* for a 2-hour ocean adventure that explores some of the remote and unspoiled sites in Hawaii. Lanai is also home to one of Hawaii's largest schools of spinner dolphins and a haven for North Pacific humpback whales. The captains and crew are Certified Island Naturalists who make each trip educational as well as entertaining, and they can usually find these wonderful and playful mammals. The cost is $75 (half-price for children 3–15), which includes soft drinks.

HIKING & CAMPING
Hiking
A LEISURELY MORNING HIKE

The 3-hour self-guided **Koele Nature Hike** starts by the reflecting pool in the backyard of the Lodge at Koele and takes you on a 5-mile loop through Norfolk Island pines, into Hulopoe Valley, past wild ginger, and up to Koloiki Ridge, with its panoramic view of Maunalei Valley and of Molokai and Maui in the distance. You're welcome to take the hike even if you're not a guest at the Lodge. The path isn't clearly marked, so ask the concierge for a free map. Do this hike in the morning; by afternoon, the clouds usually roll in, marring visibility at the top and increasing your chance of being caught in a downpour.

THE CHALLENGING MUNRO TRAIL

This tough 11-mile (round-trip) uphill climb through the groves of Norfolk pines is a lung-buster, but if you reach the top, you'll be rewarded with a breathtaking view of Molokai, Maui, Kahoolawe, the peaks of the Big Island, and—on a really clear day—Oahu in the distance. Figure on 7 hours. The trail begins at Lanai Cemetery along Keomoku Road (Hwy. 44) and follows Lanai's ancient caldera rim, ending up at the island's highest point, Lanaihale. Go in the morning for the best visibility. After 4 miles, you'll get a view of Lanai City. The weary retrace their steps from here, while the more determined go the last 1.25 miles to the top. Die-hards head down Lanai's steep south-crater rim to join the highway to Manele Bay. For more details on the Munro Trail—including information on four-wheel-driving it to the top—see "Five Islands at a Single Glance: The Munro Trail" (p. 623).

A SELF-GUIDED NATURE TRAIL

This self-guided nature trail in the Kanepuu Preserve (described below) is about a 10- to 15-minute walk through eight stations, with interpretive signs explaining the natural or cultural significance of what you're seeing. The trail head is clearly marked on the Polihua Road on the way to the Garden of the Gods. Kanepuu is one of the last remaining examples of the type of forest that once covered the dry lowlands throughout the state. There are some 49 plant species here that are found only in Hawaii. The **Nature Conservancy** (☏ 808/565-7430) conducts guided hikes every month; call for details. As we went to press, the Kanepuu Preserve was closed, but had plans for reopening, with guided hikes soon. I would definitely call the Maui Conservancy office to confirm before going. There are also plans to reconstruct the self-guided trails and signage, which have fallen into serious disrepair, but no dates or projections.

GUIDED HIKES

The **Lodge at Koele** (☏ 808/565-4552; www.fourseasons.com/lanai) offers a 2½-hour Koloiki Ridge Nature hike through 5 miles of the upland forests of Koele at 11am daily. Fee is $25. It's considered moderate, with some uphill and downhill hiking.

Camping at Hulopoe Beach Park

There is only one legal place to camp on Lanai: **Hulopoe Beach Park,** which is owned by Castle and Cooke Resorts. To camp in this exquisite beach park, with its crescent-shaped white-sand beach bordered by kiawe trees, contact **Wendell Sarme–Park Manager,** Castle and Cooke Resorts, P.O. Box 630310, Lanai City, HI 96763 (☏ 808/565-2970). There's a $25 registration fee, plus a charge of $10 per person, per night. Hulopoe has six campsites; each can accommodate up to six people. Facilities include restrooms, running water, showers, barbecue areas, and picnic tables.

GOLF & OTHER OUTDOOR ACTIVITIES

Golf

Cavendish Golf Course 🎁 This quirky par-36, 9-hole public course lacks not only a clubhouse and club pros, but also tee times, scorecards, and club rentals. To play, just show up, put a donation into the little wooden box next to the first tee, and hit away. The 3,071-yard, E. B. Cavendish–designed course was built by the Dole plantation in 1947 for its employees. The greens are a bit bumpy, but the views of Lanai are great and the temperatures usually quite mild.

Next to the Lodge at Koele in Lanai City. No phone. Greens fees $5–$10 suggested donation.

The Challenge at Manele ★★ This target-style, desert-links course, designed by Jack Nicklaus, is one of the most challenging courses in the state. Check out the local rules: "No retrieving golf balls from the 150-foot cliffs on the ocean holes 12, 13, or 17," and "All whales, axis deer, and other wild animals are considered immovable obstructions." That's just a hint of the unique experience you'll have on this course, which is routed among lava outcroppings, archaeological sites, kiawe groves, and ilima trees. The five sets of staggered tees pose a challenge to everyone from the casual golfer to the pro. Facilities include a clubhouse, pro shop, rentals, practice area, lockers, and showers.

Next to the Four Seasons Resort Lanai at Manele Bay. ☎ **800/321-4666** or 808/565-2222. Greens fees $225 ($210 for guests).

The Experience at Koele ★★ This traditional par-72 course, designed by Greg Norman with fairway architecture by Ted Robinson, has very different front and back 9 holes. Mother Nature reigns throughout: You'll see Cook Island and Norfolk pines, indigenous plants, and lots of water—seven lakes, flowing streams, cascading waterfalls, and one green (the 17th) completely surrounded by a lake. All goes well until you hit the signature hole, number 8, where you tee off from a 250-foot elevated tee to a fairway bordered by a lake on the right and trees and dense shrubs on the left. After that, the back 9 holes drop dramatically through ravines filled with pine, koa, and eucalyptus trees. The grand finale, the par-5 18th, features a green rimmed by waterfalls that flow into a lake on the left side. To level the playing field, there are four different sets of tees. Facilities include a clubhouse, pro shop, rentals, practice area, lockers, and showers.

Next to the Lodge at Koele in Lanai City. ☎ **800/321-4666** or 808/565-4653. Greens fees $225 ($210 for guests).

Biking

The **Lodge at Koele** (☎ 808/565-4552) rents mountain bikes for $10 an hour.

Horseback Riding

Horses can take you to many places in Lanai's unique landscape that are otherwise unreachable. The **Four Seasons Lanai Resort's Stables at Koele** (☎ **808/565-4424**) offers various daily rides (9am and 1:30pm), including slow, gentle group excursions starting at $95 for a 1½-hour **Paniolo Trail Ride,** which takes you into the hills surrounding Koele. You'll meander through guava groves and ironwood trees; catch glimpses of axis deer, quail, wild turkeys, and Santa

Gertrudis cattle; and end with panoramic views of Maui and Lanai. Private 2-hour rides can be arranged for $160 per person; 1½-hour sunset rides go for $200 per person. Kids will love the 15-minute pony rides; parents will love the price of $15 per person. Long pants and closed-toe shoes (like running shoes) are required, and safety helmets are provided. Bring a jacket—the weather is chilly and rain is frequent. Children must be at least 9 years old and 4 feet tall, and riders cannot weigh more than 225 pounds.

Tennis

Public courts, lit for night play, are available in Lanai City at no charge; call © 808/565-6979 for reservations. If you're staying at the Lodge at Koele or at Manele Bay, you can take advantage of the Lodge's three new Premiere Cushion outdoor hard courts, with complimentary use of Wilson racquets, balls, and bottled water. You're also invited to experience the tennis center at the Four Seasons Resort Lanai at Manele Bay, which offers a full pro shop, use of a ball machine, and weekly tennis mixers and tournaments. Courts are $20 per person for hotel guests (not open to nonguests). For information, call © 808/565-2072.

SEEING THE SIGHTS

You'll need a four-wheel-drive vehicle to reach all the sights listed below. Renting a jeep is an expensive proposition on Lanai—from $139 to $179 a day—so I suggest renting one just for the day (or days) you plan on sightseeing; otherwise, it's easy enough to get to the beach and around Lanai City without your own wheels. For details on vehicle rentals, see "Getting Around" (p. 610).

Note: You'll find the following attractions on the map on p. 607.

Garden of the Gods ★

A dirt four-wheel-drive road leads out of Lanai City, through the now uncultivated pineapple fields, past the Kanepuu Preserve (a dry-land forest preserve teeming with rare plant and animal life) to the so-called Garden of the Gods, out on Lanai's north shore. This rugged, barren, beautiful place is full of rocks strewn by volcanic forces and shaped by the elements into a variety of shapes and colors—brilliant reds, oranges, ochers, and yellows.

Ancient Hawaiians considered this desolate, windswept place an entirely supernatural phenomenon. Scientists, however, have other, less colorful explanations. Some call the area an "ongoing posterosional event"; others say it's just "plain and simple badlands." Take a four-wheel-drive ride out here and decide for yourself.

Go early in the morning or just before sunset, when the light casts eerie shadows on the mysterious lava formations. Drive west from the Lodge on Polihua Road; in about 2 miles, you'll see a hand-painted sign that'll point left down a one-lane, red-dirt road through a kiawe forest to the site.

Five Islands at a Single Glance: The Munro Trail ★

In the first golden rays of dawn, when lone owls swoop over abandoned pineapple fields, hop into a 4×4 and head out on the two-lane blacktop toward Mount Lanaihale, the 3,370-foot summit of Lanai. Your destination is the Munro Trail, the narrow, winding ridge trail that runs across Lanai's razorback spine to the summit. From here, you may get a rare Hawaii treat: On a clear day, you can see all of the main islands in the Hawaiian chain except Kauai.

When it rains, the Munro Trail becomes slick and boggy with major washouts. Rainy-day excursions often end with a rental jeep on the hook of the island's lone tow truck—and a $250 tow charge. You could even slide off into a major gulch and never be found, so don't try it. But in late August and September, when trade winds stop and the air over the islands stalls in what's called a *kona* condition, Mount Lanaihale's suddenly visible peak becomes an irresistible attraction.

When you're on Lanai, look to the summit. If it's clear in the morning, rent a four-wheel-drive vehicle and take the Munro Trail to the top. Look for a red-dirt road off Manele Road (Hwy. 440), about 5 miles south of Lanai City; turn left and head up the ridgeline. No sign marks the peak, so you'll have to keep an eye out. Look for a wide spot in the road and a clearing that falls sharply to the sea.

From here you can see Kahoolawe, Maui, the Big Island of Hawaii, and Molokini's tiny crescent. Even the summits show. You can also see the silver domes of Space City on Haleakala in Maui; Puu Moaulanui, the tongue-twisting summit of Kahoolawe; and, looming above the clouds, Mauna Kea on the Big Island. At another clearing farther along the thickly forested ridge, all of Molokai, including the 4,961-foot summit of Kamakou and the faint outline of Oahu (more than 30 miles across the sea), are visible. You actually can't see all five islands in a single glance anymore because a thriving pine forest blocks the view. For details on hiking the trail, see "Hiking & Camping" (p. 620).

☺ ESPECIALLY FOR kids

Exploring Hulopoe's Tide Pools (p. 617)   An entire world of marine life lives in the tide pools on the eastern side of Hulopoe Bay. Everything in the water, including the tiny fish, is small—kid size. After examining the wonders of the tide pool, check out the larger swimming holes in the lava rock, perfect for children.

Hunting for Petroglyphs (below)   The Luahiwa Petroglyph Field (pictured here), located just outside Lanai City, is spread out over a 3-acre site. Make it a game: Whoever finds the most petroglyphs gets ice cream from the Pine Isle Market.

Listening to Storytellers   Check with the Lanai Library, on Fraser Avenue near Fifth Street, in Lanai City

(✆ **808/565-6996**), to see if any storytelling or other children's activities are scheduled. The events are usually free and open to everyone.

The Munro Trail summit.

Luahiwa Petroglyph Field

Lanai is second only to the Big Island in its wealth of prehistoric rock art, but you'll have to search a little to find it. Some of the best examples are on the outskirts of Lanai City, on a hillside site known as Luahiwa Petroglyph Field. The characters you'll see incised on 13 boulders in this grassy 3-acre knoll include a running man, a deer, a turtle, a bird, a goat, and even a rare curly-tailed Polynesian dog (a latter-day wag has put a leash on him—some joke).

To get here, take the road to Hulopoe Beach. About 2 miles out of Lanai City, look to the left, up on the slopes of the crater, for a cluster of reddish-tan boulders (believed to form a rain *heiau,* or shrine, where people called up the gods Ku and Hina to nourish their crops). A cluster of spiky century plants marks the spot. Look for the Norfolk pines on the left side of the highway, turn left on the dirt road that veers across the abandoned pineapple fields, and after about 1 mile, take a sharp left by the water tanks. Drive for another ½ mile and then veer to the right at the V in the road. Stay on this upper road for about ¼ mile; you'll come to a large cluster of boulders on the right side. It's just a short walk up the cliffs (wear walking or hiking shoes) to the petroglyphs. Exit the same way you came. Go between 3pm and sunset for ideal viewing and photo ops.

Kaunolu Village

Out on Lanai's nearly vertical, Gibraltar-like sea cliffs is an old royal compound and fishing village. Now a national historic landmark and one of Hawaii's most treasured ruins, it's believed to have been inhabited by King Kamehameha the Great and hundreds of his closest followers about 200 years ago. It's a hot, dry, dusty, slow-going, 3-mile 4×4 drive from Lanai City to Kaunolu, but the mini-expedition is worth it. Take plenty of water, don a hat for protection against the sun, and wear sturdy shoes.

Ruins of 86 house platforms and 35 stone shelters have been identified on both sides of Kaunolu Gulch. The residential complex also includes the Halulu Heiau temple, named after a mythical man-eating bird. The king's royal retreat is thought to have stood on the eastern edge of Kaunolu Gulch, overlooking the rocky shore facing Kahekili's Leap, a 62-foot-high bluff named for the mighty Maui chief who leaped off cliffs as a show of bravado. Nearby are burial caves, a fishing shrine, a lookout tower, and many warrior-like stick figures carved on boulders. Just offshore stands the telltale fin of little Shark Island, a popular dive spot that teems with bright tropical fish and, frequently, sharks.

Excavations are underway to discover more about how ancient Hawaiians lived, worked, and worshiped on Lanai's leeward coast. Who knows? The royal fishing village may yet yield the bones of King Kamehameha. His burial site, according to legend, is known only to the moon and the stars.

Kanepuu Preserve

This ancient forest on the island's western plateau is so fragile, you can visit only once a month, and even then only on a guided hike. Kanepuu, which has 48 species of plants unique to Hawaii, survives under the Nature Conservancy's protective wing. Botanists say the 590-acre forest is the last dry lowland forest in Hawaii; the others have all vanished, trashed by axis deer, agriculture, or "progress." Among the botanical marvels of this dry forest are the remains of *olopua* (native olive), *lama* (native ebony), *mau hau hele* (a native hibiscus), and the rare *'aiea* trees, which were used for canoe parts.

Due to the forest's fragile nature, guided hikes are led only 12 times a year, on a monthly, reservations-only basis. Contact the **Nature Conservancy Oahu Land Preserve** manager at 1116 Smith St., Ste. 201, Honolulu, HI 96817 (*© 808/537-4508*), to reserve.

Off the Tourist Trail: Keomoku Village

If you're sunburned lobster red, have read all the books you packed, and are starting to get island fever, take a little drive to Keomoku Village, on Lanai's east coast. You'll really be off the tourist path here. All that's in Keomoku, a ghost town since the mid-1950s, is a 1903 clapboard church in disrepair, an overgrown graveyard, an excellent view across the 9-mile Auau Channel to Maui's crowded Kaanapali Beach, and some very empty beaches that are perfect for a picnic or a snorkel. This former ranching and fishing village of 2,000 was the first non-Hawaiian settlement on Lanai, but it dried up after droughts killed off the Maunalei Sugar Company. The village, such as it is, is a great little escape from Lanai City. Follow Keomoku Road for 8 miles to the coast, turn right on the sandy road, and keep going for 5¾ miles.

Perfect for a Rainy Day: Lanai Art Center

A perfect activity for a rainy day in Lanai City is the **Lanai Art Center,** 339 Seventh St., located in the heart of the small town. Top artists from across Hawaii frequently visit this homegrown art program and teach a variety of classes, ranging from raku (Japanese pottery), silk printing, silk screening, pareu making (creating your own design on this islanders' wrap), gyotaku (printing a real fish on your own T-shirt), and watercolor drawing to a variety of other island crafts. The cost for the 2- to 3-hour

classes is usually in the $15 to $70 range (materials are extra). For information, call *© 808/565-7503* or visit www.lanaiart.org.

Keomoku Village.

SHOPPING

Central Bakery ★ 🎁 This is the mother lode of the island's baked delights—the bakery that is, well, central to Lanai's dining pleasure. If you've noshed on the fantastic sandwiches at the Terrace at the Lodge at Koele or any of the stellar desserts at the Lodge's Main Dining Room or at the Four Seasons Resort Lanai at Manele Bay, you've enjoyed goodies from Central Bakery. The bakery supplies all breads, all breakfast pastries, specialty ice creams and sorbets, all banquet desserts, and restaurant desserts on the island. Although it's not your standard retail outlet, you can call in advance, place your order, and pick it up. The staff prefers as much notice as possible (preferably 48 hr.), but, in a pinch, will take a 24-hour order. Breads (most priced at $4.50) range from walnut onion to roasted potato bacon to olive onion. The bakery also has cookies (chocolate chip, oatmeal, coconut—all for 50¢), brownies, muffins, croissants (including chocolate croissants), Danishes, and scones, plus an assortment of breakfast pastries (pineapple turnover, hazelnut roll, mascarpone apricot Danish, pistachio chocolate roll, and others). 1311 Fraser Ave., Lanai City. ℂ **808/565-3920.**

Dis 'N Dat ★★ 🎁 Dis (Barry) and Dat (Susie) visited Lanai from Florida to look at buying a retirement home. They found their home and moved to Lanai to retire. Retirement didn't last. A few years later, outgoing Barry and his wife started searching for unusual, finely crafted teak and exotic wood sculptures and carvings. Along the way, they took a shine to mobiles and wind chimes—the more outrageous, the better. Then they started collecting handmade jewelry, stained glass, and unique garden ornaments and home decor. All this led to this eclectic store, which you have to see to believe. Meeting Barry is worth the trip alone. You'll find T-shirts, pottery, ceramics, batik scarves, hula lamps and whimsical dragonfly lamps, woven baskets, and even waterfalls. This is also the biggest collection of Hawaii slipper necklaces, earrings, anklets, and bracelets. You can't miss the vivid green shop with hanging chimes and mobiles leading the way to the front door. 418 Eighth Ave. (at Kilele St.), Lanai City. ℂ **866/DIS-N-DAT** (347-6328) or 808/565-9170.

International Food & Clothing   This store sells the basics: groceries, housewares, T-shirts, hunting and fishing supplies, over-the-counter drugs, wine and liquor, paper goods, and hardware, and even has a takeout lunch counter. I was pleasantly surprised by the extraordinary candy and bubble-gum section, the beautiful local bananas in the small produce section, the surprisingly extensive selection of yuppie soft drinks (Sobe, Snapple, and others), and the best knife sharpener I've seen. 833 Ilima Ave., Lanai City. ✆ **808/565-6433.**

Lanai Art Center ★ 📷   This wonderful center was organized in 1989 to provide a place where both residents and visitors can come to create art. The center offers classes and studio time in ceramics, painting and drawing, calligraphy, woodworking, photography, silk and textile painting, watercolor, and glass. There's an impressive schedule of visiting instructors, from writers to folk artists (quilting, lei making, and instrument making) to oil painters. Check out the reasonably priced classes (generally in the $25 range) or browse the gallery for excellent deals on works by Lanai residents. 339 Seventh St., Lanai City. ✆ **808/565-7503.** www.lanaiart.org.

Lanai Marketplace   Everyone on Lanai, it seems, is a backyard farmer. From 7 to 11am or noon on Saturday, they all head to this shady square to sell their dewy-fresh produce, home-baked breads, plate lunches, and handicrafts. This is Lanai's version of the green market: petite in scale (like the island) but charming, and growing. Dole Park, Lanai City.

The Local Gentry ★★ 📷   Jenna (Gentry) Majkus's wonderful boutique, open since 1999, is the first of its kind on the island, featuring clothing and accessories that are not the standard resort-shop fare. (Visiting and local women alike make a beeline for this store.) You'll find fabulous silk aloha shirts by Tiki, mahogany lamps, mermaids and hula girls, inexpensive sarongs, and fabulous socks. There are also great T-shirts, jewelry, bath products, picture frames, jeans, and offbeat sandals. The most recent additions are wonderful children's clothes. 363 Seventh St. (behind Gifts with Aloha, facing Ilima St.), Lanai City. ✆ **808/565-9130.**

Mike Carroll Gallery   If he is on the island, you'll find Mike Carroll at work here on his original oil paintings. After a successful 22-year career as a professional artist in Chicago, Carroll moved to Lanai and has been painting the beauty and the lifestyle of the island ever since. You'll find an extensive selection of his original work, some limited editions, prints, and notecards, plus a dozen or so of Maui's and Lanai's top artists and even some locally made, one-of-a-kind jewelry. 443 Seventh St., Lanai City. ✆ **808/565-7122.** www.mikecarrollgallery.com.

Pine Isle Market   A local landmark for two generations, Pine Isle specializes in locally caught fresh fish, but you can also find fresh herbs and spices, canned goods, electronic games, ice cream, toys, zoris, diapers, paint, cigars, and other basic essentials of work and play. The fishing section is outstanding, with every lure imaginable. 356 Eighth St., Lanai City. ✆ **808/565-6488.**

Richard's Shopping Center   The Tamashiros's family business has been on the square since 1946; not much has changed over the years. This "shopping center" is, in fact, a general store with a grocery section, paper products, ethnic foods, meats (mostly frozen), liquor, toys, film, cosmetics, fishing gear, sunscreens, clothing, kitchen utensils, T-shirts, and other miscellany. Half a wall is lined with an extraordinary selection of fishhooks and anglers' needs. Aloha shirts, aloha-print zoris, fold-up lauhala mats, and gourmet breads from the Central Bakery (see above) are among the countless good things at Richard's. 434 Eighth St., Lanai City. ✆ **808/565-6047.**

LANAI AFTER DARK

The only regular nightlife venues are the Lanai Playhouse, at the corner of Seventh and Lanai avenues in Lanai City, and the two resorts, the Lodge at Koele and Four Seasons Resort Lanai at Manele Bay.

The **Lanai Playhouse** (© **808/565-7500**) is a historic 1920s building that has won awards for its renovations. When it opened in 1993, the 150-seat venue stunned residents by offering first-run movies with Dolby sound—quite contemporary for anachronistic Lanai. The Lanai Playhouse usually, but not always, shows two movies each evening from Friday to Tuesday (to Wed in summer), at 6:30 and 8:30pm, with occasional Sunday and Monday matinees; if a 3-hour movie is on, it's shown at 7:30pm. The playhouse is also the venue for occasional special events.

The **Lodge at Koele** has stepped up its live entertainment. In front of the manorial fireplaces in the Great Hall, local artists serenade listeners, who sip port and fine liqueurs while sinking into plush chairs, with contemporary Hawaiian, classical, and other genres of music. The special programs are on weekends, but some form of nightly entertainment takes place throughout the week, from 7 to 10pm.

Occasionally, special events will bring in a few more nightlife options. During the annual **Pineapple Festival,** generally the first weekend in July, some of Hawaii's best musicians arrive to show their support for Lanai (see "Hawaii Calendar of Events," on p. 65). The **Aloha Festival** (www.alohafestivals.com) takes place in the end of September or the first week in October, and the **Christmas Festival** is held on the first Saturday in December. For details on these festivals, contact the **Lanai Visitors Bureau,** P.O. Box 631436, Lanai City, HI 96763; or 431 Seventh St., Ste. A, Lanai City, 96763 (© **800/947-4774** or 808/565-7600; fax 808/565-9316; www.visitlanai.net).

KAUAI, THE GARDEN ISLE

10

O n any list of the world's most spectacular islands, Kauai ranks right up there with Bora Bora, Huahine, and Rarotonga. All the elements are here: moody rainforests, majestic cliffs, jagged peaks, emerald valleys, palm trees swaying in the breeze, daily rainbows, and some of the most spectacular golden beaches you'll find anywhere. Soft tropical air, bird song, the smell of ginger and plumeria, sparkling waterfalls—you don't just go to Kauai, you absorb it with every sense. It may get more than its fair share of tropical downpours, but that's what makes it so lush and green—and creates an abundance of rainbows. The readers of *Travel / Leisure* magazine have voted Kauai the best island in Hawaii several years in a row.

Kauai is essentially a single large shield volcano that rises 3 miles above the sea floor. The island lies 90 miles across the open ocean from Oahu but seems at least a half-century removed in time. It's often called "the separate kingdom" because it stood alone and resisted King Kamehameha's efforts to unite Hawaii. In the end, it required a royal kidnapping to take the garden isle. After King Kamehameha died, his son, Liholiho, ascended the throne. He gained control of Kauai by luring Kauai's king, Kaumualii, aboard the royal yacht and sailing to Oahu; once there, Kaumualii was forced to marry Kaahumanu, Kamehameha's widow, thereby uniting the islands.

Today the independent spirit lives on in Kauai, which refuses to surrender its island to wholesale tourism. A Kauai rule is that no building may exceed the height of a coconut tree—between three and four stories. As a result, the island itself, not its palatial beach hotels, is the attention-grabber. There's little nightlife here, no opulent shopping malls—just the beauty of the verdant jungle, the endless succession of spectacular beaches, the grandeur of Waimea Canyon, and the drama of the Na Pali Coast.

Kauai's beauty has played a supporting role in more than 50 Hollywood films, from *South Pacific* to *Jurassic Park*. But this island is not just another pretty face: Its raw wilderness is daunting, its seas challenging, its canyons forbidding—two-thirds of the island is impenetrable. This is the place for active visitors, with watersports galore; miles of trails through rainforests and along ocean cliffs for hikers, bikers, and horseback riders; and golf options that range from championship links to local courses where chickens roam the greens and balls wind up in coconut trees.

But Kauai is also great for those who need to relax and heal jangled nerves. Here you'll find miles of sandy beaches and quiet spots in the forest, perfect for just sitting and meditating, and an endless supply of laid-back, lazy days that end with the sun sinking into the Pacific amid a blaze of glorious tropical color.

FACING PAGE: **The Napali Coast.**

ORIENTATION

Arriving

United Airlines (© 800/225-5825; www.united.com) offers direct service to Kauai, with daily flights from Los Angeles and San Francisco. **American Airlines** (© 800/433-7300; www.aa.com) has direct flights from Los Angeles. US Airways (© 800/428-4322; www.usairways.com) has direct flights to Kauai from Phoenix. **SunTrips** (© 800/514-5194; www.suntrips.com) has a charter from San Francisco or Oakland once a week that is direct. **Pleasant Holidays** (© 800/742-9244; www.pleasantholidays.com), one of Hawaii's largest travel companies, offers low-cost airfare and package deals with nonstop flights from Los Angeles and San Francisco.

All other airlines land in Honolulu (on Oahu), where you'll have to connect to a 30-minute interisland flight on **go!** (© 888/I-FLY-GO-2 [435-9462]; www.iflygo.com) or **Hawaiian Airlines** (© 800/367-5320, 808/245-1813, or 808/838-1555; www.hawaiianair.com).

You'll land at Kauai's **Lihue Airport,** located 3 miles outside the county seat of Lihue. The final approach to the airport is dramatic; try to sit on the left side of the aircraft, where passengers are treated to an excellent view of the Haupu Ridge, Nawiliwili Bay, and Kilohana Crater. There's a county visitor information kiosk located next to each baggage-claim area. All of the major car-rental companies have branches at Lihue Airport; for a complete listing, see chapter 11. For tips on insurance and driving rules in Hawaii, see "Getting There & Getting Around" (p. 74). If you're not renting a car (although you should), call **Kauai Taxi Company** (© 808/246-9554) for airport pickup.

Visitor Information

The **Kauai Visitors Bureau** is located on the first floor of the Watumull Plaza, 4334 Rice St., Ste. 101, Lihue, HI 96766 (© 808/245-3971; fax 808/246-9235; www.kauaivisitorsbureau.org). Call © 800/262-1400 for a free official *Kauai Vacation Planner* or recorded information. The **Poipu Beach Resort Association,** P.O. Box 730, Koloa, HI 96756 (© 888/744-0888 or 808/742-7444; www.poipu-beach.org), will also send you a free guide to accommodations, activities, shopping, and dining in the Poipu Beach area.

To learn more about Kauai before you go, contact the **Kauai Historical Society,** 4396 Rice St., Lihue, HI 96766 (© 808/245-3373; www.kauaihistorical society.org). The group maintains a video-lending library that includes material on a range of topics, including Hawaiian legends, ghost stories, archaeology, and travelogues on individual areas around Kauai. Mainland residents can borrow tapes for up to 3 weeks. Rates are $1 for society members, $2.50 for nonmembers; shipping and handling costs $5.

You can plan your vacation around the island's festivals and local events by checking out **www.kauaifestivals.com**.

The Island in Brief

Kauai's three main resort areas, where nearly all the island's accommodations are located, are all quite different in climate, price, and type of lodgings offered. On the south shore, dry and sunny **Poipu** is anchored by perfect beaches; it's the place to stay if you like the ocean, watersports, and plenty of sunshine. The

Orientation

KAUAI, THE GARDEN ISLE

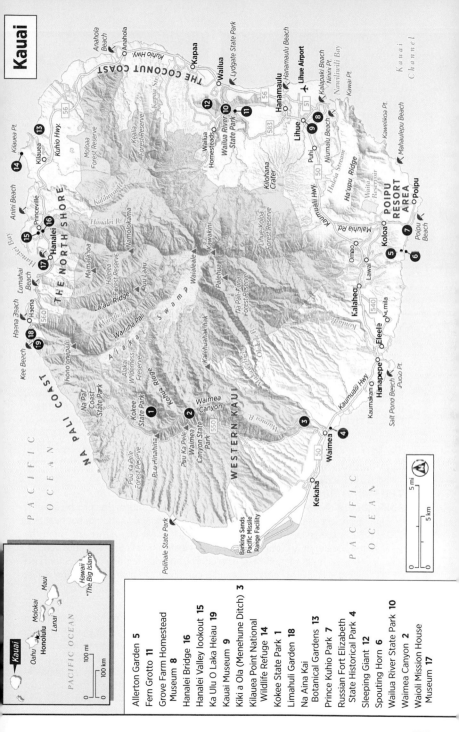

Kauai

PACIFIC OCEAN

Oahu
Honolulu ★
Molokai
★ Kauai
Maui
Lanai
Hawaii
"The Big Island"

0 100 mi
0 100 km

THE COCONUT COAST

THE NORTH SHORE

NA PALI COAST

WESTERN KAUAI

POIPU RESORT AREA

Kauai Channel

PACIFIC OCEAN

Anahola Beach
Anahola
Kuhio Hwy
Kapaa
Wailua
Lydgate State Park
Kapaa Forest Reserve
Moloaa Forest Reserve
Kilauea Pt.
Kilauea
Kuhio Hwy
Anini Beach
Princeville
Hanalei
Hanalei Bay
Lumahai Beach
Haena Beach
Kee Beach
Haena
Honoonapali

Wailua Homesteads
Wailua River State Park
Kealia Forest Reserve
Kalihiwai
Hanalei R.
Mamalahoa
Hanalei Forest Reserve
Haleleia Forest Reserve
Puu Laau
Namolokama
Kawaikini
Waialeale

Lihue Airport
Hanamaulu Beach
Hanamaulu
Lihue
Niumalu Beach
Kalapaki Beach
Ninini Pt.
Nawiliwili Bay
Kawai Pt.

Puu Hinahina
Puu Ka Pele
Waimea Canyon State Park
Kokee State Park
Na Pali Coast State Park
Alakai Wilderness Reserve
Kohua Ridge
La'au Ridge
Mamalahoa
Wainiha Park
Wainiha
Alakai Swamp
Polihale State Park

Kilohana Crater
Lihue-Koloa Forest Reserve
Na Pali-Kona Forest Reserve
Kalehuahaka
Ohaiula R.
Olokele R.
Waimea R.
Waimea Canyon
Palehua
Kalehuahakinak

Kaumualii Hwy
Puhi
Hulei Stream
Haupu Ridge
Waita Reservoir
Maluhia Rd
Knudsen
Kaumakani
Salt Pond Beach
Puolo Pt.
Hanapepe
Eleele
Kalaheo
Lawai
Omao
Koloa
Poipu
Poipu Beach
Kawelikoa Pt.
Mahaulepu Beach

Waimea
Kekaha
Barking Sands Pacific Missile Range Facility

PACIFIC OCEAN

0 5 mi
0 5 km

56
56
583
51
50
50
540
550
560

Allerton Garden 5
Fern Grotto 11
Grove Farm Homestead Museum 8
Hanalei Bridge 16
Hanalei Valley lookout 15
Ka Ulu O Laka Heiau 19
Kauai Museum 9
Kiki a Ola (Menehune Ditch) 3
Kilauea Point National Wildlife Refuge 14
Kokee State Park 1
Limahuli Garden 18
Na Aina Kai Botanical Gardens 13
Prince Kuhio Park 7
Russian Fort Elizabeth State Historical Park 4
Sleeping Giant 12
Spouting Horn 6
Wailua River State Park 10
Waimea Canyon 2
Waioli Mission House Museum 17

633

Koloa.

Hanapepe.

Coconut Coast, on the east coast of Kauai, has the most condos, shops, and traffic—it's where all the action is. Hanalei, up on the **North Shore,** is rainy, lush, and quiet, with spectacular beaches and deep wilderness. Because of its remote location, the North Shore is a great place to get away from it all—but not a great place from which to explore the rest of the island.

LIHUE & ENVIRONS

Lihue is where most visitors first set foot on the island. This red-dirt farm town, the county seat, was founded by sugar planters and populated by descendants of Filipino and Japanese cane cutters. It's a plain and simple place, with used-car lots and mom-and-pop shops. It's also the source of bargains: inexpensive lodging, great deals on dining, and some terrific shopping buys. One of the island's most beautiful beaches, **Kalapaki Beach ★★**, is just next door at **Nawiliwili,** by the island's main harbor.

The Poipu Resort Area

POIPU BEACH ★★★ On Kauai's sun-soaked south shore, this is a pleasant if sleepy resort destination of low-rise hotels set on gold-sand pocket beaches. Well-done, master-planned Poipu is Kauai's most popular resort, with the widest variety of accommodations, from luxury hotels to B&Bs and condos. It offers 36 holes of golf, 38 tennis courts, and outstanding restaurants. This is a great place for watersports and a good base from which to tour the rest of Kauai. The only drawback is that the North Shore is about 1 to 1½ hours away.

KOLOA This tiny old town of gaily painted sugar shacks, just inland from Poipu Beach, is where the Hawaiian sugar industry was born more than 150 years ago. The mill is closed, but this showcase plantation town lives on as a tourist attraction, with delightful shops, an old general store, and a vintage Texaco gas station with a 1930s Model A truck in place, just like in the good old days.

KALAHEO/LAWAI   Just a short 10- to 15-minute drive inland from the beach at Poipu lie the more residential communities of Lawai and Kalaheo. Quiet subdivisions line the streets, restaurants catering to locals dot the area, and life revolves around family and work. You can find good bargains on B&Bs and a handful of reasonably priced restaurants here.

WESTERN KAUAI

This region, west of Poipu, is more remote than its eastern neighbor and lacks its terrific beaches. But it's home to one of Hawaii's most spectacular natural wonders, **Waimea Canyon ★★★** (the "Grand Canyon of the Pacific"), and, farther upland and inland, **Kokee State Park ★★**, one of its best parks.

HANAPEPE   For a quick trip back in time, turn off Hwy. 50 at Hanapepe, once one of Kauai's biggest towns. Founded by Chinese rice farmers, it's so picturesque that it was used as a backdrop for the miniseries *The Thorn Birds*. Hanapepe makes a good rest stop on the way to or from Waimea Canyon. It has galleries selling antiques as well as local art and crafts, including Georgio's surfboard art and coconut-grams. It's also home to one of the best restaurants on Kauai, the **Hanapepe Cafe & Espresso Bar** (p. 669). Nearby, at **Salt Pond Beach Park ★** (p. 678), Hawaiians since the 17th century have dried a reddish sea salt in shallow, red-clay pans. This is a great place to swim, snorkel, and maybe even observe an ancient industry still in practice.

WAIMEA   This little coastal town, the original capital of Kauai, seems to have quit the march of time. Dogs sleep in the street while old pickups rust in front yards. The ambience is definitely laid-back. A stay in Waimea is peaceful and quiet (especially at the Waimea Plantation Cottages on the beach; p. 649), but the remote location means this isn't the best base if you want to explore the other regions of Kauai, such as the North Shore, without a lot of driving.

On his search for the Northwest Passage in 1778, British explorer Capt. James Cook dropped anchor at Waimea and discovered a sleepy village of grass shacks. In 1815, the Russians arrived and built a fort here (now a national historic landmark), but they didn't last long: A scoundrel named George Anton Scheffer tried to claim Kauai for Russia, but he was exposed as an impostor and expelled by King Kamehameha I.

Today even Waimea's historic relics are spare and simple: a statue of Cook alongside a bas-relief of his ships, the rubble foundation of the Russian fort, and the remains of an ancient aqueduct unlike any other in the Pacific. Except for an overabundance of churches for a town this size, there's no sign that Waimea was selected as the first landing site of missionaries in 1820.

THE COCONUT COAST

The eastern shore of Kauai north of Lihue is a jumble of commerce and condos strung along the coast road named for Prince Kuhio, with several small beaches beyond. Almost anything you need, and a lot of stuff you can live without, can be found along this coast, which is known for its hundreds of coconut trees waving in the breeze. It's popular with budget travelers because of the myriad B&Bs and affordable hotels and condos to choose from, and it offers great restaurants and the island's major shopping areas.

KAPAA ★   The center of commerce on the east coast and the capital of the Coconut Coast condo-and-hotel district, this restored plantation town looks just like an antique. False-front wooden stores line both sides of the highway; it looks as though they've been here forever—until you notice the fresh paint and new roofs and realize that everything has been rebuilt since Hurricane Iniki smacked the town flat in 1992. Kapaa has made an amazing comeback without losing its funky charm.

THE NORTH SHORE

Kauai's North Shore may be the most beautiful place in Hawaii. Exotic seabirds, a half-moon bay, jagged peaks soaring into the clouds, and a mighty wilderness lie around the bend from the Coconut Coast, just beyond a series of one-lane bridges traversing the tail ends of waterfalls. There's only one road in and out, and only two towns, Hanalei and Kilauea—the former by the sea, the latter on a lighthouse cliff that's home to a bird preserve. Sun seekers may fret about all the rainy days, but Princeville Resort offers elegant shelter and two golf courses where you can play through rainbows.

niihau: THE FORBIDDEN ISLAND

Just 17 miles across the Kaulakahi Channel from Kauai lies the arid island of Niihau (Knee-ee-how), "The Forbidden Island." Visitors are not allowed on this privately owned island, which until recently was home to a cattle-and-sheep ranch that employed about 200 residents living in the single town of Puuwai.

In 1864, after an unusually wet winter that turned the dry scrubland of the small island (18×6 miles) into green pasture, Eliza Sinclair, a Scottish widow, decided to buy Niihau and move her family here. King Kamehameha IV agreed to sell the island for $10,000. The next year, normal weather returned, and the green pastures withered into sparse semidesert vegetation.

Today Sinclair's great-great-grandsons, Keith and Bruce Robinson, own the island and fiercely protect the privacy of its residents. However, in 1999 they decided to close down the ranching operation (which had not been profitable for many years), thus eliminating the only source of full-time employment on the island. Since then the population has dwindled, with many families living on Kauai at least part of the year to earn a living. In order to generate some income for the island, the Robinsons have entered into a contract with the U.S. Navy, which now has a small installation on the island, and have slowly started to open up parts of the island to limited tourism in the form of helicopter tours and hunting safaris (www.niihau.us for information and prices).

Life on Niihau has not changed much in 140 years: There's no indoor plumbing, and only the school has electric power, which is supplied entirely by solar panels installed in 2007. The Hawaiian language is still spoken. The men fish and hunt, and the women specialize in gathering and stringing *pupu Niihau,* prized tiny white seashells (found only on this island), into Niihau's famous lei, which fetch prices in the thousands of dollars.

Kapaa.

Kilauea village's antique lighthouse.

KILAUEA ★ This village is home to an antique lighthouse, tropical-fruit stands, little stone houses, and Kilauea Point National Wildlife Refuge, a wonderful seabird preserve. The rolling hills and sea cliffs are hideaways for the rich and famous, including Bette Midler and Sylvester Stallone. The village itself has its charms: The 1892 Kong Lung Company, Kauai's oldest general store, sells antiques, art, and crafts; and you can order a jazzy Billie Holiday Pizza to go at Kilauea Bakery and Pau Hana Pizza.

ANINI BEACH ★ This little-known residential district on a 2-mile reef (the biggest on Kauai) offers the safest swimming and snorkeling on the island. A great beach park is open to campers and day-trippers, and there's a boat ramp where locals launch sampans to fish for tuna. On Sunday, there's polo in the park and the sizzle of barbecue on the green. Several residents host guests in nearby B&Bs.

PRINCEVILLE ★ A little overwhelming for Kauai's wild North Shore, Princeville Resort is Kauai's biggest project, an 11,000-acre development set on a high plain overlooking Hanalei Bay. This resort community includes a luxury St. Regis hotel, 10 condo complexes, new timeshare units around two championship golf courses, cliffside access to pocket beaches, and one B&B right on the golf course.

HANALEI ★★★ Picture-postcard Hanalei is the laid-back center of North Shore life and an escapist's dream; it's also a gateway to the wild Na Pali Coast. Hanalei is the last great place on Kauai yet to face the developer's blade of progress. At **Hanalei Bay,** sloops anchor and surfers play year-round. The 2-mile-long crescent beach, the biggest indentation on Kauai's coast, is ideal for kids in summer, when the wild surf turns placid. Hanalei still retains the essence of its original sleepy, end-of-the-road charm. On either side of two-lane Kuhio Highway, you'll find just enough shops and restaurants to sustain you for your visit—unless you're a hiker, surfer, or sailor, or have some other preoccupation that might keep you here the rest of your life.

HAENA ★★ Emerald-green Haena isn't a town or a beach, but an ancient Hawaiian district, a place of exceptional natural beauty, and another gateway to the Na Pali Coast. It's the perfect tropical escape, and everybody knows it: Old house foundations and temples, now covered by jungle, lie in the shadow of new million-dollar homes of movie stars and musicians like Jeff Bridges and Graham Nash. This idyllic 4-mile coast has lagoons, bays, great beaches, spectacular snorkeling, a botanical garden, and the only North Shore resort that's right on the sand, the Hanalei Colony Resort (p. 656).

Hanalei.

THE NA PALI COAST ★★★

The road comes to an end, and now it begins: the Hawaii you've been dreaming about. Kauai's Na Pali Coast (*na pali* means "the cliffs") is a place of extreme beauty and Hawaii's last true wilderness. Its majestic splendor will forever remain unspoiled because no road will ever traverse it. You can enter this state park only on foot or by sea. Serious hikers—and I mean very serious—tackle the ancient 11-mile-long trail down the forbidding coast to Kalalau Valley (see "Hiking & Camping," on p. 692). The lone, thin trail that creases these cliffs isn't for the faint of heart or anyone afraid of heights. Those who aren't up to it can explore the wild coast in an inflatable rubber Zodiac, a billowing sailboat, a high-powered catamaran, or a helicopter, which takes you for the ride of your life.

GETTING AROUND

You'll need a car to see and do everything on Kauai. Luckily, driving here is easy. However, there really is only one major road that circles the island, and during rush hour, from about 6 to 9am and 3 to 6pm, this road turns into a giant parking lot. A trip from the airport to Poipu could be as quick as 30 to 45 minutes during non-rush-hour times or as much as 1½ hours during rush hour.

From Lihue Airport, turn right and you'll be on Kapule Highway (Hwy. 51), which eventually merges into Kuhio Highway (Hwy. 56) a mile down. This road will take you to the Coconut Coast and through the North Shore before eventually reaching a dead end at Kee Beach, where the Na Pali Coast begins.

If you turn left from Lihue Airport and follow Kapule Highway (Hwy. 51), you'll pass through Lihue and Nawiliwili. Turning on Nawiliwili Road (Hwy. 58) will bring you to the intersection of Kaumualii Highway (Hwy. 50), which will take you to the south and southwest sections of the island. This road doesn't follow the coast, however, so if you're heading to Poipu (and most people are), turn south off Hwy. 50 at Maluhia Road (Hwy. 520) to get to the coast.

Kaumualii Highway (Hwy. 50) continues to Waimea, where it then dwindles to a secondary road before reaching a dead end at the other end of the Na Pali Coast.

To get to Waimea Canyon, turn north of Hwy. 50 onto either Waimea Canyon Road (Hwy. 550), which follows the western rim of the canyon and affords spectacular views, or Kokee Road (Hwy. 55), which goes up through Waimea Canyon to Kokee State Park (4,000 ft. above sea level); the roads merge together about halfway up.

CAR RENTALS All of the major car-rental agencies are represented on Kauai; for a complete list, see chapter 11. For tips on insurance and driving rules in Hawaii, see "Getting There & Getting Around" (p. 74). The rental desks are just across the street from Lihue Airport, but you must go by van to collect your car.

MOTORCYCLE RENTALS The best place to rent a motorcycle is **Kauai Harley-Davidson,** 3-1866 Kaumualii Hwy., Lihue (✆ **877/212-9253** or 808/241-7020; www.kauaiharley-davidson.com). Rates start at $175 for 24 hours.

OTHER TRANSPORTATION OPTIONS Call **Kauai Taxi Company** (✆ **808/246-9554**) for taxi, limousine, or airport shuttle service. **Kauai Bus** (✆ **808/241-6410;** www.kauai.gov, click "Transportation") operates a fleet of 15 buses that serve the entire island. Taking the bus may be practical for day trips if you know your way around the island, but you can't take anything larger than a shopping bag aboard, and the buses don't stop at any of the resort areas—but they do serve more than a dozen coastal towns from Kekaha, on the southwest shore, all the way to Hanalei. Buses run more or less hourly from 5:30am to 7:50pm. The fare is $2 for adults and $1 for seniors, children ages 7 to 18, and passengers with disabilities.

[FastFACTS] KAUAI

Dentists Emergency dental care is available from **Dr. Mark A. Baird,** 4-9768 Kuhio Hwy., Kapaa (✆ **808/822-9393**), and **Dr. Michael Furgeson,** 4347 Rice St., Lihue (✆ **808/246-6960**).

Doctors Walk-ins are accepted at **Kauai Medical Clinic,** 3-3420 Kuhio Hwy., Ste. B, Lihue (✆ **808/245-1500,** or 808/245-1831 after-hours). You can also try the **North Shore Medical Center,** Kilauea and Oka roads, Kilauea (✆ **808/828-1418**); **Koloa Clinic,** 5371 Koloa Rd. (✆ **808/742-1621**); **Eleele Clinic,** 3292 Waialo Rd. (✆ **808/335-0499**); or **Kapaa Clinic,** 4-1105 Kuhio Hwy. (✆ **808/822-3431**).

Emergencies Dial ✆ **911** for police, fire, and ambulance service. The **Poison Control Center** can be reached at ✆ **800/222-1222.** (You will automatically be directed to the Poison Control Center for the area code of the phone you are calling from, but all the centers are available 24/7, and very helpful.)

Hospitals **Wilcox Memorial Hospital,** 3420 Kuhio Hwy., Lihue (✆ **808/245-1100**), has emergency services available 24 hours a day.

Internet Access All public libraries have Internet access. Libraries are located in Hanapepe (✆ **808/335-8418**); Kapaa (✆ **808/821-4422**); Koloa

(✆ **808/742-8455**); Lihue (✆ **808/241-3222**); Princeville (✆ **808/826-4310**); and Waimea (✆ **808/338-6848**). You can go online to reserve a computer at www.librarieshawaii.org/services/pcreservation.htm. You must purchase a Hawaii Library Card for $10, which gives you 3 months of access.

Police For nonemergencies, call ✆ **808/241-1711.**

Post Office The main post office is at 4441 Rice St., Lihue. To find the branch office nearest you, call ✆ **800/ASK-USPS** (275-8777).

Weather For current weather conditions, call ✆ **808/245-6001.** For marine conditions, call ✆ **808/245-3564.**

WHERE TO STAY

You don't want to be stuck with long drives every day, so be sure to review "The Island in Brief," earlier, to choose the location that best fits your vacation needs.

Taxes of 11.42% are added to all hotel bills. Parking is free unless otherwise noted.

Lihue & Environs

VERY EXPENSIVE

Kauai Marriott Resort & Beach Club ★★ ☺ Once upon a time, this was a glitzy megaresort (the Westin Kauai) with ostentatious fantasy architecture, but then a hurricane (and new owners) toned it down. The result is grand enough to be memorable, but it's now grounded in reality—it looks like a Hawaiian hotel rather than a European palace. Water runs everywhere throughout the resort: lagoons, waterfalls, fountains, a 5-acre circular swimming pool (the largest on the island), and a terrific stretch of beach. The lagoons are home to six islands that serve as an exotic minizoo, which still lends an air of fantasy to the place and, along with the enormous pool and children's program (which includes such activities as exploring tropical gardens and learning about Hawaiian culture), makes the resort popular with families.

Guest rooms are comfortable, with fabulous views of gold-sand Kalapaki Beach, verdant gardens, and palm trees, and a recent refurbishment has them all looking brand new. The location allows for easy arrival and departure (Lihue Airport is just a mile away), but it also means you can hear the takeoff and landing of every jet. Fortunately, air traffic stops by 9pm, but it begins bright and early in the morning.

Kalapaki Beach, Lihue, HI 96766. ✆ **800/220-2925** or 808/245-5050. Fax 808/246-5149. www.marriott.com/lihhi. 356 units. $259–$459 double; from $694 suite. Room with a View Packages include deluxe accommodations and a choice of car or daily breakfast for 2 starting at $309. Extra person $40. AE, DC, DISC, MC, V. Valet parking $17; self-parking $14. **Amenities:** 4 restaurants (including Duke's Kauai, p. 662); 2 bars; free airport shuttle; babysitting; children's program; concierge; state-of-the-art fitness center; 36-hole Jack Nicklaus golf course; 5 Jacuzzis; the largest pool on the island; room service; 8 tennis courts; watersports equipment rentals. *In room:* A/C, TV/VCR, fridge, hair dryer, high-speed Internet access ($13).

MODERATE

Kauai Beach Resort Formerly the Radisson Kauai, this hotel underwent a $7-million renovation in 2006 to convert it to a condo-hotel (which means that although the hotel will continue to operate as a full-service resort for visitors, a

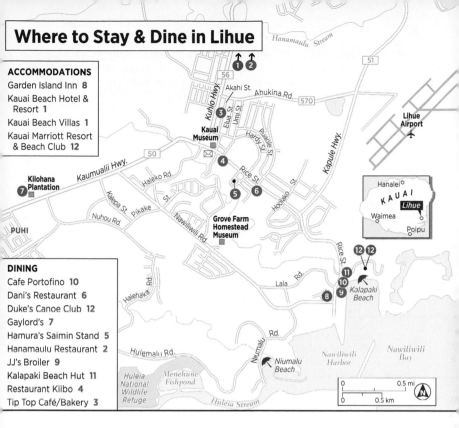

Where to Stay & Dine in Lihue

ACCOMMODATIONS

Garden Island Inn **8**

Kauai Beach Hotel & Resort **1**

Kauai Beach Villas **1**

Kauai Marriott Resort & Beach Club **12**

DINING

Cafe Portofino **10**

Dani's Restaurant **6**

Duke's Canoe Club **12**

Gaylord's **7**

Hamura's Saimin Stand **5**

Hanamaulu Restaurant **2**

JJ's Broiler **9**

Kalapaki Beach Hut **11**

Restaurant Kilbo **4**

Tip Top Café/Bakery **3**

portion of the guest rooms are available for private ownership). Then the Hilton took over the management of the property and spent another $14 million to renovate and add such amenities as a 24-hour business center, an executive-club floor, and an expanded fitness center. The property is now operated by Aqua Resorts and rates have never been lower. The 25-acre beachfront property, located 4 miles north of Lihue, is next door to a top-ranked municipal golf course and commands a 3-mile stretch of the beach (but unfortunately, it's very windy and not safe for swimming). The location is good, about equidistant from both North Shore and south-shore activities, and also close to the Wailua River, which offers kayaking, water-skiing, river tours, historical sites, and waterfalls. Guest rooms have all been updated with plush new carpeting, Balinese-style wood doors, marble bathrooms, top-of-the-line bedding, and high-speed wireless Internet service. Also new: quartzite decking at the resort's four-pool complex, a 12-foot waterfall cascading into the main pool, a flume and lava-tube water slide at the sand-bottom pool, and a new whirlpool spa in a stone grotto surrounded by ferns and a waterfall.

4331 Kauai Beach Dr., Lihue, HI 96766. (C) **888/805-3843** or 808/245-1955. Fax 808/246-9085. www.aquaresorts.com. 350 units. $104–$169 double; from $250 suite. Extra person $40. AE, DISC, MC, V. Valet or self-parking $13. **Amenities:** Free airport shuttle; babysitting; concierge; fitness room; Jacuzzi; spa; watersports equipment rentals. *In room:* A/C, TV, fridge, hair dryer, Internet access ($13).

Kauai Beach Villas These beachfront condos are a good option for families and others seeking more space and privacy than they'd get elsewhere in Lihue. Located next door to the Kauai Beach Resort (see above), this property has the same drawback: unsafe swimming conditions on the beautiful but windy white-sand beach. All units are individually owned, although most are outfitted with tropical decor and bamboo-style furniture, a fully equipped kitchen, a washer/dryer, and a lanai big enough for two lounge chairs, a table, and four chairs. The two-bedroom units have lanais off each bedroom, too. Due to the individual ownership, the prices vary widely (you can get some deals here). The immaculately landscaped grounds contain pools, tennis courts, barbecue areas, and a volleyball court. The Wailua Municipal Golf Course is next door.

4330 Kauai Beach Dr., Lihue, HI 96766. Reservations c/o Kauai Vacation Rentals, 3-3311 Kuhio Hwy., Lihue. ✆ **800/367-5025** or 808/245-8841. Fax 808/246-1161. www.kauaivacationrentals. com. 150 units. $119–$200 1-bedroom for 4; $119–$275 2-bedroom for 6. Cleaning fee $110–$160. 3- to 7-night minimum. MC, V. **Amenities:** Access to nearby health club; hot tub; outdoor pool; tennis courts. *In room:* A/C (in bedrooms), TV/VCR, hair dryer, high-speed Internet access (in some units), kitchen.

INEXPENSIVE

Garden Island Inn ★ 🏠 This bargain hunter's delight is located 2 miles from the airport, 1 mile from Lihue, and within walking distance of shops and restaurants. The spacious rooms are decorated with island-style furniture, bright prints, and fresh tropical flowers (grown right on the grounds). Each unit has a fridge, microwave, wet bar, TV, coffeemaker, shower-only private bathroom, and ocean view; some have private lanais, and the suites have sitting areas. The grounds are filled with flowers and banana and papaya trees (you're welcome to help yourself to the fruit at the front desk). There's only one caveat: The property sits on a busy street, and some units can be noisy (bring earplugs). Owner Steve Layne offers friendly service, lots of advice on activities (the entire staff happily uses its connections to get you discounts), and even complimentary use of beach gear, golf clubs (a course is nearby, as are tennis courts), and coolers. If the inn is booked, ask about the nearby two-bedroom condo ($125 per night).

3445 Wilcox Rd. (across the street from Kalapaki Beach, near Nawiliwili Harbor), Lihue, HI 96766. ✆ **800/648-0154** or 808/245-7227. Fax 808/245-7603. www.gardenislandinn.com. 21 units. $99–$119 double. Extra person $10. AE, DISC, MC, V. **Amenities:** Complimentary watersports equipment. *In room:* A/C, TV, fridge, hair dryer, high-speed Internet access.

The Poipu Resort Area

In addition to the accommodations listed below, you can try **Surf Song** (✆ **877/373-2331**; www.surfsong.com), with four units from $90 to $170 (plus a $60–$75 cleaning fee; 3-night minimum), and, closer to the beach, **Pua Hale at Poipu** (✆ **800/745-7414** or 808/742-1700; www.kauai-puahale.com), an intimate cottage within walking distance of the beach for $121 to $128 double (plus a $75 cleaning fee; 4-night minimum). At the **Garden Isle Cottages** (✆ **800/742-6711** or 808/742-6717; www.oceancottages.com), you'll overlook Koloa Landing and Waikomo Stream in an oceanfront one-bedroom apartment for $179 double, plus a $60 cleaning fee.

Where to Stay & Dine in the Poipu Resort Area

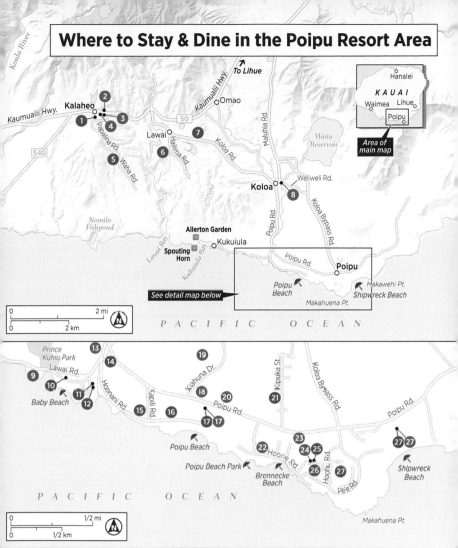

ACCOMMODATIONS

Bamboo Jungle **5**
Garden Isle Cottages **12**
Grand Hyatt Resort & Spa **28**
Hideway Cove Villas **25**
Kalaheo Inn **1**
Kauai Banyan Inn **7**
Kauai Cove **11**
Kiahuna Plantation Resort **17**
Marjorie's Kauai Inn **6**
Nini Kai Villas **26**
Poipu Crater Resort **27**
Poipu Kapili Resort **15**
Pua Hale at Poipu **21**
Sheraton Kauai Resort **16**
Surf Song **10**
Waikomo Stream Villas **14**

DINING

The Beach House **9**
Brennecke's Beach Broiler **22**
Brick Oven Pizza **2**
Casa Blanca at Kiahuna **20**
Casa di Amici **24**
Dondero's **28**
Joe's on the Green **19**
Josselin's Tapas Bar & Grill **13**
Kalaheo Coffee Co & Café **3**
Keoki's Paradise **18**
Merriman's Kauai **13**
Plantation Gardens
   Restaurant **17**
Poipu Beach Broiler **23**
Pomodoro **4**
Roy's Poipu Bar & Grill **18**
Tidepool Restaurant **28**
Tomkats Grille **8**

EXPENSIVE

Grand Hyatt Kauai Resort & Spa ★★★ ☺ Rates have dropped considerably (like $100 to $150 a night) at this "grand" resort. The Grand Hyatt Kauai is one of the top-ranked tropical resorts in *Condé Nast Traveler*'s annual readers' poll. It's hard to believe that this luxury hotel (one of Hawaii's best) could get any grander, but recent multimillion-dollar renovations have done just that. The four-story resort, built into oceanside bluffs, spreads over 50 acres that overlook Shipwreck Beach (which is too rough for most swimmers), at the end of the road in Poipu. The $250-million hotel uses the Island architecture of the mid-1920s to recapture the old Hawaii of the Matson Line steamship era.

The airy atmosphere is reminiscent of a grand plantation overlooking the sea. It's a comfortable, unostentatious place where you can bring along the kids and Grandma. The rooms are large (nearly 600 sq. ft.) and elegantly outfitted. All have marble bathrooms and spacious private lanais; most have ocean views. Club floors have their own concierge and a lounge serving continental breakfast, drinks, and snacks.

Don't leave without a treatment from the **ANARA Spa,** the best spa on Kauai. And check out the large selection of classes—some of them free—at the fitness center. The hotel is also next door to the Robert Trent Jones, Jr.–designed Poipu Golf Course. The collection of swimming pools here—freshwater and salt, with slides, waterfalls, and secret lagoons—makes this a real kids' paradise. The Camp Hyatt program offers arts and crafts, scavenger hunts, and other special activities. Plus, the Hyatt is one of the few hotels to offer "camp" in the evening, from 4 to 10pm. There may be some two dozen Grand Hyatt hotels on the planet, but frankly, I can't image any of them could be better than this.

1571 Poipu Rd., Koloa, HI 96756. ☏ **800/55-HYATT** (554-9288) or 808/742-1234. Fax 808/742-1557. www.kauai.hyatt.com. 602 units. $347–$439 double; from $397 Grand Club; from $912 suite. Extra person $75. Children 17 and under stay free in parent's room. Packages available. Daily $18 resort fee for local calls, self-parking, 1 hr. free at the tennis court, access to the ANARA Spa and fitness classes, and 10% off various on-site shops. AE, DC, MC, V. Valet parking $10. **Amenities:** 6 restaurants (including Dondero's, p. 664; and Tidepool, p. 666); 6 bars (including the partially open-air Stevenson's Library, p. 725); babysitting; bike rental; extensive Camp Hyatt kids' program; concierge; concierge-level rooms; one of the best fitness centers on the island; 3 Jacuzzis; an elaborate freshwater fantasy pool complex, plus 2 more pools and 5 acres of saltwater swimming lagoons w/islands and a man-made beach; room service; the 25,000-sq.-ft. ANARA Spa; 4 tennis courts; watersports equipment rentals. *In room:* A/C, TV/VCR (DVD players available for rent), fridge, hair dryer, high-speed Internet access ($15 per day), minibar.

Poipu Kapili Resort ★★ This quiet, upscale oceanfront cluster of condos is outstanding in every area. I like the home-away-from-home comforts and special touches: a video and book library, a spacious pool, several barbecues, tennis courts lit for night play, and an herb garden (you're welcome to take samples if you're cooking). A golf course is also nearby. The apartments are large (one-bedroom/two-bathroom units are 1,150 sq. ft.; two-bedroom/three-bathroom units are 1,820 sq. ft.) and have fully equipped kitchens, tropical furnishings, ceiling fans, and private lanais. The oceanfront two-story town houses are my favorites because they catch the trade winds. The two-bedroom units also have washer/dryers (common laundry facilities are available on the property as well). Although the Pacific is right out your window, the nearest sandy beach is a block away—which can be a blessing because it means more privacy.

2221 Kapili Rd., Koloa, HI 96756. ℂ **800/443-7714** or 808/742-6449. Fax 808/742-9162. www.poipukapili.com. 60 units. $250–$400 1-bedroom apt (sleeps up to 4); $395–$500 2-bedroom apt (sleeps up to 6), from $500 penthouse. Discounts for longer stays; package rates available. Rates include Fri continental breakfast by the pool. DISC, MC, V. **Amenities:** Oceanside pool; championship tennis courts lit for night use; barbecue area. *In room:* TV/VCR, hair dryer (on request), high-speed Internet access, kitchen.

MODERATE

Hideaway Cove Villas ★★ ⚜

Just a block from the beach, and next door to an excellent restaurant (Casa di Amici, p. 664), are these gorgeous condominium units in a plantation setting. Amenities are top-drawer, and no expense was spared in the interior decor. Units have hardwood floors, TV/VCR/DVD, comfy furniture, roomy beds (either four-poster or wood sleigh designs), spacious living areas, kitchenettes with the best appliances and granite countertops, and big lanais. You get all of this in a lush, landscaped tropical jungle at affordable prices. Owner Herb Lee is always on hand to guide you to Kauai's best spots and loan out his collection of beach toys and beach cruiser bicycles. A few of the units have Jacuzzis, so ask when you book.

2307 Nalo Rd., Poipu Beach, HI 96756. Reservations: P.O. Box 1113, Koloa, HI 96756. ℂ **866/849-2426** or 808/635-8785. www.hideawaycove.com. 7 units. $175–$210 studio double; $202–$275 1-bedroom double; $260–$320 2-bedroom for 4; $375–$405 3-bedroom for 6; from $635 5-bedroom (discount for 7 nights or more). Extra person $20. Cleaning fee $95–$345. 2-night minimum. AE, DISC, MC, V. *In room:* TV/VCR/DVD, hair dryer, kitchen, Wi-Fi.

Kiahuna Plantation Resort ★★

The downward economy has caused a big drop in rates at this plantation-style complex, loaded with Hawaiian style and sprinkled about a 35-acre garden setting with lagoons, lawns, and a gold-sand beach. Golf, shopping, and restaurants are within easy walking distance. All condo units are spacious, with full kitchens, daily maid service, and lanais. The Kiahuna Swim and Tennis Club (with the Casa Blanca at Kiahuna restaurant) is just across the street, and a championship golf course is nearby.

2253 Poipu Rd., Koloa, HI 96756. ℂ **800/OUTRIGGER** (688-7444) or 808/742-6411. Fax 808/742-1698. www.outrigger.com. 333 units. $209–$269 1-bedroom apt (sleeps up to 4); $255–$600 2-bedroom apt (sleeps up to 6). Packages available, including 5th night free, car rental, senior rates, and more. 2-night minimum. AE, DC, DISC, MC, V. **Amenities:** Restaurant (Plantation Gardens, p. 665); bar; children's program; outdoor pool; tennis courts; watersports equipment rentals; barbecue areas. *In room:* TV/VCR, hair dryer, high-speed Internet access, kitchen.

Sheraton Kauai Resort ★★ ☺

This modern Sheraton has the feel of old Hawaii and a dynamite location on one of Kauai's best beaches. It features buildings on both the ocean side and the mountain side of the road. The horseshoe-shaped, Polynesian-style lobby has shell chandeliers dangling from the ceiling. You have a choice of three buildings: one nestled in tropical gardens with koi-filled ponds; one facing the palm-fringed, white-sand beach (my favorite); or one looking across green grass to the ocean, with great sunset views. The rooms overlook either the tropical gardens or the rolling surf.

The bar here is fabulous. Even if you don't stay here, come by to sip a cocktail, nibble on appetizers, and take in the view and the Hawaiian music. A golf course is nearby. *Families, take note:* Kids eat free with a paying adult at the Shell Restaurant, at both breakfast and dinner.

One of the easiest ways to find lodging in the Poipu Beach area is to contact **Parrish Collection Kauai** (formerly Grantham Resorts), 3176 Poipu Rd., Koloa, HI 96756 (© **800/325-5701** or 808/742-2000; fax 808/742-9093; www.parrishkauai.com). Parrish handles more than 100 "handpicked" rental units for 12 different condo developments, plus dozens of vacation houses, ranging from quaint cottages to elite resort homes. The company has high standards for its rental units; if the properties are not maintained to these standards, Parrish has no problem taking the units (and, in one case, an entire condominium project) out of the pool of selected rentals. The condos start at $115 for a spacious one-bedroom, gardenview unit in low season, while vacation cottages start at $175 and go up to $1,700 for exquisite multimillion-dollar ocean estates. There's a 5-night minimum for condos and a 7-night minimum for homes. All rentals are well equipped (full kitchen, washer/dryer, wet bar, TV/DVD, phone, and most have high-speed Internet access). Check for specials on the website. Parrish offers a price-match guarantee.

If you're staying on Kauai for 5 days, ask Parrish about the **Frommer's Preferred Guest Discount** (see the reviews for Nihi Kai Villas, Poipu Crater Resort, and Waikomo Stream Villas, below). There's not a better deal on the island. Kudos to Parrish Collection Kauai for these fabulous vacation bargains.

2440 Hoonani Rd., Koloa, HI 96756. © **866/716-8109** or 808/742-1661. Fax 808/742-9777. www.starwoodhotels.com/hawaii. 413 units. $259–$449 double (maximum 4 in room); from $495 suite for 4. Extra person $50. Starwood members can get 35% off rack rates. Daily $21 resort fee for self-parking, Internet access, guest library with daily newspapers and 4 computers with Internet access, and use of fitness center and tennis courts. AE, DC, DISC, MC, V. Valet parking $9. **Amenities:** 3 restaurants; extraordinary bar; babysitting; children's program; concierge; fitness room facing the ocean (one of the most scenic places to work out on Kauai); Jacuzzi; small massage-and-skin-care center; 2 outdoor pools (1 w/water playground, 1 for children); room service; 3 tennis courts (2 night-lit); watersports equipment rentals. *In room:* A/C, TV, fridge, hair dryer, high-speed Wi-Fi.

INEXPENSIVE

Bamboo Jungle 🏠 Lucy and Terry Ryan took over this property—a jungle of verdant plants, a quaint gazebo, an 82-foot lap pool, and an impeccably decorated plantation-era house—and made the much-needed renovations to the rooms, each of which has a private entrance and French doors opening onto a private lanai with an ocean view. The netting over the beds creates a romantic mood and serves a functional purpose (it keeps Hawaii's insects on their side of the sleeping quarters). Accommodations range from a single room with deck to a studio with kitchenette. The house phone is available for guests' use. Breakfast is served in the great room inside the house. Golf and tennis courts are nearby. Note that there is no air-conditioning, which is fine 350 days of the year, but on the days the trade winds stop blowing, it's not so great.

3829 Waha Rd., Kalaheo, HI 96741. Reservations: P.O. Box 737, Kalaheo, HI 96741. © **808/332-5515.** www.kauai-bedandbreakfast.com. 3 units. $130–$170 double. Cleaning fee $35–$45. 3-night minimum (5-night minimum in Bamboo Garden Room). MC, V. From Hwy. 50, turn left at the traffic light onto Papalina Rd.; then right on Waha Rd. **Amenities:** Jacuzzi; outdoor pool. *In room:* TV, kitchenette (in 1 room), no phone, Wi-Fi.

Kalaheo Inn ★ 🏄 ☺ What a deal! Located in the town of Kalaheo, a 12-minute drive from world-famous Poipu Beach, a 5-minute drive from the Kukuiolono Golf Course, and within walking distance of shops and restaurants, the inn is a comfortable 1940s motel totally remodeled in 1999 and converted into apartment units with kitchenettes. In 2009, new owners Peggy and Leland Sun took over this budget traveler's dream inn. They couldn't be friendlier, handing out complimentary beach towels, beach toys, and even golf clubs to guests (links are nearby). They love families and have a storeroom full of games to keep the kids entertained.

4444 Papalina Rd. (just behind the Kalaheo Steakhouse), Koloa, HI 96756. 𝒞 **888/332-6023** or 808/332-6023. Fax 808/332-5242. www.kalaheoinn.com. 15 units. $87 double studio; $97–$107 1-bedroom; $137–$157 2-bedroom; $187 3-bedroom with full kitchen. Cleaning fee $8–$41. 2-night minimum. AE, MC, V. **Amenities:** Children's games; watersports equipment. *In room:* TV, hair dryer, high-speed Internet access ($10 per day), kitchen or kitchenette.

Kauai Banyan Inn ★ 🎁 This five-room inn is set on a hilltop overlooking an acre of landscaped property, a stream, and, of course, an old banyan tree. Centered by a courtyard with a burbling fountain, this is a place of peace and quiet, great for relaxation. The daughter of owner Lorna is a licensed massage therapist and can give you an in-room massage to relieve jet lag and built-up tension. Each good-size room has a terrific pastoral view of the rolling countryside, a lanai, a kitchenette (with three-quarter-size refrigerator, microwave, two-burner stove, and coffeemaker), a private bathroom, and a private entrance. Breakfast provisions are provided in your room, consisting of homemade banana bread, fruit, coffee, and juice. Lorna welcomes kids and can dig up a portable crib and highchair for families. There's a barbecue area outside. In 2009, a new studio cottage with a full kitchen, two lanais, and its own barbecue was added; it rents for $150.

3528-B Mana Hema Place, Lawai, HI 96765. 𝒞 **888/786-3855.** www.kauaibanyan.com. 6 units. $130–$150 double. Cleaning fee $45. MC, V. **Amenities:** Barbecue area; hot tub. *In room:* TV/DVD, fridge, hair dryer, free Wi-Fi.

Kauai Cove ★ 🎁 These immaculate cottages, located just 300 feet from the Koloa Landing, next to the Waikomo Stream, are the perfect private getaway. Each studio has a full kitchen, private lanai (with barbecue grill), and big bamboo four-poster bed. The cozy rooms feature beautiful hardwood floors, tropical decor, and cathedral ceilings. It's close enough that you can walk to sandy beaches, great restaurants, and shopping, yet far enough off the beaten path that privacy and quiet are assured. If the cottages are booked, ask about the two units in the Poipu Kai Resort.

2672 Puuholo Rd., Koloa, HI 96756. 𝒞/fax **800/624-9945** or 808/742-2562. www.kauaicove.com. 3 units. $99–$175 double. Cleaning fee $50–$85. 3-night minimum preferred. MC, V. **Amenities:** Use of pool, tennis courts, and hot tub nearby. *In room:* A/C, TV, CD player, kitchen, Wi-Fi.

Marjorie's Kauai Inn ★ 🎁 This quiet property, perched on the side of a hill, is just 10 minutes from Poipu Beach and 5 minutes from Old Koloa Town. From its large lanai, it offers stunning views of the rolling pastures and the Lawai Valley. Every unit has a kitchenette, dining table, ceiling fan, and lanai. The new Sunset View unit has a separate sitting area and a futon sofa for extra guests. On the

MOA BETTER: chickens & roosters

One of the first things visitors notice about Kauai is its unusually large number of *moa* (wild chickens). Kauai has always had a history of having more than its fair share of chickens and roosters running about, but after Hurricane Iniki picked up and scattered the fowl all over the island in 1992, they have been populating at a prodigious rate. Generally, having a few chickens scratching around in the dirt is quaint and downright picturesque. However, the "dark side" of the chicken population explosion is the increase in the number of roosters. In fact, a new industry has cropped up: rooster eradicators. Resorts hire these eradicators to remove the roosters from the well-manicured grounds because the large number of these male birds has led to, well, a sort of crowing contest. Roosters typically crow as the sun comes up. But on Kauai, with the population increase, the roosters crow all day long and throughout the night in some places. Just be warned that part of the "charm" of Kauai is the rooster population, so you might want to consider bringing earplugs.

hillside is a huge 50-foot pool, perfect for lap swimming. "Do more than one fun thing a day!" was the motto of the original owner, Marjorie Ketcher, who made sure that guests were out diving, snorkeling, sightseeing, hiking, dining, dancing, or enjoying one of the hundreds of other things on Kauai. Marjorie has sold her B&B, but the new owners are continuing her philosophy of living each day in paradise to the fullest. *Note:* As terrific as this property is, it is not recommended for families with children.

P.O. Box 866 (off Hailima Rd., adjacent to the National Tropical Botanical Garden), Lawai, HI 96765. ✆ **800/717-8838** or 808/332-8838. www.marjorieskauaiinn.com. 3 units. $130–$195 double. Extra person $20. Rates include continental breakfast. 3-night minimum preferred. AE, DISC, MC, V. **Amenities:** Jacuzzi; pool; barbecue. *In room:* TV, hair dryer, kitchenette, Wi-Fi.

Nihi Kai Villas ★ 🐾   The Parrish Collection Kauai (see "The King of Condos," above) is offering the deal of the decade on these well-equipped two-bedroom units, located about 600 feet from the beach. If you stay 7 nights, the rate for these oceanview apartments starts at an unbelievable $159 a night (for up to four people, which works out to just $80 per couple). You may not be getting new carpet, new furniture, new drapes, or a prime beachfront location, but you *are* getting a clean, well-cared-for unit with a full kitchen, washer/dryer, and TV/VCR; there's also an on-site barbecue and picnic area. The property is a 2-minute walk from world-famous Brennecke's Beach (great for bodysurfing) and a block from Poipu Beach Park. Within a 5-minute drive are two great golf courses, several restaurants, and loads of shopping.

1870 Hoone Rd., Koloa, HI 96756. Reservations c/o Parrish Collection Kauai, 3176 Poipu Rd., Ste. 1, Koloa, HI 96756. ✆ **800/325-5701** or 808/742-2000. Fax 808/742-9093. www.parrishkauai. com. 70 units. $145–$244 1-bedroom for up 4 guests; $159–$300 2-bedroom for up 6 guests. Ask about the Frommer's Preferred Guest Discount. 5-night minimum. AE, DISC, MC, V. From Poipu Rd., turn toward the ocean on Hoowili Rd. and then left on Hoone Rd.; Nihi Kai Villas is just past Nalo Rd. on Hoone Rd. **Amenities:** Concierge; nearby golf course; Jacuzzi; outdoor heated pool; tennis courts. *In room:* TV/DVD, free Internet access, kitchen.

Poipu Crater Resort Here's another Parrish Collection deal (see "The King of Condos," above) travelers on a budget can't beat: two-bedroom garden-view units for just $119 a night in low season (and a still-unbelievable $199 in high season). This resort consists of 15 duplexes in a tropical garden setting. Each unit is about 1,500 square feet with living area, kitchen, large lanai, bathroom, and guest bedroom downstairs, and master bedroom and bathroom upstairs. Each has a full kitchen (with microwave), as well as a washer/dryer and VCR. The complex has a swimming pool, tennis and paddleball courts, sauna, Ping-Pong tables, and barbecues. Poipu Beach is about a 10-minute walk away, and the entire Poipu Beach resort area (offering everything from restaurants to golf courses) is within a 5-minute drive. The only caveats are no maid service and no air-conditioning.

2330 Hoohu Rd., Koloa, HI 96756. Reservations c/o Parrish Collection Kauai, 3176 Poipu Rd., Ste. 1, Koloa, HI 96756. © **800/325-5701** or 808/742-2000. Fax 808/742-9093. www.parrishkauai. com. 30 units. $119–$205 2-bedroom garden view for up to 6 guests. Ask about the Frommer's Preferred Guest Discount. 5-night minimum. AE, DISC, MC, V. From Poipu Rd., turn toward the ocean on Hoowili Rd. and then left on Hoone Rd.; continue on Hoone Rd., past the bends, where the road is now called Pee Rd.; turn left off Pee Rd. onto Hoohu Rd. **Amenities:** Nearby golf course; outdoor pool; sauna; tennis courts; barbecue area. *In room:* TV/DVD, CD player, kitchen.

Waikomo Stream Villas ★ The Parrish Collection Kauai (see "The King of Condos," above) has one more fabulous trick up its sleeve: these 1,000-square-foot one-bedroom apartments, which comfortably sleep four, and larger two-bedroom units, which sleep six. Tucked into a lush tropical garden setting, these spacious, well-decorated units have everything you'll need on your vacation: full kitchen, VCR, washer/dryer, and private lanai. The complex—which has both adults' and children's pools, tennis courts, and a barbecue area—is adjacent to the Kiahuna Golf Club and just a 5-minute walk from restaurants, shopping, and Poipu's beaches and golf courses.

2721 Poipu Rd. (just after entry to Poipu, on ocean side of Poipu Rd.), Koloa, HI 96756. Reservations c/o Parrish Collection Kauai, 3176 Poipu Rd., Ste. 1, Koloa, HI 96756. © **800/325-5701** or 808/742-2000. Fax 808/742-9093. www.parrishkauai.com. 60 units. $115–$211 1-bedroom for 4; $145–$249 2-bedroom for 6. Ask about the Frommer's Preferred Guest Discount. 5-night minimum. AE, DISC, MC, V. **Amenities:** Concierge; Jacuzzi; 2 outdoor pools (1 for children, 1 for adults); complimentary tennis courts. *In room:* TV/DVD, free Internet access, kitchen.

Western Kauai

MODERATE

Waimea Plantation Cottages ★ ☺ This beachfront vacation retreat is like no other in the islands: Among groves of towering coco palms sit clusters of restored sugar-plantation cottages, dating from the 1880s to the 1930s and bearing the names of their original plantation-worker dwellers. The lovely cottages have been transformed into cozy, comfortable guest units with period rattan and wicker furniture and fabrics from the 1930s, sugar's heyday on Kauai. Each has a furnished lanai and a fully equipped modern kitchen and bathroom; some units are oceanfront. Facilities include an oceanfront pool, tennis courts, and laundry. The seclusion of the village makes it a nice place for kids to wander and explore, away from traffic. The only downsides: the black-sand beach, which is lovely but not conducive to swimming (the water is often murky at the Waimea River mouth), and the location, at the foot of Waimea Canyon Drive—its remoteness can be very appealing, but the North Shore is 1½ hours away. Golf courses and tennis courts, however, are much closer.

9400 Kaumualii Hwy. (P.O. Box 367), Waimea, HI 96796. © **866/774-2924** (Aston Hotels and Resorts) or 808/338-1625. Fax 808/338-2338. www.waimea-plantation.com. 48 units. $215–$396 1-bedroom double; $275–$461 2-bedroom (sleeps up to 4); $300–$516 3-bedroom (sleeps up to 5); from $491 4-bedroom (sleeps up to 8); from $656 5-bedroom (sleeps up to 10). Children 17 and under stay free in parent's room. AE, DC, DISC, MC, V. **Amenities:** Restaurant (Waimea Brewing Company); bar; large outdoor pool, Wi-Fi. *In room:* TV, kitchen.

INEXPENSIVE

Kokee Lodge ✦ This is an excellent choice, especially if you want to do some hiking in Waimea Canyon and Kokee State Park. There are two types of cabins here: The older ones have dormitory-style sleeping arrangements (and resemble a youth hostel), while the new ones have two separate bedrooms each. Both styles sleep six and come with cooking utensils, bedding, and linens. I recommend the newer units, which have wood floors, cedar walls, and more modern kitchen facilities (some are wheelchair-accessible as well). There are no phones or TVs in the units, but there is a pay phone at the general store. You can purchase firewood for the cabin stove at Kokee Lodge, where there's a restaurant that's open for continental breakfast and lunch every day. There's also a cocktail lounge, a general store, and a gift shop. *Warning for light sleepers:* This area is home to lots of roosters, which crow at dawn's first light.

P.O. Box 819, Waimea, HI 96796. © **808/335-6061.** 12 units. From $93 double 1st night; $73 double 2nd–5th nights. Extra person $5. 5-night maximum. AE, DC, DISC, MC, V. *In room:* Kitchen, no phone.

The Coconut Coast

This is the land of B&Bs and inexpensive vacation rentals. In addition to those reviewed below, I recommend **Opaeka'a Falls Hale,** which has two exquisite units with pool and hot tub for $110 to $130 plus a $50 cleaning fee. Reservations are available through **Hawaii's Best Bed & Breakfasts** (© 800/262-9912; www.bestbnb.com). Another excellently priced choice is **Kakalina's B&B** (© 808/822-2328; www.kakalina.com), on a 3-acre flower farm nestled in the foothills of Mount Waialeale, offering rates from $90, plus a cleaning fee of $40.

EXPENSIVE

Mahina Kai 🏠 Mahina Kai ("moon over the water") is a traditional Japanese villa (complete with teahouse next door) on 2 landscaped acres just across the road from one of the most picturesque white-sand beaches on Kauai. There are three rooms in the main house with shoji-screen doors, private bathrooms and lanais, and use of the shared kitchenette and gorgeous living room (with fish pond, vintage Hawaiian furniture, and views of Japanese gardens and Aliomanu Beach). Although this place is undeniably unique, the rooms are tiny and sparsely furnished (no TVs or phones), and the walls paper thin. I'd suggest staying at the

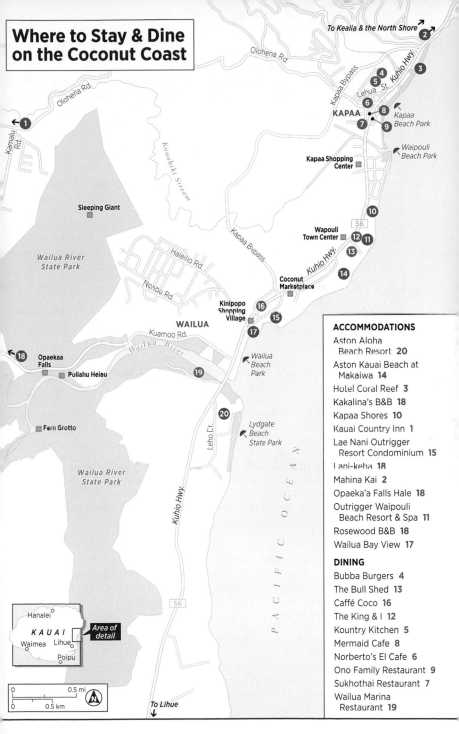

Where to Stay & Dine on the Coconut Coast

To Kealia & the North Shore

Olohena Rd.

Kapaa Bypass

Lehua St.

Kuhio Hwy.

KAPAA

Kapaa Beach Park

Waipouli Beach Park

Olohena Rd.

Kamalu Rd.

Konohiki Stream

Kapaa Shopping Center

Sleeping Giant

Wailua River State Park

Kapaa Bypass

Haleilio Rd.

Wapouli Town Center

56

Nonou Rd.

Kuhio Hwy.

Coconut Marketplace

Kinipopo Shopping Village

WAILUA

Kuamoo Rd.

Wailua River

Wailua Beach Park

Opaekaa Falls

Poliahu Heiau

Fern Grotto

Wailua River State Park

Leho Cr.

Lydgate Beach State Park

Kuhio Hwy.

PACIFIC OCEAN

56

To Lihue

Inset map

Hanalei

KAUAI

Waimea   Lihue

Poipu

Area of detail

0   0.5 mi
0   0.5 km

N

651

ACCOMMODATIONS

Aston Aloha Beach Resort 20
Aston Kauai Beach at Makaiwa 14
Hotel Coral Reef 3
Kakalina's B&B 18
Kapaa Shores 10
Kauai Country Inn 1
Lae Nani Outrigger Resort Condominium 15
Lani-keha 18
Mahina Kai 2
Opaeka'a Falls Hale 18
Outrigger Waipouli Beach Resort & Spa 11
Rosewood B&B 18
Wailua Bay View 17

DINING

Bubba Burgers 4
The Bull Shed 13
Caffé Coco 16
The King & I 12
Kountry Kitchen 5
Mermaid Cafe 8
Norberto's El Cafe 6
Ono Family Restaurant 9
Sukhothai Restaurant 7
Wailua Marina Restaurant 19

separate cottage (with kitchenette) next to the saltwater pool. Landscaped into the gardens are a lagoon-style pool and hot tub. Guests are generally gay and lesbian couples, but anyone with a sense of humor and an open mind is welcome. Sitting in the hot tub, listening to the surf across the street, and gazing at the stars is pretty darn close to heaven on earth.

4933 Aliomanu Rd. (off Kuhio Hwy. at mile marker 14), P.O. Box 699, Anahola, HI 96703. © **800/337-1134** or 808/822-9451. www.mahinakai.com. 5 units. $225–$375 double. Rates include continental breakfast. 3-night minimum. AE, MC, V. **Amenities:** Hot tub; saltwater lagoon-like swimming pool. *In room:* No phone.

Outrigger Waipouli Beach Resort ★★ ☺   The good news is rates are down! This luxurious beach resort opened at the very end of December 2006 with a $200-million condominium project on 13 acres between the historic towns of Wailua and Kapaa. The resort features six hotel rooms and 190 high-end condo units (153 two-bedroom/three-bathroom units and 37 one-bedroom/two-bathroom units), of which 130 units are in the rental pool (75% are the two-bedroom units). Each unit is furnished with top-of-the-line accouterments such as granite counters; stainless-steel appliances by Sub-Zero, Wolf, and Fisher & Paykel; a double dishwasher; a full-sized Whirlpool washer and dryer; a whirlpool tub in the master bathroom; and 37-inch flatscreen TVs. The two-bedroom units are 1,300 square feet with floor-to-ceiling windows and two lanais.

The resort features a long list of amenities: complimentary high-speed Internet access, a fitness center, and a 300,000-gallon heated saltwater fantasy pool, with flowing river, garden, dual serpentine water slides, sand-bottom children's pool, and three sand-bottom whirlpool tubs. The entire property, all the guest rooms, and the common areas are nonsmoking.

The location, across the street from the Kauai Village Shopping Center and the Waipouli Town Center, means guests are within walking distance of restaurants and shops and, more important, just across the street from a Safeway grocery store and a Longs Drug Store and pharmacy.

Unfortunately, the spa and restaurants at this property have closed.

4-820 Kuhio Hwy., Kapaa, HI 96746 © **800/OUTRIGGER** (688-7444) or 808/823-1401. Fax 808/823-1400. www.outrigger.com. 196 units. $255 hotel double; $197–$297 1-bed/2-bathroom for 4; $230–$364 2-bed/3-bathroom for 6. 2-night minimum. AE, DC, DISC, MC, V. **Amenities:** Fitness center; nearby golf course; huge oceanside outdoor pool; nearby tennis courts; 3 outdoor whirlpools. *In room:* A/C, TV/DVD, fridge, hair dryer, full kitchen (condos only), Wi-Fi.

MODERATE

Lae Nani Outrigger Resort Condominium ★   The Lae Nani ("beautiful promontory point") offers a quiet, relaxing setting right on the beach, next door to restaurants and bars, now at the best prices in years. On the point is the Kukui Heiau, where an ancient temple once stood. The one- and two-bedroom units are roomy, with large living rooms, separate dining rooms, full kitchens, and generous lanais. The two-bedroom/two-bathroom units can easily fit a family of six. Maid service is provided daily. Extras include a lava-rock-protected swimming area and barbecue facilities. Next door is the Coconut MarketPlace, with shops, restaurants, and nightlife; a golf course is nearby.

410 Papaloa Rd., Kapaa, HI 96746. © **800/OUTRIGGER** (688-7444) or 808/822-4938. Fax 808/822-1022. www.outrigger.com. 54 units. $159–$199 1-bedroom for 4; $206–$233 2-bedroom for 6. Rollaway bed/crib $20. AE, DC, DISC, MC, V. **Amenities:** Oceanfront outdoor pool; complimentary tennis courts. *In room:* TV, kitchen.

INEXPENSIVE

Aston Aloha Beach Resort ★ ☺ New ownership of this 10-acre property—next door to a 57-acre beach park and playground on one side and a very sacred historic Hawaiian site on the other side—has brought back the feel of old Hawaii. After a $10-million renovation, the entire place is rich in Hawaiian culture, from the room decor to the historical presentation given by the general manager himself to the full-time *kupuna* (senior cultural expert) who gives classes in Hawaiian arts and crafts. Every room was redone in 2006 with new carpet and furniture, Balinese mahogany doors, upgraded bathrooms, and Hawaiian-style quilts on the beds. The result is a moderately priced, family-friendly choice located right next door to Lydgate Beach Park (with Kamalani Playground for the kids) and convenient to nearby golf. Restaurants and shopping are within minutes of the resort along the Coconut Coast.

3-5920 Kuhio Hwy., Kapaa, HI 96746. © **877/997-6667** or 808/823-6000. Fax 808/823-6666. www.abrkauai.com. 216 units. $80–$157 double; $103–$240 suite; from $178 1-bedroom cottage. Extra person $30. Children 18 and under stay free in parent's room. Check the website for specials. AE, DC, DISC, MC, V. **Amenities:** Restaurant; bar; small fitness room; Jacuzzi; 2 outdoor pools; complimentary tennis court. *In room:* A/C, TV, fridge, hair dryer, high-speed Internet access (some rooms, $10 per day).

Aston Kauai Beach at Makaiwa ★ Just 10 minutes from Lihue Airport, in the town of Waipouli, this resort was totally refurbished in 2005 when Courtyard by Marriott rebranded the old Kauai Coconut Beach Resort. Then in 2006, ResortQuest took over management, and in 2009, Aston Resorts became the managers and dropped the prices considerably. The property, which sits on 10½ acres, is nestled between a coconut grove and a white-sand beach. Improvements have been made to the landscaping, the restaurants, and the open-air lobby, which now features a stained-glass depiction of a sailing canoe, a mural chronicling Kauai's sailing history, and a replica of a Hawaiian voyaging canoe. The convenient location is close to shopping and visitor attractions along the Coconut Coast, and also gives you easy access to both the North Shore and the Poipu Beach area on the south shore.

The large guest rooms have been gutted and redecorated with a Hawaiian theme, and include such amenities as hardwood furniture and a 27-inch TV. The property features a new pool, hot tub, day spa, business center, fitness center, tennis courts, jogging paths, a lounge, and an expanded restaurant.

650 Aleka Loop, Kapaa, HI 96746. © **866/77-HAWAII** (774-2924) or 808/822-3455. Fax 808/822-0035. www.astonhotels.com. 311 units. $97–$247 double; from $247 suite. Extra person $30. Children 17 and under stay free in parent's room. Daily $13 resort fee for parking, high-speed Internet access, and local calls. AE, DC, DISC, MC, V. **Amenities:** Full-service restaurant; bar; golf nearby; Jacuzzi; outdoor pool; room service; tennis nearby. *In room:* A/C, TV/VCR, fridge, hair dryer, Wi-Fi.

Hotel Coral Reef ✦ Here's a budget choice right on the beach. This small, unpretentious hotel faces a grassy lawn, coconut trees, and a white-sand beach. It offers friendly service and economical, no-frills rooms in an ideal location, within walking distance of shops, restaurants, golf, and tennis. There's even an 8-mile bike path that starts right on the grounds. In 2007, the rooms were redone with new beds, carpet, and drapes. The place is looking spiffier than ever. Of the two wings in the hotel, I prefer the oceanfront one, which has big rooms that overlook the beach through sliding-glass lanai doors.

1516 Kuhio Hwy. (at the northern end of Kapaa, btw. mile markers 8 and 9), Kapaa, HI 96746. ℂ **800/843-4659** or 808/822-4481. Fax 808/822-7705. www.hotelcoralreef.com. 19 units. $89–$245 double. Extra person $25. Children 12 and under stay free in parent's room. Packages available. AE, MC, V. **Amenities:** Pool, Wi-Fi available in public areas. *In room:* A/C, TV, fridge.

Kapaa Shores ★   These apartments are located right on the beach in the heart of Kapaa. Even the budget units have a partial view of the ocean, but oceanfront units are available for a bit more money. The one-bedrooms can comfortably sleep four, while the two-bedrooms can sleep as many as six (the sofa in each unit pulls out into a queen-size bed). All units are in excellent shape and come with fully equipped modern kitchens and large lanais, where you can enjoy a sunrise breakfast or sunset cocktails. On-site amenities include a large pool, tennis court, family-size hot tub, shuffleboard court, laundry facilities, and barbecues. Golf courses, restaurants, and bars are nearby.

900 Kuhio Hwy. (btw. mile markers 7 and 8), Kapaa, HI 96746. Reservations c/o Garden Island Properties, 4–928 Kuhio Hwy., Kapaa, HI 96746. ℂ **800/801-0378** or 808/822-4871. Fax 808/822-7984. www.kauaiproperties.com. 84 units. $850 per week 1-bedroom; $875–$1,050 per week 2-bedroom. Cleaning fee $98–$130. Reservation fee $40 (or $20 online). 5-night minimum. AE, MC, V. **Amenities:** Jacuzzi; outdoor pool; complimentary tennis courts. *In room:* TV, VCR or DVD, Internet access (in some rooms), kitchen.

Kauai Country Inn ★★ 🏠   Book this place! It's hard to believe this old-fashioned country inn exists, nestled in the rolling hills behind Kapaa. Hosts Mike and Martina Hough have taken their considerable creative talents and produced a slice of paradise on 2 acres. Each of the four suites is uniquely decorated in Hawaiian Art Deco style with a touch of humor, complete with hardwood floors, a kitchen or kitchenette, your own computer with high-speed Internet connection, and lots of little amenities. Everything is top-drawer, from the furniture to the Sub-Zero refrigerator. The grounds are immaculate, and you can pick as much organic fruit as you want from the abundance of mango, guava, lilikoi, star fruit, oranges, and lemons. Beatles fans, take note: Mike has been collecting memorabilia for decades and has the only private Beatles Museum in the state (including a Mini Cooper S car owned by Beatles manager Brian Epstein, original paintings by John Lennon, and a host of books, records, movies, tapes, T-shirts, and other interesting and unusual rare items). Annie, the house golden retriever, personally greets each guest.

6440 Olohena Rd., Kapaa, HI 96746. ℂ **808/821-0207.** www.kauaicountryinn.com. 5 units. $129–$179 1- and 2-bedroom suite double. Extra person in suite $30. Discount car rentals available. 4-night minimum preferred. AE, MC, V. **Amenities:** Hot tub. *In room:* Flatscreen TV/VCR/DVD, fridge, hair dryer, computer w/high-speed Internet access, kitchen or kitchenette.

Lani-keha ★ 🏠   Step back in time to the 1940s, when Hawaiian families lived in open, airy, rambling homes on large plots of land lush with fruit trees and sweet-smelling flowers. This gracious age is still alive and well in Lani-keha, a *kamaaina* (longtime resident) home with an open living/game/writing/dining room and oversize picture windows to take in the views. The house is elegant yet casual, with old-style rattan furniture—practicality and comfort outweigh design aesthetics. The large communal kitchen has everything a cook will need, including a dishwasher. All guests share the TV/VCR and single phone in the living area.

848 Kamalu Rd. (Hwy. 581), Kapaa, HI 96746. ☏ **808/822-1605.** Fax 808/822-2429. www.lani keha.com. 3 units. $65–$75 double. Extra person $10. Rates include continental breakfast. 2-night minimum. No credit cards. From Kuhio Hwy. (Hwy. 56), turn left at the light at Coco Palms onto Hwy. 580 (Kuamoo Rd.); go 3 miles; turn right at Hwy. 581 (Kamalu Rd.) and go 1 mile. **Amenities:** Wi-Fi on the property. *In room:* No phone.

Rosewood Bed & Breakfast ★ 🎁

This lovingly restored century-old plantation home, set amid tropical flowers, lily ponds, and waterfalls, has accommodations to suit everyone. There's a Laura Ashley–style room in the main house along with two private cottages: one a miniature of the main house, with oak floors and the same Laura Ashley decor; the other a little grass shack set in a tropical garden, with an authentic thatched roof and an outside shower. There's also a bunkhouse with three separate small rooms and a shared bathroom and toilet. In 2006, all the beds were replaced with "Heavenly Beds," and computers with Internet access were installed in each room. Hostess Rosemary Smith also has a list of other properties she manages. *Note:* Smoking is not permitted on the property.

872 Kamalu Rd., Kapaa, HI 96746. ☏ **808/822-5216.** Fax 808/822-5478. www.rosewoodkauai. com. 7 units, 3 with shared bathroom. $95 double in main house (includes continental breakfast); $50–$60 double in bunkhouse; $99 1-bedroom cottage double (sleeps up to 4); $145 2-bedroom cottage (sleeps up to 4); $200 3-bedroom home (sleeps up to 6). Cleaning fee $25–$200. 3-night minimum. No credit cards. From Kuhio Hwy. (Hwy. 56), turn left at the light at Coco Palms onto Hwy. 580 (Kuamoo Rd.); go 3 miles; turn right at junction of Hwy. 581 (Kamalu Rd.); go 1 mile and look for the yellow house on the right with the long picket fence in front. *In room:* No phone. *In cottages:* Computer w/Internet access, TV, hair dryer, kitchen, no phone. *In bunkhouse:* Kitchenette, no phone.

Wailua Bay View ★ 🗝

Located right on the ocean, these spacious one-bedroom apartments offer excellent value. All units have ceiling fans, full kitchens (including microwave and dishwasher), washer/dryers, and large lanais. The bedrooms are roomy, and the sofa bed in the living room allows you to sleep up to four. Some of the $163 garden units are close to the road and can be noisy; ask for one with air-conditioning, which generally drowns out the street sounds. The oceanview units are more expensive but still a great deal. On-site facilities include a pool and barbecue area. Restaurants, bars, shopping, golf, and tennis are nearby.

320 Papaloa Rd., Kapaa, HI 96746. ☏ **800/367-5242.** www.wailuabayview.net. 45 units. $163–$175 double. Extra person $12. 7th night free Apr 15–June 14 and Sept 1–Dec 16. Discount car rentals available. Cleaning fee $100. 4-night minimum. AE, DISC, MC, V. **Amenities:** Small outdoor pool; barbecue area. *In room:* A/C (in most units), TV/VCR/DVD, kitchen, Wi-Fi (in most units).

The North Shore

Ocean Front Realty North Shore Rentals (☏ **800/488-3336** or 808/826-6585; fax 808/826-6478; www.oceanfrontrealty.com) handles all kinds of weekly rentals—from beachfront cottages and condos to romantic hideaways and ranch houses. Renting a home is a great way to enjoy the area's awesome natural wonders, especially for those who like to avoid resorts and fend for themselves. Shopping, restaurants, and nightlife are abundant in nearby Hanalei. *Note:* The company does not accept credit cards.

In addition to the B&Bs listed below, you might consider **North Country Farms** (② **808/828-1513**; www.northcountryfarms.com), which has two private, handcrafted cottages on a 4-acre organic farm. It's a great place for families. Each cottage goes for $150 a night.

VERY EXPENSIVE

St. Regis Princeville ★★★ ☺   Palatial luxury has come to the North Shore. Formerly the Princeville Resort, the property was a palace full of marble and chandeliers, but after the multimillion-dollar massive interior renovation, it has been reborn as a luxurious reflection of the island (rather than a European castle). With the new opening comes four new restaurants, a new spa (on property), and St. Regis butler service for the suites. The location still enjoys one of the world's finest settings, between Hanalei Bay and Kauai's steepled mountains. Nearby are outstanding surfing and windsurfing areas, as well as a wonderful reef for snorkeling. The panoramic view from the lobby has to be the most dramatic vista from any hotel in the state.

The footprint of the building remains the same: stepping down a cliff, with the entrance on the ninth floor, and you take elevators down to your room and the beach. Each opulent room has such extras as a door chime, dimmer switches, bedside control panels, a safe, original oil paintings, an oversize bathtub, and a "magic" bathroom window (a liquid-crystal shower window that you can switch in an instant from clear to opaque). There are no lanais, but oversize windows allow you to admire the awesome view from your bed.

In addition to a great children's program, this property has oodles of activities not only for children but also for teens and even activities for the entire family, from horseback riding to adventures exploring the island. The hotel grounds are a fantasy land for children (and some adults), with a huge swimming pool next to a sandy beach.

Other great amenities here: daily newspaper, complimentary resort shuttle, comprehensive Hawaiiana program, riding stables, in-house cinema, arts program (from photography to painting), and a wealth of outdoor activities. Golfers may choose from two courses, both designed by Robert Trent Jones, Jr., and an on-property spa. Next door are golf and tennis courts.

P.O. Box 3069 (5520 Kahaku Rd.), Princeville, HI 96722-3069. ② **800/826-4400** or 808/826-9644. Fax 808/826-1166. www.princevillehotelhawaii.com. 252 units. $850–$1,150 double; from $1,575 suite. Extra person $135. Children 17 and under stay free in parent's room. AE, DC, DISC, MC, V. Parking $15. **Amenities:** 3 restaurants; 3 bars; babysitting; bike rental; children's program; concierge; outstanding golf on 2 courses; huge oceanside outdoor pool with outdoor whirlpools; room service; spa; 25 tennis courts; watersports equipment rentals. *In room:* A/C, TV/VCR/CD player, fridge, hair dryer, Wi-Fi.

EXPENSIVE

Hanalei Colony Resort ★ ☺   Picture this: a perfect white-sand beach just steps from your door, with lush tropical gardens, jagged mountain peaks, and fertile jungle serving as the backdrop. Welcome to Haena, Kauai's northernmost town and gateway to the famous Na Pali Coast, with miles of hiking trails, fabulous sunset views, and great beaches. This 5-acre resort is the place to stay if you're looking to experience the magic of the enchanting North Shore. The units are unbelievably spacious—six people could sleep here comfortably—making them great for families. Each has a private lanai (the less-expensive budget units

Where to Stay & Dine on Kauai's North Shore

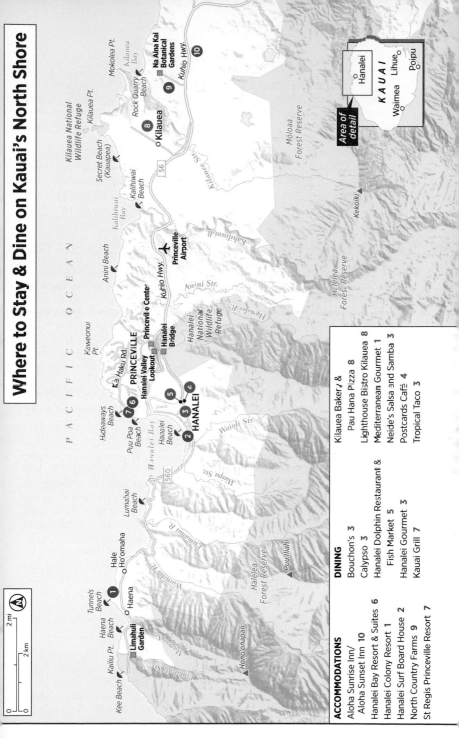

ACCOMMODATIONS

Aloha Sunrise Inn/
Aloha Sunset Inn **10**

Hanalei Bay Resort & Suites **6**

Hanalei Colony Resort **1**

Hanalei Surf Board House **2**

North Country Farms **9**

St Regis Princeville Resort **7**

DINING

Bouchon's **3**

Calypso **3**

Hanalei Dolphin Restaurant &
Fish Market **5**

Hanalei Gourmet **3**

Kauai Grill **7**

Kilauea Bakery &
Pau Hana Pizza **8**

Lighthouse Bistro Kilauea **8**

Mediterranean Gourmet **1**

Neide's Salsa and Samba **3**

Postcards Café **4**

Tropical Taco **3**

face the garden), a full kitchen, a dining area, a living room, and ceiling fans (the area is blessed with cooling trade winds, so air-conditioning isn't necessary). The atmosphere is quiet and relaxing: no TVs, stereos, or phones. The property has a large pool, laundry facilities, and a barbecue and picnic area. Guests have access to complimentary beach mats and towels, a lending library, and children's toys, puzzles, and games (plus badminton and croquet for the entire family). A full spa and an award-winning restaurant are located next door.

P.O. Box 206 (5–7130 Kuhio Hwy.), Hanalei, HI 96714. © **800/628-3004** or 808/826-6235. Fax 808/826-9893. www.hcr.com. 48 units. $225–$440 2-bedroom apt for 4. Rates include continental breakfast once a week. 2- to 3-night minimum. AE, MC, V. **Amenities:** Restaurant next door (Mediterranean Gourmet, p. 675); Jacuzzi; good-size outdoor pool; full-service spa next door; Wi-Fi. *In room:* Kitchen, no phone.

MODERATE

Aloha Sunrise Inn/Aloha Sunset Inn ★★ 🎒 Hidden on the North Shore are these two unique cottages nestled on a quiet 7-acre farm with horses, fruit trees, flowers, and organic vegetables. I highly recommend both of these darling bungalows. Each is furnished with hardwood floors, top-of-the-line bedding, tropical-island decor, a full kitchen, a washer/dryer, and more (including an excellent video and CD library). It's close to activities, restaurants, and shopping, yet far enough away to feel the peace and quiet of a Hawaii of yesteryear. Hosts Allan and Catherine Rietow, who have lived their entire lives on the islands, can help you plan your stay, give money-saving tips, and even hand out complimentary masks, snorkels, and boogie boards and point you to their favorite beaches. *Note to parents:* These cottages are not appropriate for children.

P.O. Box 79, Kilauea, HI 96754. © **888/828-1008** or 808/828-1100. Fax 808/828-2199. www.kauaisunrise.com and www.kauai-sunset.com. 2 units. $185 double (includes all taxes). Check for Internet specials. Cleaning fee $95. No credit cards. *In room:* TV/VCR (in 1 cottage), cable TV/VCR (in other cottage), hair dryer, kitchen.

Hanalei Bay Resort & Suites ★ This 22-acre resort is just up the street from the ritzy St. Regis Princeville (see above), overlooking the fabled Bali Hai cliffs and Hanalei Bay. It has the same majestic view, but for as little as half the price. The place recaptures the spirit of old Hawaii, especially in the three-story stucco units that angle down the hill to the gold-sand, palm-fringed beach it shares with its neighbor. Rooms are decorated in Island style, with rattan furnishings and lanais overlooking the bay, the lush grounds, and the distant mountains. If walking on a steep, steep hillside is difficult for you, check to see if their van-shuttle service is in operation; when we went to press, it was not running.

P.O. Box 220 (5380 Honoiki St.), Princeville, HI 96722. © **800/365-7605** or 808/826-6522. Fax 808/826-6680. www.hanaleibayresort.com. 236 units. $124–$139 double; $109–$124 studio with kitchenette (sleeps up to 4); $191–$206 1-bedroom apt (sleeps up to 4). AE, DC, DISC, MC, V. **Amenities:** Jacuzzi; 2 outdoor freshwater pools; 8 tennis courts plus pro shop and tennis school. *In room:* A/C, TV, hair dryer, kitchenette, Wi-Fi (in some rooms).

Hanalei Surf Board House ★★ 🎒 Book well in advance: This place is so fabulous, it will go fast! Just a block from the beach, these two incredibly decorated studio units are a steal at $195. Host Simon Potts is a former record-company executive from England who has "retired" to Hawaii (he's the hardest-working retired guy I've ever met). Potts has collected a bunch of surfboards from kids he coaches in soccer and lined them all standing up next to one another, creating the most unusual fenced-in yard in Hawaii. His imaginative decor choices extend to the studios, one of which sports a whimsical cowgirl theme and the other Elvis memorabilia. Both units have kitchenettes, 300-channel TVs, DVD players, Bose stereos, some 50 CDs (Simon still has connections in the music business), barbecues, and backyard lanais. But the best reason to stay here—besides a 2-minute walk to the beach and a 10-minute walk to downtown Hanalei—is Simon himself: His stories about the record industry will keep you howling with laughter for hours.

5459 Weke Rd., Hanalei, HI 96714. © **808/826-9825.** www.hanaleisurfboardhouse.com. 2 units. $195 double. Cleaning fee $75. 4-night minimum. DISC, MC, V. *In room:* TV/DVD, hair dryer, high-speed Internet access, kitchenette, MP3 docking station, private barbecue.

WHERE TO DINE

Kauai's best dining spots ring the shores: Poipu on the south, Kapaa on the east, and Hanalei on the north. While Roy's and Merriman's in Poipu, Beach House in neighboring Lawai, and Gaylord's in Kilohana remain Kauai's foodie stalwarts, there are some excellent choices at all levels of the food chain. Most of the island's newcomers are moderately priced and have cropped up along Kauai's one main road.

On your jaunt across the island, you'll find affordable choices in every town, from hamburger joints to stands dishing up saimin (noodles in broth topped with scrambled eggs, onions, and sometimes pork) to busy neighborhood diners. As long as you don't expect filet mignon on a fish and chips budget, it shouldn't be difficult to please both your palate and your pocketbook. But if you're looking for lobster, rack of lamb, or risotto to write home about, you'll find those pleasures too.

For condo dwellers preparing their own meals, I've covered a variety of markets and shops around Kauai—including some wonderful green markets and fruit stands—where you can pick up the island's best foodstuffs. These are listed under "Shops & Galleries" (p. 718). If you're looking for fresh island fruit, also see "Fruity Smoothies & Other Exotic Treats" (p. 720).

In the listings below, reservations are not required unless otherwise noted.

Lihue & Environs

Note: You'll find the restaurants in this section on the "Where to Stay & Dine in Lihue" map (p. 691).

EXPENSIVE

Gaylord's ★★ CONTINENTAL/PACIFIC RIM   One of Kauai's most splendid examples of *kamaaina* architecture, Gaylord's is the anchor of a 1930s plantation manager's estate on a 1,700-acre sugar plantation. You'll enter a complex of shops, galleries, and a living room of Hawaiian artifacts and period furniture. The main dining room, which winds around a flagstone courtyard overlooking rolling lawns and purple mountains, serves American classics (New York steak, rack of lamb, prime rib) along with pasta, fresh seafood, and lavish desserts. The ambience, historic surroundings, and soothing views from the terrace make Gaylord's a special spot for lunch, when salads, soups, fresh fish, burgers, sandwiches, and

Oliver Shagnasty's signature baby back ribs predominate. Daily specials include international dishes such as kalua pork and Mexican fajitas, plus fresh island fish in various cross-cultural preparations.

At Kilohana, 3–2087 Kaumualii Hwy., Lihue. © **808/245-9593.** www.gaylordskauai.com. Reservations recommended. Main courses $11–$15 lunch, $20–$40 dinner; Sun brunch $25. AE, DC, DISC, MC, V. Mon–Sat 11am–2pm; Sun 9am–2:30pm (brunch); daily 5:30–9pm.

JJ's Broiler ★ AMERICAN   Famous for its Slavonic steak (tenderloin in butter, wine, and garlic), JJ's is a lively spot on Kalapaki Bay, with open-air dining and a menu that covers more than the usual surf and turf. The service ranges from

---

PLATE-LUNCH pointers

If you haven't yet come face to face with the local phenomenon called the "plate lunch," Kauai is a good place to start. Like saimin, the plate lunch is more than a gastronomic experience—it's a part of the local culture. Lihue is peppered with affordable plate-lunch counters that serve this basic dish: two scoops of rice, potato or macaroni salad, and a beef, chicken, fish, or pork entree—all on a single plate. Although heavy gravies are usually de rigueur, some of the less traditional purveyors have streamlined their offerings to include healthier touches, such as grilled fresh fish. Pork cutlets and chicken or beef soaked in teriyaki sauce, however, remain staples, as does the breaded and crisply fried method called *katsu,* as in chicken katsu. Most of the time, *fried* is the operative word; that's why it's best to be ravenously hungry when you approach a plate lunch, or it will overpower you. At its best, a plate lunch can be a marvel of flavors; at its worst, it's a plate-size grease bomb. With the increasing popularity of such diets as Atkins and South Beach, many plate-lunch places are now happy to replace all those starches with a mixed green salad if you ask.

The following are the best plate-lunch counters on Kauai:

The **Koloa Fish Market** ★, 5482 Koloa Rd. (© **808/742-6199**), is in southern Kauai, on Koloa's main street. A tiny corner stand with plate lunches and prepared foods, it sells excellent fresh-fish poke, Hawaiian-food specials, and seared ahi to go. It's gourmet fare masquerading as takeout. Daily specials may include sautéed ahi or fresh opakapaka with capers. You'll get a generous portion of food for around $7–$9. For a picnic or outing on the south shore, this is a good place to start.

In east Kauai's Kapaa town, the indispensable **Pono Market,** 4–1300 Kuhio Hwy. (© **808/822-4581**), has enticing counters of sashimi, poke,

Hawaiian food, sushi, and a diverse assortment of takeout fare. It's known for its flaky *manju* (sweet potato and other fillings in baked crust), apple turnovers, sandwiches, excellent boiled peanuts, pork and chicken laulau (steamed in ti leaves), and plate lunches—shoyu chicken, sweet-and-sour spareribs, pineapple-glazed chicken, teriyaki fish, and so on. The roast pork and the potato-macaroni salad—which regulars buy by the pound for barbecues and potlucks—are top sellers. If they're available, pick up Taro Ko taro chips. They are made in Hanapepe, hard to find, and worth hand-carrying home.

Lihue, the island's county and business seat, is full of ethnic eateries serving inexpensive plate lunches. **Po's**

laudable to lamentable, but the quality of the food is consistent. The crab cakes and blue cheese–crusted rib-eye are big sellers, and the scallops Florentine are an imaginative twist on seafood. Lunchtime appetizers include potato skins, calamari rings, and other diet-buster temptations. The high ceilings, two-story dining, Kenwood Cup posters, and nautically designed rooms are enhanced by stellar views of the bay.

3416 Rice St., Nawiliwili. ☏ **808/246-4422.** www.jjsbroiler.com. Reservations recommended for dinner. Lunch sandwiches $12–$16; dinner main courses $26–$33. DISC, MC, V. Daily 11am–10pm.

Kitchen, 4100 Rice St. (☏ **808/246-8617**), offers Japanese specials: cone sushi, chicken katsu, teriyaki beef, and bentos. One block away, **Garden Island BBQ,** 4252-A Rice St. (☏ **808/245-8868**), is the place for Chinese plate lunches and local staples such as barbecued or lemon chicken and teriyaki steak, as well as soups and tofu dishes.

On the Hanamaulu side of Lihue, across the street from Wal-Mart, look for the prim, gray building that reads **Fish Express** ★, 3343 Kuhio Hwy. (☏ **808/245-9918**). It's astonishing what you'll find here for under $12: Cajun-style grilled ahi with guava basil, fresh fish grilled in a passion-orange-tarragon sauce, fresh-fish tacos in garlic and herbs, and many other delectables, all served with rice, salad, and vegetables. The Hawaiian plate lunch

(laulau or kalua pork, lomi salmon, ahi poke, rice, or poi) is a top seller, as are the several varieties of smoked fish. The owners marinate the fish in soy sauce, sugar, ginger, and garlic (no preservatives), and smoke it with kiawe wood. The fresh-fish specials, at $8.95, come in six preparations and are flavored to perfection. At the chilled counter you can choose freshly sliced sashimi and many styles of poke, from scallop, ahi, and octopus to exotic marinated crab. This is a potluck bonanza that engages even newcomers, who point and order while regulars pick up sweeping assortments of seafood appetizers on large platters. They're all fresh and reasonably priced, great for Friday-afternoon *pau hana* (after-work) parties.

At **Mark's Place,** 1610 Haleukana St., in Puhi Industrial Park (☏ **808/245-2722**), just southwest of Lihue, Island standards (Korean-style chicken, teriyaki beef, beef stew, chicken katsu) come with brown or white rice and salad for $6.75 to $8. The selection, which changes daily, always includes two salad and three entree choices, as well as hot sandwiches (chicken, beef, and hamburgers) and the ever-popular bento (rice with beef, chicken, or fish, arranged in a lidded box). Mark's is a takeout and catering operation, so don't expect table seating.

MODERATE

Café Portofino ★★ ITALIAN   This candlelit restaurant offers authentic Italian cuisine at reasonable prices. It's a good pick for a romantic dinner, with a harpist playing softly in the background. Owner Giuseppe Avocadi personally greets every guest. The menu lists appetizers ranging from ahi (or beef) carpaccio to the house special antipasto (with five daily choices). But it's the pasta that will bring you back a second time: These homemade dishes are so light you'd swear you could keep on eating all night. There are a dozen dishes to choose from, plus a few specials to make your decision all the harder. Also on the menu are fresh fish, a variety of chicken dishes, veal and beef dishes (from the traditional *osso buco* to scaloppini a la Marsala), and a few items for vegetarians. Thursday and Saturday nights are "Club Nights" with entertainment from 10pm to 3am ($5 cover charge).

3481 Hoolaulea St., Nawiliwili. ℭ **808/245-2121.** www.cafeportofino.com. Reservations recommended. Main courses $20–$44. MC, V. Daily 5–10pm.

Duke's Kauai ★ STEAK/SEAFOOD   It's hard to go wrong at Duke's. Part of a highly successful restaurant chain (including Duke's in Waikiki and three similar restaurants on Maui), this oceanfront oasis is the hippest spot in town, with a winning combination of a great view, an affordable menu, popular music, and a very happy happy hour. The noontime best seller is stir-fried cashew chicken, but the fresh mahimahi sandwich and the grilled chicken quesadilla are front-runners, too. The inexpensive fish tacos are a major attraction, and the five or six varieties of fresh catch a night are a highlight, served in several different preparations—a great value. Hawaiian musicians serenade diners nightly, while downstairs in the Barefoot Bar, traditional and contemporary Hawaiian music adds to the cheerful atmosphere. On Tropical Fridays, tropical drinks go for $6 from 4 to 6pm, when live music stirs up the joint.

At the Kauai Marriott Resort & Beach Club, 3610 Rice St., Nawiliwili. ℭ **808/246-9599.** www. dukeskauai.com. Reservations recommended for dinner. Main courses $8–$13 lunch, $19–$29 dinner. "Taco Tuesdays" 4–6pm, with $2.50 fish tacos and $3.25 draft beer. AE, DISC, MC, V. Dining room daily 5–9:30pm. Barefoot Bar daily 11am–11pm.

INEXPENSIVE

Dani's Restaurant AMERICAN/HAWAIIAN   Not a tourist spot, but a Formica-clad diner for local residents that's always packed for breakfast. Dani's is the pancake palace of Lihue: banana, pineapple, papaya, and buttermilk, plus sweetbread French toast and kalua-pig omelets. Regulars know that fried rice is offered on Thursday only and that the papaya hotcakes are always a deal. At lunch, Hawaiian specials—laulau, kalua pig, lomi salmon, and beef stew in various combinations—dominate the otherwise standard American menu of fried foods and sandwiches.

4201 Rice St., Lihue. ℭ **808/245-4991.** Main courses $5–$10 breakfast, $6–$11 lunch. MC, V. Mon–Fri 5am–1pm; Sat 5–11am.

Hamura's Saimin Stand ★ SAIMIN   If there were a saimin hall of fame, Hamura's would be it. It's a cultural experience, a renowned saimin stand where fans line up to take their place over steaming bowls of this Island specialty at a few U-shaped counters that haven't changed in decades. The saimin and teriyaki barbecue sticks attract an all-day, late-night, and pre- and post-movie crowd. The noodles come heaped with vegetables, won tons, hard-boiled eggs, sweetened pork, vegetables, and several condiment combinations. I love Hamura's casual atmosphere and the simple pleasures it consistently delivers.

2956 Kress St., Lihue. ☎ **808/245-3271.** Most items under $9. No credit cards. Mon–Thurs 10am–10pm; Fri–Sat 10am–midnight; Sun 10am–9pm.

Hanamaulu Restaurant CHINESE/JAPANESE/SUSHI   When passing this restaurant, you'd never know that serene Japanese gardens with stone pathways and tatami-floored teahouses are hidden within. You can dine at the sushi bar, American style, or in the teahouses for lunch or dinner, but you must call ahead for teahouse dining. At lunch, enter a world of chop suey, won tons, teriyaki chicken, and sukiyaki (less verve than value), with many other choices in budget-friendly Japanese and Chinese plate lunches. Special Japanese and Chinese menus can be planned ahead for groups of up to 60 people, who can dine at low tables on tatami mats in a Japanese-garden setting. Old-timers love this place, and those who came here when they were in diapers are now stopping in for after-golf pupu and beer.

3-4291 Kuhio Hwy., Hanamaulu. ☎ **808/245-2511.** Reservations recommended. Main courses $7–$19. MC, V. Tues–Fri 10am–1pm; Tues and Thurs–Sun 4:30–8:30pm.

Kalapaki Beach Hut ☺ AMERICAN   This place is tricky to find (look for the anchor chain out in front of the green building), but the money you'll save makes it worth the hunt. Started in 1990 by Steve and Sharon Gerald as Kalapaki Beach Burgers, the tiny eatery began adding more items and then evolved into serving breakfast too. This "hut" has window service and a few tables downstairs; sit upstairs for an ocean view. It's basic fare, served on paper plates with plastic cutlery at cheap, cheap prices. Breakfasts are hearty omelets, pancakes, and numerous egg dishes. Lunches are heavy on the burgers (prepared 10 ways), lots of sandwiches, a few healthy salads, and fish and chips. The kids get their own menu. This casual restaurant welcomes people in their bathing suits and flip-flops.

3474 Rice St., Nawiliwili. ☎ **808/246-6330.** Breakfast $5–$9; lunch $5–$10. MC, V. Daily 7am–8pm.

Restaurant Kiibo JAPANESE   Neither a sleek sushi bar nor a plate-lunch canteen, Kiibo is a neighborhood staple with tasty, unpretentious, home-style Japanese food served in a pleasant room accented with Japanese folk art. You can dine on sushi, ramen, sukiyaki, tempura, teriyaki, or the steamed egg-rice-vegetable marvel called *oyako donburi*. There are satisfying, affordable lunch specials and teishoku specials of mackerel, salmon, soup, dessert, and other condiments.

2991 Umi St., Lihue. ☎ **808/245-2650.** Main courses $8–$19. No credit cards. Mon–Fri 11am–1:30pm; Mon–Sat 5:30–8:30pm.

Tip Top Café/Bakery ☺ LOCAL   This small cafe/bakery (also the lobby for the Tip Top Motel) has been serving local customers since 1916. The best deal is breakfast: The macadamia pancakes are known throughout Kauai. Lunch ranges from pork chops to teriyaki chicken, but the specialty is oxtail soup. For a real treat, stop by the bakery (where you pay your bill) and take something home. (I recommend the freshly baked *malasadas*.)

3173 Akahi St., Lihue. ☎ **808/245-2333.** Breakfast items under $9; lunch entrees $5.50–$12. MC, V. Tues–Sun 6:30am–2pm.

The Poipu Resort Area

Note: You'll find the restaurants in this section on the "Where to Stay & Dine in the Poipu Resort Area" map (p. 643).

EXPENSIVE

The Beach House ★★★ HAWAII REGIONAL   This is the place to go when you want to splurge: Celebrate a birthday, anniversary, or any excuse for a romantic dinner on the beach with delicious food. The Beach House's oceanfront room remains the south shore's premier spot for sunset drinks, appetizers, and dinner—a treat for all the senses. Come early enough to see the sun set and perhaps a turtle or two bobbing in the waves. Old Hawaii Regional favorites are featured on the menu, which changes daily and may include Kauai asparagus salad, seared macadamia-crusted mahimahi with miso sauce, sea scallops with lemon grass and kaffir lime, and the Beach House crab cake with mint sambal butter sauce and grilled tomato compote. Desserts shine, too, like the molten chocolate desire and the mango crème brûlée.

5022 Lawai Rd., Poipu. © **808/742-1424.** www.the-beach-house.com. Reservations recommended. Main courses $20-$40. AE, DC, MC, V. Daily 5:30-10pm (winter), 6-10pm (summer).

Casa di Amici ★ ITALIAN/INTERNATIONAL   Former owner Chef Randall Yates and his wife, Joanna, sold this Italian restaurant in 2008 to Ray Dikilato, who had been their sous chef. Ray has faithfully kept everything the same. It's still the same free-standing wood-and-stone building in Poipu that looks like a storybook restaurant with fairy lights, high ceilings, beveled glass, and a generous open deck where you can dine among palms and heliotropes. There's even live classical piano music Saturday evenings from 7 to 9:30pm. The restaurant is worth seeking out: It's the third left turn past Brennecke's Beach, not more than 2 minutes from Poipu Beach Park, in an enclave of condos and vacation rentals.

The memorable food has strong Mediterranean and cross-cultural influences. You'll find organic greens from Kilauea, several risotto choices (quattro formaggio is my fave), black tiger prawns in orange-saffron lobster sauce, and surprises such as Thai lobster bisque and duck in a sun-dried cherry Chambord sauce. Among the nearly two dozen pasta selections is a classic fettuccine Alfredo for which Yates is deservedly famous. The set menu is Italian, but the specials showcase international influences, such as soy sauce reductions, *furikake* (seaweed sprinkle), and assertive touches of jalapeño tequila aioli on salmon and grilled tiger prawns. This is flamboyant, joyful Italian fare. Plus, you can order either light- or regular-size entrees, a policy I love.

2301 Nalo Rd., Poipu. © **808/742-1555.** www.casadiamici.com. Reservations recommended. Main courses $22-$32. DC, MC, V. Daily 5:30-9:30pm.

Dondero's ★★★ ITALIAN   If you're looking for a romantic dinner either under the stars overlooking the ocean or tucked away at an intimate table surrounded by inlaid marble floors, ornate imported tiles, and Franciscan murals, the Grand Hyatt's stellar Italian restaurant is the place for you. You get all this atmosphere at Dondero's, plus the best Italian cuisine on the island, served with efficiency. It's hard to have a bad experience here. My recommendations for a meal to remember: Start with either the organic beef carpaccio with arugula or the minestrone with oxtail ravioli. Then move on to the ricotta gnocchi with white truffle cream; the *osso buco* with gremolatta; or the Royal Hawaiian moi with fennel, cured olives, and spicy tomato broth. Save room for dessert, especially the chocolate-orange semifreddo with bittersweet chocolate sauce. Dinners are pricey but worth every penny.

At the Grand Hyatt Kauai Resort & Spa, 1571 Poipu Rd., Koloa. (C) **808/742-1234.** www.kauai. hyatt.com. Reservations are a must. Main courses $14–$36. AE, DC, DISC, MC, V. Thurs–Mon 6–10pm.

Josselin's Tapas Bar & Grill ★★★ HAWAII REGIONAL   Chef Jean-Marie Josselin, formerly of A Pacific Café, recently opened this chic, contemporary restaurant right across from Merriman's (see below), in the new Kukui'ula Village mall. The menu changes nightly and consists of a series of small and larger tapas; the idea is to order several items for your table and share. I highly recommend the meltingly tender miso-marinated butterfish if it's offered. Other recent menu items include coffee-smoked pork tonkatsu served with a crispy banana *bao* (a small pastry) and buttermilk BBQ dressing; ahi tempura roll with sweet chili soy beurre blanc, and iron plank roasted island chicken with panzanella salami salad and warm rosemary vinaigrette. Wash it all down with a litchi or pomegranate sangria, assembled tableside from the roving sangria cart.

Kukui'ula Village, 2829 Kalanikaumaka St., Koloa. (C) **808/742-7117.** www.josselins.com. Reservations recommended. Small tapas $7–$12, large tapas $17–$36. MC, V. Daily 5–10pm.

Merriman's Kauai ★★★ HAWAII REGIONAL   One of the original chefs who developed Hawaiian Regional Cuisine, and a longtime pioneer in the farm-to-table concept, Chef Peter Merriman has expanded his culinary empire (Big Island, Maui, and Oahu) to Kauai at this casual and friendly bistro with sunset views and full dining upstairs and a more affordable cafe downstairs. A dinner at Merriman's is a memorable event; every course is done to perfection and the menu identifies where he got the ingredients—their goal is to have 90% of the food they serve come from Hawaii. Reserve a table on the veranda for a romantic sunset dinner upstairs. All the famous Merriman signature items are available, from his wok-charred ahi to locally raised lamb, in a presentation that changes nightly (such as grilled leg of lamb served with asparagus and goat-cheese purée, local vegetables, and Greek olive vinaigrette). For a more casual dining experience drop in downstairs, where sandwiches (island fish tacos for $12), flat-bread pizza (alii mushroom, pesto and goat cheese for $12), soups and salads (Peter's original Caesar for $7), and happy-hour drink specials reign.

Kukui'ula Village, 2829 Kalanikaumaka St., Koloa. (C) **808/742-1234.** www.merrimanshawaii. com. Reservations are a must. Upstairs main dining room: Main courses $19–$65. AE, DC, DISC, MC, V. Daily 5:30–9:30pm. Downstairs cafe: Main courses $9–$13. AE, DC, DISC, MC, V. Daily 11am–9:30pm; happy hour 3–6pm.

Plantation Gardens Restaurant HAWAII REGIONAL   I was very disappointed when I last ate here: It's still a mix of irresistible garden ambience and a well-executed menu fashioned around fresh local ingredients, but the portions are small, everything is a la carte, and the prices are high (pupu selections in the $9–$22 range, salads $9–$11, and entrees $19–$27). The new menu comes from the culinary genius of chef Teri McLeod. The seaweed, fish, and shellfish are from local waters, and many of the fruits, herbs, and vegetables are grown on the resort premises. The historic architecture includes a generous veranda, koa trim and Brazilian cherry floors, and gracious details of a 1930s estate that belonged to the manager of Hawaii's first sugar plantation. A sprawling horticultural marvel, the property includes koi ponds, coconut and kou trees, orchids, bromeliads, and a cactus-and-succulent garden.

At the Kiahuna Plantation Resort, 2253 Poipu Rd., Koloa. ℂ **808/742-2121.** www.pgrestaurant. com. Reservations recommended. Main courses $19–$27. AE, DC, MC, V. Daily 5:30–9pm (open at 5pm for pupu and cocktails).

Roy's Poipu Bar & Grill ★★ EURO-ASIAN   This is a loud, lively room with ceiling fans, marble tables, works by local artists, and a menu tailor-made for foodies. The signature touches of Roy Yamaguchi (of Roy's restaurants in Oahu, Big Island, Maui, Tokyo, New York, and Guam) are abundantly present: an excellent, progressive, and affordable wine selection; fresh local ingredients prepared with a nod to Europe, Asia, and the Pacific; and service so efficient it can be overbearing. Because appetizers (such as blackened ahi with mustard soy sauce, grilled Szechuan baby back ribs, and crispy crab cakes with butter sauce) are a major part of the menu, you can sample Roy's legendary fare without breaking the bank. The three dozen nightly specials invariably include eight fresh-fish dishes, prepared at least five or six ways.

At the Poipu Shopping Village, 2360 Kiahuna Plantation Dr., Koloa. ℂ **808/742-5000.** www. roysrestaurant.com. Reservations highly recommended. Main courses $25–$40. AE, DC, DISC, MC, V. Daily 5:30–9:30pm.

Tidepool Restaurant ★★★ SEAFOOD   Here's another ultraromantic restaurant at the Grand Hyatt (see also Dondero's, above). A cluster of thatched bungalows overlooks the koi-filled lagoon in a dreamy open-aired restaurant with Tiki torches flickering in the moonlight. The atmosphere would be reason enough to book a table, but the cuisine is just as outstanding. The restaurant's specialty is fresh fish prepared a number of ways, but it also has juicy steaks and ribs, as well as entrees for vegetarians. My picks are the grilled local swordfish with hearts of palm, bacon, pepper coulis, and tomato marmalade; the glazed opah with coconut-crusted blue crab and lobster; and the trio of ahi, Tako, and lobster poke. Book early, and ask for a table overlooking the water.

At the Grand Hyatt Kauai Resort & Spa, 1571 Poipu Rd., Koloa. ℂ **808/742-1234.** www.kauai.hyatt. com. Reservations recommended. Main courses $23–$75. AE, DC, DISC, MC, V. Daily 5:30–10pm.

MODERATE

Brennecke's Beach Broiler ★ AMERICAN/SEAFOOD   Cheerful petunias in window boxes and second-floor views of Poipu Beach are pleasing touches at this seafood/burger house, a favorite for a couple of decades. The view alone is worth the price of a drink and pupu, but it helps that the best hamburgers on the south shore are served here, as well as excellent vegetarian selections. It's casual, so drop in before or after the beach and dine on nachos and peppers, fresh-fish sandwiches, kiawe-broiled fish and kabobs, prime rib, pasta, and build-your-own gourmet burgers. Look for happy-hour specials daily, as well as the Alaskan king crab and prime rib nights.

2100 Hoone Rd. (across from Poipu Beach Park), Koloa. ℂ **808/742-7588.** www.brenneckes. com. Main courses $10–$15 lunch, $12–$40 dinner. AE, DC, DISC, MC, V. Daily 11am–10pm (street-side deli takeout daily 7am–8pm).

Casa Blanca at Kiahuna MEDITERRANEAN   This used to be one of my favorite dining places on Kauai; I planned my trips around eating here. But it has just gotten too unreliable in recent years—either you could have the meal of your life with great service, or it could be a total fiasco, with bad service to boot. Call in advance to see if owner Elizabeth "Liz" Foley, a culinary genius, will be on-site during your visit; if not, you might want to pass, as the quality of both service and food tends to suffer when she's not here. Lunch is a creative selection of Greek and Mediterranean dishes, like lamb spiedini with couscous and mint yogurt, and even a kids' menu with such classics as PB&J and grilled cheese. There's also a delicious tapas menu: Spanish shrimp, crostini with olive tapenade, and more at happy hour. But it's at dinner that Liz's famous culinary talents really stand out, with zarzuela (Spanish stew with lobster, shrimp, mussels, tomato, and saffron), *puttanesca al tonno* (penne pasta with tomatoes, capers, olives, and fresh tuna), *agnello* (New Zealand lamb with roasted red potatoes, and nightly specials. Whatever you order, do not miss the chocolate mousse with orange for dessert. After the sun has set, it is hard to find the unlit turnoff to the restaurant, but it's worth the search.

2290 Poipu Rd. (in the Kiahuna Swim and Tennis Club), Poipu. ✆ 808/742-2929. www.casa blancakauai.com. Reservations recommended for dinner. Lunch $8–$12; tapas $6–$12; dinner entrees $16–$35. DISC, MC, V. Tues–Sat 11am–9pm, Sun 10am–9pm (brunch from 10am–2pm); happy hour 4–6:30pm.

Keoki's Paradise ☺ STEAK/SEAFOOD   A great place to take the kids—they will love the tropical ambience here. Keoki's Paradise is sprawling and lively, with lunch favorites that include a fresh-fish sandwich, fresh-fish tacos, Thai shrimp sticks, and chicken Caesar salad—all good and affordable. In the evenings, regulars tout the fresh fish baked in a garlic, lemon, and sweet basil glaze. When it's time for dessert, the original Hula pie from Kimo's in Lahaina is an ever-sinful winner. The cafe in the bar area serves lighter fare and features live Hawaiian music Sunday through Friday nights.

At the Poipu Shopping Village, 2360 Kiahuna Plantation Dr., Koloa. ✆ 808/742-7534. www. keokisparadise.com. Reservations recommended. Main courses $8.50–$15 lunch, $19–$25 dinner. AE, DC, DISC, MC, V. Daily 4:45–9:30pm in main dining room; cafe menu daily 11am–1:30pm.

Poipu Beach Broiler ☺ STEAK/SEAFOOD   Located in the former House of Seafood, this casual eatery has a relaxing atmosphere, like that of an old beach house. I love the large appetizer menu. In fact, I recommend that you drop by at sunset, have a drink, and chow down on the great variety of pupu like vegetable summer rolls, sea scallops, seared ahi sashimi, and tender calamari. Dinner entrees include fresh fish, prime rib, grilled sirloin, and baby back ribs. There's a menu for the kids too.

1941 Poipu Rd., Poipu. ✆ 808/742-6433. www.pbbroiler.com. Main courses $20–$32 dinner. AE, DC, DISC, MC. V. Daily 2–5pm for pupus, 5–9pm dinner.

Pomodoro ★★ ITALIAN   Pomodoro is the Italian magnet of the west side, a casual and intimate second-floor dining room with a bar, potted plants, soft lighting, and pleasing Italian music. It's a warm, welcoming place where Hawaiian hospitality meets European flavors: homemade garlic focaccia, chicken saltimbocca, and homemade pastas (cannelloni, manicotti, and excellent lasagna, the house specialty). Whether you order the veal, chicken, scampi, calamari, or very fresh organic salads, you'll appreciate the wonderful home-style flavor and the polite, efficient servers.

At Rainbow Plaza, Kaumualii Hwy. (Hwy. 50), Kalaheo (inland from Poipu). ✆ 808/332-5945. Reservations recommended. Main courses $16–$27. MC, V. Mon–Sat 5:30–9pm.

Tomkats Grille AMERICAN/GRILL   If you are on a low-fat or low-carb diet, this is not the place for you! Fried appetizers, inexpensive New York steak, rotisserie chicken, seafood salad with fresh catch, and sandwiches and burgers are among the offerings at the Grille, in a serene garden setting in Old Koloa Town. Old-fashioned brews are big here—everything from local microbrews to Guinness Stout, plus two dozen others to help wash down the kalua-pork quesadillas or the seared poke.

5404 Koloa Rd., Old Koloa Town. ☏ **808/742-8887.** Main courses $8–$21. AE, DC, DISC, MC, V. Daily 10:30am–10pm; happy hour daily 3–6pm. Bar daily until midnight.

INEXPENSIVE

Brick Oven Pizza PIZZA   A Kalaheo fixture for nearly 3 decades, Brick Oven is the quintessential mom-and-pop business, serving pizza cooked directly on the brick hearth, brushed with garlic butter, and topped with long-simmered sauces. You have a choice of whole-wheat or white crust, plus many toppings: house-made Italian sausage, Portuguese sausage, bay shrimp, anchovies, smoked ham, vegetarian options, and more. The result: very popular pizza, particularly when topped with fresh garlic and served with an ice-cold beer. The seafood-style pizza-bread sandwiches are big at lunch, and the "Super Pizza" with everything on it—that's *amore*.

2-2555 Kaumualii Hwy. (Hwy. 50), Kalaheo (inland from Poipu). ☏ **808/332-8561.** Sandwiches under $9; pizzas $16–$35. AE, MC, V. Mon 4–10pm; Tues–Sun 11am–10pm.

Joe's on the Green ★ 🍴 AMERICAN   Psst! I'll let you in on a secret. This "hidden" eatery is known mainly to local residents, who flock here for breakfast or for lunch after a round of golf. They don't want the secret to get out because then their local hangout will be flooded with tourists. Breakfasts are a bargain, especially if you go before 8:30am (Mon–Sat) and get the early-bird special for $7. You'll enjoy a great setting—outdoors overlooking the golf course—and a menu with everything from fluffy pancakes (banana–macadamia nut are the best) to biscuits and gravy to healthy tofu scramble. Lunch is popular for its range of sandwiches (like fresh fish, Joe Mama Burger, and a quarter-pound hot dog with sauerkraut and Cleveland stadium mustard), salads (build your own), and desserts (do not pass up the warm chocolate-chip cookie).

2545 Kiahuna Plantation Dr., at the Kiahuna Golf Club Clubhouse, Poipu. ☏ **808/742-9696.** www.ygli.bluedomino.com. Breakfast $6.75–$13; lunch $9–$13. MC, V. Daily 7am–2:30pm; happy hour 3–7pm.

Kalaheo Café & Coffee Co. ★★ 🍴 COFFEEHOUSE/CAFE   John Ferguson has long been one of my favorite Kauai chefs, and his cafe is a coffee lover's fantasy: Kauai Estate Peaberry, Kona dark roast, Guatemalan French roast, Colombian, Costa Rican, Sumatran, and African coffees—you can visit the world on a coffee bean! The coffeehouse also serves masterful breakfasts: Bonzo Breakfast Burritos (sautéed ham, peppers, mushrooms, onions, and olives scrambled with cheese and served with salsa and sour cream), veggie omelets with sun-dried tomatoes and mushrooms, and bagels. At lunch, the fabulous grilled turkey burgers (heaped with grilled onions and mushrooms on a sourdough bun) are the headliner on a list of winners that also includes fresh-from-the-garden salads and a tasty, inexpensive soup that changes daily. The cinnamon "knuckles" (baked fresh daily), apple pie, and carrot cake are more reasons to stop by. And finally, by popular demand, the cafe is serving dinner (Wed–Sat only): from pasta primavera (in vegetarian, fresh-fish, or chicken versions) and homemade turkey meatloaf to a seafood wrap and grilled New York sirloin steak.

2-2560 Kaumualii Hwy. (Hwy. 50), Kalaheo (across the street from Brick Oven Pizza). ✆ **808/ 332-5858.** www.kalaheo.com. Breakfast $5–$13; lunch $6–$11; dinner entrees $17–$26. MC, V. Mon–Sat 6:30am–2:30pm; Sun 6:30am–2pm; Wed–Sat 5:30–9pm.

Western Kauai

Hanapepe Cafe & Espresso Bar ★★ GOURMET VEGETARIAN/ITAL-
IAN   Helen Lacono (the mother of Andreas Pisciotta, the former owner) has taken over this delectable vegetarian cafe, which has a casual, winning ambience. Her new touches: adding fish to the menu, live entertainment at lunch most days, and a new bakery with wonderful baked goods and quiche. The place is packed at lunchtime, when people come for the several varieties of veggie burger, a modest staple that's elevated to gourmet status here: You can top yours with sautéed mushrooms, grilled onions, pesto, fresh-grated Parmesan, and more. Other lunch notables: fresh red-skinned home fries, a heroic grilled vegetable sandwich, and whole roasted garlic heads. They serve dinner only on Friday, which is "Art Night" in Hanapepe (p. 726). The menu changes weekly but features vegetarian and seafood specialties like lasagna *quattro formaggio* with spinach, mushrooms, and four cheeses; crepes; and the nightly special created by visiting chefs from all over the world—terrific choices all. There's no liquor license, so if you want wine, bring your own ($5 corkage fee). As we went to press, Helen was in the process of opening a deli with prepared dishes to take back to your condo or ingredients for your own masterpiece.

3830 Hanapepe Rd., Hanapepe. ✆ **808/335-5011.** Reservations recommended for dinner. Main courses $8–$15 lunch, $28–$35 dinner. DISC, MC, V. Mon–Thurs 7am–3pm; Fri 5–8:30pm.

Shrimp Station SHRIMP   Looking for a picnic lunch to take up to Waimea Canyon? Stop at this roadside eatery, which is nothing more than a kitchen with a few picnic tables outside—but the shrimp cooking up inside will make up for the lack of ambience. The shrimp is prepared a variety of ways, from shrimp taco to shrimp burger, but the star attractions are the shrimp plates (with choice of garlic shrimp, Cajun, Thai, or sweet chile garlic). If you get yours to go, make sure you grab plenty of napkins; you'll need them after munching these tasty but messy morsels.

9652 Kaumualii Hwy., Waimea. ✆ **808/338-1242.** Shrimp platters $11–$12. MC, V. Daily 11am–5pm.

Toi's Thai Kitchen THAI/AMERICAN   A west Kauai staple, Toi's has gained a following for its affordable, authentic Thai food and casual atmosphere. Tucked into a corner of a small shopping complex (look for the McDonald's on the highway), Toi's serves savory dishes using fresh herbs and local ingredients, many of them from the owner's garden. Popular items include the house specialty, Toi's Temptation (homegrown herbs, coconut milk, lemon grass, and your choice of seafood, meat, or tofu); the vegetable curries; peanut-rich satays; stir-fried Basil Delight; and ginger-sauce nua (your choice of seafood, meat, or tofu in a fresh ginger stir-fry). Most of the rice, noodle, soup, curry, and main-course selections allow you to choose from among pork, chicken, seafood, beef, and vegetarian

options. Lunch dishes come with green-papaya salad and a choice of jasmine, sticky, or brown rice; at dinner, they add dessert.

In the Eleele Shopping Center, Eleele. ✆ **808/335-3111.** Main courses $12–$19. AE, MC, V. Tues–Sat 10:30am–1:45pm and 5:30–8:45pm.

The Coconut Coast

Note: You'll find the restaurants in this section on the "Where to Stay & Dine on the Coconut Coast" map (p. 651).

EXPENSIVE

The Bull Shed STEAK/SEAFOOD   The informality and oceanfront location are big pluses, but Kauai regulars also tout the steaks and chops—prime rib, Australian rack of lamb, garlic tenderloin—and the fresh catch. The seafood selection includes broiled shrimp, Alaskan king crab, and Parmesan-drenched scallops. Dinner orders include rice and the salad bar, while combination dinners target the ambivalent, with chicken, steak, seafood, and lobster pairings. The salad bar alone is a value, and the entrees are so big they're often shared.

796 Kuhio Hwy., Waipouli. ✆ **808/822-3791.** www.bullshedrestaurant.com. Reservations recommended for parties of 6 or more. Main courses $11–$22 (many items are market price). AE, DC, DISC, MC, V. Daily 5–9:30pm.

MODERATE

Caffè Coco ★★ GOURMET BISTRO   This gets my vote for the most charming ambience on Kauai, with gourmet fare cooked to order—and at cafe prices. Caffè Coco appears just off the main road at the edge of a cane field in Wailua, its backyard shaded by pomelo, avocado, mango, tangerine, litchi, and banana trees, with a view of the Sleeping Giant Mountain. The trees provide many of the ingredients for the muffins, chutneys, and salsas that Ginger Carlson whips up in her kitchen. Seats are indoors (beyond the black-light art gallery) or on the gravel-floored back courtyard, where Tiki torches flicker at night. From interior design to cooking, this is clearly a showcase for Carlson's creativity. Food gets a lot of individual attention here. The excellent vegetarian and other healthful delights include homemade chai, Greek salad, fish wraps, seared ahi with wasabi cream, and an excellent tofu-and-roasted-veggie wrap. Service can be laid-back, to say the least. There's music most nights.

4-369 Kuhio Hwy., Wailua. ✆ **808/822-7990.** www.restauranteur.com/caffecoco. Reservations recommended for parties of 4 or more. Main courses $7–$21. AE, DISC, MC, V. Tues–Fri 11am–2pm; Tues–Sun 5–9pm.

Wailua Marina Restaurant AMERICAN   This is a strange but lovable place, anti-nouvelle to the end. I recommend the open-air seating along the Wailua River, where you can watch the riverboats heading for the Fern Grotto over sandwiches (mahimahi is a favorite) and salads. The interior is cavernous, with a high ceiling and stuffed fish adorning the upper walls—bordering on weird, but I love it anyway. The salad bar makes the place friendlier to dieters and vegetarians; otherwise, you'll find the Alaskan king crab legs with filet mignon (or filet paired with lobster tail), stuffed prawns, famous hot lobster salad, steamed mullet, teriyaki spareribs, baked stuffed Island chicken, and some 40 other down-home items heavy on the sauces and gravies. Although the open salad bar is a meal in itself, the more reckless can try the mayo-laden lobster-salad appetizer or the crab-stuffed mushrooms. ***Money-saving tip:*** The early-bird specials (5–6pm) start at $13 for a spaghetti dinner and go up to $14 for a mixed plate of shrimp tempura, or a plate of chicken yakitori, and teriyaki top sirloin for $12.

5971 Kuhio Hwy., Wailua. © **808/822-4311.** Reservations recommended. Lunch $7–$12; dinner main courses $16–$45. AE, MC, V. Tues–Sun 11am–1:30pm and 5–8:30pm.

INEXPENSIVE

Bubba Burgers AMERICAN   Here at the house of Bubba, they dish out humor, great T-shirts, and burgers nonpareil, including Boca and taro burgers for vegetarians. You can order the Slopper (open-faced with chili), the half-pound Big Bubba (three patties), the Hubba Bubba (with rice, hot dog, and chili—a Bubba's plate lunch), and others. Chicken burgers, Bubba's famous Budweiser chili, and other American standards are also served up here, where the burger is king, attitude reigns, and lettuce and tomato cost extra. For a burger joint, it's big on fish too, with a daily trio of fresh-fish specials, fresh-fish sandwiches, fish burgers, and fish and chips. You'll also find Bubba's in Hanalei (5–5161 Kuhio Hwy.) and at the new Kukui'ula Village Mall in the Poipu Resort area (2829 Kalanikaumaka St., Koloa).

4–1421 Kuhio Hwy., Kapaa. © **808/823-0069.** All items under $9. MC, V. Daily 10:30am–8pm (to 9pm in the summer).

The King and I THAI   This medium-size restaurant, in a small and nondescript roadside complex, serves reasonably priced specials and vegetarian selections, including spring rolls, salads, curries, and stir-fries using fresh herbs grown by the owners themselves. At dinner, the pad Thai noodles with shrimp have a special touch and are a popular counterpoint to the red, green, and yellow curries. The vegetarian menu is generous—with everything from noodles to curries to eggplant and tofu—but most diners come back for the Evil Jungle Prince, your choice of veggies, chicken, or fish in a sauce of coconut milk, spices, and kaffir-lime leaves.

At Waipouli Plaza, 4–901 Kuhio Hwy., Kapaa. © **808/822-1642.** Reservations recommended. Main courses $10–$16. AE, DC, DISC, MC, V. Daily 4:30–9pm.

Kountry Kitchen AMERICAN   Forget counting calories when you sit down to the brawny omelets here. You can choose your own fillings from several possibilities, among them a kimchi omelet with cream cheese and several vegetable, meat, and cheese combinations. Sandwiches and American dinners (steak, fish, and chicken) are standard coffeehouse fare, but there are sometimes fresh-fish specials that stand out. ***Warning:*** Sit as far away from the grill as possible; the smell of grease travels—and clings to your clothes.

1485 Kuhio Hwy., Kapaa. © **808/822-3511.** Main courses $7.50–$12. MC, V. Daily 6am–1:30pm.

Mermaids Cafe ★ HEALTHFUL/ISLAND   Don't you love these places that use fresh local ingredients, make everything to order, and barely charge anything for all that trouble? A tiny sidewalk cafe with brisk takeout and a handful of tables on Kapaa's main drag, Mermaids takes kaffir lime, lemon grass, local lemons (Meyers when available), and organic herbs, when possible, to make the sauces and beverages to go with its toothsome dishes. Results are lively and healthful, such as the peanut sauce made with lemon juice instead of fish sauce. It's served in the tofu or chicken satay, chicken coconut curry plate, and chicken satay wrap. The seared ahi wrap is made with the chef's special blend of garlic, jalapeño, lemon grass, kaffir lime, basil, and cilantro, then wrapped in a spinach tortilla—fabulous. The fresh-squeezed lemonade is made daily, and you can choose white or organic brown rice. These special touches elevate the simple classics to dreamy taste sensations.

4–1384 Kuhio Hwy., Kapaa. ✆ **808/821-2026.** Main courses $7–$12. DC, MC, V. Daily 7am–9pm.

Norberto's El Cafe MEXICAN   The lard-free, home-style Mexican fare here includes top-notch chilis rellenos with homemade everything, vegetarian selections by request, and, if you're lucky, fresh-fish enchiladas. All of the sauces are made from scratch, and the salsa comes red-hot with homegrown chili peppers fresh from the chef's garden. Norberto's signature is the spinachy Hawaiian taro-leaf enchiladas, a Mexican version of laulau, served with cheese and taro or with chicken.

4–1373 Kuhio Hwy., Kapaa. ✆ **808/822-3362.** Reservations recommended for parties of 6 or more. Main courses $5.50–$11; complete dinners $11–$19. AE, MC, V. Mon–Sat 5–9pm.

Ono Family Restaurant AMERICAN   Breakfast is a big deal here, with eggs Florentine (two poached eggs, blanched spinach, and hollandaise sauce) leading the pack, and eggs Canterbury (similar to eggs Benedict) following close behind. The Garden Patch, fried rice topped with fresh steamed vegetables, scrambled eggs, and hollandaise sauce, is a real conscience-buster. Steak and eggs; banana, coconut, and macadamia nut pancakes; and dozens of omelet choices also win fans. Lunch is no slouch, either, with scads of fish, veggie, steak, tuna, and turkey sandwiches to choose from, plus beef burgers with various toppings highlighting the menu. The gourmet hamburger with fries and soup demands an after-lunch siesta. Dinner is now served, as well—mostly saimin, fish plates, and burgers for $7.25 to $9.

4–1292 Kuhio Hwy., Kapaa. ✆ **808/822-1710.** Most items under $11. AE, DC, DISC, MC, V. Daily 7am–2pm.

Sukhothai Restaurant THAI/VIETNAMESE/CHINESE   Curries, saimin, Chinese soups, satays, Vietnamese pho, and a substantial vegetarian menu are a few of the features of this unobtrusive but extremely popular restaurant. Menu items appeal to many tastes and include 85 Vietnamese, Chinese, and Thai choices, along with much-loved curries and the best-selling pad Thai noodles. The coconut/lemon grass/kaffir-lime soups (eight choices) are Sukhothai highlights, along with the red and green curries.

At the Kapaa Shopping Center (next to Kapaa's Big Save Market), 4–1105 Kuhio Hwy., Kapaa. ✆ **808/821-1224.** Main courses $8–$33. AE, DC, DISC, MC, V. Daily 11am–9pm.

En Route to the North Shore

Duane's Ono-Char Burger BURGER STAND   I can't imagine Anahola without this roadside burger stand; it's been serving up hefty all-beef burgers for generations. (And now there are Boca burgers, for vegetarians.) The teriyaki sauce and blue cheese are only part of the secret of Duane's beefy, smoky, and legendary ono-char burgers, which come in several styles: teriyaki, mushroom, cheddar, barbecue, and the Special, with grilled onions, sprouts, and two cheeses. The broiled fish sandwich (another marvel of the seasoned old grill) and the marionberry ice-cream shake, a three-berry combo, are popular as well.

Kuhio Hwy., Anahola. ✆ **808/822-9181.** Hamburgers $5–$7.25. MC, V. Mon–Sat 10am–6pm; Sun 11am–6pm.

The North Shore

Note: You'll find the restaurants in this section on the "Where to Stay & Dine on Kauai's North Shore" map (p. 657).

EXPENSIVE

Kauai Grill ★★★ CONTINENTAL/PACIFIC RIM   For a romantic, splurge meal, this is it! The view (dramatic Bali Hai–like peaks in the background and the rolling surf just outside) is spectacular, but combined with the decor (spiraling lit fabric ceiling in the shape of a nautilus shell with a ruby glass hibiscus chandelier) and the amazing cuisine of Chef Jean-George Vongerichten, this is a foodie's paradise. The menu is a la carte (with a $62 tasting menu) and spotlights locally grown or raised items. Vongerichten's creative combinations include the appetizer of fresh hamachi sashimi with sweet sugarloaf pineapple with meyer lemon and wasai ($16) or an appetizer of crispy poached eggs with caviar and vodka crème fraîche ($24). Exotic salads include hearts of palm with vine-ripened tomatoes, avocado, and coconut ($14). Entrees range from steamed lobster with calamansi-jalapeño spaetzle ($48) to seared sirloin of wagyu beef in a gingered mushroom–soy caramel sauce ($48). Book a table to watch the sunset.

St. Regis Hotel, 5520 Kahaku Rd., Princeville. ℂ **800/826-4400** or 808/826-9644. Reservations recommended. Dinner entrees $26–$65. AE, DISC, MC, V. Tues–Sat 6–10pm.

Lighthouse Bistro Kilauea ★ CONTINENTAL/PACIFIC RIM/ITALIAN   Even if you're not on your way to the legendary Kilauea Lighthouse, this bistro is so good it's worth a special trip. The charming green-and-white wooden building next to Kong Lung Store has open sides, old-fashioned plantation architecture, open-air seating, trellises, and high ceilings. The ambience is wonderful, with a retro feel; it's not as polished as Poipu's Plantation Gardens but has its own casual appeal. (In fact, it's the North Shore version of Casa di Amici in Poipu, p. 664.) The food is excellent, an eclectic selection that highlights local ingredients in everything from fresh-fish tacos and fresh-fish burgers to mac nut–crusted chicken and four preparations of fresh catch. This is much more elegant than your usual lunchtime fare. (They have an all-you-can-eat pasta and sauce bar for $15 at dinner.)

At the Kong Lung Center, Kilauea Rd. (off Hwy. 56 on the way to the Kilauea Lighthouse), Kilauea. ℂ **808/828-0480.** Reservations recommended for parties of 6 or more. Lunch $6–$14; dinner main courses $15–$30. MC, V. Daily noon–2:30pm and 5:30–8:30pm.

MODERATE

Bouchon's ★ SUSHI/PACIFIC RIM   This second-floor oasis has copper tables and a copper-topped bar, large picture windows for gazing at the Hanalei waterfalls, and, most important, chefs who know their sushi. Traditional sushi, fusion sushi, and more traditional fish, beef, and pork dishes for those who aren't sushi lovers please diners of every stripe. Big hits: the temaki hand rolls, the Vegas roll (a heroic composition of ahi, hamachi, and avocado dipped in tempura batter and quickly fried, hot on the outside and chilled on the inside), the Rainbow Roll (a super-duper California roll with eight types of fish), and fresh fish prepared several ways, in fusion flavorings involving mango, garlic, sake, sesame, coconut, passion fruit, and other Pacific Rim preparations. Live music Fridays at 8pm.

At Ching Young Village, Hanalei. ✆ **808/826-9701.** www.bouchonshanalei.com. Reservations recommended for parties of 6 or more. Main courses $10–$29; sushi rolls $9 and up. MC, V. Daily 11:30am–10pm. Live music Fri–Sun from 8:30pm.

Calypso STEAK/SEAFOOD   Good food, concrete floors, window tables with flower boxes, seating on the deck with mountain views—what's not to like? Formerly Zelo's, this "beach house," spiced up with South Pacific kitsch, serves a wide variety of coffee drinks and excellent mai tais. The congenial bar area has a tin roof and ironwood poles, and a one-person canoe hangs overhead. Huge burgers, a variety of pastas, 30 microbrews and 30 tropical drinks, a wonderful salad in a large clam-shaped bowl, warm bread, and a good seafood chowder are some of the attractions. The inexpensive tap beers and tacos ensure that visitors and locals alike pack the place during happy hour (3–5:30pm). If you can, snag a table on the deck.

Kuhio Hwy. and Aku Rd., Hanalei. ✆ **808/826-9700.** Reservations recommended for parties of 6 or more. Main courses $8–$18 lunch, $9–$25 dinner. AE, MC, V. Mon–Fri 11am–9pm; Sat–Sun 8am–9pm.

Hanalei Dolphin Restaurant & Fish Market SEAFOOD   Hidden behind a gallery called Ola's are this fish market and adjoining steak-and-seafood restaurant, on the banks of the Hanalei River. Particularly inviting are the fresh-fish sandwiches, served under umbrellas at river's edge. Most appealing (besides the river view) are the appetizers: artichokes steamed or stuffed with garlic, butter, and cheese; buttery stuffed mushrooms; and ceviche fresh from the fish market, with a jaunty dash of green olives. From fresh catch to baked shrimp, from Alaskan king crab to chicken marinated in soy sauce, the Dolphin has stayed with the tried and true. On my last visit service is slow and not up to par; hopefully, this will improve. Their newest venture is the Sushi Lounge, featuring an extensive list of rolls, hand rolls, nigiri, and sakes.

5-5016 Kuhio Hwy., Hanalei. ✆ **808/826-6113.** Main courses $12–$16 lunch, $31–$60 dinner; $8–$22 sushi. AE, MC, V. Daily 11:30am–3pm and 5:30–9pm. Sushi Lounge daily 5:30–9pm. Fish market daily 10am–7pm.

Hanalei Gourmet ★ AMERICAN   The wood benches and blackboards of the old Hanalei School, built in 1926, are a haven for today's Hanalei hipsters noshing on the Waioli Salad (grilled vegetables, artichoke hearts, baby corn, and fresh greens with balsamic vinaigrette), fresh grilled fish sandwiches, roasted eggplant sandwiches, chicken-salad boats (in papaya or avocado, with macadamia nuts and sans mayonnaise), and other selections. This is an informal cross-cultural tasting, from stir-fried veggies over udon to artichoke hearts fried in beer batter. The sandwich selection, on fresh-baked bread, hits the timeless deli faves, from roast beef and pastrami to smoked turkey and chicken salad. The TV over the bar competes with the breathtaking view of the Hanalei mountains and waterfalls, and the wooden floors keep the noise level high (the music on the sound system can be almost deafening). Nightly live music adds to the fun.

At the Old Hanalei Schoolhouse, 5-5161 Kuhio Hwy., Hanalei. ✆ **808/826-2524.** www.hanalei gourmet.com. Main courses $7.50–$11 lunch, $8.50–$27 dinner. DC, DISC, MC, V. Daily 8:30am–9:30pm (open at 8am for takeout only). Bar open until 10:30pm.

Kilauea Bakery & Pau Hana Pizza ★ PIZZA/BAKERY   When owner, baker, and avid diver Tom Pickett spears an ono and smokes it himself, his catch appears on the Billie Holiday pizza, guaranteed to obliterate the blues with its brilliant notes of Swiss chard, roasted onions, Gorgonzola-rosemary sauce, and mozzarella. The much-loved bakery puts out guava sourdough; coconut cream–filled chocolate éclairs (yum!); blackberry–white chocolate scones; and other fine baked goods. The breads go well with the soups and hot lunch specials, and the pastries with the new full-service espresso bar, which serves not only the best of the bean, but also blended frozen drinks and such up-to-the-minute beverages as iced chai and Mexican chocolate smoothies (with cinnamon). I also love the fresh vegetables in olive oil and herbs, baked in a baguette; the olive tapenade; and the classic scampi pizza with tiger prawns, roasted garlic, capers, and cheeses. The Picketts have added a small dining room, and the few outdoor picnic tables under umbrellas are as inviting as ever. The macadamia-nut butter cookies and lilikoi Danishes are sublime.

At Kong Lung Center, Kilauea Rd. (off Hwy. 56 on the way to the Kilauea Lighthouse), Kilauea. © **808/828-2020.** Pizzas $11–$30. MC, V. Daily 6am–9pm.

Mediterranean Gourmet ★★ 🏨 MIDDLE EASTERN   This "hidden" restaurant, next door to the Hanalei Colony Resort and nearly at the end of the road, was awarded "Best New Restaurant on Kauai" by a local magazine and is very deserving of the distinction. The oceanfront location is the perfect backdrop for chef/owner Imad Beydoun's Middle Eastern dishes, which he embellishes with an Island twist with the help of his wife, Yarrow, a local Hanalei girl. People on Kauai have long been buying Beydoun's packaged products (hummus, baba ghanouj, falafel, and tabbouleh) at the local farmers market, so when his family opened the restaurant, they already had a following. The menu has traditional Middle Eastern cuisine (stuffed grape leaves, hand-rolled fatayer, hummus, grilled kofta, Greek salads, and various kabobs), as well as more familiar dishes like chicken quesadilla, rack of lamb, New York strip steak, and fresh fish. Do not leave until you have had the homemade baklava and a cup of Turkish coffee. Go on Thursday to see belly-dancing performances. Live music is featured Wednesday and Friday to Saturday at 6:30pm. Tuesdays they have a Luau starting at 6pm with a traditional Hawaiian buffet and a hula performance ($69 adults, $25–$59 children).

At the Hanalei Colony Resort, 5-7132 Kuhio Hwy., Hanalei. © **808/826-9875.** www.kauaimed gourmet.com. Main courses $11–$23 lunch, $22–$35 dinner. AE, DISC, MC, V. Mon–Sat 11am–8:30pm; Sun 11am–3:30pm.

Neide's Salsa and Samba BRAZILIAN/MEXICAN   Tucked away in the very back of the Hanalei Center is a "hot" eatery dishing up Brazilian cuisine like *muqueca* (fresh fish with coconut sauce), *ensopado* (baked chicken and vegetables), and *bife acebollado* (beef steak with onions), plus the usual popular Mexican dishes like enchiladas and burritos. Big portions and reasonable prices put this place on the map. But in the last year service has become slow (on a good day) to nonexistent (on a bad day). Plus they recently added a minimum $20 charge for credit cards, leaving us muttering "Es mal recibido!"

At the Hanalei Center, Hanalei. © **808/826-1851.** Entrees $11–$20. MC, V. Daily 11:30am–9pm.

Postcards Café ★ GOURMET SEAFOOD/NATURAL FOODS The charming plantation-style building that used to be the Hanalei Museum is now Hanalei's gourmet central. Postcards is known for its use of healthful ingredients, fresh from the island and creatively prepared. My picks from the ever-changing menu are the wasabi-crusted ahi, the sombrero (puff pastry filled with organic cheeses, green chilies, onions, mushrooms, and garlic), and the Shanghai (tofu with veggies and roasted cashews in a tamari-ginger sauce). Save room for the yummy chocolate silk, a chocolate pie in a crust of graham crackers, dried cherries, and cashews. In the front yard, an immense, mossy, hollowed-out stone serves as a free-standing lily pond and roadside landmark. Great menu, presentation, and ambience—a winner.

Kuhio Hwy. (at entrance to Hanalei town). ✆ **808/826-1191.** www.postcardscafe.com. Reservations highly recommended for dinner. Main courses $19–$31. AE, DC, DISC, MC, V. Daily 6–9pm.

INEXPENSIVE

Tropical Taco ★ MEXICAN For more than 25 years, Roger Kennedy has been making tacos and burritos in Hanalei. For years, you could find him working out of his green taco wagon parked alongside the road. He's still serving his tasty assortment of tacos and burritos, plus his signature "fat Jack" (a 10-in. deep-fried tortilla with cheese, beans, and beef or fish), but now from a permanent restaurant in the Halelea Building (with seating along the outside lanai). Roger does issue this warning about his tasty treats: "Not to be consumed 1 hour before surfing!" Just as he did with his taco wagon, Roger still offers "anything you want to drink, as long as it's lemonade."

At the Halelea Bldg., 5-5088 Kuhio Hwy., Hanalei. ✆ **808/827-TACO** (8226). www.tropicaltaco. com. Most items under $11. No credit cards. Daily 7–10:30am; Mon–Sat 11am–5pm; Sun 11am–4pm.

BEACHES

Eons of wind and rain have created this geological masterpiece of an island, with fabulous beaches like Hanalei, Kee, and Kalapaki. All are accessible to the public, as stipulated by Hawaii law, and many have facilities.

Lihue's Best Beach

KALAPAKI BEACH ★

Any town would pay a fortune to have a beach like Kalapaki, one of Kauai's best, in its backyard. But little Lihue turns its back on Kalapaki; there's not even a sign pointing the way through the labyrinth of traffic to this graceful half-moon of golden sand at the foot of the Kauai Marriott Resort & Beach Club. At 150 feet wide and ¼ mile long, Kalapaki is protected by a jetty and patrolled by lifeguards, making it very safe for swimmers. The waves are good for surfing when there's a winter swell, and the view from the sand of the steepled 2,200-foot peaks of the majestic Haupu Ridge that shield Nawiliwili Bay is awesome. Kalapaki is the best beach not only in Lihue, but also on the whole east coast. From Lihue Airport, turn left onto Kapule Highway (Hwy. 51) to Rice Street, turn left and go to the entrance of the Marriott, and pass the hotel's porte-cochere and turn right at the SHORELINE ACCESS sign. Facilities include lifeguards, free parking, restrooms, and showers; food and drink are available nearby at JJ's Broiler (p. 660).

Kalapaki Beach.

The Poipu Resort Area
MAHAULEPU BEACH ★★

Mahaulepu is the best-looking unspoiled beach in Kauai and possibly in the whole state. Its 2 miles of reddish-gold, grainy sand line the southeastern shore at the foot of 1,500-foot-high Haupu Ridge, just beyond the Grand Hyatt Kauai and McBryde sugar-cane fields, which end in sand dunes and a forest of casuarina trees. Almost untouched by modern life, Mahaulepu is a great escape from the real world. It's ideal for beachcombing and shell hunting, but swimming can be risky, except in the reef-sheltered shallows 600 feet west of the sandy parking lot. There's no lifeguard, no facilities—just great natural beauty everywhere you look. (This beach is where George C. Scott portrayed Ernest Hemingway in the movie *Islands in the Stream*.) See if you can find the Hawaiian petroglyph of a voyaging canoe carved in the beach rock. To get here, drive past the Grand Hyatt Kauai 3 miles east on a red-dirt road, past the golf course and stables. Turn right at the T intersection, go 1 mile to the big sand dune, turn left, and drive a half-mile to a small lot under the trees.

POIPU BEACH PARK ★

Big, wide Poipu is actually two beaches in one; it's divided by a sandbar, called a *tombolo*. On the left, a lava-rock jetty protects a sandy-bottom pool that's perfect for children; on the right, the open bay attracts swimmers, snorkelers, and surfers. And everyone likes to picnic on the grassy lawn graced by coconut trees. You'll find excellent swimming, small tide pools for exploring, great reefs for snorkeling and diving, good fishing, nice waves for surfers, and a steady wind for windsurfers. Poipu attracts a daily crowd, but the density seldom approaches Waikiki levels, except on holidays. Facilities include restrooms, showers, picnic areas, playground equipment, Brennecke's Beach Broiler nearby (p. 666), and free parking in the red-dirt lot. To get here, turn on Poipu Beach Road, and then turn right at Hoowili Road.

Mahaulepu Beach.

Surfing near Poipu Beach Park.

Western Kauai

SALT POND BEACH PARK ★

Hawaii's only salt ponds still in production are at Salt Pond Beach, just outside Hanapepe. Generations of locals have come here to swim, fish, and collect salt crystals to dry in sun beds. The tangy salt is used for health purposes and to cure fish and season food. The curved reddish-gold beach lies between two rocky points and features a protected reef, tide pools, and gentle waves. Swimming here is excellent, even for children; this beach is also good for diving, windsurfing, and fishing. Facilities include a lifeguard, showers, restrooms, a camping area, a picnic area, a pavilion, and a parking lot. To get here, take Hwy. 50 past Hanapepe and turn on Lokokai Road.

POLIHALE STATE PARK ★

This mini-Sahara on the western end of the island is Hawaii's biggest beach: 17 miles long and as wide as three football fields. This is a wonderful place to get away from it all, but don't forget your flip-flops—the midday sand is hotter than a lava flow. The golden sands wrap around Kauai's northwestern shore from Kekaha plantation town, just beyond Waimea, to where the ridgebacks of the Na Pali Coast begin. The state park includes ancient Hawaiian *heiau* (temple) and burial sites, a view of the "forbidden" island of Niihau, and the famed **Barking Sands Beach,** where footfalls sound like a barking dog. (Scientists say that the grains of sand are perforated with tiny echo chambers, which emit a "barking" sound when they rub together.) Polihale also takes in the Pacific Missile Range Facility, a U.S. surveillance center that snooped on Russian subs during the Cold War, and Nohili Dune, which is nearly 3 miles long and 100 feet high in some places.

Be careful in winter, when high surf and rip currents make swimming dangerous. The safest place to swim is **Queen's Pond,** a small, shallow, sandy-bottom inlet protected from waves and shore currents. There are facilities for

Beaches & Outdoor Activities on Kauai

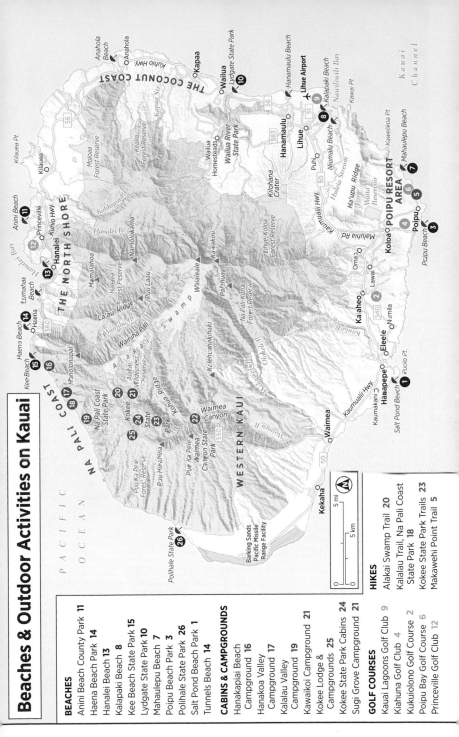

BEACHES

Anini Beach County Park **11**
Haena Beach Park **14**
Hanalei Beach **13**
Kalapaki Beach **8**
Kee Beach State Park **15**
Lydgate State Park **10**
Mahaulepu Beach **7**
Poipu Beach Park **3**
Polihale State Park **26**
Salt Pond Beach Park **1**
Tunnels Beach **14**

CABINS & CAMPGROUNDS

Hanakapiai Beach
  Campground **16**
Hanakoa Valley
  Campground **17**
Kalalau Valley
  Campground **19**
Kawaikoi Campground **21**
Kokee Lodge &
  Campgrounds **25**
Kokee State Park Cabins **24**
Sugi Grove Campground **21**

GOLF COURSES

Kauai Lagoons Golf Club **9**
Kiahuna Golf Club **4**
Kukuiolono Golf Course **2**
Poipu Bay Golf Course **6**
Princeville Golf Club **12**

HIKES

Alakai Swamp Trail **20**
Kalalau Trail, Na Pali Coast
  State Park **18**
Kokee State Park Trails **23**
Makawehi Point Trail **5**

Salt Pond Beach Park.

Polihale State Park.

camping, as well as restrooms, showers, picnic tables, and pavilions. To get here, take Hwy. 50 past Barking Sands Pacific Missile Range and follow the signs through the sugar-cane fields to Polihale. Local kids have been known to burgle rental cars out here, so don't leave tempting valuables in your car.

The Coconut Coast

LYDGATE STATE PARK ★

This seacoast park has a rock-wall fish pond that blunts the open ocean waves and provides the only safe swimming and the best snorkeling on the eastern shore. The 1-acre beach park, near the mouth of the Wailua River, is named for the Rev. J. M. Lydgate (1854–1922), founder and first pastor of Lihue English Union Church, who likely would be shocked at the public display of flesh here. This popular park is a great place for a picnic or for kite flying on the green. It's 5 miles north of Lihue on Kuhio Highway (Hwy. 56); look for the turnoff just before the Kauai Resort Hotel. Facilities include a pavilion, restrooms, outdoor showers, picnic tables, barbecue grills, lifeguards, and parking.

The North Shore

ANINI BEACH COUNTY PARK ★★

Anini is Kauai's safest beach for swimming and windsurfing. It's also one of the island's most beautiful: It sits on a blue lagoon at the foot of emerald cliffs, looking more like Tahiti than almost any other strand in the islands. This 3-mile-long gold-sand beach is shielded from the open ocean by the longest, widest fringing reef in Hawaii. With shallow water 4 to 5 feet deep, it's also the very best snorkel spot on Kauai, even for beginners; on the northwest side, a channel in the reef runs out to the deep-blue water with a 60-foot drop that attracts divers. Beach-combers love it, too: Seashells, cowries, and sometimes even rare Niihau shells can be found here. Anini has a park, a campground, picnic and barbecue facilities, and a boat-launch ramp; several B&Bs and vacation rentals are nearby. Follow Kuhio Highway (Hwy. 56) to Kilauea; take the second exit, called Kalihiwai

Lydgate State Park.

Anini Beach Country Park.

Road (the first dead-ends at Kalihiwai Beach), and drive a half-mile toward the sea; then turn left on Anini Beach Road.

HANALEI BEACH ★

Gentle waves roll across the face of half-moon Hanalei Bay, running up to the wide, golden sand; sheer volcanic ridges laced by waterfalls rise to 4,000 feet on the other side, 3 miles inland. Is there any beach with a better location? Celebrated in song and hula, and featured on travel posters, this beach owes its natural beauty to its age—it's an ancient sunken valley with posterosional cliffs. Hanalei Bay indents the coast a full 1 mile inland and runs 2 miles point to point, with coral reefs on either side and a patch of coral in the middle—plus a sunken ship that belonged to a king, so divers love it. Swimming is excellent year-round, especially in summer, when Hanalei Bay becomes a big, placid lake. The aquamarine water is also great for body boarding, surfing, fishing, windsurfing, canoe paddling, kayaking, and boating (there's a boat ramp on the west bank of the Hanalei River). The area known as **Black Pot,** near the pier, is particularly good for swimming, snorkeling, and surfing. This beach is always packed with both locals and visitors, but you can usually find your own place in the sun by strolling down the shore; the bay is big enough for everyone. Facilities include a pavilion, restrooms, picnic tables, and parking.

To get here, take Kuhio Highway (Hwy. 56), which becomes Hwy. 560 after Princeville. In Hanalei town, make a right on Aku Road just after Tahiti Nui, and then turn right again on Weke Road, which dead-ends at the parking lot for the Black Pot section of the beach; the easiest beach access is on your left.

KEE BEACH STATE PARK ★★

Where the road ends on the North Shore, you'll find a dandy little reddish-gold beach almost too beautiful to be real. Don't be surprised if it looks familiar—it was featured in *The Thorn Birds.* Kee (*Kay*-ay) is on a reef-protected cove at the foot of fluted volcanic cliffs. Swimming and snorkeling are safe inside the reef but dangerous outside; those North Shore waves and currents can be killers. This park has restrooms, showers, lifeguards, and parking (though the lot fills up quickly, so try to arrive early). To get here, take Kuhio Highway (Hwy. 56), which becomes Hwy. 560 after Princeville; Kee is about 7½ miles past Hanalei.

TUNNELS BEACH & HAENA BEACH PARK ★★

Postcard-perfect gold-sand Tunnels Beach is one of Hawaii's most beautiful. When the sun sinks into the Pacific along the fabled peaks of Bali Hai, there's no better-looking beach in the islands: You're bathed in golden rays that butter up the blue sky, bounce off the steepled ridges, and tint the pale clouds hot pink. Catch the sunset from the pebbly sand beach or while swimming in the emerald-green waters, but do catch it. Tunnels is excellent for swimming nearly year-round and is safe for snorkeling because it's protected by a fringing coral reef (the

---

FROMMER'S FAVORITE
kauai experiences

Snorkeling Kee Beach. Rent a mask, fins, and snorkel, and enter a magical underwater world (p. 689). Face-down, you'll float like a leaf on a pond, watching brilliant fish dart through water clear as day; a slow-moving turtle may even stop by to check you out. Face-up, you'll contemplate green-velvet cathedral-like cliffs under a blue sky, with long-tailed tropical birds riding the trade winds.

Hiking Waimea Canyon, the Grand Canyon of the Pacific. Ansel Adams would have loved this ageless desert canyon (p. 693), carved by an ancient river. Sunlight plays against its rustic red cliffs, burnt-orange pinnacles, and blue-green valleys. There's nothing else like it in the islands.

Wandering Around a High Mountain Forest. Kokee State Park (p. 709), through Waimea Canyon at the end of Hwy. 550, is a combination rainforest and bog at around 4,000 feet. The park's 45 miles of trails offer everything from casual nature strolls to hardy camping and hiking adventures among the redwoods.

Strolling Through Hawaiian History. Old Waimea town (p. 706, pictured here) looks so unassuming that you'd never guess it stood witness to a great many key events in Hawaii's history. This is the place where Capt. James Cook "discovered" the Hawaiian Islands, where Russians once built a fort, and where New England missionaries arrived in 1820 to save the heathens. A self-guided walking-tour brochure is available at the **Waimea Public Library,** Kaumualii Highway (✆ **808/338-6848**).

Taking a Long Walk on a Short (but Historic) Pier. First built in 1910, the pier at Hanalei Beach (below) was once a major shipping port for local farmers. Today the rebuilt pier makes a great platform for swimming, fishing, and diving. It's at Black Pot Beach, where, in the olden days, local families would camp out all summer and always have something cooking in a "black pot" on the shore. Black Pot—and all of Hanalei Beach—is great for swimming, snorkeling, and surfing.

waters can get rough in winter, though). The long, curvy beach is sheltered by a forest of ironwoods that provides welcome shade from the tropic heat.

Around the corner is grainy-gold-sand Haena Beach Park, which offers excellent swimming in summer and great snorkeling amid clouds of tropical fish. But stay out of the water in winter, when the big waves are dangerous. Haena also has a popular grassy park for camping. Noise-phobes will prefer Tunnels.

Take Kuhio Highway (Hwy. 56), which becomes Hwy. 560 after Princeville. Tunnels is about 6 miles past Hanalei town, after mile marker 8 on the highway (look for the alley with the big wood gate at the end), and Haena is just down the road. Tunnels has no facilities, but Haena has restrooms, outdoor showers, barbecue grills, picnic tables, and free parking (no lifeguard, though).

Catching a Poipu Wave. Vividly turquoise, curling and totally tubular, big enough to hang ten yet small enough to bodysurf, the waves at Poipu are endless in their attraction. Grab a boogie board—you can rent one for just dollars a day—or simply jump in and go with the flow. See p. 634 and 690 for details.

Watching for Whales. Mahaulepu Beach (p. 677), in the Poipu area, offers excellent land-based viewing conditions for spotting whales that cruise by from December to April.

Journeying into Eden. For a glimpse of the spectacularly remote Na Pali Coast, all you need to do is hike the first 2 miles along the well-maintained **Kalalau Trail** (p. 698) into the first tropical valley, Hanakapiai. Hardier hikers can venture another 2 miles to the Hanakapiai waterfalls and pools. *Warning:* Na Pali's natural beauty is so enticing that you may want to keep going—but the trail turns rugged and extremely challenging after the 2-mile mark. Contact the State Division of Parks for a permit if you want to camp along the trail.

Watching the Hula. The Coconut MarketPlace, 4–484 Kuhio Hwy. (Hwy. 56), between mile markers 6 and 7, Kapaa (© **808/245-4700**), hosts free shows every Wednesday at 5pm. Arrive early to get a good seat for the hour-long performances of both *kahiko* (ancient) and *auwana* (modern) hula. The real showstoppers are the *keiki* (children) who perform. Don't forget your camera!

Bidding the Sun Aloha. Polihale State Park (p. 678) hugs Kauai's western shore for some 17 miles. It's a great place to bring a picnic dinner, stretch out on the sand, and toast the sun as it sinks into the Pacific, illuminating the island of Niihau in the distance. Queen's Pond has facilities for camping, as well as restrooms, showers, picnic tables, and pavilions.

Hanalei Beach.

WATERSPORTS

Several outfitters on Kauai not only offer equipment rentals and tours, but also give out expert information on weather forecasts, sea and trail conditions, and other important matters for hikers, kayakers, sailors, and other backcountry adventurers. For watersports questions and equipment rental, contact **Kayak Kauai,** a mile past Hanalei Bridge on Hwy. 56 (Kuhio Hwy.), in Hanalei (© **800/437-3507** or 808/826-9844; www.kayakkauai.com). It has its own private dock (the only one on Kauai) for launching kayaks and canoes. There's now a second shop located on the east coast, at the Coconut Market Place, 4–484 Kuhio Hwy. (Hwy. 56), Kapaa. You can also go with **Snorkel Bob's,** in Kapaa at 4–734 Kuhio Hwy. (Hwy. 56), just north of Coconut MarketPlace (© **800/262-7725** or 808/823-9433; www.snorkelbob.com), and in Koloa at 3236 Poipu Rd. (just south of Poipu Shopping Village), near Poipu Beach (© **808/742-2206**).

For general advice on the activities listed below, see "Special-Interest Trips," in chapter 3.

Boating

One of Hawaii's most spectacular natural attractions is Kauai's **Na Pali Coast.** Unless you're willing to make an arduous 22-mile hike (p. 697), there are only two ways to see it: by helicopter (see "Helicopter Rides over Waimea Canyon & the Na Pali Coast," on p. 710) or by boat. Picture yourself cruising the rugged Na Pali coastline in a 42-foot ketch-rigged yacht under full sail, watching the sun set as you enjoy a tropical cocktail, or speeding through the aquamarine water in a 40-foot trimaran as porpoises play off the bow.

When the Pacific humpback whales make their annual visit to Hawaii from December to March, they swim right by Kauai. In season, most boats on Kauai—including sail- and powerboats—combine **whale-watching** with their regular adventures.

Kauai has many freshwater areas that are accessible only by boat, including the Fern Grotto, Wailua State Park, Huleia and Hanalei national wildlife refuges, Menehune Fish Pond, and numerous waterfalls. If you want a tour of these fabulous regions, **Wailua River Guides,** 4–788 Kuhio Hwy., Kapaa (℗ **866/955-2925** or 808/821-2800; www.wailuariverguides.com), has an excellent tour of the Wailua River with a brief hike to a "secret" waterfall and a swim. The price, which includes lunch, all equipment, and van transportation from its shop to the marina and back, is just $85 for adults and $75 for children 5 to 13 (not appropriate for kids 4 and under).

Captain Andy's Sailing Adventures ★ Captain Andy operates a 55-foot, 49-passenger catamaran out of two locations on the south shore. The snorkel/picnic cruise, a 5½-hour cruise to the Na Pali Coast, costs $139 for adults and $99 for children 2 to 12, and includes a continental breakfast, deli-style lunch, snorkeling, and drinks. There's also a 4-hour Na Pali Coast dinner sunset cruise that sets sail for $105 for adults and $80 for children, and a 2-hour Poipu cocktail sunset sail with drinks and pupu for $69 adults and $50 children. A 6-hour Na Pali Zodiac cruise on inflatable boats costs $139 to $159 for adults and $99 to $109 for children 5 to 12. *Tip:* Book online for a $10 discount.

Kukuiula Small Boat Harbor, Poipu; and Port Allen, Eleele. ℗ **800/535-0830** or 808/335-6833. www.napali.com. Prices vary depending on trip.

Holoholo Charters This outfitter has taken over several boats and offers swimming/snorkeling sailing charters as well as powerboat charters to the Na Pali Coast. The 5-hour sailing trips take place on a 48-foot catamaran called *Leila* and are offered in the morning (with a continental breakfast and lunch) year-round for $139 adults and $99 children 6 to 12. A 2-hour dinner sunset cruise costs $79 (passengers must be at least 18 years old). On a 7-hour trip on the 61-foot powerboat *Holoholo,* you cruise along the Na Pali Coast and then cross the channel to the forbidden island of Niihau, where you stop for snorkeling. A continental breakfast, a buffet lunch, and snorkel equipment are included in the price: $179 for adults, $129 for children. Or choose a 3½-hour sunset cruise of the Na Pali

Kee Beach State Park.

Tunnels Beach & Haena Beach Park.

Any Kauai beach is great for stargazing, almost any night of the year. Once a month, on the Saturday nearest the new moon, when the skies are darkest, the **Kauai Educational Association for the Study of Astronomy** (☎ 808/332-7827; www.keasa.org) sponsors a free star watch in Kaumakani, at the softball field (follow Hwy. 50 west past Hanapepe; after mile marker 18, look for keasa signs on the right for parking and the star-watch location). Come early to meet folks, and bring a picnic dinner, a light jacket (it gets chilly), an umbrella (the weather can change quickly), mosquito repellent, a lawn or beach chair to sit on, and a mat or blanket so you can lie down and watch the sky. I'd also suggest a flashlight with a red lens; you can pick one up at Ace Hardware, with locations in Lihue (4100 Rice St.), the Eleele Shopping Center, and the Kapaa Shopping Center. Or you can just add red cellophane (also available at Ace) to a regular flashlight to keep your night vision but allow you to navigate around the field in the dark.

Coast on a power catamaran for $99 adults, $79 for children. Complimentary shuttle service is provided to and from your hotel. *Tip:* Book online for $15 off per person.

Port Allen, Eleele. ☎ **800/848-6130** or 808/335-0815. www.holoholocharters.com. Prices and departure points vary depending on trip.

Liko Kauai Cruises ★ ☺   Liko offers more than just a typical whale-watching cruise; this is a 4½- to 5-hour combination Na Pali Coast tour/deep-sea fishing/historical lecture/whale-watching extravaganza with lunch. It all happens on a 49-foot power catamaran with only 32 passengers. In addition to seeing the whales, you'll glimpse sea caves, waterfalls, lush valleys, and miles of white-sand beaches; you'll also make stops along the way for snorkeling.

Kekaha Small Boat Harbor, Waimea. ☎ **888/SEA-LIKO** (732-5456) or 808/338-0333. Fax 808/356-0521. www.liko-kauai.com. Na Pali trips $140 adults, $95 children 4-12 (including lunch).

Body Boarding (Boogie Boarding) & Bodysurfing

The best places for bodysurfing and boogie boarding are **Kalapaki Beach** (near Lihue) and **Poipu Beach.** In addition to the rental shops listed above, one of the most inexpensive places to rent boogie boards is **Snorkel Bob's** (see above), where boards go for just $26 a week.

Fishing

DEEP-SEA FISHING   Kauai's fishing fleet is smaller and less well recognized than others in the islands, but the fish are still out there. All you need to bring is your lunch and your luck. The best way to arrange a sport-fishing charter is through the experts; the best booking desk in the state is **Sportfish Hawaii ★** (☎ **877/388-1376** or 808/396-2607; www.sportfishhawaii.com), which books boats on all the islands. These fishing vessels have been inspected and must meet rigorous criteria to guarantee that you will have a great time. Prices range from $1,250 to $1,495 for a full-day exclusive charter (you and five of your closest friends get the entire boat to yourself), $950 to $1,195 for a three-quarter-day charter, and $675 to $795 for a half-day exclusive. Frankly, the fishing is better off the Kona coast, and the prices are more reasonable, too.

FRESHWATER FISHING   Freshwater fishing is big on Kauai, thanks to its dozens of man-made reservoirs. They're full of largemouth, smallmouth, and peacock bass (also known as *tucunare*). The **Puu Lua Reservoir,** in Kokee State Park, also has rainbow trout and is stocked by the state every year. Fishing for rainbow trout in the reservoir has a limited season: It begins on the first Saturday in August and lasts for 16 days, after which you can fish only on weekends and holidays through the last Sunday in September.

Before you rush out and get a fishing pole, you must have a **Hawaii Freshwater Fishing License,** available through the **State Department of Land and Natural Resources,** Division of Aquatic Resources, 3060 Eiwa St., Room 306, Lihue, HI 96766 (© **808/274-3344;** www.hawaii. gov/dlnr) You can also get a license through any fishing-supply store; try **Wal-Mart,** 3-3300 Kuhio Hwy., Lihue (© **808/246-1599**); or **Waipouli Variety,** 4-901 1-A Kuhio Hwy., Kapaa (© **808/822-1014**). Or you can get your license online by going to www.ehawaii.gov/dlnr/fish/exe/fresh_main_page.cgi. A 7-day tourist license costs $10 (plus a $1 convenience fee if purchased online).

When you get your license, pick up a copy of the booklet *State of Hawaii Freshwater Fishing Regulations.* Another great little book is *The Kauai Guide to Freshwater Sport Fishing,* by Glenn Ikemoto, available for $2.50 plus postage from **Magic Fishes Press,** P.O. Box 3243, Lihue, HI 96766.

If you would like a guide, **Sportfish Hawaii** (© **877/388-1376** or 808/396-2607; www.sportfishhawaii.com) offers guided bass-fishing trips starting at $265 for two people for a half-day and $450 for two for a full day.

Kayaking

Kauai is made for kayaking. You can take the Huleia River into **Huleia National Wildlife Refuge** (located along the eastern portion of the Huleia Stream where it flows into Nawiliwili Bay). It's the last stand for Kauai's endangered birds, and the only way to see it is by kayak. The adventurous can head to the Na Pali Coast, featuring majestic cliffs, empty beaches, open-ocean conditions, and monster waves. Or you can just go out and paddle around Hanalei Bay.

Kayak Kauai ★, a mile past Hanalei Bridge on Hwy. 56 (Kuhio Hwy.), in Hanalei (© **800/437-3507** or 808/826-9844; www.kayakkauai.com), has a range of tours for independent souls. The shop's experts will be happy to take you on a guided kayaking trip or to tell you where to go on your own. Equipment rental starts at $29 for a one-person kayak and $54 for a two-person kayak per day. Kayak lessons are $50 per person per hour, two-person minimum. Tours (some including snacks) start at $60 per person and include transportation. Kayak Kauai also has its own private dock (the only one on Kauai) for launching kayaks and canoes.

Rick Haviland, who gained fame after he was mentioned in Paul Theroux's book *The Happy Isles of Oceania,* is the owner of **Outfitters Kauai ★,** 2827A

Poipu Rd. (in Poipu Plaza, a small five-shop mall before the road forks to Poipu/Spouting Horn), Poipu (✆ **888/742-9887** or 808/742-9667; www.outfitterskauai.com), which has a bunch of different kayaking tours. A full-day trip along the entire Na Pali Coast (summer only) costs $225 per person and includes a guide, lunch, drinks, and equipment. Another kayak tour takes you up a jungle stream and involves a short hike to waterfalls and a swimming hole; it's $98 for adults and $78 for children 5 to 14, including lunch, snacks, and drinks.

Kayaking in Huleia National Wildlife Refuge.

Ride the Huleia River through Kauai's 240-acre Huleia National Wildlife Refuge, the last stand of Kauai's endangered birds, with **True Blue,** Nawiliwili Harbor (✆ **888/245-1707** or 808/246-6333; www.kauaifun.com). You paddle up the picturesque Huleia (which appeared in *Raiders of the Lost Ark* and the remake of *King Kong*) under sheer pinnacles that open into valleys full of lush tropical plants, bright flowers, and hanging vines. Look for great blue herons and Hawaiian gallinules taking wing. The 4½-hour voyage, which starts at Nawiliwili Harbor, is a great trip for all—but especially for movie buffs, birders, and great adventurers 11 and under. It's even safe for nonswimmers. Wear a swimsuit, T-shirt, and boat shoes. The cost is $89 for adults, $69 for children 6 to 12. Prices include a picnic lunch, juice, kayak, life vest, and guide services.

Other options for kayak rentals is **Pedal 'n Paddle,** Ching Young Village Shopping Center, Hanalei (✆ **808/826-9069;** www.pedalnpaddle.com); and **Wailua Kayak & Canoe,** 169 Wailua Rd., Kapaa (✆ **808/821-1188;** www.wailuakayakandcanoe.net).

Scuba Diving

Diving on Kauai is dictated by the weather. In winter, when heavy swells and high winds hit the island, it's generally limited to the more protected south shore. Probably the best-known site along the south shore is **Caverns,** located off the Poipu Beach resort area. This site consists of a series of lava tubes interconnected by a chain of archways. A constant parade of fish streams by (even shy lionfish are spotted lurking in crevices), brightly hued Hawaiian lobsters hide in the lava's tiny holes, and turtles sometimes swim past.

In summer, when the north Pacific storms subside, the magnificent North Shore opens up, and you can take a boat dive locally known as the **Oceanarium,** northwest of Hanalei Bay, where you'll find a kaleidoscopic marine world in a horseshoe-shaped cove. From the rare (long-handed spiny lobsters) to the more common (taape, conger eels, and nudibranchs), the resident population is one of the more diverse on the island. The topography, which features pinnacles, ridges, and archways, is covered with cup corals, black-coral trees, and nooks and crannies enough for a dozen dives.

DIVE BOATS Because the best dives on Kauai are offshore, I recommend booking a two-tank dive off a dive boat. **Bubbles Below Scuba Charters,** 6251 Hauaala Rd., Kapaa (☎ **866/524-6268** or 808/332-7333; www.bubbles belowkauai.com), specializes in highly personalized small-group dives, with an emphasis on marine biology. The 36-foot *Kaimanu* is a custom-built Radon dive boat that comes complete with a hot shower. Two-tank boat dives cost $125 (if booked directly); nondivers can pay $80 to come along for the ride. In summer (May–Sept), Bubbles Below offers a three-tank trip for experienced divers only to the "forbidden" island of Niihau, 90 minutes by boat from Kauai. You should be comfortable with vertical drop-offs, huge underwater caverns, possibly choppy surface conditions, and significant currents. You should also be willing to share water space with the resident sharks. The all-day, three-tank trip costs $300 (booked directly), including tanks, weights, dive computer, lunch, drinks, and marine guide (if you need gear, it's $25 more).

On the south side of the island, call **Fathom Five Adventures,** 3450 Poipu Rd. (next to the Chevron), Koloa (☎ **808/742-6991;** www.fathom five.com).

GREAT SHORE DIVES FROM KAUAI Spectacular shoreline dive sites on the North Shore include **Kee Beach/Haena Beach Park** (where the road ends), one of the most picturesque beaches on the island. On a calm summer day, the drop-off near the reef begs for underwater exploration. **Cannons Beach,** east of Haena Beach Park (use the parking for Haena, located across the street from the Dry Cave near mile marker 9 on Hwy. 560), has lots of vibrant marine life in its sloping offshore reef. Another good bet is **Tunnels Beach,** also known as Makua Beach. It's off Hwy. 560, just past mile marker 8; look for the short dirt road (less than a half-mile) to the beach. The wide reef here makes for some fabulous snorkeling and diving, but again, only during the calm summer months.

On the south shore, head to **Tortugas** (located directly in front of Poipu Beach Park) if you want to catch a glimpse of sea turtles. **Koloa Landing** has a horseshoe-shaped reef that's teeming with tropical fish. **Sheraton Caverns** (located off the Sheraton Kauai) is also popular, due to its three large underwater lava tubes, which are usually filled with marine life.

If you want a guided shore dive, **Fathom Five Adventures** (see above) will take you out for $70 for one tank and $85 for two tanks.

Snorkeling

See the introduction to this section for locations of **Snorkel Bob's.**

For great shoreline snorkeling, try the reef off **Kee Beach/Haena Beach Park,** located at the end of Hwy. 560. **Tunnels Beach,** about a mile before the end of Hwy. 560 in Haena, has a wide reef that's great for poking around in search of tropical fish. Be sure to check ocean conditions—don't go if the surf is up or if there's a strong current. **Anini Beach,** located off the northern Kalihiwai Road (btw. mile markers 25 and 26 on Kuhio Hwy., or Hwy. 56), just before the Princeville Airport, has a safe, shallow area with excellent snorkeling. **Poipu Beach Park** has some good snorkeling to the right side of Nukumoi Point—the tombolo area, where the narrow strip of sand divides the ocean, is best. If this spot is too crowded, wander down the beach in front of the old Waiohai resort; if there are no waves, this place is also hopping with marine life. **Salt Pond Beach Park,** off Hwy. 50 near Hanapepe, has good snorkeling around the two rocky points, home to hundreds of tropical fish.

Surfing

Hanalei Bay's winter surf is the most popular on the island, but it's for experts only. **Poipu Beach** is an excellent spot to learn to surf; the waves are small and—best of all—nobody laughs when you wipe out. Check with the local surf shops or call the **Weather Service** (✆ **808/245-3564**) to find out where surf's up.

Snorkeling.

Poipu is also the site of numerous surfing schools; the oldest and best is **Margo Oberg's School of Surfing,** at the beach in front of the Kiahuna Plantation Resort (✆ **808/332-6100;** www.surfonkauai.com). Margo charges $68 for 2 hours of group instruction, including surfboard and leash; she guarantees that by the end of the lesson, you'll be standing and catching a wave.

Equipment is available for rent (ranging from $6 an hour or $25 a day for "soft" beginner boards to $8 an hour or $30 a day for hard boards for experienced surfers) from **Nukumoi Surf Shop,** across from Brennecke's Beach, Poipu Beach Park (✆ **808/742-8019;** www.nukumoisurf.com/surfshophawaii.html); **Hanalei Surf Co.,** 5–5161 Kuhio Hwy. (across from Zelo's Beach House Restaurant in Hanalei Center), Hanalei (✆ **808/826-9000**); and **Pedal 'n Paddle,** Ching Young Village Shopping Center, Hanalei (✆ **808/826-9069**).

Tubing

Back in the days of the sugar plantations, local kids would grab inner tubes and jump in the irrigation ditches crisscrossing the cane fields to get an exciting ride. Today you can enjoy this (formerly illegal) activity by "tubing" the flumes and ditches of the old Lihue Plantation with **Kauai Backcountry Adventures** (✆ **888/270-0555** or 808/245-2506; www.kauaibackcountry.com). Passengers are taken in four-wheel-drive vehicles high into the mountains above Lihue to look at vistas generally off-limits to the public. At the flumes, you will be outfitted with a giant tube, gloves, and headlamp (for the long passageways through the tunnels). All you do is jump in the water, and the gentle gravity-feed flow will carry you through forests, into tunnels, and finally to a mountain swimming hole, where a picnic lunch is served. The 3-hour tours (you'll spend about 1 hr. actually in the water) are $106 and appropriate for anyone ages 5 to 95. Swimming is not necessary, as all you do is relax and drift downstream.

☺ ESPECIALLY FOR kids

Surfing with an Expert (p. 690)   If seven-time world champ Margo Oberg, a member of the Surfing Hall of Fame, can't get your kid—or you—up on a board riding a wave, nobody can. She promises same-day results even for klutzes.

Paddling up the Huleia River (p. 687)   Indiana Jones ran for his life up this river to his seaplane in *Raiders of the Lost Ark*. You and the kids can venture down it yourself in a kayak. The picturesque Huleia winds through lush Huleia National Wildlife Refuge, where endangered species like great blue herons and Hawaiian gallinules take wing. It's ideal for everyone.

Climbing the Wooden Jungle Gyms at Kamalani Playground (p. 653, pictured here)   Located in Lydgate State Park, Wailua, this unique playground has a maze of jungle gyms for kids of all ages. Spend an afternoon whipping down slides, exploring caves, hanging from bars, and climbing all over.

Cooling Off with a Shave Ice (p. 666)   On a hot, hot day, stop by the deli at **Brennecke's Beach Broiler,** across from Poipu Beach Park (✆ **808/742-7588**), and order a traditional Hawaiian shave ice. This local treat consists of ice shavings stuffed into a paper cone and topped with a tropical flavored syrup. If you can't decide, go for the "rainbow"—three flavors in one cone.

Exploring a Magical World (p. 717)   **Na Aina Kai Botanical Gardens** sits on some 240 acres, sprinkled with around 70 life-size (or larger-than-life-size) whimsical bronze statues, hidden off the beaten path of the North Shore. The tropical children's garden features a gecko hedge maze, a tropical jungle gym, a treehouse in a rubber tree, and a 16-foot-tall Jack-in-the-Beanstalk giant with a 33-foot wading pool below. It's open only 3 days a week, so book before you leave home to avoid disappointment.

10

KAUAI, THE GARDEN ISLE

Watersports

Windsurfing & Kitesurfing

Anini Beach is one of the safest beaches for beginners to learn windsurfing. Lessons and equipment rental are available at **Windsurf Kauai** (✆ **808/828-6838**). Owner Celeste Harzel has been teaching windsurfing on Anini Beach for nearly 3 decades; she has special equipment to help beginners learn the sport. A 3-hour lesson is $100 and includes equipment and instruction. If you fall in love with windsurfing and want to keep going, she'll rent the equipment for $25 an hour. Serious windsurfers should head to **Hanalei Bay** or **Tunnels Beach** on the North Shore.

HIKING & CAMPING

Kauai is an adventurer's delight. The island's greatest tropical beauty isn't easily reachable; you've got to head out on foot and find it.

HIKING ON YOUR OWN   For more information on Kauai's hiking trails, contact the **State Division of Parks,** 3060 Eiwa St., Lihue, HI 96766 (© 808/ 274-3446; www.hawaiistateparks.org/camping/kauai.cfm); the **State Division of Forestry and Wildlife,** 1151 Punchbowl St., Room 325, Honolulu, HI 96813 (© 808/587-0166; www.dofaw.net); **Kauai County Parks and Recreation,** 4444 Rice St., Ste. 150, Lihue, HI 96766 (© 808/ 241-4460; www.kauai.gov/Government/Departments/ParksRecreation/tabid/ 515/default.aspx); or the **Kokee Lodge Manager,** P.O. Box 819, Waimea, HI 96796 (© 808/335-6061).

> ## 📎 A Warning About Flash Floods
>
> When it rains on Kauai, the waterfalls rage and rivers and streams overflow, causing flash floods on roads and trails. If you're hiking, avoid dry streambeds, which flood quickly and wash out to sea. Before going hiking, camping, or sailing, especially in the rainy season (Nov–Mar), check the weather forecast by calling © 808/245-6001.

Kayak Kauai ★, a mile past Hanalei Bridge on Hwy. 560 in Hanalei (© **800/437-3507** or 808/826-9844; fax 808/822-0577; www.kayakkauai.com), is the premier all-around outfitter on the island. It's staffed by local experts who keep track of weather forecasts as well as sea and trail conditions; they have a lot more pertinent information that hikers, campers, and other backcountry adventurers need to know. Plus, they have custom guided hiking tours starting at $81 per person for four people. If you don't plan to bring your own gear, you can rent it here or at **Pedal 'n Paddle,** in Hanalei (© **808/826-9069;** www.pedalnpaddle.com). If you want to buy camping equipment, head for **Ace Island Hardware,** at Princeville Shopping Center (© **808/826-6980**), or **Wal-Mart,** 3-3300 Kuhio Hwy. (Hwy. 56), near the airport in Lihue (© **808/246-1599**).

GUIDED HIKES   The Kauai chapter of the **Sierra Club,** P.O. Box 3412, Lihue, HI 96766 (www.hi.sierraclub.org/Kauai/kauai-hikes.html), offers four to seven different guided hikes every month, varying from an easy family moonlit beach hike to a moderate 4-mile trip up some 1,100 feet, plus 8-mile-plus treks for serious hikers only. The club also does guided hikes of Kokee State Park (see below), usually on weekends. Because there's no staffed office, the best way to contact the chapter is to check the website; outings are usually listed 3 to 6 months in advance, with complete descriptions of the hike, the hike leader's phone number, and what to wear and bring. You can also check the daily newspaper, the *Garden Island,* for a list of hikes in the "Community Calendar" section. Generally, the club asks for a donation of $5 per person per hike for nonmembers, $1 for children 17 and under and Sierra Club members. It also does service work (clearing trails, picking up trash) on the hikes, so you may spend an hour doing service work, and then 2 to 3 hours hiking. Last year, the club took three service-work trips along the Na Pali Coast trail to help maintain it.

Hawaiian Wildlife Tours ★ (② 808/639-2968; www.hawaiian wildlifetours.com) is environmental education in action. Biologist Dr. Carl Berg will take you out into the woods and down to the shoreline to see Kauai's native and vanishing species, from forest birds and flora to hoary bats, monk seals, and green sea turtles. His personalized tours last from 1 hour to 1 week and are tailored around the season and weather, your physical abilities, and what you want to see. He leads tours to Hanalei taro fields to see wetland birds, to Crater Hill to see nene geese, to Mahaulepu to see wildflowers in the sand dunes, to Kilauea Lighthouse to see oceanic birds, and much more. Rates are $50 per couple per hour.

Other options for guided hikes include **Princeville Ranch Adventures** (② 808/826-7669; www.adventureskauai.com), which offers various hikes on 2,000 acres of private property, such as a 4-hour hike to a waterfall (including swimming) for $129 adults and $89 kids 5 to 10; and **Kauai Nature Adventures** (② 888/233-8365 or 808/742-8305; www.kauainaturetours.com), which features a geological-history excursion, a tour of Kauai's environments from the mountain to the ocean, and a Mahaulepu coast hike, all led by scientists and costing $100 to $130 for adults and $75 to $85 for children 7 to 12, including lunch.

The Poipu Resort Area
MAKAWEHI POINT TRAIL ★
Like a ship's prow, Makawehi Point juts out to sea on the east side of Keoneloa Beach (known locally as Shipwreck Beach), which lies in front of the Grand Hyatt Kauai. This 50-foot-high sand-dune bluff attracts a variety of people: pole fishers, whale-watchers, those who just like the panoramic views of the Pacific, and daredevils who test their courage by leaping off the cliff into the waves (don't try it).

The trail head begins on the east end of Shipwreck Beach, past the Grand Hyatt. It's an easy 10-minute walk up to Makawehi Point; after you take in the big picture, keep going uphill along the ridge of the sand dunes (said to contain ancient Hawaiian burial sites), past the coves frequented by green sea turtles and endangered Hawaiian monk seals, through the coastal pine forest, and past World War II bunkers to the very top. Now you can see Haupu Ridge and its 2,297-foot peak, the famously craggy ridgeline that eerily resembles Queen Victoria's profile, and, in the distance, Mahaulepu Beach, one of the best-looking in Hawaii. Inland, three red craters dimple the green fields; the one in the middle, the biggest, Pu'u Huni Huni, is said to have been the last volcano to erupt on Kauai—but it was so long ago that nobody here can remember when.

Western Kauai
TRAILS IN WAIMEA CANYON
On a wet island like Kauai, a dry hike is hard to find. But in the desert-dry gulch of Waimea Canyon, known as the Grand Canyon of the Pacific (once you get here, you'll see why—it's pretty spectacular), you're not likely to slip and slide in the muck as you go.

CANYON TRAIL You want to hike Hawaii's Grand Canyon, but you don't think you have time? Take the Canyon Trail to the east rim for a breathtaking view

Waipoo Falls.

into the 3,000-foot-deep canyon. Park your car at the top of Halemanu Valley Road (located btw. mile markers 14 and 15 on Waimea Canyon Rd., about a mile down from the museum). The 3.5-mile round-trip takes 2 to 3 hours and leads to Waipoo Falls (as does the hike described below) and back. I suggest going in the afternoon, when the light is best.

HIKE TO WAIPOO FALLS ★ The 3-hour round-trip hike to Waipoo Falls is one of Kauai's best hikes. The two-tiered, 800-foot waterfall that splashes into a natural pool is worth every step it takes to get here. To find the trail, drive up Kokee Road (Hwy. 550) to the Puu Hina Hina Outlook; a quarter-mile past the lookout, near a NASA satellite tracking station on the right, a two-lane dirt road leads to the Waipoo Falls trail head. From here, the trail winds through a jungle dotted with wild yellow orchids and flame-red torch ginger before it leads you out on a descending ridgeback that juts deep into the canyon. At the end of the promontory, take a left and push on through the jungle to the falls; at the end, reward yourself with a refreshing splash in the pool.

TRAILS IN KOKEE STATE PARK ★★

At the end of Hwy. 550, which leads through Waimea Canyon to its summit, lies a 4,640-acre state park of high-mountain forest wilderness (3,600–4,000 ft. above sea level). The rainforest, bogs, and breathtaking views of the Na Pali coastline and Waimea Canyon are the draw at Kokee. Among the 45 miles of maintained trails are some of the best hikes in Hawaii. You can download a brochure of all the trails in Kokee from www.kokee.org. Official trail maps of all the park's trails are for sale for $1.60 at the **Kokee Natural History Museum** (𝄏 **808/335-9975**).

A few words of advice: Always check current trail conditions; up-to-date trail information is available on a bulletin board at the Kokee Natural History Museum. The museum staff is also very helpful. Stay on established trails, as it's easy to get lost here. Get off the trail well before dark. Carry water and rain gear—even if it's perfectly sunny when you set out—and wear sunscreen.

For complete coverage of the state park, see p. 709.

AWAAWAPUHI TRAIL This 3.25-mile hike (6.5 miles round-trip) takes about 3 hours each way and is considered strenuous by most, but it offers a million-dollar view. Look for the trail head at the left of the parking lot, at mile marker 17 between the museum and Kalalau Lookout. The well-marked, well-maintained trail now sports .25-mile markers, and you can pick up a free plant guide for the trail at the museum. The trail drops about 1,600 feet through native forests to a thin precipice right at the very edge of the Na Pali cliffs for a dramatic and dizzying view of the tropical valleys and blue Pacific 2,500 feet below. It's not recommended for anyone with vertigo (although a railing will keep you from a major slip and fall). Go early, before clouds obscure the view, or late in the day—the sunsets are something to behold.

The Awaawapuhi can be a straight-out-and-back trail or a loop that connects with the **Nualolo Trail** (3.75 miles), which provides awesome views and leads back to the main road between the ranger's house and the Kokee cabins, which is about a mile and a half from where you started. So you can hike the remaining 1.5 miles along the road or hitch a ride if you decide to do the entire loop but can't make it all the way.

HALEMANU-KOKEE TRAIL   This trail takes you on a pleasant, easy-to-moderate 2.5-mile round-trip walk through a native koa-and-ohia forest inhabited by native birds. The trail head is near mile marker 15; pick up the Faye Trail, which leads to this one. The Halemanu-Kokee links Kokee Valley to Halemanu Valley (hence the name); along the way, you'll see a plum orchard, valleys, and ridges.

PIHEA TRAIL   This is the park's flattest trail, but it's still a pretty strenuous 7.5-mile round-trip. A boardwalk that runs along about a third of the trail makes it easier, especially when it's wet. The trail begins at the end of Hwy. 550 at Puu O Kila Lookout, which overlooks Kalalau Valley; it goes down at first and then flattens out as it traces the back ridge of the valley. Once it enters the rainforest, you'll see native plants and trees. It intersects with the Alakai Swamp Trail (see below). If you combine both trails, figure on about 4 hours in and out. If that sounds too daunting, consider taking the Pihea Trail just to where it intersects with Alakai; it's about 2 miles to that point (one-way) and you'll get to see some stunning views of Kalalau Valley and the ocean, as well enjoy a few shady, wooded stretches.

ALAKAI SWAMP TRAIL ★ If you want to see the "real" Hawaii, this is it—a big swamp that's home to rare birds and plants. The trail allows a rare glimpse into a wet, cloud-covered wilderness preserve where 460 inches of rainfall a year is common. This 7-mile hike used to take 5 hours of sloshing through the bog, with mud up to your knees. Now a boardwalk protects you from the shoe-grabbing mud. Come prepared for rain. (The only silver lining is that there are no mosquitoes above 3,000 ft.)

The trail head is off Mohihi (Camp 10) Road, just beyond the Forest Reserve entrance sign and the Alakai Shelter picnic area. From the parking lot, the trail follows an old

The Alakai Swamp Trail.

World War II four-wheel-drive road. Stick to the boardwalk; this is a fragile eco-area. At the end of the 3.5-mile slog, if you're lucky and the clouds part, you'll have a lovely view of Wainiha Valley and Hanalei from Kilohana Lookout.

CAMPGROUNDS & WILDERNESS CABINS IN KOKEE

CABINS & TENT CAMPGROUNDS Camping facilities include state campgrounds (one next to Kokee Lodge, and four more primitive backcountry sites), one private tent area, and the **Kokee Lodge,** which has 12 cabins for rent at very reasonable rates. At 4,000 feet, the nights are cold, particularly in winter, and no open fires are permitted at Kokee. Also, there are a lot of roosters in this area, so you may want to bring earplugs. The best deal is the cabins, reviewed on p. 650. The **Kokee Lodge Restaurant** is open daily from 9am to 2:30pm for continental breakfast and lunch. Groceries and gas aren't available in Kokee, so stock up in advance; it's a long trip back down the mountain.

The **state campground** at Kokee allows tent camping only. Permits can be obtained from a state parks office on any island; on Kauai, it's at 3060 Eiwa St., Room 306, Lihue, HI 96766 (© **808/274-3444;** www. hawaiistateparks.org/camping/kauai.cfm). The permits are $18 per night; the time limit is 5 nights in a single 30-day period. Facilities include showers, drinking water, picnic tables, a pavilion with tables, restrooms, barbecues, sinks for dishwashing, and electric lights.

Tent camping at **Camp Sloggett,** owned by the Kauai YWCA, 3094 Elua St., Lihue, HI 96766 (© **808/245-5959;** fax 808/245-5961; www. campingkauai.com/accomodations.html), is available for $10 per person per night (children 4 and under stay free). The sites are on 1½ acres of open field, with a covered pit for fires and a barbecue area, plus volleyball and badminton nets. For a solo traveler or couple, **Caretaker's Cottage** is a one-bedroom cottage with a king-size bed, a full kitchen, and a wood-burning stove for just $85 per night on weekdays and $120 per night on weekends, for up to four people, with a 2-night minimum and $100 cleaning fee. (*Note:* If you stay only 2 nights, that cleaning fee raises the amount a couple would pay to an average of $135 a night on weekdays and $170 a night on weekends, a bit pricey for what you get.) Bring your own towels. To get here, continue on the highway past park headquarters and take the first right after the Kokee Lodge. Follow the dirt road and look for the wooden CAMP SLOGGETT sign; turn right and follow the bumpy road past the state cabins into a large clearing.

BACKCOUNTRY CAMPING The more primitive backcountry campgrounds include **Sugi Grove** and **Kawaikoi,** located about 4 miles from park headquarters on the Camp 10 Road, an often-muddy and steep four-wheel-drive road. Sugi Grove is located across the Kawaikoi Stream from the Kawaikoi campsite. The area is named for the sugi pines, which were planted in 1937 by the Civilian Conservation Corps. This is a shady campsite with a single picnic shelter, a pit toilet, a stream, and space for several tents. The Kawaikoi site is a 3-acre open grass field, surrounded by Kokee plum trees and forests of koa and ohia. Facilities include two picnic shelters, a composting toilet, and a stream that flows next to the camping area. There is no potable water—bring in your own or treat the stream water.

Permits, which are $18 per night, are available through the **State Parks Office,** 3060 Eiwa St., Room 306, Lihue, HI 96766 (**℃ 808/274-3444;** www.hawaiistateparks.org/camping/kauai.cfm). You're limited to 5 nights in any 30-day period.

BEACH CAMPING AT POLIHALE STATE PARK

Polihale holds the distinction of being the westernmost beach in the United States. The beach is spectacular—some 300 feet wide in summer, with rolling sand dunes (some as high as 100 ft.) and the islands of Niihau and Lehua just offshore. Bordered by a curtain of Na Pali cliffs on the north, razor-sharp ridges and steep valleys to the east, and the blue Pacific on the south and west, this is one of the most dramatic camping areas in the state.

The campgrounds for tent camping are located at the south end of the beach, affording privacy from the daytime beach activities. There's great swimming in summer (even then, be on the lookout for waves and rip currents—there are no lifeguards), some surfing (the rides are usually short), and fishing. The camping is on sand, although there are some kiawe trees for shade. (*Warning:* Kiawe trees drop long thorns, so make sure you have protective footwear.) Facilities include restrooms, showers, picnic tables, barbecues, and a spigot for drinking water. You can purchase supplies about 15 miles away in Waimea.

Permits, which are $18 per night, are available through the **State Parks Office,** 3060 Eiwa St., Lihue, HI 96766 (**℃ 808/274-3444;** www.hawaiistateparks.org/camping/kauai.cfm). You're limited to 5 nights in any 30-day period. To reach the park from Lihue, take Hwy. 50 west to Barking Sands Pacific Missile Range. Bear right onto the paved road, which heads toward the mountains. There will be small signs directing you to Polihale; the second sign will point to a left turn onto a dirt road. Follow this for about 5 miles; at the fork in the road, the campgrounds are to the left and the beach park is to the right.

The Coconut Coast

THE SLEEPING GIANT TRAIL

This hardy hike takes you up the fabled mountain known as Sleeping Giant (which really does look like a giant resting on his back) to a fabulous view. The hike will gain 1,000 feet in altitude on a clearly marked trail (be sure to stay on the trail). The climb is steep and steadily uphill (remember, you are climbing up a mountain), but the view at the top is well worth the constant incline. To get to the trail head, turn mauka (toward the mountain) off Kuhio Highway (Hwy. 56) onto Haleilio Road (btw. Wailua and Kapaa, just past mile marker 6); follow Haleilio Road for 1.25 miles to the parking area, at telephone pole number 38. From here, signs posted by the State of Hawaii Division of Forestry and Wildlife lead you over the 1.75-mile trail, which ends at a picnic table and shelter. The panoramic view is breathtaking. Be sure to bring water—and a picnic, if you like.

The North Shore: Na Pali Coast State Park

Simply put, the Na Pali Coast is the most beautiful part of the Hawaiian Islands. Hanging valleys open like green-velvet accordions, and waterfalls tumble to the sea from the 4,120-foot-high cliffs; the experience is both exhilarating and humbling. Whether you hike in, fly over, or take a boat cruise past, be sure to see this park.

Established in 1984, Na Pali Coast State Park takes in a 22-mile stretch of fluted cliffs that wrap around the northwest shore of Kauai between Kee Beach and Polihale State Park. Volcanic in origin, carved by wind and sea, "the cliffs" (*na pali* in Hawaiian), which heaved out of the ocean floor 200 million years ago, stand as constant reminders of majesty and endurance. Four major valleys—Kalalau, Honopu, Awaawapuhi, and Nualolo—crease the cliffs.

Unless you boat or fly in (see "Boating," on p. 684, or "Helicopter Rides over Waimea Canyon & the Na Pali Coast," on p. 710), the park is accessible only on foot—and it's not easy. An ancient footpath, the **Kalalau Trail,** winds through this remote, spectacular 6,500-acre park, ultimately leading to Kalalau Valley. Of all the green valleys in Hawaii, and there are many, only Kalalau is a true wilderness—probably the last wild valley in the islands. No road goes here, and none ever will. It's home to long-plumed tropical birds, golden monarch butterflies, and many of Kauai's 120 rare and endangered species of plants. The hike into the Kalalau Valley is grueling and takes most people 6 to 8 hours one-way.

Despite its inaccessibility, this journey into Hawaii's wilderness has become increasingly popular since the 1970s. Overrun with hikers, helicopters, and boaters, the Kalalau Valley was in grave danger of being loved to death. Strict rules about access have since been adopted. The park is open to hikers and campers on only a limited basis, and you must have a permit (though you can hike the first 2 miles, to Hanakapiai Beach, without a permit). Permits are $20 per night and are issued in person at the **Kauai State Parks Office,** 3060 Eiwa St., Room 306, Lihue, HI 96766 (© **808/274-3444;** www.hawaiistateparks.org/camping/kauai.cfm). You can also request one by writing **Kauai Division of State Parks** at the address listed above. For more information, contact **Hawaii State Department of Land and Natural Resources,** 1151 Punchbowl St., Room 325, Honolulu, HI 96813 (© **808/587-4175**).

HIKING THE KALALAU TRAIL ★★

The trail head is at Kee Beach, at the end of Hwy. 560. Even if you go only as far as Hanakapiai, bring water.

THE FIRST 2 MILES: TO HANAKAPIAI BEACH   Do not attempt this hike unless you have adequate footwear (closed-toe shoes at least; hiking shoes are best), water, a sun visor, insect repellent, and adequate hiking clothes (shorts and a T-shirt are fine; your bikini is not). It's only 2 miles to Hanakapiai Beach, but the first mile is all uphill. This tough trail takes about 2 hours one-way and dissuades many, but everyone should attempt at least the first half-mile, which gives a good hint of the startling beauty that lies ahead. Day hikers love this initial stretch, so it's usually crowded. The island of Niihau and Lehua Rock are often visible on the horizon. At mile marker 1, you'll have climbed from sea level to 400 feet; now it's all downhill to Hanakapiai Beach. Sandy in summer, the beach becomes rocky when winter waves scour the coast. There are strong currents and no lifeguards, so swim at your own risk. You can also hike another 2 miles inland from the beach to **Hanakapiai Falls,** a 120-foot cascade. Allow 3 hours for that stretch.

THE REST OF THE WAY   Hiking the Kalalau is the most difficult and challenging hike in Hawaii, and one you'll never forget. Even the Sierra Club rates the 22-mile round-trip into Kalalau Valley and back as "strenuous"—this is

The Kalalau Trail.

serious backpacking. Follow the footsteps of ancient Hawaiians along a cliffside path that's a mere 10 inches wide in some places, with sheer 1,000-foot drops to the sea. One misstep, and it's *limu* (seaweed) time. Even the hardy and fit should allow at least 2 days to hike in and out (see below for camping information). Although the trail is usually in good condition, go in summer when it's dry; parts of it vanish in winter. When it rains, the trail becomes very slippery, and flash floods can sweep you away.

A park ranger is now on-site full time at Kalalau Beach to greet visitors, provide information, and oversee campsites.

CAMPING IN KALALAU VALLEY & ALONG THE NA PALI COAST

You must obtain a camping permit; see above for details. The camping season runs roughly from May or June to September (depending on the site). All campsites are booked almost a year in advance, so call or write well ahead of time. Stays are limited to 5 nights. Camping areas along the Kalalau Trail include **Hanakapiai Beach** (facilities are pit toilets, and water is from the stream), **Hanakoa Valley** (no facilities, water from the stream), **Milolii** (no facilities, water from the stream), and **Kalalau Valley** (composting toilets, several pit toilets, and water from the stream). Keep your camping permit with you at all times.

GOLF & OTHER OUTDOOR ACTIVITIES
Golf

For last-minute and discount tee times, call **Stand-by Golf** (© **888/645-BOOK** [2665]; www.hawaiistandbygolf.com) between 7am and 9pm. Stand-by offers discounted (up to 30% off greens fees), guaranteed tee times for same-day or next-day golfing.

In the listings below, the cart fee is included in the greens fee unless otherwise noted.

LIHUE & ENVIRONS

Kauai Lagoons Golf Club   Choose between two excellent Jack Nicklaus–designed courses: the **Mokihana Course** (formerly known as the Lagoons Course), for the recreational golfer, or the **Kauai Kiele Championship Course ★**, for the low handicapper. The 6,942-yard, par-72 Mokihana is a links-style course with a bunker that's a little less severe than Kiele; emphasis is on the short game. The Kiele is a mixture of tournament-quality challenge and high-traffic playability; it winds up with one of Hawaii's most difficult holes, a 431-yard par-4 played straightaway to an island green. Facilities include a driving range, lockers, showers, a restaurant, a snack bar, a pro shop, practice greens, a clubhouse, and club and shoe rental. *Note:* At press time, Kauai Lagoons was in the middle of a long-term renovation of all courses. They are currently making "enhancements" to the Kiele course, during which you play 6 of the Mokihana holes and 12 of the Kiele holes, for a total of 18 holes open. That said, there is no completion date and work is dependent on the economy picking up.

Kalapaki Beach (less than a mile from Lihue Airport), Lihue. ✆ **800/634-6400** or 808/241-6000. www.kauailagoonsgolf.com. Greens fees: $175 ($120 for guests of the Kauai Marriott; $135 for guests of select hotels and condos on Kauai); $95 after noon. From the airport, make a left on Kapule Hwy. (Hwy. 51) and look for the sign on your left.

THE POIPU RESORT AREA

Kiahuna Golf Club   In 2004, the front 9 holes of this par-70, 6,353-yard Robert Trent Jones, Jr.–designed course underwent complete renovation. The course plays around four large archaeological sites, ranging from an ancient Hawaiian temple to the remains of a Portuguese home and crypt built in the early 1800s. This Scottish-style course has rolling terrain, undulating greens, 70 sand bunkers, and near-constant winds. The 3rd hole, a par-3 185-yarder, goes over Waikomo Stream. At any given time, about half the players on the course are Kauai residents, the other half visitors. Facilities include a driving range, practice greens, and a snack bar.

2545 Kiahuna Plantation Dr. (adjacent to Poipu Resort area), Koloa. ✆ **808/742-9595.** www.kiahunagolf.com. Greens fees: $99 for the 1st round; $75 for the rest of your stay; twilight rates $65. Take Hwy. 50 to Hwy. 520, bear left into Poipu at the fork in the road, and turn left onto Kiahuna Plantation Dr.

Kukuiolono Golf Course 🎁   This is a fun 9-hole course in a spectacular location with scenic views of the entire south coast. You can't beat the price—$8 for the day, whether you play 9 holes or 90. The course is in Kukuiolono Park, a beautiful wooded area donated by the family of Walter McBryde. In fact, you'll see McBryde's grave on the course, along with some other oddities, like wild chickens, ancient Hawaiian rock structures, and Japanese gardens. Of course, there are plenty of trees to keep you on your game. When you get to the second tee box, check out the coconut tree dotted with yellow, pink, orange, and white golf balls that have been driven into the bark. Don't laugh—your next shot might add to the decor! This course shouldn't give you many problems; it's excellently maintained and relatively straightforward, with few fairway hazards. Facilities include a driving range, practice greens, club rental, a snack bar, and a clubhouse.

Kukuiolono Park, Kalaheo. ☏ **808/332-9151.** Greens fees: $9 for the day; optional cart rental $9 for 9 holes. Take Hwy. 50 into the town of Kalaheo; turn left on Papaluna Rd., drive up the hill for nearly a mile, and watch for the sign on your right; the entrance has huge iron gates and stone pillars. No reserved tee times; no credit cards.

Poipu Bay Golf Course ★★ This 6,959-yard, par-72 course with a links-style layout was for years the home of the PGA Grand Slam of Golf. Designed by Robert Trent Jones, Jr., the challenging course features undulating greens and water hazards on eight of the holes. The par-4 16th hole has the coastline weaving along the entire left side. You can take the safe route to the right and maybe make par (but more likely bogey), or you can try to take it tight against the ocean and possibly make it in two. The most striking (and most disrespectful) hole is the 201-yard par-3 on the 17th, which has a tee built on an ancient Hawaiian stone formation. Facilities include a restaurant, a locker room, a pro shop, a driving range, and putting greens.

2250 Ainako St. (across from the Grand Hyatt Kauai), Koloa. ☏ **808/742-8711.** www.poipubay golf.com. Greens fees: $220 before noon ($150 for Grand Hyatt guests); $135 after noon; $80 after 2:30pm. Take Hwy. 50 to Hwy. 520; bear left into Poipu at the fork in the road; turn right on Ainako St. Check website for specials.

THE NORTH SHORE

Princeville Golf Club ★★ Here's your chance to play the **Prince Golf Course,** one of the best in Hawaii. This Robert Trent Jones, Jr.–designed devil of a course sits on 390 acres molded to create ocean views from every hole. Some holes have a waterfall backdrop to the greens, others shoot into the hillside, and the famous par-4 12th has a long tee shot off a cliff to a narrow, jungle-lined fairway 100 feet below. This is the most challenging course on Kauai; accuracy is key here. Most of the time, if you miss the fairway, your ball's in the drink. "The average vacation golfer may find the Prince Course intimidating, but they don't mind because it's so beautiful," Jones says. Facilities at Princeville include a restaurant, a health club and spa, lockers, a clubhouse, a golf shop, and a driving range.

The **Makai Golf Course,** under different management than the Prince Golf Course, is also designed by Robert Trent Jones, Jr., and is currently composed of two 9-hole courses, the Ocean and Lakes courses. The favorite of golfers is the Makai's par-3 7th hole, with an ocean cliff on one side and five bunkers on the green. The Woods course is under renovation and expected to open late 2010.

Prince Golf Course, Princeville. ☏ **800/826-1105** or 808/826-5070. www.princeville.com/golf. html. Greens fees: $200 ($125 after noon). Take Hwy. 56 to mile marker 27; the course is on your right. Makai Golf Course, Princeville. ☏ **808/826-1912.** www.makaigolf.com. Greens fees: $200 (guests of the Resort receive varying discounted rates, $135–$160); $160 after 1pm ($125 for Resort guests). Take Hwy. 56 to mile marker 27; the course is on your right.

Biking

There are a couple of great places on Kauai for two-wheeling: the **Poipu** area, which has wide, flat roads and several dirt cane roads (especially around Mahaulepu); and the cane road (a dirt road used for hauling sugar cane) between **Kealia Beach** and **Anahola,** north of Kapaa.

BIKE RENTALS The following places rent bikes, from a low of $20 a day (with big discounts for multiday rentals): **Outfitters Kauai,** 2827A Poipu Rd. (look for the small five-shop mall before the road forks to Poipu/Spouting Horn), Poipu (℗ **808/742-9667;** www.outfitterskauai.com); and **Kauai Cycle and Tour,** 1379 Kuhio Hwy., Kapaa (℗ **808/821-2115;** www.bike hawaii.com/kauaicycle), where bike rentals start at $20 a day. For a great selection of cruisers and hybrids at reasonable prices, it's worth the drive to **Pedal 'n Paddle,** in Hanalei (℗ **808/826-9069;** www.pedalnpaddle. com). Rentals start at $12 a day or $50 a week and include helmet, bike lock, and car rack. The knowledgeable folks here are more than happy to provide you with free maps and tell you about the best biking spots on the island. Unfortunately, they no longer rent mountain bikes.

GUIDED BIKE TOURS **Outfitters Kauai ★** (℗ **808/742-9667;** www.outfitters kauai.com) offers a fabulous downhill bike ride from Waimea Canyon to the ocean. The 12-mile trip (mostly coasting) begins at 6am, when the van leaves the shop in Poipu and heads up to the canyon. By the time you've scarfed down the fresh-baked muffins and coffee, you're at the top of the canyon, just as the sun is rising over the rim—it's a remarkable moment. You'll make a couple of stops on the way down for short, scenic nature hikes. The tour lasts about 4 to 4½ hours. The sunset trip follows the same route. Both tours cost $98 for adults, $78 for children 12 to 14.

Birding

Kauai provides some of Hawaii's last sanctuaries for endangered native birds and oceanic birds, such as the albatross. At **Kokee State Park,** a 4,345-acre wilderness forest at the end of Hwy. 550 in southwest Kauai, you have an excellent chance of seeing some of Hawaii's endangered native birds. You might spot the apapane, a red bird with black wings and a curved black bill; or the iwi, a red bird with black wings, orange legs, and a salmon-colored bill. Other frequently seen native birds are the honeycreeper, which sings like a canary; the amakihi, a plain olive-green bird with a long, straight bill; and the anianiau, a tiny yellow bird with a thin, slightly curved bill. The most common native bird at Kokee is the moa, or red jungle fowl, brought as domestic stock by ancient Polynesians. Ordinarily shy, they're quite tame in this environment. David Kuhn leads custom hikes, pointing out Hawaii's rarest birds on his **Terran Tours** (℗ **808/335-0398**), which range from a half-day to 3 days and feature endemic and endangered species.

Kilauea Point National Wildlife Refuge ★, a mile north of Kilauea on the North Shore (℗ **808/828-0168;** www.fws.gov/kilaueapoint), is a 200-acre headland habitat that juts above the surf and includes cliffs, two rocky wave-lashed bays, and a tiny islet that serves as a jumping-off spot for seabirds. You can easily spot red-footed boobies, which nest in trees, and wedge-tailed shearwaters, which burrow in nests along the cliffs. You may also see the great frigate bird, the Laysan albatross, the red-tailed tropic bird, and the endangered nene. Native plants and the Kilauea Point Lighthouse are other highlights. The refuge is open from 10am to 4pm daily (closed on federal holidays); admission is $5. Don't miss the popular 1-hour **guided hikes** up to the 568-foot summit of Crater Hill, which affords spectacular views. To get here, turn right off Kuhio Highway (Hwy. 56) at Kilauea, just after mile marker 23; follow Kilauea Road to the refuge entrance.

Peaceful Hanalei Valley is home to Hawaii's endangered Koloa duck, gallinule, coot, and stilt. The **Hanalei National Wildlife Refuge** (✆ 808/828-1413; www.fws.gov/hanalei) also provides a safe habitat for migratory shorebirds and waterfowl. It's not open to the public, but an interpretive overlook along the highway serves as an impressive vantage point. Along Ohiki Road, which begins at the west end of the Hanalei River Bridge, you'll often see white cattle egrets hunting crayfish in streams.

Horseback Riding

Only in Kauai can you ride a horse across the wide-open pastures of a working ranch under volcanic peaks and rein up near a waterfall pool. No wonder Kauai's *paniolo* (cowboys) smile and sing so much. Near the Poipu area, **CJM Country Stables,** 1731 Kelaukia St. (2 miles beyond the Grand Hyatt), Koloa (✆ 808/742-6096; www.cjmstables.com), offers 2- and 3-hour escorted Hidden Valley beach rides. You'll trot over Hidden Valley ranchland, past secluded beaches and bays, along the Haupu Ridge, across sugar-cane fields, and to Mahaulepu Beach; it's worth your time and money just to get out to this seldom-seen part of Kauai. The Secret Beach and Picnic Ride costs $125 and includes lunch. The 2-hour Scenic Valley Beach Ride is $98.

Princeville Ranch Stables, Hwy. 56 (just after the Princeville Airport), Hanalei (✆ 808/826-6777; www.princevilleranch.com), has a variety of outings. The 1½-hour country ride takes in views of the Hanalei mountains and the vista of Anini Beach ($80), while the 3-hour ($125) or 4-hour ($135) Waterfall Picnic Ride crosses ranchland, takes you on a short (but steep) hike to swimming pools at the base of waterfalls, and then feeds you a picnic lunch. Riders must be in good physical shape; don't forget to put your swimsuit on under your jeans. Other adventures offered range from wagon rides to a cattle-drive ride.

Tennis

The **Kauai County Parks and Recreation Department,** 4444 Rice St., Ste. 150, Lihue (✆ 808/244-4460), provides a list on their website (www.kauai.gov/Government/Departments/ParksRecreation/ParkFacilities/tabid/105/Default.aspx) of the 12 county tennis courts around the island, all of which are free and open to the public. Private courts that are open to the public include the **Hanalei Bay Resort,** Princeville (✆ 808/821-8225), which has eight courts available for $10 per person for 60 minutes. On the south side, try **Grand Hyatt Kauai Resort & Spa** (✆ 808/742-1234; www.kauai-hyatt.com), which has 4 courts available for $30 an hour; and **Kiahuna Swim and Tennis Club,** Poipu Road (just past the Poipu Shopping Village on the left), Poipu (✆ 808/742-9533), which has 10 courts renting for $15 per person for 60 to 90 minutes or $65 per week for two for unlimited court time.

Zip Lining

Imagine flying through the air, over the treetops, with spectacular views. Try zip lining, which essentially allows you to slide downhill from a pulley, suspended from a cable. It's like being a kid again and swimming through the air. The best zip line I've found on Kauai is **Princeville Ranch Adventures,** in Hanalei (✆ 888/955-7669 or 808/826-7669; www.adventureskauai.com). They have a range of trips, depending on your time and budget. I'd recommend the Zip Express, a 3-hour tour with nine zip lines (the last one, called King Kong, is 1,200 ft. long) for $125. If you have more time, try the Zip & Dip, which features the Zip Line adventure plus an hour at a hidden swimming hole with a picnic lunch.

SEEING THE SIGHTS

No matter how much time you have on Kauai, make it a priority to see the North Shore. No doubt about it—this is Hawaii at its best.

A Tour of the Island

Four-Wheel-Drive Backroad Adventure ★   Great for getting off the beaten path and seeing the "hidden" Kauai, this 4-hour tour follows a figure-eight path around Kauai, from Kilohana Crater to the Mahaulepu coastline. The tour, done in a four-wheel-drive van, not only stops at Kauai's well-known scenic spots, but also travels on sugar-cane roads (on private property), taking you to places most people who live on Kauai have never seen. The guides are well versed in everything from native plants to Hawaiian history. Don't forget your camera.

Aloha Kauai Tours, 1702 Haleukana St., Lihue. ℂ **800/452-1113** or 808/245-8809. www.aloha kauaitours.com. Tours $75 adults, $50 children 12 and under. Daily 7:45am and 12:45pm; reservations required.

Lihue & Environs

Grove Farm Homestead Museum   You can experience a day in the life of an 1860s sugar planter on a visit to Grove Farm Homestead, which shows how good life was (for some, anyway) when sugar was king. This is Hawaii's best remaining example of a sugar-plantation homestead. Founded in 1864 by George N. Wilcox, a Hanalei missionary's son, Grove Farm was one of the earliest of Hawaii's 86 sugar plantations. A self-made millionaire, Wilcox died a bachelor in 1933, at age 94. His estate looks much as it did when he lived here, complete with period furniture, plantation artifacts, and Hawaiiana.

4050 Nawiliwili Rd. (Hwy. 58), at Pikaka St. (2 miles from Waapa Rd.), Lihue. ℂ **808/245-3202.** www.hawaiimuseums.org/mc/isKauai_grove.htm. Admission $10 adults, $5 children 11 and under. Open only for tours on Mon and Wed–Thurs at 10am and 1pm; reservations required.

Kauai Museum ★ ☺   The history of Kauai is kept safe in an imposing Greco-Roman building that once served as the town library. This great little museum is worth a stop before you set out to explore the island. It contains a wealth of historical artifacts and

Allerton Garden of the National Tropical Botanical Garden.

The Grove Farm Homestead Museum.

information tracing the island's history from the beginning of time through contact (when Capt. James Cook landed on Kauai in 1778), the monarchy period, the plantation era, and the present. You'll hear tales of the *menehune* (the mythical elflike people who were said to build massive stoneworks in a single night) and see old poi pounders and idols, relics of sugar planters and *paniolo,* a nice seashell collection, old Hawaiian quilts, feather leis, a replica of a plantation worker's home, and much more—even a model of Cook's ship, the HMS *Resolution,* riding anchor in Waimea Bay. Vintage photographs by W. J. Senda, a Japanese immigrant, show old Kauai, while a contemporary video, shot from a helicopter, captures the island's natural beauty.

4428 Rice St., Lihue. ℂ **808/245-6931.** www.kauaimuseum.org. Admission $10 adults, $8 seniors, $6 students 13–17, $2 children 6–12. Free admission on "Family Day," 1st Sat of every month. Mon–Sat 10am–5pm. Guided tours Tues–Fri 10:30am.

The Poipu Resort Area

No Hawaii resort has a better entrance: On Maluhia Road, eucalyptus trees planted in 1911 as a windbreak for sugar-cane fields now form a monumental **tree tunnel.** The cool, leafy-green tunnel starts at Kaumualii Highway (Hwy. 50).

Allerton Garden of the National Tropical Botanical Garden ★   Discover an extraordinary collection of tropical fruit and spice trees, rare Hawaiian plants, and hundreds of varieties of flowers at the 186-acre preserve known as **Lawai Gardens,** said to be the largest collection of rare and endangered plants in the world. Adjacent **McBryde Garden,** a royal home site of Queen Emma in the 1860s, is known for its formal gardens, a delicious kind of colonial decadence. It's set amid fountains, streams, waterfalls, and European statuary. Endangered green sea turtles can be seen here (their home in the sea was wiped out years ago by Hurricane Iniki). The tours are fascinating for green thumbs and novices alike.

Visitor Center, Lawai Rd. (across the street from Spouting Horn), Poipu. ℂ **808/742-2623.** www.ntbg.org. Self-guided tours of McBryde Garden daily 9am–4pm; $20 adults and $10 children 6–12 (trams into the valley leave once an hour on the half-hour, last tram 2:30pm). Guided tour of Allerton Garden daily 9am, 10am, 1pm, and 2pm; $45 adults and $20 children 10–12. Reserve a week in advance in peak months of July–Sept.

Spouting Horn.

Prince Kuhio Park   This small roadside park is the birthplace of Prince Jonah Kuhio Kalanianaole, the "People's Prince," whose March 26 birthday is a holiday in Hawaii. He opened the beaches of Waikiki to the public in 1918 and served as Hawaii's second territorial delegate to the U.S. Congress. What remains here are the foundations of the family home, a royal fish pond, and a shrine where tributes are still paid in flowers.

Lawai Rd., Koloa. Just after mile marker 4 on Poipu Rd., veer to the right of the fork in the road; the park is on the right side.

Spouting Horn ★ ☺   This natural phenomenon is second in regularity only to Yellowstone's Old Faithful. It's quite a sight—big waves hit Kauai's south shore with enough force to send a spout of funneled saltwater 10 feet or more up in the air; in winter the water can get as high as six stories.

Spouting Horn is different from other blowholes in Hawaii, in that it has an additional hole that blows air that sounds like a loud moaning. According to Hawaiian legend, this coastline was once guarded by a giant female lizard (Mo'o) who would gobble up any intruders. One day, along came Liko, who wanted to fish in this area. Mo'o rushed out to eat Liko. Quickly, Liko threw a spear right into the giant lizard's mouth. Mo'o then chased Liko into a lava tube. Liko escaped, but legend says Mo'o is still in the tube, and the moaning sound at Spouting Horn is her cry for help.

At Kukuiula Bay, beyond Prince Kuhio Park (see above).

Western Kauai

WAIMEA TOWN

If you'd like to take a self-guided tour of this historic town, stop at the **Waimea Library,** at mile marker 23 on Hwy. 50, to pick up a map and guide to the sites.

Kiki a Ola (Menehune Ditch)   Hawaiians were expert rock builders, able to construct elaborate edifices without using mortar. They formed long lines and

passed stones hand over hand, and lifted rocks weighing tons with ropes made from native plants. Their feats gave rise to fantastic tales of *menehune*, elflike people hired by Hawaiian kings to create massive stoneworks in a single night—reputedly for the payment of a single shrimp (see "Discover the Legendary Little People," above). An excellent example of ancient Hawaiian construction is Kiki a Ola, the so-called Menehune Ditch, with cut and dressed stones that form an ancient aqueduct that still directs water to irrigate taro ponds. Historians credit the work to ancient Hawaiian engineers who applied their knowledge of hydraulics to accomplish flood control and irrigation. Only a 2-foot-high portion of the wall can be seen today; the rest of the marvelous stonework is buried under the roadbed.

From Hwy. 50, go inland on Menehune Rd.; a plaque marks the spot about 1½ miles up.

Russian Fort Elizabeth.

Russian Fort Elizabeth State Historical Park To the list of those who tried to conquer Hawaii, add the Russians. In 1815, a German doctor tried to claim Kauai for Russia. He even supervised the construction of a fort in Waimea, but he and his handful of Russian companions were expelled by Kamehameha I a couple of years later. Now a state historic landmark, the Russian Fort Elizabeth (named for the wife of Russia's Czar Alexander I) is on the eastern headlands overlooking the harbor, across from Lucy Kapahu Aukai Wright Beach Park. The fort,

Waimea Canyon.

built Hawaiian-style with stacked lava rocks in the shape of a star, once bristled with cannons; it's now mostly in ruins. You can take a free self-guided tour of the site, which affords a keen view of the west bank of the Waimea River, where Captain Cook landed, and of the island of Niihau across the channel.

Hwy. 50 (on the ocean side, just after mile marker 22), east of Waimea.

THE GRAND CANYON OF THE PACIFIC: WAIMEA CANYON ★★★

The great gaping gulch known as Waimea Canyon is quite a sight. This valley, known for its reddish lava beds, reminds everyone who sees it of the Grand Canyon. Kauai's version is bursting with ever-changing color, just like its namesake, but it's smaller—only a mile wide, 3,567 feet deep, and 12 miles long. A massive earthquake sent all the streams flowing into a single river that ultimately carved this picturesque canyon. Today the Waimea River—a silver thread of water in the gorge that's sometimes a trickle, often a torrent, but always there—keeps cutting the canyon deeper, and nobody can say what the result will be 100 million years from now.

You can stop by the road and look at the canyon, hike down into it, or swoop through it in a helicopter. For more information, see "Hiking & Camping," earlier in this chapter, and "Helicopter Rides over Waimea Canyon & the Na Pali Coast," below.

THE DRIVE THROUGH WAIMEA CANYON & UP TO KOKEE

By car, there are two ways to visit Waimea Canyon and reach Kokee State Park, 20 miles up from Waimea. From the coastal road (Hwy. 50), you can turn up Waimea Canyon Drive (Hwy. 550) at Waimea town, or you can pass through Waimea and turn up Kokee Road (Hwy. 55) at Kekaha. The climb is very steep from Kekaha, but Waimea Canyon Drive, the rim road, is narrower and rougher. A few miles up, the two merge into Kokee Road.

The first good vantage point is **Waimea Canyon Lookout,** between mile markers 10 and 11 on Waimea Canyon Road. From here, it's another 6 miles to Kokee. There are a few more lookout points along the way that also offer spectacular views, such as **Puu Hina Hina Lookout,** between mile markers 13 and 14, at 3,336 feet; be sure to pull over and spend a few minutes pondering this natural wonder. (The giant white object that looks like a golf ball and defaces the natural landscape is a radar station left over from the Cold War.)

KOKEE STATE PARK ★★

It's only 16 miles from Waimea to Kokee, but it's a whole different world because the park is 4,345 acres of rainforest. You'll enter a new climate zone, where the breeze has a bite and trees look quite continental. This is a cloud forest on the edge of the Alakai Swamp, the largest swamp in Hawaii, on the summit plateau of Kauai. Days are cool and wet, with intermittent bright sunshine, not unlike Seattle on a good day. Bring your sweater, and, if you're staying over, be sure you know how to light a fire (overnight lows dip into the 40s Fahrenheit/single digits Celsius).

The forest is full of native plants, such as mokihana berry, ohia lehua tree, iliau (similar to Maui's silversword), and imports like Australia's eucalyptus and California's redwood. Pigs, goats, and black-tailed deer thrive in the forest, but the moa, or Polynesian jungle fowl, is the cock of the walk.

Right next to Kokee Lodge (which lies on the only road through the park, about a mile before it ends) is the **Kokee Natural History Museum ★** (② **808/335-9975;** www.kokee.org), open daily from 10am to 4pm (free admission). This is the best place to learn about the forest and Alakai Swamp before you set off hiking in the wild. The museum shop has great trail information as well as local books and maps, including the official park trail map. I recommend getting the *Pocket Guide on Native Plants on the Nature Trail for Kokee State Park* and the *Road Guide to Kokee and Waimea Canyon State Park.*

A **nature walk** is the best introduction to this rainforest; it starts behind the museum at the rare Hawaiian koa tree. This easy self-guided walk of about

The view from the Kalalau Lookout.

The north shore of Kauai viewed from a helicopter.

.25 mile takes about 20 minutes if you stop and look at all the plants identified along the way.

Two miles above Kokee Lodge is **Kalalau Lookout ★**, the spectacular climax of your drive through Waimea Canyon and Kokee. When you stand at the lookout, below you is a work in progress that began at least 5 million years ago. It's hard to stop looking: The view is breathtaking, especially when light and cloud shadows play across the red-and-orange cliffs.

There's lots more to see and do up here. Anglers fly-fish for rainbow trout (see p. 687 for info on fishing licenses), while hikers tackle the 45 trails that lace the Alakai Swamp (p. 695). That's a lot of ground to cover, so you might want to plan on staying over. If pitching a tent is too rustic for you, the **Kokee Lodge** (p. 650) has wonderful cabins set in a grove of redwoods—they're one of the best lodging bargains in the islands. The restaurant at Kokee Lodge is open for continental breakfast and lunch daily from 9am to 3:30pm.

For advance information, contact the **State Division of Parks,** 3060 Eiwa St., Room 306, Lihue, HI 96766 (© **808/274-3444**), and the **Kokee Lodge Manager,** P.O. Box 819, Waimea, HI 96796 (© **808/335-6061**). The park is open daily year-round. The best time to go is early in the morning, to see the panoramic view of Kalalau Valley from the lookout at 4,000 feet, before clouds obscure the valley and peaks.

HELICOPTER RIDES OVER WAIMEA CANYON & THE NA PALI COAST ★★★

Don't leave Kauai without seeing it from a helicopter. It's expensive but worth the splurge. You can take home memories of the thrilling ride up and over the Kalalau Valley on Kauai's wild North Shore and into the 5,200-foot vertical temple of Mount Waialeale, the most sacred place on the island and the wettest spot on earth (and, in some cases, you can even take home a video of your ride). All flights leave from Lihue Airport. *Money-saving tip:* You can save 15% to 37% by booking online.

Blue Hawaiian ★★★   Blue Hawaiian has been the Cadillac of helicopter tour companies on Maui and the Big Island for more than a decade, and it has recently expanded its operations to Kauai. I strongly recommend that you try to book with Blue Hawaiian first. The operation is first class, and the equipment state-of-the-art: Blue Hawaii flies American Eurocopter ECO-Stars, which reduce noise in the helicopter by 50% and provide 23% more interior room. Plus, the craft has individual business class–style seats, two-way communication with the pilot, and expansive glass for incredible views. The 55- to 60-minute flight first journeys to Hanapepe Valley and continues on to Mana Waiapuna,

---

MAKE A PILGRIMAGE TO A hindu temple

Believe it or not, a sacred Hindu temple is being carved out of rocks from India on the banks of the Wailua River. The **San Marga Iraivan Temple** is being built to last "a thousand years or more," on the 458-acre site of the Saiva Siddhanta Church monastery. In the making for years now, the Chola-style temple is the result of a vision by the late Satguru Sivaya Subramuniyaswami, known to his followers as Gurudeva, the founder of the church and its monastery. He specifically selected this site in 1970, recognizing that the Hawaiians also felt the spiritual power of this place. The Hawaiians called it *pihanakalani*, "where heaven touches the earth."

The concrete foundation is 68×168 square feet and 3 feet thick, designed not to crack under the weight of the 3.2-million-pound temple dedicated to the Hindu god Shiva. The granite for the temple is being hand-quarried by some 70 stonemasons in India, then shipped to Kauai for final shaping and fitting on the site. The center of the temple will hold a 700-pound crystal, known as the Sivalingam, now displayed at the monastery's smaller temple on the grounds.

Hindu pilgrims come from around the globe to study and meditate at the monastery. The public is welcome to the monastery temple, open daily from 9am

to noon. There is also a weekly guided tour of the grounds that includes the San Marga Iraivan Temple. The tour time varies depending on the retreat schedule at the monastery. For information, call ✆ **808/822-3012,** ext. 1, or go to www. saivasiddhanta.com.

A few suggestions if you plan to visit: Carry an umbrella (it's very rainy here). Wear what the Hindus call "modest clothing" (certainly no shorts, short dresses, T-shirts, or tank tops); traditional Hindu dress is ideal. Also, even though this is a monastery, there are lots of people around, so don't leave valuables in your car.

To get here, turn mauka (left, inland) off Kuhio Highway (Hwy. 56) at the lights, just after crossing the bridge, onto Kuamoo Road (btw. Coco Palms Hotel and the Wailua River). Continue up the hill for just over 4 miles. A quarter-mile past mile marker 4, turn left on Kaholalele Road and go 1 block to the end of the road. The **Information Center** is at 107 Kaholalele Rd. Park on Temple Lane. Enter the open pavilion, where a guide will escort you through the monastery. You can also visit the **Sacred Rudraksha Forest,** 7345 Kuamoo Rd., for meditation (daily 6am–6pm); or the **Nepalese Ganesha Shrine** and **Bangalore Gallery,** which are located at 107 Kaholalele Rd.

commonly referred to as "Jurassic Park Falls." Next it's up the Olokele Canyon and on to Waimea Canyon, the famed "Grand Canyon of the Pacific." Most of the flight will then be along the Na Pali Coast, before heading out to the Bali Hai cliffs and the pristine blue waters of Hanalei Bay and the Princeville Resort area. If the weather gods are on your side, you'll get to see the highest point on Kauai: Mount Waialeale, the wettest spot on earth, with an average rainfall of 450 to 500 inches annually. Your flight will take you right into the center of the crater, with its 5,000-foot walls towering above and its 3,000-foot waterfalls surrounding you, something you will remember forever.

Harbor Mall staging area, 3501 Rice St., Lihue. Takeoffs from the Lihue Airport. © **800/745-2583** or 808/245-5800. www.bluehawaiian.com. 55- to 60-min. tour $226 (check for online discounts).

Island Helicopters ★ Curt Lofstedt has been flying helicopter tours of Kauai for nearly 3 decades. He personally selects and trains professional pilots with an eye not only to their flying skills, but also to their ability to share the magic of Kauai. All flights are in the six-passenger Aerospatiale A-Stars, with extralarge windows and stereo headsets to hear the pilot's personal narration.

Lihue Airport. © **800/829-5999** or 808/245-8588. www.islandhelicopters.com. 55-min. island tour $200. Ask for the Frommer's discount.

Jack Harter ★ The pioneer of helicopter flights on Kauai, Jack was the guy who started the sightseeing-via-helicopter trend. On the 60-minute tour, he flies a four-passenger Bell Jet Ranger Model 204 (with "scenic view" windows), a six-seater A-star, or a Eurocopter AS350BA A-star. The 90-minute tour (in the A-star only) hovers over the sights a bit longer than the 60-minute flight so you can get a good look, but I found the shorter tour sufficient.

4231 Ahukini Rd., Lihue. © **888/245-2001** or 808/245-3774. www.helicopters-kauai.com. 60- to 65-min. tour $259 ($229 if booked online); 90- to 95-min. tour $384 ($344 if booked online).

The Coconut Coast

FERN GROTTO

This is one of Kauai's oldest (since 1946) and most popular tourist attractions. The grotto is the source of many Hawaiian legends and a popular site for weddings. You can visit Fern Grotto by going with **Smith's Motor Boats** (© **808/821-6892;** www.smithskauai.com), which is still operating a 157-passenger motorized barge that takes people up and down the river on a 45-minute cruise, with a hula show on the return trip. Tours depart daily from 10am to 3:30pm from Wailua Marine State Park (turn off Kuhio Hwy./Hwy. 56 into the park). The cost is $20 for adults and $10 for children 3 to 12 (book online for 10% off). Reservations are recommended.

WAILUA RIVER STATE PARK

Ancients called the Wailua River "the river of the great sacred spirit." Seven temples once stood along this 20-mile river, which is fed by 5,148-foot Mount Waialeale, the wettest spot on earth. You can go up Hawaii's biggest navigable river by boat or kayak (see "Boating" and "Kayaking," earlier in this chapter), or drive Kuamoo Road (Hwy. 580), sometimes called the King's Highway, which goes inland along the north side of the river from Kuhio Highway (Hwy. 56)— from the northbound lane, turn left at the stoplight just before the ruins of Coco Palms Resort. Kuamoo Road goes past the *heiau* and historic sites to Opaekaa

Fern Grotto.

Falls and Keahua Arboretum, a State Division of Forestry attempt to reforest the watershed with native plants.

The entire district from the river mouth to the summit of Waialeale was once royal land. This sacred historic site was believed to be founded by Puna, a Tahitian priest who, according to legend, arrived in one of the first double-hulled voyaging canoes to come to Hawaii, established a beachhead, and declared Kauai his kingdom. All of Kauai's *alii* (royalty) are believed to be descended from Puna. Here, in this royal settlement, are remains of the seven temples, including a sacrificial *heiau*, a planetarium (a simple array of rocks in a celestial pattern), the royal birthing stones, and a stone bell to announce a royal birth. (You can still ring the bell—many people have—but make sure you have an announcement to make when it stops ringing.)

There's a nice overlook view of 40-foot **Opaekaa Falls** ★★ 1½ miles up Hwy. 580. This is probably the best-looking drive-up waterfall on Kauai. With the scenic peaks of the Makaleha Mountains in the background and a restored Hawaiian village on the riverbanks, these falls are what the tourist-bureau folks call an "eye-popping" photo op.

Near the Opaekaa Falls overlook is **Poliahu Heiau,** the large lava-rock temple of Kauai's last king, Kaumualii, who died on Oahu in 1824 after being abducted by King Kamehameha II. If you stop here, you'll notice two signs. The first, an official 1928 bronze territorial plaque, says that the royal *heiau* was built by *menehune*, which it explains parenthetically as "Hawaiian dwarves or brownies." A more recent hand-painted sign warns visitors not to climb on the sacred rocks.

SLEEPING GIANT

If you squint your eyes just so as you pass the 1,241-foot-high Nounou Ridge, which forms a dramatic backdrop to the coastal villages of Wailua and Waipouli, you can see the fabled Sleeping Giant. On Kuhio Highway, just after mile marker 7, around the mini-mall complex Waipouli Town Center, look mauka (inland) and you may see what appears to be the legendary giant named Puni, who, as the story goes, fell asleep after a great feast. If you don't see it at first, visualize it this way: His head is Wailua and his feet are Kapaa. For details on an easy hike to the top of the Sleeping Giant, see "The Sleeping Giant Trail" (p. 697).

HOLLYWOOD LOVES kauai

More than 50 major Hollywood productions have been shot on Kauai since the studios discovered the island's spectacular natural beauty. Here are just a few:

- Manawaiopu Falls, Mount Waialeale, and other scenic areas around the island appeared in *Jurassic Park.*

- Kauai's lush rainforests formed a fantastic backdrop for Harrison Ford in both *Raiders of the Lost Ark* and *Indiana Jones and the Temple of Doom.*

- Mitzi Gaynor sang "I'm Gonna Wash That Man Right Outta My Hair" on Lumahai Beach in *South Pacific* (pictured here).

- Elvis Presley married costar Joan Blackman near the Wailua River in the 1961 film *Blue Hawaii.*

- Beautiful Kee Beach, on the North Shore, masqueraded as Australia in the miniseries *The Thorn Birds,* starring Richard Chamberlain and Rachel Ward.

- Kauai appeared as the backdrop for *Outbreak,* the 1994 thriller about the spread of a deadly virus on a remote tropical island, starring Dustin Hoffman.

- Hoffman also appeared with Robin Williams and Julia Roberts in *Hook* (1991), in which Kauai stood in as Never Never Land.

- James Caan, Nicolas Cage, Sarah Jessica Parker, and Pat Morita shared laughs on Kauai (which appeared as itself) in *Honeymoon in Vegas.*

Now you can visit these and other Kauai locations that made it to the silver screen, plus locations from such TV classics as *Fantasy Island* and *Gilligan's Island,* with **Hawaii Movie Tours** (✆ **800/ 628-8432** or 808/822-1192; www.hawaiimovie tour.com). The commentary and sightseeing stops are supplemented by video clips of the location shots (complete with surround sound); in addition, a guide leads singalongs of movie and TV themes as you go from locale to locale in the new 14-passenger bus. All in all, there's a whole lot of fun to be had, especially for families. You'll see more of Kauai on this tour (including private estates not open to the public) than you would if you explored the island yourself. Tickets are $89 for adults and $79 for children 11 and under; lunch is included. Reservations recommended.

Paradise Found: The North Shore ★★★
ON THE ROAD TO HANALEI

The first place everyone should go on Kauai is Hanalei. The drive along **Kuhio Highway** (Hwy. 56, which becomes Hwy. 560 after Princeville to the end of the road) displays Kauai's grandeur at its absolute best. Just before Kilauea, the air and the sea change, the light falls in a different way, and the last signs of development are behind you. Now there are roadside fruit stands, a little stone church in

Sleeping Giant.

Kilauea, two roadside waterfalls, and a long, stiltlike bridge over the Kalihiwai Stream and its green river valley.

Birders might want to stop off at **Kilauea Point National Wildlife Refuge,** a mile north of Kilauea, and the **Hanalei National Wildlife Refuge,** along Ohiki Road, at the west end of the Hanalei River Bridge. (For details, see "Birding," on p. 702.) In the Hanalei Refuge, along a dirt road on a levee, you can see the **Hariguchi Rice Mill,** now a historic treasure.

Now the coastal highway heads due west and the showy ridgelines of Mount Namahana create a grand amphitheater. The two-lane coastal highway rolls through pastures of grazing cattle and past a tiny airport and the luxurious Princeville Resort.

Five miles past Kilauea, just past the Princeville Shopping Center, is **Hanalei Valley Lookout.** Big enough for a dozen cars, this lookout attracts crowds of people who peer over the edge into the 917-acre Hanalei River Valley. Seldom will you see so many shades of green in one place: The green rice, taro, and streams lace a patchwork of green ponds that back up to green-velvet Bali Hai cliffs. Don't be put off by the crowds; this is definitely worth a look. You might even see an endangered Hawaiian black-necked stilt.

Farther along, a hairpin turn offers another scenic look at Hanalei town, and then you cross the **Hanalei Bridge.** The Pratt truss steel bridge, prefabbed in New York City, was erected in 1912; it's now on the National Register of Historic Landmarks. If it ever goes out, the nature of Hanalei will change forever; currently, this rusty one-lane bridge (which must violate all kinds of Department of Transportation safety regulations) isn't big enough for a tour bus to cross.

You'll drive slowly past the **Hanalei River** banks and Bill Mowry's **Hanalei Buffalo Ranch,** where 200 American bison roam in the tropical sun; you may even see buffalo grazing in the pastures on your right. The herd is often thinned to make buffalo patties. (You wondered why there was a buffalo burger on the Ono Family Restaurant menu, didn't you?)

Just past Tahiti Nui, turn right on Aku Road before Ching Young Village and then take a right on Weke Road; **Hanalei Beach** (p. 681), one of Hawaii's most gorgeous, is a half-block ahead on your left. Swimming is excellent here year-round, especially in summer, when Hanalei Bay becomes a big, placid lake.

If this exquisite 2-mile-long beach doesn't meet your expectations, head down the highway, where the next 7 miles of coast yield some of Kauai's other spectacular beaches, including **Lumahai Beach,** of *South Pacific* movie fame, as well as **Tunnels Beach** (p. 682), where the 1960s puka-shell necklace craze began, **Haena Beach Park** (p. 682), a fabulous place to kick back and enjoy the waves, particularly in summer, and gorgeous **Kee Beach** (p. 681), at the end of the road. Once you've found your beach, stick around until sundown and then head back to one of the North Shore's restaurants for a mai tai and a fresh seafood dinner (see "Where to Dine," earlier in this chapter). Another perfect day in paradise.

ATTRACTIONS ALONG THE WAY

Ka Ulu O Laka Heiau   On a knoll above the boulders of Kee Beach (p. 681) stands a sacred altar of rocks, often draped with flower leis and ti-leaf offerings, dedicated to Laka, the goddess of hula. It may seem like a primal relic from the days of idols, but it's very much in use today. Often dancers from Hawaii's hula *halau* (schools) climb the cliff, bearing small gifts of flowers. In Hawaiian myths, Lohiau, a handsome chief, danced here before the fire goddess Pele; their passion became *Haena,* which means "the heat." Sometimes, in a revival of the old Hawaiian ways, a mother of a newborn will deposit the umbilical cord of her infant at this sacred shrine. The site is filled with what Hawaiians call *mana,* or power.

From the west side of Kee Beach, take the footpath across the big rocks almost to the point; then climb the steep, grassy hill.

Limahuli Garden of the National Tropical Botanical Garden ★

Out on Kauai's far North Shore, beyond Hanalei and the last wooden bridge, there's a mighty cleft in the coastal range where ancestral Hawaiians lived in what can only be called paradise. Carved by a waterfall stream known as Limahuli, the lush valley sits at the foot of steepled cliffs that Hollywood portrayed as Bali Hai in the film classic *South Pacific.* This small, almost secret garden is eco-tourism at its best. It appeals not just to green thumbs, but to all who love Hawaii's great outdoors. Here botanists hope to save Kauai's endangered native plants. You can take the self-guided tour to view the plants, which are identified in Hawaiian and English. From taro to sugar cane, the mostly Polynesian imports tell the story of the people who cultivated the plants for food, medicine, clothing, shelter, and decoration. In addition, Limahuli's stream is sanctuary to the last five species of Hawaiian freshwater fish.

Visitor Center, ½-mile past mile marker 9 on Kuhio Hwy. (Hwy. 560), Haena. ☏ **808/826-1053.** Fax 808/826-1394. www.ntbg.org. Admission $15 self-guided, children 12 and under free; $30 guided, $15 children 10–12 (no children under 10 on guided tour). Tues–Sat 9:30am–4pm; guided tours start 10am. Reservations required for 2½-hr. guided tour. During peak season of July–Sept, book at least a week ahead.

Na Aina Kai Botanical Gardens ★★★ 🛍   Do not miss this incredible, magical garden on some 240 acres, sprinkled with around 70 life-size (some larger-than-life-size) whimsical bronze statues, hidden off the beaten path of the North Shore. This is the place for avid gardeners, as well as people who think they don't like botanical gardens. It has something for everyone: waterfalls, pools, arbors, topiaries, colonnades, gazebos, a maze you will never forget, a lagoon with spouting fountains, a Japanese teahouse, and an enchanting path along a bubbling stream to the ocean. The imaginative, fairy-tale creativity that has gone into these grounds will be one of your fondest memories of Kauai. A host of different tours is available, from 1½ hours ($30) to 5 hours ($75) long, ranging from casual, guided strolls to rides in the covered CarTram to treks from one end of the gardens to the ocean. Currently, these tours are open to adults and children 13 and older.

For younger kids, there is a magical tropical children's garden with a gecko hedge maze, a tropical jungle gym, a treehouse in a rubber tree, and a 16-foot-tall Jack-in-the-Beanstalk giant with a 33-foot wading pool below. The 2-hour children's "Under the Rainbow" garden tour is $30 for adults and $20 for kids 13 and under, and includes the formal gardens. Book a tour before you leave for Hawaii so you won't be disappointed.

4101 Wailapa Rd. (P.O. Box 1134), Kilauea. ☏ **808/828-0525.** Fax 808/828-0815. www. naainakai.com. Tues–Thurs 8am–5pm and Fri 8am–1pm. Tours vary. Reservations strongly recommended. To get here from Lihue, drive north past mile marker 21 and turn right on Wailapa Rd. At the road's end, drive through the iron gates. From Princeville, drive south 6½ miles and take the 2nd left past mile marker 22 on Wailapa Rd. At the road's end, drive through the iron gates.

Na Aina Kai Botanical Gardens.

Waioli Mission House Museum.

Waioli Mission House Museum   If you're lucky and time your visit just right, you can visit this 150-year-old mission house, which serves today as a living museum. It's a real treasure. Others in Honolulu are easier to see, but the Waioli Mission House retains its sense of place and most of its furnishings, so you can really get a clear picture of what life was like for the New England missionaries who came to Kauai to convert the heathens to Christianity. Most mission houses are small, dark Boston cottages that violate the tropical sense of place. This two-story wood-frame house, built in 1836 by Abner and Lucy Wilcox of New Bedford, Massachusetts, is an excellent example of hybrid architecture. The house features a lanai on both stories, with a cookhouse in a separate building. It has a lava-rock chimney, ohia-wood floors, and Hawaiian koa furniture.

Kuhio Hwy. (Hwy. 560), just behind the green Waioli Huia Church, Hanalei. © **808/245-3202.** Free admission (donations gratefully accepted). Tours Mon, Wed, and Thurs 10am and 1pm. Reservations required.

THE END OF THE ROAD

The real Hawaii begins where the road stops. This is especially true on Kauai—for at the end of Hwy. 560, the spectacular **Na Pali Coast** begins. To explore it, you have to set out on foot, by boat, or by helicopter. For details on experiencing this region, see p. 692 for hiking and camping, p. 684 for boating, and p. 710 for helicopter rides.

SHOPS & GALLERIES

Shopping is a pleasure on this island. Where else can you browse vintage Hawaiiana practically in a cane field, buy exquisite home accessories in an old stone building built in 1942, and get a virtual agricultural tour of the island through city-sponsored green markets that move from town to town throughout the week, like a movable feast? At Kauai's small, tasteful boutiques, you can satisfy your shopping ya-yas in concentrated spurts around the island. This is a bonanza for the boutique shopper—particularly the one who appreciates the thrill of the hunt.

"Downtown" Kapaa continues to flourish, and Hanalei, touristy as it is, is still a shopping destination. (Ola's and Yellowfish more than make up for the hurricane of trinkets and trash in Hanalei.) Kilauea, with Kong Lung Store and the fabulous new Lotus Gallery, is the style center of the island. Basically, you can anticipate spending some of your vacation time in the great shops in Hanalei, a few art galleries and boutiques, and a handful of shopping centers—not much to distract you from an afternoon of hiking or snorkeling. The gift items and treasures you'll find in east and north Kauai, however, may be among your best Hawaiian finds.

Green Markets & Fruit Stands

The county of Kauai sponsors regular weekly **Sunshine Markets** (© **808/241-4946;** www.kauai.gov) throughout the island, featuring fresh Kauai **Sunrise papayas** (sweeter, juicier, and redder than most), herbs and vegetables used in ethnic cuisines, exotic fruit such as rambutan and atemoya, and the most exciting development in pineapple agriculture, the low-acid white pineapple called **Sugarloaf,** rarer these days but still spottily available. These markets, which sell the full range of fresh local produce and flowers at rock-bottom prices, present the perfect opportunity to see what's best and in season. Farmers sell their bounty from the backs of trucks or at tables set up under tarps. The biggest market is at **Kapaa New Town Park,** in the middle of Kapaa town, on Wednesday at 3pm.

One of Kauai's Sunshine Markets.

Kilohana Plantation.

The Sunshine Market in **Lihue,** held on Monday at 3pm at the Kukui Grove Shopping Center, in the parking lot by Star Market, 3-2600 Kaumualii Highway, is extremely popular. The schedule for the other markets: daily in **Koloa** at the Koloa Bypass Road; daily in **Poipu,** at the Poipu Road at the Cane Haul Road; and in **Hanalei** every Saturday at 9:30am at the Hanalei Neighborhood Center and Ballpark, just off the main highway, across the street from the Post Office. Go early to get the best deals.

Lihue & Environs

DOWNTOWN LIHUE The gift shop of the **Kauai Museum,** 4428 Rice St. (📞 **808/245-6931**), is your best bet for made-on-Kauai arts and crafts, from Niihau-shell leis to woodwork, lauhala and coconut products, and more.

About a mile north of the Lihue Airport, on Kuhio Highway (Hwy. 56), **Kauai Fruit & Flower** is a great stop for flowers, including the rare Kauai maile in season; coconut drums the owner makes himself; Hawaiian gourds (*ipu*); cut flowers for shipping; and Kauai fruit, such as papayas and pineapples. Other products include lauhala gift items, teas, Kauai honey, Kauai salad dressings, jams and jellies, and custom-made gift baskets.

KILOHANA PLANTATION Even if you are not interested in shopping, don't miss this, an architectural marvel that houses a sprinkling of galleries and shops. Located at 3-2087 Kaumualii Hwy., this 35-acre Tudor-style estate sprawls across the landscape in Puhi, on Hwy. 50 between Lihue and Poipu. At the **Country Store** (📞 **808/246-2778**), on the ground level, you'll find Island and American crafts of decent quality, koa accessories, pottery, and Hawaii-themed gift items.

The Poipu Resort Area

Expect mostly touristy shops in Poipu, the island's resort mecca; here you'll find T-shirts, souvenirs, black pearls, jewelry, and the usual quota of tired marine art and trite hand-painted silks.

FRUITY SMOOTHIES & OTHER
exotic treats

Fruit stands have sprouted on this island, and smoothies are gaining ground as the milkshake of the new millennium. New crops of exotic trees imported from Southeast Asia are maturing on Kauai, creating anticipation among residents and fruitful ideas for the smoothie world. "Everyone's waiting for the mangosteens and durians," comments Joe Halasey, who, with his wife, Cynthia, runs **Banana Joe's** (© **808/828-1092**), the grand-daddy of Kauai's roadside fruit-and-smoothie stands. Banana Joe's has been a Kilauea landmark since it opened in 1986 at 52719 Kuhio Hwy., between mile markers 23 and 24 heading north, on the mauka (mountain) side of the street. "They take about 12 years to start bearing, so there are a lot of maturing trees. We're all waiting for the fruit. Rambutans [with a hairy, red exterior and a translucent, litchi-like flesh] are good for the farmers here because they're available, and they're a winter fruit. In the summer, mangoes and litchis are always in high demand."

Mangosteens, reputedly the favorite fruit of Queen Victoria, have a creamy, custardy flesh of ambrosial sweetness. Though you'll have to wait for them to

Exceptions: The newly opened **Kukui'ula Village,** 2829 Ala Kalanikaumaka, just outside the Poipu resort area (© **808/742-9545;** www.kukuiulavillage.com). Some 45 restaurants and shops are located in this plantation-style shopping center set in a village atmosphere, including Lappert's Ice Cream & Coffee, Living Foods Market and Café, Hawaiian Salt, Uncle's Shave Ice & Smoothies, Bungalow 9, Quiksilver, and Relax by Tommy Bahama. Another exception is the formerly characterless **Poipu Shopping Village,** at 2360 Kiahuna Plantation Dr., which is shaping up to be a serious shopping stop. The tiny **Bamboo Lace** boutique lures the fashionistas; its resort wear and accessories can segue from Hawaii to the south of France in one easy heartbeat. Across the courtyard, **Sand People** is great for understated resort wear (such as Tencel jeans) and Indonesian coconut picture frames, while the newly renovated **Overboard** rides the wave of popularity in aloha wear and surf stuff.

The shopping is surprisingly good at the **Grand Hyatt Kauai,** with the footwear mecca **Sandal Tree, Water Wear Hawaii** for swim stuff, and **Reyn's** for top-drawer aloha shirts and the Kauai Kids line for the children.

Across the street from Poipu Beach, on Hoone Road, **Nukumoi Surf Shop** is a pleasant surprise: an excellent selection of sunglasses, swimwear, surf equipment, and watersports regalia, and not just for the under-20 crowd.

In neighboring **Old Koloa Town,** you'll find everything from **Lappert's Ice Cream** and **Island Soap and Candle Works** (where you can watch them make soap and candles) to **Crazy Shirts** and **Sueoka Store** on Koloa's main drag, Koloa Road. Just walk the long block for gifts, souvenirs, sun wear, groceries, soaps and bath products, and everyday necessities, but don't expect dazzling temptations.

On Poipu Road between Koloa and Poipu, in the tiny Poipu Plaza mini-mall, nestled next to **Sea Sport Divers** and **Outfitters Kauai,** the **Kukuiula Store** is a stop for everything from produce and sushi to paper products, sunscreen,

start appearing at Hawaii fruit stands, Banana Joe's already has a hit on its hands with Sugarloaf, the white, non-acidic, ultrasweet, organically grown pineapple popularized on the Big Island. Whether made into smoothies or frostees (frozen fruit put through the Champion juicer), or just sold plain, fresh, and whole, the Sugarloaf is pineapple at its best. For litchi lovers, who must wait for their summer appearance, new varieties such as Kaimana and Brewster are adding to the pleasures of the season. In addition to fruit smoothies, frostees, and fresh fruits such as sapodilla and star apple (round, purple, and sweet, like a creamy Concord grape), Banana Joe's sells organic vegetables, macadamia nuts, tropical-fruit salsas, jams and jellies, Anahola Granola, drinking coconuts (young coconuts containing delicious drinking water), gift items, and baked goods such as homemade papaya-banana bread. Its top-selling smoothies are papaya, banana, and pineapple.

Near the Lihue Airport, Pammie Chock at **Kauai Fruit & Flower** (© **808/245-1814;** see below) makes a pineapple–passion fruit smoothie that gets my vote as the best on the Island.

beverages, and groceries. Occasionally, when the fishermen drop by, the store offers fresh sliced sashimi and poke, quite delicious and popular for sunset picnickers and nearby condo residents.

Western Kauai

HANAPEPE   This west Kauai hamlet is becoming a haven for artists, but finding them requires some vigilance. The center of town is off Hwy. 50; turn right on Hanapepe Road just after Eleele if you're driving from Lihue. **Taro Ko Chips Factory ★**, 3940 Hanapepe Rd. (© **808/335-5586**), is located in an old green plantation house at the east end of town. These famous taro chips are handmade in a tiny, modest kitchen by the farmers who grow the taro in a nearby valley. Despite their breakable nature, these chips make great gifts to go. To really impress them back home, get the lihi mung–flavored chips.

Farther on, Hanapepe Road is lined with gift shops and galleries, including **Koa Wood Gallery** and its koa furniture, koa photo albums, and Norfolk pine bowls; and the corny but cherubic **Aloha Angels,** where everything is angel-themed or angel-related. The **Kauai Village Gallery** offers abstract and surreal paintings by Kauai artist Lew Shortridge, while nearby **Kauai Fine Arts** offers an odd mix that works: antique maps and prints of Hawaii, authentic Polynesian tapa, rare wiliwili-seed leis, old Matson liner menus, and a few pieces of contemporary Island art. Down the street, the **Kim Starr Gallery,** showing only Kim Starr's oil paintings, pastels, drawings, and limited-edition graphics, is a strong positive note in Hanapepe's art community. Taking a cue from Maui's Lahaina, where every Friday night is Art Night, Hanapepe's gallery owners and artists recently instituted the **Friday Night Art Walk** every Friday from 6 to 9pm. Gallery owners take turns hosting this informal event along Hanapepe Road. Food trucks set up next to

Hanapepe's Friday Night Art Walk.

plastic chairs and folding tables, and there's often a local musician or two providing live entertainment. Make an evening of it and have dinner at the Hanapepe Cafe & Espresso Bar (p. 669; reservations required).

A great treat to take home is **Kauai Kookies** (℗ **800/361-1126** or 808/335-5003; www.kauaikookie.com), with the factory outlet at 1–3959 Hwy. 50 in Hanapepe. Choose from eight delicious kinds of cookies (Kona coffee mac-nut, chocolate-chip mac-nut, peanut butter, guava mac-nut, and so on) to ship home, or carry a few around in your car.

WAIMEA   Neighboring Waimea is filled with more edibles than art, with Kauai's favorite native supermarket, **Big Save,** serving as the one-stop shop for area residents and passersby heading for the uplands of Kokee State Park, some 4,000 feet above this sea-level village. A cheerful distraction for lovers of Hawaiian collectibles is **Collectibles and Fine Junque,** on Hwy. 50, next to the fire station on the way to Waimea Canyon. This is where you'll discover what it's like to be the proverbial bull in a china shop (even a knapsack makes it hard to get through the aisles). Heaps of vintage linens, choice aloha shirts and muumuu, rare glassware, books, ceramics, authentic 1950s cotton-chenille bedspreads, and a back room full of bargain-priced second-hand goodies always capture my attention. You never know what you'll find in this tiny corner of Waimea.

Up in Kokee State Park, the gift shop of the **Kokee Natural History Museum** (℗ 808/335-9975) is *the* stop for botanical, geographical, historical, and nature-related books and gifts, not only on Kauai, but on all the islands. Audubon bird books, hiking maps, and practically every book on Kauai ever written line the shelves.

The Coconut Coast

As you make your way from Lihue to the North Shore, you'll pass **Bambulei** (℗ 808/823-8641), bordering the cane field in Wailua next to Caffè Coco. Watch for the sign just past the Wailua intersection, across from Restaurant Kintaro.

Bambulei houses a charming collection of 1930s and 1940s treasures—everything from Peking lacquerware and exquisite vintage aloha shirts to lamps, quilts, jewelry, parrot figurines, and zany salt and pepper shakers. If it's not vintage, it will look vintage, and it's bound to be fabulous. Vintage muumuu are often in perfect condition, and dresses go for $20 to $2,000. Closed on Sundays.

Wood-turner **Robert Hamada** (© **808/822-3229**) works in his studio at the foot of the Sleeping Giant, quietly producing museum-quality works with unique textures and grains. His skill, his lathe, and more than 60 years of experience have brought luminous life to the kou, milo, kauila, camphor, mango, and native woods he logs himself. Hamada was honored by the Kauai Museum in May 2001, when his private collection of woods was displayed in the main lobby in honor of his 80th birthday. By appointment only.

KAPAA   Moving toward Kapaa on Kuhio Highway (Hwy. 56), don't get your shopping hopes up; until you hit Kapaa town, quality goods are slim in this neck of the woods. The **Coconut MarketPlace,** 484 Kuhio Hwy., features the ubiquitous **Elephant Walk** gift shop, Gifts of Kauai, and various other underwhelming souvenir and clothing shops sprinkled among the sunglass huts. Some finds: the **Hawaiian Music Store,** with a great collection of Hawaiian music; **Auntie Lynda's Treasures,** great finds in Hawaiian music instruments (check out the Hawaiian drums), Hawaiian jewelry (including a coconut purse), wood carvings, shell jewelry, and vintage surf collectibles (from painted surfboards to surfboard clocks); and **Palm Palm,** an exquisite jewelry store with works by local designer Cherie Dori.

In the green-and-white wooden storefronts of nearby **Kauai Village,** you'll find everything from trite marine art at **Wyland Galleries** to *yin chiao* Chinese cold pills and organic produce at **Papayas Natural Foods.** Although its prepared foods are overpriced, Papayas carries the full range of health food products and is your only choice in the area for vitamins, prepared health foods to go, health-conscious cosmetics, and bulk food items. If you need Internet access or your kids need to rent a computer game, go to **Computer Web,** located here.

Less than a mile away on the main road, the **Waipouli Variety Store,** 4-901 Kuhio Hwy., is Kapaa's version of Maui's fabled Hasegawa General Store—a tangle of fishing supplies, T-shirts and thongs, beach towels, and souvenirs.

Send a Little Bit of Paradise Home

You can take paradise home with you— well, at least the outrageously beautiful flowers. The best place to order flowers to be sent home is Tropical Flowers by Charles, 3465 Lawailoa Lane, Koloa (© **800/699-7984** or 808/639-8492; www.thetropicalflowers.com). Not only is Charles a flower genius (he grows a range of tropical flowers, including some very rare and unusual varieties), but his hardy blooms and his skill at packing mean that your little bit of Kauai will live for a long, long time. All this, and extremely reasonable prices: Bouquets start at just $40, including shipping. Full arrangements in vases start at $60.

Kapaa town itself is full of surprises. On the main strip, across from Sunnyside Market, you'll find the recently expanded **Kela's Glass Gallery** (℃ 808/822-4527), the island's showiest showplace for handmade glass in all sizes, shapes, and prices, with the most impressive selection in Hawaii. Go nuts over the vases and studio glass pieces, functional and nonfunctional, and then stroll along this strip of storefronts to **Hula Girl** (℃ 808/822-1950), where a wonderful whimsy prevails: aloha shirts (very pricey), vintage-looking luggage covered with decals of old Hawaii, Patrice Pendarvis prints, zoris, sunglasses, and shells.

Down the street, **Island Hemp & Cotton** (℃ 808/821-0225), 4-1373 Kuhio Hwy., where Hawaii's most stylish selection of this miracle fabric is sold: gorgeous silk-hemp dresses, linen-hemp sportswear for men and women, hemp aloha shirts, Tencel clothing, T-shirts, and wide-ranging, attractive, and comfortable clothing and accessories that have shed the hippie image. It's also a great store for gift items, from Balinese leather goods to handmade paper, jewelry, and luxury soaps. A few doors to the north, **Orchid Alley** (℃ 808/822-0486), 1383 Kuhio Hwy., gets my vote for most adorable nursery on the island. A narrow alcove opens into a greenhouse of phalaenopsis, oncidiums, dendrobiums, and dozens of brilliant orchid varieties for shipping or hand-carrying.

The North Shore

Kauai's North Shore is the premier shopping destination on the island. Stylish, sophisticated galleries and shops, such as **Kong Lung,** in a 1942 Kilauea stone building (the last to be built on the Kilauea Plantation) off Hwy. 56 on Kilauea Road (℃ 808/828-1822), have launched these former hippie villages as top-drawer shopping spots. Save your time, energy, and, most of all, discretionary funds for this end of the island. Kong Lung, through all its changes, including pricier merchandise in every category, remains a showcase of design, style, and quality, from top-of-the-line dinnerware and bath products to aloha shirts, jewelry, ceramics, women's wear, and stationery. The book selection is fabulous, and the home accessories—sake sets, tea sets, lacquer bowls, handblown glass, pottery—are unequaled in Hawaii. It's expensive, but browsing here is a joy.

Directly behind Kong Lung is newcomer **Lotus Gallery** (℃ 808/828-9898), a showstopper for lovers of antiques and designer jewelry. Good juju abounds here. Serenity and beauty will envelop you from the moment you remove your shoes to step in the door and onto the bamboo floor. There are gems, crystals, Tibetan art, antiques and sari clothing from India, 12th-century Indian bronzes, temple bells, Oriental rugs, pearl bracelets—items from $30 to $50,000. Owners Kamalia (jewelry designer) and Tsajon Von Lixfeld (gemologist) have a staggering sense of design and discovery that brings to the gallery such things as emeralds, Brazilian amethyst crystal (immense and complex), a fine 100-strand lapis necklace ($4,000), and Kamalia's 18-karat pieces, with clean, elegant lines and gemstones that soothe and elevate.

In Hanalei, at **Ola's,** by the Hanalei River on the Kuhio Highway (Hwy. 560) after the bridge and before the main part of Hanalei town (℃ 808/826-6937), Sharon and Doug Britt, award-winning artists, have amassed a head-turning assortment of American and Island crafts, including Doug's paintings and the one-of-a-kind furniture that he makes out of found objects, driftwood, and used materials. Britt's works—armoires, tables, lamps, bookshelves—often serve as the display surfaces for others' work, so look carefully. Lundberg Studio hand-blown glass, exquisite jewelry, intricately wrought pewter switch plates, sensational handblown goblets, and many other fine works fill this tasteful, seductive shop. Be on the lookout for the wonderful koa jewel boxes by local woodworker Tony Lydgate.

From health foods to groceries to Bakelite jewelry, the **Ching Young Village Shopping Center,** in the heart of Hanalei, covers a lot of bases. It's more funky than fashionable, but Hanalei, until recently, has never been about fashion. People take their time here, and there are always clusters of folks lingering at the few tables outdoors. **Hot Rocket** is ablaze with aloha shirts, T-shirts, Reyn Spooner and Jams sportswear, flamingo china, backpacks and pareu, swimwear, and, for collectors, one of the finest collections of Bakelite accessories you're likely to see in the islands.

Next door to Ching Young Village is **On the Road to Hanalei** (© 808/826-7360), worth checking out for the unusual T-shirts (great gifts to take home because they don't take up much suitcase space), scarves, pareu, jewelry, and other unique gifts.

Across the street in the **Hanalei Center,** the standout boutique is the **Yellowfish Trading Company ★** (© 808/826-1227), where owner Gritt Benton's impeccable eye and zeal for collecting are reflected in the 1920s to 1940s collectibles: menus, hula-girl nodders, hula lamps, rattan and koa furniture, vases, bark-cloth fabric, retro pottery and lamp bases, must-have vintage textiles, and wonderful finds in books and aloha shirts.

KAUAI AFTER DARK

Suffice it to say that you don't come to Kauai to trip the light fantastic—this is the island for winding down. But there are a few nightlife options.

For action after sunset, music, dancing, and bars, the hotels and resorts are the primary players. The **Coconut MarketPlace,** 4-484 Kuhio Hwy., Kapaa (© 808/245-4700), has a free hula show every Wednesday at 5pm. The **Poipu Shopping Village,** 2360 Kiahuna Plantation Dr. (© 808/742-2831), also offers free Tahitian dance performances every Tuesday and Thursday at 5pm in the outdoor courtyard.

As the former plantation community and now county seat, Lihue is a place where local residents live and work. There are a few local places, but generally all is quiet in Lihue after dark. One option, however, is **Rob's Good Times Grill,** in the Rice Shopping Center, 4303 Rice St. (© 808/246-0311), great for dancing Thursday through Saturday nights, or karaoke Sunday through Tuesday.

At the **Kauai Marriott Resort & Beach Club,** 3610 Rice St., Nawiliwili (© 808/245-5050), the **Duke's Barefoot Bar** (© 808/246-9599) has traditional and contemporary Hawaiian music on Thursday and Friday nights, when tropical drinks go for $5.50 from 4 to 6pm and live music stirs up the joint.

The south shore, with its sunset view and miles of white-sand beaches, is a great place for nightlife. At the far end of Poipu, **Stevenson's Library** at the **Grand Hyatt Kauai Resort & Spa,** 1571 Poipu Rd., Koloa (© 808/742-1234;** www.kauai-hyatt.com), is the place for an elegant after-dinner drink, with live jazz Monday and Tuesday and Thursday through Saturday from 8 to 11pm in

Captain Andy's Na Pali Sunset Dinner Cruise.

high season (Thurs–Sat nights only the rest of the year). Come dressed in resort casual wear (no tank tops or slippers). The koa-lined bar has comfy overstuffed chairs, a big saltwater aquarium, and various activities like pool or chess. It has recently added Martini and Sushi nights every Friday, Saturday, and Sunday, with fresh sushi made to order. For literary types, Stevenson's Library houses more than 1,000 books, most of which are available to borrow and take back to your room to read.

Also in Poipu, **Keoki's Paradise,** in the Poipu Shopping Village, 2360 Kiahuna Plantation Dr. (© 808/742-7534), offers live music every night except Saturday (call for times), with the cafe menu available from 11am to 11:30pm. Hawaiian, reggae, and contemporary music draw the 21-and-over dancing crowd.

The Point, down the street at the **Sheraton Kauai Resort,** 2440 Hoonani Rd. (© 808/742-1661), on the water, is the Poipu hot spot. There's live and DJ music and dancing Friday and Saturday, with a range of artists, from contemporary Hawaiian to good ol' rock 'n' roll.

Beyond Poipu, in the old plantation community of Hanapepe, every Friday from 6 to 9pm is **Hanapepe Art Night.** Each one is unique. Participating galleries take turns acting as the weekly "host gallery," offering original performances or demonstrations, which become the theme for that Art Night. The galleries are lit up and decked out, giving this quaint, historic town a special atmosphere. Enjoy a stroll around and meet the local artists. Also in Hanapepe on Friday nights, the **Hanapepe Cafe & Espresso Bar,** 3830 Hanapepe Rd. (© 808/335-5011), is open for dinner from 5 to 8:30pm and has live music.

Up on the North Shore, Hanalei has some action, primarily at **Bouchon's,** in Ching Young Village (© 808/826-9707). Reggae, rhythm and blues, rock, and good music by local groups draw dancers and revelers Friday, from 8:30pm on. The format changes often, so call ahead to see who's playing.

Across the street, the **Hanalei Gourmet,** in the Old Hanalei Schoolhouse, 5–5161 Kuhio Hwy. (© **808/826-2524**), has live music every night except Monday, Tuesday, and Thursday. Down the road, **Tahiti Nui** (© **808/826-6277**) is a great place to experience old Hawaii with nightly live music with two acts starting at 6:30 and 9:30pm. The restaurant/bar is family-friendly, and there always seems to be someone who drops in and starts singing and playing music, just like in the old days.

FAST FACTS

FAST FACTS: HAWAII

American Express   For 24-hour traveler's check refunds and purchase information, call ✆ **800/221-7282.** For local offices, see the "Fast Facts" sections in the individual island chapters.

Area Codes   All the Hawaiian Islands are in the **808** area code. Note that if you're calling one island from another via a landline, you have to dial "1-808" before the local number. If you're calling from one island to another island, the call will be billed as a long-distance call, which can be more expensive than calling the mainland from Hawaii. Be sure to use your long-distance calling card when calling between islands to avoid adding inflated phone charges to your hotel bill.

ATM Networks/Cashpoints   All of the islands have plenty of ATMs in the major resort areas. Branches of Hawaii's most popular banks are plentiful, and all are connected to the global ATM networks. Most supermarkets also have ATMs inside, as do many convenience stores. Do yourself a favor, though, and stock up on cash before heading off to remote areas such as the North Shore of Kauai, the Big Island's North Kohala peninsula or Volcano area, or the islands of Molokai or Lanai. These areas do have ATMs, but why waste precious vacation time tracking them down and risking that they won't be in your network.

One of Hawaii's most popular banks, with branches throughout the state, is Bank of Hawaii, which is linked with all the major worldwide networks. To find the one nearest you, call ✆ **888/643-3888** or point your Web browser to the Bank of Hawaii's site (www.boh.com) and click on "Locations" in the upper navigational bar; if you don't find one near you, try First Hawaiian Bank (www.fhb.com). You can also find ATMs on the MasterCard/Maestro/Cirrus network by dialing ✆ **800/424-7787** or going online to www.mastercard.com. To find a Visa Plus ATM, call ✆ **800/843-7587** or visit www.visa.com and then click the ATM locator at the bottom of the start page. Also, see "Money & Costs," on p. 77.

Automobile Organizations   Motor clubs will supply maps, suggested routes, guidebooks, accident and bail-bond insurance, and emergency road service. The **American Automobile Association** (AAA) is the major auto club in the United States. If you belong to a motor club in your home country, inquire about AAA reciprocity before you leave. You may be able to join AAA even if you're not a member of a reciprocal club; to inquire, call AAA (© **800/222-4357;** www.aaa.com). AAA has a nationwide emergency road service telephone number (© **800/AAA-HELP** [222-4357]).

Business Hours   Most offices are open Monday through Friday from 8am to 5pm. Bank hours are Monday through Thursday from 8:30am to 3pm and Friday from 8:30am to 6pm; some banks are open on Saturday as well. Shopping centers are open Monday through Friday from 10am to 9pm, Saturday from 10am to 5:30pm, and Sunday from noon to 5 or 6pm.

Car Rentals   See "Getting Around Hawaii," p. 75, and "Airline, Hotel & Car-Rental Websites," p. 735.

Drinking Laws   The legal age for purchase and consumption of alcoholic beverages is 21; proof of age is required and often requested at bars, nightclubs, and restaurants, so it's always a good idea to bring ID when you go out.

Bars are allowed to stay open daily until 2am; places with cabaret licenses are able to keep the booze flowing until 4am. Grocery and convenience stores are allowed to sell beer, wine, and liquor 7 days a week.

Do not carry open containers of alcohol in your car or any public area that isn't zoned for alcohol consumption. The police can fine you on the spot. Don't even think about driving while intoxicated.

Driving Rules   See "Getting There & Getting Around," p. 74.

Electricity   Like Canada, the United States uses 110 to 120 volts AC (60 cycles), compared to 220 to 240 volts AC (50 cycles) in most of Europe, Australia, and New Zealand. Downward converters that change 220–240 volts to 110–120 volts are difficult to find in the United States, so bring one with you.

Embassies & Consulates   All embassies are located in the nation's capital, Washington, D.C. Some consulates are located in major U.S. cities, and most nations have a mission to the United Nations in New York City. If your country isn't listed below, call for directory information in Washington, D.C. (© **202/555-1212**) or check www.embassy.org/embassies.

The embassy of **Australia** is at 1601 Massachusetts Ave. NW, Washington, DC 20036 (© **202/797-3000;** usa.embassy.gov/au).

The embassy of **Canada** is at 501 Pennsylvania Ave. NW, Washington, DC 20001 (© **202/682-1740;** www.canadianembassy.org). Other Canadian consulates are in Buffalo (New York), Detroit, Los Angeles, New York, and Seattle.

The embassy of **Ireland** is at 2234 Massachusetts Ave. NW, Washington, DC 20008 (© **202/462-3939;** www.irelandemb.org). Irish consulates are in Boston, Chicago, New York, San Francisco, and other cities. See website for complete listing.

The embassy of **New Zealand** is at 37 Observatory Circle NW, Washington, DC 20008 (© **202/328-4800;** www.nzembassy.com). New Zealand consulates are in Los Angeles, Salt Lake City, San Francisco, and Seattle.

The embassy of the **United Kingdom** is at 3100 Massachusetts Ave. NW, Washington, DC 20008 (✆ **202/588-7800;** www.ukinusa.fco.gov.uk/en). Other British consulates are in Atlanta, Boston, Chicago, Cleveland, Houston, Los Angeles, New York, San Francisco, and Seattle.

Emergencies   Dial ✆ **911** for police, fire, or ambulance.

Gasoline   At press time, in the U.S., the cost of gasoline (also known as gas, but never petrol), is abnormally high. At this writing, average prices for regular gas in Hawaii range from $3.55 in Honolulu to $3.95 on Maui and a whopping $4.60 on Lanai. Taxes are already included in the printed price. One U.S. gallon equals 3.8 liters or .85 imperial gallons.

Holidays   Banks, government offices, post offices, and many stores, restaurants, and museums are closed on the following legal national holidays: January 1 (New Year's Day), the third Monday in January (Martin Luther King, Jr., Day), the third Monday in February (Presidents' Day), the last Monday in May (Memorial Day), July 4 (Independence Day), the first Monday in September (Labor Day), the second Monday in October (Columbus Day), November 11 (Veterans' Day/Armistice Day), the fourth Thursday in November (Thanksgiving Day), and December 25 (Christmas). The Tuesday after the first Monday in November is Election Day, a federal government holiday in presidential-election years (held every 4 years, and next in 2012).

State and county offices are also closed on local holidays. For more information, go to "Hawaii Calendar of Events" in the "When to Go" section on p. 65.

Insurance   Travel insurance is a good idea if you think for some reason you may be canceling your trip. It's cheaper than the cost of a no-penalty ticket and it gives you the safety net if something comes up, enabling you to cancel or postpone your trip and still recover the costs.

For information on traveler's insurance, trip-cancellation insurance, and medical insurance while traveling, please visit www.frommers.com/planning.

Internet Access   On every island, branches of the **Hawaii State Public Library System** have free computers with Internet access. To find your closest library, check **www.librarieshawaii.org/sitemap.htm**. There is no charge for use of the computers, but you must have a Hawaii library card, which is free to Hawaii residents and members of the military.

Visitors have a choice of two types of cards: a $25 nonresident card that is good for 5 years (and may be renewed for an additional $25) or a $10 visitor card ($5 for children 18 and under) that is good for 3 months but may not be renewed. To download an application for a library card, go to **www.librarieshawaii.org/services/libcard.htm**.

To find Internet cafes in your destination, check **www.cybercaptive.com** or **www.cybercafe.com**.

If you have your own laptop, every **Starbucks** in Hawaii has Wi-Fi. For a list of locations, go to **www.starbucks.com/retail/find/default.aspx**. To find other public Wi-Fi hotspots in your destination, go to **www.jiwire.com**; its Hotspot Finder holds the world's largest directory of public wireless hotspots.

Also see the "Fast Facts" sections in the individual island chapters for listings of local cybercafes.

Legal Aid   If you are "pulled over" for a minor infraction (such as speeding), never attempt to pay the fine directly to a police officer; this could be construed as attempted bribery, a much more serious crime. Pay fines by mail, or directly into the hands of the clerk of the court. If accused of a more serious offense, say and do nothing before consulting a lawyer. Here the burden is on the state to prove a person's guilt beyond a reasonable doubt, and everyone has the right to remain silent, whether he or she is suspected of a crime or actually arrested. Once arrested, a person can make one telephone call to a party of his or her choice. International visitors should call their embassy or consulate.

Mail   At press time, domestic postage rates were 28¢ for a postcard and 44¢ for a letter. For international mail, a first-class letter of up to 1 ounce costs 98¢ (75¢ to Canada and 79¢ to Mexico); a first-class postcard costs the same as a letter. For more information go to **www.usps.com**.

If you aren't sure what your address will be in the United States, mail can be sent to you, in your name, c/o General Delivery at the main post office of the city or region where you expect to be. (Call ℂ **800/275-8777** for information on the nearest post office.) The addressee must pick up mail in person and must produce proof of identity (driver's license, passport, and so on). Most post offices will hold your mail for up to 1 month, and are open Monday to Friday from 8am to 6pm, and Saturday from 9am to 3pm.

Always include zip codes when mailing items in the U.S. If you don't know your zip code, visit **www.usps.com/zip4**.

Newspapers & Magazines   Daily newspapers in Hawaii are as follows: on Oahu, the *Honolulu Advertiser* (www.honoluluadvertiser.com) and the *Honolulu Star-Bulletin* (www.honolulustarbulletin.com); on the Big Island, *West Hawaii Today* (www.west hawaiitoday.com) for the Kailua/Kona side, and the *Hawaii Tribune-Herald* (www. hilohawaiitribune.com) for the Hilo/Puna side; on Maui, the *Maui News* (www. mauinews.com); and on Kauai, the *Garden Island* (www.kauaiworld.com).

Publications for visitors include *This Week Oahu, This Week Big Island, This Week Maui,* and *This Week Kauai* (www.thisweek.com); *Oahu Visitor Magazine, Big Island Visitor Magazine, Maui Visitor Magazine,* and *Kauai Visitor Magazine* (www.visitormagazines. com); and *101 Things to Do* (with separate versions for Oahu, the Big Island, Maui, and Kauai).

Lifestyle magazines include *Honolulu Magazine* (www.honolulumagazine.com); business publications include *Pacific Business News* (www.bizjournals.com/pacific) and *Hawaii Business* (www.hawaiibusiness.com).

Ocean Safety   Keep these snorkel tips in mind as you don your fins and head into the water:

Always snorkel with a friend and keep an eye on each other.

Look up every few minutes to get your bearings. Check your position in relation to the shoreline and check whether there is any boat traffic.

Don't touch anything. Not only can your fingers and feet damage coral, but it can give you nasty cuts. Moreover, camouflaged fish and spiny shells may surprise you.

Before you set out, check surf conditions by calling the local dive or snorkel shops, which can give you the latest conditions and recommend alternative spots if the prime ones are too rough for snorkeling. See the "Watersports" sections in island-specific chapters for more tips.

Parks   Hawaii has several national parks and historical sites—four on the Big Island and one each on Maui, Oahu, and Molokai. The following offices can supply you with hiking and camping information (or check online at www.nps.gov):

- On the **Big Island: Hawaii Volcanoes National Park,** P.O. Box 52, Hawaii National Park, HI 96718 (© 808/985-6000); **Puuhonua O Honaunau National Historical Park,** P.O. Box 129, Honaunau, HI 96726 (© 808/328-2326); **Puukohola Heiau National Historic Site,** P.O. Box 44340, Kawaihae, HI 96743 (© 808/882-7218); and **Kaloko-Honokohau National Historical Park,** 72–4786 Kanalani St., Kailua-Kona, HI 96740 (© 808/329-6881).

- On **Maui: Haleakala National Park,** P.O. Box 369, Makawao, HI 96768 (© 808/572-9306).

- On **Molokai: Kalaupapa National Historical Park,** P.O. Box 2222, Kalaupapa, HI 96742 (© 808/567-6802).

- On **Oahu: USS *Arizona* Memorial at Pearl Harbor** (© 808/422-0561).

To find out more about Hawaii's state parks, contact the **Hawaii State Department of Land and Natural Resources,** 1151 Punchbowl St., No. 130, Honolulu, HI 96813 (© **808/587-0300;** www.hawaii.gov). The office can provide you with information on hiking and camping at the parks and will send you free topographic trail maps.

Passports   See www.frommers.com/planning for information on how to obtain a passport. See "Embassies & Consulates," above, for whom to contact if you lose yours while traveling in the U.S. For other information, please contact the following agencies:

For Residents of Australia   Contact the **Australian Passport Information Service** at © **131-232,** or visit the government website at www.passports.gov.au.

For Residents of Canada   Contact the central **Passport Office,** Department of Foreign Affairs and International Trade, Ottawa, ON K1A 0G3 (© **800/567-6868;** www.ppt.gc.ca).

For Residents of Ireland   Contact the **Passport Office,** Setanta Centre, Molesworth Street, Dublin 2 (© **01/671-1633;** www.irlgov.ie/iveagh).

For Residents of New Zealand   Contact the **Passports Office** at © **0800/225-050** in New Zealand or 04/474-8100, or log on to www.passports.govt.nz.

For Residents of the United Kingdom   Visit your nearest passport office, major post office, or travel agency, or contact the **United Kingdom Passport Service** at © **0870/521-0410** or search its website at www.ukpa.gov.uk.

For Residents of the United States   To find your regional passport office, either check the U.S. State Department website or call the **National Passport Information Center** toll-free number (© **877/487-2778**) for automated information.

Pharmacies   Longs Drugs, Hawaii's biggest drugstore chain, has convenient locations on the major islands. To locate the nearest branch, point your Web browser to www.longs.com and click "store locator" at the bottom of the home page.

Police   Dial © **911** for police.

Smoking   It's against the law to smoke in public buildings, including airports, shopping malls, grocery stores, retail shops, buses, movie theaters, banks, convention facilities, and all government buildings and facilities. There is no smoking in restaurants, bars, and nightclubs. Most bed-and-breakfasts prohibit smoking indoors, and more and more hotels and resorts are becoming nonsmoking even in public areas. Also, there is no smoking within 20 feet of a doorway, window, or ventilation intake (so no hanging around outside a bar to smoke—you must go 20 ft. away).

Taxes   The United States has no value-added tax (VAT) or other indirect tax at the national level. Every state, county, and city may levy its own local tax on all purchases, including hotel and restaurant checks and airline tickets. These taxes will not appear on price tags.

Hawaii state general excise tax is 4%. After much political hand-wringing, the Hawaii State Legislature voted (and overrode the governor's veto) to increase the hotel tax by 1% in July 2010. The tax you'll pay on a hotel room is currently 13.25%. In addition to the taxes noted above, the City and County of Honolulu (which is the entire island of Oahu) adds an additional .5% on anything purchased there (including a hotel room). These taxes will not appear on price tags.

Telephones   See "Staying Connected," p. 99.

Time   The continental United States is divided into **four time zones:** Eastern Standard Time (EST), Central Standard Time (CST), Mountain Standard Time (MST), and Pacific Standard Time (PST). Alaska and Hawaii have their own zones. For example, when it's 9am in Los Angeles (PST), it's 7am in Honolulu (HST), 10am in Denver (MST), 11am in Chicago (CST), noon in New York City (EST), 5pm in London (GMT), and 2am the next day in Sydney.

Daylight saving time is in effect from 1am on the second Sunday in March to 1am on the first Sunday in November, except in Hawaii. Daylight saving time moves the clock 1 hour ahead of standard time, making Hawaii 3 hours behind the West Coast and 6 hours behind the East Coast.

Tipping   Tips are a very important part of certain workers' income, and gratuities are the standard way of showing appreciation for services provided. (Tipping is certainly not compulsory if the service is poor!) In hotels, tip **bellhops** at least $1 per bag ($2–$3 if you have a lot of luggage) and tip the **chamber staff** $1 to $2 per day (more if you've left a disaster area for him or her to clean up). Tip the **doorman** or **concierge** only if he or she has provided you with some specific service (for example, calling a cab for you or obtaining difficult-to-get theater tickets). Tip the **valet-parking attendant** $1 every time you get your car.

In restaurants, bars, and nightclubs, tip **service staff** and **bartenders** 15% to 20% of the check, tip **checkroom attendants** $1 per garment, and tip **valet-parking attendants** $1 per vehicle.

As for other service personnel, tip **cab drivers** 15% of the fare; tip **skycaps** at airports at least $1 per bag ($2–$3 if you have a lot of luggage); and tip **hairdressers** and **barbers** 15% to 20%.

Toilets   You won't find public toilets or "restrooms" on the streets in most U.S. cities but they can be found in hotel lobbies, bars, restaurants, museums, department stores, railway and bus stations, and service stations. Large hotels and fast-food restaurants are often the best bet for clean facilities. Restaurants and bars in resorts or heavily visited areas may reserve their restrooms for patrons.

Visas   For information about U.S. visas go to **http://travel.state.gov** and click on "Visas." Or go to one of the following websites:

Australian citizens can obtain up-to-date visa information from the **U.S. Embassy Canberra,** Moonah Place, Yarralumla, ACT 2600 (📞 **02/6214-5600**), or from the U.S. Diplomatic Mission's website at http://usembassy-australia.state.gov/consular.

British subjects can obtain up-to-date visa information by calling the **U.S. Embassy Visa Information Line** (📞 **0891/200-290**) or by visiting the "Visas to the U.S." section of the American Embassy London's website at www.usembassy.org.uk.

Irish citizens can obtain up-to-date visa information through the **Embassy of the USA Dublin,** 42 Elgin Rd., Dublin 4, Ireland (📞 **353/1-668-8777,** or by checking the "Visas to the U.S." section of the website at http://dublin.usembassy.gov.

Citizens of **New Zealand** can obtain up-to-date visa information by contacting the **U.S. Embassy New Zealand,** 29 Fitzherbert Terrace, Thorndon, Wellington (📞 **644/472-2068**), or get the information directly from the website at http://wellington.usembassy.gov.

Visitor Information   For information about traveling in Hawaii, contact the **Hawaii Visitors & Convention Bureau (HVCB),** Waikiki Business Plaza, 2270 Kalakaua Ave., Ste. 801, Honolulu, HI 96815 (📞 **800/GO-HAWAII** [464-2924] or 808/923-1811; www.gohawaii.com). The bureau publishes the helpful *Accommodations and Car Rental Guide* and supplies free brochures, maps, and *Islands of Aloha* magazine, the official HVCB magazine. For information about working and living in Hawaii, contact the **Chamber of Commerce of Hawaii,** 1132 Bishop St., Ste. 402, Honolulu, HI 96813 (📞 **808/545-4300;** www.cochawaii.com).

Weather & Surf Reports   For statewide marine reports, call 📞 **808/973-4382**. For statewide coastal wind reports, call 📞 **808/973-6114**.

To check the weather forecasts online, go to www.hawaiiweathertoday.com. You can find the official National Weather Service forecast for the Hawaiian Islands online at prh.noaa.gov/pr/hnl.

For more information on Hawaii's climate and weather information, see the "When to Go" section of the Planning chapter on p. 62.

Websites   Listed below are some of the most useful Hawaii websites:

- Haleakala National Park: www.nps.gov/hale
- Hawaii Visitors & Convention Bureau: www.gohawaii.com
- Hawaii State Vacation Planner: www.hshawaii.com
- Volcanoes National Park: www.nps.gov/havo
- Planet Hawaii: www.planet-hawaii.com
- Oahu Visitors Bureau: www.visit-oahu.com
- Big Island's Kohala Coast Resort Association: www.kohalacoastresorts.com
- Big Island Visitors Bureau: www.bigisland.org

- Maui Visitors Bureau: www.visitmaui.com
- Maui Net: www.maui.net
- Maui Island Currents (arts and culture): www.islandcurrents.com
- Molokai Visitors Association: www.molokai-hawaii.com
- Lanai Visitors Bureau: www.visitlanai.net
- Kaanapali Beach Resort Association: www.kaanapaliresort.com
- Kapalua Resort: www.kapaluamaui.com
- Kauai Visitors Bureau: www.kauaivisitorsbureau.org
- Kauai's Poipu Beach Resort Association: www.poipu-beach.org.

AIRLINE, HOTEL & CAR-RENTAL WEBSITES

MAJOR AIRLINES

Air Canada
www.aircanada.com

Air France
www.airfrance.com

Air New Zealand
www.airnewzealand.com

Air Pacific
www.airpacific.com

Air Tahiti Nui
www.airtahitinui-usa.com

Alaska Airlines
www.alaskaair.com

American Airlines
www.aa.com

British Airways
www.british-airways.com

China Airlines
www.china-airlines.com

Continental Airlines
www.continental.com

Delta Air Lines
www.delta.com

go!
www.iflygo.com
(interisland Hawaii only)

Hawaiian Airlines
www.hawaiianair.com

Island Air
www.islandair.com
(interisland Hawaii only)

Japan Airlines
www.jal.co.jp

Korean Air
www.koreanair.com

Mokulele Airlines
www.mokuleleairlines.com
(interisland Hawaii only)

Philippine Airlines
www.philippineairlines.com

Qantas Airways
www.qantas.com

United Airlines
www.united.com

US Airways
www.usairways.com

CAR-RENTAL AGENCIES

Alamo
www.alamo.com

Avis
www.avis.com

Budget
www.budget.com

Dollar
www.dollar.com

Enterprise
www.enterprise.com

Hertz
www.hertz.com

National
www.nationalcar.com

Thrifty
www.thrifty.com

MAJOR HOTEL & MOTEL CHAINS

Best Western International
www.bestwestern.com

Doubletree Hotels
www.doubletree.com

Embassy Suites
www.embassysuites.com

Four Seasons
www.fourseasons.com

Hilton Hotels
www.hilton.com

Holiday Inn
www.holidayinn.com

Hyatt
www.hyatt.com

Marriott
www.marriott.com

Radisson Hotels & Resorts
www.radisson.com

Renaissance
www.renaissance.com

Sheraton Hotels & Resorts
www.starwoodhotels.com/sheraton

Westin Hotels & Resorts
www.starwoodhotels.com/westin

Wyndham Hotels & Resorts
www.wyndham.com

Index

Restaurants